LOCAL AREA NETWORKS

A CLIENT/SERVER APPROACH

JAMES E. GOLDMAN

Purdue University

John Wiley & Sons, Inc.

New York • **Chichester** • **Brisbane** • **Toronto** • **Singapore** • **Weinheim**

To Susan, Eric, and Grant

Acquisitions Editor	Beth Lang Golub
Marketing Manager	Leslie Hines
Senior Production Editor	Anthony VenGraitis
Designer	Lynn Rogan
Manufacturing Manager	Mark Cirillo
Senior Illustration Coordinator	Anna Melhorn
Illustrator	Curt Snyder

This book was set in Palatino by Digitype, and printed and bound
by Hamilton Printing. The cover was printed by Lehigh Press.

Library of Congress Cataloging-in-Publication Data:

Goldman, James E.
    Local area networks: a client/server approach / by James E.
Goldman.
      p.   cm.
    Includes bibliographical references.
    ISBN 0-471-14162-3 (paper : alk. paper)
    1. Local area networks (Computer networks)   2. Client/server
computing. I. Title.
TK5105.7.G64 1997
004.6'8—dc20   96-31290
                                           CIP

Printed in the United States of America

10 9 8 7 6 5 4 3 2 1

PREFACE

■ THE NEED FOR THIS BOOK

The field of information systems has been in a transitionary state from the mainframe-oriented, hierarchical networks of yesterday to the distributed, client-server architectures of today. The motivation for this transition was not merely economic in nature, but was also largely fueled by increased recognition of information as a corporate asset to be leveraged to competitive advantage. Businesses realized that true financial gains could be achieved by delivering the right information to the right decision maker at the right place and time for the right cost.

The distributed nature of today's information systems, enabling users to gain quick and easy access to key data regardless of location, has put increased emphasis on the importance of the networking aspects of information systems analysis and design. The often repeated phrase, "The network *is* the computer," is a reflection of the central role of networking as the foundation of today's distributed information systems.

This transition from processor-centric, mainframe-oriented computing to network-centric, client-server information systems has not been without difficulty and occasional failures. Designing distributed information systems requires business-oriented analysis, design, and problem-solving skills. Furthermore, networking can no longer be considered a technology-oriented, engineering field of study which can be dealt with in a vacuum. In order to effectively design the local area networks which form the backbone of today's distributed information systems, network analysts must thoroughly understand the business implications of their designs, as well as the characteristics of the information systems which must travel over their networks.

Designing effective local area networks to support client/server information systems requires a structured, systems engineering type of approach. Such a structured, top-down approach to network analysis and design requires thinking models or frameworks into which network analysts can organize their thoughts and questions. Just such a process-oriented, top-down model was introduced in this author's first book, *Applied Data Communications: A Business-Oriented Approach,* also published by Wiley.

The top-down model equips students with a practical, business-first, technology-last, problem solving approach with which to attack local area networking opportunities. Students are taught to use analytical models to organize local area networking requirements as well as the functionality of the technology currently available to meet those requirements. Using this methodology, this text teaches students how to *do* local area network analysis and design in a client-server information system environment, rather than merely telling students about local area networking concepts and technology.

■ UNIQUE FEATURES OF THE BOOK

Business Orientation/Problem Solving Approach

Rather than addressing business issues and decisions in isolated chapters or sections, this text adheres to a business-oriented problem solving approach throughout the entire text. In most cases, design challenges and requirements related to a particular chapter's topics are presented first, followed by alternative technology implementations which meet the outlined technical requirements. Alternative implementations are then analyzed as to advantages and disadvantages from both technical and business perspectives. The Top-Down Model is employed as a means to relate technology implementations to business objectives.

Process-Oriented Thinking Models

Local Area Networks: A Client/Server Approach provides process-oriented thinking models with which students can organize their problem solving approach. These models are reinforced and used throughout the text rather than merely being introduced in a single chapter on network design. Examples of such models include:

1. Top Down Model

2. Input-Processing-Output Model

3. Hardware-Software-Media Model

4. OSI Model

5. Client/Server Architecture Model

Most of these models are introduced in Part 1 of the text.

Business Cases

A real-world, practical approach to the industry is supported by the inclusion of business cases from professional periodicals in the text. Students are required to take real-world examples of implemented networking solutions and apply the facts of the case to the top-down model. In doing so, students are able to evaluate delivered networking functionality in terms of the implemented system's ability to deliver on stated business objectives. Additional questions are asked of the students as a means of gaining insight into the objective evaluation of real-world networking solutions. Questions also guide students toward development of analytical skills and business-oriented local area network design capabilities. Students are able to gain familiarity with the current real-world trends in local area network analysis and design while being provided with the assurance of explanations and supporting conceptual material supplied by the text.

These are not the full-blown business cases typical of MBA programs. Rather, they serve as a basis for students to organize real-world network information in a top-down model for discussion and analysis. Often, significant facts are missing from such news stories, forcing students to develop critical thinking and questioning skills.

Specialized Sections/Notations

In Sharper Focus *In Sharper Focus* sections highlight more detailed, more advanced, or background information for concepts introduced within a chapter. These sections can be included or excluded at the instructor's discretion.

Managerial Perspective *Managerial Perspective* sections take a "bottom-line" approach to local area network analysis and design. The potential business impact of management decisions in a variety of situations is highlighted in these sections which may be of particular interest to MBA audiences.

Applied Problem Solving Those sections of chapters which focus on the use of analytical models for *Applied Problem Solving* activities are highlighted for the benefit of both instructors and students. By stressing problem solving activities, students can be assured of learning how to *do* local area network analysis and design.

Practical Advice & Information Emphasizing the practical nature of the text, instances of practical advice or warnings are highlighted in order to call the reader's attention to important but often overlooked information.

■ ORGANIZATION

Overall Organization

Local Area Networks: A Client/Server Approach is divided into the following six major parts in order to maximize the flexible use of the text by a wide variety of course orientations:

1. Introduction to Local Area Networks and Client/Server Information Systems

2. Client and Server Technology

3. Local Area Networks Architectures, Hardware, & Software

4. Local Area Network Operating Systems

5. LAN Connectivity

6. Enterprise Networks

More detailed information regarding chapter headings and topics covered within these major parts can be found in the Detailed Table of Contents.

Each of the six major parts of the text begins with an introduction detailing how that part relates to the other parts of the book as well as how the chapters within that part relate to each other. The introduction provides the proverbial "big picture" so that the reader can understand how specific topics fit in the larger scheme of things. A key objective of the text is to keep the reader aware of how the information currently being read relates to previously covered material and to material yet to be covered. The Client/Server Architecture model, introduced in Chapter 2, is used as a point of reference for illustrating the relationship between concepts studied throughout the text.

Chapter Organization

Each chapter begins with an outline of new concepts introduced, previous concepts reinforced, and the learning objectives for that chapter. Section and paragraph headings help students to organize and identify key concepts introduced in each chapter. End of chapter material includes: Chapter summaries, key term listings with cross references to the page number in the chapter where the term first appeared, abundant review questions, as well as activities and problems for active student learning.

As previously mentioned, business cases from professional periodicals will be reprinted at the close of each chapter with associated analysis questions to be answered by students or used as the basis for classroom discussion. A liberal use of diagrams adds to both the usability of the text and the level of understanding of the students.

■ SUPPLEMENTS

Instructor's Resource Guide

The *Instructor's Resource Guide* recognizes the wide variance of backgrounds of instructors of local area networking courses. As a result, it is far more comprehensive than a typical instructor's guide. Additional lecture material and background information, not included in the student text, is included in the *Instructor's Resource Guide.* In addition, annotated transparency masters highlight the significance of individual diagrams and provide instructors with key points to be shared with students. In addition to providing solutions to the text's review questions and business cases, the *Instructor's Resource Guide* also provides additional test questions in a variety of formats.

Transparencies in PowerPoint Format

Included with the Instructor's Resource Guide are diskettes containing all of the diagrams and illustrations included in the text. In this manner, individual instructors have the flexibility to use these slides in their existing PowerPoint format, to print them out as transparencies, or to produce student notes versions of the illustrations with their own annotations.

■ INTENDED AUDIENCE

Due to the modular nature of this text, a variety of audiences/courses could be well served. Among the possible courses are the following:

- An introductory level course on local area networks. This may be the only data communications related course in a curriculum. The practical nature of the text would be appealing as well as its broad coverage and architectural orientation. Advanced sections of the text could be easily avoided.

- A course on information technology and architectures or client/server architectures could use the text thanks to its client server architecture organization and orientation. Local area networking issues could be covered in the summary chapters and in-depth and advanced networking chapters could be avoided.

- A junior level course on local area networks in either a lecture only or lab/lecture format. Such a course might be part of a concentration in data communications and networking or telecommunications. Advanced topics appropriate for such a course would be contained in Part 6 on Enterprise LANs. Also, one or more network operating systems could be studied in-depth in Part 4.

- As client/server information systems have taken on strategic importance to businesses, and local area networks are no longer just departmental computing solutions, the text may also have appeal in those MBA programs offering a concentration in M.I.S. The managerial perspective sections and business cases would have particular appeal to this potential audience.

- Certificate Programs offering a specialization in Client/Server Information Systems could effectively use the text for one or more courses.

■ ACKNOWLEDGMENTS

I am indebted to a number of people whose efforts were crucial in the development of this book.

For the outstanding quality illustrations which appear in the book as well as for his unwavering support, I'd like to thank Curt Snyder of Purdue University.

For his efforts in the creation of a meaningful and high quality instructors resource guide, I'd like to thank my colleague Dr. Mark Smith of the Computer Information Systems & Technology Department at Purdue University.

For overall technical support as well as the thorough review of Chapters 12 & 13, I'd like to thank Rick Smith of the Computer Information Systems & Technology Department at Purdue University.

For their collaborative efforts in turning a manuscript into a professional published book, I'd like to thank the following professionals at John Wiley & Sons:

Beth Lang Golub, Editor; Tony VenGraitis, Senior Production Editor; Dawn Stanley, Designer; Mark Cirillo, Manufacturing Manager; Anna Melhorn, Illustration Coordinator. Also, thanks to Donna King at Progressive Publishing Alternatives for her supervision of the production of the book.

Reviewers

A special debt of gratitude is owed to the professionals who were kind enough to review the manuscript of this book prior to publication. It is through your effort that an accurate text of high quality can be produced.

- Harvey Blessing, Essex Community College

- Kip Canfield, University of Maryland Baltimore County

- Mark Dishaw, University of Wisconsin-Oshkosh

- Nancy Groneman, Emporia State University
- Ross Hightower, Kansas State University
- Donald Huffman, Lorain County Community College
- Marlyn Kemper Littman, Nova Southeastern University
- Charles M. Morrison, University of Iowa
- David Preston, Eastfield College
- Julio C. Rivera, University of Alabama at Birmingham
- Sachi Sakthivel, Bowling Green State University
- Robert Schultheis, Southern Illinois University
- H. P. Stevenson, Raritan Valley Community College
- Tony Verstrate, Penn State University

CONTENTS

CHAPTER 9	LOCAL AREA NETWORK APPLICATIONS SOFTWARE	311

CHAPTER 12   WINDOWS NT   430

INTRODUCTION TO LOCAL AREA NETWORKS AND CLIENT/SERVER INFORMATION SYSTEMS

INTRODUCTION

Part 1 of *Local Area Networks: A Client/Server Approach* is intended to provide the reader with a general understanding of local area networks and client/server information systems. Chapters 1 and 2 conceptually describe the "big picture" before proceeding with more detailed technical analysis in subsequent chapters.

Most important, Part 1 introduces readers to many of the harsh realities of local area network analysis and design such as the following:

1. You will never know everything about local area networks.

2. Technology is changing so rapidly it is nearly impossible to keep your knowledge current.

3. Most, if not all, technology acquisitions must be cost-justified.

4. If the network doesn't make good business sense, it probably makes no sense.

5. Technology from different vendors often does not interoperate, despite what vendors may claim.

The problem-solving, analysis, and design skills required to cope successfully with these realities are introduced in Part 1 as well. Central to these problem-solving skills is the structured, methodical use of models and architectures.

Several models and architectures introduced in Part 1 are used periodically throughout the text.

Finally, having been introduced to *what* local area networks and client/server information systems are and *how* technology can be integrated to build such systems, Part 1 investigates *why* local area networks and client/server information systems are seen today as the vital infrastructure responsible for the successful delivery of business information.

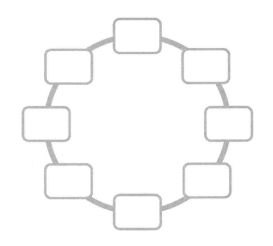

CHAPTER 1

LOCAL AREA NETWORKS: A BUSINESS PERSPECTIVE

Concepts Introduced

Local area networks	Logical network design
File transfer software	Protocols and compatibility
Printer/peripheral sharing devices	OSI seven-layer model
Network interface cards	Internet suite of protocols model
Network operating systems	I-P-O model
Top-down model	Business-oriented LAN analysis

OBJECTIVES

After mastering the material in this chapter you should:

1. Understand what a Local Area Network is.

2. Understand how hardware and software technology are combined to implement a LAN.

3. Understand the business needs and functional requirements fulfilled by a LAN.

4. Understand the use of the top-down model in business-oriented LAN analysis.

5. Understand the use of the OSI model and other models in LAN connectivity analysis.

■ WHAT IS A LOCAL AREA NETWORK?

A **Local Area Network (LAN)** is a combination of hardware and software technology that allows computers to share a variety of resources such as

- Printers and other peripheral devices.

- Data.

- Application programs.

- Storage devices.

LANs also allow messages to be sent between attached computers, thereby enabling users to work together electronically in a process often referred to as collaborative computing. The messaging capability of a LAN can be used by a variety of applications including e-mail, group scheduling, and fax servers. A category of software known as groupware supports a variety of collaborative computing applications. Groupware and other types of LAN software are explored in Chapter 9.

The local nature of a local area network is a relative rather than absolute concept. No hard and fast rule or definition of geographic limitations qualifies a network as a local area network. In general, LANs are confined to a single building or a small group of buildings.

LANs can be extended by connecting to other similar or dissimilar LANs, to remote users, or to mainframe computers. This process, generally referred to as LAN connectivity, is covered in depth in Part 5. LANs of a particular company can be connected to the LANs of trading partners such as vendors and customers. These trading partners may be located in the same town or around the globe. Arrangements linking these trading partners, commonly referred to as enterprise networks, are created by combining LANs with a variety of Wide Area Network (WAN) services. These are covered in Part 6.

Strictly speaking, the computers themselves are not part of the LAN. In other words, a single user could be productive on a standalone personal computer (PC). However, to allow sharing of information, resources, or messages with other users and their computers, a LAN must be implemented to connect these computers. The LAN is the combination of technologies that allow computers and their users to interact.

Figure 1-1 provides a conceptual illustration of a LAN.

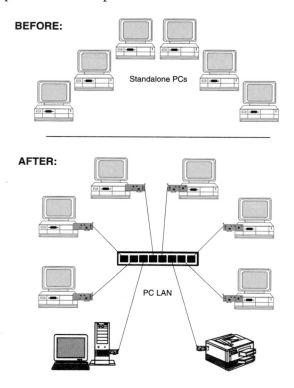

The same PCs with the addition of a Local Area Network (LAN). A LAN is a combination of hardware and software technology that enables communication and resource sharing among attached computers.

Figure 1-1   What is a Local Area Network?

Alternatives to Local Area Networks

A Local Area Network is not the only way for computers to share peripheral devices and send messages or files to each other. Two major non-LAN connectivity alternatives are

- **File transfer software.**
- **Printer/peripheral sharing devices.**

It is important to consider these LAN alternatives carefully if the functionality they offer meets stated business and functional requirements. The sophistication offered by LANs comes at a price in terms of both dollars and the level of technical expertise required to install and manage them.

File Transfer Software   Not all networking needs are of a permanent nature, requiring the installation and administration of a LAN. Not all personal computers sit on one desk or worktable all day. Recognizing both the proliferation of portable/notebook computers and the need for occasional or temporary networking of personal computers, a powerful and easy-to-use category of networking software known as file transfer software has developed.

Figure 1-2 summarizes possible business applications, currently available functionality, and technical requirements and characteristics of file transfer software. No

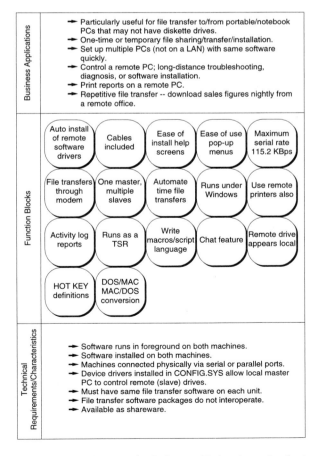

Figure 1-2   File Transfer Software Technology Analysis

single package is likely to provide all the available functionality blocks listed. The function blocks are provided to enable users to decide which are important to support their individual business applications.

Having identified required functionality, possible purchase options can be objectively reviewed by consulting either a recent product comparative review in a professional periodical or manufacturer's literature. Among the current products available in the category are LapLink and FastLynx. Both are available for about $100 to $125, with color-coded cables to connect PCs via serial or parallel ports as well as all necessary software. Some file transfer software products, such as LapLink V, can communicate simultaneously with multiple personal computers.

The key operational characteristic of all file transfer software is that it runs in the foreground on linked PCs. While the file transfer software runs over DOS or, in some cases, within Windows, no other applications programs (word processing, spreadsheets, database) can run. This need to run in the foreground limits file transfer software's business uses to temporary networking requirements such as occasional file transfer, remote file access, or remote printer access. Some file transfer software packages include the ability to control a remote PC. An entire category of software known as remote control or remote access software, such as the Norton pcAnywhere, ReachOut Remote Control, and CarbonCopy, is reviewed in Chapter 15. They sell for around $199.

Another important operational feature is that only one of the two or more linked PCs is really in control of the file transfer session. This active PC, commonly known as the "master" PC, can transfer files to or from the passive or "slave" PC and can access files or printers on the slave PC or the network to which the slave PC is attached. The passive PC merely runs the file transfer software during the session and accepts commands from the active or master PC.

FILE TRANSFER SOFTWARE APPLICATIONS

In Sharper Focus

File transfer software is popular among information systems professionals responsible for maintenance and troubleshooting of personal computers as well as among auditors and other field-service personnel. When PCs are not connected to LANs, updating software or diagnosing problems can be very time-consuming. The software's script language and transfer automation capabilities allow a PC support person to load a software upgrade on a portable PC equipped with file transfer software and move from one PC to another to update all necessary files with a single key stroke.

In some cases, portable or notebook PCs may have no diskette drive at all, or the drive's size or density may be incompatible with another PC with which it must transfer data files. File transfer software is an ideal solution to this problem, as the transfer of data actually takes place via the PC's serial or parallel ports. For ease of use and installation, some file transfer software packages also include the necessary cables to physically link PCs. Software such as Mac-in-DOS and MacLink Plus/PC Connect provide conversion between Macintosh and DOS or Windows file formats in addition to traditional file transfer capabilities.

Thanks to a piece of software known as a device driver, the slave PC's disk drives, and the files contained therein, appear on the master PC as local or virtual drives. They are called virtual drives because they appear to be attached locally although they are not actually contained in the master PC. A device driver tells the operating system how to control peripheral devices such as disk drives, printers, and network interface cards. Its name and location are added as a line in a file called CONFIG.SYS. This system configuration file is read and executed when a DOS-based PC is first powered up or booted. The device drivers are thus loaded into memory, "fooling" the local (master) PC into thinking that the remote (slave) PC's disk drives are directly attached to it and locally accessible.

It should be noted that file transfer is distinct from file sharing. File transfer sends a copy of a file from one device to another, whereas with file sharing two users have access to a file simultaneously. File sharing as a business requirement falls into the realm of Local Area Networking and exceeds the capabilities of file transfer software or peripheral sharing devices.

As you review the functionality and possible business applications of file transfer software, keep in mind its very affordable price: generally around $100 to $200. Although it can't replace a full-function LAN, it can be a real time-saver and, as the saying goes, time is money.

Printer/Peripheral Sharing Devices Printer/peripheral sharing devices are often ignored as potential connectivity solutions by uninformed users and aggressive salespeople who see LANs as the sole answer to PC connectivity requirements. Cost per connected PC can be as low as $5 for peripheral sharing devices and as high as $1000 for a sophisticated LAN. Additional costs, such as the need to hire technically oriented personnel to manage LANs, add to the overall impact of PC connectivity decision making.

The business motivation that usually brings one to non–LAN PC connectivity is the recognition of the large expense involved in equipping individual PC users with their own dedicated printers. Resource sharing is an obvious solution as users need access to a printer, but not necessarily their own individual printer.

The key challenge of PC connectivity analysis is to grant this access to shared printers while maximizing the productivity of PC–based workers. The trick is to find the best connectivity solution for a given situation in terms of both delivered functionality and cost. Incorrect analysis of the situation may yield unsatisfactory results. Potential non–LAN PC connectivity solutions range from manual switches costing as little as $10 to printer sharing systems costing several hundred dollars. Delivered functionality must always be compared with that delivered by LANs, which can cost anywhere from $100 to $1500 per connected PC.

The specific business activities involved with peripheral sharing are relatively straightforward:

1. Users may wish to share one or more printers among numerous PCs.

2. Users may wish to share one or more modems among numerous PCs. This is known as accessing a modem pool.

3. Users may also wish to send e-mail or transfer files to one another.

4. Users may wish to occasionally log onto a minicomputer or mainframe. Given the occasional nature of this use, it is important to minimize the number of minicomputer or mainframe ports dedicated to this purpose.

Beginning with these four general business uses, one should undertake a more thorough analysis of peripheral sharing needs to assist in selecting from the currently available peripheral sharing technology. Figure 1-3 outlines a series of questions to yield a more specific set of technical requirements.

These technical requirements can be compared to the non–LAN PC connectivity technology analysis grid (Fig. 1-4) for initial possible technology solutions. The technology analysis grid maps peripheral sharing functionality, on the vertical axis, against available technology alternatives on the horizontal axis. Intersections indicate whether a given feature or function is standard or occasionally included in a given device. For example, if the answer to question 12 regarding the need to transfer files and e-mail was affirmative, then referring to the technology analysis grid, only data switches and data PBXs would need to be explored further. The purpose of the technology analysis grid is not to provide definite and final answers but rather to guide product research in a time-efficient manner. Each technology alternative listed in the grid is described briefly in the following section.

Non–LAN PC Connectivity Analysis Questions

1. How many PCs will be involved in this peripheral sharing arrangement?

2. How many printers will be involved in this peripheral sharing arrangement?

3. Are the printers parallel or serial?

4. Will the PCs be linked to the printers through their parallel or serial ports?

5. Will serial-to-parallel or parallel-to-serial conversion be required?

6. Will any of the printers be laser printers?

7. What is the nature of the print jobs sent to these printers? mostly large jobs? mostly numerous small jobs?

8. Will users tolerate "printer busy" messages, or must a printer always be available?

9. Is the number of PCs or printers likely to change either totally or relatively (PC-to-printer ratio)?

10. Will simultaneous printouts be needed at more than one location?

11. Will any printers be located more than 100 ft from the PCs?

12. Will users wish to exchange files and e-mail?

13. Will users be sending graphics data to plotters or printers?

14. Will users be sharing modems or fax machines?

15. Will some printers or PCs be transmitting at different speeds than others?

16. Will PCs need occasional access to minicomputers or mainframes?

17. Will Macintosh computers be sharing peripherals as well?

18. Will any users need the ability to maintain multiple communications sessions simultaneously?

19. Will any printers be dedicated to particular forms (letterhead, envelopes, multipart invoices, etc.)?

Figure 1-3 Business Analysis Questions for Non–LAN PC Connectivity

Technology Analysis Grid

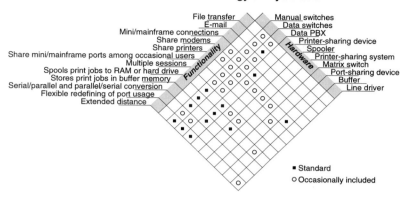

Figure 1-4   Non–LAN PC Connectivity Technology Analysis Grid

NON – LAN PC CONNECTIVITY TECHNOLOGY

The simplest of printer sharing devices is a **manual switch**, also known as a mechanical switch or an A/B switch. Up to six PCs can share a single printer in such an arrangement. The switch must be physically set to give each user access to the printer. If the printer is busy, all other users must wait.

Close physical proximity of all users to the shared printer is key to the success of such a setup. All users should ideally be within sight or talking distance of one another to efficiently coordinate the switching of printer access from one user to another. Manual switches are most often manufactured with a fixed number of serial and/or parallel ports. Input (PC) and output (printer) ports are most often of a fixed number and not interchangeable.

An important incremental improvement on the manual switch is the simple **electronic switch**. This device is especially important if a laser printer is among the printers to be shared. The small voltage spike generated with physical switching of a manual switch is potentially damaging to a laser printer's circuit boards. Electronic switches are often manufactured with built-in software, which scans attached PCs for waiting print jobs. User intervention is not necessary with these scanning electronic switches. Users either have immediate access to the printer or receive a "printer busy" message. As soon as the printer is free, the electronic switch automatically connects a waiting PC with the available printer. Buffered and non-buffered printer sharers, data switches, and data PBXs all use electronic switching.

For serial-to-parallel or parallel-to-serial conversion, a more expensive device, commonly known as a **data switch**, is a possible solution. Serial-to-parallel and parallel-to-serial conversion are also available in standalone conversion devices. Data switches also offer greater overall capacity in terms of both expandability and total number of PCs and printers that can be attached, as well as more advanced features that will be discussed shortly.

When a printer is busy printing, other users have to wait until it is available. Depending on the peripheral sharing device in use, they may get some sort of "printer busy" message. Buffer memory, spooling software, and queuing software are either added to existing peripheral sharing devices or built into standalone devices to overcome this "printer busy" message, thereby increasing worker productivity.

Buffer memory allows print jobs to be offloaded from a PC immediately, whether or not a printer is available, allowing the PC user to return to work. When an appropriate printer becomes available, the print job is downloaded from the buffer memory to the printer. This buffer memory may be in a standalone device called a **buffer** or integrated into a data switch or printer-sharing device. Additional buffer memory can usually be added to existing devices in the form of buffer memory upgrades. Specialized buffers prepare graphical data for plotters or graphics printers. These graphics buffers, sometimes called **plotter emulation buffers**, allow PCs running graphics software to download graphics output quickly, thereby freeing the PCs for more productive uses.

Spooling software works in a slightly different way to keep PCs from waiting for available printers. Rather than store copies of print jobs in buffer memory, spooling software "spools" a copy of the print job either into the PC's random access memory (RAM) or onto its hard drive. Spooling software also has the ability to simultaneously send multiple copies of a given print job to multiple printers, if this is a required peripheral sharing business activity. Standalone **spoolers** store copies of print jobs in their own buffer memory. The word spool is actually an acronym that stands for simultaneous peripheral operations on line.

Devices that send printouts to multiple printers often include **queue management** software. This software manages and monitors the distribution of print jobs to various printers. It also allows printers to be enabled, disabled, or assigned to different PCs. If business requirements dictate the need for several printers serving numerous PCs, it may be wise to look into the sophistication of the peripheral sharing device's queue management software.

Because manual switches, electronic switches, and buffered printer sharers are usually manufactured with a fixed number of serial and parallel ports, which are defined as either input (PC) or output (printer) ports, it is important to know the following:

1. How many PCs and printers are likely to be in the printer sharing arrangement?

2. Do they communicate via serial or parallel ports?

Some printer sharers are expandable, whereas others are not. It is therefore important to know the likelihood of your needing expanded peripheral sharing before you make a purchase decision.

The customary difference between buffered printer sharers and data switches, as outlined in the technology analysis grid, is the ability of data switches to redefine ports from input to output and vice-versa. In other words, data switches are more flexible, allowing port characteristics to be changed as peripheral sharing needs change. These port characteristics include port speed, which can vary widely, especially among printers. Sophisticated data switches are also able to send e-mail and transfer files between attached PCs. Some data switches also allow connection to minicomputers, mainframes, and modem pools. When users want a printout, the data switch's buffer memory and spooling software allow them to continue working, even if the requested printer is busy. In summary, the most sophisticated data switches are like "networks in a box," delivering both flexible connectivity and buffering and spooling ability.

A type of data switch known as a **matrix switch** allows all possible combinations of connections among attached input and output devices.

More sophisticated user business requirements need significantly more sophisticated peripheral sharing devices, inevitably increasing acquisition costs. Users occasionally need access from their PCs to more than printers. Common PC connectivity requirements include access to modems, fax machines, minicomputers, and mainframes.

Occasionally, Apple Macintosh computers or "dumb" asynchronous terminals may need to be part of the peripheral sharing arrangement. With the need for access to these sophisticated devices comes a need to arbitrate what is known as port contention. It would not be cost-effective to assign each of these occasional users a permanent port and connection to the minicomputer or mainframe, but port sharing orchestrates the sharing of a limited number of ports among many PC users. This port sharing feature can be incorporated into a standalone device, usually known as a **port sharing device**, or integrated into a sophisticated peripheral sharing device known as a **data PBX**. As mentioned earlier, some data switches offer minicomputer and mainframe connections as well as port sharing abilities.

Data PBXs allow flexible interconnection of PCs, Macs, printers, modems, fax machines, asynchronous terminals, minicomputers, and mainframes. They provide port sharing ability and allow for the transfer of e-mail and files among connected devices, provided that appropriate e-mail or file transfer software has been installed on the communicating PCs or computers. Data PBXs can also allow multiple sessions or multiple connections between a given PC and other available connected services.

Data PBXs may not store print jobs by either buffering or spooling. A data PBX's job, just like that of a voice PBX, is to establish, maintain, and terminate connections between devices as requested. If the requested printer is busy, a "busy message" of some type is generated. Technically, this is the major difference between data switches and data PBXs. In general, data PBXs are concerned only with creating connections between attached devices, whereas data switches provide additional buffering, spooling, and queue management capabilities. In practice, however, the terms *data switch* and *data PBX* are often used interchangeably.

Occasionally, an entire **printer sharing system**, including buffered printer sharing device, spooling and queue management software, cables, and adapters to connect the cables to the PCs and printers, is combined and sold as one product. This all-in-one approach takes the worry out of buying the correct cables to properly connect a standalone printer sharing device to all of its associated personal computers and printers.

■ HOW IS A LOCAL AREA NETWORK IMPLEMENTED?

This text is mostly dedicated to answering the previous question What is a LAN? The purpose of this section, however, is merely to introduce, in a highly conceptual manner, how a simple LAN is implemented. Complex LAN interconnectivity, LAN remote access, and LAN-to-mainframe connectivity are intentionally ignored in this discussion.

To begin with, appropriate networking hardware and software must be added to every computer or shared peripheral device that is to communicate via the LAN. Some type of network medium must physically connect the various networked computers and peripheral devices. The various connected computers and peripheral devices share this medium to converse with each other. As a result, LANs are sometimes more specifically referred to as **shared media LANs** or media-sharing LANs. Figure 1-5 provides a highly conceptual view of how a shared media LAN might be implemented.

Do not be fooled by the figure's apparent simplicity. All of the illustrated

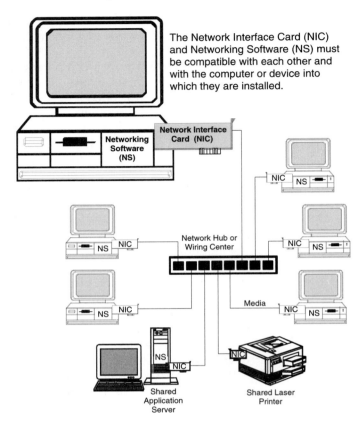

Figure 1-5   How is a Local Area Network implemented?

networking hardware and software must be compatible not only with the computer or peripheral device in which it is installed, but also with the hardware and software that compose the LAN itself and the networking hardware and software installed on all other computers and peripheral devices attached to the LAN. Compatibility refers to the ability of hardware and software, manufactured by various vendors, to work together successfully without intervention by the end user. In other words, the combination of compatible hardware and software technology is transparent to the end users who see only that they are receiving the information they need to do their job effectively.

Networking Hardware

The following are among the possible types of networking hardware employed in implementing a LAN.

- Network interface cards, which must be installed in every linked computer and peripheral device.
- Some type of network hub or wiring center into which the networked devices can be physically linked.

Most, but not all, LAN-connected PCs require specialized network interface cards (NICs). Rather than using NICs, zero-slot LANs, described and illustrated in Chapter 8, use existing serial or parallel ports of PCs and peripheral devices for communication. Given the relative slow speeds of the serial and parallel ports compared to most NICs, zero-slot LANs are usually limited to two to four users.

Appropriately named, the **network interface card** (or adapter) provides a transparent interface between the shared media of the LAN and the computer in which it is physically installed. The NIC takes messages that the computer directs it to send to other LAN-attached computers or devices and formats them in a manner appropriate for transport over the LAN. Conversely, messages arriving from the LAN are reformatted into a form understandable by the local computer. To ensure compatibility, all hardware and software technology interacting on the LAN must adhere to the same agreed upon message format.

Most LANs today use some type of **hub**, also known as a wiring hub or wiring center. The reasons most LANs use hubs as well as descriptions of LANs that don't use hubs are explained further in Chapter 7 on LAN architectures and topologies. The hub provides a connecting point through which all attached devices are able to converse with one another. Hubs must be compatible with both the attached media and the NICs that are installed in client PCs.

Networking Software

Following are some types of possible networking software employed in implementing a LAN.

- Software that allows PCs that are physically attached to the LAN to share networked resources such as printers, data, and applications.

- Software that runs on shared network devices such as printers, data storage devices, and application servers that allow them to be shared by multiple LAN-attached users.

A standalone (not LAN-attached) PC requires software to operate. Commonly referred to as the operating system, this software interfaces between application programs such as a word processing program and the client hardware (CPU, memory, disk drive). Operating systems and other client software not related to attaching to a LAN are discussed further in Chapter 4.

The software that runs on PCs and allows them to log into a LAN and converse with other LAN-attached devices is sometimes referred to as client software or client network software. A **client** PC is a computer that a user logs into to access LAN-attached resources and services. A LAN-attached client PC is sometimes characterized as a service requester. The client network software must be compatible with the network software running on all LAN-attached clients and servers. This compatibility is most easily ensured by having both the clients and the servers install the same **network operating system** software. Examples of popular network operating systems are NetWare, Vines, and Windows NT (not to be confused with Windows). LAN software is discussed in Chapters 9 through 13.

Servers such as application servers and print servers are usually dedicated computers accessed only through LAN connections. Whereas a client could be considered a service requester, servers are characterized as service providers. It stands to reason that the server's job of quickly and efficiently fulfilling the requests of multiple LAN-attached clients is more complicated than a single LAN-attached client making a single request for a service. Therefore, the server version of a particular network operating system is more complex, expensive, and larger than the client version of the same system. Client and server versions of network operating systems are purchased separately. Client licenses are usually purchased in groups (5-user,

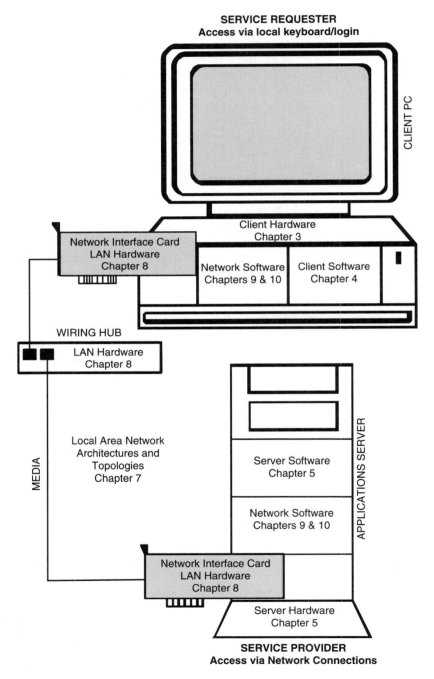

Figure 1-6 Visual Table of Contents of LAN-related Topics

25-user, 100-user), whereas server licenses are most often purchased individually. Servers occasionally require additional software beyond what the server version of the network operating system supplies. Such software is discussed in Chapter 5.

Compatibility is again an issue, because any network operating system must be compatible with the operating system and hardware of the client or server on which it is installed. Additionally, the network operating system software must be able to communicate successfully with the installed network interface card. The specifics of network operating system or network interface card compatibility are discussed further in Chapter 8. Compatibility issues and analysis in general are discussed later in this chapter, in the section entitled Introduction to Protocols and Compatibility.

Networking Media

Network media vary widely depending on required transmission speed and a variety of other factors such as network interface card type, security needs, and the physical environment in which the media are to be deployed. Even the air can serve as a LAN medium, as evidenced by the many wireless LAN alternatives currently available.

LAN media must be installed carefully and according to industry standard specifications. Something as innocent as pulling a cable tie too tightly can wreak havoc on high-speed LANs. LAN media must be compatible with network interface cards and hubs or wiring centers. LAN media alternatives and selection criteria are reviewed in Chapter 7.

Figure 1-6 offers a visual guide to further information on the elements of a LAN discussed in the previous section.

■ WHY ARE LOCAL AREA NETWORKS IMPLEMENTED?

Business Needs — The Underlying Motivation

Business needs, as articulated by management, are not inherently local area networking business needs, nor do they necessarily imply LANs as a business solution. Only by analyzing business activities and asking business analysis questions can you determine whether or not a local area networking solution is appropriate.

Business needs or perspectives provide the motivation for further business network analysis and design. Clearly understanding management's perspectives before you begin any technical analysis makes it easier to sell proposals to management afterward, with the assurance that the proposals will meet management's business objectives. These business needs and perspectives provide the network analyst with a frame of reference within which to conduct research and evaluate options. Figure 1-7 lists a few typical business needs and perspectives that may lead to local area networking solutions.

These high-level business needs and perspectives are representative examples, typical of the kinds of upper-level management priorities often articulated. Many other possible business needs or perspectives could have been listed. Business needs and perspectives are dynamic, changing in response to changing economic and competitive climates, management teams, and philosophies.

To make this exercise in business-oriented LAN analysis and design most effective, add business needs and perspectives that management has articulated to you.

- Information is a corporate asset to be leveraged to competitive advantage.

- Data accessibility must increase.

- Customer service must improve.

- Saving money, reducing expenses are priorities.

- Productivity must increase.

- More bandwidth to the desktop is needed for greater data accessibility.

- Information systems must be
  - Reliable.
  - Easy to install and use.
  - Well supported.
  - Affordable.
  - Secure.

- Information systems must minimize the need for large staffs of highly trained and high-salaried technically oriented individuals.

Figure 1-7   Business Needs and Perspectives that May Lead to Local Area Networking Solutions

Management's business needs and perspectives should be clearly documented and understood before you begin network analysis and design. These same needs and perspectives should be referred to on a continual basis, as a means of testing the feasibility of various technical networking options.

Although not all business needs and perspectives are necessarily solved by implementing LANs, it can be unequivocally stated that LANs should only be implemented if they meet stated business needs. Furthermore, the analysis and design methodology that leads to LAN implementation should be structured and documentable, to justify conclusions and recommendations. The business needs and perspectives listed in Figure 1-7 provide a basis for further business-oriented LAN analysis and design later in this chapter.

The Importance of Effective LAN Analysis and Design

Given that LANs are implemented to solve real-world business needs, as articulated by senior management, and that recommended solutions must be both justifiable and documentable, it is essential that LAN analysis and design be conducted in a structured, effective manner. As will be seen in the following section, effective LAN analysis and design can be an overwhelming task because of the number of possible pieces of hardware and software technology manufactured by different vendors that may have to interoperate. From a business perspective, senior management wants assurance that money invested in technology will have the desired business impact.

Managerial Perspective

Chief executive officers seek business solutions, not technical solutions. They are concerned with keeping information technology spending practices properly aligned with strategic business objectives. Furthermore, senior business executives realize that the most expensive technology is not always the best at delivering business solutions; in fact, less expensive technology is often sufficient. Perhaps most important, CEOs are concerned with the inevitable, constant, accelerating rate of technological change. Having a well-defined, strategic technology plan and infrastructure closely aligned with business strategic plans is the best way to prevent technological obsolescence from determining business outcomes.

Mapping business strategic plans to technological strategic plans is the purpose of LAN analysis and design. If we understand the challenges to effective LAN analysis and design, the proposed solutions and resultant methodology should be more meaningful. The remainder of this chapter explains the challenges and solutions to effective LAN analysis and design and provides an example of how to get started with business-oriented LAN analysis and design.

■ CHALLENGES AND SOLUTIONS TO EFFECTIVE LAN ANALYSIS, DESIGN, AND IMPLEMENTATION

Challenge: Information Technology Investment versus Productivity Gains, to Ensure Implemented Technology Meets Business Needs

In the past decade, business has invested over $1 trillion in information technology. Despite this massive investment, carefully conducted research indicates that little if any increase in productivity has occurred as a direct result. This dilemma is known as the **productivity paradox**. Clearly, something is wrong with an analysis and design process that recommends technology implementations that fail to meet strategic business objectives of increased productivity.

What characteristics are required in an analysis and design process to overcome the productivity paradox?

Applied Problem Solving

Solution: The Top-Down Approach

To overcome the productivity paradox, one must follow a structured methodology that ensures the implemented network meets the communications needs of the intended business, organization, or individual. One such structured methodology is known as the top-down approach. Such an approach is graphically illustrated in the **top-down model** shown in Figure 1-8. The approach is relatively straightforward.

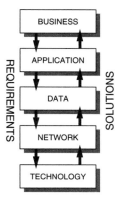

Figure 1-8   The Top-Down Model

Insisting on a top-down approach to network analysis and design should ensure that the network design implemented will meet the business needs and objectives that motivated the design in the first place.

This top-down approach requires network analysts to understand business constraints and objectives, as well as information systems applications and the data on which they run, before considering data communications and networking options.

Notice where the network layer occurs in the top-down model. It is no accident that data communications and networking form the foundation of today's sophisticated information systems. A properly designed network supports flexible delivery of data to distributed application programs, allowing businesses to respond quickly to customer needs and rapidly changing market conditions.

The Top-Down Model How does the proper use of the top-down model ensure effective, business-oriented LAN analysis and design? Figure 1-9 lists the analysis processes associated with each layer of the top-down model.

Top-Down Model Layer	Associated Analysis Processes
Business Layer	<ul><li>Strategic business planning.</li><li>Business process reengineering.</li><li>Identifying major business functions.</li><li>Identifying business processes.</li><li>Identifying business opportunities.</li></ul>
Applications Layer	<ul><li>Applications development.</li><li>Systems analysis and design.</li><li>Identifying information needs.</li><li>Relating information needs to business processes and opportunities.</li></ul>
Data Layer	<ul><li>Database analysis and design.</li><li>Data modeling.</li><li>Data distribution analysis.</li><li>Client/server architecture design.</li><li>Distributed database design.</li><li>Relating data collection and distribution to information and business needs.</li></ul>
Network Layer	<ul><li>Network analysis and design.</li><li>Logical network design (what).</li><li>Network implementation planning.</li><li>Network management and performance monitoring.</li><li>Relating logical network design to data collection and distribution design.</li></ul>
Technology Layer	<ul><li>Technology analysis grids.</li><li>Hardware-software-media technology analysis.</li><li>Physical network design (how).</li><li>Physical network implementation.</li><li>Relating physical network design to logical network design.</li></ul>

Figure 1-9 Analysis Processes of the Top-Down Model

One must start with the *business*-level objectives. What is the company (organization, individual) trying to accomplish by installing this network? Without clearly understanding business-level objectives, it is nearly impossible to configure and implement a successful network. In many cases, businesses take this opportunity to critically reexamine their business processes in an analysis methodology known as **business process reengineering** (BPR). BPR and its relationship to client/server information systems are discussed further in Chapter 2.

Once business-level objectives are understood, one must understand the *applications* that will be running on the computer systems attached to these networks. After all, the applications will be generating the traffic that travels over the implemented network.

Once applications are understood and have been documented, the *data* those applications generate must be examined. In this case, the term *data* is used in a general sense, as today's networks are likely to transport a variety of payloads including voice, video, image, and fax in addition to true data. Data traffic analysis must determine not only the amount of data to be transported, but also important characteristics about the nature of that data.

Once data traffic analysis has been completed, the following should be known:

1. Physical locations of data (Where?)

2. Data characteristics and compatibility issues (What?)

3. Amount of data generated and transported (How much?)

Given these requirements, as determined by the upper layers of the top-down model, the next job is to determine the requirements of the *network* capable of delivering these data in a timely, cost-effective manner. These network performance criteria could be referred to as *what* the implemented network must do to meet the business objectives outlined at the outset of this top-down analysis. These requirements are also sometimes referred to as the **logical network design**.

The *technology* layer analysis, in contrast, determines *how* various hardware and software components will be combined to build a functional network to meet predetermined business objectives. The delineation of required technology is often referred to as the **physical network design**.

Overall, the relationship between the layers of the top-down model could be described as follows: analysis at upper layers produces requirements that are passed down to lower layers, while solutions meeting these requirements are passed back to upper layers. If this relationship among layers holds true throughout the business-oriented network analysis, then the implemented technology (bottom layer) should meet the initially outlined business objectives (top layer)—hence the name, the top-down approach.

Challenge: Analysis of Complex LAN Connectivity and Compatibility Issues

Assuming that the proper use of the top-down model will ensure that implemented technical solutions will meet stated business requirements, the more technical challenges of LAN analysis and design must be addressed.

Introduction to Protocols and Compatibility   In previous discussions of how LANs are implemented, the term **compatibility** was introduced and explained. Solving incompatibility problems is at the heart of successful LAN implementation. Compatibility can be thought of as successfully bridging the gap or communicating between two or more technology components, whether hardware or software. This logical gap between components is commonly referred to as an **interface**.

Interfaces may be physical (hardware to hardware), as in the following examples:

- Cables physically connecting to serial ports on a computer.

- A network interface card physically plugging into the expansion bus inside a computer.

Interfaces may also be logical or software-oriented (software to software), as in the following:

- A network operating system client software (Windows for Workgroups) communicating with the client PC's operating system (DOS).

- A client-based data query tool (Microsoft Excel) gathering data from a large database management system (Oracle).

Finally, interfaces may cross the hardware to software boundary:

- Network operating system—specific software known as a driver, which interfaces to an installed network interface card (NIC).

- Operating system software known as a kernel, which interfaces to a computer's CPU chip.

These various interfaces can be bridged successfully, thereby supporting compatibility between components, because of **protocols**. Protocols are nothing more than rules for how communicating hardware and software components bridge interfaces or talk to one another. Protocols may be proprietary (used exclusively by one or more vendors) or open (used freely by all interested parties). Protocols may be officially sanctioned by international standards–making bodies such as the International Standards Organization (ISO) or purely market driven (de facto protocols). Figure 1-10 illustrates the relationship between interfaces, protocols, and compatibility.

For every potential hardware to hardware, software to software, and hardware to software interface imaginable, one or more possible protocols are likely to be supported. The sum of all the protocols employed in a particular computer is sometimes referred to as that computer's **protocol stack**. The ability to determine which protocols must be supported in which instances for the multitude of interfaces possible in a complicated LAN design is likely to make the difference between success and failure in a LAN implementation.

How can a network analyst possibly keep track of all potential interfaces and their associated protocols between all LAN-attached devices? What is needed is a framework in which to organize the various potential interfaces and protocols in such complicated internetwork designs. More than one such framework, or communications architecture, exists. Two of the most popular communications architectures are the seven-layer OSI Model and the four-layer Internet Suite of Protocols Model.

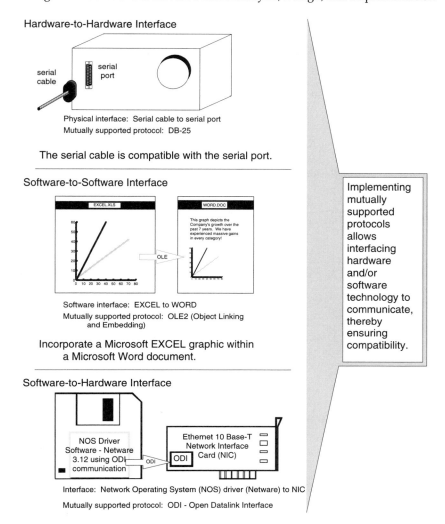

Figure 1-10   Interfaces, Protocols, and Compatibility

**Applied
Problem
Solving**

Solution: The OSI Model

Determining which technology and protocols to employ to meet the requirements determined in the logical network design, yielded from the network layer of the top-down model, requires a structured methodology. Fortunately, the ISO has developed a framework for organizing networking technology and protocol solutions known as the **Open Systems Interconnection (OSI) model,** illustrated in Figure 1-11. This section is intended to offer the reader only a brief introduction to the model's overall functionality as a network analysis tool. The OSI model is covered in greater detail throughout the remainder of the text.

The OSI model divides the communication between any two networked computing devices into seven layers or categories. Network analysts literally talk in terms of the OSI model. When troubleshooting LAN problems, the savvy network analyst inevitably starts with the physical layer (layer 1) and ensures that protocols and interfaces at each layer are operational before moving up the OSI model. The model allows data communications technology developers as well as

OSI Model Layer	Functionality	Automobile Assembly Line
7: Application	User application programs interact and receive services	Dealer-installed options: options desired by users are added at the dealership
6: Presentation	Ensures reliable session transmission between applications; takes care of differences in data representation	Painting and finish work: the vehicle is painted and trim is applied
5: Session	Enables two applications to communicate across the network	Interior: seats and dashboard are added to passenger compartment
4: Transport	Ensures reliable transmission from end to end, usually across multiple nodes	Electrical: electrical system and components are added
3: Network	Sets up the pathways or end-to-end connections, usually across a long distance, or multiple nodes	Body: passenger compartment and fenders are attached to the chassis
2: Data Link	Puts messages together, attaches proper headers to be sent out or received, ensures messages are delivered between two points	Engine/drive train: Engine and transmission components provide the vehicle with propulsion
1: Physical	Concerned with transmitting bits of data over a physical medium	Chassis/frame: steel is fabricated to form the chassis on which all other components will travel

Figure 1-11   The OSI Model

standards developers to talk about the interconnection of two networks or computers in common terms without dealing in proprietary vendor jargon.

These "common terms" are the result of the layered architecture of the seven-layer OSI model. The architecture breaks the task of two computers communicating to each other into separate but interrelated tasks, each represented by its own layer. As can be seen in Figure 1-11, the top layer (layer 7), which represents the services offered application programs running on each computer, is aptly named the application layer. The bottom or physical layer (layer 1) is concerned with the actual physical connection of the two computers or networks. The remaining layers (2 through 6) may not be as obvious, but nonetheless represent sufficiently distinct logical groups of functions required to connect two computers to justify separate layers. As you will see later in the text, some of the layers are divided into sublayers.

To use the OSI model, a network analyst lists the known protocols for each computing device or network node in the proper layer of its own seven-layer OSI model. The collection of these known protocols in their proper layers is known as the protocol stack of the network node. For example, the physical medium employed, such as unshielded twisted pair, coaxial cable or fiberoptic cable, is entered as a layer 1 protocol, while ethernet or token ring network architectures might be entered as a layer 2 protocol. As will be seen in the text covering network operating systems, a given computer may employ more than one protocol on one or more layers of the OSI model. Such computers are described as supporting multiple protocol stacks, or simply multiprotocol.

The OSI model allows network analysts to produce an accurate inventory of the protocols present on any given network node. This protocol profile represents the unique personality of each network node and gives the network analyst some insight into what **protocol conversion**, if any, may be necessary to get any two network nodes to communicate successfully. Ultimately, the OSI model provides a structured methodology for determining what hardware and software technology the physical network design will need to meet logical network design requirements.

Perhaps the best analogy for the OSI reference model, which illustrates its architectural or framework purpose, is that of an automobile assembly line. Although each process or step is managed and performed independently, each step depends on previous steps being performed according to standardized specifications or protocols for the success of the overall process, the production of a functional vehicle.

Similarly, each layer of the OSI model operates independently of all other layers, while depending on neighboring layers to perform according to specification and cooperating to complete the overall task of communication between two computers or networks.

The OSI model is not a protocol or group of protocols. It is a standardized, empty framework into which protocols can be listed to perform effective LAN analysis and design. As will be seen later, however, the ISO has also produced a set of OSI protocols that correspond to some of the OSI model layers. It is important to differentiate between the OSI model and OSI protocols.

The OSI model is used throughout the remainder of the text in analyzing the protocols stacks of various network operating systems and the analysis and design of advanced LAN connectivity alternatives.

Solution: The Internet Suite of Protocols Model

Although the OSI model is perhaps more famous than any OSI protocol, just the opposite could be said for a model and associated protocols known as the **Internet Suite of Protocols model**. Also known as the TCP/IP Protocol Suite or TCP/IP Architecture, this communications architecture takes its name from **TCP/IP (Transmission Control Protocol/Internet Protocol)**, the de facto standard protocols for open systems internetworking. As Figure 1-12 shows, TCP and IP are just two of the protocols associated with this model.

Like the OSI model, the TCP/IP model is a layered communications architecture in which upper layers use the functionality offered by the protocols of the lower layers. Each layer's protocols are able to operate independently from those of other layers. For example, protocols on a given layer can be updated or modified without having to change all other protocols in all other layers. A recent example is the new version of IP known as IPng (IP next generation), which was developed in response to a pending shortage of IP addresses. This proposed change is possible

Layer	OSI	INTERNET	Data Format	Protocols
7	Application	Application	Messages or Streams	TELNET FTP TFTP SMTP SNMP CMOT MIB
6	Presentation			
5	Session	Transport or Host-Host	Transport Protocol Packets	TCP UDP
4	Transport			
3	Network	Internet	IP Diagrams	IP
2	Data Link	Network Access	Frames	
1	Physical			

Figure 1-12   Internet Suite of Protocols versus OSI

without changing all other protocols in the TCP/IP communication architecture. The exact mechanics of TCP/IP and related protocols is explored in greater depth in Chapter 13.

Figure 1-12 compares the four-layer Internet Suite of Protocols model with the seven-layer OSI model. Either communications architecture could be used to analyze and design communications between networks. In the case of the Internet Suite of Protocols model, the full functionality of internetwork communications is divided into four layers rather than seven. Some network analysts consider this model simpler and more practical than the OSI model.

Solution: The I-P-O Model

Once the protocols are determined for two or more computers or networks that wish to communicate, the next step is to determine the type of technology required to deliver the identified internetworking functionality and protocols. To understand the basic function of any piece of networking equipment, one need only understand the differences between the characteristics of the data that came IN and those of the data that went OUT. Those differences identified were PROCESSed by the data communications equipment being analyzed.

This INPUT-PROCESSING-OUTPUT, or **I-P-O model**, is another key model that is used throughout the textbook in analyzing a wide variety of networking equipment and opportunities. By defining the difference between the data coming into a particular networked device (I) and that coming out of that same device (O), the I-P-O model documents the processing (P) performed by the device. At first glance this model may seem overly simplistic, but it is a valuable model that can assist network analysts in organizing thoughts, documenting requirements, and articulating needs.

■ GETTING STARTED WITH BUSINESS-ORIENTED LAN ANALYSIS AND DESIGN

Figure 1-7 listed examples of high-level business perspectives and needs that might lead to LAN solutions. Following is an example of how high-level business needs and perspectives can serve as a starting point for business-oriented LAN analysis and design. In compliance with the top-down model as an overall guide to LAN analysis and design, application, data, network, and technology issues must be investigated in addition to this business-layer analysis. The business layer issues are further analyzed here, and the remaining layers of the top-down model will be more thoroughly investigated and analyzed in the remainder of the text.

Business Activities Should Support Business Needs

The business activities listed in Figure 1-13 are, more precisely, the information systems or networking-related business activities identified as possibly supporting the expressed business needs and perspectives. Obviously, the term *business activities* could be more broadly defined to include sales, inventory control, marketing, research and development, accounting, and payroll, for example. Business activities in these other areas should still fulfill one or more of the identified business needs.

To ensure consistency within the top-down business model and compliance of business activities with stated business needs, a grid such as that in Figure 1-13 can be employed. For each network-related activity that must be supported in the eventual network design, check off which strategic business perspective is being satisfied. Any proposed network activities that do not support a strategic business need or perspective should be reevaluated. Modify the grid as necessary, substituting your own business needs and/or activities and evaluating them accordingly.

Assurance that possible network-related business activities fulfill specific, stated business needs is needed at this point to avoid seeking technical local area networking options that either do not support or actually conflict with these needs. As stated earlier, senior management seeks business solutions, not technology solutions.

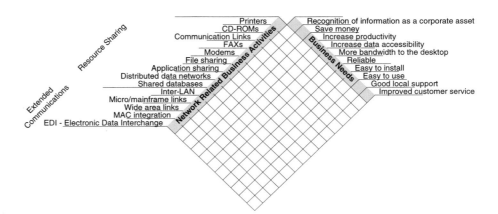

Figure 1-13   Network-related Business Activities Supporting Business Needs

Once the initial merit of the business activities has been ensured by completing an evaluation grid such as that in Figure 1-13, substantially more detailed data regarding these network-related business activities must be gathered before proceeding with the investigation of technical options through application, data, network, and technology layer analysis.

Role of the Network Analyst as a Business/Technology Intermediary

These information systems-related business activities are often expressed by nontechnical business management people, either directly or through interviews. It is important to understand that these listed activities are general, rather than technically specific. Don't expect business management to be able to articulate technical specifications.

Armed with these general business needs, the network analyst prepares a series of business analysis questions to learn more about the information system–related business activities that ensure the eventual networking proposal will adequately support the required business activities.

Subsequent analysis of available technology, through interaction with vendors and technical specialists, creates a role as intermediary for the network analyst. The network analyst must clearly understand an organization's business needs and activities, on the one hand, and the technical specifications of networking hardware and software to ideally meet those business needs, on the other hand.

Furthermore, the successful network analyst must be able to handle constant change, not just in technology, but also in the architectural design of networks and information systems required to deliver business solutions. To be specific, client/server information systems, described further in Chapter 2, require specialists with a wide background combining elements of applications development, data management, and network analysis. Technical skills must be constantly updated in response to the demands of the job market.

Business Analysis Questions Dig Deeper

Possible business analysis questions for LAN solutions are listed in Figure 1-14. Notice that these questions "dig deeper" into the more general business activities previously listed. These questions would be directed toward end users and business management and are centered on **what** the network must eventually do, rather than **how** to do it. The more technical how questions are dealt with further along this trip through the top-down model.

This list of business analysis questions is not meant to be exhaustive or all-encompassing. They result directly from the business activities and needs from the sample top-down model used in this chapter. You can add, modify, or delete questions from this list as necessary. Following are two important things to remember about any list of business analysis questions.

1. The questions should dig deep into the required information systems–related business activities.

2. The answers to these questions should provide sufficient insight to enable the investigation of possible technical solutions.

	Current	2-3 Years	5 Years
User Issues How many users? What are their business activities? What is the budgeted cost/user? Comprehensive cost of ownership? What are the security needs? (password protection levels, supervisor privileges) What are the support issues?			
Local Communication Required speed?			

Resource Sharing
 How many CD-ROMs, printers, modems, and FAXs
     are to be shared?
 What is the greatest distance from the server to each
     service?			

File Sharing Is printer/queue management required? How many simultaneous users?			
Application Sharing What is the number and type of required applications? Are e-mail services required?			
Distributed Data Access Where will shared data files be stored?			
LAN Management/Administration Will training be required to manage the network? How easy is the network to use?			

Extended Communication
 How many MACs will be part of the network?
 How many mini/mainframe connections are needed?
     (and what type, IBM, DEC, UNIX based?)
 Will this be an inter-LAN network? (LAN-LAN
     concerns. Which NOS? Must other protocols be
     considered? Are the connections local or remote
     (long-distance)?)			

Figure 1-14   LAN Business Analysis Questions

The following sections briefly explain each category of business analysis questions.

User Issues   User satisfaction is the key to any successful network implementation. To satisfy users, you must thoroughly understand their needs. Beyond the obvious questions of How many users must the network support? are the more insightful questions dealing with specific business activities of individual users:

1. Do users require large file transfers at certain times of day?

2. Do users process many short transactions throughout the day?

3. Are there certain activities that absolutely must be done at certain times of day or within a certain time?

These questions are important for establishing the amount of network communication individual users required. The levels of security required should also be addressed.

1. Are payroll files going to be accessed via the network?

2. Who should have access to these files, and what security measures will ensure authorized access?

3. What is the overall technical ability of the users?

4. Will technical staff need to be hired?

5. Can support be obtained locally from an outside organization?

Budget Reality   The most comprehensive, well-documented, and researched networking proposal is of little value if its costs are beyond the means of the funding organization or business. Initial research into possible networking solutions is often followed by the publication of feasibility option reports that outline possible network designs for varying price ranges. Senior management then dictates which options deserve further study based on availability of finances.

In some cases, senior management may have an approximate project budget in mind that could be shared with network analysts. This acceptable financial range, sometimes expressed as budgeted cost per user, serves as a frame of reference for analysts as they explore technical options. In this sense, budgetary constraints are just another overall high-level business need or perspective that helps shape eventual networking proposals.

Local Communication, e-Mail, and Messaging   Remembering that these are business, not technical analysis questions, users really cannot be asked how fast their network connections must be. Bits per second, or megabits per second, have little or no meaning for most users. If users have business activities such as CAD/CAM (computer aided design/computer aided manufacturing) or other 3-D modeling or graphics software that will be accessing the network, the network analyst should be aware that these are large consumers of network bandwidth.

Bandwidth requirements analysis as well as the bandwidth offered by various networking alternatives are explored later. It is sufficient at this point to document those information system–related business activities that may be large consumers of networking bandwidth.

Resource Sharing   The resource sharing business analysis questions for LANs are similar to business analysis questions for peripheral/printer sharing devices, outlined previously. It is important to identify which resources and how many are to be shared—printers, modems, faxes, CD-ROMs—and the preferred locations of these shared resources. The required distance between shared resources and users can have a bearing on acceptable technical options.

File Sharing, Application Sharing, and Collaborative Computing   In many cases, network versions of software packages may cost less than multiple individual licenses of the same software package for individual PCs. The network analyst is really trying at this point to compile a list of all applications programs that users will share. Not all PC-based software packages are available in network versions, and not all PC-based software packages allow simultaneous access by multiple users.

1. Which programs or software packages are users going to need to perform their jobs?

2. Which programs are they currently using?

3. Which new products must be purchased?

Once a complete list of required shared application programs has been compiled, it is important to investigate both the availability and the capability of network versions of these programs to ensure happy, productive users and the successful attainment of business needs.

Distributed Data Access   Although users cannot be expected to be database analysts, sufficient questions must be asked to determine which data are to be shared by whom, and where these users are located. This process is known as data distribution analysis. The major objective of data distribution analysis is to determine the best location on the network for the storage of various data files. That location is usually the one closest to the greatest number of the most active data users.

Some data files that are typically shared, especially in regionalized or multilocation companies, are customer files, employee files, and inventory files. Distributed data access is an even greater concern when the users sharing the data are beyond the reach of a LAN and must share the data via wide area networking (WAN) solutions. A good starting point for the network analyst might be to ask the question: Has anyone compared the business forms that are used in the various regional and branch offices to determine which data need to be sent across the network?

Extended Communications   The ability of certain local area networking solutions to communicate beyond the LAN remains a key differentiating factor among alternatives. Users should be able to articulate connectivity requirements beyond the LAN. Accomplishing these requirements is the job of the network analyst.

Extended communications might include communications to another LAN. In such a case, the network analyst must investigate all of the technical specifications of this target LAN to determine its compatibility with the local LAN. An example of such a compatibility issue is the need to connect an Apple Mac network to a PC-based network. The target LAN may be local (within the same building) or remote (across town or around the world). LAN-to-LAN connection, known as internetworking, is studied in depth in Chapter 14.

The explosive growth of mobile computing has led to a tremendous need for users to be able to access corporate information systems from home, automobiles, hotels, and even airplanes. Remote computing is explored in depth in Chapter 15.

Other examples of extended communications include the necessity for LAN users to gain access to minicomputers or mainframes, either locally or remotely. Again, users are only asked *what* they need connections to and *where* those connections must occur; it is the network analyst's job to figure out *how* to make those connections function. LAN/mainframe connectivity is explored in Chapter 14.

LAN Management and Administration   Another key differentiating factor among LAN alternatives is the level of sophistication required to manage and administer the network. If the LAN requires a full-time, highly trained manager, that manager's salary should be considered as part of the purchase cost as well as the operational cost of the proposed LAN.

Second, the users may have requirements for certain management or administration features that must be present such as user-ID creation or management, or control of access to files or user directories.

Accurate and Complete Budgets Are a Must   Detailed and accurate cost projection is a very important skill for network analysts. Management does not like large financial surprises due to unanticipated costs.

To ensure that all necessary costs have been determined, it is essential to identify all user needs (the cost generators). Thorough identification of user needs is the goal of the business analysis questions phase of the top-down model.

Anticipated Growth Is Key   User needs are not always immediate. They can vary dramatically over time. To design networking solutions that will not become obsolete in the near future, it is essential to gain a sense of the anticipated growth in user demands. Imagine the chagrin of the network analyst who must explain to management that the network that was installed last year cannot be expanded and must be replaced due to unanticipated growth of network demand.

One method of gaining the necessary insight into future networking requirements, illustrated in Figure 1-14, is to ask users the same set of business analysis questions with projected time horizons of 2 to 3 years and 5 years. Incredible as it may seem, 5 years is about the maximum projected lifetime for a given network architecture or design. Of course, there are exceptions. End users may not have the information or knowledge necessary to make these projections. Management can be very helpful in providing projected growth and informational needs, especially if the company has engaged in any sort of formalized strategic planning.

The Logical Network Design

At this point, a network analyst should have a fairly clear picture of the business networking requirements identified through the use of the top-down model. Because technology-specific issues have not been covered yet, only the logical or functional aspects of network design have been dealt with thus far. The numerous

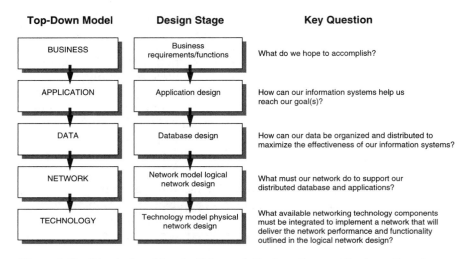

Figure 1-15   Physical and Logical Network Designs Support Business Requirements

architecture, topology, hardware, and software considerations are explored in the remaining chapters of the text.

As each area of new technology alternatives is explored, the technology that meets logical network design requirements will be investigated further for possible inclusion in a physical network design. The physical network design is a map of the actual hardware and software technology that are implemented and through which the data physically flow.

As physical network design alternatives are explored in the remainder of the text, the business requirements analyzed and determined in this chapter will be referred to less frequently. If the overall philosophy of the top-down model has been adhered to, the now complete logical network design should ensure achievement of the agree-upon business layer requirements. It should follow then, as Figure 1-15 illustrates, that as long as the physical network design (technology layer) supports the logical network design (network layer), the final implemented network should support the strategic business requirements—the ultimate goal of the top-down approach to LAN analysis and design.

SUMMARY

Perhaps the most significant conclusion that should be drawn from this chapter is that networking analysis in general, and local area network analysis in particular, must yield business solutions, not technology solutions. Given a knowledge of what a LAN is and how it is implemented, the challenge of the network analyst is to produce a documentable, justifiable network design capable of delivering stated business objectives. The key to success in this endeavor is the use of a structured methodology for LAN analysis and design. That methodology must ensure that technology investments will yield desired productivity increases or other business objectives. In addition, the analysis and design methodology must have some way to deal with the myriad of possible combinations of hardware and software protocols yielding compatibility between communicating computers or networks. The use of standardized models seems to be essential to a successful outcome of the LAN analysis and design process. Adhering to the structure and associated approach of the top-down model should ensure that the implemented physical network design will support strategic business objectives. To apply some structure to the analysis of complex internetwork communication, the OSI model or the Internet Suite of Protocols model (TCP/IP model) should offer a suitable framework for verifiable analysis and design.

KEY TERMS

buffer, 10
buffer memory, 9
business process reengineering, 19
client, 13
compatibility, 19
data PBX, 11
data switch, 9
electronic switch, 9

file transfer software, 4
hub, 13
I-P-O model, 24
interface, 20
Internet Suite of Protocols, 23
LAN, 3
local area network, 3
logical network design, 19

manual switch, 9
matrix switch, 10
network interface card, 13
network operating system, 13
NIC, 13
OSI model, 21
peripheral sharing device, 4
physical network design, 19

REVIEW QUESTIONS

1. What is a local area network?
2. What are the advantages of a LAN over a group of standalone PCs?
3. What are the potential disadvantages or negative aspects of a LAN?
4. How would a business know when it needs a LAN?
5. What are the most popular business uses of a LAN?
6. What are some alternatives to LANs?
7. Describe an appropriate application for file transfer software.
8. What are the advantages and disadvantages of printer sharing devices?
9. What is the difference between buffering and spooling?
10. What is meant by a virtual drive?
11. Describe a situation in which virtual drives would be very useful.
12. What is the difference between file transfer and file sharing?
13. What types of hardware and software technology are required to support file sharing?
14. What resources other than printers are LAN-attached computers likely to share?
15. Describe the functionality offered by a data switch.
16. In theory, what are the key differences between a data switch and a data PBX?
17. In reality, how are the terms data switch and data PBX differentiated?
18. When would queue management software represent a technology worth considering?
19. Describe the options and considerations when users need occasional access to mainframe or minicomputers.
20. What are some potential disadvantages of users getting e-mail access via software supplied with a data switch?
21. What are the advantages and disadvantages of purchasing a printer-sharing system?
22. How does a printer-sharing system differ from a printer-sharing device?
23. What is meant by the term media-sharing LAN?
24. Are all LANs media-sharing LANs? Explain.
25. Simply speaking, what hardware and software technology components are required to implement a LAN?
26. What is the function of a network interface card?
27. What is the function of a hub or wiring center?
28. In simple terms, what is the difference between an operating system and a network operating system?
29. What other technology must an NIC be able to interface with compatibly?
30. What other technology must a hub be able to interface with compatibly?
31. What is the function of a client PC operating system?
32. What is the function of a client PC network operating system?
33. How do client and server versions of the same network operating system differ?
34. What is the difference, in terms of usage and function, between client and server PCs?
35. What other technology must network media be able to interface with compatibly?
36. Why is it important for a network analyst to understand management's business needs and perspectives?
37. What are some examples of management business needs and perspectives?
38. Give examples of the potential impact of management's business needs and perspectives on network analysis and design.
39. What is the importance of a structured, documentable methodology for network analysis and design?
40. What are some typical business views of technology held by senior management?
41. What is the productivity paradox?
42. What is the top-down model and why is it important?
43. What is business process reengineering, and what is its relationship to the top-down model?
44. What is the overall relationship between the layers of the top-down model?
45. If the top-down model is used as intended, what can be assumed about implemented systems?

46. What is the difference between logical and physical network design?
47. Why is it important to allow logical and physical network designs to vary independently?
48. How are interface, protocols, and compatibility related?
49. What is meant by the term *protocol stack* in relation to its importance to internetwork design?
50. Differentiate between the following protocol-related terms: open, proprietary, de facto.
51. Describe the importance of the OSI model.
52. What is the relationship between the layers of the OSI model?
53. What is the difference between the OSI model and OSI protocols?
54. Compare and contrast the OSI model with the Internet Suite of Protocols model.
55. Describe the types of skills (technical, personal, business) required of a successful network analyst.
56. Describe the impact on networking personnel of the accelerating rate of technological change in the networking field.

ACTIVITIES

1. Prepare a chart outlining the advantages, disadvantages, and current pricing in terms of cost per user for various LANs and LAN alternatives.
2. Interview a network administrator, a network analyst, a network technician, and a director of M.I.S. Compare and contrast their perspectives on business versus technical orientation of their responsibilities.
3. Investigate and report on the possible ways in which Macs can communicate with DOS or Windows-based PCs.
4. Prepare a chart outlining the level of training and technical expertise required to implement and manage various LANs and LAN alternatives.
5. Interview senior nontechnical business administrators from a variety of companies and report on their views of the impact of technology on their operations.
6. Investigate and prepare a paper or presentation on the productivity paradox.
7. Find a description of an implemented network in a professional periodical. Place pertinent facts from the article in the appropriate layers of the top-down model. Examine your results. What questions do you have?
8. Prepare a paper on a variety of companies that have attempted business process reengineering. Has there been a variable rate of success in these efforts? Is there a right way and a wrong way to do BPR?
9. Prepare a chart with examples including employed protocols for each of the following types of interfaces: hardware/hardware, software/software, hardware/software.
10. Prepare a chart listing as many protocols as possible and categorize them as open, proprietary, officially sanctioned, or de facto.
11. Fill in a copy of the OSI model with as many OSI protocols as you can find. In another OSI model, list alternatives to the OSI protocols.
12. Interview networking personnel about how they use the OSI model or Internet Suite of Protocols model. Explain your results.
13. Prepare a chart listing the types of skills required of successful network analysts and the intended sources of those skills.

FEATURED REFERENCES

General References

Case, Thomas, and Smith, Larry (1995). *Managing Local Area Networks*. New York: McGraw-Hill.
Derfler, Frank (1995). *Guide to Connectivity*, 3rd ed. Emeryville, CA: Ziff-Davis Press.
Goldman, James (1995). *Applied Data Communications: A Business Oriented Approach*. New York: John Wiley & Sons.
Held, Gilbert (1993). *Internetworking LANs and WANs*. New York: John Wiley & Sons.
Hunter, Philip (1993). *Local Area Networks: Making the Right Choices*. Workingham, England: Addison-Wesley.
Vaskevitch, David (1993). *Client/Server Strategies: A Survival Guide for Corporate Reengineers*. San Mateo, CA: IDG Books.

Business Perspective

Allchin, Jim (November 15, 1994). The Information Network. *Network Computing*, **5**(14), 22.
Caldwell, Bruce (June 5, 1995). In the Money. *Information Week*, 530, 34.

Caldwell, Bruce (July 17, 1995). How to Align IS, Business. *Information Week*, 536, 80.

Donion, J. P. (April 1995). Creating Strategic Order from Technology Chaos. *Chief Executive*, 102, 54.

Keyes, Jessica (May 1995). So, Where's the IT Payoff? *Byte*, **20**(5), 260.

Rhodes, Wayne (June 1995). Finding Your Way. *Beyond Computing*, **4**(4), 26.

Technology Evolution/Paradigm Shift

Reinhardt, Andy (May 1995). Your Next Mainframe. *Byte*, **20**(5), 48.

CASE STUDY

Chapter 1

SOUTHWEST SOARS WITH TICKETLESS TRAVEL

Airline lures customers with its easy-to-use, network-based reservations system

In the air wars, the best way to attract travelers to your airline is to offer low fares, provide added convenience, and make it a no-hassle experience. To achieve this, Dallas-based Southwest Airlines Co. is capitalizing on network technology.

Networks are helping to maintain Southwest's low-fare structure by eliminating ticket costs, luring customers by allowing them to bypass ticket lines, and making airport check-in as easy as walking to the gate a few minutes before flight time.

Southwest, a pioneer in low-cost air transportation, is the first carrier to offer ticketless travel on all of its flights, according to Robert W. Rapp, vice president of systems for the company. "We are averaging over 15,000 ticketless passengers a day, with a lot of repeat customers. And that's before we begin advertising.

"The concept of ticketless reservations provides convenience to passengers by eliminating long lines at the ticket counters, the frustration of losing a ticket, and the anxiety of arriving late at the airport. At the same time, ticketless travel greatly decreases operating costs. It costs an airline between $15

and $30 to produce a paper airline ticket. With ticketless travel, we save the cost of sending a ticket to a customer, which eliminates paper, postage, printing, labor, and travel-agency commissions."

At the heart of Southwest's new reservations undertaking is a Hewlett-Packard Co. HP 3000 Corporate Business System Model 995. The PA-RISC-based mainframe-class server is connected in real time to more than 5,000 PCs and terminals across the country.

Southwest has 48 airports and eight reservation centers communicating with the HP server via a TCP/IP network across Novell Inc. NetWare 3.11 LANs. Other equipment on the network includes PCs, Videcom Inc. terminals, and printers.

Southwest is using an image database to store information about its ticketless passengers. Using software from Microsoft Corp., Videcom, and HP, agents move data across a private network to the appropriate location.

The system takes less than four minutes to issue a travel number to a passenger calling the airline.

Customers call the airline to reserve a flight and receive a confirmation code over the phone. Passengers then swap the code for a boarding pass at the airport.

At the boarding gate, Southwest personnel, with as few as three keystrokes, can call up the passenger's

name, record that the passenger has checked in, and enter the boarding-pass number. The information at the gate is provided via the HP 3000 computer in Dallas.

The ticketless-software program developed by Southwest is based on HP's IMAGE/SQL database-management software. Southwest first became acquainted with ticketless reservations when it acquired Morris Air, a Salt Lake City-based airline, in December 1993. "Morris Air had already been offering a ticketless alternative to customers. We were very impressed by their reservations operation," said Rapp.

"However, our needs differed enough from those of the Morris Air system, that we couldn't just turn on the switch and go. For example, we have different refund policies, agent-commission programs, and other back-office tasks that required major modifications to the Morris Air software. So we had to develop our own system."

In 1994, a development within the airlines industry accelerated Southwest's decision to offer ticketless service. Because of the actions of rival airlines that own and operate the most popular reservations computer systems, some travel agents were excluded from ticketing passengers on Southwest flights.

"This action could have impeded distribution of our service through traditional channels [for example, the travel agents]. It forced us to take a close look at what travel agencies do for us: generate and distribute tickets," said Rapp.

Southwest looked for options to counter this competitive threat. In addition to encouraging travelers to book flights directly through Southwest by telephone or via the Internet, it came up with the plan to eliminate the requirement for tickets.

Southwest began working with Dallas-based Evans Airline Information Services, a consulting service headed by Dave Evans, the prime developer of Morris Air's ticketless system.

In September of last year, four months after development began, the first ticketless passengers boarded flights in Dallas, Houston, and Little Rock, Ark. The testing was expanded to include intra-California routes in November.

Ticketless Takes Off Having produced favorable results in the areas of passenger satisfaction, cost reduction, and system reliability, the ticketless travel system is now being expanded nationwide to include all airports served by Southwest. The ticketless-travel offering is available at all 45 cities in the airline's service area. Ticketless boarding of passengers is a natural extension of the carrier's long-time policy of not issuing advance boarding passes and awarding seats strictly on a first-come, first-served basis. The new procedure continues to speed and streamline the boarding process.

Ticketless travel will improve customer service and lower operating costs, according to Rapp. "Tick-

etless reservations have been in place in the car rental and hotel business for some time, and we are definitely at the beginning of the trend in the airline industry." Industry analysts estimate that airlines could each save up to $1 billion a year by eliminating tickets.

Happy with the reliability and cost-effectiveness of the HP 3000 server, Southwest intends to expand the system into other areas. It has installed two HP 9000 midrange servers to handle passenger-revenue accounting and cargo-operations management tasks.

Hertz Rent-a-Car, Southwest, and Morris Air have based their ticketless reservations systems on HP platforms. HP is currently consulting with other national and international airlines about creating a ticketless-travel system similar to Southwest's.

Source: Ron Levine (April 24, 1995). Southwest Soars with Ticketless Travel. *LAN Times*, 12(8), 31. Reprinted with permission of McGraw-Hill, *LAN Times*.

BUSINESS CASE STUDY QUESTIONS

Activities

1. Complete a top-down model for this case by gleaning facts from the case and placing them in the proper layer of the top-down model. After completing the top-down model, analyze and detail those instances when requirements were clearly passed down from upper to lower layers of the model and solutions to those requirements were passed up from lower to upper layers of the model.
2. Detail any questions about the case that may occur to you for which answers are not clearly stated in the article.

Business

1. What are the airline's strategies to attract customers and gain market share?
2. How are networks helping Southwest Airlines achieve its business objectives?
3. What change in the competitive environment increased the priority of the ticketless travel application?
4. Did the ticketless travel application meet stated business objectives?
5. What are the future plans for this application at Southwest?

Application

1. What is ticketless travel, and how does it meet Southwest's business objectives?
2. What is the required or delivered response time of the system?
3. Why did Southwest have to develop its own system?

Data

1. How is Southwest storing information about its ticketless passengers?
2. What data management software is being used?

Network

1. What network operating system and communications protocols are being employed?
2. How many PCs are connected over what geographic area?
3. Is the transaction completed locally or is wide area transmission involved?

Technology

1. What technology has been employed to implement Southwest's ticketless travel?

CHAPTER 2

LOCAL AREA NETWORKS AND CLIENT/SERVER INFORMATION SYSTEMS

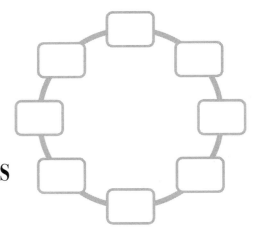

Concepts Reinforced

Local area networks
OSI model

Top-down model
Protocols and compatibility

Concepts Introduced

Client/server information systems
Client/server analysis
Client/server architectures
Distributed computing
Distributed applications
Middleware
Interprocess communications

Database distribution
Distributed transaction processing
Transaction processing monitors
Client/server management
Client/server technology and tools
Open systems
Distributed objects

OBJECTIVES

After mastering the material in this chapter you should:

1. Understand the business forces motivating the emphasis on information systems downsizing, application rightsizing, and the development of client/server information systems.

2. Understand the relationship between client/server architectures and the implementation of distributed computing, application rightsizing, database distribution, and enterprise networking.

3. Understand the major hardware and software components of a client/server architecture and the role middleware plays in integrating these components to form a working architecture.

4. Understand the additional difficulties and decision making as well as the currently available solutions implementing client/server architectures involving multiple vendor's systems and technology.

5. Understand the current state of actual implementation of client/server architectures in industry, the problem areas or limiting factors affecting these implementations, and the outlook for resolving these limiting factors.

6. Understand the unique problems encountered in managing multivendor, multiplatform client/server architectures and the current state of available distributed enterprise network management systems.

"Client/server is not just a buzzword. It's two buzzwords. Two buzzwords which, if you seek any future in computing, you cannot afford to ignore."

—Dr. Robert Metcalfe, Ethernet Inventor, Founder of 3Com and Publisher/CEO of *Infoworld*

Chapter 1 provided some familiarity with local area networks. Chapter 2 gets to the heart of their real importance, namely, their crucial role in client/server information systems. This chapter explores objectively the reasons client/server information systems are drawing so much attention, pointing out both potential positive and negative outcomes of client/server implementations. Once we complete the business analysis of client/server information systems, this chapter introduces the reader to the remainder of the book and the overall architectures and technology of client/server information systems. It supplies the proverbial "big picture," offering insight into how all the pieces of multivendor client/server information systems fit together.

The intended outcome of this introduction to client/server architectures is to provide the reader with an *introductory* understanding of the following:

- The many interacting hardware and software technology categories comprising a client/server information system.
- Examples of currently available technology within each technology category.
- The interfaces between client/server hardware and software categories and how overall compatibility is achieved across these many interfaces.

Mastery of the intricacies of client/server technology is not the intended outcome of this chapter. Many topics mentioned only briefly in this chapter are described further in later chapters.

■ BUSINESS ASPECTS OF CLIENT/SERVER INFORMATION SYSTEMS

Business Motivation

As companies sought a competitive advantage in the downturned economy of the early 1990s, information became increasingly recognized as the corporate asset to be leveraged. More precisely, the timely delivery of the right corporate information, in the right format, to the right decision maker at the right place and time can be the differentiating factor between success and failure in today's business world. It is important to add one additional criterion: this information must also be delivered at the right price. As profits have dwindled and pressures to decrease expenses have mounted, the cost of maintaining corporate information systems has come under increased scrutiny. The mainframe computer, with its associated hierarchical network and maintenance/development budget, has been singled out, perhaps unfairly, as the biggest budget item of information systems departments. As you will soon see, mainframe computers still have a place in some corporate information systems environments.

Corporate downsizing, not to be confused with **information systems downsizing,** has involved eliminating positions within a corporation through attrition, early retirement, closed operations, or forced layoffs. The duties of the eliminated positions are either assumed by remaining employees or deemed "dispensable." In many cases, the information systems of these "downsized" corporations must pick up the slack and deliver better information more efficiently to the remaining employees. "Accomplishing more with less" is one of the aims of the properly "rightsized" application.

Potential Benefits

It is important to understand that "information systems downsizing" and **"application rightsizing"** are not merely about saving money. As you will see, an entirely new **distributed architecture** for information systems processing and delivery has been produced by the combination of the following events:

- Introduction of reasonably priced, powerful personal workstations.

- Emergence of affordable powerful, multitasking server operating systems.

- Changing demands on information systems resulting from today's business climate.

Information systems constructed according to this distributed architecture paradigm are often referred to as **client/server information systems** because their overall duties are shared by client and server computers. Exactly how these client/server information systems are put together is explored in the remainder of this chapter. These distributed or rightsized information systems not only save money in many cases, but also deliver better information more flexibly while enabling quicker business-level responses to competitive situations.

Although sometimes overshadowed by more concrete benefits, such as performance improvements or budget decreases, the flexible design afforded by the distributed nature of the client/server architecture holds the key to the most significant benefits of this new computing paradigm. Following are a few examples of the potential benefits of client/server information systems.

Motorola's Computer Group has shifted in-house written applications based on an IBM mainframe to primarily packaged software running on distributed UNIX processors. In the process, they have reduced their budget by 40% and shortened application development cycles. These systems are also valued for their flexibility and ability to adapt quickly to changes in the business environment.

Flexibility and the ability to initiate new business ventures are two key outcomes sought by Kash n' Karry's 112-store grocery business' investment in a new object-oriented, distributed computing environment. These goals are not without their inherent cost, however. The new distributed information system's initiative will require a 12% increase on an annual information systems budget of 6 million dollars. The relationship between object-oriented programming and distributed computing is investigated later in this chapter.

Reader's Digest is optimizing mainframe usage while distributing information over a global LAN internetwork and, in the process, reducing its number of data centers from 17 to 3, a reduction of 82%. Improved information accessibility will be a key outcome of the project as authorized users will be able to access subscriber information on any mainframe, not just the mainframe to which they are locally connected.

Financial Guaranty Insurance Company has reduced its system budget by 80% and its programming staff by 71% as a result of its downsizing initiative from a mainframe to a client/server architecture employing 200 Intel 386–based clients and 4 Intel 486–based servers.

Finally, and perhaps most significantly, better, faster information from the City of San Antonio's Emergency Dispatch System has saved lives. Using 386–based clients and multiprocessor 486–based servers, dispatchers can get ambulances where they are needed faster due to the system's increased speed and flexibility.

Figure 2-1 summarizes the significant benefits of successful implementation of client/server information system.

Potential Negatives

Just as there are two sides to every story, information systems rightsizing efforts have drawbacks and potential pitfalls. Some of these negatives are unique to client/server or rightsizing efforts while others are true for any shift in information systems design or architecture.

Since cost savings is often the key positive attribute of client/server implementation, it is only fitting that a closer examination of these efforts often reveals this savings is minimized when **transition costs** are taken into account. If the new client/server system is replacing an existing system, both systems must be maintained and supported for some time. In addition, the cost of writing new software or converting old software should be taken into account, as should the cost of developing new user or management software "tools."

Other hidden costs have appeared only after the transition to a client/server information system has been completed. Due to the inherent distributed, multivendor nature of client/server information systems, they are often more difficult and costly to support and maintain than the single-platform, single-vendor–based platforms they replaced.

Several references cited the lack of existing management tools for the distributed computing architecture as a serious impediment to client/server deployment. Such tools must automatically and transparently cater to system backup, disaster recovery, and security issues such as user login and user access management over the entire distributed computing network. In short, users expect all of the functionality of the sophisticated operating systems of standalone mainframes on the distributed platform of the client/server architecture.

Because of the increased sophistication and processing power available to the end-user at the client workstation, increased end-user training is a reality and an additional cost that client/server architecture implementation teams must consider.

Benefit	Example/Explanation
Reduced costs in comparison to mainframe-based information systems	• Budget reductions of 40%–80% with significant staff reductions are possible
Flexibility	• Cited as a benefit in nearly every case study. Information is more accessible and display formats are more flexible thanks to the client/server architecture
Support/respond to business environment changes	• Beyond flexibility. Demonstrates potential for proactive use of information systems in business. Significantly reduced time to develop new applications is a contributing factor
Improved information accessibility	• Information stored on distributed LANs is more easily accessible to a wider user group than information stored on a mainframe-based hierarchical network
Faster information	• Distributed processing allows combined power of client PC and server PC to increase processing speed by as much as a factor of 10 over mainframe-based solutions
Better information	• The "right" information. Produced as a result of a combination of faster processing, more flexible formatting, and improved access to a wider array of information
Open architecture	• The typical PC-based client/server architecture offers unlimited potential for multivendor solutions to information systems opportunities. Mainframe-based, single-vendor information systems lock out the competition and, in many cases, innovative solutions
Empowered users	• Perhaps most significantly, users will play a larger role in information systems design and development as client-based, easy-to-use systems development tools are employed in the client/server architecture

Figure 2-1   Potential Benefits of Client/Server Information Systems

It should follow that these same more powerful end-user workstations would require increased ongoing technical support as well.

As can be seen from a thorough review of the chapter references, the shift from traditional information systems architectures to client/server architectures involves many negative aspects or potential pitfalls. Although there is little argument over the fact that the computers used in client/server information systems are significantly less expensive than the mainframes they replaced, current research indicates that when support, training, management, and maintenance costs are taken into account, no significant cost savings is achieved by the transition to client/server information systems.

Negatives	Examples/Explanation
Transition costs	• Often overlooked, these are the "hidden" costs incurred while converting to client/server architectures
High cost of training, support, maintenance, and management	• Due primarily to the open, multivendor architecture of client/server, training, support, maintenance, and management are far more complex and, therefore, more expensive
Multivendor architecture	• Also listed as a benefit, an open architecture supported by multiple vendors' technology can lead to incompatibility problems and finger pointing
Lack of management tools for distributed environment	• Although efforts are being made to fill this need, sophisticated management tools capable of managing distributed, multivendor environments are just emerging
Lack of standards	• This is especially a problem where two competing standards are backed by rival vendors or consortiums
Technology not ready for mission critical applications	• Although getting more reliable all the time, servers and server operating systems still don't guarantee the reliability and power of mainframes
Lack of software conversion tools	• Sophisticated tools which can prevent mainframe applications from having to be totally rewritten could reduce transition costs tremendously

Figure 2-2   Potential Negatives of Client/Server Information Systems

If cost savings are minimal or nonexistent, what is the key benefit to the implementation of client/server information systems? As cited in the Potential Benefits section, the most significant benefit is the ability of client/server information systems to deliver better information more flexibly, thereby enabling competitive business advantages and increased revenue. Figure 2-2 summarizes some of the potential negatives of client/server information systems.

■ ARCHITECTURES OF CLIENT/SERVER INFORMATION SYSTEMS

Evolution from Mainframe-Based Architectures to Client/Server Information Systems

What is the nature of the process that takes a mainframe-based application and redeploys that application on a distributed client/server platform? In fact, many possible processes may lead to client/server implementation. Among the commonly used terminology used to describe these processes are the following:

- Downsizing.
- Rightsizing.
- Upsizing.
- Smartsizing.

Some people consider these terms nothing more than marketing buzzwords. They are not industry standardized terms, and their use is rather arbitrary. Other terms may be used to describe similar processes. What is important is to understand the variety of possible architectural shifts in the evolution from mainframe-based architectures to client/server information systems, rather than the meaning of particular terms.

Downsizing   Downsizing implies that a mainframe-based application has been redeployed to run on a smaller computer platform. That smaller platform may or may not be a distributed client/server information system. Also, the term downsizing does not indicate the extent of redesign or reengineering. For example, the original source code could have simply been recompiled and run unaltered on the new, "downsized" platform. Alternatively, the application may have been rewritten in a new language and redeployed. Another possibility is that the programming logic was reexamined, redesigned, and reprogrammed.

Downsizing primarily seeks to take advantage of the increasingly powerful computers available at ever more affordable prices. It does not necessarily involve using that processing power more efficiently or effectively.

Rightsizing   Rightsizing implies that applications are designed for and deployed on the platform, or type and size of computer, which makes the most sense: the "right" size computer. The right computer or platform implies that the choice is based on maximizing the efficiency with which the application runs. Matching of a particular rightsized application with a particular computing platform seeks efficiency not only from a performance standpoint, but also from a cost perspective. The rightsized application is the one that will deliver the most "bang for the buck."

Because efficient execution of the application is at the heart of rightsizing, this process usually implies new development or redesign of applications, in contrast to simple downsizing efforts.

Upsizing   Upsizing might be considered a subset of rightsizing. When applications lack processing power on their existing computing platform, they may be redesigned and redeployed on larger, more powerful platforms. Whether or not the applications require reengineering before they are upsized varies from case to case.

A possible example of an upsizing need is a company that has outgrown the capabilities of a multiuser database and must move to more powerful client/server–based relational database management. Old applications may need to be redesigned and rewritten for the new database system, depending on the efficiency of the old application and the existence of a migration path from the old to the newer database system.

Smartsizing   Smartsizing implies another level of questioning or reengineering beyond rightsizing. Rather than merely reevaluating the application program, smartsizing goes a step further to reevaluate and reengineer the business process that motivated the application in the first place. Once the business process has been thoroughly and objectively reevaluated, the application programs to support that process are redesigned and rewritten. Finally, the new application is deployed on the right platform to maximize performance and cost efficiency.

Figure 2-3 illustrates the differences between downsizing, rightsizing, upsizing, and smartsizing.

Major Paradigms of the Information Age   Unique combinations of systems architectures and people architectures are often referred to as **paradigms** of the information age. There were at least two or three major paradigms in information systems before the introduction of the client/server model. Depending on which information systems philosopher is consulted, any or all of these may be major paradigms of the Information Age:

I.   Age of the mainframe

II.   Introduction of the Personal Computer

III.   Dawn of the Client/Server Architecture and Applications Rightsizing

The period during which information systems professionals are madly scrambling to gain competitive advantage for their companies by implementing the "new" paradigm is known as a **paradigm shift.** A paradigm shift is much more than the introduction of new technology. It occurs when the fundamental underlying processes and environment change to such an extent that significant changes in behavior are required. In short, a completely new way of doing things results from a completely new way of looking at the world of information systems.

Figure 2-4 highlights the major systems and corresponding people architectures of the major paradigms of the information age.

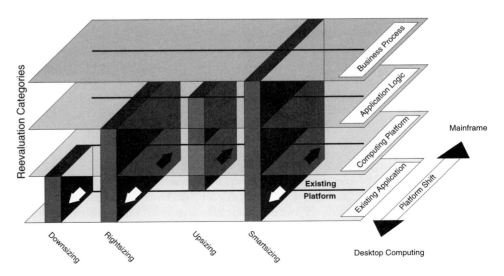

Figure 2-3   Downsizing, Rightsizing, Upsizing, and Smartsizing

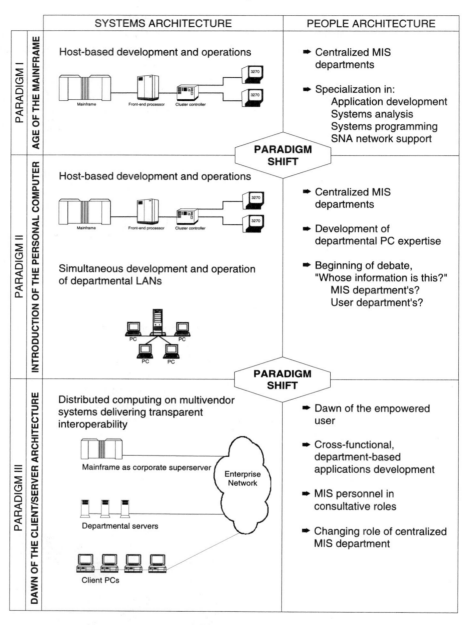

Figure 2-4   Major Paradigms of the Information Age

People Architectures Must Respond to Information Systems Architectures   The key point of paradigm shifts such as those illustrated in Figure 2-4 is to realize that major technological or systems architecture shifts are accompanied by correspondingly large shifts in people architectures. Thus, it should not be surprising that the dawn of the client/server age is uncovering a great many people-related issues as the centralized MIS departments of the "old" paradigm are faced with the reality of the distributed systems of the new paradigm. Much of the debate in today's evolving people architecture centers on which functions of an MIS department should be distributed to match the systems architecture, and which must remain centralized.

There are no easy answers to these questions. The people architecture of the client/server age is still in an evolutionary state. Figure 2-5 summarizes some of the people architecture features and issues of the client/server or applications rightsizing paradigm.

After reviewing Figure 2-5, it should be obvious that the people architecture changes resulting from the client/server or applications rightsizing paradigm shift are potentially at least as dramatic as the changes in systems architecture. For example, the distribution of processing power, coupled with the distribution of corporate data and application development via client/server architecture, can raise fundamental issues as to who owns and is responsible for different aspects of these

Feature/Characteristic	Issues/Explanation
The Dawn of the Empowered User	• Powerful, easy-to-use front-end client-based tools will empower end-users to meet many more of their own information needs thanks to easy access to distributed data via the client/server architecture and the enterprise network
Cross-functional, user department–based application development	• No longer totally centralized, application development will be distributed to end-user departments
	• Empowered users of the department, rather than MIS staff, may be project leaders
MIS personnel in consultative roles	• No longer the sole "owners" of all corporate data and applications development expertise, MIS personnel will work in a more distributed, consultative, or loaned basis for individual end-user department projects for extended periods of time
Changing role for centralized MIS department	• A smaller centralized MIS department must still be responsible for certain global information infrastructure concerns such as:
	• Centralized, coordinated user support
	• Centralized, coordinated user training
	• Maintenance of the enterprise network
	• Quality assurance in the areas of database design, applications development, and departmental networking projects
	• Data administration standards development and enforcement through definition of standard global data definitions for globally used data elements
	• Standards testing of new technology for adherence to corporate standards before allowing organizationwide deployment of that technology

Figure 2-5 The People Architecture of the Client/Server Paradigm

distributed systems. For instance, are local department personnel responsible for the maintenance, backup, and disaster recovery of local servers, or do these functions remain in the domain of the centralized MIS department? Which organization is responsible for which aspects of the enterprise network?

These people architecture changes will also cause anxiety as people worry about changing job descriptions and long-term security. The development and support of client/server information systems requires a new combination of technical skills for long-time information systems professionals. Organizations must find ways to retrain existing personnel or hire new graduates with the required skills. Current information systems professionals must also be willing to retool their skills, and colleges and universities must adjust curricula to offer this new set of required skills. A predictable reaction on the part of many is to resist the change aggressively. Coping with negativism and overall effective management of the people side of the client/server architecture is equally important as coping with rapidly changing technology.

Logical Architectures

Client/Server Information Systems   Simply stated, a **client/server information system** takes advantage of the processing power now available on desktop computers by splitting the job of delivering quality information to end-users among multiple computers. As you will soon see, much activity among interacting layers of hardware and software technology goes on behind the scenes to accomplish this task. The primary purpose of this section is to supply the reader with visual models of client/server information systems to provide a better understanding of these interacting layers of technology.

The term client/server may be a bit misleading if the reader interprets the phrase as implying a 1-to-1 ratio between clients and servers. As will be seen throughout the remainder of the text, it is far more common for multiple specialized servers to be involved with fulfilling the information and communications needs of a single client.

P-A-D Architecture   The most fundamental logical model of client/server information systems takes a closer look at what it takes to "deliver quality information to end-users." This functional perspective is illustrated in Figure 2-6, the **presentation-application-data, or P-A-D, architecture.**

As can be seen from Figure 2-6, the delivery of quality information to end-users depends on the interaction of three fundamental processes:

1. Presentation (also known as user interface).

2. Application (also known as application logic or processing).

3.   Data (also known as data management or data manipulation).

Some logical models of client/server information systems divide the application layer into the following three sublayers, highlighting the layer's interfaces with presentation and data layers:

1. Presentation logic—the part of the application program responsible for interfacing to the user interface.

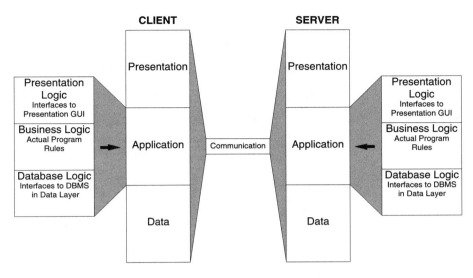

Figure 2-6   Presentation-Application-Data Logical Model

2. Business logic—the actual program rules of the application responsible for controlling program execution and enforcing business rules.

3. Database logic—the part of the application program responsible for interfacing with the database management system.

Presentation, application, and data are nothing new. These three interacting functions are at the heart of the oldest mainframe-based information systems. The only thing client/server information systems introduces to this interaction is the possibility of splitting some or all of these functions across multiple computers. As Figure 2-6 illustrates, this splitting of functions introduces the need for sophisticated communications between cooperating computers. This communication is supplied by the network, often a local area network. The importance of the network to client/server computing should be obvious. Without the network, there is no client/server computing.

In the following sections, each element of the P-A-D model, as well as the interaction between these elements, is explored in more detail.

Categories of Client/Server Information Systems

Figure 2-7 is a matrix of potential categories of client/server information systems based on a variety of combinations of the presentation, application, and data elements of the P-A-D architecture. The new variable introduced in Figure 2-7 is the executing platform for these elements. As illustrated, each function or element may be executed in three possible ways:

1. The function is performed totally on the client.

2. The function is cooperatively split between the client and server.

3. The function is performed totally on the server.

	Executing Platforms		
	Client - Only	Cooperative Client and Server	Server - Only
Presentation	Client - Based Presentation (Client GUI, Local Presentation, GUI Veneer)	Distributed Presentation (Cooperative Presentation)	Host - Based Presentation (Remote Presentation, Dumb Terminals)
Application	Client-Based Processing	Distributed Computing (Cooperative Computing, Cooperative Processing)	Host - Based Processing
Data	Client - Based Data Management (Local Data Management)	Database Distribution (Distributed Data Management, Distributed Database)	Host- Based Data Management (Remote Data Management)

Presentation - Application - Data LAYER

Figure 2-7   Potential Categories of Elements of Client/Server Information Systems

Since different terms are often used to describe the same processes, the matrix includes synonymous terms in parenthesis.

Practical Advice and Information

Remembering that a client/server information system combines presentation, application, and data functionality, a network analyst needs to know the executing platform(s) of each of these elements of the P-A-D architecture to properly categorize a particular client/server information system. However, beware. A categorization of one element of the P-A-D architecture often implies categorization of the remaining two elements as in the following:

- Host-based processing—often implies client-based presentation, host-based processing, and host-based data management.

- Client-based processing—often implies client-based presentation, client-based processing, and host-based data management.

- Cooperative processing—often implies client-based presentation, distributed computing, and distributed data management.

Figure 2-8 graphically illustrates how different variations of presentation, application, and data management elements can be combined to produce different logical client/server information systems architectures.

Many other terms are used to describe entire logical architectures of client/server information systems. The important thing for a network analyst to re-

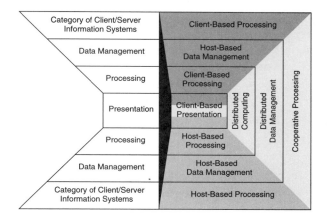

Figure 2-8   Presentation + Processing + Data Management = Logical Client/Server Architecture

member is to pay attention to the executing platforms of the constituent presentation, application, and data management elements of the client/server information system rather than to the label or name assigned to the overall logical design.

Client-Based Presentation   All three logical architectures illustrated in Figure 2-8 had only one thing in common: client-based presentation. For a system to be considered a client/server information system, the client must handle at least the first element of the P-A-D logical architecture, namely, presentation. Client-based presentation is often handled through familiar **graphical user interfaces (GUI)** such as Windows, OS/2 Presentation Manager, X Windows-based systems such as Motif and Open-Look, or the Macintosh Desktop.

As both Figures 2-7 and 2-8 illustrate, the fact that the presentation is client-based is independent of where the application logic is processed. In client-based processing client/server information systems, the applications that run on the client must be compatible with the GUI running on that client. If the client uses Windows as its GUI, then its applications must be Windows-compliant. The technical aspects of the interface between GUIs and compliant applications are studied in detail in Chapters 4 and 17.

Host-based processing client/server information systems also use client-based presentation software. With the help of a category of software known as **screen scrapers** or screen emulation software, character-based screens formerly displayed on dumb terminals are reformatted into GUI format. All that has changed is the client-based presentation. The mainframe, or host-based processing, application remains unchanged. This is often a first step on the road from mainframe-based applications to client/server computing. The GUI interface is more user-friendly than the character-based screens and probably leads to greater worker productivity. However, the key point is that the application is still running, unchanged, on the expensive mainframe computer.

Distributed Computing   Simply stated, **distributed computing,** also known as distributed processing, is nothing more than dividing an application program into two or more pieces and distributing and processing those **distributed applications** onto two or more computers, either clients or servers. The division of application programs for optimal use by a client/server environment can be a major undertaking and will be explored in greater detail later.

The client portion of the program, often called the **front-end,** is primarily used to do the following:

- Provide a user interface.

- Format requests for data or processing from the server.

- Format data received from the server for output to the user.

The server portion of the program, often called the **back-end** or **engine,** is primarily used to do the following:

- Retrieve and store data as requested.

- Perform computation and application processing.

- Provide necessary security and management functions.

In summary, the back-end does all processing except the interface and formatting-related tasks performed by the front-end. Since this back-end distributed application represents the majority of the total required processing it is referred to as the "processing engine." Figure 2-9 summarizes the key characteristics of front-end and back-end distributed applications.

Two of the most important attributes of distributed processing are **transparency** and **scalability.** The extent to which each of these attributes is present varies from one distributed processing installation to another.

Transparency refers to the ability of distributed processing systems to combine clients and servers of different operating systems, network operating systems, and protocols into a cohesive system processing distributed applications without regard to the aforementioned differences. The true measure of transparency is from the user's perspective or point of view. Distributed processing transparency exists if the combinations of multivendor hardware and software do not adversely affect a user's ability to get the information he or she needs to effectively perform the job. Complete transparency is still a largely unrealized goal of distributed processing. As you will see when specific distributed processing solutions are explored, limited transparency among a finite number or vendors' equipment, operating systems, and network operating systems is currently possible.

This transparency is achieved through a category of software known as **middleware.** Middleware resides in the middle of the distributed processing system, serving as a transparent insulator surrounding the enterprise network over which the client/server communication actually travels. Middleware is explored in more detail later.

Transparency is closely related to another frequently mentioned characteristic of distributed computing: **portability.** Portability refers to the ability for client/server applications to be developed in one computing environment and deployed in others.

Scalability refers to the ability of distributed processing systems to add clients without degrading the overall performance of the system. This is possible because as each client is added, the incremental processing power of its CPU is added to the system's overall processing power.

Characteristic	Front-End	Back-End
Also called . . .	Client-portion	Engine
Runs on . . .	Client workstation	Servers
Primary functions	User interface Format requests for data or processing from server Format data received from server	Store and retrieve data Perform computation and application processing Provide security and management functions
Runs . . .	. . . as needed or as activated by user	. . . constantly
Services . . .	. . . individual user at single client workstation	. . . multiple users sending requests for processing/data from multiple client workstations
Examples	E-Mail Systems	
	Receive, read, send personal e-mail messages as desired	Provide ongoing e-mail delivery service for all attached clients
	Database Systems	
	Format requests for data from data server	Services data requests from multiple clients

Figure 2-9 Distributed Processing Front-End versus Back-End Distributed Applications

Scalability should be contrasted with the effect on the mainframe-terminal architecture of the addition of incremental terminals. Because all processing power is concentrated in the mainframe, overall system performance is degraded for each terminal added. When overall system performance is seriously degraded, the customary solution to increase overall processing power is to buy a bigger mainframe. Obviously, the cost of a bigger mainframe is significantly more than the cost of client workstations. This is not to say that mainframes don't have their rightful place in a distributed computing environment. The changing role of the mainframe is explored in Chapter 14.

It is also worth repeating that the scalability of a distributed processing system is significant only if application programs can be split, or distributed, between clients and servers. As you will see, this is by no means a trivial task. With this distributed application hurdle overcome, massive amounts of processing power and storage capability can be merged via the enterprise backbone network to effectively form one massively powerful and flexible computer. Figure 2-10 illustrates transparency and scalability, the key attributes of distributed processing systems.

Interprocess Communications   Having succeeded in splitting the application logically between the client (front-end) and one or more servers (back-ends), the next challenge is to make these separate pieces of an application behave as if they were a single application process running on a single computer. Obviously, what is needed is

Transparency: Clients and servers cooperatively share processing load *without regard for operating system or protocol differences.*

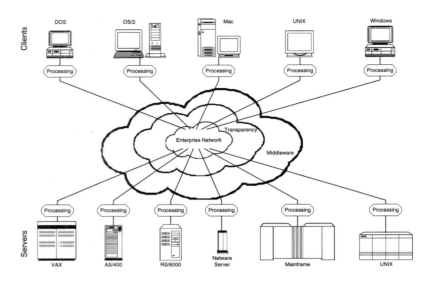

Scalability: Additional clients are added to system with little or no effect on processing load due to *incremental processing power* added by each client.

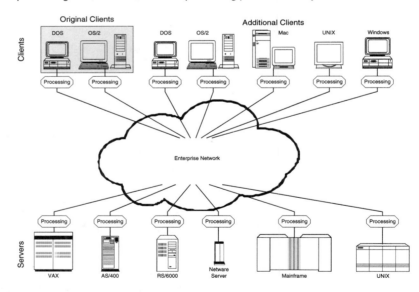

Figure 2-10   Key Attributes of Distributed Processing

a mechanism that will allow the multiple pieces of the application to communicate with each other. This communication, known as **interprocess communication (IPC),** is illustrated in Figure 2-11. Interprocess communications protocols are responsible for sending messages and commands between processes and synchronizing complicated transactions that require the execution of multiple processes on multiple computers. This interprocess communication is especially tricky when one considers

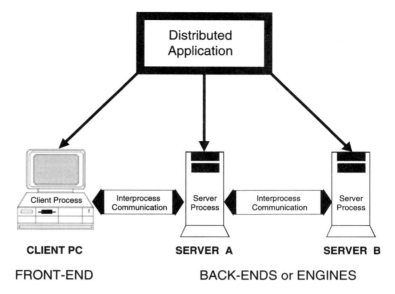

Figure 2-11 Distributed Processing Requires Interprocess Communications

that the different pieces of the distributed process may be running on computers with totally different combinations of operating systems, network operating systems, and database management systems.

Two of the most popular categories of interprocess communications protocols are **remote procedure calls (RPC)** and **message passing.** These IPC protocols are examples of middleware, previously mentioned in relation to distributed computing transparency. More examples and explanations of interprocess communications protocols are included later in this chapter as well as in Chapter 17.

Database Distribution If specially designed distributed applications are split to run as separate client (front-end) and server (back-end) portions, then it stands to reason that database management systems (DBMS) would have to be somehow specially adapted for the distributed environment as well.

In a distributed environment, data must be able to be stored in multiple physical locations, on different types of server computers in a manner which is transparent to the end-user. These multiple database servers must be able to communicate with each other, even if they are not running the same database management system. Specially designed front-end tools perform distributed database inquiry, report generation, and application development. **Distributed database management systems** and their associated front-end tools serve as an additional variable, together with application programs, operating systems, and network operating systems, which must interoperate transparently over the enterprise network.

Simply stated, to qualify as a true distributed database management system, the product in question must offer **data transparency** to the end-user. Although specific required characteristics are explored in more detail later, generally speaking, a true distributed database management system should allow a user to access data without regard for the following:

- Front-end tool or distributed application.
- Type of server computer (Intel-based, minicomputer, mainframe, etc.)

- Physical location of the server.

- Physical details and protocols of the network path to the server.

In addition to data transparency, the distribution-related characteristics largely center on the distributed database management system's ability to divide and distribute portions of databases in a flexible manner while maintaining all of the security, integrity, and control functionality of a single-site database management system. This last point, the ability to effectively manage distributed databases, is perhaps the single most important issue in implementing distributed database management systems. As you will see, financial considerations of single-site versus distributed database management systems play a large role in final purchase decisions as well.

Figure 2-12 illustrates the key components of a distributed database environment. Although each of the components illustrated is explained further either later in this chapter or in Chapters 16 or 17, following are brief descriptions:

Database Connectivity Software: Database connectivity software is concerned with connecting a variety of front-end tools with a variety of distributed DBMS engines. Key to this required functionality is a standardized database command language known as **Structured Query Language (SQL).** Database connectivity software must therefore be compatible with a specific database front-end tool or engine,

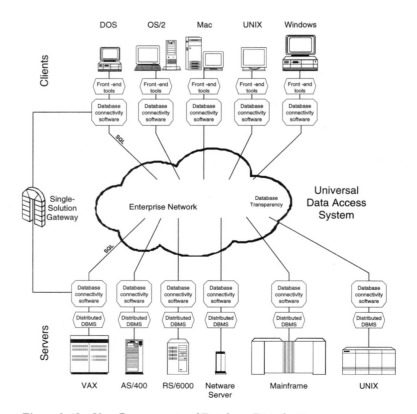

Figure 2-12   Key Components of Database Distribution

on one side, while translating to/from industry standard SQL commands on the other side.

Single-Solution Gateway: Rather than offering translation to an industry-standard neutral language such as SQL, single-solution gateways actually offer improved performance through optimally written code translating between a specific front-end tool and a specific distributed database management system or between two database engines. The downside is that single-solution gateways offer no flexibility; it works only for particular combinations of database technology.

Front-End Tools: Front-end tools for database management systems fall into two major categories:

- Database query and reporting tools.

- Multiplatform client/server application development tools.

Tools in each category depend on protocols known as **application program interfaces (API)** that allow a single application to work with multiple, different database management systems. APIs eliminate the need for programmers to write specific versions of programs for every possible combination of database management system, network operating system, and operating system for all servers to whom the front-end tool may ever wish to speak.

Universal Data Access System: A lack of standardization created by numerous vendor-specific versions of SQL provided a market opportunity for SQL middleware that could translate transparently between the many versions of SQL implemented on different platforms and databases.

A product known as EDA/SQL (Enterprise Data Access/SQL) from Information Builders Inc. has taken advantage of that market opportunity. Calling itself a **universal data access system,** EDA/SQL acts as a middleware layer, trapping SQL requests from clients and reformatting them as necessary before transporting them to the appropriate server.

EDA/SQL represents a single-vendor solution to the SQL incompatibility problem. However, any single-vendor solution can be a problem in itself. They are generally proprietary solutions, lacking in support of open systems standards and unable to guarantee wide-ranging interoperability.

Distributed Transaction Processing   In business, a transaction is an event such as purchasing a ladder, making a savings deposit, or taking out a loan. In information systems, a **transaction** is the sequence or series of predefined steps or actions taken within an application program to properly record that business transaction. Properly recording a business transaction usually implies posting changes to several files or databases. Transaction processing requires careful monitoring to ensure that all, and not just some, postings related to a particular business transaction are successfully completed. This monitoring of transaction posting is done by a specialized type of software known as transaction posting **(TP) monitors.** Whereas transactions are most often posted to databases, the integrity ensured by TP monitors depends on their ability to interact with installed database management systems. Figure 2-13 summarizes the key characteristics of transactions TP monitors must ensure.

In some cases, especially in mainframe-based systems, all of the databases that need to be updated for a given transaction are located on a single large computer. This process, known as local or nondistributed transaction posting, requires a local TP monitor. With the advent of client/server information systems, multiple geographically dispersed computers are linked, allowing transactions to be posted

Transaction Characteristic	Explanation/Importance
All or nothing	• Also known as atomicity. All of the postings related to a given transaction must be posted successfully or none must be posted. • Partial postings are not acceptable. • As far as the information system is concerned, the transaction is nonexistent until posted completely.
Synchronized lock in progress	• A transaction involving multiple postings is set up to post individual postings in a particular order. • Certain fields of information may need to be locked during these postings to prevent other programs from accessing them. • The TP monitor ensures that postings are done in the proper order and that fields of information are locked as appropriate for each posting.
Fault tolerant	• Once a transaction had been posted fully, the TP monitor ensures that these postings cannot be corrupted by other postings or system failures.

Figure 2-13 Transaction Characteristics Ensured by TP Monitors

across multiple distributed computers. This process is known as **distributed transaction processing (DTP)** and requires a distributed TP monitor. DTP is sometimes also called **enterprise transaction processing (ETP).**

As illustrated in Figure 2-14, DTP monitoring actually requires two levels of TP monitoring. First, the local TP monitor must ensure the integrity of local postings. However, these local postings are just part of a single-distributed transaction posting, which must be coordinated overall by the **DTP monitor (DTPM).** The DTPM is able to interface to the local TPM thanks to a distributed transaction processing application program interface **(DTP API)** protocol supported by both TP monitors.

Business information must be as current and up-to-date as possible. "Accurate as of the start of the business day" is often not sufficient. Information systems that give up-to-the-minute information are sometimes known as **real-time systems.** To keep information real-time, business transactions must be posted immediately, rather than in nightly batches, using **on-line transaction processing (OLTP)** systems.

The Top-Down Model Applied to Client/Server Figure 2-15 summarizes the logical or functional relationships between the elements of distributed information systems by categorizing these functions according to the top-down model. This model clearly demonstrates what a client/server information system must do (logical design). What remains to be seen is how these things can be accomplished (physical design).

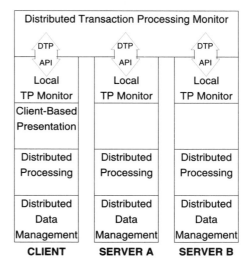

Logical Model of Local or Nondistributed Transaction Processing Monitor

Logical Model of Distributed Transaction Processing Monitor

All software installed on same system.

Local TP monitors ensure integrity of local transaction postings.
Distributed TP monitor ensures integrity of overall distributed postings.
Distributed TP monitor and local TP monitor communicate via DTP API.

Figure 2-14   Local versus Distributed Transaction Process Monitoring

Business	Increased competition on a global scale Corporate downsizing Information systems downsizing Business process redesign/reengineering		
Application	Client presentation Application rightsizing Distributed computing Distribute applications	Distributed Transaction-Process Monitors Middleware Interprocess Communication	Client/Server Architecture
Data	Distributed databases		
Network	Enterprise networks Distributed network management		
Technology	To be determined by physical client/server design		

Figure 2-15   The Top-Down Model and Logical Client/Server Architecture

To understand the full impact of client/server architectures, it is also necessary to comprehend the physical relationship or technology implementation configuration of the elements of a typical client/server architecture. The next section introduces these physical/technology architectures.

Physical/Technology Architectures

Client/Server Architecture versus Mainframe/Terminal Architecture   To understand the significant differences between a client/server architecture and a more traditional mainframe-terminal architecture, one must identify the location where each of the elements listed in Figure 2-15 is accomplished. Figure 2-16 illustrates the different locations of these key information system elements for client/server versus mainframe-based architectures.

The client/server illustration in the figure is somewhat oversimplified. First, multiple servers are commonplace in such an architecture. Second, servers are very likely to be distributed geographically, with some servers located remotely and linked to geographically dispersed clients via a wide area network (WAN), sometimes referred to as an enterprise network.

The following characteristics of client/server information systems should be evident in Figure 2-16:

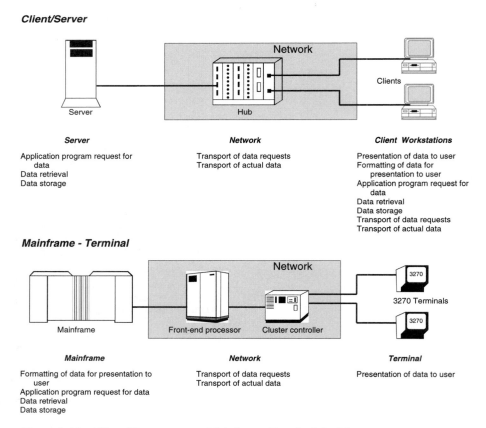

Figure 2-16   Client/Server versus Mainframe-Terminal Architectures

- Distributed Processing—the processing necessary to produce application program requests for data may take place on either the client workstation or the shared system server.

- Database Distribution—data may be stored and/or retrieved on either the client workstation or the shared system server.

- Enterprise Network—handles the transportation of data requests and actual data for the client/server architecture with the help of a specialized category of interface software known as middleware.

In contrast, Figure 2-16 shows the following characteristics of the mainframe-terminal environment:

- Requires all processing of any type to be performed on the mainframe.
- Terminals act only as "dumb" input/output devices.

Client/Server Technology Architecture   Figure 2-17 illustrates a client/server technology architecture by depicting the categories of software that may be present on client and server computers, linked via an enterprise network. This diagram is concerned primarily with software and communications, which is why only single client and server software profiles are illustrated. The fact is, any number of clients or servers may be linked via the enterprise network, but the software compatibility issues illustrated in Figure 2-17 remain. Examples of each of the technology categories listed in the figure are reviewed later in this chapter.

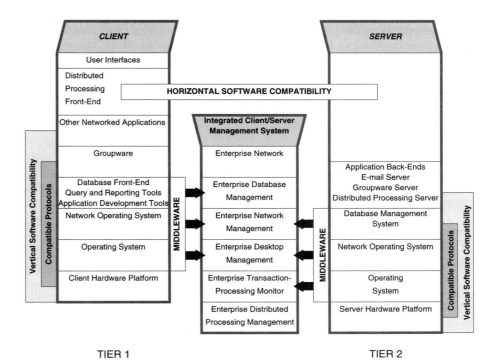

Figure 2-17   Client/Server Technology Architecture

The best way to analyze software compatibility is by direction. **Vertical software compatibility** is concerned with making sure that all necessary compatible protocols for all of the software and hardware are in place within a single client or server to operate harmoniously and transparently. The intricacies of these compatibility issues and the protocols that support vertical software compatibility are studied in depth throughout the remainder of the text. The most important thing to remember is that these are issues which must be analyzed methodically. It is not important to memorize potential compatible protocols. A structured model such as that in Figure 2-17 uncovers any potential incompatibilities before, rather than after, installation, answering such questions as:

1. How do I know that a particular version of UNIX (operating system layer) will work on my computer (server hardware platform layer)?

2. If I do get UNIX installed, how do I know which network operating systems and database management systems will be compatible with UNIX and with each other?

Whereas vertical software compatibility is concerned with transparency between *different* layers of software or hardware *within* a particular client or server, **horizontal software compatibility** is concerned with transparency between *similar* software layers *between* different clients and servers.

To elaborate, one of the benefits of a client/server architecture is its ability to incorporate hardware and software technology from multiple vendors into a transparently interoperable information system. This is easier said than done. Horizontal software compatibility is most often concerned with getting different software of the same category to interoperate transparently between clients, between clients and servers, or between servers, answering such questions as:

1. How do I get a NetWare client (network operating system layer) to interoperate with a Windows NT server (network operating system layer)?

2. How do I get an Oracle Database server (database management system layer) to query a Sybase SQL server (database management system layer)?

Horizontal software compatibility between different types of software on different types of computers is a complicated task roughly equivalent to translating between foreign languages. As a result, although vertical software compatibility was achieved by adjacent software layers, each supporting a common compatibility protocol, horizontal software compatibility is most often delivered by a category of software known as **middleware.** Middleware is an additional installed software program rather than just a set of mutually supported commands and messages. It is often specialized by software layer: database middleware, network operating system middleware, operating systems middleware, or distributed application middleware.

Occasionally, horizontal software compatibility is concerned with transparent interoperability between multiple pieces of software in the same software category layer within a single client or server. It answers such questions as:

1. How do I get my Excel spreadsheet graph into my Word document?

Remember, transparency depends on the existence of compatibility protocols or translating middleware. These may be proprietary and work only with one or a few vendors' software, or they may be open, industry-standard protocols. The important things for the network analyst to determine are where the needs for horizontal or vertical software compatibility are and what options are available to deliver that compatibility.

The Enterprise Network   Connecting the client and server in Figure 2-17 is an entity entitled the **enterprise network.** This is the transportation system of the client/server architecture. Together with middleware, it is responsible for the transparent cooperation of distributed processors and databases. The enterprise network is analogous to the system bus of a powerful standalone mainframe computer, linking the processing power of the CPU with the stored data to be processed.

The role of the enterprise network is to deliver the integration and transparent interoperability enabled by the client/server architecture. Further, it often also incorporates host-terminal traffic, voice traffic, and videoconferencing traffic in an integrated and well-managed fashion.

What exactly does an enterprise network look like? That depends on what the business enterprise looks like. If the business enterprise is composed of regional branches or subsidiaries widely dispersed geographically, then the enterprise network will obviously contain WAN links. From a physical standpoint, the enterprise network is most often the combination of network devices and connections of the following categories:

- Local area network (LAN).
- LAN-to-LAN or inter-LAN, also known as internetwork.
- Wide area network (WAN).

In addition, the enterprise network plays a key role in managing a client/server information system. Due to the distributed nature of a client/server information system composed of a multitude of widely dispersed processors, the only single location through which all traffic passes is the enterprise network. It therefore stands to reason that the enterprise network is the only sensible location from which to manage the system's numerous shared resources. A variety of management hardware and software capable of effectively supporting corporate requirements for managing distributed information systems are connected directly to the enterprise network. The enterprise network literally serves as the backbone of the client/server information system. Hopefully, this discussion clarifies the truth of the often heard statement, "The network *is* the computer."

While Figure 2-17 portrayed a conceptual or logical view of an enterprise network, Figure 2-18 shows an example of a typical physical topology. Notice the LAN, LAN-to-LAN, and WAN elements combined to form the overall enterprise network.

Management of Client/Server Information Systems   To understand the complexity of a comprehensive management system for a client/server architecture, one only needs to examine the vast array of components within that architecture which potentially require management.

Most, if not all, of the client/server architecture elements listed in Figure 2-17 are available with some sort of management system or software. The problem is

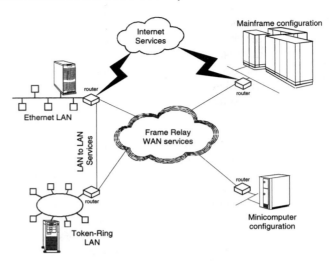

Figure 2-18   Example of an Enterprise Network Physical Topology

that there is little if any similarity or consistency in management system design among various vendors, even for elements with similar function. In addition, the multiple layers of management systems listed in Figure 2-17 under the enterprise network component present a major management system integration problem.

Users do not want "piecemeal" system management caused by the distributed nature of their information systems. They do not want separate management consoles or systems for database systems, distributed applications, operating systems, network operating systems, and networking hardware. Furthermore, since the client/server architecture can feature multiple client and server operating systems and network operating systems, one can see the potential need for an entire room just for systems consoles to manage the various client and server possibilities.

The solution to this problem comes down to two key questions regarding standards:

1. Can management system standards that lend themselves especially well to distributed information systems be developed?

2. More important, can and will the manufacturers of the various elements of the client/server architecture adhere to these standards?

In fact, open standards for sharing management information have been developed and integrated into several popular **enterprise network management systems.** The following are among the most popular:

*   HP Openview.

*   IBM NetView.

*   Sun SunNet Manager.

It is important, however, to distinguish between enterprise network management systems and **integrated client/server management systems.** In addition to managing a multivendor enterprise network, an integrated client/server management system must also be able to supply the following management capabilities:

- Enterprise database management.

- Enterprise desktop management.

- Enterprise transaction processing management.

- Enterprise distributed processing management.

Although there are many multivendor enterprise network management systems, most so-called integrated client/server management systems are still in the "vaporware" stage. Note that enterprise network management is only one component of the overall integrated client/server management. Enterprise network management systems and integrated client/server management systems are discussed in detail in Chapter 17.

Two-tiered versus Three-tiered Client/Server Architectures   Client/server physical architectures are often categorized in terms of tiers. The term "tiers" refers to the relationship between the logical sublayers of the application process of the P-A-D logical architecture (see Figure 2-6) and the physical architecture in which those sublayer processes are delivered. In other words, we know we want to implement a distributed processing information system. The question is, how will that processing be distributed? Recall that the application layer of the P-A-D logical model is subdivided into presentation logic, business logic, and database logic.

Two-tiered client/server architectures deliver the presentation logic on the client and the database logic on the server. The business logic may be distributed as follows:

- On the client in a two-tiered architecture known as **fat client.**

- On the server in a two-tiered architecture known as **fat server.**

Three-tiered client/server architectures deliver the presentation logic on the client, the business logic on a dedicated server of its own, and the database logic on a superserver or mainframe. Specialized middleware servers are often located on the second (middle) tier as well. Figure 2-19 illustrates two-tiered and three-tiered client/server architectures.

Which of the two architectures is better? The answer is the classic networking analysis answer, "It depends." Two-tiered architectures are presently far more common and work well for the type of departmental client/server systems corporations often use as pilot projects to gain experience with downsizing, application rightsizing, and client/server information systems. Development tools and database back-ends for two-tiered architectures are widely available and dependable.

Enterprisewide, distributed client/server applications require the business-logic processing to be separated from the database logic to allow multiple, different, geographically distributed database servers to all adhere to the same business logic. In these cases, three-tiered architectures are preferred. Three-tiered architectures are newer than two-tiered, and predictably have fewer development tools available and fewer successful installations as models.

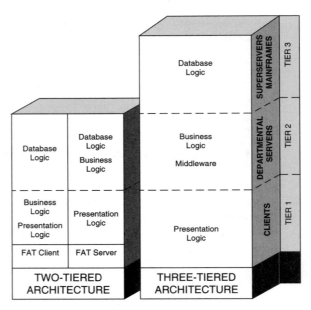

Figure 2-19   Two-Tiered versus Three-Tiered Client/
Server Architecture

From a network analyst's standpoint, philosophical arguments over the virtues of two-tiered versus three-tiered architectures should be avoided. By adhering to the top-down model, the architecture that most effectively meets the strategic business requirements of the corporation will be evident.

■ TECHNOLOGY AND TOOLS OF CLIENT/SERVER INFORMATION SYSTEMS

Technology Components and Trends

Client/server information systems require a multitude of hardware and software technology from a variety of vendors to be linked together seamlessly via an enterprise network to deliver transparent interoperability to the end-user. The term "seamlessly" implies that all software/software, software/hardware, and hardware/hardware interfaces have been successfully bridged by mutually compatible protocols. This is far from a trivial task.

Figure 2-17 illustrated the many categories of technology that must interact successfully in a client/server information system. Although many of these technology categories are elaborated on in later chapters, the following section provides some insight into the key characteristics and trends and the current products for each technology category.

SQL Databases   As previously mentioned, SQL is a standard command language supported by database vendors that allows interoperability among multivendor database front-ends and database engines. However, the problem with SQL is that individual vendors enhance the language by implementing proprietary extensions. As a result, the version of SQL all database vendors support becomes a least common denominator, or least functional version, of the database interoperability language.

One of the most important uses of SQL in a distributed client/server environment is to ensure database integrity through the use of triggers and stored procedures. **Triggers** can be built into distributed application programs that cause transactions to be posted initially. The trigger causes an "integrity-assurance subroutine" to run, which checks all of the necessary distributed database fields involved and verifies that their current contents are correct based on the latest transaction.

Rather than have the transaction posting application program trigger the integrity check, the database definition itself can be written in such a way that if any particular field in the distributed database is updated, the SQL database initiates a **stored procedure** to perform all necessary integrity checking on the distributed databases involved. Dependency tables can be included in a database definition, to indicate which fields depend on which other fields for database integrity assurance. Two of the largest vendors of SQL databases are Oracle and SyBase.

TP Monitors   Transaction-processing monitors are often considered a category of middleware that acts as a supervisor of distributed applications requiring postings to numerous distributed databases. TP monitors are currently being adapted for the multivendor, multiplatform client/server world. For example, IBM's CICS (Customer Information Control System) was originally designed for mainframe computers, and Novell's Tuxedo was originally designed for use only on UNIX platforms. Other popular TP monitors include Top End from NCR and Encina from Transarc. TP monitors can work locally, in a standalone fashion, or in a distributed environment in coordination with other TP monitors.

Numerous TP monitor standards are evolving, and interoperability among TP monitors from different vendors is by no means guaranteed. All TP monitors perform the following basic tasks:

- Oversee the successful posting(s) of the transaction.

- Route the transaction among multiple clients and/or servers.

- Load-balance the execution of the transaction.

- Restart the posting of the transaction or deal with failed postings in a predictable manner.

Groupware   Groupware is a category of software that seeks to take advantage of the fact that workers are networked together electronically to maximize worker productivity. If maximizing or increasing worker productivity was one of the top-layer business needs of the top-down model, groupware may be of some interest.

Lotus Notes is probably the best known of the currently available groupware offerings. Notes runs on Windows, Windows NT, OS/2, UNIX, and Macintosh platforms, and numerous third-party add-on products have been developed for it.

Groupware of any type depends heavily on bandwidth-intensive applications such as multimedia and videoconferencing. Network analysts should be especially careful in estimating network impact of groupware implementation.

Groupware is a general term that describes all or some of the following software categories:

- Workflow automation.

- Interactive work and electronic whiteboards.

- Group scheduling.

- Document review and management.

- Information sharing and desktop conferencing.

- Enhanced electronic mail.

Middleware   Middleware is actually a fairly general category of software which can be broken down into at least two subcategories based on the nature of the interprocess communication it enables.

Remote procedure call (RPC) middleware works in a manner similar to a locally run application program that activates, or calls a subroutine stored outside of the application program itself, but usually in a subroutine library on the same computer. The major distinguishing feature of RPCs is that the call for the execution of a subroutine is made to a remote procedure located on a remote distributed processor via the enterprise network. Where that particular server is located and how the remote procedure call is transported there are the concern of the RPC middleware rather than the applications programmer.

RPCs are like local subroutines in at least one other characteristic. When an application program branches to a subroutine, whether a local or a remote procedure, that application program waits for the local or remote procedure to complete execution and return either data or some type of status message before continuing with its own program execution. This style of interprocess communication is categorized as **send-and-wait** or **synchronous** communication.

Message passing, also known as message delivery, message queuing, and distributed messaging, differs significantly from the previously mentioned middleware subcategories in its ability to establish various types of interprocess communications modes other than the send-and-wait mode of RPCs. For instance, distributed applications programs can communicate indirectly with the help of message queues, which are roughly equivalent to post offices. In this scenario, a distributed application could generate a message for another distributed application, forward it to the message queue, and resume its own processing activity. This type of interprocess dialogue is known as **asynchronous,** not to be confused with asynchronous transmission.

Another interprocess dialogue type supported by message delivery middleware is broadcast or multicast dialogues. Broadcast sends messages to all clients and/or servers on an enterprise network, whereas multicast sends to a selected group.

Message delivery middleware is also flexible as to the content of interprocess communication messages. For instance, message-handling middleware can deliver RPC or SQL as its message. Security checking, encryption, data compression, and error recovery are all supported features of message-delivery middleware. Message-handling middleware often has the network savvy to navigate the enterprise network intelligently by responding to changing network conditions.

Middleware is an absolutely crucial component of distributed, multivendor, client/server information systems. Without it, there can be no transparent interoperability, the key operational characteristic of client/server information systems.

Operating Systems and User Interfaces   If Figure 2-17 is reviewed, the crucial role of both client and server operating systems will be immediately evident. The operating system is the first layer of software responsible for communicating with the hardware and delivering the functionality demanded by all of the upper layers of software. Although the technical aspects of present and future operating systems are reviewed in later chapters, a few key trends are worth mentioning here in non-technical terms.

First, the major differences between client and server operating systems are disappearing. Due to the demands of distributed processing in the client/server environment, both client and server operating systems must be powerful enough to run multiple applications simultaneously without allowing those applications to interfere with each other. At the same time, these futuristic operating systems should be backward-compatible, to the greatest extent possible, with users' current hardware and software technology.

Although operating systems will continue to become more complicated, to deliver this increased functionality, they need to simultaneously become more intuitive in their user interfaces. Graphical user interfaces should evolve toward **object-oriented user interfaces (OOUI),** in which users will no longer work by executing a particular application program, but will choose to accomplish a particular task. The combination of application programs required to complete that task will execute without direct actions from the user.

Server operating systems must be powerful enough to participate in the three-tiered, widely distributed architecture of tomorrow's client/server information systems. These operating systems must be very scaleable, working equally efficiently on a single processor departmental server and a multiprocessor superserver delivering real-time video and voice conferencing as well as data via a worldwide enterprise network.

Network Operating Systems   Network operating systems play a key role in the overall mission of client/server information systems to deliver transparent interoperability. These systems must serve as an insulating layer, shielding distributed applications that must interoperate transparently from the intricacies of the numerous operating systems and hardware platforms on which the network operating systems execute.

To truly deliver this transparent interoperability, present-day network operating systems must continue to develop in the following areas:

- Global services.
- NOS-to-NOS interoperability.
- Enterprisewide security.
- Middleware incorporation.

Global services, sometimes referred to as global naming services or global directory services, refer to an NOS' ability to locate a particular resource, service, or user, regardless of the location of the desired entity. This implies coordination of directory and naming services among the multiple NOSs that comprise an entire enterprise network. Sought resources may be technical, such as printers, processors, data, fax machines, and CD-ROMs, or may be human resources, such as users, coworkers, or help desk/support personnel.

For global naming services to be successfully delivered across the enterprise, different network operating systems must develop better interfaces to each other in order to deliver transparent interoperability. Although such a proposal might make perfect logical sense, it may be more difficult to accomplish from a practical standpoint as competitive pressures and market share percentages exert their influence.

As the enterprise network grows, and more mobile users require access to it, enterprisewide security becomes a key issue. Traditional userID/password schemes no longer suffice. Enterprisewide security must include the following distinct processes:

- **Authorization.**

- **Authentication.**

Authorization is the familiar userID/password process, which ensures that a certain user is authorized to access a particular enterprise resource. An authorization enhancement for remote users is callback security. Once a user has been properly authorized, authentication ensures that messages between client and servers in the distributed processing environment are genuine and have actually been sent from the processor claiming to be the source node on the network. Authentication is usually provided by a dedicated authentication server running specialized software developed specifically for distributed environments. Kerberos, developed at MIT, is a popular authentication service that will be studied further in Chapter 17.

Figure 2-20 summarizes typical current functionality of operating systems and

	Operating Systems	Network Operating Systems
Current functionality	• Interfaces between client hardware and upper layers of client software • Applications programs must be compatible with a particular operating system	• Interfaces between client operating systems and client networking hardware to communicate with network attached resources • NOS must be compatible with the operating system on the client or server • Some NOS provide their own operating systems
Future Trends	• Able to perform more than one task simultaneously (multitasking) • Able to split application across more than one CPU (multiprocessing) • Will include GUI • GUI will evolve to object-oriented interfaces • Will be included within NOS products	• Will include GUI and OS • Will be able to run on a variety of hardware platforms and operating systems • Will be able to seamlessly interoperate with other network operating systems • Will be able to seamlessly interoperate with multiple e-mail, groupware, and database management systems by including more middleware now purchased from third-party software vendors • Will include increased security

Figure 2-20 Functionality and Trends of Operating Systems and Network Operating Systems

network operating systems as well as potential future directions for each software category.

Middleware is responsible for allowing a variety of network operating systems, operating systems, and database management systems to interoperate transparently in support of distributed applications. This ability will be the responsibility of the network operating systems of tomorrow. The functionality supplied today by numerous third-party middleware vendors will be built into tomorrow's NOSs. All NOSs will be ready to support distributed processing right out of the box and will be capable of supporting the protocols necessary to deliver full horizontal software compatibility. Tomorrow's NOSs will truly be "client/server ready." The best current examples of such truly open network operating systems are DCE (Distributed Computing Environment) from the Open Software Foundation (OSF), and ONC (Open Network Computing) from Sun Microsystems.

Distributed Applications   Many of the previously described technologies represent portions of the infrastructure underlying the real purpose of client/server information systems, namely, the distributed applications. If client/server information systems are to be the absolute information systems architecture of the future, then distributed applications must become easier to develop, to implement across heterogeneous, distributed, multivendor systems, and to execute.

A key contributing factor to the achievement of many, if not all, of these goals may be the widespread development and adoption of **distributed object technology;** however, the jury is still out on the practicality and likelihood of its widespread adoption.

As a matter of background, an **object** can be thought of as a merger of the business logic, and database logic sublayers of the P-A-D model (see Figure 2-6), subsequently combined with actual data. Thus, data and the logic and rules to process that data are treated as a single, encapsulated entity which can subsequently interoperate with, or be included in (encapsulate), other objects.

Briefly stated, distributed object technology would make distributed applications easier to develop thanks to the reusability and encapsulation quality of the objects themselves. Furthermore, thanks to an entire object management architecture, objects and interobject communication could be distributed transparently across an enterprise network without application development programmers being required to know the physical location of required objects. This **object management layer** would reside between the NOS and the distributed application layers in a client/server technology architecture such as that in Figure 2-17, supposedly offering true application portability.

Applied Problem Solving

Recalling the requirements for vertical software compatibility, it should be obvious that the object management layer, or any other layer for that matter, cannot just be added to the client/server technology architecture with transparent application portability magically occurring. Each layer of software or hardware must support protocols which are understood and supported by adjacent layers in the architecture. For the object management layer to be transparently assimilated into the client/server technology architecture, network operating systems and applications layers will need to support protocols defined by the object management layer. This support is possible only if network operating systems and applications vendors are willing to commit the resources necessary to add this capability to their products. This commitment is by no means a forgone conclusion.

SUMMARY

Although many businesses may begin the exploration of client/server information systems in search of huge financial savings, the key benefit most often derived from their implementation is the flexibility of information delivery due to their distributed nature. Local area networks comprise a crucial part of the overall enterprise network infrastructure, which serves as the backbone linking the many distributed components of client/server information systems. As companies transition their information systems from mainframe-based to distributed client/server, opportunities exist to reengineer applications and the business processes they support. To analyze and design effective client/server information systems, it is essential to understand overall logical and physical architectures that model these distributed systems. The key logical elements which can be developed across a variety of clients and servers are presentation, processing, business logic, and data management. These conceptual elements are all linked via the enterprise network. Differences between heterogeneous platforms become transparently interoperable thanks to the addition of translating middleware. Designing client/server information systems requires an in-depth understanding of the interfaces between the numerous layers of hardware and software technology which must successfully interoperate. The client/server technology architecture can serve as an effective analysis tool in this regard. If client/server information systems are to become the dominant information systems architecture of the future, distributed applications must be easier to develop, implement, maintain, support, manage, and execute.

KEY TERMS

API, 55
application program interface, 55
application rightsizing, 38
asynchronous, 66
authentication, 68
authorization, 68
back-end, 50
client/server information system, 38
corporate downsizing, 38
data transparency, 53
database connectivity software, 54
distributed applications, 49
distributed architecture, 38
distributed computing, 49
distributed database management systems, 53
distributed object technology, 69
distributed transaction processing, 56
distributed transaction processing monitor, 56
downsizing, 42
DTP, 56
DTP API, 56
DTPM, 56
engine, 50
enterprise network, 61

enterprise network management system, 62
enterprise transaction processing, 56
ETP, 56
fat client, 63
fat server, 63
front-end, 50
front-end tools, 55
graphical user interfaces, 49
GUI, 49
horizontal software compatibility, 60
information systems downsizing, 38
integrated client/server management system, 62
interprocess communication, 52
IPC, 52
message passing, 53
middleware, 50
object, 69
object management layer, 69
object-oriented user interface, 67
OLTP, 56
on-line transaction processing, 56
OOUI, 67
P-A-D architecture, 46

paradigm shift, 43
paradigms, 43
portability, 50
presentation-application-data, 46
real-time systems, 56
remote procedure calls, 53
rightsizing, 42
RPC, 53
scalability, 50
screen scrapers, 49
send-and-wait, 66
single-solution gateway, 55
smartsizing, 43
SQL, 54
stored procedures, 65
structured query language, 54
synchronous, 66
three-tiered C/S architecture, 63
TP monitors, 55
transaction, 55
transition costs, 39
transparency, 50
triggers, 65
two-tiered C/S architecture, 63
universal data access system, 55
upsizing, 42
vertical software compatibility, 60

REVIEW QUESTIONS

1. Describe the fallacy of massive cost savings by implementing client/server information systems.
2. What is the key benefit of client/server information systems in terms of business impact?
3. What are transition costs, and why are they occasionally overlooked?
4. What is the difference and relationship between corporate downsizing and information systems downsizing?
5. Distinguish between the following in terms of effort, costs, and potential impact: downsizing, rightsizing, upsizing, smartsizing.
6. What is meant by the term client/server information system?
7. What are meant by the terms paradigm and paradigm shift?
8. Explain some of the impacts of the paradigm shift to client/server information systems.
9. How is a paradigm shift different from the introduction of new technology?
10. What is meant by the term people architecture, and how is it related to systems architecture?
11. What are some of the major people architecture issues surrounding the transition to client/server information systems?
12. Describe the role of each of the sublayers of the application layer in P-A-D architecture.
13. Differentiate between the following: client-based processing, host-based processing, cooperative processing.
14. What is a screen scraper, and what role does it play in the transition to client/server information systems?
15. What is the relationship between front-ends and back-ends in distributed applications?
16. Discuss the importance of each of the following terms of distributed computing: transparency, scalability, portability.
17. Why is scalability so often mentioned as a business motivation for distributed computing?
18. What is the role of interprocess communications in distributed computing?
19. Why is interprocess communications not an issue in nondistributed computing environments?
20. What are some of the variables that make interprocess communication a complicated technology?
21. What are some of the difficulties which must be overcome when data management functions are distributed?
22. What is SQL, and why is it important?
23. Why is SQL not a perfect solution for database interoperability?
24. What are the advantages and disadvantages of a single-solution gateway for database interoperability?
25. What is the outlook for universal data access systems if SQL standardization becomes more widespread and full-featured?
26. What is the difference between a transaction in business terms and in information systems terms?
27. What is the relationship between distributed transaction processing monitors and local transaction processing monitors?
28. What are the compatibility issues surrounding TP monitors and other layers of the client/server architecture?
29. What is a DTP API, and why is it important?
30. What is OLTP, and how does it differ from other TP systems?
31. Compare and contrast mainframe-terminal and client/server architectures.
32. Differentiate between vertical and horizontal software compatibility. How is each achieved?
33. What is middleware, and what is its role in distributed processing systems?
34. What is the role of the enterprise network in client/server information systems?
35. What elements or subnetworks might make up an enterprise network?
36. What types of traffic might an enterprise network carry?
37. Differentiate between enterprise network management systems and integrated client/server management systems.
38. Differentiate between two-tiered and three-tiered client/server architectures in terms of delivered functionality and physical architecture.
39. What is the difference in functionality between a fat client and a fat server?
40. Which client/server architectures are fat clients and fat servers associated with?
41. Why are triggers and stored procedures important?
42. What is the difference between a trigger and a stored procedure?
43. What types of functionality do all TP monitors have in common?
44. Why are TP monitors so important in distributed processing systems?
45. What are the major functional differences between RPCs and message-passing middleware? Which is more flexible?
46. What is the difference between GUI and OOUI?
47. What are some of the key functional

improvements necessary to make network operating systems more effectively support client/server information systems?

48. What is the difference between authentication and authorization?

49. Detail the potential benefits as well as the

obstacles facing distributed object technology.

50. What is the function of the object management layer?

51. What changes must occur in distributed applications for client/server information systems to become more widely adopted?

ACTIVITIES

1. Review trade journals and professional periodicals for information related to real-world implementation of client/server information systems. Prepare a chart or presentation summarizing stated benefits and negative impacts of the installations.

2. Find a local business in the midst of a transition from mainframe-based to client/server information systems. Prepare a presentation or chart focusing on the people issues involved with the transition.

3. After reviewing the client/server implementations for Activity 1, classify these implementations according to the categories of client/server information systems presented in Figures 2-7 and 2-8. Which is the most common category? Explain your results.

4. Prepare a presentation comparing currently available GUIs. What, if any, are the major differences?

5. Research and prepare a presentation on available front-ends and back-ends for distributed applications. Focus the presentation on compatibility between which front-ends work with which back-ends on which types of computing platforms.

6. Research and report on the latest standards-making efforts regarding SQL. How is compliance with any proposed standards ensured?

7. Research and report on database front-end tools. Prepare a chart illustrating which front-end tools work with which database engines.

8. Research and report on transaction-processing monitors. Which TP monitors work on which platforms? Which distributed TP monitors work with which local TP monitors?

9. Research and report on OLTP applications. What is the systems architecture underlying the OLTP application (distributed or local)? What TP monitors are being used?

10. Prepare a detailed client/server technology architecture for an actual client/server information system. Be sure to highlight protocols and middleware which deliver software compatibility.

11. Research and report on the latest offerings in the enterprise network management and integrated client/server management technology categories. What standards are being used to help ensure multivendor interoperability?

12. Find an example of and demonstrate or report on an OOUI. What are the key differences between GUI and OOUI? What is the potential productivity impact of these differences?

13. Research and report on the Kerberos authentication system. Report on tests to break the system as well as what steps are taken to ensure its security and integrity.

FEATURED REFERENCES

General

Alper, Alan (ed.). *Computerworld Client/Server Journal*, 2; 2 (May 1994).

Berson, Alex. *Client/Server Architecture* (New York: McGraw-Hill, 1992).

Caldwell, Bruce. In the Money, *Information Week*, no. 530 (June 5, 1995), 34.

Dewire, Dawna. *Client/Server Computing* (New York: McGraw-Hill, 1993).

Vaskevitch, David. *Client/Server Strategies: A Survival Guide for Corporate Reengineers* (San Mateo, CA: IDG Books, 1993).

Vaughn, Larry. *Client/Server Design and Implementation* (New York: McGraw-Hill, 1994).

Cases

Winchell, Jeff. Piecing Together the Client/Server Puzzle. *Network Computing*, 5; 6 (June 1, 1994), 90.

Business Aspects/Migration

Anderson, Howard. Client/Server Teams: The Art of Double Talk. *Network Computing*, 5; 14 (November 15, 1994), 26.

Borel, Sue and Milt Borel. Is Your Network Ready for

Rightsizing? *Network Computing*, 5; 9 (August 1, 1994), 140.

Chabrow, Eric. Migration Strategies: Five Who Bridged the Gap. *Communications Week*, no. 569 (August 7, 1995), 41.

Finklestein, Richard. Client-Server Woes: Who's at Fault? *Network Computing*, 5; 9 (August 1, 1994), 78.

Klein, Paula. Uncovering the Hidden Costs of Client/Server. *Network Computing*, 5; 8 (July 1, 1994), CS12.

Littman, Jonathan. Breaking Free. *Corporate Computing*, 2; 6 (June 1993), 104.

Rhodes, Wayne. Finding Your Way. *Beyond Computing*, 4; 4 (June 1995), 26.

Robinson, Teri. Emerging Technologies: Proceed with Caution. *Communications Week*, no. 565 (July 10, 1995), 44.

Sanazaro, Steven. Client-Server: Begin at the Beginning. *Business Communications Review*, 25; 1 (January 1995), 29.

Weissman, Steven. The Business End of Network Redesign. *Network World*, 12; 28 (July 10, 1995), 47.

Whiteside, John. A New Paradigm for the Millenium. *Network Computing*, 5; 14 (November 15, 1994), 115.

Technology Evolution/Paradigm Shift

Reinhardt, Andy. Your Next Mainframe. *Byte*, 20; 5 (May 1995), 48.

Client/Server Architecture

Eckerson, Wayne. Client Server Architecture. *Network World*, 12; 2 (January 9, 1995), C18.

Loosley, Chris. A Three-Tier Solution. *Database Programming & Design*, 7; 2 (February 1994), 23.

Orfall, Robert and Dan Harkey. Intergalactic Client/Server Computing. *Byte*, 20; 4 (April 1995), 108.

Tebbe, Mark. 3-Tier C/S: New Way, Not Upgrade. *PC Week*, 11; 38 (September 26, 1994), 24.

Application Splitting

Scheier, Robert. The Right Cut. *PC Week*, 12; 25 (June 26, 1995), 19.

Business Process Reengineering

Hammer, Michael and James Champy. *Reengineering the Corporation* (New York: HarperCollins, 1993).

Vacca, John and Dave Andrews. BPR Tools Help You Work Smarter. *Byte*, 19; 10 (October 1994), 24.

CASE STUDY

Chapter 2

MOVE TO LANS WITH A "MAINFRAME MENTALITY"

Faced with the prospect of migrating to a PC LAN-based computing environment, Mark Allen, director of information systems for a medical clinic and IBM Systems Network Architecture (SNA) expert, felt more than a little bit of apprehension.

His method for coping with the transition to new technology? First, avoid it as long as possible, and then get help with the move.

During 1994, the Aspen Medical Group P.A. in St. Paul, Minn., installed 10 Novell Inc. NetWare 4.x LANs supporting 150 users. These systems joined the 200 existing 3270 terminals running IBM ES 9000 mainframe and AS/400 applications.

While devising the LAN infrastructure, Allen was sure to include numerous attributes of what he calls "the mainframe mentality." To do this, he relied on outsourced expertise to help with the installation, and he continues to tap that same vendor for LAN administration and maintenance.

When You Can't Put It Off

Users at Aspen's clinics throughout the Twin Cities area had application needs that only LANs could accommodate. The breadth of applications available on LANs, as well as the quick turnaround time for LAN-based application development vs. mainframe development, dictated the migration.

Aside from the mainframe applications users were accessing, users on standalone machines at different clinics were tracking and reporting such items as patient referrals. "The clinics were like separate islands of information," Allen said. "One clinic wouldn't know when another site had created a patient referral."

Allen and his team resisted installing LANs primarily because they didn't know enough to install or manage them. "We were trying to hold off as long as we could because we didn't know how to support them," he said. "We knew very little—just enough to be dangerous."

For Allen, acquiring the LAN expertise in-house was not a viable option. "By the time we could have hired someone, trained them, and got them up to speed, we'd have spent too many resources," he said. "We have a fairly lean shop. We're constantly having to change our applications to keep pace with healthcare reform, so our resources have to go into program development."

The company Aspen ended up working with on its LANs—

Memorex Telex Corp. in Irving, Texas—was the same company that supplied equipment and support for Aspen's mainframe and midrange systems. Like many of its competitors, Memorex Telex had diversified into the growing market for network support.

Planning the Network

Allen's desire to transport mainframe techniques and advantages to the LAN-based system determined equipment choices and the architectural model. One item on his list was to choose a NOS that included directory services. "I wanted to keep the mainframe mentality of centrally controlling changes and additions," Allen explained. "That model allows us to respond to user needs faster."

The team looked at Banyan Systems Inc. VINES because they'd heard a lot of "horror stories" about NetWare 4.01, but Memorex Telex recommended NetWare despite those problems. Memorex Telex argued that 4.1, which had resolved problems with NetWare Directory Services, was due out soon (it shipped last month) and that Aspen would receive better support from their health-care system vendors because they are more familiar with NetWare than with VINES.

Allen and his team chose to run token ring LANs to simplify connectivity to the mainframe and AS/400. They also wanted the performance benefits that token ring offered compared with Ethernet.

To further the mainframe model, Memorex Telex set up a Tricord Systems Inc. superserver at Aspen's headquarters. This design allows the medical group to keep its mission-critical data in one location and to distribute only departmental data to the clinics.

"With the main server in the controlled site, we can take advantage of the UPSes [uninterruptible power supplies], fire protection, and other security measures we have in place for the mainframe," explained Allen. In addition, backup and contingency plans have been extended to the LANs.

During 1994, Aspen brought 10 clinics online running NetWare LANs with Intel Corp. Pentium- or 486/66MHz-based servers. The clinics connect to headquarters via frame relay running over T-1 or 56Kbps lines using bridges and routers from Memotec Communications Corp.

Going Forward

Aspen Medical Group intends to bring online five additional clinics during 1995, while continuing to move applications from the mainframe to the LAN environment. The group also plans to connect other business partners, such as hospitals contracted with Aspen, to the system. These connections will help streamline processes such as patient admittance.

The most far-reaching aspect of the system calls for automating medical records. "That's where our LANs will really come into play," said Allen. "Electronic records will help us perform medicine better and more efficiently." He uses the example of a patient who comes into urgent care one evening after coming in earlier that day for tests. A provider accessing the patient's records would have the test results immediately, speeding diagnosis and saving costs.

Allen will continue to depend on outside vendors to help fulfill these plans. "We'd love to support ourselves in-house, but I don't see that happening soon. We need to keep our people focused on future trends coming down the road."

Outsourcing also gives Allen peace of mind. "We have someone we can hold accountable. They're there to make sure that if we need to zig, we don't zag."

Source: Michelle Rae McLean (January 9, 1995). Move to LANs with a "Mainframe Mentality." *LAN Times*, 12(1), 9. Reprinted with permission of McGraw-Hill, *LAN Times.*

BUSINESS CASE STUDY QUESTIONS

Activities

1. Complete a top-down model for this case by gleaning facts from the case and placing them in the proper layer of the model. Then analyze and detail those instances when requirements were clearly passed down from upper to lower layers of the model and solutions to those requirements were passed up from lower to upper layers.

2. Detail any questions about the case that may occur to you for which answers are not clearly stated in the article.

3. Debate the pros and cons of outsourcing LAN installation, administration, and management.

4. Draw a diagram of the new LAN setup based on the information supplied in the article. Highlight any missing information.

Business

1. What were the key factors that necessitated the migration to LANs?

2. What were the key factors delaying the migration to LANs?

3. What criteria were used in selecting an outsourcing company?
4. What are the strategic plans from this point forward?

Application

1. What role did applications play in motivating the migration to LANs?
2. What demands of application development are unique to this industry?
3. What effect did application development demands have on the overall LAN migration plan?

Data

1. What was the problem associated with data before the installation of the LAN-based system?
2. How was data to be distributed in the proposed LAN setup?

Network

1. What were the key functional characteristics required of the network operating system to be installed on the LANs?
2. Which "mainframe mentality" network characteristics were migrated to the LAN environment?

Technology

1. Which NOSs were considered and why?
2. What was the determining factor in the final NOS choice?
3. Which data link layer technology was chosen and why?
4. Which data server technology was employed and why?

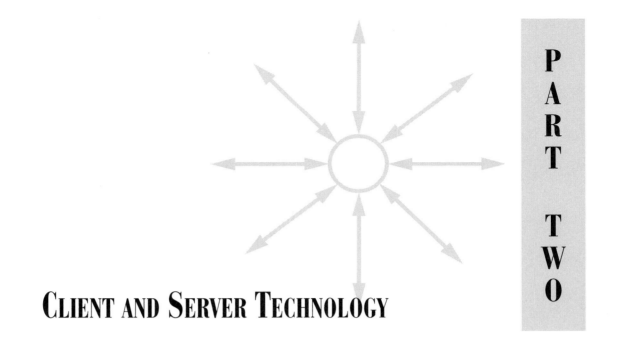

CLIENT AND SERVER TECHNOLOGY

INTRODUCTION

Having gained an introductory understanding of local area networks and client/server information systems, in Part 2 we explore in detail the technology and trends of two of the most important constituent elements of these architectures, namely, the client and the server.

In each case, both the hardware and software aspects of client and server computers are dealt with in detail. Perhaps more important, we study the vital relationship and interdependencies between hardware technology, software technology, and delivered functionality. From the latest innovations in CPU chips to the latest releases of client and server operating systems, analysis and problem-solving skills are stressed with the aid of ample models and architectures.

Figure 2-17, showing the client/server technology architecture, will help you understand how major topics in Part 2 relate both to each other and to concepts covered in Part 1. All of this technology is explored from an applied perspective, emphasizing the implications and importance of a given technological characteristic or standard.

Chapters 3, 4, and 5 explore client and server hardware and software from both conceptual and technical perspectives; Chapter 6 provides a timely application of this knowledge by exploring how clients and servers are combined with the global internet to meet business objectives.

CHAPTER 3

CLIENT HARDWARE

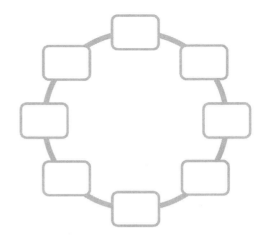

Concepts Reinforced

Client/server technology architecture
OSI model
Client/server technology and tools

Protocols and compatibility
Top-down model

Concepts Introduced

Comparative hardware platforms
PowerPC
Computer bus alternatives
Video/graphics
Computer storage

CPU chips
RISC versus CISC
PCMCIA
Computer memory
Processor fundamentals

OBJECTIVES

After mastering the material in this chapter you should:

1. Understand and differentiate between the basic internal functionality of popular CPU chips.

2. Understand the impact on overall performance of and interrelationship between the following major computer subsystems:
    *   Processor type.
    *   Memory.
    *   Disk storage.
    *   Video.

3. Understand the relationship between CPU type, clock speed, and overall performance.

4. Understand the differences between and performance impact of a variety of computer bus types.

5. Understand the differences between and implication of a variety of computer video standards.

In examining the client portion of the client/server technology architecture (see Figure 2-17), the importance of the client hardware platform should be immediately evident. The client hardware forms the foundation on which all upper-layer software depends. Regardless of how powerful or sophisticated upper-layer software such as operating systems, network operating systems, or applications might be, the ultimate limiting factor of overall client performance is the client hardware.

The treatment of the inner workings of client computing platforms in this chapter is not meant to be overly technical but takes a definite systems-oriented approach. What is most important to information systems and networking professionals is to understand how all the major technological components of a client PC—CPU chip, bus, memory, storage, and video—interact to produce the overall performance characteristics of a given computing platform. The critical outcome of this chapter is the accumulation of sufficient knowledge to ask the important analysis questions rather than rote memorization of technical specifications.

■ THE COMPUTER AS A SYSTEM

Perhaps the most important point to understand about a client computing platform is that it is really a **computer system.** The term computer system was commonly used before personal computers were introduced, and it is ultimately more descriptive, from a technological perspective, of a computer's true nature.

The following four subsystems contribute to the overall performance characteristics of any computer system:

1. Processor or CPU.

2. Memory subsystem.

3. Storage subsystem.

4. Video or input/output subsystem.

A potential fifth subsystem, which ties all of these subsystems together, is the bus subsystem. It is important to understand that a change in any one of these subsystems can profoundly affect the overall performance of the computer system as a whole. The remainder of the chapter studies each of these subsystems in detail. More detailed and highly technical information is available in many of the articles listed in the Featured References.

■ THE CPU

The feature that most uniquely identifies any computing platform is the processor chip or **central processing unit (CPU)** in which software instructions are actually executed. Today, the four predominant families of client computing platforms are categorized by their CPU chips, as follows:

CPU Chip	Computing Platform
N86 chips, Intel chips	Personal computer (PC)
PowerPC chips (RISC)	PowerPC, PowerMac

CPU Chip	Computing Platform (continued)
Motorola 68000 chips	Macintosh
RISC chips	UNIX workstations

Although there are obvious differences between these computing platforms and their installed CPUs, computer chips share a number of functional similarities.

CPU Functionality and Concepts

A generalized view of CPU functionality is important to appreciate the comparative advantages and disadvantages of alternative computing platforms and choose the right client computing platform for the right job. An information systems or network analyst must have a basic understanding of CPU functionality to evaluate alternative client hardware amid the myriad technical terms, technojargon, and marketing hype encountered.

As you review CPU technical functionality, keep in mind one simple concept: There is basically only one motivation for any technological innovation in a CPU chip—more processing speed.

The need to reliably complete more instructions in a given amount of time is behind most of the technical innovations discussed in this section. A network analyst's perspective should yield the question, "How does this innovation help the CPU operate faster and/or more reliably?" Only after answering this question can the analyst perform effective cost/benefit analysis.

The CPU Chip and Clock Speed   One of the first concepts to grasp concerning CPU chips and computing platform performance is **clock speed.** Specialized clock circuitry within the CPU chip keeps precise timing of CPU operations. Clock speed is measured in **Megahertz** (MHz), which means millions of cycles per second. A given CPU chip may be incorporated into different computing platforms at different clock speeds. The greater the clock speed, the greater the CPU performance. For example, Intel's Pentium chip is, or has been, available in at least the following clock speed options:

- 60 MHz.
- 66 MHz.
- 75 MHz.
- 90 MHz.
- 100 MHz.
- 120 MHz.
- 133 MHz.
- 166 MHz.
- 200 MHz.

For every clock speed cycle (every tick of the clock), the CPU performs one set of operations. What this set of operations consists of and how the CPU optimizes these operations is elaborated on shortly. Clock speed alone does not dictate overall performance. It is the combination of the CPU chip design and the clock speed which ultimately determines performance. For example, a 60 MHz Pentium chip may perform on a par with a 100 MHz clock speed run on a previous generation of CPU chip such as a 486DX4.

Pipelines, Scalar, and Superscalar Architectures Clock speed seeks to improve the overall performance of the CPU by making it work faster. Intuitively, it stands to reason that the only other way to increase overall performance is to have the CPU perform more than one operation simultaneously for each clock cycle. That is precisely what is achieved in many of today's CPU chips by employing variations of an architectural feature known as **pipelines.** A pipeline is analogous to an assembly line in a manufacturing plant.

In this case, what is being "manufactured" is a completed computer instruction. A pipeline typically divides the overall process of completing a computer instruction into the following five stages or subprocesses:

1. Fetch.

2. Decode.

3. Operands.

4. Execute.

5. Write back.

The purposes of each of these stages are fairly self-explanatory. The **fetch stage** brings an instruction into the pipeline from a holding area in the CPU known as the **instruction cache.**

With the next tick of the clock, the contents of the fetch stage move to the **decode stage,** and a new instruction is brought into the pipeline by the fetch stage. The decode stage converts the fetched instruction into low-level code understood by the CPU.

With the next tick of the clock, any additional data or numbers, the operands, required to complete the instruction are fetched in the **operands stage.** Meanwhile, the fetch and decode stages simultaneously work on the next instruction.

With the next tick of the clock, the instruction is executed in the **execute stage** while the fetch, decode, and operands stage work on the next instructions.

Finally, the results of the executed instruction are written out to a memory location or register, usually in a special area called a **data cache,** in the **write-back stage.** The role of caches in determining overall CPU performance is discussed shortly.

A CPU chip with a single pipeline is known as a **scalar** processor. More advanced CPU chips, employing more than one pipeline, are known as **superscalar.** More than one pipeline is analogous to more than one assembly line, resulting in more than one instruction being completed for each clock cycle. A CPU which has two pipelines can issue two instructions simultaneously and is often referred to as a **dual-issue** or two-way processor; a CPU with four pipelines is called a **quad-issue** or four-way processor.

Pipelines can be specialized in other ways to increase overall performance. For example, pipeline execution stages can be written especially to be optimized for certain operations, such as handling only floating-point operations, integer operations, or branch logic (if-then-else) operations. These operation-specific options are called **execution units.** Once a pipeline determines which type of operation is required, it forwards data and instructions to the proper execution unit. Execution units represent options for the pipeline's execute stage. As a result, CPUs often have a greater variety of execution units than pipelines. CPU chips may have more of some types of execution units than others based on anticipated demand for certain types of instructions.

Some pipelines employ more than five stages to complete a given instruction; these are called **superpipelined** architectures, not to be confused with superscalar. For example, floating point pipelines may have more than one execute stage. Intel's PENTIUM PRO chip has a 14-stage superpipeline.

Figure 3-1 illustrates pipelines, superpipelines, and scalar and superscalar architectures.

CPU Caches   Continuing with the manufacturing plant analogy, assuming that the assembly operations have been optimized for efficiency through the use of multiple, properly designed pipelines (assembly lines), what else might have a significant impact on the overall performance of the operations? What if the suppliers couldn't supply these superefficient assembly lines fast enough? The result would be that the superefficient assembly lines (pipelines) would be idle some of the time, because the suppliers (main or system memory) were unable to keep the pipelines full.

This scenario illustrates a principle of data communications in general, not just

Scalar (Single Pipeline)

➤ Each pipeline stage processes with each clock cycle.
➤ All instructions travel through a single pipeline

Superscalar (Multiple Pipelines)

➤ Each pipeline stage on every pipeline processes with each clock cycle.
➤ Instructions travel through specialized pipelines dependent on the type of processing required.

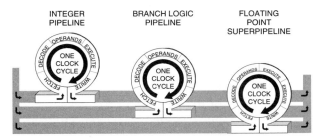

Figure 3-1   Pipelines, Superpipelines, Scalar and Superscalar Architectures

CPU design, known as the **principle of shifting bottlenecks.** The principle is really quite simple. As one aspect of a system which had been identified as a bottleneck is optimized, the bottleneck shifts to some other interacting component of the system. In this case, the CPU chip was optimized to the point where the speed of the transfer of data from the system memory into the CPU chip became the new bottleneck.

The solution to the CPU chip-to-system memory bottleneck is relatively straightforward. Include some high-speed memory directly on the processor chip, as a buffer between the slower system memory (RAM) and the fast pipelines. This on-board memory is known as **on-board cache.** On-board cache is also known as on-chip cache, **primary cache,** or **L1** (Level 1) **cache.** L1 caches are generally only 8 to 32 KB.

Just as pipelines can be specialized to increase overall efficiency, primary caches can be specialized as well. The pipelines must fetch two distinct items: data and instructions. It should come as no surprise, therefore, that some CPU chips include both a **primary instruction cache** and a **primary data cache.**

Primary cache can also be differentiated as to whether it is used just as a read-only buffer to hold data and/or instructions for the fetch stage (stage 1) of the pipeline, or also to be written to from the results of the write-back stage (stage 5). Cache that services only the fetch stage is known as **write-through cache,** while cache that also services the write-back stage is logically known as **write-back cache.**

The 8 to 32 KB generally included in L1 caches is not a great deal of buffer memory but all that can easily be fit on the limited real estate available on a CPU chip. Once again the bottleneck shifts. What is needed is a high-speed memory cache not directly on, but closely connected to, the CPU chip. This memory is known as off-chip, **secondary cache,** or **L2** (Level 2) **cache.** The L2 cache is connected to the CPU chip through a **memory bus** whose speed is also measured in megahertz. How many bits of data the CPU can read from and write to the L2 cache for each tick of the memory bus clock is determined by the **data bus width.** This is most often 32 or 64 bits. The amount of installed L2 cache is often up to 256 KB, sometimes as much as 1 MB, and consists of high-speed SRAM, or static RAM. All of the many variations of RAM memory chips available today are discussed further in the section on memory.

Figure 3-2 differentiates between primary (L1) and secondary (L2) cache, while Figure 3-3 differentiates between write-back and write-through cache.

Cache memory is the functional equivalent of a warehouse in the manufacturing analogy. As a warehouse eliminates a manufacturing operation's dependency on a supplier, by providing a buffer of readily available raw materials, cache memory eliminates the dependency of the pipelines in a superscalar CPU on the relatively slow system memory to deliver data and instructions at a rate fast enough to keep the CPU's pipelines full.

Branch Prediction   Having increased the speed of execution with higher clock speeds and decreased CPU idle time by incorporating L1 and L2 caches, what else can be done to improve the performance of the overall process? A fairly accurate answer might be, "Not much."

Many of the advanced CPU design techniques, which are beyond the scope of this book but included in referenced articles, have one thing in common. Rather than trying to improve on how *efficiently* data and instructions are moved through the pipelines, they concentrate on improving how *intelligently* data and instructions are moved. They "work smarter, not harder." The difference between moving data and instructions efficiently and intelligently is subtle but significant. Handling data

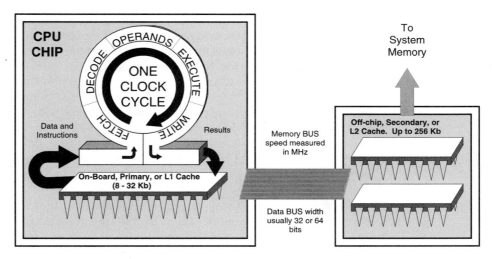

Figure 3-2   Primary versus Secondary Cache

and instructions efficiently implies improving performance without regard for the contents. Once efficiency has been maximized, the only way to increase performance is to pay attention to the *contents* of data and instructions and use the intelligence built into the CPU chip to alter pipeline behavior based on that contents.

A good, yet understandable, example of this intelligent instruction handling is a

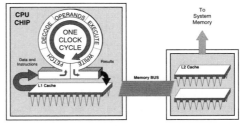

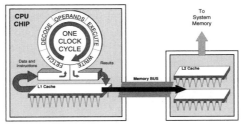

Figure 3-3   Write-back versus Write-through Cache

technique employed in many CPU chips known as **branch prediction.** A branch is a location or decision in a program's logic represented by an "if-then-else" statement (conditional branch) or a Goto or GoSub statement (unconditional branch). The problem with branches and pipelines is really a matter of timing.

Pipelines allow multiple instructions to be loaded and processed simultaneously at various pipeline stages. However, until the branch statement is evaluated in the execute stage of the pipeline, the CPU doesn't know which condition is true and, consequently, which conditional branch instruction to fetch. The simplest, but least efficient way around this problem is to evaluate the branch statement to find out which conditional branch needs to be executed, flush out all of the partially processed instructions in the pipelines, and start over again by fetching the proper conditional branch.

A more intelligent way to handle the same situation would be to have the CPU somehow predict which condition of the branch statement will be true, and automatically load the associated conditional branch statement. This is exactly what some CPU chips do with branch prediction. Like most forecasting mechanisms, the best way to predict the future is to study the past. Most branch prediction processes employ a **branch target buffer,** or branch target cache, which holds the results of as many as the last 256 branches executed in a given program. Based on the patterns observed from this past branching behavior, they predict the results of future branches.

CISC versus RISC   Although the debate between the relative merits of **CISC (complex instruction set computing)** versus **RISC (reduced instruction set computing)** once possessed all the fervor of a religious war, the differences between the two computing architectures have diminished over the years. Articles cited in the References include stories about both how CISC is becoming more RISC-like and how RISC is becoming more CISC-like. Many of the technological features cited in the earlier sections on CPU architecture as common to most, if not all, modern CPU chips were found only in RISC chips at one time.

In the purest of definitive or traditional differences between CISC and RISC, the focus is on the process to transform program instructions into executable code understandable by the CPU chip. In the case of a CISC architecture, instructions are interpreted into executable code by microcode which itself is a small computer software program running on the CPU chip. In effect, CISC required one software program to translate another software program. On the other hand, RISC architectures interpret instructions directly in the CPU chip itself without the added overhead of the executing microcode. This hardware-based decoding increased the speed of processing.

However, there is a trade-off. Initially, RISC chips worked with a reduced number of only the simplest instructions. To accomplish the same tasks a CISC architecture might do in a single complex instruction, early RISC architectures required multiple, simple instructions. As a result, so-called second-generation RISC architectures began to increase their instruction set in both number and complexity.

Key technological innovations credited to the RISC architecture are superscalar and superpipelining CPU chips. As discussed in the previous section, both of these features are now included on so-called CISC chips such as the Intel Pentium. The incorporation of floating-point units directly in the CPU chip is another RISC innovation which accounts for RISC chips' traditional superior performance in floating-point operations. The Intel 486DX was the first Intel X86 chip to incorporate a floating-point unit in the CPU chip. Prior to that, X87 math **coprocessors,** which included floating-point logic, could be purchased separately at the discretion of the computer owner. Some CPU chips discussed in the next section, on CPU technology, take X86-based CISC instructions and translate them into one or more RISC-like instructions.

Although the differences between CISC and RISC chips are diminishing, they have certainly not disappeared. Significant differences remain in terms of compatible operating systems, network operating systems, and applications software. As the following section discusses, purchasing decisions should be based on a structured methodology adhering to the top-down model, not a philosophical bias toward one chip architecture or another.

CPU Technology

This section on CPU technology examines important characteristics of and key differentiating factors between currently available CPU chips. Emphasis is on those characteristics or differences that may have a bearing on purchase recommendations of information systems or network analysts. More detailed information can be found in many of the articles cited in the Featured References.

Intel-486   To understand Intel's naming conventions for its CPU chips, it is necessary to focus on the three segments which uniquely identify each chip:

- The chip model number (486).
- The chip suffix or designator (DX).
- The clock speed (33 MHz).

Perhaps the most confusing aspect of this naming convention are the designators:

- **SX** implies no built-in math coprocessor (1989).
- **DX** implies a built-in math coprocessor (1989).
- **DX2** implies that the clock speed has been doubled above DX clock speeds (1992).
- **DX4** implies that the clock speed has been *tripled* above DX clock speeds (1994).

As a result, although 486DX4 may be the most popular 486 model currently available, at one time, any or all of these variations were available:

486**SX** 25 MHz and 33 MHz

486**DX** 33 MHz and 50 MHz

486**DX2** 50 MHz and 66 MHz

486**DX4** 75 MHz, 83 MHz, and 100 MHz

Clock Multiplying   When clock speeds on a given CPU chip are doubled or tripled, the CPU chip works at the higher rate internally only. In other words, instructions are processed in the pipelines at the new, higher rate. However, the many subsystems which interface to the CPU such as memory, bus, disk, and video were all designed to work with the CPU at its original clock speed. As a result, to avoid having to redesign all of the CPU's associated subsystems and system board, external clock speeds are not altered.

This fact offers some interesting price/performance ratios. For example, in 1994 a 50 MHz 486DX2 (clock doubled) cost substantially less than a 50 MHz 486DX (no clock doubling) but performed at 90 to 95% of the more expensive alternative. A 100 MHz 486DX4 cost about $500 more than a 33 MHz 486DX but offered about 2.5 times the performance.

Although it may be obvious that the "2" in DX2 implies a doubling of the DX clock speed, the "4" in DX4 does *not* imply quadrupling clock speeds. In fact, DX4 chips use a variety of clock multiplying factors:

- The 486DX4 75 MHz triples an input clock speed of 25 MHz.

- The 486DX4 83 MHz multiplies a 33 MHz input clock speed by a factor of 2.5.

- The 486DX4 100 MHz multiplies either a 50 MHz input clock speed by 2 or a 33 MHz input clock speed by 3.

As can be seen by the 486DX4 83 MHz example, clock multipliers do not have to be whole numbers.

Overdrive Chips   Overdrive chips are replacement CPU chips, manufactured by Intel, which offer clock multiplying capabilities. Among the 486 overdrive chips available are a 486DX2 50 MHz overdrive chip designed to double the internal processing speed of a 486SX 25 MHz, and a 486DX4 100 MHz overdrive chip designed to triple the internal processing speed of a 486DX 33 MHz.

These overdrive chips allow an existing CPU chip to be pulled from a system board and replaced by another CPU running at twice the internal clock speed without requiring any adjustments to any other components. Some system boards come with empty slots for the overdrive chip to be inserted at a later date. It is important to note that after the installation of an overdrive chip, all on-chip (CPU-based) processing runs at the clock-multiplied speed, but as soon as interaction is required with an off-chip component such as external cache (L2) memory, the processing speed slows to the original, nonmultiplied, system board speed.

Thus, the size of the internal or L1 cache has a lot to do with how much of a performance gain will be realized with an overdrive chip. The 486 SX and DX models have 8 K of L1 cache while DX4 models have 16 K. Because of this increased L1 cache size on the DX4, processing is more likely to remain on-chip, at the higher internal clock speed.

Practical Advice and Information

How does a DX4's performance compare with that of a Pentium-based unit? Several references cite a 100 MHz DX4's performance as roughly equivalent to that of a 60 MHz Pentium-based unit, all other things being equal. With this performance comparison in mind, cost/benefit or price/performance shopping should be fairly straightforward.

Overdrive chips are also available to upgrade certain 486-based computers to Pentium class machines. However, as you will see in the next section, just swapping a 486 chip with a Pentium chip does not make a Pentium computer system. Because of the numerous other changes made to the Pentium system board and surrounding subsystems, tests indicate that 486 computers using the Pentium overdrive chip perform at levels of 60 to 70% that of a native 90 MHz Pentium computer system. The Pentium overdrive chip runs at a clock speed of 83 MHz in a 33 MHz 486 system and at 63 MHz in a 25 MHz 486 system.

Intel — Pentium   The Intel Pentium chip was first shipped in 1993, and literally millions have been shipped since then. As was illustrated in the discussion on clock speed, the Pentium chip has been available at no less than seven different clock speeds. However, faster clock speeds is not all that sets the Pentium chip apart.

Among the most significant upgrades from the 486 to the Pentium was the inclusion of a 64-bit on-chip data path as opposed to a 32-bit data path on the 486 chips. This wider data bus allows twice as much information to be fetched with each tick of the CPU clock. The Pentium chip is superscalar, containing two processing pipelines with three execution units to choose from: two integer and one floating point. The Pentium contains the equivalent of 3.3 million transistors and implements branch prediction using a branch target buffer.

Heat buildup was a problem, especially with earlier (60, 66 MHz) Pentium chips. Large heat sinks and fans were the early answers to this problem. More recently, internal voltages on the chip itself dropped from 5 to 3.3 volts, leading to a significant decrease in generated heat.

The faster processing ability and wide data path offered by the Pentium challenge systems designers. System boards must be designed in such a way as to optimize the superior processing power and wide data path of the Pentium chip. Because these system board designs can vary widely, it is easy to see that all Pentium computer systems are not created equal. The most important characteristic of a Pentium-based systems board is a large (at least 256 KB) L2 external cache connected via a 64-bit data bus to the Pentium's 16 K L1 on-chip cache. The size and speed of the external cache, the size and speed of the main or system memory, and the size and speed of the data path connecting the internal and external memory components are all the responsibility of the system board designers.

Figure 3-4 highlights the differences between Intel's 486 and Pentium CPU chips.

CPU Type	486DX4	Pentium
Clock Speeds	75, 83, 100 MHz	75, 90, 100, 120, 133, 166, 200 MHz
Transistors	1.6 million	3.3 million
Pipelines	1 (5 stage)	2 (5 stage)
Execution Units	floating-point unit	3 total; 2 integer and 1 floating point
Level 1 Cache	16 K on-board unified cache	16 K total; 8 K instruction, 8 K data
Branch Prediction		yes

Figure 3-4   Intel 486 versus Intel Pentium

Intel — P6 or Pentium Pro   The biggest difference between the Pentium Pro and the Pentium chips can be seen with the naked eye. The Pentium Pro CPU chip itself is just one of two chips mounted in separate cavities in a single die or chip container, sometimes referred to as a package. This second cavity is occupied by a 256 KB SRAM L2, or secondary cache, linked directly to the neighboring Pentium Pro chip through a dedicated 64-bit bus known as the **backside bus.** This directly linked L2 cache is also known as **packaged L2 cache,** and has major implications for both system design and performance. Systems designers don't need to worry about coming up with their own unique secondary cache designs and links to the CPU. It's already taken care of. Due to the short distance and dedicated high-speed bus between the L2 cache and the CPU, less time is spent on memory access, and the CPU can be kept busy processing. In terms of performance, the Pentium Pro is one-third faster than a Pentium chip of the same clock speed.

Several functional innovations have also been included in the Pentium Pro, including the following:

- **Out-of-order execution** — A potential problem encountered in scalar or superscalar architectures is known as stalled pipelines. This condition occurs when a pipeline stage, such as an operation or data access, cannot be completed in a single clock cycle. Due to a restriction known as in-order execution, *no* pipelines can proceed if *one* is stalled. The Pentium Pro overcomes this restriction by supporting out-of-order execution, which allows other pipelines to continue processing if one stalls.

- **Speculative execution** — Speculative execution is really an extension of branch prediction. Whereas branch prediction guesses what the value of a conditional branch will be and predicts which branch will be executed, speculative execution actually goes ahead and begins to execute and store results of these predicted branches. Both speculative execution and out-of-order execution help keep the powerful Pentium Pro CPU processing as much as possible rather than sitting idle. Given that the Pentium Pro is reportedly greater than 90% accurate in branch prediction, speculative execution sounds like a fairly safe bet.

- **CISC-to-RISC decoder** — In a process which Intel refers to as **dynamic execution,** the P6 breaks complex CISC instructions down into simpler RISC-like, but not true RISC, instructions known as **micro-ops.** These simpler instructions are easier to execute in parallel in the multiple pipelines of the superscalar Pentium Pro. The reasoning behind this process is straightforward: simpler instructions can be processed more quickly and are less likely to cause pipeline stalls.

Figure 3-5 highlights the differences between Intel's Pentium Pro and Pentium CPU chips.

- **Performance** — Comparative performance of Pentium Pro versus Pentium chips depends largely on whether the software being executed is 16 or 32 bit. While the Pentium Pro outperforms the Pentium when executing 32-bit code, it actually performs more poorly than the Pentium when executing 16-bit code because of the additional overhead of running the 16-bit software in emulation mode.

Intel Clones   Competition for Intel in the X86 CPU chip market has come primarily from three companies: Advanced Micro Devices, more popularly known as AMD, Cyrix Corporation, and NexGen.

CPU Type	Pentium Pro	Pentium
Clock Speeds	133, 150, 200 MHz	75, 90, 100, 120, 133 MHz
Transistors	5.5 million in CPU, 15.5 million in 256 K L2 Cache	3.3 million
Pipelines	3 (14 stage)	2 (5 stage)
Execution Units	5 total; 2 integer, 1 FPU, 2 address	3 total; 2 integer and 1 floating point
Level 1 Cache	16 K total; 8 K instruction, 8 K data	16 K total; 8 K instruction, 8 K data
Level 2 Cache	256 K packaged	System dependent, external
Out-of-Order Execution	Yes	No
Branch Prediction	Yes, w/speculative execution	Yes, w/o speculative execution

Figure 3-5   Intel Pentium Pro versus Intel Pentium

To compete effectively in this market, Intel's competitors are basically limited to the following options:

- Offer chips of comparable performance at prices lower than Intel's.

- Offer chips of greater performance at prices similar to Intel's.

One thing these clone makers cannot afford to alter is the guarantee of 100% compatibility with Intel's CISC instruction set. Otherwise, programs written to run on Intel chips may not run correctly, or at all, on the clone chips. Although these chips may offer the full CISC instruction set, and therefore look like an Intel chip on the outside, many technical innovations have been made on the inside to meet the two options to successful competition. Detailed information regarding these competitors' chips can be found in the articles cited in the Featured References. Figure 3-6 summarizes some of the key features of the currently available Pentium clone chips.

PowerPC/PowerMac   IBM, Motorola, and Apple formed a partnership in 1991 to produce a new family of RISC chips to be incorporated into computing platforms ranging from miniature personal digital assistants (PDAs) to engineering workstations. The partnership has produced a series of chips to date, the most recent being the PowerPC 620, a 133 MHz 64-bit processor.

The PowerPC is a true RISC chip incorporating many of the previously discussed features of Pentium, PENTIUM PRO, and Intel clone chips. The PowerPC 620 features include the following:

- 64-bit internal data paths.

- 64 KB of on-chip L1 cache.

- Superscalar architecture with six execution units.

- Branch prediction, speculative execution, and out-of-order execution.

Like any other CPU chip, the PowerPC chip must be included in a computing platform. IBM, Apple, and other vendors are producing their own computing

CPU Type	AMD K5	Cyrix M1	NexGen Nx586
Pin Compatible	Pentium compatible pinout	Pentium compatible pinout	Incompatible w/Pentium pinout
Transistors	4.3 million	3 million	3.5 million
Superscalar Architecture	4-way scalar pipes	2-way scalar pipes	2-way scalar pipes
Pipelines	5 stage	7 stage	7 stage minimum
Execution Units	5 execution units, built-in FPU	4 execution units, built-in FPU	3 execution units, optional FPU
Out-of-Order Execution	Yes	Yes	Yes
Level 1 Cache	24 K total; 16 K code, 8 K data	16 K unified w/256 byte code cache	32 K total; 16 K code, 16 K data
Level 2 Cache	System dependent	System dependent	System dependent, integrated L2 cache controller

Figure 3-6   Intel Pentium Clones

platforms using the PowerPC chip. IBM has introduced a PowerPC-based RS/6000 workstation and Apple has produced a series of PowerMacs. Other companies are also producing PowerMac clones.

But the PowerPC is more than just another RISC chip. The PowerPC is also backward compatible with both Macintosh software and Intel x86-based software. Macintosh software is sometimes referred to as 68 K or 68000 compatible software, in reference to the Motorola 68000 family of CPUs that powers the Macs. On early versions of the PowerPC chip, this ability to run both Mac and Windows programs was achieved through **software emulation.**

The emulation software required to run native Macintosh applications is included in the PowerMac's operating system and runs Mac applications as well as on their native platforms. Running Windows apps on the PowerPC chip is another story, however. A third-party software emulation package called SoftWindows is available from Insignia Solutions. The performance, however, is far from Windows application performance on a high-powered Intel-based machine.

In response to this need, Apple has introduced the DOS card for the PowerMacintosh. This add-on card, containing a 486DX2 66 MHz processor, is an example of **hardware emulation.** Windows applications run quite well in this configuration. Not surprisingly, due to the RISC nature of the PowerPC chips, when it comes to floating-point operations, PowerPC chips significantly outperform Intel-based (CISC) platforms.

POWER PC MARKET ANALYSIS

Managerial Perspective

People buy computers to solve business problems. They don't buy architectures or chips and probably don't care about CISC versus RISC. The real issue is: Who is going to buy the PowerMacintosh and why will they buy them? Macintosh currently holds about 6% market share in the business community, so clearly the demand will not be from corporate America looking for an upgrade from their Macs. RISC enthusiasts have a variety of vendors to choose from including Sun, Hewlett-Packard, IBM, and Silicon Graphics to name but a few. Intel-based business applications users have no reason to abandon Intel-based architectures for the PowerPC platform.

That leaves those users who need a computing platform that can run both Windows and Macintosh applications with ease and respectable performance as the most likely prospective purchasers. This market analysis will change significantly if and when applications written specifically for the PowerPC platform become readily available. This is not to say that PowerPC-based computing platforms are not impressive. The PowerMac 9500 (Tsunami) uses a PowerPC 604 chip, runs at either 120 or 132 MHz, and runs 75 to 80% faster than a 90 MHz Pentium on floating point and integer processing.

Figure 3-7 summarizes some key information regarding PowerPC chips.

RISC Chips   True RISC functionality such as superscalar architectures, superpipelines, branch prediction, speculative execution, and out-of-order execution has been adopted by many of the chips previously discussed. The following are companies that specialize in pure RISC CPU chips, along with the names of their chip families:

- Digital Equipment Corporation (DEC): Alpha chip.
- Sun Microsystems: SPARC chip.
- Hewlett-Packard: PA-RISC.
- MIPs Technologies: MIPS.

	Introduced	Technical Specifications	Applications
PowerPC 601	1993	32-bit processor	Low-cost, initial PowerPC chip
PowerPC 602	1995	66 MHz, 1 million transistors, 4 KB cache, 4 execution units	Targeted toward PDAs & consumer electronics
PowerPC 603	1993	80 MHz, 1.6 million transistors, 8 KB cache, 5 execution units	Low power consumption, targeted at notebooks
PowerPC 603E	1995	100 MHz, 2.6 million transistors, 16 KB cache, 5 execution units	High-powered notebooks
PowerPC 604	1994	100 MHz, 3.6 million transistors, 32 KB cache, 6 execution units	High performance for high-end desktop systems
PowerPC 620	1994	133 MHz, 7 million transistors, 64 KB cache, 6 execution units	Engineering workstations and high-speed servers

Figure 3-7   Power PC Technical Specifications and Applications

More detailed technical information about each of these chip families is available in the articles cited in the Featured References. Figure 3-8 summarizes some of the key technical specifications of these RISC chips. In cases where a chip family includes multiple chips, the most recently announced chip is included.

Computing platforms based on these chips are tremendously powerful and used primarily for engineering workstations running CAD/CAM, 3-D modeling, video, or multimedia applications. These chip manufacturers do not have to worry about being backward compatible with X86 or Macintosh architectures because no one in their right mind would buy one of these workstations for that purpose.

CPU Trends

Beyond P6: P7   Although no one knows for sure what the future will bring, the next generation of Intel chips could feature any or all of the following:

- 4 to 6 superscalar pipelined architecture.

- Larger primary caches.

- Integrated secondary caches.

- More execution units.

- Larger buffers to support deeper paths of speculative execution.

- Speculative execution down both branches of conditional branch statements.

- 20 million or more transistors.

One thing that cannot change is future chips' support of the complex instructions contained in the X86 CISC instruction set. If this basic "outside" instruction set is changed, every program ever written to run on an Intel chip would have to be

Manufacturer	Hewlett-Packard	DEC	MIPS	SUN
CPU Model #	PA-8000	Alpha 21164	MIPS T5	UltraSPARC
Transistor Count		9.6 million	> 6 million	
Clock Speed	200 MHz	300 MHz	200 MHz	200 MHz
Superscalar	4-way	4-way	5-way	4-way
Execution Units	10		5	9
Bus Width	64 bit	64 bit	64 bit	64 bit
L1 Cache		16 KB	32 KB	32 KB
L2 Cache	Up to 4 MB, external	96 KB, on-chip	On-chip control of up to 16 MB, external	Integrated L2 cache support
L3 Cache		2 MB to 64 MB		

Figure 3-8   RISC Chips Technical Specifications

rewritten. As a result, although Intel's chips may get more RISC-like on the inside, they will have to stay CISC compatible on the outside.

Ever Faster   Users' need for increased computing power seems to be limitless. As more powerful processors are brought to the market, more demanding applications saturate their power. In summary, there are really only three ways to make faster CPU chips:

1. Increase the CPU's processing capacity by increasing the number of transistors—More transistors means more on-chip capacity for cache memory, specialized execution units, and deeper branch prediction buffers. The downside is that transistors take up space, consume electricity, and generate heat. As a result, current technology is quickly reaching the limit of density of transistors one chip surface can physically hold.

2. Increase the clock speed—Making the CPU work faster is a reasonable proposal as long as all of the supporting CPU infrastructure and subsystems can keep up. The main goal is to keep the CPU busy 100% of the time. As CPUs become faster and faster, keeping them busy becomes a more challenging task.

3. Work smarter, not harder—Instead of just increasing the clock speed, concentrate on accomplishing more with each tick of the clock. This is where the efforts to keep the CPU busy 100% of the time will be concentrated. Continued evolution in superscalar processes such as speculative execution, out-of-order execution, and branch prediction will be a large part of these efforts.

■   THE BUS

Bus Functionality and Concepts

Internal versus External   The term **bus** refers to a connection between components either within a CPU chip, between a CPU chip and system components, or between system components. For purposes of this discussion a bus located strictly within a CPU chip is referred to as an **internal bus** and one located outside of a CPU chip is referred to as an **external bus.** Internal buses, since they appear within a CPU chip, are most often proprietary and are called a variety of names. Some external buses, because they need to be supported by third-party hardware and software, are more likely to adhere to one of a number of industry standards for buses. In most CPU chip designs, internal buses interface to external buses in a **bus interface unit.**

Address buses and data buses are examples of internal buses that are explained in more detail later. Following are examples of external buses that are explained in more detail later:

- Main system bus, also known as the processor bus or the frontside bus.

- External cache bus, also known as external data bus, memory bus, or the backside bus.

- Input/output (I/O) bus, also known as the local bus.

- Peripheral bus, also known as the expansion bus.

Bus Width and Clock Speed Buses differ primarily according to **bus width,** which is measured in bits and refers to the number of bits that can travel in parallel down a bus. Common bus widths are 8, 16, 32, 64, and 128 bits. Bus width, however, is only one factor which contributes to the actual performance of, or amount of data traveling through, a given bus. The other factor that must be taken into account is the clock speed of the bus. The clock speed determines how often a full bus width of data is loaded onto and transferred down the bus. Bus clock speed in megahertz multiplied by the bus-width yields the bus throughput in bits/sec.

The clock speed of a bus may be the full clock speed of the CPU, measured in megahertz, or one-half, one-third, or one-fourth of the CPU clock speed, which is known as **clock-divided frequency.** External buses frequently run at a fraction of the CPU clock speed. For example, the external buses on a 100 MHz Pentium chip run at 66 MHz and the external buses on a 90 MHz Pentium chip run at 60 MHz. Part of the bus interface unit's function is to provide a buffer between the higher internal and the slower external bus speeds.

To picture the relationship between bus width and clock speed, a chairlift taking skiers to the top of a mountain serves as an excellent analogy. Each chair on the chairlift is identically wide, but chairs on different chairlifts may be of differing widths. A bus measures its width in bits, while a chairlift measures its width in butts; however, the width of the chair alone cannot measure the throughput of the chairlift. The frequency of the chairlift (how often the chairs arrive) needs to be multiplied by the chair width, yielding the throughput of the chairlift in butts delivered to the top of the mountain in a fixed amount of time.

Figure 3-9 illustrates the relationship between internal and external buses. Terms used in labeling buses are compiled from a number of CPU designs and are not reflective of any particular architecture.

Internal: Address Bus The width of the address bus is the controlling factor in how much memory a given computer system can access. Just as with street addresses, the longer the address can be, the more unique addresses are possible. Each memory location to be accessed must be assigned a unique address. If the address bus was 8 bits wide, then 2 to the 8th power, or 256 unique addresses, could possibly be transferred down the address bus. Most of the address buses in today's CPUs are 32 bits wide, yielding the ability to address 4 GB of data.

Internal: Data Bus The CPU's internal data bus is responsible for delivering data to/from the L1 cache and processing pipelines. To optimize this activity, the internal data bus nearly always runs at the full CPU clock speed. The wider the internal data bus, the more data that can be delivered to the pipelines for processing. Most CPUs have 32- or 64-bit wide internal data buses.

External: System Bus The system bus should be considered the superhighway of buses that leave the computer system's CPU. Occasionally, high-speed input/output devices such as disk drives or monitors hook directly into the system bus, but most often only other buses, such as the local, I/O, and peripheral buses, interface directly to the system bus. The memory controller which interfaces to the computer system's main memory is the primary user of the system bus, also known as the processor bus. Most system designs assume that anything which interfaces directly with the system bus must operate at the CPU's clock speed. Slower buses and their devices access the system bus via bus interface units.

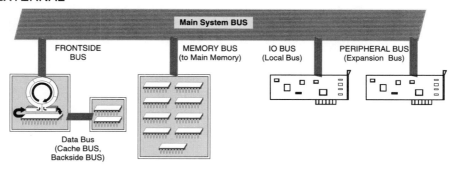

INTERNAL

EXTERNAL

Figure 3-9   Internal versus External Bus Functionality and Concepts

External: Cache Bus   The external cache bus is responsible for quickly delivering data and instructions to/from L2 cache to/from the CPU. Designs vary widely among systems vendors for the L2 cache bus. The capacity of the L2 cache bus is measured according to the bus width in bits, with most L2 cache buses being 32 or 64 bits wide. Actual throughput of the L2 cache bus can be determined only by also knowing the clock speed, sometimes called the memory bus speed. This clock speed is usually either the full CPU clock speed or some fraction thereof. For example, Pentium 66 MHz, Pentium 100 MHz, and Pentium 133 MHz CPUs all have L2 cache bus speeds of 66 MHz.

External: Local Bus   Strictly speaking, the term local bus refers to any bus which interfaces directly to the system bus. The VESA Local Bus (VL) standard is an example of a true local bus architecture. As was pointed out in the description of system buses, interfacing directly to the system bus implies that the local bus and its attached devices must operate at the CPU's clock speed. As CPU clock speeds increase, local bus devices must be able to cope with these increased clock speeds. Trying to get local bus devices to operate at faster and faster clock speeds can cause a multitude of problems. An alternative to the local bus architecture is the mezzanine architecture.

Local versus Mezzanine Architecture   A mezzanine architecture takes matters into its own hands and supplies its own clocking signal. **PCI** (peripheral component interconnect) bus, originally developed by Intel, is the best example of a mezzanine architecture. The PCI bus provides its own clocking signal at 33 MHz and has a bus width of either 32 or 64 bits. The PCI bus interfaces to the system bus via a PCI bridge, which provides buffering between the two buses. Because of the PCI bus' high capacity, typical PCI devices include high-quality video, CD-ROMs, multimedia devices, high-speed printers, and high-speed networking devices. PCI buses also interface to slower-speed expansion buses. The PCI standard as well as a variety of expansion bus standards are discussed in the Bus Technology section. Figure 3-10 differentiates between local bus and mezzanine architectures.

Local BUS Architecture

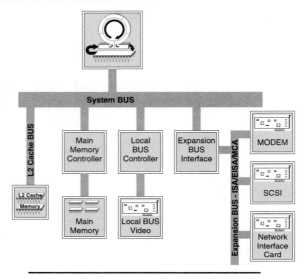

Mezzanine Architecture

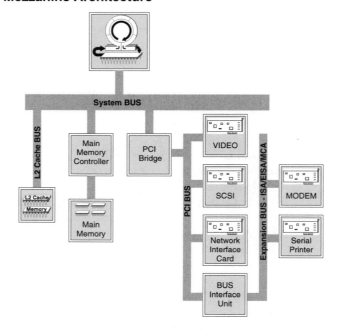

Figure 3-10   Local versus Mezzanine Bus Architectures

Expansion Bus Standard	Bus Width	Throughput
ISA	16 bit	8 MBps
EISA	32 bit	33 MBps
MCA	32 bit	20 MBps

Figure 3-11   ISA/EISA/MCA Expansion Bus Standards

External: Expansion Bus   A computer's expansion bus is for the connection of add-in cards and peripheral devices such as modems, fax boards, sound cards, additional serial ports, and additional input devices. The expansion bus interfaces to the system bus through a bus interface unit, and nearly always runs at a slower clock speed than the CPU clock. The width of the expansion bus in bits differs according to the standard of the expansion bus supported in a particular computer system. Expansion bus standards are discussed in the following section.

Bus Technology and Standards

Expansion Bus Standards: ISA/EISA/MCA   **ISA** (industry standard architecture), **EISA** (extended industry standard architecture), and **MCA** (micro channel architecture) are all expansion bus standards. EISA is backward compatible with ISA, but MCA is not compatible with either ISA or EISA. When expansion cards such as modems or network interface cards are purchased to be installed in a computer's expansion bus, those cards must be compatible with the computer's expansion bus standard. Compatibility issues and the hardware/software interface of the expansion bus are discussed further when network interface cards are covered in depth in Chapter 8. Figure 3-11 summarizes the key differences between the three expansion bus standards.

PCI, SCSI, and PCI/SCSI   Although PCI was originally developed by Intel, it is, in fact, a processor-independent bus design. RISC system designers such as DEC, Hewlett-Packard, and IBM are able to incorporate PCI buses in their computer systems as well. Recall from Figure 3-10 that all that is required to link a PCI bus to any particular system bus is a compatible PCI bridge. The beauty of PCI is that a PCI device such as a high-capacity disk drive, tape drive, or CD-ROM will work equally well on a PCI bus installed in a RISC workstation or an Intel-based computer.

PCI specifications are evolving. There are currently two PCI specifications, differing primarily in bus width: 32 and 64 bits. The PCI specifications are summarized in Figure 3-12.

Computing the throughput on a PCI bus is straightforward: 32 bits multiplied by 33 MHz divided by 8 bits/byte yields 132 MB/sec throughput. Although Figure 3-10 illustrates how expansion buses can be cascaded from a PCI bus, in fact, PCI

PCI Bus Specification	Bus Width	Clock Speed	Throughput
PCI	32 bits	33 MHz	132 MBps
PCI v2.0	64 bits	33 MHz	264 MBps

Figure 3-12   PCI Bus Specifications

buses can also be cascaded from other PCI buses. As an example, PCI buses can be put onto a single expansion card, allowing the manufacture of four-port PCI ethernet network interfaces on a single expansion card.

Small computer system interface **(SCSI)** is a specification for an expansion bus which is unique in its ability to daisy-chain up to seven SCSI devices together. SCSI can also be thought of as a truly external bus specification since SCSI devices such as disk drives, tape drives, and CD-ROMs can be standalone models, sitting totally outside of the computer system to which they are attached. SCSI specifications have changed over the years to keep up with demands for higher throughput peripheral devices. Figure 3-13 summarizes the SCSI standards.

Combining PCI and SCSI bus specifications in the form of PCI-based SCSI host adapters can achieve the benefits of both bus architectures. As a result, more than one seven-device SCSI chain per computer system can be implemented by simply installing a second PCI/SCSI host adapter card. Although the thought of multiple devices per adapter and multiple adapters per host is appealing, both PCI and SCSI specifications continue to evolve, and compatibility issues can be a problem. SCSI cards are also available for other expansion bus specifications such as ISA and EISA. However, beware of the lower throughput of ISA and EISA in comparison to PCI.

Figure 3-14 summarizes some of the technical issues to consider when purchasing a PCI/SCSI adapter.

Bus Trends

PCMCIA   **PCMCIA,** which actually stands for Personal Computer Memory Card International Association, has been more humorously defined as people can't memorize computer industry acronyms. It has been described as a general peripheral bus, a bus interface, and a bridge bus technology. Originally intended solely as a specification for memory cards in notebook computers, PCMCIA represents a tremendous potential for new and innovative technology applications. To most end-users, the PCMCIA specification is represented by the PCMCIA slots in notebook computers and the credit-card size cards of a variety of functions which slide into those slots. In addition to the originally intended use, PCMCIA cards today are used for modems, fax modems, wireless LAN adapters, network interface cards, disk drives, and SCSI ports to name but a few.

PCMCIA is actually a series of specifications representing the physical and functional/electrical standards for technology adhering to these specs. Figure 3-15

SCSI Bus Specification	Bus Width	Clock Speed	Throughput
SCSI	8 bits	5 MHz	5 MBps
Fast SCSI-2	8 bits	10 MHz	10 MBps
Wide SCSI-2	16 bits	5 MHz	10 MBps
Fast/Wide SCSI-2	16 bits	10 MHz	20 MBps
Ultra SCSI-2	32 bits	10 MHz	40 MBps

Figure 3-13   SCSI Specifications

PCI/SCSI Adapter Technical Issue	Explanation/Implication
Which PCI specification is supported?	PCI 2.0 (64 bit) is the current spec but newer specs may be forthcoming.
Does the adapter support PCI-to-PCI bridge?	Support for the PCI-to-PCI bridge (PPB) specification is important if PCI buses are to be cascaded.
Which SCSI driver specification is supported?	There are two possible driver specifications for SCSI devices: advanced SCSI programming interface drivers (ASPI), and common access method drivers (CAM)
Which operating system/network operating system drivers are included?	Commonly supported drivers: DOS, OS/2, NetWare, Windows NT, SCO UNIX
Which data transfer technique from the SCSI card to system memory is used?	Bus mastering is fastest, but programmed I/O is also used on some cards.
Is an on-board BIOS included?	This is required to simplify booting the card. BIOS is not always included.
Are the SCSI cards plug-n-play compatible?	SCSI daisy-chains require termination on the last device in the chain. Plug-n-play compatible SCSI devices are self-terminating when they are the last device in the chain.
Which interface connectors are included?	Fast and wide SCSI requires a 68-pin D-connector, other SCSI is usually 50-pin ribbon cable.

Figure 3-14   PCI/SCSI Adapter Technical Issues

summarizes the physical specifications and Figure 3-16 summarizes the functional/electrical specifications for the PCMCIA standard.

Types I through III all must support the standard PCMCIA 68-pin interface and the 85.6 × 54 mm credit-card size dimensions. Certain vendors are producing disk drives that are 16 mm thick, calling them PCMCIA Type IV. These standards are strictly proprietary as the PCMCIA Forum has not approved a Type IV specification.

The introduction of PCMCIA technology has not been without its trials and tribulations. Prior to the introduction of the V2.1 specification, incompatibility problems were very common. The card services and socket services provided a layer of transparency and compatibility between the notebook computer's hardware, the PCMCIA card, and the notebook computer's operating system software. Technical

PCMCIA Card/Slot Type	Maximum Thickness	Typical Use
Type I	3.3 mm	Memory cards
Type II	5.5 mm	Modems, network interface cards
Type III	10.5 mm	Disk drives

Figure 3-15   PCMCIA Physical Specifications

PCMCIA Spec Version	Bus Width	Clock Speed	Comments
1.0	8 bits	up to 6 MHz	Used for memory cards. No I/O functions or software drivers defined.
2.0	8–16 bits	up to 6 MHz	Introduced I/O but left software drivers up to card manufacturers.
2.1	8–16 bits	up to 6 MHz	Introduced card services and socket services.
PC Card (3.0)	32 bits	20–33 MHz	Up to 132 MBps throughput.

Figure 3-16   PCMCIA Functional/Electrical Specifications

aspects of card services and socket services are covered in the discussion of driver software in Chapter 8.

Version 2.1 is currently the most widely supported version of the PCMCIA functional/electrical specification and has minimized, although not eliminated, many of the previous incompatibility problems. Version 2.1 also introduced hot-swappable capabilities which allow PCMCIA cards to be inserted and removed with the notebook computer powered up.

Version 3.0 actually renames the cards from PCMCIA to simply PC cards. CardBus has also been mentioned as a replacement name for the much-maligned PCMCIA. More important, V3.0 vastly improves the throughput of the specification by increasing the bus width to 32 bits and the clock speed to as high as 33 MHz. The specification also adds bus-mastering capability to increase the efficiency of moving data from the card to the computer's system memory. Finally, V3.0 defines multi-function capabilities for cards so that a single card might be a fax/modem, an ethernet network interface card, and 4 MB of cache memory. In the interest of improving battery life on notebook computers, the V3.0 also outlined operations at 3.3 rather than 5 volts.

The future looks bright for PC card. PC card slots are now being included on desktop computers as well as notebooks, to allow users to make the most of their investments in peripherals. Vendors are finding new uses for the PC card such as dial-in servers. However, the reality of the situation is that today, there is no guarantee that a particular PCMCIA card will work well, if at all, with a particular computer.

■ MEMORY

Question: What is the impact of memory on CPU performance?

Answer: Research has shown that a 100 MHz Pentium runs at 8 MHz if it has to go outside of L2 cache for data.

Memory Functionality and Concepts

To appreciate recent developments in memory technology, it is first necessary to understand the motivation for those developments. The rapid advancement of CPU chip design has produced a discrepancy between how fast the CPU can accept and process data and how fast memory can supply that data. As a result, all of the memory categories discussed in the following memory technology section have contributed somehow to the same goal: Given that memory chip speeds have lagged behind CPU chip speeds, future memory chips must deliver not just more information, but more information more quickly.

As background, most of the following solutions start with one of the two major types of **RAM** (random access memory).

- **DRAM,** or **dynamic RAM,** is memory that requires refresh cycles every few milliseconds to preserve its data. DRAM requires address lines for the rows and columns of the memory address to be charged and discharged as a means of selecting particular memory locations. This time delay to allow the lines to stabilize between charges prevents immediate access to memory location contents.

- **SRAM,** or **static RAM,** in contrast, requires no refresh cycle between accesses and therefore can be accessed much faster than DRAM. SRAM is more expensive than DRAM.

More detailed technical information concerning DRAM and SRAM functionality can be found in articles cited in the Featured References.

Memory Technology

To meet the challenge of faster delivery of more information, current memory technology has taken a variety of approaches. Following is a listing of the major approaches and the names of the memory technology belonging to each category:

- Cached Approaches.
  - **CDRAM**—cached DRAM.
  - **CVRAM**—cached VRAM (video RAM).
  - **EDRAM**—enhanced DRAM.

- RAM to CPU Output Modifications.
  - **FPM**—fast page mode.
  - **EDORAM**—extended data out RAM.
  - **EDOSRAM**—extended data out SRAM.
  - **EDOVRAM**—extended data out VRAM.

- RAM to CPU Clock Synchronization Modifications.
  - **SDRAM**—synchronous DRAM.
  - **SVRAM**—synchronous VRAM.
  - **RDRAM**—rambus DRAM.

- Video RAM Specific Modifications (in addition to those previously listed).
  - **WRAM**—Windows RAM.
  - **3DRAM**—3-dimensional RAM.

- RAM Power Needs Modifications.
  - **Flash RAM.**
  - **FRAM**—ferroelectric RAM.

Cached Approaches   Cached approaches add some amount of faster SRAM to DRAM chips. The size of the SRAM cache and the width of the bus between the

SRAM and DRAM vary from one manufacturer to another. On typical 4 MB DRAM chips, the SRAM cache could be from 8 to 16 KB and the connecting bus width could be from 128 to 2048 bits. The SRAM cache fetches data from the slower DRAM and has it ready for quicker delivery to the CPU if and when requested.

RAM-to-CPU Output Modifications   Another approach to overcoming the problem of having the CPU wait for the memory is to alter the manner in which the memory outputs the data to the CPU. Extended data output (EDO) chips minimize or eliminate the time the CPU has to wait (zero-wait-state) for output from memory by reading the next stored data bit at the same time it's transferring the first requested bit to the CPU.

RAM-to-CPU Clock Synchronization Modifications   Adding clock synchronization to RAM allows memory chips to work at the same clock speed as the CPU. In addition, SDRAM solutions perform a simultaneous fetch operation as they are presenting data to the CPU. As a result, the SDRAM chip is ready to present the next bit of data to the CPU on the next tick of the CPU's clock. SDRAM works with CPU clock speeds greater than 66 MHz and can transfer data at speeds up to 500 Mbps.

Video RAM Modifications   Because video RAM is designed for a special purpose other than storing and delivering data, modifications specific to optimizing its performance for video delivery can be made. VRAM is a sort of intermediary on a video card, servicing both of the following:

- The video controller which gathers information regarding the image to be created and calculates how to display that image.

- The screen drawing or screen refresh function which actually draws the images on the video monitor.

The primary modification made by VRAM is that a portion of memory is reserved for servicing the screen refresh function to optimize performance for high-resolution graphics. RAM segmented in this manner is sometimes referred to as **dual-ported VRAM.** Other more advanced VRAM designs add intelligence to the RAM. For instance, in 3DRAM, the depth (z-axis) processing is done in RAM, making it up to nine times faster than conventional VRAM for 3D imaging.

RAM Power Needs Modification   Though most RAM requires constant voltage to maintain its data, nonvolatile RAM does not lose its data without constant voltage. Flash memory or flash RAM, which remembers its data contents until it is flashed by a larger voltage, is widely used as main memory for portable computers. The bad news is that it wears out after relatively few flashes and is therefore best for jobs that don't require data to be rewritten often. FRAM is a new type of nonvolatile memory currently under development which apparently does not degrade as quickly as conventional flash memory.

Memory Trends

Beyond the trends in memory development previously cited, equally significant trends are occurring in how memory is packaged. Originally individual dual in-line pin **(DIP)** chips were attached to circuit boards as a means of packaging and selling RAM. More recently, single in-line memory module **(SIMM)** has become the more common method of RAM packaging. SIMMs are small printed circuit boards with attached DRAMs and come in basically two varieties:

- 30-pin SIMMs, comprised of 8-bit DRAMs.
- 72-pin SIMMs, comprised of 16-bit or 32-bit DRAMs.

Looking ahead, an emerging packaging alternative is dual in-line memory module (**DIMMs**) in which the DRAMs are mounted on both sides of the small circuit board. Finally, looking further into the future, **3D memory modules,** not to be confused with 3DRAM, stack memory chips on top of each other. This packaging process is particularly appealing to the exploding portable computing market as densities of 2 GB/cubic inch are being reported using this process.

■ STORAGE

As client operating systems and application programs have grown in size, the disk drives which store these programs have had to grow in capacity as well. As CPUs have become faster and faster, disk drives have had to deliver data faster and faster.

Storage Functionality and Concepts

Basic disk drive functionality has not changed fundamentally in recent years. Although disk drives have gotten larger and faster, the basic technological design remains largely unchanged:

1. Data are stored on disks which are broken up into concentric rings, known as **tracks,** and portions of those tracks, known as **sectors.**

2. Read/write heads are attached at the ends of mechanical arms which extend and retract over given tracks of the disk.

3. Once the read/write head is positioned over the proper track, the disk platter spins until the proper sector is aligned under the read/write head.

4. Data are read from/written to the appropriate sector of the disk.

To properly evaluate disk drive alternatives, it is essential to fully understand the terminology used to categorize and describe their performance. Figure 3-17 lists disk performance terminology with their explanations and implications.

Storage Technology and Standards

The primary standards of currently available disk drives are **IDE, E-IDE,** and **SCSI.** The SCSI bus and more recent SCSI-2 standards were previously reviewed in the section on buses. Figure 3-18 compares the three primary disk standards.

Integrated drive electronics (**IDE**) disk drives are distinguished from earlier offerings by the inclusion of the drive controller in a single integrated unit and the use of a bus interface known as AT attachment (**ATA**). The key limitation of IDE drives was their capacity limitation of 528 MB and ATA's 2 to 3 MBps data transfer rate.

Disk Drive Performance Terminology	Explanation/Implication
Average Seek Time	The time it takes the mechanical arm to extend/retract so that the read/write heads are positioned over the proper track.
Average Latency	The time it takes for the disk to spin so that the proper sector is positioned under the read/write heads.
Average Access Time	Average seek time + average latency.
Data Transfer Rate	The rate at which data are transferred to/from the disk once the read/write heads are over the proper sector.
Burst Data Transfer Rate	Also known as external transfer rate. The rate at which data are read between the disk drive and the buffer memory on board the disk controller.
Sustained Transfer Rate	Also known as internal transfer rate. The rate at which data are read between the disk drive and main system memory without the use and benefit of the on-board buffer.

Figure 3-17   Disk Drive Performance Terminology

Practical Advice and Information

Disk drive advertisements, like most technology marketing, can be very misleading. Times quoted in advertisements as access times are often actually seek times, which is just a fraction of the true access time.

As a result, an improved standard known as extended IDE **(E-IDE)** was proposed by Western Digital, a major disk drive manufacturer. This proposed standard was adapted by the Small Forms Factor (SFF) Committee, an ad hoc standards proposal organization, and forwarded to American National Standards Institute (ANSI) for formal adoption. When officially adopted it will probably be known as **ATA-2.**

Given the potential throughputs of E-IDE and SCSI drives and the fact that these devices must share the bus to which they are attached with other devices, it should be obvious why it is preferable to connect these high-capacity disk

Disk Drive Standard	IDE	E-IDE	SCSI
Capacity	Up to 528 MB	Up to 8.4 GB	Up to 8.4 GB
No. of Daisy-Chained Devices	2	4	7
Compatibility with Other Device Types	Only other IDE disk drives	ATAPI compatible CD-ROMs and tape drives	SCSI CD-ROMs and tape drives
Performance	2–3 MBps	11.1 MBps	5–20 MBps

Figure 3-18   Comparison of Disk Drive Standards

drives to a local bus rather than to an ISA, EISA, or MCA expansion bus. The actual throughput of the drives, as listed on the performance line of Figure 3-18, is controlled by the choice of supported data transfer standards, otherwise known as burst data transfer rates. SCSI disk drives adhere to SCSI transfer rates as outlined in Figure 3-13. E-IDE data transfer standards fall into two general categories:

- **Processor I/O** (Input/Output)—Also known as **programmed I/O,** or PIO, this data transfer method relies on a shared memory location in system memory as a transfer point for data between the disk drive and the system or main memory. The CPU is involved with every data transfer between the disk drive and system memory.

- **Direct Memory Access** or **DMA**—This data transfer allows data to be transferred between the disk drive and system memory without intervention from the CPU. This allows for both faster data transfer and fewer CPU interruptions.

Figure 3-19 summarizes current burst data transfer standards for E-IDE disk drives.

Another issue which can have a dramatic effect on performance is the use of disk caches. A **hardware cache** is made up of memory chips placed directly on the disk controller while a **software cache** is the use of system memory in the computer reserved for a disk cache. These caches can be used for both read and write operations as follows:

- **Read-through cache** allows data stored in the cache to be forwarded directly to the CPU without performing a physical disk read.

- **Write-back cache** allows disk writes to be stored in the cache right away, so that processing can continue, rather than waiting for the disk to be idle before doing a physical write to the disk. The danger in using write-back caches is that if power is lost before physical writes are done to the disk, that data is lost.

Buffers are memory chips located on the disk drive units which can also be used to improve disk performance. By storing sequential bits of data adjacent to areas just read by the read/write heads in buffers, disk drives anticipate which data blocks the CPU will request next. Transferring data from a memory chip to the CPU is much faster than a data transfer involving a physical read/write. Some typical buffer categories follow on the next page.

Burst Data Transfer Standard	Burst Data Transfer Rate
Programmed I/O (PIO) Mode 3	11.1 MBps
Programmed I/O (PIO) Mode 4	16.6 MBps
Multiword Mode 1 DMA	13.3 MBps
Multiword Mode 2 DMA	16.6 MBps

Figure 3-19   E-IDE Burst Data Transfer Standards

- **Lookahead buffer** is the simplest or most generic buffer, implying only that a sequence of data blocks beyond that requested by the CPU is stored in anticipation of the next data request.

- **Segmented lookahead buffers** create multiple smaller buffers in which the next sequential data blocks from several reads can be stored.

- **Adaptive segmented lookahead buffers** are able to dynamically adjust the number and size of buffers depending on the situation.

Practical Advice and Information

Which type of disk drive is most appropriate for a client workstation? Disk drives should support local bus architectures such as PCI to ensure sufficient throughput. Following are some typical guidelines for capacity:

- Windows users: Not less than 720 MB.

- Average user with multiple applications: 1 GB.

- Power user with graphics applications or large data files: 1–2 GB.

As far as E-IDE versus SCSI for the single user client workstation, E-IDE is a practical choice although SCSI will also work well. SCSI is preferable in a server computer characterized by multiple users and a multitasking operating system. Server-related disk storage issues such as redundant array of inexpensive disks (RAID) are reviewed in Chapter 5.

Storage Trends

Although installation of E-IDE and SCSI disk drives is not as complicated as it once was, it is still far from simple. However, plug-n-play (PnP) disk drive technology may be available in the near future. As you will see in the next chapter, all hardware requires software to operate, and plug-n-play hardware is no exception. Windows 95 is supposed to include the necessary software support for PnP technology. Compatibility between hardware and software cannot be assumed. Disk drives or other peripherals must be certified as Windows 95 PnP compatible if the operating system is expected to reliably and automatically detect and configure the peripheral in question.

■ VIDEO

The focus of this section is on the video subsystem from the perspective of the average client workstation.

Video Functionality, Concepts, and Technology

The video needs of the average client workstation are fairly straightforward, consisting of the following:

- Monitor.

- Graphics accelerator card.

- Graphics driver software to link the video hardware with the client workstation's operating system.

Figure 3-20 illustrates the conceptual relationship of the various components of a video subsystem.

Many of the components illustrated in Figure 3-20 have been previously discussed. In fact, the only new components are the monitor, the graphics accelerator card, and whatever software may be necessary to bridge various hardware/hardware and hardware/software interfaces.

Monitors   Monitors fall into two major categories based on their technology and use:

- CRT (cathode ray tube)–based monitors for desktop use.

- LCD (liquid crystal display)–based monitors for notebook and portable computers.

Monitor performance is measured by a variety of criteria. Perhaps most familiar to the average user is the term **resolution.** Resolution refers to the number of **pixels** (picture elements) contained in the viewable area of the monitor screen and is reported as resolution height × resolution width. In simple terms, a greater number of pixels on the screen produces a sharper image. Following are common resolutions:

- 640-by-480.

- 800-by-600.

- 1024-by-768 (commonly referred to as Super VGA or SVGA).

- 1280-by-1024.

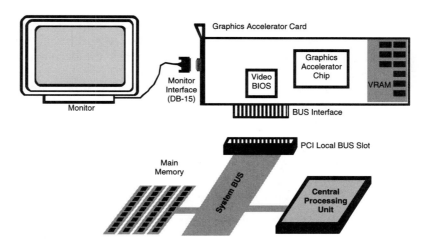

Figure 3-20   Conceptual Relationship of Video Subsystem Components

Another common monitor performance criterion is **refresh rate,** which refers to the number of times per second a screen image is redrawn or refreshed. Refresh rate is measured in hertz, with 72 Hz being the current recommended minimum refresh rate. At refresh rates of less than 72 Hz, flickering becomes perceptible, not to mention annoying, to the human eye. Interlacing is a monitor characteristic related to refresh rate. Graphics standards supported by monitors can be either interlaced or noninterlaced. Interlaced monitors update all of the pixels in even numbered horizontal rows on a screen and then update the pixels in the odd numbered horizontal rows. Noninterlaced monitors update all rows at the full refresh rate, thereby reducing perceived flicker. A performance criterion which results directly from desired resolution and refresh rate is **maximum video bandwidth,** which can be computed with the following formula:

Required video bandwidth = resolution height $\times$ resolution width $\times$ refresh rate $\times$ 1.5

As a practical example, an NEC Multisync 5FGP offers a maximum video bandwidth of 135 MHz and supports resolutions up to 1280 $\times$ 1024 with a refresh rate of 74 Hz. The term **multisync** refers to the monitor's ability to automatically adjust to the installed video card's specifications and display the desired resolution at the accompanying refresh rate. Clarity and display of greater detail is a function of pitch or dot pitch, which is the size of the dots that comprise characters and images. Dot pitches of 0.28 mm or less produce excellent clarity.

The number of displayed colors, or **color depth,** is another performance criterion that differentiates monitors. Following are common color depths:

- 16 colors.

- 256 colors.

- 65,000 colors.

- 16.7 million colors.

Color depth and resolution have a direct impact on the amount of VRAM required on the graphics accelerator card and are covered in the section on graphics accelerators.

The widespread use of notebook and portable computers has led to significant development of monitors for these computers. Although notebook monitors differ in performance level and display techniques, most start with liquid crystal display **(LCD)** technology as a foundation. Simply stated, LCD monitors employ a fluorescent backlight which shines through a "multilayer sandwich" of polarizers, liquid crystals, color filters, and an electrode grid to produce the image on the screen. There are two major categories of LCD monitors:

- **Active matrix** displays employ transistors at each point on the display grid to actively control color and intensity of each "dot" in the display. This technology enables brighter colors, sharper images, and faster response to changing images.

- **Passive matrix** displays do not employ transistors and therefore do not have individual control over each point in the display grid. As a result, screens are painted and repainted serially, a line at a time. Dual-scan passive matrix displays and active addressing passive matrix displays are two technologies that seek to improve on the shortcomings of passive matrix display technology.

Graphics Accelerator Cards   The role of the graphics accelerator card is to provide an interface between the monitor and the application software running in the CPU which is producing the images to be displayed. An important point to understand is the system-oriented nature of the video subsystem. In other words, it won't matter that an expensive monitor supports 1024 × 768 resolution with 256 colors if the installed graphics accelerator card won't perform at that specification. The performance of a typical graphics accelerator card is dictated by the specifications of the following components:

- **Graphics accelerator chip** (also known as the graphics accelerator controller chip).
- **Video memory.**
- **Bus interface.**
- **Video BIOS.**

The key performance criterion of a graphics accelerator chip is the width of its data path. In other words, how big a chunk of video information can it process and forward to/from video memory in a single tick of the clock? Most graphics accelerator cards are either 64-bit cards or 32-bit interleaved cards. **Interleaving** is a technique which allows the graphics accelerator controller chip to perform two different operations to adjacent rows of video memory with each tick of the clock. While a 32-bit interleaved chip is forwarding the contents of one row of video memory to the monitor, it is preparing the next row in a step called precharging. With the next tick of the clock, the precharged row is forwarded.

The video memory discussed in the previous paragraph is usually either VRAM or DRAM, as described earlier in the memory section of this chapter. VRAM is definitely more expensive than DRAM and is faster on high-end applications requiring high resolutions, high color depth, and high refresh rates, such as 3-D imaging. The amount of VRAM required on a graphics accelerator depends to some extent on the color depth desired. Figure 3-21 outlines some suggested VRAM amounts for given resolutions and color depths.

The data bus width of the bus interface is important to the overall performance of the video subsystem. For this reason, only a local bus architecture such as 32-bit

Resolution	Color Depth	Suggested VRAM
640-by-480	16 colors	150 KB
800-by-600	65,000 colors	960 KB
1024-by-768	16.7 million colors	2.4 MB
1280-by-1024	16.7 million colors	3.93 MB

Figure 3-21   VRAM Requirements as a Product of Resolution and Color Depth

PCI is commonly used for graphics accelerator boards. That is not to say that graphics cards are not also available for ISA, EISA, NuBUS (Macintosh), or VL-BUS, an alternative local bus architecture largely dominated by PCI.

The video BIOS (basic input output system) is contained on a chip on the graphics accelerator card. Its main function is to identify itself and its operating specifications to the computer's operating system during system startup. The video BIOS provides the interface between the graphics accelerator card (hardware) and the computer system's operating system (software).

Graphics Driver Software   How is it possible for the video BIOS on the graphics accelerator card to speak to the computer system's operating system software? The installed operating system may be any one of a number of possibilities including but not limited to the following:

- Windows NT V 3.51.

- Windows V 3.11/DOS.

- Windows 95.

- OS/2 WARP.

- UNIX.

Graphics accelerator cards should ship with specially written software drivers which understand all of the proprietary hardware controls of the particular graphics accelerator card and can also understand the commands of the particular installed operating system. These drivers act as translators between the software and hardware. In addition, most graphics accelerator cards come with specialized drivers for operation with high-powered graphics application software such as AutoCAD (revision 12). Without the appropriate drivers to bridge the graphics accelerator card–to–operating system interface, there is no communication and no functional video subsystem.

Video Trends

Plug-n-Play Monitors   An organization known as VESA (Video Electronics Standards Association) has proposed a display data channel specification which will allow a monitor to automatically transfer electronic display identification (EDID) information to the attached graphics accelerator card to enable plug-n-play monitor installation.

LCDs to FEDs   Although LCD technology for notebook computer screens continues to develop and improve, field emission display **(FED)** technology may prove to be the next generation of underlying technology for notebook computer displays. Most CRTs, and television sets, use a single electron gun to shoot electrons across the entire screen; however, FEDs use individual electron emitters arranged in a flat grid. Each FED is individually addressable and controllable by the video controller. In theory at least, FEDs should produce images as sharp as CRTs in a package small enough to fit in a notebook computer and powered by battery.

SUMMARY

Client hardware serves as the foundation for the overall processing power delivered to end-users. Operating systems, network operating systems, and applications software depend totally on client hardware to supply required computing, storage, and input/output capabilities. Client hardware is best described as a computer system, composed of processing, storage, memory, video, and bus subsystems. A key point of the systems nature of client hardware is that improvements in the technology of one subsystem, such as CPUs, have a ripple effect through other subsystems. Those other subsystems, such as memory, may or may not be equipped to cope with the advances in CPU technology.

At the heart of the client workstation is the CPU chip, the most distinguishing element of the computer system. The key trend in this area of technology is that CPU chips continue to become faster and more powerful and that major differences between CISC and RISC architectures are quickly disappearing.

Buses serve as the highway system connecting all the other systems in the client workstation. The major trend in buses is that PCI buses are gaining popularity as a method for adding high-speed peripheral devices to a variety of computing platforms.

Memory is the subsystem which probably has the most development pressure to keep up with the advances in CPU technology. Faster CPU chips are not much use if they're sitting idle because memory subsystems are not fast enough to keep the CPU supplied with data.

Bigger, faster disk drives are also required to meet the storage demands of more powerful CPUs and the larger applications programs and databases which use these advanced CPUs. These same advanced applications programs are putting increased demands on the speed and quality of the video output devices used in today's client workstation. The video subsystem's performance depends on the right combination of bus width and speed, video memory, and video processing supplied by the graphics accelerator card, in addition to the quality and capabilities of the monitor itself.

A thorough understanding of the technology which comprises the interacting subsystems of the client workstation is essential for information systems analysts and network analysts to be able to perform effective business-oriented systems analysis and design.

KEY TERMS

3D memory module, 105
3DRAM, 103
active matrix, 110
adaptive segmented lookahead
    cache, 108
address bus, 96
ATA, 106
ATA-2, 106
backside bus, 90
branch prediction, 86
branch target buffer, 86
bus, 95
bus interface unit, 95
bus width, 96
cache bus, 97
CDRAM, 103
central processing unit, 80

CISC, 86
CISC-to-RISC decoder, 90
clock multiplying, 88
clock speed, 81
clock-divided frequency, 96
computer system, 80
coprocessors, 86
color depth, 110
CPU, 80
CVRAM, 103
data bus, 96
data bus width, 84
data cache, 82
decode stage, 82
DIMM, 105
DIP, 104
direct memory access, 107

DMA, 107
DRAM, 103
dual-issue, 82
dual-ported VRAM, 104
DX, 87
DX2, 87
DX4, 87
dynamic execution, 90
dynamic RAM, 103
E-IDE, 105
EDORAM, 103
EDOSRAM, 103
EDOVRAM, 103
EDRAM, 103
EISA, 99
execute stage, 82
execution units, 82

REVIEW QUESTIONS

1. Why is a thorough knowledge of client hardware important to network analysts?
2. Name the five subsystems typically included in any computer system.
3. What is the overall role of the bus subsystem in a computer?
4. What is the major development challenge or strategic direction in CPU chip development?
5. What is the relationship behind CPU performance and clock speed?
6. Differentiate between the terms scalar, superscalar, and pipelines.
7. What is the relationship between pipelines and execution units?
8. How do pipelined architectures improve on CPU performance in comparison to nonpipelined architectures?
9. Describe the typical stages found in a pipeline.
10. What is the principle of shifting bottlenecks, and how does it apply to CPU design?
11. Why did L1 cache become necessary?
12. What is the limiting factor to the size of L1 cache?
13. What is the advantage of splitting L1 cache into separate instruction and data caches?

14. Differentiate between L1 and L2 cache.
15. What factors can affect L2 cache performance?
16. What is the difference between write-back cache and write-through cache?
17. Which cache-related design issues are the responsibility of the CPU chip designer and which are the responsibility of the system board designer?
18. What is the relationship between the data bus width and the memory bus clock?
19. How does branch prediction improve the performance of the CPU?
20. From a conceptual or theoretical perspective, what is the major difference between CISC and RISC architectures?
21. From a practical standpoint, what are the differences between currently available CISC and RISC chips?
22. Which is better, CISC or RISC?
23. Why can't Intel just abandon the CISC X86 architecture and switch to RISC chips?
24. What is the difference between a coprocessor and an integrated FPU?
25. What is clock multiplying?

26. How does clock multiplying affect internal and external clock speeds?
27. Why are internal and external clock speeds not necessarily the same?
28. Differentiate between SX, DX, DX2, and DX4.
29. What are the advantages and disadvantages of employing overdrive chips?
30. What are the significant differences between 486 chips and Pentiums?
31. What was a problem with early Pentium chips, and how was it overcome in both the short and long terms?
32. What are the significant improvements in the P6 chip?
33. How do out-of-order execution and speculative execution improve on CPU performance?
34. What are the market realities facing makers of Intel chip clones?
35. What is the PowerPC chip?
36. What advantages does the PowerPC chip possess over the Intel chips? disadvantages?
37. What is the difference between hardware and software emulation in terms of technology employed and performance?
38. What is likely to be the future direction of CPU chip development?
39. What is a clock-divided frequency, and why is it important?
40. What is the relationship between bus width and clock speed?
41. What is the major difference between the system bus and other buses such as the I/O or expansion bus?
42. Why is the PCI bus not, strictly speaking, a local bus?
43. How does a local bus architecture differ from a mezzanine architecture?
44. Which types of devices are most appropriate for PCI buses versus expansion buses?

45. Differentiate between ISA, EISA, and MCA.
46. Differentiate between the many flavors of SCSI.
47. What is the relationship between PCI and SCSI?
48. What is PCMCIA and what is it most often used for?
49. What are the differences in cost and performance between DRAM and SRAM?
50. What are the major approaches to improving memory performance?
51. What is the major distinguishing characteristic of flash RAM?
52. What are the major trends in how memory is packaged?
53. What is the difference between average seek time and average access time?
54. Differentiate between IDE, E-IDE, and SCSI.
55. Differentiate between the various terms used to categorize disk performance.
56. What is the difference between PIO and DMA?
57. What is the effect of caches and buffers on disk performance?
58. How do caches differ from buffers?
59. What are resolution and refresh rate, and what effect do they have on maximum video bandwidth?
60. What are the systems relationships or interdependencies within the video subsystem?
61. What does multisync mean?
62. What is color depth, and what effect does it have on VRAM?
63. How is resolution measured?
64. How is refresh rate measured?
65. What is the difference between active and passive matrix displays?
66. What are the four key components of a graphics accelerator card, and what role does each play?
67. What is the role of graphics software drivers, and why are they important?

ACTIVITIES

1. Divide into groups, with each group being assigned one of the subsystems of a computer system. Each group should research technical developments of their subsystem, past and present, and prepare a timeline of significant events. Get together with the other subsystem groups when timelines are completed. Compare the timing of significant events in each subsystem. Find examples of how significant developments in one subsystem led to technical developments in other subsystems.

2. Research and prepare a presentation on CPU clocks. How are they similar to the technology found in most wrist watches? How are they different?
3. Prepare a presentation on current CPU chip development highlighting pipelining. Stress the differences between the chips in terms of number of pipelines, number and type of execution units, and number of pipeline stages.
4. Find examples of the principle of shifting bottlenecks in areas other than CPU design.

5. Take the logic flowchart from a simple computer program employing if-then-else loops. Using a realistic set of data, perform structured walkthroughs on the program and save results of conditional branches in a list (branch target buffer). Begin to predict conditional branches based on the previous results contained in your branch target buffer. What percentage of accuracy does your branch target buffer produce? Repeat the experiment with different programs and different data sets.

6. Program the branch prediction logic walked through in Activity 5 in a real program and execute with a larger data set. Have the program keep statistics on branch prediction accuracy percentage.

7. Prepare graphs plotting CPU chip performance development over time. Chart items such as number of transistors, clock speed, and MIPS. What do the graphs look like? Has the rate of development been constant, or is it accelerating?

8. Trace the introduction of and sales of clones of Intel chips. Analyze the success or failure of these ventures.

9. Trace the sales of computers using the PowerPC chip. Pay particular attention to the types of applications run on these computers. Windows apps? Mac apps? RISC apps? native PowerPC apps?

10. Use data communications and computer system supply catalogs to prepare a presentation or bulletin board showing the types of devices which connect to PCI buses versus expansion buses.

11. Collect advertisements and promotional literature on disk drives. Prepare a display highlighting quoted seek times and access times. Can you find examples of when access times quoted are really just seek times?

FEATURED REFERENCES

General

Miller, Michael. The Perfect PC. *PC Magazine,* 14; 13 (July 1995), 103.

PowerPC/PowerMAC/MAC Clones

Andrews, Dave. Mac Clones—Finally. *Byte,* 20; 4 (April 1995), 22.

Andrews, Dave. PowerPC Tidal Wave. *Byte,* 20; 6 (June 1995), 25.

Halfhill, Tom. Apple's High-Tech Gamble. *Byte,* 19; 12 (December 1994), 50.

Ryan, Bob and Tom Thompson. PowerPC 604 Weighs In. *Byte,* 19; 6 (June 1994), 265.

Thompson, Tom. Apple's Tsunami: PCI Power. *Byte,* 20; 7 (July 1995), 26.

Thompson, Tom. New PowerPCs for Notebooks and PDAs. *Byte,* 20; 4 (April 1995), 211.

Thompson, Tom. New PowerPC Standard Supports MACs. *Byte,* 20; 3 (March 1995), 24.

Thompson, Tom. One Box, Two Computers. *Byte,* 20; 4 (April 1995), 165.

Thompson, Tom. Send in the Clones. *Byte,* 20; 8 (August 1995), 111.

Wittman, Art. Tuning the PowerMAC. *Network Computing,* 5; 11 (October 1, 1994), 134.

PCMCIA/PC Card

Bryan, John. PCMCIA: Past, Present, and Promise. *Byte,* 19; 11 (November 1994), 65.

Perratore, Ed. The Memory-Card Manager Grows Up. *Byte,* 19; 6 (June 1994), 32.

Rigney, Steve. PCMCIA Connectivity: Socket to Us. *PC Magazine,* 14; 2 (January 24, 1995), 207.

Wittman, Art. PCMCIA: Flexible, Yet Frustrating. *Network Computing,* 5; 12 (October 15, 1994), 52.

Bus

Apiki, Steve. SCSI Rides High on PCI. *Byte,* 19; 12 (December 1994), 163.

Carr, Eric and Jeff Newman. PCI-SCSI Hosts: Thanks for the Hospitality, We'll Stick with EISA. *Network Computing,* 6; 5 (May 1, 1995), 112.

Wittmann, Art. Battle of the Buses. *Network Computing,* 6; 2 (February 1, 1995), 140.

CPUs

Byrd, Gregory and Mark Holliday. Multithreaded processor architecture. *IEEE Spectrum,* 32; 8 (August 1995), 38.

Clyman, John. CPUs: What's Next Inside? *PC Magazine,* 14; 4 (February 21, 1995), 177.

Clyman, John. Pentium vs. Power PC: Battle for the Desktop. *PC Magazine,* 13; 10 (May 31, 1994), 114.

Clyman, John. The Perfect System Unit. *PC Magazine,* 14; 13 (July 1995), 148.

Davey, Tom. Intel Prepares P6 Successor with Clock Speeds Pushing 200MHz. *PC Week,* 12; 35 (September 4, 1995), 1.

Faust, Bruce. Designing Alpha-Based Systems. *Byte,* 20; 6 (June 1995), 239.

Grehan, Rick. Embedded Processors: Processors Proliferate. *Byte,* 19; 9 (September 1994), 67.

Halfhill, Tom. 80X86 Wars. *Byte,* 19; 6 (June 1994), 74.

Halfhill, Tom. AMD vs. Superman. *Byte,* 19; 11 (November 1994), 95.

Halfhill, Tom. Intel's P6. *Byte,* 20; 4 (April 1995), 42.

Halfhill, Tom. P6 Weakness Revealed. *Byte,* 20; 9 (September 1995), 24.

Halfhill, Tom. Pentium Overdrive = Moderate Upgrade. *Byte,* 20; 6 (June 1995), 30.

Halfhill, Tom. T5: Brute Force. *Byte,* 19; 11 (November 1994), 123.

Loudermilk, Stephen. Intel Chip Advances. *LAN Times,* 12; 13 (July 3, 1995), 1.

Mysore, Chandrika and John McDonough. 19 Pentiums at 90MHz. *Byte,* 19; 12 (December 1994), 192.

Pountain, Dick. HP's Speedy RISC. *Byte,* 20; 7 (July 1995), 175.

Pountain, Dick. Supercomputing: The Last Bastion. *Byte,* 19; 9 (September 1994), 47.

Pountain, Dick. Transport-Triggered Architectures. *Byte,* 20; 2 (February 1995), 151.

Rupley, Sebastian and John Clyman. P6: The Next Step? *PC Magazine,* 14; 15 (September 1995), 102.

Ryan, Bob. Alpha Rides High. *Byte,* 19; 10 (October 1994), 197.

Ryan, Bob. Getting CISC into RISC. *Byte,* 19; 9 (September 1994), 38.

Seymour, Jim. RISC Workstations: Ready for the Desktop? *PC Magazine,* 13; 10 (May 31, 1994), 125.

Stam, Nick. Inside the Chips. *PC Magazine,* 14; 4 (February 21, 1995), 190.

Thompson, Tom and Bob Ryan. PowerPC 620 Soars. *Byte,* 19; 11 (November 1994), 113.

VanKrieken, Roeland. Pentium's Chip's Dual Personality. *Byte,* 19; 12 (December 1994), 211.

Wayner, Peter. SPARC Strikes Back. *Byte* 19; 11 (November 1994), 105.

Video/Graphics

Bryan, John. Compression Scorecard. *Byte,* 20; 5 (May 1995), 107.

Chinnock, Chris. Color to Go. *Byte,* 20; 6 (June 1995), 115.

Corcoran, Cate. Graphics Memory Architectures: Faster Graphics Cards on the Horizon. *Byte,* 20; 4 (April 1995), 24.

Diehl, Stanford. Windows '95 Graphics Architecture. *Byte,* 20; 6 (June 1995), 241.

Kane, Jim. PCI and MAC Graphics Adapters: Lab Report on True-Color Graphics Accelerators. *Byte,* 20; 2 (February 1995), 136.

Loveria, Greg. Easing Window's Graphics Bottleneck. *Byte,* 19; 7 (July 1994), 133.

Loveria, Greg. The Matrox Triple Threat. *Byte,* 20; 8 (August 1995), 121.

Mace, Jeff. Ultrafast Graphics: The Professional's Choice. *PC Magazine,* 14; 12 (June 27, 1995), 205.

Ulanoff, Lance. The Perfect Display. *PC Magazine,* 14; 13 (July 1995), 172.

Memory

Cook, Rick. More Memory in Less Space. *Byte,* 20; 6 (June 1995), 197.

Prosise, Jeff. Memory: A PC's Most Precious Resource. *PC Magazine,* 14; 1 (January 10, 1995), 241.

Wayner, Peter. Fast, Smart RAM. *Byte,* 20; 6 (June 1995), 187.

PDAs

Nadeau, Michael. PDAs Bounce Back. *Byte,* 20; 6 (June 1995), 147.

Disk Drives/Storage

Erlanger, Leon. The Perfect Hard Disk. *PC Magazine,* 14; 13 (July 1995), 186.

Essex, David. Big, Fast IDE Drives. *Byte,* 19; 9 (September 1994), 151.

Voice Recognition/Multimedia

Bsales, Jamie. The Perfect Multimedia Add-Ons. *PC Magazine,* 14; 13 (July 1995), 202.

Richman, Dan. Speech Replaces Point and Click. *Information Week,* no. 534 (July 3, 1995), 44.

General Trends

Halfhill, Tom. The New PC. *Byte,* 20; 10 (October 1995), 52.

Wayner, Peter. Network-Ready Computers. *Byte,* 20; 3 (March 1995), 171.

CASE STUDY

Chapter 3

BANKING ON PCI FOR BANDWIDTH

Network managers craving more bandwidth and power at the desktop are changing their networks and replacing older PCs with faster PCI-equipped Intel Corp. Pentium machines.

Such is the case with Texas Commerce Bank's Investment Management Co. Just seven months ago the large, Houston-based financial institution made a big jump from ARCnet to Ethernet and from 386-based PCs to Pentium-based PCs with PCI slots.

The bank opted for a new desktop standard based on PCI for two reasons: Better network throughput and fewer I/O bottlenecks, said Henry Hudson, network administrator for the bank's technology group.

Thus, the bank overhauled its antiquated 2Mbps ARCnet LAN —which comprised 65 Tandy

Computer Corp. 4000s and a mixture of DOS-based PCs running vertical financial applications—by moving to an Ethernet network. The new scenario included 75 Summit Micro Design Inc. PCs featuring a 90MHz Pentium processor and 16MB of RAM. Each PC runs a mixture of Microsoft Windows- and DOS-based financial applications, said Hudson.

Texas Commerce changed from ARCnet to PCI Ethernet because "we were starving for bandwidth, and we're moving to Windows while we're installing video services on top of existing DOS-based [Saber Software Corp.] applications," said Hudson. The bank's administrator oversees a 90-user Novell Inc. NetWare 3.11 network, the backbone for million-dollar transactions conducted daily by portfolio managers, credit and financial analysts, and traders.

In search of extra bandwidth, Texas Commerce initially invested in Standard Microsystems Corp. Elite 16 ISA cards but found they did not perform well because of increased network traffic and more bandwidth-intensive applications, he said. The Texas Commerce Bank also investigated 100Mbps FDDI and Ethernet cards but decided those two approaches—especially FDDI—were too expensive.

The bank, which had already been using Austin, Texas-based, Thomas-Conrad Corp. ARCnet adapters and hubs, eventually decided to purchase 80 of the company's TC5048 PCI Ethernet adapters after an adapter card test drive. The TC5048 was tested against SMC's Elite 16 and outpaced its competition by more than 1,300KB per second, Hudson said.

Each Thomas-Conrad card now attaches to four Cabletron Systems Inc. MMAC-8 chassis-based hubs, two Cabletron 12-port MicroMMAC hubs, and one Compaq Computer Corp. ProLiant 4000 server.

A year ago switching to PCI adapters might not have been the best choice for Hudson.

The use of PCI-equipped products was perceived as a struggle because of electrical connection problems, and the technology was implemented differently by the systems and adapter vendors. But the bus is slowly becoming the next standard for both Ethernet and ATM NICs and other peripheral cards, according to industry observers. The 133MB per second PCI bus is at least four times faster than an EISA bus and 16 times faster than an ISA bus. For heavily loaded workstation and server environments, ISA and EISA bus technologies simply are not enough, say industry analysts.

Ease of installation was also a critical factor in making PCI Ethernet the bank's standard. The jumperless TC5048 card installed itself in seconds, sensing the network connection and media type. "We wanted something that would work for us and was easy to set up," Hudson said.

The payback for the bank has been monumental, according to Hudson. Besides saving money on adapter costs—at $150 per card—the company is increasing network performance, while freeing enough bandwidth to bring video and financial applications to the desktop, he said.

"PCI has sped up our antiquated DOS applications, improving productivity by at least 50 percent. We made a big jump when we went from ARCnet to PCI Ethernet," Hudson said. However, the only drawback in moving to PCI Ethernet was rewiring the building with Category 5 data-grade cabling, which cost the company $30,000, he said.

Next month, Texas Commerce plans to upgrade to NetWare 4.1. After that transition, the bank expects to eventually deploy fast-Ethernet technology as Microsoft Windows 95 and videoconferencing applications are deployed.

"We have 10Mbps Ethernet now, but as we move to videoconferencing, we will probably go to fast Ethernet; right now, our applications don't require much more bandwidth," Hudson said.

Source: Stephen Loudermilk (June 19, 1995). Banking on PCI for Bandwidth. *LAN Times*, 12(12), 29. Reprinted with permission of McGraw-Hill, *LAN Times*.

BUSINESS CASE STUDY QUESTIONS

Activities

1. Complete a top-down model for this case by gleaning facts from the case and placing them in the proper layer of the top-down model. After completing the top-down model, analyze and detail those instances when requirements were clearly passed down from upper to lower layers of the model and when solutions to those requirements were passed up from lower to upper layers.

2. Detail any questions that may occur to you about the case for which answers are not clearly stated in the article.

Business

1. What alternative approaches were investigated, and what was the conclusion for each of the possibilities?

2. What have been the cost/benefits of the move to PCI technology?

3. What are some of the ways in which technology impact can be measured?

4. What was the only perceived drawback to the move to PCI?
5. What are the strategic plans for future network evolution and development at Texas Commerce Bank?

Application

1. What changes in applications prompted an examination of the desktop standards?

Data

1. Describe the nature of the data and nondata traffic which needed to be transported by the network. What difficulties might the identified differences present?

Network

1. Differentiate between ARCnet and Ethernet in terms of functional characteristics.

2. What did the bank perceive as the benefits of PCI as a desktop standard?
3. What are the media requirements for PCI bus-based Ethernet network interface cards?

Technology

1. Describe the importance of bus choice to overall system throughput.
2. Which network operating system is employed?
3. Which other bus types were tested? What were the results?
4. What made the installation of the network interface cards essentially trouble-free?
5. For what types of applications are PCI bus computers especially well suited?

CHAPTER 4

CLIENT SOFTWARE

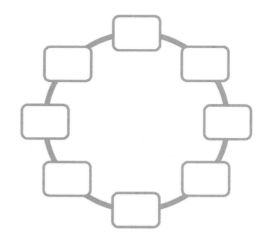

Concepts Reinforced

Client/server technology architecture
Client/server technology and tools
Client hardware platforms

Protocols and compatibility
OSI model
Processor fundamentals

Concepts Introduced

Client software architecture
Kernels and microkernels
Client operating systems
Hardware/software compatibility

Operating system architecture
Graphical user interfaces
Client network operating systems
Platform independence

OBJECTIVES

After mastering the material in this chapter you should:

1. Understand the organization and interaction of the various categories of client software from an architectural perspective.

2. Understand the concepts and architecture of a typical client operating system.

3. Understand the importance of interprocess communications and APIs to client software interoperability.

4. Understand the functionality of and major differences between currently available client software.

Having gained an appreciation for both the functionality and variety of client hardware in Chapter 3, you must now bridge the functional gap between the client hardware platform and the end-user. To deliver transparent interoperability to the end-user, many categories of client software must interact successfully. Understanding the role of each of these client software categories and, perhaps more important, how they communicate with each other to deliver the desired transparent interoperability to the end-user, is the focus of this chapter.

■ THE CLIENT SOFTWARE ARCHITECTURE

As an introduction to the different categories of client software explored in this chapter, Figure 4-1 illustrates a conceptual view of their interaction.

Several aspects of the client software architecture deserve elaboration. First, arrows between conceptual layers of the client software architecture indicate the need for a standardized protocol to successfully bridge the interface in question. The protocols used for communication between client software categories may vary, depending on which particular software technology is being used in each software category. Without agreed upon, mutually supported communications protocols between client software categories, there can be no top-to-bottom communication through the client software architecture. It therefore follows that in the absence of these mutually supported communications protocols no transparent interoperability can be delivered from the client hardware to the end-user.

The presentation, application, and data management modules of the client software architecture were introduced in Chapter 2 as the key logical elements of distributed computing, and the client hardware module that forms the foundation of the entire architecture was covered in Chapter 3. Shifting the application and data management modules into a side-by-side relationship is significant in that within the client software architecture, both of these software categories may need to interact directly with the network operating system as well as with each other.

Although the presentation, network operating system, and operating system functional models are depicted separately in the client software architecture, currently available software technology may combine these separate functional

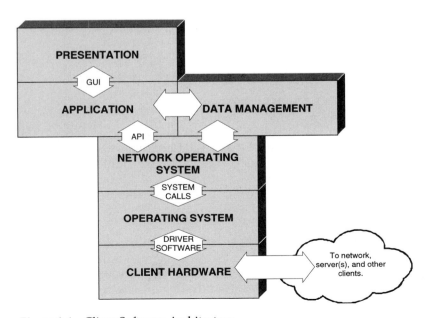

Figure 4-1   Client Software Architecture

categories into a single product. Examples of such products will be explored throughout the chapter.

Clients, and their associated client software architecture, are just part of the overall client/server architecture. As a result, Figure 4-1 depicts how the client software architecture interacts with the network, server(s), and other clients via the client hardware layer.

Interacting directly with the client hardware is the function of the operating system module. The functional concepts and current trends in this client software category begin the journey through the client software and client presentation software. Client applications software is examined only in terms of its interaction with presentation, network operating system, and operating system software. Client data management software and client application software development in a distributed computing environment are dealt with later.

■   CLIENT OPERATING SYSTEMS

Concepts and Functionality

An operating system's primary goal is to allow a user to easily execute applications programs without worrying about understanding specifics regarding the computer hardware on which those applications run. The operating system extends this hardware transparency not only to end-users, but also to the applications programmers who write the programs. Operating systems allow application programmers to include standard operating system commands or calls in their programs rather than having to write unique lower-level commands for every possible client hardware combination on which their programs may run.

An operating system can be thought of as a resource manager or resource allocator. Following are some of the resources to be managed and allocated among competing applications:

- CPU processing time.
- Memory access.
- Disk storage/retrieval and file system management.
- Input/output resources.

An additional key responsibility of operating systems is that all of these resources must be managed and allocated in a secure manner. All of these required functions of an operating system could be considered subsystems of the overall operating system. Referring back to Figure 4-1, one could say that an operating system manages and controls hardware resources on behalf of the upper layers of the client software architecture.

Operating System Architecture   The operating system is actually a computer program, at least part of which runs all of the time on any given computer. The operating system program itself is sometimes referred to as a **kernel.** Application programs request computer resources by interfacing to the operating system through mutually supported **system calls.** The operating system, or kernel, then interfaces to the various hardware components and their controllers via small software programs known as **device drivers,** which are specifically written to be compatible with a particular operating system and a particular type of hardware device.

The operating system can allocate system resources to multiple application programs and processes because of its ability to handle **interrupts** and **exceptions.** An interrupt is, quite literally, when the CPU is interrupted in doing one thing to do something else. Key hardware components such as the system bus, the keyboard, the video controller, and serial ports are all assigned interrupt numbers. Higher priority subsystems such as the system bus, keyboard, and video receive lower interrupt numbers than serial port devices such as modems. Application programs can also generate interrupts to get the CPU's attention and request services such as disk access or CPU processing time.

Exceptions are error conditions or unexpected events which the operating system must be prepared to handle appropriately. These exceptions are generally related to the operating system's responsibility to effectively manage system resources. An example of an exception that must be properly handled is when one application program tries to write into another application program's reserved memory space in an exception condition usually called a general protection fault. Protecting application program's memory space is a key differentiating factor among operating systems.

Figure 4-2 illustrates the relationship of users, application programs, operating systems, and hardware components in the operating systems architecture.

Monolithic Architecture Traditionally, operating systems were built according to a model known as a **monolithic architecture.** Required operating system components such as the file management system or the input/output and disk storage subsystem were arranged in a layered architecture, with each layer communicating directly only with the layers immediately above and below it. Maintaining or updating an operating system built with a monolithic architecture, otherwise known as a closed architecture, could be a nightmare. The closed nature of the monolithic architecture implies that all communications between the protocols on the various layers of the architecture were "hard-coded" for the specific corresponding combination of

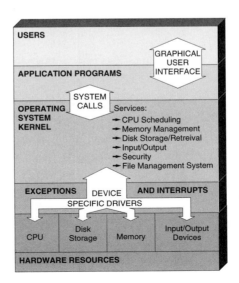

Figure 4-2 Operating System Architecture

protocols. As a result, alternative protocols could not be substituted on any given layer of the architecture. Because all communications from the application program to the device drivers had to pass through all layers of the operating system, a simple change in a single layer could have disastrous and untold consequences in other layers. New subsystems and functionality could not be easily added without rewriting several interacting layers of the operating system.

This difficulty with modification or maintenance contrasts sharply with systems developed according to open standards architectures such as the OSI model. The key difference between open and closed architectures is that open architectures define the methods or interfaces between layers of the architecture. As a result, any protocol which is able to communicate to a given layer's standardized, open interface specification is able to communicate with the protocols which reside in the neighboring layers of the open architecture.

Figure 4-3 is a conceptual representation of a monolithic operating system architecture.

Microkernel Architecture   The trend in most of today's client operating systems is toward a **microkernel-**based approach. A microkernel is a subset of the overall operating system. It could be thought of as a tiny operating system, the atomic particle of operating systems which cannot be further subdivided. It contains a minimum of hardware-specific instructions written to interact with a particular CPU chip. Although there are no laws as to what should and should not be included in the microkernel, the following CPU-related services, unique to each CPU chip, are typically included:

- CPU processor scheduling.

- Interrupt and exception handling.

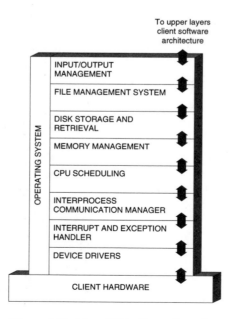

Figure 4-3   Monolithic Operating System Architecture

- Multiple processor handling.

- System crash recovery.

- Interprocess communications management.

- Virtual memory management.

The microkernel runs in what is known as **privileged mode,** which implies that it is never swapped out of memory and has highest priority for allocation of CPU cycles. The rest of the operating system is then written in separate add-on modules, or subsystems, which run in **user mode.**

The modular approach afforded by the microkernel architecture contrasts directly with the hierarchical, layered approach offered by the monolithic architecture. Surrounding the CPU-specific microkernel are modules or subsystems which offer the functionality previously offered by the layers cemented within the monolithic architecture. The operating system's modules converse with each other through the microkernel using mutually understandable message passing and interprocess communication. Figure 4-4 provides a conceptual representation of a microkernel operating system architecture in stark contrast to the monolithic architecture illustrated in Figure 4-3.

The key benefits of a microkernel operating system architecture over a monolithic operating system architecture are as follows:

- More extendible.

- More portable.

- More reliable.

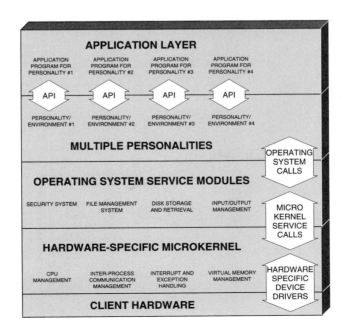

Figure 4-4   Microkernel Operating System Architecture

Extendible   As operating systems mature and the demands of information systems change, new features and subsystems are inevitably required to be added to existing operating systems. Given the small nucleus of a microkernel, with its relatively few microkernel system calls, additional modules are relatively easy to write and integrate with existing operating system modules. This characteristic can also be portrayed as being more *customizable.* Any module or service users demand can be added as long as that new subsystem communicates with the hardware resources through the microkernel via its minimal set of system calls or commands that enable its available services.

Portable   Because all of the hardware-specific code is restricted to the microkernel, modular operating systems can be ported to any processor which can communicate

RELIABLE

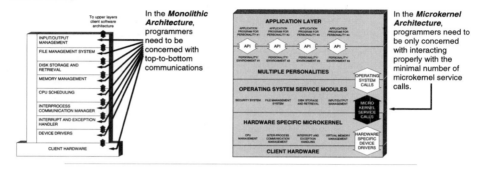

PORTABLE

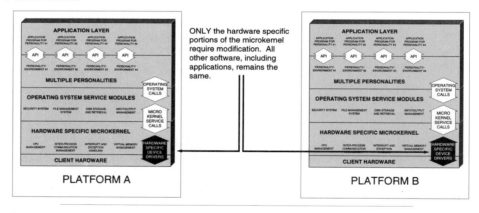

EXTENDABLE

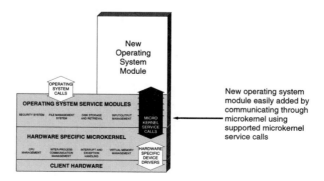

Figure 4-5   Key Benefits of Microkernel Operating System Architecture

with the microkernel on which that modular operating system is based. From a user's standpoint, this is very advantageous, as application programs written for a particular operating system could be executed on a variety of hardware platforms. Windows NT is an example of one of these so-called **hardware-independent operating systems** as it can run on Intel, MIPS, DEC Alpha, and PowerPC CPU chips.

Reliable   Increased reliability is a result of the fact that operating systems programmers only need to be concerned with interacting with the minimal number of microkernel commands. In the monolithic operating system architecture, programmers wrote layers and subsystems, which communicated only with the adjacent subsystems, and hoped that their programming would not cause unpredictable chain reactions in distant layers.

Figure 4-5 illustrates the key benefits of a microkernel operating system architecture.

Multiple Personality Operating Systems   Several current or emerging operating systems have introduced the notion of **multiple personality operating systems,** also known as **multiple workplace environments.** These multiple personality subsystems are just further examples of the extendibility or customizability of a microkernel-based operating system. As a specific example, Windows NT includes OS/2, 32-bit Windows, 16-bit Windows, and POSIX subsystems, which allow applications written for any of these environments to be run on a Windows NT platform. IBM, Apple, and Novell have all announced plans to produce multiple personality operating systems as well.

Technology and Trends

In Sharper Focus

COMPARATIVE MICROKERNELS

As illustrated in Figure 4-4, because microkernel-based operating systems can be built in a modular fashion, limited only by the requirement to interface to the microkernel through the minimal number of microkernel system calls, it is possible for different operating systems to be developed from the same microkernel. Two microkernels which have been used as the nucleus for numerous operating systems are the Mach microkernel, developed at Carnegie-Mellon University, and the Chorus microkernel, developed by Chorus Systems, located in France. Figure 4-6 lists some

Operating System	Mach Microkernel	Chorus Microkernel	Apple Microkernel	NT Microkernel
Windows NT				•
Apple System 9 (Gershwin)			•	
USL UNIX SVR4		•		
OSF OSF/1 1.3	•			
DEC	•			
NextStep	•			
Chorus/MiX		•		

Figure 4-6   Microkernels versus Operating Systems

of the operating systems currently available or under development which are based on the Mach or Chorus microkernels or on their own proprietary microkernels.

Detailed technical information regarding microkernels is available in the references cited in the Featured References. Important concepts and characteristics of the Mach and Chorus microkernels essential to a thorough understanding of operating system design are reviewed briefly.

Mach Microkernel   The following concepts or terms are not only essential to understanding the Mach microkernel, they also form the basic understanding of operating system functionality in general:

- **Task.**

- **Thread.**

- **Port.**

A **task** is the basic addressable unit of program execution. It is sometimes referred to as an execution environment to which resources such as CPU cycles or virtual memory space can be assigned. A task can be accomplished or executed through the work accomplished by one or more **threads.** Threads are the basic unit of execution and are only assigned resources through a given task. Tasks spawn threads to accomplish their instructions. The relationship between tasks and threads is sometimes characterized as a parent–child relationship. A thread is analogous to an atom whereas a task is analogous to a molecule.

Threads are essential to distributed computing environments. In a multiple-server environment, one or more threads may be required to interact simultaneously with each distributed server to accomplish the overall task as dictated by a multithreaded application. Only the parent task interacts directly with the operating system requesting system resources, as necessary to run the multithreaded application. A **port** can be thought of as a queue, or communications pipe, through which computer resources are assigned to a task.

The structure of the Mach microkernel is not unlike the generic microkernel illustrated in Figure 4-4. Specifically, the hardware-specific services included in the Mach microkernel are as follows:

- Interprocess communication management.

- Virtual memory management.

- Task and threads management.

- Host and processor sets.

- I/O and interrupt support.

All other functionality must be offered by the operating systems modules, which are written to interface to the Mach microkernel via microkernel system calls, and are free to vary from one operating system to another.

Chorus Microkernel   In a chorus-based operating system, the microkernel is correctly called the chorus **nucleus.** The chorus nucleus is functionally organized around the following concepts:

- **Actor.**

- **Thread.**

- **Port.**
- **Site.**

An **actor** is the functional equivalent of a task in a Mach microkernel or a process in a UNIX environment. **Threads,** as in the Mach environment, do not have their own address space. Threads are able to send messages through **ports.** Ports separate the communication function from the execution function and allow threads to communicate with each other without knowing physical locations of the threads to which they wish to communicate. A given hardware platform or CPU is considered a **site,** with one nucleus executing at each site.

The chorus nucleus has built-in support for multiple processors and distributed operating system servers. Embedded within the chorus nucleus itself are the following services:

- Scheduling.
- Memory management.
- Real-time events support.
- Interprocess communications management.

All other functionality is written to operate externally to the nucleus in software modules known as **servers.** Groups of servers are known as **subsystems.** Servers and subsystems interact with the minimized chorus nucleus (50 to 60 KB) via supported nucleus system calls. An entire operating system, such as UNIX V, can be run as a single subsystem as long as interaction with the hardware platform is handled by the chorus nucleus. Such is the case with the UNIX V implementation included within the Chorus/MiX operating system.

Comparative Client Operating Systems Currently available client operating systems have evolved to include graphical user interfaces and built-in networking software in addition to the traditional operating system functionality. In the following section, a variety of operating systems alternatives are analyzed from functional and application perspectives.

Following are a few important concepts, which provide important criteria for operating system comparison:

- **Multiprocessing**—An operating system which supports multiprocessing is able to split the processing demands of applications programs across more than one processor or CPU. The most common type of multiprocessing supported by current operating systems is known as **symmetrical multiprocessing,** or **SMP,** in which processing loads are split evenly among all CPUs.

- **Multiuser**—Multiuser operating systems allow more than one user to log in simultaneously. In addition, multiuser operating systems run the multiple application programs of those multiple users simultaneously.

- **Cooperative multitasking**—Multitasking implies that an operating system can be running more than one program simultaneously. Cooperative multitasking implies that a given application has access to all required system resources until that program relinquishes control. Misbehaving application programs can monopolize system resources in a cooperative multitasking environment.

- **Preemptive multitasking**—Preemptive multitasking operating systems prevent misbehaving applications from monopolizing system resources by allocating system resources to applications according to priority or timing. When a given application program's time is up, it is "swapped out" or pre-empted, and another waiting application program is given the system resources it requires.

- **Multithreaded**—Recalling the relationship between tasks and threads from the section of microkernel functionality, a multithreaded operating system allows multiple threads per task to operate simultaneously. Each thread from a single task is free to communicate individually with other threads throughout the distributed environment. Computing resources for individual threads such as CPU cycles, virtual memory, or message passing, are requested through the parent task's port.

Some of these operating systems characteristics are likely to be more important on servers supporting multiple users than on single-user client workstations.

Applied Problem Solving

Operating Systems Analysis Questions   Before reviewing important characteristics of some of today's choices for client operating systems, Figure 4-7 summarizes a few general criteria for analysis and comparison.

Analysis Criteria	Explanation/Implication/Follow-up Questions
Heritage	Was the operating system initially designed with multiuser networks in mind?
Basic Design	How, if at all, does this operating system support the following environments: multiuser, multiprocessor, multitasking, multithreaded?
Hardware Requirements	Does the operating system require a particular CPU chip? What are the memory and disk requirements for operating system installation?
Networkability	Which networking features are included as part of the operating system? What networking functionality must be added by the network operating system? How available are network operating systems that run over this operating system as clients? as servers? What is the approximate cost/user of network operating systems which run over this operating system?
Interoperability	On how many different vendors' machines will this operating system run? Will this operating system run on Macs, high-powered workstations, and minicomputers/mainframes?
Applications	How available are applications programs which run over this operating system? How easy to develop are applications programs for this operating system? Are applications development tools available for this operating system? Can this operating system run application programs written for other operating systems?

Ease of Use	Consider the ease of use and level of expertise required in the following categories:
	System installation
	System configuration
	System management
	System use
	System monitoring
	System troubleshooting and diagnosis
	Are GUIs (graphical user interfaces) available for this operating system?
Future Potential	What might the future hold for this operating system?
	Is it in the twilight or sunrise of its product life cycle?
	Is it the center of controversy among industry giants?
	Is it governed by domestic or international standards organizations?
	Is there a definite need for this operating system in the client server, open systems, distributed computing world of tomorrow?

Figure 4-7   Operating Systems Analysis Questions

MS-DOS   MS-DOS, an acronym for Microsoft disk operating system, has gone through an evolution to survive in the era of networks. Originally designed to work on standalone, single-user PCs, DOS introduced multiuser networking capabilities such as record and file locking with the release of Version 3.1. Network operating systems are able to call these DOS commands transparently to the networking operating system users.

Network operating systems that run over DOS and rely on it for file management and record locking are known as DOS-based LANs. Lantastic by Artisoft and Windows for Workgroups by Microsoft are probably the best known DOS-based LANs, also known as peer-to-peer LANs. Just because a network operating system is DOS-based does not mean it cannot support many users and offer numerous sophisticated features.

DOS 5.0, which was released in the summer of 1991, added the ability to load programs and files of various types, including device drivers, in the PC's memory above the former 640 K ceiling. Programs stored in this extended memory are often stored as **TSR**s, or terminate and stay resident, programs. TSR programs do not use any CPU processing time until they are reactivated. Many networking and interoperability software products are stored in expanded memory or extended memory. The categorization of DOS-based memory is summarized in Figure 4-8.

MS-DOS is, strictly speaking, just an operating system, with Version 6.22 being the latest release. To be a fully operational client in a client/server distributed computing environment, a graphical user interface and network operating system

DOS Memory Category	Memory Addressed
Conventional (Base)	First 640 KB
Expanded	Between 640 KB and 1 MB
Extended	Above 1 MB

Figure 4-8   DOS Memory Categorization

functionality must be added. The following have been popular options to add this functionality in the past:

- Install Microsoft Windows as the graphical user interface.

- Install Microsoft Windows for Workgroups for both a graphical user interface and networking capabilities.

- Install other DOS-based LANs such as LANtastic for networking capabilities.

Microsoft has added both a graphical user interface and networking software to DOS in an integrated fashion with the release of Windows 95. It is unclear whether new versions of standalone MS-DOS will be forthcoming or whether it will be bundled with networking and GUI software from now on.

Multilayer Client Software Products   Windows 95, Windows NT Workstation, and OS/2 Warp Connect all represent top-to-bottom client software products incorporating operating system (OS), network operating system (NOS), and graphical user interface (GUI) functionality. Other products such as Windows for Workgroups and OS/2 Warp also represent more than one layer of the client software architecture. Figure 4-9 illustrates which client software architecture layers are incorporated in a variety of multilayer client software products. Operating system capabilities of these products are compared in this section, and networking capabilities or GUI characteristics are compared in their respective sections.

Windows 95   Among the key operating system–related features incorporated in Windows 95 are the following:

- New graphical user interface.

- 32-bit API (applications program interface) in a preemptive multitasking environment.

- Plug-n-play capability.

Windows 95 could be considered an all-in-one client software product as it includes graphical user interface, network operating system, and operating system functionality in a single package. The ability to obtain all three of these layers of the client software architecture encapsulated in a single product, purchased from a single vendor, goes a long way toward eliminating potential incompatibility issues between client software layers.

	Windows NT	Windows 95	Windows	OS/2 Warp	OS/2 Warp Connect	MS-DOS	Windows for Workgroups	MAC OS	UNIX w/ TCP/IP	Motif or Open-Look
GUI	•	•	•	•	•		•	•		•
NOS	•	•			•		•	•	•	
OS	•	•		•	•	•		•	•	

Figure 4-9   Multilayer Client Software Products

The all-new graphical user interface is designed to be more intuitive and more reflective of the way people work. Users need to know less about which commands are buried beneath which menu selections within which applications. The GUI is organized around a desktop, with various folders containing users' work. The desktop is customizable, and users can drag and drop icons of their choice on the desktop. One desktop feature called "The Briefcase" is especially useful for users who take their work home or on the road as well as work in the office. When leaving the office, users can load their "briefcase" of selected files onto their notebook computer. When they get back to the office, they unpack their briefcase, and the file synchronization software automatically updates files on the office computer. The GUI is definitely different from Windows, and even if users find it more intuitive, training and transition issues and costs must be dealt with honestly.

The 32-bit API is perhaps the most strategically significant feature of Windows 95. However, only applications programmers will actually work with the Win32 API, as it is called. The primary benefits users receive from running applications supporting the Win32 API are increased reliability due to preemptive multitasking and memory protection.

Preemptive multitasking, explained earlier, prevents ill-behaved programs from monopolizing computer resources. Memory protection grants each application its own memory space, and protects that space from other applications trying to write to it. The 16-bit Windows applications run in a shared memory space in a cooperative multitasking environment. The Win32 API is also supported by Windows NT, providing a clear migration path for users who may need more computing power without rewriting application programs.

However, Windows 95 must perform the difficult task of straddling the old world of Windows' cooperative multitasking 16-bit applications and the new world of Windows NT's preemptive multitasking 32-bit applications. Inevitably in circumstances such as this, compromises must be made. As a result, although 32-bit programs run in a preemptive multitasking environment, that environment is really just a subsystem, which depends on 16-bit operating system modules retained to provide backward compatibility for 16-bit applications. Thus, when a 16-bit application is running in the Windows 95 cooperative multitasking environment, all other 16-bit and 32-bit applications are blocked from obtaining system resources.

The plug-n-play capability offered by Windows 95 requires components certified as Windows 95 plug-n-play compatible. Working with PCMCIA cards, not known for their ease of installation, is especially straightforward thanks to Windows 95's built-in card services and socket services. Windows 95 is able to automatically detect when PCMCIA cards have been added or removed, and whether drivers for those cards are available within Windows 95 or must be loaded from a vendor supplied diskette.

Windows NT Workstation   Windows NT is a top-to-bottom client software product. An alternative, more expensive version of Windows NT for servers is appropriately named Windows NT server. Windows NT is a true 32-bit, preemptive multitasking operating system. All 32-bit applications execute in protected memory space. As described previously, Windows NT is able to run applications from other platforms such as OS/2 and 16-bit Windows through specially written multiple personality subsystems. These subsystems, in which different types of applications are able to execute, are sometimes referred to as **virtual machines.**

Windows NT is a microkernel-based operating system with a minimum of hardware-specific code confined to a portion of the microkernel known as **HAL,** or the **hardware abstraction layer.** Microkernel philosophy purists argue that Windows NT cannot be considered microkernel-based because certain operating system service managers run in the kernel space in privileged mode. Philosophical arguments aside, the Windows NT architecture, as illustrated in Figure 4-10, clearly illustrates the notion of numerous modular subsystems interacting with a hardware-specific microkernel, in this case referred to as a kernel.

One of the positive attributes of a microkernel-based operating system is that once the minimum amount of hardware-specific code is rewritten, no further operating system modification should be necessary for the operating system to execute on a different CPU platform. Windows NT has been arguably more successful at being ported to multiple CPU types than any other microkernel-based operating system. Windows NT currently runs on the following:

- Intel-based chips.
- MIPS R4X00 chips.
- DEC Alpha AXP chips.

Following are additional ports either planned or underway:

- Power PC chips (available in Windows NT Version 3.51).
- HP PA-RISC chips.

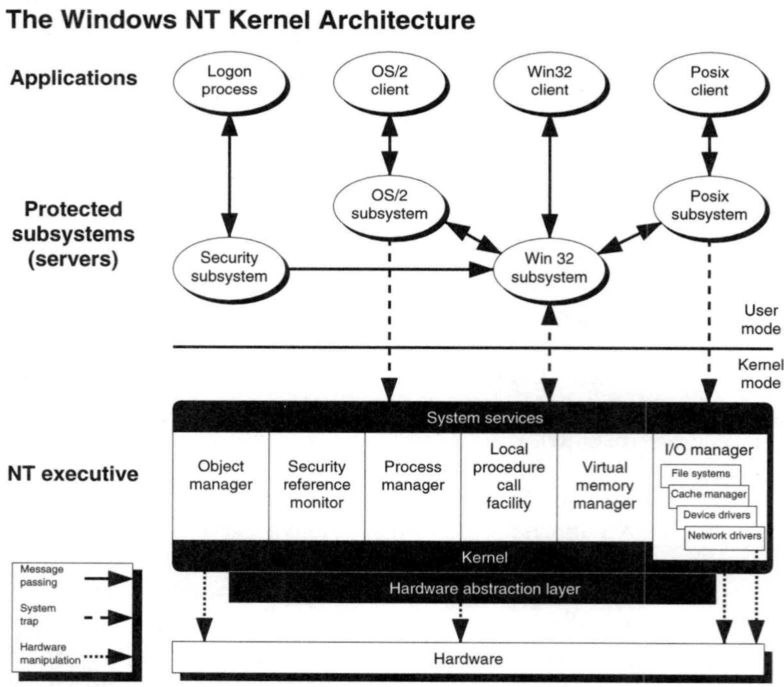

Figure 4-10   Windows NT Architecture

Windows NT is considered extremely reliable and secure. All applications must request services and interact with computer hardware resources through the local procedure call facility, thereby preventing them from interacting directly with hardware and potentially bypassing security or violating another application's memory space. The only negative aspect of this tight security is that some computer games which prefer to interact directly with hardware for performance reasons, either operate more slowly or not at all under Windows NT. Windows NT also has some significant hardware requirements: 12 to 16 MB of memory (although 32 MB is even better) and 90 to 120 MB of disk space.

In Sharper Focus

WINDOWS 32-BIT API VARIETIES

Windows applications execute over a particular operating system environment by issuing commands understood by both the application program and the operating system. This set of mutually supported commands is known as an API or application program interface. In the case of 32-bit Windows programs, this API is known as the Win32 API. Variations of the Win32 API have been created to allow 32-bit Windows applications to run in a variety of environments. The differences among the following variations of the Win32 API are subtle yet significant.

- **Win32 API**—This is the full-blown 32-bit API created for Windows NT.

- **Win32s API**—The "s" stands for subset. This API was created for applications which need the processing power of 32-bit applications but must still be able to execute under 16-bit Windows 3.1. The API in Windows 3.1 is commonly referred to as Win16. Simply stated, Win32s is a 32-bit version of Win16 without any of the Win32 API enhancements. The Win32s API is supported by a dynamic link library (DLL), which converts 32-bit API calls to the 16-bit API calls supported by Windows 3.1.

- **Win32c API**—The "c" stands for compatible. This is the API included with Windows 95 and it contains nearly all of the functionality offered by NT's Win32 API while remaining backward compatible with 16-bit Windows 3.1 applications.

Operating environments other than Windows, Windows NT, and Windows 95 can run Windows applications as long as they support the proper Win32 or Win16 API. In the case of OS/2 Warp Connect, described next, the Win32s API is supported but the full function Win32 API is not. Figure 4-11 illustrates the relationships between the various Win32 APIs and their respective GUI/operating systems.

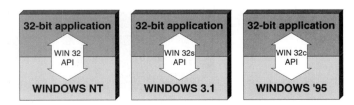

Figure 4-11   Win32 APIs

OS/2 Warp Connect   From an architectural standpoint, OS/2 Warp Connect is similar to Windows NT in that separate virtual machines are implemented for 16-bit and 32-bit applications. The 16-bit applications can run in a shared environment in which they potentially write into each other's memory area. In this arrangement, if one 16-bit application crashes, all 16-bit applications crash. Alternatively, each 16-bit application can run in its own protected virtual machine. OS/2 Warp Connect can run 16-bit Windows and DOS applications as well as native OS/2 applications. Figure 4-12 illustrates OS/2 Warp Connect's architecture and Figure 4-13 compares operating systems characteristics of Windows 95, Windows NT Workstation, and OS/2 Warp Connect.

UNIX   UNIX as a client workstation operating system is limited primarily to implementations in high-powered scientific or engineering workstations. UNIX is much more commonly used as a server operating system, with numerous implementations on minicomputers and mainframes as well. UNIX itself is actually not just a single operating system, but many, largely incompatible, variations of a single operating system. There are two main versions of UNIX:

- **AT&T System V Release 4,** commonly written as **SVR4**—Originally developed by AT&T later reorganized as USL (UNIX Systems Laboratory), which AT&T subsequently sold to Novell which Novell subsequently sold to the Santa Cruz Operation (SCO).

- **BSD** (Berkeley Software Distribution) **UNIX,** from the University of California at Berkeley.

Many other versions of UNIX, usually derived from one of these major families, are also popular. Figure 4-14 summarizes a few of the UNIX variations.

UNIX's heritage of open systems and multiplatform operation has enabled many networking features to be included in the operating system itself, precluding the need to buy an additional networking operating system to run over UNIX. Perhaps best known of these features is the Internet Suite of Protocols, more commonly known as TCP/IP, and associated protocols. TCP/IP, network file system (NFS), and other UNIX networking features are studied in detail in Chapter 13.

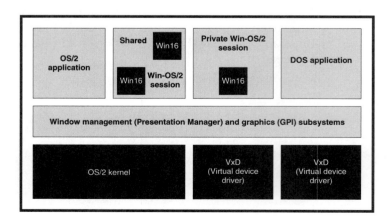

Figure 4-12   OS/2 Warp Connect Architecture

Operating System Characteristic	Windows 95	Windows NT Workstation	OS/2 Warp Connect
Preemptive multitasking—32-bit apps	•	•	•
Preemptive multitasking—16-bit apps		•	•
Supports multithreaded apps	•	•	•
Apps run in protected memory space	32 bit only	•	•
Subsystems run in protected memory space		•	•
Can run Win32sAPI applications	•	•	•
Can run Win32API applications	•	•	
Supports symmetric multiprocessing		•	•
Desktop (object-oriented) user interface	•	(Version 4.0)	•

Figure 4-13 Comparative Operating System Characteristics: Windows 95, Windows NT Workstation, OS/2 Warp

Because UNIX runs not only on PCs, but also on numerous minicomputers and larger platforms, applications written for and installed on larger UNIX machines can be downsized to smaller client-server environments. Conversely, applications can be developed on less expensive personal workstations but installed and executed on larger, more powerful computers. UNIX has become increasingly popular as the operating system of choice for LAN servers. Programs written to run on one of these versions of UNIX will not necessarily run on others.

Although variations exist between different flavors of UNIX, it can be fairly safely said that UNIX possesses the following characteristics:

- Is inherently a multiuser operating system.

- Supports symmetrical multiprocessing.

- Supports preemptive multitasking.

- Supports multithreaded applications.

- Is a kernel-based operating system which insulates hardware from misbehaving applications.

Company Name	UNIX Variant Name
Hewlett-Packard	HP-UX
Data General	DG/UX
DEC	Ultrix
Sun Microsystems	Solaris
SCO (Santa Cruz Operation)	OpenServer

Figure 4-14 UNIX Variations

UNIX was developed by and for the scientific community. Objectively, it could be called a cryptic, command-line–oriented operating system. Installation and configuration are anything but straightforward. Of course, these statements are generalizations and some versions score better than others on the user-friendliness test. Also, these traditional shortcomings of UNIX have not gone unnoticed by major UNIX system vendors. As a result, a universal desktop for UNIX known as CDE, or common desktop environment, has been developed and is elaborated on in the presentation software section. Although often appropriate as a server operating system, UNIX is presently limited as a client workstation operating system largely to high-powered engineering and scientific applications.

Novell DOS   Originally known as digital research (DR)-DOS, Novell DOS Version 7 (ND7) is an alternative to MS-DOS 6.22. ND7 is really three products in one:

- DOS.

- Universal NetWare client.

- Personal NetWare.

The DOS portion of ND7 is distinguished by its ability to run multiple applications simultaneously in a multitasking environment, thanks to a multitasking kernel. ND7 is otherwise compatible with MS-DOS and can run either Windows or Windows for Workgroups as the user interface. ND7 also comes with utilities for backup, virus detection, and network management.

The Universal NetWare Client is that portion of the client software stack required to allow a client workstation to access files and services offered by network-attached servers in a client/server environment. The term NetWare client implies that this software will allow this client to login to NetWare servers only. The term Universal indicates that this software allows clients to login to NetWare servers running versions of NetWare from 2.X to 4.X and also allows clients to use a wide variety of network interface cards. The details of client network operating system software are discussed in the next section.

Personal NetWare is a DOS-based peer-to-peer network operating system which could be considered a competitor to Microsoft's Windows for Workgroups. Peer-to-peer network operating systems allow client workstations to share resources such as disk space and printers. Simple e-mail or chat utilities are usually also included. Clients on the Personal NetWare LAN can use the universal NetWare client software to reach both Personal NetWare servers and NetWare servers.

Apple's Operating Systems   With the shift in hardware design from the Motorola 680x0 chip series in the Mac to the PowerPC chip in the PowerMacs, it was necessary to design a new operating system that could take maximum advantage of the PowerPC's RISC design. In the meantime, legacy Mac applications had to run on the PowerMacs in emulation mode, with the performance penalty of the additional emulation overhead.

With the release of Version 8.0 of the **MacOS,** code-named Copland, Apple has produced a totally new, microkernel-based operating system exhibiting the following key characteristics:

- Preemptive multitasking.

- Supports multithreaded applications.

Product	Follow-up Chapter(s)
NetWare	11
Windows NT	12
UNIX	13

Figure 4-15 Follow-up Chapters for Client Software Products

- Program execution in protected memory space.

- Microkernel foundation allowing subsystems to be easily added or modified.

- Isolation of hardware specific code to the hardware abstraction layer (HAL) portion of the microkernel.

As with Windows 95, ensuring compatibility with older applications inevitably requires compromises. As a result, although preemptive multitasking and memory protection are afforded to newer native applications, those older applications originally written to run on the 680x0 series are executed in a shared memory area in a cooperative multitasking environment. Misbehaving applications in this cooperative multitasking area can crash one another but cannot crash the individually protected programs running in the preemptive multitasking environment.

The release of MacOS Version 8.0 achieves at least three important goals for Apple:

- Creates a powerful new microkernel-based operating system.

- Runs legacy applications well.

- Removes hard-coded hardware-to-operating system links to enable Mac clone hardware vendors and third-party Mac software vendors to participate fully in the PowerMac market.

For Further Information In the interest of keeping this chapter to less than 100 pages, only the briefest of introductions have been given to the aforementioned client software products. Figure 4-15 lists follow-up chapters for selected products.

■ CLIENT NETWORK OPERATING SYSTEMS

Concepts and Functionality

Recalling Figure 4-1, it should be obvious that clients are *physically* connected to network-attached resources such as servers via the client hardware layer or, more specifically, network interface cards. However, what role does client software play in this connection to network-attached resources? Somewhere in the client software stack, at least two questions must be answered to understand how a client workstation is able to access network-attached resources:

1. Is the resource (file, disk drive, printer) requested by the client's application program physically attached to the local client or to a server or another client somewhere out on the network?

2. If the resource is network attached, how must the requesting message to that network-attached resource be formatted and delivered?

This section details the generalized logical process involved in enabling clients to access network-attached resources. More platform-specific issues related to specific network operating systems and their associated protocol stacks are discussed in Chapters 10 through 13.

Client Redirectors   For every request for services coming from an application program, a software module known as the **redirector** determines whether those requested resources are locally attached or network attached. Requests for locally attached resources are forwarded to the client's local operating system. Requests for network-attached resources are passed in proper format and properly addressed to the network interface card installed in the client PC, for subsequent delivery to the desired network attached resource.

NetBIOS API   A type of software specification known as a network **applications program interface** (API) allows requests for services from application programs to be passed along to the network-attached servers providing these services. Network basic input/output system **(NetBIOS)** is an API which has become the de facto standard of network APIs for PC-based networks.

Technically speaking, NetBIOS, or any API for that matter, is a specification outlining two major elements:

- A particular software interrupt to the client portion of the network operating system, which is executed to request network services for transportation of data or messages across the network.

- A series of standardized commands which establish network-based communication sessions, send and receive data, and name network resources.

In practice, an API such as NetBIOS allows a person running a word processing program on a client PC to retrieve a document located on a disk drive which is physically attached to a network-attached server PC. For instance, all the user knows is that the document is located on a drive known as H:, and that once he/she requests that document, it appears on the screen of the client PC ready to be edited. All the interpretation of requests between the various software layers of the client PC and server PC is of no concern to the user.

A standardized API, such as NetBIOS, allows applications programs to be written without concern for which network operating system it may eventually run over as long as that network operating system understands NetBIOS requests. Likewise, a network operating system can run transparently underneath any application program, secure in the knowledge that it will be able to understand any NetBIOS requests for network services.

NetBIOS is, by definition, a system of commands that are able to do the following:

- Interpret requests submitted to it in proper format from the application program.

- Pass these requests along to a network communications program.

NetBIOS application programs, otherwise known as NetBIOS protocols, which interface with the NetBIOS API have been developed to perform specialized tasks on client and server PCs to enable this client/server communication. Two of the most famous of these NetBIOS application programs or protocols are the NetBIOS **Redirector,** on the client, and the **server message block (SMB) server,** on the server.

Figure 4-16 illustrates the interaction of a word processing application program, the NetBIOS redirector, NetBIOS API, the SMB server, and the network operating system.

As the figure shows, the word processing program sends out a request for a particular document on a certain disk drive, not knowing whether that disk drive is on the local client PC or on the remote server PC. This request is in an agreed upon NetBIOS API format or syntax known as **NCB** or **network control block.** This network control block is received by the NetBIOS redirector and evaluated as to whether the request should be handled by the local PC and passed to the local PC's operating system or sent on to the NetBIOS API for interfacing with the network operating system running on this client PC.

If the requested document is on a remote server, the NetBIOS API tells the network operating system which server the requested document resides on by preparing a server message block for transmission. The network operating system forwards the server message block to the remote server via the local network adapter card and network media of choice.

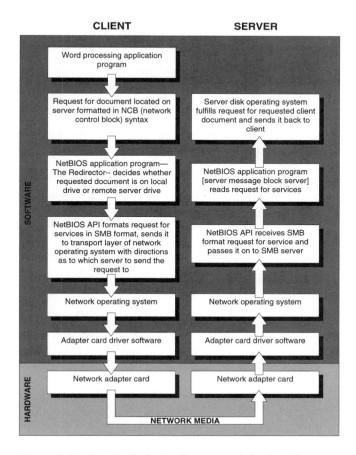

Figure 4-16   NetBIOS, the Redirector, and the SMB Server

Once the server message block is received by the remote server, it is passed by the NetBIOS API to the server message block server, which passes requests for particular files or documents on to the disk operating system of the server PC. Once the server message block receives the requested document, it sends it back to the client PC in a similar manner but opposite direction.

Notice how a particular network operating system was not referenced in Figure 4-16. Therein lies the importance of NetBIOS. It is an application program–to–application program communications protocol, which is understood by and incorporated into most network operating systems. Different versions of NetBIOS have been developed to run over different network operating systems. These varieties are summarized in Figure 4-17.

NetBIOS, with all its varieties, is not the only network communications API invented, however. Several other APIs have been implemented in various network operating systems, as outlined in Figure 4-18. In many cases, these APIs have additional commands and features not found in NetBIOS. However, even in the network operating systems which use non-NetBIOS APIs, such as NetWare or Vines, a Net-BIOS emulator is often included to ensure compatibility across varied network operating systems.

NetBIOS or some other network API is at the heart of client/server communication. Without this transparent layer of software keeping track of the location of shared resources and managing the requests for sharing them no client/server computing can occur. To be able to link client and server PCs of various network or disk operating systems, compatibility of the APIs must be ensured. NetBIOS and its derivatives are the most widely installed and supported APIs. However, beware—not even all varieties of NetBIOS are fully compatible with each other.

NOS Client Protocol Stacks   NetBIOS or a related network API properly formats messages requesting network-attached resources. However, this message must be successfully transported across the network to the destination server. This is the job of the **network operating system (NOS).** More exactly, the successful transport of messages across networks is the job of the **transport layer protocol** of the NOS.

Transportation of messages across the network physically starts with the local network interface card (NIC) interfacing to the network via the network media attached to the NIC. The software/hardware interface between the NOS and the NIC is bridged with a specially written piece of software compatible with both the NOS and the NIC, known as **NIC driver** software. Figure 4-19 summarizes the roles of the network API, the transport layer protocol, and the NIC driver in the overall task of transporting messages across networks.

It is important to note the required compatibilities in this process. The network

NetBIOS protocol	RFC 1001/1002 (request for comment)	TOP (technical office protocol)	NetBEUI (NetBIOS extended user interface)	NetBIOS/IX
Communications Network Operating Systems	TCP/IP	OSI	LAN Manager LAN Server Windows NT	UNIX

Figure 4-17   NetBIOS Protocol Varieties for Various Network Types

API (Application Program Interface)	APPC (Advanced Program to Program Communication)	Named pipes	SPX/IPX (Sequenced Packet Exchange/ Internet Packet Exchange)	Streams	Sockets	VIPC (VINES Interprocess Communications Protocol)
Network Operating System	IBM SNA	Microsoft LAN Manager	Novell Netware	AT&T UNIX System V	Berkley UNIX	Banyan VINES

Figure 4-18 Network APIs Other than NetBIOS and Their Network Operating Systems

API, such as NetBIOS, must be supported and understood by the network operating system installed in the client software architecture. The transport protocol of the installed client network operating system must be compatible with the transport protocol of the network operating system installed on the destination server. The client network operating system must support, or talk to, the locally installed network interface card. This compatibility is ensured by having the proper driver software installed. Specialized network interface card driver software, which allows more than one network operating system protocol stack to be installed in a single client or server, is reviewed in Chapter 8.

Protocol Stacks and the OSI Model   Every network operating system consists of layers of protocols which correspond in varying degrees to the seven layers of the OSI model. The transport layer (Layer 4) of the OSI model is responsible for ensuring the reliable end-to-end delivery of messages across a local area network. Exactly how the transport layer protocols ensure this reliability and how NOS protocols communicate with each other are detailed in Chapters 9 and 10.

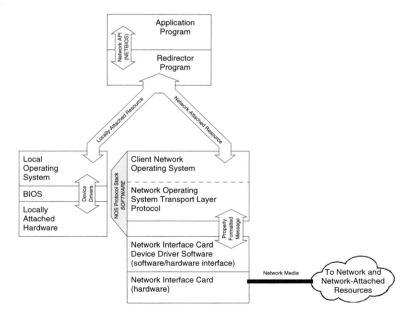

Figure 4-19 Network API, Transport Protocol, and NIC Driver Combine for Network-Based Message Transport

For a client and server to communicate successfully, they must both use the same transport layer protocol. Because clients and servers in distributed environments are likely to have different network operating systems installed with different transport layer protocols, some way must be found for them to share a common transport protocol. The following two capabilities solve most client-to-server transport layer protocol incompatibility problems:

1. Clients and servers are capable of supporting more than one network operating system transport protocol.

Network Operating System	Windows NT & Windows '95	Windows for Workgroups 3.11	Other DOS-based LANs	OS/2 Warp Connect	Novell Netware 4.1	Banyan VINES 6.0	Internet Suite of Protocols (TCP/IP)
Layer 7 Application			DOS Redirector		Netware Shell	Redirector	RFS (Remote File Service); SMB (Server Message Block); NFS (Network File System)
Layer 6 Presentation	NCP Redirector (Network Core Protocols (Netware)); SMB Redirector (Server Message Block (Microsoft))	SMB Redirector (Server Message Block (Microsoft))	DOS Redirector	NCP Redirector (Network Core Protocols (Netware)); SMB Redirector (Server Message Block (Microsoft))	NCP Redirector	VINES Remote Procedure Calls; SMB (Server Message Block)	RFS; SMB; NFS
Layer 5 Session			NetBIOS		NetBIOS Emulator	NetBIOS Service	SMTP (Simple Mail Transfer Protocol); FTP (File Transfer Protocol); TELNet (Virtual Terminal Protocol); SNMP (Simple Network Management Protocol)
Layer 4 Transport	SPX; NetBEUI; TCP (Transmission Control Protocol)	SPX; NetBEUI; TCP (Transmission Control Protocol)	NetBIOS	SPX; NetBEUI; TCP (Transmission Control Protocol)	SPX; TCP (Transmission Control Protocol)	VIPC (VINES Interprocess communications); NetBEUI; TCP (Transmission Control Protocol)	TCP (Transmission Control Protocol); UDP (User Datagram Protocol)
Layer 3 Network	IPX; IP (Internet Protocol)	IPX; IP (Internet Protocol)		IPX; IP (Internet Protocol)	IPX; IP (Internet Protocol)	VIP (VINES Internet Protocol); IP (Internet Protocol)	IP (Internet Protocol)
Layer 2 Data Link	Logical Link Control (LLC) sublayer	Multiple protocol stack NIC driver specifications: ODI, NDIS.					
	Media Access Control (MAC) sublayer	Ethernet - IEEE 802.3, 10BaseT, 10Base2, 10Base5		Fast Ethernet, 100BaseX, 100VG, AnyLAN		Token Ring IEEE 802.5 | FDDI | ATM	
Layer 1 Physical	NOTE: Protocols listed in layers 1 and 2 will operate with any upper layer protocols as long as compatible network interface card drivers are successfully installed.						

Figure 4-20   The OSI Model and NOS Protocols

2. TCP/IP is seen as a universal protocol stack and is available in versions capable of running on most client and server platforms.

The intricacies and interrelationships of network operating system protocols are detailed throughout the remainder of the text. What is important to understand at this point is the role NOS protocols, such as the transport layer protocol, play in distributed client/server computing environments. In other words, data from applications programs and program requests for network-attached services do not somehow magically get delivered to the proper network-attached server. As you will see, messages are carefully addressed and packetized within standardized NOS protocol "envelopes," to ensure proper and reliable delivery. Sometimes these messages are packaged in NetBIOS or NetBEUI envelopes, and sometimes they are packaged and addressed in a different type of transport layer protocol envelope such as TCP/IP.

Figure 4-20 serves as an introduction to NOS protocols by distributing those protocols into the seven layers of the OSI model. This distribution is not an exact science, as network operating system vendors are free to include whatever functionality they wish in a given protocol. As a result, all protocols do not correspond to a particular OSI model layer on a one-to-one basis. Also, it should be noted that Figure 4-20 does not list all of the protocols associated with each NOS. There are many additional protocols for specialized tasks such as file management, service naming, internetwork routing management, and e-mail system interoperability, which do not appear in Figure 4-20 but are covered in later chapters.

Much of the information contained in Figure 4-20 will seem extremely foreign at this point, but it is referred to throughout the remainder of the text. For a review of the role of the protocols in each of the seven layers of the OSI Model, refer to Figure 1-11.

■ CLIENT PRESENTATION SOFTWARE

Concepts and Functionality

User Interface Trends   User interfaces, like most elements of information systems design, continue to evolve. Following are the three major paradigms, or stages, or computer-to-user interface design:

- Character-based interfaces.
- **Graphical user interfaces (GUI).**
- **Social interfaces.**

Social interfaces are the emerging paradigm of computer-to-user interfaces. The overall goal of social interfaces is to provide a computer-to-user interface which is more intuitive and easier to use than the current generation of GUIs. Following are the key characteristics of a social interface which differentiate it from a graphical user interface:

- Users feel as if they're navigating through normal activities common to their life-style.

- Social interfaces offer advanced help systems which sense when a user needs help and lead them through the solutions to their problems.

- Social interfaces interact with users via on-screen characters.

Microsoft's social interface for the home market, known as **BOB,** is one of the first social interfaces to be released, but others are under development by many computer hardware and software vendors including Computer Associates, DEC, Novell, IBM, Apple, Hewlett-Packard, and Packard Bell.

One of the major motivations for the shift from graphical user interfaces to social interfaces is that the nonintuitive nature of the GUIs can prevent underlying applications and operating systems from being used to their fullest potential. This lack of use translates into a wasted software investment for corporations. As an example, Microsoft has found that only 20% of users know how to run multiple programs simultaneously in Windows, a feature which Microsoft considers Windows' most important asset.

Event-Driven Presentation for Event-Driven Applications   Event-driven, or forms-based, applications such as those developed with products like Microsoft's Visual Basic, can now be presented in an event-driven format thanks to the trend toward social interfaces. For example, Computer Associate's social interface known as Simply Village will be offered as an add-on interface for Windows 95.

The interface itself is quite literally a village scene which hides complex network links to remote servers and on-line services. To perform a banking transaction from home, for example, a user clicks on the village bank. Inside the bank is an on-screen banker, who assists the user in performing the desired transaction. Such "walk-you-through-it" help characters are commonly referred to as **wizards.** In other operating environments wizards might be known as experts or agents. Other village offerings might include clicking on specialty shops for links to home shopping networks or on the airport or travel agency to purchase airline tickets. Input devices will likely shift from keyboards to voice-recognition technology.

Social interfaces will be deployed on a variety of platforms beyond PCs, including personal digital assistants (PDAs), automatic teller machines, cable TV/video-on-demand set top boxes, and advertising/information kiosks in shopping malls and airports.

Before the arrival of these fully graphical, revolutionary social interfaces in corporations, interim or evolutionary offerings are likely to be introduced. This is where the user interfaces offered by Windows 95 and Apple's Copland are positioned. These systems will contain wizards and advanced help systems to walk users through solutions. Interim improvements on GUIs will feature **active assistance subsystems** to which users can describe what they wish to accomplish, such as purchasing an airline ticket or receiving inventory at a loading dock, and the system will lead them through the desired transaction on a step-by-step basis. Furthermore, Windows 95 will feature a task bar showing users which applications are currently running, thereby overcoming one of the previously mentioned shortcomings of the Windows GUI. The user interface portion of Windows 95 will be able to be installed over Windows NT as an alternative user interface beginning with Windows NT version 4.0.

Presentation Software for UNIX Environments   Traditionally, graphical user interfaces for the UNIX environment were supplied by software adhering to the X Windows environment standards. **X Windows** itself is not a GUI and should not be confused with Microsoft Windows. X Windows is a standardized system which defines the underlying communication between X server and X client software modules, which combine to present a multiwindowed graphical user interface on a specially designed X terminal or a client workstation running some type of X terminal emulation.

The closest equivalent to a familiar GUI such as Microsoft Windows in the X Windows environment is the X manager, which manages, sizes, and scales multiple displays from different UNIX applications and/or hosts simultaneously. **Motif** from the Open Software Foundation and **OpenLook** from Sun Microsystems are the two most popular X Window managers and communicate with X server software.

In an architectural setup which may seem to be the opposite of typical client/server relationships, the X server software, which controls display and input, runs on the user's workstation, and the X client which generates the screen drawing instructions is located on the UNIX applications host. It is important to note that X Windows systems perform strictly presentation functions. Although Microsoft Windows is characterized as a GUI, it actually performs many operating system management functions not offered by X Windows. Figure 4-21 illustrates the key components of an X Windows system.

Beyond X Windows UNIX hardware and software vendors Hewlett Packard, Sun, IBM, and Novell (UNIX Systems Laboratory) have joined together to produce a cross-platform windowing environment for UNIX named the **common desktop environment,** or **CDE.** CDE goes beyond the simple graphical presentation management of X Windows to include the following key cross-platform functionality:

- Desktop management.
- Session management.
- File management.

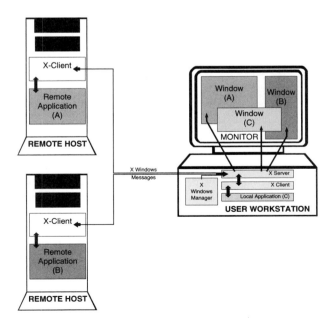

Figure 4-21 X Windows Client, Server, and Manager

- Application management.
- Productivity tools.
- Application development tools.

This top-to-bottom cross-platform suite was developed in direct response to the inroads Windows NT has made to date and is expected to continue to make in the UNIX server market. CDE will offer a single graphical environment across multiple vendors' UNIX platforms. CDE will run on nearly all versions of UNIX hardware and software and was designed to be constructed from 80% of existing "best-of-breed" software and only 20% new development. As an example, CDE employs OSF Motif as its X Window Manager. CDE has been targeted to three primary audiences:

- The end-user: CDE offers the multiprocessing, multiuser, multitasking power of UNIX while hiding its complexities.

- The software developer: CDE offers sets of common services and APIs which will allow developed software to run across a wide variety of CDE supported platforms.

- The systems administrator: CDE offers a wide variety of management tools for managing a variety of different platforms with a single suite of management tools.

The only possible bad news in all of this is that the CDE standards are meant to be least common denominators of interoperability among UNIX platforms. UNIX workstation vendors are free to enhance and extend CDE to offer product differentiation and maintain profit margins. As a result, although CDE will offer interoperability across multiple vendors' UNIX workstations, it won't necessarily deliver the full functionality offered by all of the attached workstations.

Best of Both Worlds   Multiple Windows applications can be run simultaneously in any environment supporting the Windows API such as Windows 3.1, Windows NT, Windows 95, or OS/2 Warp. Multiple UNIX applications can be run simultaneously in either an X Windows or a CDE environment. But what if an end-user has to use a combination of Windows and UNIX applications to maximize productivity?

Several solutions exist to give users the best of both worlds. Hummingbird Communications' eXceed 4 Windows NT allows an NT system to act as a PC X server by communicating with X clients, displaying screen updates, and relaying keyboard and mouse input. The UNIX applications would be running on network-attached UNIX hosts such as Sun Sparcstations, IBM RS-6000s, or Cray Supercomputers. To these remote hosts and their installed X client software, the NT workstation looks like just another X server program running on a UNIX workstation. Of course, the NT workstation can still run Windows applications and display these Microsoft Windows applications alongside the X Windows from the UNIX applications.

The previous solution allowed an NT workstation to act like a UNIX-based X server; however, Hewlett-Packard offers the HP 500 Windows Application Server, which allows Windows applications to run on UNIX workstations. The product comes in either a hardware/software option including a Pentium server or a software-only option. Windows applications are converted into X Windows and TCP/IP code and run on a version of UNIX from Santa Cruz Operation (SCO) known as OpenServer 5.0. Other Windows on UNIX implementations are available, including WinDD from Tektronix, and Windows Application Binary Interface (WABI) from Sun Microsystems. WABI is the emulation software employed in many PowerPCs and PowerMacs to allow Windows applications to run on the RISC-based PowerPC chips. DESQview/X 2.0 from Quarterdeck allows users to run any combination of DOS, Windows, or UNIX applications in an X Windows preemptive multitasking environment and is installed on a DOS-based PC.

Practical Advice and Information

In comparing Windows-over-UNIX emulation alternatives, it is important to consider both performance and compatibility. Not all emulation alternatives can run all Windows applications. Remember that software emulation is analogous to having one application program run another application program and is most often slower than hardware emulation. Any of these UNIX/Windows integrations should be considered only if a thorough top-down analysis has concluded that business objectives can be successfully met only if a combination of UNIX and Windows applications are run from a particular desktop.

SUMMARY

To understand how transparent interoperability can be delivered to an end-user through a client workstation, one must thoroughly understand the client software architecture and its inherent interprocess communication. Without complete compatibility between all software layers within the client software architecture, client workstations will not be able to communicate transparently with distant networked servers.

The first layer of software which interacts with the client hardware is the operating system. The trend in this area of software development is toward microkernel-based operating systems which offer increased extendibility, portability, and reliability over the more traditional monolithic operating system architecture. Many software products offer a graphical user interface, network operating system, and operating system all in a single integrated product. Windows 95 and OS/2 Warp Connect are two such products.

The interface between network operating systems and operating systems is bridged by redirector software conforming to a particular network

API such as NetBIOS. These network protocols are responsible for determining whether computer resources requested by applications programs are located on the locally attached computer or a distant network-attached server. The network API must be compatible with the application program, network operating system, and operating system. The request for network-attached resources is then addressed and packaged in the proper message format according to the transport layer protocol of the particular network operating system installed on the client workstation.

Client presentation software is currently evolving from graphical user interfaces to more intuitive social interfaces characterized by more active help systems which sense when users need help and walk them through solutions. UNIX-based client workstations traditionally used a GUI which supported the X Windows presentation protocol. GUIs can now integrate UNIX and Windows applications into a single presentation environment.

KEY TERMS

active assistance subsystems, 146
actor, 129
API, 140
AT&T SVR4, 136
BOB, 145
BSD UNIX, 136
CDE, 147
Chorus microkernel, 128
client software architecture, 121
common desktop environment, 147
cooperative multitasking, 129
device drivers, 123
exceptions, 123
graphical user interfaces, 145
GUI, 145
HAL, 134
hardware abstraction layer, 134
hardware-independent operating
   systems, 127
interrupts, 123
kernel, 122
Mach microkernel, 128
MacOS, 138
microkernel, 124
monolithic architecture, 123

Motif, 147
MS-DOS, 131
multiple personality operating systems, 127
multiple workplace environments,
   127
multiprocessing, 129
multithreaded, 130
multiuser, 129
NCB, 141
NetBEUI, 142
NetBIOS, 140
NetBIOS application program,
   141
network control block, 141
network operating system, 142
NIC driver, 142
NOS, 142
Novell DOS, 138
nucleus, 128
Open Look, 147
operating system architecture,
   122
OS/2 Warp Connect, 136
port, 128

preemptive multitasking, 130
privileged mode, 125
redirector, 141
server message block server, 141
site, 129
SMB, 141
SMP, 129
social interfaces, 145
subsystems, 129
symmetrical multiprocessing, 129
system calls, 122
task, 128
thread, 128
transport layer protocol, 142
TSR, 131
UNIX, 136
user mode, 125
virtual machines, 133
Win32 API, 135
Win32c API, 135
Win32s API, 135
Windows 95, 132
Windows NT Workstation, 133
Wizards, 146
X Windows, 146

REVIEW QUESTIONS

1. Explain the importance of compatible protocols to the delivery of transparent interoperability to a client workstation.
2. Describe the role of each layer of the client software architecture.
3. Why do some software products combine presentation, NOS, and OS functionality?
4. What are the primary responsibilities of any client operating system?
5. Describe the role of each component of the operating system architecture.
6. What is the difference between a system call and a device driver?
7. A device driver links which two operating system layers?
8. A system call links which two client software layers?
9. What is the advantage of using separate system calls and device drivers?
10. What is the alternative to using separate system calls and device drivers?

11. What is the difference between an interrupt and an exception?
12. What is the difference between a hardware interrupt and a software interrupt?
13. What are the disadvantages of an operating system adhering to a monolithic architecture?
14. What is a microkernel?
15. What are the supposed advantages of a microkernel-based operating system?
16. What types of services are typically confined to the microkernel?
17. Why are hardware-specific instructions confined to the microkernel?
18. Why is it important for the microkernel to run in privileged mode?
19. What is the difference between privileged mode and user mode?
20. How can a microkernel architecture enable hardware-independent operating systems?
21. How do microkernel architectures enable multiple personality operating systems?

22. Can an operating system be both hardware independent and multiple personality? Explain.
23. Distinguish between the following: task, thread, port.
24. How can one microkernel be used in different operating systems?
25. How can one microkernel be used on different CPU chips?
26. Differentiate between the following: multiuser, multiprocessing, multitasking, multithreading.
27. Differentiate between cooperative multitasking and preemptive multitasking.
28. Differentiate between conventional, expanded, and extended memory in a DOS environment.
29. What is Windows 95?
30. What are the advantages and disadvantages of Windows 95?
31. What are the key differences between Windows NT Workstation and Windows 95?
32. Why is a user most likely to choose Windows 95 over Windows NT Workstation?
33. How is Windows 95 both a preemptive multitasking and a cooperative multitasking environment at the same time?
34. What is a virtual machine?
35. Differentiate between Win32 API, Win32s API, and Win32c API.
36. Differentiate between OS/2 Warp Connect and Windows NT Workstation.
37. What are the key advantages and disadvantages of UNIX as a client operating system?
38. Differentiate between Novell DOS and MS-DOS.
39. What are the key objectives of Apple's MacOS V.8?
40. What effect can a requirement to run legacy applications have on operating system design?
41. What is HAL?

42. What is the function of the client redirector?
43. What is the NetBIOS API?
44. What is the difference between the NetBIOS API and a NetBIOS protocol?
45. What is the relationship between the NetBIOS redirector and the server message block server?
46. Why is NetBIOS the default network API for network operating systems?
47. What is the relationship between the network API and the client/server architecture?
48. How can a NOS employ a network API other than NetBIOS, and how is compatibility ensured in such a case?
49. What is meant by the term NOS protocol stack?
50. How does the OSI model relate to NOS protocol stacks?
51. What role does the client NOS play in delivering network-attached resources to the client workstation?
52. Describe the user interface evolution.
53. What are the key characteristics of a social interface?
54. Why are social interfaces necessary?
55. What is an active assistance subsystem?
56. Is a social interface required to deliver an active assistance subsystem? Why or why not?
57. What are the evolutionary steps or product features on the way to social interfaces?
58. What is X Windows?
59. How does X Windows differ from Microsoft Windows?
60. What are Motif and Open Look?
61. What is the CDE and why is it important?
62. How does CDE differ from X Windows?
63. How can UNIX and Microsoft Windows applications run simultaneously on a single client workstation?

ACTIVITIES

1. Using the client software architecture, fill in the layers with the names of actual software products, being sure to indicate which mutually supported protocols are used to bridge every software/software and software/hardware interface.
2. Research which currently available client operating systems are microkernel-based. Prepare a presentation on the rationale for this design and how well intended results have been achieved.
3. Research microkernel-based client operating systems under development. Track their progress and delivery schedules. Report on whether all initially promised subsystems are delivered.
4. Research a microkernel-based client operating system for which subsystems have been written by

a third-party vendor. Report on what effect the microkernel architecture had on this development effort.
5. Find an operating system adhering to a monolithic architecture. Report on efforts to update or revise the operating system.
6. Find examples of hardware-independent operating systems. Determine their importance and market share. Is demand likely to grow?
7. Find examples of multiple personality operating systems. What percentage of users actually use the multiple personality capability?
8. Collect sales figures and user reviews of Windows 95. Graph the sales figures over time. Calculate

market share. What are Windows 95's key competitors?

9. Track the sales of Windows 95 versus OS/2 Warp Connect. Explain your results.

10. Compare market shares of MS-DOS and Novell DOS and prepare a chart or presentation of your results.

11. Collect product information regarding technology available to integrate Windows and UNIX applications on a single client platform. Draw hardware/software architectures, indicating the interaction of the technology for the various alternative solutions. How many distinct approaches are evident?

12. Track the product releases and sales figures for social interfaces. What markets are being targeted? How are the social interfaces being received?

FEATURED REFERENCES

General

Berson, Alex. *Client/Server Architecture* (New York: McGraw-Hill, 1992).

Dewire, Dawna. *Client/Server Computing* (New York: McGraw-Hill, 1993).

Vaughn, Larry. *Client/Server Design and Implementation* (New York: McGraw-Hill, 1994).

Client Operating System Comparisons

Ayre, Rick and Amarendra Singh. OS/2 Warp 3 and Windows NT 3.5: The Future's Here Today. *PC Magazine,* 13; 22 (December 20, 1994), 221.

Panettieri, Joseph and Bob Violino. What a Mess! *Information Week,* 534 (July 3, 1995), 14.

Udell, Jon. The Great OS Debate. *Byte,* 19; 1 (January 1994), 117.

Operating System Concepts

Hayes, Frank. Personality Plus: Multiple Personality Operating Systems. *Byte,* 19; 1 (January 1994), 155.

Pountain, Dick. The Chorus Microkernel. *Byte,* 19; 1 (January 1994), 131.

Prasad, Shashi. Weaving a Thread. *Byte,* 20; 10 (October 1995), 173.

Silberschatz, Abraham and Peter Galvin. *Operating Systems Concepts,* 4th ed. (Reading, MA: Addison-Wesley, 1994).

Varhol, Peter. Small Kernels Hit It Big. *Byte,* 19; 1 (January 1994), 119.

NOS Client Protocol Stacks

Nance, Barry. Beyond DOS: IPX and NetBIOS for OS/2. *Byte,* 19; 5 (May 1994), 201.

Oggerino, Chris. Reaching Out: IP and IPX on a Windows Client. *Network Computing,* 5; 11 (October 1, 1994), 132.

Rigney, Steve. Communicating with Windows 95: Hooked and Linked. *PC Magazine,* 14; 9 (May 16, 1995), 175.

OS/2 WARP

Gerber, Barry. Warp Connect Brings Real Networking to OS/2. *Network Computing,* 6; 6 (May 15, 1995), 36.

Nance, Barry. Big Blue's Speed Trip. *Byte,* 20; 3 (March 1995), 131.

Nance, Barry. Networking at Warp Speed. *Byte,* 20; 9 (September 1995), 235.

Tamasanis, Doug. Mathematica Meets Warp. *Byte,* 20; 5 (May 1995), 137.

Udell, Jon. A Warped Perspective. *Byte,* 20; 3 (March 1995), 165.

Windows 95

Caton, Michael. Judgement Day: Network Tools Balance Windows 95 Flaws. *PC Week,* 12; 29 (July 24, 1995), 13.

Davis, Andrew. Windows Becomes DSP-Aware. *Byte,* 19; 11 (November 1994), 151.

Diehl, Stanford. Windows '95 Graphics Architecture. *Byte,* 20; 6 (June 1995), 241.

Kennedy, Randall. The Elegant Kludge. *Byte,* 20; 8 (August 1995), 54.

Linthicum, David. How Best to Migrate to Windows 95. *Byte,* 20; 7 (July 1995), 51.

Miller, Michael. Getting Ready for Windows 95. *PC Magazine,* 14; 9 (May 16, 1995), 102.

Nadile, Lisa. Migration Path Could Be Rough for Custom 16-bit Applications. *PC Week,* 12; 27 (July 10, 1995), 1.

Prosise, Jeff. Under the Hood: Windows 95 and Its Competitors. *PC Magazine,* 14; 9 (May 16, 1995), 139.

Robertson, Bruce. Windows95 Is Irresistable. *Network Computing,* 6; 7 (June 1, 1995), 56.

Sheldon, Tom. MAPI Blooms in Chicago. *Byte,* 19; 11 (November 1994), 163.

Simon, Barry. The Windows 95 User Interface. *PC Magazine,* 14; 13 (July 1995), 307.

Udell, Jon. You Can Take It with You. *Byte,* 20; 6 (June 1995), 145.

Novell DOS

Mathisen, Terje. Novell's Newest DOS. *Byte,* 19; 6 (June 1994), 241.

Plug-n-Play

Clyman, John and Nick Stam. Plug and Play: Effortless Upgrades, *PC Magazine.* 14; 9 (May 16, 1995), 159.

Halfhill, Tom. Transforming the PC: Plug and Play. *Byte,* 19; 9 (September 1994), 78.

Windows Utilities

Mace, Thomas and Barry Simon. Why Wait? Get More from Windows Now! *PC Magazine,* 14; 5 (March 14, 1995), 108.

File Systems

Proffit, Brian. OS/2's High Performance File System. *PC Magazine*, 14; 12 (June 27, 1995), 255.

Prosise, Jeff. Is VFAT Read for Prime Time? *PC Magazine*, 14; 11 (June 13, 1995), 247.

Other Operating Systems/Environments

Thompson, Tom. Apple's New Operating System. *Byte*, 20; 6 (June 1995), 59.

Thompson, Tom. Copland: The Abstract Mac OS. *Byte*, 20; 7 (July 1995), 177.

Udell, Jon. A Taligent Update. *Byte*, 19; 7 (July 1994), 183.

Varhol, Peter. QNX Forges Ahead. *Byte*, 19; 10 (October 1994), 199.

Trends

Halfhill, Tom. Inside the Mind of Microsoft. *Byte*, 20; 8 (August 1995), 48.

User Interfaces

Baker, Steven. The Power of X for Windows NT. *Byte*, 20; 7 (July 1995), 149.

Panettieri, Joseph. User Interfaces: PCs Gain Social Skills. *Information Week*, no. 534 (July 3, 1995), 32.

Seymour, Jim. The Changing Face of the Interface. *PC Magazine*, 14; 9 (May 16, 1995), 93.

Tamasanis, Doug. A Universal Desktop for UNIX. *Byte*, 20; 6 (June 1995), DM3.

APIs

Apiki, Steve. Paths to Platform Independence. *Byte*, 19; 1 (January 1994), 172.

Chernicoff, David. WinSock Expands Beyond TCP/IP. *PC Week*, 12; 27 (July 10, 1995), N1.

Hall, Martin. WinSock Specs Marry Windows Applications to Network Stacks. *Network World*, 12; 27 (July 3, 1995), 27.

CASE STUDY

Chapter 4

CDC WARDS OFF VIRUSES

Movie-goers were recently chilled by *Outbreak*, the gripping tale of a lethal and highly contagious disease threatening world health. While the job of the centers for Disease Control and Prevention in that film is to contain the cause of a deadly epidemic, administrators at the CDC are just as serious about protecting their networks from dangerous viruses.

With Headquarters in Atlanta, the CDC maintains an attitude toward network viral safety that is not far from its mission statement, "to promote health and the quality of life by preventing and controlling disease, injury, and disability."

Although the organization, comprising seven centers, standardizes on virus-protection software, the Division of Adolescent and School Health, which falls under the National Center of Chronic Disease Prevention and Health Promotion, has taken its anti-virus stance even further.

"We are a little more cognizant of it because security is a specialty of mine," said Erik Goldoff, computer specialist for the division. "I'm really satisfied with our security because we've had the server up for five years, but we haven't had one virus on the server."

Tripartite Protection

In his 60-user microcosm of the CDC's approximately 7,000-node Novell Inc. NetWare network, Goldoff oversees three levels of virus protection. In addition to Intel Corp. virus-protection software and McAfee Associates Inc. scanning software, which are licensed to the entire government agency, supervisor-level users are screened by an anti-virus TSR when logging in.

Intel's Virus Protect, included in the company's LANDesk network-management software, runs on the server as an NLM. The software's job is to prevent anybody from writing a virus to the network. Although this level of protection doesn't check floppies for infection,

at 5 A.M. every Saturday the software scans the server for an infiltrator that may have written an unauthorized executable.

Like the rest of the CDC, Goldoff's division has deployed McAfee's Virus-Scan Signature software on workstations. At the beginning of each workday the software scans the machines' local drives for viruses. In the event that something is found, the user is automatically logged out and told to notify the network administrator.

There is no bypassing this crucial step because at midnight all users are routinely knocked off the network for security and backup. Users are also required to scan any floppies created by somebody else. "The majority of [the viruses] we find are from scanning diskettes," said Goldoff.

Immunizing Resident

The third piece of anti-virus strategy is VB TSR from Thompson Network Software Division in Marietta,

Ga., which checks for suspicious virus activity in progress. Although virus alerts can be reported through the LANDesk console, Goldoff prefers the sneaker-net approach so users have time to inform one another. The three safety pieces provide Goldoff with knowledge of any virus presence—tactics that he likens to self-defense.

"A good analogy of virus signature and scanning software is as if you've been mugged and then go looking through mug shots," he explained. In comparison, with the addition of a TSR, activity would be proactively monitored like it would with "a guard and security camera at a jewelry store because it would show you when the safe was opened. You would look at anything that would change an executeable or write anything to the boot sector," he said.

In one situation, Goldoff was helping a user recover data with his own machine because the user was unable to retrieve documents from his diskette. In the process, Goldoff discovered a boot-sector infection agent on the diskette that attempted to write to his hard drive. But the Thompson TSR caught it and prevented infection before it could occur.

Because it is a target for viral attacks or accidental invasions, the CDC has taken these strong antivirus measures. Employees of the CDC often find themselves in the field alongside other health investigators, putting them at risk of contact with a contaminated floppy shared among laptops. The centers also play host to outsiders such as interns from universities, which are notorious for a nonchalant approach toward virus control, according to Goldoff.

"Universities are really lacking in virus protection; a lot of universities found out they were infected simply because we called them," he said.

In one instance, Goldoff discovered the "monkey virus," a boot-sector infection that originated from Princeton University in New Jersey. "It's not much of a threat to the network, but it would crash the local hard drive. We called them out of courtesy."

Source: Amanda Mitchell Henry (September 11, 1995). CDC Wards Off Viruses. *LAN Times,* 12(17), 53. Reprinted with permission of McGraw-Hill, *LAN Times.*

BUSINESS CASE STUDY QUESTIONS

Activities

1. Complete a top-down model for this case by gleaning facts and placing them in the proper layer of the top-down model. After completing the top-down model, analyze and detail those instances when requirements were clearly passed down from upper to lower layers of the model and when solutions to those requirements were passed up from lower to upper layers.
2. Detail any questions that may occur to you about the case for which answers are not clearly stated in the article.
3. Investigate and report on the different types of viruses currently infecting computers and the antivirus software used to detect or eliminate these viruses.
4. What was the Internet worm?

Business

1. What was the overall business motivation or strategy in relation to virus protection?
2. What is the role of users in preventing the spread of viral infection?
3. What do you think about the statement, "Universities are really lacking in virus protection"?

Application

1. What applications were run on which types of computing platform to offer overall virus protection?
2. What are the compatibility issues surrounding the choice of client virus software?
3. How and where does Intel's Virus Protect work?
4. Are there any unprotected or unchecked aspects of this virus protection plan?
5. What actions must users take if a virus is detected on their workstation?
6. What is the advantage of running virus protection as a TSR?

Data

1. Where are the majority of viruses found? Why?

Network

1. How large was the network that was to be protected from viruses?

Technology

1. Which software technology was deployed on which hardware technology to achieve the overall business objectives?

CHAPTER 5

SERVER HARDWARE AND SOFTWARE

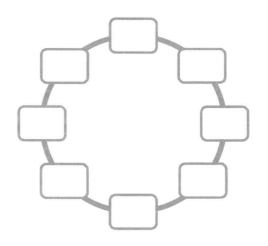

Concepts Reinforced

Client/server technology architecture   Protocols and compatibility
OSI model   Processor fundamentals
Hardware/software compatibility   Operating systems concepts
Network operating system concepts   Operating system architecture

Concepts Introduced

Multiprocessor hardware   Server specialization
Multiprocessor operating systems   Server hardware trends
Server storage alternatives   Fault tolerance

OBJECTIVES

After mastering the material in this chapter you should:

1. Understand the difference between client and server hardware technology.

2. Understand the significant trends in server hardware development.

3. Understand the relationship between server hardware and server operating systems trends.

Chapters 3 (client hardware) and 4 (client software) presented a thorough discussion of current trends in computing hardware and software; the focus of this chapter is on those aspects of computing hardware and software which are unique to servers. To afford an appreciation of the unique needs for server functionality, the chapter starts with an overview of the forces driving these hardware and software requirements. Once the originating forces have been explained, we will elaborate on the specific hardware features and requirements.

For example, one of the major jobs unique to servers is managing massive amounts of storage. Second, because of the mission-critical role servers often play, increased hardware reliability and fault tolerance are a must. Server operating systems must respond to these increased demands as well by offering the ability to work in multiprocessing environments with the reliability often associated with mainframe-based operating systems.

■ BUSINESS REQUIREMENTS DICTATE SERVER FUNCTIONALITY

As introduced in Chapter 2, the downsizing and rightsizing phenomenon has had a dramatic impact on the performance requirements of servers. The client/server architecture and the enterprise network, which provide communications between network-attached resources, are being called on to match or exceed the performance and reliability exhibited by minicomputer and mainframe-based systems. The flexibility offered by properly designed and implemented client/server information systems is an absolute necessity for corporations competing in today's rapidly changing global marketplace. Increased access to corporate information, anytime, anywhere, has boosted the needs for powerful remote computing solutions.

Flexibility and quick response to changing business needs are often associated with server-based information systems, but servers are now expected to run enormous, mission-critical, transaction-based applications formerly reserved for mainframes. The need to have these mainframe-class applications execute in an absolutely secure and reliable environment places additional requirements on server design. Figure 5-1 summarizes some of the business requirements servers are expected to fulfill, as well as the corresponding functional capabilities they offer.

As you will see in later sections, the same business requirements listed in the

Business Requirement	Server Functionality
Support downsizing, rightsizing efforts by running mainframe-class applications	• Faster processors, multiprocessor designs • Faster, wider buses linking server components such as disk I/O and memory subsystems. • Optimize servers for operation with mainframe DBMSs • High-capacity networking components for links to client/server backbone
Performance must be highly available and reliable	• Redundant components within servers, fault-tolerant design • Redundant storage designs with high-capacity links to servers • Error-correcting memory • Better monitoring and diagnostic systems
Information systems must be able to be easily and effectively managed	• Open systems designs support industry-standard, multivendor enterprise management systems
Business communication and information systems are becoming increasingly mobile and wireless	• Servers must be able to communicate with a wide variety of clients over communications links varying in protocol, bandwidth, and quality
Information systems must be able to adjust to the size and scale of the business enterprise	• Servers must be scalable, allowing the addition of more processors

Figure 5-1   Business Requirements Dictate Server Functionality

figure also put functional demands on server operating systems, network operating systems, and other aspects of the client/server architecture.

■ SERVER HARDWARE

A server is a computer whose primary function is to offer computing services or manage system resources for client PCs requesting those services. Users do not generally sit at a server and use it as a workstation. Servers have become highly specialized. Although on smaller information systems, a single server may meet all of the needs of 5 to 25 clients, it is far more common to find multiple servers performing more specific duties. Following are just a few of the types of servers reviewed here:

- Applications servers.

- File servers.

- Database servers.

- Print servers.

- Communications servers.

- CD-ROM servers.

- FAX servers.

- Video servers.

- Internet servers.

Servers communicate with and deliver services to clients via network connections. Those network connections may be strictly local or over a very great distance. Although the term server can be used generically to mean *any* type of computer offering services to client PCs, including mainframes, this chapter refers only to servers employing RISC and CISC chips. Figure 2-17 (client/server technology architecture) showed the functional relationship between clients, servers, and networks, Figure 5-2 offers a view of the physical relationship between these key components.

An important point to note about Figure 5-2 is that as applications have left the

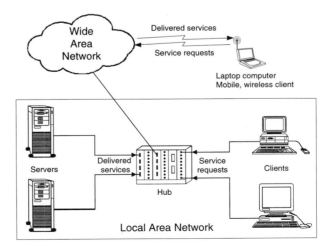

Figure 5-2   Clients, Servers, and Networks

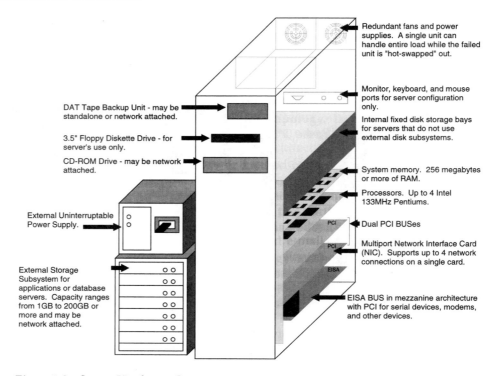

DAT Tape Backup Unit - may be standalone or network attached.

3.5" Floppy Diskette Drive - for server's use only.

CD-ROM Drive - may be network attached.

External Uninterruptable Power Supply.

External Storage Subsystem for applications or database servers. Capacity ranges from 1GB to 200GB or more and may be network attached.

Redundant fans and power supplies. A single unit can handle entire load while the failed unit is "hot-swapped" out.

Monitor, keyboard, and mouse ports for server configuration only.

Internal fixed disk storage bays for servers that do not use external disk subsystems.

System memory. 256 megabytes or more of RAM.

Processors. Up to 4 Intel 133MHz Pentiums.

Dual PCI BUSes

Multiport Network Interface Card (NIC). Supports up to 4 network connections on a single card.

EISA BUS in mezzanine architecture with PCI for serial devices, modems, and other devices.

Figure 5-3   Server Hardware Components

centralized, self-contained domain of the mainframe and migrated to the distributed architecture of the client/server information system, the network has become responsible for transporting ever-increasing amounts of various types of traffic.

Figure 5-3 illustrates how a server might combine a variety of hardware components to perform its required duties.

This figure is meant to illustrate a generalized view of server hardware components. Depending on a server's assigned specialization, hardware components could differ significantly. Having gained an appreciation for how the various server hardware components combine to produce overall server performance, individual server hardware components and characteristics are explored in more depth next.

Server Hardware Component Interaction

Applied Problem Solving

It is important to note the interaction of the server hardware components listed in Figure 5-4. Each contributes to the overall performance of the server. Remembering the principle of shifting bottlenecks, it is important to purchase a server with an effective design featuring components whose capabilities balance, rather than overwhelm, each other.

For example, file and print servers are primarily concerned with transferring large amounts of data between clients, disk drives, and printers. These applications are not particularly CPU-intensive, meaning that the CPU does not typically pose any sort of bottleneck in file and print servers. As a result, bus width and speed, disk drive size and speed, printer speed and buffer size, and the number and speed of network interface cards are more likely to have a dramatic effect on overall performance than increasing the number or performance of CPUs.

On the other hand, applications servers running on-line transaction processing (OLTP) or database servers are more likely to benefit from the increased processing power offered by multiple processors. Even in these cases, however, the systems-oriented nature of computer systems must be respected, since merely upgrading CPU capacity without paying attention to memory subsystem design or bus width could yield significant CPU idle time. Figure 5-4 summarizes some practical insights into the interaction of server hardware components.

Server Type(s)	Potential Bottleneck	Solutions/Implications
File or printer servers	Input/output bound	• Add more drives • Add I/O channels • Change to faster, wider bus • Increase size of printer buffers • Add more NICs • Add faster NICs • Add more RAM for larger cache • Segment the LAN for less LAN traffic

Applications or database servers	Compute bound	• Upgrade to faster CPU
		• Add multiple CPUs
		• Application program, NOS, and operating system must be optimized for use on multiprocessor platforms
		• To keep CPU busy, also need to:
		  • Add cache memory
		  • Add multiple, fast disk arrays

Figure 5-4   Server Hardware Component Interation

Server Hardware Components

Processors   Although the trends and development of new and more powerful CPUs was thoroughly covered in Chapter 3 (client hardware), servers differentiate themselves by the installation and simultaneous use of multiple processors. Two or four supported processors is a common number for most **multiprocessor servers;** however, some supercomputer-type multiprocessor servers can employ 64 or more CPUs and cost well over $1 million. Intel's Pentium chip at various clock speeds is perhaps the most commonly used CPU chip in multiprocessor servers, but several other chips are also employed:

- DEC Alpha chip.

- Sun SPARC, SuperSPARC and HyperSPARC chips.

- MIPS 4000 series chips.

- Motorola chips.

The important hardware/software compatibility issue to remember is that operating systems running on these multiprocessor servers must be compatible with the installed CPU chips.

As Figure 5-4 shows, adding more CPU power is not always the answer to improving server performance. Furthermore, even for compute-intensive applications, continuing to add CPUs will show diminishing incremental performance improvements. This is because of the impact of the various other subsystems that interact with the CPU such as the following:

- System architecture.
- Buses.
- Memory subsystem.
- Disk storage subsystem.

Equally important to the overall performance of multiprocessor servers is the software components that must interact with the multiprocessor hardware platform:

- Application program.
- Operating system.
- Network operating system.

All of these software components must be specifically written to take advantage of the multiple CPUs in the multiprocessor hardware platform.

System Architecture   System architecture, in the case of multiprocessor servers, refers to how the multiple CPUs within the multiprocessor server divided the processing tasks. In either case, the installed operating system must be written specifically to support the particular system architecture of the multiprocessor server. Systems which support multiple CPUs are generally referred to as **parallel processing** systems because multiple program instructions can be simultaneously executed in parallel. The two primary alternative system architectures, or subcategories of parallel processing are **symmetric multiprocessing** and **asymmetric multiprocessing.**

Symmetric multiprocessing **(SMP)** is a system architecture in which multiple CPUs are controlled by the SMP operating system and individual threads of application processes are assigned to particular CPUs on a first-available basis. In this manner, all CPUs are kept equally busy in a process known as **load balancing.** In SMP systems, the multiple CPUs generally share system memory and devices such as disk controllers. This is by far the most popular multiprocessor server system architecture, with close to 90% of all multiprocessor servers employing this option.

Asymmetric multiprocessing (**AMP** or **ASMP**) is characterized by assignments of entire applications processes, rather than threads, to a particular processor. Processor loads can become unbalanced. In AMP systems, each CPU is generally assigned its own memory and other subsystems. Because of this, AMP systems architectures can extend beyond a single computing platform to include CPU chips from multiple, separate physical machines. Two variations of the asymmetric multiprocessing system architecture take advantage of this horizontal scalability:

- **Massively parallel processing (MPP)** systems architectures employ thousands of CPUs, each with its own system memory. These MPP system architectures may be installed in a single machine or span several machines.

These types of computers are best suited for scientific and artificial intelligence applications.

- **Clustering** implies using the CPU power of multiple CPUs located in separate computing platforms to produce a single, more powerful virtual computer. Clusters are also sometimes referred to as **virtual parallel machines (VPM).** Clustering is neither a new concept nor unique to PCs. Digital Equipment Corporation (DEC) produced software to link multiple VAX minicomputers together in a VAX cluster during the 1980s. Future versions of NetWare will support clustering through a systems architecture which Novell refers to as **distributed parallel processing (DPP),** while future versions of Windows NT will support clustering thanks to collaborative efforts between Microsoft and DEC.

Systems architectures can also be categorized according to how systems resources are shared by the multiple CPUs. **Tightly coupled** systems architectures are characterized by CPUs which share a common pool of system memory as well as other devices and subsystems. Coordination among the multiple CPUs is achieved by system calls to/from the controlling operating system. Most SMP system architectures are considered tightly coupled.

Loosely coupled systems architectures are characterized by each CPU interacting with its own pool of system memory and devices. Coordination among the loosely coupled CPUs is achieved by some type of messaging mechanism, such as interprocess communication between the separate CPUs and their individual copies of the operating system. Most AMP system architectures are considered loosely coupled.

Figure 5-5 lists the key distinguishing characteristics of various system architec-

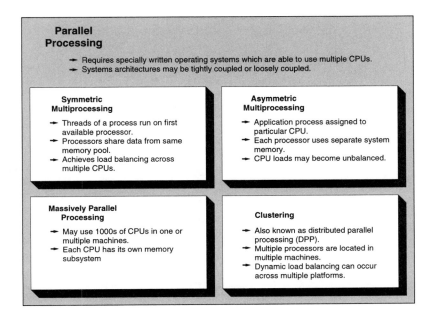

Figure 5-5 Distinguishing Characteristics of Parallel Processing System Architectures

tures and Figure 5-6 graphically depicts the difference between typical SMP and AMP system architectures.

Buses Multiple high-performance CPUs can obviously process large amounts of data. It is important that the buses connecting computer platform subsystems are both fast and wide enough to handle this large amount of data. Processing power is often measured in millions of instructions/second **(MIPs).** Following is a rule of thumb relating processing power, system memory, and bus capacity:

Each MIP of processing power requires 1 MB of memory and 128 KB of I/O bandwidth. This ratio is known as Amdahl's rule, named after Gene Amdahl, founder of Amdahl Computers, a manufacturer of IBM mainframe clone computers.

Practical Advice and Information

System buses, sometimes referred to as the processor/memory bus or host bus, are usually proprietary and vary from server to server. System buses connect the major subsystems of the server such as CPU, system memory, disk controllers, and the peripheral bus. Peripheral buses are used to connect peripherals such as network interface cards or SCSI disk controllers.

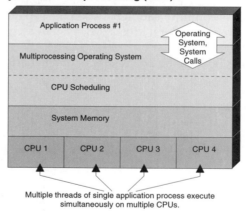

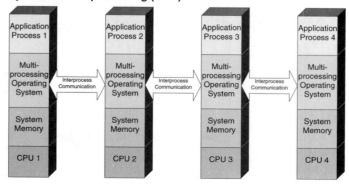

Figure 5-6 SMP versus AMP System Architectures

PCI buses seem to be the peripheral bus of choice among servers, although many high-powered multiprocessor servers use proprietary peripheral bus architectures. From a customer's perspective, the danger in purchasing a server with a proprietary bus architecture is that compatible peripheral devices and additional system memory may be available from only limited numbers of vendors at potentially higher prices.

PCI Version I has the capacity to potentially deliver up to 132 MB/sec, while PCI Version II boasts a maximum throughput of 264 MB/sec. PCI bus architectures also have the ability to expand through cascading to additional PCI buses via a PCI-to-PCI bridge or to lower-speed expansion buses such as EISA.

Figure 5-7 illustrates a typical arrangement of buses in a multiprocessor server.

Memory Memory architectures in tightly coupled multiprocessor servers can be classified as shared while memory architectures in loosely coupled multiprocessor system architectures are distributed. The memory chips themselves must be fast enough not to keep the CPU sitting idle. The relative benefits of SRAM, DRAM, EDODRAM, and a variety of other types of memory were explained in Chapter 3. Needless to say, multiprocessor servers require fast memory and plenty of it. System memory RAM capacities up to 256 MB or more are not unreasonable.

Error checking and correcting (ECC) memory, also known as error-correction code memory, is able to detect and correct errors in data stored in and retrieved from RAM memory. It is more expensive than conventional RAM but is worth the added cost for servers.

As discussed in the chapter on client hardware, L2 cache can make a tremendous difference in system performance. This is even more true with multiprocessor servers. The amount of L2 cache included in a given server is usually a design consideration controlled by the system manufacturer and not a user option. In

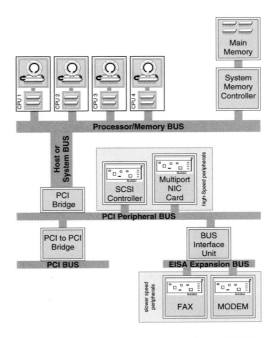

Figure 5-7 Bus Arrangement in a Multi-processor Server

symmetric multiprocessor servers, L2 cache may be dedicated to each CPU or shared by all processors.

CD-ROM   As operating system and networking operating system software continue to gain in sophistication, they also gain in sheer size. As a result, most server operating systems such as Windows NT or NetWare 4.1 are now distributed on CD-ROM rather than on 40 or more 3.5" diskettes. Not only are the one or two CD-ROMs more convenient, they are also significantly faster to install than loading 40 or more individual diskettes. For this reason, it is important to have a CD-ROM driver on a server for software installation even if the CD-ROM drive won't be shared with clients as a network-attached device. The required functionality and associated hardware requirement of dedicated, networked CD-ROM servers are outlined later in this chapter.

Because of the high capacity of a CD-ROM, it is important that the CD-ROM drive be attached to the server via a high-speed bus such as a PCI/SCSI controller, although adapters for IDE, parallel port, EISA, ISA, and MCA are available. Cache memory on the CD-ROM driver itself improves performance, with 256 KB being a common cache size. The current CD-ROM capacity standard is 680 MB of data per CD, with higher standards in the proposal stages. As with any device added to a computing platform, software drivers compatible with both the CD-ROM and the installed operating system are required. If the CD-ROM is to be used only for software installation or for seeking information on a single CD-ROM at a time, then a single-slot CD-ROM drive should suffice. CD-ROM Jukeboxes are more appropriate for specialized, networked CD-ROM servers.

A variety of standards describe CD-ROM drive performance. Figure 5-8 lists CD-ROM drive speed classifications, the most general categorization of CD-ROM driver performance.

More comprehensive standards are proposed by the Multimedia PC Marketing Council (MPC). Figure 5-9 summarizes MPC Level 1 and 2 standards.

Although many other proprietary CD-ROM standards exist, two additional standards are supported by most CD-ROM drives:

1. **XA:** Extended architecture for CD-ROM is Microsoft's Level-2 CD-ROM specification, which supports simultaneous playback of voice, video, image, and text.

2. **Photo CD:** Also known as Kodak Photo CD, this is a standard for displaying photographs proposed by Kodak.

CD-ROM Speed Specification	Sustained Average Data Throughput
Single Speed	150 KBps
Double Speed	300 KBps
Triple Speed	450 KBps
Quad Speed (4X)	600 KBps
6X	900 KBps
8X	1200 KBps

Figure 5-8   CD-ROM Drive Standards

MPC Standard Level	Sustained Transfer Rate	Average Seek Time	Max. CPU Usage	Minimum Recommended Hardware Configuration
Level 1	150 KBps	1 sec. max	40%	386SX with 2 MB RAM and 30 MB hard drive
Level 2	300 KBps	400 ms max	60%	486SX/25 with 4 MB RAM, 16 bit sound and graphics cards, 160 MB hard drive, playback support for XA files

Figure 5-9   MPC Level 1 and 2 Standards

Backup   In multiple server networked environments, backup solutions are most often network-based, rather than individually, server-by-server based. Network-based backup solutions are studied in Chapter 9. However, the following analysis is offered for those cases when a single server requires backup.

The first thing to realize about any backup solution is that it is a combination of hardware and software technology. The backup device itself, the server hardware, the third-party backup software (if applicable), and the server's operating system must all communicate transparently with each other. Figure 5-10 offers a conceptual representation of the compatibility issues involved in a single server backup solution.

Some of the compatibility requirements identified in Figure 5-10 are supplied by two standards:

1.   **Storage management system (SMS)** defines an API for third-party backup software to interoperate transparently with NetWare servers.

2.   **Storage independent data format (SIDF)** allows portability between tape media and SIDF-compliant backup devices.

A variety of backup device choices and accompanying standards are available. Choices differ in both overall capacity and backup throughput speed, as well as in price. Figure 5-11 summarizes the key characteristics of a variety of backup device possibilities.

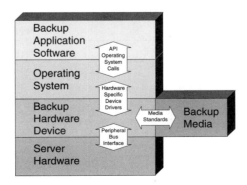

Figure 5-10   Compatibility Issues of Single Server Backup Solutions

Media Type	Explanation	Media Capacity	Throughput	Approx. Price
4mm DAT DDS 1	Digital audio tape, digital data storage	2 GB	21–23 MB/min	$800–$1700
4mm DAT DDS 2	Digital audio tape, digital data storage	4 GB	23–30 MB/min	$1000–$2000
8mm	8mm digital magnetic tape	5 GB	15–29 MB/min	$1400–$2500
DLT	Digital linear tape	10 GB	90–150 MB/min	$3100–$25,000
Magneto-Optical	Disk technology uses laser and magnetic read/write	1.3 GB	48–96 MB/min	$850–$1200
QIC	Quarter-inch cartridge magnetic tape	40 MB–25 GB	4–96 MB/min	$1200–$3500

Figure 5-11   Backup Technology Specifications

Applied Problem Solving

Although each backup situation is unique, there are some general rules of thumb for configuring backup solutions. Figure 5-12 summarizes a few scenarios, leaving the explanation of dedicated network-attached backup servers to Chapter 9.

Amount of Data to Be Backed Up	Proposed Backup Solution
Less than 2 GB	Attach a backup device to a network attached client workstation. Install and execute backup software from client workstation.
2 GB–4 GB	Attach a backup device to the server. Install and execute the backup software on the server.
Greater than 10 GB	Attach multiple backup devices to server. Install and execute backup software on server. Or consider a dedicated network-attached backup server.

Figure 5-12   Server Backup Scenarios

Each of these scenarios has trade-offs. Figure 5-13 shows the physical topology of backup solutions and lists some of the trade-offs inherent in each alternative.

Backup Device Installed on a Network Client

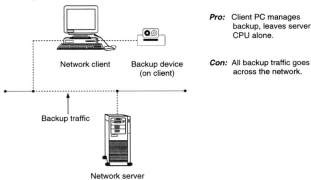

Network client

Backup device
(on client)

Pro: Client PC manages
backup, leaves server
CPU alone.

Con: All backup traffic goes
across the network.

Backup traffic

Network server

Backup Device Installed on a Network Server

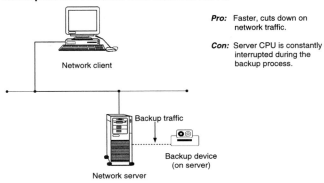

Network client

Pro: Faster, cuts down on
network traffic.

Con: Server CPU is constantly
interrupted during the
backup process.

Backup traffic

Backup device
(on server)

Network server

Figure 5-13   Trade-offs of Alternative Backup Solutions

UPS — Uninterruptable Power Supplies   Uninterruptable power supplies **(UPS)** for server PCs serve two distinct purposes:

1. They provide sufficient backup power in the event of a power failure to allow for a normal system shutdown.

2. They function as a **line conditioner** during normal operation by protecting computer equipment from "dirty" power conditions such as surges, brownouts, and static spikes.

It is important to protect servers with uninterruptable power because data can be lost, and important files can be corrupted by crashes. In their role as suppliers of uninterruptable power, UPSs must be able to respond quickly enough to a loss of normal power that the server cannot detect the power loss but continues to operate normally as if power was uninterrupted. Most servers crash with power losses of 300 milliseconds (0.3 second) or more. Most UPSs are able to supply backup power within 12 milliseconds of the power loss.

UPSs vary in the amount of backup electricity they can supply and how long they can supply it. Remember that UPSs are meant to provide only enough electricity to allow for a normal shutdown, usually about 5 minutes. Some higher priced units offer more power for longer periods of time; however, UPSs are not backup generators that allow users to continue to work for hours.

Most UPS capacities are rated in volt-amperes (VA), with 600 to 1500 volt-amperes being suitable for a single server and two to three workstations. Units in this power range are generally priced between $500 and $1500, depending on the amount of power, length of backup period, and number of additional features. Larger UPSs offer backup power in the 3000 to 5000 VA range (3 to 5 KVA) and are capable of supporting up to 22 servers or two fully loaded midrange systems.

Some UPSs are also able to link directly to servers, advising them of a loss of power and thereby triggering user notification and an orderly shutdown. This feature is known as **auto-server shutdown** and must be compatible with the particular server operating system installed. Another important management feature is the ability of the UPS to transmit status information in a standardized format understandable by enterprise network management platforms. The most common protocol for management information transmission is simple network management protocol (SNMP), a member of the TCP/IP family of protocols.

Additional technical information regarding UPS operation and selection is available in the articles cited in the Featured References.

Practical Advice and Information

EXPANDABILITY ISSUES FOR SERVERS

Expandability in a server should be considered in the following categories:

1. *RAM Expandability:* What is the maximum amount of RAM that can be installed in the server? Typical maximum amounts range from 128 MB to 1 GB. RAM memory is usually added as SIMM modules. It is therefore important to know both the total number of SIMM sockets available and how many are presently occupied.

2. *Expansion and Peripheral Bus Slot Expandability:* As servers demand faster peripherals to keep up with faster CPU performance, PCI is becoming the peripheral bus of choice. Two PCI buses bridged together are better than a single PCI bus. Six to eight empty PCI slots should be considered a desirable number. Expansion bus use will become less important as more and more peripherals shift to the PCI bus. In the meantime, however, four to six available EISA slots are desirable.

3. *Drive Bay Expandability:* Drive bays may be suitable for either 5.25" or 3.5" drives and either accessible from the front of the server or totally internal. Obviously CD-ROM drives or diskette drives need to be accessible, but fixed disk drives can easily be internal. As disk drive capacity continues to increase, the total number of available bays become less important. High demands for storage are met by external storage subsystems such as RAID. Typical servers have two 5.25" bays, seven to nine 3.5" bays, and one or two internal bays.

Network Interface Cards   Network interface cards are studied in detail in Chapter 8, however, there are a few common sense facts regarding them. To prevent them becoming the overall system bottleneck, two important decisions should be made regarding network interface cards for servers:

1. Although the server's network interface card must be compatible with the overall network architecture, that architecture should be as fast as possible. For instance, if the client/server information system's network is a 10 Mbps Ethernet network architecture, then the server must use a 10 Mbps Ethernet NIC. However, faster network architectures such as 100 Mbps Ethernet do exist. In the study of LAN design, servers can be put on faster network segments and bridged to the rest of the network.

2. The second way to prevent the server's NIC from becoming the system bottleneck is to put more than one NIC in the server. Think of the server as a building crowded with people. To get more people out of the building in a shorter time, more doors could be added. The NICs are the exits of the server. To get more data out of the server more quickly, more NICs could be added. Second, although the speed of the interface from the NIC to the network may be fixed (10 Mbps Ethernet), the speed at which data are loaded onto the NIC from within the server varies depending on the bus interface employed. As a result, PCI network interface cards are preferable to ISA or EISA NICs, and multiple PCI NICs are preferable to single PCI NICs. For convenience, four PCI Ethernet NICs can be mounted on a single card which includes a bridged PCI bus.

■ SERVER STORAGE ALTERNATIVES

RAID — Redundant Arrays of Inexpensive Disks

RAID Levels In an effort to provide large amounts of data storage combined with fault tolerance and redundancy, numerous small disk drives were joined together in arrays and controlled by software which could make these numerous disks appear to server operating systems as one gigantic disk. Exactly how these numerous disks were physically and logically linked was defined by a series of standards known as **RAID.** RAID originally stood for redundant array of inexpensive disks, but now often refers to redundant array of independent disks.

RAID is not the first method used to provide fault-tolerant or redundant data storage. Individual network operating systems previously offered two closely related methods for ensuring data availability for mission-critical applications:

1. **Disk mirroring** involves two disks attached to the same controller acting as mirror images of one another. Everything written to one disk is identically written to the other. In the event that one disk fails, the other disk immediately takes over. The single point of failure in this scheme is the single disk controller which controls the two mirrored disks. If the single controller fails, both disks become unreachable.

2. **Disk duplexing** seeks to overcome the single point of failure inherent in disk mirroring by linking a separate disk controller to each mirrored disk drive.

RAID incorporates, but also goes beyond, disk mirroring and disk duplexing, including six different RAID levels. These levels serve as standards for hardware and software vendors selling RAID technology. RAID standards are maintained by the RAID Advisory Board (RAB). Figure 5-14 (page 170) lists key facts concerning the six RAID levels officially recognized by RAB.

The text in the comments column in Figure 5-14, attributed to Joe Molina, the RAID Advisory Board chairman, are included for insight into the practical, rather than theoretical, significance of the various RAID levels. Figure 5-15 (page 171) lists other RAID level definitions used by some RAID technology vendors but not officially sanctioned by the RAB.

RAID Level	Definition	Comment	Application	Advantages	Disadvantages
Level 1 Disk Mirroring	Disk mirroring, also known as shadowing	Mirroring	System drives, critical files	High reliability	Writing to both mirrored disks degrades write performance, expensive
Level 2 Striped Array Plus Hamming Code	Writes data across multiple disks, adding Hamming code for error detection and correction	Doesn't exist for all practical purposes because it requires a modified disk drive that's too expensive to implement	None	High data transfer rate, high reliability	Not commercially viable
Level 3 Striped Array Plus Parity Disk	Stripes data a byte at a time. Parity is calculated on a byte by byte basis and stored on a dedicated parity drive	Parallel access for high read and write rates	Large I/O request applications such as imaging, CAD	Good for large block data transfers	Entire array acts as a single disk and can handle only one I/O request at a time. If parity disk is lost, so is error detection and correction
Level 4 Independent Striped Array Plus Parity Disk	Stripes data in sectors. Parity stored on parity drive. Disks can work independently	Forget it. The write penalty is too high	Not widely available	Good read performance	Poor write performance. If parity disk is lost, so is error detection and correction
Level 5 Independent Striped Array Plus Striped Parity	Stripes data in sectors. Parity is interleaved and striped across multiple disk	Striping across the disks with parity data	High request rate, read-intensive data lookups where write performance is not critical	High data reliability, good read performance	Poor write performance because data has to be striped across multiple disks
Level 6 Independent Striped Array Plus Striped Double Parity	Striped data and parity with two parity drives	Level 5 with data duplication to provide for extra redundancy	High request rate, read-intensive data lookups where write performance is not critical	High data reliability, good read performance	Worse write performance than level 5 due to added parity calculation

Figure 5-14   RAID Levels Officially Recognized by RAB

RAID Level	Definition	Application	Advantages	Disadvantages
Level 0 **Disk Striping**	Stripes data across multiple disks without redundancy	High performance for noncritical data	Fast I/O at low cost	No data redundancy. Not really RAID
Level 10 **Level 1 Plus 0**	Disk mirroring plus disk striping	Any critical response time application	Excellent I/O performance and data reliability	High hardware cost. Not widely used
Level 7 **Independent** **Striped Array** **Plus Dual** **Parity Disks**	Stripes data in sectors. Parity stored on two parity drives. Disks work independently	High request rate, read-intensive data lookups where write performance is not critical	High data reliability, good read performance	Poor write performance
Level 53 **Level 0 Plus 3**	Combines disk striping and RAID 3	Large I/O request apps such as imaging, CAD	High performance and high data transfer rates	Poor write performance

Figure 5-15   RAID Levels Not Officially Recognized by RAB

RAID Technology   Nearly all RAID storage subsystems support RAID levels 0, 1, and 5, and fewer RAID technology vendors support levels 3, 6, 7, and 10. Figure 5-16 graphically illustrates the categorization of the major types of RAID systems.

The key differentiating factors among the various categories of RAID technology depicted in Figure 5-16, can be summarized by answering the following key questions:

1. Where is the RAID software executed?
    - In the CPU of the server (software-based RAID).
    - In a dedicated CPU embedded within the RAID controller board (hardware-based RAID).

2. In the case of hardware-based RAID, where is the RAID controller board that contains the dedicated CPU installed?
    - In an available expansion slot in the host system (host-controller RAID).
    - In the RAID subsystem cabinet linked to the host via a standard SCSI controller (SCSI-to-SCSI RAID).

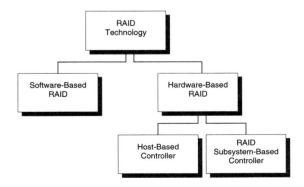

Figure 5-16   RAID Technology Categorization

Software-based RAID uses the CPU of the server to execute the RAID software, which controls the multiple disk drives contained in the redundant array of independent disks. The RAID level implemented is determined by the logic contained within the RAID application software executed on the server. The disadvantage of this approach is that it takes valuable server CPU cycles to control the RAID subsystem, especially in the event of a catastrophic event such as a disk rebuild. Another potential disadvantage is that another ill-behaved application also running on the same server on which the RAID software is executing could interfere with or crash the RAID application, resulting in data corruption. RAID software written as a server application must be written for a particular operating system or network operating system. The advantage of software-based RAID is that it is usually less expensive than hardware-based RAID. Software-based RAID could actually be implemented by purchasing a NetWare loadable module (NLM) with RAID functionality and executing it on a NetWare server. Of course, an array of disk drives would also be required.

Hardware-based RAID is more expensive than software-based RAID but is also more reliable and able to support more operating systems. In the case of **host-controller RAID,** the controller board which contains the RAID intelligence is installed in an available expansion slot. This requires bus interface compatibility. Most RAID controllers support ISA, EISA, MCA, and PCI bus interfaces. Several also support NuBus (Apple) and various minicomputer bus interfaces as well. The RAID software contained in firmware on the host-controller RAID card must make system calls to the host's operating system and/or network operating system to control the disks in the RAID subsystem. Operating system specific drivers unique to each host controller card must therefore be supplied by the host controller card vendor. Most host controller cards are available with drivers for the following:

- NetWare (multiple versions).
- Windows NT.
- OS/2.
- Vines.
- Appleshare.
- UNIX and its numerous vendor specific varieties.

SCSI-to-SCSI RAID keeps all the RAID intelligence in the disk array cabinet. The controller card is installed with the RAID subsystem cabinet and connects to the host server via a standard SCSI controller. SCSI RAID controllers vary as to which SCSI standards are supported (fast, wide, fast/wide, ultra). The advantage of SCSI-to-SCSI RAID is that the RAID portion of the software is operating system independent. All that is required for communication are standard SCSI drivers. To the operating system running on the server, the RAID subsystem appears to be one massive SCSI disk drive. SCSI-to-SCSI RAID is ideal for less frequently supported operating systems such as Macintosh or some flavors of UNIX.

RAID Technology Analysis   Armed with a knowledge of RAID level standards and the broad classifications of RAID technology, a variety of other issues are important to ensuring that selected RAID technology will meet the data storage needs of a particular information system. Figure 5-17 summarizes a few of the RAID technology analysis issues which deserve investigation.

Applied Problem Solving

RAID Technology Analysis Issue	Questions/Implications
RAID Levels Supported	Look for at least levels 0, 1, and 5. Make sure that you can mix and match RAID levels within the subsystem, that is, support multiple different RAID levels simultaneously.
Subsystem Enclosures	Cabinets should have room for at least seven drives and support hot-swappable components including fans and power supplies. Is there also room for tape drives or optical drives in the cabinet?
Disk Drives	Are disk drives for the subsystem restricted to a particular vendor's drives? Although this may aid compatibility, it may reduce the ability to get the largest, fastest, or least expensive drives if all drives must come from particular vendor.
Subsystem Capacity	Can the subsystem support more than one controller? How many drives or what size can be supported? What are the expansion capabilities?
Embedded CPU and BUS	A faster, wider bus such as PCI is preferred. RAID controllers often employ specialized CPUs such as the Intel I960 RISC chip.
Cache Memory	On-board cache will assist system performance. Write-back cache is acceptable if a method has been devised to save data left in the cache in the event of a power failure.
Management Utilities	Can the RAID subsystem output status information to an enterprise network management system in SNMP format? How easy is it to initiate a drive rebuild? How is the RAID subsystem configured? Is a setup utility included? What platform does the configuration software run on?
Operating System Compatibility	Host-based controllers must be physically compatible with the host server in terms of the peripheral or expansion bus. Controller software must be fully compatible with the operating system/network operating system installed in the host server.
Vendor-Related Issues	What is the vendor's policy on parts replacement? What type of warranty or on-site support is offered at what cost? What is the quality and availability of vendor technical support? What is the cost of technical support? Is an 800 number available? Will this vendor still be in business in 5 years?

Figure 5-17   RAID Technology Analysis Issues

HSM — Hierarchical Storage Management

Although technologies such as RAID are able to keep tremendous amounts of data on-line and immediately available to users, at some point one needs to ask whether this is necessary. At what point does sales history no longer need to take up valuable disk space? When are other storage media such as optical jukeboxes or tape libraries appropriate?

Hierarchical storage management (HSM) is a technology which seeks to make optimal, or most effective, use of available storage media while minimizing the need for human intervention. HSM starts by looking at information in terms of its urgency or frequency of access, and then stores that information on the most cost-effective storage medium that meets performance requirements. Levels of urgency/ access and corresponding storage technologies are organized into the hierarchical model illustrated in Figure 5-18.

As the figure shows, the most frequently accessed data are stored on the fastest on-line media. Less frequently accessed information is stored on **near-line** or near-on-line devices such as optical jukeboxes, and the least frequently accessed data are stored in off-line media such as tape libraries.

HSM software automates the process of migrating data between the various stage storage devices. HSM software does not replace backup/restoral software, it merely manages stored data in an overall organizational scheme that properly uses storage technology. Executing HSM software enables a multilevel system for mass storage characterized by automatic, transparent migration of data between available storage technologies. Initial setup and configuration of HSM software is time-consuming, however, as network managers must set numerous thresholds for moving data between storage devices before the software can take over and run automatically.

LAN-based HSM technology is relatively new, having migrated from the mainframe and minicomputer domains. HSM software must be compatible with a server's operating system and network operating system to transparently manage network-attached storage technology. Compatibility with existing backup application software can also be a problem. LAN-based HSM technol-

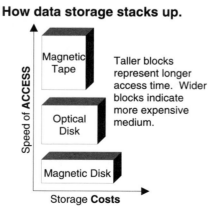

Figure 5-18   Hierarchical Storage Management Model

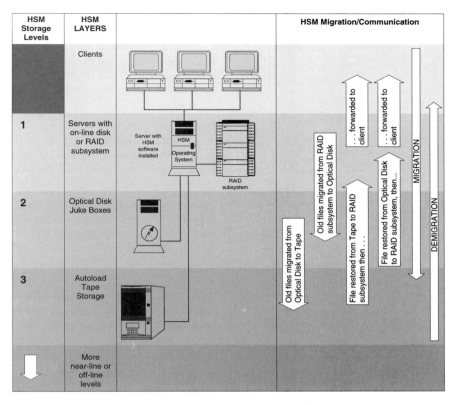

Figure 5-19   Hierarchical Storage Management Technology

ogy, currently available primarily for NetWare LANS, differ in the following ways:

- Number of HSM hierarchical tiers supported: varies from two to unlimited.

- Storage media supported: some support only optical disk or optical disk and 8 mm tape, while others also support 4 mm tape and DLT tape.

- Execution mode: some HSM software runs as an NLM on a NetWare server while other products require a dedicated server.

- Price: ranges as well as criteria vary widely. Many products charge between $1000 and $10,000 *per server.*

Figure 5-19 illustrates the relationship among HSM software, servers, and hierarchical storage technology.

In Sharper Focus

HSM software varies widely in features and functionality. To differentiate between HSM products' management capabilities, the five-layer hierarchy of HSM levels presented in Figure 5-20 was proposed by a company named Peripheral Strategies and adopted by HSM vendors. The layers of the hierarchy increase in complexity from 1 through 5, and products supporting higher HSM levels are understandably more expensive.

HSM Level	Required Functionality
1	Simple automatic file migration with transparent retrieval.
2	Real-time dynamic load-balancing of disk space based on multiple predefined thresholds. Manages two or more levels in the storage hierarchy, for example, an optical jukebox and an automated tape library.
3	Transparent management of three or more levels in the storage hierarchy. Storage thresholds between different levels in the hierarchy are dynamically balanced and managed. Volume management, including media management, job queuing, and device performance optimization. Supports optical and tape devices.
4	Policy management and administration at all levels of the hierarchy. Storage management of diverse platforms, from file servers to workstations to application servers. Maintains the ownership, attributes, and location of data, thus enabling multiplatform (DOS, Macintosh, OS/2) HSM. Can migrate files based on data type, as dictated by policies.
5	Object management, including structured or nonstructured records, and nonfile structures. Preserves the relationships of objects at all levels of the hierarchy. Can work with database management systems to migrate portions of a database, rather than the entire file, to and from secondary storage.

Figure 5-20   HSM Levels of Functionality

■ SERVER FUNCTIONALITY AND SPECIALIZATION

Before deciding which particular hardware features are most important to include in a given server, it is important to specify the intended use of that server. As LANs have grown and users have demanded more services from those LANs, servers have become increasingly specialized. The overall class of network-attached servers can be subdivided into two major categories:

- Servers that provide access to network-attached resources.

- Servers that provide computational services by running back-end applications of one type or another.

The difference between the two subcategories of servers is significant, as it has major implications for the required hardware and operating systems which must be included in a given server. Servers which provide access to network-attached resources require little processing power, but servers expected to run back-end engines can use all the processing power they get. Figure 5-21 categorizes many of the specialized servers available today, which are described in more depth in the articles cited in the Featured References.

In the early days of local area networks, servers were called on to function primarily as file and printer servers. Novell NetWare gained a large share of the local area network operating system market by doing an excellent job at supplying network-based file and print services. As downsizing and rightsizing efforts have con-

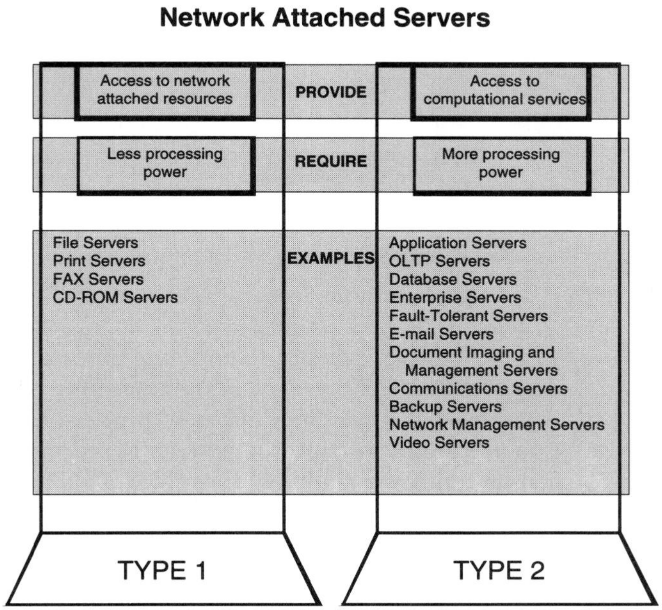

Network Attached Servers

Access to network attached resources	PROVIDE	Access to computational services
Less processing power	REQUIRE	More processing power
File Servers Print Servers FAX Servers CD-ROM Servers	EXAMPLES	Application Servers OLTP Servers Database Servers Enterprise Servers Fault-Tolerant Servers E-mail Servers Document Imaging and Management Servers Communications Servers Backup Servers Network Management Servers Video Servers
TYPE 1		**TYPE 2**

Figure **5-21**   Network-Attached Server Functional Categorization

tinued, applications servers requiring large amounts of processing power have become more available and affordable, thereby allowing applications formerly deployed on minicomputers and mainframes to execute on multiprocessor, LAN-based application servers.

■ SERVER SOFTWARE

Being able to successfully execute mission-critical, transaction-based, high-end applications on powerful LAN-based multiprocessor servers requires compatible server operating systems, which are able to take full advantage of the multiprocessor powered servers. As LAN-based server hardware has developed and become more powerful and affordable, server operating systems have had to become more powerful as well. The key aspect of this power is the ability to take full advantage of the server's multiple processors and transparently pass this power along to the application program.

Server Operating Systems

It is difficult to distinguish between server operating systems and server *network* operating systems. A server must be a LAN-attached device to properly service its clients, but the server operating system nearly always also includes the required functionality for the server to communicate over the network to which it is attached.

Characteristics   The key criteria by which server operating systems can be evaluated are as follows:

- Price.
- Performance.
- Management.
- Security.
- Applications integration.

Price: Price is difficult to compare among server operating systems because pricing schemes vary widely. Some operating systems vendors charge more for their software based on the number of processors installed in the multiprocessor server. Others charge in fixed increments based on the number of users. For example, licenses might be available for 5, 25, 50, 100, 250, 1000, or an unlimited number of users. The problem with **fixed-step license pricing,** as illustrated in the preceding increments, is that a 250 user license would have to be purchased to enable 101 users. In response to this dilemma, some vendors, such as Novell with their NetWare 4.1 software, have initiated an alternative pricing mechanism known as **additive license pricing.** With additive license pricing, any combination of license increments may be combined to allow businesses to buy only the number of user licenses they really need. When computing comparative pricing of operating systems, it is important to consider upgrade costs as well as initial costs.

Performance: To take advantage of the increased processing powers of multiple processors, server operating systems must be specially written to operate in a symmetrical multiprocessing (SMP) environment. Server operating systems can differ as to the maximum number of processors they can support. Figure 5-22 summarizes the number of processors supported by some currently available server operating systems.

UNIX-based server operating systems such as Solaris and others have been offering SMP capabilities for many more years than operating systems developed in the Intel chip environment. As a result, UNIX-based server operating systems tend to be more stable with servers having more than 16 or 32 processors.

To allow greater freedom of choice in matching SMP server hardware with SMP server operating systems, Intel has proposed a SMP specification for the hardware/software interface known as **MultiProcessing Specification 1.1 (MPS)** which is widely supported by SMP hardware and software vendors. As stated earlier in

Server Operating System	Vendor	Number of Processors Supported
Windows NT Server	Microsoft	2–32
OS/2 SMP	IBM	2–16
Solaris	Sun Microsystems	2–64
UnixWare 2	Novell	2–16
OpenServer MPX	SCO (Santa Cruz Operation)	2–30
NetWare 4.1 SMP	Novell	2–32

Figure 5-22   Number of Processors Supported by Server Operating Systems

the chapter, clustering, now largely confined to minicomputer operating systems and high-powered database engines, will begin to become available for LAN-based servers as more powerful and performance-hungry applications migrate from the mainframe environment to client/server architectures. By truly distributing applications on a thread level, as well as associated data, over multiple CPUs physically located on multiple machines, clustering-capable operating systems can truly harness all of the available computing power in a fault-tolerant client/server environment.

Practical Advice and Information

When it comes to optimizing performance in a symmetrical multiprocessing environment, the most important thing to remember is that the operating system and application program must support not only SMP but also multithreading, to ensure that the application program runs as efficiently as possible. Applications or operating systems which do not support multithreading may leave some CPUs idle, thereby negating the positive impact of SMP.

Management: As more mission-critical applications are deployed on LAN-attached servers, server operating systems must offer more sophisticated management tools to manage those applications effectively. Monitoring ability is essential in determining where potential performance bottlenecks might occur and reacting accordingly. Among the server attributes which should be easily monitored in a graphical display are the following:

- Processors.
- Network I/O.
- Disk I/O.
- Memory usage including L2 cache.
- Individual application performance and system impact.
- Process and thread performance.

The monitor tool should be able to display data in a variety of ways:

- As graphs.
- As reports.
- As alarms or alerts if preset thresholds are crossed.

A strong and flexible alert system is essential to keeping applications running and users happy. Some alert systems have the ability to dial particular pagers for particular alerts and can forward system status information to that pager as well.

A monitoring tool should support multiple open monitoring windows simultaneously for observing multiple attributes or applications. The monitoring or management tool should be open and support industry standard management protocols and APIs so that application-specific management tools can be easily integrated into the overall operating system monitor.

Security: Overall security features fall into three broad categories:

1. Authorization.

2. Encryption.

3. Authentication.

Authorization is concerned with user accounts and passwords. Systems differ in level of access allowed before a valid userID and password must be entered. Authorization also controls user access rights to disks and files. Assignments of user rights varies widely from system to system. An important security management feature is the level of integration, if any, between applications' security systems and the operating system's security system. For example, does e-mail require a separate userID and login from the system login? In many cases, the answer is yes. Also, considerable time is saved if userIDs can be created or modified with a template or group name instead of having to answer numerous questions for each userID.

Encryption is especially important when passwords are entered. Encrypted passwords are unreadable while being transmitted between a client workstation and the authorizing server.

Authentication involves ensuring that messages supposedly received from a certain client workstation are really from that properly authorized workstation. Authentication security is necessary because of a process called spoofing, in which bogus network messages which appear to be authentic and properly authorized are sent to servers requesting data or services. Authentication security is complicated and usually implemented by a dedicated authentication server running the Kerberos authentication system.

In Sharper Focus

Security can be classified by security level. Server operating systems often claim to implement **C2 level security.** C2 level security is actually part of a specification known as "Trusted Computer System Evaluation Criteria," which is specified in a Department of Defense document commonly known as *The Orange Book.* The book concentrates on seven levels of data confidentiality, from D (low) to A1 (high).

In C level security, users can control the access to their own files. C2 level security more specifically implies that, although users can control access to their files, all file access can be monitored and recorded, or audited. Furthermore, these file-access audit records are reliable and verifiable and therefore able to track and prove unauthorized file access. C2 level systems can also do the following:

- Identify and authenticate users.

- Have hidden passwords.

- Provide for resource isolation.

- Audit user activity.

Systems claiming to be C2 *compliant* are judged so by the vendor, whereas systems (hardware and software) claiming to be C2 *evaluated* or *certified* have undergone rigorous testing, taking as long as two years.

The Orange Book addressed only security concerning file access and confidentiality of data. The security of networked systems is addressed in another Department of Defense document known as *The Red Book.* Encrypting passwords before transmitting them from client to server is a *Red Book* specification. Some server operating systems also claim *Red Book compliance.*

Applications Integration: Applications integration refers to the extent to which applications program are able to integrate or take advantage of the capabilities of the operating system to optimize application program performance. Successful applications integration with the operating system can yield both increased convenience and performance.

From a convenience standpoint:

1.   Does the application integrate with the operating system's security system, allowing single userIDs and user accounts, or must two separate security databases be maintained?

2.   Does the application integrate with the operating system's monitoring capabilities, allowing it to be monitored from within the operating system?

3.   Can the application be configured and maintained from within the operating system's control panel or setup subsystem?

From a performance standpoint:

1.   Can the application take advantage of the multithreaded capabilities of the operating system?

2.   Can the application automatically detect the presence of multiple processors and respond accordingly?

3.   Can the application use the multitasking capabilities of the operating system, or does it supply its own multitasking environment?

4.   How easily, and to what extent, can adjustments be made to the operating system to optimize the performance of the application?

5.   Does the application run as a 32-bit or a 16-bit application?

Managerial Perspective

New versions of server operating systems are released annually, if not more frequently. When in the market for a server operating system, one should take a fresh look at all currently available products while bearing in mind current technology investments, business objectives, and the characteristics of the application programs to be executed in the proposed server environment, as well as the stability and strategic product development direction of the operating system vendor.

■ SERVER HARDWARE AND SOFTWARE TRENDS

Fault-Tolerant Servers

One of the initial objectives or proposed benefits of client/server information systems was the ability to migrate mainframe-based applications onto right-sized applications servers. An underlying assumption of such a migration is that these applications servers will be able to offer the same levels of performance and reliability as the mainframes.

With the right combination of symmetrical multiprocessing hardware and software, it is now possible to match the performance levels of the mainframe. However, the ability to match their reliability and fault tolerance is a challenge for today's application servers. This reliability and fault tolerance is required for so-called mission-critical applications. On-line transaction processing (OLTP) systems such as banking or airline reservation systems are good examples of mission-critical applications. Control systems involved with military applications or nuclear power plants could also be considered mission-critical applications.

A server that is considered fault tolerant and capable of supporting mission-critical applications must exhibit all or most of the following characteristics:

- Fully redundant processors.

- Processor auditing to check calculations each clock cycle.

- Automatic correction of memory errors up to 8 bits long.

- Hot swappable redundant components such as fans or power supplies.

A **redundant processor architecture** goes beyond traditional symmetrical multiprocessing design. In a redundant processor architecture, each primary CPU is shadowed by a secondary identical tandem processor which executes the exact same instructions. This secondary tandem processor is only used in the event of a primary CPU failure. Third and fourth audit processors perform the same instructions as the primary and secondary CPUs, respectively, and compare the results of every clock cycle for consistency. Thus, to deliver two-way (two CPU) SMP in a fault-tolerant redundant processor architecture, a total of eight CPUs (2 primary, 2 secondary, 4 audits) is required.

To ensure superb performance, additional processors may be dedicated to I/O processing or application processing. Each processor would run its own copy of the server's network operating system and a back-end application program such as an e-mail server. To be scalable and cost-effective, the fault-tolerant servers should be able to run standard SMP network operating systems such as Windows NT or NetWare 4.1 SMP. Figure 5-23 illustrates a possible fault-tolerant server layout featuring a redundant processor architecture.

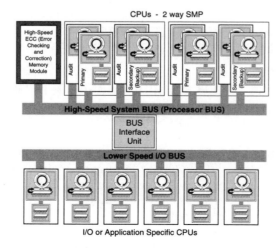

Figure 5-23   Fault-Tolerant Server Architecture

Routing Servers

One of the stated underlying business motivations for client/server information systems is the ability to deliver the right information to the right decision maker at the right place and time for the right cost. One of the dilemmas in achieving this lofty goal is finding a suitable way to deliver full information systems access cost-effectively to users or decision makers in remote branch offices and to mobile computing users.

Although networks can certainly be designed and installed to link every location in an enterprise, one of the great ongoing costs in such a network is for training and supporting highly technical networking personnel to be stationed at every remote branch office and location. Deploying highly paid networking personnel in this manner is simply not cost-effective. As a result, applications servers including integrated internetworking capabilities are being developed.

These hybrid networking/applications servers should be able to transparently link remote branch information systems with corporate headquarters' operating systems while simultaneously supporting dial-in access from mobile computing corporate personnel. Several applications server manufacturers are teaming with internetworking equipment vendors in this effort. A key to this server integration is that these additional networking duties must not degrade the overall server performance in executing application programs. Second, managing the networking aspects of these servers must be transparently integrated with enterprise network management programs executing at corporate headquarters or centralized network operations control centers.

When easily manageable hybrid servers combining networking and applications server capabilities are widely available and affordable, client/server information systems will have made significant progress toward achieving the overall goal of supplying the right information to the right decision maker at the right place and time for the right cost.

SUMMARY

To deliver on the applications rightsizing benefits of client/server information systems, servers must be able to deliver high performance in a fault-tolerant, reliable manner if they are to be trusted with mission-critical applications formerly reserved for mainframe computers. High performance expectations require new, scalable system architectures employing parallel processing techniques such as symmetrical multiprocessing. More important, no single aspect or subsystem of the server can be allowed to overwhelm or act as a bottleneck for other subsystems. As a result, bus architectures, memory subsystems, CD-ROMs, and backup subsystems must all be on a par with each other from a performance perspective.

Servers must be reliable. In some cases this implies the need for redundant, hot-swappable components such as fans or powers supplies. Reliable electrical power should be ensured with a properly sized uninteruptable power supply.

Server data storage needs must also be met in a high-performance, reliable manner. RAID, redundant array of independent disks, is a technology which allows a reliable, redundant storage subsystem to be linked to an applications server.

Servers have become more specialized as client/server information systems have matured.

Two major subcategories of servers have developed: those servers which offer access to network attached resources, such as printers, and those servers which process back-end applications engines, such as e-mail servers or database servers.

Server operating systems must complement server hardware architectures by maximizing the effective use of the symmetrical multiprocessing systems architectures in a secure, reliable fashion while integrating fully with applications programs.

KEY TERMS

4 mm DAT DDS 1, 166
4 mm DAT DDS 2, 166
8 mm, 166
additive license pricing, 178
AMP, 160
ASMP, 160
asymmetric multiprocessing, 160
auto-server shutdown, 168
c2 level security, 180
clustering, 161
disk duplexing, 169
disk mirroring, 169
distributed parallel processing, 161
DLT, 166
double speed, 164
DPP, 161
ECC memory, 163
fixed step license pricing, 178
hardware-based RAID, 172
hierarchical storage management, 174
host-controller RAID, 172

HSM, 174
line conditioner, 166
load balancing, 160
loosely coupled, 161
Magneto-Optical, 166
massively parallel processing, 160
MIP, 162
MPC level 1, 165
MPC level 2, 165
MPP, 160
MPS, 178
multiprocessor server, 159
multiprocessing specification 1.1, 178
near-line, 174
parallel processing, 160
photo CD, 164
QIC, 166
quad speed, 164
RAID, 169
RAID level 0, 171
RAID level 1, 170
RAID level 2, 170

RAID level 3, 170
RAID level 4, 170
RAID level 5, 170
RAID level 6, 170
redundant processor architecture, 182
SCSI-to-SCSI RAID, 172
SIDF, 165
single speed, 164
SMP, 160
SMS, 165
software-based RAID, 172
storage independent data format, 165
storage management system, 165
symmetric multiprocessing, 160
tightly coupled, 161
triple speed, 164
uninterruptable power supply, 166
UPS, 166
virtual parallel machines, 161
VPM, 161
XA, 164

REVIEW QUESTIONS

1. What are some of the business requirements underlying the importance of client/server information systems?
2. What are some of the server functionalities required to meet the demands of client/server information systems?
3. What are the two major categories of servers?
4. How do the two major categories of servers differ in functionality and potential bottlenecks?
5. Why does a multiprocessor architecture alone not guarantee a high-performance server?
6. Differentiate between the two major subcategories of parallel processing.
7. What is load balancing, and how is it achieved?
8. What are some of the future directions of parallel computing?

9. Which is more efficient and why: loosely coupled or tightly coupled systems architectures?
10. Which bus architecture is preferred in servers and why?
11. Why is ECC memory important in servers?
12. What are the advantages of having a CD-ROM installed in a server?
13. What are some of the acceptable backup media for servers?
14. What compatibility issues are associated with designing a backup solution for servers?
15. What are the two major functions of a UPS?
16. What are some of the more advanced communications-related features of UPSs?
17. What are the three major categories of

expandability to be ensured in a computer, and why are they important?

18. What is the difference between disk mirroring and disk duplexing?
19. Practically speaking, which RAID levels are commercially viable?
20. Differentiate between the cost and performance of software-based versus hardware-based RAID.
21. Differentiate between host-controller RAID and SCSI-to-SCSI RAID performance and compatibilities.
22. What are some of the important features to look for when purchasing a RAID subsystem, and why are they important?
23. What is HSM?
24. How is HSM related to RAID, if at all?
25. What is the difference between HSM storage hierarchy levels and HSM functionality levels?
26. What are the major differences between the two major subcategories of server functionality?
27. What are the overall requirements of server software?
28. What are some of the key criteria by which server software can be evaluated, and why are they important?
29. What are some of the different license pricing schemes available today?
30. Why is the prospect of clustering operating systems for client/server architectures so exciting?
31. What are the major areas of security for server operating systems to support?
32. What is C2 level security?
33. What is the difference between C2 compliant and C2 certified?
34. Why is the ease and extent of applications integration important to server operating systems?
35. Why are fault-tolerant servers important to the increased adoption of client/server information systems?
36. What are the significant architectural features of a fault-tolerant server?
37. Why are internetworking or routing features being integrated with applications server functionality?

ACTIVITIES

1. Find examples of as many different kinds of mission-critical applications as possible in real business situations. What do all mission-critical applications seem to have in common? How do they differ?
2. What types of computer platforms are the real-world mission-critical applications running on today? Describe any migration plans.
3. What are the requirements or criteria for migrating mission-critical applications from their present platform?
4. Gather product literature and prepare a presentation on SMP versus AMP platforms. Which are more common? more expensive? What types of applications and operating systems are run on each?
5. Investigate and prepare a presentation on some of the future parallel processing platforms such as MPP, VPM, and clustering.
6. Investigate and prepare a presentation on CD-ROM drives. What are the current important standards?
7. Investigate and prepare a presentation on CD-ROM recorders. What are the current important standards?
8. Investigate and prepare a presentation on backup solutions for servers. Pay careful attention to hardware/software compatibility issues.
9. Investigate and prepare a presentation on UPSs. What are the environmental issues, if any, regarding the batteries contained in the UPS? Is special handling or storage required?
10. Investigate available RAID technology and report on RAID levels supported as well as any other significant technical differences.
11. Investigate and prepare a presentation about available HSM technology. Pay particular attention to the cost and the number of hierarchy levels and HSM functionality levels supported.
12. Investigate and prepare a presentation on multiprocessor operating systems. Pay particular attention to price, number of processors supported, and number and type of available applications programs. Compare UNIX-based products and non-UNIX–based products.
13. Compare security features of multiprocessor operating systems. Compare UNIX-based products and non-UNIX–based products.
14. Find examples of fault-tolerant servers. Examine product literature to determine actual architectural features which deliver fault tolerance. Compare the prices of fault-tolerant and "normal" servers.

FEATURED REFERENCES ....

Cases

Bucholtz, Chris. Taming Design Data with HSM. *LAN Times*, 12; 13 (July 3, 1995), 54.

Server Trends

Groff, James. Five Drivers of Computing Change. *Network Computing*, 5; 14 (November 15, 1994), 104.

Lapolla, Stephanie. Routers Find a Way to Serve. *PC Week*, 12; 27 (July 10, 1995), 101.

Loudermilk, Stephen. App Server Features Power Boost. *LAN Times*, 12; 13 (July 3, 1995), 30.

Loudermilk, Stephen. Intel Chip Advances. *LAN Times*, 12; 14 (July 24, 1995), 1.

Loudermilk, Stephen. Servers Bulk Up for Enterprise Nets. *LAN Times*, 12; 14 (July 24, 1995), 7.

Roelandts, Willem. The Big Five. *Network Computing*, 5; 14 (November 15, 1994), 76.

Samper, Phil. View from the Sun. *Network Computing*, 5; 14 (November 15, 1994), 102.

Stam, Nick and Tami Peterson. RISC Servers: One Size Does Not Fit All. *PC Magazine*, 13; 10 (May 31, 1994), 175.

Stimac, Gary. Bundling It Together. *Network Computing*, 5; 14 (November 15, 1994), 98.

Fault-Tolerant Servers

Saunders, Stephen. A PC-Based Platform Takes Aim at the Big Time. *Data Communications*, 24; 1 (January 1995), 96.

Storage

Andrews, Dave. Storage Technologies: 15MB in a Matchbook. *Byte*, 20; 1 (January 1995), 30.

Asthana, Praveen and Blair Finklestein. Superdense Optical Storage. *IEEE Spectrum*, 32; 8 (August 1995), 25.

Carr, Eric. RAID Without Compromise. *Network Computing*, 6; 10 (September 1, 1995), 44.

Carr, Eric. tRAIDoff. *Network Computing*, 5; 15 (December 1, 1994), 52.

Gerber, Barry. Hierarchical Storage Management for NetWare. *Network Computing*, 6; 3 (March 1, 1995), 66.

Guy, Michelle. 16 Fast, Reliable RAID Subsystems. *Byte*, 20; 9 (September 1995), 248.

Loudermilk, Stephen. A Fresh Look at RAID. *LAN Times*, 11; 12 (June 5, 1995), 71.

Lubell, Peter. The Gathering Storm in High-Density Compact Disks. *IEEE Spectrum*, 32; 8 (August 1995), 32.

Milne, Jay. RAID Storage Solutions: Which Is Right for You? *Network Computing*, 6; 5 (May 1, 1995), 154.

Nance, Barry. Network Storage Economizers. *Byte*, 20; 3 (March 1995), 137.

Reinhardt, Andy. Managing Storage. *Byte*, 19; 6 (June 1994), 153.

Saunders, Stephen. HSM Tries to Tame the LAN Storage Tiger. *Data Communications*, 23; 11 (August 1994), 73.

Saunders, Stephen. LAN Storage Rx: 60 Gbytes, No Waiting. *Data Communications*, 24; 1 (January 1995), 98.

Tannenbaum, Todd. HSM: Is This Technology for You? *Network Computing*, 5; 11 (October 1, 1994), 129.

Internet Servers

Johnson, Johna. Corporate Internet Server, Hold the Hassles. *Data Communications*, 24; 1 (January 1995), 100.

NetWare Servers

Saunders, Stephen. NewWare Servers: New Rules, Tougher Choices. *Data Communications*, 23; 12 (September 1994), 85.

FAX Servers

Bolles, Gary. Fax Headaches? Think About a FAX Server. *Network Computing*, 5; 6 (June 1, 1994), 178.

Carr, Eric. A FAX Server Solution that Fits. *Network Computing*, 6; 9 (August 1, 1995), 128.

Carr, Eric. Plug-n-Play FAX Servers More Trouble Than They're Worth. *Network Computing*, 5; 11 (October 1, 1994), 106.

Salamone, Salvatore. Brooktrout Cuts the Cost of Internal Faxing. *Byte*, 20; 2 (February 1995), 32.

CD-ROM Servers

Danielle, Diane. Choosing CD-ROM Hardware for the Network. *Network Computing*, 5; 9 (August 1, 1994), 164.

Drews, James. Serving Up CD-ROM with Everything on Your Network. *Network Computing*, 6; 8 (July 1, 1995), 128.

Kohlhepp, Robert. Netting a CD-ROM Server. *Network Computing*, 6; 9 (August 1, 1995), 108.

Rigney, Steve. Networked CD-ROMs Made Simple. *PC Magazine*, 14; 14 (August 1995), NE25.

Shannon, Ronald. Networked CD-ROMs: Big, Fast, Easy. *Network Computing*, 6; 8 (July 1, 1995), 154.

NT Servers

Lipschutz, Robert. Pentiums and Windows NT: A Wining Combination. *PC Magazine*, 14; 1 (January 10, 1995), NE1.

Morse, Stephen. Choosing an NT Platform: You Pay Your Money and You . . . *Network Computing*, 5; 11 (October 1, 1994), 56.

Printers/Print Servers

Adams, Jay and Robert Kohlhepp. All the New Printers that Fit. *Network Computing*, 5; 15 (December 1, 1994), 86.

Boardman, Bruce. Sizing Up Your Printer. *Network Computing*, 5; 12 (October 15, 1994), 70.

Koegler, Scott. Affordable Network Printers Output High Quality Color. *Network Computing*, 6; 5 (May 1, 1995), 118.

Kohlhepp, Robert. New Ways to Network Your Old Printers. *Network Computing*, 6; 4 (April 1, 1995), 118.

Milne, Jay. Pulling Your Print Needs Together. *Network Computing,* 6; 8 (July 1, 1995), 160.

Communications Servers

Larsen, Amy. Communications Server Clears Up LAN Bottlenecks. *Data Comunications,* 24; 10 (August 1995), 117.

Video Servers

Halhed, Basil. Video Server Technology and Applications Evolve. *Business Communications Review,* 25; 8 (August 1995), 29.

Morse, Stephen. As Seen on TV: NetWare Based Video Servers. *Network Computing,* 5; 13 (November 1, 1994), 104.

Pentium Servers

Adams, Jay and Eric Carr. Pentium Servers: Intangibles Matter. *Network Computing,* 5; 13 (November 1, 1994), 80.

Multiprocessor Servers

Milne, Jay. Multiprocessor Servers. *Network Computing,* 5; 15 (December 1, 1994), 138.

Enterprise Servers/SuperServers

Gerber, Barry. Enterprise Servers: Making the Quantum Leap. *Network Computing,* 6; 6 (May 15, 1995), 46.

Workgroup Servers

Boyle, Padraic. Born to Serve. *PC Magazine,* 14; 6 (March 28, 1995), 218.

Low-End Servers

Perratore, Ed. Low End Servers Grow Up. *Byte,* 20; 4 (April 1995), 23.

File Servers

Boyle, Padraic. Service with Style. *PC Magazine,* 14; 12 (June 27, 1995), 167.

Application Servers

Fisher, Sharon and Marcia Jacobs. PC App Servers Take Hold in Enterprise Nets. *Communications Week,* no. 565 (July 10, 1995), 1.

Shimmin, Bradley. Apps Servers Take Off. *LAN Times,* 12; 4 (February 27, 1996), 1.

Streeter, April. Applications Servers Bulk Up. *LAN Times,* 12; 4 (February 27, 1996), 48.

FAX Server Software

Carr, Eric. Fax Server Software Gets the FAX Right. *Network Computing,* 6; 4 (April 1, 1995), 104.

Web Server Software

Tabibian, O. Ryan. Internet Servers: Publish or Perish? *PC Magazine,* 14; 9 (May 16, 1995), NE1.

Tabibian, O. Ryan. Web Server Software: Electronic Businesses. *PC Magazine,* 14; 3 (February 7, 1995), NE1.

SMP/Multiprocessor Operating Systems

Chacon, Michael. More Horsepower: Designed from the Ground Up to Support SMP, Windows NT Can Work with One Processor or 16. *LAN Magazine,* 9; 12 (November 1994), 53.

Cole, Barb. Database Vendors Taking Alternate Routes to Support Parallel Processing. *Network World,* 12; 27 (July 3, 1995), 24.

Farrow, Rik. C2 Sounds Good, But What Does It Mean? *InfoWorld,* 16; 51 (December 19, 1994), 76.

Kogan, Michael. Retrofitting OS/2 for SMP. *Byte,* 19; 6 (June 1994), 267.

Lamb, Jason. The New NetWare: SMP Workhorse. *LAN Magazine,* 9; 12 (November 1994), 42.

Pountain, Dick. Parallel Course. *Byte,* 19; 7 (July 1994), 53.

Shimmin, Bradley. SMP: Building for Power. *LAN Times,* 12; 4 (February 27, 1995), 9.

Operating Systems

Foley, Mary Jo. PC Operating Systems Come of Age on Servers. *PC Week,* 12; 27 (July 10, 1995), 22.

Harper, Eric. Applications Server Operating Systems. *LAN Times,* 12; 7 (April 10, 1995), 63.

Uninterruptable Power Supplies

Gill, Philip. When Lightning Strikes. *Information Week,* no. 539 (August 7, 1995), 70.

Kirvan, Paul. Are You Up on UPS? *Communications News,* 31; 12 (December 1994), 48.

Rosch, Winn. Keeping Up with UPSs. *PC Magazine,* 12; 15 (September 14, 1993), 309.

Staino, Patricia. Protect Yourself: No One Else Will. *Teleconnect,* 12; 5 (May 1994), 48.

Chapter 5

RAIDING THE STORAGE CLOSET

A service bureau's migration from a hardware- to a software-based RAID solution yields savings, reliability

Michael Sanders got a dose of double jeopardy with his previous RAID system that he wasn't willing to repeat: At roughly the same time that his system began experiencing crashes, his system vendor went belly up.

"Under peak utilization the system would sometimes crash," said Sanders, senior programmer/analyst at Atlanta-based service bureau Datamatx Inc. Sanders was backing up his service bureau's files on an Ultrastore Corp. 124F hardware-based RAID system, and he had been generally pleased with it, until one day he was unable to reboot after a routine crash. "Unfortunately for me, that was at about the exact time that Ultrastore decided to go out of business."

Although Sanders got some assistance from his systems integrator in getting the system back online, the company's demise and the RAID's crash pattern forced him to scout down a new RAID supplier.

Sanders knew he needed a more reliable system fast—the company absolutely depended on fast and secure storage and retrieval of client data for day-to-day operations. High-volume mailings—between 60,000 to 100,000 pieces—and bulk print jobs are handled with a variety of applications running on the company's two Novell Inc. NetWare 3.12 servers, which support about 30 PC clients. The company's larger customers expect to submit these bulk printing jobs and mailings online and store addresses at Datamatx, so a lack of data-access or storage capacity could cost the company dearly.

Fortunately, the ailing system went down on a Saturday and went largely unnoticed. "None of my clients knew about the failure. But we needed a system that would keep us up and going all the time," Sanders said.

Cost was a concern that Sanders had to keep in mind as he scrambled to secure a fast, economical replacement that still supported his NetWare network. "We don't have a big corporate budget. . . . Everything we do is based on fractions of a penny per page. We couldn't go to our customers and say, 'We're raising your fees to pay for new hardware,'" he said. "Generally, I have to find a place to add value and then slowly build up enough budget to pay for new equipment, so price was a big consideration in the new system. I had to shop around."

Gun-shy from his experience with Ultrastore, Sanders also wanted to find a solid, mainstream RAID vendor that wouldn't go out of business in the foreseeable future. "I did feel a little bit burned," he said. He also looked to his chosen vendor to provide easy replacement parts.

Sanders chose Conner Peripherals Inc. in Lake Mary, Fla., and its CR-6 RAID subsystem, priced at $10,995. Although his Ultrastore solution had been based on a hardware controller, Sanders saw the cost advantage of going with a software-controlled RAID.

"I was a little nervous, but it actually took me only about 45 minutes to get the system up and running," he said. "There were no glitches in the beginning, and as long as I don't let NetWare run out of disk space, there aren't any glitches now."

Although software-based solutions tend to be slightly slower in lab testing than hardware-based RAID systems, Sanders said he finds performance of both old and new systems "roughly equivalent." His new system has four of Conners' FilePro hot-swappable 1 GB drives and uses RAID Level 5. Sanders wanted RAID 5 because its data-striping capabilities allow the company to be online even if a disk drive fails. The CR-6 lets him monitor the system through Conner's included Array Management Software.

Thus far, however, not much management has been necessary, Sanders said. He hasn't yet experienced a failure in the six months he's had the system, although he said he runs the RAID to about 95 percent of its capacity. He also hasn't yet seen the need to use the included diagnostic utilities.

Looking to the future, Sanders could add two more 1 GB drives to the system. But because of Datamatx's expansion into new client services such as a BBS, he said he's hoping to put another server on the network and complement it with another CR-6.

Although NetWare 4.x is not completely out of the running as the new server's NOS, especially if compression could help him get more storage out of his accompanying RAID solution, Microsoft Windows NT is also a consideration.

"I'm looking hopefully at NetWare's compression features, as I might be able to pick up 30 to 50 percent more space," Sanders said. "That's the only thing about 4.x that would really intrigue me."

In the interim, the CR-6 gives Sanders more than adequate peace of mind. "I'm extremely pleased," he said. "I've got enough to worry about just keeping our different software up and running, so it's good this system has been plug and play from the beginning."

Source: April Streeter (June 5, 1995). RAIDing the Storage Closet. *LAN Times,* 12(11), 77. Reprinted with permission of McGraw-Hill, *LAN Times.*

BUSINESS CASE STUDY QUESTIONS

Activities

1. Complete a top-down model for this case by gleaning facts from the case and placing them in the proper layer of the top-down model. After completing the top-down model, analyze and detail those instances when requirements were clearly passed down from upper to lower layers of the model and solutions to those requirements were passed up from lower to upper layers.

2. Detail any questions that may occur to you about the case for which answers are not clearly stated in the article.

Business

1. What aspects of the company's business market and expected profit margins had an impact on technology decisions?

2. What types of business services did this company provide?

3. What strategic "business event" triggered the search for a new RAID solution?

4. What impact did the strategic "business event" have on establishing evaluation criteria or system requirements?

5. List all of the evaluation criteria for the new RAID system mentioned in the article.

6. What new business services might the company be offering in the future, and what impact might these new services have on required technology?

Application

1. What types of applications were used to provide the company's business services?

Data

1. What were the important criteria established for evaluating potential replacement RAID systems?

2. How do large customers expect to deliver and store data?

3. What effect did customer expectations have on system requirements?

4. Which RAID level was required in this application and why?

Network

1. How many servers and clients were linked via the LAN?

2. What was the advantage of software-controlled RAID versus hardware-controlled RAID?

3. What, if any, were the expected or actual disadvantages of software-controlled RAID versus hardware-controlled RAID?

4. What role does the network play in a software-controlled RAID implementation?

Technology

1. What network operating system was employed at the time the article was written?

2. What other network operating systems were under consideration for possible future implementation?

3. What was the motivation for looking into other network operating systems?

4. How expandable was the chosen RAID system?

CHAPTER 6

INTERNET CLIENTS AND SERVERS

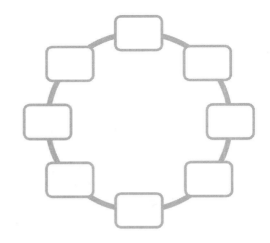

Concepts Reinforced

Client/server technology architecture
OSI model
Top-down model

Protocols and compatibility
Hardware/software compatibility
Server hardware fundamentals

Concepts Introduced

Internet business considerations
Internet connectivity services
Internet/web client software
Internet client/server design

Internet/web client hardware
Internet/web server software
Internet/web server hardware
Internet security

After mastering the material in this chapter you should:

1. Understand how Internet clients and servers are able to connect to the Internet.

2. Understand available hardware and software technology for building client/server connections to the Internet and the worldwide web.

3. Understand the business implications of Internet use.

4. Understand the security implications of Internet use.

5. Understand the important comparative characteristics of commercial Internet and WWW connectivity services.

6. Understand how Internet access technology integrates with a corporation's overall client/server information system.

The **Internet** is a wide area network linking over 4 million host computers. Originally developed as a means for the research, education, and scientific communities to share information, the Internet has been opened up in recent years to more commercial uses as well as to access by individuals. The purpose of this chapter is to explore the use of the Internet from a business perspective. Specifically, this chapter deals with the following questions:

- What does the Internet have to offer business?

- What are the various ways in which businesses can access Internet services?

- How can a business integrate the Internet with its LANs in a client/server architecture?

This chapter does not deal with how to surf the net or navigate the Web. Many books have been written on the best ways to travel through cyberspace on the Internet. Rather, this chapter offers business-oriented network analysts and management a top-down approach to objectively evaluating the merits of connecting to the Internet, as well as a methodology to develop the logical and physical network designs to do so.

More specifically, after reviewing the potential advantages and disadvantages the Internet offers business, the chapter continues with a study of the use of the Internet as a client/server platform. Both the client/server architecture and technology for Internet connectivity are thoroughly explored in keeping with the client/server approach to local area networks stressed throughout this text.

■ BUSINESS PERSPECTIVE ON THE INTERNET

Why Connect to the Internet?

From a business perspective, the Internet is currently being used primarily as a marketing tool rather than a sales tool. Millions of dollars in sales transactions are not presently taking place on the Internet. Most companies currently using the Internet for marketing purposes are doing so for image building rather than direct profit increases.

A recent survey of businesses currently using the Internet for marketing produced the following results:

- 72% of companies surveyed said the purpose of their Internet use was to enhance their company's image.

- 22% said their Internet usage was financially rewarding.

- 40% didn't expect financial rewards for 12 to 24 months.

- Fewer than 6% of companies conduct credit-card transactions over the Internet.

From the potential customer perspective, four to five times more people use the Internet for browsing rather than for buying.

Managerial Perspective

Strategically speaking, when should a company start to think about developing a presence on the Internet?

- If existing or potential customers are Internet users, it would probably be advantageous, for public relations reasons if nothing else, to establish a presence on the Internet.

- If enterprise partners such as key vendors or suppliers have an Internet presence, it may be advantageous for a company to also be connected.

The Internet customer market is small in comparison to other, more general markets. For example, there are an estimated 11 million Internet users in the United States and over 200 million television viewers. Internet users are a highly specialized, technically knowledgeable market segment. At the present time, the Internet offers a means to develop specially targeted marketing for this relatively small but significant market segment. For a variety of reasons to be discussed in the remainder of the chapter, however, it does not yet provide a lucrative untapped market for on-line electronic commerce and credit-card transactions.

What Are the Available Services/Resources?

The Internet is currently in a state of major transition from a government-funded entity designed for a research and education audience, to a privately funded entity catering increasingly to commercial concerns. The Internet offers three major service categories:

1. The WorldWide Web.

2. Information servers.
    - FTP servers.
    - Gopher servers.
    - WAIS servers.
    - UseNet servers.

3. Global e-mail.

The WorldWide Web   The **WorldWide Web (WWW)** is a collection of servers accessed via the Internet which offer graphical or multimedia (audio, video, image) presentations about a company's products, personnel, or services. WWW servers are accessed via client-based front-end software tools, commonly referred to as **Web browsers.** Companies wishing to use the WorldWide Web as a marketing tool establish a **web site** on the Internet and publicize its address. Web presentations can be interactive, inviting visitors to the web site to register their visit, complete marketing surveys, watch product demos, download available software, and a variety of other multimedia activities. The web site and web server presentation design, implementation, and management can be done in-house or contracted out to professional web site development and management services.

Information Servers   Text-based information stored in Internet-connected servers can be assessed by remote users logging into these servers via a TCP/IP protocol known as **Telnet.** Once they are successfully logged into an Internet-based information server, using either previously assigned user accounts and passwords or general access "anonymous" user accounts, users can execute programs on the remote computer as if they were locally attached.

To download, or transfer, information back to their client PCs, users would access another TCP/IP protocol known as file transfer protocol **(FTP).** Servers that support such activity are often called **FTP servers** or anonymous FTP servers. Users can access FTP servers directly or through Telnet sessions. The difficulty with searching for information in this manner is that a user must know the Internet address of the specific information server (Telnet or FTP) they wish to access.

A menu-based client/server system which features search engines that comb through all of the information in all of these information servers is referred to as the **Gopher** system, named after the mascot of the University of Minnesota where the system was developed. The key difference between Gopher and the WorldWide Web is that Gopher's information is text-based whereas the World-Wide Web is largely graphical. Also, web sites tend to be more interactive whereas using the Gopher subsystem is more analogous to searching for information in a library and then extracting or checking out the desired information. Gopher client software is most often installed on a client PC and interacts with software running on a particular **Gopher server,** which transparently searches multiple FTP sites for requested information and delivers it to the Gopher client. Gopher users do not need to know the exact Internet address of the information servers they want to access.

A third type of information server offers a text-searching service known as **WAIS** or **wide area information services.** WAIS indexers generate multiple indexes for all types of files that organizations or individuals wish to offer access to via the Internet. **WAIS servers** offer these multiple indexes to other Internet-attached WAIS servers. WAIS servers also serve as search engines which have the ability to search for particular words or text strings in the indexes located across multiple Internet-attached information servers of various types.

Usenet servers, or newsgroup servers, share text-based news items over the Internet. Over 10,000 newsgroups covering selected topics are available. Usenet servers update each other on a regular basis with news items that are pertinent to the news groups housed on a particular server. Usenet servers transfer news items between each other using a specialized transfer protocol known as **network news transport protocol** (NNTP) and are also known as NNTP servers. Users who want to access NNTP servers and their newsgroups must have NNTP client software loaded on their client PCs.

Global E-Mail   Millions of users worldwide are connected to the Internet via the **global e-mail** subsystem. From a business perspective, Internet e-mail offers one method of sending intercompany e-mail. Most companies have private networks which support e-mail transport to fellow employees but not necessarily to employees of other companies. By adding Internet e-mail gateways to a company's private network, e-mail can potentially be sent to users all over the world. However, Internet e-mail gateways are a double-edged sword. Unauthorized access from the Internet into a company's private network is also possible unless proper security precautions are taken. Such security issues as firewall servers are discussed later in the chapter.

Global e-mail users can subscribe to e-mail mailing lists of their choice on various topics of interest. Companies can easily e-mail to targeted audiences by sending a single e-mail message to a list server and allowing the list server to forward that e-mail message to all subscribed users. Targeted list servers provide the best commercial use of global e-mail for marketing or sales purposes. Global e-mail also affords access to specifically targeted electronic magazines **(E-zines)** and topical discussion groups often referred to as "frequently asked question" groups, or **FAQ groups.** FAQ groups are similar to ListServe groups that users can subscribe to via e-mail.

What Are the Potential Advantages?

To gain the maximum benefit from Internet connectivity, a company would probably want to avail itself of the services of all three of these Internet subsystems rather than choosing just one. By combining the benefits offered by the WorldWide Web, Gopher, and global e-mail a company could have access to highly focused marketing campaigns, almost limitless research data, and access to peers, partners, and customers throughout the world. Figure 6-1 highlights more specific examples of benefits, advantages, and trends supporting increased Internet access by business, which are elaborated on in the chapter.

Benefit/Advantage/Supporting Trend	Implication/Explanation
More Readily Accessible Internet Access	Local, regional, and national Internet access providers are now plentiful leading to competitive pricing. AT&T, Sprint, and MCI as well as most RBOCs (regional bell operating companies) offer Internet access services of some type.
Realistic Bandwidth	Mere access to the Internet is not enough. The "pipe" (bandwidth) into the Internet must be wide enough to accommodate desired traffic. Graphical traffic from the WWW is especially bandwidth intensive. Advances in modem technology support 28.8 Kbps over dial-up lines while Integrated Services Digital Network (ISDN) offers up to 144 Kbps and is becoming more widely available.
Improved Front-End Tools	Improved front-end tools or browsers mean that even novices have a reasonable chance of finding what they're looking for on the Internet. Many of these tools will be integrated into more familiar products such as word processors and presentation graphics packages.
Improved Server Tools	Internet access gateways and Internet server software will be increasingly integrated into mainstream server operating systems from companies such as IBM, Novell, and Microsoft. This will make the software easier to use, more tightly integrated, and more reliable.
Improved Information Services	The types of information and services which can be accessed on the Internet continue to improve and broaden in scope. Airline reservations, stock trading and quotations, weather forecasts, publishers, government agencies, and high-tech companies are but a few of the types of information and services available.

Figure 6-1   Benefits, Advantages, and Supporting Trends of Internet Access for Business

Disadvantage/Obstacle	Implication/Explanation
Bandwidth Availability	Although ISDN is becoming more widely available, it is still not universally available. Bandwidth must be reasonably priced as well. Also, local providers of Internet access bandwidth vary in their financial backing and commitment to provide adequate bandwidth as user traffic demands grow.
Search Abilities	The information on the Internet is rather loosely organized. If it is to be commercially viable, information must be organized and cataloged in such a way that it is easier to find. Busy business people do not have a lot of time to "surf" for information. Sophisticated search agents and global search engines would suggest best and/or nearest sources of desired information. Although front-end tools are improving, they are still new and largely unproven.
Internet Ownership	The management and funding of the Internet is transitioning from government to the private sector. Questions remain as to who is (and will be) responsible for network maintenance, upgrades, management, and policy development and enforcement.
Internet Regulation	The Internet is unregulated. Questions are being raised in the U.S. Congress as to what represents acceptable use of and behavior on the Internet. It is uncertain whether the Internet will remain unregulated. Certain information available on the Internet may be considered offensive to certain people. The Internet is accessed by millions of users, most of them "surfers," not buyers.

Figure 6-2   Disadvantages and Obstacles to Widespread Use of the Internet by Business

What Are the Potential Disadvantages?

From a business perspective, the current major concern of widespread business use of the Internet is probably a perceived lack of adequate security. As you will see later in the chapter, several alternative methods have been proposed to deal with this perception. If the Internet is to succeed as a viable commercial communications link for business, financial transactions of any magnitude must be able to be conducted in an absolutely secure and confidential manner. Figure 6-2 summarizes other potential disadvantages or obstacles to widespread use of the Internet by business.

■   A CLIENT/SERVER APPROACH TO INTERNET CONNECTIVITY

Before deciding which combination of technology and network services to employ to provide the desired Internet access, one must determine the nature of that Internet access by a business. When it comes to Internet access, companies can be **information consumers, information providers,** or a combination of the two. Depending on the nature of the Internet access, technology requirements can vary dramatically.

Overall Client/Server Architecture for Internet Connectivity

Figure 6-3 illustrates an overall view of some of the ways in which businesses can access Internet services as either information consumers or providers. Elements of the overall architecture are explained here, and more specific alternative connectivity options for WorldWide Web, information server, and global e-mail access follow.

As is explained further in the section on Internet connectivity services, a company should be able to purchase as much or as little Internet connectivity assistance as it deems appropriate. Although there are no hard and fast rules, Internet service providers are often categorized as follows:

- **Internet Access Providers (IAP)**—Also known as Internet connectivity providers (ICP) or Internet Service Providers (ISP), are primarily concerned with getting a subscriber company physically hooked up to the Internet. The IAP may provide for additional hardware acquisition and maintenance, but are unlikely to provide programming services. IAPs may be the local or long distance phone company or may be a business entirely independent of established phone companies. IAPs are most concerned with the infrastructure required to provide Internet access for subscriber companies.

- **Internet Presence Providers (IPP)**—Are primarily concerned with designing, developing, implementing, managing, and maintaining a subscriber company's presence on the Internet. IPPs may depend on IAPs for actual

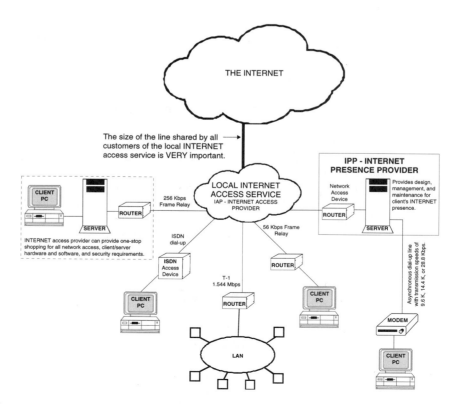

Figure 6-3   Overall Client/Server Architecture for Internet Connectivity

physical access to the Internet. If a company wanted a web page on the WorldWide Web but did not want to invest in the required hardware and personnel to launch such a venture in-house, it would be likely to contract with an IPP.

Clients, servers, and local area networks are connected to the Internet via a **network access device** such as a modem, as ISDN network access device, or a router. Which particular network access device is required in each case is a function of the type and bandwidth of the access line and the characteristics of the client or server to which the network access device must interface. All of the network access devices illustrated in Figure 6-3 are explained in greater detail later.

Those companies that wish to be only Internet information consumers require a properly configured client PC to be connected to the Internet. Companies wishing to be only information providers on the Internet require a properly configured server to be connected to the Internet. Those wishing to both consume and provide Internet information must have both client(s) and server(s) properly attached.

Service-Specific Client/Server Architectures for Internet Connectivity

Configurations of client and server hardware and software varies depending on which Internet services a company wishes to access. Alternative configurations for each major category of Internet services are explained next.

WorldWide Web Connectivity Alternatives Internet information consumers who want to access the WorldWide Web require a client PC configured with a front-end software tool or web browser such as **Mosaic** or **Netscape.** Several connectivity alternatives exist for those companies that want to establish a presence or web site on the WorldWide Web. The characteristics of these alternatives are detailed in Figure 6-4. Each alternative connectivity option listed in Figure 6-4 is broken down into the major processes involved in establishing and maintaining a web site. Depending on the connectivity alternative chosen, these processes may be the responsibility of the company (C) that wishes to establish the web presence or the vendor (V) providing the web connectivity service. Approximate costs are also included for each connectivity alternative.

Each of the alternatives for establishing a web site outlined in Figure 6-4 has its advantages and disadvantages. There is no single best way for all businesses to establish a WorldWide Web presence. A company must first understand the business objectives of establishing such a presence. Following are some possibilities:

- Improved customer service to existing customers.

- Increased or more focused marketing opportunities toward potential customers.

- Response to competitive pressures.

- Web presence should (or should not) be financially profitable.

While the first alternative listed in Figure 6-4, "post customer-designed page on access provider's server," is relatively inexpensive, the sophistication of the web presentation will not match those of the more expensive web connectivity

Connectivity Alternative	Design, Develop, and Maintain Web Page	Establish and Maintain Internet Node	Establish, Maintain, and Manage Network Access	Configure and Maintain the Web Server	Approximate Cost, Both Recurring (RC) and Nonrecurring (NRC)
Post Customer-Designed Page on Access Provider's Server	C	V	V	V	$20–$40/month (RC)
Hire Web Service Provider	V	V	V	V	$100–$1000 (NRC) $25–$10,000/month (RC)
In-House Development and Deployment	C	C	C	C	$1,000s/month (RC) —Depends on number of staff assigned

Figure 6-4   Web Server Connectivity Alternatives

alternatives. For example, it is less likely that such web pages would be highly interactive and possess the ability to prompt and store customer responses.

Hiring a web service provider to perform all aspects of establishing and managing a web site is certainly a quicker and more certain way to get on the web but obviously can run into a substantial financial investment. The experience offered by at least some of these providers enables the production of professional-quality presentations, which can then be incorporated into **cybermalls** with other professional-quality web pages adhering to the standards established by the cybermall management.

Hiring, training, and keeping an in-house staff to maintain a company's web site is a third alternative. Hiring experienced web site developers can be costly, but the learning curve of new hires will delay the establishment of a web site. Operation costs for maintaining the web server and access to the Internet also need to be considered, as does the security concerns of anonymous access to corporate network facilities.

Finally, a mix of these three approaches is also possible. Perhaps a web service provider could be hired on a fixed length contract to quickly establish a quality web site. Depending on customer response and potential profitability of the web site, in-house staff could be hired and trained as management of the web site is gradually transitioned into their realm of responsibility.

Information Server Connectivity Alternatives   Information servers such as FTP/Telnet, Gopher, Usenet, and WAIS servers are not mutually exclusive of each other or of web servers. A company does not need to make a strategic decision to implement one of the three types of information servers. They all share a common goal to present primarily text-based information to Internet users. They differ in the manner in which that information is organized and accessed. In some cases, one type of information service can be integrated within another. Figure 6-5 illustrates the complementary nature of the various types of information servers.

The diagrams in Figure 6-5 represent logical or functional design alternatives. The section on client/server technology for Internet connectivity elaborates on how each of these logical designs are physically implemented.

Global E-Mail Connectivity Alternatives   A company has an abundance of alternatives for connecting to the Internet for global e-mail services. As with other Internet service connectivity alternatives already reviewed, options vary primarily in cost, available functionality, ease of use, and security. Figure 6-6 (page 200) summarizes some of the functional features of selected global e-mail connectivity alternatives, and Figure 6-7 (page 201) compares the physical connectivity of each of these alternatives.

Internet Transport Protocols   Transmission control protocol/Internet protocol (TCP/IP) is the transport protocol used within the Internet which allows different types of computers and network access devices to exchange messages and deliver data and e-mail. In Figure 6-7, the network access devices, most often routers, which connect to Internet services, package their messages according to the Internet-standard TCP/IP protocols. The phone lines which connect the network access devices to the Internet are direct or leased lines which are constantly connected. It is as if the remote network access device is directly connected to the devices on the Internet and can therefore converse with the Internet attached computers (nodes, hosts) using the native transport protocol, TCP/IP.

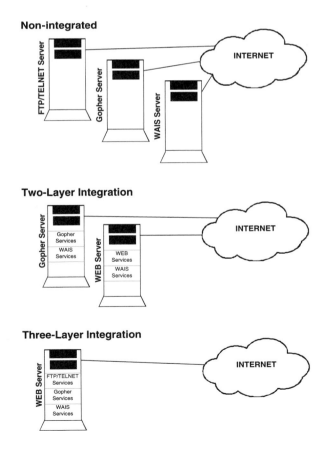

Figure 6-5   Information Server Connectivity Alternatives

Global E-Mail Connectivity Alternative	Required Technology	Company Responsibilities	Approximate Cost
E-Mail Client Front-End	Internet e-mail front-end software, modem, dial-up line, Internet connection. Single user at a time solution.	Supply all required technology for each client to be connected to global e-mail. Maintain network connections.	Software: $50–$200 Modem: $150–$250 Connection: $30–$50/mo plus phone charges.
E-Mail Server Gateway	Can use existing LAN server hardware, e-mail gateway software often included with either e-mail software or network operating system. Need a network access device such as a router that will allow more than one LAN user to access e-mail services simultaneously.	Maintain gateway software and authorization for access to/from gateways. Gateways are two-way devices. They allow users into a company's LAN as well as allowing company employees to access global e-mail. Security may be an issue. Make sure size of network access line is sufficient to support required number of simultaneous users.	Software: E-mail gateway probably included. Hardware: $5000–$15,000 for server if existing one is not available, plus $3000–$5000 for router, plus network connection.
E-Mail Commercial Service	Allows individuals to connect via front-end software and modems or corporations to connect via gateways. Software is usually supplied by the service, but many e-mail packages, network operating systems, and communications software already contain software to link to specific commercial services.	Commercial e-mail service is responsible for maintaining network connections and may also offer hardware and software support at user or corporate sites. Commercial services often offer value-added services beyond simple e-mail such as news and information services, fax, or full internet connection to WWW.	Monthly fees of $30 to several hundred dollars per month, depending on number of users and level of usage.

Figure 6-6   Functionality of Global E-Mail Connectivity Alternatives

However, expensive leased-line connections to Internet access providers are not cost effective for individual client PCs. Instead, these standalone PCs which need only occasional access to the Internet use dial-up circuits of one type or another. Transport protocols which belong to the TCP/IP family of protocols, more properly known as the Internet Suite of Protocols, that support communication over serial or dial-up lines are **serial line Internet protocol (SLIP)** and the more recently released and more functional **point-to-point protocol (PPP)**. The entire suite of TCP/IP protocols is explained further in Chapter 13.

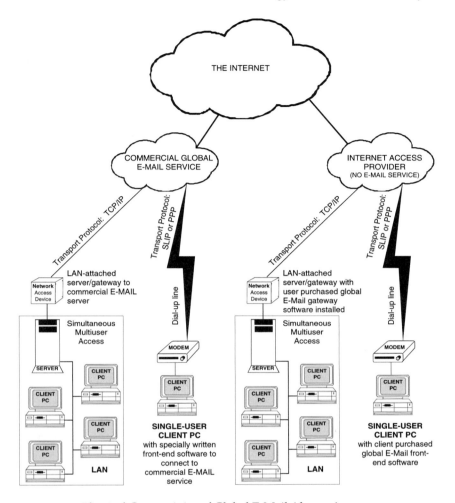

Figure 6-7   Physical Connectivity of Global E-Mail Alternatives

■ CLIENT/SERVER TECHNOLOGY FOR INTERNET CONNECTIVITY

Web browser software, otherwise known as web client software, is executed on client hardware for the purpose of accessing previously developed web pages available on Internet-attached web servers. These web servers run specialized web server software which supports **hypertext transport protocol (HTTP)** to handle servicing the multiple web client requests for web pages. These web pages are collections of text, graphics, sound, and video elements programmed using web publishing software which may run on either client or server platforms. The web pages are programmed using text formatted with **hypertext markup language (HTML).** Because HTML is text-based, any text editor could be used to generate the HTML code, which would then be interpreted by the HTTP server software.

When a web client running web browser software requests a web page or constituent element from a web server by clicking on a hyperlink, a TCP/IP message is sent to the web server identified in the **uniform resource locator (URL).** Included in this message is the identity of the requested web page file noted with a HTML extension, and a version indicator identifying which version of HTML the requesting client understands. In response, the web server retrieves the requested file and transfers it to the web client. Figure 6-8 distinguishes between web browsers, web servers, and web publishers.

Internet/Web Clients

Web Browsers   Web browsers are a client-based category of software which is undergoing tremendous development due to the vast interest in the WorldWide Web. The scope of web browser software is expanding horizontally to include access to not only Internet-attached resources but also the following:

- Local client-attached resources.

- Local area network-attached resources.

- Enterprise or corporate network-attached resources.

A network composed of corporate information that is accessible to only authorized employees is referred to as an **Intranet.** The latest web browser products display all reachable resources, from the local Intranet to the worldwide Internet, on a

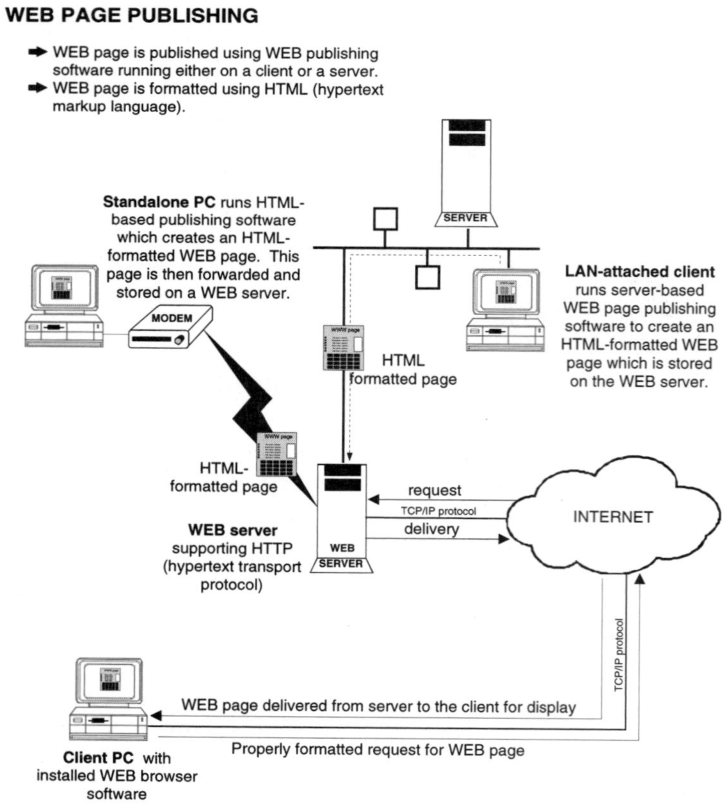

Figure 6-8   Web Clients, Web Servers, and Web Publishers

single hierarchical file tree display. The scope of web browser software is also expanding vertically as well by including access to all Internet-attached resources and services in addition to the WorldWide Web. By combining navigation features of traditional web browsers and search features of information server front-ends, the latest web browsers make the following resources directly accessible:

- Global e-mail.

- Search agents.

- FTP.

- Gopher.

- WAIS and other index and search engines.

- Usenet newsgroups.

Web browsers' transition to managing locally attached hardware resources means that they must be more closely integrated with client operating systems than before. In the past, web browsers were just another application program executing over a particular operating system via APIs and operating system calls, but they are now more like a single integrated piece of software with a particular client operating system embedded within the web browser software. This is an interesting phenomenon to observe as web browser software vendors such as NetScape and Wollongong attempt to embed operating systems within their web browsers and traditional operating systems vendors such as Microsoft, IBM, and Novell, attempt to embed web browsers within their operating systems. For example, Windows 95 features an add-on known as the Internet Explorer Browser and OS/2 Warp includes the Web Explorer.

It should be noted that many high-quality web browsers can be downloaded from the Internet and are available at little or no charge. In general, all web browsers offer transparency to users from the following concerns and compatibility issues:

- Geography—users do not need to know the web address or physical location of the destination web server.

- Storage file format—users do not need to know the file format of the target web page feature regardless of whether the web page feature is text, sound, video, or image.

- Hardware characteristics and operating system of the destination web server.

- Type of network or transport protocol involved with the destination web server.

Figure 6-9 summarizes the key comparative criteria to consider when evaluating web browser software.

One thing to bear in mind about web browsers and their ability to search the WorldWide Web for a particular web page or topic is that web browsers still require a master web index service or home page. The LYCOS home page at Carnegie-Mellon University is an example of such a master web indexing service. Indexed web pages which may be located throughout the Internet are accessible through LYCOS via hot-clickable links known as URLs, or uniform resource locators.

Web Browser Characteristic	Explanation/Implication
Vertical Integration	• Does the web browser software supply access to all Internet-attached resources including global e-mail?
Ease of Setup and Use	• How easy is the software to install and configure? • Is technical support available and helpful? • Can the web browser handle dial-up connections using SLIP/PPP as well as LAN-attached connections using TCP/IP?
Performance	• Can multiple sessions be executed simultaneously? • Can the web browser be easily customized with user bookmarks which remember paths to particular Internet resources? • Can graphics be partially displayed while they are still being downloaded? • Can the web browser link easily to other programs such as word processing, spreadsheet, or presentation graphics programs? • Can downloaded material be easily transferred into other applications programs? • Can the web browser support a variety of sound and video compression and storage formats? • Can URL for new resources be added easily? • Can hot lists (local lists of bookmarks for favorite web pages) be annotated with user notes? • Which versions of HTML does the browser support?
Horizontal Integration	• Does the web browser organize access only to Internet-attached resources or are locally and network-attached resources also accessible through the browser?

Figure 6-9   Web Browser Differentiating Criteria

URLs are also used within a given web page to allow **hypertext links** to other related web pages, documents, or services such as e-mail. The term hypertext merely refers to documents with the ability to link to other documents. In web pages, hypertext is usually highlighted in a different color and hot-clickable for instant access to the linked document.

Internet E-Mail Front-Ends   Although Internet or global e-mail front-end functionality may be included in web browser software, the unique nature of the protocols and functionality involved with Internet e-mail front-ends warrants a separate discussion. Figure 6-10 illustrates the relationship between mail clients, mail servers, Internet post offices, and associated protocols.

A key feature of Internet e-mail front-ends is their ability to allow attached documents of various types such as reports, spreadsheets, or presentations to be attached to the Internet e-mail. The e-mail recipient on the destination client is able to unattach the previously attached documents from the received e-mail message. A protocol known as **multipurpose Internet mail extension (MIME)** allows documents to be attached to e-mail regardless of the source application program, operating system, or network operating system. Figure 6-11 (page 206) highlights some of

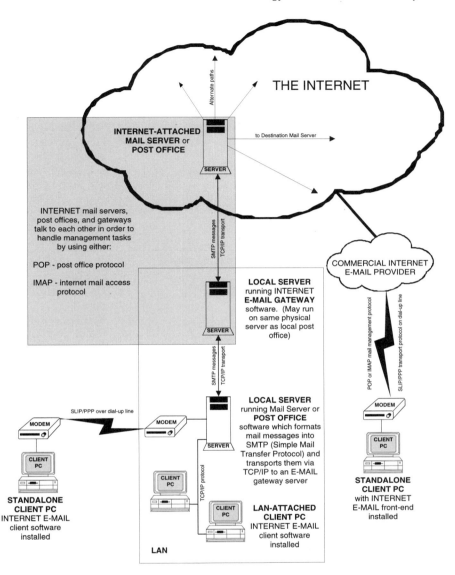

Figure 6-10   Internet E-Mail Clients, Servers, Post Offices, and Protocols

the key comparative criteria to consider when evaluating Internet e-mail front-ends. Depending on the operating system or network operating system installed on a client PC, a separate Internet e-mail front-end may not be required. For example, Microsoft Mail client is included with Windows NT, Windows for Workgroups, Windows 95, and the Microsoft Office application suite.

Mail server management protocols may be either **post office protocol (POP)** or **Internet mail access protocol (IMAP).** IMAP is a more recent standard and possesses features added in response to increased remote connectivity and mobile computing. To minimize the amount of time and bandwidth required to download one's e-mail for review, a standalone Internet e-mail client connected via a dial-up line to an Internet e-mail server can download just the headers of received e-mail,

Internet E-Mail Client Characteristic	Explanation/Implication
Setup and Installation	• How easy is it to set-up this Internet e-mail client? • What are the memory and disk requirements? • What client operating systems is this e-mail software compatible with?
Mail Creation and Editing	• How flexible is the address book creation? • How easy is it to CC: or send to multiple recipients? • Is the mail creation editor nearly as powerful as a word processor? • Is spell checking available? • Can different types of documents be attached to e-mail? • Is MIME supported?
Mail Handling and Management	• Can mail be routed as well as sent to multiple recipients? • How easy is it to reply to, forward, or print mail? • Can just e-mail headers be downloaded from remote locations? • How many ways can incoming or sent mail be sorted? • Can you create private folders in which to sort mail? • Can the folders be arranged hierarchically? • How easy is it to create and maintain public and private address lists, including groups? • What levels of security are provided? passwords? encryption? • Can other applications which correspond to attached documents be launched from within the e-mail client software?

Figure 6-11   Internet E-Mail Clients Differentiating Criteria

stating the e-mail sender, date, subject, and hopefully file size. The remotely connected e-mail user can then selectively download only those e-mail messages they wish to deal with immediately.

Internet/Web Gateways

Internet E-Mail Gateways   LAN-based mail servers act as post offices delivering mail to intended LAN-attached recipients and forwarding nonlocal destination mail onto other distant mail servers (post offices) for eventual delivery to clients. Mail servers run a particular type of mail server software such as Microsoft Mail or cc:Mail. When clients on the LANs to which these mail servers are attached run the same type of e-mail client software, no translation between mail systems is necessary. However, when a Microsoft Mail client wants to send e-mail via the Internet to a cc:Mail client, translation is required. This translation is supplied by an **Internet**

e-mail gateway. This gateway acts as a translator, speaking a LAN-specific e-mail software protocol on one side and the Internet's **Simple Mail Transport Protocol (SMTP)** on the other. Depending on the transport protocol used by the LAN, the Internet e-mail gateway may also have to translate between transport protocols, since the Internet uses strictly TCP/IP.

Figure 6-12 illustrates the relationship between LAN-based mail servers, Internet e-mail gateways, and the Internet.

A key differentiating factor among Internet e-mail gateway products is their ability to support document attachment through protocols such as MIME. Some e-mail gateways also limit the number of attachments per e-mail message. Whether or not the Internet e-mail gateway software can be monitored by the local area network's system monitoring or performance monitoring is also important. Gateways are a likely bottleneck because of the amount of processing involved in translating between mail protocols, especially at high traffic levels.

The Internet e-mail gateway product itself is actually strictly software. It is installed like any other application over a particular operating system, most often DOS or OS/2. The required power of the hardware on which the gateway software must execute depends on the amount of Internet e-mail which must be translated by the gateway. In some cases, the gateway software may be physically installed on the same server as the LAN-based e-mail server software. In other cases, increased Internet-bound e-mail traffic warrants a dedicated server.

Internet Gateways versus Internet Servers   While Internet e-mail gateways offer translation strictly between different LAN-based e-mail packages, **Internet gateways**

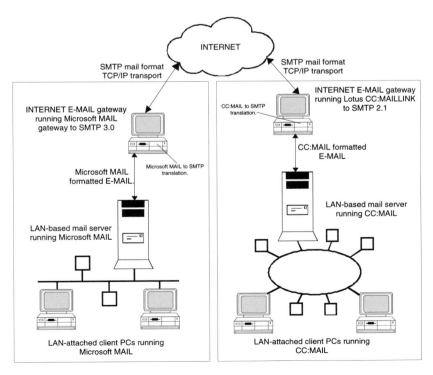

Figure 6-12   LAN-Based Mail Servers, Internet E-Mail Gateways, and the Internet

offer a LAN-attached link for client PCs to access a multitude of Internet-attached resources including e-mail, FTP/Telnet, newsgroups, Gopher, and the WorldWide Web. An Internet gateway is a software product which includes multiuser versions of the client front-ends for each supported Internet-attached resource. The Internet gateway also translates between the local area network's transport protocol and TCP/IP. It is an *access*-oriented product.

Internet gateways offer no Internet-attached services for users from distant corners of the Internet to avail themselves of. They are strictly on-ramps into the Internet. LAN-attached client PCs accessing the Internet through the Internet gateway must seek the Internet services they desire from an **Internet server.** This server runs a server application and offers e-mail, Gopher, newsgroup, or WorldWide Web services to all Internet-attached users.

As an alternative to an Internet gateway, LAN-attached client-PCs can also set up individual links to Internet servers via a shared router. Each client PC must be loaded with TCP/IP software and Internet client software for whatever Internet services the user wants to access. Figure 6-13 differentiates between the connectivity

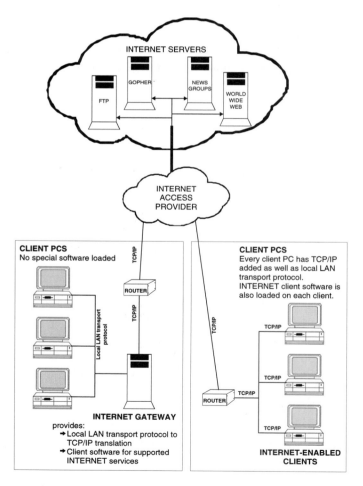

Figure 6-13   Internet Gateways, Internet Servers, and Internet Enabled Clients

	Internet Gateway	**Internet-Enabled Clients**
Advantages	• Single location of TCP/IP and client front-ends easier to implement and manage than multiple client locations.	• Eliminates gateway as potential bottleneck.
Disadvantages	• Gateway can become a bottleneck with large number of users.	• Every client requires its own TCP/IP software and Internet client front-ends. • Each client PC must be individually configured and managed. • Client PCs also need to be able to use local LAN transport protocol.

Figure 6-14   Internet Gateways versus Internet-Enabled Clients

of Internet gateways, Internet servers, and Internet-enabled clients; Figure 6-14 highlights the advantages and disadvantages of Internet gateways versus Internet-enabled clients.

Internet/Web Servers

An Internet server requires a combination of hardware and software to offer the following:

- Web services.
- Global e-mail.
- FTP/Telnet services.
- Usenet newsgroup services.

A **web server** combines hardware and software components to offer primarily web services, but increasingly web servers are also offering links to Gopher, FTP, and news services, making the terms web server and Internet server more and more synonymous. Web servers may or may not also contain software to develop or program web pages and web applications.

Server Hardware/Software Analysis   Any Internet or web server implementation requires four basic components:

1. A link to the Internet via an appropriately sized (sufficient bandwidth) access transmission line.

2. An IP address which uniquely identifies the intended server among all Internet-attached servers.

3. The server hardware which will connect to the Internet and fulfill client requests.

4. The server software which will run on the server hardware. In the case of a web server, this server software is usually based on the HTTP server from the National Center for Supercomputing Applications (NCSA).

The link to the Internet is purchased from a local telecommunications company and terminated at a chosen Internet access provider (IAP). In some cases, the IAP makes the arrangements for the access line with the local telecommunications vendor. The IP address to uniquely identify an Internet or web server could be provided by either the IAP or the InterNIC, which is the sole official authority in charge of issuing Internet IP addresses.

To understand the types of hardware and software required to successfully implement an Internet or web server, one must first examine intended objectives of the server, focusing especially on the server's intended audience and what services will be offered to that audience. As stated previously, the server may strictly offer access to web pages or it may also offer gateway services to file transfer and search resources such as FTP, Gopher, Usenet, and WAIS.

For example, a company that wishes to offer only product information could suffice with a web server, while a gateway to file transfer and search engines would be required for a company that wanted to offer on-line technical support as well. Because proposals for implementing security protocols to ensure the confidentiality of financial transactions over the Internet are pending, companies should be wary of implementing widespread financial dealings via the Internet. Web security is discussed shortly in the section on Internet/web application development. Some companies may only wish to display product information on web pages, while others may want customer input for demographic or product development purposes. The ability to handle customer input forms is a web server software capability that cannot be assumed.

Server Software   Internet/web server software differs in its ability to deliver any or all of the following capabilities:

- Web page display and management.

- Gateway to Internet file transfer and search engines such as FTP, Gopher, Usenet, and WAIS.

- Level of security supported.

- Ability to develop and manage customer input forms.

- Ability to monitor and report on web page or Internet resource usage. This feature is important to be able to justify the cost of investment in server hardware and software. Is the intended customer audience responding in the intended fashion?

- Ability to integrate management functions with the enterprise management system of the server's operating system.

Besides just displaying web pages, web servers may also possess the ability to execute interactive web applications such as the previously mentioned customer input forms. Some servers offer a standardized API known as **common gateway interface,** or **CGI,** which allows web applications to be written and potentially executed on multiple web servers.

Some web server software supports **proxy servers,** which act as holding bins or repositories for previously requested web pages from distant Internet servers. If a request from a local client is received for a previously requested web page which is still in the local proxy server, that web page can be delivered quickly to the local client without the normal delay associated with downloading the web page again in its entirety across the Internet.

Perhaps most significant among the differentiating characteristics of server software is the supporting operating system. Due to the high processing demands of a web server, UNIX in its many variations has been the standard operating system, although Windows NT-based web server software is now available. For lower-end applications, web server software is also available for Macintosh computers.

Server Hardware   Retrieving and transmitting the highly graphical web pages with a good response time to multiple users simultaneously calls for high-performance server hardware. To know a recommended hardware configuration, a web server manager (Web Master) must really know how many inquiries per day are anticipated on the web server. In general, the following minimum recommendations are generally agreed upon for web server hardware configuration:

- CPU: 120 MHz (or faster) Pentium is acceptable, but higher speed RISC chips such as the DEC Alpha or Mips R4600 are required for high-performance servers.

- Storage: Graphical images, and digitized voice and video take up a lot of space, so provision should be made for numerous drive bays or attachment to a RAID subsystem.

- Bus: PCI bus for fast internal transfer of images.

- Memory: 128 MB installed is not unusual for web servers, with potential capacities up to 1024 MB desirable.

- Network Interface Cards: 100 Mbps Ethernet or multiple 10 Mbps Ethernet cards should be sufficient. Remember, Internet-attached users will be accessing this server via telecommunications lines of various bandwidths. These transmission lines are usually the narrowest bandwidth of the entire system.

As demands for server performance increase to 250,000 or more inquiries per day, high-end UNIX workstations with over 128 MB RAM and 1 GB of disk are recommended.

Server Trends   The web server software market is very young and changing rapidly. Although many of the original web server software offerings were shareware or offered by third-party vendors, mainstream software vendors such as IBM, Microsoft, and Novell are aggressively pursuing this market. The advantage of web server software produced by the leaders in software development is increased integration with that vendor's enterprise management system and application suites.

Internet Connectivity Services

A Top-Down Approach to Internet Connectivity Needs Analysis   Internet service providers vary widely in the levels of services they provide and in the fees they charge for these services. To ensure that purchased Internet services meet the business objectives of a given company, it is essential that a top-down approach to Internet connectivity needs analysis be executed. By starting with business objectives and detailing, in writing, all of the performance requirements associated with each layer of the top-down model, the network analyst will possess detailed documentation which can serve as the basis for negotiations with Internet service providers. This leaves no doubt as to what is expected of the Internet service provider and that provided Internet services will meet stated business objectives. Figure 6-15 divides the numerous issues surrounding Internet connectivity needs analysis into their respective top-down model layers.

Top-Down Model Layer	Internet Connectivity Needs Analysis Issues

Business	• What are the business objectives for Internet connectivity?
	  • Increased market exposure
	  • Improved customer service
	  • Response to competitive pressures
	  • Increased market share
	  • New market entry
	  • Improved market research capabilities
	  • Improved intra- and intercompany communications
	• What are the budgetary limitations of this connectivity, if any?
	• Does senior management have a preference between outsourcing or in-house development, support, management?
	• What are the availability requirements? (24 hrs/day?)
	• What are the reliability requirements? (length of acceptable downtime?)
	• What are the security requirements regarding this Internet connection?
	• What are the acceptable uses of the Internet by employees?

Application	• What applications are required to support identified business objectives?
	  • Global e-mail
	  • World Wide Web
	  • Information/news services
	  • FTP/Telnet
	  • Gopher
	• Will the company be offering Internet services (web pages) for Internet users or strictly accessing Internet services?
	• How many users will be offered access to which services?
	• What is an acceptable response time for the various required Internet services? Remember, literally millions of users are sharing the same network on the Internet.

Figure 6-15   Internet Connectivity Needs Analysis

(continued)

Data	• Depending on the applications required, how much data (in KB) is likely to be required to be transported and/or stored? • Graphical applications (WWW) have much higher bandwidth demands than text-based services.

Network	• Complete a logical network design outlining the required functionality of the network which will successfully support the data, application, and business layer requirements of the top-down model.
	• Depending on the amount of data required to be transferred and the acceptable response time, what is the minimum size (Kbps or Mbps) of the access line to the Internet services provider required?
	• What is the anticipated growth of bandwidth demand for Internet connectivity access?
	• What will be the Internet connectivity network configuration?
	  • Internet (TCP/IP) enabled clients
	  • Internet gateway
	  • Dial-up links into Internet service provider's Internet server
	• Reliability issues:
	  • What kind of redundant circuits are required?
	  • What kind of redundant or hot-swappable networking hardware is required?

Technology	• Produce a physical network design which will support the logical network design completed in the network layer of the top-down model.
	• Depending on the choice of Internet connectivity services provider, any or all of these technology issues may or may not be handled by that provider.
	  • Installation, management, troubleshooting of access line
	  • Size of access line between Internet provider and the Internet
	  • Choice of Internet front-ends, web browsers
	  • Choice of web page development software
	  • Choice of web/Internet server software
	  • Use of proxy servers and/or local domain name servers
	  • Choice of network access devices, routers
	  • Development of firewalls and other security capabilities
	• Who is responsible for ensuring integration and compatibility of all of the hardware and software technology?
	• Who is responsible for ensuring a reasonable migration and upgradability path for acquired technology?
	• What types of data transmission services are available from local telecommunications providers at each corporate site? (ISDN?, T-1?, T-3?, ATM?)
	• What are the local telecommunications provider's plans for deploying high-speed data services?

Figure 6-15   (*continued*)

As is always true of top-down analysis, if business objectives of Internet connectivity are clearly stated and verified by senior management, and each successive layer of the top-down model successfully meets the requirements of the preceding layer, the physical network design produced on the technology layer will produce an Internet connectivity network capable of meeting initial business objectives.

Differences Between Internet Connectivity Service Providers   Once the Internet connectivity needs analysis has been completed and documented using the top-down model, the next step is to find the Internet connectivity service provider which best matches the business objectives and technological needs of the company. Although the range of services offered by potential Internet service providers is constantly changing, basically three categories of vendors are involved in this market:

- Internet presence providers.

- Internet access providers.

- Telecommunications companies.

Internet presence providers are full-service organizations offering everything from web page setup to 24 hr/day monitoring of Internet links. Examples of such high-end providers are BBN Planet, InternetMCI, and IBM Global Network. AT&T has combined its worldwide networking expertise with the Internet experience of BBN Planet to become a major player in the Internet presence provider arena.

Practical Advice and Information

Numerous local and regional Internet access providers have emerged since the recent explosion of interest in the Internet in general and the WorldWide Web in particular. It is important to evaluate the financial stability of Internet service providers. Many such newly formed operations may not be sufficiently capitalized to afford necessary upgrades to maintain satisfactory service levels. Especially important is the bandwidth of the access line between the Internet access provider and the Internet itself. That access line is shared by all subscribers of a particular Internet access provider. If the access line between the Internet access provider and the Internet becomes a bottleneck, then the size of the company's access line to the Internet access provider is irrelevant. Such companies may lack sufficient technical expertise to diagnose or troubleshoot compatibility or technology integration issues. It is important to have written agreements as to the division of user and Internet service provider responsibilities for technology integration.

If the development, installation, and management of Internet access and services is to be handled by an in-house operation, then arranging with the local telecommunications vendor for installation of a data line for Internet access may be the only interaction with outside vendors required. Outside of large metropolitan areas, the availability of data transmission services from local telecommunications vendors can vary widely. Increased deregulation of the local access market may have a dramatic effect on the availability of local data transmission services. Some local and regional telecommunications companies have developed Internet presence provider and Internet access provider services in addition to their basic data transmission services. Ameritech and PacTel are two of the more aggressive Regional Bell Operating Companies (RBOCs) in the Internet presence provider market.

Figure 6-16 lists the typical activities required to complete a connection to the Internet and which of those activities are typically provided by Internet presence providers, Internet access providers, and local telecommunications vendors. The term local telecommunications vendors in this case refers to those companies or divisions which offer only basic data transmission services, without any Internet-related value-added services.

Internet Connectivity Activity	Internet Presence Provider	Internet Access Provider	Local Telecom Provider
Provide local access line for Internet connectivity	•	•	•
Monitor and manage local access	•	•	
Provide terminating equipment for local access	•	•	•
Security services offered	•		
Design and develop web page	•		
Manage and monitor web/Internet activity	•		
Guarantee sufficient bandwidth/growth path	•		
Provide web server hardware	•		
Provide web server software	•		
Provide client front-end software	•		
Provide Internet (IP) address	•	•	
Resolve incompatibility issues	•		
Manage global e-mail addressing issues	•		

Figure 6-16 Internet Connectivity Activities and Providers

Beyond Internet Connectivity Connectivity to the Internet does not necessarily meet all the wide area communication needs of a global enterprise. Another category of services, commonly known as **business communications services,** goes beyond Internet connectivity to include the following additional services:

- Videoconferencing.
- Simultaneous document sharing.
- Electronic data interchange (EDI).
- Global FAX service.
- Electronic document distribution.
- Paging.
- E-mail.
- News and information services.

These additional services enable globally dispersed enterprises to function as if all network-attached users were physically located in the same building. In other words, anything coworkers in the same building can accomplish ought to be able to be accomplished via the business communications services network. The deliverance of this capability is sometimes referred to as a **virtual corporation.** Business communications services can differ widely in the exact services offered, but following are some examples:

- AT&T Easylink Services.
- GE Information Services Business Network.

- NetworkMCI Business.

- Sprint Mail.

Some of these business communications services include access to global e-mail via the Internet. It is likely that the same vendor will integrate these services with Internet presence provider services at some future time.

■ INTERNET APPLICATION DEVELOPMENT

Web Page Publishing Software

A web page is a document, transferred from web servers to web clients for execution, which contains a variety of text, graphics, sound, and video elements. The web page itself contains embedded hypertext markup language (HTML) commands which indicate links to other web pages or constituent elements located on either the local server or anywhere else on the global Internet. These links are formatted according to a syntax known as URL. As an example of this syntax, following is the URL for my web page: http://www.tech.purdue.edu/cpt/goldman.html. The "www.tech.purdue.edu" is the name of the web server, and the remaining information leads to the proper directory and file.

HTML software is currently divided into two major product categories:

- **HTML conversion utilities.**

- **HTML hyperlink maintenance software.**

HTML conversion utilities are add-on products which work with existing word processing packages such as Microsoft Word. For example, the Internet Assistant for Word for Windows automatically creates HTML documents from Word documents, without the need for users to learn the intricacies of HTML.

HTML is actually a subset of **standard generalized markup language (SGML).** HTML supports a predefined set of core elements of a web page such as headlines, paragraphs, chapter headings, hyperlink anchors, and footnotes identified by **tags;** SGML allows higher-level programming which defines its own **document type definitions (DTDs).** Add-on products such as SGML Author for Word are able to produce both HTML documents and SGML documents supporting DTDs and tags.

Conversion utilities address only the issue of producing the initial web page. A separate, and arguably more complicated, issue is how to reasonably maintain web pages and all of their associated hyperlinks. Interleaf's Cyberleaf maintains an internal database of all hyperlinks within and among maintained web pages. As web pages change and hyperlinks must be updated to reflect those changes, automated hyperlink maintenance software ensures that all hyperlinks for web pages contained in the hyperlink database are automatically updated. This eliminates old hyperlinks on web pages whose associated URLs are no longer valid.

HTML continues to evolve as standards and features for new versions are proposed. While HTML Version 1.0 is currently the most popular, HTML Version

2.0 has been approved by the Internet Engineering Task Force (IETF) and adds significant capabilities in the area of interactive forms. HTML Version 3.0 is under development with features such as the following:

- Increased numbers and types of tags to allow increased access by information searching programs.

- Additional defined elements including math, tables, and combination graphics/text objects.

- Ability to have text flow around graphics objects.

Although HTML is currently the most popular language for web page development, two other powerful web page development languages exist. **Virtual reality modeling language (VRML)** and VRML+ have the capability to produce graphical programs which portray three-dimensional images, allowing the user to seem to move in three-dimensional space when programs are executed. A virtual joystick in the middle of the screen serves as the navigating device. VRML is a language in which VRML application programs are written. Executing or viewing these programs requires a browser-type of software which is able to load and execute VRML programs. SGI's (Silicon Graphics Inc.) WebSpace is a product which supports VRML applications. Understandably, executing full-motion three-dimensional graphics programs is hardware intensive, requiring at least a 90MHz Pentium with 32MB RAM and Windows NT, or a UNIX workstation.

Another emerging web environment programming language, **Java,** is included in a browser from Sun Microsystems named Hot Java. Java is an object-oriented language which adds animation and real-time interaction through the use of independently executed miniprograms called **applets.** The object-oriented nature of the language allows the applets to be run in a variety of different orders, depending on the interaction with the user. Such an object-oriented programming environment will allow for more powerful interactive applications to be executed via the WorldWide Web. Java is a high-level, full-function programming language which is much more difficult to work with than the presentation-oriented HTML. A hardware and operating–specific Java interpreter provides a layer of transparency between the portable applets and a specific hardware/operating system environment. If the Internet is to be used extensively for wide-ranging commercial applications, then highly flexible, portable, and interactive languages such as Java will be part of the requirements.

Security

The other major prerequisite to widespread use of the Internet for commercial transactions is the development and deployment of increased security for those transactions. Security of Internet transmissions actually involves several processes such as the following:

- **Encryption** renders data indecipherable to any unauthorized users who might be able to examine packets of data traffic. Encryption is especially important when transmitting credit card numbers or other confidential information.

- **Authorization** screens users by userIDs and passwords and examines **access control lists (ACL)** to determine whether or not a given user is authorized to access requested files or system resources.

- **Authentication** uses **digital signatures** attached to transmitted documents to ensure both the authenticity of the author and the document's **message integrity,** which verifies that the document has not been tampered with.

Firewalls   When a company links to the Internet, it creates a two-way access point both out of and *into* that company's confidential information systems. To prevent unauthorized access to confidential data from the Internet, companies often employ specialized software known as a **firewall.** Firewall software usually runs on a dedicated server which is connected to, but outside of, the corporate network. All network packets entering the firewall are filtered, or examined, to determine whether or not those users have authority to access requested files or services.

Filtering   Every packet of data on the Internet is uniquely identified by the source address of the computer which issued the message and the destination address of the Internet server to which the message is bound. These addresses are included in a portion of the packet called the header. More details about Internet addressing and the TCP/IP protocol are covered in Chapter 13.

A **filter** is a program that examines the source address and destination address of every incoming packet to the firewall server. Network access devices known as routers are also capable of filtering data packets. **Filter tables** are lists of addresses whose data packets and embedded messages are either allowed or prohibited from proceeding through the firewall server and into the corporate network. Filter tables can also limit the access of certain IP addresses to certain directories. This is how anonymous FTP users are restricted to only certain information resources. It obviously takes time for a firewall server to examine the addresses of each packet and compare those addresses to filter table entries. This filtering time introduces **latency** to the overall transmission time. A filtering program which only examines source and destination addresses and determines access based on the entries in a filter table is known as a **port-level filter** or **network-level filter.**

Application-level filters, otherwise known as **assured pipelines,** go beyond port-level filters in their attempts to prevent unauthorized access to corporate data. While port-level filters determine the legitimacy of the party asking for information, application-level filters ensure the validity of what they are asking for. These filters examine the entire request for data rather than just the source and destination addresses. When secure files are marked, application-level filters will not allow those files to be transferred, even to users authorized by port-level filters. Understandably, assured pipelines are more complicated to configure and manage, and they introduce increased latency compared to port-level filtering.

Encryption

Encryption involves the changing of data into an indecipherable form before transmission. In this way, even if the transmitted data is somehow intercepted, it cannot be interpreted. The changed, unmeaningful data is known as **ciphertext.** Encryption must be accompanied by decryption, to change the unreadable text back into its original form.

The decrypting device must use the same algorithm or method to decode or decrypt the data as the encrypting device used to encrypt it. Although proprietary standards do exist, a standard known as **Data Encryption Standard (DES),** originally approved by the National Institute of Standards and Technology (NIST) in 1977, is often used, allowing encryption devices manufactured by different manufacturers to interoperate successfully. The **DES** encryption standard actually has two parts which serve to offer greater overall security. In addition to the standard algorithm or method of encrypting data 64 bits at a time, the DES standard also uses a 64-bit key.

The encryption key customizes the commonly known algorithm to prevent anyone without this **private key** from possibly decrypting the document. This private key must be known by both the sending and receiving encryption devices, and it allows so many unique combinations (nearly 2 to the 64th power) that unauthorized decryption is nearly impossible. The safe and reliable distribution of these private keys among numerous encryption devices can be difficult. If this private key is somehow intercepted, the integrity of the encryption system is compromised.

As an alternative to the DES private key standard, **public key encryption** can be utilized. Public key encryption could perhaps more accurately be named public/private key encryption, as the process actually combines use of both public and private keys. In public key encryption, the sending encryption device encrypts a document using the intended recipient's public key. This public key is readily available in a public directory or is sent by the intended recipient to the message sender. However, to decrypt the document, the receiving encryption/decryption device must be programmed with the recipient's private key. In this method, only the receiving party needs to know the private key, eliminating the need for transmission of private keys between sending and receiving parties.

As an added security measure, **digital signature encryption** uses this public key encryption methodology in reverse as an electronic means of guaranteeing authenticity of the sending party and assurance that encrypted documents have not been tampered with during transmission. The digital signature has been compared to the wax seals of old, which (supposedly) guaranteed tamper-evident delivery of documents.

With digital signature encryption, a document digital signature is created by the sender using a private key and the encrypted document. To validate the authenticity of the received document, the recipient uses a public key associated with the apparent sender to regenerate a digital signature from the received encrypted document. The transmitted digital signature is then compared by the recipient to the regenerated digital signature produced by using the public key and the received document. If the two digital signatures match, the document is authentic and has not been tampered with.

In Sharper Focus

WORLDWIDE WEB SECURITY

Following are the two primary standards for encrypting traffic on the WorldWide Web:

- **S-HTTP: Secure Hypertext Transport Protocol.**
- **SSL: Secure Sockets Layer.**

Secure HTTP is a secure version of HTTP which requires both client and server S-HTTP versions to be installed for secure end-to-end encrypted transmission. S-HTTP is described as providing security at the document level, since it works with the actual HTTP applications to secure documents and messages. S-HTTP uses digital signature encryption to ensure that the document possesses both authenticity and message integrity.

SSL is described as wrapping an encrypted envelope around HTTP transmissions. Whereas S-HTTP can be used only to encrypt web documents, SSL can be wrapped around other Internet service transmissions such as FTP and Gopher as well as HTTP. SSL is a connection-level encryption method that provides security to the network link itself.

SSL and S-HTTP are not competing or conflicting standards, although they are sometimes viewed that way. Using a postal service analogy, SSL provides the locked postal delivery vehicle while S-HTTP provides the sealed, tamper-evident envelope which allows only the intended recipient to view the confidential document contained within.

Another Internet security protocol directed specifically toward securing and authenticating commercial financial transactions, known as **Secure Courier,** is offered by the market leader in web software, Netscape. Secure Courier is based on SSL and allows users to create a secure digital envelope for transmission of financial transactions over the Internet. Secure Courier also provides consumer authentication for the cybermerchants inhabiting the commercial Internet.

An Internet e-mail–specific encryption standard which also uses digital signature encryption to guarantee the authenticity, security, and message integrity of received e-mail is known as **PGP,** or **Pretty Good Privacy.** PGP overcomes inherent security loopholes with public/private key security schemes by implementing a web of trust in which e-mail users electronically sign each other's public keys to create an interconnected group of public key users. PGP as well as other network-related security issues are discussed in more detail in Chapter 17.

SUMMARY

The Internet is a wide area network linking over 4 million host computers. Originally developed as a means for the research, education, and scientific communities to share information, the Internet has been opened up in recent years to more commercial uses as well as to access by individuals. Before investing in the required technology to link to the Internet, a business should first have a thorough understanding of the types of services available on the Internet and what business objectives can be achieved by such a link.

The WorldWide Web is a fully graphical Internet service which has generated a great deal of interest recently. Other Internet services include global e-mail, FTP servers, Gopher servers, and Usenet groups. Depending on how much support is required, a company may choose to enlist the services of either an Internet presence provider or an Internet access provider. These Internet connectivity services differ dramatically in the level of services offered and, in some cases, the level of technical expertise and financial stability.

With the Internet itself acting as a global LAN, an Internet-based client/server architecture would require specialized client hardware and software and server hardware and software. The particular software required depends on which Internet service a company wishes to access or offer. Clients are Internet services consumers and servers are Internet services providers.

To develop a presence on the Internet, a company needs four basic elements: an access transmission line of sufficient bandwidth, an IP Internet address, server hardware, and appropriate server software designed for a particular Internet service.

If the Internet is ever to become a viable medium for widespread commercial financial transactions, security issues must be addressed. Security on the Internet goes beyond just encrypting credit card numbers. When a company links to the Internet, it is opening up its own corporate network to any of the estimated 10 to 20 million Internet users, unless proper procedures are implemented to prevent such access. A thorough security program should address all three major security areas: encryption, authorization, and authentication. The digital signature encryption standard and its derivations are among the most popular today. Security solutions for the Internet continue to evolve. Given the enormous potential for commercial use of the Internet for financial transactions, it is likely that security issues will be dealt with in a manner satisfactory to both the consumers and merchants of the Internet's cybermalls.

KEY TERMS

REVIEW QUESTIONS

1. What are some of the reasons why a business might be interested in connecting to the Internet?
2. What are some bad reasons for a company to connect to the Internet?
3. Distinguish between the information available, ease of access, and most probable uses/users of available Internet services.
4. What is the WorldWide Web?
5. How does the WorldWide Web differ from other Internet services in the information it offers and its hardware/software requirements?
6. Distinguish between the major types of information servers available on the Internet.
7. What are the business advantages of global e-mail?
8. What are some of the trends which have combined to produce this increased interest in corporate access to the Internet?
9. What are some of the potential pitfalls of corporate access to the Internet?
10. Differentiate between IAP and IPP.
11. Differentiate between WWW connectivity alternatives.
12. What is a cybermall?
13. Differentiate between global e-mail connectivity alternatives.
14. When are transport protocols such as SLIP or PPP used?
15. What is the difference between HTTP and HTML?
16. What is a web browser?
17. Name two popular web browsers.
18. Differentiate between web client, web browser, web page, and web server.
19. Describe and differentiate between hypertext links and URLs.
20. What is the importance of MIME to global e-mail?
21. Differentiate between POP and IMAP.
22. Differentiate between Internet gateways and Internet e-mail gateways.
23. What are the advantages and disadvantages of an Internet gateway?
24. Differentiate between accessing Internet services via an Internet gateway and Internet-enabled clients.
25. Differentiate between an Internet server and a web server.
26. What are the most likely sources for web browser and web server software?
27. What is the potential value of CGI?
28. What is the impact of proxy servers on network performance?
29. Differentiate between the services offered by Internet presence providers, Internet access providers, and local telecommunications providers.
30. How do business communications services differ from Internet services?
31. What is a virtual corporation, and how is it related to business communications services?
32. Differentiate between the two major categories of web page publishing software.
33. What is the difference between HTML and SGML?
34. What increased capabilities do VRML and Java offer over HTML?
35. What is an applet, and how does it relate to increasingly interactive web pages?
36. Differentiate between encryption, authorization, and authentication.
37. What two assurances does authentication offer?
38. What is a firewall, and what function does it serve?
39. What is filtering?
40. Differentiate between port-level filters and application-level filters in terms of function, effectiveness, and introduced latency.
41. Differentiate between public and private key encryption schemes.
42. Explain how digital signature encryption works and what security assurances it delivers.
43. Differentiate between the two primary WWW encryption methods.
44. Why should SSL be considered a more flexible encryption method?
45. Are SSL and S-HTTP competing standards? Why or why not?
46. What features does Secure Courier offer beyond SSL?
47. Which market is Secure Courier aimed at?

ACTIVITIES

1. Prepare a position paper or organize a debate on any or all of the following questions:
    a. What should a company's policy be regarding employee use of corporate Internet accounts after business hours?
    b. Should employees have to distinguish,

disclaim, or otherwise identify personal opinions and messages posted to the Internet from corporate accounts?

c. Should an official company spokesperson be designated to represent a company's on-line position and image?

d. Should employees be able to upload or download software of their choice to/from the Internet via corporate Internet accounts?

e. Should "cyberporn" sites be declared off-limits or restricted from corporate Internet accounts regardless of time of day?

f. Should the federal government regulate the use of the Internet?

2. Gather statistics and prepare a graph, chart, or presentation regarding the growth of the Internet in general and the WWW in particular.

3. Try to access the following WWW home pages or others of your choice:

a. For general information regarding the WWW: http://akebono.stanford.edu/yahoo/bin/menu?95,7

b. For information about the Internet in general: http://www.cc.gatech.edu/gvu/stats/NSF/merit.html

c. For information about web server security: http://www.commerce.net/software/Shttpd/Docs/manual.html

d. For information about building a home page: http://www.ncsa.uiuc.edu/demoweb/html-primer.html

e. For information about building a web server: http://info.cern.ch/hypertext/WWW/Daemon/JanetandJohn.html

f. For an index of available home pages: http://www.biotech.washington.edu/WebCrawler/WebQuery.html

g. For information about web browsers and clients: http://www.ncsa.uiuc.edu/SDG/Software/Mosaic/NCSAMosaicHome.html

h. For information about getting an Internet IP address: http://www.internic.net/

FEATURED REFERENCES

Business Perspective

Arnum, Eric. Doing Business on the Internet—A Question of Balance. *Business Communications Review,* 25; 8 (August 1995), 35.

Arnum, Eric. The Move to Electronic Commerce Gets Under Way. *Business Communications Review,* 24; 12 (December 1994), 28.

Ayre, Rick and Don Willmott. The Internet Means Business. *PC Magazine,* 14; 9 (May 16, 1995), 195.

Baran, Nicholas. The Greatest Show on Earth. *Byte,* 20, 7 (July 1995), 69.

Dern, Daniel. The Internet, Your Company, and You. *Network Computing,* 5; 14 (November 15, 1994), 50.

Rendleman, John. No Rush to the Web. *Communications Week,* no. 566 (July 17, 1995), S23.

Internet Front-Ends/Web Browsers

Ayre, Rick and Kevin Reichard. Web Browsers: The Web Untangled. *PC Magazine,* 14; 3 (February 7, 1995), 173.

Clark, Jim and Marc Andreessen. The Pattern in the Mosaic. *Network Computing,* 5; 14 (November 15, 1994), 44.

Dern, Daniel and Barry Gerber. Navigating the Web Navigators. *Network Computing,* 6; 4 (April 1, 1995), 52.

Johnson, Johna. Netscape: A Fast (and Secure) Track to Hypertext. *Data Communications,* 24; 1 (January 1995), 112.

Mullet, Kevin. Surfing the Worldwide Web with Mosaic. *Network Computing,* 5; 9 (August 1, 1994), 156.

Pickering, Wendy. Oracle to Play Internet Card with SmartClient 10 Launch. *PC Week,* 12; 27 (July 10, 1995), 1.

Raynovich, R. Scott. Complex Browsers Seek to Expand Role. *LAN Times,* 12; 13 (July 3, 1995), 1.

Reichard, Kevin. Internet E-Mail Front-Ends. *PC Magazine,* 14; 8 (April 25, 1995), 111.

Stevenson, Ted. The Perfect Internet Toolkit. *PC Magazine,* 14; 13 (July 1995), 246.

Vacca, John. Mosaic: Beyond Net Surfing. *Byte,* 20; 1 (January 1995), 75.

Internet Connectivity and Services

Adam, John. Upgrading the Internet. *IEEE Spectrum,* 32; 9 (September 1995), 24.

Bragen, Michael. Four Paths to Messaging. *PC Magazine,* 14; 8 (April 25, 1995), 139.

Cummings, Joanne and Fred Knight. Internet Service Providers to Ride a Familiar Roller Coaster. *Business Communications Review,* 25; 1 (January 1995), 67.

deVries, Peter and Karl Auerbach. Guide to Selecting an Internet Provider. *Network Computing,* 6; 6 (May 15, 1995), 120.

Gareiss, Robin. A Comprehensive Package for Corporate Internet Access. *Data Communications,* 24; 7 (May 21, 1995), 29.

Gonzalez, Sean. Mail Services for Hire. *PC Magazine,* 14; 8 (April 25, 1995), 177.

Reichard, Kevin. Leveraging E-Mail. *PC Magazine,* 14; 9 (May 16, 1995), 241.

Stevenson, Ted. The Perfect Internet Toolkit. *PC Magazine,* 14; 13 (July 1995), 246.

Udell, Jon. Live Wire. *Byte,* 20; 8 (August 1995), 103.

Internet Servers/Web Servers Hardware and Software

Fogarty, Kevin. Novell Reveals Internet Strategy for NetWare. *Network World,* 12; 31 (July 31, 1995), 1.

Gonzalez, Sean. Building a Web Presence. *PC Magazine,* 14; 9 (May 16, 1995), 205.

Johnson, Johna. Corporate Internet Server, Hold the Hassles. *Data Communications,* 24; 1 (January 1995), 100.

Levitt, Jason. Windows NT Serves the Net. *Information Week,* no. 544 (September 11, 1995), 60.

Platt, Stephen and Anthony Lennon. 5 Internet Servers Go Head-to-Head. *Byte,* 20; 8 (August 1995), 134.

Reichard, Kevin. Letting Customers Dig Through Your Data. *PC Magazine,* 14; 9 (May 16, 1995), 233.

Snyder, Joel. Putting Your Web Site into Orbit: Five Servers that Help Fire It Up. *Network World,* 12; 31 (July 31, 1995), 1.

Streeter, April. Apple Enters Internet Race. *LAN Times,* 12; 14 (July 24, 1995), 29.

Tabibian, O. Ryan. Internet Servers: Publish or Perish? *PC Magazine,* 14; 9 (May 16, 1995), NE1.

Tabibian, O. Ryan. Web Server Software: Electronic Businesses. *PC Magazine,* 14; 3 (February 7, 1995), NE1.

Internet Gateways/E-Mail Gateways

Garris, John. IP/IPX Internet Gateways: Hassle-Free Internet. *PC Magazine,* 14; 13 (July 1995), NE1.

Lipschutz, Robert. Internet Mail Gateways: Extending E-Mail's Reach. *PC Magazine,* 14; 8 (April 25, 1995), 155.

Rizzo, Joe. Opening the Internet Gate. *Network Computing,* 6; 9 (August 1, 1995), 104.

Security

Baron, Talia. Internet Commerce: Safer Than You Think. *Communications Week,* no. 561 (June 12, 1995), 57.

Baron, Talia. Netscape Protocol Improves Internet Security. *Communications Week,* no. 567 (July 24, 1995), 12.

Baron, Talia. New Security Fear May Hinder "Net Commerce." *Communications Week,* no. 571 (August 21, 1995), 1.

Cobb, Stephen. Internet Firewalls. *Byte,* 20; 10 (October 1995), 179.

Mier, Edwin. Another Brick in the Firewall. *Communications Week,* no. 575 (September 18, 1995), 65.

Reichard, Kevin. Will Your Business Be Safe? *PC Magazine,* 14; 9 (May 16, 1995), 218.

Wilder, Clinton and Bob Violino. Online Theft. *Information Week,* no. 542 (August 28, 1995), 30.

Internet Application Development

Gonzalez, Sean. HTML: Nothing but Net. *PC Magazine,* 14; 3 (February 7, 1995), 156.

Karney, James. SGML and HTML: Tag Masters. *PC Magazine,* 14; 3 (February 7, 1995), 144.

Kay, Alan. Close-up: Interactive Applications, Banking on the Net. *Communications Week,* no. 570 (August 14, 1995), 35.

Kohlhepp, Robert. Next Generation Web Browsing. *Network Computing,* 6; 9 (August 1, 1995), 48.

Messmer, Ellen. Electronic Commerce Enters Third Dimension. *Network World,* 12; 33 (August 14, 1995), 8.

Morro, David. Demystifying Web Hyperlinks. *Network World,* 12; 31 (July 31, 1995), 41.

Vaughan-Nichols, Steven. Dialects of the Web. *Byte,* 20; 3 (March 1995), 30.

Vaughan-Nichols, Steven. Internet Publishing Tools Proliferate. *Byte,* 20; 3 (March 1995), 30.

CASE STUDY

Chapter 6

SUN'S WEB LINKS COMPANY'S WORLD

Perhaps proving the maxim that says information wants to be free, Sun Microsystems Inc. unconsciously adopted WorldWide Web technology to allow individuals and groups within Sun to more freely share information specific to the company.

Taking advantage of a user-inspired movement to publish information via the WorldWide Web (WWW), Sunnyvale, Calif.-based Sun over the past two years has organized and optimized what is now a worldwide, 600-node network of Web servers and many more Mosaic clients.

Unlike other Web servers, which are used predominantly on the Internet as a means for simplifying data access, these Web servers can only be accessed by Sun personnel over the company's Sun Wide-Area Network (SWAN). They are strictly for internal use because they provide Sun employees with information about human resources, copyrights, education, and other Sun-specific matters.

Initially, Sun's Web network evolved without the direct and deliberate involvement of the company, said Carl Meske, Internet technical program manager at Sun. "Slowly it started as a grassroots effort of individuals sharing information," he said. "But larger and larger groups started putting them together."

Organizing the Wealth

The result of such unchecked growth was an uncoordinated mass of information that was available yet unreachable because nobody knew how to obtain the network's Universal Resource Locator (URL), Meske said. To organize this wealth of information, Meske installed a single Sun SPARCstation 10, equipped it with a Web server from the National Center for Supercomputing Applications (NCSA), and began gathering URLs.

"I wanted to group the URLs and put them together to make sense," Meske said. "So the SunWeb server started out as a bunch of repositories for URLs to corporate, sales offices, engineering, and pointers to 'How to build Web server pages.'"

Initially, Meske wanted to build a centralized repository for all of Sun's information. However, he soon found out that as more individuals and groups contributed information to the single SunWeb server, the burden of updating that information became too time-consuming. "We did not want the Sun-Web to be a repository that aged and was disposed of," he said. "So we wanted the individuals who were responsible for the data to maintain their data."

Meske therefore made SunWeb into an index server containing pointers to other internal Web servers containing users' Hyper-Text Markup Language (HTML) documents. "We started putting pointers in there," Meske said, "and we tried to find owners of information and ask them to convert their information into HTML."

The idea of converting information into the HTML standard met with some opposition at first, noted Judy Lindberg, Internet program manager for Sun. "Most of our people had information in Frame or In-terleaf format," she said, "and how to get that into HTML format was a problem."

Users unwilling or unable to translate existing information into HTML, however, could make their information available without modification through the Web's capability to transparently access multiple data formats. "Mosaic is a complexity integrator; before, you had to know how to use WAIS [Wide-Area Information Service], gopher, etc.," said Meske, "But now you can just point and click."

For example, by incorporating a Practical Extraction and Report Language (Perl) scripting utility, Meske was able to let users publish a database without changing it from its initial form. Also, for users not wanting to translate information, they could make directories and files available through Mosaic's built-in ftp client. All other formats, such as images or spreadsheets, could be accessed in their native format.

Change Is Good?

Despite WWW's capability to make information easily accessible, the decision to give publishing powers to the authors met with limited support, said Lindberg. First, because control of the information passed from management to the information authors, many within Sun felt that there would be a loss of control over the information. Second, in transmitting information such as voice, video, images, and text over WWW, many felt that it would negatively affect Sun's network performance.

"What I had to do was get the information-resources people not to worry about managing a limited resource, its security, and bandwidth," said Lindberg, "because nobody knew how much bandwidth Mosaic would eat up."

Concerning security, Sun openly published only freely available information. For sensitive material, Sun adopted password protection through WWW's built-in scripting utilities.

Erasing performance problems was a bit more difficult because the Web server and Mosaic clients can exchange bandwidth-intensive information, such as voice files, said Meske. "One of our concerns in deploying this is how do we minimize network activity," he said. "With an audio message, if 1,400 people hit that one machine, it would kill the network."

To void such problems, Sun implemented a unique staging approach in which universal information that would have been stored centrally was transferred to software-distribution servers residing closer to the users. "We took the audio files and distributed them to the distribution servers," said Meske. "Then you don't have to have this major traffic across the network."

Once beyond the initial performance and political difficulties, the SunWeb server let Sun streamline its information distribution, said Meske. By giving people the chance to make information available instead of distributing that information, users can lessen E-mail and paper-based memorandum usage.

"Now people are starting to use the pull model instead of the push model; it is a much more diplomatic way to get information across," Meske said. "Instead of sending information via E-mail, you can just send the URL asking people to come to your site."

"This shows the power of the Web and the Internet," said Lindberg, "because we were able to put the information from the minds of many into a product quickly."

Source: Bradley F. Shimmin (April 24, 1995). Sun's Web Links Company's World. *LAN Times,* 12(8), 31. Reprinted with permission of McGraw-Hill, *LAN Times.*

BUSINESS CASE STUDY QUESTIONS

Activities

1. Complete a top-down model for this case by gleaning facts from the case and placing them in the proper layer of the top-down model. After having completed the top-down model, analyze and detail those instances when requirements were clearly passed down from upper to lower layers of the model and solutions to those requirements were passed from lower to upper layers.
2. Detail any questions that may occur to you about the case for which answers are not clearly stated in the article.

Business

1. From a business perspective, what is different about the use of web servers at Sun from typical web server installations?
2. How did Sun's web network start and grow initially? What were some of the shortcomings of this method?
3. What were some of management's concerns with allowing information to be published on the company's web?
4. What were the perceived positive impacts of the web network after initial installation?

Application

1. What types of information are available on Sun's web servers?

2. What types of traffic other than data are transmitted over the network?
3. How was the effect of bandwidth-intensive applications on overall network traffic minimized?

Data

1. What is the importance of URLs to overall information organization on a web server?
2. What was the perceived shortcoming of storing all data in a centralized repository?
3. Which standardized web data formatting language was chosen and why?
4. How were security issues handled?

Network

1. How are these web servers networked together?
2. How does the network connecting these web servers differ from the way in which most web servers are connected?
3. How did the proposed network design overcome the shortcomings of a single, centralized data repository?

Technology

1. What hardware and software technologies were employed in this web server installation?
2. Which web client software was employed, and what important special features did it offer?

LOCAL AREA NETWORKS ARCHITECTURES, HARDWARE, AND SOFTWARE

INTRODUCTION

Part 2 provided an understanding of clients and servers. In Part 3 we explore the LAN hardware and software technology which links clients and servers.

In Chapter 7, local area network architectures and concepts are studied. Functionality, standards, advantages, disadvantages, and proper business application of each alternative network architecture are addressed. The OSI model is reintroduced as a means of organizing information concerning alternative network architectures.

In Chapter 8, the hardware technology required to install a LAN is studied in detail. The numerous technological changes affecting network interface cards are explored as well as the trend toward LAN switches as a means to meet the ever-increasing demands for LAN bandwidth. The hardware/software interface between network interface cards and the LAN software studied in Chapter 9 is given particular attention as a key point in protocol compatibility.

Finally, Chapter 9 addresses the LAN application software which is responsible for helping to achieve the required business objectives. The software is divided into two major categories: LAN productivity software, which is concerned with directly increasing the productivity of its users; and LAN resource management software, which is more concerned with providing access to shared network resources and services.

CHAPTER 7

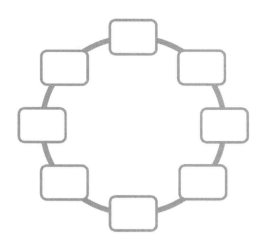

LOCAL AREA NETWORK ARCHITECTURES

Concepts Reinforced

OSI model
Client/server technology architecture
Protocols and standards

Top-down model
Hardware/software compatibility
Local area networks

Concepts Introduced

Access methodologies
Logical topologies
Physical topologies

Network architectures
IEEE 802 standards
High-speed network architectures

OBJECTIVES

After mastering the material in this chapter you should:

1. Understand how access methodologies, logical topologies, and physical topologies combine to form alternative network architectures.

2. Understand the similarities and differences between and the advantages and disadvantages of current network architectures such as Ethernet, Token Ring, and FDDI.

3. Understand the similarities and differences between and the advantages and disadvantages of emerging high-speed network architectures such as 100BaseT, 100VG-AnyLAN, and isoEthernet.

4. Understand the value of the OSI model in analyzing network architecture alternatives.

5. Understand how proper LAN analysis can help determine which network architecture is most appropriate in any given situation.

Clients and servers are able to communicate and share information thanks to the combined components of the local area network which links them. These local area network components can offer transparent network transmission services to clients and services because of their adherence to standards and protocols. One of the key distinguishing characteristics of a particular LAN is the network architecture it adheres to. This chapter first explores the components of a network architecture and then provides comparative evaluations of the numerous network architectures either currently available or emerging in the networking marketplace.

The OSI model, first introduced in Chapter 1, is reintroduced as a means of organizing comparative information on alternative network architectures.

■ THE OSI MODEL REVISITED

Overall Structure and Characteristics

The **OSI model** consists of a hierarchy of seven layers loosely grouping the functional requirements for communication between two computing devices. The power of the OSI model lies in its openness and flexibility. It can be used to organize and define protocols involved in communicating between two computing devices in the same room as effectively as two devices across the world from each other.

Each layer in the OSI model relies on lower layers to perform more elementary functions and offer total transparency to the intricacies of those functions. At the same time, each layer provides the same transparent service to upper layers. In theory, if this transparency model is supported, changes in the protocols of one layer should not require protocol changes of other layers. A **protocol** is a set of rules which govern communication between hardware and/or software components.

Physical Layer

The **physical layer,** also known as layer 1, is responsible for establishing, maintaining and terminating physical connections between communicating devices. These connections are sometimes referred to as **point-to-point data links.** The physical layer transmits and receives a stream of bits. There is no data recognition at the physical layer.

Specifically, the physical layer operation is controlled by protocols which define the electrical, mechanical, and procedural specifications for data transmission. The RS232-C specification for serial transmission is an example of a physical layer protocol. Strictly speaking, the physical layer does not define the specifications for connectors and cables, which are sometimes referred to as belonging to layer 0.

Data-Link Layer

The **data-link layer** is responsible for providing protocols which deliver reliability to upper layers for the point-to-point connections established by the physical layer protocols. The data-link layer is of particular interest to the study of LANs because this is where network architecture standards are defined. These standards are debated and established by the **Institute of Electrical and Electronic Engineers (IEEE) 802** committee and will be introduced and explained later in this chapter. The number 802 is derived from the date of the committee's formation, in February (2) 1980 (80).

The data-link layer provides the required reliability to the physical layer transmission by organizing the bit stream into structured **frames,** which add addressing and error-checking information. Information added to the front of data is called a **header,** and information added to the back of data is called a **trailer.** Data-link layer protocols provide error detection, notification, and recovery.

The data-link layer frames are built within the **network interface card** installed in a computer according to the predetermined frame layout particular to the network architecture of the installed network interface card. Network interface cards are given a unique address in a format determined by their network architecture. These addresses are usually assigned and preprogrammed by the NIC manufacturer. The network interface card provides the connection to the LAN, transferring any data frames addressed to it to the computer's memory for processing.

The first two layers of the OSI model, physical and data-link, are manifested as hardware (media and NICs, respectively), and the remaining layers are all installed as software protocols.

Sublayers

To allow the OSI model to more closely adhere to the protocol structure and operation of a local area network, the IEEE 802 committee split the data-link layer into two sublayers.

Media Access Control   The **media access control** or **MAC sublayer,** interfaces with the physical layer and is represented by protocols which define how the shared local area network media is to be accessed by the many connected computers. As will be explained more fully later, Token Ring (IEEE 802.5) and Ethernet (IEEE 802.3) networks use different media access methodologies and are therefore assigned different IEEE 802 protocol numbers.

Logical Link Control   The upper sublayer of the data-link layer which interfaces to the network layer is known as the **logical link control,** or **LLC sublayer,** and is represented by a single IEEE 802 protocol (IEEE 802.2). The advantage to splitting the data-link layer into two sublayers and having a single, common LLC protocol is that it offers transparency to the upper layers (network and above) while allowing the MAC sublayer protocol to vary independently. In terms of technology, the splitting of the sublayers and the single LCC protocol allows NetWare to run equally well over Token Ring or Ethernet NICs.

Network Layer

The **network layer** protocols are responsible for establishing, maintaining, and terminating **end-to-end network links.** Network layer protocols are required when computers which are not physically connected to the same LAN must communicate. Network layer protocols are responsible for providing network layer (end-to-end) addressing schemes and enabling internetwork routing of network layer data **packets.** The term "packets" is usually associated with network layer protocols and the term "frames" with data-link layer protocols. Unfortunately, not all networking professionals or texts adhere to these generally accepted conventions. Addressing schemes and routing are thoroughly reviewed in the remainder of the text.

Network layer protocols are part of a particular network operating system's protocol stack. Different networking operating systems may use different network layer protocols. Many network operating systems are able to use more than one network layer protocol. This capability is especially important to heterogeneous, multiplatform, multivendor client/server computing environments.

Transport Layer

Just as the data-link layer was responsible for providing reliability for the physical layer, the **transport layer** protocols are responsible for providing reliability for the end-to-end network layer connections. Transport layer protocols provide end-to-end error recovery and flow control. Transport layer protocols also provide mechanisms for sequentially organizing multiple network layer packets into a coherent **message.**

Transport layer protocols are also supplied by a given network operating system and are most often closely linked with a particular network layer protocol. For example, NetWare uses IPX/SPX in which Internet packet exchange (IPX) is the network layer protocol and sequenced packet exchange (SPX) is the transport layer protocol. Another popular transport/network protocol duo is TCP/IP, in which transmission control protocol (TCP) provides reliability services for Internet protocol (IP).

Session Layer

The **session layer** protocols are responsible for establishing, maintaining, and terminating sessions between user application programs. Sessions are interactive dialogues between networked computers and are particularly important to distributed computing applications in a client/server environment. As the area of distributed computing is in an evolutionary state, the session layer protocols may be supplied by the distributed application, the network operating system, or a specialized piece of additional software known as middleware, designed to render differences between computing platforms transparent.

Presentation Layer

The **presentation layer** protocols provide an interface between user applications and various presentation-related services required by those applications. For example, data encryption/decryption protocols are considered presentation layer protocols as are protocols which translate between encoding schemes such as ASCII to EBCDIC. A common misconception is that graphical user interfaces such as Windows and Presentation Manager are presentation layer protocols. This is not true. Presentation layer protocols deal with network communications whereas Windows and Presentation Manager are installed on end-user computers.

Application Layer

The **application layer,** layer 7 of the OSI model, is also open to misinterpretation. Application layer protocols do not include end-user application programs. Rather, they include utilities which support end-user application programs. Some people include network operating systems in this category. Strictly speaking, the best examples of application layer protocols are the OSI protocols X.400 and X.500. X.400 is an open systems protocol which offers interoperability between different e-mail programs, and X.500 offers e-mail directory synchronization among different e-mail systems.

Figure 7-1 offers a conceptual view of the OSI model and summarizes many of the previous comments.

LAYER	USER APPLICATION			DATA FORMAT	ENABLING TECHNOLOGY	
7 APPLICATION	Provides common services to user applications. ➡ X.400 E-MAIL interoperability specification ➡ X.500 E-MAIL directory synchronization specification ➡ Strictly speaking, does *not* include user applications	Higher layer protocols — independent of underlying communications network	Node-to-node sessions			SOFTWARE
6 PRESENTATION	Provides presentation services for network communications. ➡ Encryption ➡ Code translation (ASCII to EBCDIC) ➡ Text compression *Not* to be confused with ➡ Graphical user interfaces(GUIs)					
5 SESSION	Establishes, maintains, terminates node-to-node interactive sessions.			sessions / Interactive, real-time dialogue between 2 user nodes	Distributed applications, middleware, or network operating systems.	
4 TRANSPORT	Ensures reliability of end-to-end network connections.		End-to-end user network connection.	messages / Asembles packets into messages.	Network operating systems	
3 NETWORK	Establishes, maintains, and terminates end-to-end network connections.		Network	packets / Embedded within frames.	Network operating systems.	
HARDWARE/SOFTWARE INTERFACE					**NIC DRIVERS**	
2 DATA LINK	Logical link control sublayer. / Media access control sublayer.	Specified by 802.X protocols. ➡Ensures reliability of point-to-point data links.	Communications / Point-to-point data link	frames / Recognizable as data.	Network interface cards.	HARDWARE
1 PHYSICAL	Establishes, maintains, and terminates point-to-point data links.			bits / Unrecognizable as data.	Media	

Figure 7-1   OSI Model — A Conceptual View

Encapsulation/Deencapsulation

The previous discussion highlighted the roles of the various OSI model layer proto-cols in a communication session between two networked computers. How the various protocol layers actually interact to enable an end-to-end communication session is highlighted in Figure 7-2.

As the figure illustrates, a data message emerges from a client front-end pro-gram and proceeds down the protocol stack of the network operating system in-stalled in the client PC in a process known as **encapsulation.** Each successive layer of the OSI model adds a header according to the syntax of the protocol which occupies that layer. In the case of the data-link layer, both a header and a trailer are added. The bit stream is finally passed along the shared media, which connects the two computing devices. This is an important point. Although the

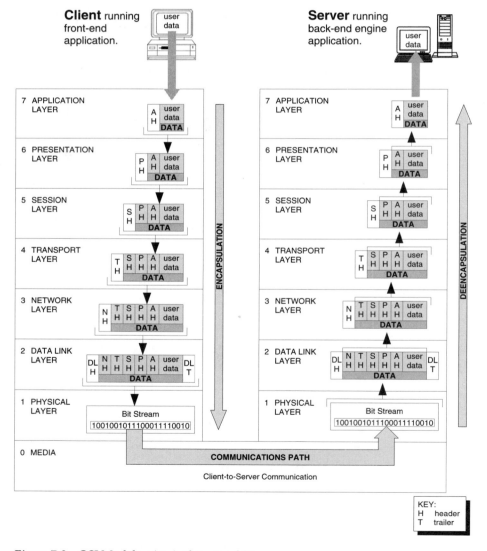

Figure 7-2   OSI Model—An Architectural View

OSI model may seem to imply that given layers in a protocol stack talk directly to each other on different computers, the computers are actually physically connected only by the media, which is the only layer that talks directly between computers.

When the full bit stream arrives at the destination server, the reverse process of encapsulation, **deencapsulation,** takes place. In this manner, each successive layer of the OSI model removes headers and trailers and processes the data passed to it from the corresponding layer protocol on the source client. Once the server has processed the client's request for data in the server back-end engine application, the whole process is reversed and the requested data will be encapsulated by the server's protocol stack, transmitted over the communications media, and deencapsulated by the client PC's protocol stack before being ultimately delivered to the client front-end application which requested it.

■ THE LOCAL AREA NETWORK ARCHITECTURE MODEL

Although not all network architectures are standardized by the IEEE or some other standards-making organization, all network architectures are made up of the same logical components. To accurately describe a given network architecture, one needs to know the following:

- Access methodology.
- Logical topology.
- Physical topology.

These three major components are discussed in each case as the numerous network architectures are evaluated later in the chapter. The only other variable added to the network architecture of choice is the particular medium over which a given network architecture can operate. As you will see, most network architectures are able to operate over a variety of media types. These combinations of variables can be summarized in the following manner:

- Network architecture = access methodology + logical topology + physical topology.
- Network configuration = network architecture + media choice.

Access Methodology

Realizing that more than one user is likely to be sending requests onto the shared local area network media at any one time, the need for some way to control which users get to put their messages onto the network and when should be obvious. If the medium is to be shared by numerous PC users, there must be some way to control access by multiple users. These media-sharing methods are properly known as **access methodologies.** Sharing the media is an important concept to LANs, which are sometimes referred to as **media-sharing LANs.**

Logically, there are really only two philosophies for controlling access to shared media. The analogy of access to a crowded freeway provides a vivid illustration of access methodology choices.

CSMA/CD One philosophy says, "Let's just let everyone onto the media whenever they want and if two users access the media at the exact same split second, we'll work it out somehow." Or, using the analogy, "Who needs stop lights! If we have a few collisions, we'll work it out later!"

The access methodology based on this model is known as **carrier sense multiple access with collision detection,** or **CSMA/CD.** A clearer understanding of how this access methodology works can be achieved by examining its name one phrase at a time.

Carrier sense means that the PC wishing to put data onto the shared media listens to detect if other users are "on the line," by trying to sense a neutral electrical signal known as a carrier. If no transmission is sensed, then "multiple access" allows anyone onto the media without requiring further permission. Finally, if two user PCs both sense a free line and access the media at the same instant, a collision occurs; "collision detection" lets the user PCs know their data was not delivered and controls retransmission in such a way as to avoid further data collisions. Another possible factor leading to data collisions is the **propagation delay,** which is the time it takes a signal from a source PC to reach a destination PC. Because of this propagation delay, it is possible for a workstation to sense there is no signal on the shared media when, in fact, another distant workstation has transmitted a signal that has not yet reached the carrier-sensing PC.

In the event of a collision, the station which first detects a collision sends out a special jamming signal to all attached workstations. Each workstation is preset to wait a random amount of time before retransmitting, thus reducing the likelihood of recurring collisions. If successive collisions continue to occur the random timeout interval is doubled.

CSMA/CD is obviously most efficient with relatively little contention for network resources. The ability to allow user PCs to access the network easily without a lot of permission requesting and granting reduces overhead and increases performance at lower network usage rates. As usage increases, however, the increased number of data collisions and retransmissions can negatively affect overall network performance.

Token Passing The second philosophy of access methodology is much more controlling. It says, "Don't you dare access the media until it's your turn. You must first ask permission, and only if I give you the magic token may you put your data onto the shared media." The highway analogy is the controlled access ramps to freeways in which a driver must wait at a stop light, then somehow immediately reach 60 mph to merge with the traffic.

Token passing ensures that each PC user has 100% of the network channel available for data requests and transfers by insisting that no PC accesses the network without a specific packet (24 bits) of data known as a **token.** The token is generated by a designated PC known as the **active monitor** and passed among PCs until one PC would like to access the network.

At that point, the requesting PC seizes the token, changes its status from free to busy, puts its data frame onto the network, and doesn't release the token until it is assured that its data was delivered successfully. Successful delivery of the data frame is confirmed by the destination workstation setting **frame status flags** to indicate successful receipt of the frame and continuing to forward the original frame around the ring to the sending PC. Upon receipt of the original frame with frame status flags set to "destination address recognized, frame copied successfully," the sending PC resets the token status from busy to free and releases it. After the sending PC releases the token, it is passed along to the next PC, which may either grab the free token or pass it along.

16-Mbps Token Ring network architectures use a modified form of token passing access methodology in which the token is set to free and released as soon as the transmission of the data frame is completed, rather than waiting for the transmitted data frame to return. This is known as the **early token release mechanism.** The software and protocols which actually handle the token passing and token regeneration, in the case of a lost token, are usually located in the chips on the network adapter card. Figure 7-3 illustrates a simple token passing access methodology LAN.

Token passing's overhead of waiting for the token before transmitting inhibits overall performance at lower network usage rates. However, because all PC users on a token passing access control network are well behaved and always have the magic token before accessing the network, there can be no collisions, making this a more efficient access methodology at higher network utilization rates.

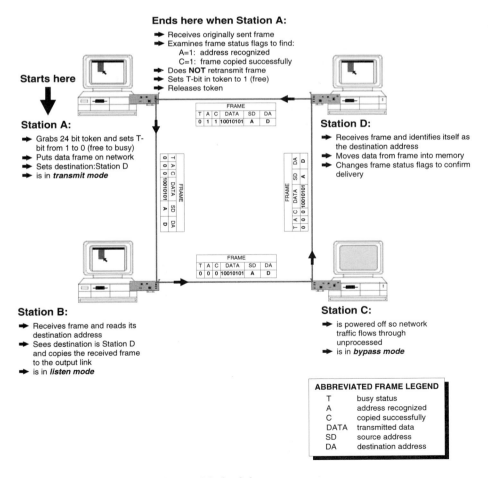

Figure 7-3 Token Passing Access Methodology

Logical Topology

Once a data message is on a shared LAN medium which is connected to numerous workstations, it must be determined how that message will be passed from workstation to workstation until it ultimately reaches its intended destination workstation. The particular message passing methodology employed is more properly known as a network architecture's **logical topology**. Logical topologies are described by an analogy of putting out a fire in a PC user's wastebasket.

Sequential   The first logical topology or method of delivering data is known as **sequential**. In a sequential logical topology, also known as a **ring** logical topology, data is passed from one PC (or node) to another. Each node examines the destination address of the data packet to determine if this particular packet is meant for it. If the data was not meant to be delivered at this node, it is passed along to the next node in the logical ring.

This is the bucket brigade logical topology method of putting out a fire. A bucket of water is filled by one PC user and passed to the neighboring PC user, who determines if his/her wastebasket is on fire. If it is, the user douses the flames with the bucket of water. Otherwise, the user passes the bucket along to the next user in the logical ring.

Broadcast   The second logical topology, or method of delivering data, is known as **broadcast.** In a broadcast logical topology, a data message is sent simultaneously to all nodes on the network. Each node decides individually if the data message was directed to it. If not, the message is simply ignored. There is no need to pass the message along to a neighboring node. They've already gotten the same message.

This is the sprinkler system method of putting out a fire. Rather than worry about passing a bucket of water around a logical ring until it finally reaches the engulfed wastebasket, the water is just broadcast over the entire network to put out the flame in the right wastebasket.

Physical Topology

Finally, the clients and servers must be physically connected to each other according to some configuration and be linked by the shared medium of choice. The physical layout of this configuration, known as a network architecture's **physical topology,** has a significant impact on LAN performance and reliability.

Bus   The **bus** topology is a linear arrangement with terminators on either end and devices connected to the "bus" via connectors and/or transceivers. The weak link in the bus physical topology is that a break or loose connection anywhere along the entire bus will bring the whole network down.

Ring   The **ring** topology suffers from a similar Achilles heel. Each PC connected via a ring topology is actually an active part of the ring, passing data packets in a sequential pattern around the ring. If one of the PCs dies, or a network adapter card malfunctions, the "sequence" is broken, the token is lost, and the network is down.

Star   The **star** physical topology avoids these two aforementioned potential pitfalls by employing some type of central management device. Depending on the network architecture and the sophistication of the device, it may be called a hub, a wiring center, a concentrator, a multistation access unit (MAU), a repeater, or a switching hub. All of these devices are studied later. With each PC or node isolated on its own leg or segment of the network, any node failure affects only that leg, leaving the remainder of the network functioning normally.

Since all network data in a star topology goes through one central location, this is a marvelous spot to add system monitoring, security, or management capabilities. On the other side of the coin, since all network data goes through this one central location, it is a marvelous networking no-no known as a **single point of failure.** The good news is any node can be lost and the network will be fine. The bad news is if the hub is lost, the whole network goes down.

As we will see shortly in the section on hubs, vendors have risen to the occasion by offering such reliability extras as redundant power supplies, dual buses, and "hot-swappable" interface cards. Figure 7-4 highlights the differences between these physical topologies.

Bus topology

Star topology

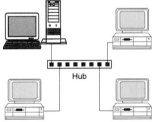

Hub

Ring topology

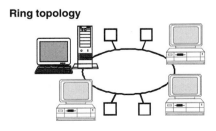

Figure 7-4   LAN Physical Topology Choices

■ NETWORK ARCHITECTURES

Ethernet

Origins   The invention of **Ethernet** is generally credited to Robert Metcalfe, who went on to become the founder of 3COM Corporation. Although strictly speaking, Ethernet and **IEEE 802.3** are conflicting standards, the term Ethernet is commonly used to refer to any IEEE 802.3–compliant network. Differences between the two standards are outlined shortly.

Functionality

- Access methodology: CSMA/CD.

- Logical topology: Broadcast.

- Physical topology: Traditionally, bus; currently, most often star.

Standards   The first Ethernet standard was developed by Digital, Intel, and Xerox Corporation in 1981 and was known as DIX 1.0, or sometimes Ethernet I. This standard was superseded in 1982 by DIX 2.0, the current Ethernet standard, also known as Ethernet II. The frame layouts for **Ethernet II** and IEEE 802.3 are illustrated in Figure 7-5.

As the figure illustrates, both Ethernet II and IEEE 802.3 frames can vary in length from 64 to 1518 octets. An **octet** is eight bits of data. Whereas a byte is eight bits representing a particular character or number, an octet is merely eight bits of digital data potentially representing digitized voice, video, image, or other digital information.

Ethernet II   The Ethernet II frame layout consists of the following fields:

- The Ethernet II frame starts with a preamble of 8 octets. The purpose of the preamble is to alert and synchronize the Ethernet network interface card to the incoming data.

Ethernet II Frame Layout

Preamble	Destination Address	Source Address	Type	Data Unit	Frame Check Sequence
8 Octets	6 Octets	6 Octets	2 Octets	46 to 1500 bytes	4 Octets

The overall frame length varies from 64 to 1518 Octets

IEEE 802.3 Frame Layout

Preamble	Start Frame Delimiter	Destination Address	Source Address	Length	Logical Link Control IEEE 802.2 Data	Frame Check Sequence
7 Octets	1 Octet	2 or 6 Octets	2 or 6 Octets	2 Octets	46 to 1500 bytes	4 Octets

The overall frame length varies from 64 to 1518 Octets

NOTE: 1 Octet = 8 bits

Figure 7-5   Ethernet and IEEE 802.3 Standards

- The destination and source addresses are each 6 octets long and are also known as MAC layer addresses. These addresses are permanently burned into the read only memory (ROM) of the Ethernet II network interface card at the time of manufacture. The first 3 octets of the address identify the manufacturer of the network interface card and are assigned by the IEEE. The last 3 octets are assigned by the manufacturer, producing unique MAC layer addresses for all Ethernet network interface cards.

- The type field identifies which network protocols are embedded within the data field. For example, if the data field contained network IPX/SPX protocols, then the type field would have a value of 8137(hexadecimal), and if the data field contained TCP/IP protocols, then the type field would contain a value of 0800(hexadecimal). These type values are assigned by the IEEE. The type field is important to enable multiple protocols to be handled by a single network interface card, which allows multiple protocol stacks to be loaded in a given client or server. Once the network interface card identifies which protocol is embedded within the data field, it can forward that data field to the proper protocol stack for further processing. Multiple protocol stacks allow communication between clients and servers of different network operating systems, which is essential to transparent distributed computing.

- The data unit field contains all of the encapsulated upper layer (network through application) protocols and can vary in length from 46 to 1500 bytes. The 46-byte minimum data field length combines with the 18 octets of fixed overhead of all of the other fields to produce the minimum frame size of 64 octets.

- The **frame check sequence (FCS)** is an error detection mechanism generated by the transmitting Ethernet network interface card. A 32-bit **cyclical redundancy check (CRC)** is generated over the address, type, and data fields. The receiving Ethernet network interface card regenerates this same CRC on the address, type, and data fields in the received frame and compares the regenerated CRC to the transmitted CRC. If they match, the frame was received error free. Thirty-two bit CRCs have the ability to detect error bursts of up to 31 bits with 100% accuracy.

IEEE 802.3   The IEEE 802.3 frame layout is very similar to that of Ethernet II. Highlights of the IEEE 802.3 frame layout are as follows:

- The 7-octet preamble plus the 1-octet starting frame delimiter perform the same basic function as the 8-octet Ethernet II preamble.

- Address fields are defined and assigned in a similar fashion to Ethernet II frames.

- The 2-octet length field in the IEEE 802.3 frame takes the place of the type field in the Ethernet frame. The length field indicates the length of the variable-length **logical link control (LLC)** data field, which contains all upper-layer embedded protocols.

- The type of embedded upper-layer protocols is designated by a field within the LLC data unit and is explained more fully in the following In Sharper Focus section.

- The frame check sequence is identical to that used in the Ethernet II frame.

In Sharper Focus

IEEE 802.2 AND ETHERNET SNAP

For an IEEE 802.3–compliant network interface card to be able to determine the type of protocols embedded within the data field of an IEEE 802.3 frame, it refers to the header of the IEEE 802.2 LLC data unit. Figure 7-6 illustrates the fields contained in the IEEE 802.2 data unit.

More specifically, the types of protocols embedded within the data unit are identified within the destination and source service access point fields (DSAP and SSAP). These fields are analogous to type field in the Ethernet frame. SAP codes which identify a particular protocol are issued by the IEEE to those companies which register their IEEE-compliant protocols. For example a SAP code of E0 identifies a Novell protocol, and a SAP code of 06 identifies a TCP/IP protocol. NetWare frames adhering to this standard are referred to as NetWare 802.2 (802.3 plus 802.2).

However, in some cases, rendering network protocols to be IEEE 802 compliant was not an easy task. To ease the transition to IEEE 802 compliance, an alternative method of identifying the embedded upper-layer protocols was developed, known as **SNAP, or sub network access protocol.** Any protocol can use SNAP with IEEE 802.2 and appear to be an IEEE 802–compliant protocol. In some cases, network operating systems vendors such as NetWare used SNAP until modifications were made to bring protocols into compliance with IEEE standards. Now that NetWare is IEEE 802 compliant and has a designated SAP code, NetWare users can choose a NetWare 802.2 frame layout.

A single SAP code of AA in both the DSAP and SSAP, and a control code of 03 are used to identify all noncompliant protocols. To differentiate which particular noncompliant protocol is embedded, any packet with AA in the DSAP and SSAP fields also has a 5-octet SNAP header known as a **protocol discriminator** following the control field, as illustrated in Figure 7-6. The first 3 octets of the protocol discriminator are called the organization ID and indicate to which company the embedded protocol belongs, while the last 2 octets are called the EtherType field and indicate which protocol is embedded. All zeroes in the organization ID field indicates that it is a generic Ethernet frame, not unique to any particular company. Examples of EtherType values are 08-00 for TCP/IP and 81-37 for NetWare. NetWare frames adhering to this specification are known as NetWare 802.2 SNAP (802.3 plus 802.2 plus SNAP).

Media-Related Ethernet Standards   Ethernet can run over numerous media types. The unshielded twisted pair media employed in an Ethernet standard known as **10BaseT** sells for as little as 6 cents per foot. The "10" in 10BaseT refers to 10Mbps capacity, the "Base" refers to **baseband transmission,** meaning that the entire bandwidth of the media is devoted to one data channel, and the "T" stands for twisted pair, the medium. Another important distinction of 10BaseT is that it specifies the use of a star topology with all Ethernet LAN segments connected to a centralized wiring hub. Other Ethernet standards and associated media are listed in Figure 7-7.

Application   The potential for collisions and retransmission on an Ethernet network, thanks to its CSMA/CD access methodology, has already been mentioned. In some cases, Ethernet networks with between 100 and 200 users barely use the 10-Mbps capacity of the network. However, the nature of the data transmitted is the key to determining potential network capacity problems. Character-based transmissions, such as typical data entry, in which a few characters at a time are typed and sent over the network, are much less likely to cause network capacity problems than the

IEEE 802.3 frame layout
IEEE 802.2 LLC data unit layout

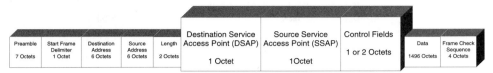

IEEE 802.2 HEADER FIELDS

SAP codes indicate the type of IEEE 802
compliant embedded protocols.

IEEE 802.3 frame layout
IEEE 802.2 LLC data unit layout with SNAP

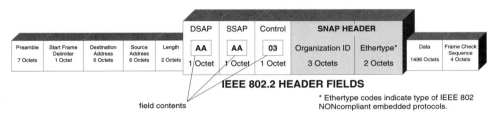

IEEE 802.2 HEADER FIELDS

field contents

* Ethertype codes indicate type of IEEE 802
NONcompliant embedded protocols.

Figure 7-6   IEEE 802.2 and Ethernet SNAP

transfer of GUI, or graphical user interface screen-oriented transmissions such as Windows-based applications. CAD/CAM images are even more bandwidth intensive.

Simultaneous requests for full-screen Windows-based transfers by 30 or more workstations on a single Ethernet LAN segment can cause collision and network capacity problems on an Ethernet network. As with any data communication

Standard	Popular Name	Speed	Media	Maximum Segment Length
10Base5	Frozen yellow garden hose	10Mbps	Thick coaxial cable (RG-8)	500 meters
10Base2	ThinNet, CheaperNet	10Mbps	Thin coaxial cable (RG-58)	185 meters
10BaseT	10BaseT, twisted pair Ethernet	10Mbps	Unshielded twisted pair	100 meters
10BaseFL	Fiber Ethernet FOIRL (Fiber Optic Inter Repeater Link)	10Mbps	Multimode fiber-optic cable	Described by IEEE 802.1j-1993 standard (1000 meters)
1Base5	StarLAN	1Mbps	Unshielded twisted pair	500 meters
10BaseT	StarLAN10	10Mbps	Unshielded twisted pair	100 meters

Figure 7-7   Ethernet Media-Specific Standards

problem, there are always solutions or ways to work around them. The point of these examples is to provide some assurance that, although Ethernet is not unlimited in its network capacity, in most cases, it provides more than enough bandwidth.

Token Ring

Origins   Credit for the first token ring network architecture has been given to Olaf Soderblum, who proposed such a network in 1969. IBM was the driving force behind the standardization and adoption of Token Ring, with a prototype in IBM's lab in Zurich, Switzerland, serving as a model for the eventual **IEEE 802.5** standard.

Functionality

- Access methodology: token passing.
- Logical topology: sequential.
- Physical topology: traditionally, ring; currently, most often star.

Standards   Unlike IEEE 802.3 Ethernet networks, which have a speed of 10 Mbps specified as part of the IEEE standard, the IEEE 802.5 Token Ring standard does not include a speed specification. IBM, the leading advocate of the Token Ring network architecture, has specified Token Ring network architectures which operate at 4 and 16 Mbps.

As mentioned earlier in the discussion of the token passing access methodology, the token, illustrated in Figure 7-8 along with the IEEE 802.5 Token Ring MAC sublayer frame layout, is actually a 24-bit formatted data packet.

IEEE 802.5 Token Frame Layout

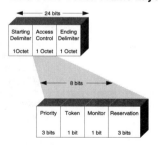

IEEE 802.5 MAC Sublayer Frame Layout

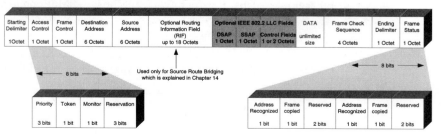

Figure 7-8   IEEE 802.5 Token Ring Token and MAC Sublayer Frame Layout

The IEEE 802.5 Token frame layout consists of the following fields:

- The starting delimiter field alerts the Token Ring network interface card installed in a workstation that a Token Ring frame is approaching. Notice that both the token frame and the MAC sublayer frame both start with the starting delimiter.

- Once the access control field is received, the workstation can distinguish between tokens and MAC sublayer frames. If the token bit within the access control field (see Figure 7-8) is set to 0, then the received frame represents a free token, in which case the access control field would be immediately followed by an ending delimiter. The workstation is welcome to receive the full token frame and change the token bit from 0 to 1 to indicate a busy token. The received starting delimiter field plus the access control field with the T (token) bit now set to 1 form the first two fields of an IEEE 802.5 MAC sublayer data frame, allowing the sending workstation to just append address information, data, and the remaining fields in the data frame layout and transmit this frame onto the ring.

- If the token bit on the received frame was set to 1, then the next field is the frame control field, which indicates whether this frame contains data or is a special network management frame.

- Following the frame control field are the destination and source address fields. The receiving network interface card reads the destination address to determine if it is the frame's intended recipient. If it is, then the workstation reads the rest of the frame into memory. If not, the NIC simply passes the rest of the bits of the frame along the ring without transferring them to the workstation's memory.

- The routing information field is used with devices known as source routing bridges, which are able to link together multiple Token Ring LANs. Source route bridging and other LAN-to-LAN connectivity options are discussed in Chapter 15.

- The IEEE 802.2 header fields are used in an identical manner as they are used with IEEE 802.3 Ethernet MAC sublayer frames. Likewise, IEEE 802.2 SNAP is also supported within the IEEE 802.5 MAC sublayer frame.

- The data field contains data in the form of embedded upper-level protocols if this is a data frame, and network management information if it is a network management frame, as indicated by the frame control field. The data field does not have a fixed maximum length, as in the case of Ethernet, but is effectively controlled by a timing limit as to how long any workstation can hold onto a token. The timing limit of 10 ms (milliseconds) imposes a practical limit on the size of the data field in a 4-Mbps Token Ring network to about 4500 bytes or to about 16,000 to 18,000 bytes on a 16-Mbps Token Ring network.

- The frame check sequence uses a 32-bit cyclical redundancy check in an identical manner to IEEE 802.3.

- The ending delimiter not only lets the workstation know that the end of the frame has arrived but also lets the workstation know if this was an intermediate frame with more related data to follow immediately behind.

The ending delimiter can also indicate if another station has found an error in a frame and has indicated that it should be ignored and returned around the ring to the source address workstation for removal from the ring.

- The frame status field serves an important role in letting the sending workstation know whether or not the frame was delivered successfully. If the destination workstation recognized its address, then the A (address recognized) bits are set to 1, and if the frame was successfully copied into the destination workstation's memory, the C (frame copied) bits are set to 1. There are two sets of A and C bits for redundancy, to help eliminate errors. To be more specific, since the A and C bits are set by the destination station after the frame has been received, they are not covered by the frame check sequence error detection mechanism.

One workstation on every Token Ring LAN is designated as the active monitor and acts as a kind of caretaker of the Token Ring network architecture. Being the active monitor requires no special hardware or software, and all other workstations are designated standby monitors. Among the tasks which can be performed by the active monitor are the following:

- Removes frames from the ring which have not been removed by their sending workstations.

- Regenerates lost or damaged tokens.

- Provides a special 24-bit buffer if the physical ring is so small that it does not have enough delay or latency to hold the 24-bit token. (For more information, see the In Sharper Focus: Token Ring and Timing.)

- Controls the master clock.

- Makes sure that there is only one designated active monitor on this ring.

Application IBM's Token Ring network architecture, adhering to the IEEE 802.5 standard, uses a star configuration, sequential message delivery, and a token-passing access methodology scheme.

Remembering that the sequential logical topology is equivalent to passing messages from neighbor to neighbor around a ring, the Token Ring network architecture is sometimes referred to as **logical ring, physical star.**

The Token Ring's use of the token-passing access methodology furnishes one of its key positive attributes. The guarantee of no data collisions, with assured data delivery afforded by the token-passing access methodology is a key selling point in some environments where immediate, guaranteed delivery is essential.

The second attribute in Token Ring's favor is the backing of a computer company of the magnitude of IBM. For those businesses facing integration of PCs with existing IBM mainframes and minicomputers, IBM's Token Ring network architecture offers assurance of the possibility of such an integration.

Although Token Ring is IBM's PC networking architecture, it is neither a closed system nor a monopoly. Third-party suppliers offer choices in the network adapter card and wiring hub (multistation access unit) markets, while numerous network operating systems run over the Token Ring architecture. Competition encourages research and development of new technology and may eventually drive prices down. Price is an important consideration with Token Ring. Network adapter cards for a Token Ring network tend to cost between one and one-half to two times as much as Ethernet network adapter cards.

ADDRESS BIT-ORDER REVERSAL

One small but significant difference between Ethernet and Token Ring networks is known as **address bit-order reversal**. As illustrated in Figure 7-9, both Ethernet and Token Ring refer to the first (leftmost) octet of the address as byte 0. Also, both Ethernet and Token Ring believe that bit 0 on byte 0, referred to as the **least significant bit,** should be transmitted first. However, in the case of IEEE 802.3, the least significant bit is the rightmost bit of the byte, and in the case of IEEE 802.5, it is the leftmost bit of the byte. This bit-order reversal is especially troublesome for translating bridges which must translate between Token Ring and Ethernet frames.

TOKEN RING AND TIMING

For the Token Ring network architecture to operate correctly, the 24-bit token must circulate continuously even if no workstations are in need of transmitting data. Therefore, the entire network must possess enough delay or latency to hold the entire 24-bit token. This latency or required delay can be computed by dividing the length of the token (24 bits) by the ring's transmission speed (4 Mbps), yielding a required latency of 6 microseconds. The next question is how far can an electrical signal travel in 6 microseconds? The answer to that question depends on the media through which the signal is traveling, with different media possessing different propagation velocities. For example, unshielded twisted pair has a propagation velocity of 0.59 times the speed of light, denoted as "c." The speed of light is equal to

Original Data Stream of 6 bytes

6 BYTES					
11110101	00110111	10111011	10000110	01110010	01010110

IEEE 802.3 Transmission

DESTINATION ADDRESS CONSISTING OF 6 BYTES

BYTE 0	BYTE 1	BYTE 2	BYTE 3	BYTE 4	BYTE 5
1 1 1 1 0 1 0 1	0 0 1 1 0 1 1 1	1 0 1 1 1 0 1 1	1 0 0 0 0 1 1 0	0 1 1 1 0 0 1 0	0 1 0 1 0 1 1 0
bit 7 bit 6 bit 5 bit 4 bit 3 bit 2 bit 1 bit 0	bit 7 bit 6 bit 5 bit 4 bit 3 bit 2 bit 1 bit 0	bit 7 bit 6 bit 5 bit 4 bit 3 bit 2 bit 1 bit 0	bit 7 bit 6 bit 5 bit 4 bit 3 bit 2 bit 1 bit 0	bit 7 bit 6 bit 5 bit 4 bit 3 bit 2 bit 1 bit 0	bit 7 bit 6 bit 5 bit 4 bit 3 bit 2 bit 1 bit 0

Note that in the IEEE 802.3 transmission the least significant bit (BIT 0) is transmitted last.

IEEE 802.5 Transmission

DESTINATION ADDRESS CONSISTING OF 6 BYTES

BYTE 0	BYTE 1	BYTE 2	BYTE 3	BYTE 4	BYTE 5
1 0 1 0 1 1 1 1	1 1 1 0 1 1 0 0	1 1 0 1 1 1 0 1	0 1 1 0 0 0 0 1	0 1 0 0 1 1 1 0	0 1 1 0 1 0 1 0
bit 0 bit 1 bit 2 bit 3 bit 4 bit 5 bit 6 bit 7	bit 0 bit 1 bit 2 bit 3 bit 4 bit 5 bit 6 bit 7	bit 0 bit 1 bit 2 bit 3 bit 4 bit 5 bit 6 bit 7	bit 0 bit 1 bit 2 bit 3 bit 4 bit 5 bit 6 bit 7	bit 0 bit 1 bit 2 bit 3 bit 4 bit 5 bit 6 bit 7	bit 0 bit 1 bit 2 bit 3 bit 4 bit 5 bit 6 bit 7

Note that in the IEEE 802.5 transmission the least significant bit (BIT 0) is transmitted first.

Figure 7-9 Address Bit-Order Reversal in Ethernet and Token Ring

300,000,000 meters/sec. Finally, the minimum ring size to introduce the required 6 microseconds of delay can be calculated as follows:

$$
\begin{aligned}
\text{Minimum ring size} &= \text{Required latency} \times \text{Propagation velocity of media} \\
&= 0.000006 \text{ sec} \times 0.59 \times 300,000,000 \text{ meters/sec} \\
&= 1062 \text{ meters} \\
&= 1.062 \text{ kilometers}
\end{aligned}
$$

According to this calculation, the minimum length of a Token Ring network, even for three or four workstations, would have to be over a kilometer. This is obviously not practical. As mentioned earlier, the active monitor station adds a 24-bit delay buffer to the ring to ensure that regardless of the size of the ring, the token will be able to circulate continually.

Managerial Perspective

TOKEN RING OR ETHERNET?

Discussions as to the relative merits of Token Ring or Ethernet network architectures were conducted at one time with all the fervor of a religious war. There seems to be less argument now, as estimates put the ratio of Ethernet to Token Ring networks at about 3 to 1. This is not to say that Ethernet is a better network architecture. The significant advantage of Ethernet in market share probably has more to do with the affordability and availability of its hardware. Ethernet cards sell for $20 to $150 while Token Ring cards sell for $219 to $475. A 12-port Ethernet hub sells for around $529 while the equivalent Token Ring MAU sells for $1459.

In terms of performance, Ethernet works just fine in most installations. Although Ethernet is said to offer 10 Mbps, when collisions and overhead are taken into consideration, actual throughputs of 6 Mbps are more the norm. There is no argument that Token Ring's deterministic access methodology eliminates collisions at higher traffic levels. However, with the overhead associated with the token management, performance at lower traffic levels can suffer. Research performed on 16-Mbps Token Ring, which features the early token release mechanism, has shown conflicting results. Some studies show that network performance is not significantly greater than 10 Mbps, while others show nearly a full 16 Mbps throughput. If one considers cost/Mbps of throughput rather than just pure equipment cost differences, Token Ring begins to look more favorable.

At one time, Token Ring network architectures were more easily integrated with minicomputer and mainframe environments. This is no longer true, as the mainframe/minicomputer world has evolved to embrace open systems, TCP/IP, and Ethernet.

In conclusion, the biggest difference between Token Ring and Ethernet continues to be the initial expense of the Token Ring hardware and the overwhelming market share of Ethernet. Performance is not significantly different and interoperability between the two network architectures is possible, although challenges do exist. Ethernet/Token Ring bridges, which provide transparent interoperability between the two network architectures, are detailed in Chapter 15.

FDDI

Origins   Fiber distributed data interface (FDDI) is a 100-Mbps network architecture which was first specified in 1984 by the American National Standards Institute

(ANSI) subcommittee entitled X3T9.5. It is important to note that FDDI is not an IEEE standard. However, it does support IEEE 802.2 logical link control protocols, offering it transparent interoperability to IEEE-compliant upper-layer protocols (layers 3 to 7).

Functionality

- Access methodology: modified token passing.
- Logical topology: sequential.
- Physical topology: dual counterrotating rings.

Built-in Reliability and Longer Distance   FDDI supplies not only a great deal (100 Mbps) of bandwidth, but also a high degree of reliability and security while adhering to standards-based protocols not associated with or promoted by any particular vendor.

FDDI's reliability comes not only from the fiber itself, which is immune to both electromagnetic interference **(EMI)** and radiofrequency interference **(RFI).** An additional degree of reliability is achieved through the design of its physical topology.

FDDI's physical topology is composed of not one, but two, separate rings around which data moves simultaneously in opposite directions. One ring is the primary data ring and the other is a secondary or backup data ring to be used only in the case of the failure of the primary ring or an attached workstation. Both rings are attached to a single hub or concentrator, which means a single point of failure remains in the hub while redundancy is achieved in the network media. Figure 7-10 illustrates some of the key features of the FDDI network architecture and technology, and Figure 7-11 more specifically illustrates the self-healing capabilities of its dual counterrotating rings network architecture.

In addition to speed and reliability, distance is another key feature of an FDDI LAN. Up to 500 nodes at 2 km apart can be linked to an FDDI network. The total media can stretch for a total circumference of up to 200 km (125 miles) if repeaters are used at least every 2 km. This increased distance capability makes FDDI an excellent choice as a high-speed backbone network for campus environments.

Another positive attribute of FDDI, illustrated in Figure 7-10, is its ability to interoperate easily with IEEE 802.3 10-Mbps Ethernet networks. A business does not have to scrap its entire existing network to upgrade part of it to 100 Mbps FDDI. An FDDI-to-Ethernet bridge is the specific technology employed in such a setup.

The technology involved with FDDI network architectures is similar in function to that of other network architectures and is illustrated in Figure 7-10. PCs, workstations, minicomputers, or mainframes that want to access the FDDI LAN must be equipped with either internal FDDI network adapter cards or external FDDI controllers.

One way in which some network managers cut down on the cost of FDDIs while still benefiting from the 100-Mbps bandwidth is to connect to only one of FDDI's two fiber rings. This type of connection is sometimes called **single-attachment stations,** or **SAS,** as opposed to **dual-attachment stations,** or **DAS,** in which both FDDI rings are accessed. Obviously, if a device is attached to only one FDDI ring, it loses the reliability afforded by the redundant secondary data ring.

At the heart of the FDDI LAN is the FDDI concentrator or hub. The design of these hubs is often modular, with backbone connections to both FDDI rings, management modules, and device attachment modules in various media varieties available for customized design and ease of installation.

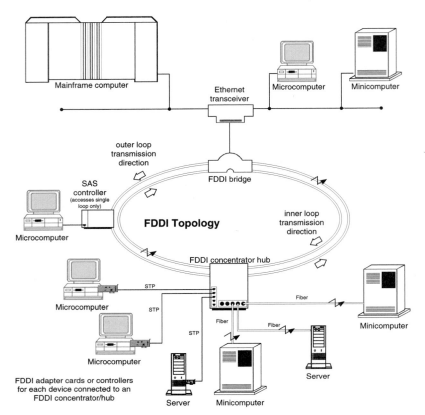

Figure 7-10 FDDI Network Architecture and Technology

Another key piece of FDDI technology is the FDDI-to-Ethernet bridge, which allows 10-Mbps Ethernet LANs to interface with the 100-Mbps FDDI LANs. The Ethernet LANs are often department-based networks, while the FDDI is more likely to be a campuswide backbone. Bridges may be able to connect either a single Ethernet or several Ethernets to the FDDI LAN.

Standards FDDI uses a modified token passing access methodology. The word "modified" is used here because the methodology is different from IEEE 802.5 Token Ring–type token passing in at least two key respects:

- First, because of the great potential distances on an FDDI LAN, it was impractical to turn "free" tokens into "busy" tokens and let a single station monopolize that token until it received confirmation of successful delivery of its data. Instead, unlike Token Ring which just flipped the T bit in the access control byte from 0 to 1 and appended a data frame, FDDI physically removes the token from the ring and transmits a full data frame. Upon completion of transmission, it immediately releases a new token. Recall that Token Ring waits until the transmitted frame returned before releasing the token. Collisions are still avoided, as only one station can have the free token at a time, and stations cannot put data messages onto the network without a token.

Dual-Attached Workstations in *Normal Operation*

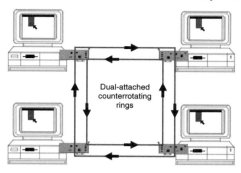

Self-healed after *Link Failure*

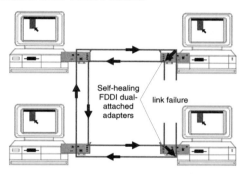

Self-healed after *Station Failure*

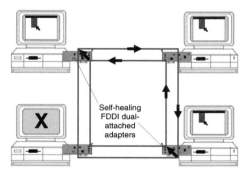

Figure 7-11   FDDI's Self-Healing Ability

- A second token passing modification in FDDI is that numerous messages may be sent by a single PC before the token is relinquished, as opposed to the "one message per token per customer" philosophy of the IEEE 802.5 token passing access methodology. Frames transmitted in a continuous stream are known as **synchronous frames** and are prioritized according to a methodology known as **synchronous bandwidth allocation (SBA),** which assigns fixed amounts of bandwidth to given stations. While synchronous frames are being transmitted, any unused network capacity can still be used by other workstations transmitting **asynchronous frames.**

Figure 7-12 illustrates both an FDDI token layout and an FDDI data frame layout.

An alternative to fiber-based FDDI is to run FDDI over copper wiring, either shielded or unshielded twisted pair, as used in Ethernet and Token Ring installations. Cost savings of UTP over fiber amount to about 33 percent. Because running a fiber-based architecture over copper sounds a little strange, this variation of FDDI has been dubbed **copper distributed data interface (CDDI).** It still supports 100 Mbps, but distance is limited to 100 meters per segment compared with the 2 km per segment of fiber-based FDDI. The official ANSI standard for CDDI is known as twisted pair–physical media dependent **(TP-PMD).** The pinouts or wiring patterns for TP-PMD are not the same as for 10BaseT Ethernet over twisted pair pinouts.

Application   To understand all the fuss about FDDI and CDDI, it is necessary to first understand why 10-Mbps Ethernet and 16-Mbps Token Ring may not contain sufficient bandwidth for the bandwidth-hungry applications of the not too distant future. The major bandwidth drivers fall into two major categories:

1. Network architecture trends.

2. Network application trends.

As far as trends in network architecture go, as more and more users are attached to LANs, the demand for overall network bandwidth increases. LANs are increasing in both size and overall complexity. Internetworking of LANs of various protocols via bridges and routers means more overall LAN traffic. FDDI is frequently used as a high-speed backbone network architecture servicing multiple lower-speed network segments, each of which supports multiple workstations.

Network applications are driving the demand for increased bandwidth as well. Distributed computing, data distribution, and client/server computing all rely on a network architecture foundation of high bandwidth and high reliability. Imaging, multimedia, and data/voice integration all require large amounts of bandwidth to transport and display these various data formats in "real" time.

In other words, for full-motion video to be transported across the LAN as part of a multimedia program, sufficient bandwidth must be available on that LAN for the video to run at full speed and not in slow motion. Likewise, digitized voice

FDDI Token Layout

Preamble	Starting Delimiter	Frame Control	Ending Delimiter
8 Octets	1 Octet	1 Octet	1 Octet

FDDI Data Frame Structure

Preamble	Starting Delimiter	Frame Control	Destination Address	Source Address	DATA up to	Frame Check Sequence	Ending Delimiter	Frame Status
8 Octets	1 Octet	1 Octet	6 Octets	6 Octets	4500 Octets	4 Octets (32 bit CRC)	.5 Octet (4 Bits)	1.5 Octets (12 Bits)

Figure 7-12   FDDI Token and Data Frame Layouts

transmission should sound "normal" when transported across a LAN of sufficient bandwidth.

The uses of the FDDI network architecture seem to fall into three categories:

1. **Campus backbone**   Not necessarily implying a college campus, this implementation is used for connecting LANs located throughout a series of closely situated buildings. Remember that the total ring circumference can equal 200 km, and multiple FDDI LANs are also always a possibility. Building backbones fall into this category as well, with perhaps a 100-Mbps FDDI building backbone going between floors connecting numerous 10-Mbps Ethernet LANs located on the various floors via routers. High bandwidth devices such as servers can be connected to the FDDI backbone via concentrators. Multiple concentrators attaching multiple devices to the FDDI rings, as illustrated in Figure 7-13, is known as a **dual**

Backbone

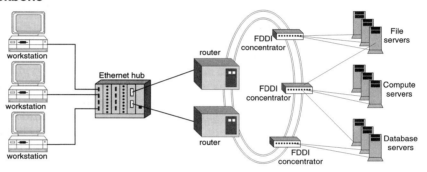

Workgroup

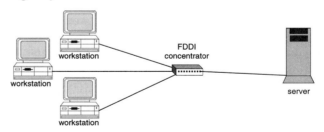

Sub-workgroup

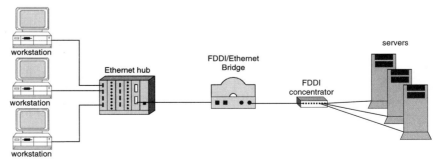

Figure 7-13   Alternative Applications of the FDDI Network Architecture

ring of trees. In some cases, a given server may be connected to more than one FDDI concentrator to provide redundant connections and increased fault tolerance. Using dual-connecting servers in this manner is known as **dual homing.**

2. **High-bandwidth workgroups**   The second application category is when the FDDI LAN is used as a truly local area network, connecting a few (less than 20) PCs or workstations which require high-bandwidth communication with each other. Multimedia workstations, engineering workstations, or CAD/CAM workstations are all good examples of high-bandwidth workstations. As "power users" turn increasingly toward GUIs such as Windows and OS/2, this constituency's bandwidth requirements will rise as well.

3. **High-bandwidth subworkgroup connections**   In some cases, only two or three devices, perhaps servers, need high-bandwidth requirements. As distributing computing and data distribution increase as part of the downsizing and applications rightsizing trends sweeping the information systems industry, an increasing demand for high-speed server-to-server data transfer will be seen. Figure 7-13 illustrates alternative applications of the FDDI network architecture.

After all of these positive features, surely there must be something negative to say about FDDI network architecture. Chief among the negatives is price, although how long this will be a negative remains to be seen. As with any other shared media network architecture, for a PC to access an FDDI LAN, it must be equipped with an FDDI network adapter card. These cards range in price from $1500 to $7500, with the lower priced cards able to attach to and use only one of the two FDDI data rings. Compare these prices with the average Ethernet card, at $75 to $200, and the average Token Ring card at roughly twice that price.

As FDDI gains in popularity and competition increases in the FDDI technology market, prices will undoubtedly fall, although it is doubtful they will ever reach Ethernet price levels. The fiber media itself is seen as a negative factor by some as well. Although fiber is lightweight and can be packed more densely than copper wire, it is made of glass and can break. Also, connecting, terminating, and splicing fiber-optic cables requires special tools and training. These obstacles can be overcome and, at least in some cases, the "fear of fiber" may be nothing more than the fear of the unknown.

Managerial Perspective

FDDI'S FUTURE

Occasionally in the field of data communications and networking, one technology is eclipsed or replaced by a newer technology which might be cheaper, easier to work with, or both. This may be the fate of FDDI. At one time, FDDI was the only network architecture alternative to turn to when Ethernet and Token Ring could no longer meet demands for bandwidth capacity. As you will see in the next section, numerous alternative high-speed network architectures able to exceed FDDI in terms of price, performance, and ease of use now exist. That is not to say that FDDI is dead, but the handwriting may be on the wall.

■ HIGH-SPEED NETWORK ARCHITECTURES

100BaseT

The 100BaseT network represents a family of fast Ethernet standards offering 100-Mbps performance and adhering to the CSMA/CD access methodology. The details of the operation of 100BaseT are in the **IEEE 802.3u** proposed standard. The three media-specific physical layer standards of 100BaseT are as follows:

- **100BaseTX** — This is the most common of the three standards and the one for which the most technology is available. It specifies 100-Mbps performance over two pair of Category 5 UTP (unshielded twisted pair) or two pair of Type 1 STP (shielded twisted pair).

- **100BaseT4** — Physical layer standard for 100 Mbps transmission over four pair of Category 3, 4, or 5 UTP.

- **100BaseFX** — Physical layer standard for 100 Mbps transmission over fiber-optic cable.

Network Architecture   The 100BaseT standards use the same IEEE 802.3 MAC sublayer frame layout and yet transmit it at 10 times faster than 100BaseT. Obviously, there must be a trade-off somewhere. The trade-off comes in the maximum network diameter:

- 10BaseT's maximum network diameter is 2500 meters, with up to 4 repeaters/hubs between any two end nodes.

- 100BaseT's maximum network diameter is 210 meters, with up to only 2 repeaters/hubs between end nodes.

The 100BaseT network architecture is implemented as a shared-media LAN which links 100BaseT workstations via 100BaseT hubs and repeaters.

In Sharper Focus

TIMING ISSUES AND 100BASET NETWORK DIAMETER

Collisions are a fact of life with any CSMA/CD-based network architecture. The time required for a given workstation to detect a collision is known as **slot time** and is measured in bits. When collisions occur, the transmitting station must be notified of the collision so that the affected frame can be retransmitted. However, this collision notification and retransmission must occur before the slot time has expired. The slot time for both 10BaseT and 100BaseT is 512 bits.

The speed of 100BaseT is obviously 10 times as fast as 10BaseT. To be certain that collision notifications are received by 100BaseT network-attached workstations before their constant slot time expires, the maximum network diameter has to be reduced proportionally to the increase in network speed. As a result, the maximum network diameter shrinks from 2500 meters to 210 meters.

Technology   Most of the 100BaseT NICs are called **10/100 NICs,** which means they are able to support either 10BaseT or 100BaseT, but not both simultaneously. These cards cost not much more than quality 10BaseT only cards, allowing network managers to buy 100BaseT capability now and enable it later when the requisite 100BaseT hubs are installed.

The 10BaseT and 100BaseT networks can interoperate only with the help of internetworking devices such as 10/100 bridges and routers. These types of technology are discussed in more depth in Chapter 15.

Some Ethernet switches, which are discussed in Chapter 8, have the capability to support 100BaseT connections and to autosense, or distinguish between, 10BaseT and 100BaseT traffic. Figure 7-14 illustrates a representative 100BaseT installation.

100VG-AnyLAN

The **100VG-AnyLAN** network architecture is a 100-Mbps alternative to 100BaseT which replaces the CSMA/CD access methodology with **demand priority access,** or **DPA,** otherwise known as **demand priority protocol (DPP).** Details of the 100VG-AnyLAN network architecture are contained in the proposed **IEEE 802.12** standard. The "AnyLAN" part of this network architecture's name refers to its ability to deliver standard IEEE 802.3 or IEEE 802.5 MAC layer frames. However, both of these frame types cannot be delivered simultaneously by the same 100VG-AnyLAN network.

IEEE 802.3 and IEEE 802.5 Support   The 100VG-AnyLAN's ability to support IEEE 802.3 and IEEE 802.5 frame types and networks more specifically means the following:

- If current cabling for existing 10BaseT or Token Ring LANs meets the respective cabling specifications for those LANs, then 100VG-AnyLAN will run over the existing LAN cabling without changes to network design or cabling.

- Current network systems and application programs do not have to be modified to operate with the upgraded 100VG-AnyLAN network interface cards.

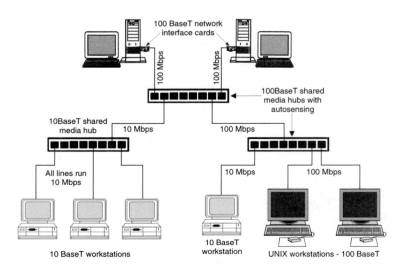

Figure 7-14   100BaseT Network Architecture Implementation

- 10BaseT and Token Rings LANs can communicate with 100VG-AnyLANs by linking the respective LANs with internetworking devices such as bridges and routers.

Figure 7-15 illustrates the integration of IEEE 802.3, IEEE 802.5, and 100VG-AnyLAN network architectures.

Network Architecture   The 100VG-AnyLAN is able to match 100BaseT's speed performance and offer the following network architecture characteristics:

- Supports a network diameter of up to 2500 meters between any two end nodes. This is the same as 10BaseT and over 10 times the maximum diameter of 100BaseT.

- Supports up to four hubs/repeaters between any two end nodes while 100BaseT supports up to two.

Obviously, 100VG-AnyLAN cannot offer these gains in network architecture compared to 100BaseT without some sort of trade-off.

The major difference is in the cabling requirements. Whereas, 10BaseT and 100BaseT require only two pair of UTP to operate, 100VG-AnyLAN requires four pair of either Category 3, 4, or 5 UTP using a signaling methodology known as quartet signaling or channeling. Cabling standards have also been defined for two pair of Type 1 shielded twisted pair as well as single-mode and multimode fiber-optic cable.

Demand Priority Access   Perhaps the most unusual aspect of the 100VG-AnyLAN network architecture is the demand priority access access methodology, also known as demand priority media access (DPMA). This unique access methodology eliminated

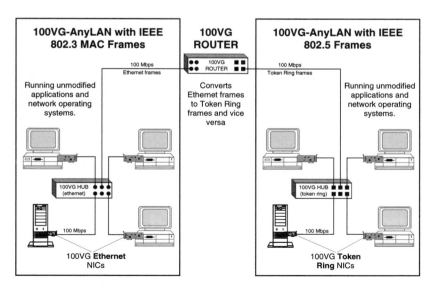

Figure 7-15   IEEE 802.3, IEEE 802.5, and 100VG-AnyLAN Network Architectures

the collisions and retransmissions characteristic of Ethernet and the token rotation delays of Token Ring. Following are the key points of this access methodology:

- Specialized 100VG-AnyLAN hubs control all access to the network.

- Using a **round robin polling scheme,** the hubs scan each port in sequence to see if the attached workstations have any traffic to transmit. The round robin polling scheme is distributed through a hierarchical arrangement of cascaded hubs.

- Ports can be designated as high priority, thereby giving priority delivery status to time-sensitive types of traffic such as video or voice which require guaranteed delivery times for smooth presentation. This makes 100VG-AnyLAN especially well suited for multimedia traffic.

- These high and low priorities can be assigned by application programs as well as ports.

- High-priority ports cannot permanently monopolize the entire network. Once lower-priority ports have been timed out for 250 to 300 milliseconds, they are boosted to high priority.

In Sharper Focus

CASCADING HUBS AND THE ROUND ROBIN POLLING SCHEME

As illustrated in Figure 7-16, the central hub, also known as the controlling hub or the root hub, controls access to the network, while all lower-level hubs maintain communication with attached workstations and maintain address tables identifying which workstations are attached to which ports. When a workstation requests permission of its locally attached hub to load a message onto the network, that request for permission is passed up through the hierarchy of hubs until it reaches the designated controlling hub. The corresponding granted permission to transmit onto the network is passed down through the hub hierarchy to the initially requesting workstation. Remember, a maximum of only four hubs or repeaters can lie between any two end nodes or workstations.

Technology The implementation of a 100VG-AnyLAN requires compliant NICs, driver software, and hubs. 100VG-AnyLAN NICs cost between $225 and $300 while hubs cost about $300 per port. For ease of migration 10/100 Ethernet 100VG-AnyLAN NICs are available for generally less than $300. When it comes to technology, attention must be paid to whether this 100VG-AnyLAN technology will be transporting Ethernet frames or Token Ring frames. Specific NICs and hubs must be purchased for each of the two transported frame types, with Ethernet 100VG-AnyLAN technology being more readily available than Token Ring 100VG-AnyLAN technology.

Isochronous Ethernet

Although the ability to transport time-sensitive traffic such as voice, video, or multimedia is one of the advantages of 100VG-AnyLAN, other network architectures such as **isochronous Ethernet,** also known as **Iso-Ethernet,** can also effectively transport such traffic although not at 100-Mbps performance. Details of the Iso-

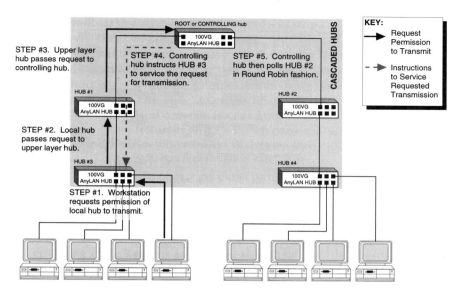

Figure 7-16 Cascading Hubs and the Round Robin Polling Scheme

Ethernet network architecture are contained in the **IEEE 802.9a** standard, which is officially known as Isochronous Ethernet Integrated Services. The term **isochronous** refers to any signaling system in which all connections or circuits are synchronized using a single common clocking reference. This common clocking mechanism allows such systems to offer guaranteed delivery times which are very important to streaming or time-sensitive traffic such as voice and video.

Network Architecture   One unique feature of the Iso-Ethernet network architecture is its close relationship with **integrated services digital network (ISDN)** wide area network services. Iso-Ethernet offers a combination of services by dividing the overall 16.144-Mbps bandwidth delivered to each workstation into several service-specific channels:

- A 10-Mbps ISDN **P channel** is reserved for Ethernet traffic and is completely compatible with 10BaseT Ethernet. In fact, this P channel can be used by 10BaseT NICs, allowing network managers to selectively or gradually migrate to Iso-Ethernet offering the multimedia capabilities to only those workstations which require it.

- A 6.144-Mbps ISDN **C channel** is reserved for streaming time-sensitive traffic such as multimedia applications.

The 6.144-Mbps C channel is further subdivided:

- Ninety-six 64-Kbps ISDN **B channels** carry the actual multimedia traffic. Applications are able to aggregate these B channels as needed up to the 6.144-Mbps limit.

- One 64-Kbps ISDN **D channel** is used for management tasks such as call control and signaling.

The 6.144-Mbps C channel which carries the multimedia traffic uses the same 8-KHz clocking signal as the commercial ISDN WAN services offered by long distance carriers, enabling a transparent interface between the Iso-Ethernet LAN and WAN segments. This "same clocking signal" is the derivation of the term isochronous (Iso = "Same as" and chronous = "timing").

The network diameter of an Iso-Ethernet network is limited to 100 meters from the most distant LAN workstation to the WAN interface. Iso-Ethernet runs over two pair of Category 3 or 5 unshielded twisted pair, allowing it to operate over existing network wiring in many cases.

Iso-Ethernet networks operate in three different service modes:

1. **10BaseT Mode**   uses only the 10-Mbps P channel for Ethernet traffic.

2. **Multiservice Mode**   uses both the 10-Mbps P channel for Ethernet and the 6.144-Mbps C channel for video/multimedia.

3. **All Isochronous Mode**   uses all 16.144 Mbps (248 × 64-Kbps channels) for streaming protocols. This amount of isochronous bandwidth supports real-time video or voice distribution.

Figure 7-17 illustrates an implemented Iso-Ethernet architecture including WAN links, transparent interoperability with 10BaseT workstations, and simultaneous transmission of Ethernet and multimedia traffic. Figure 7-18 illustrates the breakdown of the 16.144-Mbps Iso-Ethernet bandwidth.

Technology   Iso-Ethernet hubs, known as **attachment units (AU),** cost between $400 and $500 per port while Iso-Ethernet NICs cost between $200 and $300 each. Most Iso-Ethernet AUs include an integrated WAN port configured to be linked to commercial ISDN services available from long distance carriers. A workstation with an Iso-Ethernet NIC installed is properly referred to as **integrated services terminal equipment (ISTE).** To transmit isochronous traffic, 10BaseT NICs and hubs must be replaced. However, not all 10BaseT NICs and hubs have to be replaced at once.

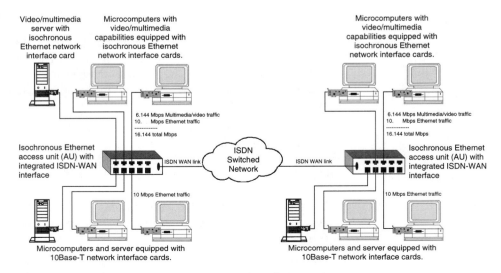

Figure 7-17   Isochronous Ethernet Network Architecture

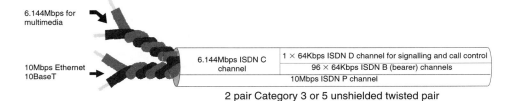

6.144Mbps for multimedia

10Mbps Ethernet 10BaseT

6.144Mbps ISDN C channel	1 × 64Kbps ISDN D channel for signalling and call control
	96 × 64Kbps ISDN B (bearer) channels
	10Mbps ISDN P channel

2 pair Category 3 or 5 unshielded twisted pair

Figure 7-18   Isochronous Ethernet Bandwidth Profile

A TOP-DOWN APPROACH TO NETWORK ARCHITECTURE ANALYSIS

Many of the shared media network architectures reviewed in this chapter are ideal in certain situations. There is no one "best" network architecture. In addition to all of the shared media network architectures reviewed in this chapter, another entire category of network architectures known as switched network architectures are reviewed in the next chapter. Deciding which network architecture is best in any given situation requires a top-down approach:

- What types of applications are required to meet business objectives?
  - Multimedia?
  - Collaborative computing?
  - Large or frequent distributed database lookups?
  - Specialized applications such as CAD/CAM, medical imaging, or video editing?

- What are the bandwidth and network delivery requirements of the data produced by these applications?
  - High bandwidth needs?
  - Guaranteed delivery times for time-sensitive or streaming traffic?

- What is the cost threshold for upgrading to a high-speed network architecture?
  - FDDI NICs traditional cost about $1000 each and offer 100 Mbps.
  - 100VG-AnyLAN NICs cost about $300 each and offer 100 Mbps. At these prices, perhaps a company doesn't even need a high bandwidth or time-sensitive application to justify upgrading to a high-speed network architecture. Even traditional applications will be transported much more quickly.

- Which upgrade philosophy is preferred?
  - Replace all NICs, hubs, and possibly cabling?
  - Replace hubs and NICs gradually?
  - Replace just the hubs and leave the NICs and cabling alone? This option is really available only with switched network architectures, which are studied in the next chapter.

- When considering an upgrade to a particular high-speed network architecture, these are just some of the issues that may require attention:
  - New NICs.
  - New NIC drivers—can be a real problem. Where is the source of these drivers? As will be explained later, drivers must be compatible with a

particular NIC and the network operating system and operating system of the computer in which the NIC is installed.

- Proper cabling to meet new cable specifications.
- New hubs.
- Management software.
- New distance limitations.
- New rules for cascading hubs or maximum number of repeaters between two end nodes.
- Availability of internetworking hardware, such as bridges and routers, which are compatible with this particular high-speed network architecture. Without such hardware, the network cannot be extended beyond the immediate local network.

SUMMARY

To properly analyze and design local area networks, it is absolutely essential to have a thorough understanding of the OSI model and its constituent layers. Of particular interest is the data-link layer which serves as the home of the IEEE LAN standards and is subdivided into the MAC and LLC sublayers for that purpose. Encapsulation and deencapsulation as OSI model processes are the basis of understanding communication between two computing devices. The importance of protocol compatibility to network communications can be modeled using the OSI model as an open framework for protocol compatibility design.

The local area network architecture model distills all network architectures into three basic components: access methodology, logical topology, and physical topology. Network architectures applied to a variety of media alternatives are known as network configurations. Key access methodologies are CSMA/CD and token passing, logical topologies are either broadcast or sequential, and physical topologies are most often star, though bus and ring are also possible.

Two of the most popular network architectures are Ethernet (IEEE 802.3) and Token Ring (IEEE 802.5). Debates as to the relative merits between the two are no longer as great as they once were given Ethernet's market dominance and significant price advantage. The most popular current implementation of Ethernet is 10BaseT, which uses unshielded twisted pair as media.

FDDI is the most stable traditional high-speed network architecture offering 100-Mbps performance over dual counterrotating rings of fiber-optic cable. The dual counterrotating network architecture affords FDDI exceptional fault tolerance, redundancy, and reliability.

More recent high-speed network architectures have been proposed. The 100BaseT network is a CSMA/CD-based 100 Mbps network architecture that operates over two pair of twisted pair but is limited to a network diameter of only 210 meters. The 100VG-AnyLAN network is compatible with both IEEE 802.3 Ethernet and IEEE 802.5 Token Ring, but requires four pair of unshielded twisted pair to operate and is championed primarily by a single vendor: Hewlett-Packard. The 100VG-AnyLAN network uses demand priority protocol as an access methodology allowing time-sensitive traffic such as voice, video, and multimedia to be delivered effectively. An alternative method of delivering multimedia traffic is isochronous Ethernet, which is closely aligned with ISDN standards. Iso-Ethernet offers both a 10-Mbps channel for Ethernet and a 6.144-Mbps channel for multimedia or time-sensitive traffic.

No single network architecture can be considered the best in all situations. Top-down analysis examining business, application, and data issues is required to determine which network architecture is most appropriate in each situation.

KEY TERMS

10/100 NICs, 255
100BaseFX, 255
100BaseT4, 255
100BaseTX, 255
100VG-AnyLAN, 256
10Base2, 243
10Base5, 243
10BaseFL, 243
10BaseT, 242
1Base5, 243
access methodologies, 235
active monitor, 236
address bit-order reversal, 247
applications layer, 232
asynchronous frames, 252
attachment units, 260
AU, 260
B channel, 259
baseband transmission, 242
broadcast, 238
bus, 238
C channel, 259
Carrier sense multiple access with
  collision detection, 236
CDDI, 252
Copper distributed data interface, 252
CRC, 241
CSMA/CD, 236
cyclical redundancy check, 241
D channel, 259
DAS, 249
data-link layer, 230
deencapsulation, 235
demand priority access, 256
demand priority protocol, 256
DPA, 256
DPP, 256
dual attachment station, 249

dual homing, 254
dual ring of trees, 253
early token release mechanism, 237
EMI, 249
encapsulation, 234
end-to-end network links, 231
Ethernet, 240
Ethernet II, 240
FDDI, 248
fiber distributed data interface, 248
frame check sequence, 241
frame status flags, 236
frames, 231
header, 231
IEEE, 230
IEEE 802.12, 256
IEEE 802.2, 231
IEEE 802.3, 240
IEEE 802.3u, 255
IEEE 802.5, 244
IEEE 802.9a, 259
Institute of Electrical and Electronic
  Engineers, 230
integrated services digital network,
  259
integrated services terminal equipment, 260
ISDN, 259
Iso-Ethernet, 258
isochronous, 259
isochronous Ethernet, 258
ISTE, 260
least significant bit, 247
LLC, 241
LLC sublayer, 231
logical link control, 231
logical ring, physical star, 246
logical topology, 238

MAC sublayer, 231
media access control, 231
media sharing LANs, 235
message, 232
network interface card, 231
network layer, 231
octet, 240
OSI model, 230
P channel, 259
packets, 231
physical layer, 230
physical topology, 238
point-to-point data links, 230
presentation layer, 232
propagation delay, 236
protocol, 230
protocol discriminator, 242
RFI, 249
ring, 238
round robin polling scheme, 258
SAS, 249
SBA, 251
sequential, 238
session layer, 232
single attachment station, 249
single point of failure, 239
slot time, 255
SNAP, 242
star, 239
subnetwork access protocol, 242
synchronous bandwidth allocation,
  251
synchronous frames, 251
token, 236
token passing, 236
TP-PMD, 252
trailer, 231
transport layer, 232

REVIEW QUESTIONS

1. What is the importance of the OSI model to local area network analysis and design?
2. What is a protocol?
3. What is the relationship between protocols and the OSI model?
4. What is the overall purpose of the physical layer?
5. What are the major differences between a point-to-point link and an end-to-end link?
6. Why is the data-link layer of particular interest to LAN network architectures?
7. Define the relationship between the two data-link layer sublayers.
8. What does the introduction of data-link layer sublayers offer in terms of increased interoperability options?
9. In general, what are the purposes of the header and trailer added to data-link layer frames?

10. Where are data-link layer frames built, and why is this an appropriate place?
11. What is the relationship between the network layer and the data-link layer?
12. What is the relationship between the transport layer and the network layer?
13. Why is the session layer of more interest to client/server information systems?
14. Name at least two misconceptions in interpretating layer functionality.
15. Briefly explain the purpose of encapsulation/deencapsulation.
16. What are the three elements which make up any network architecture?
17. Compare and contrast CSMA/CD and token passing as access methodologies.
18. What are two potential causes of collisions in Ethernet networks?
19. What does the early token release mechanism accomplish?
20. What actually is a token?
21. What is the difference between a logical and a physical topology?
22. Differentiate between the broadcast and sequential logical topologies.
23. Differentiate between the bus, star, and ring physical topologies.
24. Differentiate between Ethernet II and IEEE 802.3 Ethernet.
25. What is the relationship between IEEE 802.2 and IEEE 802.3?
26. Differentiate between IEEE 802.2 and Ethernet SNAP.
27. What is a protocol discriminator?
28. Differentiate between the various media-specific alternative configurations of Ethernet.
29. What are the unique characteristics of a Token Ring network architecture?
30. What is the role of the active monitor in a Token Ring network?
31. How are timing issues significant to Token Ring networks?
32. Differentiate between Ethernet and Token Ring in terms of performance at various traffic levels.
33. What advantages does FDDI offer over Ethernet and Token Ring?
34. Explain the self-healing powers of FDDI.
35. What are FDDI's primary negative attributes?
36. What are the three primary uses of the FDDI network architecture?
37. What are the advantages and disadvantages of CDDI over FDDI?
38. What is the advantage of dual homing?
39. Compare the advantages and disadvantages of 100BaseT versus FDDI.
40. Describe the three standards defined for 100BaseT.
41. What is the advantage of buying 10/100 NICs?
42. Describe demand priority protocol.
43. How does demand priority protocol ensure that low-priority traffic does not get permanently shut out of network access?
44. Compare the advantages and disadvantages of 100BaseT versus 100VG-AnyLAN.
45. Compare the advantages and disadvantages of isochronous Ethernet versus 100VG-AnyLAN.
46. What are some unique attributes of isochronous Ethernet compared to other high-speed network architectures?
47. What does isochronous mean?
48. Describe the relationship between isochronous Ethernet and ISDN.

ACTIVITIES

1. Prepare a presentation or bulletin board consisting of an empty OSI seven-layer model. As local area networks or network operating systems are encountered, place the protocols in the proper layers of the OSI model.
2. From the previous activity, determine which categories of protocols do not conform well to a particular layer of the OSI model.
3. Design an alternative network communications protocol model to the OSI model. Justify why the new model is more effective than the OSI model.
4. Choose a particular protocol stack and outline the frame layouts for each protocol in each layer of the OSI model. Be sure to indicate relationships between protocols as to which protocols are encapsulated by which other protocols.
5. Investigate the IEEE 802.4 Token Bus standard. Report on its history, implementation, available technology, current status, and an explanation of this current status.
6. Survey the local area network implementations in your school or business. Report on the physical topologies found. Explain your results.
7. Investigate the daisy-chain physical topology. Is it truly a unique physical topology or a variation of one of the three primary physical topologies?
8. Conduct a survey of Ethernet networks in your school or business. What is the medium of choice

in each installation? Why was each medium chosen in each situation?

9. Survey schools or companies which have installed Token Ring networks. Report on the reasons for their choice and add your own analysis of the results.

10. Survey schools or businesses which employ FDDI network architectures. Gather information regarding motivation, installation date, satisfaction, problems, and the outcome of a similar decision on network architecture made today.

11. Investigate the availability and cost of technology for the three standards defined for 100BaseT. Analyze your results.

12. Investigate the availability and cost of technology for 100VG-AnyLAN varieties. Analyze your results.

13. Compare the availability and cost of 100BaseT technology versus 100VG-AnyLAN technology. Analyze your results.

14. Investigate the cost and availability of isochronous Ethernet technology. Analyze your results.

FEATURED REFERENCES

General References

Goldman, James. *Applied Data Communications: A Business Oriented Approach* (New York: John Wiley & Sons, 1995).

Hardy, James. *Inside Networks* (Englewood Cliffs, NJ: Prentice-Hall, 1995).

Leidigh, Christopher. An 802 LAN Standards Primer. *Communications Systems Design*, 1; 5 (September 1995), 30.

Naugle, Matthew. *Network Protocol Handbook* (New York: McGraw-Hill, 1994).

Shimada, K. Karl. High Speed LAN Shoot-out. *Data Communications*, 24; 4 (March 21, 1995), 97.

Shimada, K. Karl. High Speed LAN Shoot-out II. *Data Communications*, 24; 10 (August, 1995), 91.

Tolly, Kevin. Token Ring vs. Ethernet: The Real Cost Story. *Data Communications*, 24; 7 (May 21, 1995), 23.

LAN Architecture and Design

Charney, Howard. Ever Faster Goes the LAN. *Network Computing*, 5; 14 (November 15, 1994), 88.

Derfler, Frank. The Pefect Network. *PC Magazine*, 14; 13 (July 1995), 224.

Eng, John and James Mollenauer. IEEE Project 802.14: Standards for Digital Convergence. *IEEE Communications*, 33; 5 (May 1995), 20.

Garris, John. The Greed for Speed. *PC Magazine*, 14; 8 (April 25, 1995), NE1.

Husselbaugh, Brett. (Mis)Using Bandwidth. *Byte*, 19; 12 (December 1994), 117.

Jeffries, Ron and Art Whitmann. The Great ATM-FDDI Debate. *Network Computing*, 5; 15 (December 1, 1994), 131.

Parnell, Tere. Shopping for a High-Speed Vehicle. *LAN Times*, 11; 12 (June 5, 1995), 81.

Shimmin, Bradley. LAN Technologies: Sharing the Workload. *LAN Times*, 12; 1 (January 9, 1995), 58.

Fast Ethernet

Chiang, Al. A Look at 100BASE-T. *Communications Systems Design*, 1; 4 (August 1995), 43.

Costa, Janis. *Planning and Designing High Speed Networks Using 100VG-AnyLAN* (Englewood Cliffs, NJ: Prentice-Hall, 1994).

Drews, James and Joel Conover. Fast Ethernet: Let Those Heavy-Bandwidth Apps Fly! *Network Computing*, 6; 5 (May 1, 1995), 108.

Finneran, Micheal. Life in the Fast LAN. *Business Communications Review*, 25; 5 (May 1995), 62.

Forbath, Theo and Christine Morrison. 100Mbps Ethernet Eases the Bandwidth Blues. *Business Communications Review*, 25; 4 (April 1995), 29.

Melatti, Lee. Fast Ethernet: 100Mbit/s Made Easy. *Data Communications*, 23; 16 (November 1994), 111.

Rauch, Peter and Scott Lawrence. 100VG-AnyLAN: The Other Fast Ethernet. *Data Communications*, 24; 3 (March 1995), 129.

Tolly, Kevin. Testing the Speed Limit for Fast Ethernet. *Data Communications*, 24; 3 (March 1995), 41.

FDDI

Axner, David. Field Experience with FDDI. *Business Communications Review*, 24; 12 (December 1994), 35.

Restivo, Ken. The Boring Facts About FDDI. *Data Communications*, 23; 18 (December 1994), 85.

Token Ring

Guruge, Anura. Token Ring—The Next Generation. *Business Communications Review*, 24; 9 (September 1994), 48.

Ethernet/Isochronous Ethernet

Brand, Richard. Iso-Ethernet: Bridging the Gap from WAN to LAN. *Data Communications*, 24; 9 (July 1995), 103.

Fritz, Jeffrey. Video Connections. *Byte*, 20; 5 (May 1995), 113.

Miastkowski, Stan. Daisy-Chain Ethernet. *Byte*, 20; 1 (January 1995), 229.

Pickett, Scott. Isochronous Ethernet for Multimedia Design. *Communications Systems Design*, 1; 5 (September 1995), 41.

Sodergren, Mark. Pumping Up 10Base-T with IsoEthernet. *Network World*, 12; 32 (August 7, 1995), 33.

CASE STUDY

Chapter 7

NETWORK CALLS FOR 100MBPS

Manager Goes to 100VG-AnyLAN to Process 40GB Hourly

In an age in which a company's ability to access and process information determines its success, Scott Armstrong, systems manager for a call-center organization, is constantly scrambling to provide more efficient access to crucial contact databases.

Armstrong is network systems manager for Infocision Management Corp., a company that manages fund-raising and telemarketing campaigns for political and nonprofit entities.

When Armstrong joined the Akron, Ohio-based company six years ago, he helped two people manage a small network with one 386-based file server and 15 workstations processing 600MB of data. Today, Armstrong is one of 28 people overseeing a Novell Inc. NetWare LAN with nine file servers and 155 workstations processing 40GB of data hourly.

"We're processing millions and millions of records each day," said Armstrong. "With all that data, we always need to provide more bandwidth, more disk space, faster machines."

To help alleviate the bandwidth crunch in one department, Armstrong and his team upgraded the workgroup to 100VG-AnyLAN technology.

The departments most plagued by performance problems are the two responsible for transferring client data to and from the call-management system. At the start of each new phone campaign, Infocision employees on the NetWare LAN must translate contact information from a variety of media and format types to one the XENIX call-management system can use. At the end of the campaigns, clients require reports and new databases containing the results.

"I had segmented all I could," said Armstrong. "Any way we can minimize the amount of traffic between the workstations and the server, or speed up the flow of that data, is a benefit. So we took the easiest step, increasing the size of the pipe between the server and stations. We put the workgroup on VG."

Armstrong had considered revamping the network with a switched architecture, giving each user dedicated 20Mbps and having a 100Mbps pipe to the server.

"The cost per port for those devices was too high," said Armstrong. "I was looking at spending $60,000. Instead, we opted for VG, which, for not a lot of money, gave us a lot faster throughput."

Armstrong has installed one 100VG-AnyLAN hub on which he has put seven workstations. He said this has resulted in an average performance increase of 30 percent. He plans to increase the number of stations and 100VG segments.

Trying to Keep Up

Armstrong is pleased with the performance of the upgraded segment, but the company's growth, which has averaged 35 percent every year, will require more improvements.

Infocision maintains one office in Akron that runs two phone centers and two offices 20 miles away in Green Township that run three phone centers; additional offices are anticipated. The sites are connected with Newport Systems Solutions Inc. routers that send data over switched-56Kbps links.

Every hour, employees generate status reports about each campaign. That process sends 5MB to 10MB of data over the lines from the remote site to headquarters. Upgrading those links is among Armstrong's top priorities. He's investigating T-1 lines.

Armstrong also is looking into upgrading the network backbone. Currently, 15 segments on 13 Accton Technology Corp. Ethernet concentrators, as well as the VG segment, feed into a 10Mbps backbone.

"We definitely need a 100Mbps backbone," explained Armstrong. "I don't want to use any of the fast-Ethernet solutions because I don't think they can support a backbone." He's considering a more centralized routing system, and eventually he may put in a switch.

Armstrong also said he needs to upgrade the database technology itself. Today, the company stores its information in Borland International Inc.'s dBASE III Plus format. The MIS team builds all its own applications in-house. Armstrong wants to move to a SQL server architecture but notes that the current investment in dBASE equipment, software, and training will make that difficult. He plans to begin the transition in the next few quarters.

In addition to technological hurdles, Armstrong has problems finding downtime to work on the system. The call centers run from 8 a.m. to midnight; at 2 a.m. the fulfillment center starts to generate letters confirming the day's donations.

Evidently, the pace suits him, though: "There's always something we need to be doing; another problem we need to solve. I'd hate it if things moved slowly around here," he said.

Source: Michelle Rae McLean (February 13, 1995). Network Calls for 100Mbps. *LAN Times*, 12(3), 31. Reprinted with permission of McGraw-Hill, *LAN Times*.

BUSINESS CASE STUDY QUESTIONS

Activities

1. Complete a top-down model for this case by gleaning facts from the case and placing them in the proper layer of the top-down model. After you have completed the top-down model, analyze and detail those instances when requirements were clearly passed down from upper to lower layers of the model and solutions to those requirements were passed up from lower to upper layers.
2. Detail any questions that may occur to you about the case for which answers are not clearly stated in the article.

Business

1. What is the importance of quick access to data for the company profiled in this case study?
2. What are the typical types of business activities conducted by this company?
3. What was the business motivation for investigating higher bandwidth networking technology?
4. What is the company's growth rate and what effect does that have on strategic network planning?

Application

1. What types of applications were run by this organization in support of their business activities?
2. Are applications primarily purchased or developed in-house?

Data

1. What is the volume of data processed on an hourly basis?
2. How many records are processed on a daily basis?

3. What is the effect of these data volumes on required networking and technology resources?
4. What processes and technology are involved in transferring client data to/from the call management system?
5. How much, how often, and what type of data is transferred between various corporate locations?
6. What database format is data currently stored in?
7. What are the strategic plans for new database technology adoption?

Network

1. How many servers and workstations are linked to this network?
2. How can segmenting temporarily relieve network congestion?
3. What technology is required for segmenting?
4. What alternative upgrade paths were considered, and why was 100VG-AnyLAN chosen?
5. What is the current network configuration for linking corporate branches?
6. What is the difference between a 100-Mbps segment and a 100-Mbps backbone?
7. What alternatives are being considered for backbone upgrades?

Technology

1. Which portion of the network was put onto the 100VG-AnyLAN hub and why?
2. What type of network services and technology are being considered to link various corporate locations in the future?

CHAPTER 8

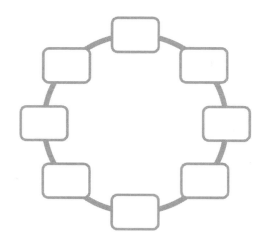

LOCAL AREA NETWORK HARDWARE

Concepts Reinforced

OSI model
Network architectures
IEEE 802 standards
Protocols and standards

Top-down model
Physical topologies
High-speed network architectures
Hardware/software compatibility

Concepts Introduced

LAN technology architecture
Switched LAN architectures
Network interface card technology
Network interface card drivers

Shared-media LAN wiring centers
LAN switches
Desktop ATM
LAN media alternatives

OBJECTIVES

After mastering the material in this chapter you should:

1. Understand the interaction between the various hardware and software components of the local area network technology architecture.

2. Understand the differences between switched LAN architectures and shared-media LAN architectures.

3. Understand the importance of compatible network interface card drivers to overall network implementation.

4. Understand the comparative differences between and proper application of available network interface cards.

5. Understand the comparative differences between and the proper application of available hubs, MAUs, switching hubs, concentrators, and similar devices.

6. Understand the comparative differences between and the proper application of the various available types of LAN media.

In Chapter 7 we reviewed the relative merits of the various network architectures that can be implemented to link clients and servers; Chapter 8 focuses on the hardware technology one must employ to implement a given network architecture. The transition from shared-media network architectures to hardware-based switched network architectures is a development of major proportions, of which informed network analysts must be aware. As applications demand more and more bandwidth, numerous alternatives exist for upgrading network capacity. Choosing the right upgrade path requires a thorough understanding of the local area network hardware described in this chapter.

To provide an appreciation of the interaction of all the various LAN hardware components, Chapter 8 begins by introducing the reader to the local area network technology architecture. To help you understand the role of LAN switches in network architectures, the chapter outlines the differences between switched-based and shared-media LAN architectures before reviewing in detail the local area network hardware alternatives.

The issues, technology, and protocols involved with managing LAN hardware are covered in Chapter 17.

■ THE LOCAL AREA NETWORK TECHNOLOGY ARCHITECTURE

In general terms, any local area network, regardless of network architecture, requires the following components:

- A central wiring concentrator of some type serves as a connection point for all attached local area network devices. Depending on the particular network architecture involved and the capabilities of the wiring center, this device is known alternatively as a hub, MAU, CAU, concentrator, LAN switch, or a variety of other names.

- Media such as shielded or unshielded twisted pair, coaxial cable, or fiber-optic cable must carry network traffic between attached devices and the wiring center of choice.

- **Network interface cards (NIC)** are installed either internally or externally to client and server computers to provide a connection to the local area network of choice.

- Finally, network interface card drivers are software programs which bridge the hardware/software interface between the network interface card and the computer's network operating system. Figure 8-1 summarizes the key components of the local area network technology architecture.

Zero Slot LANs

A subset of LANs known as **zero slot LANs** do not require all of the hardware listed in the local area network technology architecture. The term "zero slot" indicates that by using existing serial or parallel ports for network communications, zero expansion slots are occupied by network interface cards. Zero slot LANs offer a simple connectivity alternative for small workgroups while still offering more capabilities than the non-LAN connectivity devices mentioned in Chapter 1.

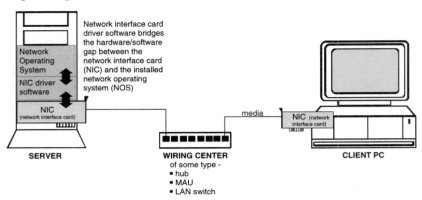

Figure 8-1   The Local Area Network Technology Architecture

For example, the key difference between file transfer software and software-based zero slot LANs is that file transfer software runs in the foreground on connected PCs, and the software-based zero slot LAN software runs in the background, allowing other application software to run in the foreground. The two technologies share similar benefits: local access to virtual drives from the remote PC, file transfer, and remote printing capabilities.

A hardware-based zero slot LAN is centered on a central wiring center with attached PCs connected via their serial or parallel ports. The wiring center provides the physical connections which allow any attached device to communicate with any other attached device. Hardware zero slot LANs usually include software to be loaded onto each connected PC, offering more sophisticated capabilities such as e-mail, file transfer, and perhaps virtual drive access. In addition, the software portion of these zero slot LANs usually runs in the background, transparent to the user.

As network interface card prices have plummeted to $50 and below, and two-user and five-user network operating system licenses have fallen below $100, the market for zero slot LANs has been seriously reduced.

■ MEDIA-SHARING LAN ARCHITECTURES VERSUS SWITCHED LAN ARCHITECTURES

As client/server information systems and distributed computing applications have put increasing demands on the local area network infrastructure for data traffic transfer, network architects and technology providers have responded with alternative solutions.

As you saw in Chapter 7, one solution to the network bandwidth crunch is to offer higher-speed **shared-media network architectures** such 100BaseT, 100VG-AnyLAN, and isochronous Ethernet. Each of these alternatives possess the same basic shared-media structure as Ethernet and Token Ring; the only difference is that the higher-speed alternatives offer more bandwidth for all attached workstations to share. Media-sharing network wiring centers such as hubs offer all attached workstations shared access to a single LAN segment. If the hub happens to be a 10BaseT Ethernet hub, then all attached workstations must share access to the single 10-Mbps LAN segment, while 100BaseT hubs offer shared access for all attached workstations to a single 100-Mbps LAN segment. The shared media approach is the same in both cases, except for the amount of available bandwidth to be shared.

Switched LAN architectures depend on wiring centers called LAN switches or switching hubs, which offer all attached workstations access to a switching matrix that provides point-to-point, rather than shared, connections between any two ports. Each port on the LAN switch is effectively a dedicated LAN segment, with dedicated bandwidth offered to attached devices. Each port on the LAN switch may be assigned to a single workstation, or to an entire LAN segment linked by a media-sharing network architecture (nonswitching) hub. Although shared-media LAN segments can link to a LAN switch to take advantage of its dedicated connections and guaranteed bandwidth, the switched LAN architecture itself has no shared media or shared bandwidth. The limiting factor in a switch-based LAN architecture is the number of simultaneous point-to-point connections a given switch can support. Figure 8-2 contrasts the differences in wiring center functionality between media-sharing and switch-based LAN architectures.

Shared-Media LAN Architecture

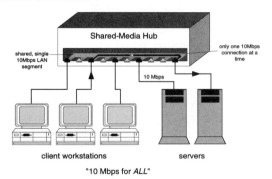

Switch-Based LAN Architecture

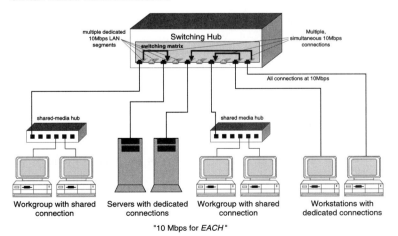

Figure 8-2 Switched LAN Architectures Versus Media-Sharing LAN Architectures Wiring Center Functionality

ADVANTAGES OF SWITCHED LAN ARCHITECTURES

It is important to note that implementation of switched LAN architectures only changes the wiring center technology and, as a result, the manner in which workstations set up point-to-point communications to each other. In other words, network interface cards, network interface card drivers, and media do not change. For this reason, installing a LAN switch is often the first, and easiest alternative chosen when network bandwidth demands exceed current supply. To go from an Ethernet shared-media architecture to an Ethernet switch-based architecture, one only needs to replace the shared-media hub with an Ethernet LAN switch. To migrate from a Token Ring shared-media environment to Token Ring switch-based architecture, one only needs to replace the shared-media MAUs with a Token Ring LAN switch.

LAN SWITCH TRAFFIC ANALYSIS

It is important to analyze the traffic patterns between attached clients and servers before swapping out hubs and installing switches. To minimize the interswitch traffic, which represents a potential bottleneck, the author suggests the following:

- It is important to have those workstations and servers that communicate most often with each other on the same switch, since switches differ in cascadability and speed of interswitch communications connection.

- Another benefit of analyzing traffic patterns before installing the switch is the ability to identify those users and workstations that need a dedicated switch port and those that can reside on a shared LAN segment attached to a switched port.

Following are a few general guidelines for switch port allocation:

- Servers and UNIX workstations should ideally have their own switch ports.

- Distributed computing power users with frequent queries to servers should be able to connect to switch ports via shared LAN segments of up to eight users.

- Casual or light traffic users accessing only e-mail and terminal, character-based programs can be connected to switch ports via shared LAN segments of 50 or more users.

The ability of LAN switches to support multiworkstation LAN segments on a single switch port may vary among switches. The number of workstation addresses which can be supported by a given switch port may vary as well.

Implementation Scenarios for Switched LAN Architectures

Depending on switch capacity and installed components, LAN switches can be implemented to fulfill a variety of roles.

- **Standalone Workgroup/Departmental LAN Switches**—offer dedicated connections to all attached client and server computers via individual switch ports. Such an implementation is appropriate for multimedia or videoconferencing workstations and servers. In some cases, such as a distributed computing environment, dedicated ports are necessary only for servers, while client workstations share a switch port via a cascaded media-sharing hub. This variation is sometimes referred to as a **server front-end LAN switch.**

• **Backbone-Attached Workgroup/Departmental LAN Switches**—offer all of the local switching capabilities of the standalone workgroup/departmental LAN switch plus switched access to higher-speed backbone networks. This higher-speed backbone connection may be to a higher-capacity backbone switch or to a higher-speed shared-media device such as a backbone router.

• **Backbone/Data Center Switches**—offer high-capacity, fault-tolerant, switching capacity with traffic management capabilities. These high-end switches are really a self-contained backbone network sometimes referred to as a **collapsed backbone network.** These backbone switches most often offer switched connectivity to other workgroup switches, media-sharing hubs, and corporate servers which must be accessed by multiple departments/workgroups. They are often modular in design, allowing different types of switching modules such as Ethernet, Token Ring, fast Ethernet, and asynchronous transfer mode (ATM) to share access to a high-capacity switching matrix or backplane.

Figure 8-3 highlights differences between these switched-LAN architecture implementation scenarios.

In Sharper Focus

FULL DUPLEX NETWORK ARCHITECTURES

Switched LAN architectures provide dedicated point-to-point links between communicating clients and servers. In the case of Ethernet switches, for example, since the point-to-point link between two communicating PCs is dedicated, no data collisions can occur and there is no longer any need for an access methodology such as CSMA/CD, since no other workstations are contending for this dedicated bandwidth connection. As a result, the two computers which serve as the end-points of this switched dedicated connection can both send and receive data between each other simultaneously. This switch-dependent capability is known as **full duplex Ethernet** and requires specialized full duplex Ethernet NICs, NIC drivers, and full duplex Ethernet switches. Many Ethernet switches allow certain ports, such as those attached to servers, to be set for full duplex Ethernet. In such an implementation, only the servers attached to full duplex switch ports require full duplex NICs. In theory, full duplex Ethernet should allow twice the normal Ethernet performance speed by offering a dedicated 10 Mbps communication channel in each direction, for a total available bandwidth of 20 Mbps.

In practice, the throughput, or actual data transferred, on full duplex Ethernet connections is not nearly 20 Mbps. The chief reason for this is that the amount of network transmission is a product of application program design. Most distributed application programs tend to exhibit short requests for services from clients to servers followed by large transfers of data from the server back to the client. This is not to say, however, that the technology lacks the ability to deliver higher performance. Controlled tests involving high-bandwidth applications have produced throughput of 20 Mbps. As a result, the most likely implementation scenarios for full duplex Ethernet is in switch-to-switch connections and switch-to-server connections.

Standalone Workgroup/Departmental LAN Switches

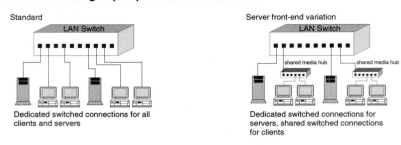

Backbone-Attached Workgroup/Departmental LAN Switches

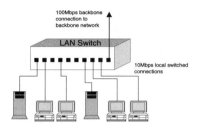

Backbone/Data Center Switches

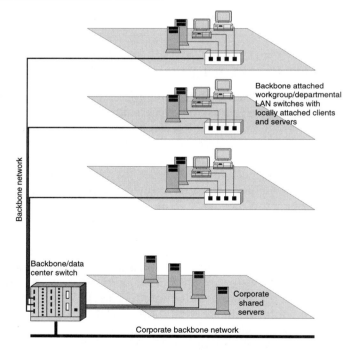

Figure 8-3   Implementation Scenarios for Switched LAN Architectures

Since the full duplex NIC installed in the computer is both sending and receiving data simultaneously, a multithreaded operating system and network operating system are required to take full advantage of this technology. Examples of such multithreaded operating systems and network operating systems are Windows NT, OS/2, NetWare 3.11 and 4.1, and most varieties of UNIX. Full duplex Ethernet has gathered sufficient interest from the networking technology vendor and user communities to warrant the formation of the **IEEE 802.3x** committee to propose standards for it. Full duplex technology is also either under development or available in full duplex Token Ring (32 Mbps) and full duplex FDDI (200 Mbps) varieties.

■ NETWORK INTERFACE CARDS

Functionality

Network adapter cards, also known as network interface cards (NICs), are the physical link between a client or server PC and the shared media of the network. Providing this interface between the network and the PC or workstation requires that the network adapter card have the ability to adhere to the access methodology (CSMA/CD or token passing) of the network architecture (Ethernet, Token Ring, FDDI/CDDI, etc.) to which it is attached. These software rules, which are implemented by the network adapter card and control the access to the shared network media, are known as media access control (MAC) protocols; they are represented on the MAC sublayer of the data-link layer (layer 2) in the OSI seven-layer reference model.

Because these are MAC-layer interface cards, and therefore the keepers of the MAC layer interface protocol, it's fair to say that it is the adapter cards themselves that determine network architecture and its constituent protocols more than any other component. Take an Ethernet adapter card out of the expansion slot of a PC and replace it with a Token Ring adapter card, and you have a Token Ring workstation. The medium may not even need to be changed because Ethernet, Token Ring, and FDDI/CDDI often work over the same media.

A network adapter card is a bit like a mediator or translator. On one side are the demands of the client or server PC in which it is installed for network-based services; on the other side is the network architecture, with its rules for accessing the shared network media or LAN switch. The network adapter card's job is to get the PC all the network services it desires while adhering to the rules (MAC layer protocols) of the network architecture.

Technology Analysis

Listed here are some of the key differences in adapter design and available features:

- Bus type.
  - ISA (8 or 16 bit).
  - EISA (16 or 32 bit).
  - MCA.
  - NuBus.
  - PCI.
  - PCMCIA.

- On-board processor capabilities.

- Amount of on-board memory.

- Data transfer techniques.
  - Bus mastering DMA.

  - DMA.
  - Shared memory.
  - Programmed I/O.
- Media interfaces.
- System memory requirements.
- Internal adapters versus external adapters.
- Network architecture(s) supported.

Applied
Problem
Solving

NETWORK INTERFACE CARD TECHNOLOGY ANALYSIS GRID

Many of these features are listed in Figure 8-4, the network interface card technology analysis grid. A technology analysis grid is a structured analysis tool for mapping functional networking requirements, identified by the logical network design of the networking layer in the top-down model, to the technical capabilities and characteristics of available technology. It allows technology to be comparatively evaluated in an objective fashion. Recalling the basic premise of the top-down model, assuming that each lower layer offers solutions that meet the requirements of the immediate upper layer, the chosen technology incorporated in the physical network design should meet the original business goals and objectives identified in the business layer.

As a practical example, because servers need to transfer large quantities of data more quickly than client PCs, to minimize potential bottlenecks technology analysis should be performed to purchase more powerful, faster NICs for servers than for clients.

	Bus Type								Drivers				Cabling Type (media interface)						Data transfer				
	Internal/external	ISA — 8 bit/16	MCA — 32	EISA — 32 bit	PCI — 32 bit/64 bit	Macintosh — NUBUS	External interface to parallel port	PCMCIA (laptops)	NDIS	ODI	NETBIOS	IPX	UTP	STP	Thin COAX	Thick COAX	Fiber	Wireless	BUS mastering	DMA	Programmed I/O	Shared memory	Prices
Ethernet																							
Token Ring (4 Mbps)																							
Token Ring (16 Mbps)																							
FDDI																							
CDDI																							
100Base-T																							
100VG-AnyLAN																							
ISO-ethernet																							
Full duplex Ethernet																							
ATM																							

Figure 8-4 Network Interface Card Technology Analysis Grid

Bus Type   As described in Chapter 3, the bus into which a network adapter card is attached allows many different types of add-in cards to be attached to this data transfer pipeline leading to the CPU and RAM memory. The expansion bus in a PC is a lot like a straight line of empty parking spaces waiting to be filled by PC expansion cards of one type or another. These expansion cards draw electricity from and transfer data between other system components, such as the CPU or memory, through the expansion bus. NICs are manufactured to physically interface to a particular type of bus.

Because the PCI bus offers its own clocking signal and low CPU utilization, it seems to be the bus of choice for high-performance NICs. PCI bus–compatible NICs are now available for a variety of network architectures, with some taking advantage of the PCI bus's ability to cascade buses by delivering four network interface ports on a single network interface card. Some PCI-based cards also have full duplex capabilities. Such high-capacity cards are most appropriate for servers with high data transfer demands.

The important choice related to bus architecture is to select a network adapter card that not only "fits," or is compatible with, the installed bus, but more important, takes full advantage of whatever data transfer capability that bus may afford.

Data Transfer Method   The key job of the network adapter is to transfer data between the local PC and the shared network media. Ideally, this should be done as quickly as possible, with a minimum of interruption of the PC's main CPU. Two hardware-related network adapter characteristics which can have a bearing on data transfer efficiency are the amount of on-board memory and the processing power of the on-board CPU contained on the network adapter card. Figure 8-5 summarizes four network adapter card–to–PC memory data transfer techniques:

- Programmed input/output (I/O).
- Direct memory access (DMA).
- Shared memory.
- Bus mastering DMA.

Network adapter cards may support more than one of these techniques. Some of these data transfer techniques are possible only with more sophisticated buses such as EISA, MCA, or PCI, with certain network architectures, or with a certain level of CPU power.

Remembering that one of the objectives of network-to-PC data transfer was to minimize the number of interruptions of the system CPU, one can see in Figure 8-5 that only the **bus mastering DMA** data transfer technique leaves the system CPU alone to process other applications. In bus mastering DMA, the CPU on the network adapter card manages the movement of data directly into the PC's RAM memory without interrupting the system CPU by taking control of the PC's expansion bus. PCI bus-based NICs also exhibit low utilization of the main CPU thanks to the intelligence of the PCI bus itself.

Bus mastering DMA requires the PC expansion bus to support being "mastered" by the CPU on the network adapter card. Some buses are more sophisticated (MCA, EISA, and PCI) in relation to bus mastering, maintaining more control and management over how the network adapter card CPU handles mastering of the expansion bus. The CPU and operating system must also be capable of relinquishing

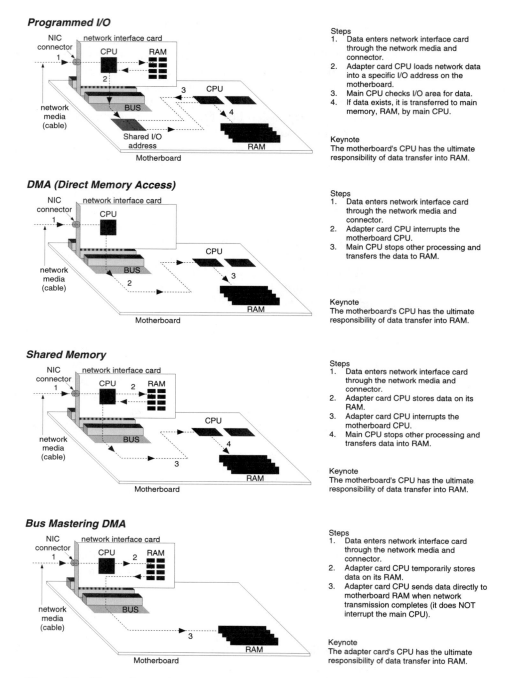

Figure 8-5 Network Interface Cards Data Transfer Methods

control of the expansion bus for bus mastering network adapter cards to function correctly.

Media Interfaces A network adapter card must worry about hardware compatibility in two directions. First, the card must be compatible with the expansion bus into which it is inserted. Second, it must be compatible with the chosen medium of a particular network architecture implementation. Supported media types depend on standards defined for a particular network architecture. Not all NICs support all media types. In addition to the type of media, the physical connector that interfaces between the NIC and the media varies.

Several network adapter cards come with interfaces for more than one media type, with "jumpers" or switches enabling one media type or another. Ethernet adapter cards with interfaces for both 10BaseT (**RJ45** or 8 pin Telco plug) and thin coax connections known as **BNC connectors,** or with both thick and thin coax connections, are quite common. Thick coax connectors are 15-pin interfaces (DB-15), also called **AUI** (Attachment Unit Interface) connectors. AUI connectors allow Ethernet NICs to be attached to thin or thick coax Ethernet backbone networks via **transceivers** (transmitter/receivers) and AUI or transceiver cables. Figure 8-6 illustrates the three common Ethernet media interfaces and an Ethernet NIC connection to an Ethernet backbone network via transceivers.

The discussion thus far regarding installing network adapter cards has assumed that the adapters are internal or connected directly to the system expansion bus. Alternatively, network adapters can be connected externally to a PC via the PC's parallel port. This market has grown considerably with the proliferation of laptop or notebook computers which lack internal expansion capability. In these cases, **external adapters** as small as a pack of cigarettes interface the PC's parallel port with the network media. External adapters cannot draw electricity from the expansion bus like internal adapters and therefore require a power source of their own, most often an AC adapter. Some external adapters can draw power from the keyboard jack on the notebook computer, eliminating the need for bulky and inconvenient AC adapters.

As an example of the principle of shifting bottlenecks, although NICs can transfer data at rates of several megabits per second, throughput on existing parallel ports hovers around 130 Kbps while a newer **high-performance parallel port,** also known as **enhanced parallel port (EPP),** delivers a throughput of up

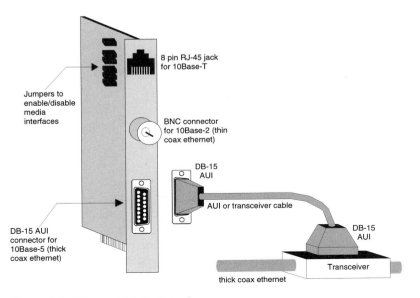

Figure 8-6   Ethernet Media Interfaces

to 2 Mbps. Remember that the parallel port is a component of the laptop PC, not the external adapter. An alternative to parallel port external adapters is **PCMCIA adapters.** The top-rated PCMCIA Ethernet adapters typically deliver throughputs of between 800 and 900 Kbps. PCMCIA standards were reviewed in Chapter 3.

Network Interface Card Trends

Following are some of the trends in network interface cards which are either emerging or under development:

- Dual-Speed Cards—Some 10/100 Ethernet cards feature autosensing, which can automatically determine whether traffic is being transmitted and received at 10 or 100 Mbps through a single media interface connector. Others, especially 100VG-AnyLAN 10/100 cards, have two separate media interface connectors, one for 10 Mbps Ethernet and one for 100VG-AnyLAN; 10/100 cards are important as a means of easing migration from a 10-Mbps network architecture to a 100-Mbps network architecture.

- Integrated or On-Board NICs—Some computer manufacturers such as Hewlett-Packard, now include an Ethernet NIC right on the PC's motherboard, thereby saving a slot on the expansion bus.

- Multiport NICs—The cascading ability, otherwise known as the mezzanine architecture of the PCI bus, allows multiport NICs to be manufactured on a single card. This allows servers with high traffic demands to have up to four links to the network while using only a single expansion slot.

- On-NIC Virus Protection and Security—As security and virus protection have become more important issues, focus had shifted to the NIC as the entry point for network communications. Some NICs now offer encryption, virus protection, or both as means of protection against network infiltration.

- Integrated Repeater Modules—Some NICs have incorporated integrated repeater modules which allow up to seven additional devices to be cascaded from the NIC and attached to the network via a single 10BaseT hub port.

- Full Duplex Mode—Some Ethernet NICs have full duplex capability which can be enabled. Recall that implementation of full duplex Ethernet depends on the full duplex Ethernet NIC being directly connected to a port on a full duplex Ethernet switch.

- Performance Improvements—Several manufacturers of Ethernet NICs have implemented **packet overlapping** or **fast-packet forwarding** technology to improve overall NIC performance by as much as 50%. Traditionally, Ethernet NICs forwarded only one packet at a time from the CPU bus, through the NIC buffer memory, to the network media. Packet overlapping technology allows the next packet of information to be forwarded as soon as its start of frame is detected, rather than waiting for the previous frame to be totally onto the network media.

▦ NETWORK INTERFACE CARD DRIVERS

Role of Adapter Card Drivers

Insuring that a purchased network interface card successfully interfaces both the bus of the CPU and the chosen network architecture medium ensures hardware connectivity. Full interoperability, however, depends on compatibility between the NIC and the network operating system installed in a given computer, and is delivered by **network interface card drivers.** Any driver software must be compatible with the hardware card itself, which is why many adapter card manufacturers ship numerous drivers from which to choose. A network adapter card may also need to be compatible with a number of network operating systems. The network operating systems use the adapter card drivers to communicate with the adapter cards and the network beyond. Without the proper adapter card drivers, no communication can occur through the adapter card and, as a result, no network exists.

Driver Availability

Initially, drivers were written for specific combinations of a particular adapter card and a particular version of an operating system or network operating system. It was to an adapter card vendor's advantage to ship drivers for as many operating systems and network operating systems as possible. Following are examples of drivers typically included:

- LANtastic.
- LANManager.
- LANServer.
- Pathworks.
- PowerLAN.
- NetWare Version 2.X, NetWare Version 3.X, NetWare 4.X for DOS and OS/2.
- Vines.
- Windows.
- OS/2.
- Windows NT.
- UNIX (many variables).

This is obviously a fairly long list, and drivers may well have to be rewritten for each new version of an operating system or network operating system. Drivers written for specific adapter card/network operating system combinations are known as **monolithic drivers.** Network interface card drivers were also supplied by network operating system vendors. In these cases, the competition centered on which network operating system vendor could include drivers for the largest number of network interface cards. As the number of possible combinations of network interface cards and network operating systems continued to increase, network interface card vendors and network operating system vendors found themselves spending ever-increasing amounts of time and money on driver development.

A more generic approach to the problem was for adapter card manufacturers to supply drivers which could interact successfully with either NETBIOS or TCP/IP. The reasoning is that most network operating systems communicate with either NETBIOS (PC environment) or TCP/IP (UNIX environment). These drivers were generally successful, except for the occasional incompatibilities among NETBIOS versions, as long as the operating system supported NETBIOS or TCP/IP. Specifically written, monolithic drivers were also more efficient and performed better in most cases.

Another approach is for network adapter card manufacturers to emulate the adapter interface specifications of market-leading network interface cards for which drivers are most commonly available. The NE2000 adapter card, originally manufactured by Eagle Technologies and since purchased by Novell, is often emulated by other manufacturers who claim that their adapters are NE2000 compliant.

Multiprotocol Network Interface Card Drivers

Novell produced the first network operating system that attempted to break the need for specially written drivers for every possible adapter card/network operating system combination. By allowing adapter card vendors to develop one file, called IPX.COM, which was linked with a Novell file called IPX.OBJ through a process known as WSGEN, unique drivers could be more easily created and updated. However, even these "bound" drivers were still monolithic in the sense that only a single protocol stack, Novell's IPX/SPX, could communicate with the installed network adapter card.

Thus, an industry initiative was undertaken to develop driver software to accomplish two major objectives:

1. To develop adapter card–specific drivers independently from network operating system–specific protocol stack drivers, and bind the two drivers together into a unique driver combination.

2. To develop driver management software allowing for installation of both multiple network adapter cards and multiple protocol stacks per adapter card.

This initiative was undertaken by two independent industry coalitions:

-   Microsoft and 3Com, a major adapter card manufacturer developed **network driver interface specification (NDIS).**

-   Novell, producers of NetWare, and Apple joined forces to develop **open data-link interface (ODI).** Most adapter cards are now shipped with both NDIS and ODI drivers.

The significant operational difference these two driver specifications offer is the ability to support multiple protocol stacks over a single adapter card. For example, a network adapter card with an ODI driver installed could support communications to both a NetWare server via IPX protocols and a UNIX host via TCP/IP protocols. Network operating systems and their protocol stacks are detailed in Part 4.

NDIS

NDIS is a driver specification which offers standard commands for communications between NDIS-compliant network operating system protocol stacks (NDIS protocol driver) and NDIS-compliant network adapter card drivers (NDIS MAC drivers). In addition, NDIS specifies a **binding** operation which is managed by a separate program known as the **protocol manager** (PROTMAN.DOS in DOS-based systems). As you will see, the protocol manager program does much more than just supervise the binding of protocol drivers to MAC drivers. NDIS also specifies standard commands for communication between the protocol manager program and either protocol or MAC drivers.

Protocol drivers and MAC drivers which adhere to the NDIS specification work as follows:

1. When a DOS-based computer is first booted or powered up, a configuration file known as CONFIG.SYS is executed. One line in this file specifies that the protocol manager program (PROTMAN.DOS) should be initiated.

2. The first job of the protocol manager is to access a text file known as PROTOCOL.INI, which contains
    *   setup information about protocol drivers and MAC drivers, and
    *   binding statements which link particular protocol drivers to particular MAC drivers.

3. Having read PROTOCOL.INI and parsed its contents into usable form, the protocol manager program loads the PROTOCOL.INI information into a memory-resident image.

4. As new protocol drivers or MAC drivers are loaded, they
    *   ask the protocol manager program for the location of the memory-resident image of PROTOCOL.INI,
    *   look in PROTOCOL.INI for setup information about the MAC driver or protocol driver with which they wish to bind, and
    *   identify themselves to the protocol manager program which adds their information to the PROTOCOL.INI file.

5. Binding takes place when the protocol manager program oversees the exchange of characteristic tables between protocol drivers and MAC drivers.

6. Once bound and operating, packets of a particular protocol are forwarded from the adapter card to the proper protocol stack by a layer of software known as the **vector**.

Figure 8-7 illustrates many of the concepts and components of the NDIS specification.

ODI

Like NDIS, ODI allows users to load several protocol stacks simultaneously for operation with a single network adapter card and supports independent development with subsequent linking of protocol drivers and adapter drivers. In ODI, users enter configuration information regarding network adapter settings and protocol driver information into a file named NET.CFG. Operations of ODI are

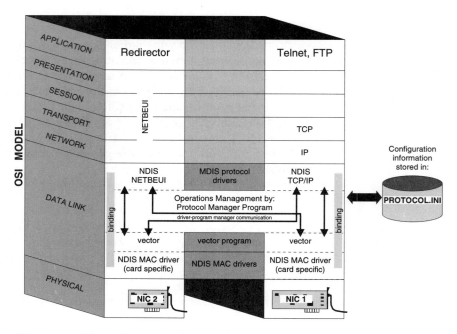

Figure 8-7   Network Device Interface Specification (NDIS) Architecture

similar to the basic functionality of NDIS and are orchestrated by a program known as LSL.COM, in which **LSL** stands for **link support layer.** Network interface card drivers are referred to as **multilink interface drivers,** or **MLID,** in an ODI-compliant environment. Figure 8-8 illustrates the basic architecture of an ODI-compliant environment.

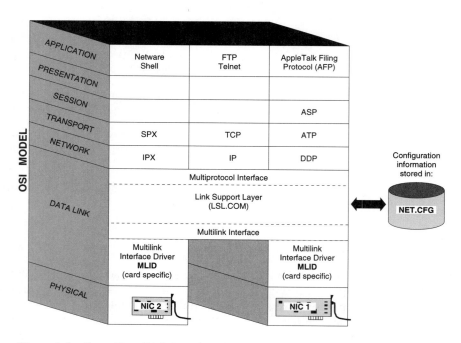

Figure 8-8   Open Data-Link Interface (ODI) Architecture

PCMCIA Drivers

When network interface cards are PCMCIA-based, two levels of driver software are required:

1. Drivers to interface to operating systems and network operating systems such as NDIS 2.0 for DOS and OS/2 and ODI for DOS and OS/2. Occasionally, NetWare-specific drivers may also be available with certain PC cards.

2. Drivers to interface the PCMCIA controller to the PCMCIA card and to the aforementioned client software drivers.

As noted in Chapter 3, with the introduction of PCMCIA Specification Version 3.0, the term PCMCIA has been replaced by the terms PC card and card bus.

Compatibility problems and lack of standardized driver software were common with PCMCIA-based network interface cards before the release of PCMCIA version 2.1 with its **card and socket services** driver specification. **CSS** is supposed to be relatively self-configuring and enables the following capabilities:

- Hot swappable devices allowing PCMCIA cards to be removed and inserted while the notebook computer is powered up.

- Automatic PCMCIA card configuration.

- Multiple PCMCIA card management.

- Standby mode.

- I/O conflict management.

CSS is split into two logical sublayers:

1. The **card services** sublayer is hardware independent and interfaces to the client operating system or network operating system driver software. Card services deliver error messages and enable resource management and configuration.

2. The **socket services** sublayer is written specifically for the type of PCMCIA controller included in a notebook computer. Among the common varieties of controllers are Intel, Cirrus Logic, Databook, Vandem, Toshiba, VLSI, and Ricoh. Socket services are more hardware oriented and provide information concerning insertion and removal of cards from available slots.

If compatible CSS drivers are not available for a particular PC card/controller combination, or if the amount of memory CSS drivers require is unacceptable, then lower-level drivers known as **direct enablers** must be configured and installed. Direct enablers, like the socket services of CSS, are controller specific and must be configured for each PC card/controller combination, unlike the card and socket services drivers, which allow multiple cards to be swapped in and out of a given PCMCIA slot without the need for reconfiguration. Direct enabler drivers are often supplied on diskette, along with CSS drivers by the PCMCIA card vendors.

Practical Advice and Information

It is in best interests of adapter card manufacturers to include as many drivers as possible with adapter cards to ensure that they will work with as many network operating systems as possible. However, before you purchase any adapter card, be sure that proven software drivers compatible with the installed or chosen network operating system(s) are included.

Remember that drivers for various cards are often supplied with the installed networking operating system as well. One of these drivers may be more efficient in terms of operation or required memory than another.

■ SHARED-MEDIA LAN WIRING CENTERS

The most common network physical topology employed today is the star topology, the heart of which is the wiring center. A wiring center is alternatively known as a hub, a concentrator, a repeater, a MAU, or a variety of other terms. In this section, wiring center functionality, technology, management, and analysis for shared-media network architectures are examined; LAN switches and switching hubs appropriate for switch-based network architectures are covered in the next section.

Wiring Center Categories

Token Ring wiring centers are known as **MAUs** (Multistation Access Units) whereas wiring centers for all other network architectures are known as **hubs.** All hubs or MAUs are basically just multiport digital signal repeaters. They do not make logical decisions based on the addresses or content of messages. They merely repeat all digital data received at connected ports. In terms of the OSI model, repeaters or hubs are Layer 1 or physical layer devices that deal only with bit streams.

The functionality and features of wiring centers can be separated into three broad categories:

1. **Standalone hubs** are fully configured hubs offering a limited number (12 or fewer) of ports of a particular type of network architecture (Ethernet, Token Ring) and media. They are fully configured and include their own power supply but are not generally expandable, do not include management software, and are the least expensive of the three wiring center categories.

2. **Stackable hubs** add expandability and manageability to the basic capabilities of the standalone hub. Stackable hubs can be linked together, or cascaded, to form one larger virtual hub of a single type of network architecture and media. Given the larger number of ports, management software becomes essential. Most stackable hubs offer some type of local management software as well as links to enterprise management software platforms such as HP OpenView, Sun's SunNet Manager, IBM NetView, and Novell's NMS.

3. **Enterprise hubs,** also known as **modular concentrators,** differ from stackable hubs in both physical design and functionality. Rather than being fully functional self-contained units, enterprise hubs are modular, offering a chassis-based architecture into which a variety of modules can be inserted. In some cases, these modules can be inserted and/or removed while the

hub remains powered-up, a capability known as **hot-swappability.** Among the possible modules supported by enterprise hubs are the following:
* Ethernet, Token Ring, and FDDI port modules in a variety of port densities and media choices.
* Management modules.
* Router modules.
* Bridge modules.
* WAN link modules.
* Multiple power supplies for redundant power.

These broad categories are not standards, and they are not universally adhered to by manufacturers. Signaling standards defined as part of the IEEE or ANSI LAN standards allow hubs and NICs of different vendors to interoperate successfully in most cases. Figure 8-9 illustrates some of the physical differences between the three major categories of hubs, and Figure 8-10 (page 288) differentiates between the functionality of the major categories of wiring centers.

Standalone hubs

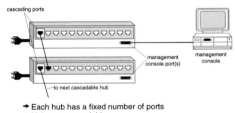

➨ Fixed number of ports
➨ Single network architecture
➨ Not expandable
➨ Single media type

Stackable hubs

➨ Each hub has a fixed number of ports
➨ Hubs are cascadable
➨ Single network architecture and media
➨ Provides management software and link
　to network management console

Enterprise hubs

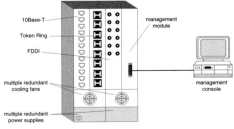

➨ Modular chassis-based design
➨ Supports multiple network architectures and media types
➨ Integrated management module
➨ May include internetworking or WAN modules

Figure 8-9　Major Categories of Hubs

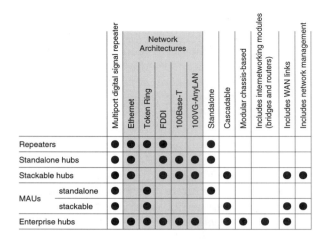

	Multiport digital signal repeater	Ethernet	Token Ring	FDDI	100Base-T	100VG-AnyLAN	Standalone	Cascadable	Modular chassis-based	Includes internetworking modules (bridges and routers)	Includes WAN links	Includes network management
		Network Architectures										
Repeaters	●	●	●	●			●					
Standalone hubs	●	●		●	●	●	●					
Stackable hubs	●	●		●	●	●		●			●	●
MAUs standalone	●		●				●					
MAUs stackable	●		●					●			●	●
Enterprise hubs	●	●	●	●	●	●			●	●	●	●

Figure 8-10   Wiring Center Functional Comparison

Repeaters

A repeater, as its name implies, merely "repeats" each bit of digital data it receives. This repeating action actually "cleans up" the digital signals by retiming and regenerating them before passing this repeated data from one attached device or LAN segment to the next. Repeaters can only link devices or LAN segments of similar network architectures.

Hubs

Hubs are a subset of repeaters which allow attachment of single devices rather than LAN segments to each hub port. The terms "hub" and "concentrator" or "intelligent concentrator" are often used interchangeably. Distinctions can be made between these broad classes of wiring centers, although there is nothing to stop manufacturers from using the terms as they wish.

The term hub is often reserved for describing a standalone device with a fixed number of ports which offers features beyond that of a simple repeater. The type of media connections and network architecture offered by the hub is determined at the time of manufacture as well. For example, a 10BaseT Ethernet hub offers a fixed number of RJ-45 twisted pair connections for an Ethernet network. Additional types of media or network architectures are not usually supported.

Stackable Hubs

Hubs can also be cascadable or stackable via **cascading ports,** which may be specialized ports on the hub or switch-configurable "normal" ports that allow repeated data to flow out of a cascading port to the next hub rather than the normal inbound-only port traffic flow. Specialized hub-to-hub cascading cables may also be required, and the maximum allowable distance between stacked hubs varies as well. Stackability also varies, with the number of stackable hubs ranging from 4 to 20 and the total number of stacked ports ranging from 48 to 768. Cost per port can range from $35 to $147, with most ports costing $60 to $70.

MAUs

MAU is IBM's name for a Token Ring hub. A MAU is manufactured with a fixed number of ports and connections for unshielded or shielded twisted pair. IBM uses special connectors for Token Ring over shielded twisted pair (STP) connections to a MAU known as Type 1 connectors. Some MAUs support RJ-45 connectors rather than the Type 1 connectors which are bulkier and more difficult to work with. MAUs typically have eight ports with two additional ports labeled RI (ring in) and RO (ring out). These specialized cascading ports allow multiple MAUs to be linked in a single logical ring. MAUs can also be cascaded to each other via fiber-optic cable instead of shielded twisted pair.

MAUs offer varying degrees of management capability. **Active-management MAUs** can send alerts to management consoles regarding malfunctioning Token Ring adapters and also forcibly remove these misbehaving adapters from the ring. The ability to remove malfunctioning nodes is especially critical in Token Ring LANs due to the possibility of a malfunctioning node becoming disabled while holding onto the token. Such an event would be inconvenient, but it would not be a catastrophe as the active monitor workstation is capable of regenerating a new token.

Enterprise Hubs

The terms concentrator, intelligent concentrator, smart hub, and enterprise hub are often reserved for a device characterized by both flexibility and expandability. A concentrator starts with a fairly empty, boxlike device, often called a chassis. This chassis contains one or more redundant power supplies and a "built-in" network backbone. This backbone might be Ethernet, Token Ring, FDDI, Appletalk, 100BaseT, 100VG-AnyLAN, or some combination of these. Into this backplane, individual cards or modules are inserted.

For instance, an 8- or 16-port twisted pair Ethernet module could be purchased and slid into place in the concentrator chassis. A network management module supporting simple network management protocol (SNMP) could then be purchased and slid into the chassis next to the previously installed 10BaseT Port module. In this "mix and match" scenario, additional cards could be added to connect PCs with Token Ring adapters, PCs or workstations with FDDI adapters, or "dumb" asynchronous terminals. These modules are most often hot-swappable, allowing modules to be added or removed without shutting down the entire enterprise hub. Obviously, the capacity of these enterprise hubs is as important as the flexibility of their modular design. In fact, they often support several hundred ports of varying network architectures.

This "network in a box" is now ready for workstations to be hooked up to it through twisted pair connections to the media interfaces on the PC or workstation network interface cards. Its ability to allow different media types to be intermixed in the concentrator was one of its first major selling points. Remember that Ethernet can run over UTP, STP, and thick and thin coax as well as fiber-optic cable.

Additional modules available for some, but not all, concentrators may allow data traffic from this network in a box to travel to other local LANs via bridge or router add-on modules. Bridges and routers are discussed later. These combination concentrators are sometimes called Internetworking hubs. Communication to remote LANs or workstations may be available through the addition of other specialized cards, or modules, designed to provide access to wide area network services purchased from common carriers such as the phone company. All local network traffic travels through this single enterprise hub, but it is also an ideal location for security modules to be added for either encryption or authorization functionality.

Backplane design within enterprise hubs is proprietary, and as a result, the modules for enterprise hubs are not interoperable. It is therefore important to ensure that the enterprise hub purchased has available all required types of modules for network architecture, media type, management, internetworking, WAN interfaces, or security. Don't depend on the vendor's promised delivery dates for required modules.

Hub Management

Because all local area network traffic must pass through the hub, it is an ideal place for installing management software to monitor and manage network traffic. As previously stated, standalone hubs are rarely manufactured with management software. In the case of stackable and enterprise hubs, two layers of management software are most often involved:

1. First, **local hub management software** is usually supplied by the hub vendor and runs over either DOS or Windows. This software allows monitoring and management of the hub from a locally attached management console.

2. Second, because these hubs are just a small part of a vast array of networking devices that might have to be managed on an enterprise basis, most hubs are also capable of sharing management information with **enterprise network management systems** such as HP OpenView, IBM NetView, Sun SunNet Manager, or Novell NMS (network management system).

Although Chapter 17 covers enterprise network management in more detail, a small explanation of how hub management information is fed to the enterprise network management system is appropriate here.

Network management information transfer between multivendor network devices and enterprise network management systems must be characterized by standards-based communication. The standards which govern this network management communication are part of the TCP/IP family of protocols more correctly known as the Internet suite of protocols. Specifically, network management information is formatted according to **SNMP** (Simple Network Management Protocol). The types of information to be gathered and stored have also been defined as **management information bases (MIBs).** Numerous MIBs are actually defined, with the one most often used for network monitoring and management known as the **remote monitoring (RMON) MIB.** Network statistics and information are first gathered and packetized in SNMP format by specialized software known as **agents,** which reside within the monitored network device and are supplied by the network device's manufacturer. Enterprise network management systems such as HP OpenView, can interpret, consolidate, and display information and alarms from a variety of networking equipment manufactured by a variety of vendors, thanks to standards-based communication protocols. Figure 8-11 illustrates the relationship of the various aspects of the standards-based network management communications protocols.

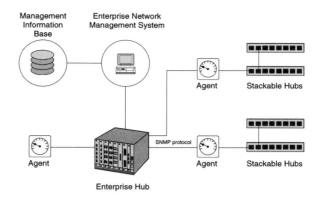

Figure 8-11   Standards-Based Network Management
Communications Protocols

Some hub management issues are particular to stackable and/or enterprise hubs:

- Many stackable hubs offer network management capabilities as an optional hardware or software upgrade. It is important to fully understand how easily this upgrade can be accomplished and whether or not the hubs must be powered off while doing so.

- The network management traffic may exit the hub via a separate serial port or travel along a separate bus within the hub, so as not to diminish the amount of bandwidth available for data. These options are sometimes referred to as out-of-band management connections.

- The entire stack of hubs should be viewed, monitored, and managed by the network management software as a single, virtual hub.

- The local hub management software should be simple, easy to use, and preferably Windows-based, with the capability to talk to enterprise network management system platforms if the need arises.

- If at all possible, management modules or upgrades should be included with the original purchase to avoid potential upgrade hassles. Buying management modules at purchase time is often more economical than buying upgrades later, thanks to vendor discount packages.

- An issue particular to Token Ring modules included in enterprise hubs is the need for management software to be able to dynamically assign ports located on the same physical module onto different logical rings, to optimize network performance.

WIRING CENTERS TECHNOLOGY ANALYSIS

Some of the major technical features to be used for comparative analysis are listed in Figure 8-12. Before purchasing a wiring center of any type, consider the implications of the various possible features listed in this wiring center technology analysis.

Wiring Center Characteristic	Implications/Options
Expandability	Most standalone hubs are neither expandable nor cascadable. Stackable hubs are cascadable and enterprise hubs are expandable by adding more LAN modules. Enterprise hubs vary in the number of open slots from approximately 5 to 20. Total backplane capacity (speed) is important, as this network media must be shared by all attached modules.
Network Architectures	Options: Ethernet, Token Ring, FDDI, Appletalk, 100Base-T, 100VG-AnyLAN. Not all types of network architecture modules are available in all enterprise hubs.
Media	Options: UTP, STP, thin coax, thick coax, fiber-optic cable. Modules also differ in supported media. Remember that an NIC is on the other end of the connection to the hub module. Is this hub module media type and connector compatible with installed NICs?
Macintosh Communications	Can an Apple Macintosh be linked to the hub?
Terminal Communications	Can "dumb" asynchronous terminals be connected directly to the hub? What is the physical connector and serial transmission specification? (DB-25?, RS-232?)
Internetworking	Are bridging and/or routing modules available to redirect traffic from module to module? Across different types of network architecture modules? Across which different network architecture modules will traffic need to be bridged?
Wide Area Networking	Is this hub connected to other hubs remotely through the use of carrier-based data services? If so, which WAN services are supported? Options: frame relay, ISDN, switched 56K, digital leased lines from 9.6 Kbps to 1.544 Mbps (T-1).
Management	Is a local hub management program available? Are SNMP management protocols supported? Can individual ports be managed? Is monitoring software included? What security services are available? Can ports be remotely enabled/disabled? Can the hub be controlled by a port-attached workstation or only by a special management console? Can the hub be controlled remotely? via modem? Are management statistics and alarms graphically displayed? How are alarm thresholds set? How are faults managed? Can port access be limited by day and/or time? What operating systems can the management software run on? Options: DOS, OS/2, Windows, Windows NT, UNIX, Mac, etc. Can a map of the network be displayed? Which enterprise network management systems are supported? Options: HP OpenView, IBM NetView, Sun SunNet Manager, Novell NMS.
Reliability	Is an integrated UPS included? Are power supplies redundant? Are modules hot-swappable? Are cooling fans redundant? Which components are capable of being replaced by the user?

Figure 8-12 Wiring Centers Technology Analysis

■ LAN SWITCHES

The "network in a box" or "backbone in a box" offered by concentrators and hubs shrinks the length of the network backbone but doesn't change the architectural characteristics of a particular network backbone. For instance, in an Ethernet concentrator, multiple workstations may access the built-in Ethernet backbone via a variety of media, but the basic rules of Ethernet, such as CSMA/CD access methodology at 10 Mbps, still control performance on this Ethernet in a box. Only one workstation at a time can broadcast its message onto the shared 10-Mbps backbone.

Switch Classification

Supported Network Architectures   A **switching hub,** or **LAN switch,** seeks to overcome this "one at a time" broadcast scheme, which can potentially lead to data collisions, retransmissions, and reduced throughput between high bandwidth–demanding devices such as engineering workstations or server-to-server communications. By adding the basic design of a data PBX to the modular concentrator, numerous manufacturers have delivered simultaneously "switched" Ethernet connections at 10 Mbps to multiple users through a process known as parallel networking.

The Ethernet switch is actually able to create connections, or switch, between any two attached Ethernet devices on a packet-by-packet basic in as little as 40 milliseconds. The "one-at-time" broadcast limitation previously associated with Ethernet is overcome with an Ethernet switch. Figure 8-2 illustrated the basis functionality of an Ethernet switch. Ethernet is not the only network architecture for which LAN switches are available. Standalone versions and slide-in modules for enterprise switches are also available for Token Ring, FDDI, and fast Ethernet.

In addition, many high-end LAN switches also support **asynchronous transfer mode (ATM),** a type of switching that not only allows the previously mentioned LAN network architectures to be switched extremely quickly but can also switch voice, video, and image traffic equally well. In fact, ATM can switch any type of digital information over LANs or WANs with equal ease and at speeds currently in the 622-Mbps range and rapidly approaching the gigabit/second range.

Superswitches or megaswitches support multiple LAN architectures, ATM, and interface to WAN services.

Functional Differences   Switches can vary in ways other than just the types of network architecture frames that are switched. Significant functional differences between switches can have a dramatic effect on switch performance. The first major functional difference has to do with how the network architecture frames are processed before they are switched to their destination:

- **Cut-through switches** read only the address information in the MAC layer header before they begin processing. After reading the destination address, the switch consults an address lookup table to determine which port on the switch this frame should be forwarded to. Once the address lookup is completed, the point-to-point connection is created and the frame is immediately forwarded. Cut-through switching is very fast. However, because the frame check sequence on the forwarded frame was not checked, bad frames are forwarded. As a result, the receiving station must send a request for retransmission followed by retransmission of the original frame, which leads to overall traffic increases.

- **Store-and-forward switches** read the entire frame into a shared memory area in the switch. The contents of the transmitted frame check sequence field is read and compared to the locally recalculated frame check sequence. If the results match, then the switch consults the address lookup table, builds the appropriate point-to-point connection, and forwards the frame. As a result, store-and-forward switching is slower than cut-through switching but does not forward bad frames.

- **Error-free cut-through switches** read both the addresses and frame check sequences for every frame. Frames are forwarded immediately to destination nodes the same as with cut-through switches. However, if bad frames are forwarded, the error-free cut-through switch is able to reconfigure the individual ports producing the bad frames to use store-and-forward switching. As errors diminish to preset thresholds, the port is set back to cut-through switching for higher-performance throughput.

SWITCH TECHNOLOGY ISSUES

Practical Advice and Information

Switch Flow Control   Switches are often employed to make switched connections between multiple network architectures. A common role of LAN switches is to provide switched connections between 10- and 100-Mbps network architectures. However, when servers on high-speed (100 Mbps) switched connections blast high-bandwidth data traffic back to clients on shared 10-Mbps port connections, data traffic can get backed up and data frames may be lost once buffers designed to hold overflow data become filled.

Switch vendors have attempted to respond to this situation in a variety of ways. Some switches include so-called deep buffers, which allow more overflow traffic to be buffered before it is discarded. The dilemma with this approach, however, is that memory is expensive and it is difficult to determine how much buffer memory is enough while still keeping switch costs reasonable.

A second approach involves implementing a feedback mechanism known as **backpressure.** In the case of Ethernet switches, backpressure prevents lost frames during overload conditions by sending out false collision detection signals to get transmitting clients and servers to time-out long enough to give the switch a chance to forward buffered data. It is somewhat ironic that the CSMA/CD access methodology the switch sought to overcome is being used to improve switch performance. The difficulty with backpressure mechanisms in the case of multiple-device LAN segments being linked to a single-switch port is that the false collision detection signal stops all traffic on the connected LAN segment, even peer-to-peer traffic which could have been delivered directly without the use of the switch. One possible solution to this shortcoming is to enable backpressure only on those switch ports connected to single devices such as servers.

Switch Management   Another major issue to be faced by network managers before jumping blindly onto the LAN switch bandwagon is the matter of how to monitor and manage switched-LAN connections. Unlike shared-media LAN management tools, which can access all network traffic from a single interface to the shared-media hub, switched architecture management tools must be able to monitor numerous short-lived point-to-point dedicated connections simultaneously. In a switched-LAN architecture, each port is the equivalent of a dedicated LAN, which must be individually monitored and managed. Switch vendors currently offer three basic approaches to the switch management dilemma:

1. **Port mirroring** copies information from a particular switch port to an attached LAN analyzer. The difficulty with this approach is that it allows only one port to be monitored at a time.

2. **Roving port mirroring** creates a roving remote monitoring (RMON) probe which gathers statistics at regular intervals on multiple switch ports. The shortcoming with this approach remains that at any single point in time, only one port is being monitored.

3. **Simultaneous RMON view** allows all network traffic to be monitored simultaneously. Such a monitoring scheme is possible only on those switches which incorporate a shared-memory multigigabit bus as opposed to a switching matrix internal architecture. Furthermore, unless this monitoring software is executed on a separate CPU, switch performance is likely to degrade.

There is little doubt that, properly deployed, LAN switches can greatly improve network performance. However, management tools for LAN switches continue to evolve, and network managers should be wary of introducing technology into an enterprise network whose impact cannot be accurately monitored and managed.

Applied
Problem
Solving

LAN SWITCH TECHNOLOGY ANALYSIS

Figure 8-13 highlights some of the important analysis issues surrounding LAN switch selection.

LAN Switch Characteristic	Implications/Options
Switching Architecture	Options include cut-through, store-and-forward, and error-free store-and-forward.
Token Ring Switches	Some Token Ring switches also employ store-and-forward switching with buffering on the outbound port so that the outbound port has time to wait until the token reaches that switch port when multiple Token Ring devices are attached to a single switch port.
Network Architectures	Switches may support one or more of the following: Ethernet, Token Ring, FDDI, fast Ethernet, ATM. Network architectures may be available in a variety of different media types.
Port Configuration	Switches can vary in both the number of MAC addresses allowed per port and the total number of MAC addresses supported for the entire switch. Some switches allow only single devices to be attached to each LAN switch port. How easily can devices be assigned/reassigned to switch ports? Can devices which are physically attached to different switch ports be assigned to the same virtual LAN?

Figure 8-13 LAN Switch Technology Analysis

(continued)

LAN Switch Characteristic	Implications/Options
Full Duplex	Some switches allow some ports to be enabled for full duplex operation. Full duplex switch ports communicate only with full duplex NICs whereas "normal" switch ports communicate with existing NICs.
Switch-to-Switch Connection	Some switches use Ethernet or Token Ring–switched ports while others use higher-speed architectures such as FDDI or ATM to connect to other switches. These interswitch connections are sometimes referred to as the fat pipe.
Internetworking	In addition to merely establishing switched connections and forwarding traffic, some switches can also examine the addressing information contained within the data frames and perform bridging and routing functions. Token Ring switches may or may not perform source route bridging specific to the Token Ring architecture. Some routing models can also examine embedded protocols and make routing and filtering decisions based on that criteria.
Management	Does the switch support both SNMP and the RMON MIB? Does the switch contain a management port and management software? Which type of RMON probe is supported? Is a separate CPU provided for processing system monitoring software? Does the local management software support enterprise network management software such as HP OpenView, IBM NetView, or Sun SunNet Manager? Is a port provided to which a protocol analyzer can be attached?

Figure 8-13 *(continued)*

ATM for the LAN

ATM is a connection-oriented switched transmission methodology which holds great promise for becoming a single solution for transmitting data, voice, and video over both local and wide area networks. The word "promise" is significant. Any technology that seems to be the ultimate solution to the world's transmission needs would obviously require an enormous amount of standards-making and interoperability planning efforts. Such is the case with ATM.

One of the characteristics of ATM which affords it the capability of delivering a variety of traffic over both local and wide area networks is the fixed-length 53-byte cells into which all traffic is segmented. This uniform length allows timed, dependable delivery for streaming traffic such as voice and video, while simplifying troubleshooting, administration, setup, and design. Standards-making activities are divided into two major efforts:

1. **User-network interface (UNI)** defines standards for interoperability between end-user equipment and ATM equipment and networks. These standards are well-defined and equipment is fairly widely available.

2. **Network-network interface (NNI)** defines interoperability standards between various vendors' ATM equipment and network services. These standards are not as well-defined as UNI.

As a result, single vendor solutions are currently the safest bet for network managers requiring ATM's speed and flexibility. Technology supporting the following cabling/speed specifications is currently available for ATM as shown in Figure 8-14:

ATM Speed	Cabling Type
25 Mbps	STP, UTP3, or better
100 Mbps	UTP5
155 Mbps	Multimode fiber-optic cable

Figure 8-14   Available ATM Speed/Cabling Specifications

Costs for ATM technology vary widely and should decrease significantly with increased demand. Following are some typical cost ranges:

- 25-Mbps adapter cards: $400–$1500 each.

- 100-Mbps and 155-Mbps adapter cards: $1200–$3000 each.

- Per-port cost on ATM hubs/switches: $1000–$5000 each.

As with any high-speed network architecture, migration strategies from existing network architectures to ATM are of critical importance. Two basic migration approaches have been defined:

1. **IP over ATM,** otherwise known as **classical IP,** adapts the TCP/IP protocol stack to employ ATM services as a native transport protocol directly. This is an IP-specific proposal and is not an option for LANs using other protocol stacks such as NetWare's IPX/SPX.

2. **LAN emulation** provides a translation layer which allows ATM to emulate existing Ethernet and Token Ring LANs and allows the ATM services to transport all current upper-layer LAN protocols in an unmodified form. With LAN emulation, ATM networks become nothing more than a transparent, high-speed delivery service. LAN emulation is most often implemented by the ATM vendor by installing an **address resolution server** which provides translation between the ATM addressing scheme and the addressing scheme native to a particular emulated LAN. LAN emulation is discussed in greater detail in Chapter 16.

Figure 8-15 illustrates a typical ATM implementation featuring an ATM local workgroup, connection of legacy LANs to a local ATM network, the local ATM switched network itself acting as a local high-speed backbone, and access to wide area ATM services which may be either a private network or purchased from an ATM WAN service provider.

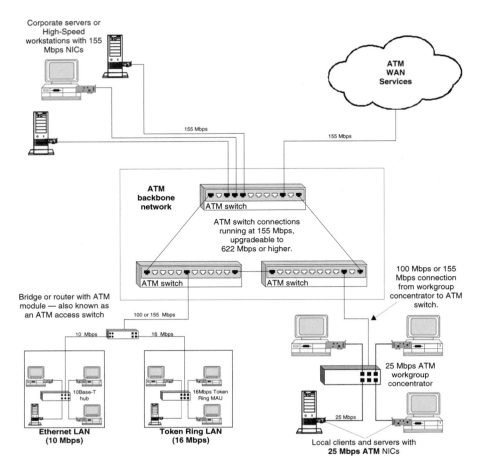

Figure 8-15   ATM Implementation

■ LAN MEDIA ALTERNATIVES

This section reviews a variety of wire and fiber media alternatives, and Chapter 15 explores wireless alternatives for LAN media.

Not Twisted Pair

The type of phone wire installed in most homes, consisting of a tan plastic jacket containing four untwisted wires—red, yellow, green, and black—is also known as **4 conductor station wire,** or **RYGB.** This type of wire is not suitable for data transmission and is not the unshielded twisted pair (UTP) which is so often referred to.

Another popular type of phone wiring is referred to as **flat gray modular** wiring, also known as gray satin or silver satin. Inside this flat gray jacket are either 4, 6, or 8 wires which are crimped into RJ-11 (4 wire), RJ-12 (6 wire), or RJ-45 plugs (8 wire) by a specialized crimping tool. Premises phone wiring as well as phones, crimp tools, RJ-11 plugs, and flat gray modular wire are attainable at nearly any hardware or department store.

Flat gray modular wire is not the same as twisted pair and is suitable only for carrying data over short distances. For instance, this type of cable is often used between a PC or workstation and a nearby RJ-11 jack for access to premises wiring systems or LAN backbones. Modular adapters with RJ-11 input jacks mounted within RS-232 hoods are available to quickly construct data cables of various pinout configurations without the need to crimp RS-232 pins on individual conductors.

Unshielded Twisted Pair

Twisted pair wiring consists of one or more pairs of insulated copper wire which are twisted at varying lengths, from 2 to 12 twists per foot, to reduce interference both between pairs and from outside sources such as electric motors and fluorescent lights. Interference can cause data errors, necessitating retransmission. These individually twisted pairs are then grouped together and covered with a plastic or vinyl covering or jacket. No additional shielding is added before the pairs are wrapped in the plastic covering. Thus, the completed product is known as **unshielded twisted pair,** or **UTP.** Two, 3, 4, and 25 pairs of twisted copper wire are the most common numbers of pairs combined to form the unshielded twisted pair cables.

All UTP is not created equal. One of the appeals of UTP is that it is often already installed in modern buildings to carry voice conversation through the voice PBX. Most often, when the twisted pair wiring for the voice PBX was installed, extra pairs were wired to each office location. Some people conclude that they don't need to invest in any new wiring to carry data transmission throughout their buildings, but can just use the existing extra pairs of unshielded twisted pair wiring. The problem is that there are five categories of UTP, as specified by **EIA/TIA 568** of the Electronics Industry Association/Telecommunications Industry Association. In addition to providing UTP specifications, EIA/TIA 568 also specifies the following:

- The topology, cable types, and connector types to be used in EIA/TIA 568-compliant wiring schemes.

- The minimum performance specifications for cabling, connectors, and components such as wall plates, punch down blocks, and patch panels to be used in an EIA/TIA 568-compliant installation.

Although Category 1 UTP, otherwise known as voice-grade, need only carry voice conversations with reasonable clarity, Categories 3 to 5 (data-grade) cable must meet certain predefined electrical characteristics which ensure transmission quality and speed. Before assuming that the UTP in a building is just fine for data transmission, have its transmission characteristics tested, to ensure these characteristics meet listed data-grade UTP specifications. Figure 8-16 summarizes the specifications for Categories 1 to 5 UTP.

Wire thickness is measured by gauge, represented with the unit **AWG** (American Wire Gauge). The higher the gauge number, the thinner the wire. UTP wiring of different categories must meet specifications for resistance to different forces which interfere with signal strength. Following are two of the more common sources of interference or loss of signal strength:

1. **Attenuation** is the decrease in the power of signal over a distance in a particular type of wire or media.

UTP Category	Specifications/Applications
Category 1	22 or 24 AWG. Not recommended for data.
Category 2	22 or 24 AWG. Suitable only for data transmission of less than 1 Mbps.
Category 3	24 AWG. Very common in existing installations. Most often used for voice-only installations. Suitable for data up to, but not including, 16 Mbps. As a result, it can be used reliably for 4-Mbps Token Ring and 10-Mbps Ethernet. Tested for attenuation and near-end crosstalk up to 16 MHz.
Category 4	22 or 24 AWG. Tested for attenuation and near-end crosstalk up to 20 MHz. Not widely used in favor of Category 5 UTP.
Category 5	22 or 24 AWG. Tested for attenuation and near-end crosstalk to 100 MHz. Capable of transmitting up to 100 Mbps when strictly installed to EIA/TIA 568 specifications. Currently the most commonly installed category of UTP.

Figure 8-16   Unshielded Twisted Pair Specifications

2. **Near-end crosstalk (NExT)** is signal interference caused by a strong signal on one pair (transmitting) overpowering a weaker signal on an adjacent pair (receiving).

Practical Advice and Information

COMMON UTP INSTALLATION MISTAKES

As mentioned in the definition of Category 5 UTP in Figure 8-16, strict adherence to EIA/TIA 568 installation standards is essential to successful transmission at 100 Mbps over UTP Cat. 5. Because a less-than-perfect installation will probably transport 10-Mbps traffic without any problem, noncompliant installations may not surface until upgrades to 100-Mbps network architectures are attempted. Among the most common installation mistakes are the following:

- Untwisting the UTP wire more than the maximum 13mm to secure the UTP to wallplates or punch-down blocks.

- Exceeding the maximum bend radius specified for UTP. Overbending the wire increases crosstalk between stretched pairs of wires.

- Bundling the groups of UTP together too tightly with cable ties. Excessively pinching the UTP together increases crosstalk between pairs.

Shielded Twisted Pair

Data transmission characteristics, and therefore the data transmission speed, can be improved by adding **shielding** around each individual pair as well as around the entire group of twisted pairs. This shielding may be a metallic foil or copper braid. Its function is rather simple. It "shields" the individual twisted pairs as well as the entire cable from either electromagnetic interference (EMI) or radiofrequency interference (RFI). Installation of shielded twisted pair can be tricky.

Remember that the shielding is metal and therefore a conductor. The shielding is often terminated in a drain wire which must be properly grounded. The bottom line is that improperly installed shielded twisted pair wiring can actually increase rather than decrease interference and data transmission problems. STP was commonly specified for Token Ring installations. However, recent specifications for CDDI, fast Ethernet, ATM, and other high-speed network architectures are using Category 5 UTP rather than STP.

Coaxial Cable

Coaxial cable, more commonly known as coax or cable TV cable, has specialized insulators and shielding separating two conductors to allow reliable, high-speed data transmission over relatively long distances. Figure 8-17 is a cross-section of a typical coaxial cable. Coax comes in various thicknesses, as specified by RG (radio government) standards, and historically has been used in Ethernet network architectures. In some cases, these network architecture specifications include required characteristics of the (physical layer) coaxial cable over which the (data-link layer) MAC layer protocol is transmitted.

Ethernet 10Base5 specifies coaxial cable known as thick coax (RG-8), or more affectionately "frozen yellow garden hose," which gives a hint as to how easy it is to work with.

Fiber — The Light of the Future

Coax was at one time the medium of choice for reliable, high-speed data transmission. But times and technology change, and people now often turn to fiber-optic cable when seeking reliable, high-bandwidth media for data transmission beyond the capabilities of Category 5 UTP. Price is still a factor, however, as Figure 8-19 shows, fiber-optic cable is still the most expensive medium option available. This expensive medium delivers high bandwidth in the range of several gigabytes (billions of characters) per second over distances of several kilometers.

Fiber-optic cable is also one of the most secure of all media. It is relatively untappable, transmitting only pulses of light, unlike all other media which transmit varying levels of electrical pulses. Fiber-optic is a thin fiber of glass rather than copper and is immune to electromagnetic interference, which contributes to its high bandwidth and data transmission capabilities. It is important to remember that it is glass and requires careful handling. Fiber-optic cable made of plastic is under development but it does not deliver nearly the speed and bandwidth of the glass fiber cable. Fiber-optic cable comes in a number of varieties. Figure 8-18 shows a cross-section of a fiber-optic cable.

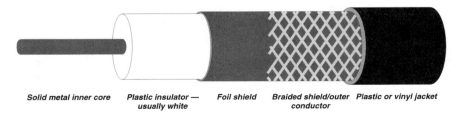

Solid metal inner core   Plastic insulator —   Foil shield   Braided shield/outer   Plastic or vinyl jacket
                           usually white   conductor

Figure 8-17   Coax Cable: Cross-Section

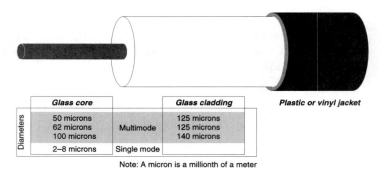

	Glass core		Glass cladding	
Diameters	50 microns		125 microns	
	62 microns	Multimode	125 microns	
	100 microns		140 microns	
	2–8 microns	Single mode		

Note: A micron is a millionth of a meter

Figure 8-18   Fiber-Optic Cable: Cross-Section

Light Transmission Modes   Once a pulse of light enters the core of the fiber-optic cable, it behaves differently depending on the physical characteristics of its core and cladding. In a **multimode** or **multimode step index** fiber-optic cable, the rays of light bounce off of the cladding at different angles and continue down the core while others are absorbed in the cladding. These multiple rays at varying angles cause distortion and limit the fiber's overall transmission capabilities. This type of fiber-optic cable is capable of high-bandwidth (200 Mbps) transmission but usually over distances of less than 1 km.

Gradually decreasing a characteristic of the core known as the refractive index from the center to the outer edge focuses the reflected rays along the core more efficiently, yielding a higher bandwidth (3 GBps) over several kilometers. This type of fiber-optic cable is known as **multimode graded index fiber.**

The third type of fiber-optic cable focuses the rays of light even further, so that only a single wavelength can pass through at a time. This fiber type is known as **single mode.** Without numerous reflections of rays at multiple angles, distortion is eliminated and bandwidth is maximized. Single mode is the most expensive fiber-optic cable, but it can be used over the longest distances.

Core Thickness   The thickness of fiber-optic cable's core and cladding is measured in microns [millionths of a meter (about $\frac{1}{25,000}$ inch)]. The three major core thicknesses are 50, 62, and 100 microns, with associated claddings of 125, 125, and 140 microns, respectively. The increasing core thicknesses, however, generally allow transmission over longer distances at a greater expense.

Light Source Wavelength   The wavelength of the light which is pulsed onto the fiber-optic cable is measured in nanometers (nm), with the optimal light transmitting wavelengths coming in three distinct windows of 820 nm, 1310 nm, 1500 nm. Wavelengths of 820 nm and 1310 nm are most often used for local and campuswide networking such as FDDI, and 1310 nm and 1500 nm are used by carriers to deliver high-bandwidth fiber-based service over long distances. The higher frequency light emitting sources carry a higher price tag.

Applied Problem Solving

LAN MEDIA TECHNOLOGY ANALYSIS

Figure 8-19 summarizes important characteristics of a variety of LAN media including network architecture applicability.

Media Type	Also Called	Bandwidth	Distance Limits	Connectors	Comments/Applications	Architectures Token Ring	Ethernet	FDDI	CDDI	Fast Ethernet	ATM	Price ($)
4-wire phone station wire	Quad RYGB	3 Kbps	200 feet	RJ-11 jacks	4 insulated wires—red, green, yellow, black. Home phone wiring. Voice applications							0.09/foot
Flat gray modular	Flat satin, telephone cable, silver satin	14.4 Kbps	10–20 feet	RJ-11 or RJ-45 plugs	Comes with 4,6,8 conductors. Used for short data cables using modular (mod-tap) adapters	■	■		■	■	■	0.09–0.18/foot
Unshielded twisted pair	UTP	100 Mbps	100 feet	RJ-45	5 designated categories. Twists prevent interference, increase bandwidth. Voice grade usually not suitable for data	■	■		■	■	■	0.10/foot
Shielded twisted pair	STP	16 Mbps	100 feet	RJ-45 or IBM data connectors	Shielding reduces interference but complicates installation	■	■		■	■	■	0.42/foot
Coax- thick	RG-8 Frozen yellow garden hose	10 Mbps	500 feet	AUI (attachment unit interface)	Original Ethernet cabling		■					1.10 foot
Coax-thin	RG-58, thinnet, cheaper net	10 Mbps	200 feet	BNC connector	Looks like cable TV cable. Easier to work with than thick coax.		■					0.32/foot
Coax-thin	RG-62	2.5 Mbps	200 feet	BNC or IBM data connector	Similar to RG-58 (thinnet) but different electrical characteristics make these cables NOT interchangeable	■						0.32/foot
Fiber-optic cable	Fiber glass	Several Gbps	Several kilometers	SI or SMA 905 or SMA 906	Difficult to install but technology is improving. High bandwidth, long distance, virtually error free, high security	■	■	■			■	1.00/foot

Figure 8-19 LAN Media Technology Analysis

SUMMARY

The hardware required to implement any local area network architecture falls into one of a relatively few broad categories: network interface cards, media, and wiring centers. Linking this hardware to the network operating system and operating system software is the network interface card driver. Advances in wiring center technology have enabled an entirely new, switch-based LAN architecture. LAN switches are extremely popular as an upgrade strategy for bandwidth-hungry networks because they require no changes to network interface cards, drivers, or media. Preupgrade traffic analysis is prudent, however, since interswitch bottlenecks can actually degrade, rather than improve, performance.

PCI-based network interface cards are emerging as the high-performance NIC of choice, thanks largely to PCI's own clock, CPU, and mezzanine architecture. The key operational characteristics of network interface card drivers are the ability to support multiple protocol stacks on a single network adapter card and the need to avoid writing monolithic drivers for every possible network interface card/network operating system combination. NDIS and ODI are the two most popular multiprotocol NIC drivers.

Shared-media wiring centers include

standalone hubs, stackable hubs, enterprise hubs, and MAUs. These shared-media hubs merely collapse the shared-media LAN backbone into a single enclosure, while maintaining the one-at-a-time access methodologies. Hub management is especially important as the number of users grows into the 100s. Hub management software should be able to tie into enterprise network management software.

LAN switches offer multiple simultaneous connections to attached workstations as opposed to the one-at-a-time access schemes of the shared media hubs. However, LAN switches are a relatively new technology and have definite drawbacks. For one, when high-speed ports transfer large amounts of data to shared lower-speed ports, data overflow and lost data can occur. Second, managing switched connections which may last for only fractions of a second is not nearly as straightforward as managing a shared media hub. Each of these challenges is being addressed by LAN switch vendors.

LAN media can differ significantly in cost, supported speeds, ease of use, and network architectures supported. Although fiber-optic cable was once considered the only medium suitable for speeds of 100 Mbps and greater, Category 5 unshielded twisted pair seems to be a common media option for high-speed network standards.

KEY TERMS

4 conductor station wire, 298
active management MAUs, 289
address resolution server, 297
agents, 290
asynchronous transfer mode, 293
ATM, 293
attenuation, 299
AUI, 279
AWG, 299
backbone-attached LAN switch, 273
backbone/data center switch, 273
backpressure, 294
binding, 283
BNC connectors, 279
bus mastering DMA, 277
card and socket services, 285
card services, 285
cascading ports, 288
classical IP, 297
collapsed backbone network, 273
CSS, 285
cut-through switches, 293
direct enablers, 285
EIA/TIA 568, 299
enhanced parallel port, 279
enterprise hubs, 286
enterprise network management systems, 290
EPP, 279
error-free cut-through switches, 294
external adapters, 279
fast packet forwarding, 280
flat gray modular, 298
full duplex Ethernet, 273

high performance parallel port, 279
hot-swappable, 287
hubs, 286
IEEE 802.3x, 275
IP over ATM, 297
LAN emulation, 297
LAN switch, 293
link support layer, 284
local hub management software, 290
LSL, 284
management information base, 290
MAU, 286
MIB, 290
MLID, 284
modular concentrators, 286
monolithic drivers, 281
multilink interface drivers, 284
multimode, 302
multimode graded index, 302
multimode step index, 302
multistation access unit, 286
NDIS, 282
near-end crosstalk, 300
network device interface specification, 286
network interface card drivers, 281
network interface cards, 269
network-network interface, 296
NExT, 300
NICs, 269
NNI, 296
ODI, 282

open data-link interface, 282
packet overlapping, 280
PCMCIA adapters, 279
port mirroring, 295
protocol manager, 283
remote monitoring, 290
RJ45, 279
RMON, 290
roving port mirroring, 295
RYGB, 298
server front-end LAN switch, 273
shared-media network architecture, 270
shielding, 300
simple network management protocol, 290
simultaneous RMON view, 295
single mode, 302
SNMP, 290
socket services, 285
stackable hubs, 286
standalone hubs, 286
standalone LAN switches, 272
store-and-forward switches, 294
switched LAN network architecture, 271
switching hub, 293
transceivers, 279
UNI, 296
unshielded twisted pair, 299
user-network interface, 296
UTP, 299
vector, 283
zero slot LANs, 269

REVIEW QUESTIONS

1. What are the unique characteristics of zero-slot LANs?
2. How do zero slot LANs compare functionally to "normal" LANs?
3. List the broad functions and interrelationships of each of the major categories of technology cited in the LAN technology architecture.
4. Differentiate between the advantages and disadvantages of shared-media network architecture versus a switched-based network architecture.
5. What are some of the potential drawbacks or cautions to upgrading to a LAN switch?
6. Differentiate between the delivered functionality and corresponding required switch technology for the three major implementation scenarios for LAN switches.
7. Describe the advantages and disadvantages of a collapsed backbone network.
8. What are the advantages and disadvantages of full duplex network architectures?
9. What hardware and software do full duplex architectures require, beyond normal switch-based LAN architectures?
10. What applications are full duplex network architectures especially well-suited for?
11. What is the meaning of the phrase "The NIC is the keeper of the MAC layer protocol"?
12. What unique advantages can PCI bus NICs offer?
13. Which NIC data transfer method is most efficient and why?
14. Why is it not safe to assume that a bus mastering DMA NIC will work on any computer?
15. What is the disadvantage of using external adapters on notebook or laptop computers?
16. What is the functional role of a network interface card driver?
17. What are the disadvantages of monolithic drivers?
18. What are the two major advantages of multiprotocol network adapter card drivers?
19. Compare and contrast the architecture and functionality of NDIS and ODI.
20. What is the significance of binding in a NDIS environment?
21. Which files and programs are involved in a binding operation?
22. How are protocols actually directed to the proper protocol stack in an NDIS environment?
23. What are the differences between PCMCIA card services and socket services?
24. What are the differences between PCMCIA CSS and direct enablers?
25. Differentiate between delivered functionality and required technology features of the three major categories of hubs.
26. What important advantages does an active management MAU offer?
27. Why can't modules from one vendor's enterprise hub be used in another vendor's enterprise hub even if both modules support the same network architecture?
28. What are the differences between the two levels of management software which hubs should support?
29. How is it possible for an enterprise network management system to compile statistics from networking equipment manufactured by a variety of different vendors?
30. What are the major functional differences between how LAN switches process and forward packets? What are the advantages and disadvantages of each method?
31. In what types of LAN switch implementations is backpressure likely to be an issue?
32. Why is traffic monitoring and management more of a challenge in LAN switches than in shared-media hubs?
33. Differentiate between the three major LAN switch traffic monitoring and management techniques.
34. What are the advantages and disadvantages of assigning multiple workstations per switch port?
35. What switching issues are unique to Token Ring switches?
36. What roles can ATM play in a local area network?
37. How can "legacy LANs" be integrated into an ATM network?
38. What unique capabilities of ATM account for all of the interest in this technology?
39. What is LAN emulation, and why is it important?
40. Why is twisted pair twisted?
41. What is the importance of EIA/TIA 568?
42. What is the most common category of UTP installed today and why?
43. Why is UTP category 5 favored over shielded twisted pair, coax, and fiber-optic cable for many high-speed network architectures?
44. Why is shielded twisted pair considered trickier to install than UTP?

ACTIVITIES

1. Review data communications product catalogs for zero slot LAN advertisements. Report on the results of the search in terms of total number found, number of hardware-based versus software-based, and maximum number of users. Comment on the results.
2. Research the relative market sizes of hubs versus LAN switches over the past three years. Interpret your results.
3. Find actual LAN switch implementations and analyze and compare the various implementation scenarios. What function is the LAN switch serving in each case? Are there implementation categories beyond those listed in this chapter? Were examples found of each scenario listed?
4. Find actual implementations of full duplex network architectures and report on the applications served by this technology. Is traffic level measured in this application? If so, report on the findings.
5. Research the network interface card market and report on the features or functions offered by the most advanced NICs.
6. Locate a computer which uses NDIS drivers. Print out the CONFIG.SYS and PROTOCOL.INI files. Trace the binding operation between MAC drivers and protocol drivers.
7. Locate a computer which uses ODI drivers. Print out the CONFIG.SYS and the NET.CFG files. Determine how multiple protocol stacks can be assigned to a single NIC.
8. Research data communications catalogs, buyers' guides, and product literature for the latest information on PCMCIA adapters. Report on the latest trends and capabilities. Are multiple functions, such as modems and NICs, being included on a single card?
9. Research data communications catalogs, buyers' guides, and product literature for the latest information on hubs. Pay special attention to the availability of management features, especially ties to enterprise management systems.
10. Research the topic of the RMON MIB. Which standards-making organization is responsible for the definition? What types of information are collected in the RMON MIB? What are RMON probes, and how do they function?
11. Research data communications catalogs, buyers' guides, and product literature for the latest information on LAN switches. Pay special attention to how the switches handle flow control issues, and report on the alternative methods.
12. Research data communications catalogs, buyers' guides, and product literature for the latest information on LAN switches. Pay special attention to how the switches handle monitoring and management of LAN switch traffic and report on the alternative methods.
13. Research data communications catalogs, buyers' guides, and product literature for the latest information on ATM technology for the LAN. What is the availability and cost range for ATM NICs of various speeds? Which vendors seem to have the most complete "single-vendor solutions"?
14. Prepare a display including electrical specifications of the various types of LAN media cited in this chapter. Detail network architectures and maximum transmission speeds to which each medium type is assigned.

FEATURED REFERENCES

General References

Derfler, Frank. The Perfect Network. *PC Magazine*, 14; 13 (July 1995), 224.
Hardy, James. *Inside Networks* (Englewood Cliffs, NJ: Prentice-Hall, 1995).

Case Studies

Loudermilk, Stephen. Banking on PCI for Bandwidth. *LAN Times*, 12; 12 (June 19, 1995), 29.
McLean, Michelle. Bayer's Switching Eases Net Aches. *LAN Times*, 12; 11 (June 5, 1995), 39.
Moeller, Michael. Government Goes Wireless in Indiana. *PC Week*, 12; 26 (July 3, 1995), 23.
Saunders, Stephen. Lessons Learned from Ethernet Switching Pathfinders. *Data Communications*, 24; 9 (July 1995), 77.

LAN Switches

Bryan, John. LANs Make the Switch. *Byte*, 19; 9 (September 1994), 113.
Dell'Oro Tam. Switching into the Future. *Business Communications Review*, 25; 7 (July 1995), 29.
Giorgis, Tadesse. 29 Switching Hubs Save the Bandwidth. *Byte*, 20; 7 (July 1995), 162.
Haber, Lynn. Switching Hub Technology: Too Awesome to Manage? *Communications Week*, no. 568 (July 31, 1995), 45.
Newman, David. LAN Switches Leave Users Looking

for Trouble. *Data Communications*, 24; 3 (March 1995), 103.

Salamone, Salvatore. Merging ATM and Ethernet. *Byte*, 20; 8 (August 1995), 155.

Saunders, Stephen. A Mix-and-Match Switch for Ethernet and ATM. *Data Communications*, 24; 3 (March 1995), 43.

Saunders, Stephen. Cell Switching: Dollars and Sense. *Data Communications*, 24; 1 (January 1995), 88.

Saunders, Stephen. LAN Switch Pulls Double Duty. *Data Communications*, 24; 5 (April 1995), 49.

Saunders, Stephen. Traffic Jam at the LAN Switch. *Data Communications*, 23; 17 (November 21, 1994), 53.

Wittmann, Art. Mega Switches, Mega Gold. *Network Computing*, 6; 9 (August 1, 1995), 56.

Wittmann, Art. The Switching Hub Era Begins!. *Network Computing*, 5; 10 (September 1, 1994), 62.

Wittman, Art and Robert Kohlhepp. The New Network Frontier. *Network Computing*, 6; 4 (April 1, 1995), 66.

Ethernet Switches

McLean, Michelle. Switch Monitor Tangle. *LAN Times*, 12; 11 (June 5, 1995), 1.

Salamone, Salvatore. Ethernet Switching Hubs: Sorting Through the Offerings. *Business Communications Review*, 24; 7 (July 1994), 38.

Saunders, Stephen. An Ethernet Switch with a View. *Data Communications*, 24; 4 (March 21, 1995), 37.

Saunders, Stephen. Full-Duplex Ethernet: More Niche than Necessity? *Data Communications*, 23; 4 (March 1994), 87.

Saunders, Stephen and Bruce Levy. Industrial-Strength Testing for Ethernet Switches. *Data Communications*, 24; 9 (July 1995), 54.

Tolly, Kevin. Full Speed Ahead for Full-Duplex Ethernet. *Data Communications*, 23; 4 (March 1994), 39.

Token Ring Switches

Gerber, Barry. Switching to Token Ring. *Network Computing*, 6; 10 (September 1, 1995), 50.

Guruge, Anura. Token Ring Switches Come of Age. *Business Communications Review*, 25; 8 (August 1995), 38.

Haugdahl, J. Scott. Token-Ring Switching. *Network Computing*, 5; 15 (December 1, 1994), 126.

Passmore, David. A Closer Look at Token-Ring Switching. *Business Communications Review*, 25; 6 (June 1995), 20.

Saunders, Stephen. The Switch Is on for Token Ring. *Data Communications*, 24; 1 (January 1995), 75.

Saunders, Stephen. Token Ring Switches Make It to Market. *Data Communications*, 24; 4 (March 21, 1995), 49.

Tolly, Kevin. Token Ring Switching: The Design Challenge. *Data Communications*, 24; 2 (February 1995), 97.

Hubs/MAUs

Axner, David. Intelligent Hubs—What Makes Them So Smart? *Business Communications Review*, 25; 1 (January 1995), 40.

Gerber, Barry. Token-Ring Hubs Have Come a Long Way, Baby. *Network Computing*, 5; 15 (December 1, 1994), 100.

Kohlhepp, Robert. The Great Network Stack Attack. *Network Computing*, 5; 13 (November 1, 1994), 68.

Salamone, Salvatore. PC Switching Hub Cards: Ethernet Switching at a Fraction of the Cost. *Byte*, 19; 10 (October 1994), 36.

Network Interface Cards

Adams, Jay. PC Card NICs: Small Differences. *Network Computing*, 6; 4 (April 1, 1995), 92.

Boyle, Padraic. Riding the First Wave of 100VG. *PC Magazine*, 14; 15 (September 1995), NE21.

Conover, Joel. Get More from Your Network with High-Performance Ethernet Cards. *Network Computing*, 6; 5 (May 1, 1995), 124.

Conover, Joel. Security Vendors Put Virus Protection in the Network Hardware. *Network Computing*, 6; 6 (May 15, 1995), 106.

Danielle, Diane. Getting the Knack of 32-Bit NICs. *Network Computing*, 5; 10 (September 1, 1994), 184.

Kohlhepp, Robert. More Ethernet Solutions for PowerBooks. *Network Computing*, 5; 9 (August 1, 1994), 118.

MacAskill, Skip and Melinda LeBaron. Adapting to Dual-Speed Ethernet Interface Cards. *Network Computing*, 12; 25 (June 19, 1995), L18.

Saunders, Stephen. Desktop ATM: It's in the Cards. *Data Communications*, 24; 1 (January 1995), 94.

Tolly, Kevin and David Newman. FDDI Adapters: A Sure Cure for the Bandwidth Blues. *Data Communications*, 23; 10 (July 1994), 60.

PCI NICs

Conover, Joel. PCI-Based NICs. *Network Computing*, 6; 8 (July 1, 1995), 136.

Drews, James and Joel Conover. Ethernet Cards Take the PCI Bus to Better Server Performance. *Network Computing*, 5; 13 (November 1, 1994), 98.

Koegler, Scott. PCI FDDI Cards: Making the Cut. *Network Computing*, 6; 7 (June 1, 1995), 128.

Loudermilk, Stephen. Cogent's Four-Port Fast-Ethernet Board Boosts Performance of PCI Bus. *LAN Times*, 12; 1 (January 9, 1995), 1.

Media

Germain, Arthur. More than Just Plumbing. *Communications Week*, no. 566 (July 17, 1995), S16.

Pike, Tyrone and Stanley Ooi. Taking Sides on 155Mbit/s Over Category 3 UTP. *Data Communications*, 24; 5 (April 1995), 105.

Saunders, Stephen. Bad Vibrations Beset Category 5 UTP Users. *Data Communications*, 23; 9 (June 1994), 49.

LAN Alternatives/Zero Slot LANs

Nance, Barry. File Transfer on Steroids. *Byte*, 20; 2 (February 1995), 129.

ATM

Jeffries, Ron. 25-Mbps ATM—Can It Fly? *Business Communications Review*, 24; 8 (August 1994), 29.

Johnson, B.J. The ATM Deskset. *Network Computing*, 5; 14 (November 15, 1994), 94.

McQuillan, John. Can ATM Make It to the Desktop? *Business Communications Review*, 25; 5 (May 1995), 10.

Newman, David and Kevin Tolly. Are PC LANs Ready for ATM? *Data Communications*, 23; 12 (September 1994), 95.

Newman, Peter. Traffic Management for ATM Local Area Networks. *IEEE Communications*, 32; 8 (August 1994), 44.

CASE STUDY

Chapter 8

LAYER 3 SWITCHING CURES MEDICAL CENTER'S ILLS

Multilayer switches keep the data flowing at the University of Pittsburgh Medical Center through a complex arterial network that connects 5,000 devices. The medical center's five major hospital wings span a half-mile radius. This central site connects to a primary-care center at Pittsburgh International Airport and 26 affiliated clinics and patient-care facilities. And the system will grow even more this summer as the medical center extends deeper into the suburbs.

John Bregar, director of telecommunications, said Cisco Systems Inc.'s Catalyst 5000 switch with built-in routing capabilities helps his limited staff respond quickly to the changing needs of the medical center.

"We can dedicate a 10Mbps pipe from the Catalyst for each of our servers," he said. "That avoids the major cabling nightmare of having to break out additional LAN segments as network traffic grows." Currently there are two Catalysts within the system, and two more are on order to handle future expansion projects.

The magnetic resonance imaging (MRI) research department and various medical groups are connected through a 100Mbps Layer 3 switch. This speeds the flow of medical images and research data between doctors and technicians, who had previously been on a single Ethernet segment. Increased traffic and unacceptable throughput forced Bregar to upgrade the system.

A second multilayer switch will be installed soon to push through imaging from various radiology groups across the network. Doctors sitting at any terminal will be able to access any department in the network, remotely monitor patient care, and even receive X-rays and radiology scans from any trauma facility for analysis. Bregar said the switch will also provide additional bandwidth when the medical center needs to install a new scanner or receive large images.

"Once they come up with a location for this equipment," he said, "we'll simply dedicate a 10Mbps pipe off the Catalyst switch." The multilayer switches are used to move data between high-traffic workstations, for general capacity relief, and to avoid additional costly segmentation.

Anatomy 101

The medical center is anchored by a dual-ring FDDI backbone. A five-node FDDI collapsed-Ethernet backbone, supported by Cisco HES Plus and Cisco 7000 routers, links the five major hospital wings and creates a separate subnetwork for each wing that protects one ring from another and from other traffic and users. A Chipcom Corp. intelligent-management hub on the backbone feeds Category 5 UTP cable to all users.

All told, there are 75 LANs on the network hosted by various legacy and client/server systems. An IBM 4090 mainframe is the big iron on the network, devoted primarily to systems used for patient billing and for scheduling lab tests.

A cluster of seven Digital Equipment Corp. VAX processors support a variety of imaging systems for the radiology and MRI departments. This cluster is also utilized as a database server and applications server for clinical applications, which include a pharmacy system, anatomic pathology system, and lab system.

Remote-radiology applications running on servers located in rural hospital, clinics, emergency rooms, and patient-care facilities require high-speed data and imaging transfers to the network backbone. For example, when trauma patients come into any rural facility, emergency-room personnel can transmit X-ray images to radiologists whether a patient should be treated locally or be flown to Pittsburgh. One such primary-care center, located at Pittsburgh's International Airport, is connected to the main medical campus by T-1 fiber lines.

A variety of Sun Microsystems Inc. SPARCstation model 10 and model 20 workstations and servers are at the top of the network. Underneath them are Compaq Computer Corp. 486 and Intel Corp. Pentium processor workstations and servers running on Novell Inc. NetWare LANs.

The network supports TCP/IP, IPX/SPX, and Digital DECnet.

When John Bregar came to the medical center eight years ago, the computing hardware consisted of 88 IBM dumb terminals connected to an IBM mainframe through SNA-type controllers. There were also 40 Digital terminals connected to a single VAX processor that served as a billing system.

Most of the medical center's spectacular growth has taken place only in the last three to four years. "As technology decreased in cost," Bregar explained, "it became easier to justify replacing a dumb terminal with a smart terminal." Since then, the implementation of new technology has quickly progressed.

Coping with the changing information technology requirements of such a vast medical complex often tests the skills and resources of Bregar's limited staff. He is assisted by only 21 technicians for all voice and data communications facilities.

Eight of these technicians make up the PC support staff, which installs PC workstations and servers, performs hardware upgrades, installs new software, and supports the Novell LANs. Another seven are dedicated to network support and handling the day-to-day help-desk calls. Two of this group also oversee upcoming network planning and network tuning. The remaining six staff members install network voice and data cables. Outside contractors install cabling at locations other than the main campus.

Interoperability Is Key

Bregar uses only Cisco and Chipcom equipment for the backbone network and Sun and Compaq servers and workstations. "We know their respective systems work well together, and we have the added advantage of always having spare parts and systems on hand."

The current task is connecting four new remote medical facilities to the backbone with additional Cisco Catalyst switches. There are also plans to connect all the doctors' offices and to install a patient billing and scheduling system. Connections will be made via the most appropriate method: dial-up, frame relay, or ISDN.

Bregar is taking a wait-and-see approach to ATM. "I'm keeping in touch with what all the vendors are doing and where the standard is going." He said the network has been positioned so that he can upgrade the Cisco switches and move into the ATM arena when the time comes. He's waiting to evaluate the applications driving ATM.

"There's no immediate need to jump into ATM," he concludes. "Our facilities aren't widely enough dispersed to justify the cost of voice, data, and video. There would have to be a compelling application or a compelling need for such an investment."

Source: Peter Ruber (July 24, 1995). Layer 3 Switching Cures Medical Center's Ills. *LAN Times*, 12(14), 84. Reprinted with permission of McGraw-Hill, *LAN Times*.

BUSINESS CASE STUDY QUESTIONS ·······················

Activities

1. Complete a top-down model for this case by gleaning facts from the case and placing them in the proper layer of the top-down model. After you complete the top-down model, analyze and detail those instances when requirements were clearly passed down from upper to lower layers of the model and solutions to those requirements were passed up from lower to upper layers.
2. Detail any questions that may occur to you about the case for which answers are not clearly stated in the article.
3. Prepare an OSI seven-layer model outlining as many protocols on as many platforms as possible from the information supplied in the article.

Business

1. What type of business activities required special treatment by the network resources?
2. What factors had forced the system upgrade?

3. What are the strategic plans for technology upgrades?
4. What are some of the elements of a strategic business plan?
5. How do strategic technology upgrades relate to strategic business plans?

Application

1. What types of applications are run in support of primary business activities?
2. Which applications are executed on the mainframe?
3. Which applications are executed on the VAX minicomputers?
4. Which types of applications are run at remote locations?

Data

1. What types of data unique to this business had to be catered to by networking functionality?
2. What types, and how much, traffic is transmitted to/from remote locations?

Network

1. How many devices are connected to the University of Pittsburgh Medical Center Network?
2. How many different geographically dispersed locations are connected to the network?
3. How did the network technology chosen in this case make it easy to cater to the unique data requirements?
4. What are the network architecture and physical topology of the backbone network?

5. How are remote locations linked to the corporate network? What are the potential options for WAN services?

Technology

1. How do network switches meet the unique networking requirements of this business?
2. How many LANs are linked via the backbone network?
3. What additional functionality did Layer 3 switching offer that routing did not?

CHAPTER 9

LOCAL AREA NETWORK APPLICATIONS SOFTWARE

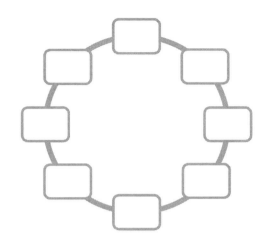

Concepts Reinforced

OSI model
Protocols and standards
Client/server technology model

Top-down model
Hardware/software compatibility
Network architectures

Concepts Introduced

LAN software architecture
LAN productivity software
e-mail
Groupware
LAN resource management software

Network backup
Multiprotocol network printing
Network faxing
Electronic software distribution
License and inventory management

OBJECTIVES

After mastering the material in this chapter you should:

1. Understand the categorization of LAN productivity software and LAN resource management software.

2. Understand the analysis involved in properly applying LAN productivity and LAN resource management software.

3. Understand the compatibility issues involved with implementing LAN software.

4. Understand the functionality and potential business impact of LAN productivity and LAN resource management software.

Chapter 7 provided an understanding of LAN network architectures and Chapter 8 covered LAN hardware. Chapter 9 explores the critical role played by LAN software. LAN software is distinguished from the server software alternatives described in Chapter 5 by its ability to communicate across the LAN between clients

311

and servers, between two or more servers, and to enterprise management workstations. In other words, the server software explored in Chapter 5 required only a server to operate whereas the software explored in this chapter requires a LAN over which to communicate.

■ LAN SOFTWARE ARCHITECTURE

To organize and illustrate the interrelationships between the various categories of LAN software, a **LAN software architecture** can be constructed. In fact, this LAN software architecture could serve as a graphical outline of the major topics included in this chapter. As Figure 9-1 illustrates, LAN software is divided into two major categories: (1) network operating systems and (2) application software.

Network operating systems are concerned with providing an interface between LAN hardware, such as network interface cards, and the application software installed on a particular client or server. The network operating system's job is to provide transparent interoperability between client and server portions of a given application program. More detailed explanations of network operating system functionality as well as the differences between peer-to-peer and client/server networking operating systems are provided in Chapter 10.

Applications software on a LAN is divided into client front-ends and server back-ends or engines and is concerned with accomplishing a specific type of task or

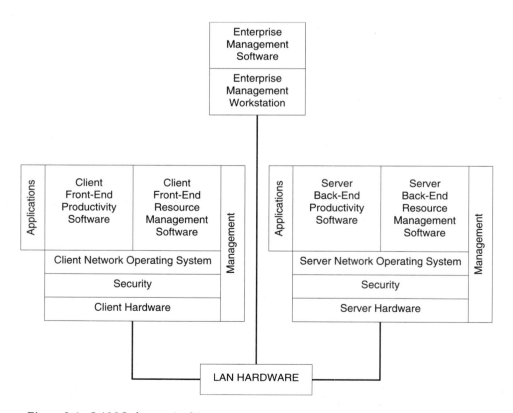

Figure 9-1 LAN Software Architecture

transaction. LAN applications software can be divided into two major subcategories:

1. LAN productivity software.

2. LAN resource management software.

LAN productivity software is application software that contributes directly to the productivity of its users. In other words, this is the software people use not only to get their work done, but more important, to get it done more quickly, effectively, accurately, or at a lower cost. Examples include e-mail, scheduling software, groupware, and a variety of other types of software which will be explained further.

LAN resource management software is more concerned with providing access to shared network resources and services. Examples of such shared network-attached resources include printers, fax machines, CD-ROMs, modems, and a variety of other devices and services.

Two overlying elements required in any LAN software configuration are security and management.

Security is especially important in networked, LAN software environments because logged-in users can be physically dispersed over large areas. Increased deployment of remote workers has led to increased need for remote access to corporate information resources. As important corporate data is transferred over network links, precautions must be taken to prevent unauthorized access to transmitted data, as well as to corporate networks and computer systems.

Finally, management software must be incorporated to provide a single, consolidated view of all networked resources, both hardware and software. From a single location, all of the distributed elements comprising today's client/server information systems must be effectively monitored and managed. This single enterprise management platform must be able to integrate management information from not just networking components, but also application programs, database management systems, and client and server hardware.

■ LAN PRODUCTIVITY SOFTWARE

Because it is impossible to give an exhaustive review of each of the major categories of LAN productivity software within the constraints of a reasonably sized text, we offer a practical approach from the perspective of a network analyst, focusing primarily on the following key areas:

- Key current issues and trends in each LAN productivity software category which are important to the network analyst.

- Examples of how each category of LAN productivity software actually increases worker productivity.

- Key criteria on which product decisions and recommendations should be made.

The scope of coverage in this chapter is restricted to LAN-specific issues for each software category, and wide area, internetworking, and enterprisewide issues are left for discussion in Chapter 17.

E-Mail

Most surveys show e-mail to be the second most popular use of local area networks, following printer and file services. Although many new e-mail users balk at the technology at first, they quickly become convinced of the positive attributes of LAN-based e-mail, such as the following:

- Correspondence can be handled at one's convenience rather than having to coordinate face-to-face meetings or catch a person at his or her desk for a phone call. It eliminates the old game of telephone tag.

- E-mail enables more concise correspondence. People tend to get more to the point in e-mail messages, and concise answers can be quickly returned.

- Overall productivity is increased as specific issues are handled via e-mail rather than through a never-ending series of meetings, appointments, and lengthy conversations.

E-mail could be considered a **store-and-forward messaging** technology, as messages are sent, received, replied to, and delivered in discrete steps performed in a disjointed fashion over a period of time. This series of events is sometimes also described as an asynchronous messaging system. In contrast, a phone conversation would be considered a synchronous messaging system, as calling parties speak to each other simultaneously in a "live" fashion.

Important functionality or features of e-mail systems can be divided into two major subcategories, differentiated by the intended recipient of the functionality: end-user features and administration features.

End-User Features   To understand which features are important in an e-mail system, one needs only to examine the types of things one ordinarily does when creating, mailing, receiving, sorting, storing, and retrieving paper-based correspondence. Effective e-mail systems should deliver all of the same functionality plus increased productivity enabled by its electronic, computer-based nature. End-user–related features of e-mail can be logically divided into four general categories:

1. Features related to the ease with which e-mail can be created, addressed, and edited.

2. Features related to how flexibly a variety of different types of files and documents can be attached to e-mail messages.

3. Features related to how easily received e-mail can be organized for retrieval at a later time.

4. Integration with supplementary or advanced systems such as scheduling systems or workflow automation systems.

Figure 9-2 summarizes some important end-user e-mail features based on this categorization.

Remote End-User Features   With the increased emphasis on mobile computing and virtual offices, the needs and constraints of remote or mobile e-mail users are becoming increasingly important. Chief among the constraints faced by remote e-mail users is the comparatively limited bandwidth dial-up telecommunications services

End-User Features Category	Features/Importance
E-Mail Creation, Editing, and Addressing	• Group addressing capabilities to easily send the same e-mail to a number of individuals. • E-mail routing capabilities to control the order in which users receive, revise, and pass along e-mail. • E-mail flags and options: urgent, return receipt requested, message delivery confirmation versus message open and read confirmation. • Private electronic Rolodex organization. • Automatic e-mail replies "I won't be able to check e-mail for two weeks." • E-mail easily forwarded and/or replied to. • Separate login, authentication, and security system for e-mail system. • Is the e-mail desktop environment customizable? Can custom toolbars be created for individual users which include icons for features most often used by a particular user? • Can rules be established which automatically handle incoming or outgoing messages? • Can e-mail be screened by administrative assistants or by the e-mail system? • Carbon copy, blind copy, priority setting. • Can individual messages be encrypted or password protected?
E-Mail Attachments	• Several types of files can be attached to both sent and received mail. • Multiple files can be attached to single e-mail message. • Attachments can be saved and edited. • Attachments can be encrypted.
E-Mail Organization and Retrieval	• Multiple hierarchical folders for organization of e-mail by topic or project. • Received e-mail can be sorted or selected by date, sender, topic, keywords, or message content.
Integration with Supplementary Systems	• Integrated with scheduling system so that meeting requests are sent via e-mail system. • Integrated with workflow automation software for automatic routing of attached documents. • Integrated with FAX server subsystem so that messages and documents may be either faxed or e-mailed from a single screen. • Integrated with voice-mail system so that voice messages can be digitized, stored on disk, listed along with e-mail in a single received messages in-box, and replayed. • Integrated with forms design software so that customized forms can be created and routed via the e-mail system.

Figure 9-2   E-Mail End-User Features

offer compared to local area network bandwidth. As a result, some e-mail systems offer specialized **remote e-mail client software** which offers such specialized features as:

- Built-in phone number storage and communications software.

- Support of large number of types of modems and/or wide area network services.

- The ability to download only the headers of received e-mail indicating the source, data, time, size, and subject of e-mail. Subsequently, the remote user can download the entire body of only selected e-mail messages he or she chooses to deal with immediately. This feature conserves both bandwidth and time.

- The remote end-user client software can be updated and synchronized automatically with corporate-based e-mail which might be installed in a docking station or workstation at corporate headquarters.

Administration Features   Administration features can be logically divided into three subcategories:

1. Installation features are concerned with such issues as how many platforms the e-mail system can operate or how easily it can be established.

2. Operation features are concerned with how easily the system can be maintained on an ongoing basis, including ease of user administration, troubleshooting, security management, and message delivery management.

3. Interoperability features are concerned with how easily this e-mail system can exchange e-mail and attachments with a variety of other e-mail systems.

E-Mail System Interoperability   Although e-mail system interoperability and protocols, both among different e-mail systems and between e-mail systems and mail-enabled application software, are studied in detail in Chapter 17, a few key concepts of e-mail interoperability are reviewed here to better understand the administration features listed in the interoperability section of Figure 9-3.

The client portion of any e-mail system software is the portion that runs on a particular type of client workstation to send and receive e-mail messages. **Multiplatform e-mail client software,** the first stage of interoperability for e-mail systems, can be objectively evaluated by the number of computing platforms for which it is available. Similarly, the post office portions of most e-mail systems can use the file management systems of numerous different network operating systems.

When e-mail messages created on one system need to be sent to a destination workstation running a different type of e-mail, some translation between the two systems is obviously necessary. This system-to-system translation is accomplished by specially written software known as **e-mail gateways.** E-mail systems vary in the number of gateways they support and whether or not the gateway software must be run on a dedicated server.

Figure 9-3 summarizes key e-mail administration features.

E-Mail Systems Architectures   Although the end-user and administration features listed in the previous sections are the most overt evidence of e-mail system functionality, the system's underlying messaging architecture can determine both how

Administration Features Category	Features/Importance
Installation	• Can e-mail system read network operating system userID directories such as the NetWare bindery to ease establishment of e-mail userIDs? • Are user directories integrated so that only a single user account needs to be maintained? • Can a single e-mail user profile be copied to create multiple new e-mail userIDs? • How easy is the e-mail server installation? • Is there a maximum number of mailboxes per post office?
Operation	• Is a separate login required to access the e-mail system? • Must separate e-mail system user accounts be maintained? • Are users automatically notified of newly received mail? • Can the administrator manage the e-mail system remotely? • Can the administrator manage multiple e-mail systems from single management console? • Can the administrator read all user e-mail? • Can the administrator limit connect times to/from remote post offices? • Can the administrator monitor statistics on links to remote post offices or clients? • Can the administrator track system usage by individuals or groups? • Can the administrator delete old messages? • Is a remote client module available to allow access via modem? • Does the remote client module interface match the local client interface? • Does the remote client module cost additional money? • Can the mail system files be backed up while users are logged in? • Can the post office disks be compressed while the system is up?
Interoperability	• Is client software available for Macintosh, OS/2, UNIX, and VAX workstations? • Which network operating systems can the post office run over? Options: NetWare, LANmanager, LANserver, Vines, Windows NT, various flavors of UNIX. • Are gateways available to NetWare E-mail (MHS), AT&T Mail, CompuServe, DEC All-in-One, DEC VMS Mail, IBM DISOSS, IBM PROFS, MCI Mail, Wang MailWay. X.400? • What options are supported for interpost office links: LAN-to-LAN, leased lines, dial-up lines, X.25, ISDN?

Figure 9-3   E-Mail Administration Features

efficiently it operates as the number of users increases and how easily it may be managed. There are two primary messaging architectures for LAN-based e-mail products:

1. **Shared-file e-mail systems.**

2. **Client/server e-mail systems.**

In a shared-file e-mail system architecture, the e-mail software uses the native file system included with each network operating system over which it executes. This setup allows a single e-mail package to run over multiple network operating systems. Often, a single file server can be used for e-mail system operation for a given network, thereby affording relative ease of installation and operation. E-mail messages are just files which are transferred to the proper destination post office or file server by **message transfer agent (MTA)** software, which is usually executed on a dedicated workstation. The file server or post office is generally used only as a storage device in a shared-file e-mail system architecture and does not execute back-end e-mail engine software. As a result, it is the client-based e-mail software which must poll the post office (file server) periodically to see if any new mail (file) has arrived.

In client/server e-mail systems, the server plays a more active role in operating and managing the e-mail system. Rather than serving as a passive file-server used only for storage purposes, it executes back-end e-mail engine software which supports real-time communication links to e-mail clients and other post offices via remote procedure calls (RPC). Client/server e-mail systems interact with a network operating system's communication protocols rather than merely with its file management system. Allowing real-time communication between e-mail clients and servers on an as-needed basis eliminates the need for polling and its associated bandwidth usage. The processing power provided by the server-based e-mail engine makes client/server e-mail messaging architectures more efficient for more users in terms of installation, operation, and interoperability. Figure 9-4 illustrates some of the key architectural differences between shared-file and client/server e-mail messaging architectures.

Groupware

Groupware is a category of software which seeks to take advantage of the fact that workers are networked together electronically to increase communication and maximize worker productivity. The overall category of groupware can first be divided into two subcategories based on the characteristics of the information shared between group members:

1. **Communication-based groupware** deals with establishing, maintaining, and managing a variety of ad-hoc communications between networked group members. Among the types of groupware represented by this category are the following:
   - E-mail (previously reviewed).
   - Group scheduling.
   - Electronic conferencing and meeting support.
   - Electronic whiteboard software.
   - Videoconferencing.

2. **Document-based groupware** deals with managing, storing, retrieving, and transporting structured documents among participating networked co-workers. Among the types of groupware represented by this category are the following:
   - Workflow automation.
   - Document management, imaging, and conferencing.

Shared-File E-Mail System

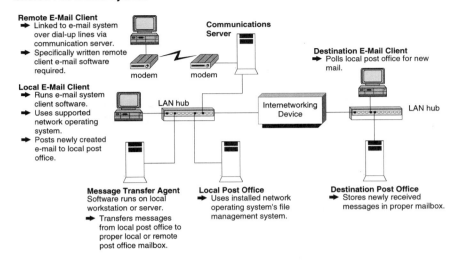

Client/Server E-Mail System

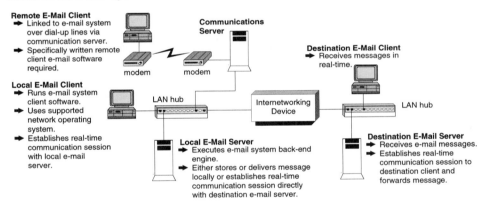

Figure 9-4   Shared File Versus Client/Server E-Mail Systems

Group Scheduling   **Group scheduling software,** or calendar packages, can be a very efficient means of scheduling electronic or face-to-face meetings or conferences. By simply listing with whom one wishes to meet, you can schedule a meeting without making a single phone call. Some scheduling software even has the ability to work over internetworks or wide area networks, allowing meetings to be scheduled with people across the country or around the world. Group scheduling software is often integrated with e-mail systems, allowing requests for meetings to be automatically sent and replied to via e-mail. Most of the differences between group scheduling packages can be divided into the following categories:

- Platforms supported/installation.
- Personal schedule management.

- Group calendar management.
- Group meeting scheduling.

Figure 9-5 summarizes some of the key features included in group scheduling software based on these categories.

Practical Advice and Information

Although this electronic scheduling process may sound simple, be forewarned! Implementation of group scheduling software can fail miserably because of people factors, not software bugs. If everyone in a given organization does not make a firm commitment to keep their electronic schedule and calendar accurate and up-to-date, the product simply cannot work. Also, inevitably, controls must be set as to who has the authority to add commitments to someone else's schedule. The politics of group scheduling can turn out to be much more complicated than the software.

Electronic Conferencing and Meeting Support   **Electronic conferencing and meeting support** software offers opportunities for workers to interact electronically. Brainstorming or idea generating sessions are conducted via the network and managed by the **workgroup conferencing software** package. Ideas can be generated on "private" screens and then shared with the group. Meetings can be held electronically, and thereby anonymously, allowing more honest interaction not subject to the political pressures of many face-to-face meetings. Ideas can be prioritized, consensus reached, action items established, and meeting minutes electronically recorded, edited, and approved.

Workgroup conferencing software may be a standalone application or integrated with other groupware modules such as document management or workflow automation. In addition to the obvious technical issue of which computing platforms are supported, three major functional categories for electronic meeting support software correspond to the natural flow of meeting events:

1. **Meeting creation**—Meetings must first be created or established.

2. **Idea generation**—The major purpose of an electronically supported meeting is to generate ideas in a nonthreatening, politically neutral environment.

3. **Meeting results reporting**—To benefit fully from the ideas generated at the meeting, results must be easily, accurately, and flexibly reported.

Electronic meeting support software has a unique vocabulary and many software packages function in an overall similar manner. Discussion groups are called **forums.** Each forum probably contains multiple topics for discussion, known alternatively as **discussion categories** or **sections.** Specific discussion topics, on which participants are welcome to comment, are generally referred to as **threads.** User comments on topics are made up of a series of **messages** which may contain supporting material or documents known as **enclosures.** Meetings may be held in specially equipped **decision support rooms** in which all forum participants gather in what is known as a **same-place, same-time meeting,** or they may convene via a local or wide area network according to participants' availability, in what is known as a **different-place, different-time meeting.** Figure 9-6 (page 322) summarizes some of the key features to look for when purchasing electronic meeting support software.

Group Scheduling Feature Category	Feature/Implication
Platforms Supported/ Installation	• Which network operating systems can this group scheduling software run over? Options: NetWare, Vines, LANManager, Windows NT, AppleShare, LANtastic, and other DOS-based LANs. • Does the scheduling package support out-bound and in-bound wide area network links? Is this feature included or optional? • What options can be performed remotely? edit or view schedule including appointments? • If a schedule is kept on a remote workstation, can the scheduling package automatically synchronize the remote schedule with new meetings and appointments from the server? • Is the group scheduling system designed to integrate tightly with a particular e-mail or groupware package? Options: Lotus Notes, GroupWise, cc:Mail, Microsoft Mail. • Are e-mail gateways available to send meeting and appointment messages across a variety of different e-mail platforms? • Can the scheduling package communicate directly with **PDAs (personal digital assistants)**? • Can the scheduling system output be incorporated into other documents such as word processing or spreadsheets?
Personal Schedule Management	• Can recurring appointments be easily and flexibly defined? • Are reminder alarms available and programmable? • Can tasks or projects be scheduled as well as meetings? • Can prospects or contacts be managed within the scheduling system? • Is an address book module integrated? • Can appointments be easily changed or rescheduled? • Are reports available in a variety of formats such as daily planner pages or to-do lists? • Are a variety of access levels available to control who can request meetings of whom? • Can administrative assistants be given control of one's schedule? • Can notes be attached to appointments?
Group Calendar Management	• Are reports available to show group activities and meetings scheduled for a given date range? • Can tasks and activities as well as meetings be assigned to groups? • Can other group members' calendars be viewed? • How are holidays and length of business day defined and displayed?
Group Meeting Scheduling	• Can rooms and resources be reserved/assigned as meetings are scheduled? • How powerful are the querying tools to find available meeting times for multiple attendees? • Does the program allow users to set up automated rules for response to meeting requests? • How are conflicts or double-bookings handled? • Can confirmed replies be requested? • How are nonresponses to meeting requests handled?

Figure 9-5   Key Features of Group Scheduling Software

Electronic Meeting Support Feature Category	Feature/Importance
Platforms Supported	• Over what network operating system does the information sharing take place? NetWare, Windows for Workgroups, Windows NT? • What clients are supported for meeting participation? Macintosh, Windows, DOS?
Meeting Creation	• Can facilitators designate in advance and structure the meeting's agenda and topics for discussion ahead of time? • Can threads be easily moved from one forum to another? • What are the security procedures for entry into a forum? • Can forums be built across multiple servers? • Can existing forums be merged or segmented? • Can users participate in forums via dial-up access? • Are tools available for agenda creation? • Can different-place, different-time meetings be supported as well as same-place, same-time meetings?
Idea Generation	• What types of functionality are supported during the meeting? Options: workflow automation, document management, interactive workgroup discussions, idea generation via collaboration and feedback. • Support for integrating documents with document tracking and version control may be very important as group discussion often centers on historical or proposed documentation. • Are "viewers" for different types of documents included, or must every forum participant have every document software package installed on his or her workstation? • Are tools available for alternative consolidation, evaluation, and voting? • Can ad-hoc surveys of participants be quickly created and executed and results evaluated?
Meeting Results Reporting	• Can reports be easily generated and interpreted for meeting agendas as well as meeting results and follow-up?

Figure 9-6   Electronic Meeting Support Software

Managerial Perspective

Electronic meeting support software is no substitute for effective leadership and excellent communications skills. This software must be looked upon as an enabling technology which, when properly implemented by trained individuals, can encourage open, unbiased discussion and idea generation leading to better overall collaboration and consensus building. When properly planned and implemented, electronic meetings tend to stay more focused on agenda items, generate more alternative ideas, reach consensus more quickly, and provide immediate electronic documentation of the entire meeting's proceedings. Electronic meeting support software can make good group leaders even better but will do little to improve ineffective leadership skills.

Electronic Whiteboard Software   **Electronic whiteboard software** is a hybrid category of groupware software combining elements of electronic meeting support, document conferencing, and videoconferencing. As a result, many electronic whiteboard software packages are incorporated into a variety of software packages. Functionality of the electronic whiteboard software aspects of these alternatives differs primarily in the level of collaboration required among session participants:

- **Collaborative or interactive work sessions** allow users connected via networks to participate in joint work sessions as if they were all in the same room working at the same whiteboard or conference table. These sessions may involve intensive document creation and modification work or may be more discussion-oriented, in which case documents may only need to be displayed for all participants. The whiteboard aspects of the session allow participants to use the equivalent of whiteboard markers to annotate and draw on the networked whiteboard which appears on all participants' workstations. When electronic whiteboard software sessions involve collaborative development or review of documents by multiple users linked via LAN or WAN links, the software category is occasionally referred to as **document conferencing software.**

- **Networked group presentations** allow one individual to present a graphically oriented presentation to multiple network-attached group members as if all seminar participants were seated in a single room. Collaborative interaction is minimal compared to the collaborative work sessions.

Because of the bandwidth demands involved with electronic whiteboard software, one of the key technical differences among products is whether they support multipoint conferences or are limited to two-user point-to-point links. As a result, the number of supported work session participants can vary widely from 2 to more than 50. Figure 9-7 (page 324) summarizes the key features of electronic whiteboard software.

Videoconferencing   LAN-based desktop videoconferencing adds live video images between communicating parties to the collaborative computing functionality offered by electronic whiteboard software. The level to which users can collaboratively share applications or documents varies among desktop videoconferencing systems. Some videoconferencing systems support full application sharing, allowing users to simultaneously edit a single document with full application functionality, while others support only file transfer between parties or highlighting a noneditable document on an electronic whiteboard with electronic marking pens.

Most current LAN-based videoconferencing technology supports only two-party, point-to-point connections, although standards for multipoint conferences do exist. One of the key problems with LAN-based videoconferencing is the basic incompatibility between the video traffic and the LAN access methodologies and bandwidth. Video and its associated voice transmission are time-sensitive, streaming types of traffic that depend on guaranteed bandwidth and delivery times for smooth transmission. Neither Ethernet nor Token Ring network architectures possess the access methodology or sufficient bandwidth to ensure such guaranteed delivery times. As a result, alternative network architectures such as Iso-Ethernet, 100BaseT, and 100VG-AnyLAN, which claim the ability to satisfactorily deliver video payloads, have been developed. Even on these more advanced network architectures, however, more than a few simultaneous videoconferences will saturate the network and render it unusable for data-only users.

Furthermore, if the videoconference extends beyond the LAN, then sophisticated wide area network services such as ISDN or switched 56 K must be available at all end points of the conference. The availability of such data services at all corpo-

Electronic Whiteboard Software Feature Category	Feature/Importance
Network Communications	• What types of network connections are supported for work sessions? Options: dial-up modems, ISDN, LAN-to-LAN connections. • For dial-up communications, are address books and autodialers included? • For LAN communications, what types of network operating systems are supported? Options: NetWare (IPX), Windows for Workgroups (NetBEUI), DOS-based LANs (NetBIOS), UNIX (TCP/IP). • Given the amount of network communications, what types of video compression are supported? Options: JPEG, MPEG, proprietary.
Work Sessions	• How many work session participants are possible? Options: from 2 to 50+. • Does the work session software support facilitator functionality? • Can session participants join and leave once the session has started? • What is the nature of the security controlling access to sessions? • Can application programs be shared or controlled remotely as part of the work session?
Whiteboard and Tools	• Are slide sorters and slide show software available for networked group presentations? • How many participants can be writing on the electronic whiteboard simultaneously? • How many markers or different types of annotation tools (eraser, etc.) are available? • How many different marker colors are available? • Can typed text be edited with annotation tools? • Can whiteboard contents be easily saved and printed? • Can certain regions of whiteboard be highlighted, saved, and printed? • How many different types of file formats can be imported into the whiteboard? Options: ASCII, .BMP, .DIB, .GIF, .PCX, TIFF, JPEG.

Figure 9-7 Electronic Whiteboard Software

rate locations is by no means a forgone conclusion. Another consideration is the quality of the transmitted video signal, usually measured in frames per second (fps). As a reference, standard broadcast television in the United States displays 30 fps. In comparison, most LAN-based videoconferencing systems achieve only half that number, with some displaying less than 1 fps.

At the heart of the videoconferencing system is the video **CODEC (COder-DECoder),** which digitizes not only analog video signals but also analog voice signals. **Video digitization** is a process by which a sample of a video signal is digitized into an 8-bit binary code. To maximize the amount of video and audio information transmitted over limited bandwidth, the CODEC probably also compresses and decompresses digitized video and audio. The following additional equipment, beyond the "normal" workstation, is required:

- A communications adapter card to merge the digitized video and voice signal with the digital data stream from the workstation and communicate this integrated stream of digital traffic over a specialized WAN link such as an ISDN or switched 56 K line.

- A microphone for audio input and speakers for audio output.

- A camera for video input.

The International Telecommunications Union (ITU) has overseen the development of a family of videoconferencing standards, known collectively as **H.320.** Figure 9-8 summarizes these standards.

LAN-based desktop videoconferencing systems differ primarily in the LAN network architectures over which they operate, the number of simultaneous users supported, and the extent to which they support application sharing and collaborative computing. Figure 9-9 (page 326) summarizes the major feature categories of these systems.

Managerial Perspective

LAN-based videoconferencing workstations cost between $6000 and $8000, plus substantial monthly charges for network usage if the videoconferences use public network facilities. You should take a careful top-down approach to purchasing LAN-based videoconferencing equipment. What is the business objective to be achieved by such an acquisition? Will reduced travel expenses and travel time justify such a purchase? On this basis, what would the payback period be? Videoconferencing should not be used casually for everyday, unscheduled communications

Videoconferencing Standard	Purpose/Explanations
H.221	Framing and synchronization specification, which standardizes the CODEC's handshaking and interface to WAN services such as ISDN used for videoconference transmission.
H.230	Multiplexing specification, which describes how audio and video information should be transmitted over the same digital WAN link.
H.231	Multipoint control unit (MCU) specification, which defines standards for a device to bridge three or more H.320-compliant CODECs together on a single multipoint videoconference.
H.233	Specification for encryption of video and audio information transmitted through H.320-compliant CODECs, also known as H.KEY.
H.242	Specification for call setup and tear-down for videoconference calls.
H.261	Also known as Px64, describes compression and decompression algorithms used for videoconferencing. Also defines two screen formats: **CIF (common intermediate format),** 288 lines x 352 pixels/line, and **QCIF (quarter common intermediate format),** 144 lines x 176 pixels/line.

Figure 9-8   H.320 Family of Videoconferencing Standards

Videoconferencing Feature Category	Feature/Importance
Hardware	• What hardware is included with the videoconferencing workstation? Required: microphone, camera. • Is the CODEC included? • What computer bus types is the CODEC compatible with? Options: ISA, EISA, PCI. • Is the CODEC H.320 compliant?
Network	• What wide area network services are supported? Options: ISDN, switched 56 K, T-1, fractional T-1, analog dial-up. • Is an ISDN adapter included? • Over which LAN architectures can the videoconference be transmitted? Options: Ethernet, Token Ring, FDDI, Iso-Ethernet, 100BaseT, 100VG-AnyLAN. • Is a separate phone circuit required for audio transmission?
Application	• What is the maximum resolution of the video frames? • What is the maximum number of frames/second possible? • Can incoming and outgoing video be displayed simultaneously? • What is the maximum number of users per videoconference? • Is real-time application and collaborative computing supported? • Is electronic whiteboard highlighting supported? • Is file transfer supported? • Can linked application objects be embedded within other applications?

Figure 9-9 LAN-Based Desktop Videoconferencing Systems

when it is not certain that the called party will be present. Considering how often callers are transferred to a person's voice mail because the individual is away from the desk, what is the benefit of placing videoconference calls to an empty chair?

Workflow Automation **Workflow automation software** allows geographically dispersed coworkers to work together on project teams as documents and information are automatically routed according to preprogrammed rules or workflow directives. As project assignments change, there is no need to move offices or workstations. The work from the new project simply flows to the current worker location, thanks to workflow automation. Workflow automation also tracks the time individuals spend on given projects, to simplify client chargeback and billing for professional or consulting organizations. Workflow automation software encourages reevaluating and/or reengineering of business processes before they are programmed into the workflow automation software.

Workflow automation software varies widely in both cost and capabilities, and it can be categorized in a number of ways. One criterion for categorization is the type of business process it is attempting to automate. Three major categories emerge:

1. **Production workflow** This category of workflow software automates complicated business processes which are performed regularly, perhaps daily. These processes are at the heart of a business's production capability.

Examples include building an automobile and custom-made vinyl replacement windows.

2. **Ad-hoc workflow**   This category automates more open-ended, creative, or flexible business processes which are done occasionally or on an unscheduled basis. Product design, marketing plan design, application software design, network design, or other brainstorming-based activities are examples of such processes.

3. **Administrative workflow**   This category automates routine business processes which nearly all businesses have in common. Examples include purchase order requisition and approval, accounts payable approval, review of job applicants' files, or expense report approval.

Related to the business process categorization is categorization based on the extent of routing the workflow product supports:

1. **Sequential routing** is the simplest of the routing schemes; business processes follow predictable paths, with individual steps following each other in a linear fashion.

2. **Conditional branch routing** introduces multiple possible routes that depend on the results or outcomes at each particular step in the process. Exception handling and sophisticated rules-based or expert systems are all supported or integrated into conditional branch routing workflow automation software.

3. **Parallel routing** adds a layer of sophistication to workflow automation software by allowing subprocesses to be completed simultaneously by multiple users. Parallel routing may be combined with conditional branch routing.

Figure 9-10 (page 328) summarizes a few additional functional issues to consider when contemplating the purchase of workflow automation software.

**Managerial
Perspective**

In truth, workflow automation software only mirrors the business processes designed by humans. It will not improve a poorly designed or inefficient work process. Poorly implemented workflow automation software can actually have the opposite of intended impacts by increasing headcount and decreasing worker productivity. Workflow automation software should be viewed as more of a toolkit for developing automated processes than a type of off-the-shelf, ready-to-go application software. Most workflow automation software requires setup and programming by properly trained individuals knowledgeable not only in the syntax of the particular workflow automation software package, but also in business process engineering in general. There are currently no interoperability standards between different workflow automation packages, and not all workflow automation software runs on all available computer platforms. A good method for evaluating the applicability of workflow automation software is to first map out a business process that needs automation, then directly inquire whether vendors' software can automate this business process. If the answer is in the affirmative, get it in writing.

Document Management and Imaging   When workflow automation involves a great deal of handling, storage, indexing, and retrieval of documents, an ancillary **document**

Workflow Automation Software Feature Category	Feature/Importance
Platform/Scalability	• How many simultaneous users will the workflow automation software support? • Over which LAN network operating systems will the software execute? • Will the software perform over a variety of WAN links? • How many different computer platforms will the system run over? • Is this a standalone product or an add-on for Lotus Notes? • Does this software include a programming language? • Does this software integrate or include document management and imaging capabilities? • Does this software integrate or include faxing and scanning management capabilities? • What is the impact on network bandwidth of adding users and more complicated processes?
Workflow Development	• How intuitive or easy to use are the workflow design tools? • How easily and flexibly can tasks or processes be assigned to individuals or groups of individuals? • How complicated can links and rules between dependent sub-processes be? • Can workflow rules be stored in a Notes database? • Does the software support a variety of security settings that can be varied for each step in the overall workflow process? • Can batch moves and updates be processed between databases either as work is completed or at timed intervals? • Does the system integrate with existing e-mail system for delivery of forms and work in process? If so, which e-mail systems? • Can complicated conditional branching algorithms written in other languages such as Visual Basic be integrated with this product?

Figure 9-10 Workflow Automation Software

management and imaging software package may be required. These software packages, also known as **departmental image management** software, seek to bring new levels of electronic efficiency to the classic manual filing cabinet by storing key information about stored documents which can then be queried, searched, and reported on by a multitude of differentiating indexing criteria. In some cases, the document management and imaging software includes workflow automation capabilities as well. Productivity gains from this software are achieved by eliminating long searches through desks and filing cabinets for a given document.

Interoperability standards among document management packages are contained in a specification known as **document management alliance,** or **DMA.** The DMA interoperability standard actually defines a series of common APIs and middleware which will enable interoperable document management and services, such as the following:

• **Query services** which support access to documents stored in any DMA-compliant document management system.

- **Library services,** which include interoperable version control and access control.

- **Multilevel security services,** which provide a variety of security levels for individual documents regardless of which DMA-compliant document management system they are stored in.

Figure 9-11 summarizes some of the key features of document management and imaging software.

Document Management and Imaging Feature Category	Feature/Importance
Platform/Scalability	• Does the document management package include, or is it integrated with, workflow automation software? • How many users can simultaneously be supported by the software? • Would this software be considered a workgroup or enterprise solution? both? • What is the network impact at various levels of the number of users and documents? • How easy is the software to install and manage? • Is the software DMA compatible?
Document Management	• Is the software integrated with e-mail systems for delivery of documents? If so, which ones? • What is the nature or sophistication of the search engine or database used to categorize and search for documents? • Can searches be performed for keywords embedded within stored documents? • Is there a limit to the number of documents the system can efficiently handle? • Is the query tool for finding documents intuitive and easy to use with a natural interactive language interface, or does it require entering search strings in a particular syntax? • How flexible is the security system? Can different security levels be assigned to individual documents? • Are documents arranged logically in electronic files or folders? • Is the database in which document indexing information is stored open or proprietary? • Is the database accessible by other query, report generation, and application tools? • What is the nature and sophistication of the version control features?
Document Input/Output	• Does the software include **optical character recognition (OCR)** software to turn faxed images into editable documents? • Can audio and video objects also be stored, indexed, and retrieved? • How well integrated is the system with fax machines, fax servers, and scanners? • Are optical storage devices supported?

Figure 9-11   Document Management and Imaging

LAN Productivity Software Trends

Most of the types of LAN productivity software reviewed to this point are readily available today. Some other types which are just beginning to emerge hold the potential for even greater improvements in worker productivity.

Agents/Smart Software   **Intelligent software,** also known as **smart software,** uses **agents** which assist end-users in their quest for increased productivity in at least two ways:

1. **Advisory agents** or **wizards** assist users as they learn their way around new software packages, thereby easing frustration and shortening the learning curve. Advisory agents can sense when a user is performing a repetitive task which could perhaps be automated or done more efficiently. Wizards are able to walk users through complicated tasks one step at a time.

2. **Assistant agents** act much as human administrative assistants by performing specific tasks on behalf of, but out of the direct control of, the end-user. Examples of assistant agents' tasks include:
   - Screening, managing, and reformatting received e-mail and faxes.
   - Surfing the Internet in search of articles or research on a given topic.

Assistant agents must be initially trained and continually monitored at intervals determined by the end-user. As the agent-user relationship matures, the agent increases in competence to act on behalf of the user. Uses for software agents will only be limited by the imaginations of their users or mentors. Eventually agents will become interoperable as specialized interagent languages are developed. At that point, it may become difficult to determine if e-mail was really sent by the end-user or by that person's assistant agent. In any case, it might be wiser just to let one's assistant agent handle the whole situation.

Computer Telephony Integration   **Computer Telephony Integration (CTI)** seeks to integrate the two most common productivity devices, the computer and the telephone, to enable increased productivity not otherwise possible by using the two devices in a nonintegrated fashion. CTI is not a single application, but an ever-widening array of possibilities spawned by the integration of telephony and computing. Two LAN-based standards for CTI are emerging:

1. **TSAPI,** or **telephony services API,** was jointly developed and sponsored by Novell and AT&T.

2. **TAPI,** or **telephony API,** was jointly developed and sponsored by Intel and Microsoft.

Applications written to use either of these APIs should be able to operate transparently in either a NetWare (TSAPI) or Windows (TAPI) environment. Both Novell and Microsoft are developing their own CTI application software as well. Figure 9-12 briefly describes some of the subcategories of CTI applications.

CTI Application Category	Application Description
Call Control	• Using computer-based applications, users can more easily use all of the features of their phone system or PBX, especially the more complicated but seldom used features. • Includes use of features such as on-line phone books, auto-dialing, click-and-point conference calls, on-line display, and processing of voice-mail messages.
Automated Attendant	• Allows callers to direct calls to a desired individual at a given business without necessarily knowing the extension number.
Automated Call Distribution	• Used primarily in call centers staffed by large numbers of customer service agents, it automatically distributes incoming calls to the first available rep, or in some cases, the rep who serves a given geographic region, as automatically determined by the computer based on the incoming phone number.
Audiotex	• These systems deliver audio information to callers based on responses on the touch-tone keypad to prerecorded questions. Primarily used for information hotlines.
Fax-on-Demand	• By combining computer-based faxing with interactive voice response, users can dial in and request that specific information be faxed to their fax machine.
Interactive Voice Response	• Interactive voice response systems differ from audiotex systems in that IVR systems support on-line transaction processing rather than just information hotline applications. As an example, banks use IVR systems to allow users to transfer funds between accounts by using only a touch-tone phone.
Unified Messaging	• Perhaps the most interesting feature for the LAN-based user is **unified messaging.** Also known as the **universal in-box,** unified messaging allows voice mail, e-mail, faxes, and pager messages to be displayed on a single graphical screen. Messages can then be forwarded, deleted, or replied to easily in point-and-click fashion. Waiting calls can also be displayed in the same universal in-box.

Figure 9-12 Computer Telephony Integration

■ LAN RESOURCE MANAGEMENT SOFTWARE

Multiprotocol Network Printing

Certainly one of the first motivations for installing a local area network was the need to share networked printers. As a result, the software required to offer LAN-based shared printing services is nearly always included in network operating systems software. Network operating system functionality is reviewed in Chapter 10.

When shared printing services are required across multiple, different network operating systems, specialized **multiprotocol network printing** hardware and software are required. Multiprotocol network printing software is not generally included with most network operating systems. As illustrated in Figure 9-13 (page 332), multiprotocol printer servers need to be able to support multiple network op-

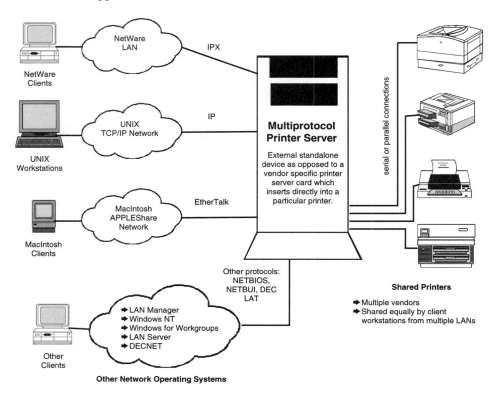

Figure 9-13   Multiprotocol Printer Servers Implementation

erating systems protocols, multiple network architectures, and multiple vendors' printers.

Figure 9-14 summarizes some of the functional differences between multiprotocol printer servers of which network analysts should be aware.

Printer Management

Printer management in a multiprotocol, multivendor environment is in a state of evolution. Several of the larger printer vendors such as HP and LexMark have their own printer management software packages. However, they work very little, if at all, with printers from other vendors. As printers have become another distributed resource to be managed in a multiprotocol networked environment, the need for printer management standards has become evident. At least three organizations are involved with developing printer management standards:

1. The **Desktop Management Task Force (DMTF)** has developed a common management environment for the management of desktop devices known as the **desktop management interface (DMI).** Specific aspects of the DMI are contained in **management information file (MIF)** definitions.

2. The **Internet Engineering Task Force (IETF)** is the group in charge of seeking approval for a printer management management information base (MIB) which would transport printer management information over TCP/IP networks in simple network management protocol (SNMP) format.

Multiprotocol Printer Server Feature	Feature/Implication
NetWare Support	• NetWare supports two printing methods: PSERVER and RPRINTER. PSERVER spools print jobs to the NetWare file server while RPRINTER transmits print jobs directly to the print server. • Multiprotocol print servers should support both PSERVER and RPRINTER.
UNIX Support	• UNIX print services are performed via LPD, or line printer daemon. • Multiprotocol print servers should support LPD.
Macintosh Support	• Apple's print services protocol is known as PAP, or printer access protocol. • Apple also expects bidirectional communication with printers. • Multiprotocol printer servers should support both PAP and bidirectional communication.
Network Architectures	• Which network architectures are supported? Options: Ethernet (10Base2, 10BaseT), Token Ring (4 Mbps, 16 Mbps). • Is more than one network architecture supported in a single multiprotocol print server?
Management	• Is the management console PC-based or UNIX workstation-based? • Does the management protocol support SNMP and MIBs? • Are the MIB and management system proprietary? • Evaluate management systems based on ease of configuration, installation, and monitoring. • Do the management systems support existing or emerging standards?
Price Range	• Prices can vary between $500 and $1000.

Figure 9-14   Multiprotocol Printer Servers Functionality

3. A group known as the Printer Working Group is sanctioned by both the DMTF and the IETF to develop printer management specifications in both MIF and MIB formats.

These management protocols are studied in more detail in Chapter 17. Standardized printer management protocols would allow users with proper authorization to change paper trays or printer setup from their network-attached desktop computer. Users would see a replica of the printer control panel on their computer monitor. Multiprotocol printer management systems would also be able to monitor printer usage by user to spot abuse or for chargeback purposes.

Network Backup

Network Backup Objectives   Server backup devices and analysis issues were introduced in Chapter 5; the discussion in this section is limited to those issues specific to multiple server, networked environments. To evaluate network-based backup solutions, it is important to first establish objectives or expected outcomes of such a system. Among the possibilities are the following:

- Network backup systems should be designed in such a way as to minimize the amount of required operational support.

- Network backup systems should be expandable or scalable, so that additional clients and servers can easily be added to the backup plan.

- Since the entire purpose of backup systems is to be able to restore critical files in the event of a problem, file restoral must be efficient and effective.

- Network backup systems should be interoperable, so that all backup can be managed from a single location regardless of the operating systems or network operating systems of backed-up devices.

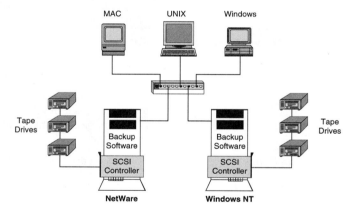

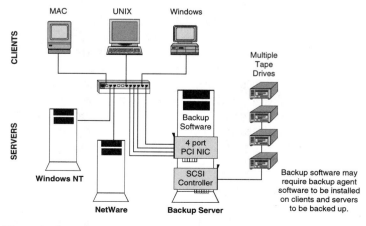

Figure 9-15   Network Backup Architectures

Network Backup Architectures   Multiple server environments have two primary network backup architecture alternatives:

1. **Locally attached multiple tape drives** are attached directly to each server. The multiple tape drives provide both faster backup performance and fault tolerance. Depending on the capabilities of the backup software, multiple backup devices may be operational simultaneously. Locally attached tape devices perform at bus speeds rather than network backbone speeds.

2. **Dedicated backup server** architectures allow multiple servers to be backed up across the network backbone onto a dedicated backup server linked to multiple backup devices. Dedicated backup servers provide the added benefit of being able not only to restore files but also to serve as a contingency server for executing restored files in the event of primary server failures. Such an architecture is appropriate if multiple gigabytes of data must be backed up across multiple servers. Dedicated backup servers require multiple, high-speed, network connections to the network backbone. **Tape changers** are also required, to swap tapes into/out of backup devices for multigigabyte backup sessions.

Figure 9-15 illustrates these alternative network backup architectures.

Applied Problem Solving

NETWORK BACKUP ANALYSIS

Figure 9-16 summarizes some of the key issues involved in analyzing and designing an effective network backup solution, in addition to the primary issue of network backup architecture previously described.

Network Backup Analysis Issue	Importance/Implication
Potential Bottlenecks	• Network backup analysis must be performed with an eye for end-to-end system performance. Among the potential bottlenecks in a network backup solution are tape drive/media capacity, tape drive speed, hard disk I/O speed, network bandwidth.
Tape Drives-to-Server Ratio	• It is possible, depending on backup software capability, to have multiple tape drives attached to a single server simultaneously performing backup duties. The number of backup devices is limited by the number of SCSI controllers per server a particular backup software package will support. Each SCSI controller supports 6 tape drives.
Servers-to-Tape Drive Ratio	• It is possible, depending on backup software capability, to have multiple servers (or clients) being backed up by a single tape device through a process known alternatively as **interlacing, interleaving,** or **tape streaming.**

Figure 9-16   Network Backup Analysis

(continued)

Network Backup Analysis Issue	Importance/Implication
Scheduling Backup Sessions	• Backups may be performed either during or after business hours. This decision can have a serious impact on available network bandwidth for dedicated backup server architectures. During business hours, 20% to 30% of network capacity may be consumed by backup jobs, whereas up to 50% of network bandwidth may be available after business hours. • If backups are performed during business hours, is the backup software capable of retrying to back up open files?
Computing Required Backup Time and Capacity	• To determine amount of backup capacity required to complete network-based system backups in an acceptable amount of time, multiply the available network bandwidth in bits per second by 60 seconds per minute and divide by 8 bits per byte. The result is expressed in megabytes per minute. Most of today's servers contain storage capacities of gigabytes (1000 megabytes), leading to the need for substantial backup capabilities.
System Restoral	• How easy and fast is the system, or selected files to restore? • Can the restoral process be easily tested and benchmarked? • Can users restore their own files?
Fault Tolerance	• If a tape drive fails, can the backup software automatically shift the backup responsibilities of the failed drive to another functional drive?
Tape Library Management	• Can the backup software keep databases or lists of all files contained on all backup volumes? • Can the backup software keep multiple versions of the same files organized and display multiple versions for possible restoral?
Multiplatform Support	• Which client operating systems are compatible with server-based backup software? Options: Windows, Windows NT, DOS, UNIX, OS/2, Macintosh, NetWare 3.12 or 4.1. • Does the backup software support interoperability standards such as NetWare's SMS and SIDF? (see Chapter 5) • Can multiple locally attached tape drives, attached to multiple servers, be centrally administered from one location?
Tape-to-Tape Backups	• Can the software automatically perform tape-to-tape backups between tape drives for redundant storage?

Figure 9-16   *(continued)*

Network Faxing

Network Faxing Objectives   To choose a particular network faxing architecture or analyze network faxing requirements, it is necessary to first identify the objectives, or desired outcomes, of the implemented network faxing solution. Among the possible objectives are the following:

- Allow users to share fax modems and phone lines to maximize worker productivity while simultaneously minimizing investment in modems and phone lines.

- Allow users to fax directly from PCs and workstations.

- Allow users to receive faxes directly at PCs and workstations.

Network Faxing Architecture   Providing fax services to network-attached workstations requires network-aware fax software in combination with fax boards or fax modems. PCs equipped with fax boards or fax modems and specially written faxing software dedicated to network faxing are known as **fax servers.** Network faxing architectures can be divided into three basic alternatives:

1. **Software-only solutions,** in which the user supplies the PC to execute the fax software as well as compatible fax boards or modems. The fax software purchased for such an architecture must be network-aware or LAN-enabled. Such is not always the case, as most fax software originated as single-server versions.

2. **Hardware/software solutions,** in which the user supplies the PC to which vendor-supplied fax boards and bundled software are loaded.

3. **Turnkey solutions,** which are specially made LAN-attached devices pre-configured with both software and all necessary fax hardware.

Which of these three architectures is correct for any given situation varies according to the budget and performance needs determined by the network faxing needs analysis. In general, turnkey solutions are easier to configure, install, and operate, but are also more expensive than the other two options. Figure 9-17 (page 338) illustrates these alternative network faxing architectures.

Network Faxing Standards   Network faxing software must adhere to two sets of standards:

1. Standards for fax software APIs, which define interfaces between fax software and hardware components.

2. Fax transmission international standards, known commonly as fax Group I through Group IV, as defined by the CCITT.

There are two **fax APIs:**

1. **Communications applications specification (CAS)** was developed by Intel and DCA. This API allows software vendors to integrate fax capabilities

Software Only Solution

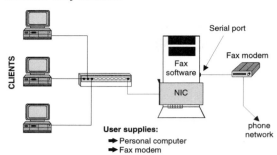

Hardware/Software Solution

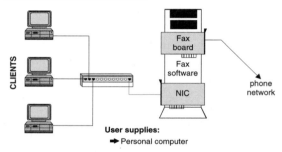

Turnkey Fax Server

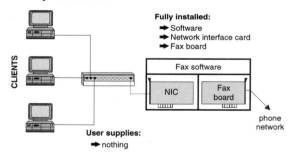

Figure 9-17   Network Faxing Architectures

into their application software by allowing the software to include standardized, embedded commands which are understood by fax boards and fax modems.

2. **FaxBIOS** is an alternative fax API developed and supported by the FaxBIOS Association, which is composed of fax circuit board vendors.

Figure 9-18 summarizes fax transmission standards.

CCITT Fax Standard	Description/Features
Group 1	• Transmits an 8.5 x 11 inch page in 6 minutes. • Outdated.
Group 2	• Transmits an 8.5 x 11 inch page in 3 minutes. • Outdated.
Group 3	• Most common fax standard. • Transmits an 8.5 x 11 inch page in 20 sec. • Resolutions: 203 x 98 dots per inch (dpi) and 203 x 196 dpi. • 9600 bps transmission rate.
Group 3 bis	• Resolution: 406 x 196 dpi. • 14.4 Kbps transmission rate.
Group 4	• Transmission rate: 64 Kbps. • Requires ISDN switched digital service. • Transmits an 8.5 x 11 inch page in 6 seconds.

Figure 9-18   Fax Transmission Standards

Applied Problem Solving

NETWORK FAXING ANALYSIS

Figure 9-19 summarizes some of the key analysis issues which must be examined before recommending network faxing architectures.

Networking Faxing Analysis Issue	Importance/Implication
Incoming vs. Outgoing Faxes	• Allowing multiple users to access shared fax modems for outgoing faxes is far less complicated than automatically routing faxes to users' network-attached workstations. • Not all fax software packages or fax servers can provide both outgoing and incoming fax capability.
Application Integration	• How easily/transparently does the fax software integrate with application software such as word processing, spreadsheet, presentation graphics, and e-mail? • Can fax capabilities be transparently accessed from within Windows applications? • Does the fax software execute in the background allowing the user to continue working? • Is a fax viewer included? • Is optical character recognition (OCR) software included to convert fax images to editable documents? • Does the fax client run as a terminate and stay resident (TSR) program, thereby always taking up memory?
Hardware Interface	• Are users able to choose modems and phone lines manually, or are outgoing lines automatically selected by the software?

Figure 9-19   Network Faxing Analysis

(continued)

Networking Faxing Analysis Issue	Importance/Implication
	• Can a fax be sent to multiple destinations simultaneously by using multiple modems simultaneously? • Does the fax software require a dedicated fax server? • How many different types of fax modems and fax boards are supported? • How many modem setup strings are included? • Can the modems be shared for data transmission as well as fax transmission?
Capacity/Expandability	• What is the maximum number of fax modems per server, workgroup, and LAN? • How easily can additional modems and phone lines be added?
Licensing	• What is the licensing policy? server-based or client-based? • Are client licenses available in only fixed increments such as 10, 25, 50? • Are unlimited client licenses available?
NOS Compatibility	• How many network operating systems are supported? NetWare, Windows for Workgroups, LANtastic, Windows NT, Windows 95. • Is a 32-bit version available for Windows NT networks? • Does the NT version support multitasking? symmetrical multiprocessing?
E-Mail Compatibility	• Which e-mail systems and associated e-mail protocols does the fax software support? Microsoft Mail (MAPI), Lotus cc:Mail (VIM), NetWare (MHS).
Management Capabilities	• What is the extent of administrative features? Call logging, summary reports, departmental chargeback reports.
Scheduling	• Can faxes be scheduled for transmission at later dates and times to accommodate reduced phone rates and changing time zones?
Internet Capabilities	• Does the fax software include Telnet, FTP, and TCP/IP support for transparent interfacing to the Internet?
Security	• Can faxes be secured by password protection?

Figure 9-19   (continued)

Electronic Software Distribution

As the client/server architecture has taken hold as the dominant information systems paradigm, the increased processing power possessed by client workstations had been matched by increasing amounts of sophisticated software installed on them. The distribution of client software to multiple locally and remotely attached client workstations would be very personnel-intensive and expensive were it not for a new category of LAN-enabled software known as **electronic software distribution** or **ESD.** ESD software varies widely in the types of services and features offered as

ESD Software Functional Category	Description/Implication
NOS Support	• Since ESD software distributes software via the LAN, it is important to know which network operating systems are supported. Options: NetWare, LANManager, Vines, LANServer, Windows NT, Windows for Workgroups, PathWorks, LANtastic.
Update Control	• Can updates be scheduled? • Can updates be selectively done based on hardware configuration? • Can updates be done only on selected machines? • Can only certain files be searched for and replaced? • Can files be edited or updated? Examples: CONFIG.SYS, AUTOEXEC.BAT, WIN.INI, SYSTEM.INI. • Can files in use be replaced? • Can files be moved and renamed? • Can the update be done in the background on client workstations? • How secure is the update control? • Can updates be scripted? • Can update keystrokes be captured and converted to an automated update control file? • Can users perform their own selected updates from a distribution server? • Are unattended updates possible? • Are in-progress status screens available? • Can outside distribution lists be imported? • Can remote workstations be shut down and rebooted? • How extensive are the update reporting and logging capabilities?
Interoperability	• Is the ESD software integrated with license metering or LAN hardware/software inventory software? • Are other software packages required to execute the ESD software?
Licensing	• Are licensing fees based on number of clients or number of distribution servers?

Figure 9-20   Electronic Software Distribution Functionality

well as the costs for the convenience offered. For example, in addition to simply delivering software to LAN-attached clients, ESD software may also do the following:

- Update configuration files.340
- Edit other files.
- Capture commands entered during a manual software installation and convert the captured text into an automated script to control subsequent electronic software distribution.

Figure 9-20 summarizes some of the key functional characteristics of ESD software.

License Metering Software

Although **license metering software** was originally intended to monitor the number of executing copies of a particular software package versus the number of li-

LAN Inventory Management Functional Category	Description/Functionality
Platforms	• Client platforms supported: DOS, Macintosh, Windows, OS/2. • Server platforms supported: NetWare, LANManager, LANServer, PathWorks, Vines, NetBIOS (DOS-Based), Windows NT.
Data Collection	• Scheduling: How flexibly can inventory scans be scheduled? • Can inventory scans of client workstations be completed incrementally during successive logins? • Does the inventory software flag unknown software which it finds on client workstations? • How large a catalog of known software titles does the inventory software have? 6000 titles is among the best. • Can software titles be added to the known software list? • Are fields for data collection user-definable? • Can the software audit servers as well as client workstations? • Are hardware and software inventory information stored in the same database? • What is the database format? • Can the software differentiate between and track the assets of multiple laptop computers which share a single docking bay?
Reporting	• How many predefined reports are available? • Are customized reports available? • How easy is it to produce a customized report? • Can reports be exported in numerous formats such as popular word processing, spreadsheet, and presentation graphics formats?
Query	• How user-friendly and powerful are the query tools? • Can queries be generated on unique hardware and software combinations? • Can inventory information be gathered and displayed on demand?

Figure 9-21 LAN Inventory Management Software Functionality

censes purchased for that package, an interesting and beneficial side effect has occurred, in recognition of which this software is now sometimes called **license management software.** The beneficial side effect stems from the realization that at any one time, less than 100% of the workstations possessing legitimate licenses for a given software product are actually executing that software product.

As a result, with the aid of license management software, fewer licenses can service an equal or greater number of users, thereby reducing the number of software licenses purchased and the associated cost of software ownership. License management software can dynamically allocate licenses to those users wishing to execute a particular software package in a process known as **license optimization.** Following are three of the more popular license optimization techniques:

1. **Dynamic allocation** gives out either single user or suite licenses based on the number of suite applications used. As an example, if a user starts a word processing package within an application suite, a single user license would be issued for the word processing package. However, if this user subsequently also executed a spreadsheet package within the same suite, a suite license would be issued rather than a second single user license.

2. **Load balancing** shifts licenses between servers to meet demands for licenses put on those servers by locally attached users. Licenses are loaned between servers on an as-needed basis. In this way, not every server needs a full complement of licenses to meet all anticipated user demands. This technique is also known as **license pooling.**

3. **Global license sharing** recognizes the opportunity for license sharing presented by the widely distributed nature of today's global enterprise networks. While users on one side of the globe are sleeping, users on the other side can share the same pool of licenses.

License metering and management software have traditionally been supplied as add-on products written by third-party software developers. However, this trend may change abruptly. Novell and Microsoft have cooperated (an unusual circumstance in itself) on a **licensing server API (LSAPI).** This API would build license metering capability into Microsoft's and Novell's network operating systems, eliminating the need for third-party license metering software.

LSAPI-compliant applications communicate with a specialized **license server** which issues **access tokens,** more formally known as **digital license certificates,** based on the license information stored in the license server database. Application programs wishing to take advantage of the NOS-based license metering service would need only to include the proper commands, as specified in the LSAPI.

LAN Inventory Management Software

LAN inventory management software is often included or integrated with electronic software distribution or license metering software. However, it has a unique and important mission of its own in a widely distributed client/server architecture in which hardware and software assets are located throughout an enterprise network. A quality LAN inventory management software system is especially important for planning network hardware and software upgrades. An enormous amount of human energy and associated expense spent going from workstation to workstation, figuring out the hardware and software characteristics of each, can be saved by LAN inventory management software which does the job automatically and reports gathered data in useful and flexible formats.

Although the two key operational characteristics are accuracy and ease of use, the functional characteristics of LAN inventory management software, summarized in Figure 9-21, can vary significantly from one package to another. This is a developing, relatively immature, category of LAN-based software offering enormous promise but currently characterized by products of varying degrees of accuracy and usefulness.

SUMMARY

Local area network software categories include network operating systems and LAN-enabled application software. LAN-enabled application software written specifically to take advantage of the networked nature of clients and servers can be further subdivided into LAN productivity software and LAN resource management software categories.

LAN-based e-mail systems are currently in architectural transition from simple shared-file architectures to more complex client/server messaging-based e-mail systems. Interoperability features to allow any e-mail system to interoperate with any other e-mail system and the ability to attach multiple diverse documents to e-mail messages are among the key functional e-mail developments.

Groupware is a category of LAN productivity software which offers a collection of integrated software packages to enable geographically dispersed coworkers to be at least as productive as if they all worked at a single location. Groupware is an emerging category of software which may contain any or all of the following software modules: e-mail, group scheduling, electronic conference and meeting support, electronic whiteboard software, videoconferencing, workflow automation, and document management and imaging. From a network analyst's standpoint, sufficient bandwidth is a key concern for supporting the many bandwidth-intensive groupware applications.

LAN resource management software seeks to optimize the use of network-attached hardware resources such as printers, fax modems, and backup devices. The LAN resource management software written for this optimization must be compatible with the installed network operating systems and their associated communications protocols as well as with the network-attached hardware which the software seeks to manage.

LAN-based software resources represent a significant capital investment and can potentially benefit from the use of LAN resource management software as well. Electronic software distribution seeks to reduce the time it takes to distribute software to widely dispersed client workstations on an enterprise network by using the network itself as a distribution mechanism. License management software uses a variety of license optimization techniques to allow users to execute desired applications while minimizing the number of purchased software licenses. The final LAN resource management category, LAN inventory management software, automatically scans network-attached workstations and inventories their hardware and software assets. By knowing exactly what hardware and software is currently installed, users can make more cost-effective planning and purchasing decisions.

KEY TERMS

access tokens, 343
ad-hoc workflow, 327
administrative workflow, 327
advisory agents, 330
agents, 330
applications software, 312
assistant agents, 330
audiotex, 331
automated attendant, 331
automated call distribution, 331
call control, 331
CAS, 337
CIF, 325
client/server e-mail systems, 317
CODEC, 324
collaborative worksessions, 323

common intermediate format, 325
communications applications specification, 337
communications-based groupware, 318
computer telephony integration, 330
conditional branch routing, 327
CTI, 330
decision support room, 320
dedicated backup server, 335
departmental image management, 328
desktop management interface, 332
desktop management task force, 332
different-place, different-time meeting, 320

digital license certificates, 343
discussion categories, 320
DMA, 328
DMI, 332
DMTF, 332
document conferencing software, 323
document management and imaging, 328
Document Management Alliance, 328
document-based groupware, 318
dynamic allocation, 342
electronic conferencing and meeting support, 320
electronic software distribution, 340

REVIEW QUESTIONS

1. How can LAN-enabled application software be developed to interoperate with a variety of different network operating systems?
2. What types of services does network applications software request from network operating systems?
3. Differentiate between the intended benefits of LAN productivity software versus LAN resource management software.
4. What are the areas of compatibility with which remote e-mail client software must be concerned?
5. What is the importance of attachment capabilities to overall e-mail system usefulness?
6. What are some of the e-mail features or functions important to remote e-mail client software?
7. Why are e-mail interoperability features important?
8. In which types of corporate environments would e-mail interoperability features be most important?

9. Differentiate between the two major e-mail system messaging architectures' complexity, interoperability with a variety of network operating systems, and scalability.
10. What nontechnical issues can interfere with an effective implementation of group scheduling software?
11. What unique benefits can electronic conferencing support software offer over regular face-to-face meetings?
12. What are some of the limitations of electronic meeting support software?
13. What other types of groupware modules might electronic meeting support software integrate with, and what additional functionality would each of these integrated modules offer?
14. Differentiate between electronic whiteboard software and electronic meeting support software.
15. Differentiate between collaborative work sessions and networked group presentations.

16. List the issues surrounding videoconferencing which should be of concern to a network analyst.
17. Why are ISDN and switched 56K popular WAN services for videoconferencing?
18. What is the business justification for purchasing workflow automation software?
19. Differentiate between the types of workflow automated by the different workflow automation software. Is one type of workflow more likely to benefit from automation than another?
20. What is the relationship between business process reengineering and workflow automation software?
21. Why is interoperability important to document management systems from a business perspective?
22. What is the intended business impact of computer telephony integration software?
23. Differentiate between advisory agents and assistant agents.
24. What are the various levels of compatibility which multiprotocol printer servers must address?
25. Differentiate between the advantages, disadvantages, and delivered functionalities of alternative network backup architectures.
26. What are some of the key network backup issues with which network analysts should be concerned?
27. Differentiate between the ease of installation and expense of the alternative network faxing implementation solutions.
28. Why would shared network access for incoming faxes be more difficult to automate than shared network access for outgoing faxes?
29. What is the purpose of a fax API?
30. What is the business justification for purchasing and implementing electronic software distribution software?
31. What types of issues should a network analyst be concerned with regarding the implementation of electronic software distribution?
32. Why has license metering software now taken on more of a license management or license optimization role?
33. What business benefits can be gained through implementing LAN inventory management software?

ACTIVITIES

1. Research the topic of e-mail etiquette and report on your findings, or prepare a brochure for distribution of e-mail etiquette tips.
2. Consult buyer's guides or product directories regarding e-mail systems. Differentiate between available products' architectures. Focus on messaging protocols and services used in each system, and relate your findings to the level of interoperability offered by each e-mail system.
3. Investigate and report on installed e-mail systems at a school or business. Pay particular attention to interoperability with other e-mail systems. How is mail prepared for transmission over the internet? Are e-mail gateways employed?
4. Investigate groupware as a category of software in terms of market size, market growth, and leading vendors. What percentage of the market is held by the number one vendor? How widely do groupware products vary in the software modules included?
5. Investigate the electronic whiteboard software category of groupware. Pay particular attention to functionality delivered and bandwidth requirements. Report on the relationship between bandwidth requirements, network architectures and WAN service supported, and number of simultaneous users supported.
6. Prepare a survey of schools or companies which employ videoconferencing. Report on videoconference network infrastructure, videoconference usage or applications, and payback or cost/benefit analysis. Is the video traffic sharing network bandwidth with data transmission?
7. Find a school or business which has implemented workflow automation software. Analyze the type of workflow, type of routing, implementation history, and perceived benefits of the implementation.
8. Investigate the current market size, estimated market growth, key vendors, standard efforts, and intended business impact of computer telephony integration software, and report on your results.
9. Investigate and report on the current status of printer management standards development efforts.
10. Investigate network faxing software, paying special attention to comparative abilities to support automatic routing of incoming faxes. Contrast the various approaches found for autorouting of incoming faxes.
11. Investigate and report on the current status of efforts to develop a standardized license server embedded within popular network operating systems.

FEATURED REFERENCES

General References

Case, Thomas and Larry Smith. *Managing Local Area Networks* (New York: McGraw-Hill, 1995).

Goldman, James. *Applied Data Communications: A Business Oriented Approach* (New York: John Wiley & Sons, 1995).

Enterprise Network Operating Systems

Finklestein, Richard. Skyscrapers on Quicksand? *Network Computing,* 5; 8 (July 1, 1994), CS3.

Harrison, David. Client/Server Operating Systems: Challenges on All Fronts. *Network Computing,* 5; 8 (July 1, 1994), CS1.

Johnson, Johna. Enterprise NOSs: Now's the Time. *Data Communications,* 24; 7 (May 21, 1995), 40.

Peer-to-Peer Network Operating Systems

Chernicoff, David. Gains in Peer Networking Bring Muscle to the Mix. *PC Week,* 12; 30 (July 31, 1995), N1.

Miastkowski, Stan. Peer Power Upgrade. *Byte,* 20; 3 (March 1995), 135.

Nance, Barry. Four Peer Operating Systems, *Byte,* 19; 12 (December 1994), 169.

Rigney, Steve. Small-Business Networks: Breaking Through. *PC Magazine,* 14; 10 (May 30, 1995), NE1.

Sullivan, Kristina. Measuring Peer-to-Peer Pressure. *PC Week,* 12; 30 (July 31, 1995), N1.

Wilson, Linda. Peer-to-Peer Networks: Here Today, Gone Tomorrow? *Communications Week,* no. 562 (June 19, 1995), 39.

Backup/Fault Tolerance

Carr, Eric. Tape Backup: Network Protection Requires Planning. *Network Computing,* 5; 8 (July 1, 1994), 152.

Carr, Eric. Windows Doesn't Ease the Pain of Backup. *Network Computing,* 5; 6 (June 1, 1994), 94.

Danielle, Diane. Server- vs. Workstation-Based Backup. *Network Computing,* 5; 6 (June 1, 1994), 108.

Garris, John. Network Backup: Flexing Your Backup Muscle. *PC Magazine,* 14; 11 (June 13, 1995), NE1.

Giorgis, Taadesse and John McDonough. 24 Safeguards Against Data Loss. *Byte,* 20; 3 (March 1995), 144.

Marks, Howard. Forgiving Network Faults. *Network World,* 12; 27 (July 3, 1995), 31.

Nadeau, Michael. Network Backup: Vendors Work to Cure Incompatibility Blues. *Byte,* 19; 6 (June 1994), 32.

Stone, M. David. QIC-3010/QIC-3020 Drives: The Bigger Backup. *PC Magazine,* 14; 3 (February 7, 1995), 237.

Yamkowy, Shane. Developing Network Backup Solutions. *Network Computing,* 6; 5 (May 1, 1995), 151.

FAX

Baldazo, Rex and David Essex. Software Roundup: Industrial-Strength FAX Servers. *Byte,* 20; 10 (October 1995), 137.

Bolles, Gary. Fax Headaches? Think about a FAX Server. *Network Computing,* 5; 6 (June 1, 1994), 178.

Robertson, Bruce. DID Delivers Incoming Faxes Directly to the Desktop. *Network Computing,* 5; 6 (June 1, 1994), 170.

Electronic Software Distribution

Drews, James and Eddie Correia. Special Delivery— Automatic Software Distribution Can Make You a Hero. *Network Computing,* 5; 8 (August 1, 1994), 80.

Software Metering/Inventory

Drews, James. Software Vendors Keep the Meter Running. *Network Computing,* 5; 11 (October 1, 1994), 98.

Graziano, Claudia. License Servers on the Way. *LAN Times,* 12; 13 (July 3, 1995), 1.

Lisle, Reggie. Software-Metering Tools. *LAN Times,* 12; 13 (July 3, 1995), 65.

Marks, Kristin. Making a List and Checking It Twice. *Network Computing,* 6; 7 (June 1, 1995), 116.

Philips, Ken. Keeping Tabs on Apps. *PC Week,* 12; 25 (June 26, 1995), N1.

Salamone, Salvatore. You're Saving Money When the Meters Runnning. *Byte,* 20; 3 (March 1995), 26.

Sullivan, Kristina. Surveying the Lay of the LAN. *PC Week,* 12; 32 (August 14, 1995), N3.

Multiprotocol Peripherals/Printers

Kay, Emily. Taming the Intelligent Peripheral. *Information Week,* no. 544 (September 11, 1995), 50.

NOS Interoperability

Oggerino, Chris. Reaching Out: IP and IPX on a Windows Client. *Network Computing,* 5; 11 (October 1, 1994), 132.

Imaging Application Software

Hurwicz, Michael. The Paperless Office. *Network Computing,* 6; 9 (August 1, 1995), 70.

Storage Management Software

Arnett, Matthew. Storage-Management Solutions. *LAN Times,* 12; 15 (August 14, 1995), 75.

E-Mail

Arnum, Eric. New Servers Will Alter LAN-Based E-Mail Market. *Business Communications Review,* 24; 7 (July 1994), 42.

Blum, Daniel and Gary Rowe. Plan Now for Smoother E-Mail Migration. *Network World,* 12; 27 (July 3, 1995), 35.

Burns, Nina. E-Mail Beyond the LAN. *PC Magazine,* 14; 8 (April 25, 1995), 102.

Butler, Cheryl. DMA: Document Management Made Easy. *Network World,* 12; 29 (July 17, 1995), 51.

Carr, Eric. Global E-Mail Communications Through SMTP. *Network Computing,* 5; 12 (October 15, 1994), 36.

Cullen, Alex. Message Architectures in Transition. *Network World,* 12; 26 (June 26, 1995), 35.

Devers, Linda. Uncovering the Hidden Costs of E-Mail. *Network Computing,* 5; 9 (August 1, 1994), 142.

Dorshkind, Brent. Messaging Vendors Wary of NDS. *LAN Times,* 12; 14 (July 24, 1995), 22.

Eglowstein, Howard and Ben Smith. E-Mail from Afar. *Byte,* 19; 5 (May 1994), 122.

Fogarty, Kevin and Peggy Watt. ODSI: NOS Vendors Cave In. *Network World,* 12; 29 (July 17, 1995), 1.

Girishankar, Saroja. It's in the E-Mail. *Communications Week,* no. 567 (July 24, 1995), 67.

Johnson, Johna. Document Sharing Without E-Mail Barriers. *Data Communications,* 24; 1 (January 1995), 107.

Morse, Stephen. E-Mail Management in Disarray. *Network Computing,* 5; 15 (December 1, 1994), 122.

Morse, Stephen. Super E-Mail: New Applications and Architectures Enhance Services. *Network Computing,* 5; 12 (October 15, 1994), 30.

Myer, Ted. Straight Talk about E-Mail Connectivity. *Business Communications Review,* 25; 7 (July 1995), 35.

Robertson, Bruce. Mail-Enabling Databases. *Network Computing,* 6; 7 (June 1, 1995), 154.

Robertson, Bruce. MIME Speaks Volumes. *Network Computing,* 5; 13 (November 1, 1994), 135.

Rooney, Paula and Paula Musich. Universal Client to Link Mixed E-Mail. *PC Week,* 12; 25 (June 26, 1995), 1.

Sheldon, Tom. MAPI Blooms in Chicago. *Byte,* 19; 11 (November 1994), 163.

Snyder, Joel and Jan Trumbo. E-Mail Directories—Directory Assistance. *Network Computing,* 6; 7 (June 1, 1995), 88.

Stahl, Stephanie. Pumping Up Corporate E-Mail. *Information Week,* no. 531 (June 12, 1995), 46.

Tolly, Kevin. E-Mail Gateways: What's Missing from the Link. *Data Communications,* 24; 9 (July 1995), 35.

Tolly, Kevin and David Newman. Grow Up!: Evaluating LAN-Based E-Mail for the Enterprise. *Data Communications,* 23; 16 (November 1994), 70.

Desktop Videoconferencing/Multimedia

Bryan, John. Compression Scorecard. *Byte,* 20; 5 (May 1995), 107.

Davis, Andrew. Videoconferencing: Face to Face. *Byte,* 20; 10 (October 1995), 69.

Fritz, Jeffrey. Video Connections. *Byte,* 20; 5 (May 1995), 113.

Haight, Timothy. Does Videoconferencing Matter? *Network Computing,* 5; 8 (July 1, 1994), 64.

Halhed, Basil. Standards Extend Videoconferencing's Reach. *Business Communications Review,* 25; 9 (September 1995), 52.

Henderson, Tom. Maybe You Have a Case of the BLOBs. *Network Computing,* 6; 4 (April 1, 1995), 138.

Quait, Barry and Timothy Haight. Let's Meet! Desktop to Desktop. *Network Computing,* 5; 8 (July 1, 1994), 62.

Sullivan, Joe. T.120 Conferencing Standards Ease Data Sharing. *Network World,* 12; 25 (June 19, 1995), 49.

Taylor, Kieran. Desktop Videoconferencing: Not Ready for Prime Time. *Data Communications,* 24; 5 (April 1995), 65.

Tolly, Kevin. Networked Multimedia: How Much Bandwidth Is Enough? *Data Communications,* 23; 13 (September 21, 1994), 44.

Groupware

Baldazo, Rex and Stanford Diehl. Workgroup Conferencing. *Byte,* 20; 3 (March 1995), 125.

Bartholomew, Doug. A Better Way to Work. *Information Week,* no. 544 (September 11, 1995), 32.

Dorschkind, Brent. Orchestrating Notes. *LAN Times,* 12; 12 (June 19, 1995), 61.

Hahn, Eric. Groupware Comes of Age. *Network Computing,* 5; 14 (November 15, 1994), 68.

Hsu, Meichun and Mike Howard. Work-Flow and Legacy Systems. *Byte,* 19; 7 (July 1994), 109.

Layland, Robin. Is Your Network Ready for Notes? *Data Communications,* 24; 5 (April 1995), 83.

Marshak, David. Competing Platforms. *Byte,* 20, 8 (August 1995), 84.

May, Thornton. Know Your Workflow Tools, *Byte,* 19; 7 (July 1994), 103.

Newman, David and Kevin Tolly. Document Conferencing: Real Time, Real Data. *Data Communications,* 24; 8 (June 1995), 81.

Pompili, Tony. The Best Notes Server. *PC Magazine,* 14; 12 (June 27, 1995), NE1.

Pompili. Tony. Closing the Workflow Gap. *PC Magazine,* 14; 2 (January 24, 1995), NE1.

Seachrist, David. Work-Free Workgroup Schedulers. *Byte,* 20; 8 (August 1995), 128 NA2.

Sullivan, Kristina. Step Up to the Whiteboard Please. *PC Week,* 12; 23 (June 12, 1995), N3.

Timmins, Annmarie. Beta Report: Lotus Notes 4 Proves to Be Enterprise-Saavy. *Network World,* 12; 31 (July 31, 1995), 1.

Tolly, Kevin. A Real World Benchmark for Lotus Notes. *Data Communications,* 24; 8 (June 1995), 35.

Trammel, Kelly. Under Construction. *Byte,* 20; 8 (August 1995), 93.

Wallace, Scott. Working Smarter. *Byte,* 19; 7 (July 1994), 100.

Yavin, David. Replication's Fast Track. *Byte,* 20; 8 (August 1995), 88A.

Security

Barrus, Karl. Protecting Your Privacy. *Network Computing,* 6; 4 (April 1, 1995), 146.

Bellovin, Steven and William Cheswick. Network Firewalls. *IEEE Communications,* 32; 9 (September 1994), 50.

Brown, Patrick. Digital Signatures: Are They Legal for Electronic Commerce? *IEEE Communications,* 32; 9 (September 1994), 76.

Bryan, John. Build a Firewall. *Byte,* 20; 4 (April 1995), 91.

Bryan, John. Firewalls for Sale. *Byte,* 20; 4 (April 1995), 99.

Chokhani, Santosh. Toward a National Public Key Infrastructure. *IEEE Communications,* 32; 9 (September 1994), 70.

Denning, Dorothy and Miles Smid. Key Escrowing Today. *IEEE Communications,* 32; 9 (September 1994), 58.

Kay, Russell. Distributed and Secure. *Byte,* 19; 6 (June 1994), 165.

Moskowitz, Robert. Firewalls: Building in that Peaceful, Easy Feeling. *Network Computing,* 5; 6 (June 1, 1994), 159.

Neuman, B. Clifford and Theodore Tso. Kerberos: An Authentication Service for Computer Networks. *IEEE Communications,* 32; 9 (September 1994), 33.

Sandhu, Ravi and Pierangela Samarati. Access Control: Principles and Practice. *IEEE Communications,* 32; 9 (September 1994), 40.

Schwartz, Jeffrey. Group Agrees on Method to Secure E-Mail. *Communications Week,* no. 567 (July 24, 1995), 1.

Stallings, William. Pretty Good Privacy. *Byte,* 19; 7 (July 1994), 193.

Wayner, Peter. Corporations Eye Private Security Schemes. *Byte,* 20; 8 (August 1995), 36.

Wayner, Peter. Software Key Escrow Emerges. *Byte,* 19; 10 (October 1994), 40.

Yesil, Magdalena. Securing Electronic Payments over the "Net." *Network World,* 12; 28 (July 10, 1995), 35.

EDI

Hendry, Mike, *Implementing EDI* Boston: Artech House, 1993).

Wayner, Peter. EDI Moves the Data. *Byte,* 19; 10 (October 1994), 121.

Agents/Smart Software

Indermaur, Kurt. Baby Steps. *Byte,* 20, 3 (March 1995), 97.

Wayner, Peter. Free Agents. *Byte,* 20; 3 (March 1995), 105.

Packaged Client/Server Application Software

Cox, John. Making Packaged Applications Fit In. *Network World,* 13; 23 (June 5, 1995), 36.

Dolgicer, Max. Tools of Choice for Client/Server Development. *Data Communications,* 24; 8 (June 1995), 31.

Scheier, Robert. Tailor Made. *PC Week,* 12; 23 (June 12, 1995), 19.

CASE STUDY

Chapter 9

METERING CAN CUT COSTS

Not long ago SEMATECH, a semiconductor manufacturers' consortium, had a nagging problem: Outdated software revisions and a shortage of applications hampered productivity. Although the nearly 1,000 PC users clamored for software updates, the IS staff was unable to meet their demands. By the time support staff visited each workstation and installed Microsoft Excel 3.0 in late 1993, for example, version 4.0 was already available.

Limited funding prevented Austin, Texas-based SEMATECH, which works with academia and the federal government to sponsor and conduct semiconductor research, from adequately responding to its users' needs. SEMATECH PC Support Manager Kevin Hyatt looked to Simpler-Webb Inc., a systems integrator, also in Austin, for help.

"By the end of 1993 we were actively looking for a way to automate the [distribution] process to give people what they needed and when," said Hyatt.

Simpler-Webb partner, Jeff Simpler, recommended that SEMATECH implement On Demand Software and Services Inc.'s WinINSTALL software-distribution application and Express Systems Inc.'s Express Meter metering software to help automate its distribution system.

Hyatt estimated the implementation of this project has saved SEMATECH about 4,500 hours of IS staff time and more than $225,000 in software costs in the past year alone.

But the savings came about only after anticipating and remedying barriers that would prevent SEMATECH from effectively distributing applications across its network. Simpler was faced with a complex set of challenges.

Because the consortium receives a large portion of its funding from the federal government, financial resources were limited. However, the scientists and engineers, who are employed by the member companies but work at SEMATECH on two-year rotations, were accustomed to having a more current and wider selection of software.

Maximizing Resources

When Simpler walked into SEMATECH, he found a varied network environment. Most employees were running no more than three applications locally on each of the approximately 900 IBM PS/2s, most of which were 386es with 60MB hard drives. Another 150 Unix workstations were used to run Unix-only semiconductor modeling-process software. All of the PCs were connected to IBM AS/400s, Digital Equipment Corp. VAXes, and two PS/2 386/20 file servers, which were running Microsoft LAN Manager 2.0 and Novell Inc. WordPerfect for Windows 5.1.

SEMATECH had already anticipated its older PCs and slow file servers would need upgrading in the near future. Therefore prior to the distribution and metering rollout, SEMATECH upgraded its workstations from 4MB to 8MB of RAM and began a gradual replacement of the PS/2s to Digital DECpc XL 486es. Three more servers were added and eventually replaced as performance complications presented themselves during test runs.

"If you want to distribute applications and you're dealing with resource-limited PCs," Simpler said, "you want to minimize the impact on the local hard disk." For this reason, Simpler wanted a software-distribution package that would let SEMATECH run applications from the network servers rather than just copying them from the servers to the local hard disks.

He recommended WinINSTALL for its ease of use and because it minimized the total number of configuration files needed to be loaded locally to run applications from the server.

Painless Implementation for Users

Simpler and SEMATECH's IS staff designed WinINSTALL's implementation so that it was totally transparent to users. The only visible difference was a new WinINSTALL icon that let them install or delete other applications.

As Simpler anticipated, even with just three applications automatically distributed, the strain was too much for the outdated file servers. "We quickly went from two to three and then to four servers," he said. Then after adding about 35 new installations and upgrades, Simpler moved on to the metering software.

Before SEMATECH brought Simpler in, it was buying a higher number of applications even though concurrent usage was very low. Not having an effective way to track and log executions forced them to buy more software than they really needed.

"Originally, we didn't see metering as part of the solution or the problem," said Hyatt. "But it quickly became clear that we could save a lot of money on licensing. Now we can . . . roll out [Shapeware Corp.'s] Visio, for example, with 20 licenses to be used by 100 people."

As with WinINSTALL, Express Meter is totally transparent to users—it runs in the background as a Microsoft Windows device driver. The IS staff appreciates its capability to let them track all their applications, not just the ones provided by WinINSTALL.

Soon after the new applications were installed, the servers were overloaded and no one server was large enough to house all the metering data.

The IS staff decided to replace all four servers with dual-processor Compaq Computer Corp. ProLiant 4000s with 2GB of hard disk space and 64MB of RAM.

After installing the new servers, it became obvious SEMATECH had to migrate to something more robust than LAN Manager. Simpler

recommended the company migrate to Microsoft Windows NT because it allowed the metering data to be housed on one server and afforded more connections per server as well as memory for running applications.

The major thrust of the project was completed six months later, by mid-1994. The total cost for the distribution and metering software, consultation, and integration was $62,500.

Investment Yields Big Savings

SEMATECH bases its $375,000 in savings on the resources available to be spent on new applications and updates, plus the total man-hours saved by automatic distribution. Using WinINSTALL, total installations numbered 4,500. Manual installation of these applications would not have been possible because the cost would have exceeded SEMATECH's budget.

"Intelligent automation was the fundamental key to the success of this project," Simpler said. "We eliminated a lot of manual labor and maximized the inevitable investment SEMATECH made in upgrading its PCs and replacing the servers."

New applications and upgrades are now rolled out as needed, but for the most part, the focus is on utilizing the metering data more effectively with better tools.

"We give people more choices and have increased our response time to their requests," said Hyatt. "In the future, metering software will drive our decision making about how many licenses we need or if we want to continue [the application] at all."

Source: Jill Marts (May 8, 1995). Metering Can Cut Costs. *LAN Times,* 12(9), 55. Reprinted with permission of McGraw-Hill, *LAN Times.*

BUSINESS CASE STUDY QUESTIONS ··

Activities

1. Complete a top-down model for this case by gleaning facts from the case and placing them in the proper layer of the top-down model. After completing the top-down model, analyze and detail those instances when requirements were clearly passed down from upper to lower layers of the model and solutions to those requirements were passed up from lower to upper layers.
2. Detail any questions that may occur to you about the case for which answers are not clearly stated in the article.

Business

1. What business problem was the company in this case facing?
2. What were some of the challenges which needed to be addressed before a successful technology implementation?
3. What was the business motivation for investigating software metering software?

Application

1. What type of application software was investigated in hopes of solving the identified business problem?
2. What performance criteria or functionality requirements were established for the application software in terms of its impact on local workstations?
3. How does software metering software actually work? How is it executed on a local PC?

Network

1. What is the impact on the network of running applications on a server rather than on local workstations?

Technology

1. Did the implemented technology solve the previously identified business problems? Defend your answer.
2. What amounts of financial and manpower savings have been attributed to the technology implementation?
3. What was the initial network configuration in terms of numbers of PCs, workstations, servers, minicomputers, operating systems, and network operating systems?
4. What changes were made to hardware technology prior to the implementation of the software solutions?
5. What changes were made to hardware technology after the initial implementation of the software distribution solutions?
6. How can the implementation of software metering software potentially save substantial amounts of money?
7. What changes were made to hardware technology after the initial implementation of the software metering solution?
8. What changes were made to software technology after the initial implementation of the software metering solution?
9. Do you think that some of the required hardware and software changes could have been better anticipated? Why or why not? Defend your answer.
10. How did the combination of software distribution and software metering applications combine to offer solutions to an identified business problem?

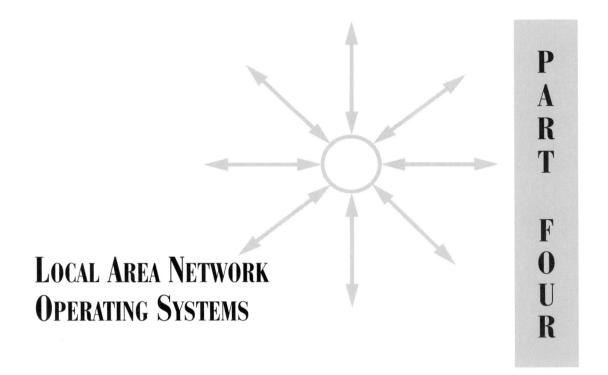

LOCAL AREA NETWORK OPERATING SYSTEMS

INTRODUCTION

Part 3 covered local area network architectures, hardware, and application software; in Part 4 we cover network operating systems in detail.

Chapter 10 studies local area network operating systems from architectural and functional perspectives. Comparisons are made between currently available network operating system technologies which are representative of such network operating system categories as peer-to-peer, small business, client, and server. This chapter serves as a suitable overview of network operating systems in general.

Chapters 11 through 13 study specific network operating systems in much greater detail. Particular attention is paid to the internal operations of each network operating system including transport protocols, interoperability, memory management, file systems, directory services, and application program support services. Each chapter stands on its own, covering a particular network operating system:

- Chapter 11 covers NetWare
- Chapter 12 covers Windows NT.
- Chapter 13 covers Unix and Network File System (NFS), which forms a popular network operating system combination with the TCP/IP suite of transport protocols.

CHAPTER 10

LOCAL AREA NETWORK OPERATING SYSTEMS

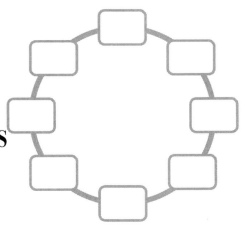

Concepts Reinforced

OSI model
Protocols and standards
Client/server technology model
LAN software architecture

Top-down model
Hardware/software compatibility
Network architectures

Concepts Introduced

Network operating systems
   architectures
Peer-to-peer network operating systems
Client/server network operating
   systems
Client network operating systems

Server network operating systems
Network operating systems
   functionality
Network technology analysis
Functional network analysis

OBJECTIVES

After mastering the material in this chapter you should:

1. Understand the compatibility issues involved with implementing LAN software.

2. Understand the basics of network operating system functionality.

3. Understand the important differences between peer-to-peer and client/server network operating systems architectures.

4. Understand the emerging role of the client network operating system and the universal client.

5. Understand how to analyze functional networking requirements and match those requirements to available technology.

Network operating systems, like most other aspects of data communications, are undergoing tremendous change. As a result, before you examine the operational characteristics of a particular network operating system, it is important to gain an overall perspective of network operating systems in general. In particular, network operating systems architectures are in a state of transition from closed environments, in which only clients and servers running the same network operating system could interact, to open environments, in which universal clients are able to interoperate with servers running any network operating system.

Network operating system functionality is examined for both client and server network operating systems. The functionality examined is representative of current network operating systems in general rather than any particular product. This review serves as a basis of comparison for the more detailed analyses of particular network operating systems offered in Chapters 11 through 13.

■ NETWORK OPERATING SYSTEMS ARCHITECTURES

Traditional Differentiation: Peer-to-Peer versus Client/Server

Traditionally, network operating systems were divided into two major product categories:

- **Peer-to-peer network operating systems,** also known as DOS-based LANs or low-cost LANs, offered easy to install and use file and print services for workgroup and departmental networking needs.

- **Client/server network operating systems** offered more powerful capabilities including the ability to support hundreds of users and the ability to interact with other network operating systems via gateways. These client/server network operating systems were both considerably more expensive and considerably more complicated to install and administer than peer-to-peer network operating systems.

Peer-to-Peer   One of the early appeals of peer-to-peer network operating systems was their relatively minimal hardware requirements for memory and disk space. In addition, the fact that they ran as a background application over the DOS operating system made them considerably less complicated to install and administer than client/server network operating systems. When printer sharing and file sharing for less than 50 users were the major functional requirements of a network operating system, peer-to-peer network operating systems such as Artisoft's LANtastic and Performance Technology's PowerLAN were popular choices in this technology category.

In most peer-to-peer LANs, individual workstations can be configured as a service requester (client), a service provider (server), or a combination of the two. The terms client and server, in this case, describe the workstation's functional role in the network. The installed network operating system is still a peer-to-peer system, because all workstations in the network are loaded with the same networking software. Most peer-to-peer network operating systems lacked the ability to access servers of client/server network operating systems and suffered from diminished performance as large numbers (more than 50) of users were added to the system. As a result, traditional peer-to-peer network operating systems were characterized as lacking interoperability and scalability.

Client/Server   In contrast, traditional client/server network operating systems require two distinct software products to be loaded onto client and server computers, respectively. The specialized client software required less memory and disk space, and was less expensive than the more complicated, more expensive server software. NetWare 3.12 and Microsoft LANManager are examples of traditional client/server network operating systems. The client software was made to interact with the corresponding server software. As a result, although traditional client/server network operating systems overcame the scalability limitation of peer-to-peer network operating systems, they did not necessarily overcome the interoperability limitation. Functionally, client/server network operating systems offered faster, more reliable performance than peer-to-peer LANs and improved administration and security capabilities. Figure 10-1 illustrates the key differences between traditional peer-to-peer and client/server network operating systems.

Current Differentiation: Client NOS versus Server NOS

Functional Requirements of Today's Network Operating Systems   Although traditional peer-to-peer and client/server network operating systems met the functional requirements for workgroup and departmental computing, their limitations became evident when these departmental LANs needed to be integrated into a single, cohesive, interoperable, enterprisewide information system.

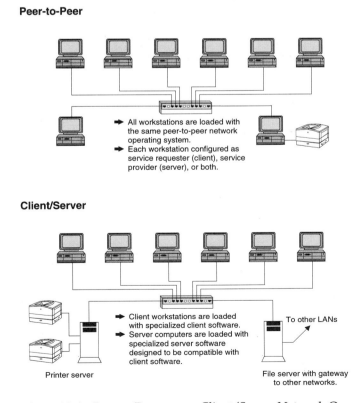

Figure 10-1   Peer-to-Peer versus Client/Server Network Operating Systems

To understand the architectural specifications of today's network operating systems, it is first necessary to understand the functional requirements these network operating systems must deliver. In a top-down analysis of network operating system requirements, one might ask, "What services do users of an enterprisewide information system demand of a network operating system?" The answer lies in the application layer of the top-down model. Since distributed applications enable enterprisewide productivity and decision making, the underlying network operating systems must support these distributed applications by supplying the message services and global directory services required to execute them in an enterprisewide, multiple-server environment.

Figure 10-2 illustrates these functional requirements and contrasts them with the requirements traditionally demanded of client/server and peer-to-peer network operating systems.

As the figure illustrates, the following new or emerging demands are being put on network operating systems:

- Application services.

- Directory services.

- Integration/migration services.

Key points about each of these emerging required services are bulleted in Figure 10-2. To successfully meet these functional requirements, network operating system architectures have shifted from integrated, single-vendor client/server network operating systems, as illustrated in Figure 10-1, to distinct independent, multivendor, client and server network operating systems. The functional characteristics of these distinct client and server network operating systems are described in detail later in this chapter. Figure 10-3 illustrates this architectural shift in NOS development.

Client Network Operating Systems: The Universal Client   Client network operating systems, as illustrated in Figure 10-3, integrate traditional operating system functional-

Traditional Requirements		All services delivered seamlessly across multiple server platforms regardless of installed network operating system		
		Emerging Requirements		
FILE SERVICES	PRINTER SERVICES	APPLICATION SERVICES	DIRECTORY SERVICES	INTEGRATION/MIGRATION SERVICES
		➡ Database back-end engines ➡ Messaging/communication back-end engines SUPPORT FOR: ➡ 32-bit symmetrical multi-processing ➡ Preemptive multitasking ➡ Applications run in protected memory mode ➡ Multithreading	➡ Global directory or naming services ➡ All network objects defined in single location and shared by all applications ➡ Directory information is stored in replicated, distributed databases for reliability, redundancy, fault tolerance	➡ Allow multiple different client network operating systems to transparently interoperate with multiple, different server network operating systems ➡ Provide easy-to-implement paths for upgrades to more recent versions or migration to different network operating systems

Figure 10-2   Required Services of Network Operating Systems: Traditional versus Emerging

Client/Server Network Operating System

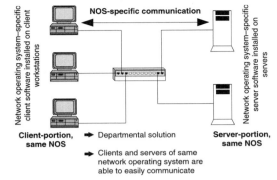

Client Network Operating System
- and -
Server Network Operating System

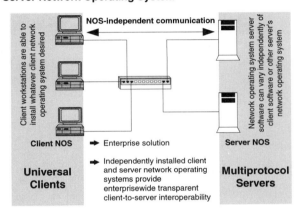

Figure 10-3 Client/Server Network Operating Systems versus Client *and* Server Network Operating Systems

ity with advanced network operating system features to enable communication with various types of network operating system servers. This client workstation's ability to interoperate transparently with a number of different network operating system servers without the need for additional products or configurations is described as a **universal client** capability.

Server Network Operating Systems   **Server network operating systems** can be chosen and installed based on their performance characteristics for a given required functionality. For example, NetWare servers are often employed as file and print servers whereas Windows NT, OS/2, or Unix servers are more likely to be employed as application servers. Because of the universal client's ability to communicate with any server, and the server network operating system's ability to communicate with a variety of client network operating systems, the choice of server network operating system can be based more on optimizing functional performance than on delivering required communication protocols.

Small Business Network Operating Systems Traditional peer-to-peer network operating systems have undergone both functional and architectural transitions in response to new functional requirements. Peer-to-peer networking functionality such as file sharing, printer sharing, chat, and e-mail is now included in most client network operating systems. As a result, traditional peer-to-peer network operating systems products such as LANtastic and PowerLAN have had to differentiate themselves from emerging client network operating systems such as Windows 95 and IBM OS/2 Warp Connect.

Architecturally, today's small business network operating systems have changed from closed, identically configured, peer-to-peer environments to offer interoperability with server network operating systems via universal client capabilities. In addition, they offer their own 32-bit server software to offer greater performance than the 16-bit peer software configured as a server.

One important characteristic of the latest **small business network operating systems** is that they continue to exhibit all of the positive attributes of the peer-to-peer network operating systems from which they evolved such as the following:

- DOS-based, low memory and disk requirements.

- Easy installation, configuration, and management.

- High-quality file and print services.

Peer-to-Peer Network Operating System

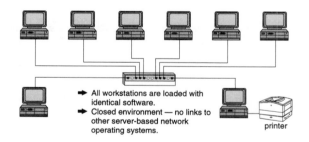

Small Business Network Operating System

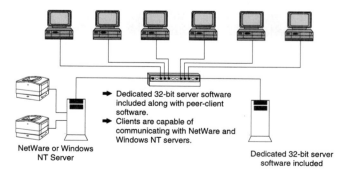

Figure 10-4 Architectural Transition from Peer-to-Peer to Small Business Network Operating Systems

Small business network operating systems have also had to differentiate themselves from client network operating systems, by offering more advanced features, including the following:

- Dedicated 32-bit server software.

- Bundled workgroup software.

- Easy migration path to server-based network operating systems.

Small business network operating systems seem to be getting squeezed between the client and server network operating systems and are functionally situated to offer a migration path between the two markets. Figure 10-4 illustrates the architectural transition from traditional peer-to-peer network operating systems to today's small business network operating system, and Figure 10-5 summarizes some of the key functional characteristics of small business network operating systems.

Small Business NOS Functional Category	Importance/Implication
Platform Issues	• How much memory is required for client functionality? server functionality? both? • Are standard network interface cards supported or are proprietary NICs required? • Are multiprotocol specifications such as NDIS and ODI supported? • Which network architectures are supported? Ethernet, Token Ring, Arcnet, LocalTalk?
Interoperability	• Is NetWare client software included? • Is Windows client software included? • Is remote access software to enable remote clients included?
Workgroup Software	• Is e-mail software included? • Is group scheduling software included? • Is fax gateway software included? • Is CD-ROM sharing software included?
File Sharing	• What extent of security is available? • Can files be hidden? • Can users share (mount) multiple remote disks? • Can applications be executed on remote shared clients?
Printer Sharing	• How many printers can be attached to a given computer? • How many printers can be managed overall? • What is the extent of management capabilities available to the administrator? • How much printer management can users do on their own? • Can printers be assigned to classes based on performance characteristics with jobs queued to printer classes rather than to specific printers? • Are printer usage statistics by user available?

Figure 10-5   Small Business Network Operating Systems Functional Characteristics

(continued)

Small Business NOS Functional Category	Importance/Implication
Scalability	• Is a 32-bit compatible server program available? • Are any client changes necessary to interoperate with the 32-bit server? • Is there a maximum number of client nodes supported?
Management	• Is a centralized management facility available? • What is the management platform? DOS, Windows? • Does the management facility keep a log of all network events? • Is an SNMP agent available to link to enterprise management systems? • How much information is available about active users and processes? • Can logon time restrictions or password expiration dates be set?

Figure 10-5   (continued)

■ CLIENT NETWORK OPERATING SYSTEMS FUNCTIONALITY

Figure 10-3 in the previous section provided an understanding of the new architectural arrangement of network operating systems, consisting of distinct, interoperable, multivendor, client and server network operating systems; this section explains in detail the functional aspects of client network operating systems categories, and the next section covers server network operating systems.

Client network operating systems such as Windows 95, OS/2 Warp Connect, and Windows NT Workstation offer three major categories of functionality:

- Operating system capabilities.

- Peer-to-peer networking capabilities.

- Client software for communicating with a variety of server network operating systems.

The logical relationship of these three distinct yet complementary categories of functionality is illustrated in Figure 10-6, which also points out potential areas for

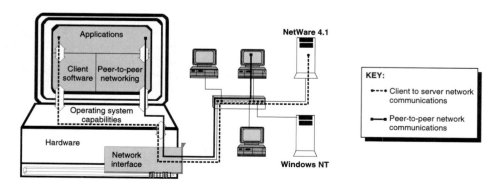

Figure 10-6   Logical Relationship of Client Network Operating System Functional Categories

compatibility and protocol consideration where the various software and hardware layers interface.

In the following sections, each of these major categories of functionality of client network operating systems are reviewed from the perspective of the network analyst. The importance of each functional category to the overall network operating system is explained, as are key differences in the implementation among available technology of any given functionality. From such a review of network operating system functionality, the network analyst should be able to construct a logical network design listing the functionality required to meet business objectives.

This logical network design can then be used as an evaluation mechanism for comparison with the delivered functionality of available technology. Logical network design functionality can be compared to available technology's delivered functionality in a technology analysis grid such as that in Figure 10-13 (Client Network Operating System Technology Analysis Grid). As stated in previous chapters, the advantage to employing a technology analysis grid in such an endeavor is that it ensures that purchase decisions or recommendations are based on facts rather than creative packaging or effective marketing.

Operating System Capabilities

Client operating systems concepts and capabilities were reviewed in Chapter 4. The following desirable operating systems characteristics, which were thoroughly explained in Chapter 4, are listed and briefly explained here from the perspective of importance of each characteristic to overall network operating system performance:

- Thirty-two-bit operating system—32-bit operating systems will allow more sophisticated and higher-performance 32-bit applications to execute more quickly.

- Preemptive multitasking—Preemptive multitasking prevents misbehaving programs from monopolizing systems resources at the expense of the performance of other applications.

- Protected memory space—Protected memory space prevents application programs from accidentally writing into each other's or the operating system's memory space causing general protection faults or system crashes.

- Support for symmetrical multiprocessing (SMP)—SMP is especially important for server network operating systems because of the processing load imposed by multiple simultaneous requests for services from clients. Some high-powered client applications such as 3-D modeling or simulation software may warrant SMP on client platforms as well.

- Multithreading—Multithreaded applications are able to achieve performance increases only if they are executed by an operating system which supports multithreaded applications, allowing more than one subprocess to execute simultaneously.

User Interface   Object-oriented user interfaces present the user with a graphical desktop on which objects such as files, directories, folders, disk drives, programs, or devices can be arranged according to the user's whim. More important, as objects are moved around the desktop, they retain their characteristic properties. As a result, when you click on a desktop object, only legitimate actions presented in context-sensitive menus appropriate for that class of objects can be executed.

Unlike object-oriented user interfaces, Windows-based user interfaces, although graphical, do not allow icons representing directories, files, or disk drives to be broken out of their particular Window and placed directly on the desktop. Figure 10-7 contrasts Windows-based user interfaces and object-oriented user interfaces.

Application Program Support A very important aspect of any migration plan to a new client network operating system is the extent of support for **backward compat-**

Windows-based User Interface (Windows 3.1)

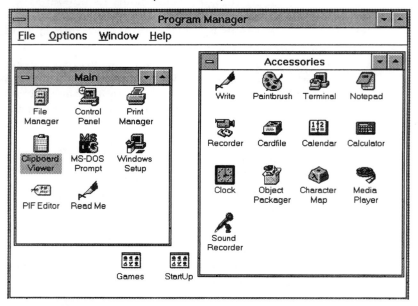

Object-oriented User Interface (Windows '95)

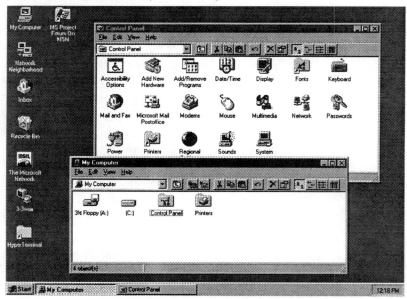

Screen shot(s) reprinted with permission from Microsoft Corporation

Figure 10-7 Windows-based User Interfaces versus Object-oriented User Interfaces

ibility with applications, also known as **legacy application** support. It stands to reason that most companies cannot afford to replace or rewrite all of their application software to upgrade to a new client network operating system.

Although we stated previously that 32-bit client network operating systems are desirable, the vast majority of network-based applications are still 16-bit applications. In addition, many of these 16-bit application programs, commercially produced as well as "home-grown," bypass supported API calls and commands in favor of conversing directly with or controlling hardware devices. In most cases, this type of programming was done initially in the interest of increased performance. Programs or subroutines which write directly to computer hardware are sometimes referred to as employing **real-mode device drivers.**

Many 32-bit network operating systems do not allow application programs to address or control hardware directly, in the interest of security and protecting applications from using each other's assigned memory spaces and causing system crashes. Instead, these more secure 32-bit operating systems control access to hardware and certain system services via **virtual device drivers,** otherwise known as **VxDs**. Windows NT is perhaps the best example of a 32-bit network operating system which prevents direct hardware addressing. As a result, many 16-bit applications, particularly highly graphical computer games, will not execute over the Windows NT network operating system. On the other hand, Windows NT is extremely stable.

Another issue concerning the execution of 16-bit applications is whether or not they execute in a shared memory address space, sometimes referred to as a **16-bit subsystem.** If they do, a single misbehaving 16-bit application can crash the 16-bit subsystem and all other executing 16-bit applications. Some 32-bit operating systems allow each 16-bit application to execute in its own protected memory execution area.

Client network operating systems may execute 32-bit applications in their own address space, otherwise known as **protected memory mode.** However, if all these protected mode 32-bit applications execute over a single 32-bit subsystem, a single misbehaving 32-bit application can crash the entire 32-bit subsystem and all other associated 32-bit applications.

Whether or not an application is executable over a particular network operating system depends on whether or not it issues commands and requests for network-based services in a predetermined format defined by the network operating system's **application program interface (API).** Each network operating system has its own unique API or variation. For example, as documented in Chapter 4, Windows, Windows NT, and Windows 95 all support variations of the Win32 API.

Some client network operating systems, such as Windows NT, have the ability to support multiple APIs and multiple different operating system subsystems, sometimes known as **virtual machines.** This feature allows applications written for a variety of operating systems such as OS/2, DOS, or POSIX to all execute over a single client network operating system.

Figure 10-8 (page 366) illustrates some of the concepts of application program support by client network operating systems.

Plug-n-Play Features   **Plug-n-play (PnP)** features are included, to varying degrees, in most client network operating systems. The goal of plug-n-play is to free users from the need to understand and worry about such things as interrupt requests (IRQs), direct memory access (DMA) channels, memory addresses, COM ports, and editing CONFIG.SYS whenever they want to add a device to their computer.

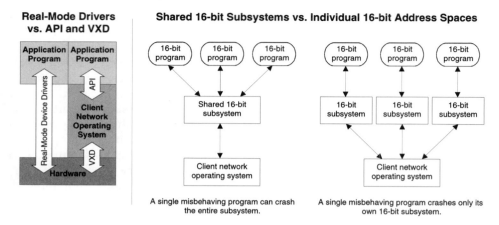

Figure 10-8   Application Program Support by Client Network Operating Systems

Although that goal has not been fully realized, definite progress has been made. Ideally PnP functionality will do the following:

- Automatically detect the addition or removal of PnP devices.

- Set all of the previously mentioned settings so that they do not conflict with other devices.

- Automatically load necessary drivers to enable the particular device.

PnP standards also include support for **dynamic reconfiguration** which will enable such things as the following:

- PCMCIA cards being inserted into and removed from computers without a need to reboot.

- Hot docking (powered up) of laptop computers into docking bays or stations.

- Dynamic reconfiguration-aware applications software which respond automatically to changes in system configuration.

Eventually, PnP devices will include not just network interface cards but also controllers of many types, SCSI devices, monitors, printers, and a variety of input-output devices. SCSI controllers will be configured according to a PnP standard known as **SCAM** or **SCSI configured automatically.** PnP compliant monitors will be controlled and configured according to the PnP **data display channel (DDC)** standard.

Compatibility issues are important to achieving full PnP functionality. To be specific, three distinct elements must support PnP standards:

1. A **PnP** basic input-output system **(BIOS)** is required to interface directly to both PnP and non-PnP–compliant hardware.

2. PnP capabilities must be supported by the client network operating system through interaction with the PnP BIOS. Windows 95 possesses the most PnP capability among currently available client network operating systems.

3. The devices which are to be installed must be PnP compliant. This basically means that the manufacturers of these devices must add some software and processing power to allow these devices to converse transparently with the PnP operating system and BIOS. In some cases, PnP-compliant device drivers may also need to be supplied.

To cater to the vast majority of legacy (non-PnP–compliant) devices, many PnP-compliant client network operating systems also assist in easing configuration hassles with these non-PnP–compliant devices. Using a variety of detection techniques, non-PnP devices are detected by the client operating system which then executes an assistant agent program, sometimes referred to as a hardware wizard, which walks the user through the configuration routine. Such programs are often capable of detecting and displaying IRQs and DMA addresses used by other devices, often allowing users to accept supplied default answers in this semiautomatic configuration scenario.

Peer-to-Peer Networking Capabilities

Many of the same functional capabilities discussed previously in the section on the evolution of the small business network operating system are included as part of the peer-to-peer capabilities of client network operating systems. In fact, it is this inclusion of workgroup application software which forced the vendors of traditional peer-to-peer network operating systems such as LANtastic and PowerLAN to add more advanced features to their offerings.

File and Printer Sharing   Perhaps the most basic of peer-to-peer network functions is file and printer sharing. In many cases, other resources such as CD-ROM drives can also be shared. Network operating systems supporting peer-to-peer networking can vary widely in their ability to limit access to certain drives, directories, or files. How finely access can be controlled (by disk, directory, or file level) is sometimes referred to as the **granularity** of the access control scheme. In addition, access must be controlled to drives, directories, or files by user groups or individual users. Sophistication of the printer management facility can also vary from one client network operating system to another.

Not all client network operating systems include peer-to-peer networking capabilities. For example, the Windows for Workgroups 3.11 upgrade offers Windows 3.1 its peer-to-peer networking, and only the IBM OS/2 Warp Connect version offers peer-to-peer networking. As client network operating systems have grown in sophistication, file and printer sharing services have become available to client platforms other than those configured with identical client network operating systems. Figure 10-9 (page 368) illustrates some of the cross-platform peer-to-peer file and printer sharing capabilities of Windows 95.

Practical Advice and Information

Following is one very important point to be made regarding the type of cross-platform interoperability illustrated in Figure 10-9:

Interoperability solutions cannot be assumed to be two-way or reversible. For example, as the figure illustrates, although NetWare clients are able to connect to a Windows 95 client running file and print services for NetWare, the converse is not true. Windows 95 clients cannot log into or share the disks and files of the NetWare clients.

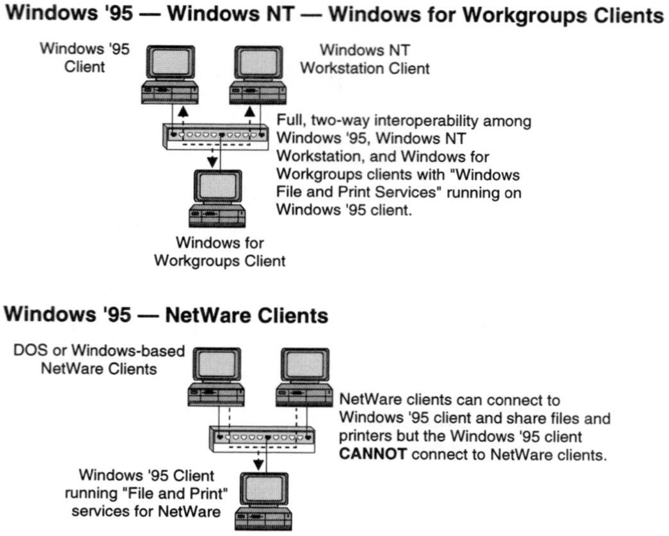

Windows '95 — Windows NT — Windows for Workgroups Clients

Windows '95
Client

Windows NT
Workstation Client

Full, two-way interoperability among
Windows '95, Windows NT
Workstation, and Windows for
Workgroups clients with "Windows
File and Print Services" running on
Windows '95 client.

Windows for
Workgroups Client

Windows '95 — NetWare Clients

DOS or Windows-based
NetWare Clients

NetWare clients can connect to
Windows '95 client and share files and
printers but the Windows '95 client
CANNOT connect to NetWare clients.

Windows '95 Client
running "File and Print"
services for NetWare

Figure 10-9 Cross-Platform File and Printer Sharing

Workgroup Applications   Ever striving to find new ways to differentiate themselves from the competition, client network operating systems are being offered bundled with the following types of workgroup application software:

- Terminal emulation.
- Calculator.
- Clock.
- Games.
- Paintbrush.
- Sound recorder.
- Remote access software.
- CD player.
- Backup.
- Chat.
- Phone dialer.
- Performance and network monitors.
- Diagnostic software.
- Screen savers.
- Web browsers.
- Fax access software.

Some client operating systems also offer more sophisticated workgroup applications in bonus packs which are sold for a modest charge. For example, IBM sells the BonusPak for OS/2 Warp Connect, and Microsoft sells Win 95 Plus!.

Managerial Perspective

The client network operating systems which offers the greatest number of workgroup applications is not necessarily the best or most appropriate choice. Although free application software is nice, priority should be given to the following types of client network operating systems characteristics:

- Application program support and operating system characteristics.
- Peer-to-peer networking capabilities.
- Flexibility and ease of installation and use in acting as a client to a variety of server network operating systems.

Client network operating systems which are able to connect to a great many server operating systems are sometimes called universal clients. In supporting multivendor, multiplatform, distributed information systems, this is perhaps the most important evaluation criterion of all for selecting a client network operating system.

Client Networking Capabilities

As illustrated architecturally in Figure 10-10, there are three distinct elements of networking functionality, in addition to the previously mentioned application support capabilities, which must be included in a client network operating system. In some cases, more than one alternative is offered for each of the following elements:

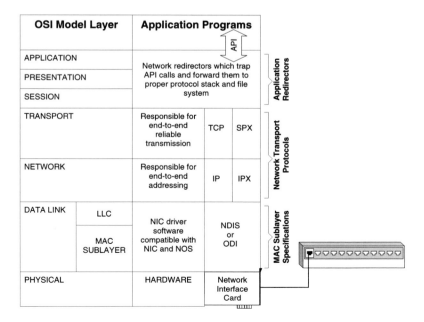

Figure 10-10   Client Networking Functionality

- Client software and network drivers which allow a particular client to communicate with a compatible server. These are media access control (MAC) protocol specifications such as NDIS and ODI.

- Network transport protocols which package and transport messages between clients and servers. These protocols correspond to the network and transport layers of the OSI model.

- Network redirectors which trap API calls and process them appropriately. Redirectors are concerned with providing file system–related services in support of application programs.

As stated, more than one alternative protocol may be provided in a given client network operating system for each of these three network protocol categories. Figure 10-11 displays the protocol stacks for Windows for Workgroups, Windows NT Workstation, Windows 95, and OS/2 Warp Connect. Rather than organize protocols in an OSI model architecture, the figure divides the protocols into layers based on networking functionality.

Network Client to Multiple Servers   In most client network operating systems, the combination of these three elements of network functionality allows client platforms to automatically find and connect to reachable, compatible servers. For example, a properly configured Windows NT client is able to automatically display network connections and connect to physically reachable Windows NT and NetWare servers to which the client has been assigned access privileges. The client software does not have to be preconfigured with any information about these servers. The

	Windows for Workgroups	Windows NT Workstation	Windows '95	IBM OS/2 Warp Connect
Application Support	WIN16 API 16-bit Windows applications supported	WIN32 API 32-bit and some 16-bit Windows applications supported	WIN32 API 32-bit and most 16-bit Windows applications supported	Supports DOS applications, 16-bit Windows applications, and native OS/2 applications
Application Redirectors and File Systems	SMB Server Message Block Redirector (Microsoft); FAT File Allocation Table File System (DOS/Windows)	NCP Netware Core Protocol Redirector (Novell); SMB Server Message Block Redirector (Microsoft); FAT File Allocation Table File System (DOS/Windows); NTFS NT File System	NCP Netware Core Protocol Redirector (Novell); SMB Server Message Block Redirector (Microsoft); FAT File Allocation Table File System (DOS/Windows)	NCP Netware Core Protocol Redirector (Novell); SMB Server Message Block Redirector (Microsoft); NFS Network File System (UNIX); HPFS High-Performance File System (OS/2)
Network Transport Protocols	IPX/SPX; NETBEUI NetBIOS Extended User Interface (Microsoft); TCP/IP	IPX/SPX; NETBEUI NetBIOS Extended User Interface (Microsoft); TCP/IP; Apple-Talk	IPX/SPX; NETBEUI NetBIOS Extended User Interface (Microsoft); TCP/IP	IPX/SPX; NETBEUI NetBIOS Extended User Interface (Microsoft); TCP/IP
MAC SubLayer Specifications	NDIS Network Data-Link Interface Specification (Microsoft/3Com); ODI Open Data-Link Interface (Novell)	NDIS Network Data-Link Interface Specification (Microsoft/3Com)	NDIS Network Data-Link Interface Specification (Microsoft/3Com); ODI Open Data-Link Interface (Novell)	NDIS Network Data-Link Interface Specification (Microsoft/3Com); ODI Open Data-Link Interface (Novell)

Figure 10-11   Client Network Operating Systems Protocol Stacks of Networking Functionality

server discovery and access is all handled transparently by the client network operating system.

In addition to offering network operating system client software such as Net-Ware 3.x and 4.x, client network operating systems often also include specialized application-oriented client software such as the following:

- File transfer protocol (FTP) client software.

- E-mail client software.

- Scheduling systems client software.

- Web browsers and gopher clients.

In the case of the e-mail and scheduling clients, compatible e-mail and scheduling application servers must be available. The client portion is merely the front-end to a back-end application engine executing in another network-accessible location.

Remote Access Specialized client software written to allow remote access to network operating systems servers is included with or available for most client network operating systems. These remote-access clients must access a specialized portion of the server network operating system specifically designed to handle incoming remote-access clients. The most popular server-based remote-access software to which client portions are generally available are **Windows NT Remote Access Server (RAS)** and **NetWare Connect.** Both of these products execute on a typical server platform either as a dedicated communications server or in conjunction with applications server duties. An alternative to server-based remote access software is a standalone device, known as either a **dial-up server** or a **remote node server.** Such a self-contained unit includes modems, communications software, and NOS-specific remote-access server software in a turnkey system. Shiva is perhaps the best known vendor of dial-up servers. As a result, some client operating systems include remote-access client software written especially to interface to Shiva dial-up servers.

Some client network operating systems include not only remote-access client software, but also remote-access server software. With this capability, other remote-access clients can dial-in to each other for file sharing, e-mail exchange, schedule synchronization, and so on. Windows NT Workstation extends this scenario by offering limited local server capability as well as remote-access server capability. Figure 10-12 (page 372) illustrates the relationship between remote-access client and remote-access server software as well as the architectural differences between applications server–based and remote-node server–based remote access.

Laptop Synchronization As mobile computing on laptop and notebook computers has grown exponentially, a need to synchronize versions of files on laptops and desktop workstations has quickly become apparent. Such **file synchronization software** was initially available as a standalone product or included as a feature on remote access or file transfer packages. Also known as **version control software** or **directory synchronization software,** this valuable software is now often included as a standard or optional feature in client network operating systems.

Laptops may be linked to their related desktop system in a number of ways:

- The laptop and desktop computer systems may be locally linked directly via serial or parallel cables.

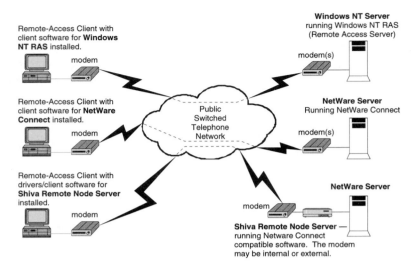

Figure 10-12   Remote-Access Client Software

- The laptop and desktop computer systems may be remotely linked via modems and a dial-up line.

- The laptop and desktop computer system may be remotely linked via a local area network running a network operating system such as NetWare, Windows for Workgroups, or Windows NT.

Client network operating systems should support laptop synchronization in all of the aforementioned connectivity options, especially LAN-based alternatives. Laptop synchronization should happen automatically when the laptop computer is docked in its docking station. E-mail clients and scheduling system client software should synchronize automatically with the LAN-attached e-mail and scheduling application servers.

Following are some of the important functional characteristics of and differences among laptop synchronization software:

- Copy by Date Option—Files and directories can be selectively synchronized by selected data range.

- Bidirectional Option—File synchronization can occur from just laptop to desktop, desktop to laptop, or both (bidirectional).

- Cloning Option—The contents of a directory on one system are guaranteed to exactly match the contents of the same directory on another system.

- Refresh Option—Only newer versions of files already located on both systems are copied from one system to another.

- **Delta File Synchronization**—This is perhaps the most significant file synchronization option in its potential impact on reducing required bandwidth and file transfer time. Rather than send entire files across the dial-up or LAN link, delta file synchronization transfers only the changes to those files.

CLIENT NETWORK OPERATING SYSTEM TECHNOLOGY ANALYSIS

Figure 10-13 is a technology analysis grid comparing key architectural and functional characteristics of the following client network operating systems:

- Windows for Workgroups.

- Windows NT Workstation.

- Windows 95.

- OS/2 Warp Connect.

This grid is included as an example of how technology analysis grids can be used to effectively map required networking functional requirements to available technology solutions in an objective manner. This technology analysis grid is not meant to be absolutely authoritative or all-inclusive. Its primary purpose is to provide a concrete example of the type of analysis tool used in a professional, top-down, network analysis and design methodology. It is expected that network analysts will create new technology analysis grids for each networking analysis opportunity based on their own networking functional requirements and the latest technology specifications available from buyer's guides or product reviews.

The client network operating system technology analysis grid is divided into the following major sections:

- Hardware/platform-related characteristics.

- Operating system capabilities.

- Peer-to-peer networking capabilities.

- Client networking capabilities.

Client Network Operating System Category	Windows for Workgroups	Windows NT Workstations	Windows 95	OS/2 Warp Connect
Hardware and Platform				
Required-Recommended Memory	4 MB–8 MB	16 MB–32 MB	8 MB–16 MB	8 MB–16 MB
16 or 32 bit	16 bit	32 bit	32 bit	32 bit
User Interface	Windows	Windows (Object-oriented Version 4.0)	Object-oriented desktop	Object-oriented desktop
Operating System Capabilities				
Preemptive Multitasking	No	Yes	Yes	Yes
Supports SMP	No	Yes	No	No
Protected Memory Program Execution	No	Yes	Yes	Yes

Figure 10-13 Client Network Operating System Technology Analysis Grid

(continued)

Client Network Operating System Category	Windows for Workgroups	Windows NT Workstations	Windows 95	OS/2 Warp Connect
Multithreading	No	Yes	Yes	Yes
Runs 32-bit apps	No	Yes	Yes	Yes, but not Win 95 or Win NT 32-bit apps
Runs 16-bit apps	Yes	Some. Won't support real-mode drivers	Yes	Some. Won't support real-mode drivers
Peer-to-Peer Networking				
File and Printer Sharing	Yes	Yes	Yes	Yes
Workgroup Applications	Yes	Yes	Yes	Yes
Client Networking				
Network Clients	Windows NT, Microsoft Mail and Schedule	NetWare, FTP, Internet	Windows NT, NetWare, Microsoft Exchange	NetWare, Internet, Gopher, LANServer
Network Transport Protocols	NetBEUI	NetBEUI, TCP/IP, IPX/SPX, AppleTalk	NetBEUI, TCP/IP IPX/SPX	TCP/IP
Remote Access	Yes	Yes	Yes	Yes
Laptop Synchronization	No	No	Yes	No

Figure 10-13   *(continued)*

■ SERVER NETWORK OPERATING SYSTEM FUNCTIONALITY

Changing Role of the Server Network Operating System

Traditionally, file and printer sharing services were the primary required functionality of server-based network operating systems. However, as the popularity of client/server information systems has boomed, **application services** have become the criteria by which server network operating systems are judged. The distributed applications of the client server model require that distinct client and server portions of a given application interact to execute the application as efficiently as possible. The server network operating system is responsible for not only executing the back-end engine portion of the application, but also supplying the messaging and communications services to enable interoperability between distributed clients and servers. Figure 10-14 illustrates the evolving role of the server network operating system from an architectural perspective.

The examination of server network operating system functionality in the remainder of the chapter focuses on those aspects of functionality which are most important to the support of distributed applications and their associated distributed clients and users. Although NetWare 3.12 is unquestionably the most widely installed server network operating system, with somewhere between 60 and 70% market share currently, its functional strength has always been file and print services rather than application services.

As a result, the market for the so-called next-generation network operating sys-

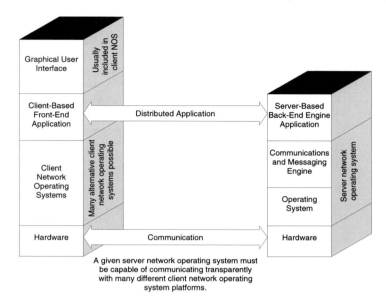

Figure 10-14   Role of Server Network Operating Systems in Distributed Applications

tems featuring application services is more wide open. Understandably, one of the key features of these advanced server-based network operating systems is the ease of migration and upgrade from market-dominating NetWare 3.12 or Windows NT Server 4.0. The two most popular next-generation server network operating systems for applications servers are NetWare 4.1 and Windows NT Server 3.51.

Various flavors of Unix combined with TCP/IP as a network protocol and NFS as a file system have also been popular choices of applications server platforms. However, this combination of operating system, network protocols, and file system is not as integrated or feature-rich as NetWare 4.1 or Windows NT Server 3.51 4.0 and probably does not deserve the label of "next-generation" NOS.

NetWare 4.1, Windows NT 3.51, and Unix–TCP/IP are each explored individually in detail in Chapters 11, 12, and 13, respectively.

Directory Services

Network operating systems have always depended on some sort of naming service or directory in which to store information about users as well as systems resources such as disks, servers, and printers. NetWare 3.x servers stored this type of information in a **bindery.** NetWare 4.1 employs a **global directory service** known as **Net-Ware Directory Services (NDS),** and Windows NT uses a **domain directory service.**

Global Directory Services versus Domain Directory Services   Global and domain directory services differ primarily in how they organize information concerning network users and resources. Global directory services organize all network user and resource data into a single hierarchical database, providing a single point of user and resource management. The hierarchical database is based on an organizational hierarchical tree structure of the network, which must first be designed. All servers which are part of this global hierarchical network can see all other parts of the hierarchical network. In this sense, the hierarchical directory database is merely a reflection of the hierarchical network itself.

This global directory database may well be **distributed,** meaning that different portions of the data are physically stored on multiple distributed servers linked via the network. In addition, it can be **replicated,** with multiple copies of identical data being stored on multiple servers for redundancy and fault-tolerance purposes. Logically, global directory services provide a view of a single, enterprise network.

In contrast, domain directory services see the network as a series of linked subdivisions called **domains.** Domain directory services associate network users and resources with a primary server known as a **primary domain controller (PDC).** Each domain's directory must be individually established and maintained. Domains can also be controlled as to how much of other domains can be seen.

Directory services can also vary in the type of information stored in their database. In some cases, all users and network resources are considered **network objects** with information concerning them stored in a single database, arranged by object type. Object attributes can be modified and new network objects can be defined. In other cases, network users and network resources are kept in separate databases. Frequently, separate databases are maintained for network user account information and e-mail user account information.

In Sharper Focus

DIRECTORY SERVICES COMMUNICATION

When a user wants to access resources on a remote or foreign server in a global directory service such as NetWare 4.1's NDS, the server performs a lookup in the NDS database to authenticate the user's right to the requested service. This NDS database lookup is repeated for every request for service from remote users. Recalling that the NDS database is distributed, the physical location of the server which contains the rights information of the requesting user may be located anywhere in the hierarchical distributed network.

In the case of a domain directory service such as Windows NT 3.51, the remote or foreign server receives the user authentication from the user's primary domain controller (local server) in a process known as **interdomain trust (IT).** Having servers act on behalf of their local users when verifying authenticity with remote and foreign servers eliminates the need for every user ID to be entered and maintained in every domain's directory service. In addition, once the interdomain trust has been established for a particular user, the remote domain server does not repeat the request for authentication.

As enterprise networks become more heterogeneous, composed of network operating systems from a variety of different vendors, the need will arise for different network operating systems to share each other's directory services information. A directory services specification known as **X.500** offers the potential for this directory services interoperability. NetWare 4.1's NDS is based on X.500 with proprietary extensions.

Applications Services

Recalling that the primary objective of the next-generation server NOS is to provide high-performance application services, the most important enabling characteristic of the NOS is its ability to support symmetrical multiprocessing. As numbers of users and sophistication of application programs continue to increase, the only real solution is for the application to be able to utilize more processing power simultaneously. Not all server network operating systems support symmetrical multiprocessing, and those that do may vary in the maximum number of processors supported. The following other server network operating system characteristics are essential to optimizing application program performance:

- Preemptive multitasking.

- 32-bit execution.

- Multithreaded application support.

- Program execution in protected memory space.

File Services Applications programs are stored in a particular file system format. In addition, when these application programs execute, they may request additional services from the resident file system via API calls. Server network operating systems vary in the types and number of supported file systems. Some network operating systems, such as Windows NT, can have multiple partitions on a disk drive, with one partition supporting file allocation table (FAT) file systems and another supporting the NT file system (NTFS). Figure 10-15 lists some file systems supported by server network operating systems.

Other file services offered by some server network operating systems include file compression utilities and **data migration** utilities, which manage the migration of data among different types of storage devices as part of a comprehensive hierarchical storage management (HSM) program. Finally, just as client network operating systems either bundled or offered optional workgroup software as part of their package, server network operating systems offer a variety bundled back-end engines. For example, as an option or add-on to Windows NT server, a bundled product known as Microsoft Back-Office offers the following suite of server applications:

- System management server.

- SQL server.

- Mail and schedule (Exchange) server.

- SNA gateway to IBM mainframe networks.

File System Name	Associated Network Operating System
FAT—file allocation table	Windows NT server
HPFS—high performance file system	OS/2 LAN server
NetWare file system	NetWare 3.12 and 4.1
NFS	Unix (native), most other NOS:optional
NTFS—NT file system	Windows NT server
Vines file system	Banyan Vines 5.54

Figure 10-15 File Systems and Associated Server Network Operating Systems

Networking and Connectivity Services

Network Clients Supported In addition to the client network operating systems previously reviewed, server network operating systems may also have to communicate with client platforms with only the following operating systems installed:

- DOS.
- Windows.
- Macintosh.
- OS/2.
- Unix (implies support for NFS file system).

Because these operating systems possess no native networking functionality, the server network operating system in these cases must be able to generate diskettes with the necessary operating system–specific network communications capabilities. These diskettes are then loaded on the intended networking client, and the required network communication capabilities are merged with the native operating system.

Network Protocols Supported The key question concerning network protocols and server network operating systems is not just how many network protocols are supported, but more important, how many can be supported simultaneously? In these days of heterogeneous multivendor enterprise networks, it is essential that a server network operating system be able to support multiple network protocols simultaneously to maximize not only the number of client types, but also the number and type of other servers with which it can communicate. The ease with which multiple network protocols can be supported or whether multiple network protocols can be supported at all, varies among server network operating systems.

Related to the ability of a server network operating system to simultaneously support multiple protocols is its ability to support multiple network interface cards. If a single NIC is the bottleneck to network communications, additional NICs can be added as long as the computer's bus can support multiple NICs and network operating system can communicate with them. As PCI buses and PCI-based NICs have increased in popularity, PCI cards containing up to four NICs are being produced. Unless the server network operating system is able to communicate with four NICs simultaneously, this four-NIC PCI card is of little use.

Multiprotocol Routing Underlying a server network operating system's ability to process multiple protocols simultaneously is the presence of **multiprotocol routing** software. This software may be either included, optional, or not available, depending on the server network operating system in question. Multiprotocol routing provides the functionality necessary to actually process and understand multiple network protocols as well as translate between them. Without multiprotocol routing software, clients speaking multiple different network protocols cannot be supported. Routing in general and multiprotocol routing in particular are covered in greater detail in Chapter 14. Figure 10-16 illustrates the relationship between multiple network protocols, multiple network interface cards per server, and multiprotocol routing software.

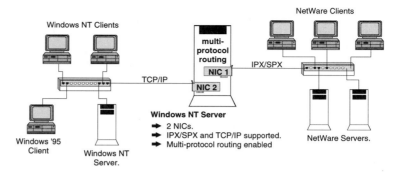

Figure 10-16 Multiple Network Protocols and Server Network Operating Systems

Remote Access and Gateway Services Just as client network operating systems supplied the client portion of a remote-access communication, server network operating systems may or may not supply the server side of the remote access communication. These remote-access servers may be included with the server NOS or available for an additional fee. It is important that these remote-access servers are well integrated with the server network operating system to ensure remote users both reliable performance and the full functionality offered to locally connected users. Windows NT RAS (remote-access server) is integrated with Windows NT Server 3.51, and NetWare Connect is the remote-access server that integrates with NetWare 4.1.

In some cases, it may be necessary for either clients or servers to access IBM mainframe computers or AS/400s linked on IBM's proprietary network architecture known as **Systems Network Architecture (SNA).** In such cases, it makes more sense for the translation software necessary to access the SNA network to reside on a single server than on multiple clients. The server with the SNA translation software installed becomes a gateway to the SNA network. Windows NT's product for IBM mainframe access is called SNA Gateway and NetWare's is called NetWare for Systems Application Architecture (SAA).

Management and Administration Services

Installation, Configuration, and Administration Recent reviews of server network operating systems consistently list **autodetection** and **configuration** of installed controllers, interface cards, and peripherals as the most important installation-related feature. The ability of a server NOS to automatically configure a controller, adapter, or peripheral depends on the NOS possessing a compatible driver for that device. It stands to reason that the greater the number of drivers a network operating system supports, the greater the probability that autoconfiguration will be successful.

Another hardware compatibility issue related to installation is the number of different CPUs on which a given server network operating can operate. For example, although NetWare 4.1 can operate only on Intel chips, Windows NT server can operate on Intel chips, DEC Alpha chips, PowerPC chips, and MIPs RISC chips.

To appreciate the differences in ease of administration server network operating systems offer, it is important to scale the network to be administered to a multiserver enterprise network serving hundreds if not thousands of users. With this scenario in mind, consider the following pertinent questions:

- How many steps are involved in creating a new user account?

- What is involved in giving a user access to remote servers?

- How easily can a user profile be copied and used as a template to automatically generate other user profiles? This feature is particularly important in academic settings where user profiles must be constantly generated in large numbers.

- What tools are available to assist in managing multiple servers simultaneously?

Server network operating systems can vary widely in the sophistication of the **performance monitoring** software included or available as an add-on. Ideally, the monitoring software should offer the ability to set thresholds for multiple system performance parameters. If these thresholds are exceeded, alerts or alarms should notify network management personnel of the problem and advise on possible diagnoses or solutions. Event logging and audit trails are often included as part of the performance monitoring package.

In multiple-server environments, it is particularly important that all servers can be monitored and managed from a single management console. Desktop and server management software offers capabilities beyond the monitoring software included in server network operating systems. For example, performance statistics are often gathered and stored in databases known as **management information base (MIBs).** In addition, this performance management information can be communicated to enterprise management systems such as HP OpenView or IBM SystemView in the proper **simple network management protocol (SNMP)** format. Microsoft's desktop and server management product is known as System Management Server (SMS) and Novell's is called ManageWise.

Integration and Migration Integration and migration features of next-generation network operating systems are clearly aimed at one audience: the 60+% of servers currently running NetWare 3.12. **Migration** features are aimed at easing the transition from NetWare 3.12 to either NetWare 4.1 or Windows NT. Key among the migration concerns is the conversion of the directory services information stored in the NetWare 3.12 bindery into either NetWare 4.1 NDS or Windows NT domain directory services. Utilities available from third-party software vendors as well as Novell and Microsoft at least partially automate the bindery conversion.

Integration refers to that transitionary period in the migration process when both network operating systems must be running simultaneously and interacting to some degree. Integration utilities or strategies include the following:

- NetWare File and Print Services for NT—allows a Windows NT server to appear to be a NetWare server by offering native file and print services to NetWare clients.

- NW-Link—Allows Windows NT Workstation clients and Windows 95 clients to communicate with NetWare 3.12 servers.

- File Access Protocols for NetWare Core Protocol (NCP) and Server Message Block (SMB)—Can be loaded simultaneously as redirectors, allowing execution of either NetWare- or Windows-compatible programs.

SERVER NETWORK OPERATING SYSTEM TECHNOLOGY ANALYSIS

**Applied
Problem
Solving**

A network analyst's job is to always seek out the latest information the industry has to offer before recommending purchases which could have a significant bearing on the company's prosperity as well as personal job security. The following server networking operating system technology analysis grid (Figure 10-17) provides an example but is not meant to be either authoritative or all-inclusive. NetWare 4.1 and Windows NT Server 3.51 are covered in greater detail in Chapters 11 and 12, respectively. The technology analysis grid is divided into the following major categories:

- Hardware/platform characteristics.
- Installation and configuration.
- Networking and connectivity.
- Management and administration.

Server Network Operating System Characteristic	Windows NT Server 3.51	NetWare 4.1
Hardware/Platform		
Min/max memory	16MB–4GB	8MB–4GB
Min/max disk space	90MB–1700TB	75MB–32TB
CPUs	Intel, DEC Alpha, MIPs, RISC, PowerPC	Intel
Symmetrical multiprocessing	Yes	No
Preemptive multitasking	Yes	Yes
Multithreading	Yes	Yes
Protected memory app execution	Yes	Yes, but not with NLMs
Installation and Configuration		
Automatic detection and configuration of adapters and peripherals	Yes	No
Requires a separate administrator console	No	Yes
Number of included NIC drivers	98	68
Networking and Connectivity		
Clients supported	DOS, Windows, Windows for Workgroups, OS/2, Windows NT, Mac, Unix	DOS, Windows, Windows for Workgroups, Unix, OS/2, Windows NT, Mac

Figure 10-17 Server Network Operating System Technology Analysis Grid

(continued)

Server Network Operating System Characteristic	Windows NT Server 3.51	NetWare 4.1
Network protocols supported	TCP/IP, IPX, NetBEUI, AppleTalk, TCP/IP encapsulated NetBIOS	TCP/IP, IPX, AppleTalk, TCP/IP encapsulated IPX, IPX encapsulated NetBIOS
Routing supported	TCP/IP, IPX	TCP/IP, IPX, AppleTalk
Remote access services	Windows NT RAS included	NetWare Connect optional
E-mail gateways	Mail server optional	MHS included
Clients able to access remote resources	Yes	Yes
Management and Administration		
Can act as SNMP agent for enterprise mgmt system	Yes	Optional
Can set performance thresholds and alerts	Yes	Yes with ManageWise (optional)
Central management of multiple servers	Yes	Yes
Audit trails and event logs	Yes	Yes
RAID levels supported	0,1,5	0,1

Figure 10-17 *(continued)*

SUMMARY

Network operating systems have traditionally provided shared file and print services among networked clients. With the increase in client/server architectures and the associated increase in distributed applications, network operating systems are being called on to provide application services, directory services, and messaging and communications services to support these distributed applications.

Network operating systems were once categorized as either peer-to-peer or client/server. Their evolution shows peer-to-peer network operating systems evolving into small business NOSs and client/server network operating systems evolving into distinct, independent, client and server NOSs.

Functionality of client network operating systems can be categorized into operating systems capabilities, peer-to-peer networking capabilities, and client networking capabilities. Client network-ing capabilities are largely measured by the number of different server network operating systems with which the client can transparently interoperate. Remote access capability is also important.

Server network operating systems are now primarily concerned with high-performance application services for back-end application programs. Enterprisewide directory services must also be provided. The two major approaches to enterprise directory services are global directory services and domain directory services. To communicate with numerous client platforms, server network operating systems must support a variety of network clients as well as network transport protocols. Multiprotocol routing and remote-access services are also essential to deliver transparent interoperability to the greatest number of client platforms. In the multiple server environments of the enterprise network, monitoring, management, and administration tools play a critical role.

KEY TERMS

16-bit subsystem, 365
application program interface, 365
application services, 374
autodetection and configuration, 379
backward compatibility, 364
bindery, 375
client network operating systems, 358
client/server network operating systems, 356
data display channel, 366
data migration, 377
DDC, 366
delta file synchronization, 372
dial-up server, 371
directory synchronization software, 371
distributed, 376
domain directory services, 375
domains, 376
dynamic reconfiguration, 366
file synchronization software, 371
global directory services, 375

granularity, 367
integration, 380
interdomain trust, 376
IT, 376
legacy applications, 365
management information base, 380
MIB, 380
migration, 380
multiprotocol routing, 378
NDS, 375
NetWare Connect, 371
NetWare Directory Services, 375
network objects, 376
object-oriented user interfaces, 363
PDC, 376
peer-to-peer network operating systems, 356
performance monitoring, 380
plug-n-play, 365
PnP, 365
PnP BIOS, 366
primary domain controller, 376
protected memory mode, 365

real-mode device drivers, 365
remote node server, 371
replicated, 376
SCAM, 366
SCSI configured automatically, 366
server network operating systems, 359
simple network management protocol, 380
small business network operating systems, 360
SNA, 379
SNMP, 380
systems network architecture, 379
universal client, 359
version control software, 371
virtual device drivers, 365
virtual machines, 365
VxDs, 365
Windows NT Remote Access Server, 371
X.500, 376

REVIEW QUESTIONS

1. What effect has the adoption of client/server architectures and distributed applications had on network operating systems architectures?
2. Differentiate between peer-to-peer network operating systems and client/server network operating systems.
3. Differentiate between today's client network operating system and the client portion of client/server network operating systems.
4. How does the combination of today's client and server network operating systems differ from a client/server network operating system implementation?
5. What is a universal client?
6. Why is a universal client important to enterprise computing?
7. What new demands for services are being put on today's server network operating systems?
8. Describe the importance of the following service categories in more detail: directory services, applications services, integration/migration services.
9. Differentiate between peer-to-peer NOS and small business NOS.

10. What forces have caused the transition from peer-to-peer to small business NOS?
11. Describe the major categories of functionality of client network operating systems.
12. What are the major differences between an object-oriented user interface and a graphical user interface?
13. Explain the difficulty in supporting legacy applications while offering protected memory mode execution.
14. What are real-mode device drivers, and how do they differ from applications that interact with the operating system via APIs?
15. Why do many computer games use real-mode device drivers?
16. Why don't some client and server network operating systems support real-mode device drivers?
17. Describe how 16-bit or 32-bit applications running in their own protected memory space can still cause system crashes.
18. What is the objective of PnP standards?
19. Describe the components required to deliver a PnP solution and the relationship of the described components.

20. Which client network operating system is most PnP compliant?
21. What is meant by the statement, "Interoperability is not two-way"?
22. Describe the three elements of networking functionality that belong to client network operating systems, paying particular attention to the relationship between the elements.
23. Why is it important for a client network operating system to be able to support more than one network transport protocol?
24. Describe the importance of laptop synchronization as a client network operating system feature.
25. Describe the major differences in architecture and functionality between global directory services and domain directory services.
26. What is accomplished by having directory services databases be both distributed and replicated? Differentiate between the two techniques.
27. What is interdomain trust?
28. How does interdomain trust save on network administration activity?
29. What is X.500?
30. What is the relationship between file systems, APIs, and application services?
31. Why might it be important for a network operating system to support more than one file system?
32. What is the role of NCP and SMB redirectors in offering application services?
33. What is the difference in functionality and communication between a client running only an operating system such as Windows and one running a network operating system such as Windows 95?
34. What is the role of multiprotocol routing in a server network operating system?
35. What is the role of gateway services such as SNA server?
36. What are some important functional characteristics of server network operating systems related to installation and configuration?
37. What are some important functional characteristics of server network operating systems related to integration and migration?

ACTIVITIES

1. Using back issues of a publication such as *PC Magazine*, prepare a presentation tracing the functionality of peer-to-peer LANs from 1992 to the present. Prepare a graph detailing price, number of supported users, and required memory over the research period.
2. Using back issues of a publication such as *PC Magazine*, prepare a presentation tracing the functionality of client/server LANs from 1992 to the present. Prepare a graph detailing price, number of supported users, and required memory over the research period.
3. Gather current market share statistics for the following market segments and prepare a presentation: peer-to-peer NOS, small business NOS, client NOS, server NOS.
4. Analyze the results of the previous activity. Which products are gaining market share and which are losing market share? Relate the market shifts to product functionality. Present your results in a top-down model format.
5. Prepare a presentation on the comparative functionality of Windows 95 versus OS/2 Warp Connect. Compare marketing campaigns and current market share.
6. Conduct a survey of users of object-oriented user interfaces (Win 95, OS/2 Warp) and graphical users interfaces (Windows). What are users' impressions of the two? Does one really make users more productive than the other? Is this increase in productivity measurable?
7. Review advertisements and catalogs for devices which support the PnP standard. Prepare a list detailing which types of devices have the most PnP offerings. Which network operating system (if any) do devices claim to be compatible with?
8. Prepare a product review of dial-up or remote node servers, paying special attention to the source and compatibility of client software. Are most dial-up servers NOS specific? Why or why not?
9. Research and prepare a presentation on X.500. What software categories supported X.500 specs originally? currently? What key vendor groups or standards bodies (if any) support X.500? What is your prediction as to the widespread adoption of X.500?
10. Compare the performance monitoring capabilities of various server network operating systems. Which are best at monitoring a single server? multiple servers? Which are best at setting thresholds and alerts? Which are best at linking to enterprise management systems such as HP OpenView or IBM NetView?

11. Compare the functionality of Microsoft Systems Management Server and Novell Managewise. Contrast the functionality and price of these programs with those of enterprise management systems such as HP OpenView and IBM SystemView.

12. Investigate and compare the structures of NetWare 3.12 bindery and NetWare 4.1 NDS database.

13. Prepare a product review of software tools designed to automate the migration from the 3.12 bindery to the 4.1 NDS database.

FEATURED REFERENCES

NOS Comparisons

Giorgis, Tadesse. Software Roundup: Networks for the Enterprise. *Byte,* 20; 2 (February 1995), 119.

Lipshutz, Robert. The Versatile Network Operating System. *PC Magazine,* 14; 10 (May 30, 1995), 228.

Mier, Edwin. The Great NOS Shoot-Out. *Communications Week,* no. 562 (June 19, 1995), 46.

Miller, Michael. Getting Ready for Windows 95. *PC Magazine,* 14; 9 (May 16, 1995), 102.

Miller, Michael. Your Next Operating System. *PC Magazine,* 14; 16 (September 26, 1995), 102.

Morse, Stephen. The NOS Report Card: Are We There Yet? *Network Computing,* 5; 11 (October 1, 1994), 75.

Rigney, Steve. Communicating with Windows 95: Hooked and Linked. *PC Magazine,* 14; 9 (May 16, 1995), 175.

Tabibian, O. Ryan. NOS: The Next Generation. *PC Magazine,* 13; 22 (December 20, 1994), NE1.

CASE STUDY

Chapter 10

HOSPITAL'S CLIENT/SERVER CURE

Mainframe-to-VINES Migration Speeds Workflow

Greenwich Hospital in Greenwich, Conn., boasts a state-of-the-art network, with automatic inventory ordering and frame-relay links to other hospitals in the area. But in the hospital's move from a mainframe to a client/server environment, the biggest challenges came not from adopting new technology but from changing the way people thought about workflow.

Two years ago, an IBM 4381 formed the cornerstone of the hospital's computing infrastructure. It ran accounting and administrative programs but supported no medical applications. "There were no applications of any clinical value on it," said Eric Disilvestro, director of network systems at the 290-bed community hospital.

Because the mainframe didn't run necessary programs, depart-ments throughout the hospital developed their own systems tailored to fit their special needs. "We were charged with breaking down all these independent systems and creating an environment to share the information," said Disilvestro.

The hospital's MIS staff includes just Disilvestro and two other people, so the team needed to select products their limited resources could tackle.

Disilvestro and staff installed a 10Base-T Banyan Systems Inc. VINES network with an FDDI backbone. In particular, they wanted the features in Banyan's directory services, StreetTalk. "If we were using Novell, we never could have achieved what we've been able to do," said Disilvestro. They said they could manage their print and file services and deploy E-mail far more easily with StreetTalk than with NetWare.

Looking to build a system that could meet future needs, Disilvestro had Category 5 cable installed throughout the four-building campus. The network has 250 clients, but Disilvestro had the company install 500 termination points.

For an applications platform, the team selected Medical Information Technologies Inc.'s Meditech software to run such clinical programs as pharmaceutical; scheduling; billing; and admissions, discharges, and transfers. Four Digital Equipment Corp. Alpha machines run the Meditech software.

Porting Meditech applications to the VINES environment has proved challenging. The administrative features of the NOS are very strong, but few medical applications are written for the environment. The MIS staff often found they were working with contractors who were porting their software to VINES for the first time.

Working with staff to determine the appropriate flow of information throughout departments has presented the biggest challenge in building the system. The departments' closed programs were fine-tuned for their needs, but the general system had to support all of the departments.

"We had to change the mind-set of all the users," said Disilvestro. "Everybody had to give up something because the hospital system couldn't provide each one of the elements their closed system had. That was our biggest challenge, but the departments realized they had to make sacrifices for the benefit of the hospital as a whole."

The staff also needed to limit the hardware and desktop software they would support. They selected Compaq Computer Corp. file servers, desktops, and portables and Xyplex Inc. hubs, switches, and routers.

"From a maintenance, support, and administrative standpoint, I can't afford to learn more than just one basic system," said Disilvestro. The team also limited desktop applications to Novell Inc.'s WordPerfect; Microsoft's Excel, Access database, PowerPoint, and Project; and Banyan's Beyond Mail. Disilvestro contracted with an outside company to provide help-desk services for those applications.

The departments' capability to share information has streamlined such processes as billing and ordering, for example. When the pharmacy fulfills a prescription, the inventory database is automatically updated; if supply levels fall below a set threshold, the transaction automatically triggers a supply order. Prescription fulfillment also generates a bill for the patient.

One of the most dramatic space savings has been with the hospital's inventory. "We used to stock all our supplies in a warehouse, but now we're online with a supplier," said Disilvestro. "What we ordered yesterday comes today. It's critical that the network stays up—otherwise, that scheduled hip replacement won't have all the necessary parts."

Future plans include outfitting staff with wireless communicators, upgrading the system to support real-time image transfer, readdressing network for Internet access, and adding services to the statewide frame-relay network currently linking 10 hospitals.

Disilvestro is proud of the progress his team made, "We see hospitals five times our size that we absolutely dwarf in technology."

Source: Michelle Rae McLean (March 13, 1995). Hospital's Client/Server Cure. *LAN Times,* 12(5), 29. Reprinted with permission of McGraw-Hill, *LAN Times.*

BUSINESS CASE STUDY QUESTIONS

Activities

1. Complete a top-down model for this case by gleaning facts from the case and placing them in the proper layer of the top-down model. After completing the top-down model, analyze and detail those instances when requirements were clearly passed down from upper to lower layers of the model and solutions to those requirements were passed up from lower to upper layers.
2. Detail any questions that may occur to you about the case for which answers are not clearly stated in the article.

Business

1. What were the biggest challenges in the migration from the mainframe environment to client/server architectures?
2. Why were individual departments allowed to develop their own information systems?
3. What was the impact on individual departments when their independent systems had to be linked to the overall client/server architecture?
4. How did the MIS department implement a support mechanism which could function as efficiently as possible?

5. What improvements in business processes has the shared information made possible by the client/server architecture enabled?
6. What other business partners were included in the client/server information system?
7. What are the business benefits of including links to vendors as part of a network design?
8. What are some of the strategic future business directions, and how do they relate to stated future technological directions?

Application

1. Which types of applications were run on the mainframe?
2. What applications were run on the new client/server architecture?
3. What challenges did the chosen network operating system pose for application development? Could these challenges have been minimized or avoided? If so, how?

Data

1. What was the result of letting departments develop information systems independently?
2. Why was document and process flow analysis

important as a means of designing a client/server architecture which allowed sharing of the information from all the independent systems?

Network

1. What was the proposed solution to allow information from independently developed information systems to be shared?
2. What network operating system functionality was particularly important and served as a major evaluation criteria? Why was this functionality important in this case?

3. What were the network requirements to enable linking the hospital's vendors into the information system?

Technology

1. Describe the implemented network including network architectures, backbone networks, and network operating systems.
2. How were future needs taken into consideration in the network design and installation?
3. What types of computers were used as servers in the client/server architecture?

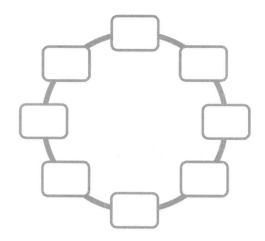

CHAPTER 11

NOVELL NETWARE

Concepts Reinforced

OSI model
LAN software
Network architecture
Network operating system
   architectures

Client/server technology model
Protocols and standards
Network operating system functionality

Concepts Introduced

NetWare loadable modules
Bindery
NetWare protocols

NetWare directory services
Virtual loadable modules
NetWare 3.12 migration

OBJECTIVES

After mastering the material in this chapter you should:

1. Understand the major architectural and functional similarities and differences between NetWare 3.12 and NetWare 4.1.

2. Understand the communications protocols underlying the NetWare network operating system.

3. Understand the issues and options surrounding migration from NetWare 3.12 to NetWare 4.1.

4. Understand the interoperability options between NetWare and other network operating systems such as Windows NT.

5. Understand the remote access options associated with NetWare.

Chapter 10 provided an overall understanding of network operating systems architecture and functionality, and this chapter explores the intricacies of Novell's NetWare operating system architecture and functionality. Although NetWare 4.1 is the most recent version of NetWare, pre-Version 4.1 characteristics are reviewed for comparison's sake. Special attention is paid to the communications protocols which perform the bulk of the work in any network operating system. Remote access and interoperability with other network operating systems such as Windows are explored from both architectural and functional perspectives. Finally, issues and options surrounding the migration from NetWare 3.12 to NetWare 4.1 are detailed.

This chapter provides the reader with an in-depth knowledge of the underlying architecture and protocols which deliver NetWare functionality. It is not intended to be a "how-to" guide of installation and configuration and will not list particular NetWare commands required to accomplish certain tasks. Suggestions for references on these subjects are included in sections on installation and configuration in the Featured References.

■ LEGACY NETWARE

Overall Architecture

Figure 11-1 illustrates many of the key features of a typical single-server NetWare architecture.

Clients   NetWare client software is available for the following types of client workstation:

- DOS.
- Windows.

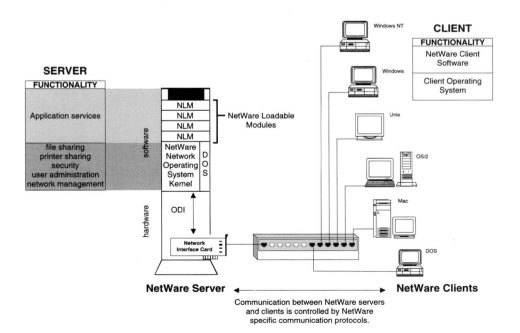

Figure 11-1   Generalized Overall NetWare Architecture

- Windows NT (NetWare Version 4.1).

- Unix.

- OS/2.

- Macintosh.

The native operating system of a particular client workstation serves as the foundation for the operating system–specific version of the NetWare client software. A more detailed explanation of the interaction between NetWare client software and a DOS workstation will provide insight into how NetWare client software interacts with workstation operating systems in general.

Up through NetWare Version 3.11, the NetWare client software for DOS clients was usually referred to as the **NetWare Shell,** or NETx, in reference to NETx.COM which was the primary file involved in creating the NetWare DOS client shell. The "x" refers to the version of DOS with which the NetWare client software is used. The shell executes as a client terminate and stay resident program (TSR) and acts as a redirector of commands generated by application programs and the keyboard by intercepting them and deciding whether they should be handled by the NetWare network operating system or passed to the client's local DOS operating system. The shell was really an independent, monolithic operating system of its own, passing only those commands and requests it deemed appropriate to the local operating system. The NETx shell builds its own tables to keep track of the location of network-attached resources rather than using DOS tables. Figure 11-2 illustrates the relationship between the NetWare shell and DOS in a DOS-based client.

Servers   Various NetWare client platforms communicate with the NetWare servers via predetermined communication protocols supported or understood by both the NetWare clients and servers. Open data-link interface (ODI), reviewed in Chapter 8, allows network interface cards in NetWare servers to support multiple transport protocols, such as IPX/SPX and TCP/IP, simultaneously. In the case of Ethernet net-

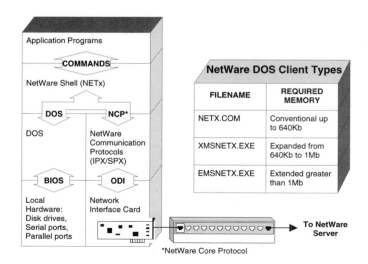

Figure 11-2   The NetWare Shell and DOS Client

work interface cards, ODI also allows the NICs to simultaneously support multiple Ethernet frame types such as Ethernet 802.3, Ethernet 802.2, Ethernet II, and Ethernet SNAP. NetWare communication protocols are described later in detail in a dedicated section.

The NetWare server is able to offer clients such services as file and printer sharing thanks to the NetWare network operating system engine, or kernel. The NetWare kernel resides in a section of the server's disk drive known as the **NetWare partition.** This is the only portion of the disk the NetWare kernel is physically able to access. However, to install the NetWare server software in the first place, the native operating system of the server must be present in its own disk partition. The example in Figure 11-1 shows a **DOS partition,** but the native operating system could have just as easily been Unix or Windows NT.

NetWare Loadable Modules (NLMs)   Additional functionality can be added to the basic NetWare kernel through the use of **NetWare loadable modules,** or **NLMs.** NLMs are programs specially written to interact with and add functionality to the NetWare kernel. Because the specification for program interaction with the NetWare kernel is available to third-party software developers, a wide variety of NetWare NLMs are available. These NLMs fall into three major categories:

1. **Operating system enhancements:**   The NetWare kernel itself needs additional operating system features such as virus protection, network interface card drivers, and disk drivers to be fully operational and ready to interact with client workstations. This additional operating system functionality can be added in a platform-specific fashion, thanks to the use of NLMs.

2. **Application programs:**   Application programs which actually execute on the NetWare server, rather than being transferred to the client for execution, are written in the form of NLMs. As a result, they are loaded into memory only as called for and dynamically removed from memory following program execution, allowing the memory to be reused by other applications.

3. **Relational Database Management Systems:**   Perhaps considered a subcategory of application programs, an entire RDBMS engine can be loaded in the form of an NLM, allowing a NetWare server to act as a database server.

Bindery Services   The primary job of the server network operating system is to fulfill requests for services as received from NetWare clients. To fulfill such requests, the network operating system must have some method to keep track of individual users, user groups, file and directory access rights, print queues and printers, and other available resources and services clients may request. In a NetWare 3.12 environment, this type of security and network resource information is stored in **bindery files.**

All requests for services are first verified for authorization against the information in the bindery files. User logins and password verification are also handled by the bindery. In a multiple server environment, servers advertise available services via a specialized communication protocol known as the service advertising protocol, or SAP, which is described in detail in the communication protocol section of this chapter. Bindery services on a particular server can receive SAP broadcasts and update bindery files with the latest information regarding available services on other reachable servers.

NetWare's bindery service is organized around the relationship of three important concepts:

1. **Objects** can be thought of as the system to be controlled or managed. User groups, users, printers, print servers, print queues, and disk volumes can all be considered objects by bindery services.

2. **Properties** are associated with objects and those aspects of objects which can or must be controlled. Examples of properties include such things as login time restrictions, network address restrictions, e-mail address, print job configuration, file and directory access rights, or user group membership.

3. **Values** are associated with properties and, in turn, with objects. For example, a value of Monday through Friday, 8:00 a.m. to 5:00 pm., would be associated with the login time restriction property of a particular user or user group object.

The information related to these three important bindery services concepts are stored in three separate files linked by pointers on every NetWare server:

1. NET$OBJ.SYS contains object information.

2. NET$PROP.SYS contains property information.

3. NET$VAL.SYS contains value information

An important point to remember is that these bindery service files are associated with a single NetWare server. In multiple server environments, bindery files on each server must be established and maintained independently if users are to have access to multiple servers. This implies that when user information or other system resource information changes, these changes must be made to all associated servers to keep the bindery services of the overall server environment synchronized. This manual synchronization across multiple servers can be a management nightmare as the number of servers continues to grow. This dilemma was addressed in NetWare 4.1 with the introduction of NetWare directory services. Figure 11-3 summarizes some of the key points regarding NetWare bindery services.

Communications Protocols

All network communications between clients and servers, regardless of installed network operating system, depend on standardized communications protocols. Communications protocols represent the standardized delivery mechanisms for the actual requests and data flowing between clients and servers.

In a NetWare environment, the following communications protocols correspond directly to OSI model layers:

- **Internet packet exchange,** or **IPX,** which is the OSI network layer protocol.

- **Sequenced packet exchange,** or **SPX,** which is the OSI transport layer protocol.

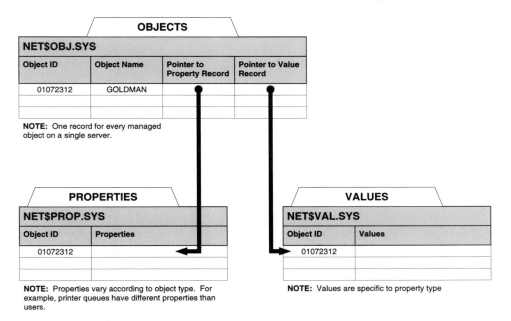

Figure 11-3   NetWare Bindery Services

Following are other service-specific communications protocols which don't necessarily correspond to a particular layer of the OSI model:

- **Routing information protocol (RIP).**

- **Service advertising protocol (SAP).**

- **NetWare core protocols (NCP).**

IPX   IPX, like most OSI network layer protocols, serves as a basic delivery mechanism for upper layer protocols such as SPX, RIP, SAP, and NCP. This delivery
mechanism is accomplished through encapsulation of upper layer protocols within
properly addressed IPX "envelopes." Network layer protocols are generally characterized as follows:

- **Connectionless**—Individual, fully addressed packets, or datagrams, are
free to negotiate their way through the network in search of their final destination.

- **Unreliable**—IPX does not require error checking and acknowledgment of
error-free receipt by the destination host.

The entire IPX packet is, in turn, encapsulated within a data-link layer frame,
which corresponds to the installed network interface card. For example, if the workstation in question has a token ring card, then the entire IPX packet will be inserted
into the data field of the Token Ring frame; if an Ethernet card is present, then the
encapsulation of the IPX packet will be into the data field of the designated type of
Ethernet frame. Figure 11-4 (page 394) illustrates the layout for an IPX packet and
encapsulation of upper layer protocols in the IPX data field.

The role of each field in the IPX packet layout is detailed in Figure 11-5 (page 394).

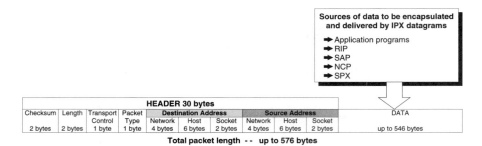

Figure 11-4 IPX Packet Layout (Network Layer)

IPX Packet Fields	Function/Importance
Checksum	Not used by IPX. No error-checking in IPX, hence its "unreliable" characterization. IPX depends on upper layer protocols such as SPX for error-checking and proper sequencing of messages and file transfers, which span multiple IPX packets.
Length	Length of the entire IPX packet in bytes.
Transport Control	Also known as a hop-counter or "time-to-live" timer. Ensures that free-floating datagrams do not meander infinitely around the network, occupying bandwidth. Every time an IPX packet is processed by a router, this counter is incremented by 1. When this field reaches 16, the packet is deleted to avoid further aimless wandering. This is one reason why IPX packets may never reach their intended destination.
Packet Type	As illustrated in Figure 11-4, the data field of an IPX packet may contain a variety of upper layer protocols, each of which needs to be processed in its own unique way. By identifying the embedded upper layer protocol in the header's packet type field, the upper layer protocols can be properly processed.
Addressing	Both source and destination addresses are composed of three segments: • Network address. • Host (computer) address. • Socket address. NetWare uses a hierarchical addressing scheme in which multiple hosts can be independently addressed within multiple networks. Since many processes or applications can be running on a given host, a socket address identifies to which specific process the IPX datagram is to be delivered. IPX supports up to 50 sockets per computer. Upper layer protocols such as NCP, SAP, RIP, and NetBIOS, to which IPX transfers data frequently via encapsulation, have reserved socket numbers.
Data	As previously described and illustrated in Figure 11-4, upper layer protocols are encapsulated within the data field.

Figure 11-5 IPX Field Descriptions and Explanations

SPX   SPX is the upper layer protocol which, among other things, makes up for IPX's shortcomings; that is, unlike IPX, the key characteristics of SPX are as follows:

- **Connection-oriented**—Specific paths known as **virtual circuits** are explored and determined before the first packet is sent. Once the virtual circuit is established directly from the source host or node to destination node, all packets bound for that address follow each other in sequence down the same physical path. Virtual circuits are especially important when the source host and destination host reside on different networks.

- **Reliable**—SPX requires error-checking and acknowledgment to ensure reliable receipt of transmitted packets. Because transfer of a single file may be broken up across multiple IPX packets, SPX adds sequence numbers to ensure that all pieces are received and reconstructed in the proper order. To ensure that packets are not lost accidentally because hosts or routers suffer from buffer overflow, SPX also has mechanisms to institute flow control.

SPX accomplishes this functionality by the fields contained with a 12-byte header. Figure 11-6 illustrates an SPX packet, including the fields in the SPX header, and shows the relationship between SPX and IPX. As you can see, SPX is encapsulated within IPX and therefore depends on IPX for delivery to the destination workstation via the local network interface card.

The role of each field in the SPX packet layout is detailed in Figure 11-7 (page 396).

RIP   Although routers are studied in detail in Chapter 14, it is necessary to understand a little bit about them to understand the function of NetWare's routing information protocol, or RIP.

Routers are specialized network processors which act as dedicated "direction-givers" in large networks composed of numerous linked LANs. Routers can receive

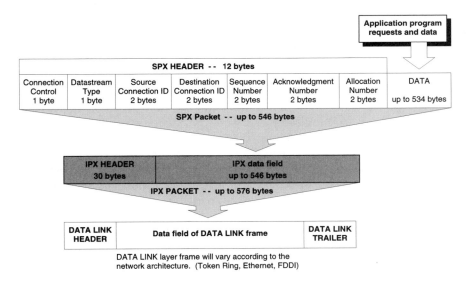

Figure 11-6   SPX Packet Layout and Encapsulation

SPX Packet Fields	Function/Importance
Connection Control	Different 1-byte flags inserted into this field assist with the overall flow control and reliability for which SPX is responsible. Examples include end-of-message flags and acknowledgment request flags.
Datastream Type	This 1-byte field allows upper layer protocols to offer hints as to the protocols or information contained within the SPX data field so that it might be processed more efficiently. This field is analogous to including an Attention: line on the outside of an envelope. It allows that envelope to be properly routed for processing without having to examine the contents (data) contained within the envelope.
Connection IDs	Source and destination connection IDs are used to identify communication sessions between two communicating processes. A connection ID is another layer in the hierarchical addressing scheme introduced in IPX. Just as multiple-socket IDs were possible for each host ID, multiple-connection IDs can be associated with each socket ID.
Sequence Number	As the name implies, this field is used to ensure the proper sequencing of packets in multipacket file transfers.
Acknowledgment Number	This field is incremented by the destination host as it receives sequenced packets. When the next packet is received, it will be error-checked and the acknowledgment will be sent to the source workstation with this number included.
Allocation Number	This number is used in implementing the flow control mechanism. It informs the source workstation of the number of buffers the destination workstation can afford to allocate to SPX connections.

Figure 11-7 SPX Field Descriptions and Explanations

IPX packets and, depending on the destination address of the workstation written in the IPX destination address field, forward that packet along the "best route" possible toward its ultimate destination. The "best route" at any time is based on information kept in a routing table. Obviously, especially in large networks, network conditions can change over time as reachable destinations come and go and "best routes" change according to variable network traffic conditions. It is therefore necessary to keep routing tables up to date and provide some standardized mechanism for routers to exchange current routing table information with each other.

NetWare's routing information protocol, or RIP, is a router-to-router protocol used to keep routers on a NetWare network synchronized and up to date. RIP information is delivered to routers via IPX packets. Figure 11-8 illustrates the fields of information included in a RIP packet.

As the figure shows, the RIP packet can request or report on multiple reachable networks in a single RIP packet. Alternatively stated, a RIP packet can transport multiple routing table entries in a single packet. Although there is only one operation field per RIP packet, the network number, number of router hops, and number of tick fields are repeated as often as necessary up to the length limit of the RIP packet. This group of three fields (network number, number of router hops, number of ticks), which represent a routing table entry for a single network, is sometimes called a tuple.

Figure 11-9 details the role of each field in the RIP packet layout.

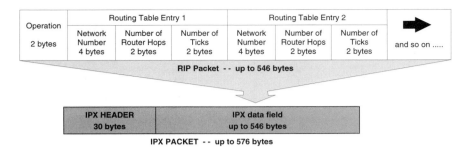

Figure 11-8   RIP Packet Layout and Encapsulation

In terms of generated network traffic, one of the undesirable qualities of RIP is that every router broadcasts its entire routing table every 60 seconds to all other routers to which it is directly attached. As you will see, NetWare 4.1 has dealt with this shortcoming. One very desirable quality of NetWare's RIP protocol is that routing table entries to particular networks can be updated and replaced if faster delivery routes are discovered based on the contents of the number of ticks field. The contents of routing tables and routing logic are reviewed in depth in the chapter on LAN-to-LAN connectivity (Chapter 14).

SAP   All network servers use service advertising protocol, or SAP, to advertise the services they provide to all other reachable networked servers. Servers broadcast this information every 60 seconds. Networked servers receiving SAP broadcasts store that information in their NetWare bindery for future reference. Local workstations requiring a particular service can query their local server, which consults its updated bindery, to provide the latest information on the closest availability of any

RIP Packet Fields	Function/Importance
Operation	This field indicates whether this RIP packet is a request for routing information on a particular network or a response supplying routing information. Request is indicated by a hexadecimal 01 and response is indicated by a hexadecimal 02. This operation field applies to the entire RIP packet.
Network Number	This is the assigned address number of the network for which routing information is being either requested or supplied.
Number of Router Hops	This field indicates how many routers the packet must pass through to reach the desired destination network. Each additional router represents one additional hop.
Number of Ticks	This field indicates the length of time it will take for a given packet to reach its desired destination network. In this case, time is measured in ticks, which are roughly equal to one-eighteenth of a second. This field was added because the route with the smallest number of router hops may not be the fastest, depending on the traffic characteristics of the circuits linking the routers.

Figure 11-9   RIP Field Descriptions and Explanations

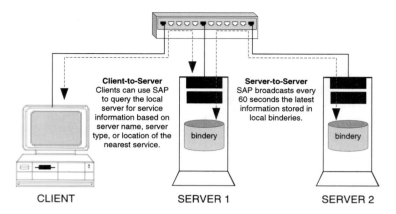

Figure 11-10   Uses of SAP in a NetWare Network

network service. IPX packets are the means of delivering SAP service advertising requests or responses throughout the network. Figure 11-10 provides a physical representation of the uses of SAP and Figure 11-11 illustrates the fields of information included in a SAP packet.

In a manner similar to RIP, information regarding multiple servers can be either requested or supplied within a single SAP packet. Although only one operation type field per SAP packet is permitted, the remaining six fields can be repeated up to seven times in a single SAP packet. The role of each field in the SAP packet layout is detailed in Figure 11-12.

NCP   NetWare core protocols (NCP) provide a standardized set of commands or messages which can be used to communicate requests and responses for services between clients and servers. As Figure 11-2 illustrated, when the NETx shell determines that a request from an application program should be directed over the network to the server, it encapsulates that message in an NCP packet, which in turn, is encapsulated within an IPX packet for delivery. NCP fulfills a role for NetWare networks very similar to that of NetBIOS for DOS-based LANs, extending the client workstation's operating system capabilities onto the network. Figure 11-13 illustrates the packet layout and encapsulation of an NCP packet, and Figure 11-14 (page 400) describes and explains the fields within the NCP packet.

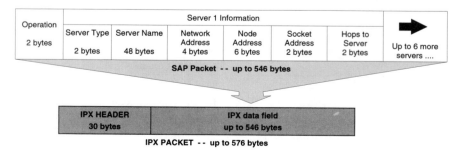

Figure 11-11   SAP Packet Layout and Encapsulation

SAP Packet Fields	Function/Importance
Operation Type	This field defines whether this SAP packet contains a request for service information or a broadcast of existing or changed information. Only one operation type is allowed for each SAP packet.
Server Type	This field identifies the particular type of service offered by a server. One server can offer multiple services. The valid service types are defined by Novell and identified by unique hexadecimal values in this field. Following are a few of the defined service types and their hex values:

Service Type	Hex Value
File server	4
Job server	5
Gateway	6
Print server	7
Archive server	9
SNA gateway	21
Remote bridge server	24
TCP/IP gateway	27
NetWare access server	98

SAP Packet Fields	Function/Importance
Server Name	This field identifies the server or host offering the type of service identified in the service type field.
Network Address	This is the address of the network on which the server resides.
Node Address	This is the address of the server itself.
Socket Address	This is the socket address on this particular server, to which requests for this particular type of service must be addressed.
Hops to Server	This field indicates how far from the local server this particular service is located. This field is used on queries from workstations that desire the nearest available service of a particular type.

Figure 11-12   SAP Field Descriptions and Explanations

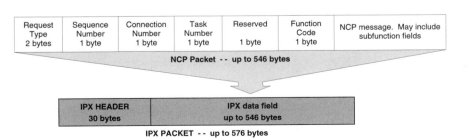

Figure 11-13   NCP Packet Layout and Encapsulation

NCP Packet Fields	Function/Importance
Request Type	This field indicates the general category of NCP communication contained within this packet, as distinguished by different hexadecimal values. Among the possible types are

Request Type	Hex Value	
Create a service connection	1111	Created at login time
Service request from workstation	2222	
Service response from server	3333	
Terminate a service connection	5555	Performed at logout time
Busy message	9999	

NCP Packet Fields	Function/Importance
Sequence Number	This field is incremented for each request sent from a particular workstation. The server uses this same number in its response so that the client knows which request is being responded to.
Connection Number	This number is associated with the connection established when the user first logged into the server. It is used along with the sequence and task numbers to uniquely identify requests and associated responses.
Task Number	This number identifies which particular program on a workstation issued the request for services.
Reserved	
Function Code	This field indicates which of the over 100 standard NCP messages or commands is being executed or requested in this packet. Entries are indicated by hexadecimal numbers representing requested services. An extended listing of subfunctions will always insert 16 hex in this field and then list the desired subfunction later in the NCP message packet. Following are some possible functions:

Function	Hex Value
Get file size	40
Close a file	42
Delete a file	44
Rename a file	45
Open a file	4C
Create a file	4D
Get a directory entry	1F

NCP Packet Fields	Function/Importance
NCP Message	This field contains additional information transferred between clients and servers, including possible subfunction hex codes.

Figure 11-14 NCP Field Descriptions and Explanations

■ NETWARE 4.1

Managerial
Perspective

OVERALL ARCHITECTURE

Having covered traditional aspects of NetWare in the previous section, we next explore the unique architectural and functional changes NetWare 4.1 introduced. Whenever new technology of any type is introduced, it is important to evaluate that technology with a somewhat skeptical, business-oriented perspective. As we explore the new features of NetWare 4.1, therefore, we should keep a few key questions in mind:

1. What functional features are being newly delivered?

2. What are the benefits of these features?

3. Do these features offer potential cost savings?

4. Are migration or installation issues involved, to take advantage of these new features, or are they implemented transparently to the user?

NetWare Directory Services   **NetWare directory services,** or **NDS,** is arguably the most significant new feature of NetWare 4.1. With the release of NetWare 4.11, NDS is now known as Novell Directory Services. NDS is a single logical database containing information about all network-attached resources which replaces the independently maintained, server-specific bindery files. The term "single logical database" is used because portions of the NDS database may be physically distributed on different servers throughout the network. This section familiarizes the user with the key features of NDS, and is not meant as a tutorial on how to design an NDS database structure.

From a user perspective, the single-database design allows a single user login for access to all authorized network-attached resources rather than separate logins for each server. In other words, with NetWare 4.1, a user really logs into the NDS database from any network-attached server whereas in previous NetWare versions, the user would log in multiple times into particular servers. From a management perspective, NDS allows administrative tasks to be performed only once rather than numerous times on multiple servers as was required with bindery-based administration. Figure 11-15 summarizes some of the differences between the bindery and NDS.

One thing NDS and bindery services have in common is the organization of

	Bindery	NDS
Logical Structure	Flat	Hierarchical
Users/Groups	Single server	Networkwide
Volumes	Single server	Global objects
Login	Password for each server	Systemwide login with single password
Location	Single server	Distributed

Figure 11-15   Bindery versus NDS

network resources by objects, properties, and values. The following are examples of network resources:

- Users or user groups.
- File servers.
- Volumes on a file server.
- Printers.
- Printer queues.
- Print servers.
- NetWare servers.
- Communications servers.
- Database servers.

Categories of information which can be used to describe or control objects are referred to as properties. The following are some of the properties which can, but aren't required to, apply to user objects:

- Identification.
- Environment.
- Login restrictions.
- Login time restrictions.
- Network address restrictions.
- Mailbox.
- Foreign e-mail address.
- Intruder lockout.
- Group memberships.
- Rights to files/directories.
- Postal address.
- Login script.
- Print job configuration.

Entries for a specific object (user) for any of these properties are known as values.

NDS actually defines two types of objects. Network resources are considered **leaf objects** while organizational units such as companies, divisions, and departments are **container objects.** Container objects can be cascaded and can contain leaf objects. Leaf objects cannot be cascaded.

Because NDS is a **global directory service,** organizing and managing all networked resources over an entire enterprise, a method had to be found to organize this myriad of network resources in some logical fashion. As a result, the NDS database is organized **hierarchically,** like a tree. The hierarchical design of the NDS database is roughly equivalent to the hierarchical and geographical organization of the corporation in question. The tree hierarchy starts at the top with the **root** object. There is only one root object in an entire global NDS database. Branches off of the root object are represented by container objects. Container objects were added to NDS to allow leaf objects to be logically organized into container objects such as buildings, campuses, departments, or divisions. Figure 11-16 represents a sample NDS database including root, container, and leaf objects.

NDS STRUCTURES DO NOT HAVE TO MAP ORGANIZATIONAL STRUCTURES

Practical Advice and Information

One important thing to remember when developing the NDS structure is that the structure does not have to perfectly mirror the organizational structure of the corporation. Early adopters of NetWare 4 were overwhelmed trying to create massive NDS database structures designed to exactly match the proper placement of every employee in a corporate structure. The purpose of the NDS database structure is to logically organize network resources, including users, in a manner that optimizes both the ease of administration by the network manager and the ease of use by the network users. The NDS structure does not need to reflect reporting responsibilities or corporate hierarchy and does not need to be approved by the human resources department. The design of the NDS structure should be simply organized, with network resources logically grouped from a network management perspective.

Continuing with the metaphor of a tree to describe the overall hierarchical structure of the NDS database, utilities are provided within NetWare 4.1 to modify the structure as necessary. Entire branches of the tree, designated as **partitions,** and including all subordinate container objects and leaf objects, can be **pruned** (removed) from one point in the NDS structure and **grafted** to another branch. In fact, two entire trees can be merged into a single tree.

One of the key characteristics of the NDS database is its ability to **replicate,** or physically store, a given partition on multiple file servers. Replication implies that these multiple copies of the same NDS partition are kept synchronized. Replicating NDS partitions offers two primary benefits:

1. Fault tolerance is achieved by the availability of a second copy of the NDS partition if the file server on which the primary copy is stored fails.

2. In situations where portions of the enterprise network are linked over long distances by a wide area network, it is advantageous for user authentication at login to be able to access a replica of the NDS partition on the local side of the WAN link.

One final benefit to NDS' one-stop shopping for network resource information is that application programs such as e-mail are also able to use the same NDS databases. Although this may seem obvious from a commonsense standpoint, the fact is that most e-mail programs have their own separate databases of userIDs, passwords, and security restrictions which must be set for every user. These **integrated**

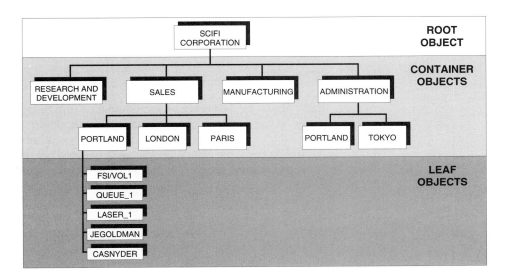

Figure 11-16   NDS Database Structure with Root, Container, and Leaf Objects

messaging services offered by NDS allow network managers to maintain a single database of user information for both network and e-mail services.

Client Changes and Upgrades   Unlike the DOS client software of previous NetWare versions, known as the NETx shell which acted as a replacement redirector, the DOS client software for NetWare 4.1 is referred to as the **requester.** The change in name is relatively minor compared to the architectural changes to the NetWare client software. Rather than remaining as a monolithic, standalone operating system, the requester has taken on a more flexible modular appearance. NetWare client functionality can be added or updated incrementally, thanks to the introduction of **virtual loadable modules,** or **VLMs.** Some VLMs depend on other VLMs, and must be loaded in a particular order, while other VLMs are totally optional.

In fact, the **NetWare DOS requester** actually works through DOS, having a VLM management program known as VLM.EXE interrupt DOS as appropriate to request services. The DOS requester uses DOS tables of network-attached resources rather than creating and maintaining its own, as was the case with the NETx shell. DOS serves as the primary redirector, passing only those requests for network-attached resources on to the NetWare DOS requester. The DOS requester also uses DOS file handlers to open files on network-attacked volumes. In this manner, the NetWare DOS requester combines with DOS to make a transparently interoperating client operating system. Numerous VLM modules are loaded separately onto the DOS client to offer the following types of combined functionality:

- IPX and NCP protocol stacks.
- TCP/IP and NCP protocol stacks.
- Security function calls.
- NDS services.
- Bindery-based services.
- NetWare protocol multiplexer for handling multiple protocol stacks.
- File management.
- DOS redirector.
- Printer redirection to network print queues.
- NETx shell emulation.

An upgrade to the NetWare DOS requester known as the **Client32 Requester** offers a wider variety of VLM-based services while using client memory resources more efficiently. DOS, Windows, and Windows 95 versions are based on a new 32-bit architecture known as **NetWare I/O Subsystem,** or **NIOS.** Figure 11-17 illustrates a conceptual view of the relationship between the NetWare DOS requester and DOS.

Functionality

Although printer services and file services have always been NetWare's traditional strengths, improvements have been made in these areas in NetWare 4.1. Additional improvements have been made to help NetWare 4.1 compete more effectively in the

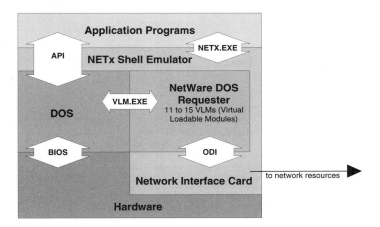

Figure 11-17   The NetWare DOS Requester

applications services arena with network operating systems such as Windows NT and Unix. In response to some well-publicized security holes in NetWare 3.11, security has also been beefed up in NetWare 4.1. Each of these feature upgrades is explained in more detail in the following sections.

Application Services   Until NetWare 4.1, the operating system or kernel portion of NetWare ran in the same general memory area or ring as the application programs loaded as NLMs. In this scenario, a misbehaving NLM could write into the operating systems memory space and crash the entire system. NetWare 4.1 introduces **ring memory protection,** which seeks to isolate and protect the operating system from potentially dangerous NLMs. The area reserved for the operating system is known as **Ring 0,** otherwise known as **domain** operating system **(OS)**. The area reserved for NLMs is known as **Ring 3** or **domain** operating system protected **(OSP)**. NLMs executing in Ring 3 access operating systems service in Ring 0 by issuing structured **interring gate calls,** thereby protecting the operating system from misbehaving NLMs overwriting its memory space.

Practical Advice and Information

Ring memory protection should not be confused with protected memory as implemented in Windows NT or Unix. First, some NLMs must still run in Ring 0 and, therefore, still have the potential to crash the operating system. Second, if an NLM running in Ring 3 crashes, it has the potential to crash all other NLMs running in Ring 3. True protected memory means that each application runs in its own protected memory space rather than in a shared protected memory ring.

In Sharper Focus

NETWARE 4.1 SMP

High-powered application servers require network operating systems which can support multiple CPUs, otherwise known as **symmetrical multiprocessing,** or **SMP.** Since the original NetWare 4.1 did not have SMP capability, some way needed to be found to support SMP while still ensuring backward compatibility with all existing NLMs. This was done by having **NetWare 4.1 SMP** load a second operating system kernel, known as the **SMP kernel,** which works cooperatively with the first or native operating system kernel. The native kernel works on processor 1 while the SMP

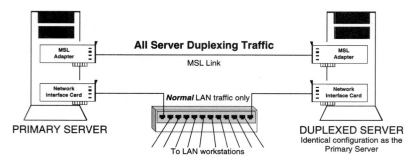

Figure 11-18   Server Duplexing with NetWare 4.1 SFT III

kernel works on processors 2 through 4. Since the SMP kernel has to be able to take full advantage of multiple processors, it must also support multithreading, although the native kernel does not. SMP capability is included in NetWare 4.11.

The two kernels need to cooperate when data must be shared between threads executing on the two kernels. If data needed by a thread executing in the SMP kernel belongs to code executing in the native kernel, that thread must be migrated from the SMP kernel to the native kernel to retrieve the required data. Once the required data have been retrieved, the thread is returned to the SMP kernel for further processing on CPUs 2 through 4.

Fault Tolerance   Fault tolerance is another characteristic which is increasingly important to corporate application services. Such fault-tolerance features as disk duplexing and disk mirroring were reviewed in Chapter 5, but **NetWare 4.1 SFT III** offers a unique fault-tolerant feature known as **server duplexing.** Not only are the contents of the disks synchronized, but also the contents of the servers' memory and CPUs. In case of the failure of the primary server, the duplexed server takes over transparently.

The synchronization of the servers is accomplished through a dedicated link known as the **mirrored server link** (MSL). The use of the dedicated MSL link and dedicated MSL adapters prevents the server duplexing from adversely effecting LAN traffic. The largest cost of such an arrangement is obviously the second identical duplexed server. However, the fact remains that this feature offers a level of fault tolerance not achieved by other network operating systems. Figure 11-18 illustrates server duplexing with NetWare 4.1 SFT III.

File Services Upgrades   Several enhancements have been added to the files services offered by NetWare 4.1. **File compression** is incorporated into NetWare 4.1 and is controllable on a file-by-file basis. The file compression process is highly customizable with adjustable settings for how often compression takes place as well as minimum acceptable disk space gained by compression. Since the number of simultaneous file compressions, as well as compression time of day can be controlled to minimize system impact, this entire file compression process is transparent to the user both for file access time and CPU performance.

Disk block suballocation is a process aimed at optimizing the use of disk space for file storage. Disks in a NetWare environment are divided into **disk allocation blocks** which can range in size from 4 to 64 KB. In the past, when a file needed a portion of a disk allocation block to complete file storage, the remainder of the partially occupied disk allocation block could not be used by other files and was effectively wasted. By dividing all disk allocation blocks into 512-byte (0.5-KB) **suballocation blocks,** multiple files are allowed to occupy single disk allocation blocks and disk storage efficiency is maximized. Figure 11-19 illustrates how disk block suballocation can minimize wasted disk space.

Support of CD-ROMs has become increasingly transparent to the user in NetWare 4.1. CD-ROMs are mounted as just another disk volume and can be accessed like any other network-attached resource. NetWare 4.1 supports popular CD-ROM file systems such as ISO 9660, High Sierra (DOS), and HFS (Macintosh). Driver software included with NetWare 4.1 supports approximately 95% of all CD-ROM readers.

This transparent integration of CD-ROMs into the NetWare 4.1 file system has enabled the use of the **DynaText on-line help** system as the means of accessing all of the NetWare 4.1 manuals. In applications involving large sequential accesses such as reading manuals via CD-ROM, another NetWare 4.1 feature known as **read-ahead cache buffering** improves performance by reading ahead in the sequentially accessed file and caching that information in anticipation of the next request for information from the user. In the case of the DynaText help system, the read-ahead caching buffers the next few pages of a document, to avoid the delay of a physical disk seek to retrieve the next page the user wishes to read. It is important to note that read-ahead caching is likely to have a positive effect only on performance on large sequential accesses.

The improved support of access to optical drives includes access to optical storage devices such as optical jukeboxes. As a result, **data migration** features have been added to NetWare 4.1 to allow files to be automatically migrated and archived

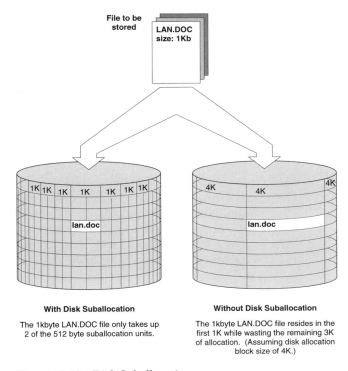

With Disk Suballocation	**Without Disk Suballocation**
The 1kbyte LAN.DOC file only takes up 2 of the 512 byte suballocation units.	The 1kbyte LAN.DOC file resides in the first 1K while wasting the remaining 3K of allocation. (Assuming disk allocation block size of 4K.)

Figure 11-19   Disk Suballocation

in a structured fashion to the archival storage media of choice such as optical drives. Which files get migrated and when are totally controlled by parameters the system manager sets.

Printer Services Upgrades   The print server program known as PSERVER.NLM has been improved to support up to 255 printers in addition to executing up to three times faster than older versions. Part of the reason for this improved performance is that printer services information is stored in the NetWare directory services database rather than in bindery files. Print queues can also be more flexibly managed in NetWare 4.1. In past versions of NetWare, the printer queues had to be stored as subdirectories in SYS:SYSTEM with sufficient disk space allocated to handle any print job. In NetWare 4.1, the location of the print queue subdirectories is up to the network manager and can be changed as necessary, should disk space issues warrant it.

Security   Several important security enhancements have been added to NetWare 4.1. Due to a well-publicized security hole in NetWare 3.x, which allowed impostors to gain supervisory privileges, **authentication** is perhaps the most important of the security innovations. Using a combination of private encryption keys and passwords, the VLM requester security agent on the client workstation and NDS file server combine to ensure that users are properly authenticated before being logged in. If even higher security is required, every packet transmitted from a particular client workstation can have a unique, encrypted digital signature attached which can be authenticated only by the server in a process known as **packet signing.** However, the increased security costs a performance price of 5 to 7% with valuable CPU cycles spent encrypting and decrypting digital signatures.

While authentication and packet signing ensure that only valid users are accessing system resources, an extensive **auditing system** monitors and reports on what those valid users are doing. The auditor acts independently of the supervisor in an effort to ensure a proper system of checks and balances in which no single person could remain undetected while performing potentially harmful acts. The auditing system separately monitors activity on both the file system, as defined by volumes, and the NetWare directory services database, as defined by container units. Figure 11-20 illustrates the organization and capabilities of the NetWare auditing system.

Communications Protocols

NetWare was originally designed when local area networks emphasized the term "local" in their architectures. Little consideration was given to the impact of NetWare communications protocols on the limited bandwidth, relatively expensive wide area network (WAN) links which connect multiple LANs. As a result, NetWare 4.1 introduced a number of new communications protocols in an effort to make more efficient use of WAN links.

Packet Bursts   Error detection and correction has always been important in data communications. Most error detection/correction schemes depend on the sending workstations waiting for acknowledgment from the receiving station of the error-free receipt of a packet of data before it is allowed to send the next packet of data. This is sometimes referred to as a stop-and-wait protocol.

In large file transfers or other high-volume data broadcasts, a considerable

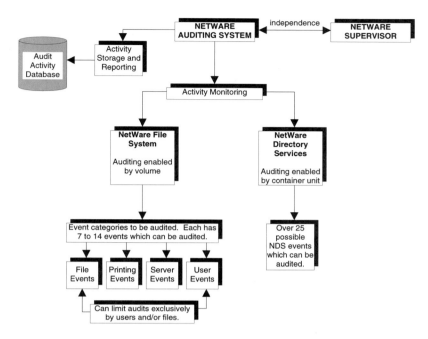

Figure 11-20   Organization of the NetWare Auditing System

amount of time is wasted waiting for acknowledgments, and a nontrivial amount of bandwidth is consumed by the multitudes of acknowledgments. To alleviate both of these situations, NetWare 4.1 introduced **packet bursts,** otherwise known as **burst mode IPX.** This capability is built into the NetWare kernel and allows the NetWare 4.1 VLM requester on the clients and the NetWare 4.1 kernel on the servers to negotiate how many packets can be transmitted before an acknowledgment is required; 10 to 20 packets before acknowledgment is not uncommon. By allowing multiple packets to be transmitted before requiring acknowledgment, NetWare 4.1 can significantly reduce idle waiting time as well as remove a significant number of acknowledgments from the data traffic stream, leading to greater overall transmission efficiency. Burst mode IPX has a positive impact on both local area and wide area traffic.

LIP   Large Internet packets or **LIP** applies only to NetWare 4.1 LANs linked to each other via a wide area network through routers. LIP, also known as **large packet IPX,** allows NetWare clients to negotiate with the routers as to the size of the IPX frame. From the NetWare client's perspective, the larger the IPX frame, the larger the IPX frame's data field, and the greater the amount of data that the client can cram into a single IPX frame. This philosophy leads to greater efficiency as long as the packet doesn't become too long, thereby introducing data errors which would necessitate retransmission of the large packet and negating the previous gains in efficiency. Recall that IPX frames are normally limited to 576 bytes.

One potential drawback of LIP is that it must be supported by the installed routers. Although Novell's software-only router, known as **multiprotocol router (MPR),** supports LIP, there is no guarantee that large router vendors such as Cisco or Bay Networks (formerly Wellfleet) will support such a NOS–specific protocol.

NLSP   NetWare link services protocol, or **NLSP,** is included in NetWare 4.1 in an effort to overcome the inefficiencies introduced by RIP. When dealing strictly with local area networks and their megabit-per-second bandwidths, protocols such as RIP and SAP which broadcast every 60 seconds are really nothing more than a slight nuisance. However, when expensive, limited-bandwidth WAN links are involved, chatty protocols such as RIP and SAP become intolerable.

To be specific, the major problem with RIP is that all Novell file servers broadcast their entire routing table every 60 seconds, whether or not anything has changed since the last broadcast. In contrast, NLSP broadcasts only as changes occur, or every 2 hours at a minimum. Real-world implementations of NLSP have reported reductions of 15 to 20 times (not percent) in WAN traffic, with Novell claiming up to 40-fold decreases in router-to-router traffic as possible. Obviously, these data traffic reductions are possible only if communicating routers both support NLSP. Again, Novell's MPR currently supports NLSP, but other vendor's routers need to be carefully reviewed.

Another limitation of RIP was its maximum of 16 hops before the RIP packet was discarded. This 16-hop limit effectively limited the physical size of the internetwork linking NetWare LANs. NLSP has also addressed this shortcoming by increasing the maximum hop count to 128. NLSP is interoperable or backward compatible with RIP, allowing gradual migration by network segment to the more efficient NLSP. This feature is especially important to large internetworks typically manned by small networking staffs.

NLSP is known as a link-state routing protocol whereas RIP is a distance vector routing protocol. Although the full differentiation between these two categories of routing protocols is explored later in Chapter 14, suffice to say at this point that link-state protocols offer more efficient updates of routing tables and more intelligent routing directions recommendations for data packets than distance vector protocols.

To eliminate the every-60-second broadcast of SAP packets, an associated feature of advanced IPX known as **SAP filtering** ensures that SAP broadcasts are synchronized to take place only with NLSP updates.

TCP/IP   As introduced in Chapter 1, transmission control protocol/internet protocol (TCP/IP) is the protocol of choice for internetworking a variety of LANs together over wide area network links. As interoperability with other network operating systems over internetworks has become more important to NetWare customers, NetWare has been forced to support TCP/IP in conjunction with or as a replacement for its own communication protocols: IPX/SPX.

NetWare/IP Version 2.1 is currently included with NetWare 4.1, and layers NetWare core protocols (NCP) over TCP/IP. NetWare/IP can be implemented in a variety of ways, as illustrated in Figure 11-21.

As the figure shows, NetWare/IP clients can support IP, IPX, or both as their network communications protocols. Depending on the protocols supported by internetwork routers, NetWare/IP servers may support both IP and IPX, or just IP. In the case of a full IP-only implementation on clients and servers, Novell claims NetWare IP experiences about an 8% decrease in performance compared with NetWare 4.1 using IPX.

NetWare/IP allows its TCP/IP stack to be swapped with other commercially available TCP/IP products at the users' discretion. Novell's LAN Workplace TCP/IP protocol stack is included with NetWare/IP, but Chameleon TCP/IP from NetManage, Inc., and Microsoft's Windows 95 TCP/IP protocol stacks also work with NetWare IP.

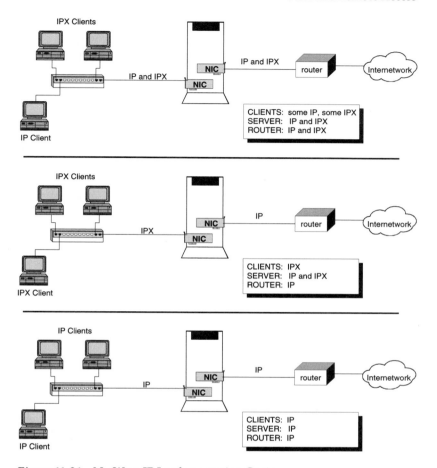

Figure 11-21   NetWare IP Implementation Options

■ NETWARE REMOTE ACCESS

As telecommuting and an increasingly mobile workforce have become more commonplace, network operating system architectures have had to adjust to these business-level requirements. LAN remote access solutions are explored in depth in Chapter 15, but NetWare's current approach to remote access is briefly discussed here. NetWare currently offers or supports three distinct product categories that cater to the remote-access needs of NetWare clients:

- NetWare Connect.
- Mobile NetWare.
- AT&T NetWare Connect Services.

NetWare Connect

NetWare Connect is NetWare's software-only remote-access server solution that provides both dial-in and dial-out capabilities for up to 128 simultaneous users.

While the server portion of NetWare Connect runs as an NLM, client versions are available for DOS, Windows, Mac, and OS/2 client workstations. Remote access implies that the same functionality is available to a dialed-in client as to a locally attached client. NetWare Connect allows the establishment and support of modem pools, which preclude the need for every client workstation to have a directly attached modem and phone line. Following are some of the key operational features and advantages of NetWare Connect:

- *Installation:* Autodetection of modems provides easy installation. Ordinarily, linking modems and communications software can be a tedious chore, requiring the correct modem set-up string of Hayes AT commands unique to a particular modem.

- *Management:* Multiple NetWare Connect servers can be managed from a single console. In addition, the auditing software provided tracks system statistics such as users, port usage, line conditions, call duration, and modem speed. NetWare Connect is integrated with NDS, thereby allowing network managers to control and assign both remote and local user access rights from a single location.

- *Security:* Since the passwords between the remote clients and local server must traverse public phone networks, the passwords are encrypted.

- *Supported Protocols:* To support the goal of remote access to grant remote clients the same functionality as local clients, specialized protocols are required to encapsulate upper layer protocols such as IPX/SPX and NCP and deliver them over the serial WAN links between remote clients and local servers. In other words, in a totally local setting, upper layer protocols are encapsulated in data link layer protocol frames such as Ethernet or Token Ring, depending on the installed network interface card. In the case of WAN-attached remote access clients, that data-link layer protocol is either **point-to-point protocol (PPP)** or **serial line internet protocol (SLIP),** both members of the TCP/IP family more correctly referred to as the internet suite of protocols. NetWare Connect also supports packet bursting, which allows more efficient use of potentially expensive WAN links while improving overall performance.

- *Usage Analysis:* An add-on product known as **ConnectView** allows network managers to analyze usage trends to spot possible abuse or prepare reports for cost analysis or chargeback purposes.

- *Supported WAN Services:* In addition to normal phone service, otherwise known as plain old telephone service (POTS) or public switched telephone network (PSTN), NetWare Connect also supports integrated services digital network (ISDN) which can deliver up to 144 Kbps of digital bandwidth over long distances.

NetWare Mobile

To meet the information needs of a branch of remote computing sometimes referred to as **nomadic computing,** Novell combined the functionality of NetWare Connect with a new communications protocol known as **mobile IPX,** which supports remote-access clients that must frequently change locations. NetWare Mobile consists of a client VLM portion and a server NLM portion. Interestingly, the remote-access functionality offered by NetWare Connect can be replaced by other remote-access communications packages, thanks to the modular design of Net-Ware Mobile.

The key functional characteristic NetWare Mobile attempts to deliver to mobile computer users is the illusion of access to full network functionality whether or not they are physically linked to their home network. To be more specific, NetWare mobile delivers the following features:

- **Automatic resynchronization** of data on return to the office or when dialed in to the headquarters file servers.

- **Quick synchronization** allowing only the changed portions of files to be transmitted during file resynchronization.

- **Password authentication** still enforced on laptop computers as if they were attached to the file server, to prevent unauthorized access. Password encryption is supported with overall security still managed by NDS.

- **Location managers** to detect the closest network-attached resources such as printers for nomadic computer users that may be unaware of local network resources.

- **Deferred printing** allowing requests for document printing to be queued within the laptop until it is linked back to the network with access to a printer.

AT&T NetWare Connect Services

In partnership with AT&T, Novell has launched **AT&T NetWare Connect Services (ANCS).** ANCS is a network of access servers running NetWare Connect remote-access software and offering support for both IP and IPX network layer protocols. NetWare NDS servers provide networkwide directory and security services. Plans call for the ANCS network to be linked via NDS to similar networks offered by other telecommunications service providers. In addition, applications servers running Lotus Notes groupware software will offer application-level connectivity between remote clients.

Some businesses currently running NetWare 4.1 are interested in the possibility of linking remote sites or remote users via ANCS for the following reasons:

- They would no longer have to maintain and upgrade private wide area networks.

- In theory, ANCS should be able to offer tighter security than the internet.

One potential hurdle to widespread intercarrier use of ANCS is that, unlike the Internet where all IP addresses have been controlled from a single international organization, the NetWare community has no such address coordination. For a business to use ANCS, its NetWare address must be unique among all ANCS users worldwide.

Figure 11-22 (page 414) illustrates the variety of NetWare's remote access solutions.

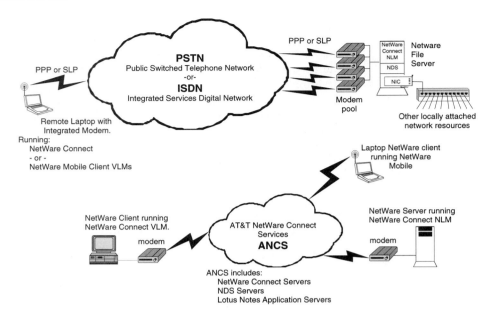

Figure 11-22   NetWare's Remote Access Solutions

■ NETWARE INTEROPERABILITY

Because of increased demands to be able to share information more quickly and easily within a company, as well as the increased number of corporate mergers and acquisitions, interoperability between different types of network operating systems has become an increasingly important functional characteristic. Interoperability can be separated into at least three levels:

- **Client-to-server interoperability** allows various client platforms such as Windows NT, Windows, DOS, Mac, and OS/2 to function fully as directly connected NetWare client workstations. Client-to-server interoperability is determined strictly by the availability of NetWare client software for the client workstation operating system in question. In this case, the servers are strictly NetWare servers.

- **Server-to-server file system interoperability** allows servers of different network operating systems and their respective clients to share each other's files. Server-to-server interoperability is not automatically two-way. For example, one interoperability product may be required to allow server A to share server B's file system, while a distinct product may be required to allow server B to share server A's file system.

- **Server-to-server directory system interoperability** allows two different network operating systems to share and synchronize their respective directory systems. As with the server-to-server file system interoperability, two separate products may be required to ensure two-way directory systems interoperability.

Client-to-Server Interoperability

As previously stated, NetWare client software is available for Windows NT, Windows, DOS, Mac, and OS/2. NDS client support is now integrated into Windows 95. Unix clients can access NetWare file servers via server-to-server file system interoperability software such as NetWare NFS or UnixWare.

Server-to-Server File System Interoperability

TCP/IP is the communications protocol stack most often associated with Unix, and NetWare/IP offers interoperability between TCP/IP and NetWare's native communication protocols, IPX/SPX. However, there are other levels of Unix/NetWare interoperability besides communications protocols. **Network file system (NFS)** is the file system most often associated with Unix. To offer interoperability between NFS and NetWare 's native file system, Novell offers the following additional products:

- **NetWare NFS** allows Unix systems to access NetWare file servers as if they were native NFS servers. NetWare NFS is actually a group of NLMs which run on a NetWare server. This software allows Unix workstations to access NetWare servers via TCP/IP, without requiring any software changes to the Unix clients.

- **NetWare NFS Gateway** allows NetWare users to access NFS file systems on Unix servers as if they were NetWare file servers. The gateway software is available for DOS, OS/2, or Macintosh computers.

- **UnixWare** is a full implementation of NetWare which runs over Unix. The advantage of such an implementation is that the inherent capabilities of Unix such as symmetrical multiprocessing are immediately available. UnixWare clients can access NetWare servers via IPX without any additional client software.

NetWare to Windows NT server-to-server file system interoperability is not nearly as open as Unix to NetWare. Windows NT server software includes interoperability to NetWare servers. Once installed, the software is able to automatically find and offer services to reachable NetWare file servers. Files, directories, and print queues attached to NetWare file servers are available to both the NT servers and clients attached to the NT servers. Unfortunately, as of the publication of the book, no such interoperability was available in the opposite direction, from a NetWare server to a Windows NT server.

Figure 11-23 (page 416) illustrates the options for server-to-server file system interoperability.

Server-to-Server Directory System Interoperability

Server-to-server directory system interoperability is also directional and dependent on distinct products. Windows NT's directory system is a domain-based naming service while NetWare's enterprisewide directory system is known as NetWare directory services.

Microsoft offers the **Microsoft Directory Services Manager for NetWare,** which

NetWare NFS

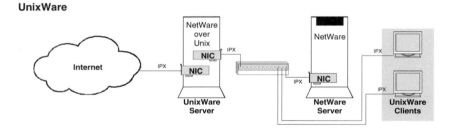

NetWare NFS Gateway

UnixWare

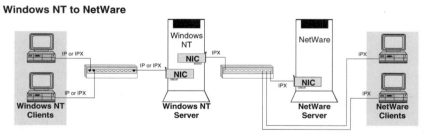

Windows NT to NetWare

NOTE: NT clients and server can see NetWare files but the reverse is NOT true.

Figure 11-23   Server-to-Server File System Interoperability

uses NT to centrally manage NetWare 2.x or 3.x servers that would normally need to be individually managed. Because NetWare 4.1 includes NDS, the Microsoft Directory Services Manager for NetWare cannot also manage NetWare 4.1 directory services.

Novell has introduced the **NDS Agent for NT,** which allows an NT server to act as an NDS client on either a NetWare NDS server or on Unix servers such as HP or SCO, running NetWare services over Unix. This software allows NT's domain-based naming service and NetWare's NetWare directory services to exchange and synchronize directory information. In this manner, the NDS agent for NT really acts as a gateway between the two directory systems.

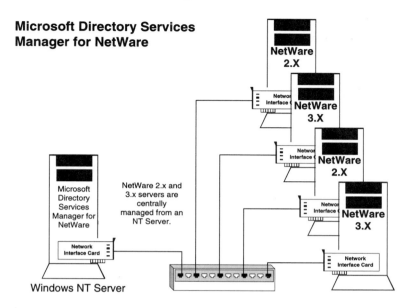

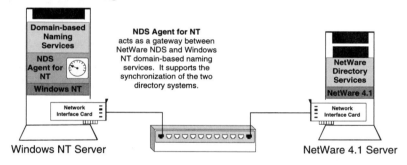

Figure 11-24   Server-to-Server Directory System Interoperability

Rather than synchronizing different directory services databases through custom-written platform specific gateways, support of open application program interfaces (APIs) for directory services allows transparent interoperability between all directory services supporting such an API. Unfortunately yet predictably, Microsoft and Novell differ in their opinions of what that open directory service API should be. Microsoft is promoting its own **Open Directory Services Interface (ODSI),** and Novell is promoting its **Net2000 Universal API,** explained further in the section on NetWare future directions.

Figure 11-24 illustrates the options for server-to-server directory system interoperability.

■ MIGRATION FROM NETWARE 3.12 TO NETWARE 4.1

Rather than present a how-to discussion of migrating from NetWare 3.12 to NetWare 4.1, this section discusses major options and issues to consider before planning such a migration. Migration from NetWare 3.12 to NetWare 4.1 involves the following four major steps:

1. Transfer the 3.12 bindery objects to corresponding directory services objects.
2. Upgrade the file server volumes to 4.1.
3. Install new utilities, NLMs, and drivers.
4. Install the new 4.1 server software.

Novell supplies programs to assist in the migration effort and has identified three alternative approaches using these supplied utilities. All three approaches assume that full system backups have been completed before the migration is started:

1. **In-place migration** uses the INSTALL program included in NetWare 4.1. After the NDS structure is built, NetWare 3.x bindery users and groups are moved to the NetWare 4.1 NDS database.

2. **Across-the-wire migration** is used to install NetWare 4.1 on a new computer rather than one currently running NetWare 3.x. In addition to the new computer and the existing NetWare 3.x server, a DOS client is also required so that the MIGRATE utility can be run between the two servers. The MIGRATE utility transfers NetWare 3.x bindery users and groups directly to the NetWare 4.1 NDS database and produces a migration report. Two other utilities are then run: MIGPRINT, to convert print queues and servers, and UIMPORT, to convert user login scripts to NDS format.

3. **Same-server migration** is used if the current 3.x server must be the 4.1 server but in-place migration is not an option. In this case, the DOS-based client becomes a temporary repository for 3.x system files while the 3.x server is reformatted and has 4.1 installed. Once 4.1 is installed and the volumes are configured for optimal performance, the 3.x information is migrated back to the new 4.1 server.

Bindery Synchronization and Emulation

NetWare 4.1 offers two distinct features which ease the transition from NetWare 3.12 to NetWare 4.1. In large multiserver environments, it is often not practical to migrate all 3.12 servers to NetWare 4.1 simultaneously. At the same time, it would be nice if migrating even a few servers to 4.1 made the multitude of 3.12 servers more manageable. **Bindery synchronization** allows a single NetWare 4.1 server to be automatically and transparently synchronized with up to 12 NetWare 2.x or 3.x servers. By running NETSYNC NLMs on both the NetWare 4.1 and NetWare 3.12 servers, all administration of the NetWare 3.12 servers, or **NetSync cluster,** is done through NDS on the NetWare 4.1 server, with changes automatically replicated to the binderies on the NetWare 3.12 servers. The only caveat is that when the NetSync cluster is created, the binderies of the 3.12 servers must be searched for duplicate object names, which must be eliminated. The entire NetSync cluster is seen as a single bindery context container unit within NDS, and no duplicate object names can exist within the same container unit. Figure 11-25 illustrates bindery synchronization.

While bindery synchronization allows NetWare 4.1 servers to manage NetWare

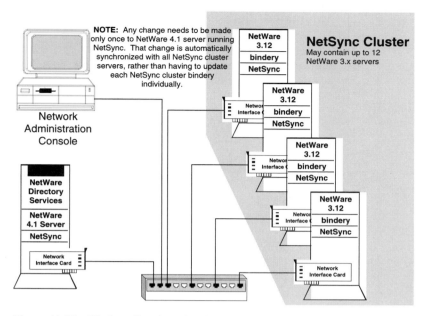

Figure 11-25   Bindery Synchronization

3.12 servers, **bindery emulation** allows newly migrated NetWare 4.1 servers to enjoy most of the benefits of NetWare 4.1 without fully converting NetWare 3.12 bindery objects into a NetWare 4.1 NDS database. Bindery emulation allows the use of NetWare 2.x or NetWare 3.x software, NLMs, and NETx shells but still offers many NetWare 4.1 benefits. NDS users are still able to access files and services managed by bindery emulation. In bindery emulation, NetWare 4.1 NetWare directory services emulates the flat, nonhierarchical structure of the bindery, thereby allowing transition time to develop the hierarchical NDS database structure. Figure 11-26 summarizes the availability of NetWare 4.1 features under bindery emulation.

Effect of Bindery Emulation on Availability of NetWare 4.1 Features	NetWare 4.1 Features
Available only in NDS	• NetWare directory services • Enhanced security
Available in Bindery Emulation But Enhanced by NDS	• Virtual loadable modules • Improved print services • Network auditor
Available in Both Bindery Emulation and NDS	• Improved memory usage • Suballocation block • File compression • Data migration • Better administative tools • LIP • Packet bursts • CD-ROM support • DynaText on-line documentation

Figure 11-26   Bindery Emulation

Automated Migration Tools

To ease the creation of the NetWare directory services database from NetWare 3.12 bindery objects, **automated migration tools** have been developed to allow the creation and manipulation of the NDS database structure in a safe, off-line environment, without the danger of corrupting live global NDS database structure information.

Two such tools are DS Standard from Preferred Systems, Inc. and RexxWare Migration Toolkit from SimWare. These tools are able to capture bindery-based server information from multiple servers and merge that information into an NDS database structure. Among their features are the following:

- The tools contains their own database, allowing work to proceed safely in an off-line environment with real data.

- Editing tools such as global search and replace make it easier to merge the information from numerous file servers' binderies.

- Log files are kept to record all changes.

- An assistant, wizard, or intelligent software agent can walk users through difficult procedures.

- Pruning and grafting of sections of the NDS tree can be done graphically with drag-and-drop functionality.

- Similar objects, such as multiple printers in a single area, can be automatically consolidated, or the software can prompt the user for advice.

- Preset parameters warn users if they are constructing an NDS structure which might adversely affect system performance or exceed a design limitation of NetWare 4.1.

Managerial Perspective

The combination of automated migration tools with bindery synchronization and bindery emulation provides a more realistic migration path for the transition from NetWare 3.12 to NetWare 4.1. Although the transition is still not without potential pitfalls, it is not the 100%, all-or-nothing, hot-cut, do-or-die migration nightmare many network managers feared.

▪ NETWARE FUTURE DIRECTION

Although strategic plans can change drastically at a moment's notice, two major initiatives define Novell's strategic direction for the foreseeable future. It is essential for network analysts and managers responsible for planning the strategic networking direction for a company or clients to understand the strategic direction of the major vendors on whom the company or clients depend.

Novell Embedded Systems Technology (NEST)

Novell talks about a view of the future known as **pervasive computing** in which not just computers but household and industrial appliances are all part of the same communications network, NetWare-based of course. By having vending machines, environmental controls, printers, and electric meters attached to networks, remote monitoring for the purposes of billing or inventory replacement is easy.

To attach this wide variety of devices to networks, all the devices must be made network-aware by embedding some type of network intelligence within them. Novell wants that embedded networking technology to be **Novell embedded systems technology (NEST).** This common networking communications architecture allows noncomputing devices to interact transparently with distributed information systems, providing centralized monitoring and control capabilities.

By embedding NEST within their devices, vendors can selectively enable the level of networking intelligence they desire. Since many of these devices already have proprietary operating systems and communications protocols running over a variety of CPU chips, NEST must be independent of hardware and operating system.

The NEST architecture, illustrated in Figure 11-27, consists of the following components:

- Portable operating system extension (POSE) is an API which provides links to all of the services NEST provides to the particular device. A version of this API must be specifically written to interface to a device's proprietary operating system.

- Application layer contains the programs which control the operation of the embedded system. This is where device-specific application control programs are installed. In addition, NEST supplies two printer control programs in this layer.

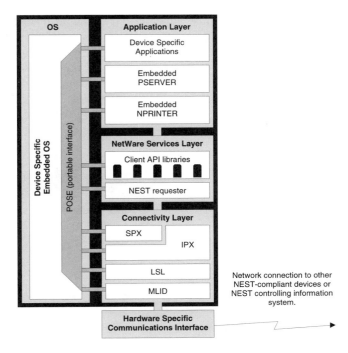

Figure 11-27 NetWare Embedded Systems Technology (NEST) Architecture

- NetWare services layer offers the typical NetWare services for the use of the device-specific application programs. These include file, print, directory (NDS), security, and communications services. The advantage to the developer of the device-specific application software is that all of these services are available through simple, standardized API commands. In the past, all of these services would have been included in the application program, adding substantially to the length and complexity of the application development project.

- Connectivity layer provides the communications protocols which deliver device-specific information. This layer is composed of familiar communications protocols such as IPX/SPX. Link support layer (LSL) and multilink interface driver (MLID) are part of the open data-link interface (ODI) specification detailed in Chapter 8.

Net2000 APIs

Another of Novell's strategic initiatives is to create an application development environment in which the support of multiple distributed applications standards and operating systems is rendered transparent through the use of a single set of high-level, network-aware APIs. This single interface to all networking services has been called the **Net2000** APIs. In essence, Novell is selling its core networking services to distributed application developers rather than competing directly in the distributed application market.

Through this single set of APIs, application developers are able to access file, print, security, directory, and communications services. From the application developers' perspective, the beauty of this approach is that only one version of an application needs to be developed. Hardware or operating system–specific versions are no longer necessary. Distributed applications will execute across a variety of client and server platforms.

By sending all calls for networking services through the Net2000 API, applications developers gain hardware independence but add a layer of processing and protocol translation which may lead to slight decreases in overall performance. The Net2000 APIs communicate through and consolidate a number of competing

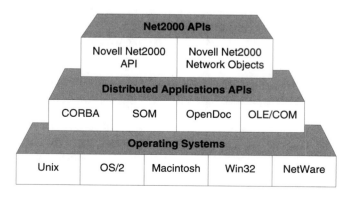

Figure 11-28   Net2000 APIs

and/or conflicting distributed application API standards. Among the distributed application development standards illustrated in Figure 11-28 are the following:

- Common object request broker architecture (CORBA) is the communications component of the object management architecture (OMA) which manages the communications of messages between objects in a distributed environment.

- Systems object model (SOM) is IBM's object architecture providing full implementation of the CORBA standard.

- OpenDoc is a compound document architecture that allows multiple data structures such as text, graphics, and sound to be embedded in a single document. This standard is supported by Apple, IBM, Novell, and Sun, among others.

- Object linking and embedding/common object model (OLE/COM) is Microsoft's standard for compound documents (OLE) combined with an updated version (COM) supported by Microsoft and DEC.

SUMMARY

With nearly 70% of the local area network operating system market, Novell's NetWare has undergone significant changes in the transition to NetWare 4.1. Most significant among the architectural changes is the introduction of a new directory service known as NetWare directory services (NDS), which is based on a single distributed, replicated, object-oriented database.

The single control point characteristics of NDS contrast sharply with previous versions of NetWare, which required bindery information on each server to be individually maintained. Print and file services have always been the functional strength of NetWare. Although some changes have been made in NetWare 4.1 to allow more effective support of applications services, other operating systems such as Windows NT, Unix, or even Novell's UnixWare are more efficient and more secure in their applications services support.

Security was significantly enhanced in Version 4.1, in an effort to overcome negative publicity generated from the revelation that users could spoof a NetWare 3.x server into thinking they had supervisor privileges. As internetworking continues to depend more on limited-bandwidth, expensive WAN links, NetWare has vastly improved communications protocols to make more efficient use of both LAN and WAN links.

As business conditions have forced more and more workers to take to the road, NetWare has responded by offering a variety of remote-access options including NetWare Connect, NetWare Mobile, and AT&T NetWare Connect Services.

Interoperability with other network operating systems is becoming increasingly important as enterprise networks must deliver transparent interoperability to users with different installed network operating systems. Although NetWare exhibits excellent interoperability with Unix servers, its interoperability with Windows NT servers is limited.

Looking to the future, NetWare envisions pervasive computing in which NetWare will not only be the dominant purveyor of network services for distributed applications but also will be embedded in every household and industrial appliance imaginable, all linked by NetWare-based networks.

KEY TERMS

across-the-wire migration, 418
ANCS, 413
AT&T NetWare Connect Services, 413
auditing system, 408
authentication, 408
automated migration tools, 420
automatic resynchronization, 413
bindery emulation, 419
bindery files, 391
bindery synchronization, 418
burst mode IPX, 409
Client32 Requester, 404
connection-oriented, 395
connectionless, 393
Connectview, 412
container objects, 402
data migration, 407
deferred printing, 413
disk allocation blocks, 406
disk block suballocation, 406
domain OS, 405
domain OSP, 405
DOS partition, 391
DynaText on-line help, 407
file compression, 406
global directory service, 402
grafted, 403
hierarchical, 402
in-place migration, 418
integrated messaging services, 404
interring gate calls, 405
Internet packet exchange, 392
IPX, 392
large internet packets, 409
large packet IPX, 409
leaf objects, 402
LIP, 409
location managers, 413

Microsoft Directory Services, Manager for NetWare, 415
mirrored server link, 406
mobile IPX, 412
MPR, 409
MSL, 406
multiprotocol router, 409
NCP, 393
NDS, 401
NDS agent for NT, 416
NEST, 421
NET2000 APIs, 422
Net2000 universal API, 417
NetSync cluster, 418
NetWare 4.1 SFT III, 406
NetWare 4.1 SMP, 405
NetWare Connect, 411
NetWare core protocol, 393
NetWare directory services, 401
NetWare DOS requester, 404
NetWare I/O subsystem, 404
NetWare link services protocol, 410
NetWare loadable module, 391
NetWare NFS, 415
NetWare NFS gateway, 415
NetWare partition, 391
NetWare shell, 390
NetWare/IP, 410
network file system, 415
NFS, 415
NIOS, 404
NLMs, 391
NLSP, 410
nomadic computing, 412
Novell embedded systems technology, 421
objects, 392
ODSI, 417
open directory services interface, 417

packet bursts, 409
packet signing, 408
partitions, 403
password authentication, 413
pervasive computing, 420
point-to-point protocol, 412
PPP, 412
properties, 392
pruned, 403
quick synchronization, 413
read-ahead cache buffering, 407
reliable, 395
replicate, 403
requester, 404
Ring 0, 405
Ring 3, 405
ring memory protection, 405
RIP, 393
root object, 402
routing information protocol, 393
same server migration, 418
SAP, 393
SAP filtering, 410
sequenced packet exchange, 392
serial line internet protocol, 412
server duplexing, 406
service advertising protocol, 393
SLIP, 412
SMP, 405
SMP kernel, 405
SPX, 392
suballocation blocks, 407
symmetrical multiprocessing, 405
UnixWare, 415
unreliable, 393
values, 392
virtual circuits, 395
virtual loadable modules, 404
VLMs, 404

REVIEW QUESTIONS

1. What is the NetWare shell and what is its relationship to DOS?
2. What is the purpose of the separate NetWare and DOS partitions on a NetWare server?
3. What is the functional difference between NLMs and VLMs?
4. What is the relationship between objects, properties, and values in a bindery?

5. What is a bindery?
6. What is the difference between IPX and SPX?
7. Why is IPX referred to as connectionless and unreliable?
8. Why is SPX referred to as connection-oriented and reliable?
9. What is the major function of RIP?
10. What is the major shortcoming of RIP?

11. What is the function of SAP?
12. What is the major shortcoming of SAP?
13. What is the function of NCP?
14. What are the major functional differences between NDS and bindery-based directory services?
15. What are the major architectural differences between NDS and bindery-based directory services?
16. What are the benefits of distribution of the NDS database?
17. What are the benefits of replication of the NDS database?
18. Differentiate both architecturally and functionally between the NETx shell and the NetWare DOS requester.
19. Describe NetWare 4.1's attempts at memory protection for the operating system kernel.
20. What are the shortcomings of this memory protection scheme?
21. Describe the implementation of SMP in NetWare SMP.
22. Why is the SMP implementation in NetWare 4.1 somewhat unique?
23. Evaluate the pros and cons of server duplexing.
24. What is the benefit of disk suballocation?
25. Differentiate between encryption, authentication, and packet signing.
26. What are the potential benefits and drawbacks of NetWare 4.1's auditing system?

27. What are the benefits of packet bursts?
28. What are the benefits of LIP?
29. Compare the functional characteristics and benefits of NLSP to those of RIP.
30. What functionality is delivered by NetWare Connect?
31. What additional benefits does NetWare Mobile offer beyond NetWare Connect?
32. Why would a company be interested in ANCS?
33. Compare the three levels of interoperability discussed in the text. Why is interoperability considered directional?
34. Compare the functionality, architecture, and installed software options of Unix/NetWare interoperability.
35. Compare the functionality, architecture, and installed software options of Windows NT/NetWare interoperability.
36. Compare the migration options suggested by Novell from NetWare 3.12 to NetWare 4.1.
37. Describe the differences between bindery synchronization and bindery emulation.
38. What are the primary benefits of automated migration tools?
39. What is pervasive computing?
40. What is NEST?
41. What is the significance of the Net2000 APIs?

ACTIVITIES

1. What are the hardware requirements for a NetWare 4.1 server?
2. How large must the NetWare and DOS partitions be on a NetWare 4.1 server?
3. Find examples of NLMs from sources other than Novell.
4. Draw an OSI diagram, properly placing all communications protocols associated with NetWare.
5. Find installations currently running NetWare 4.1, and interview networking personnel. Focus questioning on migration issues and perceived benefits. Include as much measurable, objective data in your report/presentation as possible.
6. Find and interview installations currently running NetWare 3.x. Focus questioning on migration planning, timetables, and perceived benefits. Why (or why not) is this installation migrating to NetWare 4.1?
7. Interview NetWare 4.1 network managers that have fully implemented NDS. Next, interview Windows NT 3.51 network managers that have

implemented NT's domain-based naming services. Focus questioning on the managers' perceptions of the benefits/shortcomings of each directory service. Analyze your results.

8. Research the implementation of SMP in either Windows NT or Unix. Compare and contrast this implementation with the SMP implementation in NetWare 4.1. Analyze your results.
9. Prepare a budget for server duplexing. How available are the mirrored server link adapters? Are they actually special adapters? How much do they cost? Name some vendors that sell them.
10. Prepare a payback period or breakeven analysis for investment in NetWare 4.1 SFT III, including hardware and software. State assumptions as to mean time between failures (MTBF) and lost revenue per hour.
11. Research the cost of hot sites and compare that cost and functionality to the cost of the NetWare 4.1 SFT implementation.
12. Interview a NetWare 4.1 network manager to investigate the use of the auditing system. What

features are being audited? What have the benefits been?

13. Find an installation of NetWare IP. Why was this product chosen? Report on the benefits, draw protocol stacks for both clients and servers, and draw a network architecture map highlighting the communication protocols.

14. Find an installation of NetWare Connect. Interview the people that use NetWare Connect remotely as well as the network manager. Report on functional benefits and drawbacks, and draw a detailed network architecture highlighting communications protocols.

15. Investigate pricing information and equipment requirements for ANCS as well as for any competing network services. Compare functionality and pricing.

16. Find a NetWare 4.1 installation supporting bindery synchronization and/or bindery emulation. Investigate the motivations for implementing this functionality as well as the perceived benefits.

17. Investigate which device vendors are supporting NEST. Contact these vendors and report on the timetable for releasing NEST-enabled devices. Pay particular attention to the networking aspects of these devices.

18. Research Novell's plans for and subsequent abandonment of the idea of a SUPERNOS. What caused the change in strategic direction? Provide your own analysis of the situation.

FEATURED REFERENCES

General References

Fisher, Sharon. NetWare 4.X: Overcoming a Slow Start. *Communications Week*, no. 566 (July 17, 1995), S6.

Installation and Configuration

Bierer, Doug. *Inside NetWare 4.1* (Indianapolis: New Riders Publishing, 1994).

Cases

Streeter, April. NetWare 4.1 Shines. *LAN Times*, 12; 13 (July 3, 1995), 29.

Migration

Berg, Al. Breaking Through the 250-User Barrier. *LAN Times*, 12; 14 (July 24, 1995), 110.

Dausman, Jack and Gary Bolles. Plan Your NetWare v4 Directory. *Network Computing*, 5; 6 (June 1, 1994), 168.

Garris, John. Is There Life After NetWare 3.12? *PC Magazine*, 14; 18 (October 24, 1995), NE1.

Johnson, Johna. NetWare for the Enterprise, Take Two. *Communications*, 24; 2 (February 1995), 45.

Yamkowy, Shane. Bindery Emulation: Your Stepping Stone to NDS. *Networking Computing*, 5; 13 (November 1, 1994), 142.

NLMs

Robertson, Bruce. Dawn of a New Age for NLMs. *Network Computing*, 5; 8 (July 1, 1994), 82.

Willis, David and David Cox. NLM-Based Job Control Languages Make Your Job Easier. *Network Computing*, 5; 11 (October 1, 1994), 113.

Management/Design

Yamkowy, Shane. Consolidate Your NetWare File Servers. *Network Computing*, 5; 8 (July 1, 1994), 144.

NetWare 4.1/NDS

Allen, John. Novell's Enterprise NOS. *Network World*, 12; 37 (September 11, 1995), 63.

Dorshkind, Brent. Messaging Vendors Wary of NDS. *LAN Times*, 12; 14 (July 25, 1995), 22.

Liebing, Edward. The Client32 Requester Module. *LAN Times*, 12; 22 (October 23, 1995), 116.

Nance, Barry. NetWare 4.1 Forges Ahead. *Byte*, 20; 5 (May 1995), 175.

Rosenfield, David. Backing Up and Restoring NDS Databases. *LAN Times*, 12; 14 (July 24, 1995), 116.

Schultz, Keith. NDS Takes Managers One Step Closer to Networking Nirvana. *Communications Week*, no. 577 (September 28, 1995), 23.

Wittman, Art and James Drews. Netware 4.1 Puts Novell in the Spotlight. *Network Computing*, 6; 1 (January 15, 1995), 50.

NetWare SMP

Shimmin, Bradley. NetWare Powers Up. *LAN Times*, 12; 19 (September 25, 1995), 1.

UnixWare

Doering, David. Novell Boosts UnixWare2. *LAN Times*, 12; 4 (February 27, 1995), 60.

Garris, John. UNIX for the NetWare Masses. *PC Magazine*, 14; 10 (May 30, 1995), NE15.

Linthicum, David. Network Operating Systems: Serving Up Apps. *PC Magazine*, 14; 18 (October 24, 1995), 205.

HSM

Gerber, Barry. Hierarchical Storage Management for NetWare. *Network Computing*, 6; 3 (March 1, 1995), 66.

Interoperability

Chernicoff, David. Novell's Windows NT Tool Gives

Users Control of NDS. *PC Week*, 12; 25 (June 28, 1995), 1.

Fisher, Sharon. Novell's NT Client Woes. *Communications Week*, no. 564 (July 3, 1995), 1.

Graziano, Claudia. Solaris Powers NetWare. *LAN Times*, 12; 7 (April 10, 1995), 1.

Henry, Amanda. Integration Tools Stop Short. *LAN Times*, 12; 14 (July 24, 1995), 29.

Leach, Norvin. Novell Prepares to Ship NT-NetWare Client. *PC Week*, 12; 22 (June 5, 1995), 8.

Leach, Norvin. Users Praise Speed, Criticize Glitches in NetWare NT Client. *PC Week*, 12; 26 (July 3, 1995), 1.

Communication Protocols

Berg, Al. RIP the SAP from Your Server. *LAN Times*, 12; 13 (July 3, 1995), 93.

Chernicoff, David. NetWare/IP Weds IPX/SPX, TCP/IP. *PC Week*, 12; 38 (September 25, 1995), N29.

Fogarty, Kevin. Novell Reveals Internet Strategy for NetWare. *Network World*, 12; 31 (July 31, 1995), 1.

Garris, John IP/IPX Internet Gateways: Hassle-Free Internet. *PC Magazine*, 14; 13 (July 1995), NE1.

Gillooly, Caryn. Novell Protocol Speeds Nets. *Information Week*, no. 533 (June 26, 1995), 100.

Raynovich, R. Scott. IPX-to-IP Products Proliferate. *LAN Times*, 12; 13 (July 3, 1995), 37.

NetWare Connect/Mobile NetWare

Henry, Amanda. Novell Sends LANs Packing. *LAN Times*, 12; 20 (October 2, 1995), 1.

Leach, Norvin. NetWare Connect Acquires Security, Management Aids. *PC Week*, 12; 23 (June 12, 1995), 23.

Sweet, Lisa. NetWare Connect Gains Power Plus Flexibility. *PC Week*, 12; 27 (July 10, 1995), N1.

Future Direction

Buerger, David. Novell Solves the Vision Puzzle. *Network World*, 12; 37 (September 11, 1995), 54.

Cummings, Joanne. An Up-Close Look at Novell's Next-gen OS. *Network World*, 12; 28 (July 10, 1995), L1.

Fisher, Sharon. Novell's SuperNOS Strategy Details Emerge. *Communications Week*, no. 566 (July 17, 1995), 88.

Fogarty, Kevin. Novell Goes Back to its Network Roots. *Network World*, 12; 36 (September 4, 1995), 1.

Fogarty, Kevin. Novell Plots Three Sequels to NetWare. *Network World*, 12; 40 (October 2, 1995), 1.

Gillooly, Caryn. NetWare at the Crossroads. *Information Week*, no. 544 (September 11, 1995), 14.

Gillooly, Caryn. Novell Tries for the Simpler Approach. *Information Week*, no. 546 (September 25, 1995), 20.

Henry, Amanda. More Vendors Lay NEST Plans. *LAN Times*, 12; 14 (July 24, 1995), 30.

Salamone, Salvatore. Novell Builds a NEST. *Byte*, 20; 8 (August 1995), 151.

Udell, Jon. Novell's Campaign. *Byte*, 20; 2 (February 1995), 42.

CASE STUDY

Chapter 11

NETWARE 4.1 SHINES

Easy Corporate Conversion Made on Faith

The decision to migrate from an IBM LAN Server environment to Novell Inc.'s NetWare 4.1 transformed the Western Reserve Life Assurance Co. from LAN-laggard to corporate standard-bearer.

Western Reserve, an insurance/ financial services company in Largo, Fla., previously ran the IBM LAN Server 3.0 Advanced on its eight-ring, 800-node token-ring network. Although the company was not dissatisfied with LAN Server, David Arroyo, manager of production ser-

vices, found he had difficulty recruiting qualified technicians. "We were having a devil of a time finding people well-versed in OS/2 and LAN Server," he said.

Western Reserve's parent company, Baltimore-based Aegon USA, had long ago switched its U.S. locations to NetWare, leaving Western as the odd LAN out in the corporate structure. Late last year Arroyo decided the time had come to plan the NetWare leap.

Although there was no doubt NetWare would be Western's new network operating system, the question remaining was which version to implement. Aegon ran Net-Ware 3.12 servers, but Arroyo was

attracted to NetWare 4.1's main feature: NDS.

"We eventually chose NetWare 4.1 because our LAN administrators had been trained in a domain-like concept, and [with 4.1] we felt we could continue with just one person managing the 800 users' logons and access to devices," he said. Single logon was essential, and access to improved compression and backup also attracted Arroyo to version 4.1.

Faith in NetWare 4.1

At the time Arroyo was contemplating conversion, however, bug reports on version 4.01 abounded in the media. Novell assured Arroyo in onsite meetings that the upcoming 4.1 revision would correct most malfunctions, which gave Arroyo confidence to leapfrog the rest of Aegon and migrate to the enterprise platform.

Arroyo is not alone in his assumption that 4.1 is ready for prime time. According to figures from market-analyst Computer Intelligence InfoCorp in La Jolla, Calif., more than 5,000 companies have enough confidence in NetWare 4.x's stability to start implementation this year.

But Arroyo also decided to ensure the success of his company's migration through a number of safeguards. With help from Clearwater, Fla.-based integrator Dataflex Corp., Arroyo formed a team that dedicated months to detailed planning of the eventual over-the-weekend migration. "The best thing we did was dedicate a team to the changeover, telling them, 'This is your only task for the next six months,'" he said. Reviewing Western's application requirements, the team was happy to note only one IBM OS/2 application, Script Language Processor from Decision Technology Inc., was unavailable for the setup, which was to include 600 converted OS/2-to-Windows 3.11 users.

The group then designed the 4.1 servers to run temporarily alongside the old LAN Server environment. "We set up our [new] server structure in a pristine environment because we thought it was better to be safe as far as 4.1 was concerned," said Dataflex's Joe Provenza, manager/ consultant on the Western project.

Early this spring 10 users in the company's actuarial department served as guinea pigs for a 4.1 test server. To the surprise of both Arroyo and Provenza, there were few glitches. "I don't think any of the network's problems have been related to NetWare 4.1," Arroyo said. "We were ready to shoot down problems, and there's been nothing to shoot at."

Provenza admitted that, in the final weeks leading up to the conversion, a hardware technician spent most of his days on the phone to Novell's technical support ironing out inevitable compatibility issues. "You'd find an odd problem on a 4.1 server, but never anything that would take the world down," he said. "In most cases, Novell said, 'There's a patch, here's how to download it,' and that was it."

As Western's projected switchover date approached, all the company's technicians were trained and ready for an instantaneous cutback to LAN Server should NetWare 4.1 show serious signs of failure.

But Provenza described the migration as "remarkably smooth." He said moving to the new platform let the company institute new administrative standards, such as mandatory password changes and diskspace usage limits.

Arroyo sites the dearth of good NetWare reporting and management software as one missing tool in Western's managerial repertoire. But he thinks ManageWise, the joint effort from Novell and Intel Corp., will help.

"We want to do what any administrator wants to do, i.e., reduce support costs on the net; to do that we need electronic-software upgrades and inventory control—the ability to change AUTO.EXEC and CONFIG files easily," he said. "I hope ManageWise will start moving us in that direction."

In a May presentation to the rest of Aegon regarding Western's 4.1 migration, Dataflex's Provenza highlighted the long planning and test time as key to its success and speculated that it will make the rest of Aegon's transition to 4.1 that much easier. "By taking our deliberate time, we can now really recommend 4.1 as a stable platform," he said. "And once you've seen what it can do, [NetWare] 3.12 begins to look antiquated."

BUSINESS CASE STUDY QUESTIONS

Activities

1. Complete a top-down model for this case by gleaning facts from the case and placing them in the proper layer of the top-down model. After completing the top-down model, analyze and detail those instances when requirements were clearly passed down from upper to lower layers of the model and solutions to those requirements were passed up from lower to upper layers.

2. Detail any questions that may occur to you about the case for which answers are not clearly stated in the article.

Business

1. What was the business motivation for choosing NetWare 4.1?

2. Describe the migration planning process used in this case, as well as the impact of such a process.

3. What was credited as the key to the success of the migration effort?

Application

1. What applications-related issues needed to be dealt with when migrating from one network operating system to another?
2. Was the change in network operating systems a major problem for applications programs? Why or why not?

Network

1. How many users were supported on this network?
2. Which network operating system did the parent company run?
3. Which network operating system functionality available only on NetWare 4.1 was of particular interest to the business in this case?

4. What are some of the new LAN administrative standards enabled by NetWare 4.1?
5. Which area of functionality did the user feel that NetWare 4.1 was lacking?

Technology

1. What was the technology profile of the network before migration, including operating system, network operating system, and network architecture?
2. Describe some of the safeguards included for the actual switchover from one network operating system to the other.
3. Did the installed technology meet the objectives of the business in this case? Defend your answer.

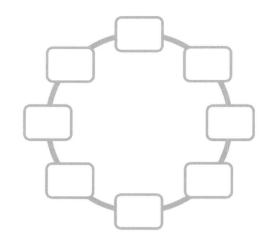

CHAPTER 12

WINDOWS NT

Concepts Reinforced

OSI model
LAN software
Network architecture
Network operating systems
  architectures

Client/server technology model
Protocols and standards
Network operating systems
  functionality

Concepts Introduced

NT architecture
Hardware abstraction layer
NT functionality
NT servers

NT communications protocols
NT interoperability
NT clients
NetWare/NT interoperability

After mastering the material in this chapter you should:

1. Understand the major architectural and functional features of Windows NT.

2. Understand the communications protocols underlying the Windows NT network operating system.

3. Understand the options and limitations for interoperability between Windows NT and other platforms such as Unix, NetWare, and Macintosh.

4. Understand the remote-access options associated with Windows NT.

Like NetWare, Windows NT is a fully integrated network operating system incorporating operating system and network operating system functionality into a single integrated product. Unlike NetWare, Windows NT was designed from the outset to be both portable and scalable. **Portability** is evidenced by Windows NT's unique ability to execute over multiple CPUs such as Intel x86, MIPs RISC, DEC Alpha, and

PowerPC. **Scalability** is evidenced by the ability of Windows NT to support symmetrical multiprocessing. Portability and scalability are only two of the important architectural characteristics Windows NT exhibits which are explored further in this chapter. Functionally, Windows NT distinguishes itself from NetWare by its ability to successfully support high-powered applications such as database engines, in addition to admirably performing print and file services.

The overall purpose of this chapter is to introduce the reader to the important architectural and functional characteristics of Windows NT. NetWare and Windows NT are directly compared throughout the chapter, and the chapter follows an outline similar to that of the chapter on NetWare to ease further comparison.

Having carefully reviewed the chapters on NetWare and Windows NT as part of an overall top-down, business-oriented networking analysis, the reader should feel comfortable recommending whether either of these two powerful and popular network operating systems will meet networking needs they identify.

■ WINDOWS NT ARCHITECTURE

Figure 12-1 illustrates the overall Windows NT architecture.

In addition to scalability and portability, stability is a very important functional characteristic of Windows NT. Unlike Windows 3.1, Windows NT is, for all intents and purposes, crash proof. This system stability can be largely attributed to rigid enforcement of structured access to hardware resources. Application programs and APIs are prohibited from interacting directly with hardware resources in Windows

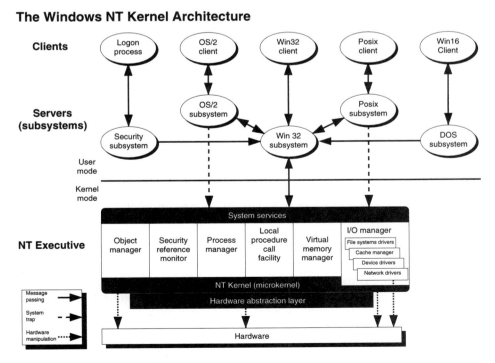

Figure 12-1   Windows NT Architecture

NT. Instead, applications and APIs must access hardware resources by requesting services through the collection of system services known as the **NT Executive.** Communications between the various NT executive subsystems and the I/O manager are controlled by the **NT kernel,** sometimes referred to as a microkernel. Communications with hardware resources are allowed to occur in either of the following methods:

- Through the systems services layer, through the NT kernel, through the hardware abstraction layer, to the hardware resources.

- Through the systems services layer, through the I/O manager and its subsystems, through the hardware abstraction layer, to the hardware resources.

This stable architecture with structured communications between subsystems affords NT another architectural characteristic known as **modularity of design,** which allows entire subsystems to be easily added or replaced. For example, the replacement of the current Windows NT security subsystem with the Kerberos authentication system would be a relatively straightforward modification.

Hardware Abstraction Layer

As Figure 12-1 illustrates, most of the hardware-specific portions of Windows NT are isolated in a subsection known as the **hardware abstraction layer,** or **HAL.** In Windows NT the HAL provides functionality similar to the BIOS in DOS. It is the hardware (CPU)–specific HAL which affords Windows NT its portability. As a practical example, to be able to execute Windows NT on any given CPU chip, the following major steps are required:

- Develop a hardware (CPU)-specific version of the hardware abstraction layer.

- Supply a compatible Microsoft C compiler, since Windows NT is written in C.

- License the Windows NT source code from Microsoft.

- Recompile the Windows NT source code on the C compiler, which executes on this new CPU.

Routines or system calls embedded within HAL can be called from either the NT kernel or device drivers included in the NT I/O manager.

NT Kernel

The NT kernel, which is concerned with the overall traffic flow of messages throughout the operating system, runs over the hardware abstraction layer. The NT kernel is more specifically concerned with handling interrupts and exceptions for communications between subsystems and between hardware resources and the operating system. As part of the management of all intersubsystem communication, it is responsible for constantly checking with the NT executive's security subsystem to ensure that requests for services have been properly authorized. More specifically, the NT kernel is responsible for the following:

- Thread scheduling in NT's multithreaded environment.

- Multiple processor synchronization when NT runs on an SMP-capable computer.

- Interrupt and exception handling.

- System crash recovery.

- Security checking and enforcement.

Interrupt handling occupies most of the NT kernel's time, as an interrupt to the NT kernel is generated for every NT executive subsystem interaction. The NT kernel runs in **privileged mode** and is therefore never paged out of memory.

NT Executive

The NT executive is composed of the NT kernel plus a variety of subsystems known collectively as system services. Among these system services are the following:

- I/O manager.

- Local procedure call manager.

- Object manager.

- Process manager.

- Virtual memory manager.

- Security reference monitor.

I/O Manager   The **I/O manager** is in charge of managing all input and output for the Windows NT operating system. As Figure 12-1 illustrates, the I/O manager is particularly concerned with managing the communications between device drivers, network drivers, cache manager, and file systems drivers.

Device drivers, otherwise known as hardware device drivers, are specifically written to support a particular hardware device such as a printer, keyboard, or mouse. Windows NT provides a standardized environment within the I/O manager in which these device drivers can execute. Thanks to this standardized environment, device drivers operate on any platform which supports Windows NT. Device drivers are written in C, like Windows NT, and can be easily swapped or added.

Network drivers are discussed in more detail in the Communications Protocols section. Many of the network drivers supported by Windows NT were mentioned previously including the following:

- NetBIOS, redirector, and the SMB server interface to applications and file systems.

- Communication protocols such as TCP/IP, NetBEUI, and IPX/SPX provide transport services.

- NDIS provides the ability for a network interface card to support multiple protocols as well as the ability for a network operating system to communicate with more than one NIC in a single computer.

The **cache manager** works closely with the file systems supported by NT to optimize the file services offered to applications. By effectively managing cache memory, it minimizes the number of physical read/writes to disks, thereby optimizing the performance of applications programs. Cache management is especially critical with the overall increase in processing speed afforded by NT's support for SMP.

As will be discussed later in the chapter, NT supports multiple file systems including its own native NTFS, FAT (DOS), and HPFS (OS/2). For NT to communicate with these multiple different file systems, an intermediate layer of software which can interact with both NT and the particular file system must be written. These specially written intermediate layers of software are known as **file system drivers.** When applications require file systems services, the particular file system in question is accessed by the I/O manager via the proper file system driver.

The modular design of the I/O manager allows these categories of drivers to be swapped or changed and also allows multiple file systems and drivers to be supported simultaneously. Often, requests for I/O services come indirectly from applications programs via the Win32 subsystem. The I/O manager oversees the interaction among the various categories of drivers to ensure that requested services to applications programs are delivered in a timely fashion. Communication among these various drivers is standardized by the I/O manager through the use of **I/O request packets.**

Local Procedure Call Facility   Window NT adheres to a client/server model internally. Application programs which request services of the NT operating system via subsystem services are considered clients, while the NT operating subsystems which service those requests are considered servers. Within Windows NT the internal communication between internal client requests and server responses is controlled by a message passing environment known as the **local procedure call facility.** The exact nature of the message passing between application programs and NT system services is explored further in the section on applications services.

Object Manager   Objects in the context of Windows NT are anything the NT operating system or any of its subsystems can manipulate, access, or use in any way. Files, directories, and application program threads are all examples of objects. All of these object categories differ in the types of operations which can be performed on them and in the required level of authorization to perform any given operation. The **object manager** in Windows NT is responsible for overall management of all NT objects, including enforcement of naming conventions and authorization for accessing and manipulating any object. In a very real sense, the object manager is responsible for object security.

Process Manager   A process can be thought of as the application program's execution environment, including its executable code as well as the required memory space in which to execute that process. The **process manager** is ultimately responsible for creating, maintaining, and terminating processes within Windows NT, and it communicates with the object manager and virtual memory manager to provide required resources and protection for the process in question.

Virtual Memory Manager To allow application programs easy access to large amounts of memory despite limited physically installed memory, Windows NT uses portions of the disk drive as a swap file that offers up to 4GB of memory to every process. The fact that some of a process' allocated memory is physically located on a disk drive rather than in RAM is kept transparent to the process by the **virtual memory manager.** In a process known as **demand paging,** the virtual memory manager moves program code and data between assigned physical RAM and the disk-based paging or swap file unbeknownst to the unsuspecting process. The virtual memory manager is also responsible for ensuring that processes do not write into each other's memory space. Much like the object manager and the process manager, the virtual memory manager also ensures that processes are protected from each other.

Security Reference Monitor   Yet another source of security for processes and the objects they manipulate is the **security reference monitor,** which is primarily concerned with authorization or authentication for processes that wish to access objects and users who wish to access the system via the logon process. The security reference monitor also generates audit reference messages so that proper records, which accurately record a wide variety of system activity, are available at a later date.

Multiprocessing, Multitasking, Multithreading

Thanks to its limited functional focus on the management of overall traffic flow through the operating system, the NT kernel can be executed on any CPU in a symmetrical multiprocessing (SMP) computer. This arrangement allows any processor in a NT multiprocessor arrangement to offer full multithreaded operating system functionality. This contrasts with other SMP arrangements such as NetWare 4.1 SMP in which the native NetWare kernel, which did not support multithreading, must run on only the first CPU while the SMP kernel runs on CPUs two and higher. Windows NT is able to run on as many as 32 processors simultaneously.

Windows NT is a preemptive multitasking operating system, which implies that applications are preempted or replaced with other application programs once they've consumed their allotted amount of CPU cycles. In this scenario, the Windows NT operating system never relinquishes full control of the CPU or memory resources to the application programs. Windows NT retains the ability to interrupt any application program.

Memory Management and Process Execution

In contrast to NetWare, which uses memory Ring 0 to run both the NetWare kernel and NetWare NLMs, Windows NT offers protected memory application execution via the use of Ring 0 and 3 assignments. Although some NetWare NLMs can operate in Ring 3, this is still not equivalent to NT's protected memory execution since a single misbehaving Ring 3 NLM can cause all other Ring 3 NLMs to terminate abnormally.

Windows NT applications are normally executed in Ring 3, known as **user mode,** in which they are limited to their own protected memory area. This prevents applications from writing into each other's memory space and thereby causing general protection faults and system crashes. To access the I/O manager portion of the

NT executive, applications must enter Ring 0, or **kernel mode** execution. User mode and kernel mode processes and subsystems are architecturally illustrated in Figure 12-1.

MULTITHREADED KERNELS AND SMP SCALABILITY

SMP scalability refers to the percentage of increased performance achieved for each additional CPU. For example, 100% SMP scalability implies that adding a second CPU will double the computer's original performance or computing power, and a third CPU will triple the original performance. In reality, because of the operating system overhead of coordinating the efforts of multiple CPUs, the highest achievable SMP scalability is something less than 100%.

Not all network operating systems achieve the same level of SMP scalability. Network operating systems vary in their level of SMP scalability depending on whether or not the network operating system's kernel is multithreaded. For example, although OS/2 and Windows NT are both considered multithreaded operating systems capable of SMP, only Windows NT's kernel is multithreaded. In other words, although multiple threads can execute simultaneously across multiple CPUs in user mode in OS/2, when a thread requires I/O services and is required to enter kernel mode, only a single thread can be in kernel mode at any point in time. In contrast, multiple threads in Windows NT can execute on multiple CPUs in kernel mode simultaneously due to its multithreaded kernel. Figure 12-2 illustrates the effects of single-threaded and multithreaded kernels within multithreaded operating systems.

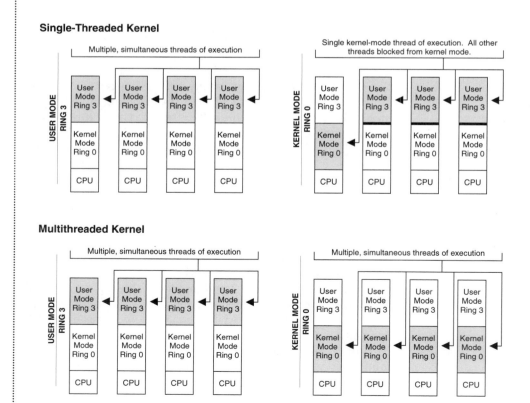

Figure 12-2   Single-Threaded versus Multithreaded Kernels

■ WINDOWS NT FUNCTIONALITY

Windows NT Server versus Windows NT Workstation

To further illustrate differentiation between client and server NOS, Windows NT is available in two distinct versions:

- Windows NT workstation.

- Windows NT server.

Windows NT workstation is just one of the possible client platforms which can interact with Windows NT server. In addition, several computers running Windows NT workstation can be linked together in a peer-to-peer network architecture.

File Systems

As previously stated, NT supports the following file systems:

- **FAT** (file allocation table)—DOS operating system, only file system for diskettes.

- **HPFS** (high-performance file system)—OS/2 operating system.

- **NTFS** (NT file system)—Windows NT.

- **CDFS** (CD file system).

In fact, Windows NT can also support simultaneous access to NetWare files stored on NetWare servers, thanks to a layer of software acting as a sort of redirector for file system requests known as the **multiple provider router (MPR).** The MPR is an open interface which accepts requests to any supported file system from application programs adhering to the Win32 API. It is the MPR's responsibility to examine each request for file system services and to route that request to the proper server housing the requested file system.

FAT   File names in the FAT file system are limited to eight characters plus a three-character extension, while file names in Windows NT can be up to 256 characters in length. To make files created in NTFS by the FAT file system easier to use, NTFS creates a FAT-compatible eight-plus-three conventional directory name for the file. For example, although this chapter was created as CHAPTER12.DOC on an NT computer with NTFS, when it is edited on a laptop running Windows for Workgroups with FAT, the file is loaded as CHAPTE~1.DOC. FAT and NTFS partitions can be created on the same disk and files can be easily copied between the two file systems with a utility such as file manager. NT's FAT file system allows file names of up to 256 characters on floppy diskettes.

HPFS   Support for HPFS is primarily for backward compatibility to the file system rather than transparent interoperability with the OS/2 operating system. In other words, rather than support many of the advanced features of HPFS, NTFS merely implements advanced features similar to its own; among these are the following:

- Support of long file names up to 255 characters.

- Disk organization to maximize contiguous storage of files and minimize file fragmentation, thus improving file storage and retrieval performance.

- Directories of files organized into quickly searched hierarchical B-tree structures.

Although NTFS may not implement all of these features identically, it does offer equivalent or greater functionality.

NTFS NTFS attempted to take the positive attributes of the FAT and HPFS file systems and add features required for the very large files and disk drives typical today along with features for increased security, reliability, and recoverability. Figure 12-3 summarizes the key features of NTFS.

NTFS Feature	Explanation/Importance
Access Control	Access control permissions can be assigned to individual files as well as to directories
Master File Table	• Contains records for each file and directory in NTFS • Records concerning the organization of NTFS and the MFT are redundant in case the primary record becomes corrupted • Small files (less than 1500 bytes) are stored entirely within the MFT for faster access
NTFS File Attributes	File attributes are contained with a file's MFT record. The list of file attributes can be customized for particular environments (Mac, Unix) and added to in order to extend NTFS functionality
File Names	NTFS allows file names up to 255 characters, but also generates 8-plus-3 names for FAT/DOS compatibility
POSIX Compliance	POSIX compliance allows Unix applications to access files stored in NTFS on Windows NT. To do this, NTFS needs to support some unique POSIX file attributes such as: • Case-sensitive file names • Hard-links which allow a given file to be accessed by more than one file name • Additional time stamp attributes to show when a given file was last accessed or modified
Macintosh Support	• Windows NT services for Macintosh allows files to be accessed by both Macintosh users and Windows NT clients. To the Mac users, the NT server looks like an AppleShare server. NTFS supports unique Mac file attributes such as resource and data forks as well as the Finder utility. Macintosh access control permissions are also supported
Hot Fixing	If NTFS finds a bad sector on a SCSI disk, it will automatically move the affected files and mark that segment as bad without the need for any user intervention
File System Recovery	NTFS uses the cache manager to buffer disk writes in a process known as lazy-write, and also runs a transaction log on all disk writes to allow NTFS to recover quickly from system crashes

Figure 12-3   NTFS Features

MASTER FILE TABLE DESIGN ENSURES FAST ACCESS AND RELIABILITY

The design of the **Master File Table (MFT)** is intended to accomplish two key objectives, which are often contradictory:

- Fast performance and lookups, especially on small files and directories.

- Reliable performance, thanks to numerous redundant features.

Interestingly, the **MFT** can accomplish both of these objectives quite well. First, the definition of the records within the MFT allows small files and directories to actually be included on its record, thereby precluding the need for any further searches or disk accesses. For larger directory files, NTFS uses a hierarchical B-tree structure to ensure fast performance and directory lookups on larger directories as well.

Reliability is ensured through the relationship of the following redundant features, as illustrated in Figure 12-4:

- Redundant MFT master records—MFT mirror record.

- Redundant MFT files and data segments—MFT mirror file.

- Redundant boot sectors.

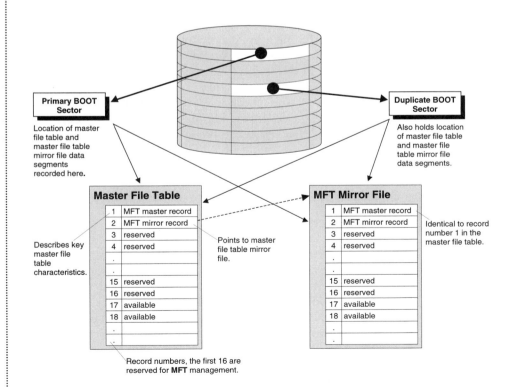

Figure 12-4   Built-in Reliability in the Master File Table Design

NTFS FILE SYSTEM RECOVERABILITY

NTFS treats its file system activity like most corporations treat the transactions which update their corporate databases. Special care is taken to see that all transactions are fully and correctly completed. If they are not successfully completed for any reason, mechanisms are in place to either repost or rollback those transactions to maintain database integrity.

The same applies to NTFS as well. File system activity is looked on as a series of transactions which are documented by the **log file service** of NTFS. In the unlikely event of a Windows NT system crash, two types of file system transactions would require further scrutiny:

- Transactions which were being held in disk cache for lazy-write posting and were therefore not physically written to disk when the system crashed.

- Transactions which were in the midst of posting when the system crashed.

The log file service records two types of information:

- Redo information allows transactions which were still sitting in disk cache to be reposted. Periodically, NTFS checks the cache to note the status of transactions which had been physically written to disk. In the event of a system crash, these checkpoints make the recovery process more expedient.

- Undo information allows transaction entries which were in the midst of posting to be rolled back or undone.

The NTFS file system is selfrecovering. No file clean-up utility needs to be run by the users. NTFS comes up knowing it has crashed and performs an analysis pass with the help of the log file service to determine where it left off when the system crashed. NTFS then proceeds to repost file system transactions based on the log file service's redo and checkpoint information, and to remove partial or corrupted transactions based on the log file service's undo information. The amazing part of all of this is that the entire file system recovery takes only a matter of seconds. In contrast, a file recovery of 1.2 GB with the OS/2 operating system takes approximately 35 minutes.

Printer Services

Recalling that printer sharing is a key NOS application, as well as NetWare's claim to fame, it should come as no surprise that Windows NT does an especially good job of offering managed print services to client workstations. In keeping with the overall modular design of Windows NT, printer services are organized around the Windows NT printing model, as illustrated in Figure 12-5.

The importance of the modular design of the Windows NT printing model should be clearly evident from the figure. At many layers of the model, a variety of options are available, depending on the particular environment of the user. For example, choices can be made for the following:

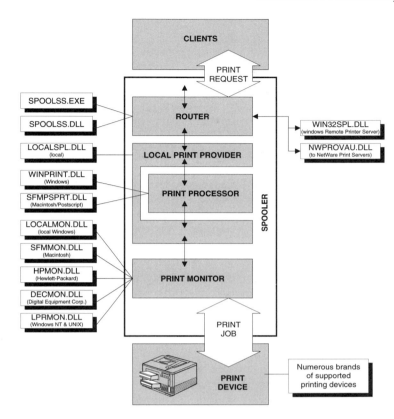

Figure 12-5   Windows NT Printing Model

- Print providers for interoperability with Macintosh, NetWare, or Unix-based printers.

- Printing monitor programs compatible with a variety of management platforms.

- A wide variety of types and brands of printers.

If it weren't for the modular design of the Windows NT printing model, monolithic printing spoolers would have to be developed for every possible unique combination of spooler, monitor, and printer—a truly unthinkable undertaking. Following are the basic building blocks of the Windows NT printing model:

- Clients are any application program which has the ability to produce a request for print services and pass that request to the spooler. The clients may be local or network-attached.

- The router receives all requests for print services and determines whether this print request can be fulfilled locally or if it must be shipped out to another print provider more qualified to deal with this print request.

- Print providers, whether local or remote, examine the spooled print request and determine which print processor should be used to process the print job. In addition, the print provider determines which print monitor is in charge of dealing with printer port output.

- Finally, the appropriate print monitor actually forwards the print job to the proper print device, whether local or network-attached.

Windows NT Domains

Domains and Workgroups   Unlike NetWare 4.1, Windows NT does not have a single, universal database in which all user and network resource information is stored and maintained. Instead, Windows NT networks are organized around the concept of **domains.** A domain is a collection of Windows NT servers which share a single security subsystem that controls access to all resources in that domain. Information concerning domain resources is tracked by the NT server directory services, formerly known as domain services.

Information concerning the network resources in a domain and the users allowed access to those resources is housed in a Windows NT server designated as the **primary domain controller.** All domains must have one, and only one, primary domain controller. Other NT servers in the domain can be designated as backup domain controllers for increased reliability or simply as servers, to offer a variety of services to authorized users.

Windows NT computers, especially Windows NT workstation clients, can alternatively belong to **workgroups** rather than domains. The key difference between workgroups and domains is that in a workgroup, there is no domain controller, and therefore, each workgroup computer must maintain its own security subsystem. In a workgroup, users log into a particular computer, whereas in domains, users log into a domain. This difference is not unlike the differences between logging into particular servers in NetWare 3.11 and into the universal NDS database in NetWare 4.1. Figure 12-6 illustrates some key features of domains and workgroups.

Trust Relationships   To provide access to network resources beyond local domains without having all user account and security information for every domain on all domain controllers, domains interact in a relationship known as trust. As long as **trust relationships** have been established between the Windows NT primary domain controllers in a multidomain environment, authorized users within those domains can access the resources on the multiple domains without the user accounts established on all domains. Users allowed into domains based on the trust relationships established by domain controllers are authorized by **passthrough authentication.**

Interdomain trust relationships are defined separately for each direction. That is to say, domain A granting trust to domain B and its users is separate from domain B granting similar trust to domain A. Interdomain trust relationships are strictly point-to-point. The fact that domains A and B have a two-way trust relationship and domain B also has a two-way trust relationship with domain C does not imply that users on domain A have access to domain C.

Interdomain trust accounts which allow NT server domain controllers to perform passthrough authentication to other domains are only one of three types of trust accounts supported by Windows NT. The following are the other two:

Domain

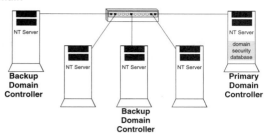

➤ All security and access control list information is maintained on the *primary domain controller*. Copies are stored on *backup domain controllers* for reliability.
➤ *Backup domain controllers* promoted in case of *primary domain controller* failure.
➤ Any *primary* or *backup domain controller* can log you in.

Workgroup

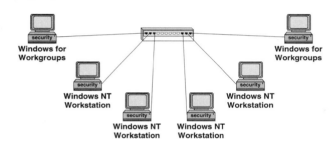

➤ Files and directories can be shared among the workgroup, but each workstation is responsible for maintaining its own user accounts and access control lists.

Figure 12-6   Domains and Workgroups

- **Workstation trust accounts,** which allow the workstation to connect to a domain by providing passthrough authentication for a Windows NT server in the domain. In essence, the workstation is able to authenticate itself or remote users which have logged directly into the workstation and now want to access domain-based resources.

- **Server trust accounts,** which allow NT servers to download copies of the master domain database from a domain controller. This trust relationship is what enables backup domain controllers.

Figure 12-7 illustrates a variety of trust relationships supported by Windows NT.

DOMAIN ARCHITECTURES

In Sharper Focus

The number and structure of domains and interdomain trust relationships can vary significantly from one organization to another. Decisions as to the proper domain architecture for a given organization hinge largely on the number and location of users, and the number and location of network management personnel. Following

Workstation Trust Accounts

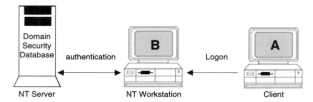

➡ NT Workstation **"A"** wishes to access Workstation **"B"**
➡ Workstation **"B"** passes login information to the domain controller for authentication.

Server Trust Accounts

➡ The Backup Domain Controller is able to receive a copy of the Domain Security Database due to Server Trust Account.

Interdomain Trust Accounts

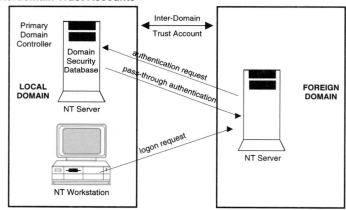

➡ Local workstation requests access to Foreign Domain Server.
➡ Foreign Server Requests authentication from Local Domain Controller
➡ Local Domain Controller performs pass-through authentication.

Figure 12-7   Trust Relationships in Windows NT

are descriptions of five major models for possible domain architectures as well as some key positive and negative attributes of each:

- **Single-Domain Architecture**—As the name implies, all users and network resources are organized into a single domain of up to 10,000 users. This is a flat architecture with no interdomain trust relationships involved. All security management is performed from a single location.

- **Multiple Nontrusting Domains Architecture**—If multiple divisions or departments within a given organization do not need access to each other's data or network resources, then multiple independently managed domains can be established without the need to define any trust relationships between the domains.

- **Master Domain Architecture**—This is a hierarchical architecture with a single master domain into which all users are defined. Multiple subdomains offer interdomain trust accounts to the single master domain, but the master domain does not allow trusted access from the subdomains. The advantage of this architecture is that access to departmental data can be controlled by trust relationships, and all management is performed from a single centralized location. Since all user information is managed by the single master domain, this architecture is limited to 10,000 total users.

- **Multiple Master Domains Architecture**—This two-tiered architecture supports multiple master domains, with up to 10,000 users each. All subdomains offer interdomain trust accounts to all master domains. Appropriate for very large organizations, this architecture involves increased maintenance of the multiple master domains and the interdomain trust relationships.

- **Multiple Trust Architecture**—In this idealistic, flat architecture, all domains offer interdomain trust accounts to all other domains. The difficulty with this architecture is that all domains are independently administered, and trust relationships must be established for every possible domain–domain combination. This architecture can grow quite large, as 10,000 users per domain are permitted. However, the totally decentralized management of the domains may not be appropriate for all organizations.

Figure 12-8 illustrates these various alternative domain architectures.

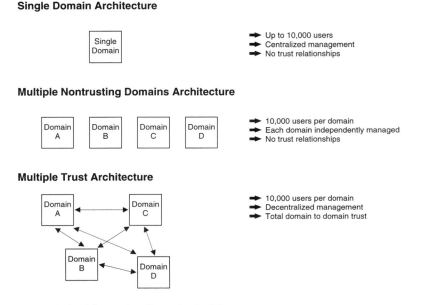

Figure 12-8   Alternative Domain Architectures

(continued)

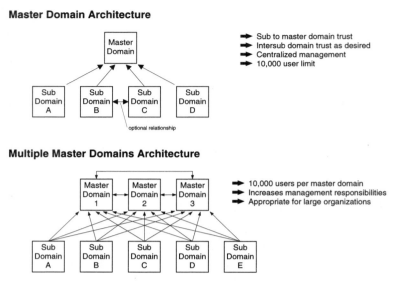

Figure 12-8   (continued)

Network Services

Windows NT network services provide the transport mechanism by which other services such as printing, security, file systems, and applications support are delivered. These multipurpose network services are the result of a structured, modular architecture of interacting components, as illustrated in Figure 12-9.

Following is a layer-by-layer description of the Windows NT network services architecture:

- The network interface card at the base of the Windows NT Network Services Architecture provides the physical connectivity from every Windows NT client and server to the Windows NT network.

- The first layer of software in the architecture is the network device interface specification (NDIS) driver software, which supports both multiple transport protocols per network interface card and multiple network interface cards per computer.

- Support for a variety of transport protocols allows Windows NT to interoperate successfully with most popular client and server networking platforms. These protocols are explained in more detail in the section on communications protocols.

- The **transport driver interface** is actually a protocol specification which provides a layer of transparency between session layer redirectors and transport layer protocols. It fulfills a role similar to the NDIS specification between the network and data-link layer protocols. This allows session layer redirector software to be written independently of the particular transport layer software with which it needs to communicate.

- Windows NT is able to support a variety of redirectors simultaneously as well as multiple transport protocols. It is the redirector's job to determine

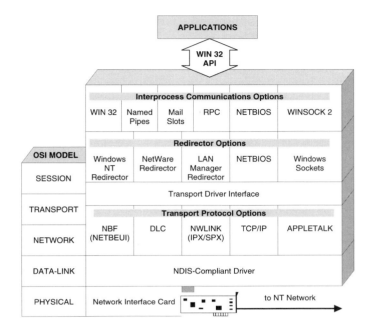

Figure 12-9 Windows NT Network Services Architecture

whether requests for files and services can be handled on the local computer, or if they must be forwarded to a particular remote computer via the appropriate transport protocol. Redirectors in Windows NT can also request additional services from any of the systems services available in the NT executive. The various options for redirectors are described further in the section on applications services.

- Finally, Windows NT applications must have some way to pass their requests for files and services to the redirector layer. The Win32 API, described in previous chapters, is the standard interface specification by which NT applications pass requests for services to the NT network operating system.

Application Services

Application services within Windows NT are concerned primarily with providing support for distributed or client/server applications. More specifically, Windows NT provides communications services between the client and server portions of distributed applications. These communications fall into two major categories:

- **Synchronous I/O,** or interprocess communication, refers to a client application spawning a thread for information or processing and waiting for the results of that thread before continuing to execute the client application. Synchronous I/O is sometimes also called connection-oriented communication.

- **Asynchronous I/O** refers to a client application spawning a thread for information or processing and proceeding with the execution of the client application, without waiting for the results. Depending on how the client application is written, the server portion may notify the client application when the requested information has been delivered, or the client program may be required to check back regularly for any new information. Asynchronous I/O is sometimes also called connectionless communication.

As illustrated in earlier chapters on client/server software architectures, distributed applications interact with network operating systems via application program interfaces (APIs). In the case of Windows NT, this API is the Win32 API.

Interprocess Communications The next requirement in establishing a distributed application between a client and server is some type of mechanism for interprocess communication. A way needs to be offered for the application to spawn threads and establish links from clients to servers to receive requested files and services. Windows NT offers at least six options for establishing interprocess communications, as illustrated in Figure 12-9.

The **Windows Sockets** interprocess communications mechanism, more commonly known as **WinSock,** is the most flexible interprocess mechanism currently supported by Windows NT. The term sockets reflects this protocol's derivation from Berkeley Unix sockets. Earlier versions of the WinSock protocol allowed programs written to support this protocol to operate transparently over a variety of vendors' TCP/IP protocol stacks. **WinSock2** added to this functionality by allowing WinSock-compliant applications to operate transparently over IPX/SPX, AppleTalk, DECnet, and OSI transport protocols as well. The importance of this multiprotocol support from an application developer's standpoint is that only one version of an application needs to be developed and maintained, rather than several network protocol–specific versions.

A WinSock-compliant application uses the WinSock interprocess communication mechanism by loading the WinSock.DLL file. A DLL or **dynamic link library** file is loaded into memory by Windows NT as needed at run time rather than being compiled into, and permanently added to the applications programs themselves. As Figure 12-10 illustrates, the WinSock.DLL file includes two distinct interfaces:

- The WinSock API, used by applications developers for including appropriate commands in their WinSock-compliant applications.

- The WinSock service provider interface (SPI), which translates the API calls to enable WinSock-compliant applications to access multiple network transport protocols through the transport driver interface.

NetBIOS can also be used by applications to establish client-to-server or interprocess communication. NetBIOS is an API which allows NetBIOS-compliant applications to communicate with the NetBIOS redirector which, in turn, establishes communications via the NetBEUI frame (NBF) transport protocol. The NetBIOS API is implemented by the NetBIOS DLL. NetBIOS establishes sessions between client and server computers which can then exchange messages that adhere to the server message block (SMB) format.

Following are two other interprocess communications mechanisms included in Windows NT primarily for backward compatibility with applications written for other network operating systems:

- **Named pipes** is included as an interprocess communication mechanism used by the OS/2 operating system.

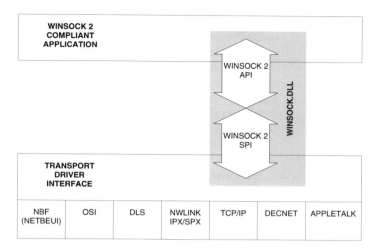

Figure 12-10 WinSock2 Provides Network Transport Independence

- **Mailslot** is an interprocess communication mechanism used by the OS/2 LAN manager network operating system.

The Open Software Foundation (OSF) has developed an entire architecture for the development of distributed applications, known as the **distributed computing environment (DCE).** DCE is explored in detail in the chapter on enterprise network application development. The interprocess communication service defined within DCE is known as **remote procedure call,** or **RPC.** Windows NT, along with many other operating systems, supports RPC, which is like a "super" interprocess communication mechanism in that it can use other interprocess mechanisms such as named pipes, NetBIOS, or WinSock, if a particular application requires it. Client and server programs that wish to use the RPC service simply issue program calls for that service via specialized calls to the RPC mechanism known as **stubs.**

While the stub calls are compiled within the program, the interprocess communications are actually executed with the help of the RPC runtime module. All computing platforms which support the RPC interprocess communication mechanism must have a compatible RPC runtime module. This makes the RPC runtime module the common interprocess communication mechanism across all computing platforms attempting to communicate with each other.

Security

Overall Functionality   Security is an integral part of the Windows NT operating system rather than a shell or subsystem. As a result, security in Windows NT offers not only user authorization services typically associated with network operating system security, but also an assurance that the programs and processes launched by those authorized users will access only system resources to which they have the appropriate level of permission. In Windows NT, no interprocess communication takes place without the knowledge and approval of the Windows NT security system.

The overall security system is organized around the concept of objects, not unlike NetWare 4.1's view of the NetWare directory services' object-oriented database. In Windows NT, examples of objects are files, directories, print queues, and other networked resources. All objects are assigned permission levels, which are then associated with individual users or user groups. Following are examples of permission levels:

- Read.
- Delete.
- Execute.
- Take ownership.

- Write.
- Change permission level.
- No access.

By monitoring permission levels, NT security can monitor and control who accesses which objects as well as how those objects are accessed. In addition to monitoring and control, NT security also audits and reports on these object accesses by users, according to permission level. The components of the Windows NT security model are illustrated in Figure 12-11.

Components of the Windows NT Security Model   A logical start for introducing the interacting components of the Windows NT security model might be the **logon process,** which is responsible for the interaction with the user in whatever computer platform on which they may log in. This is really a client presentation layer function, identified as a separate component to allow login processes for a variety of computer platforms to interact with the Windows NT security model in a standardized manner.

The platform-specific login process interacts with the **local security authority** which actually provides the user authentication services. Specifically, the local security authority generates a **security access token** for authorized users, which con-

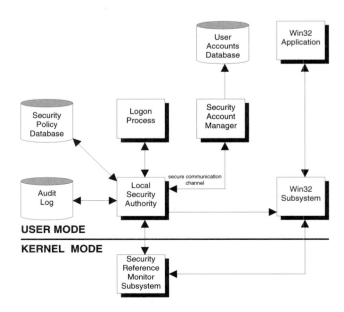

Figure 12-11   Windows NT Security Model

tains **security IDs (SID)** for this user and all of the user groups to which the user belongs. This security access token accompanies every process or program the user launches and serves as a means to reference whether or not the user and the processes spawned have sufficient permission to perform requested services or access requested resources. The local security authority also controls the security model's audit policy and generates audit messages which are stored in the audit log.

All of the user and user group ID and permission level information is stored in and maintained by the **security account manager,** which interacts with the local security authority to verify user IDs and permission levels. The **user accounts database** is physically stored on the primary domain controller, except when an individual workstation may need to verify specific user IDs for remote access to that workstation. The links between components of the NT security model involved in the logon process are designed as secure communication channels to ensure that traffic supposedly received from a given workstation or computer is actually from that computer. This authentication is accomplished in Windows NT by a process very similar to the challenge handshake authentication protocol (CHAP) employed in NetWare 4.1 for a similar purpose. Passwords are encrypted before being transmitted during the logon process.

The only kernel mode portion of the NT security model is the **security reference monitor (SRM),** which really serves as the security engine or back-end application for all of the previously mentioned security client applications. It is the security reference monitor that has the ultimate responsibility to ensure that users have the proper authority to access requested network resources. The SRM is able to meet this responsibility by comparing the requested object's security description as documented in **access control lists (ACL),** with the requesting user's security information as documented on their security access token. Besides access validation, the SRM is also responsible for audit checking and generating audit messages.

Fault Tolerance

Windows NT offers the following fault-tolerant features, most of which have been described in detail in previous chapters:

- Disk mirroring—all data written to one disk is also written to a second redundant disk. In the event that the primary disk fails, the redundant disk takes over immediately.

- Disk duplexing—Improves on disk mirroring by ensuring that the two mirrored disks are also supported by separate disk controllers, thereby eliminating another potential point of failure.

- Software-based RAID 5—Otherwise known as disk striping with parity, this allows data to be reconstructed from among the redundant array of disks in the event of a disk failure. Software-based RAID offers a less expensive alternative to hardware RAID subsystems available from a variety of vendors.

- UPS support—Especially important because of the function of the cache manager within Windows NT. To optimize system performance, physical writes to disk are not always performed immediately on the execution of a "save" command. This information is often stored in cache memory until it is convenient to access the disk. If the system shuts down unexpectedly, all information stored in cache memory is lost. With the ability to support uninterruptable power supplies, NT can execute an orderly system shutdown when necessary, thereby saving all cached information.

■ WINDOWS NT COMMUNICATIONS PROTOCOLS

Overall Architecture and Functionality

As illustrated in Figure 12-12, Windows NT offers not just a choice of multiple communications protocols, but the ability to run multiple communications protocols simultaneously. Windows NT supports some of these communications protocols for backward compatibility and others for interoperability purposes.

IPX/SPX

IPX/SPX is the traditional communications protocol stack for NetWare network operating systems. Operational details on IPX/SPX were included in Chapter 11. IPX/SPX is supported in the Windows NT environment through a protocol stack known as **NWLink,** which allows IPX/SPX to serve as the native communications protocol for all communications between NT clients and servers. As a result of having IPX/SPX serve as NT's native transport protocol, interoperability with NetWare clients and servers is more easily enabled through the following NetWare interoperability products available from Microsoft:

- Gateway service for NetWare.
- Client service for NetWare.
- File and print services for NetWare.
- Directory service manager for NetWare.

Each of these NetWare interoperability products is described in more detail in the section on Windows NT interoperability.

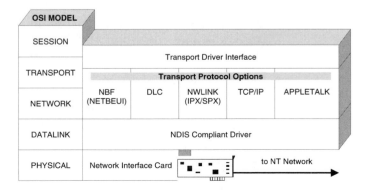

Figure 12-12   NT Communications Protocols Architecture

NetBEUI (NBF)

NetBEUI frame (NBF) is the Windows NT version of the NetBEUI protocol stack included for backward compatibility with such NetBEUI-based network operating systems as Microsoft LAN manager and OS/2 LAN server. As the expansion of Net-BEUI (NetBIOS extended user interface) implies, NetBEUI is merely an extended version of the original NetBIOS API. NBF can also be chosen as the native transport protocol for Windows NT, supplying transport services for all communications between NT clients and NT servers.

NetBEUI frame provides compatibility with NetBEUI while making at least two significant improvements to the native NetBEUI protocol stack.

Like most communications protocol stacks, NBF is able to establish communications sessions between a client and a server to exchange information. The reliable transport of data across this connection-oriented session is the responsibility of the employed transport protocol. Transport protocols such as NetBEUI ensure reliable data transfer through error checking and acknowledgment of the successful receipt of data on a packet-by-packet basis. In such a scenario, the sending computer must wait for a positive acknowledgment from the receiving computer on each packet before it sends the next packet. This error-checking method requires both the sending and receiving computers to spend a considerable amount of time waiting. NBF improves on NetBEUI's data transfer performance in connection-oriented sessions by adopting an **adaptive sliding window protocol** which allows for more efficient data transfer.

NBF adjusts how many packets can be sent by the sending computer before an acknowledgment must be received. Ideally, the sending computer wants to send the maximum number of packets possible while avoiding the need to retransmit packets due to transmission errors. The number of packets that can be sent before acknowledgment determines the size of the **send window.** If a negative acknowledgment is received, necessitating a packet retransmission, the sending window slides back to the packet which was received in error and retransmits it.

The second major improvement of NBF over NetBEUI has to do with **session limits.** Since NetBEUI is NetBIOS-based, it was forced to support the 254-session limit of NetBIOS. The source of this limit is a variable within NetBIOS known as the **local session number.** The local session number is a 1-byte (8-bit) field with a limit of only 256 possible entries (2 to the eighth = 256, less reserved numbers = 254). Since Windows NT servers using the NBF communications protocol could easily need to support more than 254 sessions, the 254 session limit had to be overcome. Although a detailed explanation of the mathematical algorithms behind the solution is beyond the scope of this chapter, the key is a two-dimensional matrix maintained by NBF which maps 254 logical session numbers against the network address of each computer with which it may establish a session. The result of maintaining and translating the various matrices is that each client-to-server connection can support 254 sessions, rather than only 254 sessions for all connections together.

AppleTalk

AppleTalk is included as a communications protocol to support NT's **Services for Macintosh (SFM).** These independently controlled services, which include file server for Macintosh and print server for Macintosh, allow an NT server to act as an

AppleShare server for Macintosh clients. Mac clients can easily retrieve and maintain files from the NT server. To the Mac clients, the connection is totally transparent; no additional software needs to be added. At the same time, the files stored in the AppleShare section of the NT server are also accessible to NT clients with proper permission levels. Thus, services for Macintosh plus the AppleTalk communications protocol provide a transparent interoperability environment for NT and Mac clients.

DLC

Data-link control, or **DLC,** is a Windows NT communication protocol traditionally reserved for communication with IBM mainframe computers. Recently, this communication protocol has been used to communicate between Windows NT servers and printers which are attached directly to the network by network interface cards, such as the Hewlett-Packard LaserJet 4Si equipped with a JetDirect card. To successfully complete such a communication, the mainframe or network-attached printer must also support the DLC protocol.

DLC adheres to the OSI model principal of independence of the functional layers by running equally well over Ethernet or Token Ring network interface cards and attached network architectures. In addition, DLC is also compatible with the IEEE 802.2 LLC (Logical Link Control) specification and frame layout.

DLC is also the communications protocol used to support the Microsoft SNA Gateway for Windows NT, which allows transparent interoperability between Windows NT clients and IBM mainframe computers. Using a gateway server eliminates the need for hardware or software modifications for Windows NT clients to communicate with the IBM mainframe.

Figure 12-13 is a functional illustration of the use of the IPX/SPX, NBF, AppleTalk, and DLC communications protocols.

TCP/IP and Related Protocols

Although the intricacies of TCP/IP and the related protocols of the Internet suite of protocols are thoroughly reviewed in the chapter on Unix and TCP/IP, a brief description of supported protocols and services is discussed here. In addition, significant issues related to Windows NT's implementation of TCP/IP-related protocols such as **dynamic host configuration protocol,** or **DHCP,** and its associated **Windows Internet Naming Service (WINS)** are also discussed. Figure 12-14 summarizes some of the TCP/IP protocols and services supported by Windows NT.

Practical Advice and Information

TCP/IP can be used as the native communications protocol between all NT clients and servers. However, this is not the real advantage to using TCP/IP as a communications protocol. The real benefits to TCP/IP are apparent only when one looks outside the local NT clients and servers. TCP/IP is the communications protocol of the Internet, as well as most other public and private internetworks. As a result, communications outside of the local NT network becomes much easier when TCP/IP is chosen as the communications protocol. In addition, TCP/IP has become the de facto common communications protocol across nearly every computing platform imaginable. Although many computers use communications protocols other than TCP/IP, nearly all computers are also able to speak to each other using TCP/IP.

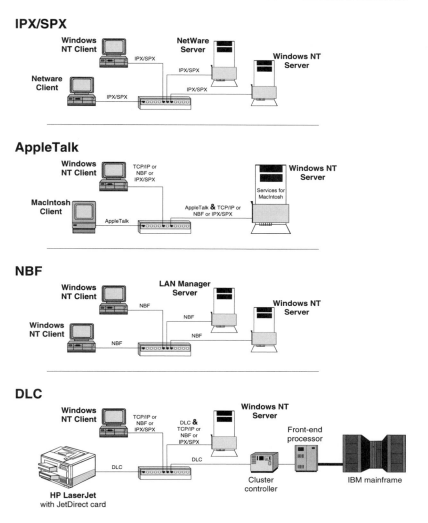

Figure 12-13   Use of IPX/SPX, NBF, AppleTalk, and DLC in Windows NT

DHCP and WINS   TCP/IP, like any network operating system communications protocol, depends on an organized addressing scheme to know where to find intended recipients of interprocess communications. Traditionally, IP addresses were associated with the network interface cards within computers and were therefore more or less permanently associated with a physical machine. Two forces contributed primarily to the need for an alternative to the permanent, physically oriented IP addressing scheme:

- An overall lack of possible IP addresses, due to the explosive growth of the Internet, which depends on IP addressing. As a result, a solution was sought to assign IP addresses dynamically, as needed, from a pool of available addresses, rather than having them permanently assigned to computers which were not being used.

- The explosive growth of remote and mobile computing. Some way needed to be found to give remote and mobile users IP addresses as needed, without permanently assigning unique IP addresses to everyone's office computer as well as their laptop or notebook computer.

Protocol/Service Category	Details/Explanation
Communications Protocols	• TCP—transmission control protocol: transport layer protocol which ensures reliability of IP transmission • IP—Internet protocol: network layer communications protocol which provides end-to-end addressing and communication • UDP—user datagram protocol: transport layer alternative protocol to TCP for transmission of short datagram messages which don't require reliability checking overhead of TCP
Special Delivery Protocols	• ARP—address resolution protocol • ICMP—Internet control message protocol
Remote Access Protocols	• PPP—point-to-point protocol • SLIP—serial line internet protocol • Both PPP and SLIP can be used for remote access of TCP/IP-based computers
APIs	• Windows Sockets 1.1 and 2.0
Utilities	• FTP—file transfer protocol • TFTP—trivial ftp: simpler version of FTP • Telnet—remote terminal login protocol • LPR—line printer protocol: used to print a file to a host print server • RCP—remote copy protocol • REXEC—Remote execution protocol, allows commands to be executed on remote hosts • Note: some utilities may be available only from add-on product—Windows NT Resource Kit
Diagnostics	• LPQ—used to obtain status of a print queue • PING—used to verify connections to a particular host • Tracert—used to trace the route of a packet from source to destination • Netstat—displays protocol statistics and network connections • Nbtstat—displays protocol statistics and network connections using NetBIOS over TCP/IP
Services	• WINS—Windows Internet name service • DHCP—dynamic host configuration protocol
Management Protocols	• SNMP—simple network management protocol: NT actually supplies an SNMP agent which is able to forward network statistics in SNMP format to enterprise network management systems such as HP OpenView, Sun Sunnet Manager, and IBM Systemview

Figure 12-14   TCP/IP Protocols and Services in Windows NT

The solution was the Internet Engineering Task Force (IETF) Request for Comment (RFC) 1541, better known as dynamic host configuration protocol, or DHCP. Dynamic host configuration protocol allows NT servers using TCP/IP to dynamically assign TCP/IP addresses to NT workstations, Windows for Workgroups clients, Win 95 clients, or DOS clients running the TCP/IP-32 protocol stack. The

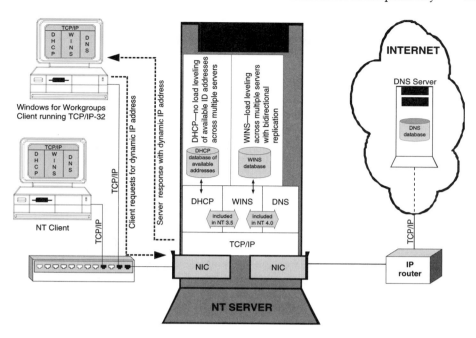

Figure 12-15   DHCP, WINS, and DNS

DHCP server is included as part of the TCP/IP protocol stack for NT server, and references a DHCP database for lists of available IP addresses. IP addresses issued by DHCP are leased, rather than being permanently assigned, and the length of time the IP addresses can be kept by DHCP clients is known as the **lease duration.** Dial-in users are typically assigned an IP address only for the duration of their call. If necessary, specific IP addresses can be reserved for specific clients. DHCP must be enabled on Windows clients supporting the TCP/IP protocol stack to be able to request IP addresses from the DHCP server.

Because users and their workstations are easier to remember and access by name than by address, NT keeps track of user names and associated IP addresses with a service known as Windows Internet Name Service (WINS). The Internet uses a different naming service, known as **domain name system (DNS).** The utilities to translate between these two naming services will be included with the Windows NT server TCP/IP protocol suite with NT version 4.0. As a result, users assigned DHCP addresses who are logged into the WINS database will still be accessible from the internet via the DNS database. The DHCP server, WINS server, and DNS server can all be physically located on different server computers. Figure 12-15 illustrates the interaction of DHCP, WINS, and DNS clients and servers.

■ WINDOWS NT INTEROPERABILITY

INTEROPERABILITY ANALYSIS

Transparent interoperability between different network operating systems does not happen by magic. Compatibilities on a variety of levels must be reconciled. The OSI model provides an excellent organizational tool for determining how identified incompatibilities are to be dealt with. A separate seven-layer OSI model protocol stack profile should be completed for each representative client and server computer which is to interoperate transparently. Figure 12-16 illustrates sample OSI model profiles for an NT client, a NetWare client, an NT server, and a NetWare server.

Once the layer 1 media (UTP, Fiber, Coax) and layer 2 network architecture (Ethernet, Token Ring, FDDI, Fast Ethernet) incompatibilities have been settled, the options for eliminating remaining incompatibilities are really quite straightforward. Incompatibilities on layers 4 through 7 can be dealt with in combinations of any of the following:

- Communications protocols: In the case of NetWare/NT interoperability, IPX/SPX or TCP/IP can be supported by both network operating systems, depending on NOS version numbers.

- Client-side software: Which clients need access to which servers? Does NetWare or Microsoft offer a way for NT clients to access NetWare servers? for NetWare clients to access NT servers?

- Server-side software or gateways: Can NT or NetWare clients access each other's servers without adding any client software? Are server-based gateway products available to give clients access to foreign servers?

Although not specifically noted on a particular layer of the OSI model, at least two other areas of NOS functionality must be dealt with before true transparent interoperability can be achieved:

- File systems—clients and servers of different network operating systems must be able to access each other's file systems.

	NetWare Client 3.11	NetWare Client 4.1	NetWare Server 3.11	NetWare Server 4.1	NT Client		NT Server	
LAYER 7 APPLICATION								
File Systems	NetWare Proprietary	NetWare Proprietary	NetWare Proprietary	NetWare Proprietary	NTFS		NTFS	
Directory Services	Bindery Files	NDS	Bindery Files	NDS	NT Server Directory Services		NT Server Directory Services	
LAYER 6 PRESENTATION	NetWare Shell		NetWare Shell		NCP Redirector	SMB Redirector	NCP Redirector	SMB Redirector
LAYER 5 SESSION	NCP Redirector		NCP Redirector					
	NETBIOS Emulator		NETBIOS Emulator					
LAYER 4 TRANSPORT	SPX	TCP or SPX	SPX	TCP or SPX	TCP or SPX		TCP or SPX	
LAYER 3 NETWORK	IPX	IP or IPX	IPX	IP or IPX	IP or IPX		IP or IPX	
LAYER 2 DATA-LINK	ODI	ODI	ODI	ODI	NDIS		NDIS	
	Either NetWare or Windows NT will operate on a variety of network architectures as long as the network interface card drivers have been written to the ODI (NetWare) and NDIS (NT) specifications.							
LAYER 1 PHYSICAL	Physical media chosen will depend on which media the chosen network architecture is defined for.							

Figure 12-16 OSI Model Protocol Profiles for NetWare and NT Clients and Servers

- Directory services—as in file system interoperability, if clients can't find what they're looking for due to incompatible directory services, transparent interoperability has not been achieved.

Having spoken in general terms about how transparent interoperability between network operating systems can be analyzed and implemented, we now explore a few NT interoperability scenarios in more detail.

Applied Problem Solving

NETWARE/NT INTEROPERABILITY

As one examines Figure 12-16 to focus on the incompatibilities between NetWare and NT which must be overcome, the following are among the more important observations:

- Interoperability issues differ depending on which version of NetWare is involved. For example, NetWare's VLMs are not interoperable with NT, although NT 4.0 includes an NDS-aware NetWare client that supports NetWare login scripts.

- Communications protocols incompatibilities are fairly easily solved thanks to Windows NT's ability to run IPX/SPX as its native communications protocol.

- File systems and directory services incompatibilities must be overcome.

Figure 12-17 summarizes some of the NetWare/NT interoperability solutions currently available. In evaluating any interoperability solution, one should ask several key questions:

1. What level of interoperability is offered?
2. Is this service included in the NOS or is it a separately purchased product?
3. Is the product installed on every client or just on servers?
4. How difficult is the product to install, configure, and manage?
5. Is the product designed to offer interoperability, or is it actually designed to provide a transition or migration path from one product or platform to another?

Product Name	Functionality/Explanation
NWLink	Windows NT's IPX/SPX protocol stack is NDIS compliant and allows Windows NT servers to be accessed by NetWare clients without requiring any additional hardware or software on the NetWare clients. This is especially appropriate when the NT server is required to function as a powerful applications or database server.
Client Service for Netware	This service allows a Windows NT client to access file and print services from a NetWare server. Clients can access NetWare 4.1 servers only in bindery emulation mode. NDS-aware 32-bit clients for NT are available in NT 4.0.

Figure 12-17 NT/NetWare Interoperability Alternatives

(continued)

Product Name	Functionality/Explanation
Gateway Service for NetWare	This service allows a Windows NT server to access file and print services from NetWare servers and also offer these NetWare services to attached NT clients which are not running their own client service for NetWare software. NT servers can access NetWare 4.1 servers only in bindery emulation mode.
NetWare Requestor for Windows NT	Available from Novell, this product allows NT clients to access NetWare servers. It allows NT clients to access NetWare 4.1 NDS databases through NT's file manager utility and NT clients to login to NetWare 4.1 servers as NetWare users.
Directory Service Manager for NetWare	Available from Microsoft, this product is intended for networks transitioning from NetWare 3.x to NT rather than ongoing network interoperability. Requires Gateway Service for NetWare. This product is able to import NetWare bindery files and transform them into databases on NT primary and backup domain controllers. From that point forward, all of the former bindery information can be maintained from Windows NT.
File and Print Service for NetWare	Available from Microsoft, this service allows a Windows NT server to offer file and print services to NetWare clients. The NetWare clients are unmodified and think they are interacting with a native NetWare server. The product is aimed at allowing NetWare users who wish to use NT as an application server also use NT for file and print services.
BW-Multiconnect for Windows NT	Available from Beame & Whiteside, a traditional TCP/IP client developer, this product offers similar functionality to Microsoft's File and Print Service for NetWare. It has slightly less functionality than the Microsoft product, such as a lack of support for NetWare login scripts and client print utilities.

Figure 12-17   (*continued*)

As you examine the array of products available from Microsoft, you should see that although these products can certainly achieve interoperability with NetWare, their primary purpose is to form a suite of products that make the transition from NetWare to NT as painless as possible.

Unix/NT Interoperability

Unix as an operating system is bonded to TCP/IP as its native communications protocol. Windows NT's support of TCP/IP communications protocols, utilities, and services has already been well documented, substantiating the basis for NT/Unix interoperability.

Client-to-Server Interoperability   Recalling that interoperability is a two-way affair, the following client-to-server combinations are possible:

- Windows NT Client to Unix Server—Using the Telnet utility included in the Windows NT TCP/IP protocol stack, NT clients are able to login to Unix servers as if they were Unix terminals. With the use of third-party software,

NT clients can run X Windows and X Windows-based applications on Unix servers.

- Unix client to Windows NT Server—Third-party software developers are offering software that allows X Windows-based Unix clients to access applications on Windows NT servers.

File System and Application Interoperability   Network **file system,** or **NFS,** is Unix's native network file system. Companies such as Beame & Whiteside, Intergraph, Process Software, and NetManage have developed versions of the NFS file system which run on Windows NT, thereby offering file system interoperability as well as client and server interoperability. These products should be reviewed carefully as they can differ in several ways:

- Level of compatibility with standard NFS functionality.

- Performance on reads, writes, copies, and deletes, which varies significantly.

- Number of simultaneous clients supported.

- Support for multithreaded architecture.

- Support for advanced CPUs such as DEC's Alpha.

- Pricing policy, which varies significantly as some products are priced per server and others per user. General range is from $295 to $695 per server.

In terms of application program interoperability, third-party software from Bristol Technologies allows Windows applications to run on Unix machines while software from Consensys Portage allows Unix applications to run on Windows NT servers.

Future Interoperability Possibilities   Most talk of further interoperability possibilities centers on applications. By developing applications which can execute over multiple platforms, application developers can reap the most potential benefit for their investment. End-users who purchase applications software are able to buy the application which best meets their needs without concern for whether or not it will execute over their installed network operating system.

Microsoft is making a conscious effort to promote the Win32 API as an open applications program interface, supported by many network operating systems besides Windows NT. To some extent at least, Microsoft's efforts are paying off. Unix applications written in C can be relatively easily modified and recompiled to comply with the Win32 API, with the aid of porting tools available on the Internet or from third-party vendors. In addition, Microsoft and DEC have reached an agreement which will enable DEC's operating system, known as **OpenVMS,** to also support the Win32 API.

■ WINDOWS NT REMOTE ACCESS

Windows NT RAS Functionality

As more and more workers find themselves working from home (remote computing) or on the road (mobile computing) there has been an increasing need for network operating systems capable of delivering the full power of the network operating system to these remote users. Ideally, the fact that these users are not situated in the same building as the server connected via a LAN should be totally transparent. All services available to local clients such as printing, database access, applications services, and directory services should be equally accessible to remote clients. Windows NT offers a service known as **remote access service, or RAS,** which consists of both client and server software. The client software is able to operate on any of the following computing platforms:

- Windows NT.
- Windows for Workgroups.
- MS-DOS 3.1 or higher.

In addition, the network services connecting the remote client with the local server can be any of the following:

- Dial-up phone service, sometimes referred to as plain old telephone service **(POTS).**
- Integrated services digital network (ISDN).
- X.25 packet switched network.

The RAS server software, which runs only on an NT server, is basically responsible for authenticating remote users and overseeing the communications sessions established with remote clients.

In simple terms, the RAS server sees to it that the remote client is provided all the services it requires, as if it were a local client. The actual servicing of the remote client's requests is performed by the NT network operating system. The RAS is responsible for seeing that the remote client's requests successfully reach the NT server and that server responses successfully reach the remote client. The RAS server is able to support up to 256 simultaneous connections and also supports data compression to optimize the throughput of information between the local server and the remote client. Figure 12-18 illustrates the interaction of the components of a RAS architecture. More details on the hardware, media, and network services required to enable remote access to LANs in general are covered in the chapter dedicated to LAN remote access.

RAS Communications Protocols

In keeping with the initial objective of RAS to allow the remote client all the functionality of local clients, RAS allows remote clients to run NBF, TCP/IP, or IPX/SPX communications protocols either alone or simultaneously. The data-link layer protocol is the only one which must change for the trip over the WAN link. In this case, the wide area data-link layer protocols which encapsulate the upper layer protocols are **point-to-point protocol (PPP)** or serial line Internet protocol (SLIP), which are part of TCP/IP's internet suite of protocols.

The fact that RAS supports TCP/IP, NBF(NetBEUI), and IPX/SPX also means that NetWare applications, NT applications, and NetBIOS applications can all be accessed and executed by the remote client. NetWare servers available to local clients

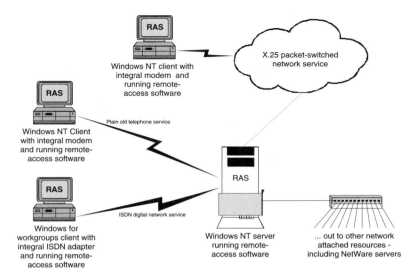

Figure 12-18   Windows NT Remote-Access Service Architecture

are equally available to remote clients. Any additional gateway services offered by the local NT server, such as Internet gateways or SNA gateways to IBM mainframes, are equally accessible by remote clients. Figure 12-19 illustrates a communications protocol architecture of RAS clients and servers.

RAS Security

Windows NT remote clients benefit from the same security features afforded local NT clients. In addition, due to the vulnerability of communications between the remote RAS clients and the local NT servers, additional security precautions are available. These precautions fall into two categories: authentication and encryption.

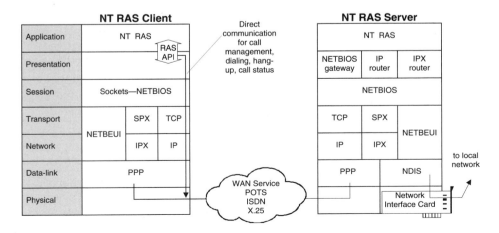

Figure 12-19   NT RAS Client and Server Communication Protocols

Authentication   The first control over remote access to NT servers is the need for explicit authorization of users to access RAS remotely. Just because a person is a valid NT user does not mean he/she is authorized for remote access. Once authorized users have accessed the RAS server, they must be authenticated. RAS supports encrypted authentication to prevent passwords from being intercepted during transmission. Three methods of encrypted authentication are supported by RAS and are listed from most secure to least secure:

- Challenge handshake authentication protocol, or CHAP, is the most secure, during both the actual authentication process and the session. Windows NT RAS clients and RAS servers will always authenticate via CHAP.

- Shiva password authentication protocol, or SPAP, is supported by the Windows NT RAS server if the Windows NT RAS client used a Shiva LAN Rover LAN modem as a remote-access device. SPAP is not as secure as CHAP.

- In some cases, client workstations may want to access the NT RAS server while running third-party RAS client software. In these cases, if the client software will not support CHAP or SPAP, then password authentication protocol, or PAP, also known as clear-text authentication, is employed.

Encryption   If desired, all remote client to local server communications can be encrypted as well as authenticated. This is accomplished by a setting on the RAS server, which encrypts all communications destined for transmission over the WAN link.

■ FUTURE DIRECTIONS

Although Windows NT currently offers a unique combination of functionality among network operating systems with its graphical user interfaces, SMP capability, reliability, fault tolerance, security, interoperability with NetWare, and other features, the future direction of Windows NT promises ever more impressive functionality. Figure 12-20 summarizes some of the reported functional enhancements which may be on the horizon.

NT Future Feature	Functionality/Implication
Clustering	A clustering API is under development for NT which will eventually allow two or more servers to be clustered offering fault-tolerant mirrored servers as well as distributed memory and loosely coupled multiprocessing.
Plug-n-Play	Already included in Windows 95, PnP allows computers to self-discover and self-configure PnP network interface cards, controller cards, and peripherals.
Object File System	The object file system is NT's next-generation object-oriented file system which should support a directory system similar to NetWare's NDS among other capabilities.
Microsoft Network	Like Windows 95, client software and server gateway software for interfacing to Microsoft's own information services network should be included in a future release of NT.

Figure 12-20   Windows NT Future Directions

(continued)

NT Future Feature	Functionality/Implication
Win 95 Explorer	Otherwise known as the Win 95 shell, the next release of NT should include the object-oriented, desktop interface which allows users to organize documents of all types into folders regardless of the applications used to develop those documents.
Platform of Choice for Enterprise Management Systems	Recently, enterprise network management systems such as HP Openview, Cabletron Spectrum, Computer Associate's CA-Unicenter and DEC's Polycenter NetView have migrated their network management platforms from Unix to Windows NT. This is a significant migration as, until now, Unix has been looked upon as the only operating system powerful and reliable enough to handle these enormous, mission-critical applications.
Exchange Messaging Client	The next generation of Microsoft mail and schedule, known as Exchange, represents a major shift in architecture to a true client/server messaging approach complete with remote procedure calls. The new architecture will offer improved performance as well as increased security.
Microsoft Internet Information Server	This web server software interoperates with NT workstation 4.0 peer web services and Internet Explorer to provide web publishing and browsing capabilities.
Point-to-Point Tunneling Protocol (PPTP)	Allows secure remote sessions to be established via RAS using the Internet as the connecting WAN service. Such a connection is known as a virtual private LAN.
RAS Multilink	This bandwidth aggregation utility allows RAS to combine multiple physical WAN links into a single virtual WAN link.

Figure 12-20   *(continued)*

SUMMARY

Windows NT is a powerful network operating system gaining significant market share thanks to its ability to serve as a powerful applications server as well as offer file and print services. The reliability, scalability, and portability which characterize Windows NT are directly attributable to its architecture including a CPU-specific hardware abstraction layer and strict enforcement of program access to hardware resources through the NT kernel. One of NT's big advantages over market leader NetWare is its ability to support SMP with its multithreaded kernel.

Windows NT is designed for interoperability or extensibility on a number of levels. For example, NT supports numerous file systems including FAT, HPFS, NTFS, and AppleShare. In addition, it is also able to communicate with native NetWare file systems. In terms of communications protocols, NT supports TCP/IP, IPX/SPX, or NBF (NetBEUI Frame) as its native communication protocol providing all transport services between NT clients and servers. In addition, NT supports DLC and AppleTalk communications protocols for interoperability with IBM mainframes, networked printers, and Macintosh computers.

Unlike NetWare 4.1, which organizes an entire enterprise network's objects into a single NDS database, an NT enterprise network is divided into numerous independent domains. User accounts and access lists for each domain are administered by designated computers known as primary domain controllers. Users can access network-attached resources on numerous domains thanks to specialized trust relationships established between domain controllers.

Interoperability between NT and NetWare is more precisely focused on providing a reasonable migration or transition path from NetWare 3.x to Windows NT.

In recognition of the increased emphasis on remote and mobile computing, NT includes remote-access services which provide outstanding security as well as sophisticated interoperability, thanks to support of multiple communications protocols. In short, NT RAS offers full functionality to remote clients equivalent to that available to locally attached NT clients.

Market surveys consistently show increased interest in Windows NT as an enterprise network operating system particularly well-suited to high-end applications or database server roles.

KEY TERMS

access control lists, 451
ACL, 451
adaptive sliding window protocol, 453
AppleTalk, 453
asynchronous I/O, 447
cache manager, 434
CPFS, 437
data-link control, 454
DCE, 449
demand paging, 435
device driver, 433
DHCP, 454
distributed computing environment, 449
DLC, 454
DNS, 457
domain name system, 457
domains, 442
dynamic host configuration protocol, 454
dynamic link library, 448
FAT, 437
file system drivers, 434
HAL, 432
hardware abstraction layer, 432
HPFS, 437
I/O manager, 433
I/O request packets, 434
interdomain trust accounts, 442
kernel mode, 436
lease duration, 457
local procedure call facility, 434
local security authority, 450
local session number, 453

log file service, 438
logon process, 450
mailslot, 449
master domain architecture, 445
master file table, 438
MFT, 438
modularity of design, 432
MPR, 437
multiple master domains architecture, 445
multiple nontrusting domains architecture, 445
multiple provider router, 437
multiple trust architecture, 445
named pipes, 448
NBF, 453
NetBEUI frame, 453
network driver, 433
network file system, 461
NT executive, 432
NT kernel, 432
NTFS, 437
NWLink, 452
object manager, 434
OpenVMS, 461
passthrough authentication, 442
point-to-point protocol, 462
portability, 430
POTS, 462
PPP, 462
primary domain controller, 442
privileged mode, 433
process manager, 434
RAS, 462

remote access service, 462
remote procedure calls, 449
RPC, 449
scalability, 431
security access tokens, 450
security account manager, 451
security IDs, 451
security reference, 435
security reference monitor, 435
send window, 453
server trust accounts, 443
Services for Macintosh, 453
session limits, 453
SFM, 453
single domain architecture, 444
SMP scalability, 436
SRM, 451
stubs, 449
synchronous I/O, 447
transport driver interface, 446
trust relationship, 442
user accounts database, 451
user mode, 435
virtual memory manager, 435
Windows Internet Naming Service, 454
windows sockets, 448
WINS, 454
WinSock, 448
WinSock 2, 448
workgroup, 442
workstation trust accounts, 443

REVIEW QUESTIONS

1. What is meant by the NT characteristic of portability? Give examples.

2. What is meant by the NT characteristic of scalability? Give examples.

3. Differentiate between the following: NT executive, NT kernel, hardware abstraction layer.
4. What is the function of the I/O manager?
5. How does the NT kernel ensure system reliability?
6. Describe the role of each of the components of the I/O manager.
7. What is the function of the local procedure call facility?
8. What is the function of the object manager?
9. What is the function of the process manager?
10. What is the function of the virtual memory manager?
11. What is the function of the security reference manager?
12. How do the various subsystems of the kernel interact, and what controls this interaction?
13. How does SMP in NT differ from SMP in NetWare SMP, both architecturally and functionally?
14. Differentiate between user and kernel mode in NT.
15. Explain the implication of SMP scalability.
16. How is it possible for NT to support multiple file systems simultaneously?
17. What are some of the unique functional characteristics of NTFS?
18. Describe both the importance and functionality of NTFS file system recoverability.
19. What is the importance of the modularity of the NT printing model?
20. Describe the function of each module or layer of the NT printing model.
21. Differentiate between domains and workgroups in NT.
22. Why are trust relationships important to domain-based user accounts?
23. What is the alternative to trust relationships for users that need resources from multiple domains?
24. What is passthrough authentication?
25. Differentiate between the various domain architectures in terms of domain management, number of users supported, functionality offered, and target organization.

26. Describe each layer of the NT network services architecture. How does each layer contribute to NT's ability to support multiple transport protocols?
27. Differentiate between synchronous and asynchronous I/O.
28. What is the role of interprocess communication in general, and what advantage, if any, does WinSock 2 offer over alternative IPC protocols?
29. Explain the relationship between the various modules of the NT security model.
30. How does NBF differ from NetBEUI?
31. What functionality is offered by Services for Macintosh?
32. What architectural elements are required on NT to implement Services for Macintosh without requiring any hardware or software changes to the Mac clients?
33. What is DHCP, and why is it important?
34. What is the relationship between WINS and DNS? When would each or both be employed?
35. Name and describe the issues surrounding at least five areas on NOS functionality which must be addressed when designing interoperability solutions.
36. What is NFS, and what alternatives are available for support of NFS by NT?
37. What is the importance of the Win32 API and WinSock2 to future interoperability possibilities?
38. What are the business layer issues behind the demand for tightly integrated remote-access services?
39. Describe NT RAS in terms of supported communication protocols, WAN services, functionality, and architecture.
40. How is it possible for remote clients to still support the same network and transport layer protocols as locally attached clients?
41. What are the additional security concerns involved with remote access clients? How are they addressed in NT?

ACTIVITIES

1. Interview several organizations which have implemented NT. Determine the domain architecture employed in each case. Describe the organization structure and relate the organization size and structure to the chosen domain architecture. In your opinion, was the domain architecture implemented the best alternative? Why or why not?
2. Interview several organizations which have implemented NT. Document the chosen communications protocol in each case. Draw network diagrams indicating the communications protocols which must be supported at clients and servers. Determine why each communication protocol was chosen in each case. Were there alternatives which could have implemented in any cases?
3. Interview several organizations which have implemented NT. Determine the functional use of NT. Is it being used as an application server?

database server? file server? print server? more than one? What other network operating systems are being employed for which function?

4. Investigate DLC as implemented on network-attached printers such as the HP 4Si. What functionality does DLC offer? What is required on both the printer and NT to implement it? Are alternatives to DLC available?

5. Interview several organizations which have implemented NT. Focus especially on those organizations which have implemented DHCP. What was their motivation? What has been their experience with DHCP to date? What unique requirements come into play when DHCP must be supported across networks using internetworking devices such as routers?

6. Interview several organizations which support both NT and NetWare LANs. Which interoperability products are employed, and what functionality is delivered by each product? Is each product employed more for interoperability or transition? Be sure to note whether NetWare LANs are 3.x or 4.x.

7. Investigate several organizations which have implemented NT RAS. Draw detailed diagrams of their architecture, including any additional hardware or software required. Be sure to also include business motivation and delivered functionality. Were alternatives to NT RAS considered?

8. Research the future directions of NT listed in the chapter as well as any others discovered in professional periodicals. Which do you think are most significant? Survey industry professionals as to which they think are most significant. Present and explain your results.

9. Gather information concerning comparative market share of NetWare and NT from professional periodicals. Present your findings in graphical format. Explain your results. What trends are developing? Is NetWare or NT being adopted more in some market segments than others? As a network manager, what would your strategic plan for network operating system be, given the results of your research?

FEATURED REFERENCES

IP/DHCP

Enck, John. Take a Number. *Windows NT Magazine* (October 1995), 31.

Johnson, Johna. TCP/IP without Tears. *Data Communications,* 24; 1 (January 1995), 114.

Wayner, Peter. Automating TCP/IP in NT. *Byte,* 19; 11 (November 1994), 189.

DNS

Reich, Richard. DNS Strategies. *Windows NT Magazine* (October 1995), 27.

NT 3.5/3.51

Allen, John et al. Serving Up Windows on the Network. *Network World,* 12; 39 (September 25, 1995), 87.

Linthicum, David. Network Operating Systems: Serving Up Apps. *PC Magazine,* 14; 18 (October 24, 1995), 205.

Prasad, Shashi. Windows NT Threads. *Byte,* 20; 11 (November 1995), 253.

Robertson, Bruce. Microsoft Windows NT 3.5: Nice Touch, New Technology, Now Try. *Network Computing,* 5; 15 (December 1, 1994), 72.

Robertson, Bruce. NT 3.51 Adds a Few Frills. *Network Computing,* 6; 6 (May 15, 1995), 32.

Streeter, April. NT Forges Corporate Foothold. *LAN Times,* 12; 4 (February 27, 1996), 56.

NT Network Architecture/API/WinSock

Amaru, Chris. When SMP Isn't SMP. *IT/IS BackOffice* (November 1995), 23.

Chan, Chuck. Write an NT WinSock Service. *Byte,* 19; 12 (December 1994), 89.

Custer, Helen. *Inside Windows NT* (Redmond, WA: Microsoft Press, 1993).

Custer, Helen. *Inside the Windows NT File System* (Redmond, WA: Microsoft Press, 1994).

Fisher, Sharon. Apple to Bring Windows Sockets API to the Mac. *Communications Week,* no. 567 (July 24, 1995), 20.

Foley, Mary Jo. Win NT Tackles Clustering. *PC Week,* 12; 41 (October 16, 1995), 120.

Gaskin, James. WinSock Opens Wider. *Information Week,* no. 531 (June 12, 1995), 60.

Vaughan-Nichols, Steven. WinSock2 Enhances Connectivity. *Byte,* 20; 8 (August 1995), 30.

NT/NetWare Interoperability and Transition

Auditore, Peter and Patrick Higbie. Unix-to-NT Migration. *IT/IS BackOffice* (November 1995), 39.

Feniello, Mark. Open(ing) VMS to Win32. *Byte,* 20; 11 (November 1995), 251.

Fisher, Sharon and Marcia Jacobs. Microsoft Drawing NetWare Users to NT. *Communications Week,* no. 562 (June 19, 1995), 1.

Gaskin, James. Faux-NetWare on Windows NT. *Information Week,* no. 537 (July 24, 1995), 72.

Katz, William. Microsoft's New Manager for NT Simplifies Cross-NOS User Handling. *PC Week* 12; 25 (June 26, 1995), 91.

Udell, Jon. Microsoft Furthers NetWare-to-NT Transition. *Byte,* 20; 4 (April 1995), 26.

NT/NFS

Phillips, Ken. NFS Server Spreads NT Wealth. *PC Week,* 12; 27 (July 10, 1995), N3.

Sedore, Christopher. NT Meets NFS. *Network Computing*, 6; 9 (August 1, 1995), 96.

Networking

Graziano, Claudia. Management Moves to NT. *LAN Times*, 12; 15 (August 14, 1995), 1.

Johnson, Johna. Windows95 on the Net: Handle with Care. *Data Communications*, 24; 14 (October 1995), 47.

Levitt, Jason. Windows NT Serves the Net. *Information Week*, no. 544 (September 11, 1995), 60.

Ruley, John. *Networking Windows NT* (New York: John Wiley & Sons, 1994).

Fault Tolerance

Carr, Eric. Making NT Fault Tolerant. *Network Computing*, 6; 9 (August 1, 1995), 124.

Future Directions

Panettieri, Joseph. What Next for NT? *Information Week*, no. 544 (September 11, 1995), 26.

CASE STUDY

Chapter 12

THE NT DECISION

A User's Move from Netware Hinges on Stability and Cost

Late in 1991, with two weeks to build a 24-node network, Jeff Compton turned to Novell Inc.'s NetWare 3.11. But as the network grew to its current 200 nodes, management and reliability problems drove Compton to abandon NetWare and adopt Microsoft Windows NT.

As the director of MIS for Financial Alliance Processing Services Inc., a Louisville, Ky.-based credit-card processing company, Compton oversees a network infrastructure that includes 200 Windows for Workgroup users on four 16-Mbps token-ring networks and a fiber ring that ties a Cisco Systems Inc. 7000 router to an FDDI hub. The hub connects eight copper distributed data interface (CDDI)-based servers running Windows NT 3.5.

But in 1991, as Financial Alliance's ninth employee, Compton inherited an IS infrastructure that comprised an electric typewriter and a two-line telephone system. With Rosa's Inc., a systems integrator in Richmond, Ind., Compton set about installing the first 24 nodes. But before deployment began, Compton had to decide among NetWare, Microsoft LAN Manager, and Banyan Systems Inc. VINES.

"I was the most familiar with NetWare, and we were on a very, very short time frame. I was hired on the 23rd of December, 1991, and by Jan. 6, we had 24 workstations up on a network," said Compton, explaining his choice of network operating system. "We were on NetWare, but basically what I wanted to do was a Windows solution."

The familiarity that let Compton deploy his network in two weeks did not prevent the ensuing NetWare-related growing pains.

Network stability and reliability were primary concerns. Compton found that certain Microsoft Access queries made against data sitting on a NetWare-based Access server would cause an abnormal end (ABEND) error and bring down the fraud-monitoring system. "Every time we would kick off a query on data that was sitting on the Novell server, we would repeatedly kill the Novell server—bring it to its knees—and get an ABEND error."

With the mission-critical fraud-monitoring and settlement systems running on NetWare, the company couldn't afford the resulting network downtime. Acting as a middleman between merchants and banks, Financial Alliance verifies credit-card transactions, and the fraud-monitoring application watches for and alerts the company of suspicious or fraudulent credit-card use. When this system is down, Financial Alliance is responsible for any money lost as a result.

"We can very easily have $75,000 of fraudulent transactions run through our system in an afternoon if our fraud-monitoring system happens to be down because of a Novell server," said Compton.

Network administration, for instance, included mundane but time-consuming chores. By the time Financial Alliance was running multiple NetWare servers in September 1992, network managers were entering redundant information as they set up user accounts and access rights on each server.

Other factors led Compton to abandon his NetWare infrastructure. The costs of implementing fault tolerance under NetWare 3.11 were prohibitive. Network manageability and reliability would become increasingly important to Financial Alliance, which was acquired by Shoreview, Minn.-based financial services company Deluxe Corp. in January. Over the next few years, Deluxe plans to expand Financial Alliance into a company five times its current size of 520 employees and approximately $50 million in revenue.

Frankly, Compton didn't see

that growth happening under NetWare, even version 4.x with its single, enterprisewide login, NDS, and Virtual Loadable Modules (VLMs). By the time Microsoft made its first NT beta code available, Compton was migrating Financial Alliance to the all-Windows network he wanted from the beginning.

As Fast As We Could

Financial Alliance's move to NT began in August 1993, and the mission-critical applications were the first to migrate. Compton ran the fraud-monitoring application and the settlement system, which reconciled merchant accounts of $2.2 billion last year, on NT beta code in parallel with NetWare 3.11 servers that ran as hot-standby units in case NT crashed. It didn't.

Satisfied with Windows NT's stability, Compton moved file and print services over to NT a few months later. "We were moving to NT as fast as we could," said Compton. "Our business was going to crater if we didn't."

Last fall, Financial Alliance moved its Systems Network Architecture (SNA) gateway, which it uses to communicate with the mainframes of the vendors it represents, from NetWare for SAA to Microsoft's SNA Server 2.1. The switch marked the end of NetWare service on the network, and the company hasn't looked back.

The biggest bang for Financial Alliance's NT buck is the built-in RAID Level 5 support, said Compton. Unlike NetWare, which requires hardware-level RAID, NT performs the RAID functions, so users can assemble RAID with off-the-shelf disk drives.

Compton recently bought six 9GB drives for $2,900 each, giving him a 54GB RAID 5 drive for $17,400. He figures a hardware-based RAID 5 would have cost him over $50,000.

Except for scheduled maintenance or problems unrelated to the NOS, Compton hasn't seen any NT-caused network downtime.

NT administration is another boon, according to Compton. Network managers enter user information once, at one console, and set access to servers and applications for the entire NT domain. Bundled utilities such as Performance Monitor improve Financial Alliance's network troubleshooting.

For Compton, the NT price is right. "If I would have bought everything under Novell to get me to where I'm at with my NT stuff, including RAID, centralized administration, and Performance Monitor, we would have spent tens of thousands of dollars more than what we spent on a $900 package that has all that stuff built in."

Beyond the Windows NT feature set lies network peace of mind. "I'm very confident that we're not going to have to switch operating systems because we're going to have a thousand users," Compton said. "We're not going to have to totally redo things. The operating systems we've put in place are key to us being able to grow like they want us to grow over the next five years."

Source: Brent Dorschkind (March 13, 1995). The NT Decision. *LAN Times,* 12(5), 1. Reprinted with permission of McGraw-Hill, *LAN Times.*

BUSINESS CASE STUDY QUESTIONS

Activities

1. Complete a top-down model for this case by gleaning facts from the case and placing them in the proper layer of the top-down model. After completing the top-down model, analyze and detail those instances when requirements were clearly passed down from upper to lower layers of the model and solutions to those requirements were passed up from lower to upper layers.
2. Detail any questions that may occur to you about the case for which answers are not clearly stated in the article.
3. Based on the information supplied in the article, draw a network topology diagram including all installed network hardware and software.

Business

1. What were the motivating business factors which led to the migration to Windows NT?

2. What were the motivating factors in the choice of NetWare in the first place?
3. What are the key business activities and services this company provides?
4. What impact on required network functionality did the company's business requirements have?
5. What would be the business impacts on this company if the network goes down?
6. What were the strategic business plans of this company, and what impact did they have on strategic network plans?
7. What financial comparisons were made by the network manager regarding NetWare vs. NT implementation costs?

Application

1. Which types of applications were run on the NetWare servers?

2. What are some of the difficulties of using Windows as a GUI on NetWare clients?
3. What is meant by the term mission-critical application?
4. Were the applications executed by this company mission-critical? Defend your answer.
5. What types of applications are running on the NT server?

Data

1. Which database management system was used in this case?
2. Was the use of this database management system a problem in a NetWare environment? Why or why not?
3. What are the key differences between the ways in which NetWare and NT support RAID?
4. How can differences in RAID implementations translate into financial impact?

5. Why is RAID an important complement to mission-critical applications?

Network

1. Describe the growth of the network in the case.
2. Describe the network topology and transmission speed which services both clients and servers.
3. What were the company's requirements in the area of LAN administration?
4. How would the LAN administration capabilities of NT (administer entire LAN with single entry from single console, etc.) compare with NetWare 4.1?
5. What do you think are the two most important functional characteristics in the mind of the network manager in this case? Justify your answer.

Technology

1. Describe the migration process. What safeguards were implemented?
2. What was the purpose of the SNA gateways?

CHAPTER **13**

Unix, TCP/IP, and NFS

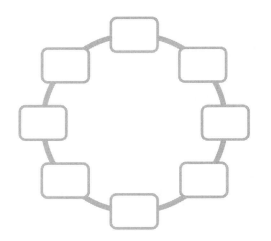

Concepts Reinforced

OSI model
Internet suite of protocols model
Network operating systems functionality

Network operating systems architecture
Protocols and standards
Interoperability

Concepts Introduced

Unix architecture
Unix functionality
Unix implementations
TCP/IP

Network addressing
TCP/IP and WANs
NFS functionality
NFS architecture

OBJECTIVES

After mastering the material in this chapter you should:

1. Understand how Unix, TCP/IP, and NFS can combine to offer functionality equivalent to a fully integrated network operating system.

2. Understand the unique functional and architectural aspects of Unix.

3. Understand the individual functionality as well as the relationship between the many members of the Internet suite of protocols.

4. Understand the pressures and trends contributing to the need for changes in the Internet suite of protocols.

5. Understand the functionality, application, advantages, and disadvantages of the currently available versions of Unix, TCP/IP, and NFS.

Although not distributed as a ready-to-run single product, Unix as an operating system, combined with the TCP/IP family of protocols for network communications, and NFS for a network-aware file system constitute a very common combina-

472

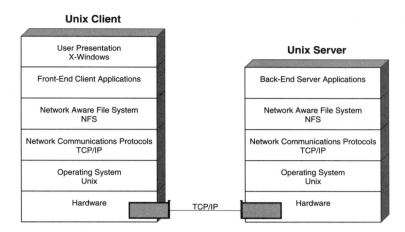

Figure 13-1   Unix, TCP/IP, and NFS as a Network Operating System

tion of elements which offer all the functionality of commercially available single-product network operating systems.

In this chapter, each of the following key elements is explored from both architectural and functional perspectives:

- Unix operating system.
- TCP/IP family of protocols, more properly known as the Internet suite of protocols.
- Network file system (NFS).

Figure 13-1 conceptually illustrates how Unix, the Internet suite of protocols (TCP/IP), and NFS can be combined to offer full network operating system functionality to network-attached clients and servers.

■ UNIX

Unix is a large family of related operating systems descended from the work of Ken Thompson and Dennis Ritchie at Bell Laboratories in the late 1960s and early 1970s. The name Unix is derived from a play on words on another Bell Labs/MIT project of the same era which produced a mainframe computer utility known as Multics. Although many innovations have been introduced in Unix implementations as Unix has evolved, all variations still share much of the original Unix architecture and functionality.

Unix Architecture

Figure 13-2 illustrates the basic components of the Unix operating system architecture. Unix is a two-layered operating system consisting of the following:

- **Unix systems programs.**
- **Unix system kernel.**

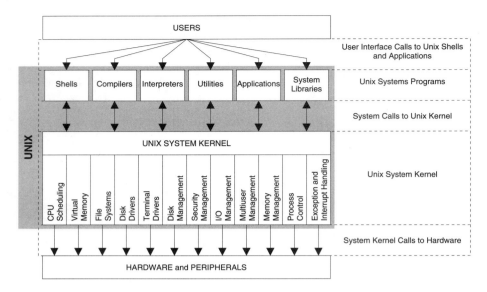

Figure 13-2   Overall Unix Architecture

Most Unix systems programs and kernels are written in C, allowing for easy portability to any hardware platform with a compatible C compiler. Unix systems programs and utilities deliver requested functionality to users by issuing system calls to the Unix system kernel. The kernel then fulfills these requests by interacting with the hardware layer and returning requested functionality to the systems programs and utilities. In this layered architecture, only the Unix system kernel needs to be concerned with the particular hardware devices with which it must interact. Even within the kernel, most hardware-specific code is confined to device drivers. Unix system programs, utilities, and end-user applications are hardware-independent and are only required to issue standardized system calls to the Unix kernel.

Most of the functionality of the Unix kernel is concerned with managing files or some type of device. To simplify and standardize system calls, Unix treats devices as a special type of file.

Perhaps the most significant characteristic of the Unix operating system is the availability of the source code, which allows individual programmers to enhance and modify Unix over the years. Modifications and enhancements are possible because of Unix's layered, modular, design, as illustrated in Figure 13-2. New utilities or systems programs can be added as long as they issue standard system calls to the kernel. The kernel can be modified as long as the modifications are compatible with the locally installed hardware, including the local C compiler.

One could conclude from this discussion that the following are the chief positive attributes of the Unix operating system:

- Portability—A characteristic of Unix on two distinct levels. First, Unix itself is portable across numerous hardware platforms. Second, application programs written for Unix are inherently portable across all Unix platforms dependent on the level of similarity between Unix kernels and system programs.

- Modularity—Unix is a viable, dynamic, operating system to which functionality can be added in the form of new system utilities or programs. Even modifications to the Unix kernel itself are possible.

Unix Shells In Unix, the command interpreter, which is the user's interface to the system, is a specialized user process known as a **shell.** Following are popular Unix shells:

- Bourne shell.

- C shell.

- TC shell.

- Korn shell, combining features of Bourne and C shells.

Each of these shells has its own associated shell scripts, and users are also able to write their own shells.

Cross-shell, cross-platform scripts and programs can be developed using either of the following languages:

- The **Perl language** (Practical Extraction and Reporting Language) adds the following functionality to that offered by the Korn and Bourne shells:
  1. List processing.
  2. Associative arrays.
  3. Modern subroutines and functions.
  4. More control statements.
  5. Better I/O.
  6. Full function library.
  7. In addition, Perl is free via download from the Internet. On the negative side, Perl is similar in syntax and commands to the more cryptic Unix shells it sought to improve on. As a result, for Unix nonexperts, Perl may still not be the answer.

- The **Rexx** scripting language is an easier to learn and use alternative which supports structured programming techniques such as modularity while still offering access to shell commands.

Unix File System Unix implements a hierarchical, multilevel tree file system starting with the root directory, as illustrated in Figure 13-3. In fact, Unix is able to support multiple file systems simultaneously on a single disk. Each disk is divided into **slices,** each of which can accommodate a file system, a swap area, or a raw data area. A Unix slice is equivalent to a partition in DOS. Each disk has only one root file system, and each file system has only one root directory.

In Unix, files are treated by the kernel as just a sequence of bytes. In other words, although application programs may require files of a particular structure, the kernel merely stores files as sequenced bytes and organizes them in directories. In the Unix file system, directories are treated as specially formatted files containing information on the location of listed files. The basic job of the file system is to offer file services as a consistent interface without requiring user application programs to worry about the particulars of the physical storage hardware used.

Unix uses **path names** to identify the specific path through the hierarchical file structure to a particular destination file. **Absolute path names** start at the root directory in the listing of the path to the destination directory, and **relative path names** start at the current directory. Figure 13-3 illustrates the difference between absolute and relative path names.

Links are another unique aspect of the Unix file system which allow a given file

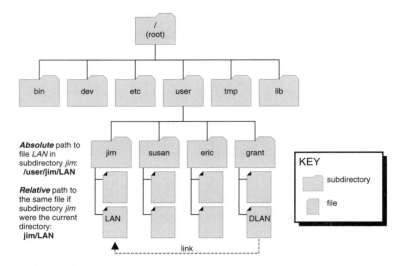

Figure 13-3   Unix File System

to be known by, and accessed by, more than one name. A link is nothing more than an entry in a directory which points to a file stored in another directory or to another whole directory. Links are also illustrated in Figure 13-3.

Unix Functionality

Unix exhibits the following functional characteristics, the significance of which has been detailed in previous chapters:

- Multiuser.
- Preemptive multitasking.
- Multiprocessing.
- Support of multithreaded applications.

Memory Management   Following are the two primary methods employed by Unix systems to manage memory:

- Swapping.
- Paging.

Swapping allows entire processes to be swapped in and out of physical memory and onto the swap space partition of one or more disk drives. When multiple processes are contending for the same limited amount of primary memory not occupied by the nonswappable Unix kernel, the **scheduler process,** also known as the **swapper,** decides which processes should be removed from primary memory to the swap partition and which should be moved from the swap partition into main memory. One of the major problems with swapping is that enough contiguous memory must be found in which to fit the swapped processes to optimize the speed and efficiency of the swapping process. The difficulty with this process is that continuously cutting out contiguous memory blocks of varying sizes from a finite amount of primary memory causes **fragmentation,** leaving numerous small pieces of unused contiguous memory.

Paging seeks to eliminate or at least minimize fragmentation, by allowing processes to execute with only portions of the process being physically present in primary memory. These fixed-size portions of the process loaded into primary memory on demand are known as **pages,** and the entire process is sometimes referred to as a **demand-paged virtual memory system.**

I/O System   It is the job of the I/O system to minimize the amount of hardware-specific interaction required of the Unix kernel. As a result, most of the hardware-specific device drivers are located in the I/O system. Figure 13-4 shows a representative Unix I/O system.

The Unix I/O system is composed of three major types of I/O:

- The sockets interface, used for interprocess communications.

- The block-device driver, used for communicating with block-oriented devices such as disk drives and tape drives. Block-oriented devices transfer data back and forth in fixed-length blocks, often 512 or 1024 bytes.

- The character-device driver, used for communicating with character-oriented devices such as terminals, printers, or other devices which don't transfer data in fixed-length blocks.

Both block-oriented and character-oriented I/O may use buffers and queues to organize the transfer of data from the operating system to the hardware device in question, through their respective **cooked interfaces.** Alternatively, both block-oriented and character-oriented I/O may bypass all buffers and queues and interact directly with hardware devices through their respective **raw interfaces.** In the case of character I/O, terminals and editing programs which must interact on a keystroke-by-keystroke basis would use the raw TTY interface. The acronym **TTY** refers to terminals in general, but actually stands for teletypewriter, a holdover from the days before terminals had video monitors.

Device drivers for specific block and character–oriented devices are stored outside of the kernel, in arrays accessed with the assistance of pointers known as device numbers that point to the correct array location, or entry point, of a particular

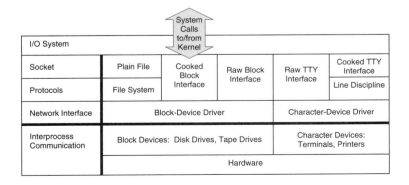

Figure 13-4   Unix I/O System

device driver. Storing device drivers outside of the kernel contributes to the portability of the Unix kernel.

Process Control   Processes in Unix are controlled by the **fork** system call, initiated through the shell interface, which allows **parent processes** to spawn multiple subprocesses known as **child processes.** Access to system calls is controlled by both userID and groupID privileges. The kernel checks these privilege levels before fulfilling requested system calls.

The exception and interrupt handling facility in Unix is known as **signals.** Besides handling exceptions, this facility is also used in starting and stopping subprocesses and allowing one shell to manage more than one process simultaneously. Processes may be organized into a **process group** to more easily or effectively accomplish a common goal, and they may communicate with each other via an interprocess communication mechanism known as pipes.

Interprocess Communications   **Pipes** is an interprocess communication mechanism which allows the output of one process to be used as the input for another process. Pipes is limited to communication between two processes executing on the same local computer and is initiated by a pipes system call. The two processes which communicate via the pipes interprocess communications mechanism must be related (parent-child), as enabled by the fork system call.

Sockets is a more powerful and flexible interprocess communications mechanism able to provide interprocess communications across network interfaces to processes running on widely distributed computers. Sockets can also be used as a more generalized interprocess mechanism for other interprocess communications mechanisms such as pipes. Sockets IPC is implemented through a series of sockets system calls which, among other things, establish the network addresses of the processes that communicate via the sockets IPC mechanism. Sockets is the IPC mechanism used to establish communications between a process on a server and multiple processes on multiple clients in a client/server architecture. Different types of sockets can be established for specific types of interprocess communications. Some of these are described in Figure 13-5.

Socket Type	Explanation
Stream Sockets	Provides reliable, connection-oriented, two-way (full-duplex), sequenced packet interprocess communications through use of TCP as the transport layer protocol.
Datagram Sockets	Provides unreliable, connectionless, datagram interprocess communications through the use of UDP (user datagram protocol) as the transport layer protocol.
Raw Sockets	Provides direct interprocess communication from sockets to other layer protocols such as IP on the network layer or Ethernet on the data-link layer. Raw sockets is sometimes called the **do-it-yourself (DIY)** interface since the programmer must supply the functionality provided by higher (transport) layer protocols such as TCP or UDP.

Figure 13-5   Socket Types

Unix Implementations

There are two major families of Unix:

- Unix System V Release 4, commonly known as SVR4 or V.4. This version is descended from the original model developed at Bell Laboratories, later known as Unix Systems Laboratory (USL), and recently sold by Novell to SCO (Santa Cruz Operation).

- BSD (Berkeley Software Distribution) version 4.4, commonly known as 4.4BSD.

Information concerning current Unix implementations on a variety of hardware platforms is summarized in Figure 13-6.

Although all of these implementations are considered Unix, they may not be 100% compatible. Two efforts launched by Unix vendors to improve on Unix variant compatibility are as follows:

- **Common Desktop Environment (CDE)** — An effort by a consortium of Unix vendors to establish standards for a unified graphical user interface allowing those Unix varieties which support the CDE to present an identical interface to users. Applications developers will be able to write applications to the CDE API rather than developing separate versions of their application for each Unix variant.

- In attempting to standardize the operating system elements of Unix, a consortium of vendors has been working on the **single Unix specification,** otherwise known as the **Spec 1170 APIs.** This is a collection of over 1000 APIs which, hopefully, all versions of Unix will support.

Compliance with both the CDE and Spec 1170 API specifications will be certified by **X/Open,** an independent Unix standards organization located in Menlo Park, CA.

Unix Implementation	Hardware Platform	Vendor
A/UX	Macintosh	Apple Computer
OSF/1 and Ultrix	DEC VAX and Alpha workstations	Digital Equipment Corporation
HP-UX	HP RISC workstations and servers	Hewlett-Packard Corporation
AIX	IBM workstation, RS/6000, and mainframes	IBM
NextStep	Intel 486 or Pentium, Next	Next Computer
SCO OpenServer	Intel 486 or Pentium	Santa Cruz Operation
Solaris	Sun Sparcstations and Intel x86	SunSoft
Linux	Intel x86	Shareware
UnixWare	Intel 486 or Pentium	Novell

Figure 13-6   Unix Implementations

■ THE INTERNET SUITE OF PROTOCOLS: OVERALL ARCHITECTURE AND FUNCTIONALITY

Transmission control protocol/Internet protocol (TCP/IP) refers to an entire suite of protocols that provide communication on a variety of layers between widely distributed types of computers. Strictly speaking, TCP and IP are just two of the protocols contained within the family of protocols, more properly known as the **Internet suite of protocols.** TCP/IP was developed during the 1970s and widely deployed during the 1980s under the auspices of the Defense Advanced Research Projects Agency **(DARPA),** to meet the Department of Defense's need for a wide variety of computers able to interoperate and communicate. TCP/IP became widely available to universities and research agencies and has become the de facto standard for communication between heterogeneous networked computers.

Overall Architecture

TCP/IP and the entire family of related protocols are organized into a protocol model. Although not identical to the OSI seven-layer model, the **TCP/IP model** is no less effective at organizing protocols required to establish and maintain communications between different computers. Figure 13-7 illustrates the TCP/IP model, its constituent protocols, and its relationship to the seven-layer OSI model.

As the figure shows, the OSI model and TCP/IP model are functionally equivalent, although not identical, up through the transport layer. The OSI model continues with the session, presentation, and applications layers, but the TCP/IP model has only the application layer remaining, with utilities such as Telnet (terminal emulation) and FTP as examples of application layer protocols. As Figure 13-7 illustrates, the functionality equivalent to the OSI model's session, presentation, and application layers is added to the TCP/IP model by combining it with the network file system (NFS) distributed by Sun Microsystems. As a result, to offer equivalent functionality to that of the full OSI seven-layer model, the TCP/IP family of protocols must be combined with NFS, sometimes known as the open network computing (ONC) environment.

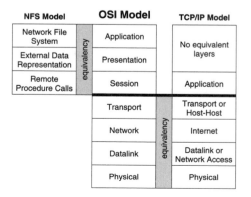

Figure 13-7   The TCP/IP Model

■ INDIVIDUAL PROTOCOLS: ARCHITECTURE AND FUNCTIONALITY

Figure 13-8 illustrates the placement of many of the TCP/IP family of protocols in their respective layers of the TCP/IP model. Each of these protocols, as well as several others, will be explained in detail. Many protocols involved with network management, routing, and remote access do not fit logically into any of the layers of the TCP/IP model and are therefore not listed. Not all protocols in the OSI model have proper layers in which to be placed either.

Communications Protocols

Internet Protocol (IP)   **Internet protocol (IP)** is the network layer protocol of the TCP/IP suite of protocols. It is primarily responsible for providing the addressing functionality necessary to ensure that all reachable network destinations can be uniquely and correctly identified. The IP addresses included within the header of the IP packets are used by routers to determine the best path to be taken by each individual packet to reach its ultimate destination. IP allows each packet to be processed individually within the network and does not provide any guarantees that packets will arrive at their intended destination in sequence, if at all. As such, IP is described as a **connectionless, unreliable** protocol. Assurance of reliable receipts of packets in the proper sequence require the use of upper layer protocols such as TCP.

IP packets have a minimum length of 576 bytes and a maximum length of 64 Kbytes. Depending on the network architecture (Ethernet, Token Ring, etc.) employed, larger IP packets may need to be fragmented into multiple data-link layer frames. Figure 13-9 illustrates the IP packet layout.

As the figure shows, the IP header can be either 20 or 24 bytes long, with the bits actually being transmitted in **network byte order,** or from left to right. The significance of each field in the IP header is as follows:

- IP Version—It is important for computers and internetwork devices processing this IP packet to know the IP version with which it was written to preclude any potential cross-version incompatibility problems.

- Header Length—The header can be either five or six 32-bit words (20 or 24 bytes), depending on whether or not the options field is activated.

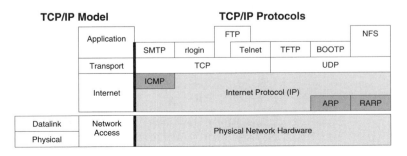

Figure 13-8   TCP/IP Family of Protocols

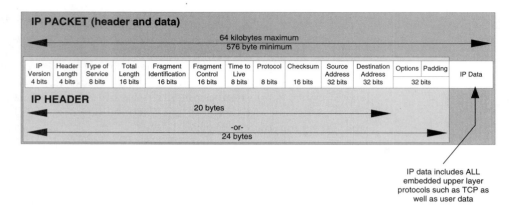

Figure 13-9   IP Packet Layout

- Type of Service—The flags in this field can be used to indicate eight levels of precedence as well as different types of service for low delay, high throughput, or high reliability. Unless routers can read this field and respond accordingly, they are of no use.

- Total Length—This is the total length of the IP packet, including the header and the IP data.

- Fragment Identification—This is a 16-bit integer ID of a fragment. IP packets must be fragmented as dictated by the limitations of lower layer (data-link) network architectures.

- Fragment Control (Flags and Offset)—Fragment flags (3 bits) are used to indicate the last fragment of an original datagram as well as if a datagram should not be fragmented. Fragment offset (13 bits) indicates the relative position of this fragment in the original IP datagram.

- Time to Live—This field is a simple hop counter which is decremented every time this IP packet is handled by a router. When the time to live counter reaches 0, the packet is discarded so that it does not wander around the network for infinity, monopolizing bandwidth. The counter can be initialized as high as 255 but is typically set to 32 or 16.

- Protocol—This is an important field that indicates which protocol is embedded with the IP data area. By reading this field, the IP software is able to forward the IP data to the proper transport layer protocol stack for further processing. Typical values and their corresponding protocols are as follows:
    1. 17   UDP.
    2. 6   TCP.
    3. 1   ICMP.
    4. 8   EGP.
    5. 89   OSPF.

- Checksum—This field is more correctly known as the IP header checksum, because it provides error detection only for the IP header. Reliability checks for the IP data is provided by upper layer protocols.

- Source Address—32-bit IP address of source computer.

- Destination Address—32-bit IP address of ultimate destination computer.

- Options—Used for diagnostics purposes, these fields are sometimes set by other TCP/IP family utilities such as Ping or TraceRte. Security and source routing options can also be set using this field. These features must be supported by all workstations and routers in a given network to be implemented fully and effectively.

- Padding—Depending on how many options are selected, padding of zeroes may need to be added to bring the IP header to the full 6×32-bit word (24 byte) length.

Network Addressing with IP   As previously mentioned, one of the chief jobs of the IP protocol is to provide a structured addressing scheme so that computers and internetwork routers can be uniquely and correctly identified. In general, the 32-bit IP address is divided into three components:

- Address class.

- Network ID.

- Host ID.

IP Address Classes   IP addresses are categorized into **address classes** A, B, C, D, or E. Class D addresses are reserved for multicast systems such as routers, and Class E addresses are reserved for future use. Class A, B, and C addresses vary in the number of bits allocated for network IDs versus host IDs. As a result, address classes vary in the ratio of available network IDs to available host IDs, as Figure 13-10 illustrates.

Assigning address classes and network ID ranges to a particular organization that wants to connect to the Internet is the responsibility of the Internet Activities Board (IAB). The IAB ensures that all organizations using the Internet for network communications have unique IP addresses for all of their workstations. If an organization has no intention of ever accessing the Internet, there may be no need to register with the IAB for an IP address class and range of valid network IDs. However,

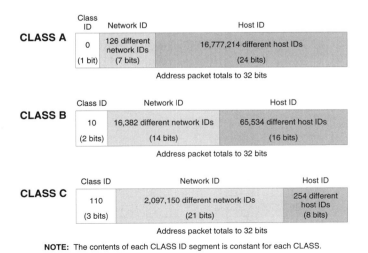

NOTE: The contents of each CLASS ID segment is constant for each CLASS.

Figure 13-10   IP Address Classes

even in this case, all workstations on all communicating networks must have unique IP addresses within the internal corporate network.

Subnetworks   In many cases, a given organization may be issued a single class B network ID address with its associated 65,534 host IDs. This may seem like more than enough addresses until one considers that most organizations are distributed across multiple geographic locations. Internetworking devices known as routers (explained further in Chapter 14) must be employed to ensure that information traveling from one corporate location to another is properly routed. The difficulty with this scenario is that each network connected to the routers must have a unique network ID, allowing the router to distinguish one destination network from another. As previously stated, however, the IAB issued the organization in question only a single network ID.

The solution to this dilemma is **subnetworking.** By applying a 32-bit **subnet mask** to a class B IP address, a portion of the bits which comprise the host ID can be reserved for denoting subnetworks, with the remaining bits being reserved for host IDs per subnetwork. If the first 8 bits of the host ID were reserved for subnetwork addresses and the final 8 bits for hosts per subnetwork, this would allow the same class B address to yield 254 subnetworks with 254 hosts each, as opposed to one network with 65,534 hosts. Figure 13-11 provides examples of subnet masks.

Domain Name System   Because it is easier to remember and address destinations by name rather than by IP address, the **domain name system,** or **DNS,** has been created to provide the following key services:

- Uniquely identify by name all hosts connected to the Internet.

- Resolve, or translate, host names into IP addresses (and vice versa).

- Identify which services are offered by each host, such as gateway or mail transfer, and to which networks these services are offered.

To implement DNS, naming conventions needed to be established. One element of this convention is the use of standard suffixes for internet naming such as .edu for educational institutions, .com for commercial entities, and .gov for government agencies. Private institutions are welcome to establish their own naming schemes for use within corporate networks.

DNS is physically implemented in a client/server architecture in which client-based DNS software known as the DNS or name **resolver,** sends requests for DNS name resolution to a **DNS** (or name) **server.** The address of the nearest (primary) DNS server, as well as at least one backup (secondary) DNS server, is entered into a

Binary Subnet Mask	Decimal Subnet Mask	Number of Subnetworks	Number of Hosts per Subnetwork
11111111 11111111 **00000000** 00000000	255.255.0.0	1	65,534
11111111 11111111 **11111111** 00000000	255.255.255.0	254	254

Figure 13-11   IP Subnet Masks

configuration file when TCP/IP is installed on the local client. Networks which connect to the Internet must supply both a primary and a backup DNS server, to process name queries from Internet-attached hosts. DNS is a hierarchical service in that, if a given DNS server cannot resolve a name as requested, it will reply with the address of a DNS server of a higher authority which may have more information available. Alternatively, the local DNS server may contact the higher authority DNS server itself, thereby increasing its own knowledge while meeting the client request, in a process known as **recursion.** The scope of coverage, or collection of domains, for which a given DNS server can resolve names is known as a DNS **zone.**

Transmission Control Protocol (TCP)   **Transmission control protocol,** or **TCP,** is a transport layer protocol which provides **connection-oriented, reliable** transmission for upper layer application programs or utilities. This reliability is ensured through the additional fields contained within the TCP header, which offer the following functionality:

- Flow control.

- Acknowledgments of successful receipt of packets after error checking.

- Retransmission of packets as required.

- Proper sequencing of packets.

The fact that TCP is considered connection-oriented implies that a point-to-point connection between source and destination computers must be established before transmission can begin and that the connection will be torn down after transmission has concluded.

TCP offers reliable transport services to applications through the use of **ports.** Ports are specific 16-bit addresses which are uniquely related to particular applications. Source port and destination port addresses are included in the TCP header. The unique port address of an application combined with the unique 32-bit IP address of the computer on which the application is executing is known as a **socket.** Some typical port numbers for popular TCP/IP applications are listed in Figure 13-12.

TCP/IP Application	Port Number
Telnet	23
FTP	21
SMTP	25
BootP client	68
BootP server	67
TFTP	69
Finger	79
NetBIOS session service	139
X.400	103
SNMP	161

Figure 13-12   Selected TCP/IP Applications and Port Numbers

It should be pointed out that not all applications require reliable, connection-oriented connections and could therefore alternatively avail themselves of the connectionless, unreliable transport protocol known as UDP, which is further explained shortly.

The TCP header layout, illustrated in Figure 13-13, is composed of the following fields:

- Source and destination port addresses: As previously described, the port addresses are part of the socket address which uniquely identifies the particular application on the particular computer to or from which this packet is sent.

- Sequence number: Proper sequencing of packets is one of the jobs of TCP, and the sequence number in the TCP header holds the sequence number of the first octet of data in this segment. This allows TCP at the destination address to properly resequence the data stream if IP happens to deliver the segments out of order.

- Acknowledgment number: To meet its objective of ensuring reliable transmission, the transmitting computer must know the sequence number of the segment last successfully received by the receiving computer. The transmitted acknowledgment number is, in fact, the segment number of the last successfully received segment plus 1. This lets the transmitting computer know which segment the receiving computer is waiting for. If the acknowledgment number does not increment before a preset retransmission timer expires, then the transmitting computer assumes that the repeated acknowledgment number's segment never arrived and it must retransmit that segment.

- Data offset (4 bits): This is another means of stating the length of the TCP header, in terms of the number of 32-bit words before the TCP data starts. The entry in this field is 5 (20 bytes) if options and padding are not enabled or 6 (24 bytes) if they are enabled.

- Reserved (6 bits): Set to all zeroes.

- Codes (6 bits): Also known as flags, codes are used for connection setup, management, and termination. There are six possible codes:
    1. SYN—Used to initially set up connections and synchronize sequence numbers.
    2. ACK—Indicates validity of acknowledgment number, especially important at connection setup time.
    3. URG—Indicates validity of urgent pointer field.
    4. PSH—The push flag causes TCP to immediately flush data buffers, to

IP HEADER	IP DATA									
	TCP HEADER									TCP DATA
	Source Port 16 bits	Destination Port 16 bits	Sequence Number 32 bits	Acknowledgement Number 32 bits	Data Offset and Codes 16 bits	Window 16 bits	Checksum 16 bits	Urgent Pointer 16 bits	Options and Padding 32 bits	Upper Layer Protocols and User Data
20 or 24 bytes	24 bytes									

Figure 13-13   TCP Header Layout

push this packet directly to the application whose port number is indicated in the TCP header.

5. FIN—Terminates connections normally.

6. RST—Resets the connection, thereby forcing a connection termination.

- Window: The window field is used by TCP as a means of flow control. The window value is sent from a destination node to a source node, advertising how many bytes of free buffer space are available on the destination node for this connection. This number then becomes the limit on how much data can be sent by the source before an acknowledgment must be received from the destination node.

- Checksum: This is a calculated checksum on the TCP header and data which is transmitted to the destination node for error detection.

- Urgent pointer: This field tells the destination where to look in the data field for an urgent message, such as a break signal or some other type of interrupt.

- Options and padding: The only option typically set with TCP is a value for maximum segment size which lets the destination node know the largest acceptable segment length. Padding extends the options field to a full 32-bit word, and is used only if options are set.

Note that the TCP header plus the TCP data, consisting of the embedded upper layer protocols and user data from applications, are all embedded within the data area of the IP packet.

User Datagram Protocol (UDP)   **User datagram protocol,** or **UDP,** provides unreliable, connectionless messaging services for applications. Because UDP does not need to offer a great deal of functionality in addition to that already offered by IP, it requires only an 8-bit header, as illustrated in Figure 13-14. The main purpose of the header is to allow UDP to keep track of which applications it is sending a datagram to/from through the use of port addresses, and to pass those messages along to IP for subsequent delivery.

The fields of the UDP header are as follows:

- Source and destination port addresses: Addresses of applications to and from which UDP datagrams are sent.

- Length: Length of the UDP datagram.

- Checksum: Calculated on both the UDP header and UDP data.

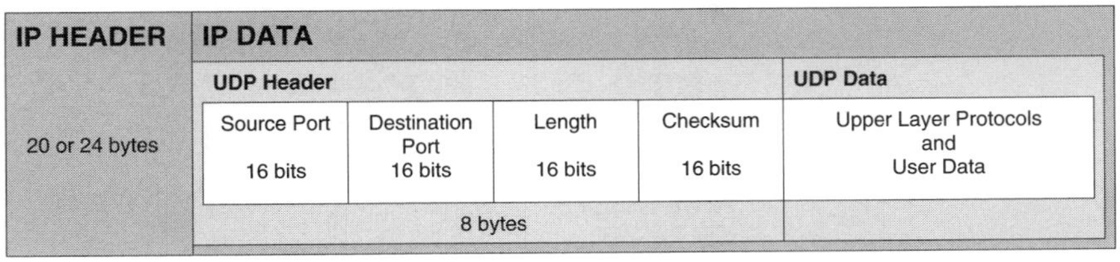

IP HEADER	IP DATA				
	UDP Header				UDP Data
20 or 24 bytes	Source Port 16 bits	Destination Port 16 bits	Length 16 bits	Checksum 16 bits	Upper Layer Protocols and User Data
	8 bytes				

Figure 13-14   UDP Header Layout

WAN or Remote-Access Protocols

Two protocols within the TCP/IP family can be used to connect TCP/IP supporting computers or internetworking devices via wide area links, including dial-up links:

- **Serial line Internet protocol,** or **SLIP.**
- **Point-to-point protocol,** or **PPP.**

Serial Line Internet Protocol (SLIP)   SLIP is the older of the two TCP/IP WAN protocols and lacks some of the advanced functionality of PPP. SLIP can establish asynchronous serial links between two computers which support both SLIP and TCP/IP over any of the following connections:

- Modems and a dial-up line.
- Modems and a point-to-point private or leased line.
- Hard-wired or direct connections.

In terms of the OSI model, SLIP is really providing an alternative data-link layer protocol frame in which to embed IP packets. In a local area network environment, these IP packets would have been embedded in Ethernet, Token Ring, FDDI, or some other network architecture's data-link layer frames. Unlike most LAN data-link layer protocols, SLIP does not provide any error-detection mechanism. Figure 13-15 illustrates some of the characteristics of SLIP-based connections.

Point-to-Point Protocol (PPP)   PPP is a WAN data-link layer protocol established to overcome some of the shortcomings of SLIP. As the demand for remote access to TCP/IP-based networks has increased, due to industry's increased interest in telecommuting, PPP has played an increasingly important role. Strictly speaking, PPP is actually a collection of protocols extended over time with the issuance of ad-

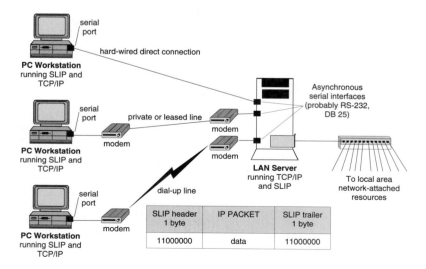

Figure 13-15   SLIP Connections

ditional request for comments (RFCs). Although the extendibility of PPP is a positive attribute, it is somewhat of a double-edged sword as claims of PPP compatibility must be carefully investigated to determine exactly which PPP features are supported.

Perhaps the most important distinction between SLIP and PPP is that, although SLIP can transport only IP packets, PPP is able to deliver multiple network layer protocols including IP, IPX, Vines (VIP), DECnet, XNS, AppleTalk, and OSI. To be more specific, PPP supports multiple network layer protocols simultaneously over a single WAN connection.

In addition, PPP is able to establish connections over a variety of WAN services including ISDN, Frame Relay, SONET, X.25, and synchronous and asynchronous serial links.

Figure 13-16 illustrates the PPP frame layout as well as potential implementation scenarios.

The fields included in the PPP frame layout are as follows:

- Flags—A specific sequence of bits (01111110) is used to indicate both the beginning and end of the PPP frame.

- Address—Since PPP creates only point-to-point connections, there is no need for addressing on the data-link layer; therefore this field is set to all

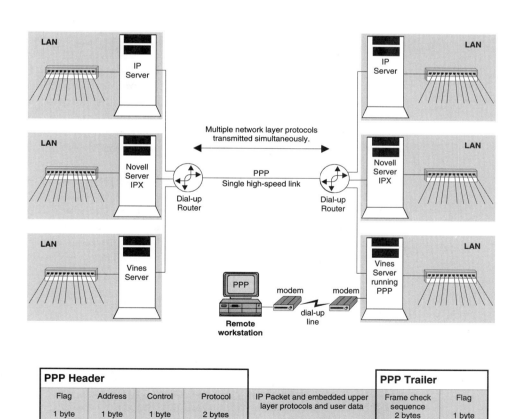

PPP Header				IP Packet and embedded upper layer protocols and user data	PPP Trailer	
Flag 1 byte	Address 1 byte	Control 1 byte	Protocol 2 bytes		Frame check sequence 2 bytes	Flag 1 byte
01111110	11111111	00000011				01111110

Figure 13-16 PPP Protocol Layout and Implementation Scenarios

ones. Don't forget, the IP address is essential to successful delivery of this packet and is embedded within the data payload section of the PPP frame.

- Protocol—Three major protocol types are required to support PPP connections:
  - LCP—Link control protocol is responsible for creating and terminating the connection. It negotiates with the distant PPP node on such issues as data encapsulation format, packet size, link quality, and authentication (PAP and CHAP).
  - IPCP—IP control protocol is in charge of negotiating with the remote IP node for IP addresses to be used once LCP has established the connection.
  - NCP—Once LCP and IPCP have established the connection, network control protocol then transports the multiple network layer protocols between the two end-nodes of the connection. A different type of NCP protocol is defined for each network layer protocol transported.
- Frame Check Sequence—This is the standard 16-bit frame check sequence used by the PPP protocol at either end of the connection, to detect errors prior to passing embedded information on to the local node for further processing.

Multilink Point-to-Point Protocol (MLPPP)   Although PPP was an improvement on SLIP, **multilink point-to-point protocol,** or **MLPPP** (RFC 1717), improves on PPP by supporting multiple simultaneous physical WAN links. MLPPP doesn't replace PPP. It is an additional protocol which sits between PPP and the network layer protocols to be transported. Besides being able to support more than one physical WAN link simultaneously, MLPPP also combines multiple channels from a variety of WAN services into a single logical link. Examples of such WAN services are multichannel switched service such as integrated services digital network (ISDN) as well as packet-switched services such as frame relay and cell-based services such as ATM. PPP links are identified with a particular MLPPP group identifier during PPP connection setup.

By acting as a separate logical link layer responsible for combining a variety of WAN services between two end-points of a connection to deliver required bandwidth, MLPPP-compliant devices can deliver "bandwidth on demand" in a process referred to as **inverse multiplexing.** This is a particularly important feature for unpredictable, bursty, LAN-to-LAN traffic. Figure 13-17 illustrates the relationship between PPP, MLPPP, network layer protocols, and WAN services.

Routing Protocols

Routing Is Address Processing   Although routing is explained in detail in the chapter on LAN-to-LAN connectivity, it is important to understand some basic routing concepts to appreciate routing protocol functionality. Perhaps the most important thing to understand about routing is that it is nothing more than address processing performed when messages need to travel beyond the local LAN. By keeping track of the following address-related issues, the entire routing process can be largely demystified:

- As illustrated in Figure 13-18, the first logical step in the routing process would be for the source workstation to fill in the source address field in the

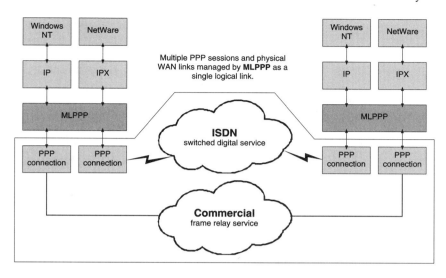

Figure 13-17   Multilink Point-to-Point Protocol

Physical Topology

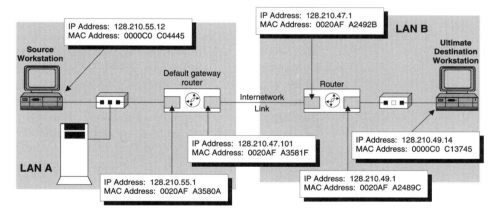

Address Processing

From source workstation to default gateway router found on LAN A:

Data-Link		IP	
destination	source	destination	source
0020AF A3580A	0000C0 C04445	128.210.49.14	128.210.55.12

From LAN A router to next hop router towards ultimate destination as noted in routing table:

Data-Link		IP	
destination	source	destination	source
0020AF A2492B	0020AF A3581F	128.210.49.14	128.210.55.12

From LAN B router to locally attached ultimate destination workstation:

Data-Link		IP	
destination	source	destination	source
0000C0 C13745	0020AF A2489C	128.210.49.14	128.210.55.12

Figure 13-18   Routing Is Address Processing

IP header with its own IP address and the destination address field in the IP header with the IP address of the ultimate destination workstation. Since the destination workstation is not on the local LAN, the IP packet must be forwarded to the local gateway, or router, which will have sufficient information to forward this packet properly.

- The source workstation looks in its IP configuration information to find the IP address of its default gateway. The default gateway is the only way out for IP packets on the local LAN. To deliver this IP packet to the local router for further processing, the IP packet must be wrapped in a data-link layer frame such as Ethernet, Token Ring, or FDDI. Addresses included in the data-link layer header are known as media access control (MAC) addresses. Although the source workstation has the IP address of the default local router in its IP configuration file, it does not know the MAC address of that router. As a result, the source workstation broadcasts a request for that MAC address using a special protocol known as **address resolution protocol,** or **ARP.** More detailed information regarding ARP is supplied in the section on control protocols.

- Once the source workstation has been supplied with the MAC address of the default gateway, thanks to ARP, it encapsulates the IP packet in a data-link layer frame with the MAC address associated with its own NIC as the source address in the data-link layer frame and the MAC address of the default gateway in the destination address of the data-link layer frame.

- The default gateway or local router receives the data-link layer frame explicitly addressed to it, discards the data-link layer frame and examines the ultimate destination address held in the IP packet. The router then consults its routing tables to see if it has an entry for a known path to the ultimate destination workstation. That known path may be via another router, or the ultimate destination workstation may be part of a different LAN connected to this same router through a different NIC. In either case, the IP packet and its addresses are not modified but are reencapsulated in a fresh data-link layer frame, with the MAC layer destination address of either the ultimate destination workstation or the next router along the path to that workstation. The source address field on the fresh data-link layer frame is filled in with the MAC layer address of the default router, which has just completed processing the IP packet.

Routing Information Protocol (RIP)   Once you have gained a basic understanding of how routing works, the importance of router-to-router communication for establishing, maintaining, and updating routing tables should be obvious. One such router-to-router protocol associated with TCP/IP is **routing information protocol,** or **RIP.** A routing table in a router serviced by RIP contains multiple records with the following fields:

- Address—IP address of the network about which this record contains information.

- Gateway—IP address of the next hop router, or directly reachable router along the path to the network identified in the address field. RIP broadcasts its routing table to these directly connected routers every 30 seconds. In larger networks, these routing table broadcasts can amount to substantial network traffic.

- Interface—The MAC layer address or port number of the physical interface on this router connected to the link that leads to the next hop gateway identified in the previous field.

- Metric or Hop Count—Total number of hops, or intermediate routers, between this router and the destination network. RIP limits the number of intermediate hops between any two networks to 15, thereby limiting the physical size of RIP-supported networks. Hop counts of 16 indicate that a network is unreachable.

- Timer—Age of this entry. Two separate timers are actually used. One is usually set to 180 seconds when an entry is first updated and counts down to 0, when the entry is marked for deletion. Remember that entries are normally updated every 30 seconds. The second timer controls when the entry is physically deleted from the table.

RIP uses UDP as a transport protocol and broadcasts its routing tables to all directly connected routers every 30 seconds. Those directly connected routers then propagate the new routing table information to the routers, which are directly connected to them. This pattern continues, and after a matter of about 7 minutes (30-sec intervals × 15 hop max), all routing tables have been updated and, for the moment, are synchronized. However, the delay, known as **slow convergence,** which occurs while all of the routers are propagating their routing tables could allow certain routers to think that failed links to certain networks are still viable. To reduce the convergence time, the following optional approaches have been added to RIP:

- **Split horizon** and **reverse poison** prevent routers from wasting time broadcasting routing table changes back to the routers which just supplied them with the same changes in the first place.

- **Triggered updates** allow routers to immediately broadcast routing table updates regarding failed links rather than having to wait for the next 30-sec periodic update.

It should be pointed out, however, that even with these improvements RIP is not as efficient as other routing protocols which will be explored shortly. Figure 13-19 illustrates the fields of RIP protocol.

Following are the field-by-field descriptions of the RIP protocol:

- Command—This field identifies whether this RIP packet is an explicit request for routing information (1) or the associated response (2), as opposed to the default 30-sec interval broadcasts.

UDP	RIP Protocol Layout											
Header	Command	Version	reserved	Family of NET 1	NET 1 Address	Number of Hops to NET 1	Family of NET2	NET2 Address	Number of Hops to NET2	and so on	Family of NET25	NET25 Address	Number of Hops to NET25
	8 bits	8 bits	16 bits	16 bits	112 bits	32 bits	16 bits	112 bits	32 bits	...	16 bits	112 bits	32 bits
	1st tuple			2nd tuple						25th tuple			

Figure 13-19 RIP Protocol

- Version—This field identifies the version of RIP supported, to avoid possible incompatibilities due to RIP upgrade versions.

- Family of Net 1—This field is used to identify the network layer protocol used in the network described in this routing table entry. RIP can build routing table entries for networks with network layer protocols other than IP. Net 1 refers to the first network entry in the routing table update being broadcast by RIP. RIP is limited to either 25 network entries per RIP packet or a maximum packet length of 512 bytes.

- Net 1 Address—This is the network address of this network entry in the RIP routing table update. The address format corresponds to the network layer protocol identified in the family of Net 1 field.

- Number of Hops to Net 1—This field indicates the number of hops, or intermediate routers, between the router broadcasting this routing table update and Net 1.

Open Shortest Path First (OSPF)   Router-to-router protocols, such as RIP, which consider only the distance between networks in hops in determining the best internetwork path, are known as **distance vector protocols.** A more sophisticated category of routing protocols known as **link state protocols** takes into account other factors regarding internetwork paths such as link capacity, delay, throughput, reliability, or cost.

Open shortest path first (RFC 1247), or **OSPF,** is an example of a link state protocol which was developed to overcome some of RIP's shortcomings, such as the 15 hop limit and full routing table broadcasts every 30 seconds. OSPF uses IP for connectionless transport.

In Sharper Focus

LINK STATE PROTOCOLS

Link state protocols such as OSPF (TCP/IP) and NLSP (NetWare) are able to overcome slow convergence and offer a number of other performance enhancements as well. One important distinction between distance vector and link state routing protocols is that distance vector routing protocols only use information supplied by directly attached neighboring routers, whereas link state routing protocols employ network information received from all routers on a given internetwork.

Link state routing protocols are able to maintain a complete and more current view of the total internetwork than distance vector routing protocols by adhering to the following basic processes:

- Link state routers use specialized datagrams known as link state packets (LSP) to determine the names of and the cost or distance to any neighboring routers and associated networks.

- All information learned about the network is sent to all known routers, not just neighboring routers, using LSPs.

- All routers have all other routers' full knowledge of the entire internetwork via the receipt of LSPs. The collection of LSPs are stored in an LSP database. This full internetwork view is in contrast to only a view of one's immediate neighbors using a distance vector protocol.

- Each router is responsible for compiling the information contained in all of the most recently received LSPs in order to form an up-to-the-minute view of the entire internetwork. From this full view of the internetwork, the link state routing protocol is able to calculate the best path to each destination network as well as a variety of alternate paths with varying costs.

- Newly received LSPs can be forwarded immediately whereas distance vector routing protocols had to recalculate their own routing tables before forwarding updated information to neighboring routers. The immediate forwarding of LSPs allows quicker convergence in the case of lost links or newly added nodes.

Controls and Support Protocols

Internet Control Message Protocol (ICMP)   Although IP is, by definition, an unreliable transport mechanism, **Internet control message protocol,** or **ICMP,** does deliver a variety of error status and control messages related to the ability of IP to deliver its encapsulated payloads. ICMP uses IP as a transport mechanism and delivers a variety of error and control messages through the use of type and code fields, as illustrated in Figure 13-20.

Figure 13-21 details the 13 different message types of ICMP.

ARP and RARP   Given the importance of addresses to the successful delivery of messages, it should come as no surprise that the TCP/IP family includes a pair of protocols to assist in the discovery and resolution of data-link and IP addresses. Network layer addresses such as IP are used for end-to-end addressing from original source to ultimate destination while data-link layer, or MAC addresses, are used for hop-to-hop addressing. IP addresses are assigned by a network administrator and MAC layer addresses are often burned into the ROM of the network interface cards by the card vendor.

These address resolution protocols are analogous to the use of directory assistance services to find a desired phone number. Two address resolution protocols differ only in the type of address to be resolved:

- **Address resolution protocol** (RFC 826), or **ARP,** is used if an IP address of workstation is known but a data-link layer address for the same workstation is required.

- **Reverse address resolution protocol,** or **RARP,** is used if the data-link layer address of the workstation is known but the IP address of the same workstation is required.

IP Header	IP Payload			
	ICMP Packet			ICMP Data
	Message Type	ICMP Code	Checksum	
	8 bits	8 bits	16 bits	

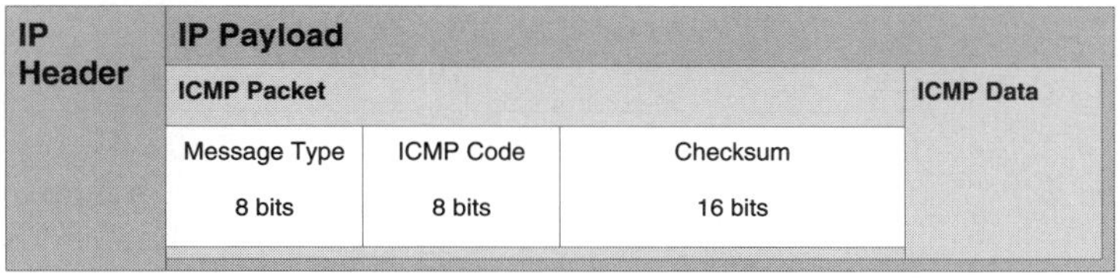

Figure 13-20   ICMP Protocol Layout

ICMP Type	Name	Explanation/Use
0	Echo reply	This is the ICMP message expected from a workstation which has been "pinged" by an ICMP type 8 message.
3	Destination unreachable	This message would be returned by a router to the source workstation or router along with a code indicating a more specific reason why the destination was unreachable. In this case, unreachable means that the network identified in the IP address could not be found. Possible reason codes are • 0—Network unreachable. • 1—Host unreachable. • 2—Protocol unreachable. • 3—Port unreachable. • 4—Fragmentation needed but the "Do not fragment" bit is set. • 5—Source route failed.
4	Source quench	This is how IP's version of flow control is implemented. The source quench message is a request from a computer or router to a source of IP datagrams to slow down the flow of IP datagrams to avoid data loss.
5	Redirect a route	Also known as route change request, this ICMP message is used by routers only when they receive an IP packet they believe could be handled more quickly or efficiently by a different router. In that case, the originating workstation or router is notified of the new suggested route, and the original message is also forwarded to the preferred router to expedite the delivery of the original IP packet.
8	Echo request to a remote station	This is the ICMP message sent out by the ping utility. ICMP message type 0 is the expected return from a successful ping.
11	Time exceeded for datagram	This message is usually sent from routers to originating workstations if the time to live field (TTL) in the IP header has been decremented to 0. This can be caused if a hop count has been exceeded or a network failure has occurred causing an IP packet to be processed by more routers than usual.
12	Parameter problem with a datagram	This message is fairly serious, as it indicates that a parameter within the IP header could not be understood. Luckily, the message includes an indication of where the parameter problem occurred in the IP header, to more easily diagnose the problem.
13	TimeStamp request	This message is used to request the time of day from a networked host.

Figure 13-21   ICMP Message Types

(continued)

ICMP Type	Name	Explanation/Use
14	TimeStamp reply	This is the reply message type for message type 13 requests.
15	Information request	This message is used to request the network number of the network to which the requesting host is attached. The most likely scenario when a host wouldn't know the network to which it is attached is in remote-access situations using SLIP or PPP.
16	Information reply	This is the ICMP message type used to reply to ICMP message type 15.
17	Address mask request	This message type is used to request the subnetwork mask of the network to which a host is connected. It is likely to be used in the same situations as ICMP message type 15.
18	Address mask reply	This is the ICMP message type used to reply to ICMP message type 17.

Figure 13-21   *(continued)*

ARP and RARP requests for addresses are broadcast throughout an entire IP network. Obviously this could represent a significant traffic burden. Routers do not rebroadcast ARP or RARP packets, and thereby act as a filter to prevent infinite propagation of ARP/RARP broadcasts. Responses to ARP and RARP requests are sent directly to the requesting workstation rather than being broadcast to all attached workstations. The ARP response is sent by the workstation whose IP address is found in the destination address field of the broadcast ARP packets. ARP responses are also stored in an ARP cache, so that it will not be necessary to rebroadcast for the same address.

Utilities and Application Layer Services

TCP/IP utilities, otherwise known as application layer services, adhere to a distributed processing or client/server model in that it takes two distinct pieces of software—a client piece and a server piece—running on two different computers to deliver a given application layer service. The server piece, usually referred to as a **daemon,** includes a "d" suffix in its name. For example, the client piece of the FTP utility is known as FTP while the server piece is known as ftpd. The following sections offer brief descriptions of several popular application layer services.

File Transfer Protocol (FTP)   **File transfer protocol,** or **FTP,** provides a common mechanism for transferring files between a variety of types of networked computers. Strictly speaking, FTP does not provide a user interface but rather an API for FTP services. An application program must be written to invoke the FTP commands and execute the FTP services. To accomplish this, FTP client and ftpd server software must be available to communicate with any given networked computer.

FTP is the language, or in this case the file transfer protocol, all of the computers have in common though they differ in a variety of other ways, such as underlying operating system commands. For example, a user may type "dir" on a DOS-based terminal, which translates locally and travels across the network as an FTP "list" command, where it is translated by FTP into an "ls" command for the local Unix operating system. The only commands actually defined by the FTP protocol are those which are exchanged between the FTP client and FTP server. FTP user commands vary according to the vendor of the FTP user software, but generally conform to the commands of the operating system on which the FTP user software is installed. FTP uses TCP for its reliable transport services. The need for reliable transport services for file transfer should be evident. Figure 13-22 differentiates between FTP client software, FTP server software, and FTP user software.

Trivial File Transfer Protocol (TFTP)   **Trivial file transfer protocol,** or **TFTP,** was designed to be a simpler and less memory-intensive alternative to FTP. It does not offer nearly the sophistication or functionality of FTP, but is primarily used for computer-to-computer communication of small messages. TFTP uses UDP rather than TCP and, as a result, must provide its own error-correction mechanism.

Telnet   Strictly speaking, **Telnet** is a terminal access API which allows remote terminals to connect to hosts running Telnetd (the Telnet server program). If the remote terminal accessing the Telnet server is not truly a "dumb" terminal, then terminal emulation software must be executed to make it appear as a "dumb" terminal to the Telnet server host. The real purpose of Telnet is to make this remote terminal, which may be something other than a typical terminal, appear to be a normal terminal to the login host.

Because Telnet must be able to operate with a variety of terminal types, it contains an adaptive negotiation mechanism known as **Telnet negotiation.** This allows Telnet to establish sessions assuming very basic functionality, known as the **net-**

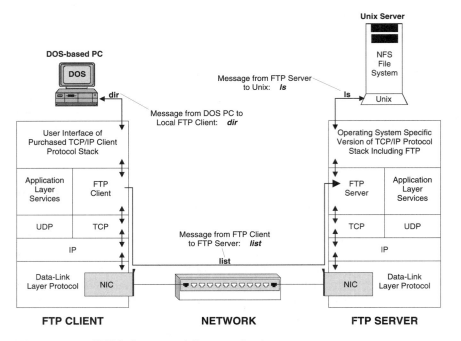

Figure 13-22   FTP Software and Communication

work virtual terminal, and progressively negotiate the more advanced terminal features that must be supported for the particular terminal and application in question.

Simple Mail Transfer Protocol (SMTP) Just as the FTP client required a separately written application program to provide an interface with users, the **simple mail transfer protocol,** or **SMTP,** client also requires a separately written user front-end. SMTP allows different computers which support the TCP/IP protocol stack to exchange e-mail messages. It is important to understand that SMTP is only able to establish connections, provide reliable transport of e-mail messages via TCP, notify users of newly received e-mail, and terminate connections. SMTP establishes reliable point-to-point connections between SMTP clients and their destination SMTP servers.

Sophisticated e-mail translation must be provided by the end-user's e-mail application. Strictly speaking, SMTP only defines communication between the SMTP client service (requests) and the SMTP server service (responses). Extensions to SMTP such as **multipurpose Internet mail extension,** or **MIME,** allow binary files to be attached to SMTP-delivered e-mail messages. Enterprisewide e-mail systems are explored further in the chapter on enterprise network applications.

R Commands **R commands** are a group of application layer service commands which can be executed remotely. For example, rlogin allows a user to remotely login to another computer, and rexec allows the same user to execute a program on that remote computer. The major problem with the R commands is their lack of sophisticated authentication and security features. As a result they are often disabled, especially on PC-based TCP/IP clients.

Line Printer Services **Line printer services,** or **LPS,** are also available in client (requests) and server (responses) versions. The client portion runs on the client PC requesting services, and the server portion runs on the print server. Basically, LPS supplies the printer services typically supplied by network operating systems such as NetWare, Windows for Workgroups, or Windows NT. LPS utilities allow users to send or remove a print job to/from a print queue attached to another computer or to display the status of the print jobs in a print queue, among other typical print queue management commands.

Management

Simple Network Management Protocol (SNMP) As client/server architectures have been implemented using a variety of server platforms and internetworking devices from a multitude of vendors, a need has developed for a way to effectively manage all of these multivendor network-attached devices. Although enterprise network management systems are discussed in detail in Chapter 17, the role of the TCP/IP family's **simple network management protocol,** or **SNMP,** in the successful implementation of enterprise network management systems is introduced here.

A multivendor enterprise network management system requires the interaction of a number of components, as illustrated in Figure 13-23.

SNMP offers a standardized protocol for transporting management information such as device status, device activity, and alarm conditions. The decision as to which information should be requested, transported, and stored for a variety of devices is defined by a protocol related to SNMP, known as **management information**

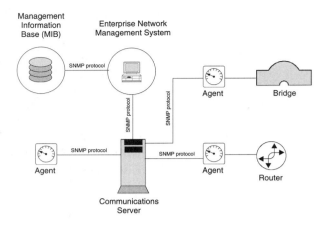

Figure 13-23 SNMP, MIB, Agents, and Enterprise Network Management Systems

base, or **MIB.** These defined fields and quantities, which are encapsulated by SNMP and delivered via UDP, are known as MIB objects. Individual vendors have added their own fields or MIB extensions to the standardized MIB definitions. Although these extensions offer product differentiation and increased functionality, they can also make SNMP interoperability difficult. Each network-attached device which is to be SNMP-compliant must be equipped with software capable of reporting required performance statistics in standardized SNMP format. This embedded SNMP reporting software is known as a software **agent,** SNMP agent, or management agent.

SNMP-compliant agents report statistics from their managed nodes in SNMP format to the MIB for storage and eventual access by enterprise network management systems. Enterprise network management systems use the MIB objects to present network configuration and operational status in a meaningful manner. In some cases, enterprise network management systems can be programmed to react to certain SNMP reported conditions by dialing pager or cellular phone numbers of network managers.

■ TCP/IP EVOLUTION

Internet Address Pressures

The recent boom in the use of the Internet by commercial entities has put a serious strain on the availability of IP addresses. Recall that connection to the Internet requires use of an absolutely unique IP address. Although the current version of IP could theoretically support 4.3 billion host addresses, far fewer addresses than that are actually available. The reason for this has largely to do with the IP address classes reviewed earlier. Class C addresses, with only 256 host IDs, are too limiting for many corporations, while Class B addresses, with 65,534 host IDs, provide far more host IDs than necessary, often leading to wasted and subsequently unavailable addresses. Several alternatives for dealing with these Internet address pressures are possible. Subnetworking, described previously, is one way to stretch a limited number of IP addresses across several subnetworks.

DHCP   Dynamic host configuration protocol, or **DHCP,** is one way in which a limited number of IP addresses can be shared by multiple IP clients. Typically, IP addresses are permanently or statistically assigned to a given workstation or server, becoming associated with the physical location of that workstation. In contrast, DHCP assigns an IP address dynamically on request from clients. With DHCP, IP addresses are leased for a fixed length of time rather than being permanently assigned. The next time a given DHCP client requests an IP address, it is likely to be different from the previously assigned IP address. DHCP allows a range of reusable IP addresses to be shared as needed by multiple hosts, rather than permanently assigning addresses to hosts which may be idle a great deal of the time. This dynamic address assignment is especially important for mobile or remote laptop users who may need to connect at a variety of locations or docking stations on a given network. With DHCP, roaming computing is not a problem, as IP addresses can be assigned on the fly.

DHCP is implemented in a client/server architecture with DHCP requester software being installed on clients and DHCP server software installed on the DHCP server that will deal out IP addresses. In larger, router-based internetworks, a third piece of DHCP software, known as a DHCP relay agent, must be supported by intermediate routers to allow DHCP requests for IP addresses to be broadcast from one network to another. DHCP does not imply that all IP addresses in a given domain are dynamic. IP addresses for servers can still be permanently assigned by issuing an infinite lease. Figure 13-24 outlines the process of DHCP address request and assignment.

Step #	From	To	DHCP Command	Description
1	DHCP client	Broadcast	DHCPDISCOVER	• DHCP client broadcasts request for IP address. Message includes the client's own MAC address.
2	DHCP server	DHCP client	DHCPOFFER	• DHCP server able to fulfill request responds directly to the requesting client (using previously broadcast MAC address) with an offer of IP address, subnet mask, and address expiration.
3	DHCP client	DHCP server	DHCPACCEPT	• DHCP client responds directly to the offering DHCP server with acceptance of the offer.
4	DHCP server	DHCP client	DHCPACK	• DHCP server ACKnowledges the acceptance and supplies additional information on the location of the nearest DNS server and available gateways.

Figure 13-24 DHCP Address Request and Assignment

Practical Advice and Information

One current limitation with DHCP is its lack of ability to automatically and dynamically update or integrate with DNS servers. This can be a problem as, more often than not, hosts are known by their name rather than their IP address. With IP addresses constantly changing in DHCP, it is even more important to be able to simply address hosts by name. Although Microsoft has integrated DHCP and DNS along with WINS in Windows NT, that integration is currently limited to the Windows NT environment.

BootP   DHCP can be thought of as an enhancement to **BootP,** which was originally designed to configure local diskless workstations that were not able to store IP configuration information locally. In the case of BootP, the MAC address of the BootP client had to be known beforehand, entered into a database in the BootP server, and permanently associated with an IP address. Thus, each time the BootP client broadcast a request for an IP number, the BootP server would look up the client's MAC address in its table and assign it the same IP address each time. While DHCP's address assignment is automatic and dynamic, BootP's address assignment is automatic and static. Similarly to DHCP, BootP can be supported across internetworks provided that intermediate routers are capable of forwarding BootP broadcasts.

IPng   An alternative to doing more with fewer addresses, as in DHCP, is to redesign IP entirely to provide more address space, and, consequently, more addresses. **IP next generation (IPng),** otherwise known as **IPv6** (IP version 6), offers significant increases in functionality as well as increased address space compared to **IPv4** (current version, IP version 4). Among the significant features of IPng are the following:

- 128-bit addresses (as opposed to IPv4's 32 bit).

- Hierarchical addressing adds fields for Internet provider and Internet subscriber in addition to network and host IDs.

- Broadcasts have been eliminated in favor of multicasts directed at specified hosts through the use of cluster addresses.

- The IP header has been optimized to improve router performance by including only those fields required by routers in a fixed-length header. All other information has been moved to subheaders.

- Allows end-users to label packets as "high-priority," to better support voice, video, and multimedia applications.

- Supports automatic address configuration to simplify IP address assignment.

- Supports authentication and encryption to prevent users from masquerading with false host IDs.

One of the greatest challenges to implementing IPv6 is the transition from IPv4. Several issues have been identified, and solutions proposed for many. Among the migration issues are the following:

- Upgrades can be done incrementally. Clients, routers, and servers can all be upgraded to IPv6 independently since IPv6 devices can also process IPv4 IP addresses and packets. IPv4 32-bit addresses will be zero-padded to IPv6's 128-bit addresses. However, IPv4 devices will not be able to process IPv6 packets.

- DNS will need to be upgraded to accommodate resolving names to the 128-bit IPv6 addresses.

- A new MIB will need to be developed to link IPv6 devices to enterprise network management systems.

- Routing IPv6 packets can be done by either upgrading hybrid IPv4/IPv6 routers or encapsulating IPv6 packets within an IPv4 packet and routing over the IPv4 routers.

■ TCP/IP IMPLEMENTATION

Client TCP/IP Software

Now that we have thoroughly reviewed the functionality of TCP/IP, we can explore implementation of TCP/IP on a client workstation. Numerous vendors offer TCP/IP client stacks, including the following:

- Pathway Access from Wollongong.
- PC-NFS from Sun.
- Chameleon from NetManage.
- LAN Workplace from Novell.
- Air NFS from Spry.
- Super TCP/NFS from Frontier.
- B&W TCP with NFS from Beame & Whiteside.
- Reflections 2, The TCP Connection from WRQ.

The prices of these packages generally vary from $350 to $595, with some packages available for less than $100. Issues of functionality to be considered when purchasing a TCP/IP package are summarized in Figure 13-25.

Functional Category	Explanation/Implication

Setup and Software Interface	• Can installation routine automatically detect driver software (NDIS, ODI) and adjust installation and configuration accordingly?
	• How much, if any, manual editing of configuration files is required?
	• Does the software need to be a TSR, thereby consuming memory resources?
	• Is the software written to be compliant with any of the following:
	  • VXD—Microsoft Virtual Device Driver.
	  • DLL—Dynamic Link Library.
	  • WinSock API—1.0 or 2.0
	• Are DHCP and/or BootP supported?

Figure 13-25 Functional Issues of TCP/IP Software

(continued)

Functional Category	Explanation/Implication
	• Is SNMP supported?
	• Which MIB definitions are supported? (MIB I, MIB II, RMON MIB)
	• Is an uninstall utility included?
TCP/IP Application and Protocol Support	• Is NFS included? (client and server?)
	• Are SLIP and PPP supported?

	• Which of the following applications are included?
	  • Ping.
	  • Line printer commands.
	  • R commands.
	  • TFTP.
	  • Finger.
	  • Talk.
	  • Traceroute.

	• Applications which deserve close scrutiny include
	  • Telnet.
	  • What is the most sophisticated terminal emulated? (VT220, VT320?)
	  • Are both client and server versions included?
	  • Is a scripting language included?
	  • How well are specialized keyboard features of the "real" keyboard emulated by Telnet? (user-definable button bars, macro keys)
	  • Can host profiles be saved and recalled?
	  • Is TN3270 (IBM mainframe) and/or TN5250 (IBM minicomputer) supported?

	• Mail
	  • Are both SMTP client and server included?
	  • UUencode (Unix-to-Unix encoding converts binary files to/from ASCII) and decode included?
	  • Attachments supported?
	  • Is MAPI supported?
	  • Is MIME supported?

	• FTP
	  • Are both FTP clients and servers included?
	  • How extensive are server access controls?
	  • Can remote files, directories be viewed?
	  • Can the type of remote FTP server be detected?
	  • Is a file transfer progress indicator included?
	  • Drag-and-drop interface?

Internet Support	• Which of the following Internet-related applications are included?
	  • Mosaic or NetScape for WWW.
	  • Gopher.
	  • FTP (client and server).
	  • Telnet (client and modem server).
	  • News.
	    • How easily can articles be saved?
	    • Can articles be sorted by date and subject?
	  • Firewall software included?

Figure 13-25   *(continued)*

It is important to realize that although the TCP/IP family of protocols themselves are standardized, there can be a wide range of variance in the functionality offered by the commercially available versions of client TCP/IP products.

■ NETWORK FILE SYSTEM (NFS)

Network file system, or **NFS,** was originally developed by Sun Microsystems as part of their Open Network Computing (ONC) environment. NFS allows multiple computing platforms to share files. To all of the heterogeneous computers which support NFS, the NFS file system appears as a transparent extension to their local operating system or file system by making remote disk drives appear as local. Print jobs can also be redirected from local workstations to NFS servers. Although originally developed for the Unix operating system and TCP/IP transport protocols, NFS is now supported on a variety of platforms, including PCs. This allows network operating systems such as NetWare and Windows NT to transparently support NFS as well, offering transparent interoperability with Unix workstations, minicomputers, and mainframes.

Although NFS is often considered functionally equivalent to the file systems of fully integrated network operating systems such as NetWare or Windows NT, in fact, NFS derives much of its functionality from the native operating system of the platform on which it is installed. Additionally, although NFS is capable of supporting file sharing between different computing platforms, more advanced file management features such as user and group access rights, file and record locking, and conversion between different file types may not be universally supported. In other words, in some cases, NFS can implement only those features which are common to all linked file systems and computing platforms, not the most advanced file management functionality of any particular computing platform.

NFS Architecture

NFS generally refers to a collection or suite of three major protocols:

- Network file system, or NFS.
- **External data representation**, or **XDR.**
- **Remote procedure call**, or **RPC.**

Strictly speaking, NFS is only the API portion of a collection of programs and utilities which offer the transparent file management interoperability typically associated with the NFS suite of protocols. Transparency is a key factor, as the client application requesting files does not know that the NFS client software will be used to communicate with a remote NFS server to deliver the requested files. Each NFS client protocol stack interacts with the native operating system and file system of the computing platform on which it is installed and translates requests and responses for NFS services into standardized NFS protocols for communication with similarly configured NFS servers. NFS could be considered an example of an OSI Layer 7 protocol.

External data representation (XDR) is a presentation layer protocol responsible

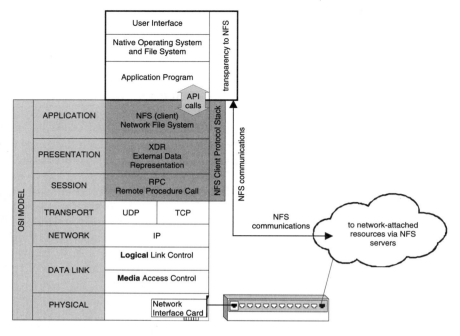

Figure 13-26 NFS Architecture

for formatting data consistently so that all NFS clients and servers can process it, regardless of the computing platform or operating system on which the NFS suite may be executing.

Remote procedure call (RPC) is a session layer protocol responsible for establishing, maintaining, and terminating communications sessions between distributed applications in an NFS environment. NFS protocols may use either UDP or TCP for transport layer services. The architectural relationship among the NFS suite of protocols, the TCP/IP suite of protocols, and the OSI Model is illustrated in Figure 13-26.

SUMMARY

Although not truly a single product, fully integrated network operating system, Unix plus TCP/IP, and NFS do offer equivalent functionality to many fully integrated network operating systems. The standardized, open systems orientation of Unix, TCP/IP, and NFS have made this combination of technology a popular choice for high-performance network-based computing. While Unix offers a preemptive multitasking operating system, TCP/IP offers the network communications and management

functionality, and NFS offers the ability for a variety of network-attached computers to share disk drives and file systems.

The architecture of the Unix operating system is hierarchical, consisting of the Unix systems programs and the Unix kernel. User interfaces are known as Unix shells. The two key functional characteristics enabled by this architecture are portability and modularity. Unix has a native file system of its own. NFS is added to offer a networked file system which can be shared by a variety of distributed computing platforms.

TCP/IP is the name most commonly used to refer to a family of open, standardized protocols, more properly known as the Internet suite of protocols. In fact, TCP/IP supports its own four-layer model which is roughly equivalent to the OSI seven-layer model.

IP is the network layer protocol and is most concerned with network and host addressing. If computers are to be attached to the Internet, they must be issued unique IP addresses. TCP is the transport layer protocol offering connection-oriented reliable transmission, and UDP offers connectionless, unreliable transmission. Remote access to TCP/IP hosts can be accomplished by using either SLIP or PPP. Routers can keep each other's routing tables updated with either RIP or OSPF.

To deal with the pending IP address shortage, two solutions are available. DHCP shares a pool of available IP addresses among numerous hosts on a dynamic, as-needed basis. IPng (IPv6) offers an upgrade of the IP protocol, extending IP addresses from 32 bits to 128 bits.

KEY TERMS

REVIEW QUESTIONS

1. How is the combination of Unix, TCP/IP, and NFS functionally equivalent to a fully integrated network operating system such as Windows NT?
2. What is the relationship between the Unix systems programs, Unix system kernel, Unix shells, and Unix applications programs?
3. Describe which architectural features of Unix contribute to its portability.
4. Describe which architectural features of Unix contribute to its modularity.
5. Describe some of the unique features of the Unix file system.
6. What is the relationship between the Unix file system and NFS?
7. Differentiate between swapping and paging. Which do you feel is more efficient? Justify your answer.
8. What is the relationship between the fork system call and the multithreading capabilities of Unix?
9. What is the difference between pipes and sockets?
10. Differentiate between the functionality and proper application of various types of sockets.
11. What is the relationship between TCP/IP, the Internet suite of protocols, and the TCP/IP model?
12. Why is IP referred to as a connectionless, unreliable protocol?
13. Differentiate between address classes A, B, and C.
14. What is the importance of IP addresses to routing?
15. Why are unique IP addresses important only if a company wishes to connect to the Internet?
16. How does subnetworking allow more efficient usage of IP addresses?
17. How is subnetworking implemented?
18. What is the importance of DNS?
19. Describe the relationship between the DNS resolver and the DNS server.
20. What is recursion?
21. What is the difference between TCP and UDP?
22. What is the purpose of ports and sockets in TCP?
23. Differentiate between SLIP and PPP.
24. Which applications is MLPPP particularly well suited for?
25. Explain the use of MAC addresses and IP addresses by a router.
26. What are some of the shortcomings of RIP, and how are they overcome?
27. What type of information is stored in a RIP routing table?
28. What is the role of ICMP, and which other protocol does it work most closely with?
29. Differentiate between ARP and RARP.
30. When is ARP most likely to be used?
31. What is a negative side effect of ARP, and how can it be minimized?
32. Why are TCP/IP application layer services considered to be running in a client/server architecture?
33. What is a daemon?
34. Describe the relationship between an FTP client, an FTP server, and the operating systems of the computing platforms on which each is installed.
35. Differentiate between FTP and TFTP.
36. Why is SMTP not considered to be a fully functional e-mail system?
37. Describe the relationship between SNMP, MIB, agents, and enterprise network management systems.
38. What are the benefits of DHCP?
39. Describe the relationship between DHCP client, a DHCP server, and a DHCP relay agent.
40. Differentiate between DHCP and BootP.
41. Differentiate between IPng and IPv4.
42. What are the important migration issues from IPv4 to IPv6, and how have they been addressed?
43. What are some of the key issues concerning analysis and purchase of a client-based TCP/IP protocol stack?
44. Explain the relationship between the various layers of the NFS architecture.

ACTIVITIES

1. Draw a diagram comparing the functionality of a fully integrated network operating system such as Windows NT and the combination of Unix, TCP/IP, and NFS. Use the OSI model as a frame of reference.

2. Draw a diagram illustrating the relationship between Unix systems programs, Unix system kernel, Unix shells, and Unix applications programs.

3. Investigate and report on the differences between the various Unix shells as well as languages such as Perl and Rexx. What is the relationship between Unix and languages such as C, C++, and Visual C++?

4. What is the relationship between sockets in Unix and sockets in TCP/IP?

5. Prepare a chart or timeline showing the major events in the history of Unix. Pay particular attention to standardization efforts or other efforts to make Unix more commercially acceptable.

6. Research and report on any current efforts to offer increased standardization to the Unix environment.

7. Prepare a diagram comparing the TCP/IP model with the OSI model. Place all protocols possible in their proper layers. Which protocols are the most difficult to place in a particular layer?

8. Research and report on the depletion of Internet addresses and what steps are being taken to rectify the situation.

9. Prepare a chart listing those protocols which use TCP as a transport protocol and those protocols which use UDP as a transport protocol. What do the members of each group have in common?

10. Perform a survey of technical specifications for routers. What percentage of the routers investigated support DHCP? Explain your results.

11. Research and report on the current status of industry acceptance of and migration to IPv6. What are the key stumbling blocks to widespread acceptance?

12. Review product specifications or buyers guides for TCP/IP software, and prepare a technology analysis grid to display your findings.

FEATURED REFERENCES

General References/Future Directions

Comer, Douglas and David Stevens. *Internetworking with TCP/IP Vol. III: Client — Server Programming and Applications* (Englewood Cliffs, NJ: Prentice-Hall, 1993).

Foley, John. Unifying UNIX: Now It's Hewlett-Packard's Turn. *Information Week*, no. 553 (November 13, 1995), 22.

Foley, John. UNIX Gets Hot. *Information Week*, no. 546 (September 25, 1995), 14.

Foley, John. The UNIX World Comes Together. *Information Week*, no. 549 (October 16, 1995), 52.

Kapustka, Paul. Link to the Future. *Information Week*, no. 533 (June 26, 1995), 60.

Rhodes, Wayne. UNIX Drives Business. *Beyond Computing*, 4; 6 (September 1995), 38.

Rodbell, Mike. TCP/IP: Internet Transport Services. *Communications Systems Design*, 1; 7 (November 1995), 66.

Washburn, K. and J.T. Evans. *TCP/IP: Running a Successful Network* (Workingham, England: Addison-Wesley, 1993).

Yager, Tom. OS Paradise. *Byte*, 20; 11 (November 1995), 81.

IP Addresses/DHCP

Johnson, Johna. IP Addresses: Easing the Crunch. *Data Communications*, 24; 1 (January 1995), 76.

Layland, Robin. TCP/IP Needs More Directory Assistance. *Data Communications*, 24; 3 (March 1995), 33.

Passmore, David. Quick Fixes for the Internet Address Shortage. *Business Communications Review*, 24; 12 (December 1994), 24.

Phaltankar, Kaustubh. Subnets Make the Most of Your IP Addresses. *Network Computing*, 5; 13 (November 1, 1994), 140.

Robertson, Bruce. DHCP: Dynamic IP Address Assignment on the Desktop. *Network Computing*, 5; 12 (October 15, 1994), 10.

Winston, Tim. Create More IP Addresses. *Byte*, 20; 4 (April 1995), 217.

Client TCP/IP Software/X Windows

Kay, Emily. The Incredible Shrinking Client. *Information Week*, no. 553 (November 13, 1995), 50.

Levitt, Jason. Desktop TCP/IP with a Twist. *Information Week*, no. 549 (October 16, 1995), 62.

Molta, Dave and Ron Anderson, Peter Morrissey. TCP/IP Vendors Blow Their Stacks. *Network Computing*, 5; 10 (September 1, 1994), 102.

Newman, David and Kevin Tolly. TCP/IP Applications: Easy Does It. *Data Communications*, 24; 2 (February 1995), 85.

Phillips, Ken. WRQ Clips Hummingbird's Wings. *PC Week*, 12; 40 (October 9, 1995), N1.

Sullivan, Kristina. TCP/IP: Old Faithful Still Has Broad Appeal. *PC Week,* 12; 27 (July 10, 1995), N14.

Tristram, Claire. TCP/IP on PC LANs. *Open Computing,* 12; 11 (November 1995), 46.

Unix SVR4

Fordyce, Wayne. Making the Leap to UNIX SVR4. *Network Computing,* 5; 6 (June 1, 1994), 166.

IP Routing

Waclawsky, John. TCP/IP Congestion Control: Can You Win the Battle? *Business Communications Review,* 25; 11 (November 1995), 75.

Wittman, Art. TCP/IP, Bridging and Packet Sizes. *Network Computing,* 5; 10 (September 1, 1994), 65.

IPng

Callon, Ross. Migrate to Ipng or Retrofit IP? *Network World,* 12; 23 (June 5, 1995), 41.

Cooney, Michael. Is IPng at a Fork in the Road? *Network World,* 12; 43 (October 23, 1995), 24.

Moskowitz, Robert. Planning for a New Protocol. *Network Computing,* 6; 5 (May 1, 1995), 144.

Passmore, David. Next Generation IP: Construction Ahead. *Business Communications Review,* 25; 3 (March 1995), 18.

File Systems/NFS

Alderson, Bill and J. Scott Haugdahl. NFS Woes Creating Work Nightmare. *Network Computing,* 6; 6 (May 15, 1995), 134.

Phillips, Ken. NFS Server Spreads NT Wealth. *PC Week,* 12; 27 (July 10, 1995), N3.

Sedore, Christopher. Use NFS to Integrate UNIX and Windows NT. *Network Computing,* 6; 8 (July 1, 1995), 146.

Tabibian, O. Ryan. NFS Servers: A Universal Language for Your Network. *PC Magazine,* 14; 6 (March 28, 1995), NE1.

Yager, Tom. The Great Little File System. *Byte,* 20; 2 (February 1995), 155.

PPP

Conant, George. Multilink PPP: One Big Virtual WAN Pipe. *Data Communications,* 24; 13 (September 21, 1995), 85.

Smith, Ben. From Here to There. *Byte,* 19; 6 (June 1994), 271.

WABI/Windows–Unix Integration

Conover, Joel. A Moment in the Sun. *Network Computing,* 6; 9 (August 1, 1995), 110.

Fisher, Sharon. New Devices Boost PC–UNIX Integration. *Communications Week,* no. 565 (July 10, 1995), 22.

Foley, John. More Windows on UNIX. *Information Week,* no. 553 (November 13, 1995), 90.

Foley, May Jo. SCO Tools integrate UNIX and Windows. *PC Week,* 12; 46 (November 20, 1995), 21.

Tabibian, O. Ryan. WinDD:In a Class by Itself. *PC Magazine,* 14; 13 (July 1995), NE29.

Tamasanis, Doug. A Less Wobbly Wabi. *Byte,* 20; 7 (July 1995), 159.

Internet Connectivity

Garris, John. IP/IPX Internet Gateways: Hassle-Free Internet. *PC Magazine,* 14; 13 (July 1995), NE1.

Unix Shells

Fosdick, Howard. Winning the UNIX Shell Game. *Information Week,* no. 538 (July 31, 1995), 70.

Unix Implementations

Comparisons

Cheek, Martin. UNIXes Must Keep Competitive Edge. *LAN Times,* 12; 4 (February 27, 1995), 58.

Jacobs, Marcia. New LAN Man Ported to UNIX. *Communications Week,* no. 583 (November 6, 1995), 23.

Linux

Dawson, J. Bruce. Power of Cooperation. *Byte,* 19; 9 (September 1994), 167.

HP-UX

Sontag, John. HP-UX 10.0. *Byte,* 20; 4 (April 1995), 213.

Johnston, D. Britton. Sometimes UNIX Is Best. *Byte,* 20; 4 (April 1995), DM5.

Solaris

Foley, John. SunSoft Upgrades Solaris. *Information Week,* no. 554 (November 20, 1995), 184.

Galvin, Peter. Solaris Comes of Age. *Byte,* 20; 4 (April 1995), DM17.

Tamasanis, Doug. Springtime at Sun. *Byte,* 20; 9 (September 1995), 271.

Common Desktop Environment (CDE)

Foley, John. UNIX Finds Common Ground. *Information Week,* no. 538 (July 31, 1995), 90.

Tamasanis, Doug. A Universal Desktop for UNIX. *Byte,* 20; 6 (June 1995), DM3.

OpenServer

Fiedler, David. SCO Fights Back on UNIX Front. *Information Week,* no. 534 (July 3, 1995), 50.

Garris, John. SCO Gets Serious with OpenServer. *PC Magazine,* 14; 16 (September 26, 1995), NE47.

Koegler, Scott. OpenServer is Still King of the UNIX-on-Intel Mountain. *Network Computing,* 6; 8 (July 1, 1995), 60.

AIX

Pawliger, Marc. UNIX with No Excuses. *Byte,* 20; 8 (August 1995), 123.

UnixWare

Garris, John. Unix for the NetWare Masses. *PC Magazine,* 14; 10 (May 30, 1995), NE15.

Streeter, April. UnixWare Under the Gun. *LAN Times,* 12; 17 (September 11, 1995), 69.

CASE STUDY

Chapter 13

IS THERE LIFE AFTER MAINFRAME?

UNOCAL 76 forgoes IBM's es900 820 for Intel-based SMP

When UNOCAL 76 Corp. faced a systemwide software upgrade for its IBM mainframe in 1992, it did the unexpected and dropped 20 years of mainframe dependence for Intel Corp.-based applications servers and relational databases.

Since 1992, the Brea, Calif.-based petroleum-refining and marketing company has been slowly moving away from its IBM es900 820 mainframe to escape the costs of upgrading its COBOL applications, said John Mount, manager of technical services for UNOCAL 76. "We were so behind the times. To upgrade, the cost would have been ridiculous."

Being behind the times did not mean a flaw in traditional mainframe architecture, explained Mount. Rather, it indicated shortcomings in the COBOL programs that were too expensive to fix.

The first step in downsizing for UNOCAL 76 was to recruit hardware and software vendors that could step in with integration services as well as products. To this end, Oracle Corp. provided UNOCAL 76 with relational databases, engines, and user interfaces, as well as a set of custom financial applications with an ideal combination of support and flexibility, said Mount. Through Oracle's help, UNOCAL 76 was able to call in an initial development team to assist in the creation of financial applications, while leaving UNOCAL 76 free to enhance and support the code at a later time.

To maintain mainframelike performance with Oracle applications, Mount purchased three Sequent Computer Systems Inc. Symmetry 2000/790 symmetrical multiprocessing (SMP) servers, which came with a total of 28 Intel Pentium processors and DYNIX/ptx, a proprietary System 5, release 3 UNIX OS designed specifically for SMP.

With this combination, Mount found it easy to move UNOCAL 76's 1,500 employees off the mainframe. He gradually replaced individual Customer Information Control System (CICS) services with corresponding client/server applications by installing the new applications servers on the active IBM mainframe network. This enabled incoming financial and marketing data to simultaneously flow from UNOCAL 76's employees to both the mainframe and the applications servers.

Because UNOCAL 76's network already ran on both TCP/IP and IBM's Systems Network Architecture (SNA) over Ethernet, Mount simply removed the existing 3270 dumb terminals and used Wall Data Inc.'s Rumba tools to install both protocols on each workstation.

Over a three-month period, Mount moved financial information on to both systems through both Microsoft Corp. Visual Basic front ends and terminal-emulation sessions, ensuring that the new Oracle applications functioned properly.

Although capable of distributed processing through remote procedure calls (RPCs), not all applications are spread across the three Sequent Symmetry 2000/790 machines, said Mount. Each server functions individually. The primary machine, containing 16 processors, maintains the

financial database application. The second machine, containing eight processors, holds applications development and testing tools. And the third, containing four processors, houses decision-support data gathered from both the mainframe and the financial application in a data warehouse.

In structuring the three Sequent servers, Mount discovered that duplicating financial information in a data warehouse allowed marketing users to query financial information without disrupting the primary applications server's transaction throughput.

The data warehouse also makes the transition from mainframe to client/server much easier because it provides a single data set for mainframe data that has not yet been transferred to the Sequent machines.

More important, downsizing with Oracle and Sequent has not only saved UNOCAL 76 money in applications development but also saved its users processing time for report generation. "Some users were complaining about waiting two hours for reports," said Mount. "But it took them 15 hours to get the same reports on the mainframe."

Although UNOCAL 76 has not completely downsized its applications, the company plans to have them 70 percent downsized by year end.

UNOCAL 76's only regret in this process, however, is that now the same amount of data must be maintained with fewer management tools, said Mount. "MVS was a very robust operating system," he said. "If you needed a product to do something, you had to fight vendors off. On the UNIX operating system, the companies are coming along, but it is not as robust."

Source: Bradley F. Shimmin (February 27, 1995). Is There Life After Mainframe? *LAN Times*, 12(4), 19. Reprinted with permission of McGraw-Hill, *LAN Times*.

BUSINESS CASE STUDY QUESTIONS

Activities

1. Complete a top-down model for this case by gleaning facts from the case and placing them in the proper layer of the top-down model. After completing the top-down model, analyze and detail those instances when requirements were clearly passed down from upper to lower layers of the model and solutions to those requirements were passed up from lower to upper layers.
2. Detail any questions that may occur to you about the case for which answers are not clearly stated in the article.

Business

1. What were the business considerations which led UNOCAL 76 to consider the Intel SMP solution as an alternative to mainframes?
2. What have been the benefits, in both finance and productivity, of the transition from the mainframe to a SMP server–based environment?

Application

1. What impact did the mainframe applications have on the decision to migrate to a server-based environment?
2. Why were SMP servers chosen as application and database servers?
3. Describe how the migration process tested the SMP servers and new applications for reliability before actual cutover.

4. Which applications run on each of the three SMP servers?
5. Is this the only way applications can be run on SMP servers?

Data

1. Which relational database management system was chosen and why?
2. What were the benefits of constructing and maintaining a data warehouse?

Network

1. Which network transport protocols were employed on the enterprise backbone?
2. How did the support of multiple protocols on the enterprise backbone network aid in the migration from mainframe to SMP servers?
3. How could the use of remote procedure calls alter how applications are run on SMP servers?
4. Which types of functionality was the mainframe operating system (MVS) able to offer that Unix is not?

Technology

1. What was used for processing power to replace the mainframe?
2. Which operating system was employed? Why?
3. What technology was installed where, to allow user workstations to converse with both the IBM mainframe and the Sequent servers?

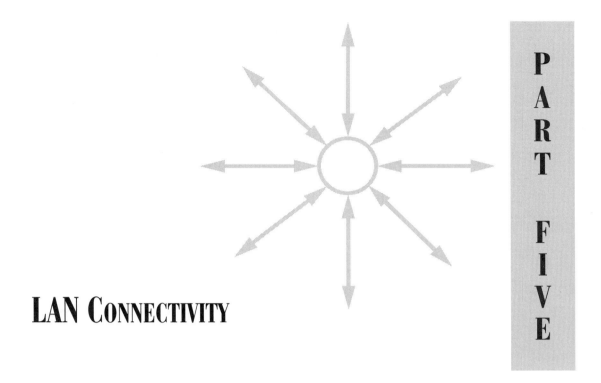

LAN Connectivity

INTRODUCTION

After concluding Part 4 on Local Area Network Operating Systems, the reader should be familiar with both the business motivation and technological implications of building a local area network to support a client/server information system. Part 5 recognizes the need to share the information contained within these individually built LANs.

Sharing information across heterogeneous LANs poses a significant challenge when one considers all of the potential variables of the hardware and software LAN technology which have been explored to this point. Connecting LANs together or with mainframe-based information systems, taking into account all of the differences in hardware and software protocols to transparently share information, is known as internetworking.

Chapter 14 focuses on the design of internetworking solutions for transparently linking LANs composed of a variety of hardware and software technologies. The functionality and proper application of internetworking hardware such as repeaters, bridges, and routers are explored in detail. In addition, the design issues and technology involved in linking LANs to mainframe-based information systems are also explored.

Chapter 15 focuses on the need for individual users to connect occasionally to LANs from remote locations. As mobile computing and telecommuting have increased in popularity, the need for transparent interoperability solutions for remote access to LANs has increased proportionately. LAN remote access design and technology alternatives are explored in detail.

CHAPTER **14**

LAN INTERNETWORKING

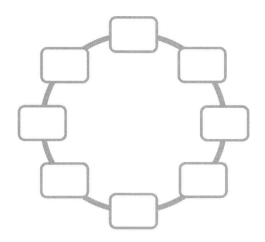

Concepts Reinforced

OSI model	Internet suite of protocols model
Protocols and standards	Interoperability
Network operating systems architecture	Network operating systems functionality
Network addressing	TCP/IP protocols

Concepts Introduced

Internetwork design	Bridges
Bridging	Bridging protocols
Routing	Routers
Switching versus routing	Routing protocols
Internetworking technology	SNA/SDLC
Repeaters	SNA/LAN integration

OBJECTIVES

After mastering the material in this chapter you should:

1. Understand why an organization would want to implement LAN-to-LAN internetworking.

2. Understand the basics of internetwork design, including decisions about bridging, routing, or switching.

3. Understand the importance of protocols to successful internetworking design and implementation.

4. Understand the functionality and proper application of the following types of internetworking technology: repeaters, bridges, branch office routers, edge routers, boundary routers, route servers, distributed routers, dial-up routers, ISDN bridges and routers, wireless bridges, source routing bridges, and software-only routers.

5. Understand the options available for integrating LAN traffic with SNA/SDLC mainframe traffic.

This chapter has two basic purposes:

- To introduce the reader to the complexities and basic principles of internetwork design.

- To introduce the reader to the available technology with which to implement designed internetworking solutions.

These internetwork design and technology issues are explored for both LAN-to-LAN internetworking and LAN-to-mainframe internetworking. To understand the importance of internetworking in general, one must first understand the business motivation for seeking internetworking solutions in particular.

■ INTERNETWORKING DESIGN

Managerial
Perspective

BUSINESS MOTIVATION AND INTERNETWORKING CHALLENGES

Local area networks tend to grow by a natural process until the shared media network architecture (Ethernet, Token Ring, FDDI, etc.) becomes too congested and network performance begins to suffer. This scenario is one of the two primary reasons for investigating **internetworking** solutions. The other situation which often leads to internetworking design is when independently established and operated LANs wish to begin to share information. Each of these scenarios really boils down to business issues. The poor performance of the overloaded share media LAN leads to a decrease in worker productivity with potential ripple effects to decreased customer satisfaction, sales, market share, and so on.

The ability to provide decision makers with instantaneous access to the right information at the right place and time, regardless of the location of that information, is really the key motivation for internetworking. The key challenge or stumbling block to achieving transparent information access are the numerous incompatibilities caused by the multiple vendor hardware and software technologies which comprise the individual LANs to be linked. The operational characteristics of LANs are defined by protocols, which when organized into a layered model such as the OSI model, are referred to as a protocol stack. A LAN's protocol stack really defines its personality. In other words, to achieve transparent LAN-to-LAN interoperability, each protocol in a given LAN's protocol stack must be either matched or converted to transparently interoperate with the corresponding protocol in the LAN to which the LAN is being linked. Overall LAN-to-LAN transparent interoperability is achieved only when corresponding protocols are able to achieve transparent interoperability.

Overall Internetworking Design Strategies

To improve performance on overburdened shared media LANs, several proven design strategies can be followed:

- **Segmentation** is usually the first approach to reducing shared media congestion. Fewer workstations per segment results in less contention for the shared bandwidth. Segmentation improves performance for both CSMA/CD (Ethernet) and token passing (Token Ring) access methodologies. Some type of internetworking device, such as a bridge or router, is required to link the LAN segments.

- Taking segmentation to the extreme of limiting each LAN segment to only a single workstation is a design strategy known as **microsegmentation.** A microsegmented internetwork requires a LAN switch compatible with the NICs installed in the attached workstations. Both Ethernet and Token Ring switches are readily available.

- In a design strategy known as **server isolation,** instead of assigning all workstations to their own LAN segment as in microsegmentation, only selected high-performance devices such as servers are assigned to their own segment. Isolating servers on their own segments guarantees access to network bandwidth.

- **Hierarchical networking** isolates local LAN traffic on a local network architecture such as Ethernet or Token Ring while transmitting internetwork traffic over a higher-speed network architecture such as FDDI or fast Ethernet. Servers are often directly connected to the **backbone network** while individual workstations access the backbone network through routers, only as needed.

Figure 14-1 illustrates these overall internetworking design strategies.

Bridging, routing, and switching are the three primary internetworking processes which offer LAN segmentation and isolation of network resources. All three internetworking processes are basically address processors that decide how to forward internetwork traffic based on data-link layer and network layer addresses. The three processes differ in their use of network addresses, overall sophistication, and advantages and limitations. The bridging, routing, and switching internetworking processes are reviewed here, and differences between their associated internetworking technologies later in the chapter.

Bridging

Bridging is often the first internetworking or LAN segmentation strategy employed because of its ease of installation and effective results. Dividing a single overburdened LAN into two LAN segments linked by a bridge must be done with some forethought to minimize the amount of internetwork traffic and avoid producing an internetwork bottleneck. The 80/20 rule is often used to decide which workstations and servers should be assigned to each side of the bridge. The goal should be for 80% of all LAN traffic to stay local, with no more than 20% of overall traffic requiring processing and forwarding by the bridge.

Addressing   Bridging is a data-link layer process, making forwarding decisions based on the contents of the MAC layer or data-link layer addresses. Bridges are passive or transparent devices, receiving every frame broadcast on a given LAN. Bridges are called **transparent** because of their ability to process only data-link layer

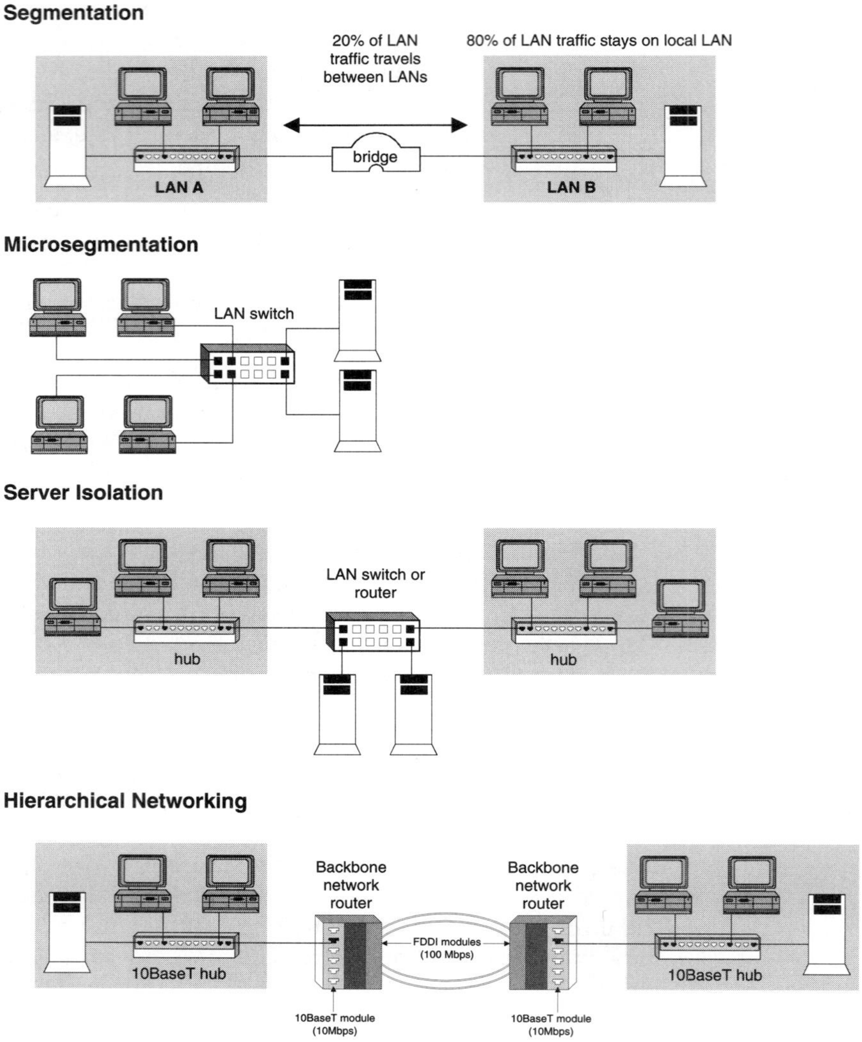

Segmentation

20% of LAN
traffic travels
between LANs

80% of LAN traffic stays on local LAN

bridge

LAN A

LAN B

Microsegmentation

LAN switch

Server Isolation

LAN switch or
router

hub

hub

Hierarchical Networking

Backbone
network
router

Backbone
network
router

FDDI modules
(100 Mbps)

10BaseT hub

10BaseT hub

10BaseT module
(10Mbps)

10BaseT module
(10Mbps)

Figure 14-1   Overall Internetworking Design Strategies

addresses while transparently forwarding any variety of upper layer protocols safely embedded within the data field of the data-link layer frame. Not merely transferring all data between LANs or LAN segments, a bridge reads the **destination address** (MAC layer address of destination NIC) of each data frame on a LAN, decides whether the destination is local or remote (on the other side of the bridge), and allows only those data frames with nonlocal destination addresses to cross the bridge to the remote LAN.

Data-link protocols such as Ethernet contain **source addresses** as well as the destination addresses within the predefined Ethernet frame layout. A bridge checks the source address of each frame it receives and adds that source address to a table of **known local nodes.** In doing so, the bridge is learning, without being manually reconfigured, about new workstations which might have been added to the local LAN. Some bridges broadcast requests to all locally attached workstations, thereby forcing responses which can then be stored in the known local nodes table.

After each destination address is read, it is compared with the contents of the Known Local Nodes table, to determine whether or not the frame should be allowed to cross the bridge (whether or not the destination is local). Since only frames with destination addresses not found in the known local nodes table are forwarded across the bridge, bridges are sometimes called **forward-if-not-local** devices. Figure 14-2 illustrates the use of data-link layer frame addresses by bridges.

Advantages   With their ability to learn, bridges are relatively easy to install and configure, for quick, cost-effective relief of overburdened network segments. In addition to providing logical segmentation of LAN traffic, bridges also extend network segment length by repeating, retiming, and regenerating received signals before forwarding them across the bridge. Bridges are also able to translate between different network architectures (Token Ring to Ethernet) and different media types (UTP to fiber).

Bridges are most often used to segment either traffic between LANs or traffic between a LAN and a higher-speed backbone network.

Limitations   The primary limitation of bridges is also one of their strengths. Because bridges learn and do not require ongoing configuration, they can only forward all packets addressed to nonlocal nodes. In the case of a destination node many LANs and connecting bridges away from its source workstation, all workstations between the source and destination workstation will be broadcast with the frame bound for the distant destination. Forwarding messages to all workstations on all intermittent LANs is known as **propagation.** Frames improperly addressed or destined for nonexistent addresses can be infinitely perpetuated or flooded onto all bridged LANs in a condition known as a **broadcast storm.** Bridges are generally not able to support networks containing redundant paths, since the multiple active loops between LANs can lead to the propagation of broadcast storms.

Routing

Although both processes examine and forward data packets discriminately, routing and bridging differ significantly in several key functional areas:

Data-Link Layer Frame

Data-Link Header		Data-Link Data Field	Data-Link Trailer
Source Address	Destination Address	Upper layer protocols including network layer address information	
Contains MAC address of original source workstation	Contains MAC address of ultimate destination workstation		
These address are used by bridges to determine whether or not packets should be forwarded across the bridge.			
Data-link layer addresses are **NOT** changed by bridges.			

Figure 14-2   Use of Data-Link Addressing by Bridges

- Although a bridge reads the destination address of every data packet on the LAN to which it is attached, a router examines only those data packets specifically addressed to it.

- Rather than just merely allowing the data packet access to the internetwork like a bridge, a router is more cautious as well as more helpful.

Before indiscriminately forwarding a data packet, a router first confirms the existence of the destination address as well as the latest information on available network "paths" to reach that destination. Next, based on the latest network traffic conditions, it chooses the best path for the data packet to reach its destination and sends the data packet on its way.

Addressing   While bridges base their forwarding decisions on the contents of the MAC layer addresses contained in the header of the data-link layer frame, routers base them on the contents of the network layer addresses embedded within the data field of the data-link layer frame.

The router itself is a data-link layer destination address, available to receive, examine, and forward data packets from anywhere on any network to which it is either directly or indirectly internetworked.

How do data packets arrive at a router? The destination address on an Ethernet or Token Ring packet must be the MAC address of the router which will handle further internetwork forwarding. Thus, a router is addressed in the data-link layer destination address field. The router then discards this MAC sublayer "envelope" which contained its address and proceeds to read the contents of the Ethernet or Token Ring frame data field. Data-link layer addressing is functionally referred to as point-to-point addressing.

As with the data-link layer protocols, network layer protocols dictate a bit-by-bit data frame structure which the router understands. What the data-link layer internetworking device, the bridge, sees as just "data" and ignores, the router "unwraps" and examines thoroughly to determine further processing.

After reading the network layer destination address, which is actually the network address of the ultimate destination workstation, the router consults its **routing tables** to determine the best path on which to forward this data packet. As described in discussions of routing protocols in the chapters on NetWare and TCP/IP, routing tables contain at least some of the following fields on which to base their "best path" decisions:

- Network number of the destination network. This field serves as the key field or lookup field used to find the proper record with further information concerning the best path to this network.

- MAC address of the next router along the path to this target network.

- Port on this router out of which the readdressed data-link layer frame should be sent.

- Number of hops, or intermediate routers, to the destination network.

- The age of this entry, to avoid basing routing decisions on outdated information.

Once it's found the best path, the router has the ability to repackage the data packet as required for that delivery route (best path). Although the network layer addresses remain unchanged, a fresh data-link layer frame is created. The destination address on the new data-link layer frame is filled in with the MAC address of the next router along the best path to the ultimate destination and the source address on the new data-link layer frame is filled in with the MAC address of the router which has just completed examination of the network layer addresses. Network layer addressing is functionally referred to as end-to-end addressing.

Unlike the bridge, which merely allows access to the internetwork (forward-if-not-local logic), the router specifically addresses the data packet to a distant router. However, before it releases a data packet onto the internetwork it confirms the existence of the destination address. Only when the router is satisfied with the viability of the destination address and the quality of the intended path, does it release the carefully packaged data packet. This meticulous processing activity is known as **forward-if-proven-remote** logic. Figure 14-3 illustrates routers' use of data-link and network layer addresses, and Figure 14-4 illustrates a simple logic flow diagram for the addressing aspects of the routing process.

Advantages   Compared with bridging, routing makes more efficient use of bandwidth on large networks containing redundant paths. The effective use of a network's redundant paths allows routers to perform **load balancing** of total network traffic across two or more links between two given locations. Routers' choice of the "best path" can be determined by a variety of factors, including number of hops, transmission cost, and current line congestion. Routers dynamically maintain routing tables, adjusting performance to changing network conditions. Thanks to the forward-if-proven-remote logic, routers can better keep misbehaving or misaddressed traffic off the network by filtering network layer addresses. In this role, they can be considered firewalls between connected networks. Router-based networks are much more scalable than bridge-based networks. Routers can forward more sophisticated and informative management information to enterprise network management systems via SNMP.

When LANs are connected over a long distance via WAN links, routers are more likely than bridges to be employed to interface to the WAN link. Thanks to the router's ability to more accurately identify upper layer protocols, unnecessary or unwanted traffic can be kept off the relatively low-speed, high-cost WAN links.

Perhaps routers' most significant advantage is their ability to process multiple

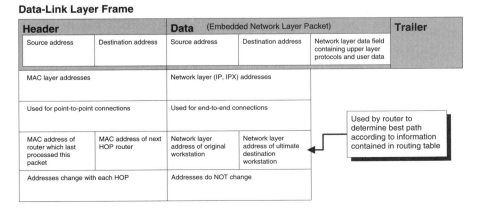

Figure 14-3   Router's Use of Data-Link and Network Layer Addresses

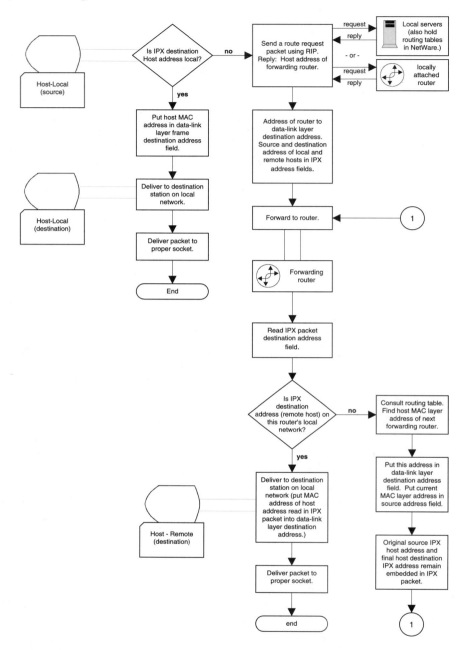

Figure 14-4   Logic Flow for Address Processing by Routers

network layer protocols simultaneously. A properly configured router can process IP, IPX, and AppleTalk packets simultaneously while forwarding each protocol type to the proper destination network. In addition, some routers are also able to handle nonroutable protocols, such as NetBIOS, LAT, or SNA/SDLC, which possess no network layer addressing scheme. In these cases, either the data-link layer frames are bridged or upper layer protocols are encapsulated in a network layer envelope such as IP.

To summarize, routers provide the internetwork with the following services:

- Create firewalls to protect connected LANs.

- Filter unwanted broadcast packets from the internetwork.

- Discriminate and prioritize packet processing according to network layer protocol.

- Provide security by filtering packets by either data-link or network layer addresses.

- Provide transparent interconnection between LANs.

Limitations   Because of their sophisticated processing, routers are considerably more complicated to configure and manage than bridges. As the number of routers increases in a router-based network, the complexity of network management increases proportionally. To be able to process multiple network layer protocols, they must have all supported protocol stacks installed and properly configured.

The router's sophisticated processing also has an impact on the sophistication and cost of the router technology compared with bridging technology.

Switching

Switching, otherwise known as LAN switching, is very similar in function to bridging. The key difference is that switching is done in hardware, or application-specific integrated circuit (ASIC) chips and is extremely fast compared to bridging. The primary purpose of a switch is to increase available bandwidth within a shared-media LAN by implementing microsegmentation on the local LAN. Since the switch creates point-to-point connections for each packet received, shared-media LANs that employ switches become switched-media LANs.

Addressing   Switching uses addresses in a manner similar to bridging. LAN switches read the destination MAC addresses on incoming data-link layer frames and quickly build a switched connection to the switched LAN segment which contains the destination workstation. The switch ports for LAN segments which contain multiple workstations can discriminate between traffic between locally attached workstations and traffic which must be switched to another LAN switch port.

Switches work best when traffic does not have to leave the LAN segments linked to a particular LAN switch. In other words, to minimize the use of expensive WAN links or filter the traffic allowed onto high-speed backbone networks, layer 3 protocols need to be examined by a router. In some cases, this routing functionality is being incorporated into the LAN switch. Basic LAN switches are layer 2 devices which must be complemented by either external layer 3 routers or internal layer 3 routing functionality.

Much like a bridge would handle "nonlocal" traffic, when a LAN switch receives a data-link frame bound for a destination off the local network, it merely builds a switched connection to the switch port to which a router is connected, or to a virtual router within the switch where the switch's routing functionality can be accessed.

Practical Advice and Information

In discriminating between the proper roles of switching and routing, the best advice may be to switch for bandwidth and route for filtering and internetwork segmentation.

Advantages   LAN switches produce dramatic increases in bandwidth compared to shared-media LANs if sufficient thought has gone into logically organizing workstations and servers on LAN switch segments.

Virtual LANs, which are thoroughly explored in Chapter 16, are enabled by the LAN switch's ability to quickly make any two workstations or servers appear to be physically attached to the same LAN segment. Virtual LANs take advantage of this switching capability by logically defining the workstations and computers which belong to the same virtual LAN regardless of their physical location. A given workstation or server can belong to more than one virtual LAN.

Limitations   A LAN switch's limitations are largely a result of its bridging heritage. Switching cannot perform sophisticated filtering or security based on network layer protocols because LAN switches are unable to read network layer protocols. Switches cannot discriminate between multiple paths and make best path decisions. Management information LAN switches offer enterprise network management systems is minimal compared with that available from routers.

Perhaps more important, because switched LAN connections may exist for only a matter of microseconds, monitoring and managing traffic within the LAN switch is considerably more challenging than performing similar tasks on routers. Traditional LAN analyzers constructed for use on shared-media LANs are useless on switched-media LANs. Potential solutions to this and other switching limitations, such as buffering between high- and low-speed network architectures within a single switch, are covered in the LAN switch technology analysis section of Chapter 8.

■ INTERNETWORKING TECHNOLOGY

Internetworking Technology and the OSI Model

Internetworking technology can be categorized according to the OSI model layer corresponding to the protocols a given internetworking device can process. The following internetworking devices can be categorized in this way with the following OSI layers:

- Repeaters   OSI layer 1   Physical layer

- Bridges   OSI layer 2   Data-link layer

- Routers   OSI layer 3   Network layer

Each of these categories of internetworking devices are explored in more detail in the following sections. Although switching was dealt with in this chapter as an internetworking design issue based on future directions such as virtual LANs and integrated routing, LAN switch technology was explored in the chapter on LAN hardware because of its current use largely in local area networks rather than internetworks.

A few characteristics are true of all internetworking devices in relation to the protocols of the OSI layer with which they are associated:

- Any network device can translate or convert protocols associated with OSI layers lower than or equal to the OSI layer of the internetworking device.

- No network device is able to process protocols associated with OSI layers higher than the OSI layer of the internetworking device.

Figure 14-5 illustrates the relationship between the OSI model and internetworking devices.

Repeaters

Functionality   All data traffic on a LAN is in a digital format of discrete voltages of discrete duration traveling over some type of physical medium. The only exception to this is wireless-based LANs in which case the transmission is through the air in an analog format. Given this, a **repeater**'s job is fairly simple to understand:

- Repeat the digital signal by regenerating and retiming the incoming signal.

- Pass all signals between all attached segments.

- Do not read destination addresses of data packets.

- Allow for the connection of and translation between different types of media.

- Effectively extend overall LAN distance by repeating signals between LAN segments.

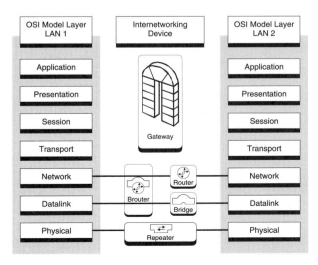

Figure 14-5 Relationship between the OSI Model and Internetworking Devices

A repeater is a nondiscriminatory internetworking device. It does not discriminate between data packets. Every signal which comes into one side of a repeater is regenerated and sent out the other side. Repeaters are available for both Ethernet and Token Ring network architectures for a wide variety of media types. A repeater is a physical layer device concerned with physical layer signaling protocols relating to signal voltage levels and timing. Following are the primary reasons for employing a repeater:

- To increase the overall length of the network media by repeating signals across multiple LAN segments. In a Token Ring LAN, several MAUs can be linked together by repeaters to increase the size of the LAN.

- To isolate key network resources onto different LAN segments, to ensure greater survivability.

- To translate between different media types supported for a given network architecture.

Figure 14-6 illustrates typical installations of repeaters.

REPEATER TECHNOLOGY ANALYSIS

Applied Problem Solving

Figure 14-7 outlines some of the technology analysis issues to consider before you purchase Ethernet or Token Ring repeaters.

Installation — Ethernet Fiber-Optic Multiport Repeater

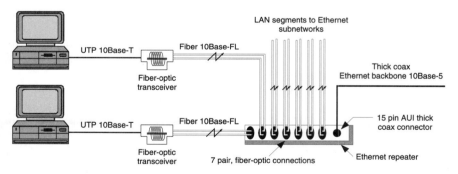

Installation — Token Ring Repeaters

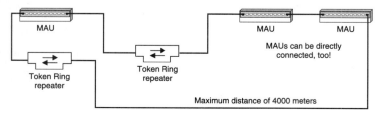

Figure 14-6   Repeater Installations

Network Architecture	Technology Analysis Issue	Importance/Implications
Ethernet	Media type/interface support	• 10BaseT: UTP, RJ-45 • 10Base2: Thin coax, BNC • 10Base5: Thick coax, AUI • 10BaseFL: Fiber-optic cable, ST or SMA connectors
	Long/extended distance repeaters	• Work over single pair telephone wire • Extend Ethernet LANs up to 1250 ft • Must be used in pairs • Fiber-optic links yield distances of up to 1.2 miles
	Local repeaters	• Used to extend and segment local LANs
	Modular repeaters	• Hot-swappable modules allow flexible use for a variety of different media types and interfaces
	Workgroup repeaters	• Used for media conversion • All possible media combinations are available
	Autopartitioning	• An important feature which prevents failure of one connected segment from affecting other segments • Autorestoral upon segment reestablishment is often also included
	Number of segments per repeater	• Repeaters vary in segment capacity • Typical segment capacities range from 2 to 8
	Cascadability	• Some repeaters can be daisy-chained or cascaded to increase overall LAN length
	Price range	• $250–$2500
Token Ring	Transmission speed	• Token Ring is available in 4Mbps and 16Mbps • Some repeaters are able to convert between speeds • Repeaters must support proper speed
	MAU ring length vs. lobe length	• Token Ring repeaters can extend either the overall ring length, as measured by the distance between MAUs, or the lobe length, which is the distance from the workstation to the MAU. • Some Token Ring repeaters can be used to extend either ring length or lobe length
	Fiber-optic repeaters	• Token Ring fiber-optic repeaters can extend ring length to 8200 ft
	Media type/interface support	• Type 1 cabling: STP, Type 1 connectors • Type 3 cabling: UTP, RJ-45 connectors
	Price range	• $815–$2300

Figure 14-7   Repeater Technology Analysis

Bridges

Functionality   When users on one LAN need occasional access to data or resources from another LAN, an internetworking device which is more sophisticated and discriminating than a repeater is required. Comparing the functionality of **bridges** versus repeaters, one could say that bridges are more discriminating.

This reading, processing, and discriminating indicates the bridge's higher level of sophistication, afforded by installed software, and also implies a higher price tag (repeaters: $250–$2500; bridges: $2,000–$6,000). Bridges come in many varieties, as determined by the characteristics of the two LANs joined by a particular bridge. Physically, bridges may be network interface cards which can be plugged into a PC expansion slot along with additional bridging software, or they may be standalone devices.

Bridge performance is generally measured by two criteria:

- **Filtering Rate:** Measured in packets/sec or frames/sec. When a bridge reads the destination address on an Ethernet frame or Token Ring packet and decides whether or not that packet should be allowed access to the internetwork through the bridge, the process is known as **filtering.** Filtering rates for bridges range from 7000 to 60,000 frames per second.

- **Forwarding Rate:** Also measured in packets/sec or frames/sec. Once it's been decided whether or not to grant a packet access to the internetwork in the filtering process, the bridge must perform a separate operation of **forwarding** the packet onto the internetwork medium, whether local or remote. Forwarding rates range from as little as 700 packets per second for some remote bridges to as much as 30,000 packets per second for RISC-based high-speed local bridges.

Although bridging functionality has already been reviewed in the section in internetwork design, two issues specific to bridging deserve further explanation:

- Dealing with redundant paths and broadcast storms.

- Source route bridging.

Spanning Tree Algorithm   The **spanning tree algorithm (STA)** has been standardized as **IEEE 802.1** for the purpose of controlling redundant paths in bridged networks to reduce the possibility of broadcast storms. When installing multiple bridges in a complex internetworking arrangement, a looping topology containing multiple active loops could be accidentally introduced into the internetwork architecture. The spanning tree algorithm (IEEE 802.1), implemented as software installed on STA-compliant bridges, senses multiple paths and disables all but one. In addition, should the primary path between two LANs become disabled, the spanning tree algorithm can reenable the previously disabled redundant link, thereby preserving the inter-LAN link. STA bridges accomplish this path management by communicating with each other via **configuration bridge protocol data units** (configuration BPDU). The overall effect of STA-compliant bridges is to enable the positive aspects of redundant paths in bridged networks while eliminating the negative aspects.

Source Route Bridging   **Source routing bridges** should not be confused with routers since the routing information which delineates the chosen path to the destination address is captured by the source device, usually a LAN-attached PC, and not the bridge. The PC sends out a special **explorer packet** which determines the best path to the intended destination of its data message. The explorer packets are continually propagated through all source routing bridges until they reach their destination workstation. Along the journey, each source routing bridge enters its address in the routing information field of the explorer packet. The destination workstation sends the completed RIF field back directly to the source workstation. All subsequent data messages include the suggested path to the destination embedded within the header of the Token Ring frame. Having determined the best path to the intended destination, the source PC sends the data message along with the path instructions to the local bridge, which forwards the data message according to the received path instructions.

Data messages arrive at a source routing bridge with a detailed map of how they plan to reach their destination. One very important limitation of source routing bridges as applied to large internetworks is the **7 hop limit.** Because of the limited space in the **router information field (RIF)** of the explorer packet, only seven hop locations can be included in the path to any remote destination. As a result, routers with larger routing table capacity are often employed for larger internetworks.

To avoid constantly flooding the network with explorer packets seeking destinations, source routing bridges may employ some type of **address caching** or RIF caching, so that previously determined routes to known destinations are saved and reused.

BRIDGE TECHNOLOGY ANALYSIS

Bridges can be categorized in a number of different ways. Perhaps the major criteria for categorizing bridges is the network architecture of the LANs to be joined by the bridge.

First and foremost, are the two LANs to be bridged Ethernet or Token Ring? Bridges that connect LANs of similar data-link format are known as **transparent bridges.** Transparent bridges exhibit the following characteristics:

- **Promiscuous listen** means that transparent bridges receive all data packets transmitted on the LANs to which they are connected.

- Store-and-forward bridging between LANs means that messages not destined for local workstations are forwarded through the bridge as soon as the target LAN is available.

- Learning is achieved by examining all MAC source addresses on data-link frames received, to understand which workstations are locally attached to which LANs through which ports on the bridge.

- The IEEE 802.1 spanning tree algorithm is implemented to manage path connectivity between LANs.

A special type of bridge which includes a **format converter** can bridge between Ethernet and Token Ring. These special bridges are also called **multiprotocol bridges** or **translating bridges.**

A third type of bridge, somewhat like a translating bridge, is used between Ethernet and FDDI networks. Unlike the translating bridge, which must actually manipulate and rewrite the data-link layer frame, the **encapsulating bridge** merely

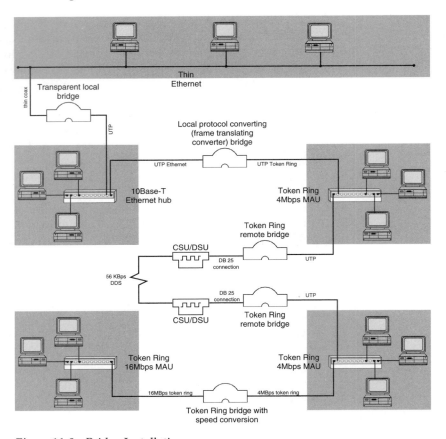

Figure 14-8 Bridge Installations

takes the entire Ethernet data-link layer frame and stuffs it in an "envelope" (data frame), which conforms to the FDDI data-link layer protocol.

Source routing bridges are specifically designed for connecting Token Ring LANs which have source routing enabled. Not all Token Ring LANs are source routing LANs, but only Token Ring LANs can be source routing LANs. Bridges which support links between source routing Token Ring LANs or transparent LANs, are known as **source routing transparent (SRT) bridges.** These bridges are able to identify whether frames are to be bridged transparently or source routed by reading the flags setting in the data-link frame header.

Figure 14-8 illustrates typical bridge installations, and Figure 14-9 identifies some of the technology analysis issues to consider before purchasing bridge technology.

Bridge Technology Analysis Issue	Importance/Implication
Network Architectures to Be Connected	• Bridges for Ethernet and Token Ring are common • Bridges for FDDI, 100BaseT, and 100VGAnyLAN are less common • Network architecture determines LAN speed

Figure 14-9 Bridge Technology Analysis

(continued)

	• Network architecture determines supported network media
Transparent Bridges	• Used for connecting Ethernet to Ethernet or nonsource routing Token Ring to nonsource routing Token Ring • Must be able to support promiscuous listen, store-and-forward bridging, learning, and spanning tree algorithm
Translating Bridges	• Ethernet/Token Ring is the most common translating bridge • Can become a serious network bottleneck due to incompatibilities between Ethernet and Token Ring frame layouts, transmission speeds, and frame lengths
Source Routing Bridges	• Used to connect two or more source routing enabled Token Ring LANs • Source routes are determined by explorer packets broadcasts • Explorer packet broadcasts can negatively affect network performance • Routes are limited to 7 hops (intermediate bridges)
Source Routing Transparent Bridges	• An intelligent bridge which is able to distinguish between transparent bridge traffic and source routing bridge traffic and to bridge each appropriately

Bridge Performance Testing	• Bridge performance can be measured in any of the following ways:
	  • Throughput: maximum sustained transmission rate with zero errors or lost packets
	  • Packet Loss Rate: % of packets lost at maximum theoretical transmission speed of the bridge
	  • Latency: the time it takes for a bridge to process a single packet; in other words, the delay per packet introduced by the bridge

Local Bridges	• Local bridges connect two or more LANs directly via network media • Local bridges contain two or more network interface cards • Local bridges are used to translate between media types
Multiport Bridges	• Multiport bridges contain more than two network interface cards • If the bridge has learned which ports a destination workstation is attached to (by building a known local nodes table for each port), it will forward the data-link layer frame to that port • If the bridge does not know which port a destination workstation is attached to, it will broadcast the data-link layer frame to all ports except the one from which it came
Remote Bridges	• Remote bridges contain network interface cards as well as serial ports for connection to WAN links via modems or CSU/DSUs • Most remote bridges contain one network interface card, specific to a particular network architecture, and one serial interface (RS-232 or V.35) • A compatible remote bridge must be used on the far end of the WAN link to complete the LAN-to-LAN connection

Figure 14-9   *(continued)*

Bridge Technology Analysis Issue	Importance/Implication
	• Data compression is particularly important to remote bridges as the WAN links possess significantly less bandwidth than the LANs. Although compression rates depend on the file being compressed, 3:1 compression ratios are possible • SNMP management information from remote bridges is important to allow these bridges to be monitored and managed by an SNMP-compliant enterprise network management system • To be able to configure remote bridges from a centralized support location, the remote bridges must support Telnet login
WAN Services for Remote Bridges	• Among the WAN services available for remote bridges are 56K DDS, ISDN, T-1 (1.544 Mbps)
Hot-Swappable Modules	• Some bridges may support hot-swappable modules, allowing users to flexibly configure the network interfaces in a bridge without disabling the network
RISC Processors	• Bridge performance is directly related to the speed of the processor within the bridge • RISC processors produce superior performance results
Price range	• $2000–$6000

Figure 14-9   *(continued)*

Wireless Bridges   When corporate LAN locations are up to 3 miles apart, remote bridges linked by WAN services such as 56 Kbps or faster lines are a common internetworking solution. This design implies monthly recurring expenses of approximately $500 for the WAN services in addition to fixed costs for the acquisition of the remote bridges and associated transmission equipment. **Wireless bridges** are an increasingly popular alternative for bridging remote LANs within 3 miles of each other. They use spread spectrum radio transmission between LAN sites and are primarily limited to Ethernet networks at this time.

Like most Ethernet bridges, most wireless bridges support the spanning tree algorithm, filtering by MAC addresses, protection against broadcast storms, SNMP management, encryption, and a variety of Ethernet network media. Like other remote bridges, wireless bridges must be used in pairs. List prices can range from $2700 to $13,500, with the majority of wireless bridges falling in the $4000 to $5000 range. Initial costs of wireless bridges are comparable to those of remote WAN bridges, but no ongoing monthly expense for WAN services is required.

Routers

Functionality   Among the advanced functionality offered by routers, perhaps the most important is their ability to discriminate between multiple network layer protocols. For instance, remembering that multiple protocols can be "sealed" within Ethernet data-link layer "envelopes," a router may be programmed to open the Ethernet envelopes and forward all NetWare (IPX) traffic to one network and all TCP/IP (IP) or AppleTalk (AFP) to another. In some cases, a certain protocol may require "priority" handling due to session time-out restrictions or the time sensitivity of the embedded data.

Routers are made to read specific network layer protocols to maximize filtering and forwarding rates. If a router has to route only one type of network protocol, it knows exactly where to look for destination addresses every time and can process packets must faster. However, realizing that different network layer protocols have different packet structures, with destination addresses of various lengths and positions, some more sophisticated routers known as **multiprotocol routers** have the capability to interpret, process, and forward data packets of multiple protocols.

In the case of an Ethernet data-link frame, the multiprotocol router knows which network layer protocol is embedded within the data-link frame's information field by the contents of the TYPE field in the Ethernet frame header.

Following are some common network layer protocols and their associated network operating systems or upper layer protocols:

- IPX   NetWare
- IP   TCP/IP
- VIP   Vines
- AFP   AppleTalk
- XNS   3Com
- OSI   Open Systems

Other protocols processed by some routers are actually data-link layer protocols without network layer addressing schemes. These protocols are considered **nonroutable.** Routers can process nonroutable protocols by either acting as bridges or encapsulating the nonroutable data-link layer frame's upper layer protocols in a routable network layer protocol such as IP. At one time, specialized devices which could either bridge or route were referred to as **brouters;** however, today most advanced routers include bridging functionality. Following are some of the more common nonroutable protocols and their associated networking environments:

- LAT   Digital DecNet
- SNA/SDLC   IBM SNA
- NetBIOS   DOS-based LANs
- NetBEUI   LAN Manager

In Sharper Focus

ROUTING PROTOCOLS

Routers manufactured by different vendors need a way to talk to each other to exchange routing table information concerning current network conditions. Every network operating system contains an associated routing protocol as part of its protocol stack. Figure 14-10 lists common routing protocols and their associated protocol suites or network environments.

Routing Protocol		Network Environment
RIP	Routing information protocol	XNS, NetWare, TCP/IP
OSPF	Open shortest path first	TCP/IP
NLSP	NetWare link state protocol	NetWare 4.1
IS-IS	Intermediate system to intermediate system	DECnet, OSI
RTMP	Routing table maintenance protocol	AppleTalk
RTP	Router table protocol	Vines

Figure 14-10   Router-to-Router Protocols

Routing information protocol (RIP), at one time the most popular router protocol standard, is largely being replaced by **open shortest path first (OSPF).** OSPF offers several advantages over RIP, including its ability to handle larger internetworks as well as a smaller impact on network traffic for routing table updates.

A major distinction between routing protocols is in the method or algorithm by which up-to-date routing information is gathered by the router. For instance, RIP uses a **distance vector** algorithm which measures only the number of hops to a distant router, to a maximum of 16, while the OSPF protocol uses a more comprehensive **link state** algorithm which can decide between multiple paths to a given router based on variables other than number of hops such as delay, and capacity, throughput, and reliability of the circuits connecting the routers. Perhaps more important, OSPF uses much less bandwidth to keep routing tables up to date.

Distance vector routing requires each router to maintain a table listing the distance in hops, sometimes referred to as link cost, between itself and every other reachable network. These distances are computed by using the contents of neighboring routers' routing tables and adding the distance between itself and the neighboring router that supplied the routing table information. Routing tables must be kept up-to-date to reflect any changes in the network. The key problem with distance vector routing protocols is that all routers don't always know of changes in the network immediately because of the delays caused by routers recalculating their own routing tables before retransmitting updated information to neighboring routers. This phenomenon is referred to as **slow convergence.**

Link state protocols such as OSPF (TCP/IP) and NLSP (NetWare) can overcome slow convergence and offer a number of other performance enhancements as well. One important distinction between distance vector and link state routing protocols is that distance vector routing protocols use only information supplied by directly attached neighboring routers, whereas link state routing protocols employ network information received from all routers on a given internetwork.

Link state routing protocols are able to maintain a complete and more current view of the total internetwork than distance vector routing protocols by adhering to the following basic processes:

- Link state routers use specialized datagrams known as **link state packets (LSP)** to determine the names of and the cost or distance to any neighboring routers and associated networks.

- All information learned about the network is sent to all known routers, not just neighboring routers, using LSPs.

- All routers have all other routers' full knowledge of the entire internetwork via the receipt of LSPs. The collection of LSPs is stored in an LSP database. This full internetwork view contrasts with a view of only the immediate neighbors, using a distance vector protocol.

- Each router is responsible for compiling the information contained in all of the most recently received LSPs to form an up-to-the-minute view of the entire internetwork. From this full view of the internetwork, the link state routing protocol is able to calculate the best path to each destination network as well as a variety of alternate paths with varying costs.

- Newly received LSPs can be forwarded immediately whereas distance vector routing protocols had to recalculate their own routing tables before forwarding updated information to neighboring routers. The immediate forwarding of LSPs allows quicker convergence in the case of lost links or newly added nodes.

Applied Problem Solving

ROUTER TECHNOLOGY ANALYSIS

The most significant distinguishing factor among routers is directly related to the location and associated routing requirements into which the router is to be deployed. As a result, **central site routers,** otherwise known as **enterprise** or **backbone routers,** are employed at large corporate sites, while **boundary** or **branch office routers** are employed at remote corporate locations with less routing requirements and fewer technical support personnel. For branch offices the amount of whose internetwork traffic does not warrant the constant bandwidth and higher cost of leased lines, **dial-up routers** are often employed. Figure 14-11 illustrates the installation of various types of routers.

Boundary Routers and Branch Office Routers   In the case of boundary or branch office routers, all routing information is kept at the central site router. This

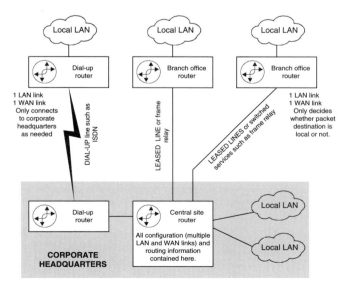

Figure 14-11   Router Installations

allows the boundary router to require less technical configuration and to be available for a lower cost than central site routers. Boundary routers generally have just two interfaces: one WAN link and one LAN link. A boundary router's logic is fairly simple. All locally generated packets are either destined for the local LAN, in which case they are ignored, or nonlocal, in which case they are forwarded over the single WAN link to the central site router for further processing.

The obvious limitation of such a topology is that there is no direct communication between boundary routers and the central routers must include redundancy, since all internetwork communication depends on them. Also, a particular vendor's boundary routers must be matched with that vendor's central office routers because this configuration has no interoperability standards. Figure 14-12 outlines some of the technical analysis issues to be considered with boundary routers.

Technical Analysis Issue	Importance/Implication
Ability to Deal with Nonroutable Traffic	• Must be able to deal with nonroutable protocols such as SNA/SDLC and NetBIOS • Must be able to deal with timing requirements such as SDLC's session time-out limitation
Remote Configuration Support	• Must be able to be remotely configured • Software upgrades must be able to be performed remotely from central site • What happens if the transmission line or power fails during a remote update?
SNMP Compatibility	• Must be able to output SNMP-compatible management information for interaction with enterprise network management systems
WAN Services Supported	• May be any of the following: 56K DDS, T-1, frame relay
Frame Relay Support	• If frame relay is to be used as the WAN service, can the device interact properly with frame relay's congestion control mechanism to avoid packet loss?
Backup WAN Services	• Are switched WAN services available for backup if the leased line fails? • Examples: ISDN, dial-up async, switched 56K
WAN Protocols Supported	• Examples: HDLC, X.25, frame relay, PPP
LAN Network Architectures Supported	• Examples: Ethernet, Token Ring. Others?
LAN Protocols Routed	• Examples: IP, IPX, DECnet, AppleTalk, Vines, XNS, OSI
LAN Protocols Filtered	• Some LAN protocols are very chatty and can waste precious WAN bandwidth • Boundary routers should be able to filter these protocols to keep them off the WAN link: SAP, RIP, NetBIOS broadcasts, Source Routing explorer packets

Figure 14-12 Boundary Routers Technology Analysis

Dial-Up Routers   In cases when the amount of inter-LAN traffic from a remote site does not justify the cost of a leased line, dial-up routers may be the appropriate choice of internetworking equipment. This is especially true if the dial-up digital WAN service known as integrated services digital network (ISDN) is available at the two ends of the LANs to be linked. ISDN basic rate interface (BRI) provides up to 144 Kbps of bandwidth on demand, and ISDN primary rate interface (PRI) provides up to 1.536 Mbps of usable digital bandwidth on demand. There are currently no interoperability standards for dial-up routers. As a result, dial-up routers should always be bought in pairs from the same manufacturer.

In addition to all of the technical features which are important to boundary routers, perhaps the most important feature of dial-up routers is **spoofing.** Spoofing is a method of filtering chatty or unwanted protocols from the WAN link while ensuring remote programs that require ongoing communication from these filtered protocols are still re-assured via emulation of these protocols by the local dial-up router. Following are some of the chatty protocols most in need of filtering:

- Routing information protocol (RIP): NetWare & TCP/IP

- Service advertising protocol (SAP): NetWare

- Watchdog, otherwise known as keep-alive messages: NetWare

- Serialization, looking for duplicate license numbers: NetWare

The reason filtering is so important to dial-up routers is that these unwanted protocols can easily establish or keep a dial-up line open, leading to excessive line charges. Spoofing as a combination of filtering and emulation is illustrated in Figure 14-13.

Occasionally, updated information such as session status or service availability must be exchanged between dial-up routers so that packets are not routed in error and sessions are not terminated incorrectly. The manner in which these required updates of overhead information are performed can make a significant difference in the efficiency of the dial-up routers and the size of the associated charge for the use of dial-up bandwidth. It is important to remember that these routers communicate only via dial-up connections, and it would be economically unwise to create or maintain immediate dial-up connections for every update of overhead information.

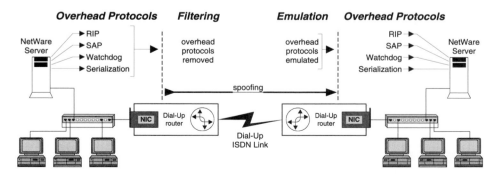

Figure 14-13   Dial-Up Router Spoofing

Different dial-up routers use different update mechanisms. Three primary methods for efficient updating are as follows:

- **Timed updates**—performed at regular predetermined intervals.

- **Triggered updates**—performed whenever a certain programmable event, such as a change in available services, occurs.

- **Piggyback updates**—performed only when the dial-up link has already been established for exchanging user data.

Routing Evolution   Although no one knows for sure what the future of internetworking design and technology holds, most people seem to agree that some combination of switching and routing is the likely scenario for the foreseeable future. Although

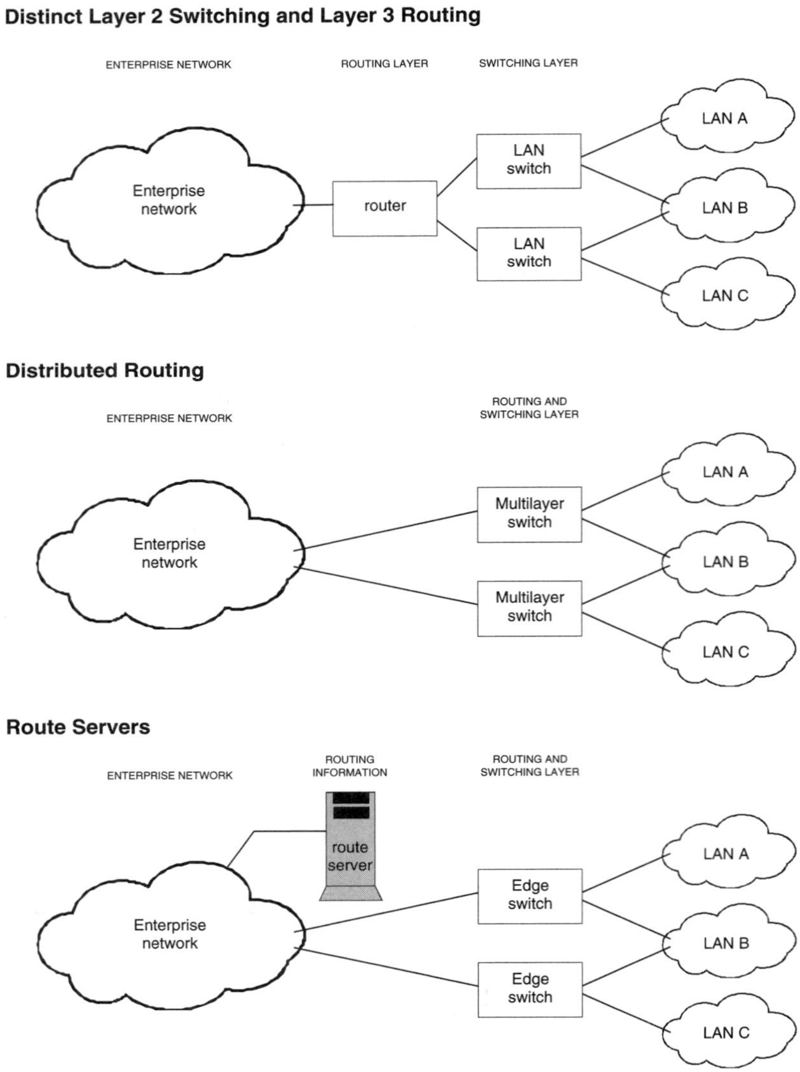

Distinct Layer 2 Switching and Layer 3 Routing

Distributed Routing

Route Servers

Figure 14-14   Routing Evolution Scenarios

switching provides large amounts of switched LAN bandwidth, it is a layer 2 technology and cannot offer the advanced filtering, security, and internetwork segmentation associated with layer 3 routing technology.

Three possible internetwork design evolutionary scenarios are as follows:

- **Distinct layer 2 switching and layer 3 routing,** in which separate layer 2 switches and layer 3 routers cooperatively contribute what each does best to deliver internetwork traffic as efficiently as possible.

- **Distributed routing,** in which layer 2 switching and layer 3 routing functionality combine into a single device sometimes referred to as a **multilayer switch.**

- **Route servers,** which provide a centralized repository of routing information while **edge switches** deployed within the LANs are programmed with minimal routing information. Edge switches will consult distributed route servers for "directory assistance" when they encounter routing situations they are not equipped to handle. In this scenario, routing information and processing overhead is kept to a minimum at the switches primarily responsible for providing local bandwidth.

Practical Advice and Information

In different ways, each of these scenarios implements the future of internetwork design as described by the currently popular phrase, "Switch when you can, route when you must." These three internetworking design scenarios are illustrated in Figure 14-14.

■ LAN-TO-MAINFRAME INTERNETWORKING

Introduction

Micro-Mainframe Connectivity vs. Peer-to-Peer Internetworking   Strictly speaking, micro-mainframe connectivity and internetworking are two different concepts. In **micro-mainframe connectivity,** the micro (standalone or LAN-attached PC) pretends to be or "emulates" a mainframe terminal such as an **IBM 3270** attached and logged into the mainframe. Although file transfer utilities may allow more capability than mere remote login, this is not the peer-to-peer networking implied by the term internetworking.

With full **peer-to-peer internetworking,** the PC can exchange data with any mainframe or any other PC on a host-to-host level rather than acting like a "dumb" terminal, as in micro-mainframe connectivity. Although these two mainframe connectivity alternatives have their differences, they still have much in common. The truth is that most "IBM shops" have a mixture of 3270 terminal connections, mainframes, and LANs, which must communicate with each other on a number of levels.

Hierarchical Networks and Peer-to-Peer Communications Networks   A hierarchical network structure such as the "classic" Systems Network Architecture (SNA) centers on the mainframe. If two devices other than the mainframe on an SNA network wanted to communicate, they would have to establish, maintain, and terminate that communication through the mainframe. This model directly contrasts with a peer-to-peer network communications structure, typical of most LANs, in which any device can communicate directly with any other LAN-attached device.

Classic SNA Architecture

Figure 14-15 illustrates a simple SNA architecture and introduces some key SNA network elements.

This figure illustrates the following two devices in a classic SNA environment:

- **Front-end processor** (FEP)—(IBM 3745, 3746) A front-end processor is a computer that offloads the communications processing from the mainframe, allowing the mainframe to be dedicated to processing activities. A high-speed data channel connects the FEP to the mainframe locally, although FEPs can be deployed remotely as well. The FEP, also known as a communications controller, can have devices such as terminals or printers connected directly to it, or these end-user devices may be concentrated by another device known as a cluster controller. There are two options for high-speed data channels between FEPs and IBM mainframes:
  - **Bus and tag** has a transmission rate of 4.5 Mbps and has been available since 1967.
  - **ESCON II (Enterprise System CONnection)** has a maximum transmission rate of 70 Mbps, has been available since 1990, and can transmit up to 30 miles over fiber-optic cable.
- **Cluster controller**—(IBM 3174, 3274) A cluster controller is a device which allows connection of 3270 terminals as well as LANs, with possible wide area links to packet switched networks (X.25) or high-speed leased lines. A cluster controller concentrates the transmissions of its numerous input de-

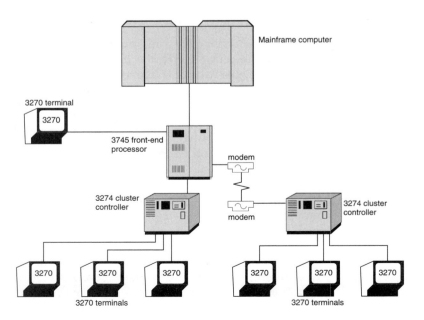

Figure 14-15   Classic SNA Architecture

vices and directs this concentrated data stream to the FEP, either locally or remotely.

The hierarchical nature can be seen in Figure 14-15 as data received from the lowly terminals is concentrated by multiple cluster controllers for a front-end processor, which further manages the data for the almighty mainframe. As additional processors and minicomputers such as an IBM AS/400 are added, the hierarchical nature of classic SNA is even more clear.

The network illustrated in Figure 14-15 is modified one step at a time, until the goal of an architecture which seamlessly transports SNA as well as LAN traffic is reached.

Micro-Mainframe Connectivity

PCs as 3270 Terminals   The first step of PC or LAN integration with classic SNA is to allow a standalone PC to emulate a 3270 terminal and conduct a communication session with the mainframe. This is accomplished through **protocol conversion,** which allows the PC to appear as a 3270 terminal to the mainframe.

A **3270 protocol conversion card** is inserted into an open PC expansion slot. Additional protocol conversion software, which may or may not be included with the protocol conversion card, must be loaded onto the PC to make the PC keyboard behave like a 3270 terminal keyboard (keyboard remapping). The media interface on the card is usually RG-62 thin coax for local connection to cluster controllers. Synchronous modems could also be employed for remote connection. Figure 14-16 illustrates possible configurations for standalone PC–3270 terminal emulation.

LAN-based SNA Gateways   The next scenario to be dealt with is how to deliver mainframe connectivity to LAN-attached PCs. One way is to mimic the method for

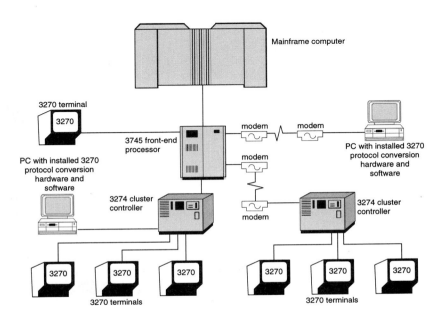

Figure 14-16   Standalone PC 3270 Terminal Emulation

attaching standalone PCs; that is, for every LAN-attached PC, buy and install the 3270 protocol conversion hardware and software and provide a dedicated link to a cluster controller. Since most of these LAN-attached PCs need mainframe connectivity only occasionally, this would not be a very cost-effective solution. It is wasteful not only in terms of the number of PC boards purchased, but also in the number of cluster controller ports monopolized but underutilized.

It would be wiser to take advantage of the shared resource capabilities of the LAN to share a protocol conversion attachment to the mainframe. Such a LAN server–based, shared protocol–converted access to a mainframe is known as a **gateway.** Two popular SNA gateway software packages associated with LAN network operating are Microsoft SNA server, for linking to Windows NT LANs, and NetWare for SAA, for linking to NetWare LANs. Figure 14-17 illustrates a LAN-based local gateway and a remote gateway.

As the figure shows, a gateway configuration can allow multiple simultaneous 3270 mainframe sessions to be accomplished via a single gateway PC and a single port on the cluster controller. A remote PC-based LAN gateway needs additional hardware and software to emulate not only the 3270 terminal but also the 3274 clus-

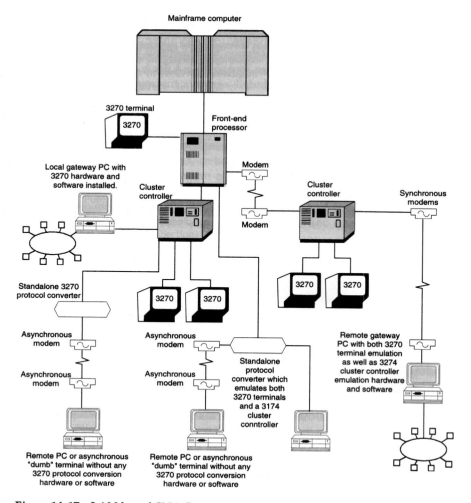

Figure 14-17   LAN-based SNA Gateways

ter controller. Such remote 3274 cluster controller boards and software are as readily available as 3270 terminal emulation hardware and software. As a slight variant on PC-based emulation hardware and software, standalone protocol conversion devices for both 3270 terminal and 3274 cluster controller emulation are available, as illustrated in Figure 14-17.

Mainframe Channel-Attached Gateways As an alternative to LAN-based gateways, **channel-attached gateways** interface directly to the mainframe's high-speed data channel, bypassing the FEP entirely. Physically, the channel-attached gateways are often modules which are added to enterprise routers. Depending on the amount of actual 3270 terminal traffic required in a given network, the use of channel-attached gateways may either preclude the need for additional FEP purchases or allow FEPs to be replaced altogether.

The price difference between channel-attached gateways and FEPs is significant. An ESCON-attached IBM 3745 FEP costs approximately $225,000, while an equivalent router-based Cisco channel interface processor costs approximately $69,000. Figure 14-18 illustrates the installation of channel-attached gateways for linking LAN-based PCs as 3270 terminals to mainframes.

The SNA Architecture

Figure 14-19 illustrates a seven-layer model of the SNA hierarchy. Like the OSI model, the SNA model starts with media issues in layer 1—the physical control layer—and ends up at layer 7—the transaction services layer, which interfaces to the end-user. The layers in between, however, do not match up perfectly with the corresponding numbered layer in the OSI model, although general functionality at each layer is similar. "Similar general functionality" does not suffice when it comes to internetworking. As a result, options will be seen for merging SNA (SDLC) and OSI (LAN-based) data transmissions on a single internetwork involving various methods to overcome the discrepancies between the two architectures.

The SDLC Protocol Figure 14-20 illustrates the structure of the **synchronous data-link control (SDLC)** protocol. Although the protocol structure itself does not look

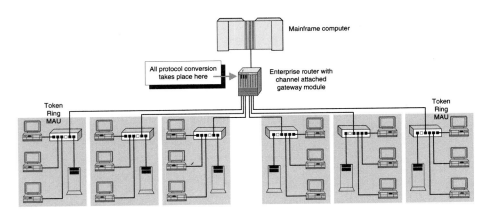

Figure 14-18 Channel-attached LAN/SNA Gateways

Layer number	Sublayer number	Layer/Sublayer Name	Function
7		Transaction services	Provide network management services. Control document exchange and distributed database access.
6		Presentation services	Formats data, data compression, and data transformation.
5		Data flow control	Synchronous exchange of data supports communications session for end-user applications, ensures reliability of session.
4		Transmission control	Matches the data exchange rate, establishes, maintains, and terminates sessions. Guarantees reliable delivery of data between end points. Error control, flow control.
3		Path control	Overall layer: creates the link between two endpoints for the transmission control protocols to manage. Divided into 3 sublayers.
	3	Virtual route control	Create virtual route (virtual circuit), manage end-to-end flow control.
	2	Explicit route control	Determines actual end-to-end route for link between end nodes via intermediate nodes.
	1	Transmission group control	If multiple possible physical paths exist between the endpoints, this protocol manages to use these multiple lines to ensure reliability and load balancing.
2		Data-link control	Establishes, maintains, and terminates data transmission between two adjacent nodes. Protocol is SDLC.
1		Physical control	Provides physical connections specifications from nodes to shared media.

Figure 14-19   The SNA Architecture Model

all that unusual, it is the fact that the information block of the SDLC frame contains nothing equivalent to the OSI network layer addressing information for use by routers which makes SDLC a **nonroutable protocol.** SDLC is nonroutable because there is simply no network layer address information available for the routers to process. This shortcoming can be overcome in a number of ways. It is important, however, to understand that this nonroutability is one of the key challenges facing SNA-LAN integration.

Given that SDLC cannot be routed, network managers had no choice but to implement multiple networks between corporate enterprises. One network carries SDLC traffic between remote cluster controllers and FEPs to local cluster controllers, FEPs, and mainframes; a second network supports remote bridged/routed LANs linking with local LANs between the same corporate locations. Such an implementation is sometimes referred to as a **parallel networks model.** Obviously, it would be advantageous, from both business and network management perspectives, to somehow combine the two traffic streams into a single network. Figure 14-21 illustrates this multiple network scenario.

Challenges to SNA/LAN Integration

To understand how SNA and LAN traffic can be integrated, we must first delineate the incompatibilities between SNA networks and local area networks:

Flag	Address	Control	Information	Frame Check Sequence	Flag
1 byte	1 byte	1 byte		2 bytes	1 byte

Figure 14-20   SDLC Data-Link Control Frame Layout

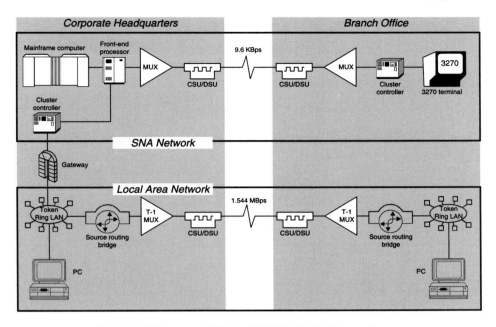

Figure 14-21 SNA/LAN Incompatibilities Yield Multiple Networks

- The first characteristic of SNA which can cause trouble on a LAN is the great amount of **acknowledgment and polling traffic** between SNA processors and SNA end-user devices. This constant chatter could quickly monopolize LAN bandwidth.

- The second SNA characteristic which can cause problems over a shared LAN backbone is that SNA has **timing limitations** for transmission duration between SNA hosts and end-user devices. Thus, on wide area internetworked LANs over shared network media, SNA sessions can "time-out," effectively terminating the session.

- Another traffic contributor which can easily monopolize internetwork bandwidth comes from the LAN side. As described earlier in this chapter, Token Ring LANs use an internetworking device known as a source routing bridge. To define their source-routed internetworking paths, source PCs send out numerous explorer packets to gain a sense of the best route from source to destination. All of these discovery packets mean only one thing — significantly more network traffic.

- As previously stated, SDLC is a nonroutable protocol. To maximize the efficiency of the integrated SNA/LAN network, some way must be found to route SDLC or otherwise transparently incorporate it with LAN traffic.

Given the aforementioned incompatibilities, it seems clear that there are three major challenges to allowing SNA and LAN traffic to share an internetwork backbone:

- To reduce unnecessary traffic (source routing explorer packets and SDLC polling messages).

- To find some way to prioritize SNA traffic to avoid time-outs.
- To find a way to allow internetwork protocols to transport or route SDLC frames.

SNA/LAN Integration Solutions

Several major categories of SNA/LAN integration solutions are currently possible:

- Adding a Token Ring adapter to a compatible cluster controller.
- TCP/IP encapsulation.
- SDLC conversion.
- APPN—advanced peer-to-peer networking.

Each varies in both approach and the extent to which SNA/LAN incompatibilities are overcome.

Token Ring Adapter into Cluster Controller   The first method, illustrated in Figure 14-22, is the least expensive and, predictably, also the least effective in meeting the SNA/LAN integration challenges. A Token Ring network adapter is attached to an available cluster controller port, and attached to a Token Ring network. The SNA traffic is transported using the standard source route bridging (SRB) to its destination.

However, that is only one of the three challenges to be met. The failure to deal with unnecessary traffic and prioritization of SNA traffic makes this a less than ideal solution. This bridged approach deals only with OSI layer 2 protocols. Notice, how-

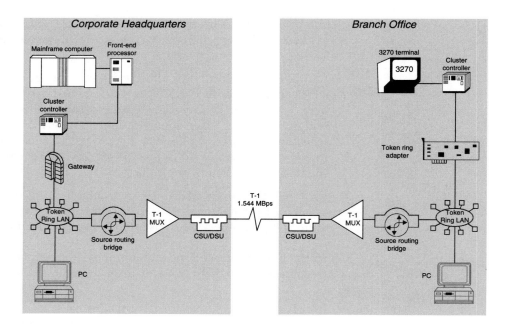

Figure 14-22   Token Ring Adapter into Cluster Controller

ever, the significant potential reduction of hardware and networking costs with this simple approach.

TCP/IP Encapsulation   The second method is known alternatively as **TCP/IP encapsulation,** passthrough, or tunneling. Simply stated, each upper layer SNA packet is "stuffed" into an IP "envelope" for transport across the network and processing by routers supporting TCP/IP internetworking protocol. This IP passthrough methodology for SDLC transport is a common feature or option on internetworking routers. In this methodology, IP supplies the network layer addressing the native SDLC protocol lacks, thereby enabling routing. Figure 14-23 illustrates a passthrough architecture. On close examination of the figure, one may see that, in fact, there is no SNA/LAN integration. What the SNA and LAN traffic share is the T-1 wide area network between routers. The SNA traffic never travels over shared LAN media. Cost savings over the parallel networks model (see Figure 14-21) result from eliminating one wide area link and associated internetworking hardware. The actual TCP/IP encapsulation may take place in either a gateway or a router.

IBM's version of TCP/IP encapsulation, known as **Data-Link Switching** or **DLSw,** has been proposed as an IETF (Internet Engineering Task Force) standard as RFC (Request for Comment) 1434. DLSw does not propose anything radically new but incorporates many vendor-specific TCP/IP encapsulation features into a single standard which will hopefully be widely supported. DLSw is implemented as a software feature on supported routers.

In addition to encapsulating SNA packets in IP addressed envelopes, DLSw also deals with the polling traffic and session time-out issues of SDLC traffic. **Poll spoofing** is the ability of an internetworking device, such as an SDLC converter or router, to respond directly to, or acknowledge, the FEP's constant polling messages to the remote cluster controller. Answering these status check messages locally prevents

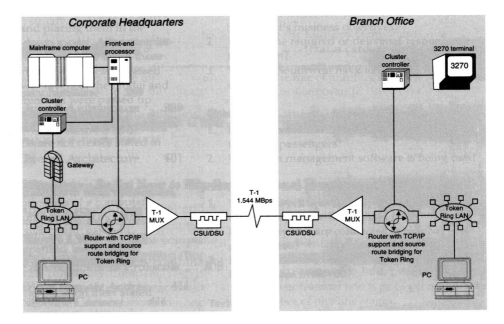

Figure 14-23   TCP/IP Encapsulation

the inquiry and its answer from entering the wide area link portion of the internetwork. **Proxy polling,** on the other hand, emulates the FEP's polling messages on the remote side of the network, thereby ensuring that the remote cluster controller is still in touch with an FEP.

Broadcast filtering addresses a bad habit of the LAN side of SNA/LAN integration. In Token Ring source route bridging, individual PCs send out multiple broadcast packets or explorer packets, causing potential congestion on the internetwork links. Instead of allowing these packets onto the internetwork, routers can filter them out of the traffic, read the destination address to which the PC is seeking a route, and directly supply the PC with that information after consulting its own routing tables.

SDLC Conversion   The third possible solution to SNA/LAN traffic integration, known as **SDLC conversion,** is characterized by SDLC frames actually being converted to Token Ring frames by a specialized internetworking device known as a **SDLC converter.** The SDLC converter may be a standalone device or integrated into a bridge/router. As you can see in Figure 14-24, in the SDLC conversion configuration, the cluster controller is attached to the Token Ring LAN via a standalone or integrated SDLC converter.

SDLC frames are converted to Token Ring frames, transported across the Token Ring internetwork, and routed to a gateway which transforms the Token Ring frames back into SDLC frames and forwards them to the mainframe. Also notice the absence of the FEP from the illustration, potentially saving several thousand dollars. Eliminating the FEP assumes that all 3270 traffic could be routed through attached LANs and gateways.

APPN: IBM's Alternative to LAN-Based SNA/LAN Integration   **Advanced peer-to-peer network (APPN)** is IBM's answer to multiprotocol networking on a peer-to-peer basis, using the SNA architecture, rather than a LAN-based network architecture. Simply put, attached computers, whether PCs, AS/400s, or mainframes, are welcome to talk directly with each other without having the communications session estab-

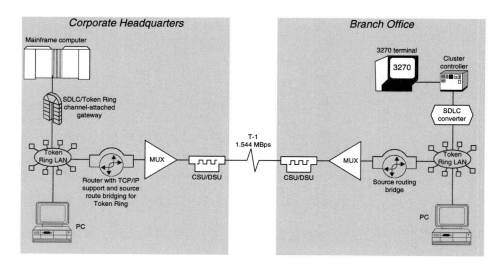

Figure 14-24   SDLC Conversion

lished, maintained, and terminated by the almighty mainframe as the classic SNA architecture required. Recent enhancements to APPN, known as **high performance routing (HPR)/AnyNET,** now allow multiple transport protocols such as IP and IPX to travel over the APPN network simultaneously with SNA traffic. In such an implementation, APPN rather than TCP/IP serves as the single backbone protocol able to transport multiple LAN protocols as well as SNA traffic simultaneously. The specific APPN protocol which deals with SNA/LAN integration is known as **dependent logical unit requester/server (DLUR/S).**

APPN is a software-based solution consisting of only three basic components:

- **End nodes** are end-user processing nodes, either clients or servers without any information on the overall network, available internetwork links, or routing tables.

- **Network nodes** are processing nodes with routing capabilities. They have the ability to locate network resources, maintain tables of information regarding internetwork links, and establish a session between the requesting end node and the internetwork service requested.

- The **central directory server** can save time as well as network traffic for the network nodes. Instead of each network node on an internetwork doing its own information gathering and internetwork exploration and inquiry, it simply consults the central directory server.

A simple example of an APPN network with HPR/AnyNET is illustrated in Figure 14-25.

If the functionality of APPN sounds a lot like what was just reviewed in the other SNA/LAN integration solutions, that should come as no surprise. IBM is not proposing any radical new methodologies. Rather, they are offering an IBM-backed migration from the hierarchical SNA network to a more effective peer-to-peer environment. Put another way, APPN runs TCP/IP and other protocols over an SNA mainframe-based internetwork, rather than running SNA over a TCP/IP-based LAN internetwork.

More significant than IBM's APPN announcement is the blueprint of **the new**

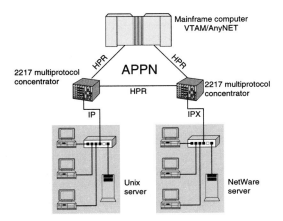

Figure 14-25 APPN with HPR/AnyNET for SNA/LAN Integration

		Systems Management			
Conversation	Remote procedure call	Message queueing	Standard applications	Distributed services	**Applications**
CPI-C	RPC	MQI			
APPC OSI/TP	OSF DCE		FTAM X.400 TELNET FTP	Data directory security recovery time	**Multivendor application support**
Common Transport Semantics					
SNA APPN*	TCP/IP	OSI		NetBIOS IPX	**Multiprotocol transport networking**
LANs frame relay		X.25 cell packet			**Network architecture**
Physical					**Media**

Figure 14-26   The New SNA

SNA. It seems that IBM has realized customers want to be able to integrate multivendor, multiplatform, multiprotocol information systems rather than being locked into one vendor's proprietary network architecture.

The new SNA architecture is illustrated in Figure 14-26. The protocols on the **multiprotocol transport networking layer** should be somewhat familiar. Significantly, SNA/APPN is just one of several transport protocols supported in the new SNA.

The **common transport semantics** layer offers independence between the applications and the transport protocols which deliver those applications across the internetwork.

Managerial Perspective

Although it now supports multiple protocols, APPN should not be misconstrued as an open architecture. APPN is a single-vendor solution with only limited support from third-party internetworking hardware vendors.

One other thing to bear in mind: the new SNA is only a blueprint. When the bricks and mortar to support this proposed architecture start to appear, it may warrant closer attention.

SNA/LAN Integration and Frame Relay   Although all of the SNA/LAN integration solutions illustrated thus far have used a leased T-1 (1.544 Mbps) as their WAN service, this is by no means the only option. A WAN packet switched network service known as **frame relay** has become a popular alternative SNA/LAN integration WAN service. Its key positive attribute is that charges are based on actual amounts of traffic transmitted rather than fixed monthly rates. The key negative aspect of using frame relay as a WAN service for SNA/LAN integration is that this network is being shared with numerous subscribers and is subject to congestion. The access device to the frame relay network, known as a **frame relay access device** or **FRAD**, must be able to respond to requests from the frame relay network to "throttle back" or slow down the input to the network or risk losing transmitted packets due to network overload.

The IETF RFC 1490 contains specifications for the transmission of integrated SNA/LAN traffic over frame relay networks, including proper reaction to congestion notification.

SUMMARY

Internetworking represents an evolutionary stage of LAN development brought on by either poor network performance or a need to share information between two LANs. Internetworking design includes techniques such as segmentation and hierarchical networking as well as processing methodologies such as bridging, routing, and switching.

Bridging is an OSI layer 2 process which bases forwarding decisions on the contents of data-link layer addresses. Routing is an OSI layer 3 process which bases forwarding decisions on the contents of network layer addresses. Switching is actually an implementation of microsegmented bridging designed to supply ample bandwidth to a local area network.

Switching and routing functionality must be combined to deliver optimal performance on the internetwork. Switching supplies bandwidth while routing provides security, filtering by network layer protocols, and internetwork segmentation.

Repeaters are physical layer internetworking devices that extend LAN segment length and convert between media types. Bridges are data-link layer internetworking devices used to logically segment LANs, thereby supporting fewer workstations and more bandwidth on each LAN. Division of workstations onto bridged LANs should be done with some forethought to avoid making the bridge an internetwork bottleneck.

Routers are network layer devices which deal with larger internetworks than bridges and determine best paths to destination workstations. Routers must keep routing tables up to date with the latest internetwork status through the use of routing protocols. Routing protocols can add significantly to bandwidth usage.

LAN-mainframe connectivity can be as simple as 3270 terminal emulation or as sophisticated as SNA/LAN integration via a single backbone protocol. In either case, alternatives are available with varying ability to meet the challenges of SNA/LAN integration as well as cost and complexity.

KEY TERMS

REVIEW QUESTIONS

1. What is internetworking?
2. What are some of the factors which lead an organization to seek internetworking solutions?
3. Differentiate between proper applications of the four basic internetwork design strategies.
4. Describe the use of data-link layer addresses by bridges.
5. What is meant by the phrase "forward if not local"?
6. What are some of the key limitations of bridges?
7. How do routers overcome some of the key limitations of bridges?
8. Describe the use of data-link layer addresses by routers.
9. Describe the use of network layer addresses by routers.
10. What is meant by the phrase "forward if proven remote"?
11. What are some of the key services routers provide to the internetwork?
12. Is switching more like bridging or routing? Explain.
13. What types of functionality are switches not able to deliver?
14. What can be said of all internetworking devices in relation to the OSI model layers and protocols?
15. What types of functionality can a repeater deliver?
16. What is autopartitioning, and why is it important to repeaters?
17. What is the difference between ring length and lobe length in Token Ring networks?
18. What is the difference between filtering and forwarding in bridge functionality?
19. What is the importance of the spanning tree algorithm?
20. What are the advantages and disadvantages of source route bridging?
21. Name and describe the functional characteristics of transparent bridges.
22. Differentiate between translating bridges and encapsulating bridges.
23. Differentiate between source routing bridges and source routing transparent bridges.
24. What implementation scenario is particularly well suited to wireless bridges?
25. What makes a protocol nonroutable?
26. What is slow convergence, and why is it a problem?
27. Differentiate between the delivered functionality of distance vector and link state routing protocols.
28. From a business standpoint, when should boundary routers and dial-up routers be employed?

29. What functionality is particularly important to boundary or branch office routers? Why?
30. What functionality is particularly important to dial-up routers? Why?
31. What is spoofing, and why is it important?
32. Differentiate between the three major methods for updating spoofed protocols on dial-up routers.
33. Differentiate between the three major alternatives for combining routing and switching functionality.
34. Differentiate between micro-mainframe connectivity and peer-to-peer internetworking in terms of where presentation, data management, and application processing take place in each alternative.
35. Why is a classic SNA architecture considered hierarchical?
36. What is the difference in functionality between a front-end processor and a cluster controller?
37. Differentiate between cost and functionality of LAN-based SNA gateways and channel-attached SNA gateways.
38. What is SDLC?
39. Why is SDLC considered nonroutable?
40. What is the parallel networks model, and what causes it?
41. Describe each of the challenges to SNA/LAN integration introduced by either SDLC or LAN protocols.
42. Differentiate between the ability of the four major SNA/LAN integration solutions to meet the previously identified SNA/LAN integration challenges.
43. What is DLSw? Describe its functionality.
44. What is the importance of poll spoofing and proxy polling to DLSw?
45. Differentiate between the functionality, advantages, and disadvantages of TCP/IP encapsulation and SDLC conversion.
46. What are some of the major differences between APPN and TCP/IP encapsulation?

ACTIVITIES

1. Find an organization which has implemented internetworking solutions. Interview the individuals who initiated the internetwork design. What were the motivating factors? Were they primarily business-oriented or technology-oriented?
2. Survey a number of organizations with internetworks to determine how many use primarily bridges versus routers. Explain your results.
3. Research the expected market forecast for bridges, routers, and other internetwork technology. Many professional periodicals publish such surveys in January. Report the results of your study.
4. Research broadcast storms and the spanning tree algorithm. Draw diagrams depicting how broadcast storms are created, and how the spanning tree algorithm controls multiple active loops.
5. Print out the contents of a routing table from two different routers on the same internetwork. Trace the logical path which a packet would take from a local workstation on a LAN connected to either router.
6. Survey organizations with internetworks. Research how many are currently employing or plan to implement LAN switches. What do all of the situations have in common? How do they differ?
7. Research the topic of source route bridging. What percentage of Token Ring LANs employ source route bridging? Is this percentage increasing or decreasing? How is source route bridging being dealt with in multiprotocol internetworks by either bridges or routers?
8. Conduct a survey of organizations with router-based internetworks as to the router-to-router protocol currently employed and planned within the next year. What percentage use RIP versus OSPF? What percentage are planning a change? Analyze and present your results.
9. Review trade magazines, professional periodicals, and product literature to determine the alternative methods for combining switching and routing technology. Is one method dominant? Report on and explain your results.
10. Survey organizations with both SNA/SDLC traffic and LAN internetwork traffic. What percentage run parallel networks? What percentage have achieved SNA/LAN integration? How was it achieved? What are the plans for the one-year horizon? Report on and explain your results.

FEATURED REFERENCES ···

General References

Perlman, Radia. *Interconnections: Bridges and Routers* (Reading, MA: Addison-Wesley, 1992).

Steenstrup, Martha (ed.). *Routing in Communications Networks* (Englewood Cliffs, NJ: Prentice-Hall, 1995).

Case Studies

Nicastro, Linda. Making the Grade at Nebraska's ESU #3. *Network Computing*, 6; 8 (July 1, 1995), 112.

Network Design

Ben-Yosef, Glenn. Toward a New Model: Where to Switch? Where to Route? *Business Communications Review*, 25; 9 (September 1995), 41.

Bruno, Charles. Checking the Routing Structure of the Switching Blueprints. *Network World*, 12; 39 (September 25, 1995), 79.

Glick, Steve and Paul McNab. Internetworking between High Speed Networks. *Communications Systems Design*, 1; 4 (August 1995), 20.

Haber, Lynn. Routing Trends. *Communications Week*, no. 575 (September 25, 1995), 123.

Husselbaugh, Brett. Break Up Your Network. *Byte*, 20; 6 (June 1995), 91.

McLean, Michelle. Routing in a Switched World. *LAN Times*, 12; 14 (July 24, 1995), 77.

Nolle, Tom. Routing and ATM. *LAN Times*, 12; 14 (July 24, 1995), 82.

Passmore, David. Network Architectures Grow Even More Vendor Specific. *Business Communications Review*, 25; 7 (July 1995), 18.

Roberts, Erica. Internetworking: Prepare to Be Switched. *LAN Times*, 12; 1 (January 9, 1995), 62.

Roberts, Erica. Users See Reasons to Retain Routing. *Communications Week*, no. 586 (November 27, 1995), 1.

Branch Office Routers/Edge Routers/ Boundary Routers

Birembaum, Eric. Multi-purpose, Multiprotocol Branch Office Box. *Data Communications*, 23; 9 (June 1994), 37.

Morrisey, Peter. How to Reduce Your Remote Routing Costs. *Network Computing*, 5; 8 (July 1, 1994), 132.

Newman, David and Kevin Tolly. Branch-Office Routers: No Match for Frame Relay. *Data Communications*, 24; 10 (August 1995), 61.

Saunders, Stephen. Closing the Price Gap Between Routers and Switches. *Data Communications*, 24; 2 (February 1995), 49.

Saunders, Stephen. The Incredible Shrinking Price Tag. *Data Communications*, 24, 1 (January 1995), 82.

Snyder, Joel and Ehud Gavron. Branch Office Routers: Extending the Enterprise. *Network Computing*, 6; 1 (January 15, 1995), 62.

Tolly, Kevin and David Newman. The New Branch Office Routers. *Data Communications*, 23; 11 (August 1994), 58.

Routers/Route Servers

Bradner, Scott. The Bradner Report 1995: Bridges and Routers. *Network Computing*, 6; 6 (May 15, 1995), 61.

Bradner, Scott. The Exclusive Bradner Report: Routers. *Network Computing*, 5; 10 (September 1, 1994), 74.

Heywood, Peter. Compression and Routers: Together at Last. *Data Communications*, 24; 5 (April 1995), 55.

Miller, Mark. Buyer's Guide: Which Route for Routers? *Network World*, 12; 35 (August 28, 1995), 55.

Saunders, Stephen. A Router Design that Stacks up Savings. *Data Communications*, 24; 1 (January 1995), 92.

Saunders, Stephen. Route Server Spells End to Table Service. *Data Communications*, 24, 6 (May 1995), 39.

Wittmann, Art. State of the Router: Evolving or Dissolving. *Network Computing*, 6; 2 (February 1, 1994), 52.

Distributed Routers/Virtual Network Routing

Roberts, Erica. Digital Ships Distributed Routers. *Communications Week*, no. 546 (July 3, 1995), 1.

Dial-Up Routers/ISDN Bridges and Routers

Kafaipour, Shawn. ISDN Routers: ISDN Picks Up the Pace. *PC Magazine*, 14; 16 (September 26, 1995), NE1.

Larribeau, Bob. ISDN Routing Made Simple. *Network World*, 12; 49 (December 4, 1995), 47.

Mandeville, Robert. Who's Fooling Who? Evaluating ISDN Routers. *Data Communications*, 23; 16 (November 1994), 88.

Mandeville, Robert and David Newman. ISDN Bridges and Routers: Ready for Central-Site Service? *Data Communications*, 24; 15 (November, 1995), 63.

Saunders, Stephen. A Low-Cost Entry to ISDN Routing. *Data Communications*, 24; 4 (March 21, 1995), 127.

Tolly, Kevin and David Newman. Testing Dial-Up Routers: Close, but No Cigar. *Data Communications*, 23; 9 (June 1994), 69.

Security

Saunders, Stephen. Making the Public Network Safe for Private Enterprise. *Data Communications*, 24; 6 (May 1995), 35.

Bridges

Bradner, Scott. The Exclusive Bradner Report on Bridges. *Network Computing*, 5; 11 (October 1, 1994), 66.

Ketchersid, John. Bridges Go Wireless. *Network World*, 12, 24 (June 12, 1995), 53.

Molta, Dave. The Bridges of Wireless County. *Network Computing*, 6; 13 (October 15, 1995), 76.

Sullivan, Kristina. Bridging Employees the Wireless Way. *PC Week*, 12; 41 (October 16, 1995), N18.

Routing Protocols

Gerber, Barry, OSPF Routing: Coming Soon to a TCP/IP Router Near You. *Network Computing*, 5; 12 (October 15, 1994), 16.

Software Only Routers

Riggs, Brian. Microsoft Eyes Enterprise WANs. *LAN Times,* 12; 23 (November 6, 1995), 22.

Wittman, Art. The Soft Route: A Complimentary Approach to Hardware Solutions. *Network Computing,* 5; 12 (October 15, 1994), 28.

SNA/LAN Integration/APPN/TCP/IP

Cooney, Michael. Bank Invests in APPN Network Savings Plan. *Network World,* 12; 29 (July 17, 1995), 1.

Cooney, Michael. Enhanced APPN Arrives with a Twist. *Network World,* 12; 22 (May 29, 1995), 1.

Cooney, Michael. IBM Big Iron Prepped for TCP/IP Traffic Duty. *Network World,* 12; 34 (August 21, 1995), 1.

Cooney, Michael. Vendors Look to Expand APPN. *Network World,* 12; 35 (August 28, 1995), 19.

Enck, John. SNA Connectivity Solutions. *Windows NT Magazine,* no. 4 (December 1995), 41.

Gillooly, Caryn. Microsoft to Offer SNA Link. *Information Week,* no. 558 (December 18, 1995), 24.

Guruge, Anura. TCP/IP and SNA: Can They Get Along? *Business Communications Review,* 24; 10 (October 1994), 33.

Hoffman, Guy. Hey, Big Blue, You Have SNA Visitors. *IT/IS Backoffice* (December 1995), 17.

Layland, Robin. The SNA Connectivity Challenge Solutions Showcase. *Data Communications,* 24; 7 (May 21, 1995), DC1.

Layland, Robin. The SNA Internetworking Challenge Solutions Showcase. *Data Communications,* 24; 2 (February 1995), DC1.

Passmore, David. APPN: The Once and Future SNA. *Business Communications Review,* 25; 5 (May 1995), 16.

Passmore, David. SNA Internetworking to the Desktop. *Business Communications Review,* 25; 8 (August 1995), 20.

Riggs, Brian. Apps Makers Rally Behind SNA over IP. *LAN Times,* 12; 25 (December 4, 1995), 1.

Roberts, Erica. APPN Spec to Meld SNA Nets with ATM. *Communications Week,* no. 583 (November 6, 1995), 1.

Routt, Thomas. Integration Strategies for APPN and TCP/IP. *Business Communications Review,* 25; 3 (March 1995), 43.

Routt, Thomas and Deric Villanueva. Microsoft's SNA Server vs. Novell's NetWare for SAA. *Business Communications Review,* 25; 6 (June 1995), 57.

Salamone, Salvatore. Pruning Branch-Office Problems. *Byte,* 20; 7 (July 1995), NA4.

Taylor, Kieran. SNA and LANs, Together at Last. *Data Communications,* 24; 1 (January 1995), 51.

Tolly, Kevin. TCP/IP's Rise Has APPN on the Ropes. *Data Communications,* 24; 2 (February 1995), 37.

Waclawsky, John. Thinking Strategically about TCP/IP and SNA. *Business Communications Review,* 25; 5 (May 1995), 51.

Wilson, Linda. SNA TCP/IP Network Magic. *Communications Week,* no. 586 (November 27, 1995), 41.

SNA Routers

Arnette, Wendy and Ralph Case. Advanced Routing Spec Clears Net Paths. *Network World,* 12; 34 (August 21, 1995), 37.

Loudermilk, Stephen. Prime Paths for SNA Routing. *LAN Times,* 12; 14 (July 24, 1995), 86.

Tolly, Kevin and David Newman. Routers and SNA: Improving the State of the Art. *Data Communications,* 23; 14 (October 1995), 60.

Network Services

Heywood, Peter. SITA's SNA Token Ring Access Service: Freeing the FEP: Step by Step. *Data Communications,* 24; 1 (January 1995), 70.

DLSw

Boardman, Bruce. Datalink Switching: Keeping Its Promise. *Network Computing,* 5; 13 (November 1, 1994), 144.

Riggs, Brian. DLSw Earns Respect as SNA Fix. *LAN Times,* 12; 23 (November 6, 1995), 47.

Saunders, Stephen. One Giant Step Towards Integrated Networks. *Data Communications,* 24; 1 (January 1995), 80.

Channel Attached Devices

Bruno, Charles and Anura Guruge. Channel Gateways Threaten FEP Future. *Network World,* 12; 43 (October 23, 1995), 45.

Johnson, Johna. Avoiding the Big Iron Middle Man. *Data Communications,* 24; 1 (January 1995), 84.

McLean, Michelle. Hubs Simplify SNA/SAA Access. *LAN Times,* 12; 23 (November 6, 1995), 49.

Morin, Jim and Gene Misukanis. Changing Channels for Corporate Connectivity. *Data Communications,* 23; 9 (June 1994), 93.

Database Interoperability

Taylor, Charles. The Long and Winding Road from Mainframe DB2 to SQL Server. *Network Computing,* 5; 11 (October 1, 1994), 120.

Windows/Mainframe Interoperability

Cooney, Michael. Microsoft Teams with Proginet to Deliver Windows to Hosts. *Network World,* 12; 28 (July 10, 1995), 1.

Ohlsson, Ann. InfoSessions Puts the PC Into MVS. *Network Computing,* 6; 10 (September 1, 1995), 112.

Scott, Brendan. Windows Puts 3270 Emulators in the Right Frame of Mind. *Network Computing,* 6; 10 (September 1, 1995), 84.

Yasin, Rutrell. Faster Access to Hosts. *Communications Week,* no. 565 (July 10, 1995), 1.

Client/Server

Cooney, Michael. IBM Mainframes Get a Client/Server Boost. *Network World,* 12; 25 (June 19, 1995), 17.

AS/400 Connectivity

Tabibian, O. Ryan. AS/400 Connectivity: Kiss SNA Goodbye! *PC Magazine,* 14; 15 (September 1995), NE1.

CASE STUDY

Chapter 14

THE TIME FOR A SWITCH

In 1991, One Net Manager Shunned Routers, Bet on Switching

In 1991, when most people still considered routers the best technology for segmenting LAN networks, Stephen Lopez, network manager for the National Board of Medical Examiners, took a chance. He placed his bets on switching because he believed it would deliver the scaleability and high performance he needed.

Based in Philadelphia, the National Board of Medical Examiners serves as the exclusive source for creating, maintaining, and recording all U.S. and Canadian physician-licensing examinations.

Lopez is currently converting 80 years worth of registrations, transcripts, and candidate files into an image database that will be retrievable from any platform, anywhere on the network. Because of this, Lopex stressed that the network needs to be scaleable and flexible.

This is not the first time Lopez has had to tackle these goals. In fact, the initial network, which was composed of Bay Networks' (then SynOptics Communications Inc.) 3000 shared-media Ethernet hubs also required these attributes.

At that time, the growing demand for bandwidth came primarily from the growing number of PC users, although increased experimentation with distributed applications also contributed.

Then, the National Board of Medical Examiners still had separate, Digital Equipment Corp. VAX and IBM environments. To improve connectivity for the PC users, Lopez consolidated the VAX and IBM environments using terminal emulation for VAX access and gateways for accessing the IBM mainframes.

But during consolidation, users discovered that it was easier to manipulate data in the PC environment than the VAX and IBM environments. "So we integrated and created an infrastructure that would support all three platforms."

As Lopez considered integration options, switching became more appealing because of its perceived "unlimited" high performance at that time. So Lopez selected the first 3Com Corp. (then Synernetics Inc.) LANplex 5000 switching hub for the network.

By introducing the LANplex switches, Lopez saw immediate performance improvement and was also able to link previous performance problems of the 3000 hubs to the low-speed, 10Mbps connections between hubs.

"We ended up placing the LANplex 5000 in one spot and running a direct 10Mbps line to each floor to increase network segmentation," said Lopez.

The file server on each floor was connected to a 3000 hub on that floor, which minimized network backbone traffic.

Lopez discovered a second wave of performance improvements when the servers were given direct attachments to the LANplex 5000 switches, instead of the 3000s.

In 1992, the National Board of Medical Examiners bought its first LANplex 5012 to introduce a backbone hub between two floors with a LANplex 5004 and a second 5012 for floor distribution.

Using the new switches, Lopez decided to increase the floor segmentation of the LANs and separate the servers, which had grown from four to 10. He also gave each server a dedicated 10Mbps link.

The success of the initial switches encouraged Lopez to design a structured wiring system for both vertical and floor distribution. He also redesigned the network so he could beta test the newer LANplex 6000s.

"When we designed this building, we decided to 'future-proof' it, and the only way we could think of doing that was by putting fiber everywhere with Category 5 cabling," he explained.

Although the copper was installed for future use, it is helpful now, said Lopez: "It allows me a little flexibility to create private internetworks within the building."

Lopez also uses the copper cabling to tie in Bay Networks' 2000 hubs to the company's FDDI ring that connects all of the LANplex switching hubs.

The LANplex hubs can be managed through Telnet connections from any workstation on the network. "I run the diagnostics that are in the box," he said. "I can completely manage the box—right down to the port—from anywhere on the network." Lopez also uses a Network General Corp. Sniffer to monitor the bandwidth utilization on the fiber backbone, which he says has never risen above 5 percent.

What's in Store

For Lopez, future work is focused on downsizing the applications to remove the IBM mainframe from the network and to move the VAX applications into a distributed client/server environment.

"To do that, we're going to need fast throughput," he said, explaining that the new applications would require item analysis for the candidate-registry database, scanning, and digital imaging.

"We've been mandated to create and distribute a completely paper-less exam by the year 2000," said Lopez. "This means a lot of scanning and digital images will be coming across the network."

For the first time, Lopez is also considering using IP routing, an integral feature of the LANplex switching hubs, to provide filtering and a fire wall for securing Internet access.

Lopez is also hoping to extend the use of his switching hubs to provide T-1, wide-area connectivity and, by doing so, alleviate the need for separate routers or bridges for wide-area access.

Lopez said he believes the network will meet his future needs, even if that means going to ATM.

"Switching is a lot of common sense. It doesn't take nearly the thought or planning that a router-based network does. If you buy the right switch, it handles the bridging and routing functions automatically," said Lopez. "There isn't one router on the entire network. I have one logical network number for everything."

Source: Erica Roberts (January 9, 1995). The Time for a Switch. *LAN Times,* 12(1), 29. Reprinted with permission of McGraw-Hill, *LAN Times.*

BUSINESS CASE STUDY QUESTIONS

Activities

1. Complete a top-down model for this case by gleaning facts from the case and placing them in the proper layer of the top-down model. After completing the top-down model, analyze and detail those instances when requirements were clearly passed down from upper to lower layers of the model and solutions to those requirements were passed up from lower to upper layers.
2. Detail any questions that may occur to you about the case for which answers are not clearly stated in the article.
3. Do you feel that switching successfully met the internetworking needs of this organization? If not, why not? If so, what changes in networking requirements would have increased the need for routing capabilities?

Business

1. What were the major business activities of this organization?
2. What business directive for the year 2000 is driving strategic application planning?

Application

1. What impact did applications have on the growing demand for bandwidth?
2. What is the strategic plan for applications, and what impact might this have on strategic network planning?

Data

1. What were the unique requirements of data storage and retrieval in this case?

2. Which computing platform did users feel was the easiest in which to manipulate data?

Network

1. What network requirements did the individual in this case believe switching would deliver?
2. From where did the data need to be able to be retrieved?
3. What were the primary sources of the growing demands for bandwidth?
4. How were separate PC, VAX, and IBM environments integrated?
5. Which internetwork design strategies were employed in this case? Give examples.
6. Describe the management capabilities of the switched internetwork.
7. What role might routing have to play in future internetwork design?
8. What role in WAN connectivity support is planned for the switches?

Technology

1. Which switching technology was first chosen, and what were the results of the implementation?
2. List the switching technology introduced in chronological order, along with the associated network impact of each phase.
3. What is being used as a backbone network? How is it implemented?
4. How will routing be implemented in this switched internetwork environment?

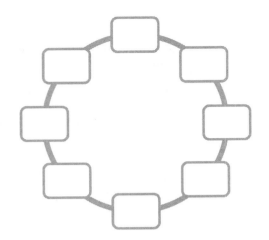

CHAPTER 15

LAN REMOTE ACCESS

Concepts Reinforced

OSI model
Top-down model
Internetwork design
Network operating systems

Internet suite of protocols model
Protocols and compatibility
Internetworking technology

Concepts Introduced

Remote access
Mobile computing
Remote access network design
Remote control
Remote node

Remote access security
Remote access technology
Wireless LANs
Wireless WAN services

After mastering the material in this chapter you should:

1. Understand the difference between and proper application of remote node and remote control computing.

2. Understand the business motivation behind the need for remote access network design.

3. Understand the importance of and networking implication of mobile computing.

4. Understand how to successfully design logical and physical topologies for remote access networks.

5. Understand how to evaluate remote access technology including hardware, software, and WAN services.

6. Understand the unique security issues introduced by remote access and mobile computing.

Chapter 14 explored remote access to corporate LANs and mainframes from remote offices via boundary or dial-up routers. In this chapter we explore remote access from individuals to corporate information resources. To understand the importance of this category of technology, it is important to first appreciate the business forces which have created the increased demand for such technology.

One of the most important things to understand about LAN remote access is the relatively limited bandwidth of the wide area network links individuals use to connect to corporate information resources. Although the goal of LAN remote access may be to offer transparent remote LAN connectivity, decreases in bandwidth by a factor of 100 on WAN links compared to LAN links cannot be ignored.

The goal of this chapter is to outline a methodology for the proper design of remote access solutions based on a thorough understanding of user needs, network architecture alternatives, available technology, and available WAN services.

Managerial Perspective

BUSINESS ISSUES OF REMOTE ACCESS

As information has come to be seen as a corporate asset to be leveraged to competitive advantage, the delivery of that information to users working at remote locations has become a key internetworking challenge. Corporate downsizing has not only increased remaining employees' responsibilities, but pushed those responsibilities ever closer to the corporation's customers. As a result, the voice mail message, "I'll be virtual all day today," is becoming more and more common. The business-oriented motivations for remote access to local LAN resources fall into three general categories:

The first category of remote LAN access is **telecommuting,** that is, working from home with all the information resources of the office LAN at one's fingertips. This category of connectivity and computing is often referred to as **small office home office,** or **SOHO.**

Studies have indicated that the following are some of the ways telecommuting can increase overall worker productivity:

- Better, quicker, more effective customer service.

- Increased on-time project completion and quicker product development.

- Increased job satisfaction among highly mobile employees which can lead to both greater productivity and employee retention.

- Decreased worker turnover, which leads to decreased training and recruiting budgets.

- Increased sales.

A variation of telecommuting, **mobile computing,** addresses the need for field representatives to be able to access corporate information resources to offer superior customer service while working on the road. These field reps may or may not have a corporate office PC into which to dial.

Although some of the positive results of enabling remote access to corporate data for mobile workers are similar to those of telecommuters, the increased customer focus of the mobile worker is evident in the following benefits:

- Faster responses to customer inquiries.

- Improved communications with coworkers and support staff at corporate offices.

- Better, more effective customer support.

- Increased personal productivity by the mobile workers, such as being able to complete more sales calls.

- Increased ability to be "on the road" in front of customers.

- Ability of service personnel to operate more efficiently.

The third major use of remote computing is for **technical support** organizations which must be able to dial in to client systems able to appear as a local workstation, or take control of those workstations, to diagnose and correct problems remotely. Being able to diagnose and solve problems remotely can have significant impact, such as the following:

- Quicker response to customer problems.

- Increased ability to avoid sending service personnel for on-site visits.

- More efficient use of subject experts and service personnel.

- Increased ability to avoid revisits to customer sites due to a lack of proper parts.

- Greater customer satisfaction.

The market for remote access technology was expected to grow by 600%, between 1994 and 1998, to a yearly revenue level of $4.4 billion.

■ ARCHITECTURAL ISSUES OF REMOTE ACCESS

There are basically only four steps to designing a dial-in/dial-out capability for a local LAN:

- Needs analysis.

- Logical topology choice.

- Physical topology choice.

- Current technology review and implementation.

Logical Design Issues

Needs Analysis   As dictated by the top-down model, before designing network topologies and choosing technology, it is essential to first determine what is to be accomplished in terms of LAN-based applications and use of other LAN-attached resources. Following are among the most likely possibilities for the information-sharing needs of remote users:

- Exchange e-mail.

- Upload and download files.

- Run interactive application programs remotely.

- Utilize LAN-attached resources.

Examining information-sharing needs in this manner validates the need for the remote PC user to establish a connection to the local LAN which offers all of the capabilities of locally attached PCs. In other words, if the ability to upload and download files is the extent of the remote PC user's information-sharing needs, then file transfer software, often included in asynchronous communications software packages, would suffice at a very reasonable cost. A network-based bulletin-board service (BBS) package is another means of easily sharing information with remote users. Likewise, e-mail gateway software loaded on the LAN would meet the requirement e-mail if exchange is the total information-sharing need.

To run LAN-based interactive application programs or use LAN-attached resources such as high-speed printers, CD-ROMs, mainframe connections, or FAX servers, however, a full-powered remote connection to the local LAN must be established. From the remote user's standpoint, this connection must offer transparency. In other words, the remote PC should behave as if it were connected locally to the LAN. From the LAN's perspective, the remote user's PC should virtually behave as if it were locally attached.

Logical Topology Choice: Remote Node versus Remote Control   In terms of logical topology choices, two logical methods for connecting remote PCs to LANs are possible. Each method has advantages, disadvantages, and proper usage situations. The two major remote PC operation mode possibilities are remote node and remote control.

The term **remote access** most often describes the process of linking remote PCs to local LANs, without implying the particular functionality of that link (remote node vs. remote control). Unfortunately, remote access is also sometimes used as a synonym for remote node.

Figure 15-1 outlines some of the details, features, and requirements of these two remote PC modes of operation, and Figure 15-2 highlights the differences between remote node and remote control installations.

Remote node or remote client computing implies that, in theory, the remote client PC should be able to operate as if it were locally attached to network resources. In other words, the geographic separation between the remote client and the local LAN resources should be transparent. That's a good theory, but in practice, the comparative bandwidth of a typical dial-up link (28.8 Kbps for a V.34 modem) compared with the Mbps bandwidth of the LAN is anything but transparent. Whereas a NIC normally plugs directly into an expansion slot in a computer, a remote node connection merely extends that link via a relatively low-speed dial-up link. Client applications run on the remote client rather than a local LAN-attached client.

Client/server applications which require large transfers of data between client and server will not run well in remote node mode. Most successful remote node applications are rewritten to minimize large data transfers. For example, modified remote node e-mail client software allows just the headers of received messages, which include sender, subject, and date/time to be transferred from the local e-mail

Functional Characteristic	Remote Node	Remote Control
Also called	Remote client Remote LAN node	Modem remote control
Redirector hardware/ software required?	Yes	No
Traffic characteristics	All client/server traffic	Keystrokes and screen images
Application processing	On the remote PC	On the LAN-attached local PC
Relative speed	Slower	Faster
Logical role of WAN link	Extends connection to NIC	Extends keyboard and monitor cables
Best use	With specially written remote client applications which have been optimized for execution over limited bandwidth WAN links	DOS applications. Graphics on Windows apps can make response time unacceptable

Figure 15-1   Remote Node versus Remote Control Functional Characteristics

server to the remote client. The remote client selects which e-mail messages should have the actual e-mail message body and attachments transferred. Local e-mail client software, which assumes plenty of LAN bandwidth, does not bother with such bandwidth-conserving modifications. Other client/server applications must be similarly modified to execute acceptably in remote node mode.

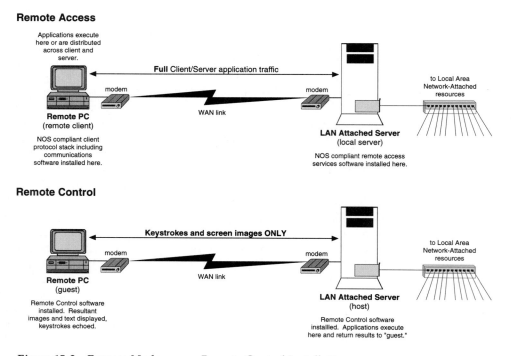

Figure 15-2   Remote Node versus Remote Control Installations

**Practical Advice
and Information**

Although transparent interoperability was discussed as one of the goals of remote access, that does not necessarily mean a worker's mobile computer programs must be identical to those running on one's desktop at the price of terrible performance. One of the most commonly overlooked aspects of deploying remote access solutions is the need to customize applications for optimal performance in a remote access environment.

Remote node mode requires a full client network operating system protocol stack to be installed on the remote client. In addition, wide area network communication software must be incorporated with the remote client NOS protocol stack. Remote node software also often includes optional support of remote control functionality.

Remote control differs from remote node mode in both technology involved and the degree to which existing LAN applications must be modified. In remote control mode, the remote PC is merely supplying input and output devices for the local client, which interacts as normal with the local server and other locally attached LAN resources. Client applications still run on the local client which is able to communicate with the local server at native LAN speeds, precluding the need to rewrite client applications for remote client optimization.

Remote control mode requires only remote control software to be installed at the remote PC rather than a full NOS client protocol stack, which is compatible with the NOS installed at the local LAN. The purpose of the remote control software is only to extend the input/output capabilities of the local client to the keyboard and monitor attached to the remote PC. The host version of the same remote control package must be installed at the host or local PC. There are no interoperability standards for remote control software.

**Practical Advice
and Information**

One of the most significant difficulties with remote control software is confusion of end-users over logical disk assignments. Recalling that the remote PC supplies only the keyboard and monitor functionality, remote users fail to realize that a C: prompt refers to the C: drive on the local LAN-attached PC and not the C: drive of the remote PC they are sitting in front of. This can be particularly confusing with file transfer applications.

Protocols and Compatibility   At least some of the shortcomings of both remote node and remote control modes result from the underlying transport protocols responsible for delivering data across the WAN link.

In the case of remote control, the fact that proprietary protocols are used between the guest and host remote control software is the reason remote control software from various vendors is not interoperable.

In the case of remote node, redirector software in the protocol stack must take LAN-based messages from the NDIS or ODI protocols and convert them to proper format for transmission over asynchronous serial WAN links.

Some remote node software uses TCP/IP as its protocol stack and PPP as its data-link layer WAN protocol. In this manner, remote node sessions can be easily established via TCP/IP, even using the Internet as the connecting WAN service should that connection satisfy the security needs of the company in question. Once the TCP/IP link is established, the remote control mode of this software can be executed over TCP/IP as well, overcoming the proprietary protocols typically associated with remote control programs. In addition, due to PPP's ability to transport upper layer protocols other than TCP/IP, these remote node clients can support communications with a variety of servers.

Figure 15-3 illustrates the protocol-related issues of typical remote control and remote node links as well as TCP/IP-based links.

Security Although security from an enterprisewide perspective is dealt with in the chapter on enterprise network management (Chapter 17), security issues specifically related to remote access of corporate information resources are introduced here. Security-related procedures can be logically grouped into the following categories:

• Password assignment and management—Change passwords frequently, even considering single-use passwords. Ideally passwords should not be actual words found in a dictionary, but a random or meaningless combination of letters and numbers.

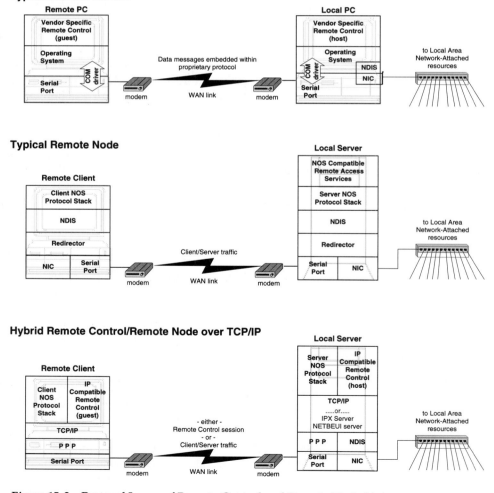

Figure 15-3 Protocol Issues of Remote Control and Remote Node Links

- Intrusion responses—User accounts should be locked after a preset number of unsuccessful logins. These accounts should be able to be unlocked only by a system administrator.

- Logical/physical partitioning of data—Separate public, private, and confidential data onto separate physical servers to avoid users with minimum security clearances gaining unauthorized access to sensitive or confidential data.

- Encryption—Although it is important for any sensitive or proprietary corporate data to be encrypted, it is especially important that passwords be encrypted to avoid interception and unauthorized reuse.

- Dial-back systems—After remote users enter proper user ID and passwords, these systems terminate the call and dial the authorized user back at preprogrammed phone numbers.

- Remote client software authentication protocols—Remote client protocol stacks often include software-based authentication protocols such as password authentication protocol (PAP) or challenge handshake authentication protocol (CHAP).

One remote access security category which deserves further explanation is hardware-based **token authentication.** Although exact implementation details may vary from one vendor to the next, all token authentication systems include server components linked to the communications server and client components which are used with the remote access clients. Physically, the token authentication device employed at the remote client location may be a handheld device resembling a calculator, a floppy disk, or an in-line device linked to either the remote client's serial or parallel port. Figure 15-4 illustrates the physical topology of a typical hardware-based token authentication remote access security arrangement.

In Sharper Focus

TOKEN AUTHENTICATION

Logically, token authentication schemes work in either of two ways:

- **Token response** authentication schemes work as follows:
  1. Remote user dials in and enters private identification number (PIN).
  2. Authentication server responds with a challenge number.

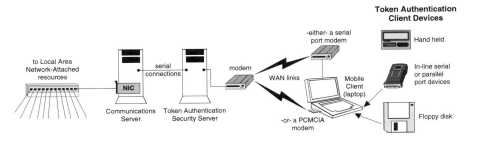

Figure 15-4   Token Authentication Physical Topology

3. The number is entered by remote user into handheld client authentication unit, or it is received automatically by in-line client authentication unit.
4. Client authentication unit generates challenge response number which is either automatically transmitted back to the authentication server or entered manually by the remote user.
5. Transmitted response is received by the authentication server and compared to the expected challenge response number generated at the server. If they match, the user is authenticated and allowed access to network-attached resources.

- **Time synchronous** authentication schemes work as follows:
  1. Random authentication numbers are generated in time-synchronous fashion at both the authentication server and client.
  2. Remote user enters PIN number and the current random authentication number displayed on the client authentication unit.
  3. Due to time synchronization, the server authentication unit should have the same current random authentication number, which is compared to the one transmitted from the remote client.
  4. If the two authentication numbers match, the authentication server authenticates the user and allows access to the network-attached resources.

Following are a few other important operational issues concerning token authentication security systems for remote access:

- Most authentication servers have a management console which provides supervisory access to the authentication security system. Transmission between the management console and the authentication server should be encrypted.

- Valid passwords and user IDs may be stored on either the management console or the authentication server. In either case, security-related data such as user IDs and passwords should be stored in encrypted form.

- The authentication server's response to failed attempts at remote login should include both account disabling and the ability to generate an alarm, preferably both audible and as a data message to the management console. Ideally, the authentication server should pass alarms seamlessly to enterprise management systems via SNMP, to avoid having separate management consoles for every management function.

- Although this functionality is also supplied by such remote access server products as Windows NT RAS, the authentication server should also be able to limit access from remote users to certain times of day or days of the week.

- As Figure 15-4 shows, the authentication server must be able to transparently interoperate with the communications or remote access server. This should not be assumed, but demonstrated or guaranteed by the authentication server vendor.

Physical Design Issues

Physical Topology: Alternative Access Points As Figure 15-5 illustrates, a remote PC user can gain access to the local LAN resources in three basic ways:

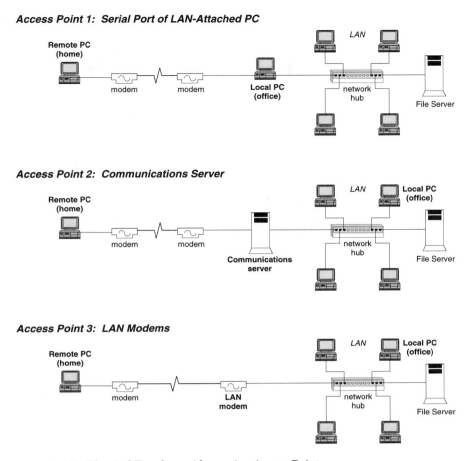

Figure 15-5   Physical Topology: Alternative Access Points

- Serial port of a LAN-attached PC—Perhaps the simplest physical topology or remote access arrangement is to establish a communications link to a user PC located in the corporate office. However, many field representative or mobile computing users no longer have permanent offices and workstations at a corporate building and must depend on remote access to shared computing resources.

- Communications server—As an alternative to having a dedicated PC at the corporate office for each remote user to dial into, remote users could attach to a dedicated multiuser server, known as an **access server** or **communications server,** through one or more modems. Depending on the software loaded on the communications server, it may deliver remote node functionality, remote control functionality, or both.

- LAN modem—Another alternative is to install a specialized device known as a **LAN modem** or **dial-in server,** to offer shared remote access to LAN resources. LAN modems come with all necessary software preinstalled, and therefore require no additional remote control or remote node software. LAN modems are often limited to a single network architecture such as Ethernet or Token Ring, and/or to a single network operating system protocol such as IP, IPX (NetWare), NetBIOS, Net BEUI, or AppleTalk.

The physical topology using the communications server (Illustration 2 in Figure 15-5) actually depicts two possible remote LAN connections. Most communications servers answer the modem, validate the user ID and password, and log the remote user onto the network. Some communications servers go beyond this to allow a remote user to access and/or remotely control a particular networked workstation. This scenario offers the same access capabilities as if the networked workstation had its own modem and software, but also offers the centralized management, security, and possible financial advantage of a network-attached communications server.

The three access arrangements illustrated are examples of possible physical topologies and do not imply a given logical topology, such as remote node, remote control, or both. It is important to understand that the actual implementation of each of these LAN access arrangements may require additional hardware and/or software. They may also be limited in their ability to use all LAN-attached resources, or to dial out of the LAN through the same access point.

■ REMOTE ACCESS TECHNOLOGY

Hardware

Communications Servers and Remote Access Servers   As is often the case in the wonderful but confusing world of data communications, communications servers are also known by many other names. In some cases these names may imply, but don't guarantee, variations in configuration, operation, or application. Following are some of these varied labels for the communications server:

- Access servers.
- Remote access servers.
- Remote node servers.
- Telecommuting servers.
- Network resource servers.
- Modem servers (usually reserved for dial-out only).
- Asynchronous communications servers.

A communications server offers both management advantages and financial payback when large numbers of users wish to gain remote access to and from a LAN. Perhaps more important than the cost savings of power, modems, phone lines, and software licenses are the gains in control over the remote access to the LAN and its attached resources. By monitoring the use of the phone lines connected to the communications server, one can more easily determine exactly how many phone lines are needed to service users who require remote LAN access.

Multiple remote users can dial into a communications server simultaneously. Exactly how many users can gain simultaneous access varies with the sophistication and cost of the communications server and the installed software. Most communications servers service at least four simultaneous users.

Figure 15-6 provides an input–processing–output (I-P-O) diagram to illustrate options for the key functional components of a communications server.

As the figure shows, the key hardware components of the communications

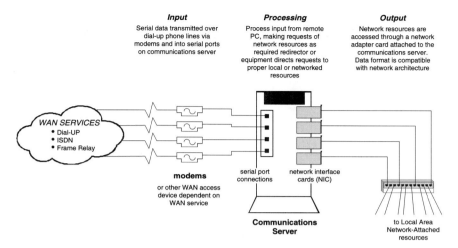

Figure 15-6   Communications Server Components

server are serial ports, CPU(s), and network interface card(s). The relative number of each of these components included in a particular communications server is a key differentiating factor in communications server architectures or configurations. Although not guaranteed, the communications and remote node servers are generally differentiated by the following:

- Communications servers include several CPU boards inside a single enclosure. These servers combine applications server and remote node server functionalities. Applications are physically loaded and executed on the communications server. Communications servers are often used for remote control functionality as an alternative to having several separate desktop PCs available for remote control. Consolidating the CPUs into a single enclosure provides additional fault tolerance and management capabilities over the separate PCs model. Following are examples of communications servers and vendors:

Communications Server	Vendor
J&L Chatterbox	J&L Information Systems
CubixConnect Server	Cubix Corp.
CAPServer	Evergreen Systems

- **Remote node servers** are concerned strictly with controlling remote access to LAN-attached resources and acting as a gateway to those resources. Applications services are supplied by the same LAN-attached applications servers that are accessed by locally attached clients.

The functional differences between communications servers and remote node servers are illustrated in Figure 15-7.

Currently, remote node server solutions fall into three major categories:

- Software-only solutions, in which the user supplies a sufficiently powerful server and adds a remote node server software package such as Windows

Communications Server

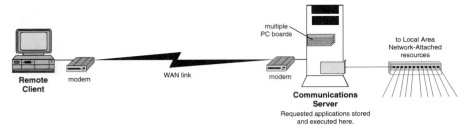

Remote Node Server

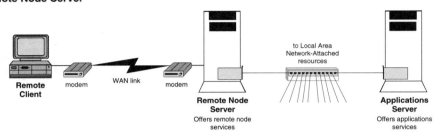

Figure 15-7 Communications Servers versus Remote Node Servers

NT RAS or NetWare Connect or other third-party remote node software package. In some cases, a multiport serial board may be included with the software to add sufficient serial ports to the user's server. The section on remote node software offers more information about software-only solutions.

- Turnkey or hard/software solutions, in which fully configured remote node servers are compatible with existing network architectures and operating systems. Integrated modems may or may not be included. The remote node server software included on these turnkey systems must be compatible with the installed network operating system. Among the more popular remote node servers are the following:

Remote Node Server	Vendor
LANexpress 4000	Microcom
RLN Turnkey Server	Attachmate
LAN Rover/E Plus 3.5	Shiva
NetBlazer	Telebit
AccessBuilder 2000	3Com
Remote Annex 2000	Xylogics

- LAN modems, also occasionally known as dial-up servers, could be thought of as remote node servers with one or more integrated modems. Included security and management software are also installed on the LAN modem.

Given the rapid increase in modem transmission speeds with evolving modem transmission standards, integrating a modem which cannot be upgraded within a remote node server may be less beneficial than using external modems which are more easily upgraded. Perhaps in a response to this need for convenient modem upgrades, some remote node servers now come with four or eight PC card (PCMCIA) slots into which the latest modem technology can be easily inserted. LAN modems are generally included in reviews of remote node servers rather than being regarded as a distinct product category.

When employing a self-contained remote node server, including both hardware and software, compatibility with existing network resources on a number of levels must be taken into account. Figure 15-8 outlines these compatibility issues as well as key functional issues of remote node servers.

Remote Node Server Compatibility/Functional Issue	Importance/Implication
Network architecture compatibility	• Since the remote node server includes network interface cards, these must be compatible with the network architecture (Ethernet, Token Ring) of the network in which it is to be installed. • Most remote node servers have Ethernet models, while fewer offer Token Ring models. • Media compatibility must also be ensured. For example, Ethernet may use AUI, BNC, or RJ-45 interfaces.
Network operating system compatibility	• The remote node server software installed in the server must be compatible with the network operating system installed in the network-attached applications servers. • Since these are third-party hardware/software turnkey systems, the remote node server software is not the same as the native software-only solutions, such as Windows NT RAS or NetWare Connect, which imply guaranteed compatibility with their respective network operating systems. • The remote node server must also be compatible with the underlying transport protocols used by the installed network operating system. • Can the remote node server access the network operating system's user authorization files to avoid having to build and maintain a second repository of user IDs and passwords? • In the case of NetWare LANs, integration with NetWare Bindery (3.12) or NDS (4.1) should be provided.
Remote client software compatibility	• The remote node server software must be compatible with the remote node software executed on the remote clients.

Figure 15-8   Compatibility and Functional Issues of Remote Node Servers

(continued)

Remote Node Server Compatibility/Functional Issue	Importance/Implication
	• This remote client software must be compatible with the native operating system on the remote client. • If compatible remote client software is not supplied with the remote node server, is compatibility with third-party PPP client or remote client software guaranteed? • Cost of remote client software may be included in remote node server purchase cost, or may be an additional $50/client.
Physical configuration	• Number of serial ports: most models start at 8, some are expandable up to 128. • Serial port speed: most support serial port speeds of 115.2 Kbps while some support speeds of 230.4 Kbps.

Transmission optimization	• Use of the limited bandwidth WAN link can be optimized in a variety of ways:
	  • Compression—Are both headers and data compressed?
	  • Spoofing—Are chatty protocols restricted from the WAN link?
	  • Are users warned before launching remote applications which may bog down the WAN link and offer poor performance?

Routing functionality	• Routing functionality would allow LAN-to-LAN or remote server-to-local server connectivity rather than connection from a single remote client to the local server. • Routing functionality allows the remote node server to also act as a dial-up router. Dial-up routers must be used in pairs.
WAN services supported	• Is connectivity to ISDN, X.25, frame relay as well as dial-up lines supported? • Some remote node servers have high-speed serial ports for connection to higher-speed WAN services such as T-1 (1.544 Mbps).
Call management	• Are dropped calls automatically redialed? • Can connect-time limits be enforced? • Can status of all remote access calls be viewed and controlled from a single location? • Are event logs and reports generated? • Are status and alarm messages output via SNMP agents? • Is fixed and variable callback supported? • Is encryption supported?

Figure 15-8   (continued)

DIALING-OUT FROM THE LAN

Normally, when a modem is connected directly to a PC, the communications software expects to direct information to the local serial port to which the modem is attached. However, in the case of a pool of modems attached to a remote node server, the communications software on the local clients must redirect all information for modems through the locally attached network interface card, across the local LAN, to the remote node server, and ultimately to an attached modem. This ability to redirect information for **dial-out** modem applications from LAN-attached PCs is a cooperative task accomplished by the software of the remote node server and its corresponding remote client software. Not all remote node servers support dial-out functionality.

The required redirection is accomplished through the use of industry standard software redirection interrupts. The interrupts supported or enabled on particular remote node servers vary:

- **Int14,** or Interrupt 14, is one of the supported dial-out software redirectors and is most often employed by Microsoft network operating systems. Int14 is actually an IBM BIOS serial port interrupt used to redirect output from the local serial port. A terminate-and-stay-resident (TSR) program running on the client intercepts all the calls and information passed to Int4 and redirects that information across the network to the modem pool.

- NetWare asynchronous services interface, or **NASI,** is a software interrupt which links to the NetWare shell on NetWare clients. As with the Int14 implementation, a TSR intercepts all the information passed to the NASI interrupt and forwards it across the network to the dial-out modem pool.

Figure 15-9 illustrates some of the issues involved in dialing out from the LAN.

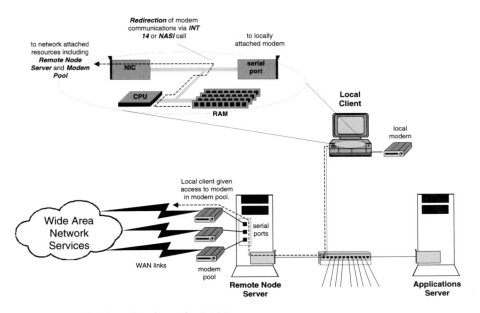

Figure 15-9   Dialing Out from the LAN

Wireless LANs   Although not strictly limited to use in a remote access setting, wireless LANs do play a role in the overall objective of untethering workers to increase productivity and customer satisfaction. Although wireless LANs may have been initially marketed as a means of replacing wire-bound LANs, that marketing strategy has not been reflected in their applied uses to date.

Mobile computing can be performed within the confines of a corporate or campus environment as well as over longer distances, with the assistance of wireless bridges or WAN services. Portable or notebook PCs equipped with their own wireless LAN adapters can create an instant LAN connection merely by getting within range of a server-based wireless LAN adapter or wireless hub. In this way, a student or employee can sit down anywhere and log into a LAN as long as he/she is within range of the wireless hub and has the proper wireless adapter installed in a portable PC. These implementations are especially helpful in large warehouse or inventory settings.

Meeting rooms could be equipped with wireless hubs to allow spontaneous workgroups to log into network resources without running cables all over the meeting room. Similarly, by quickly installing wireless hubs and portable PCs with wireless adapters, one can quickly handle temporary expansion needs or emergency/disaster recovery situations with relative ease. No rerunning of wires, or finding the proper cross-connects in the wiring closet is necessary.

Finally, wireless LAN technology allows entire LANs to be preconfigured at a central site and shipped "ready to run" to remote sites. The nontechnical users at the remote site literally just have to plug the power cords into the electrical outlets to have an instant LAN. For companies with a great number of remote sites and limited technical staff, such a technology is ideal. No preinstallation site visits are necessary. Also avoided are costs and supervision of building wiring jobs and troubleshooting building wiring problems during and after installation.

Wireless LANs are a relatively new technological phenomenon. Although they have been called a technology looking for a market or, perhaps more aptly, a solution looking for a problem, they do offer significant flexibility and spontaneity not possible with traditional wire-bound LANs.

Following are two currently popular wireless transmission technologies in local area network technology:

- **Spread spectrum transmission.**
- **Infrared transmission.**

FREQUENCY HOPPING VERSUS DIRECT SEQUENCE SPREAD SPECTRUM

In Sharper Focus

Spread spectrum transmission, as its name implies, spreads a data message across a wide range, or spectrum, of frequencies. This technique was originally employed as a security measure, since a receiver would need to know exactly how the message was spread across the frequency spectrum to intercept the message in a meaningful form. Spread spectrum transmission for wireless LANs is limited to two frequency ranges: 902 to 928 MHz and 2.4 to 2.4835 GHz. In addition, the FCC allows only two spread spectrum techniques for wireless LANs:

- **Frequency hopping spread spectrum.**
- **Direct sequence spread spectrum.**

As Figure 15-10 shows, direct sequence spread spectrum is more commonly employed in wireless LAN technology and, in general, is capable of delivering higher data throughput rates than frequency hopping spread spectrum. Direct sequence spread spectrum (DSSS) transmits at a particular frequency within the allowable range. To distinguish between transmissions from multiple wireless workstations, DSSS adds at least 10 bits to the data message to uniquely identify a particular transmission. DSSS receivers must be able to differentiate between these bits, known as chips, to properly distinguish transmissions. The addition, removal, and interpretation of chips in DSS adds complexity, cost, and processing overhead. Nonetheless, DSSS generally delivers superior throughput to FHSS.

Frequency hopping spread spectrum (FHSS) hops from one frequency to another throughout the allowable frequency range. The pattern of frequency hopping must be known by the wireless receiver so that the message can be reconstructed correctly. A given wireless transceiver's signal is on a given frequency for less than 1 second. Another desirable effect of all of the hopping from one frequency to another is that the transmission tends to be less effected by interference, an especially desirable characteristic for mobile computing applications.

Practical Advice and Information

Interference with wireless LANs using the 2.4 to 2.4835 GHz frequency range can be generated by microwave ovens.

Interference with wireless LANs using the 902–928 MHz frequency range can be generated by cordless phones or portable bar code scanners using the same frequency range.

Wireless LAN	Manufacturer	Network Architecture	Wireless Transmission Technology	Data Throughput	Maximum Distance
AirLAN	Solectek Corp.	Ethernet	Direct sequence spread spectrum 902–928 MHz	2 Mbps	800 ft
ArLAN	Aironet Wireless Communications Inc.	Ethernet or Token Ring	Direct sequence spread spectrum 902–928 MHz	860 Kbps	1000 ft
			Direct sequence spread spectrum 2.4–2.4835 GHz	2 Mbps	500 ft
Collaborative	Photonics Corp.	Ethernet	Diffuse infrared	1 Mbps	30 ft radius
FreePort	Windata	Ethernet	Direct sequence spread spectrum 902–928 MHz	5.7 Mbps	260 ft
InfraLAN	InfraLAN Wireless	Ethernet	Line-of-sight infrared	10 Mbps	90 ft
NetWave	Xircom Inc.	Ethernet	Frequency hopping spread spectrum 2.4–2.4835 GHz	1.6 Mbps	750 ft
RangeLAN2	Proxim Inc.	Ethernet	Frequency hopping spread spectrum 2.4–2.4835 GHz	1.6 Mbps	1000 ft
Roamabout	Digital Equipment Corp.	Ethernet	Direct sequence spread spectrum 2.4–2.4835 GHz	2 Mbps	800 ft
WaveLAN	AT&T G.I.S.	Ethernet	Direct sequence spread spectrum 902–928 MHz	2 Mbps	800 ft

Figure 15-10   Wireless LAN Functional and Technical Analysis

Although spread spectrum and infrared are the primary wireless transmission methods today, Motorola produced a wireless LAN product known as Altair until 1995 using microwave transmission on frequencies which it had licensed with the FCC. Some of the technical and functional differences between these wireless LAN technologies are summarized in Figure 15-10.

Internetworking devices which are able to link wireless LANs with wire-based LANs, known as wireless bridges or wireless access points, were reviewed in Chapter 14.

Following are some functional issues of wireless LANs not addressed in Figure 15-10:

- Network interface cards—Since wireless LAN technology seems to be shifting toward an emphasis on mobile computing via laptops and portables, it should come as no surprise that most wireless LAN network interface cards are available as PC cards (PCMCIA). In such a case, card and socket services compatibility should be verified. Parallel port adapters which can also be attached to portable computers are also available on some wireless LANs, as are ISA adapters.

- Encryption—Since data are being sent through the air, it is especially important to consider security with wireless LANs. Some wireless LANs support data encryption standard (DES) encryption directly on the network interface card, usually through installation of an optional encryption chip.

In Sharper Focus

WIRELESS LAN STANDARDS: IEEE 802.11 AND MOBILE IP

One of the key shortcomings of wireless LANs found to date has been a lack of interoperability among the wireless LAN offerings of different vendors. In an effort to address this shortcoming, a proposal for a new wireless LAN standard known as **IEEE 802.11** has been proposed. Key points included in the standard are as follows:

- Physical layer—The standard defined physical layer protocols for each of the following transmission methods:
  - Frequency-hopping spread spectrum.
  - Direct-sequence spread spectrum.
  - Pulse position modulation infrared.

- Media access control layer—The standard defined **carrier sense multiple access with collision avoidance (CSMA/CA)** as the MAC layer protocol. The standard is similar to CSMA/CD except that collisions cannot be detected in wireless environments as they can in wire-based environments. CSMA/CA avoids collisions by listening to the network prior to transmission and not transmitting if other workstations on the same network are transmitting. Before transmitting, workstations wait a predetermined amount of time to avoid collisions, and set up a point-to-point wireless circuit to the destination workstation. Data-link layer header and information fields such as Ethernet or Token Ring are sent to the destination workstation. It is the responsibility of the wireless LAN access device to convert IEEE 802.3 or 802.5 frames into IEEE 802.11 frames. The wireless point-to-point circuit remains in place until the sending workstation receives an acknowledgment that the message was received error-free.

- Data rate—Either 1 or 2 Mbps, selectable by either the user or the system, depending on transmissions conditions.

One important issue not included in the IEEE 802.11 standard is **roaming** capability, which allows a user to transparently move between the transmission ranges of wireless LANs without interruption. Many wireless LAN vendors currently offer proprietary roaming capabilities. **Mobile IP,** under consideration by the IETF, may be the roaming standard which wireless LANs require. Mobile IP, limited to TCP/IP networks, employs two pieces of software to support roaming:

- A mobile IP client is installed on the roaming wireless client workstation.

- A mobile IP home agent is installed on a server or router on the roaming user's home network.

The mobile IP client keeps the mobile IP home agent informed of its changing location as it travels from network to network. The mobile IP home agent forwards any transmissions it receives for the roaming client to its last reported location.

Software

Remote Control Software   **Remote control software,** especially designed to allow remote PCs to "take over" control of local PCs, should not be confused with the asynchronous communications software used for dial-up connections to asynchronous hosts via modems. Modem operation, file transfer, scripting languages, and terminal emulation are the primary features of asynchronous communications software.

Taking over remote control of the local PC is generally only done via remote control software. Remote control software allows the remote PC keyboard to control the actions of the local PC, with screen output reflected on the remote PC screen. The terms remote and local are often replaced by **guest** (remote) and **host** (local), when referring to remote control software.

Operating remote control software requires installation of software programs on both the guest and host PCs. Various remote control software packages do not interoperate. The same brand of remote control software must be installed on both guest and host PCS. Both the guest and host pieces of the remote control software may or may not be included in the software package price. Remote control software must have modem operation, file transfer, scripting language, and terminal emulation capabilities similar to those of asynchronous communications software. However, in addition, remote control software should possess features to address the following situations unique to its role:

- Avoid lockups of host PCs.

- Allow the guest PC to disable the keyboard and monitor of the host PC.

- Provide additional security precautions to prevent unauthorized access.

- Include virus detection software.

Additionally, Windows-based applications pose a substantial challenge for remote control software. The busy screens of this graphical user interface can really bog down with V.32bis or V.34 modems. Some remote control software vendors have implemented proprietary Windows screen transfer utilities which allow Windows-based applications to run on the guest PC as if they were sitting in front of the host PC, while others do not support Windows applications remotely at all.

Figure 15-11 summarizes the important features of remote control software as well as their potential implications. Following are some of the more popular packages:

Software	Vendor
CO/Session for Windows 3.0	Triton Technologies
PCAnywhere for DOS 5.0	Symantec
PCAnywhere for Windows 2.0	Symantec
Close Up 6.0	Norton/Lambert
Carbon Copy for Windows 3.0	Microcom
LapLink for Windows	Traveling Software
LapLink for Windows 95	Traveling Software

Prices range from $65 to $188 with most in the $99 range.

Feature Category	Feature	Importance/Implication
Protocol compatibility	Windows support	• How are Windows applications supported? Are full bit-mapped screens transmitted or only the changes? • Proprietary coded transmission of Windows screens?
	Windows 95 support	• Are Windows 95 applications supported?
	Network operating system protocols	• Which network operating system protocols are supported? (IP, IPX, NetBIOS)
LAN compatibility	LAN versions	• Are specific multiuser LAN server versions available or required?
	Host/guest	• Are both host and guest (local and remote) versions included?
	Operating system	• Some remote control packages require the same operating system at host and guest PCs while others do not.
Operational capabilities	Printing	• Can remote PC print on local or network attached printers?
	File transfer	• Which file transfer protocols are supported? (Kermit, XModem, YModem, ZModem, proprietary) • **Delta file transfer** allows only changes to files to be transferred. • Automated file and directory synchronization is important to mobile workers who also have desktop computers at home or at the office.
	Drive mapping	• Can guest (remote PC) drives be mapped for host access? • Can local (host PC) drives be mapped for guest access?

Figure 15-11   Remote Control Software Technology Analysis

(continued)

Feature Category	Feature	Importance/Implication
	Scripting language	• Allows repetitive call setups and connections to be automated.
	On-line help system	• Context sensitive which gives help based on where the user is in the program is preferable.
	Color/resolution limitations	• Different packages vary from 16 to 16 million colors and 800 × 600 to 2048 × 1280 pixels resolution.
	Terminal emulation	• How many different terminals are emulated? Most common are VT100, VT102, VT320, TTY.
	Simultaneous connections	• Some packages allow more than one connection or more than one session per connection, for example, simultaneous file transfer and remote control.
Security	Password access	• This should be the minimum required security for remote login.
	Password encryption	• Since passwords must be transmitted over WAN links it is more secure if they were encrypted.
	Keyboard disabling	• Since the local PC is active but controlled remotely, it is important that the local keyboard be disabled to prevent unauthorized access.
	Monitor blanking	• Similar to the rationale for keyboard disabling, since output is being transmitted to the remote PC it is important to blank the local monitor so that processing cannot be viewed without authorization.
	Call-back system	• Added security, although not hacker-proof, hangs up on dial-in, and calls back at preprogrammed or entered phone number.
	Access restriction	• Are remote users able to be restricted to certain servers, directories, files, or drives? Can the same user be given different restrictions when logging in locally or remotely?
	Remote access notification	• Can system managers or enterprise network management systems be notified when remote access or password failures have occurred?
	Call logging	• Can information about all calls be logged, sorted, and reported?
	Remote host reboot	• Can the remote PC (guest) reboot the local host if it becomes locked up?
	Limited logon attempts	• Are users locked out after a given number of failed login attempts?
	Virus protection	• This feature is especially important given file transfer capabilities from remote users. • Can remote users be restricted to read-only access?
	Logoff after inactivity time-out	• To save on long distance charges, can users be logged off (and calls dropped) after a set length of time?

Figure 15-11   (continued)

The remote control software loaded onto a communications server for use by multiple simultaneous users is not the same as the remote control software loaded onto single remote (guest) and local (host) PCs. Communications servers' remote control software can handle multiple users and, in some cases, multiple protocols. Because of this, it is considerably more expensive than the single PC variety. Prices range from $399.00 for 2 users to $6,850.00 for 16 users. Following are examples of LAN remote control software:

Software	Vendor
Remote LAN Node (RLN)	Digital Communications Associates
Close Up/LAN Pro	Norton/Lambert
WinView for Networks 2.3	Citrix Systems

Remote Node Software   Traditionally remote node client and server software were supplied by the vendor of the network operating system on the server to be remotely accessed. **Windows NT** remote access service **(RAS)** and **NetWare Connect** are two examples of such NOS-specific **remote node server** software. Third-party software vendors have also offered remote node server products which vary as to operating system or network operating system compatibility. It is important to note that these are software-only solutions, installed on industry standard, Intel 486, or higher application servers as opposed to the proprietary hardware of specialized remote access or communications servers. Representative remote node server software, required operating system or network operating system, and vendors are listed in Figure 15-12.

Figure 15-13 lists some of the important functional characteristics of remote node server software other than operating system/network operating system compatibility.

Most of the remote node server software packages also included compatible **remote node client** software. A problem arises, however, when a single remote node client needs to login to a variety of servers running a variety of network operating systems or remote node server packages. What is required is some sort of universal remote access client. In fact, such remote node clients are available.

Remote Node Server Software	Required Operating System or Network Operating System	Vendor
Windows NT RAS	Windows NT 3.5	Microsoft
NetWare Connect	NetWare 3.12 or 4.1	Novell
IBM LAN Distance	OS/2	IBM
Remote Office Communications Server	DOS	Stampede Technologies
Enterprise Wide Foray PPP Server	DOS	TechSmith
Wanderlink	NetWare 3.1x or 4.1	Funk Software

Figure 15-12   Remote Node Server Software Operating System Compatibility

These standardized remote clients with the ability to link to servers running a variety of network operating systems are sometimes referred to as **PPP clients.** In general, they can link to network operating systems which support IP, IPX, Net-BEUI, or XNS as transport protocols. Those that support IPX are generally installable as either NetWare virtual loadable modules (VLMs) or NetWare loadable modules (NLMs). In addition, these PPP client packages include sophisticated authentication procedures to ensure secure communications, compression to ensure

Remote Node Server Software Functional Characteristic	Importance/Implication
NOS protocols supported	• While most remote node server software supports IP and IPX, support of NetBIOS, NetBEUI, AppleTalk, Vines, LANtastic, and SNA was more limited. • If IP is supported, is the full IP protocol stack supplied including applications and utilities?
WAN data-link layer protocol	• Most remote node server software now supports PPP, while others support proprietary protocols. Proprietary protocols are fine in single-vendor environments.
Modem support	• How many serial ports can be supported simultaneously? Numbers vary from 32 to 256. • How many modem setup strings are included? If the setup string for a particular type of modem is not included, configuration could be considerably more difficult. Numbers vary from 75 to over 400. • Does the remote node server software support modem pools, or does there have to be a modem dedicated to every user? • Does the remote node server software support dial-out functionality over the attached modems?
Management	• How is the remote node server managed? via a specialized console or any attached workstation with proper software? • Does the remote node server software output management information in SNMP format? • Can remote users be limited as to connect time or by inactivity time-out?
Security	• Is forced password renewal (password aging) supported? • Are passwords encrypted? • Is the remote node server software compatible with third-party security servers such as token authentication servers? • Does the remote node server support call-back (dial-back) capabilities?
Client support	• Which types of client platforms are supported? (DOS, Mac, Windows, Windows for Workgroups, Windows 95, Windows NT, OS/2) • Are both NDIS and ODI driver specifications supported?

Figure 15-13 Remote Node Server Software Functional Characteristics

optimal use of the WAN link, as well as most of the important features of remote control software. The inclusion of remote control software allows users to choose between remote node and remote control for optimal performance.

Following are some of the specialized compression and authentication algorithms included with a majority of these PPP clients:

- **CIPX**—for compression of IPX headers.
- **VJ**—for compression of IP headers.
- **CHAP MD 5**—for PPP encrypted authentication.
- **CHAP MD80**—authentication for Windows NT RAS.
- **SPAP**—Shiva's proprietary authentication protocol which includes password encryption and call-back capability.

Although not all include both fully functional remote control software and full TCP/IP stacks and utilities, the following are some of the available PPP clients and their vendors:

Software	Vendor
Remotely Possible	Avalan Technology
Timbuktu Pro	Farallon Computing
WanderLink PPP Client	Funk Software
PPP	Klos Technologies
LAN Express PPP Client	Microcom
TCP Pro	Network TeleSystems
ShivaPPP	Shiva Corp.
Remote Office Gold	Stampede Technologies

Mobile-Aware Operating Systems   The mobile computer user requires flexible computing functionality to easily support at least three possible distinct computing scenarios:

- Standalone computing on the laptop or notebook computer.
- Remote node or remote control computing to corporate headquarters.
- Synchronization of files and directories with desktop workstations at home or in the corporate office.

Operating systems which easily adapt to these different computing modes with a variety of included supporting accessory programs and utilities are sometimes referred to as **mobile-aware operating systems.** Windows 95 is perhaps the best current example of such an operating system. Among the key functions offered by such mobile-aware operating systems are the following:

- Autodetection of multiple configurations—If external monitors or full-size keyboards are used when at home or in the corporate office, the operating system should automatically detect them and load the proper device drivers.

- Built-in multiprotocol remote node client—Remote node software should be included which can automatically and transparently dial into a variety of network operating system servers, including Windows NT RAS or NetWare Connect. The remote node client should support a variety of network protocols including IP, IPX, and NetBEUI as well as open data-link WAN protocols such as SLIP and PPP.

- Direct cable connection—When returning from the road, portables should be easily linked to desktop workstations via direct connection through existing serial or parallel ports. The software utilities to initiate and manage such connections should be included.

- File transfer and file/directory synchronizations—Once physical connections are in place, software utilities should be able to synchronize files and directories between either the laptop and the desktop or the laptop and the corporate LAN server.

- Deferred printing—This feature allows printed files to be spooled to the laptop disk drive and saved until the mobile user is next connected to corporate printing resources. At that point, instead of having to remember all of the individual files that require printing, the deferred printing utility automatically prints all of the spooled files.

- Power management—Since most mobile computing users depend on battery-powered computers, anything the operating system can do to extend battery life would be very beneficial. The demand for higher resolution screens has meant increased power consumption in many cases. Power management features offered by operating systems have been standardized as the **Advanced Power Management (APM)** specification.

- Infrared connection—To avoid the potential hassle of physical cable connections, mobile-aware operating systems are including support for infrared wireless connections between laptops and desktops. To ensure multivendor interoperability the infrared transmission should conform to the **Infrared Data Association (IrDA)** standards.

Mobile-Aware Applications Beyond the shortcomings of remote node applications already delineated, mobile applications which depend on inherently unreliable wireless transmission services must be uniquely developed or modified to optimize performance under these circumstances.

Oracle Mobile Agents, formerly known as Oracle-in-Motion, is perhaps the best example of the overall architecture and components required to produce **mobile-aware applications.** As illustrated in Figure 15-14, the Oracle Mobile Agents architecture adheres to an overall **client–agent–server** architecture, as opposed to the more common LAN-based client/server architecture. The overall objective of such an architecture is to reduce the amount of client-to-server network traffic by building as much intelligence as possible into the server-based agent so that it can act on behalf of the client application. Oracle's testing of applications developed and deployed in this wireless architecture have produced performance improvements of up to 50:1.

The agent portion of the client–agent–server architecture consists of three co-operating components:

- The **message manager** executes on the mobile client and acts as an interface between client applications requesting services and the wireless link over which the requests must be forwarded. It keeps track of requests pending on various servers which are being handled by intelligent agents. Oracle Mobile Agents also operates over LAN links or PPP-based dial-up links.

- The **message gateway** can execute on the local server or on a dedicated Unix or Windows workstation, and acts as an interface between the client's message manager and the intelligent agent on the local server. The gateway also acts as a holding station for messages to and from mobile clients which are temporarily unreachable. The client-based message manager and the message gateway communicate with each other via a communications protocol Oracle developed to provide reliable message delivery over wireless transmission services while minimizing acknowledgment overhead.

- The **agent event manager** is combined with a customer written transaction handler to form an entity known as the **intelligent agent,** which resides on the local server. Once the agent event manager receives a request from a mobile client, it acts on behalf of that client in all communications with the local server until the original client request is totally fulfilled. During this processing time, in which the intelligent agent is representing the mobile client, the wireless connection can be dropped. Once the original client request has been fulfilled, the entire response is sent from the intelligent agent to the client-based message manager in a single packet, thereby conserving bandwidth and transmission time. Having received the response to a pending request, the client-based message manager deletes the original request from its pending request queue.

Mobile Middleware   An emerging category of software which seeks to offer maximum flexibility to mobile computing users while optimizing performance is **mobile middleware.** Although specific products within this software category vary significantly, the ultimate goal of mobile middleware is to offer mobile users transparent client/server access independent of the following variables:

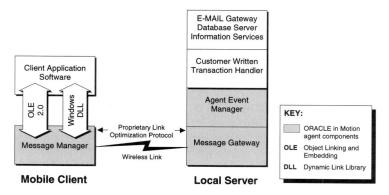

Figure 15-14   Client–Agent–Server Architecture Support Mobile-Aware Applications

- Client or server platform (operating system, network operating system).

- Applications (client/server or client/agent/server).

- Wireless transmission services.

Figure 15-15 illustrates the basic components and interactions of mobile middleware.

As the figure shows, the primary purpose of mobile middleware is to consolidate client/server traffic from multiple applications for transmission over a variety of potential wireless (or wire-based) transmission services. Consolidating client requests from multiple applications into a single transmission can reduce overall transmission time and expense. In some cases, the mobile middleware has sufficient intelligence to inform clients or servers if the intended destination is currently reachable or not, thereby preventing wasted time and transmission expense. Some mobile middleware can also evaluate between available wireless services for the mobile client and the local server, and choose an optimal wireless transmission service based on performance and/or expense.

Mobile middleware is an emerging category of software characterized by proprietary APIs and a resultant lack of interoperability. As a result, applications written to interact with one vendor's mobile middleware probably won't interact with another vendor's mobile middleware. As Figure 15-15 shows, mobile middleware interacts with two sets of APIs: one between the mobile middleware and the applications, and one between the middleware and the wireless transmission services. Two efforts to standardize wireless APIs for mobile middleware are currently underway:

- The Winsock 2 Forum is developing standardized Winsock 2 APIs for linking mobile middleware with Windows-based applications. This API would deliver transmission-related information such as signal strength and transmission characteristics to the applications themselves. Such information could make the applications more intelligent and responsive to changing transmission quality.

- The Portable Computer and Communications Association (PCCA) is developing the standardized API to link mobile middleware to a variety of wireless

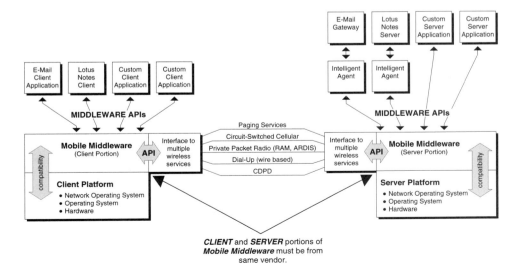

Figure 15-15   Mobile Middleware

transmission services. This API will provide extensions to existing multiproto-col data-link layer device specifications such as NDIS and ODI.

Among the currently available mobile middleware packages and their vendors are the following:

Software	Vendor
MobileSync	Adaptive Strategies
MobileWare	MobileWare
WorldLink	Technology Development Systems
RemoteWare	XcelleNet
Transnet II	Teknique
Mobilera	Business Partners Solutions
Via	Moda Systems

Management and Configuration of Remote Access Technology

Practical Advice and Information

OPTIMIZING REMOTE NODE AND REMOTE CONTROL SOFTWARE PERFORMANCE

As previously described in the section on the remote node logical topology, suitable performance of remote client applications is severely hampered by the limited transmission speed of the WAN links combined with the high bandwidth demands of client/server applications. Besides rewriting the client/server application to min-imize the amount of remote client–to–local server traffic, several other opportuni-ties are available to improve overall remote access performance. These optimization techniques will also improve performance of remote control applications:

- Use V.34 modems. This new modem specification can support transmission speeds of up to 28.8 Kbps over dial-up lines.

- Use integrated services digital network (ISDN) services, if available, as an alternative to asynchronous dial-up with the V.34 modem. ISDN basic rate interface (BRI) delivers up to 144 Kbps of switched digital bandwidth. Using ISDN requires ISDN terminal adapters, the equivalent of an ISDN modem, and compatible communications software.

- Use 16550 universal asynchronous receiver transmitters (UARTs) and matching serial port drivers. The UART transmits and receives data to and from a PC's serial port which interfaces to the modem. The 16550 UART in-cludes increased buffering capacity to match the performance of faster modems such as the V.34. Transmission via serial ports and UARTS is con-trolled by operating system software known as serial or COM drivers. Some of these COM drivers have limitations of 19.2 Kbps. More recent operating systems, such as Windows 95, and many asynchronous communications packages support serial transmission rates of at least 115.2 Kbps.

- Use data compression software/hardware and set communications software transmission speed to/from the modem to the PC (DTE rate) high enough to take full advantage of the compression software's capabilities. V.34 modems include V.42bis built-in data compression capabilities which can yield compression ratios of up to 4:1, depending on file content. Since V.34 modems have a maximum transmission speed of 28.8 Kbps and V.42bis supplies 4:1 data compression, PC hardware and software should support maximum serial transmission rates of 115.2 Kbps (28.8 $\times$ 4).

- Make sure that the remote control or remote node software being used supports **screen caching,** which allows transmission of only changes to screens, rather than entire screens, over the limited bandwidth WAN links. Screen caching will reduce the amount of actual traffic transmitted over the WAN link.

- Not to be confused with screen caching software, **network caching** or **LAN caching** software improves overall remote node performance up to five times by caching repetitive applications commands and systems calls. These add-on packages are composed of both client and server pieces which work cooperatively to cache application commands and reduce network traffic over relatively low-speed WAN links. Network caching software is network operating system and protocol dependent, requiring that compatibility be ensured before purchase. The following are two network caching software packages and their vendors:

Software	Vendor
Powerburst	AirSoft, Inc.
Shared LAN Cache	Measurement Techniques, Inc.

Mobile MIB   To integrate the management of mobile computing users into an overall enterprise network management system such as HP Openview or IBM Systemview, a specialized MIB was required to store configuration and location information specific to remote users. The Mobile Management Task Force (MMTF) has proposed a **mobile MIB** capable of feeding configuration and location information to enterprise network management systems via SNMP. A key to the design of the mobile MIB was to balance the amount of information required to effectively manage remote clients while taking into account the limited bandwidth and expense of the remote links over which the management data must be transmitted. From the enterprise network management system's side, controls on how often remote clients are to be polled via dial-up or wireless transmission to gather up-to-date management information need to be installed. Among the fields of information included in the proposed mobile MIB are the following:

- Current user location.
- Type and speed of connection device.
- Type of remote client or remote control software installed on remote device.
- Battery power.
- Memory.

Network Services

Wireless WAN Services   While wireless LANs offer mobility to users across a local scope of coverage, a variety of wireless services are available for use across wider geographic spans. These **wireless WAN services** vary in many ways including availability, application, transmission speed, and cost. Among the available wireless WAN services explained further are the following:

- Circuit-switched analog cellular.
- Cellular digital packet data (CDPD).
- Private packet radio.
- Enhanced paging and two-way messaging.
- Enhanced specialized mobile radio (ESMR).
- Microcellular spread spectrum.
- Personal communications services (PCS).

Applied Problem Solving

A TOP-DOWN APPROACH TO WIRELESS WAN SERVICES ANALYSIS

Due to the many variable factors concerning these wireless WAN services, it is important to take a top-down approach when considering their incorporation into an organization's information systems solution. Questions and issues to be considered on each layer of the top-down model for wireless WAN services are summarized in Figure 15-16.

Top-Down Layer	Issues/Implications
Business	• What is the business activity which requires wireless transmission? • How will payback be calculated? Has the value of this business activity been substantiated? • What are the anticipated expenses for the 6 month, 1 year, and 2 year horizons? • What is the geographic scope of this business activity? localized? national? international?
Application	• Have applications been developed especially for wireless transmission? • Have existing applications been modified to account for wireless transmission characteristics? • Have training and help-desk support systems been developed?
Data	• What is the nature of the data to be delivered via the wireless WAN service? short bursty transactions, large two-way messages, faxes, file transfers? • Is the data time-sensitive or could transmissions be batched during off-peak hours for discounted rates? • What is the geographic scope of coverage required for wireless data delivery?
Network	• Must the WAN service provide error correction? • Do you wish the WAN service to also provide and maintain the access devices?
Technology	• Which wireless WAN service should be employed? • What type of access device must be employed with the chosen WAN service? • Are access devices proprietary or standards-based?

Figure 15-16 Top-Down Analysis for Wireless WAN Services

As a practical example of how to use the top-down model for wireless WAN services analysis, start with the business situation which requires wireless support and examine the applications and data characteristics which support the business activity in question. For example, which of the following best describes the data to be transmitted by wireless means?

- Fax.

- File transfer.

- E-mail.

- Paging.

- Transaction processing.

- Database queries.

The nature of the content, geographic scope, and amount and urgency of the data to be transmitted will have a direct bearing on the particular wireless WAN service employed. Unfortunately, no single wireless WAN service fits all application and data needs. Once a wireless WAN service is chosen, compatibility with existing local area network architectures and technology must be ensured. Typical uses of the currently most widely available wireless WAN services are as follows:

- Transaction processing and database queries: CDPD.
  - Advantages: Fast call setup, inexpensive for short messages.
  - Disadvantages: Limited availability but growing, expensive for large file transfers.

- Large file transfers and faxes: Circuit-switched cellular.
  - Advantages: Widely available, call duration pricing is more reasonable for longer transmissions than per kilopacket pricing.
  - Disadvantages: Longer call setup time than CDPD (up to 30 sec vs. less than 5 sec), expensive for short messages.

- Short bursty messages and e-mail: Private packet radio.
  - Advantages: Wide coverage area and links to commercial e-mail systems.
  - Disadvantage: Proprietary networks, expensive for larger file transfers.

The key characteristics of these and other wireless WAN services are summarized in Figure 15-17.

Two-Way Messaging

Two-way messaging, sometimes referred to as **enhanced paging,** allows short text messages to be transmitted between relatively inexpensive transmission devices such as personal digital assistants (PDAs) and alphanumeric pagers. Two distinct architectures and associated protocols have the potential to deliver these services.

One such architecture, based on **cellular digital packet data (CDPD),** is being proposed and supported by AT&T Wireless Services, formerly known as McCaw Cellular. CDPD is a service which uses idle capacity in the circuit-switched cellular

Wireless WAN Service	Geographic Scope	Directionality	Data Characteristics	Billing	Access Device	Standards and Compatibility
Circuit Switched Cellular	National	Full-duplex circuit switched	14 Kbps max	Call duration	Modems with specialized error correction for cellular circuits	MNP-10 (adverse channel enhancements) and ETC (enhanced throughput cellular)
Private Packet Radio	Nearly national, more cities than CDPD but fewer than circuit-switched cellular	Full duplex packet switched digital data	4.8 Kbps	Per character	Proprietary modem compatible with particular private packet radio service	Proprietary. Two major services: RAM Mobile Data and Ardis
CDPD	Limited to large metropolitan areas	Full duplex packet switched digital data	19.2 Kbps max	Flat monthly charge plus usage charge per kilopacket	CDPD modem	Compatible with TCP/IP for easier internetwork integration
Enhanced Paging	National	One or two-way relatively short messages	100 characters or less	Flat monthly charges increasing with coverage area	Pagers	
ESMR	Currently limited	One or two-way, voice, paging, or messaging	4.8 Kbps	Unknown. Service is under devel-opment	Proprietary integrated voice/data devices	
Microcell Spread Spectrum	Limited to those areas serviced by microcells. Good for college and corporate campuses	Full duplex	10–45 Mbps	Monthly flat fee	Proprietary modem	Most provide access to internet, e-mail services.
PCS	Under development. Should be national	Full duplex, all digital voice and data services	up to 25 Mbps		Two-way pagers, personal digital assistants, PCS devices	Standards-based, should assure device/ service interoperability

Figure 15-17 Wireless WAN Services Technology Analysis

network to transmit IP-based data packets. The fact that CDPD is IP-based allows it to easily interface to IP-based private networks as well as the internet and other e-mail services.

By adding a protocol known as **limited size messaging (LSM),** CDPD will be able to transport two-way messaging which will offer the following key services be-yond simple paging:

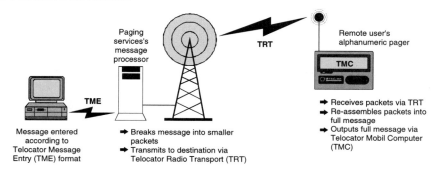

Figure 15-18   Two-Way Messaging Protocols: LSM and TDP

- Guaranteed delivery to destination mobile users even if those devices are unreachable at the time the message was originally sent.

- Return receipt acknowledgments to the party which originated the message.

An alternative two-way messaging architecture is proposed by the Personal Communicator Industry Association (PCIA). Rather than building on existing IP-based networks as the CDPD/LSM architecture did, the **Telocator Data Protocol (TDP)** architecture is actually a suite of protocols defining an end-to-end system for two-way messaging to and from paging devices. Figure 15-18 illustrates the differences between the LSM and TDP two-way messaging protocols.

SUMMARY

Remote access to LANs has taken on increased importance in response to major changes in business conditions. As indicated by the top-down model, network functionality must respond to changing business conditions. Expectations of

LAN remote access are significant. Remote users expect the same level of data accessibility, application services, and performance on the road as they receive at the office. Delivering this equivalent functionality is the challenge faced by networking professionals today. The major obstacle to this lofty objective is the bandwidth, availability, and quality of the wide area network services which are expected to deliver remote connectivity to mobile users. Increasingly, wireless WAN services are at the forefront of remote access solutions.

In designing remote access solutions, it is essential to start with a thorough understanding of the needs of remote users. These needs dictate both the logical and physical topologies of the remote access network.

There are two basic logical topologies for remote access. Remote control allows a remote PC to take over or control a local PC. Processing occurs on the local PC and only keyboard strokes and screen images are transported over the WAN link. Remote node allows the remote PC to act as a full-fledged LAN client to the local LAN server. In this case, full client/server traffic travels over the WAN link as the application executes on the remote client PC. No one logical topology is preferable in all cases. Each situation must be analyzed on an individual basis.

Physical topologies include accessing a local LAN-attached PC directly via modem, accessing a shared communications server which might include PC boards for embedded shared computing power, or accessing a LAN modem that provides access to local LAN computing resources.

Mobile computing requires specialized software, including mobile-aware operating systems, mobile-aware applications, and mobile middleware to interface between multiple applications and multiple possible wireless WAN services.

Wireless WAN services vary widely in availability, bandwidth, reliability, and cost. No single wireless WAN service is appropriate for all mobile computing applications. It is important to understand the application needs and data characteristics of mobile applications before choosing a wireless WAN service.

KEY TERMS

access server, 567
advanced power management, 583
agent event manager, 584
APM, 583
carrier sense multiple access with collision avoidance, 576
CDPD, 589
cellular digital packet data, 589
CHAP MD5, 582
CHAP MD80, 582
CIPX, 582
circuit-switched cellular, 590
client–agent–server, 583
communications server, 567
CSMA/CA, 576
delta file transfer, 578
dial-in server, 567
dial-out, 573
direct sequence spread spectrum, 574
enhanced paging, 589
ESMR, 590
frequency hopping spread spectrum, 574
guest, 577
host, 577

IEEE 802.11, 576
Infrared Data Association, 583
infrared transmission, 574
Int14, 573
intelligent agent, 584
IrDA, 583
LAN caching, 587
LAN modem, 567
limited size messaging, 590
LSM, 590
message gateway, 584
message manager, 584
microcell spread spectrum, 590
mobile computing, 559
mobile IP, 577
mobile MIB, 587
mobile middleware, 584
mobile-aware applications, 583
mobile-aware operating systems, 582
NASI, 573
NetWare Connect, 580
network caching, 587
Oracle Mobile Agents, 583
PCS, 590
PPP clients, 581
private packet radio, 590

remote access, 561
remote control, 563
remote control software, 577
remote node, 561
remote node client software, 580
remote node server software, 580
remote node servers, 569
remote node software, 580
roaming, 577
screen caching, 587
small office home office, 559
SOHO, 559
SPAP, 582
spread spectrum transmission, 574
TDP, 591
technical support, 560
telecommuting, 559
telocator data protocol, 591
time synchronous authentication, 566
token authentication, 565
token response authentication, 565
two-way messaging, 589
VJ, 582
Windows NT RAS, 580
wireless WAN services, 588

REVIEW QUESTIONS

1. What are some of the key business trends which have led to an increased interest in LAN remote access?
2. What is the importance of needs analysis to LAN remote access design?
3. Differentiate between the functionality and network impact of remote node and remote control.
4. What is the major limitation in delivering transparent access to remote LAN users?
5. Describe how it is possible to run remote control software via a remote node connection. What are the advantages of such a setup?
6. What are some of the security issues unique to remote access situations?
7. What added security capability can token authentication systems offer?
8. What advantages does a communications server offer over separate remote access links to multiple PCs? What disadvantages?
9. What is the common differentiation between communications servers and remote node servers?
10. Differentiate between the three major categories of remote node servers.
11. Why are dial-out solutions for remote node servers different from dial-in solutions?
12. How can dial-out solutions be implemented on LANs equipped with remote node servers?
13. Differentiate between the functionality and applications of the two spread spectrum transmission techniques approved by the FCC.
14. Why are wireless LAN NICs most often PCMCIA?
15. Differentiate between CSMA/CD and CSMA/CA.
16. What is roaming, and why is it important to remote access users?
17. How does mobile IP work?
18. What is the relationship between the guest and host remote control software?
19. Why is remote control software not interoperable?
20. Differentiate between the transport protocols and client protocol stacks of remote control and remote node software.
21. Differentiate between LAN (multiuser) remote control software and point-to-point remote control software.
22. What are some of the unique functional requirements of remote control software beyond being able to control local (host) PCs?
23. What are some of the unique functional requirements of remote node server software?
24. What advantage do PPP clients offer?
25. What are some of the unique functional requirements of mobile-aware operating systems?
26. Differentiate between the client–agent–server architecture and the client/server architecture.
27. How do mobile-aware applications need to adjust to or compensate for wireless transmission services?
28. Describe the interaction between the components of Oracle Mobile Agents.
29. What two distinct interfaces do mobile middleware products transcend?
30. What are the functional objectives of mobile middleware?
31. How can the proprietary nature of mobile middleware products be overcome?
32. Describe standards development efforts which may affect mobile middleware.
33. What are some ways to optimize remote node or remote control applications?
34. What is the difference between screen caching and network caching?
35. What unique information is required in a mobile MIB, and why?
36. What are the conflicting objectives or limitations of mobile management software and the mobile MIB?
37. Why is CDPD of such interest to circuit-switched cellular vendors?
38. What standards are important to a person wishing to purchase a "cellular-ready" modem?
39. Match each of the following to the most appropriate wireless WAN service and justify your answer: transaction processing, short messages, large file transfers.
40. What are the advantages of two-way messaging systems for data transfer?

ACTIVITIES

1. Gather articles regarding business trends which have contributed to the rise in LAN remote access. Relate these business trends to market trends for remote access technology and wireless WAN services. Use graphical presentation wherever possible.
2. Find an organization currently supporting LAN remote access. Analyze the situation from a

business perspective. Analyze the situation from a business perspective. Which business activities are being supported? Was cost/benefit or payback period analysis performed or considered?

3. In the organization being studied, what physical topology is employed? links to multiple PCs? communications server? LAN modems? Prepare a diagram of the physical topology, including all software components such as network operating systems and transport protocols.

4. In the organization being studied, is remote node functionality supported? If so, which remote client software is installed? Are remote users able to access servers with multiple different network operating systems? Are PPP clients installed?

5. In the organization being studied, are dial-out capabilities supplied? If so, how?

6. In the organization being studied, has any effort been made to optimize the performance of remote node or remote control applications? If so, what

were those adjustments, and what impact did they have?

7. What types of additional security precautions, if any, are instituted for remote users?

8. Investigate infrared wireless LANs. What is the difference between line-of-sight and diffuse infrared? Where are infrared wireless LANs being deployed? What is the percentage market share of infrared wireless LANs vs. spread spectrum wireless LANs?

9. Why did the FCC choose the frequency bands they did for spread spectrum transmission?

10. What devices other than wireless LANs use the 902- to 928-MHz frequency range? Could this be a problem?

11. What is the difference between the CSMA/CA employed in IEEE 802.11 and that employed in AppleTalk networks?

12. What is the current status of IEEE 802.11? What are the perceived shortcomings of the standard?

FEATURED REFERENCES

General References

Derfler, Frank. *Guide to Connectivity*, Third Edition (Emeryville, CA: Ziff-Davis Press, 1995).

Goldman, James. *Applied Data Communications: A Business Oriented Approach* (New York: John Wiley & Sons, 1995).

Case Studies

Pappalardo, Denise. Weather Service Uses Remote Ware. *Communications Week*, no. 563 (June 26, 1995), 53.

Business Impact/Architecture Design

Borthick, Sandra. Who's Reaching for Remote Access? *Business Communications Review*, 25; 12 (December 1995), 29.

Bransky, Jonathan and Marvin Chartoff. Finding the Best Path to the Branch Office. *Business Communications Review*, 25; 3 (March 1995), 35.

Durr, Michael. Buyer's Guide: Remote Control—Alive and Well. *LAN Times* 12; 20 (October 2, 1995), 75.

Durr, Michael. Optimizing for Speed in Remote Access. *LAN Times*, 12; 20 (October 2, 1995), 83.

Durr, Michael. Users Clamor for Connections. *Communications Week*, no. 587 (December 4, 1995), S2.

Fitzgerald, Susan. Remote Office Access—What Does It Really Mean? *Network Computing*, 6; 6 (May 15, 1995), 114.

Frezza, Bill. Wireless Awaiting. *Network Computing*, 5; 14 (November 15, 1994), 30.

Hallberg, Bruce. Oceans Apart: Remote Access International Style. *Network Computing*, 6; 11 (September 15, 1995), 138.

Heller, Paul. Fingers on the Wireless Pulse. *Network Computing*, 5; 14 (November 15, 1994), 34.

Hindin, Eric and John Morency. The Branch-Office Balancing Act. *Data Communications*, 23; 9 (June 1994), 60.

Hufnagel, Ellen and Joe McVey. What!? That Remote Site's Down Again!? *Network Computing*, 6; 2 (February 1, 1995), 136.

Ingari, Frank. Real Convergence Without the Hype. *Network Computing*, 5; 14 (November 15, 1994), 38.

Korzrniowski, Paul. Telecommuting—A Driving Concern. *Business Communications Review*, 25; 2 (February 1995), 45.

Molta, Dave. A Bit of a Twist on Remote Control. *Network Computing*, 6; 16 (December 15, 1995), 112.

Molta, Dave. Remote Control or Remote Node: Which Is Right for You? *Network Computing*, 5; 10 (September 1, 1994), 170.

Morency, John and Eric Hindin. A Close Look at Remote Access. *Business Communications Review*, 25; 5 (May 1995), 32.

Morse, Stephen. On the Road Again: Remote Computing Your Lifeline. *Network Computing*, 5; 12 (October 15, 1994), 46.

Moskowitz, Robert. Remote Access Strategy. *Network Computing*, 6; 3 (March 1, 1995), 43.

Nadeau, Michael. Remote Connections. *Byte*, 19; 6 (June 1994), 197.

Purdy, J. Gerry. Remote Access Dominates Market. *Communications Week*, no. 587 (December 4, 1995), S14.

Stone, Jordan and Michael Howard. The High Price of Remote Access. *LAN Times*, 12; 20 (October 2, 1995), 16.

Tam, Terry and Huy Nguyen. Pushing the Envelope of Remote Access. *PC Week*, 12; 27 (July 10, 1995), N1.

Tolly, Kevin. No Easy Answers for Remote Access. *Data Communications*, 24; 16 (November 21, 1995), 27.

Wong, William. Choosing a Remote Access Method That's the Right Fit. *Communications Week*, no. 577 (September 28, 1995), 13.

Modems

Anderson, Ron. 22 V.32bis PC Card Modems: The Glory of Choice. *Network Computing*, 6; 2 (February 1, 1994), 84.

Bing, George. PCMCIA Modems: Little Beauties or Beasts? *Network Computing*, 5; 11 (October 1, 1994), 140.

Boardman, Bruce. Get More Mileage from V.34 Modems. *Network Computing*, 6; 4 (April 1, 1995), 154.

Boardman, Bruce. V.34 Modems: They're Here! They're Fast! Some Are Scary! *Network Computing*, 6; 3 (March 1, 1995), 96.

Brown, Bruce. Hooking Up with Home Modems. *PC Magazine*, 14; 18 (October 24, 1995), 371.

Davis, Andrew. The V.34 Standard. *Communications Systems Design*, 1; 1 (June 1995), 47.

Krechmer, Ken. Catching Up with V.34 Modems. *Business Communications Review*, 25; 3 (March 1995), 62.

Reinhardt, Andy. Multimode Modems: Doing It All on One Line. *Byte*, 20; 1 (January 1995), 145.

Snell, Monica. Single-Line Voice/Data Options Emerge. *LAN Times*, 12; 16 (August 28, 1995), 10.

Surkan, Michael. Fax Modems Allow Users to Cruise at ISDN Speeds. *PC Week*, 12; 39 (October 2, 1995), N14.

Taylor, Kieran. V.34 and Then Some. *Data Communications*, 24; 1 (January 1995), 52.

Taylor, Kieran. V.34 Modems: You Get What You Pay For. *Data Communications*, 24; 8 (June 1995), 62.

Taylor, Kieran. V.34 Modems: Watch the Fine Print. *Data Communications*, 23; 16 (November 1994), 99.

ISDN Access Devices/Services

Amidon, David and Lisa Robertson. Internet Connectivity Via ISDN—A Perfect Match? *Business Communications Review*, 25; 4 (April 1995), 55.

Chernicoff, David. Moving to ISDN? It's Time to Set a Strategy. *PC Week*, 12; 22 (June 5, 1995), N1.

Dippert, Jonathan. Exploring ISDN. *LAN Times*, 12; 19 (September 25, 1995), 79.

Fritz, Jeffrey. Digital Remote Access. *Byte*, 19; 9 (September 1994), 125.

Fritz, Jeffrey. Switching ISDN. *Byte*, 19; 11 (November 1994), 251.

Fritz, Jeffrey. Tuning into ISDN. *Byte*, 20; 9 (September 1995), 273.

Fritz, Jeffrey. You Can Take It with You. *Byte*, 20; 9 (September 1995), 41.

Garris, John. ISDN Slight of Hand. *PC Magazine*, 14; 5 (March 14, 1995), NE1.

Heywood, Peter. ISDN LAN Links: Easy Does It. *Data Communications*, 24; 1 (January 1995), 59.

Kalman, Steve. So You Want to Use ISDN. *Network World*, 12; 49 (December 4, 1995), 43.

Kohlhepp, Rob and Jeff Newman. ISDN Routers Link Branch Offices on the Cheap. *Network Computing*, 6; 12 (October 1, 1995), 92.

Newman, Jeff. ISDN Services and Products. *Network Computing*, 6; 3 (March 1, 1995), 152.

Park, Sung-Yong. Internetworking ISDN and ATM. *Communications Systems Design*, 1; 4 (August 1995), 30.

Rash, Wayne. 3COM's Big Impact on ISDN. *Communications Week*, no. 560 (June 5, 1995), 12.

Robertson, Bruce. Choose an ISDN Flavor: NIC or Digital Modem. *Network Computing*, 5; 10 (September 1, 1994), 174.

Robertson, Bruce and Jeff Newman. ISDN Does It All! *Network Computing*, 6; 4 (April 1, 1995), 62.

Salamone, Salvatore. ISDN and Analog Access in One Package. *Byte*, 20; 7 (July 1995), 181.

Sullivan, Kristina. ISDN Moves Toward the Mainstream. *PC Week*, 12; 49 (December 11, 1995), N1.

Remote Access and Remote Control Hardware/Servers/Software

Alwang, Greg and Padraic Boyle. Remote Node Servers. *PC Magazine*, 14; 17 (October 10, 1995), NE19.

Bing, George. Buyer's Guide: Remote Access Servers. *Network Computing*, 6; 6 (May 15, 1995), 126.

Boardman, Bruce. Remote Access Without the Hassle. *Network Computing*, 5; 11 (October 1, 1994), 86.

Boardman, Bruce. Remote Possibilities. *Network Computing*, 6; 8 (July 1, 1995), 66.

Cooke, Kevin. Controlling the Remote. *Network Computing*, 6; 9 (August 1, 1995), 84.

Cooke, Kevin and Bruce Boardman. Remote Node Servers: It's in the Software. *Network Computing*, 6; 14 (November 1, 1995), 64.

Derfler, Frank. The Art of Remote Access. *PC Magazine*, 14; 14 (August 1995), 279.

Henry, Amanda. Novell Sands LANs Packing. *LAN Times*, 12; 20 (October 2, 1995), 1.

Johnson, M. Harry. Remote Access for Any Net. *LAN Times*, 12; 24 (November 20, 1995), 102.

Kramer, Matt. Going Beyond the Beep. *PC Week*, 12; 49 (December 11, 1995), N5.

Mier, Edwin and Robert Smithers. Remote LAN Access, Making the Right Connection. *Communications Week*, no. 571 (August 21, 1995), 41.

Schwartz, Jeffrey. Duo Tries to Ease Remote Access. *Communications Week*, no. 560 (June 5, 1995), 1.

Sweet, Lisa. pcAnywhere Host Manages Many Remote Sessions. *PC Week*, 12; 22 (June 5, 1995), N1.

Taylor, Kieran. Remote Frame Relay and ISDN Access Is in the Cards. *Data Communications*, 24; 7 (May 21, 1995), 31.

Williams, Dennis. Remote Control Apps for Windows 95. *LAN Times*, 12; 25 (December 4, 1995), 89.

Williams, Gerald. Review: Communications Cluster. *Network World*, 12; 29 (July 17, 1995), 63.

Willams, Gerald. Software Roundup: Remote Control Windows. *Byte*, 19; 9 (September 1994), 137.

Williams, Gerald and Jonathan Torta. Ready, Set, Go Remote. *Network World*, 12; 42 (October 16, 1995), 41.

Network Services/Remote Access Outsourcing

Gareiss, Robin. AT&T's NetWare Connect: The Future Starts Here. *Data Communications*, 24; 1 (January 1995), 60.

Gareiss, Robin. AT&T's Personalink: A Value-Added Service with Brains. *Data Communications*, 24; 1 (January 1995), 66.

Schurr, Amy. Remote-Access Outsourcing Is In. *PC Week*, 12; 28 (July 17, 1995), N3.

Wireless Mobile Computing/Wireless LANs

Bryan, John. Data Over Cellular. *Byte*, 19; 9 (September 1994), 59.

Carlson, Susan and Craig Mathias. Big Guns Target Mobile Middleware. *Business Communications Review*, 24; 11 (November 1994), 51.

Coffee, Peter. Techniques Spread Wireless Benefits. *PC Week*, 12; 27 (July 10, 1995), 72.

Edney, John. 802.11: The New Wireless Standard. *Data Communications*, 24; 12 (September, 1995), 77.

Frezza, Bill. Converging Standards for Wide Area Wireless Data. *Network Computing*, 6; 12 (October 1, 1995), 45.

Frezza, Bill and Emily Andren. Wide Area Wireless All Over the Spectrum. *Network Computing*, 6; 4 (April 1, 1995), 82.

Gareiss, Robin. Wireless Data: More than Wishful Thinking. *Data Communications*, 24; 4 (March 21, 1995), 52.

Johnson, Johna. Middleware Makes Wireless WAN Magic. *Data Communications*, 24; 4 (March 21, 1995), 67.

Johnson, Johna. Oracle in Motion: Wireless Data Gets the Business. *Data Communications*, 24; 1 (January 1995), 104.

Johnson, Johna. A Standards Boost for Wireless Software. *Data Communications*, 24; 5 (April 1995), 49.

Juodikas, Al. Wireless LANs: Considerations and Implementation. *Communications Systems Design*, 1; 5 (September 1995), 48.

Larsen, Amy. Wireless LANs: Worth a Second Look. *Data Communications*, 24; 15 (November 1995), 95.

Lipoff, Stuart. Up in the Air. *Business Communications Review*, 25; 9 (September 1995), 61.

Loudermilk, Stephen. Wireless LANs Seek Mass Appeal. *LAN Times*, 12; 20 (October 2, 1995), 29.

Mier, Edwin. Cellular Phone Modems. *Communications Week*, no. 569 (August 7, 1995), 52.

Reinhardt, Andy. From Here to Mobility. *Byte*, 20; 6 (June 1995), 100.

Robertson, Bruce. How to Go Wireless with Microsoft Mail and Lotus cc:Mail. *Network Computing*, 6; 3 (March 1, 1995), 148.

Salamone, Salvatore. Radio Days. *Byte*, 20; 6 (June 1995), 107.

Salamone, Salvatore. Untangling Wireless. *Byte*, 20; 12 (December 1995), 96NA1.

Snell, Monica. Digital Promises Virtual Access for Remote Users. *LAN Times*, 12; 12 (June 19, 1995), 1.

Snell, Monica. Radio to Get Data Boost. *LAN Times*, 12; 11 (June 5, 1995), 1.

Streeter, April. A MIB to Keep Track of the Mobile. *LAN Times*, 12; 20 (October 2, 1995), 51.

Wayner, Peter. Oracle Hits the Road. *Byte*, 20; 6 (June 1995), 207.

Wittman, Art. Will Wireless Win the War? *Network Computing*, 5; 6 (June 1, 1994), 58.

Wireless LANs

Baldazo, Rex. Local Air Networks. *Byte*, 20; 6 (June 1995), 201.

Boyle, Padraic. Wireless LANs: No Strings Attached. *PC Magazine*, 14; 1 (January 10, 1995), 215.

Carlson, Susan. Wireless LANs Take on New Tasks. *Business Communications Review*, 25; 2 (February 1995), 36.

Cohen, Jodi. Wireless LANs Hope to Get Second Wind with Upcoming Standard. *Network World*, 12; 24 (June 12, 1995), 32.

Fernandes, Jose et al. Wireless LANs: Physical Properties of Infra-Red Systems vs. Mmw Systems. *IEEE Communications*, 32; 8 (August 1994), 68.

Frezza, Bill. Making Wide Area Wireless Work. *Business Communications Review*, 25; 11 (November 1995), 65.

Hills, Alex and Richard Hovey. CDPD Puts IP Networks on the Move. *Business Communications Review*, 25; 5 (May 1995), 58.

Hubbard, Barbara. Taking CDPD's Measure: A Primer. *LAN Times*, 12; 20 (October 2, 1995), 39.

Links, Cees. Universal Wireless LANs. *Byte*, 19; 5 (May 1994), 99.

Mathias, Craig. Wireless LANs: The Top 10 Challenges. *Business Communications Review*, 24; 8 (August 1994), 42.

Molta, Dave and Josh Linder. Wireless Act: Wireless LANs Making Big Sense. *Network Computing*, 6; 8 (July 1, 1995), 82.

Newman, David and Kevin Tolly. Wireless LANs: How Far? How Fast? *Data Communications*, 24; 4 (March 21, 1995), 77.

Pahlavan, Kaveh and Thomas Probert. Trends in Local Wireless Networks. *IEEE Communications*, 33; 3 (March 1995), 88.

Snell, Monica. Service to Give CDPD Wider Development. *LAN Times*, 12; 23 (November 6, 1995), 1.

Tam, Terry. Wireless LAN Yields Horizontal Mobility. *PC Week*, 12; 41 (October 16, 1995), N1.

Vaughan-Nichols, Steven. Infrared Gets Real. *Byte*, 20; 1 (January 1995), 30.

Wallace, Hank and Bud Simciak. Wireless Design: Options for the 90s. *Communications Systems Design*, 1; 1 (June 1995), 18.

Yang, Thomas. Ensuring Wireless Security. *Communications Systems Design*, 1; 1 (June 1995), 30.

Security

Davis, Beth. Products to Secure Remote Net Links. *Communications Week*, no. 566 (July 17, 1995), 1.

Johnson, Johna and Kevin Tolly. Token Authentication: The Safety Catch. *Data Communications*, 24; 6 (May 1995), 62.

Stephenson, Peter. Remote Access Security. *Network Computing*, 6; 2 (February 1, 1994), 130.

Sullivan, Eamonn. Scrambler Software Protects Data from Prying Eyes. *PC Week*, 12; 42 (October 23, 1995), N1.

File Synchronization

Kohlhepp, Robert. Keeping in Sync. *Network Computing*, 5; 12 (October 15, 1994), 58.

Remote Access Protocols/Operating Systems

Boardman, Bruce. Pillars of PPP Connectivity. *Network Computing*, 6; 10 (September 1, 1995), 62.

Chernicoff, David. MultiLink PPP Offers Route to Channel Bonding. *PC Week*, 12; 22 (June 5, 1995), N18.

Rigney, Steve. Windows 95: The One for the Road. *PC Magazine*, 14; 17 (October 10, 1995), 375.

Schwartz, Jeffrey. IP Key to Plan to Tie CDPD, Private E-Mail. *Communications Week*, no. 566 (July 17, 1995), 1.

Schwartz, Jeffrey. Standards Proposal Readied. *Communications Week*, no. 562, (June 19, 1995), 31.

Smith, Ben. From Here to There. *Byte*, 19; 6 (June 1994), 271.

Tam, Terry. Caching in on Performance. *PC Week*, 12; 42 (October 23, 1995), N1.

Williams, Dennis. Mobile Middleware Reaches Out. *LAN Times*, 12; 20 (October 2, 1995), 63.

Communications Servers

Larsen, Amy. Communications Server Clears Up LAN Bottlenecks. *Data Communications*, 24; 10 (August 1995), 117.

Mier, Edwin. Communications Servers: Dialing for Data. *Communications Week*, no. 572 (August 28, 1995), 44.

CASE STUDY

Chapter 15

BP STRIKES REMOTE SUCCESS

Company Deploys Human-Resources Applications Server

One of the biggest challenges facing today's network administrator is how to manage users who travel frequently or work at satellite offices.

The task for network administrators at British Petroleum PLC's Oil Division, headquartered in Cleveland, was to install a client/server database application to be distributed to multiple remote offices.

On Jan. 1, BP Oil made its New Year's resolution: to find one high-performance, low-priced remote-access product through which a fleet of more than 100 mobile users could be managed.

The company wanted to deploy a PeopleSoft Inc. application called HMRS, an all-in-one human-resources, benefits, and payroll system with links to four remote satellite offices located in Houston; Lima and Toledo, Ohio; and Bell Chase, La.

Working within the confines of a budget, Ken Fox, technical manager for the PeopleSoft project, wanted to provide quick and easy remote access to the central PeopleSoft application. Fox said he was immediately overwhelmed with a variety of remote-access solutions, including remote-control software such as Symantec Corp.'s PCAnywhere, communications servers from companies such as Cubix Corp., and remote-node software.

Fox's problem was such: How do you support a mobile work force equipped with a hodgepodge of 286- and 386-based machines when the PeopleSoft application requires 386- and 486-based machines with at least 8MB of RAM?

"We couldn't afford to upgrade PCs at remote sites, especially slow-speed PCs that could not run Windows," Fox said.

With more than 50 remote users and plans to add 70 more users to 20 remote sites, remote control required that every dial-in line be dedicated to a single PC. This solution was unappealing because of BP Oil's large installed base of remote users. BP looked at communications servers, which list for $25,000 to $30,000 for eight users. The company then turned to remote-node software from companies such as TechSmith Corp., but found that flat-file databases perform ineffectively over WAN links.

Citrix Systems Inc., based in Coral Springs, Fla., stepped in to provide applications-server software called WinView for Networks. For its first 50 remote users, BP Oil bought five copies of WinView for Networks, each supporting 10 users, for a total of $60,000. BP Oil estimates that it saved about $90,000—or 60 percent of its capital expenditures—on what it would have spent upgrading mobile workstations.

With a Novell Inc. NetWare 3.12 file server in Cleveland, BP had to find a better way to load and execute dynamic link libraries and executable files. Once WinView for Networks was loaded on five separate IBM OS/2-based servers and connected to the file server, performance increased dramatically because only screen changes were sent over the WAN. With remote-node and remote-control solutions, entire files are sent.

Human-resources personnel in the remote offices were able to receive quick updates on employee changes throughout the day.

"With Citrix [and its WinView for Networks applications software], there was no need to download software out in Cleveland and no need to change files," said Fox.

Remote users can now execute DOS and Microsoft Windows applications, even on 286-based machines.

Overall, BP Oil's implementation of WinView for Networks software has centralized the management of remote dial-in connections. Because each WinView for Networks server supports 10 users, data sent over WAN links has been reduced substantially, thus controlling phone-line charges.

"Now we don't have to upgrade and travel around the country to do an update," said Fox. "No single file for the PeopleSoft [database] needs to go outside the building."

Source: Stephen Loudermilk (February 27, 1995). BP Strikes Remote Success. *LAN Times*, 12(4), 25. Reprinted with permission of McGraw-Hill, *LAN Times*.

BUSINESS CASE STUDY QUESTIONS

Activities

1. Complete a top-down model for this case by gleaning facts from the case and placing them in the proper layer of the top-down model. After completing the top-down model, analyze and detail those instances when requirements were clearly passed down from upper to lower layers of the model and solutions to those requirements were passed up from lower to upper layers.
2. Detail any questions that may occur to you about the case for which answers are not clearly stated in the article.

Business

1. What business activities were to be distributed to the remote offices via remote access?
2. What were the cost savings of the chosen technology versus upgrading mobile workstations?
3. What were the business-related benefits of the technology acquisition and implementation?

Application

1. What application was to be distributed to multiple remote offices?
2. What performance requirements were established for the remote access products to be purchased?

3. Where does the application processing take place in the implemented solution?

Data

1. With WinView for Networks, what is actually transmitted over the WAN links?
2. Where is data for the applications stored?
3. Is data transferred to remote sites? If so, how? If not, why not?

Network

1. What is one of biggest challenges facing today's network administrator?
2. What computing resources at headquarters would a remote control solution have required?
3. What other remote access technologies did BP investigate, and what were their findings?
4. To which category of remote access technology does WinView for Networks belong?
5. Describe the hardware and software platform over which WinView executes.
6. How are remote access users managed in the implemented solution?

Technology

1. How did the current computer technology in place at remote sites influence the strategic technology acquisition and implementation plan?

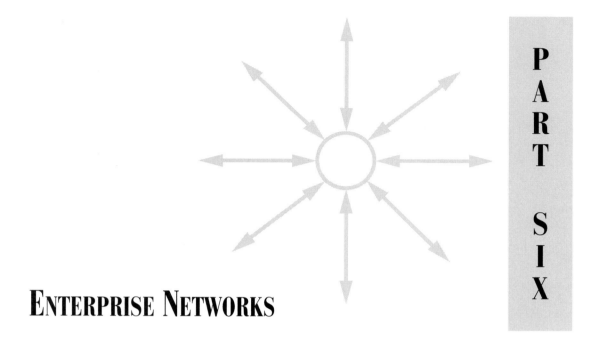

ENTERPRISE NETWORKS

INTRODUCTION

At this point, the reader should be familiar with the business motivations for building local area network–based client/server information systems, the benefits derived from such information systems, and the requisite knowledge to analyze, design, and implement such networks.

Enterprise networking seeks to extend the benefits of local area networking to an entire enterprise, regardless of its geographic scope. One of the terms most often associated with enterprise networks is "virtual LANs."

Virtual LANs seek to allow any group of users, regardless of geographic location, to interact via voice, video, and information systems as if they were all members of the same local area network. Although descriptions of virtual LANs such as this may sound simple, designing and implementing virtual LANs can be anything but simple. Part 6 of the text serves as an introduction to the issues surrounding the analysis, design, implementation, and management of enterprise networks.

Chapter 16 on Enterprise Network Architecture and Topology introduces the overall architecture of enterprise networks, the components which comprise the overall architecture, and the interaction between those components.

Chapter 17 on Enterprise Network Applications and Management introduces the unique issues involved with designing, developing, and deploying applications in a multiplatform, multivendor, multiprotocol enterprise network and the issues surrounding management of these complex, worldwide, integrated enterprise networks.

CHAPTER **16**

ENTERPRISE NETWORK ARCHITECTURE AND TOPOLOGY

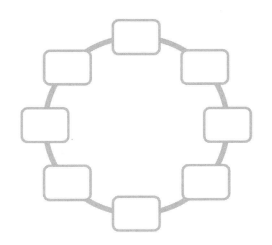

Concepts Reinforced

OSI model
Internetwork design
Switching versus routing

Internet suite of protocols model
Internetworking technology
Top-down model

Concepts Introduced

Virtual workgroups
Virtual LANs
Distributed computing environment
Middleware
Enterprise network logical design

ATM
Enterprise network physical design
LAN emulation
Relational networks

OBJECTIVES

After mastering the material in this chapter you should:

1. Understand the business motivation for the analysis, design, and implementation of enterprise networks.

2. Understand the importance of virtual LANs to enterprise networks.

3. Understand the issues surrounding the analysis, design, implementation, and management of virtual LANs.

4. Understand the differences between, as well as the advantages and disadvantages of, alternative physical topologies for enterprise networks.

5. Understand the importance of ATM to virtual LANs and enterprise networks.

6. Understand the issues surrounding the analysis, design, and implementation of ATM LAN emulation as a means of building virtual LANs and enterprise networks.

Having gained an appreciation of the type of services well-designed LANs deliver as well as their business-related benefits, network managers wanted to extend these benefits to the entire business enterprise including, in some cases, vendors and customers. Although LANs may be local in geographic scope, the data they generate and store are an enterprisewide asset which must be quickly and easily accessible by the entire enterprise. Beyond the obvious challenges of building international networks, more important network design hurdles such as the following need to be overcome to realize the competitive advantage of enterprise networks:

- There is a relative lack of affordable wide area network bandwidth required to carry integrated voice, data, video, and multimedia applications.

- The multivendor, multiplatform, multiprotocol reality of the numerous nodes of a typical enterprise network need to be transparently integrated.

- Due to the quickly changing nature of the competitive business environment combined with downsized human resources, enterprise networks need to be extremely flexible to allow collaboration between individuals on projects regardless of geographic location.

- Data required for decision making need to be accessed quickly and easily regardless of physical location or data management system. This ease of access is especially critical for data locked away in mainframe computers.

These are just some of the challenges which must be addressed to effectively analyze, design, and implement enterprise networks. This chapter introduces the reader to the numerous issues surrounding enterprise network design by exploring alternative enterprise network architectures, topologies, and technologies.

Applied Problem Solving

BUSINESS MOTIVATIONS FOR ENTERPRISE NETWORKS

As dictated by the top-down model, to understand the functionality required of an enterprise network, the network analyst must first understand the business-related issues and requirements the enterprise network will be expected to fulfill. Figure 16-1 uses the top-down model to summarize the factors influencing the required functionality of enterprise networks.

Top-Down Model Layer	Enterprise Network Implications
Business	• Dawn of the virtual corporation • Dynamic work teams, virtual workgroups • Matrix management, centers of excellence • More workers telecommuting or working on the road with increased customer contact • Extending the enterprise to include customers and vendors • Minimizing expenses to increase profits
Application	• Remote users require full access to corporate information resources. • Remote users require intelligent agent-based software to act on their behalf when they are not logged in.

Figure 16-1 Top-Down Model for Enterprise Networks

(continued)

Top-Down Model Layer	Enterprise Network Implications
	• Virtual workgroups require specialized collaborative software for cooperative development and design projects.
Data	• Remote users require data and files to be automatically synchronized each time they log in to corporate information resources. • Collaborative application software often transmits video, image, and voice as well as traditional data. • Collaborative application software often requires database replication across numerous geographically distributed databases.
Network	• Collaborative application software has high bandwidth demands and time-sensitive delivery constraints. • Distributed database replication imposes high bandwidth demands on the network. • Enterprise network services have become mission-critical requiring absolute 7 day/wk, 24 hr/day availability. • Because of constant relocation of workers in virtual workgroups, the network services must be more active and intelligent by being able to provide appropriate services for each workgroup member regardless of physical location. • Virtual LANs are required to provide the flexible, dynamic workgroup connections for virtual workgroups.
Technology	• More powerful SMP servers • LAN switches for local bandwidth • ATM for high-speed backbone switching • SONET for high-speed WAN transmission • Open, standards-based technology helps ensure multivendor, multiplatform, multiprotocol interoperability

Figure 16-1 (*continued*)

A business phenomenon known as the **virtual corporation** is a business partnership among cooperating business entities which is electronically enabled via an **enterprise network.** In most cases, these business entities are sufficiently distant from one another that constant travel between locations to accomplish business objectives would be impossible. In other words, without the enterprise network, the virtual corporation would not exist.

If the virtual corporation is considered a strategic business initiative, the tactical fulfillment of that strategic objective is fulfilled via the establishment and support of **virtual workgroups.** By dynamically allocating people to projects based on expertise rather than location, the most qualified people can be more easily assigned to appropriate projects without concern for the expense and wasted productivity caused by extensive travel or frequent relocation.

Virtual workgroups require specialized application software which will allow them to cooperatively function as if they were all in the same geographic location. Collaborative computing software such as groupware is required to support the need for multiple simultaneous forms of communication (voice, video, data, image, multimedia).

The enterprise network which must support these virtual workgroups consisting of numerous remote computing users must be able to be dynamically defined to mirror the dynamic definition of the virtual workgroups themselves. In other

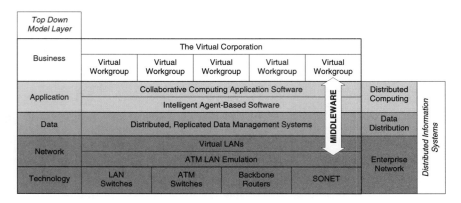

Figure 16-2   Overall Enterprise Network Architecture

words, although members of virtual workgroups may be geographically dispersed, when they log in to corporate information resources, the enterprise network must treat them as if they are all connected to the same local LAN. Networks which make geographically distributed users appear to be connected to the same local LAN are known as **virtual LANs.**

■ OVERALL ENTERPRISE NETWORK ARCHITECTURE

Figure 16-2 presents a logical model for how an enterprise network supports a virtual corporation.

   As the figure shows, the virtual corporation requires a **distributed information system** composed of a number of major interacting components or subsystems. The applications layer functionality of the top-down model is delivered by a **distributed computing** solution which can interact successfully with the numerous virtual workgroups. Data from this distributed computing environment is distributed and replicated as needed through the functionality delivered by the **data distribution** or data management subsystem. The client-to-server messaging from the distributed computing subsystem must be transparent to differences in computing platforms, operating systems, network operating systems, or data management systems. This messaging transparency is delivered by an important category of software known as **middleware.** All client-to-server and server-to-server messages are actually delivered via the enterprise network.

■ DISTRIBUTED ENTERPRISE APPLICATIONS

Given all the interacting component layers illustrated in Figure 16-2 and the possibility of numerous technologies, products, or protocols being employed on any given layer, guaranteeing transparent interoperability between the various components of an enterprise-based distributed information system seems to be a daunting task. To bring some standardization to distributed information systems architectures to help ensure enterprisewide interoperability, the **Open Software Foundation (OSF)** has introduced the **distributed computing environment (DCE)** model.

The DCE Architecture

The Distributed Computing Environment architecture is illustrated in Figure 16-3.

DCE ARCHITECTURE COMPONENTS

In Sharper Focus

DCE is actually a collection of operating system and network operating system–independent services that allow distributed applications to be developed, deployed, and managed in a secure environment. Among its key components are the following:

- **Distributed file services (DFS)**—The purpose of DFS is to offer a consistent interface and consistent services for allowing users to access files from any node on the DCE-based enterprise network. DFS acts as a sort of translator between the native file system of the DCE host node and the DCE requesting client by using other DCE services such as the DCE naming service, which guarantees a consistent naming convention for all DFS-accessible files. Likewise, DFS depends on the DCE security services to provide authorization and authentication controls over file access by any DCE client. The RPC messaging subsystem is used to set up point-to-point connections between client and server to optimize file transfer efficiency. To further improve file transfer efficiency, a DFS cache manager resides on the client workstation to minimize the amount of client-to-server communication. Since the file system is distributed and the possibility exists for more than one client to request access to the same file simultaneously, a token manager is used to ensure that file updates are synchronized to prevent unintentional file corruption.

- **Naming service or directory service**—Just as DFS was responsible for presenting a consistent interface for file access regardless of the native file system of the DCE node, consistent directory services are also required for all DCE-compliant clients to quickly and easily access required services. DCE's

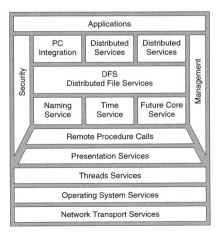

Figure 16-3 Distributed Computing Environment Architecture

directory service is not unlike Novell's NDS. Any service or device which can be accessed is referred to as an object, described by a series of attributes, and listed as an entry in a directory. Directories themselves are considered objects and can therefore be listed as entries in other directories, thereby supporting a hierarchical directory structure. Through a gateway service known as the global directory agent, local or cell directory services are linked to global directory services such as the X.500 international directory service.

- **Remote procedure calls service** is the interprocess communications mechanism supplied with DCE. To ensure consistency and interoperability, the RPC services in DCE are not alterable by users or licensees of DCE. As a result, some proprietary RPC services may offer more sophisticated interprocess communications services. As illustrated in Figure 16-3, RPC provides the basic transport or messaging mechanism for all DCE services as well as for DCE-compliant client applications. RPC provides consistent support for communications via distributed enterprise network connections regardless of the platform or protocol of either the source or destination node. This transparency means that programmers do not have to worry about platform-specific network communications while developing distributed applications for the DCE environment. RPC works with the DCE security services to provide for secure client/server communications across the enterprise network.

- **Threads services** are provided to offer multithreaded capabilities to DCE nodes whose native operating systems are not multithreaded. Threads services are stored as functions which can be called from within a threads library. Although not as efficient as a native multithreaded capability contained within an operating system kernel, the threads service does provide a homogeneous multithreaded environment supported by all DCE nodes. Like most multithreaded environments, DCE threads allow multiple subprocesses of a single application to execute simultaneously. This is particularly useful when RPCs have created a link to a distant server, allowing the local application to continue processing in the interim. Other DCE services such as RPC, security, time, and directory services use the threads service.

- **Distributed time service (DTS)**—DCE services such as DFS and security services depend on time and date stamps as part of their functionality. It is important, given the distributed, multinode nature of a DCE implementation, that there is a source for an "official" time by which all connected systems can be synchronized. DCE provides three types of time servers to coordinate system time across a DCE environment. Local time servers coordinate with other local servers on the same LAN while global time servers offer similar services across WAN or inter-LAN links. A courier time server is responsible for coordinating with global time servers at regular intervals.

- **Security services** for DCE are divided into two general categories. Authorization grants users access to objects based on the contents of access control lists (ACLs) while authentication guarantees the identity or authenticity of a user or object. Authentication in DCE is based on **Kerberos** authentication system which provides multilevel authentication and encryption services depending on the level of security required. Authentication can be established only at connection time or can be enforced for every network message that traverses the connection.

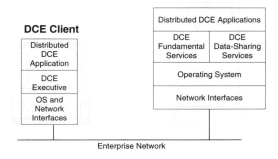

Figure 16-4   DCE Implementation in a Client/
Server Environment

DCE Implementation   Figure 16-4 illustrates a logical model of how DCE is actually
implemented in a client/server environment.

DCE services are included or embedded within **DCE-compliant** client or server
operating system or network operating system environments. As a result, end-user
companies or organizations do not purchase or implement DCE codes or services
directly. Rather, end-users purchase DCE-compliant software technology from software developers who have purchased licenses to incorporate standardized DCE services within their products. Figure 16-5 lists some DCE-compliant products available.

DCE Software	Software Category	Vendor
DCE client and server software	DCE compliant OS/NOS	Most Unix vendors
PC-DCE	DCE client software for Windows NT, Windows 95, Novell UnixWare, and Macintosh System 7 clients	Gradient Technologies
DCE for OS/2	DCE client software for OS/2 platforms	IBM
DE-Lite	DCE gateway software	Transarc
Connection/DCE	Data access middleware to Informix, Oracle, and SyBase databases	Open Horizon
Tuxedo	DCE-compliant OLTP monitor software	Novell
Encina	DCE-compliant OLTP monitor software	Transarc/IBM
DCE for MVS	DCE server software for IBM mainframes	IBM
SQL*Net/DCE	DCE-compliant data messaging service	Oracle

Figure 16-5   DCE-Compliant Software Products

DCE ACCEPTANCE

Although some potential adopters of DCE point to limitations of the DCE RPC messaging services as a reason for their reluctance, the truth is that because Microsoft and Novell have not given whole-hearted support to producing fully DCE-compliant client software, users are understandably reluctant to jump on the DCE bandwagon. Although both Windows NT and Windows 95 support **DCE-compatible** RPC messaging services, the Microsoft client platforms do not include other DCE services for distributed computing and therefore cannot be considered DCE-compliant. Given the percentage of client workstations running either Microsoft or Novell software, it is doubtful that DCE will be universally deployed or accepted until either or both of these software industry giants, commit their resources to producing a fully DCE-compliant client software platform.

■ MIDDLEWARE

The term middleware is used to describe a wide variety of types of software which enable transparent interoperability across enterprise networks.

Middleware Architecture

Architecturally, middleware fits between client/server applications and the enterprise network which delivers the messages linking them. Middleware's overall function is to provide whatever services are required to allow client/server applications to transparently interoperate across a variety of computing platforms and networks. Figure 16-6 illustrates both an overall and a detailed view of middleware architecture.

A product does not have to deliver all services and functionality included in this architectural drawing to be considered middleware. A few comprehensive middleware products, or suites of products, however, deliver most of the services illustrated. The entire DCE architecture, as well as common object request broker architecture (CORBA) and object linking and embedding (OLE) are examples of complete suites of middleware functionality.

Middleware Functionality

Before one can fully understand the functionality of middleware, one must first understand how distributed applications would communicate with each without the benefit of middleware. To make client/server application programs network-aware, network protocol-dependent communications programming must be added to the applications programming.

A fitting analogy might be if each telephone user had to delineate which central office switches and interswitch protocols should be employed to establish the connection for a long distance call before beginning a conversation. In this case, the phone switch software which reads the source and destination phone numbers and establishes the circuit-switched connection transparently to the user is fulfilling the role of middleware.

To return to the client architecture, each network transport protocol offers an application program interface (API) to which commands can be passed from application programs. The syntax of this command includes sufficient information to

Overall Architecture

Architectural

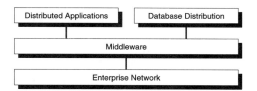

Functional

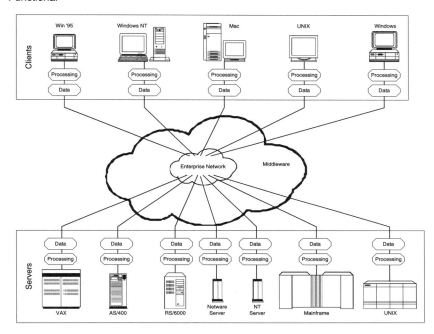

Detailed Architecture

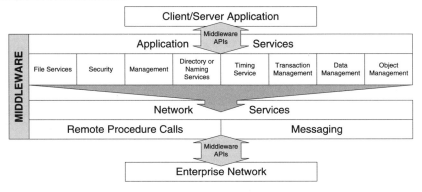

Figure 16-6   Middleware Architecture

indicate the location of and path to the destination server, establish a session to the destination server, and authorize the requesting application's authority to access that destination server. The real drawback to this approach is that each of the network transport protocol APIs follows a different syntax, obligating application programmers to customize application programs depending on the network operating system and network transport protocols of each client and server platform on which the application must execute. Figure 16-7 illustrates network transport APIs and their relationship to API-specific application programs.

Some of these network transport protocol APIs are quite complicated, employing more than 30 commands, or verbs, as well as several possible error conditions for every verb. In comparison, most middleware employs fewer than 10 verbs, with some products featuring fewer than 5. This full-functionality without overcomplication is compounded by the fact that these same few middleware verbs are used regardless of the network protocol API or server platform. The real demand for middleware stems from the impracticality of developing and supporting several unique versions of every distributed application, depending on client, network, and server combinations.

As a matter of fact, it is probably safe to say that, were it not for middleware, the widespread deployment of client/server architectures would be called into serious question. Middleware delivers network transparency by offering a single set of commands which, in turn, interface to the various network protocol APIs previ-

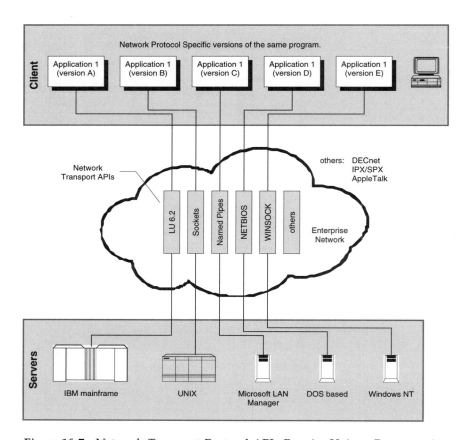

Figure 16-7 Network Transport Protocol APIs Require Unique Programming

ously mentioned, and write the network protocol-specific commands on behalf of the end-user.

Middleware itself is really a "super-API" which interfaces to the network-specific APIs. By delivering network transparency to distributed applications, middleware eliminates the need for and expense of developing network-specific distributed applications. Client and server portions of distributed applications can be developed independently. In fact, client-based applications can be developed without regard for the server which will interact with this client. Figure 16-8 illustrates how middleware interacts with a variety of network protocol APIs to yield network transparency for distributed applications.

Middleware Categorization

When middleware categorization is more focused on available middleware products, the most common middleware categories are as follows:

- Database middleware.
- Remote procedure call (RPC) middleware.
- Message-oriented middleware.

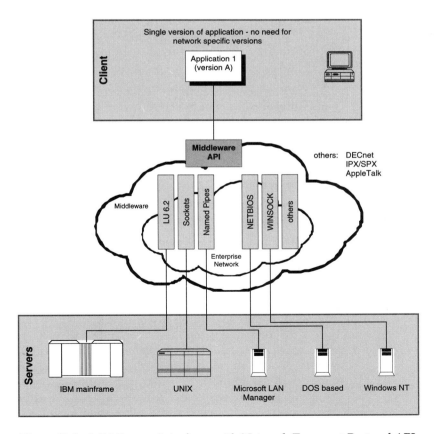

Figure 16-8   Middleware Interfaces with Network Transport Protocol APIs

- Object middleware.

- Transaction processing monitors (OLTP monitors).

Database Middleware **Database middleware** offers transparent database interoperability between clients and database servers executing a variety of database engines. **Structured query language (SQL)** is a standardized data manipulation and query language supported by most databases which is roughly equivalent to a database-specific remote procedure call. Rather than just initiate a remote application or procedure, SQL initiates database interaction with remote database servers and returns database server responses to the inquiring client.

Database connectivity products, or database middleware, is often supplied by the vendors of the databases themselves. For instance, Oracle's SQL*Net allows clients on virtually any platform to access databases on nearly any server, via any network protocol. Alternatively, third-party software developers also offer database middleware. A product known as enterprise data access/SQL **(EDA/SQL)** from Information Builders Inc., calling itself a universal data access system, acts as a database middleware layer trapping SQL requests from clients and reformatting them as necessary before transporting them to the appropriate server.

Portions of the specially written software are deployed on clients, to interface to PC-based products such as Lotus 1-2-3. Server portions of the software are also available for IBM mainframes, DEC and HP minicomputers, Unix processors such as IBM RS/6000, Sun, Pyramid, DEC, NCR, and Data General, and IBM OS/2 LAN server and Novell NetWare Servers. SQL data access to over 50 databases deployed on these servers is supported. EDA/SQL routing software, which runs on the mainframe, mini, and Unix servers listed; is able to transport EDA/SQL queries to their appropriate servers on widely distributed database management systems.

Managerial Perspective

EDA/SQL represents a single-vendor solution to the database incompatibility problem. However, any single-vendor solution can be a problem in itself. Single-vendor solutions are generally proprietary solutions, lacking in support of open systems standards and unable to guarantee wide-ranging interoperability. Be sure to carefully weigh the pros and cons of proprietary solutions such as EDA/SQL versus the standards-based solutions proposed by the SQL access group before making any purchase decisions.

Messaging-Oriented Middleware versus Remote Procedure Calls **Remote procedure calls, RPC,** and **message-oriented middleware,** or **MOM,** are the two subcategories of a broader category of interoperability software known as **messaging middleware.**

Remote procedure call middleware works in a manner similar to a locally run application program which activates, or calls, a subroutine stored outside of the application program itself, but usually in a subroutine library on the same computer. The major difference within the remote procedure call is that the call for the execution of a subroutine is made to a remote procedure located on a distributed processor via the enterprise network. Where that particular server is located and how the remote procedure call is transported there are the concern of the RPC middleware rather than the applications programmer.

RPCs are like local subroutines in at least one other characteristic. When an application program branches to a subroutine, whether a local or a remote procedure, that program waits for the local or remote procedure to complete execution and return either data or some type of status message before continuing with its own program execution. This style of interprocess communication could be categorized as **send-and-wait.** Send-and-wait messaging is also referred to as **synchronous communication,** because the requesting program and responding program remain synchronized, executing simultaneously in real time. Send-and-wait messaging assumes total network and client/server platform reliability, as the client program will wait indefinitely or terminate without a response from the requested server.

MOM, also known as message delivery, message passing, message queuing, and distributed messaging, differs significantly from remote procedure call middleware in its ability to establish various types of interprocess communications modes other than RPC's send-and-wait or synchronous mode.

For instance, distributed applications programs can communicate indirectly with the help of message queues, which are roughly equivalent to post offices. In this scenario, a distributed application could generate a message for another distributed application, forward it to the message queue, and resume its own processing activity. This type of interprocess dialogue is known as **asynchronous message passing,** or asynchronous communication, and does not assume or rely on total network reliability.

Another interprocess dialogue type supported by message-oriented middleware is broadcast or multicast dialogues. Broadcast sends messages to all clients and/or servers on an enterprise network, whereas multicast sends to a selected group.

Message-oriented middleware is flexible as to the content of interprocess communication messages as well. For instance, it can deliver RPC or SQL as its message. Security checking, encryption, data compression, and error recovery can all be supported features of message delivery middleware. Message handling middleware often has the network savvy to navigate the enterprise network intelligently by responding to changing network conditions.

Object Middleware   An emerging category of middleware known as **object middleware** allows objects created in multiple vendors' environments to communicate and request services of each other via the mediation services of an **object request broker (ORB).** An **object** is a software entity which describes data in terms of its attributes, contained in fields, and its behavior, as defined by the methods or procedures which can alter the object's attributes. Objects could be thought of as miniature, free-standing software components which interact in a structured manner, to produce overall application software functionality.

Unfortunately, there are two rival standards for object middleware:

- **Common object request broker architecture (CORBA),** as proposed by the industry coalition known as the Object Management Group (OMG).

- **Object linking and embedding (OLE)** developed by Microsoft.

Regardless of which object middleware standard is used, either RPC or MOM messaging middleware actually transports the object requests between requesting objects and the object request broker. Interoperability between object request brokers from different vendors can be achieved by compliance with the **CORBA 2.0** specification, otherwise known as **universal networked objects, or UNO.**

Applications software programs which employ objects are referred to as object-oriented or event-driven programs as opposed to traditional, procedure-oriented programs.

Transaction Processing Monitors   Predating the creation of the term middleware, **transaction processing monitors,** sometimes referred to as **on-line transaction processing (OLTP)** monitors, were developed to monitor and control the posting of numerous simultaneous transactions across multiple computing platforms. IBM's **Customer Information Control System (CICS)** was among the original mainframe-based transaction process monitoring systems. **Tuxedo** from Novell and **Encina** from Transarc are two of the more popular multiplatform OLTP monitors suitable for client/server applications.

In evolving toward a middleware role, OLTP monitors provide a single middleware API for developing applications to execute in a distributed computing environment and integrate with existing messaging middleware, such as RPC and MOM, for message delivery. Because of their mainframe-based heritage, OLTP monitors generally include a complete set of management tools which ensure reliable execution of distributed applications in a client/server environment.

In multiserver distributed environments, in which a single transaction can require updates to multiple database servers, the OLTP monitor middleware ensures that all updates to all required databases are completed successfully to guarantee database integrity. OLTP monitors often do this by employing a control known as **two-phase commit.** When multiple distributed databases physically located on widely dispersed servers must all be updated as part of a transaction update, two-phase commit basically ensures that either all or none of the required databases will be updated. What happens to the "failed" two-phase commit transactions varies from one OLTP monitor to another, and should be examined very carefully.

If one server on a multiserver network, or the network link to a particular server goes down, no transactions will be posted during that time with a two-phase commit transaction process in place. This may not be acceptable in every business situation. Some businesses may prefer to continue posting to distributed servers that can successfully be reached.

Figure 16-9 lists some middleware products by category, along with their respective vendors.

Middleware Application Development Tools

Because of the multiple categories of middleware, and the multiple proprietary middleware products and APIs within each category, **middleware application development tools** must be able to transparently integrate with a wide variety of middleware products. More important, it is essential that a selected enterprise application development tool support an organization's middleware platform.

Middleware application development tools provide the functionality to build separate client and server-based distributed applications with embedded remote procedure calls. **Stubs** are specially coded lines of applications program that the middleware application development tool adds to allow the client and server portions of distributed applications to interface with the enterprise network connecting them.

In some cases, the middleware vendor provides the middleware application development tool, while in other cases third-party middleware application development tool vendors provide products which support numerous middleware products. Alternatively, middleware applications development tools support only their own proprietary middleware solutions in one or more middleware product categories.

Middleware Category	Middleware Product	Middleware Vendor
Database middleware	SQL*Net	Oracle
	EDA/SQL	Information Builders
RPC middleware	DCE	Open Software Foundation and numerous vendors which incorporate DCE into client and server operating systems
	NetWise RPC	NetWise
	Open Network Computing (ONC)	SunSoft
MOM middleware	Communications Integrator	Covia Technologies
	ISIS Reliable SDK	ISIS Distributed Systems
	Pipes	Peerlogic
	DECMessageQ	DEC
	XIPC, Message Express	Momentum
Object middleware	Orbix	Iona Technologies
	XShell	Expersoft
Transaction monitoring middleware	CICS	IBM
	Encina	Transarc
	TopEnd	AT&T G.I.S.
	Tuxedo	Novell

Figure 16-9   Middleware Products by Category

Managerial
Perspective

MIDDLEWARE REALITIES

Managers must deal with realities of the middleware market such as the following:

- Standards are evolving or nonexistent.

- Product categorization is arbitrary.

- Support for various client and server platforms varies significantly among middleware products.

- There is no single product that meets all middleware needs.

- Middleware vendors are often relatively small, start-up firms.

- Middleware application development tools vary widely in middleware product support and sophistication.

- Some middleware standards or products are merely protocol definitions, while others are complete suites of services.

In view of these realities, it is essential that applications development and network management teams work cooperatively to choose the best products for a given organization's environment. The top-down approach should be followed, with business requirements dictating application requirements. Given the types of applications which must be distributed and the distribution of the data which must support those applications, management should be able to choose the correct middleware product to deliver required functionality while remaining compatible with enterprise network protocols.

ENTERPRISE NETWORK LOGICAL DESIGN

The logical design of the enterprise network must deliver the required functionality to allow businesses to respond to rapidly changing business requirements by supporting the rapid formation of dynamic workgroups and project teams. Organizations must be able to quickly and efficiently bring together in-house knowledge and resources on an as-needed basis. A virtual LAN, rather than physically rewiring network connections for each change in workgroup configurations, allows dedicated network resources to be flexibly assigned to virtual workgroups by grouping users logically rather than by physical network connections.

Virtual LANs

Basic Functionality   The logical network design known as a virtual LAN depends on a physical device, the LAN switch, for its functionality. Though the original LAN switches delivered abundant bandwidth to locally attached workstations and segments, they lacked the ability to partition the switch into multiple segregated broadcast zones and segment users into corresponding separate workgroups.

Virtual LANs are software definable through configuration software contained within the LAN switch. The use of virtual LANs allows workgroup members to be assigned to more than one workgroup quickly and easily, if necessary. Subsequently, each virtual workgroup is assigned some portion of the LAN switch's backplane capacity. LAN switches which support virtual LANs use OSI layer 2 bridging functionality to logically segment the traffic within the switch into distinct virtual LANs.

Any message received by a LAN switch destined for a single workstation is delivered to that destination workstation via an individual switched network connection. The key difference between a LAN switch which does not support virtual LANs and one that does is how it treats broadcast and multicast messages. In a virtual LAN, broadcasts and multicasts are limited to the members of that virtual LAN only, rather than to all connected devices. This prevents propagation of data across the entire network and reduces network traffic. To simply, virtual LANs are nothing more than logically defined broadcast/multicast groups within layer 2 LAN switches, since point-to-point traffic is handled by switched dedicated connections.

Limitations   A key limitation of virtual LANs is that when members of the same virtual LAN are physically connected to separate LAN switches, the virtual LAN configuration information must be shared among multiple LAN switches. Currently, no interoperability standards exist for transmitting or sharing virtual LAN information between layer 2 LAN switches. As a result, only proprietary switch-to-switch protocols between a single vendor's equipment is possible for multi-switch virtual LANs.

Virtual LANs are more difficult to manage and monitor than traditional LANs because of the virtual LAN's dependence on LAN switches for physical connectivity. Because the switched LAN connections are established, used, and terminated in a matter of microseconds for most transmissions, it is difficult if not impossible to monitor these transmissions in real time by traditional means. One solution to this dilemma is **traffic duplication,** in which traffic between two switch ports is duplicated onto a third port to which traditional LAN analyzers can be attached.

Figure 16-10 illustrates the differences between a LAN switch, a virtual LAN, and a multiswitch virtual LAN.

LAN Switch

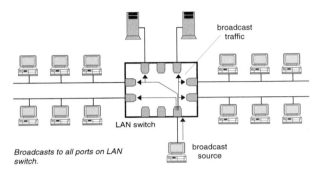

Single Switch Virtual LANs

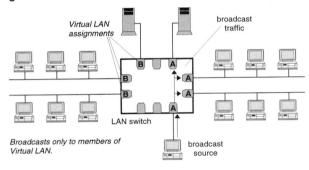

Multi-Switch Virtual LANs

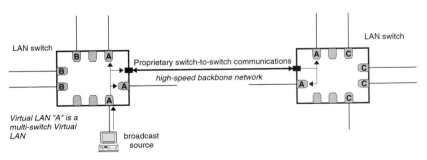

Figure 16-10   LAN Switches and Virtual LANs

TRANSMISSION BETWEEN LAYER 2 LAN SWITCHES

Following are among the alternative methods used by switch vendors to share virtual LAN information across layer 2 LAN switches:

- Signaling message—Switches inform each other whenever new workstations come on line as to the MAC address and virtual LAN number of that workstation. To keep all switches' information synchronized, each switch's virtual LAN tables are broadcast periodically to all other switches. In larger switched networks, this virtual LAN table transfer can introduce significant amounts of broadcast traffic.

- Frame tagging—A tag indicating the virtual LAN number of the source workstation is appended to every data-link layer frame which must travel between LAN switches. In this way, the recipient switch knows immediately to which virtual LAN workstations the received frame must be forwarded. One difficulty with frame tagging is that the added bits may exceed the maximum frame length of the data-link layer protocol, thereby requiring additional proprietary methods to cope with this limitation.

- Time division multiplexing—Each virtual LAN is assigned a specific portion of the bandwidth available on the LAN switches' backplanes. Only the assigned virtual LAN is allowed to use designated bandwidth. Each virtual LAN has a virtual private backplane, and traffic from various virtual LANs do not interfere with each other. However, assigned but unused bandwidth cannot be shared among other virtual LANs.

IEEE 802.10 is one possibility for standardizing switch-to-switch communication to support virtual LANs which span multiple switches. Originally conceived as a standard for secure data exchange on LANs which would allow workstations to set encryption and authentication settings, this standard is of interest to virtual LAN switch vendors because of the addition of a 32-bit header to existing MAC sublayer frames. Instead of just holding security information, this additional 32-bit header could hold virtual LAN identifiers. To overcome the limitation on maximum data-link layer frame length, IEEE 802.10 also includes specifications for segmentation and reassembly of any frames which should exceed maximum length with the addition of the 32-bit header.

Transmission Between Virtual LANs   Virtual LANs are built using LAN switches which are OSI layer 2 devices able only to distinguish between MAC layer addresses. As a result, LAN switches can offer only the "forward-if-not-local" internetworking logic of bridges. To selectively transmit traffic between virtual LANs, routing functionality is required. This routing functionality may be supplied by an external router or by specialized router software included in the LAN switch. LAN switches with built-in routing capabilities are sometimes referred to as **layer 3 switches.** Since traffic cannot move selectively between virtual LANs without the benefit of routing, the virtual LAN logical design has been credited with offering firewall functionality due to the filtering capabilities of intermediary routers.

Classification of Virtual LANs   Virtual LANs are often classified by the OSI layer which represents their highest level of functionality:

   Layer 2 virtual LANs are built using LAN switches which act as microsegmenting bridges. A LAN switch which supports a layer 2 virtual LAN distinguishes only between the MAC addresses of connected workstations. No differentiation is possible based on layer 3, network layer, protocols. One or more workstations can be connected to each switch port.

Layer 3 virtual LANs are built using LAN switches which can process layer 3 network addresses. Such devices may be called IP switches or **routing switches.** Since these devices perform filtering based on network layer protocols and addresses, they can support multiple virtual LANs using different network layer protocols.

In other words, one virtual LAN might support only TIP/IP while another might support only IPX/SPX. Since layer 3 switches understand layer 3 addressing schemes, they use the subnetwork numbers embedded within layer 3 addresses to organize virtual LANs. Since these subnetwork numbers are previously assigned to workstations, some layer 3 switches can query all connected workstations and autoconfigure or automatically assign workstations to virtual LANs based on these subnetwork numbers. Workstations using nonroutable protocols such as LAT, NetBEUI, or NetBIOS are likewise segregated into their own virtual LANs.

Figure 16-11 illustrates the architectural differences between layers 2 and 3 virtual LANs, and Figure 16-12 details the functional differences between the two virtual LAN designs.

Managerial Perspective

VIRTUAL LAN REALITIES

Depending on which network expert one listens to, virtual LANs are either a passing fad or the greatest thing to happen to networking in the past 10 years. As is most often the case, the truth probably lies somewhere in between. Virtual LANs are not the ultimate network architecture for all organizations. It is important to differentiate between the switched bandwidth capabilities delivered by the LAN switch and the broadcast domain limitation added by virtual LAN definitions. The lower cost of moves, adds, and changes most often credited to virtual LANs is significant only if a given organization is constantly moving, adding, and changing users among workgroups and from LAN to LAN. Virtual LANs remove the architectural constraint that all members of a given local area network must exist in close physical proximity to each other. This property allows all servers to be maintained at a secure, centralized location with technical support personnel, while users of that LAN server may be physically located at another location. As virtual LANs grow in sophistication, configuration and management become more of an issue. The trend toward autoconfiguring LAN switches and more sophisticated monitoring and management reporting tools should allow virtual LANs to be more easily integrated into an enterprise network. From a management perspective, perhaps the biggest stumbling block to widespread acceptance of virtual LANs and the LAN switches on which they are deployed is the current lack of open, industrywide standards for multivendor LAN switch and virtual LAN interoperability.

Bandwidth Hierarchy

One of the overriding principles of the logical design of enterprise networks is the creation and management of a structured **bandwidth hierarchy.** Creating a bandwidth hierarchy as part of a strategic network design, allows required bandwidth to be upgraded incrementally in a planned fashion rather than replacing networking technology wholesale, in reaction to a crisis crippling network performance.

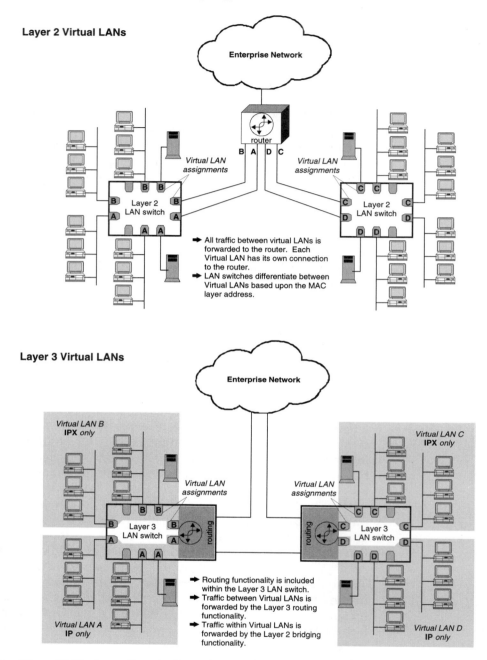

Figure 16-11   Layer 2 versus Layer 3 Virtual LANs: An Architectural Comparison

Adherence to the top-down model should produce anticipated bandwidth requirements as an outcome of the analysis of the applications and their associated data which must traverse various levels of the enterprise network. As one calculates application and data requirements for each location and groups of locations on the enterprise network, the required bandwidth necessary to produce required response times falls within the range of one of the available network services con-

Virtual LAN Characteristic	Layer 2 Virtual LAN Functionality	Layer 3 Virtual LAN Functionality
Configuration	Simpler	More difficult
Expense	Less expensive, but may require external routers	More expensive, but include internal routing capability
Performance	Faster since they only process layer 2 addresses	Up to 30% slower since they must process layer 3 protocols
Nonroutable protocols	No problem since this is a layer 2–only device	May be able to segregate into a separate VLAN or may not be able to handle
Routable protocols	No ability to differentiate between layer 3 protocols	Can differentiate between layer 3 protocols and build separate virtual LANs based on the layer 3 protocol. Layer 3 switches vary in the number of routable protocols supported
Multiswitch virtual LANs	Must use proprietary switch-to-switch communication, which adds to network traffic congestion in most cases	Able to use subnetwork numbers in network layer addresses to keep track of virtual LANs, which span multiple switches without the need for proprietary switch-to-switch protocols
Broadcasts	Broadcasts to all segments which belong to a particular virtual LAN	Can broadcast to only appropriate subnetwork within a virtual LAN
Filtering	No filtering on network layer addresses or protocols possible	Filtering on network layer addresses and protocols for security and virtual LAN segmentation by protocol
Routing capabilities	Must be supplied by external router	Included with built-in routing software, which provides traffic management and protocol isolation; some layer 3 switches are able to communicate with routers via RIP or OSPF while others are not

Figure 16-12   Layer 2 versus Layer 3 Virtual LANs: A Functional Comparison

tained in an enterprise network's bandwidth hierarchy. Figure 16-13 illustrates one example of an enterprise network bandwidth hierarchy.

Other bandwidth hierarchies for other enterprise networks are possible and equally correct. No single correct bandwidth hierarchy applies universally to all enterprise networks. As a result, taking a top-down approach to each enterprise networking opportunity is absolutely essential.

As the figure illustrates, the bandwidth needs of local area networks are often initially met by a shared-media LAN network architecture such as Ethernet or Token Ring. Once local area network traffic begins to burden given network segments,

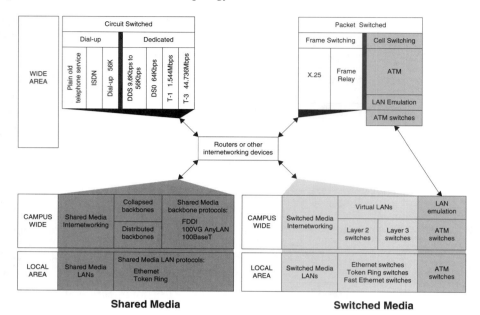

Figure 16-13   Enterprise Network Bandwidth Hierarchy

logical segmentation through the use of bridges will reduce the amount of traffic on each segment. Bridges are an example of shared-media internetworking. Physically, shared-media internetworking can be accomplished via two backbone architectures:

- **Distributed backbones** were once the norm in which individual LAN segments are linked to a backbone LAN media via bridges and transceivers. These backbone networks often ran vertically between floors of a building while multiple, horizontal LAN segments were distributed throughout the building and attached to the backbone via bridges.

- **Collapsed backbones,** a more recent innovation, collapse the entire network backbone, which once spanned several floors of a building, into the backplane of a single internetworking device such as a router. The backplane of the router shared by numerous internetworking modules has enormous bandwidth capacity, usually in the gigabits per second range.

Figure 16-14 contrasts distributed and collapsed backbone architectures for shared-media internetworking.

Higher-speed backbone network architectures such as FDDI, 100BaseT, or 100VGAnyLAN offer incremental upgrades to overburdened LAN segments as well as serving as a backbone protocol for linking internetworking devices such as routers. Servers can be linked directly to the higher-speed backbone network rather than to a LAN segment of Ethernet or Token Ring.

Another upgrade alternative when shared LAN segments running Ethernet or Token Ring become overburdened is to install switched LAN media technology such as a LAN switch. As described in the previous section, LAN switches can also support virtual LANs which can be linked via layer 2 or 3 LAN switches. In some cases, LAN switches support proprietary higher-speed switch-to-switch transmission links. Ethernet switches are by far the most common LAN switch, although

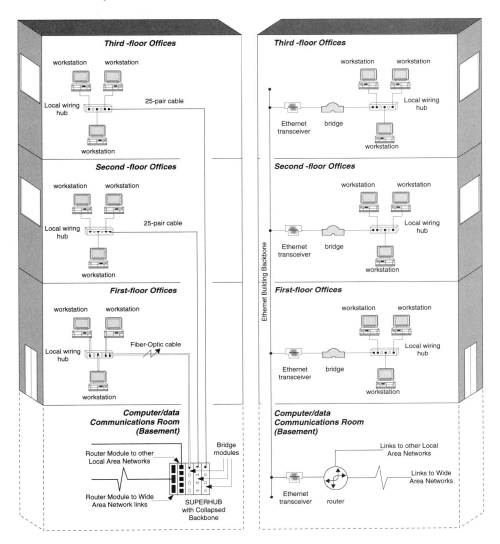

Figure 16-14 Collapsed versus Distributed Backbones

Token Ring and FDDI switches are also available. Some LAN switches also support more than one network architecture, with Ethernet switches supporting both 10 and 100 Mbps speeds being the most common example of this type of switch.

If the switched bandwidth offered by traditional LAN switches is not sufficient, a faster switching technology known as **asynchronous transfer mode,** or **ATM,** is also available. One of the real benefits of ATM is its ability to switch LAN traffic without the need to make any hardware or software changes to LAN clients or servers. This transparent delivery of LAN information via ATM, known as **LAN emulation** is explained in more detail later. Another key benefit of ATM is its scalability in terms of both transmission speed and geographic scope of coverage. While ATM transmission speeds have been defined up to 2.4 Gbps (Gigabits per second), its geographic scope of coverage spans from LAN-based switches to wide area ATM network services offered by long distance carriers. The net effect of ATM's availability from the LAN to the WAN is that virtual LANs can be established over long distances using ATM switches as the virtual LAN bandwidth provider. In addition, ATM can simultaneously transmit voice, video, data, and image between network locations.

Alternatively, as local area network information needs to be shared over the wide area, more traditional circuit-switched and packet-switched WAN services can be purchased from a variety of WAN service providers. As a network analyst, it is important to know which WAN services are available at each corporate location, including remote branches and telecommuting sites.

Managerial Perspective

The importance of a bandwidth hierarchy as part of a strategic network plan is that network segments can be offered required bandwidth as needed without having to rewrite or modify the applications that use them. In addition, due to the availability of incrementally increasing levels of bandwidth in a bandwidth hierarchy, bandwidth requirements can be met with a minimum of service disruption, an increasingly important issue as networks become mission-critical to corporate survival.

■ ENTERPRISE NETWORK PHYSICAL DESIGN

Architectures versus Marketectures

As network managers and strategic network planners have sought strategic migration paths for enterprise network architectures, vendors of internetworking equipment have been quick to respond with their individual views of the future of enterprise network design. To persuade potential customers to commit to today's technology, savvy internetworking technology vendors articulate migration paths to the higher performance enterprise network architectures of tomorrow while preserving customers' current technology investments. These single-vendor migration paths through increasingly sophisticated and high-performance enterprise network architectures are commonly referred to as **marketectures.** Although many competing internetworking technology vendors have proposed their own individual plans, these plans tend to have a great deal in common when the marketing hype is removed revealing the actual enterprise network architectures and physical topologies beneath. Among the enterprise network marketectures and their vendors are the following:

Marketecture Name	Vendor
HPSN (high-performance scalable networking)	3Com Corp.
Baysis	Bay Networks, Inc.
Securefast Virtual Networking	Cabletron Systems, Inc.
Ciscofusion	Cisco Systems Inc.
Clearpath	Crosscomm Corp.
EnVisn (enterprise virtual intelligent switched networks)	DEC
SVN (switched virtual networking)	IBM
Vivid	Newbridge

ATM as a Common Switching Platform

One characteristic the various vendors' views of the future of enterprise networking share is that ATM will serve as the high-speed switched backbone network service to connect geographically dispersed corporate networks. As a result, all of the previously listed physical topologies depend on ATM as their wide area switching platform, sometimes referred to as an underlying switching fabric. As was previously discussed in the section on virtual LANs, layer 2 switching, no matter how fast, is not by itself a sufficient enterprise network platform. As a result, routing capabilities must be added to the underlying switching capabilities ATM offers. How the routing capabilities are added to the ATM switching fabric, and the subsequent enterprise network performance characteristics exhibited as a result of those routing capabilities, are the basic differences between alternative enterprise network physical topologies.

ATM LAN Emulation   Since ATM acts as a layer 2 switching service, and since layer 2 LAN switches support virtual LANs, it stands to reason that ATM switches ought to be able to support virtual LANs as well. In fact, through a process known as **ATM LAN emulation,** virtual LANs can be constructed over an ATM switched network regardless of the geographic scope of that network. ATM LAN emulation is considered a bridging solution, like LAN switch–based virtual LANs, since traffic is switched based on MAC layer addresses. Unlike LAN switch–based virtual LANs, however, MAC layer addresses must be translated into, or resolved into, ATM addresses in a process known as **ATM address resolution.** In ATM LAN emulation, the ATM switching fabric adds an entire layer of its own addressing schemes, which it uses to forward virtual LAN traffic to its proper destination.

ATM LAN EMULATION ARCHITECTURE

In Sharper Focus

How MAC layer addresses are resolved into ATM addresses is defined by an ATM forum specification known as LAN emulation or more formally as LANE or LAN emulation user to network interface (L-UNI). The ATM LAN emulation specification actually defines an entire architecture of interacting software components to accomplish the ATM-to-MAC layer address resolution. Among the interacting components which cooperate to accomplish ATM LAN emulation, as illustrated in Figure 16-15, are the following:

- **LAN emulation client (LEC)** software may physically reside within ATM-to-LAN conversion devices or be included within a router that supports ATM interfaces. The job of the LEC is to appear to be an ATM end-station on behalf of the LAN client it represents. As a result, the LEC is sometimes referred to as a proxy ATM end-station. The LEC is also responsible for converting the LAN's data-link layer protocols (Ethernet, Token Ring, FDDI) into fixed-length ATM cells. Once the local LEC knows the ATM address of the remote LEC which is acting as an ATM proxy for the remote LAN destination, it sets up a switched virtual circuit, or switched network connection, to the remote LEC which subsequently delivers the information payload to the remote LAN workstation in a **unicast** (point-to-point) transmission.

- **LAN emulation server (LES)** software resides on a server or workstation directly attached to the ATM network with a unique ATM address. The LES

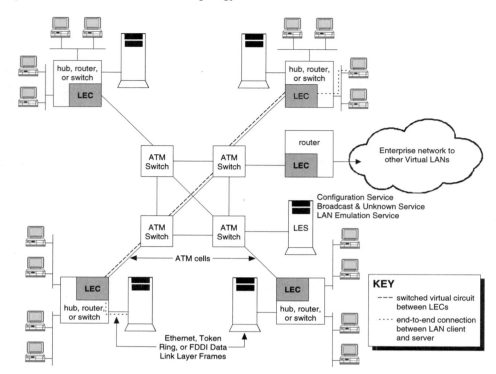

Figure 16-15 ATM LAN Emulation Architecture

software performs three major tasks or services, which can actually be accomplished by separate software programs executed on separate servers:

- LES **configuration services** are responsible for keeping track of the types of virtual LANs being supported over the ATM switching fabric and of which LECs belong to which type of LAN. MAC addresses and corresponding ATM addresses of attached workstations are stored by the configuration server. Keeping track of LAN type (Ethernet, Token Ring, FDDI) is important because of the variability of the maximum frame length that workstations attached to each type of LAN accept.

- LES **broadcast and unknown services (BUS)** are responsible for handling requests for broadcasts and multicasts within the virtual LANs which exist across the ATM switching fabric. In addition, if a LEC does not know the destination ATM address of a destination LAN workstation, it forwards that frame to the broadcast and unknown server, which broadcasts it throughout the virtual LAN on behalf of the LEC.

- LES **LAN emulation services** receive address resolution protocol (ARP) requests from LECs seeking the ATM addresses of destination LAN workstations for which the MAC address is known. Once the LES responds to the LEC with the requested ATM address, the LEC can set up the point-to-point connection to the destination LEC. If the LES does not respond right away, the LEC continues to use the BUS to broadcast the destination frame throughout the virtual LAN.

It is important to understand that ATM emulation, like other virtual LAN architectures built on layer 2 switching, is basically a bridged topology which suffers from the same limitations as other layer 2 switched networks:

- Flat network topology.

- Broadcast storms (although limited to a particular virtual LAN).

- No layer 3 filtering for security or segmentation.

On the other hand, because it does not discriminate between network layer (layer 3) protocols, ATM LAN emulation supports, or transports, multiple network layer protocols between virtual LANs.

Perhaps more important, however, ATM LAN emulation offers no routing capability. As a result, each virtual LAN which is emulated using ATM emulation, must still have a dedicated connection to a router which can process layer 3 addresses and make appropriate route determination and forwarding decisions between virtual LANs.

Layer 3 Protocols over ATM Networks   A variety of initiatives are underway by both the Internet Engineering Task Force (IETF) and the ATM Forum to somehow integrate layer 3 functionality with ATM networks. IETF Request for Comment (RFC) 1577 is known as **classical IP over ATM.** The goal of classical IP over ATM is to allow IP networks, as well as all upper layer TCP/IP protocols, utilities, and APIs encapsulated by IP, to be delivered over an ATM network without requiring modification to the TCP/IP protocols. Classical IP treats the ATM network like just another subnet or data-link protocol such as Ethernet or Token Ring. IP routers see the entire ATM network as only a single hop, regardless of the actual size of the ATM network. IP subnets established over ATM networks using this protocol are known as **logical IP subnets,** or **LIS.**

A significant limitation of classical IP over ATM is that it works only within a given subnet. As a result, an IP router must still be employed to use IP addresses to properly route data between classical IP subnets. Just as with ATM LAN emulation, classical IP over ATM also requires address resolution. In this case a new protocol known as **ATM address resolution protocol (ATMARP)** runs on a server in the logical IP subnet and provides address resolution between IP and ATM addresses. ATM addresses may actually be the virtual circuit ID numbers of the virtual circuits or connections established on the ATM network between two ATM end-points.

Understandably, classical IP over ATM supports only IP as a network layer protocol over ATM networks. Other initiatives are underway to support multiple network layer protocols over ATM. The ATM Forum is currently working on **Multiprotocols over ATM (MPOA)** which not only will support IP, IPX, AppleTalk and other network protocols over ATM, but also will be able to route data directly between virtual LANs, precluding the need for additional external routers. Routing implemented on switches using protocols, such as MPOA, is sometimes referred to as **cut-through routing** and uses ATM LAN emulation as its layer 2 switching specification. Like ATM LAN emulation, MPOA operates transparently to end-devices and does not require any hardware or software changes to those end-devices or their applications. Multiprotocol over ATM is actually an entire architecture, as illustrated in Figure 16-16, composed of the following key components:

- **Edge devices** might be a kind of hybrid hub, switch, and router acting as interfaces or gateways between LANs and the ATM network. Once the ATM

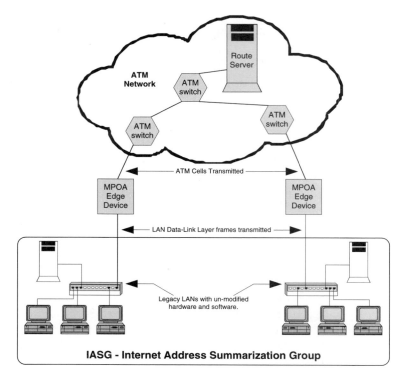

Figure 16-16 Multiprotocol over ATM Architecture

address is known, edge devices are capable of establishing new virtual circuits over the ATM network.

- A **route server** supplies edge devices with their routing information, including ATM addresses and virtual circuit IDs. The route server may actually be located within one of the ATM switches in the ATM backbone. Routing tables within the route server are organized according to layer 3 protocol-specific subnets, referred to as **internet address summarization groups (IASG).**

While MPOA defines multiprotocol communications between ATM end-stations and a given route server, another ATM forum specification known as **integrated private network-to-network interface (IPNNI)** defines how route servers are able to communicate path and address information to each other and to/from ATM switches over an ATM network. If multiple route servers are required on a given enterprise network, then a protocol such as IPNNI must be implemented to share the layer 3 information between ATM switches and route servers to allow the best path through the network to be selected dynamically.

The IETF is currently working on RFC 1483, **Multiprotocol Encapsulation over ATM Adaptation Layer 5.** One of the significant contributions of this proposal is that it defines two ways in which multiple network layer protocols can be transmitted simultaneously over an ATM network. The first method, LLC/SNAP encapsulation, places indicators in the ATM data-link layer frame to identify which network layer protocols are embedded within that data-link layer frame. The second method, virtual channel-based multiplexing, establishes a separate virtual circuit, or connection, through the ATM network, for each network layer protocol transported from one workstation to another.

Alternative Physical Topologies

Most of the vendor-specific enterprise network marketectures previously listed view the following physical topologies as viable migration paths for the enterprise network:

- **Layer 2 switches plus independent routing.**
- **Distributed routing.**
- **Route servers.**

Although migration between the alternative physical topologies is possible and, in some cases, desirable, each physical topology has advantages and disadvantages, and is optimally implemented in distinct situations. These alternative physical topologies vary in the hardware technology required for their implementation. Not all marketecture vendors offer, or plan to offer, all three of these predominant views of the future of enterprise networking.

Layer 2 Switches Plus Independent Routing   The first alternative physical topology alternative has already been discussed in both the virtual LAN and ATM LAN emulation sections. Layer 2 switches are employed to provide bandwidth and control broadcasts within virtual LANs while independent routers are employed to control traffic between virtual LANs and connect the switched virtual LANs to the enterprise backbone. One problem with this topology is that the routers add significant latency to the intervirtual LAN traffic, thereby constituting both a potential network bottleneck and single point of failure. To be specific, routers can add as much as a 5-millisecond delay for processing each packet while layer 2 switches typically add only 100 microseconds of delay. One of the advantages of this architecture is that existing routers can be used to provide routing capabilities while relatively inexpensive layer 2 switches are added for increased LAN bandwidth. Figure 16-17 illustrates the physical topology of a layer 2 switch plus independent routers.

Distributed Routing   Rather than concentrating the routing functionality into a single device, distributed routing spreads the routing functionality across several devices. Using devices known alternatively as **layer 3 switches** or **multilayer switches,** routing functionality between virtual LANs is performed without the need for conventional routers. Routing tables must be maintained in the multilayer switches just as in conventional routers. Traffic is transferred between VLANs when the multilayer switch uses the subnet numbers embedded in the layer 3 address to search routing tables for the switch port to which the destination virtual LAN is attached. Creating switched connections based on subnet numbers by the multilayer switch is significantly less sophisticated than the complicated route determination, security, and filtering functions conventional routers perform. As a result, the minimal routing by the multilayer switch does not add nearly the latency of a conventional router. Most multilayer switch vendors report a maximum performance drop of between 1 and 30% when layer 3 switching must transfer data between, rather than within, virtual LANs.

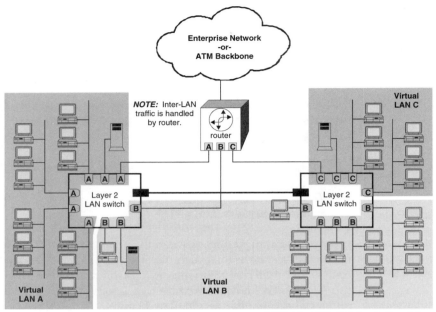

Figure 16-17   Layer 2 Switches Plus Independent Routing

Since the multilayer switches are used only for connecting virtual LANs, a smaller number of conventional routers are still required in the distributed routing topology to link switched virtual LANs with wide area network interfaces or to the enterprise network backbone. Figure 16-18 illustrates a distributed routing physical topology.

Route Servers   A route server–based physical topology actually employs both a route server and a number of auxiliary devices known as **edge switches**. The route server–based physical topology is also sometimes referred to as **virtual routing**. A route server physical topology recognizes that routing is actually not one, but two, distinct functions: route determination and packet forwarding. The route server's primary job is to maintain all routing information in a single centralized location and service the edge switches requests for routing information. The route server also handles any required route discovery.

Since the primary task of the edge switches is packet forwarding, they are loaded with only a minimum of routing information which is most often kept in fast cache memory. Like multilayer switches, edge switches make routing decisions based on the subnet IDs in the network layer destination addresses embedded within the data-link layer frames. Edge switches query the route server when they encounter unknown addresses. A route server–based physical topology, as illustrated in Figure 16-19, is best for a large distributed network with numerous virtual LANs.

Although the route server may represent a single point of failure, redundant servers and fault-tolerant systems should be able to overcome that shortcoming. One good aspect of the route server is that all routing information only needs to be maintained from a single location since edge switches are updated from the route

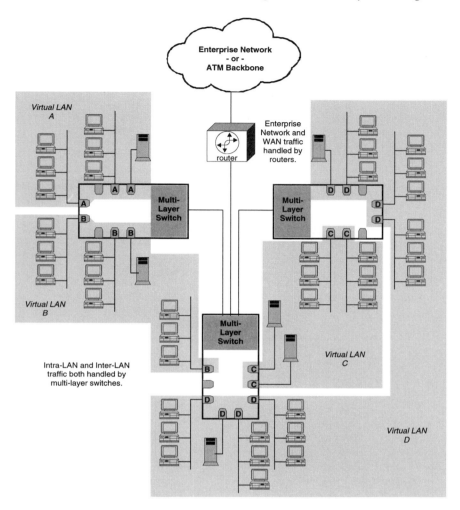

Figure 16-18   Distributed Routing

server. However, the impact on network traffic of the route server updating multiple edge switches may be worth investigating. These updates between route servers and edge switches are via proprietary communications protocols which limits route server physical topologies to single-vendor solutions.

Relational Networks   A final enterprise network topology, known as **relational networks,** seeks to overcome the need to manually configure and maintain virtual LAN configuration tables in multilayer switches and route servers through a process known as **automatic configuration.** This automatic configuration is possible only with the use of a hybrid hardware device known as a **relational switch,** which combines the capabilities of multilayer switches and ATM switches. Alternatively stated, virtual LANs plus automatic configuration yield relational networks.

Automatic configuration in relational switches is possible thanks to sophisticated software which can automatically detect not only the MAC layer addresses of attached devices, but also the layer 2 and layer 3 network protocols executing on

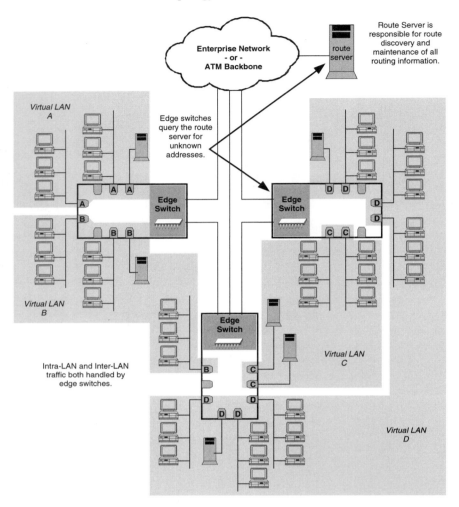

Figure 16-19   Route Servers

those devices. Workstations and servers using similar network protocols are auto-matically grouped together into relational networks. Separate relational LANs are established for each layer 3 protocol, and all nonroutable protocols are included in a single relational LAN. Newly added or moved workstations or servers can be auto-matically detected and added to the appropriate relational LAN. Although the rela-tional switches handle traffic delivery within the relational networks, conventional routers are still required to direct traffic between relational networks.

SUMMARY

As competitive pressures have forced businesses to accomplish more with fewer employees, distributed information systems and the

underlying enterprise networks which link businesses with their trading partners, as well as with telecommuting and remote employees, have taken on mission-critical roles. The analysis, design, and implementation of enterprise networks must deal not only with the wide area geographic scope of such networks but also with the multiplatform, multiprotocol, multivendor reality of the distributed information systems they must deliver.

To bring some structure to this apparent myriad of choices, distributed computing architectures such as DCE offer transparently interoperable services for distributed applications. A broad category of software known as middleware provides more specific interoperability services for databases, messaging, objects, and transaction monitoring. In general, middleware's role is to act as an insulator between distributed client/server applications and the enterprise network which must deliver them.

The most significant trend in the logical design of enterprise networks is the virtual LAN. By added configuration capabilities to existing LAN switches, virtual LANs are able to offer switched bandwidth on demand while confining broadcasts and multicasts to designated

workstations. Virtual LANs which span multiple switches do so by proprietary protocols. Since virtual LANs depend on layer 2 LAN switches for bandwidth management, routing capabilities between virtual LANs must be supplied by either independent routers or specialized multilayer switches which create switched connections based on network layer subnet addresses.

Nearly all enterprise network physical designs include ATM as their basic underlying switching fabric. Designs differ primarily in how routing capabilities are added to ATM's switching capabilities. Some designs favor independent routers while others prefer hybrid multilayer switches which can both switch and route. Route server or virtual routing designs concentrate all routing maintenance and configuration in a single server, which is responsible for providing routing services to edge switches. Finally, relational networks start with the premise that beyond combining routing and switching in a single device, enterprise networks should also be automatically configured by such devices without the need for constant configuration maintenance by networking personnel.

KEY TERMS

REVIEW QUESTIONS

1. Describe some of the business motivations for the development of enterprise networks.
2. Describe the relationship between virtual corporations, virtual workgroups, and virtual LANs.
3. What is the importance of architectures in the development of distributed applications such as the DCE environment?
4. What is the overall purpose of the services available within the DCE environment?
5. How does the DCE threads service differ from multithreaded operating systems?
6. What is the difference between DCE-compliant and DCE-compatible? Give an example of each.
7. What is middleware, and what is its relationship to distributed applications and the enterprise network?
8. From an application development standpoint, what is the alternative to middleware?
9. Describe the major categories of middleware.
10. Differentiate between the functionality, advantages, and disadvantages of RPC middleware and message-oriented middleware.
11. Why is transaction processing monitor middleware especially important in the distributed client/server environment?
12. What are some of the current limitations characteristic of the middleware market in general?
13. What is two-phase commit, and why is it important?
14. What is the relationship of middleware application development tools to middleware, and why are they important?

15. How does the functionality of a virtual LAN differ from that offered by a simple LAN switch?
16. What are the advantages of a virtual LAN over a shared media LAN?
17. What are some of the key limitations of virtual LANs?
18. What are some of the ways in which the limitations of virtual LANs can be overcome?
19. Why is transmission between layer 2 switches important, and what is the current status of protocol standardization for such communications?
20. What is IEEE 802.10?
21. Why must routing be used to transmit selectively between virtual LANs?
22. What are some of the alternative ways in which routing can be used to transmit between virtual LANs?
23. What are the key functional differences between layer 2 and layer 3 switches?
24. What is the importance of developing a bandwidth hierarchy to enterprise network design?
25. Differentiate between distributed and collapsed backbones.
26. What are some of the advantages of ATM?
27. What is a marketecture, and how can network analysts effectively compare them?
28. What is ATM LAN emulation, and what are its advantages and limitations?
29. How is ATM LAN emulation actually implemented?
30. How are ATM addresses mapped to LAN addresses?

31. What is the purpose of the configuration service?
32. What is the purpose of the broadcast and unknown service?
33. Compare the advantages, disadvantages, and limitations of the alternatives being developed for routing over ATM.
34. What is the difference between routing and cut-through routing?
35. Differentiate between the three enterprise network physical topologies described within the chapter in terms of proper application, advantages, disadvantages, limitations, required hardware, and level of required support, maintenance, management.
36. What is virtual routing?
37. How does a relational network differ from a virtual network?
38. What are some of the key advantages of a relational network?
39. What are the unique hardware requirement of relational networks?
40. What are the advantages and limitations of automatic configuration?

ACTIVITIES

1. Research and report on the results of the relationship between business trends and enterprise network design. Cite specific examples of how enterprise networks have taken on increasingly mission-critical roles.
2. Research virtual corporations and describe the technology required to enable them.
3. Research the current status of both the OSF and DCE. How is the OSF funded? What is the current strategic mission of the OSF compared with when it was founded? How widely adopted is DCE, and what are its future prospects? What are the key benefits and limitations of DCE?
4. Research Novell's and Microsoft's current commitment to DCE. What is the effect of these commitments?
5. Using buyers guides and product specifications, prepare a comparative analysis of the middleware market. What are the product categories and market leaders within each category? What are the important functional trends in middleware?
6. Prepare a survey of businesses or organizations in your area. How many are employing LAN switches? Of this number, what percentage are employing virtual LANs? What was their reason for implementing virtual LANs? What kinds of benefits have the virtual LANs offered? Were there any complications, either anticipated or unanticipated?
7. Research and report on the results of your investigation into the development of the IEEE 802.10 standard or other standards development efforts for layer 2 switch communication.
8. Research the current marketectures being proposed as enterprise network design visions by a variety of vendors. Report on the similarities and differences among their respective visions.
9. Research the topic of relational networking, and report on the level of their acceptance in terms of the number of vendors shipping technology that supports it as well as the level of implementation.

FEATURED REFERENCES

General References

Held, Gilbert. *Interconnecting LANs and WANs: Concepts, Techniques and Methods* (New York: John Wiley & Sons, 1993).

Enterprise Network Architecture/Design

Adam, Joel et al. Media-Intensive Data Communications in a "Desk Area" Network. *IEEE Communications*, 32; 8 (August 1994), 60.

Ball, D. Integrating Voice and Data over Frame Relay. *Telecommunications*, 29; 12 (December 1995), 56.

Ben-Yosef, Glenn. Toward a New Model: Where to Switch? Where to Route? *Business Communications Review*, 25; 9 (September 1995), 41.

Hart, John. Speeding Up and Reaching Out. *Network Computing*, 5; 14 (November 15, 1994), 81.

Kaufman, H. PBXs, Computers, and the Trend Toward ATM. *Telecommunications*, 29; 12 (December 1995), 51.

Korzeniowski, Paul. ATM Provides Therapy for Aching Network Backbones. *Network World*, 12; 37 (September 11, 1995), 1L.

Marshall, William. Virtual, Relational, Ubiquitous Networking. *Network Computing*, 5; 14 (November 15, 1994), 109.

McQuillan, John. Planning Networks without Network

Planning. *Business Communications Review,* 25; 7 (July 1995), 10.

Molta, Dave. Confessions of a Network Evangelist. *Network Computing,* 5; 14 (November 15, 1994), 111.

Morency, John and Nick Lippis. The Cost of Network Complexity. *Network World,* 12; 31 (July 31, 1995), 44.

Olsen, R.P. Relational Networking: A New Model for Local Backbones. *Telecommunications,* 29; 12 (December 1995), 33.

Pieper, R. Building Your Enterprise Network Using a Bandwidth Hierarchy. *Telecommunications,* 29; 9 (September 1995), 37.

Routt, Thomas. ATM Essentials—Switched Network Integration. *Business Communications Review,* 25; 9 (September 1995), ATM2.

Routt, Thomas. IBM's Switched Virtual Networking Strategy. *Business Communications Review,* 25; 9 (September 1995), ATM9.

Saunders, Stephen. Next-Generation Routing: Making Sense of the Marketectures. *Data Communications,* 24; 12 (September 1995), 52.

Schmidt, Ronald. Redoing the Enterprise. *Network Computing,* 5; 14 (November 15, 1994), 84.

Schwartz, Jeffrey. What Drives the Network? *Communications Week,* no. 566 (July 17, 1995), S12.

Violino, Bob. Bringing Harmony to Business Systems. *Information Week,* no. 547 (October 2, 1995), 34.

Wickre, P. Branch Networks: Evaluating Frame Relay vs. Data Link Switching. *Telecommunications,* 29; 12 (December 1995), 45.

DCE

Dickman, Alan. How to Engineer DCE Deployment. *Information Week,* no. 536 (July 17, 1995), 58.

Johnson, Johna. Distributed Computing Comes to the Mainframe. *Data Communications,* 24; 14 (October 1995), 39.

Millikin, Michael. DCE: Building the Distributed Future. *Byte,* 19; 6 (June 1994), 125.

Robertson, Bruce, DCE: Night of the Living Dead, or Dawn? *Network Computing,* 6; 10 (September 1, 1995), 119.

ATM Switches and Access Devices

Bellman, B. ATM Edge Switched: Evaluating Features and Functionality. *Telecommunications,* 29; 9 (September 1995), 29.

Gage, Beth. Frame Relay, Meet ATM. *Network World,* 12; 45 (November 6, 1995), 57.

Mandeville, Robert. The ATM Stress Test. *Data Communications,* 24; 3 (March 1995), 68.

Mandeville, Robert. ATM Switches: The Great Unknowns. *Data Communications,* 24; 5 (April 1995), 99.

Mier, Edwin and Robert Smithers. ATM to the Desktop. *Communications Week,* no. 575 (September 25, 1995), 129.

Taylor, Kieran. ATM Switching: Freedom of Choice. *Data Communications,* 24; 1 (January 1995), 46.

Taylor, Kieran. Concentrating on Keeping ATM Prices Down. *Data Communications,* 24; 4 (March 21, 1995), 45.

Taylor, Kieran. Starting Small with ATM. *Data Communications,* 24, 1 (January 1995), 56.

TCP/IP and ATM

Chao, H. Jonathan et al. IP on ATM Local Area Networks. *IEEE Communications,* 32; 8 (August 1994), 52.

Marshall, George. Classical IP over ATM: A Status Report. *Data Communications,* 24; 17 (December 1995), 103.

McQuillan, John. TCP/IP and ATM: Sibling Rivalry or Generation Gap? *Business Communications Review,* 24; 11 (November 1994), 10.

Sammartino, Fred. ATM Design Issues. *Communications Systems Design,* 1; 8 (December 1995), 15.

Witt, Michael. Running TCP/IP over ATM Networks. *Telecommunications,* 29, 7 (July 1995), 53.

Virtual LANs/LAN Emulation

Bellman, Robert. Evolving Traditional LANs to ATM. *Business Communications Review,* 24; 10 (October 1994), 43.

Chernicoff, David. Making the Switch to Virtual Networking. *PC Week,* 12; 26 (July 3, 1995), N/1.

Cohen, Jodi. VLANs Set to Enhance Their Value Through Policy-based Management. *Network World,* 12; 33 (August 14, 1995), 23.

Duffy, Jim. Cisco Spearheads Industry Push for Multivendor VLANs. *Network World,* 12; 24 (June 12, 1995), 1.

Jeffries, Ron. ATM LAN Emulation: The Inside Story. *Data Communications,* 23; 13 (September 21, 1994), 95.

King, Steven. Switched Virtual Networks. *Data Communications,* 23; 12 (September 1994), 66.

Kroder, Stan and Robert Mercer. VSATs Link Far-Flung LANs. *Business Communications Review,* 24; 10 (October 1994), 51.

Layland, Robin. Virtual LANs Reality Check. *Data Communications,* 24; 4 (March 21, 1995), 23.

Lippis, Nick and Rolf McClellan. Gauging Service Options for Global LAN Interconnect. *Data Communications,* 23; 14 (October 1994), 78.

McLean, Michelle. Windows '95 Highlights Potential Virtual LAN, DHCP Address Conflict. *LAN Times,* 12; 14 (July 24, 1995), 1.

Morency, John. Do VLANs Really Deliver? *Business Communications Review,* 25; 7 (July 1995), 39.

Olsen, Bob. The One, Two, Three of Building Virtual LANs. *Network World,* 12; 44 (October 30, 1995), 49.

Peri, Ron. What It Will Take to Make Virtual LANs a Net Reality. *Communications Week,* no. 577 (September 28, 1995), 47.

Ruber, Peter. Router Aims to Redirect vLAN Traffic. *LAN Times,* 12; 25 (December 4, 1995), 47.

Salamone, Salvatore. Virtual LANs Get Real. *Byte,* 20; 5 (May 1995), 181.

Saunders, Stephen. Making Virtual LANs a Virtual Snap. *Data Communications,* 24; 1 (January 1995), 72.

Schurr, Amy. Buying into a Virtual Plan. *PC Week,* 12; 26 (July 3, 1995), N/4.

Swallow, George. Transparency Key to Multiprotocol over ATM. *Network World,* 12; 42 (October 16, 1995), 37.

Truong, Hong et al. LAN Emulation on an ATM Network. *IEEE Communications,* 33; 5 (May 1995), 70.

Wittman, Art. LAN Emulation, Virtual LANs and the Reality of ATM. *Network Computing,* 6; 4 (April 1, 1995), 150.

Wittman, Art. VLANs: Dispelling Myths. *Network Computing,* 6; 13 (October 15, 1995), 120.

Frame Relay

Gareiss, Robin. The Frame Relay Explosion. *Data Communications,* 24; 2 (February 1995), 58.

Taylor, Kieran. From Frames to Cells: Low-Speed Access to ATM. *Data Communications,* 24; 6 (May 1995), 47.

ATM Services/Standards

Gareiss, Robin. An ATM Service for Wide Open Spaces. *Data Communications,* 24; 4 (March 21, 1995), 43.

Jeffries, Ron. Enough Hype About ATM—What's Real Today? *Network Computing,* 5; 6 (July 1, 1994), 136.

Kavak, Nail. Data Communication in ATM Networks. *IEEE Network,* 9; 3 (May/June 1995), 28.

McLean, Michelle. ATM Growing Pains. *LAN Times,* 12; 26 (December 18, 1995), 1.

Nielsen, Jim. ATM Standard Promises Switch Interoperability. *Network World,* 12; 35 (August 28, 1995), 49.

Swallow, George. PNNI: Weaving a Multivendor ATM Network. *Data Communications,* 23; 18 (December 1994), 102.

Vickers, Brett and Tatsuya Suda. Connectionless Service for Public ATM Networks. *IEEE Communications,* 32; 8 (August 1994), 34.

Wayner, Peter. On the Road to ATM. *Byte,* 19; 9 (September 1994), 103.

Security

Johnson, Johna. Proper Protection for Proprietary Traffic. *Data Communications,* 24; 7 (May 21, 1995), 97.

Liebmann, Lenny. How to Protect Distributed Data. *Communications Week,* no. 577 (September 28, 1995), 53.

Moore, Mitchell. The Role of Cryptography in Network Security. *Business Communications Review,* 25; 9 (September 1995), 67.

Middleware/Distributed Objects

Dolgicer, Max. Messaging Middleware: The Next Generation. *Data Communications,* 23; 10 (July 1994), 77.

Dorshkind, Brent. Apps Get Networked Services. *LAN Times,* 12; 14 (July 24, 1995), 56.

Eckerson, Wayne. Searching for the Middle Ground. *Business Communications Review,* 25; 9 (September 1995), 46.

Girishankar, Saroja. Distributed Object Technology: Objects of Frustration. *Communications Week,* no. 560 (June 5, 1995), 43.

Greenbaum, Joshua. Middleware. *LAN Times,* 12; 16 (August 28, 1995), 67.

Hayes, Frank. Object Lesson in Patience. *Information Week,* no. 536 (July 17, 1995), 40.

Johnson, Johna. Software Guarantees Data Delivery. *Data Communications,* 24; 5 (April 1995), 45.

Leach, Norvin. PeerLogic Widens Pipes Platform. *PC Week,* 12; 41 (October 16, 1995), 29.

Mann, John. Message-Oriented Middleware. *Network Computing,* 5; 14 (November 15, 1994), 72.

Marshall, Martin. Microsoft, OMG Take New Steps. *Communications Week,* no. 563 (June 26, 1995), 15.

Orfali, Robert and Dan Harkey. Client/Server with Distributed Objects. *Byte,* 20; 4 (April 1995), 151.

Passmore, David. DCE vs. NDS: Will Middleware Worlds Collide? *Business Communications Review,* 24; 9 (September 1994), 24.

Rao, Bindu. Making the Most of Middleware. *Data Communications,* 24; 12 (September 1995), 89.

Robertson, Bruce. APIware vs. Middleware. *Network Computing,* 5; 15 (December 1, 1994), 120.

Tibbitts, Fred, CORBA: A Common Touch for Distributed Applications. *Data Communications,* 24; 7 (May 21, 1995), 71.

CASE STUDY

Chapter 16

UTILITY MIGRATES TO WIRELESS

Jacksonville Electric's Mobile System Saves Time, Paperwork

One year ago, the Jacksonville Electric Authority (JEA) in Jacksonville, Fla., decided to augment its audio communications network with wireless technology. For Paul Bodenstein, the company's professional engineer, the decision was complex and risky, especially because wireless-data network technology is still in its infancy.

Officials at JEA wanted a cost-effective solution that eliminated radio conversations and paperwork between central-site dispatchers and mobile troubleshooters, who restored power to customer sites as needed. The electric company also wanted an alternative communications network that could be used during storm emergencies.

After wireless packet-radio coverage was expanded to the Jacksonville area in January 1994, JEA enlisted the support of RAM Mobile Data in New York and Telepartner International Inc. in Farmington, Conn. RAM operates a nationwide wireless-data network, called Mobitex. The network lets mobile users transmit data through wireless links to central-site LANs.

JEA's installed base of 315,000 customers covers a 1,000-square-mile area in northeastern Florida. Executives decided to replace the utility's old field-dispatch system with an easy-to-use, wireless data-terminal system that could generate trouble tickets.

Before the new system, called Distribution System Restoration (DSR), JEA utility personnel would contact the mobile troubleshooters about a particular project several times. "Now, the dispatcher handles a piece of work once. More information is given to our troubleshooters without delays," said Bodenstein.

RAM's partner, Telepartner helped create JEA's wireless-data network. Telepartner's Mobi/3270 software provided the utility with a 50-user gateway that was compatible with JEA's IBM mainframes and front-end processors. Essentially, software troubleshooters see the same DSR software as if they were at the central site, said Bodenstein.

"The main reasons we were interested in RAM was because it saved us money in the infrastructure, such as base stations," said Bo-

denstein. "We could find nothing else that was reliable."

JEA has equipped each troubleshooter with a GRiD Systems Inc. 1680, DOS-compatible laptop and wireless-enabled Ericsson GE Mobile Communications Inc. C719 modems. The Telepartner Mobi/3270 software runs on the laptops and acts as the main driver for the trouble-ticket information returned to the dispatchers.

Bodenstein couldn't quantify the time saved by using the wireless-data trouble-ticket system. However, he said six out of nine trouble tickets are now done without radio communications.

"The dispatcher assigns the trouble ticket, and it appears on the individual's terminal immediately," said Bodenstein. "We have made it so the dispatcher can focus attention on the more critical things, such as the routing of power."

For troubleshooter Ronni Dicks, the learning curve associated with the wireless system has not been steep, and the system is a practical way for dealing with dispatchers.

"If there are problems in the coverage area, we can move antennas around. If we have trouble with the calls, we can fall back to radio [voice] communication," he said.

JEA is also working with the South Florida-based utility Florida Power and Light. When possible, the utilities assist each other during catastrophic disasters, such as hurricanes, by activating wireless-modem identifications. This lets people use the RAM network for identification of new wireless-modem subscribers.

The benefits for JEA from the new system have been tremendous. More than 35 vehicles (26 of which are trucks) and more than 40 employees use the wireless system.

Besides getting a corporate discount on the initial installation fee for the Mobitex network, JEA has eliminated a lot of paperwork, said Bodenstein. "We are able to provide people a lot more information and use critical communications on other channels," he added.

In addition to improving the communications of dispatch operations, JEA is expanding the use of its wireless system to other applications and operations.

The utility plans to create a more efficient system for repairing street lights. Currently, when street lights break or burn out, tickets are generated from the central office and given to troubleshooters.

Eventually, troubleshooters will have everything they need in one vehicle, from a customer's address to a power-source location. Now, information on damaged street lights is reported to troubleshooters instantly and is entered into their GRiD 1680 laptops after repairs, a process that also eliminates paperwork between dispatchers and troubleshooters. Other plans include providing wireless terminals to service-center workers and on-call customer-service representatives.

"We are trying to make it so every customer-service representative can take home his or her portable office in a briefcase," said Bodenstein.

JEA has not finished tinkering with wireless technology. In fact, its next step is to look into deploying a system based on the emerging Cellular Digital Packet Data (CDPD) network once CDPD coverage reaches the Jacksonville area and it meets JEA's strict pricing and performance standards, said Bodenstein.

Source: Stephen Loudermilk (February 13, 1995). Utility Migrates to Wireless. *LAN Times,* 12(3), 23. Reprinted with permission of McGraw-Hill, *LAN Times.*

BUSINESS CASE STUDY QUESTIONS

Activities

1. Complete a top-down model for this case by gleaning facts from the case and placing them in the proper layer of the top-down model. After completing the top-down model, analyze and detail those instances when requirements were clearly passed down from upper to lower layers of the model and solutions to those requirements were passed up from lower to upper layers.
2. Detail any questions that may occur to you about the case for which answers are not clearly stated in the article.

Business

1. What were some of the strategic business issues which brought about this change to the enterprise network?
2. What are some of the perceived benefits to date from the implementation of the enterprise network solution?
3. What specific business processes were streamlined in this case and how?
4. How did this enterprise network design extend and improve the current enterprise network?
5. What are some other ways in which the enterprise network might be further extended or improved?
6. How does the business enterprise expand during catastrophic disasters, and how must the enterprise network respond?

7. How did the implemented technology meet strategic business objectives?

Application

1. What special applications, if any, needed to be developed for the enterprise network?
2. How did the mobile clients link with legacy applications residing on the mainframe?
3. What other applications are slated to be delivered over the same enterprise network?
4. What might be the application implications of "trying to make it so every customer-service representative can take home his or her portable office in a briefcase"?

Data

1. What types of data are transmitted between mobile clients and corporate headquarters?

Network

1. What were some of the required functional characteristics for the enterprise network?
2. What emerging network service is the business in question considering and why?

Technology

1. Which network technology was chosen for the enterprise network and why?
2. What type of hardware is each mobile troubleshooter equipped with?

ENTERPRISE NETWORK APPLICATIONS AND MANAGEMENT

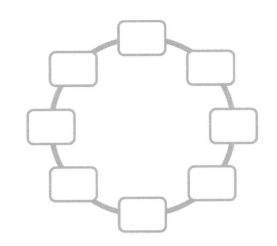

Concepts Reinforced

OSI model
Enterprise network architectures
Distributed information systems

Top-down model
Middleware
Protocols and interoperability

Concepts Introduced

Enterprise network applications
Enterprise e-mail interoperability
Enterprise database interoperability

Enterprise network security
Enterprise network management
Desktop management

OBJECTIVES

After mastering the material in this chapter you should:

1. Understand the interoperability issues and protocols involved with deploying applications across an enterprise network architecture.

2. Understand the interoperability issues and protocols involved with deploying distributed data management across an enterprise network architecture.

3. Understand the security issues and protocols involved with ensuring proper security for enterprise network applications.

4. Understand the functional requirements of desktop management and enterprise network management software.

5. Understand the interoperability and protocol issues involved with desktop management and enterprise network management software.

6. Understand the currently available technology for delivering desktop management and enterprise network management functionality.

The purpose of this chapter is to provide an awareness of the interoperability issues and protocols involved with deploying and managing applications across an enterprise network architecture. The perspective taken is that of a network analyst rather than an applications development or data management specialist. As a result, the discussion of enterprise network applications focuses on their impact on the enterprise network and how they interoperate and are properly managed. By understanding the impact of distributed applications and distributed data management on an enterprise network, a network analyst can help application development and data management specialists ensure successful deployment and management of their respective areas of responsibility across the enterprise network.

■ ENTERPRISE NETWORK APPLICATIONS

Enterprise Network Applications: A Network Analyst's Perspective

Figure 17-1 illustrates a conceptual view of the relationship between distributed applications, distributed data management, and the enterprise network. The challenge for the network analyst is to determine what types of services the enterprise network must provide to properly support distributed applications and distributed data management.

Following are some of the objectives of the enterprise network in supporting distributed applications and distributed data management:

- Enable anywhere, anytime access to data.

- Support current business paradigms such as virtual corporations, virtual offices, and virtual workgroups.

- Since distributed applications have become mission critical, the networks on which these applications depend are also mission critical, implying a need for the following:
  - Redundant network designs and deployment to avoid critical or catastrophic network failures.
  - Effective proactive rather than reactive monitoring and management of enterprise networks.
  - Effective association of the most appropriate available network service with each distributed application based on traffic type, bandwidth need, and delivery requirements.

Enterprise Network Applications: Overall Characteristics

Distributed applications that are delivered via enterprise networks are characterized by separate client and server portions of applications which are executed on a wide variety of computing platforms. The fact that any client portion can communicate with any server portion of a distributed application regardless of computing platform is an important characteristic of distributed computing known as **transparency.** In fact, transparency goes beyond just any client to any server communication, to include elements of fault tolerance as well. In other words, thanks to replicated servers and automated cut-over programs, a distributed client application program could shift communication to a replicated backup server in the event of primary server failure without ever being aware of the primary server failure.

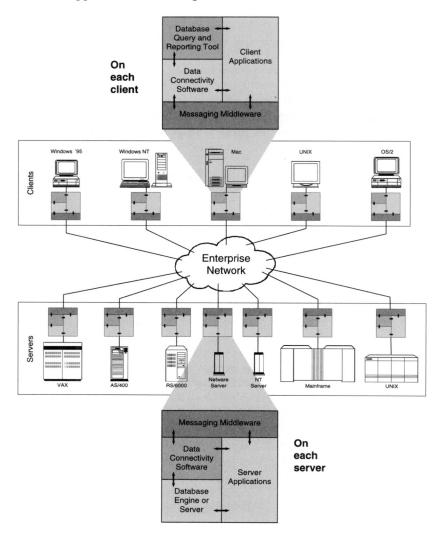

Figure 17-1   Enterprise Networks, Distributed Applications, and Distributed Data Management

Second, distributed computing is characterized by its **scalability.** If a given distributed application requires more processing power, additional servers can be added to the pool of processing power without any changes to client portions of the distributed applications. Adding servers for additional processing power is more specifically known as **horizontal scalability.** Applications which support horizontal scalability must be able to support multiserver directory synchronization, naming services, and replication. Alternatively, a server of lesser processing power can be replaced by a more powerful server if the distributed applications executing on that server support **vertical scalability.** Vertical scalability requires a given application to be able to operate over a variety of computing platforms and operating systems.

Enterprise Directory Services   All of this transparency and scalability, regardless of computing platform, requires a centralized source of information about all services and computing platforms attached to a given enterprise network. This central repository of information is called **enterprise directory services.** In addition to providing a single location for the storage and retrieval of network-related information, enterprise or centralized directory services also play a key role in supporting the fault-tolerant aspects of distributed applications. For example, if a given server crashes, the enterprise directory services knows which applications were running on that server, where replicated versions of that software and data currently reside, and which users are authorized to access each of the applications on the failed server and its replicated backup servers. Enterprise directory services are also essential in the support of virtual workgroups, providing a single point of login and allowing users to access services as desired by logical name, without keeping track of their varying physical locations.

Each client and server in a distributed information system must have the same view or understanding of the entire distributed information system. That single view is provided by the enterprise directory services. Physically, a copy of the enterprise directory services data is usually stored as part of the server network operating system. Clients query this server-based directory via client/server messaging. All servers in an enterprise network must keep their enterprise directory services' data synchronized by replicating changes throughout the enterprise network. In other words, all servers must share a common view of available enterprise directory services, regardless of the native platform or operating system of clients and servers. Figure 17-2 conceptually illustrates the relationship between distributed applications, enterprise directory services, and the enterprise network.

As is often the case in multivendor enterprise networks, multiple standards exist for enterprise directory services. Some are open standards supported by international standards-making organizations, and others are proprietary vendor-specific options. Figure 17-3 illustrates some of alternative enterprise directory services currently available.

Following are the vendors or standards-making organizations associated with each of the enterprise directory services listed in the figure:

Enterprise Directory Service	Vendor
X.500	Open Software Foundation
NetWare directory services	Novell
NT server directory services	Microsoft
Vines StreetTalk	Banyan
NetWare bindery	Novell
Notes	IBM/Lotus

The difficulty with multiple enterprise directory standards is that within a given organization, multiple proprietary enterprise directory services may exist. In such cases, it is essential that these enterprise directory services be able to interoperate, to reduce manual configuration and reconciliation of multiple, independent enterprise directory services. An overall directory service which could insulate client applications from these multiple enterprise directory services is known as a **metadirectory.** Microsoft has developed an enterprise directory API known as **Open Directory Services Interface (ODSI),** which interfaces between Windows clients and multiple enterprise directory services supporting the ODSI API.

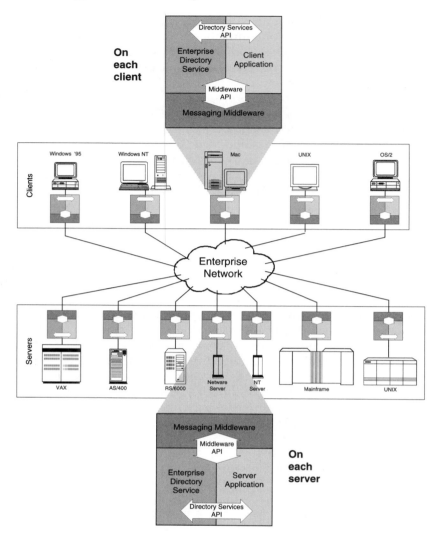

Figure 17-2 Distributed Applications, Enterprise Directory Services, and the Enterprise Network

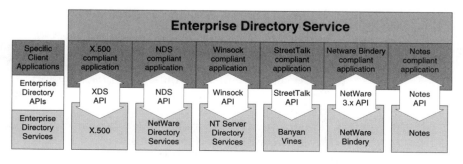

Figure 17-3 Enterprise Directory Services: Multiple Standards

X.500   Some might argue that a metadirectory already exists in the form of **X.500.** Strictly speaking, X.500 is an open specification for enterprise directory services which can be deployed in a distributed, replicated, hierarchical manner. X.500-compliant products are developed by a variety of vendors. However, because of selective implementation of portions of the X.500 specification, along with proprietary extensions to the standard, there is no guarantee that X.500-compliant directory services from different vendors will even interoperate. In addition, at least two major versions of the X.500 specification have been issued: one in 1988 and the most recent in 1993. It is important to know which version a given X.500 product supports.

X.500 products also vary according to the type of database in which the network directory information is stored. For example, some X.500 products may store directory information in Oracle or Informix databases while others use proprietary database formats. In addition, X.500 does not define the types of information, or **directory schema** which should be stored in these directory databases. This allows design flexibility for X.500 product vendors but leads to interoperability problems for the purchasers.

X.500 specifications also include a feature known as **certificate management,** which keeps track of which users are allowed to access which network resources. Figure 17-4 illustrates a conceptual view of both the architecture and protocols of X.500 enterprise directory services.

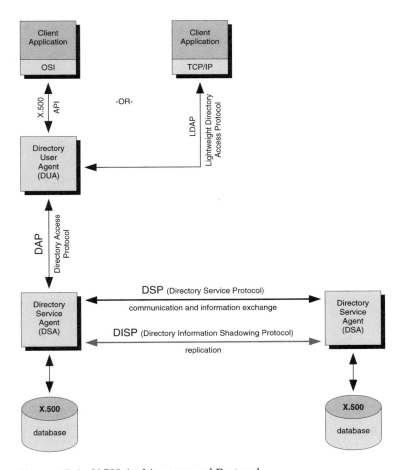

Figure 17-4   X.500 Architecture and Protocols

Enterprise E-Mail Issues

Objectives One of the first applications that required enterprisewide distribution and support of enterprise directory services is **enterprise e-mail**. Enterprise e-mail applications have undergone significant architectural change to take full advantage of the distributed nature of client/server architectures. The following are some of the functional objectives these architectural changes seek to achieve:

- Client and server portions of enterprise e-mail applications should be able to execute on a variety of computing platforms.

- Enterprise e-mail applications should be both horizontally and vertically scalable.

- Enterprise e-mail applications should be able to transparently integrate with other mail-enabled applications.

- Enterprise e-mail applications should support industry standard security procedures.

- Enterprise e-mail applications should support industry standard messaging architectures.

Architectures Support of industry standard messaging architectures is a key objective in understanding the architectural transition of enterprise e-mail applications. Traditionally, e-mail applications were monolithic, relying on network operating system–specific file systems and transport protocols for message storage and delivery.

However, the strategic role of enterprise e-mail has evolved from a single-purpose, monolithic application to an enterprisewide **messaging infrastructure.** Enterprise e-mail has become an enabling technology for other applications, providing standardized, real-time intelligent transport services. Allowing other applications to access enterprise e-mail messaging services enables enterprisewide collaborative work environments in which documents can be electronically routed transparently from within the application where the documents were created. Enterprise e-mail messaging systems enable group scheduling enterprise applications, as requests and replies for meetings are transparently delivered by the e-mail system from within the scheduling application.

Figure 17-5 illustrates the architectural transition from **shared file e-mail** systems, which depended on **store-and-forward messaging,** to **real-time e-mail** systems, which depend on **remote procedure call messaging,** and functional aspects of the two architectures are compared in Figure 17-6.

Managerial Perspective

From a network analyst's perspective, the key focus of enterprise e-mail systems should be on their basic architectural elements and the protocols employed to communicate between those architectural elements. Higher-level functional requirements can vary significantly from one enterprise e-mail system to another. These functional requirements are the result of business layer analysis and are the concern of applications development specialists and systems analysts. A network analyst is most concerned with the impact of the enterprise e-mail system on network performance.

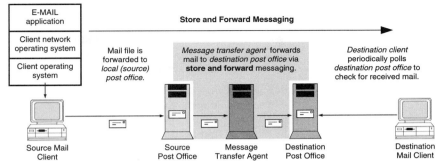

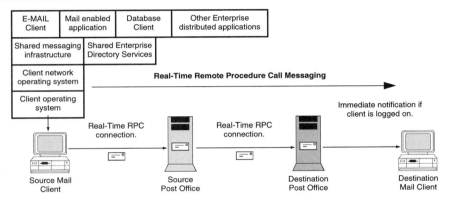

Figure 17-5   E-Mail Messaging Architectures: Shared-File versus Client/Server

E-Mail Architecture Characteristic	Shared-File Architecture	Client/Server Architecture
Application	Monolithic, single-purpose e-mail applications	Enterprisewide messaging infrastructure for use by e-mail application as well as mail-enabled applications and other client-server applications
Basic architecture	Shared-file relies on native file system of the network operating system over which it is installed	Client-server messaging delivers messages between client and server applications in real-time
Client role	Periodically polls local post office server to check for any newly received mail	Destination post office immediately notifies client of newly received mail. No client polling means less unnecessary traffic
Server role	Acts as depository of mail message files using native file system. Message transfer agent	Establishes real-time connections to destination post offices via remote procedure calls. Notifies

Figure 17-6   E-Mail Messaging Architectures: Functional Differences

(continued)

E-Mail Architecture Characteristic	Shared-File Architecture	Client/Server Architecture
	server software may need to execute on a separate server to route and forward messages to destination post offices	destination clients of receipt of new mail
Message delivery	Messages are treated like files and transferred between servers and stored in shared directories by message transfer agents (store-and-forward)	Remote procedure calls are used to deliver messages directly from the source e-mail client to the destination post office (real-time)
Connection time orientation	Not real time	Real time
Security	Based on access control mechanisms of network operating system's native file system	Enforced by servers at applications level as to both access control and allowed actions (read, write, append, delete)
Management and monitoring	More difficult, since message transfer is not real-time	Monitoring is easier due to real-time nature of connections and mail delivery. Among key management and monitoring issues are the following: • Ability to control connect time with remote post offices • Ability to monitor connection status • Ability to monitor traffic status • Ability to prepare usage or chargeback accounting reports • Ability to track usage logging
Suitable use	Smaller networks with all clients running the same e-mail package and the same network operating system	Larger heterogeneous networks where interoperability between multiple e-mail systems and network operating systems is required in a carefully monitored and managed environment
Example	Microsoft Mail	Microsoft Exchange

Figure 17-6 (*continued*)

Most enterprise e-mail systems are composed of the following architectural elements:

- **Post offices** for storage of received messages and initial hops for outbound messages. Post offices are server-based and may also be required to maintain and store user profiles and routing information to other post offices. Some e-mail systems share a network operating system's user profile directory while others require their own redundant user profile directory.

- **Message transfer agents** are responsible for forwarding messages between post offices and to destination clients. Some e-mail systems require the message transfer agent software to execute on a separate physical server from the local post office software. Because message transfer agents are likely to be asked to forward more than one message simultaneously, it is important that this application support multitasking, which means it must be able to execute over a multitasking operating system.

- **Gateways** are sometimes included as part of the message transfer agent functionality. Designed to translate fully between two e-mail systems, they must translate between different e-mail addressing schemes, messaging protocols, and file attachment types. From a network analyst's perspective, an e-mail gateway's performance and expected traffic levels should be evaluated carefully, as they represent likely network bottlenecks.

- **E-mail clients** may be either LAN-attached or linked to post offices via remote access. Advanced e-mail client capabilities include **rules-based message handling,** which allows the e-mail client to act as an agent on behalf of the user by automatically returning e-mail during vacation periods or screening e-mail by source or priority. E-mail clients should also support encryption and the ability to attach a wide variety of different file types. E-mail clients must be compatible with e-mail post offices in a number of protocol categories including the following:
  - e-mail APIs
  - messaging protocols
  - network transport protocols

The key architectural elements and variables of enterprise e-mail architectures are illustrated in Figure 17-7.

E-Mail Protocol Issues As Figure 17-8 illustrates, enterprise e-mail systems must deal with numerous categories of messaging protocols. Within each category, enterprise e-mail systems may differ according to the number of different protocols supported.

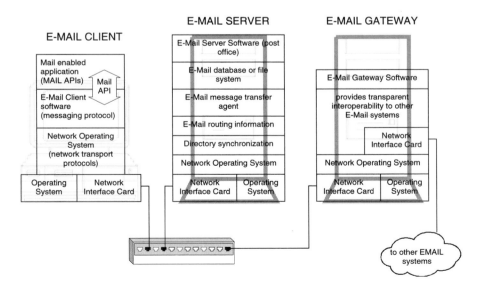

Figure 17-7 Key Elements and Variables of Enterprise E-Mail Architectures

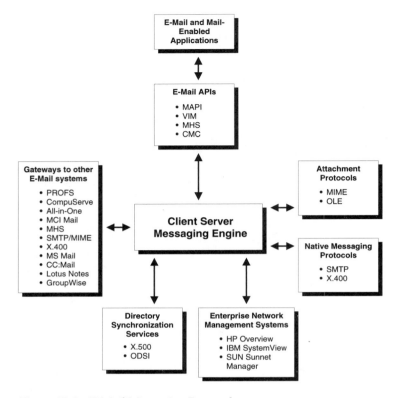

Figure 17-8   E-Mail Messaging Protocols

Native messaging protocols are concerned with how the e-mail messages are addressed, encapsulated, and delivered. Although proprietary messaging protocols are satisfactory in closed environments, open enterprisewide environments require a widely supported messaging protocol. Currently two such open enterprise messaging protocols exist. It should come as no surprise that one of the rival standards is an internet protocol from the IETF and the other is an OSI protocol from the ISO:

- **Simple mail transfer protocol (SMTP)** is defined in two RFCs; RFC 822 defines the structure of an SMTP message and RFC 821 defines how SMTP messages are delivered from source to destination workstations. Some enterprise e-mail systems use SMTP as their native messaging protocol while others use SMTP gateways to translate native messaging protocols into SMTP.

- **X.400** is an OSI e-mail messaging protocol which defines both addressing and message delivery standards. X.400 defines two entities to accomplish message delivery: a user agent, which interfaces to client e-mail programs and formats messages into X.400 format, and a message transfer agent, which is responsible for delivering the message to the intended recipient. Like SMTP, some enterprise e-mail systems are able to use X.400 as the native messaging protocol while others translate into X.400 through the use of gateways.

Attachment protocols are concerned with how additional files such as documents, spreadsheets, sound bites, video images, or faxes can be attached to e-mail messages and then successfully detached and viewed at the destination workstation. Following are two dominant e-mail attachment protocols:

- **Object linking and embedding (OLE)** is a Microsoft protocol which allows documents, spreadsheets, graphical presentations, and other types of attachments to be linked with e-mail messages. By clicking on the attachment at the destination workstation, the associated application required to support it is launched, assuming it is present on the destination workstation. Sophisticated translation capabilities allow attachments to be viewed by other compatible applications.

- **Multipurpose internet mail extension (MIME)** is actually an extension of SMTP which provides each part of a multimedia e-mail message with its own header that defines not only the type of information it contains but also the method used to encode that information. For example, video clips may be compressed with either joint photographic expert group (JPEG) or motion picture experts group (MPEG) compression algorithms. This information allows the correct viewer to be enabled at the destination workstation.

E-mail APIs are required to allow e-mail and other mail-enabled applications to access the messaging infrastructures established by enterprise e-mail systems. It is important that mail-enabled applications are chosen which support the proper e-mail APIs, to interoperate transparently with underlying network operating systems and messaging infrastructures. Among the popular e-mail APIs and their associated operating environment are the following:

E-Mail API	Operating Environment
MAP (messaging API)	Microsoft Part of WOSA (Windows Open Services Architecture).
VIM (vendor-independent messaging)	Lotus, Apple, Novell, and Borland developed this vendor-independent e-mail API.
MHS (message handling service)	Novell NetWare. Often used as a common e-mail gateway protocol.
CMC (common mail call)	E-mail API associated with the X.400 native messaging protocol.

Gateway protocols are specific to the e-mail systems the gateway is translating between. Among the more popular gateway protocols and their operating environments are the following:

Gateway Protocol	Operating Environment
PROFS (professional office system)	IBM mainframes and minis
CompuServe	CompuServe
All-in-One	DEC minicomputers
MCI Mail	MCI Mail

(continued)

Gateway Protocol	Operating Environment
MHS	Novell NetWare
SMTP.MIME	Internet
X.400	X.400
MS Mail	Microsoft Mail
cc:Mail	cc:Mail
Lotus Notes	Lotus Notes
GroupWise	Novell/Wordperfect

Directory synchronization services protocols are particularly important in enterprise e-mail environments in which multiple e-mail systems are supported with accompanying independent directories. As described previously, two primary directory synchronization protocols are X.500, which is part of the OSI suite of protocols, and Microsoft's ODSI.

As enterprise e-mail systems have taken on expanded roles as enterprise messaging infrastructures for numerous applications, it is essential to carefully monitor their impact on network performance. Like most enterprise network applications and devices, enterprise e-mail systems link to enterprise network management systems via simple network management protocol (SNMP).

Enterprise Database Issues

Architectures   As an enterprise's demand for data grows, strategic decisions as to the architecture of the enterprise's data management system are inevitable. Two primary nonexclusive architectures are most often used in describing today's enterprise data management systems:

- **Database distribution.**
- **Database replication.**

Managerial Perspective

Each of these respective enterprise database management system architectures can have a significant impact on the design and performance of enterprise networks. It is the job of the network analyst to cooperate with database design professionals to ensure that whichever enterprise data management architecture is chosen is compatible with the protocols and performance capabilities of the enterprise network.

Database distribution implies that while an enterprise's entire database is viewed as a single logical, centrally managed database, it is in fact, physically distributed across multiple servers which may or may not be widely separated geographically. The motivation for database distribution is to ensure that data are always as close as possible to the applications most likely to access them. A key attribute of a properly designed distributed database is transparency to users and programmers who don't need to worry about the physical location of data. Distributed databases can be implemented only if an enterprise's database management system is capable of globally managing distributed database servers from a single location.

While database distribution produces a single copy of a database distributed across multiple servers, in database replication multiple copies of a database are stored on multiple servers. Database replication also assumes that sufficient data management routines are implemented to ensure that these multiple copies of the same database are synchronized to maintain data integrity and consistency. One of the key benefits of database replication is fault tolerance. If the primary database server becomes unavailable, a replicated secondary server can be transparently accessed by the user application. This fault tolerance is a characteristic of the replicated data management system and does not have to be specially programmed by the applications programmer. Figure 17-9 contrasts database distribution and database replication.

While the fault tolerance delivered by database replication is certainly a positive attribute, the network analyst must consider the bandwidth required to keep multiple copies of enterprise databases synchronized at all times. Replication strategies employed by data management systems can be characterized in two primary ways:

- **Synchronous replication.**

- **Asynchronous replication.**

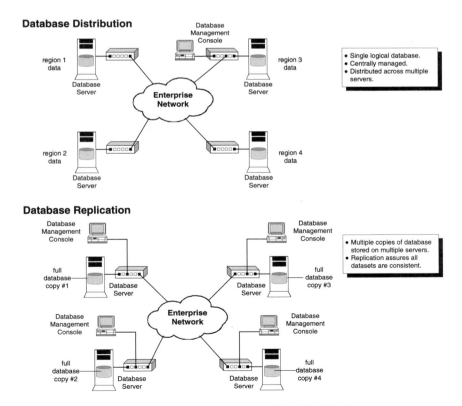

Figure 17-9 Database Distribution versus Database Replication

Some data management systems can employ either replication strategy while others support only one or the other.

Synchronous replication assumes 100% network reliability. This is an important underlying assumption from the network analyst's perspective. To support synchronous replication, all network links will have to be redundant with either leased or dial-up WAN backup facilities. Synchronous replication uses a process known as **two-phase commit** to ensure that all replicated database servers are properly updated. The two phases are as follows:

- First, each replicated database server to be updated is queried about its availability and readiness to accept database updates. Unless all intended recipients of database updates are ready, the transaction or database replication is not posted.

- Given that all intended recipients of the database update answer in the affirmative, the actual database replication takes place in the second phase of the two phase commit. If a network failure occurs during this commit phase, most data management systems perform a **transaction rollback** and remove all previously made updates from this replication, returning all replicated servers to their previous state.

Synchronous replication places high demands on networks and database servers. However, in those industries where all replicated database servers must have a single view of enterprise data on a real-time basis, synchronous replication may be the only way to ensure up-to-the-second consistency across the enterprise.

Asynchronous replication, also known as store-and-forward replication, does not guarantee that all replicated servers are totally synchronized at all times. However, it does not require the same 100% network reliability as synchronous replication does. If a server which must be updated is unavailable, the database management system keeps track of the updates to be done and updates the server when it becomes available. Depending on the data management system in which it is implemented, asynchronous replication may be implemented with either or both of the following methods:

- **Periodic replication** on a timed basis. All new transactions which have accumulated since the last replication update are stored and forwarded all at once to all replicated servers. This method of replication can have serious network implications as well. Because a significant number of transactions may be stored and transmitted during periodic replications, these updates may cause network performance problems if sufficient network bandwidth is not allocated. One possible solution is to perform periodic replication at nonpeak network usage times such as at night. Even this proposal may not be suitable, however, as it limits periodic updates to only once per day and given the international nature of most enterprise networks, there may never be a nonpeak period of usage.

- **Triggered replication** as necessary, determined by certain programmable events such as the number of queued database updates to be replicated. Triggered replication can be more flexible than periodic updates and may be programmed to be more responsive to changes in demand for database replication.

Enterprise Security Issues

Enterprise security issues can be logically divided into three major areas, each of which is characterized by both associated protocols and technology.

- **Authentication.**

- **Authorization.**

- **Encryption.**

Authentication   Authentication is concerned with ensuring that only legitimate users of enterprise network resources are allowed to gain access to those resources. In its simplest form, this is done with user IDs and passwords. However, passwords can be stolen, forgotten, or shared, compromising restriction of access to the enterprise network.

One way in which authentication technology and protocols improve on the security offered by simple passwords is by implementing **single-use passwords.** The technology used to generate and authenticate these single-use passwords, known as **intelligent token authentication technology,** may be either hardware-based or software-based. Following are some of the hardware based token authentication options:

- **Smart Cards** or **SmartIDs,** which are creditcard sized devices that generate a one-time nonreusable password.

- In-line token authentication devices that are installed between computers and modems.

- SmartDisks, which incorporate SmartCard technology into a 3.5″ diskette that can be read by standard disk drives.

In some cases, the token authentication can be performed by software known as Softokens, installed in the user's PC.

Logically, token authentication schemes work in either of two ways:

- **Token response** or **challenge response** authentication schemes work as follows:
    1. Remote user dials in and enters private identification number (PIN).
    2. Authentication server responds with a challenge number.
    3. Remote user enters that number into handheld client authentication unit or in-line client authentication unit receives it automatically.
    4. Client authentication unit generates challenge response number, which is either automatically transmitted back to the authentication server or entered manually by the remote user.
    5. Transmitted challenge response is received by the authentication server and compared to the expected challenge response number generated at the server. If they match, the user is authenticated and allowed access to network-attached resources.

- **Time synchronous** authentication schemes work as follows:
    1. Random authentication numbers are generated in time-synchronous fashion at both the authentication server and client.

2. Remote user enters PIN number and the current random authentication number displayed on the client authentication unit, which are both transmitted to the authentication server.

3. Due to time synchronization, the server authentication unit should have the same current random authentication number, which is compared to the one transmitted from the remote client.

4. If the two authentication numbers match, the authentication server authenticates the user and allows access to the network-attached resources.

If the security offered by token authentication is insufficient, **biometric authentication** can authenticate users based on fingerprints, palm prints, retinal patterns, voice recognition, or other physical characteristics. Passwords or SmartCards can be stolen, but fingerprints and retinal patterns cannot.

Authorization   Sometimes perceived as a subset of authentication, authorization is concerned with ensuring that only properly authorized users are able to access particular network resources or corporate information resources. In other words, while authentication ensures that only legitimate users can log into the network, authorization ensures that these properly authenticated users access only the network resources for which they are properly authorized. This assurance that users can log into only a network, not individual servers and applications, and access only resources for which they are properly authorized is known as **secure single login.**

The authorization security software can be either server-based **(brokered authorization)** or workstation-based **(trusted node).**

In Sharper Focus

KERBEROS

Perhaps the best known combination authentication/authorization software is **Kerberos,** developed originally at Massachusetts Institute of Technology and marketed commercially by a variety of firms. The Kerberos architecture is illustrated in Figure 17-10.

As the figure shows, a Kerberos architecture consists of three key components:

- Kerberos client software.
- Kerberos authentication server software.
- Kerberos application server software.

To be able to ensure that only authorized users can access a particular application, Kerberos must communicate directly with that application. As a result, the source code of the application must be "Kerberized" or modified to be compatible with Kerberos. If source code is not available, perhaps the software vendor sells Kerberized versions of their software. Kerberos cannot offer authorization protection to applications with which it cannot communicate. Kerberos enforces authentication and authorization through the use of a ticket-based system. An encrypted **ticket** is issued for each server-to-client session and is valid for only a preset amount of time. The ticket is valid only for connections between a designated client and server, thus precluding users from accessing servers or applications for which they are not properly authorized. Logically, Kerberos works as follows:

1. Users are first authenticated by the Kerberos authentication server, which consults its database and grants a ticket for the valid user to communicate

Enterprise Network Applications **657**

with the ticket granting server (TGS). This ticket is known as a **ticket-granting ticket**.

2. Using this ticket, the user sends an encrypted request to the TGS for a ticket to access a particular applications server.

3. If the TGS determines that the request is valid, a ticket is issued allowing the user to access the requested server. This ticket is known as a **service-granting ticket.**

4. The user presents the validated ticket to the application server, which evaluates its validity. If the application determines that the ticket is valid, a client/server session is established.

Enterprise networks implementing Kerberos are divided into Kerberos **realms,** each served by its own Kerberos server. If a client wishes to access a server in another realm, it requests an **inter-realm** ticket granting ticket from its local ticket granting server to authorize access to the remote ticket granting server which can authorize access to the remote applications server.

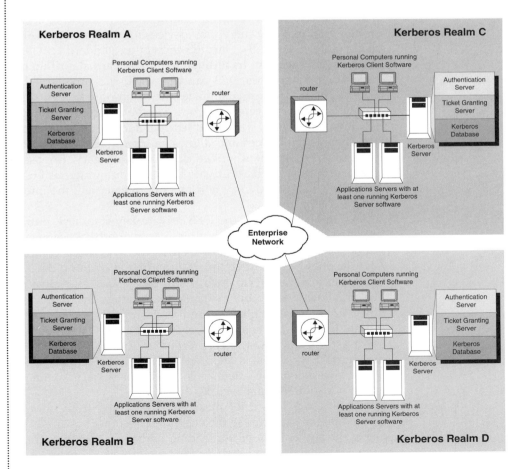

Figure 17-10   Kerberos Architecture

From a network analyst's perspective, concern should be centered on the amount of overhead or network bandwidth consumed by the addition of Kerberos security. Research has indicated that, in fact, the network impact is minimal. However, the additional administrative responsibility of maintaining the Kerberos databases indicating which users are authorized to access which network resources should not be ignored.

An open API which allows applications to communicate with a variety of security authorization programs, known as **generic security service–applications program interface (GSS-API),** is documented in RFCs 1508 and 1509.

Encryption   Encryption is a security process complimentary rather than mutually exclusive to authentication and authorization. As one-time token-generated passwords are traversing networks, encryption ensures that the contents of the transmission would be meaningless if they were intercepted. Likewise, Kerberos tickets are encrypted before transmission as well.

Encryption involves changing data into an unreadable or meaningless form before transmission. In this, way, even if the transmitted data is somehow intercepted, it cannot be interpreted. The changed, unmeaningful data is known as **ciphertext.** Encryption must be accompanied by decryption, to change the unreadable text back into its original form.

Although proprietary standards do exist, **Data Encryption Standard (DES),** originally approved by the National Institute of Standards and Technology (NIST) in 1977, is often used to allow encryption devices manufactured by different manufacturers to interoperate successfully. The DES encryption standard actually includes two parts for greater overall security. In addition to the standard **algorithm** or method of encrypting data 64 bits at a time, the DES standard also uses a variable 64-bit key.

The encryption key customizes the commonly known algorithm to prevent anyone without this **private key** from possibly decrypting the document. This private key must be known by both the sending and the receiving (encrypting and decrypting) encryption devices and allows so many unique combinations (nearly 2 to the 64th power), that unauthorized decryption is nearly impossible. The safe and reliable distribution of these private keys among numerous encryption devices can be difficult. If this private key is somehow intercepted, the integrity of the encryption system is compromised.

As an alternative to the DES private key standard, **public key encryption** can be used. Public key encryption could perhaps more accurately be named public/private key encryption, as the process actually combines public and private keys. In public key encryption, the sending encryption device encrypts a document using the intended recipient's public key and the originating party's private key. This public key is readily available in a public directory. To decrypt the document, however, the receiving encryption device must be programmed with the recipient's private key and the sending party's public key. This method requires only the receiving party to possess their private key and eliminates the need for transmission of private keys between sending and receiving parties. One of the most popular public key encryption schemes is the Rivest-Shamir-Adelman (RSA) encryption algorithm from RSA Data Security.

As an added security measure, **digital signature encryption** appends an encrypted digital signature to the encrypted document as an electronic means of guaranteeing the authenticity of the sending party and assurance that encrypted documents have not been tampered with during transmission. The digital signature is regenerated at the receiving encryption device from the transmitted document and compared to the transmitted digital signature. If the digital signatures match, the document is still in its original condition. The digital signature has been compared to the wax seals of old which (supposedly) guaranteed tamper-evident delivery of documents.

A public domain encryption system known as **pretty good privacy (PGP)** combines digital signature encryption with public key encryption. Digital signature encryption is provided using a combination of RSA and **MD5** (Message Direct Version 5) encryption techniques. Combined documents and digital signatures are then encrypted using **International Data Encryption Algorithm (IDEA),** which makes use of one-time 128-bit keys known as **session keys.**

Managerial Perspective

Due to patent and national security issues, many encryption algorithms cannot be exported from the United States. It is important for network analysts working in the international arena to be intimate with regulations concerning export of encryption algorithms.

■ ENTERPRISE NETWORK MANAGEMENT

As local area networks, internetworks, and wide area networks have combined to form enterprise networks, the management of all these elements of the enterprise has been a key concern. LANs, internetworks, and WANs have traditionally each had their own set of management tools and protocols. Once integrated into a single enterprise, these disparate tools and protocols do not necessarily meld together into an integrated cohesive system. The overall network and system management requirements and associated technology are most often divided into two major categories:

- Enterprise network management systems.

- Desktop or system management systems.

Figure 17-11 summarizes the key functional differences between these two categories and lists some representative technologies as well.

	Functionality	Technology
Enterprise network management	• Monitor and manage internetwork technology—switches, routers, bridges, hubs • Monitor and manage WAN links	• HP Openview • IBM SystemView • Sun Solstice Enterprise Manager
Desktop or system management	• Track hardware and software inventory • Perform license metering • Monitor LAN and server activity • Software distribution • Asset management • Server monitoring	• SaberLAN Workstation—McAfee • Brightworks—McAfee • LANDesk Suite—Intel • Norton Administrator for Networks—Symantec • Frye Utilities for Desktops—Seagate • System Management Server—Microsoft • ManageWise—Novell

Figure 17-11   Desktop Management versus Enterprise Network Management

Enterprise Network Management Systems

Enterprise Network Management Architecture and Protocols   As Figure 17-12 illustrates, enterprise network management architectures are composed of a relatively few elements.

Agents are software programs which run on networking devices such as servers, bridges, and routers to monitor and report the status of those devices. Agent software must be compatible with the device that it is reporting management statistics for, as well as the protocols supported by, the enterprise network management system to which those statistics are fed. Agents from the numerous individual networking devices forward this network management information to **enterprise network management systems,** which compile and report network operation statistics to the end-user, most often in some type of graphical format. Enterprise network management systems are really management application programs running on a management server.

The network management information gathered must be stored in some type of database with an index and standardized field definitions so that network management workstations can easily access this data. A **management information base,** or **MIB,** as these databases are known, differs in the fields defined for different vendor's networking devices. These fields within the MIBs are known as **objects.** One fairly standard MIB is known as the **RMON MIB,** which stands for remote network monitoring MIB. Finally, a protocol is required to encapsulate the management data for delivery by network and transport layer protocols. Partly because of the dominance of TCP/IP as the internetworking protocol of choice, **simple network management protocol (SNMP)** is the de facto standard for delivering enterprise management data.

Which SNMP Is the Real SNMP?   The original SNMP protocol required internetworking device-specific agents to be polled for SNMP encapsulated management data. Alarm conditions or exceptions to preset thresholds could not be directly reported on an as-needed basis from the agents to the enterprise network management software. The inability of agents to initiate communications with enterprise network

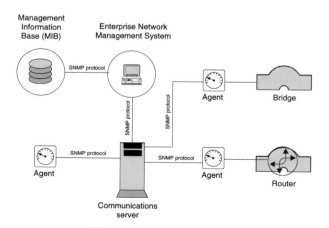

Figure 17-12   Enterprise Network Management Architecture

management systems requires constant polling of agents, consuming considerable network bandwidth.

Also, the original SNMP protocol did not provide for any means of manager-to-manager communication. As a result, only one enterprise network manager could be installed on a given network, forcing all internetworked devices to report directly to the single enterprise network manager. Hierarchical arrangements in which regional managers are able to filter raw management data and pass only exceptional information to enterprise managers is not possible with the original SNMP.

Another major shortcoming of the original SNMP is that it was limited to TCP/IP as its transport protocol. It was therefore unusable on NetWare (IPX/SPX), Macintosh (AppleTalk), or other networks. Finally, SNMP does not offer any security features which would authenticate valid polling managers or encrypt traffic between agents and managers.

The need to reduce network traffic caused by the SNMP protocol as well as to deal with other SNMP shortcomings led to a proposal for a new version of SNMP known as **SNMP2,** or **simple management protocol (SMP).**

SNMP2's major objectives can be summarized as follows:

- Reduce network traffic.

- Segment large networks.

- Support multiple transport protocols.

- Increase security.

- Allow multiple agents per device.

Through a new SNMP2 procedure known as **bulk retrieval mechanism,** managers can retrieve several pieces of network information at a time from a given agent. This precludes the need for a constant request and reply mechanism for every piece of network management information desired. Agents have also been given increased intelligence, which enables them to send error or exception conditions to managers when requests for information cannot be met. With SNMP, agents simply sent empty datagrams back to managers when requests could not be fulfilled. The receipt of the empty packet merely caused the manager to repeat the request for information, thus increasing network traffic.

SNMP2 allows multiple manager entities to be established within a single network. As a result, SNMP2 manages large networks that were managed by a single manager under SNMP by multiple managers in a hierarchical arrangement. Overall network traffic is reduced as network management information is confined to the management domains of the individual network segment managers. Information is only passed from the segment managers to the centralized network management system via manager-to-manager communication at the request of the central manager or if certain predefined error conditions occur on a subnet. Figure 17-13 illustrates the impact of SNMP2 manager-to-manger communications.

SNMP was initially part of the internet suite of protocols and therefore was deployed on only those networks equipped with the TCP/IP protocols. SNMP2 works transparently with AppleTalk, IPX, and OSI transport protocols.

Increased security in SNMP2 allows not just monitoring and management of remote network devices, but actual **remote configuration** of those devices as well. Furthermore, SNMP2 or a variation of SNMP known as **secure SNMP,** allows users

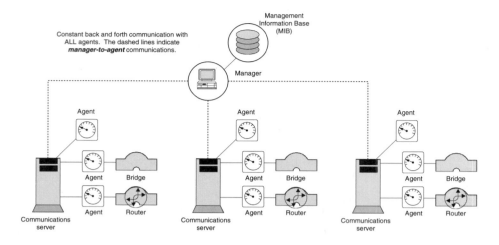

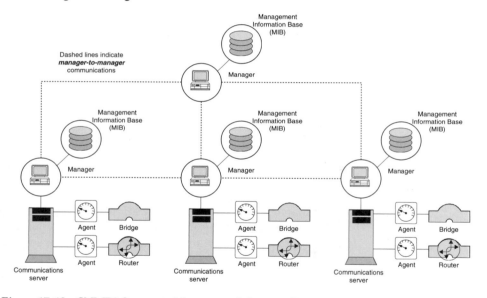

Figure 17-13   SNMP2 Supports Manager-to-Manager Communications

to access carriers' network management information and incorporate it into the wide area component of an enterprise network management system. This ability to actually access data from within the carrier's central office has powerful implications for users and enables many advanced user services such as software-defined network, SDN.

Perhaps the most significant SNMP2 development in its implication for distributed client-server management is the ability to deploy multiple agents per device. As a practical example, on a distributed server, one agent could monitor the processing activity, a second could monitor the database activity, and a third could monitor the networking activity, with each reporting back to their own manager. In this way, rather than having merely distributed enterprise network management, the entire distributed information system could be managed, with each major element of the client/server architecture managed by its own management infrastructure.

Unfortunately, considerable debate over portions of the SNMP2 protocol have delayed its deployment for years. Some people feel that features of SNMP2, especially the security aspects, are too difficult to implement and use, while others blame the delay on concerns over marketing position and competitive advantage from technology vendors. In the interim, alternative upgrades to SNMP have been proposed by officially sanctioned organizations such as the IETF as well as ad hoc forums. Figure 17-14 summarizes key points of the various SNMP2 alternatives.

MIBs   Management information bases serve as repositories for enterprise network performance information to be displayed in meaningful format by enterprise network management systems. The original RMON MIB standard which was developed in 1991 has been updated as **RMON2.** While the original RMON MIB required only compatible technology to be able to collect and analyze statistics on the physical and data-link layers, RMON2 requires collection and analysis of network layer protocols as well. In addition, RMON2 requires compatible technology to be able to identify from which applications a given packet was generated. RMON2-compatible agent software which resides within internetworking devices and reports performance statistics to enterprise network management systems is called **RMON probe.** Overall, RMON2 should enable network analysts to more effectively pinpoint the exact sources and percentages of the traffic which flows through their enterprise networks. Figure 17-15 summarizes some of the key functional areas of the RMON2 specification.

SNMP Standard	Also Known As	Advantages	Disadvantages
SNMP		• Part of TCP/IP suite • Open standard • Works with defined MIBs	• Excessive polling • No manager-to-manager communication • Supports only TCP/IP • No security
SNMP2	• SMP • Secure SNMP	• Supports bulk retrieval • Supports manager-to-manager communication • Supports multiple protocols • Provides security • Remote configuration	• Never implemented due to squabbling among standards bodies
Updated SNMP2	• SNMP2t • SNMP2c • SNMP1.5	• Supposedly easier to implement due to removal of security features	• No security features • No manager-to-manager communications • No remote configuration
SNMP3	• SNMP2	• Adds security features back into SNMP2	• Lack of support from official standards-making organization • Vendor-specific solutions are being offered as alternatives

Figure 17-14   Alternative SNMP2 Proposals

RMON2 Function	Explanation/Importance
Protocol distribution	• Tracks and reports data-link layer protocols by percentage • Tracks and reports network layer protocols by percentage • Tracks and reports application source by percentage
Address mapping	• Maps network layer addresses to MAC layer addresses • Maps MAC layer addresses to hub or switch port
Network layer host table	• Tracks and stores in table format network layer protocols and associated traffic statistics according to source host
Network layer matrix table	• Tracks and stores in a matrix table format network layer protocols and associated traffic statistics according to sessions established between two given hosts
Application host table	• Tracks and stores in table format application-specific traffic statistics according to source host
Application matrix table	• Tracks and stores in a matrix table format application-specific traffic statistics according to sessions established between two given hosts
Probe configuration	• Defines standards for remotely configuring probes which are responsible for gathering and reporting network activity statistics
History	• Tracks and stores historical traffic information according to parameters determined by the user

Figure 17-15   RMON2 Specifications

While the RMON2 specification may be able to track traffic generated by a particular application, it does not provide the functionality to determine whether or not the application is performing appropriately. To effectively manage distributed information systems, distributed applications must be manageable in a manner similar to enterprise network components. Proposals for such an **application MIB** identify three key groups of variables for proper application tracking and management:

- **Definition variables** would store background information concerning applications, such as application name, manufacturer, version, release, installation date, license number, and number of consecutive users.

- **State variables** would report on the current status of a given application. Three possible states are up, down, and degraded.

- **Relationship variables** would define all other network-attached resources on which a given distributed application depends. This includes databases, associated client applications, and other network resources.

One of the major difficulties with developing and implementing an application MIB is the vast difference among distributed applications.

Distributed database management is also important to overall enterprise information system management. Although most distributed data management platforms provide their own management system for reporting performance statistics, there is currently no way to consolidate these separate management systems into a single enterprisewide view. The IETF has been working on a **database MIB** specification which would allow any enterprise data management system to report performance statistics back to any SNMP-compliant enterprise network management system.

Enterprise Network Management Technology   Enterprise network management systems must be able to gather information from a variety of sources throughout the enterprise network and display that information in a clear and meaningful format. Furthermore, enterprise network management systems are being called on to monitor and manage additional distributed resources such as the following:

- Workstations and servers.

- Distributed applications.

- Distributed data management systems.

One of the current difficulties with actually implementing enterprise network management systems is a lack of interoperability between different enterprise network management systems and third-party or vendor-specific network management systems. As Figure 17-11 notes, the following are popular enterprise network management systems:

- HP Openview.

- IBM SystemView.

- Sun Soft Solstice Enterprise Manager.

Following are examples of third-party or vendor-specific network management systems:

- Seagate NerveCenter.

- Cisco CiscoWorks.

- Bay Networks Optivity.

- UB Networks UB Network Director.

- Xyplex ControlPoint.

- American Power Conversion PowerNet.

Manifestations of the lack of interoperability between third-party applications and enterprise network management systems include the following:

- Separate databases maintained by each third-party application and enterprise network management system.

- Redundant polling of agent software to gather performance statistics.

- Multiple agents installed and executed on networked devices to report to multiple management platforms.

The lack of interoperability between different enterprise network management systems makes it difficult if not impossible to exchange network topology information and maps or threshold performance parameter and alarm information.

The major cause of all of this lack of interoperability is the lack of common APIs between both enterprise network management systems and a given enterprise network management system and a variety of third-party network management systems. Figure 17-16 illustrates an architectural view of how enterprise network management systems interface to other enterprise network components. Interoperability APIs included in the figure are either proposed or under development.

In addition to the interoperability issues previously discussed, Figure 17-17 lists key functional areas of enterprise network management software.

Desktop Management Systems

Desktop Management Architecture and Protocols It is important to distinguish between the strategic intents of enterprise management and desktop management systems. While enterprise management systems are primarily concerned with shared network resources, desktop management is more concerned with the configuration and support of desktop workstations.

While enterprise network management systems were standardized by the IETF, desktop management systems rely on an architecture and associated protocols proposed by the **Desktop Management Task Force (DMTF),** composed of over 50 companies including Intel, Microsoft, IBM, Digital, Hewlett-Packard, Apple, Compaq, Dell, and Sun. The overall desktop management architecture, illustrated in Figure 17-18, is known as the **desktop management interface,** or **DMI.**

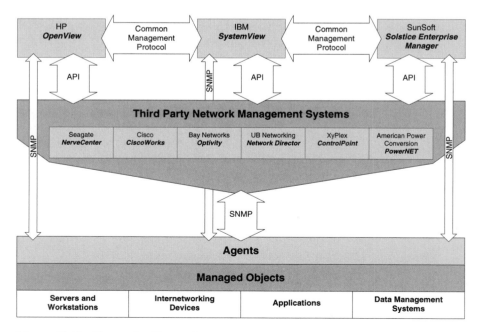

Figure 17-16 Enterprise Network Management System Architecture

Functional Category	Importance/Implication

Operating system compatibility	• Over which operating systems does the enterprise network management system run?
	  • HP UX
	  • Sun OS
	  • Solaris SPARC
	  • IBM AIX
	  • Windows NT
	• How many simultaneous operators of the enterprise network management system are supported?
	• Can multiple operators be distributed across the enterprise network?

Database compatibility	• Which databases can the enterprise network management system interoperate with?
	  • Oracle
	  • Ingres
	  • SyBase
	  • Informix
	  • Proprietary
	  • DB2
	  • Flat file

Network size and architecture	• Is there a limit to the number of nodes supported? • Can the software map all network architectures? Ethernet, Token Ring, FDDI, Switched LANs, WANs, ATM • Can mainframes be integrated into the enterprise network management system? • Can IPX as well as IP devices be managed?
Third-party application support	• How many third-party applications are guaranteed to interoperate with this enterprise network management system?
MIB and management protocol support	• How many different MIBs are supported? MIBs can be both IETF sanctioned and vendor specific. Enterprise network management systems can easily support more than 200 different MIBs. • Are management protocols other than SNMP supported? CMIP (common management information protocol), proprietary, SNMP2
Self-configuration	• To what extent is the enterprise network management software able to self-configure or autodiscover the enterprise network topology? • Can the self-configuration process be customized or controlled?
Cascading or effect alarms	• Is the system able to identify and report alarms triggered by other alarms to more easily pinpoint the cause of problems? This capability is also known as event correlation.

Figure 17-17   Functional Categories of Enterprise Network Management Systems

Although differing in both strategic intent and governing standards-making organizations, it is still important for desktop management and enterprise management systems to be able to interoperate transparently. Since DMI-compliant desktop management systems store performance and configuration statistics in a **management information format (MIF),** and enterprise management systems employ an

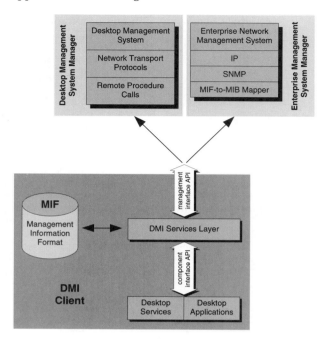

Figure 17-18 Desktop Management Interface Architecture

MIB, an MIF-to-MIB mapper is required to link desktop and enterprise management systems. The DMI architecture is composed of four primary components:

- **DMI services layer** is the DMI application which resides on each desktop device to be managed. The DMI services layer does the actual processing of desktop management information on the client platform and serves as an interface to two APIs.

- The **management interface API** is designed to interface to the desktop system management program which will consolidate the information from this client with all other desktop information.

- The **component interface API** is designed to interface to the individual application programs or desktop components to be managed and monitored on the local client.

- Information about the local desktop components is stored locally in a management information format, or MIF.

Desktop Management Technology   Desktop management technology offerings from different vendors are best characterized as suites of associated desktop management applications. Current offerings differ in the variety of management modules included within a given suite as well as the extent of integration between suite modules. Among the modules some, but not necessarily all, desktop management suites include are the following:

- Hardware and software inventory.

- Asset management.

- Software distribution.

- License metering.
- Server monitoring.
- Virus protection.
- Help desk support.

Key functional characteristics of desktop management systems are listed in Figure 17-19.

Functional Category	Importance/Implication
Integration	• Are all desktop management applications tied together through a single interface to a single console? • Do all desktop management applications share information with each other via a single database? • Can software modules be added individually as needed? Suites may be either modular or tightly integrated in design. • Does the system support the DMI architecture? output data in MIF format?
Network operating system compatibility	• Which network operating system must the desktop management console or server run over? • Which network operating systems is the desktop management system able to monitor? Some desktop management systems can monitor only a single NOS. For example, some versions of Novell ManageWise are able only to monitor NetWare networks and Microsoft's System Management Server only manages Microsoft networks. • Examples of supported network operating systems include NetWare, Windows NT, IBM LAN Server, Banyan Vines, Artisoft LANtastic, DEC Pathworks, and AppleTalk
Desktop compatibility	• Since the primary objective of this software category is to manage desktops, it is essential that as many desktop platforms as possible are supported. • Examples of supported client platforms include DOS, Macintosh, OS/2, Windows 95, Windows NT Workstation, Windows for Workgroups, or Windows 3.11
Hardware and software inventory (asset management)	• Can the inventory software autodetect client hardware and software? • Can changes in files or configure be tracked? • Can versions of software be detected and tracked? • How many applications can be identified? Libraries of 6,000 are not uncommon. • Can CPU types and speeds be correctly identified? • Is a query utility included to identify workstations with given characteristics?
Server monitoring	• Does the software support the setting of threshold limits for CPU activity, remaining disk space, etc? • What server attributes can be tracked? CPU activity, memory usage, free disk space, number of concurrent logins or sessions

Figure 17-19   Functional Categories of Desktop Management Systems

(*continued*)

Functional Category	Importance/Implication
Network monitoring	• Can data-link layer traffic be monitored and reported on? • Can network layer protocol traffic activity be monitored and reported on? • Can MAC layer addresses be sensed and monitored? • Can activity thresholds be established for particular data-link or network layer protocols?
Software distribution	• Can software be distributed to local client drives as well as network servers? • Can updates be automatically installed? • Can the system track which software needs to be updated through ties with the software inventory system? • Can updates be uninstalled automatically? • Can progress and error reports be produced during and after software distribution?

License metering	• Where can software licenses be tracked?
	    • Clients
	    • Server
	    • Across multiple servers
	• Can license limit thresholds be set?
	• Will the manager be notified before the license limit is reached?
	• Will users be notified if license limit has been reached?
	• Will users be put into a queue for next available license after the license limit has been reached?

Virus protection	• Can virus protection be provided for both clients and servers? • Can diskette drives as well as hard drives be protected? • Can viruses embedded within application programs be detected?
Help desk support	• Are trouble ticketing and call tracking utilities included? • Are query capabilities included to search for similar problems and solutions? • Are reports available to spot trends and track help desk effectiveness and productivity?
Alarms	• Can managers be notified of changes to files or configuration? • Can violations or preset thresholds be reported? • Can alarms be sent by e-mail, pager, fax, cellular phone?
Remote control management	• Can managers take over remote client workstations for monitoring or troubleshooting purposes? • Can this be done via modem as well as over the local LAN? • Can files be transferred to/from the remote client? • Can files on remote client be viewed without taking over complete control of the remote client? • Can remote reboots be initiated?
Reporting capabilities	• How many predefined reports are available? • Can users define their own reports? • Can information be exported to documents, spreadsheets, or databases? • Which export file formats are supported?

Figure 17-19 (*continued*)

SUMMARY

To effectively analyze, design, implement, and manage the enterprise network, a network analyst must understand the impact of enterprise application and data management systems. It is the responsibility of the network analyst to ensure that the enterprise network supports the protocol and bandwidth requirements of these enterprise applications and data management systems.

Enterprise applications require a common directory service regardless of differing computing platforms across the enterprise. X.500 is one such standardized enterprise directory service, whereas ODSI is a standardized API to a variety of different directory services.

Enterprisewide e-mail has evolved from a monolithic application to a strategic messaging infrastructure which can be accessed from a variety of mail-enabled applications. Among the e-mail protocol issues that network analysts must deal with are native messaging protocols, attachment protocols, e-mail APIs, and gateway protocols.

Enterprise data management design issues can have a dramatic impact on enterprise network design and performance. Database distribution implies the use of a single logical database, physically distributed across multiple servers throughout the enterprise. Database replication implies that multiple copies of corporate databases are kept in a consistently updated state throughout the enterprise.

Enterprise security issues involve implementation of procedures in three primary areas: authentication, authorization, and encryption. Authentication ensures that only legitimate users gain access to the enterprise network. Authorization ensures that legitimate users access only those resources for which they are properly authorized, and encryption ensures that transmitted messages cannot be deciphered by anyone but intended recipients.

Managing the enterprise network involves a combination of enterprise network and desktop management systems. While desktop management systems are more concerned with hardware and software inventory, software distribution, and license metering, enterprise network management is more concerned with internetworking devices and the LAN and WAN architectures which constitute the information highway of the enterprise.

KEY TERMS

REVIEW QUESTIONS

1. What are the responsibilities of a network analyst when it comes to enterprise applications and enterprise data management?
2. Differentiate between horizontal and vertical scalability.
3. Why are enterprise directory services important to enterprise applications?
4. What is one difficulty with implementing enterprise directory services?
5. What is a metadirectory?
6. Differentiate between X.500 and ODSI.
7. Describe the current transition of e-mail infrastructures.
8. Differentiate between store-and-forward and remote procedure call message-based e-mail.
9. What is rules-based messaging?
10. Describe the basic function of each of the key components of an e-mail system architecture.
11. Differentiate between the available options for native e-mail messaging protocols.
12. Differentiate between e-mail attachment protocol options.
13. Why should e-mail gateways be of special concern to network analysts?
14. Differentiate between database replication and database distribution.
15. What are some of the potential network impacts of database distribution?
16. What are some of the potential network impacts of database replication?
17. Differentiate between the network impact of synchronous and asynchronous replication.
18. Differentiate between the network impact of periodic and triggered replication.
19. What is the overall objective of authentication?
20. What is the overall objective of authorization?
21. How are authentication and authorization related?
22. What is the overall objective of encryption?
23. How does the use of intelligent token authentication technology improve security?
24. Differentiate between token response and time synchronization token authentication schemes.
25. How does Kerberos offer authorization as well as authentication services?
26. What does it mean for an application to be kerberized?
27. Differentiate between public key encryption and private key encryption.
28. What are the disadvantages of private key encryption?
29. Differentiate between public key encryption and digital signature encryption.
30. Describe the role of each element of an enterprise network management system architecture.
31. Describe some of the key shortcomings of SNMP.
32. What are some of the ways in which SNMP2 overcomes SNMP's shortcomings?

33. What are some of the key differences between RMON and RMON2 MIBs?
34. What is the importance of application and database MIBs?
35. What are some of the key limitations of today's enterprise network management systems?

36. What are the key functional objectives of desktop management systems?
37. Differentiate between the purpose of desktop management systems versus enterprise network management systems.

ACTIVITIES

1. Research X.500 in terms of its level of acceptance and implementation on enterprise networks. What functionality was added in the 1993 release of X.500? What are some of X.500's shortcomings? Analyze your results.
2. Research X.400 in terms of its level of acceptance and implementation on enterprise networks. What are some of the common criticisms of X.400?
3. Survey current and planned use of e-mail in businesses or other organizations. Which e-mail products are being used? Do your results support the trend of transitioning to real-time message based e-mail? Analyze and report on your results.
4. Survey the enterprise data management architecture of businesses or other organizations. What percentage implement database distribution or database replication? How did the business and application requirements dictate the data management design decisions? Do any organizations implement both database distribution and replication?
5. Survey the enterprise security implementation of businesses or other organizations. Why might organizations be reluctant to share this information? How could you overcome these objections? What percentage of organizations surveyed employ authentication? authorization? encryption?
6. Research the architecture and implementation issues of Kerberos. Differentiate between the various commercial versions of Kerberos available and the public domain versions available from

MIT. Are there any shortcomings or disadvantages to Kerberos?
7. Investigate the current status of the Clipper chip. Prepare an historical account highlighting debate over the Clipper chip. What are some of the key objections to the Clipper chip? What is the government's motivation for its adoption as an encryption standard?
8. Investigate the current status of SNMP2. Is the IETF still working on the standard? What are businesses doing in the meantime? What are the key issues causing debate?
9. Survey businesses or organizations that have implemented enterprise network management systems. Which enterprise network management system was chosen? Why? Which third-party network management systems (if any) does the enterprise system interface with? What functionality of the enterprise network management system has actually been implemented? What do the organizations feel has been the benefit of these systems? What personnel investment has been made to implement and support these systems?
10. Investigate the current state of the desktop management systems market. What percentage of products support the DMI architecture? What percentage of products interface directly to enterprise network management systems? Does one product have a dominant market share? Analyze and report on your results.

FEATURED REFERENCES

General References

Case, Thomas and Larry Smith. *Managing Local Area Networks* (New York: McGraw-Hill, 1995).

Goldman, James. *Applied Data Communications: A Business Oriented Approach* (New York: John Wiley & Sons, 1995).

Trends

Caron, Jeremiah. Distributed Technology Gets Real. *LAN Times*, 12; 1 (January 9, 1995), 55.

Cummings, Joanne. New Tools for Collaboration Emerge in the Public Network. *Telecommunications*, 29; 12 (December 1995), 25.

Dejesus, Edmund. Big OOP, No Oops. *Byte*, 20; 8 (August 1995), 74.

Linthicum, David. The End of Programming. *Byte*, 20; 8 (August 1995), 69.

Applications Network Services

Curtis, Walt. The Electronic Wallet. *Network Computing*, 5; 14 (November 15, 1994), 56.

Freeze, James. Sizing up Public Network Notes Services. *Network World*, 12; 30 (July 24, 1995), 33.

Gareiss, Robin. MCI Ties Applications in a Tidy Bundle. *Data Communications*, 23; 16 (November 1994), 121.

Gareiss, Robin. Networking Notes for the World. *Data Communications*, 24; 1 (January 1995), 62.

E-Mail/Interoperability/MIME/MAPI/MHS

Arnum, Eric. New Servers Will Alter LAN-Based E-Mail Market. *Business Communications Review*, 24; 7 (July 1994), 42.

Blum, Daniel and Gary Rowe. Plan Now for Smoother E-Mail Migration. *Network World*, 12; 27 (July 3, 1995), 35.

Burns, Nina. E-Mail Beyond the LAN. *PC Magazine*, 14; 8 (April 25, 1995), 102.

Butler, Cheryl. DMA: Document Management Made Easy. *Network World*, 12; 29 (July 17, 1995), 51.

Carr, Eric. Global E-Mail Communications Through SMTP. *Network Computing*, 5; 12 (October 15, 1994), 36.

Chernicoff, David. Integration of NDS and MHS Yields Benefits. *PC Week*, 12; 36 (September 11, 1995), N10.

Connor, John. Getting the Message Across. *Network Computing*, 6; 11 (September 15, 1995), 144.

Cullen, Alex. Message Architectures in Transition. *Network World*, 12; 26 (June 26, 1995), 35.

Cullen, Alex. SNMP Finds a New Home in Electronic Messaging Systems. *Network World*, 12; 37 (September 11, 1995), 2L.

Devers, Linda. Uncovering the Hidden Costs of E-Mail. *Network Computing*, 5; 9 (August 1, 1994), 142.

Dorshkind, Brent. Messaging Vendors Wary of NDS. *LAN Times*, 12; 14 (July 24, 1995), 22.

Eglowstein, Howard and Ben Smith. E-Mail from Afar. *Byte*, 19; 5 (May 1994), 122.

Fogarty, Kevin and Peggy Watt. ODSI: NOS Vendors Cave In. *Network World*, 12; 29 (July 17, 1995), 1.

Gerber, Barry. Client/Server Messaging: Delivering the Enterprise. *Network Computing*, 6; 15 (November 15, 1995), 68.

Gerber, Barry. Exchange Delivers the Message. *Network Computing*, 6; 15 (November 15, 1995), 40.

Girishankar, Saroja. It's in the E-Mail. *Communications Week*, no. 567 (July 24, 1995), 67.

Gonzales, Sean. Choosing an E-Mail Protocol. *PC Magazine*, 14; 21 (December 5, 1995), 407.

Johnson, Johna. Document Sharing without E-Mail Barriers. *Data Communications*, 24; 1 (January 1995), 107.

Kramer, Matt. Exchange Server Beefs up Features. *PC Week*, 12; 36 (September 11, 1995), N1.

Morse, Stephen. E-Mail Management in Disarray. *Network Computing*, 5; 15 (December 1, 1994), 122.

Morse, Stephen. Super E-Mail: New Applications and Architectures Enhance Services. *Network Computing*, 5; 12 (October 15, 1994), 30.

Myer, Ted. Straight Talk about E-Mail Connectivity. *Business Communications Review*, 25; 7 (July 1995), 35.

Robertson, Bruce. Mail-Enabling Databases. *Network Computing*, 6; 7 (June 1, 1995), 154.

Robertson, Bruce. MIME Speaks Volumes. *Network Computing*, 5; 13 (November 1, 1994), 135.

Rooney, Paula and Paula Musich. Universal Client to Link Mixed E-Mail. *PC Week*, 12; 25 (June 26, 1995), 1.

Sheldon, Tom. MAPI Blooms in Chicago. *Byte*, 19; 11 (November 1994), 163.

Snyder, Joel and Jan Trumbo. E-Mail Directories-Directory Assistance. *Network Computing*, 6; 7 (June 1, 1995), 88.

Stahl, Stephanie. Pumping Up Corporate E-Mail. *Information Week*, no. 531 (June 12, 1995), 46.

Tolly, Kevin. E-Mail Gateways: What's Missing from the Link. *Data Communications*, 24; 9 (July 1995), 35.

Tolly, Kevin and David Newman. Grow Up!: Evaluating LAN-Based E-Mail for the Enterprise. *Data Communications*, 23; 16 (November 1994), 70.

Vins, David. Inside Exchange. *IT/IS Back Office* (December 1995), 47.

Desktop Videoconferencing/Multimedia

Bryan, John. Compression Scorecard. *Byte*, 20; 5 (May 1995), 107.

Cassidy, Peter. The Next Best Thing to Being There. *LAN Times*, 12; 25 (December 4, 1995), 79.

Fritz, Jeffrey. Video Connections. *Byte*, 20; 5 (May 1995), 113.

Haight, Timothy. Does Videoconferencing Matter? *Network Computing*, 5; 8 (July 1, 1994), 64.

Henderson, Tom. Maybe You Have a Case of the BLOBs. *Network Computing*, 6; 4 (April 1, 1995), 138.

Labriola, Don. Videoconferencing: The Next Best Thing. *PC Magazine*, 14; 21 (December 5, 1995), NE1.

Quait, Barry and Timothy Haight. Let's Meet! Desktop to Desktop. *Network Computing*, 5; 8 (July 1, 1994), 62.

Sullivan, Joe. T.120 Conferencing Standards Ease Data Sharing. *Network World*, 12; 25 (June 19, 1995), 49.

Taylor, Kieran. Desktop Videoconferencing: Not Ready for Prime Time. *Data Communications*, 24, 5 (April 1995), 65.

Tolly, Kevin. Networked Multimedia: How Much Bandwidth Is Enough? *Data Communications*, 23; 13 (September 21, 1994), 44.

Middleware/Distributed Objects

Dolgicer, Max. Messaging Middleware: The Next Generation. *Data Communications*, 23; 10 (July 1994), 77.

Dorshkind, Brent. Apps Get Networked Services. *LAN Times*, 12; 14 (July 24, 1995), 56.

Girishankar, Saroja. Distributed Object Technology: Objects of Frustration. *Communications Week*, no. 560 (June 5, 1995), 43.

Greenbaum, Joshua. Middleware. *LAN Times*, 12; 16 (August 28, 1995), 67.

Hayes, Frank. Object Lesson in Patience. *Information Week*, no. 536 (July 17, 1995), 40.

Johnson, Johna. Software Guarantees Data Delivery. *Data Communications*, 24; 5 (April 1995), 45.

Mann, John. Message-Oriented Middleware. *Network Computing*, 5; 14 (November 15, 1994), 72.

Marshall, Martin. Microsoft, OMG Take New Steps. *Communications Week*, no. 563 (June 26, 1995), 15.

Orfali, Robert and Dan Harkey. Client/Server with Distributed Objects. *Byte*, 20; 4 (April 1995), 151.

Passmore, David. DCE vs. NDS: Will Middleware Worlds Collide? *Business Communications Review*, 24; 9 (September 1994), 24.

Rao, Bandu. Making the Most of Middleware. *Data Communications*, 24; 12 (September 1995), 89.

Robertson, Bruce. APIware vs. Middleware. *Network Computing*, 5; 15 (December 1, 1994), 120.

Tibbitts, Fred. CORBA: A Common Touch for Distributed Applications. *Data Communications*, 24; 7 (May 21, 1995), 71.

Williams, Dennis. Mobile Middleware Reaches Out. *LAN Times*, 12; 20 (October 2, 1995), 63.

Database Interoperability/Replication/Distribution

DePompa, Barbara. There's Gold in Database. *Information Week*, no. 561 (January 8, 1996), 52.

Dorschkind, Brent. What's Up OpenDoc? *LAN Times*, 12; 13 (July 3, 1995), 45.

Edelstein, Herb. Mining Data Warehouses. *Information Week*, no. 561 (January 8, 1996), 48.

Hall, Jeff. Adventures in Data Replication. *Network Computing*, 6; 3 (March 1, 1995), 134.

Hansen, Mark and James LaFollette. Getting in Front of Lotus Notes Replication. *Business Communications Review*, 25; 5 (May 1995), 38.

Kay, Emily. Taming the Paper Jungle. *Information Week*, no. 534 (July 3, 1995), 58.

Keating, Paul. Migrate Your SQL Server to Windows NT. *Network Computing*, 5; 15 (December 1, 1994), 116.

Mier, Edwin. One Database, Many Pieces. *Communications Week*, no. 567 (July 24, 1995), 70.

Rao, Bindu. Distributed Applications? Don't Forget the Database. *Data Communications*, 24; 14 (October 1995), 113.

Richter, Jane. Distributing Data. *Byte*, 19; 6 (June 1994), 139.

Robertson, Bruce. Information Builders' EDA/SQL: Middleware Everywhere. *Network Computing*, 5; 6 (September 1, 1994), 156.

Robertson, Bruce. Many Roads Through the Middle. *Network Computing*, 6; 2 (February 1, 1995), 68.

Robertson, Bruce. Sniffing Microsoft SQL Server 6.0 DB-Library. *Network Computing*, 6; 12 (October 1, 1995), 132.

Robertson, Bruce. To DB2 from the Desktop: Too Many Ways. *Network Computing*, 7; 1 (January 15, 1996), 152.

Schulman, Marc. OLE, OpenDoc Vie to Shape the Future of Computing. *Network World*, 12; 26 (June 26, 1995), 37.

Shimmin, Bradley. OLE to Span Platforms. *LAN Times*, 12; 23 (November 6, 1995), 1.

Taschek, John. ODBC Emerges as a Top Option for Enterprise Data Access. *PC Week*, 12; 22 (June 5, 1995), 70.

Taschek, John. OLE DB to Cut Limits of Legacy Systems. 12; 25 (June 26, 1995), 86.

Walsh, Brian. Client Application's First Deadly Sin. *Network Computing*, 6; 6 (May 15, 1995), 45.

Yavin, David. Optimizing Notes Replication. *Byte*, 19; 9 (September 1994), 201.

Database/Data Access Tools

Butler, Brian and Thomas Mace. SQL Query and Reporting: Straight Answers, Limited Risk. *PC Magazine*, 14; 11 (June 13, 1995), 209.

Johnson, Johna. Workgroup Oracle: Fast and Mobile. *Data Communications*, 24; 3 (March 1995), 137.

McKee, Dan. Simple Cross-Platform Apps with DataEdit. *Network Computing*, 5; 13 (November 1, 1994), 126.

Groupware

Baldazo, Rex and Stanford Diehl. Workgroup Conferencing. *Byte*, 20; 3 (March 1995), 125.

Dorschkind, Brent. Orchestrating Notes. *LAN Times*, 12; 12 (June 19, 1995), 61.

Hahn, Eric. Groupware Comes of Age. *Network Computing*, 5; 14 (November 15, 1994), 68.

Hsu, Meichun and Mike Howard. Work-Flow and Legacy Systems. *Byte*, 19; 7 (July 1994), 109.

Layland, Robin. Is Your Network Ready for Notes? *Data Communications*, 24; 5 (April 1995), 83.

Marshak, David. Competing Platforms. *Byte*, 20; 8 (August 1995), 84.

May, Thornton. Know Your Workflow Tools. *Byte*, 19; 7 (July 1994), 103.

Newman, David and Kevin Tolly. Document Conferencing: Real Time, Real Data. *Data Communications*, 24; 8 (June 1995), 81.

Pompili, Tony. Closing the Workflow Gap. *PC Magazine*, 14; 2 (January 24, 1995), NE1.

Pompili, Tony. The Best Notes Server. *PC Magazine*, 14; 12 (June 27, 1995), NE1.

Schrage, Michael. Groupware Requires Much More than Bandwidth. *Business Communications Review*, 25; 11 (November 1995), 35.

Seachrist, David. Work-free Workgroup Schedulers. *Byte*, 20; 8 (August 1995), 128 NA2.

Sullivan, Kristina. Step Up to the Whiteboard Please. *PC Week*, 12; 23 (June 12, 1995), N3.

Timmins, Annmarie. Beta Report: Lotus Notes 4 Proves to Be Enterprise-Saavy. *Network World*, 12; 31 (July 31, 1995), 1.

Tolly, Kevin. A Real World Benchmark for Lotus Notes. *Data Communications*, 24; 8 (June 1995), 35.

Trammel, Kelly. Under Construction. *Byte*, 20; 8 (August 1995), 93.

Wallace, Scott. Working Smarter. *Byte*, 19; 7 (July 1994), 100.

Yavin, David. Replication's Fast Track. *Byte*, 20; 8 (August 1995), 88A.

X.500/Directory Integration

Allison, Jeff. X.500 Directory Services: One Big Happy Network. *Data Communications*, 24; 7 (May 21, 1995), 55.

Gillooly, Caryn. Directory Services: Finding the Way. *Information Week*, no. 560 (Jaunary 1, 1996), 24.

Gillooly, Caryn. Let Your Fingers Do the Walking. *Information Week*, no. 552 (November 6, 1995), 65.

Horwitt, Elizabeth. Bringing It All Together, Enterprise Style. *Network World*, 12; 35 (August 28, 1995), C13.

Johnson, Johna. An X.500 Method to Directory Madness. *Data Communications*, 24; 7 (May 21, 1995), 27.

O'Brien, Timothy and Remi DuBois. Getting a Grip on Directory Services. *Business Communications Review*, 25; 12 (December 1995), 44.

Surkan, Michael. How Directory Services Standards Stack Up. *PC Week*, 13; 3 (January 22, 1996), N14.

Surkan, Michael. Net Directories Mature. *PC Week*, 13; 3 (January 22, 1996), N1.

Security

Barrus, Karl. Protecting Your Privacy. *Network Computing*, 6; 4 (April 1, 1995), 146.

Bellovin, Steven and William Cheswick. Network Firewalls. *IEEE Communications*, 32; 9 (September 1994), 50.

Brown, Patrick. Digital Signatures: Are They Legal for Electronic Commerce? *IEEE Communications*, 32; 9 (September 1994), 76.

Bryan, John. Build a Firewall. *Byte*, 20; 4 (April 1995), 91.

Bryan, John. Firewalls for Sale. *Byte*, 20; 4 (April 1995), 99.

Chokhani, Santosh. Toward a National Public Key Infrastructure. *IEEE Communications*, 32; 9 (September 1994), 70.

Denning, Dorothy and Miles Smid. Key Escrowing Today. *IEEE Communications*, 32; 9 (September 1994), 58.

Kay, Russell. Distributed and Secure. *Byte*, 19; 6 (June 1994), 165.

Moskowitz, Robert. Firewalls: Building in that Peaceful, Easy Feeling. *Network Computing*, 5; 6 (June 1, 1994), 159.

Neuman, B. Clifford and Theodore Tso. Kerberos: An Authentication Service for Computer Networks. *IEEE Communications*, 32; 9 (September 1994), 33.

Sandhu, Ravi and Pierangela Samarati. Access Control: Principles and Practice. *IEEE Communications*, 32; 9 (September 1994), 40.

Schwartz, Jeffery. Group Agrees on Method to Secure E-Mail. *Communications Week*, no. 567 (July 24, 1995), 1.

Stallings, William. Pretty Good Privacy. *Byte*, 19; 7 (July 1994), 193.

Stallings, William. The PGP Web of Trust. *Byte*, 20; 2 (February 1995), 161.

Wayner, Peter. Corporations Eye Private Security Schemes. *Byte*, 20; 8 (August 1995), 36.

Wayner, Peter. Software Key Escrow Emerges. *Byte*, 19; 10 (October 1994), 40.

Yesil, Magdalena. Securing Electronic Payments over the Net. *Network World*, 12; 28 (July 10, 1995), 35.

Fault Tolerance

Callaway, Erin. No-Fault Insurance. *PC Week*, 12; 22 (June 5, 1995), 19.

EDI

Hendry, Mike. *Implementing EDI* (Boston: Artech House, 1993).

Wayner, Peter. EDI Moves the Data. *Byte*, 19; 10 (October 1994), 121.

OLTP Monitors

Cole, Barb. Novell Plans to Gussy Up Tuxedo. *Network World*, 12; 22 (May 29, 1995), 16.

Cox, John. Novell Jazzes up Tuxedo to Manage Bigger Nets. *Network World*, 12; 45 (November 6, 1995), 37.

Fogarty, Kevin. Novell to Dress up Tuxedo. *Network World*, 12; 35 (August 1995), 1.

Gray, Jim and Jeri Edwards. Scale Up with TP Monitors. *Byte*, 20; 4 (April 1995), 123.

Hudgins-Bonafield, Christine. Tuxedo Becomes Novell's Secret Weapon. *Network Computing*, 6; 5 (May 1, 1995), 34.

Johnson, Johna. Client-Server's Magic Bullet? *Data Communications*, 24; 10 (August 1994), 44.

Johnson, Johna. Flexibility Comes to Transaction Management. *Data Communications*, 24; 17 (December 1995), 39.

Peterson, David. The Great Debate: OLTP vs RDBMS. *Business Communications Review*, 25; 4 (April 1995), 62.

Richman, Dan. Transaction Monitors: The Open View. *Information Week*, no. 543 (September 4, 1995), 45.

Rogers, Amy. New Version of Tuxedo Integrated with NDS. *Communications Week*, no. 560 (June 5, 1995), 4.

Application Interoperability/OLE/Applications Development/Software Testing

Apiki, Steve. OLE Controls from the Ground Up. *Byte*, 20; 3 (March 1995), 169.

Burke, Bill. Building Applications Component by Component. *Network World*, 12; 40 (October 2, 1995), 43.

Cox, John. Special Focus: Software Testing. *Network World*, 12; 31 (July 31, 1995), 33.

Gallagher, Sean. Visual Tools: Constructing Better Visuals. *Information Week*, no. 560 (January 1, 1996), 50.

Halfhill, Tom and Salvatore Salamone. Components Everywhere. *Byte*, 21; 1 (January 1996), 97.

Hayes, Frank. Bridging the Object Gap. *Information Week*, no. 540 (August 14, 1995), 70.

Henry, Amanda. Novell Upstages Microsoft OLE. *LAN Times*, 12; 17 (September 11, 1995), 1.

Linthicum, David. And One for All. *Byte*, 20; 11 (November 1995), 131.

Linthicum, David. Integration, Not Perspiration. *Byte*, 21; 1 (January 1996), 83.

Malone, Ian. Getting Real about Client-Server Design.

Business Communications Review, 26; 1 (January 1996), 31.

Plain, Stephen. Prepackaged Power: New OCX Controls. *PC Magazine*, 15; 2 (January 23, 1996), 203.

Plain, Stephen. Prepackaged Power II: More New OCX Controls. *PC Magazine*, 15; 3 (February 6, 1996), 211.

Pleas, Keith. Extending the Reach of OLE. *Byte*, 19; 11 (November 1994), 199.

Robertson, Bruce. Too Many Directories and Too Many Applications. *Network Computing*, 6; 14 (November 1, 1995), 119.

Shimmin, Bradley. General Magic Waves Its Wand. *LAN Times*, 12; 25 (December 4, 1995), 61.

Shimmin, Bradley. Splitting Apps Speeds Development. *LAN Times*, 12; 23 (November 6, 1995), 59.

Sturm, Rick and John Weinstock. Application MIBs: Taming the Software Beast. *Data Communications*, 24; 15 (November 1995), 85.

van Kirk, Doug. Diamond in the Rough. *Information Week*, no. 538 (July 31, 1995), 34.

Wong, William. Network Divided by Three. *Communications Week*, no. 575 (September 18, 1995), 56.

Agents/Smart Software

Indermaur, Kurt. Baby Steps. *Byte*, 20; 3 (March 1995), 97.

Shimmin, Bradley. General Magic Waves Its Wand. *LAN Times*, 12; 25 (December 4, 1995), 61.

Wayner, Peter. Free Agents. *Byte*, 20; 3 (March 1995), 105.

Packaged Client/Server Application Software

Cox, John. Making Packaged Applications Fit In. *Network World*, 13; 23 (June 5, 1995), 36.

Dolgicer, Max. Tools of Choice for Client/Server Development. *Data Communications*, 24; 8 (June 1995), 31.

Scheier, Robert. Tailor Made. *PC Week*, 12; 23 (June 12, 1995), 19.

OLAP—On-Line Analytical Processing

Callaway, Erin. The Flavors of OLAP. *PC Week*, 12; 28 (July 17, 1995), 14.

Gill, Philip and Gael Core. OLAP: A Great Concept in its Infancy. *Open Computing*, 12; 12 (December 1995), 61.

Pickering, Wendy. Financial Vendors Drilling into OLAP. *PC Week*, 12; 25 (June 26, 1995), 33.

Pickering, Wendy. Financial Vendors Drilling into OLAP. *PC Week*, 12; 25 (June 26, 1995), 33.

CASE STUDY

Chapter 17

KARAT RUNS SMALL-TIME SHOW

Enterprise Platform Manages LAN for Cable TV-Guide Publisher

When people think of management platforms, many think of high-powered, high-priced systems reserved for managing only the largest of client/server networks. But the reality is that even small networks need to be managed efficiently. Implementing a heavy-duty network-management platform can be a practical investment for growing companies that need to get unruly networks under control.

In the case of TVSM Inc., a modest-sized publishing company that specializes in cable-TV guides and services, implementing IBM's SystemView management platform helped keep IS staff requirements to a minimum and provide a solution for handling network growth.

Before beta testing SystemView, John Spiewak, information services director at TVSM in Horsham, Pa., said he used few, if any, tools for managing the company's 100-plus IBM OS/2 PCs, Apple Computer Inc. Macintoshes, and Digital Equipment Corp. 5000 workstations.

"A firehose" was Spiewak's answer when asked what tools he used to help him detect and resolve problems with the network. However, Spiewak conceded to using IBM's ADSTAR Distributed Storage Management software for managing data backup and restore and IBM's LoadLeveler/60000 software for balancing data-processing jobs among various workstations.

Spiewak found himself enrolled in the Karat beta-testing program last year after learning that TVSM's lone RS/6000 server was about to be joined by three additional RS/6000 servers, with another two servers to be added by June.

"All of a sudden we had six servers instead of one," said Spiewak.

A key priority was to manage the backup and recovery process for all six servers, he said. With only one staff member in charge of backups, TVSM needed a way to automate the process. "Our goal is to have a complete, lights-out operation," Spiewak said.

Among the first management tasks Spiewak used Karat to accomplish was scheduling and monitoring backup processes. With an IBM 3494 robotic tape library connected to the Karat server, Spiewak or one of the IS staff members could immediately detect backup errors or make changes to backup schedules.

However, Spiewak quickly came up to speed on Karat's other functions. "After [attending] one three-day class on Karat, I was able to use all of the applications it came with," he said. Using Karat's NetView for AIX component, Spiewak and his team were able "to find network problems we didn't even know we had."

Easy to Use

Karat's simple, object-oriented interface particularly impressed Spie-wak. "Everything is work-oriented vs. application-oriented, which makes [Karat] easy for anyone to learn how to use." Performing tasks from the Karat control panel is "easy as dragging an icon and dropping it on a folder," he explained.

Spiewak said another plus is that "I can access Karat from anywhere on the network—any OS/2 machine, for example, provided I have the access rights to do it." In addition, he can use Karat to monitor TVSM's IBM DB2/6000 database. With some customization on his part, Spiewak was able to configure Karat to automatically react to certain problems. Aside from automatically generating a trouble ticket when the DB2 server fails, Karat will either restart the server, run a custom program and restart the server, or page the system programmer.

According to Spiewak, implementing an end-to-end system for managing TVSM's network has saved the company significantly in terms of staff expenditures. "We thought we'd need multiple administrators when we added more machines. The truth is, we aren't going to need more people now," he said. "The next step [is] going to be to try to manage our remote sites using Karat."

Source: Claudia Graziano (May 8, 1995). Karat Runs Small-Time Show. *LAN Times*, 12(9), 22. Reprinted with permission of McGraw-Hill, *LAN Times*.

BUSINESS CASE STUDY QUESTIONS

Activities

1. Complete a top-down model for this case by gleaning facts from the case and placing them in the proper layer of the top-down model. After completing the top-down model, analyze and detail those instances when requirements were clearly passed down from upper to lower layers of the model and solutions to those requirements were passed up from lower to upper layers.
2. Detail any questions that may occur to you about the case for which answers are not clearly stated in the article.

Business

1. From a strategic perspective, what did the implementation of IBM's SystemView enterprise network management system provide?
2. After reading the article, do you agree with the contention that enterprise network management systems are appropriate for small or growing business?
3. What was the overall goal of the network operations management?
4. How difficult or complicated is it to implement required training for an enterprise network management system?
5. According to the article, what was the most significant business layer benefit?

Application

1. What were the operation management priorities?
2. Which particular network management applications were employed in this environment?
3. What were some of the reported benefits from these applications?
4. What is the orientation of the user interface in IBM SystemView?
5. What was the customer's reaction to the interface orientation?
6. Were any help desk features implemented?
7. What were some of the optional actions which could be taken in the event of an alarm condition?

Data

1. Does IBM SystemView possess the capability to manage databases? If so, how?

Network

1. What impending changes in network configuration motivated the network manager in the article to investigate enterprise network management software?
2. What was the somewhat surprising outcome of the NetView for AIX component?
3. From where on the network can the enterprise network management system be accessed? Why might this be important?
4. What is the likely next step for further implementation of the enterprise network management system?

Technology

1. Describe the variety of workstations to be managed in this network environment.

Glossary

10/100 NICs Most of the 100BaseT NICs are called 10/100 NICs which means that they are able to support either 10BaseT or 100BaseT, but not simultaneously

100BaseFX physical layer standard for 100Mbps transmission over Fiber optic cable

100BaseT4 physical layer standard for 100Mbps transmission over 4 pair of Category 3, 4, or 5 UTP

100BaseTx this is the most common of the three 100BaseX standards and the one for which the most technology is available. It specifies 100Mbps performance over 2 pair of Category 5 UTP (Unshielded Twisted Pair) or 2 pair of Type 1 STP (Shielded Twisted Pair)

100VG-AnyLAN 100VG-AnyLAN is a 100Mbps alternative to 100BaseT which replaces the CSMA/CD access methodology with Demand Priority Access or DPA, otherwise known as Demand Priority Protocol or DPP

10Base2 A 10Mbps Ethernet standard for thin coaxial cable media

10Base5 A 10Mbps Ethernet standard for thick coaxial cable media

10BaseF A 10Mbps Ethernet standard for fiber optic cable media

10BaseT A 10Mbps Ethernet standard for unshielded twisted pair media

16-bit sub-system A shared memory address space, sometimes referred to as a 16-bit sub-system, allows 16bit applications to execute in a 32 bit operating environment

1Base5 A 1Mbps Ethernet standard for unshielded twisted pair

3270 protocol conversion card 3270 Protocol Conversion card is inserted into an open expansion slot of a PC. Additional protocol conversion software, which may or may not be included with the protocol conversion card, must be loaded onto the PC in order to make the PC keyboard behave like a 3270 terminal keyboard

3D Memory Module 3D Memory Modules, not to be confused with 3DRAM, stack memory chips on top of each other.

3DRAM 3 Dimensional RAM

4 conductor station wire The type of phone wire installed in most homes consists of a tan plastic jacket containing four untwisted wires: red, yellow, green, and black and is also known as 4 conductor station wire or RYGB

4mm DAT DDS 1 Digital Audio Tape Backup device with 2GB capacity & 21-23MB/min throughput

4mm DAT DDS 2 Digital Audio Tape Backup device with 4GB capacity & 23-30MB/min throughput

7 Hop limit One very important limitation of source routing bridges as applied to large internetworks is known as the 7 Hop Limit. Because of the limited space in the RIF (Router Information Field) of the explorer packet, only 7 hop locations can be included in the path to any remote destination

8mm 8mm digital magnetic tape backup device with 5GB capacity & 15-29MB/min throughput

absolute path names In Unix, Absolute path names start at the root directory in the listing of the path to the destination directory while relative path names start at the current directory

access control lists See ACL

access methodologies Since the LAN media is to be shared by numerous PC users, then there must be some way to control access by multiple users to that media. These media sharing methods are properly known as access methodologies.

access server See Communications server

access tokens See token authentication

acknowledgment & polling traffic The first characteristic of SNA which can cause trouble on a LAN is the great amount of acknowledgement and polling traffic between SNA processors and SNA end-user devices. This constant chatter could quickly monopolize the better part of the LAN bandwidth.

ACL Authorization screens users according to UserIDs and passwords and determines by examining Access Control Lists (ACL) whether or not a given user is authorized to access requested files or system resources. NT's security reference monitor compares the requested object's security description as documented in access control lists (ACL), with the requesting user's security information as documented on their security access token

Across the Wire Migration   Across the Wire Migration would be used to install NetWare 4.1 on a new computer rather than one currently running NetWare 3.x. In this case, in addition to the new computer and the existing NetWare 3.x server, a DOS client is also required so that the MIGRATE utility can be run between the two servers

active assistance sub-systems   active assistance sub-systems allow users to describe what they wish to accomplish, such as purchasing an airline ticket or receiving inventory at a loading dock, and the system will lead them through the desired transaction on a step-by-step basis

active management MAUs   Active management MAUs are able to send alerts to management consoles regarding malfunctioning token ring adapters and can also forcibly remove these misbehaving adapters from the ring.

active matrix   Active Matrix displays employ transistors at each point on the display grid to actively control color and intensity of each "dot" in the display. This technology enables brighter colors, sharper images, and faster response to changing images

active monitor   In a token passing access methodology, the token is generated in the first place by a designated PC known as the active monitor and passed among PCs until one PC would like to access the network.

actor   The term actor is specific to the Chorus microkernel and is the functional equivalent of a task in a Mach microkernel or a process in a UNIX environment

ad hoc workflow   This category of workflow software automates more open-ended, creative, or flexible business processes which are done occasionally or in an unscheduled manner.

adaptive segmented lookahead cache   Adaptive Segmented Lookahead buffers are able to dynamically adjust the number and size of buffers dependent on the situation.

adaptive sliding window protocol   NBF improves on NetBEUI's data transfer performance in connection-oriented sessions by adopting an adaptive sliding window protocol which allows for more efficient data transfer.

address bit order reversal   In the case of IEEE 802.3, the least significant bit is the right-most bit of the byte and in the case of IEEE 802.5, the least significant bit is the left-most bit of the byte. This bit order reversal is especially troublesome for translating bridges which must translate between token ring and Ethernet frames

address bus   The width of the address bus is the controlling factor as to how much memory a given computer system can access

address caching   In order to avoid constantly flooding the network with explorer packets seeking destinations, source routing bridges may employ some type of address caching or RIF caching, so that previously determined routes to known destinations are saved and re-used.

address classes   IP addresses are categorized into address classes A, B, C, D, or E

address resolution protocol   See ARP

address resolution server   LAN emulation is most often implemented by the ATM vendor by the installation of an address resolution server which provides translation between the ATM addressing scheme and the addressing scheme which is native to a particular emulated LAN

administrative workflow   This category of workflow software automates routine business processes which nearly all businesses have in common. Examples include purchase order requisition and approval, accounts payable approval, review of job applicants' files, or expense report approval.

Advanced Peer to Peer Networking   See APPN

Advanced Power Management   See APM

advisory agents   Advisory agents or wizards assist users as they learn their way around new software packages thereby easing frustration and shortening the learning curve. Advisory agents can sense when a user is performing a repetitive task which could perhaps be automated or done more efficiently

agent   Each network-attached device which is to be SNMP-compliant must be equipped with software capable of reporting required performance statistics in standardized SNMP format. This embedded SNMP reporting software is known as a software agent, SNMP agent, or management agent. Network statistics and information are gathered in the first place and packetized in SNMP format by specialized software known as agents which reside within the monitored network device and are supplied by the network device's manufacturer

agent event manager   One of three cooperating components of the agent portion of the client/agent/server architecture. The agent event manager is combined with a customer written transaction handler to form an entity known as the intelligent agent which resides on the local server. Once the agent event manager receives a request from a mobile client, it acts on behalf of that client in all communications with the local server until the original client request is totally fulfilled

agents   Intelligent software, also known as smart software, utilizes agents which assist end-users in their quest for increased productivity

agents Agents are software programs which run on networking devices such as servers, bridges, and routers to monitor and report the status of those devices. Agent software must be compatible with the device that it is reporting management statistics for as well as with the protocols supported by the enterprise network management system to which those statistics are fed

algorithm The DES encryption standard actually has two parts which serve to offer greater overall security. In addition to the standard algorithm or method of encrypting data 64 bits at a time, the DES standard also uses a 64 bit key.

AMP Asymmetric multiprocessing (AMP) or (ASMP) is characterized by entire applications processes, rather than threads, being assigned to a particular processor. Processor loads can become unbalanced. In AMP systems, each CPU is generally assigned their own memory and other sub-systems

ANCS AT&T NetWare Connect Services (ANCS) is a network of access servers running NetWare Connect remote access software and offering support for both IP and IPX network layer protocols. NetWare NDS servers provide network-wide directory and security services.

API Application Program Interfaces (API) allow a single application to work with multiple, different database management systems. APIs prevent programmers from having to write specific versions of programs for each unique database management system, network operating system, operating system combination possible for all servers to whom the front-end tool may ever wish to speak.

API A type of software specification known as a network Applications Program Interface (API) allows requests for services from application programs to be passed along to the network attached services from application programs to be passed along to the network attached servers which provide these services

APM Power management features offered by operating systems have been standardized as the Advanced Power Management (APM) specification.

Appletalk Appletalk is included as a communications protocol in order to support NT's Services for Macintosh (SFM)

applets Java is an object-oriented language which adds animation and real-time interaction through the use of independently executed mini-programs called applets. The object-oriented nature of the language allows the applets to be run in a variety of different orders depending on the interaction with the user.

application level filter Application level filters, also known as assured pipelines, examine the entire request for data rather than just the source and destination ad-dresses. Secure files can be marked as such and application level filters will not allow those files to be transferred, even to users authorized by port level filters

application MIB In order to effectively manage distributed information systems, distributed applications must be able to be managed in a manner similar to enterprise network components through the use of an Application MIB

application program interface See API

application program interface Whether or not an application is executable over a particular network operating system is dependent upon whether or not that application issues commands and requests for network-based services in a pre-determined format defined by the network operating system's application program interface

application rightsizing Applications rightsizing implies that applications are designed for and deployed on the platform, or type and size of computer, which makes the most sense: the "right" size computer. The right computer or platform implies that the choice is based on maximizing the efficiency with which the application runs

application services It is the server network operating system which is responsible for application services which includes not only executing the back-end engine portion of the application, but also supplying the messaging and communications services to enable interoperability between distributed clients and servers.

applications layer The application layer, layer 7 of the OSI Model is also open to misinterpretation. Application layer protocols do not include end-user application programs. Rather, they include utilities which support end-user application programs. Some people include network operating systems in this category. Strictly speaking, the best examples of application layer protocols are the OSI protocols X.400 and X.500

applications software Applications software on a LAN is divided into client front-ends and server back-ends or engines and is concerned with accomplishment of a specific type of task or transaction. LAN applications software can be divided into two major sub-categories: LAN productivity software & LAN resource management software

APPN APPN-Advanced Peer to Peer Network is IBM's answer to multiprotocol networking on a peer to peer basis using the SNA architecture, rather than a LAN-based network architecture.

ARP ARP or Address Resolution Protocol (RFC 826) is used if an IP address of workstation is known but a datalink layer address for the same workstation is required.

ASMP See AMP

assistant agents Assistant agents act much like a human administrative assistant by performing specific tasks on behalf of, but out of the direct control of, the end-user. Examples of assistant agents' tasks might be: to screen, manage, and re-format electronic received e-mail and faxes, to surf the Internet in search of articles or research on a given topic

assured pipeline   See application level filter

asymmetric multi-processing   See AMP

asynchronous   A distributed application could generate a message for another distributed application, forward it to the message queue, and resume its own processing activity. This type of inter-process dialogue is known as asynchronous

asynchronous frames   In FDDI, while synchronous frames are being transmitted, any unused network capacity can still be used by other workstations transmitting asynchronous frames.

asynchronous I/O   Asynchronous I/O refers to the situation when a client application spawns a thread for information or processing and proceeds with the execution of the client application without waiting for the results of the spawned thread

asynchronous message passing   A distributed application could generate a message for another distributed application, forward it to the message queue, and resume its own processing activity. This type of inter-process dialogue is known as asynchronous message passing or asynchronous communication and does not assume nor rely upon total network reliability

asynchronous replication   Asynchronous replication, also known as store-and-forward replication, does not guarantee that all replicated servers are totally synchronized at all times. However, asynchronous replication does not require the same 100% network reliability of synchronous replication

asynchronous transfer mode   See ATM

AT&T NetWare Connect Services   See ANCS

AT&T SVR4   One of the two popular versions of Unix. AT&T System V Release 4, commonly written as SVR4-Originally developed by AT&T later reorganized as USL, (UNIX Systems Laboratory) which AT&T subsequently sold to Novell

ATA   IDE (Integrated Drive Electronics) Disk drives are distinguished from earlier offerings by the inclusion of the drive controller with the disk drive in a single integrated unit and the use of a bus interface known as ATA (AT Attachment). The key limitation of IDE drives was their capacity limitation of 528MB and ATA's 2-3MBps data transfer rate

ATA-2   See E-IDE

ATM   ATM (Asynchronous Transfer Mode) which is a type of switching which allows not only LAN net-

work architectures to be switched extremely quickly but can also switch voice, video, and image traffic equally well. In fact ATM can switch any type of digital information over LANs or WANs with equal ease and speeds which are currently in the 622Mbps range and rapidly approaching the gigabit/second range.

ATM   If the switched bandwidth offered by traditional LAN switches is not sufficient, then a faster switching technology known as ATM or Asynchronous Transfer Mode, is also available. One of the real benefits of ATM is its ability to switch LAN traffic without the need to make any hardware or software changes to LAN clients or servers

ATM address resolution   In ATM LAN Emulation, unlike LAN switch-based virtual LANs, MAC layer addresses must be translated into, or resolved into, ATM addresses in a process known as ATM address resolution

ATM Address Resolution Protocol   See ATMARP

ATM LAN emulation   In ATM LAN Emulation, virtual LANs are able to be constructed over an ATM switched network regardless of the geographic scope of that network. ATM LAN emulation is considered a bridging solution, like LAN switch-based virtual LANs, since traffic is switched based on MAC layer addresses.

ATMARP   ATMARP (ATM Address Resolution Protocol) runs on a server in the logical IP subnet and provides address resolution between IP addresses and ATM addresses

attachment protocols   attachment protocols are concerned with how additional files such as documents, spreadsheets, sound bites, video images, or faxes can be attached to e-mail messages and then successfully detached and viewed at the destination workstation

Attachment Units   See AU

attenuation   Attenuation is the decrease in the power of signal over a distance in a particular type of wire or media.

AU   Iso-Ethernet hubs are known as Attachment Units (AU) and cost between $400 - $500 per port

audiotex   These systems deliver audio information to callers based on responses on the touch-tone keypad to pre-recorded questions. Primarily used for information hot-lines.

auditing system   In NetWare 4.1, an extensive auditing system monitors and reports on what valid users are doing. The auditor acts independently of the supervisor and separately monitors activity on both the file system and the NetWare Directory Services database

authentication   Authentication assures that messages between client and servers in the distributed processing environment are genuine and have actually been sent from the processor claiming to be the source node on the network. Authentication is usually provided by a dedicated authentication server running specialized software developed specifically for distributed environment

authentication Authentication uses digital signatures which are attached to transmitted documents in order to assure both the authenticity of the author and the document's message integrity which verifies that the document has not been tampered with

authentication Authentication in NetWare 4.1 uses a combination of private encryption keys and passwords, while the VLM requester security agent on the client workstation and NDS file server combine to assure that users are properly authenticated before being logged in

authentication Authentication is concerned with assuring that only legitimate users of enterprise network resources are allowed to gain access to those resources

authorization Authorization is the familiar UserID/Password process which assures that a certain user is authorized to access a particular enterprise resource.

authorization Authorization screens users according to UserIDs and passwords and determines by examining Access Control Lists (ACL) whether or not a given user is authorized to access requested files or system resources

authorization Authorization assures that properly authenticated users only access the network resources for which they are properly authorized

auto-detection & configuration Auto-detection & configuration of installed controllers, interface cards and peripherals by network operating systems is dependent on the network operating system possessing a compatible driver for that device

auto-server shutdown Some UPSs also have the ability to link directly to servers, advising them of a loss of power, thereby triggering user notification and an orderly shutdown. This feature is known as auto-server shutdown, and must be compatible with the particular server operating system installed

automated attendant Allows callers to direct calls to a desired individual at a given business without necessarily knowing their extension number

automated call distribution Used primarily in call centers staffed by large numbers of customer service agents, incoming calls are automatically distributed to the first available rep, or in some cases, the rep which serves a given geographic region as automatically determined by the computer based on the incoming phone number

automated migration tools In order to ease the creation of the NetWare Directory Services database

from NetWare 3.12 bindery objects, automated migration tools have been developed which allow the creation and manipulation of the NDS database structure in a safe, off-line environment without the danger of corrupting live global NDS database structure information.

automatic configuration See relational networks

automatic resynchronization A feature of NetWare Mobile which automatically resynchronizes data upon return to the office or when dialed in to the headquarters file servers.

AWG Wire thickness is measured by gauge and represented with the unit AWG (American Wire Gauge).

B channel In Isochronous Ethernet, The 6.144 Mbps C channel is in fact further subdivided into 96 64Kbps ISDN B channels which carry the actual multimedia traffic. Applications are able to aggregate these B channels as needed up to the 6.144 Mbps limit.

back-end The server portion of the program is often called the back-end or engine

backbone network In a hierarchial enterprise network design, the high speed inter-LAN portion of the network is often referred to as the backbone network

backbone-attached LAN switch offer all of the local switching capabilities of the stand-alone workgroup/departmental LAN switch plus switched access to higher speed backbone networks.

backbone/data center switch offer high capacity, fault tolerant, switching capacity with traffic management capabilities. These high-end switches are really a self-contained backbone network which is sometimes referred to as a collapsed backbone network.

backpressure In the case of Ethernet switches, backpressure prevents lost frames during overload conditions by sending out false collision detection signals in order to get transmitting clients and servers to time-out long enough to give the switch a chance to forward buffered data.

backside bus In a P6 CPU, the second cavity is occupied by a 256KB SRAM L2, or secondary cache, linked directly to the neighboring Pentium Pro chip through a dedicated 64 bit bus known as the backside bus.

backward compatibility A very important aspect of any migration plan to a new client network operating system is the extent of support for backward compatibility is terms of application support, also known as legacy application support. In other words, will current applications run without modification on the new network operating system?

bandwidth hierarchy By creating a bandwidth hierarchy as part of a strategic network design, required bandwidth can be upgraded incrementally in a planned fashion rather than facing wholesale replacement of networking technology in reaction to a crisis of crippling network performance.

baseband transmission baseband transmission means that the entire bandwidth of the media is devoted to one data channel

bindery Network operating systems have always depended on some sort of naming service or directory in which to store information about users as well as systems resources such as disks, servers, and printers. NetWare 3.x servers stored this type of information in a bindery

bindery emulation Bindery emulation allows newly-migrated NetWare 4.1 servers to enjoy most of the benefits of NetWare 4.1 without having to fully convert NetWare 3.12 bindery objects into a NetWare 4.1 NDS database. Bindery emulation allows the use of NetWare 2.x or NetWare 3.x software, NLMs and Netx Shells but still offers many NetWare 4.1 benefits.

bindery files In a NetWare 3.12 environment, this type of security and network resource information is stored in bindery files.

bindery synchronization Bindery synchronization allows a single NetWare 4.1 server to be automatically and transparently synchronized with up to twelve NetWare 2.x or 3.x servers.

binding NDIS specifies a binding operation which is managed by a separate program known as the Protocol Manager that combines separate NDIS compliant driver software supplied by NIC and NOS vendors.

biometric authentication Biometric authentication can authenticate users based on fingerprints, palm prints, retinal patterns, voice recognition or other physical characteristics

Bob Microsoft's social interface for the home market, known as BOB is one of the first social interfaces to be released

BootP BootP which was originally designed to configure local diskless workstations that were not able to store IP configuration information locally. In the case of BootP, the MAC address of the BootP client had to be known beforehand, entered into a database in the BootP server, and permanently associated with an IP address

boundary router In the case of boundary or branch office routers, all routing information is kept at the central site router. This allows the boundary router to require less technical configuration and to be available for a lower cost than central site routers

branch prediction An intelligent instruction handling technique employed in many CPU chips in which the CPU predicts which condition of the branch statement will be true, and automatically loads the associated conditional branch statement.

branch target buffer Most branch prediction processes employ a branch target buffer, or branch target cache which holds the results of as many as the last 256 branches executed in a given program

bridge A bridge uses MAC layer addressing to logically segment traffic between attached LANs

broadcast In a broadcast logical topology, a data message is sent simultaneously to all nodes on the network. Each node decides individually if the data message was directed toward it. If not, the message is simply ignored

Broadcast & Unknown Services See BUS

broadcast filtering Instead of allowing explorer packets onto the internetwork, routers can filter those broadcast packets out of the traffic, read the destination address to which the PC is seeking a route, and supply the PC directly with that information after consulting its own routing tables.

broadcast storm In the case of improperly addressed frames or frames destined for non-existent addresses, frames can be infinitely perpetuated or flooded onto all bridged LANs in a condition known as a broadcast storm

brokered authorization The authorization security software can be server-based, also known as brokered authorization.

brouters At one time, specialized devices which could either bridge or route were referred to as brouters, however, today most advanced routers include bridging functionality

BSD UNIX One of the two popular versions of Unix. BSD (Berkeley Software Distribution) UNIX from the University of California at Berkeley

buffer A device which allows print jobs to be off-loaded from a PC immediately, whether or not a printer is available, allowing the PC user to return to work

buffer memory Buffer memory may be in a stand-alone device called a buffer or may be integrated into a data switch or printer sharing device. Additional buffer memory can usually be added to existing devices in the form of buffer memory upgrades

bulk retrieval mechanism Through a new SNMP2 procedure known as Bulk Retrieval Mechanism, managers can retrieve several pieces of network information at a time from a given agent. This precludes the need for a constant request and reply mechanism for each and every piece of network management information desired.

burst mode IPX NetWare 4.1 introduced packet bursts otherwise known as Burst Mode IPX. This capability is built into the NetWare kernel and allows the NetWare 4.1 VLM requester on the clients and the NetWare 4.1 kernel on the servers to negotiate how many packets can be transmitted before an acknowledgment is required. 10 to 20 packets prior to acknowledgment is not uncommon.

bus The term bus refers to a connection between components either within a CPU chip, between a CPU chip and system components, or between system components

bus The bus topology is a linear arrangement with terminators on either end and devices connected to the "bus" via connectors and/or transceivers.

BUS LES Broadcast & Unknown Services (BUS) are responsible for handling requests for broadcasts and multicasts within the virtual LANs which exist across the ATM switching fabric

bus and tag A standard for high speed data channels between FEPs and IBM mainframes, Bus and Tag has a transmission rate of 4.5 Mbps and has been available since 1967.

bus interface The data bus width of the bus interface is important to the overall performance of the video sub-system. For this reason, only a local bus architecture such as 32-bit PCI is commonly used for graphics accelerator boards

bus mastering DMA In Bus Mastering DMA, the CPU on the network adapter card manages the movement of data directly into the PC's RAM memory without interruption of the system CPU by taking control of the PC's expansion bus.

bus width bus width is measured in bits and refers to the number of bits which can travel in parallel down a bus. Common bus widths are 8, 16, 32, 64 and 128 bits.

business communications services Business Communications Services go beyond Internet connectivity to include such additional services as: Videoconferencing, Simultaneous document sharing, Electronic Data Interchange (EDI), Global FAX service, Electronic Document Distribution, Paging, E-Mail, News & Information Services

business process reengineering an analysis methodology which provides an opportunity to critically re-examine business processes

C channel In Isochronous Ethernet, A 6.144 Mbps ISDN C channel is reserved for streaming time sensitive traffic such as multimedia applications.

C2 level security Server operating systems often claim to implement C2 level security. C2 level security is ac-

tually part of a specification known as "Trusted Computer System Evaluation Criteria" which is specified in a Department of Defense document commonly known as "The Orange Book". The book concentrates on 7 levels of data confidentiality from D (low) to A1 (high).

cache bus The external cache bus is responsible for quickly delivering data and instructions to/from L2 cache to/from the CPU

cache manager The cache manager works closely with the file systems supported by NT to optimize the file services offered to applications. By effectively managing cache memory, the cache manager can minimize the number of physical read/writes to disks, thereby optimizing the performance of applications programs.

Call control Using computer-based applications users are more easily able to use all of the features of their phone system or PBX, especially the more complicated but seldom used features. Includes use of features like on-line phone books, autodialing, click-and-point conference calls, on-line display and processing of voice mail messages

card and socket services See CSS

card services The Card services sub-layer of PCMCIA Card & Socket Services is hardware independent and interfaces to the client operating system or network operating system driver software

Carrier Sense Multiple Access with Collision Avoidance See CSMA/CA

Carrier Sense Multiple Access with Collision Detection See CSMA/CD

CAS Communications Applications Specification is a FAX API that was developed by Intel and DCA. This API allows software vendors to integrate FAX capabilities into their application software by allowing the software to include standardized, embedded commands which are understood by FAX boards and FAX modems.

cascading ports Hubs may also be cascadable or stackable via cascading ports which may be specialized ports on the hub or may be switch configurable "normal" ports allowing repeated data to flow out of a cascading port to the next hub rather than the normal inbound-only port traffic flow

CDDI Copper Distributed Data Interface employs FDDI over twisted pair media. The official ANSI standard for CDDI is known as TP-PMD (Twisted Pair-Physical Media Dependent).

CDE UNIX hardware and software vendors Hewlett Packard, Sun, IBM and Novell (UNIX Systems Laboratory) have joined together to produce a cross-platform windowing environment for UNIX named the Common Desktop Environment or CDE

CDE   Common Desktop Environment (CDE) is an effort by a consortium of Unix vendors to establish standards for a unified graphical user interface which allows those Unix varieties which support the CDE to present an identical interface to users.

CDFS   CDFS (CD File System)

CDPD   Cellular Digital Packet Data (CDPD) is a service which uses idle capacity in the circuit-switched cellular network to transmit IP-based data packets. The fact that CDPD is IP-based allows it to easily interface to IP-based private networks as well as to the Internet and other e-mail services.

CDRAM   Cached DRAM

Cellular Digital Packet Data   See CDPD

Central Directory Server   In APPN, The Central Directory Server can save time as well as network traffic for the Network Nodes. Instead of each Network Node on an internetwork doing their own information gathering and internetwork exploration and inquiry, they can simply consult the Central Directory Server.

Central Processing Unit   See CPU

central site router   Central site routers, otherwise known as enterprise or backbone routers are employed at large corporate sites, while boundary or branch office routers are employed at remote corporate locations with less routing requirements and fewer technical support personnel

certificate management   X.500 specifications also include a feature known as certificate management which keeps track of which users are allowed to access which network resources

CGI   Some servers offer a standardized API known as CGI or Common Gateway Interface which allows web applications to be written and potentially executed on multiple different Web servers.

challenge response   See token response

channel-attached gateways   As an alternative to LAN-based gateways, channel-attached gateways are able to interface directly to the mainframe's high speed data channel, thereby bypassing the FEP entirely. Physically, the channel attached gateways are often modules which are added to enterprise routers

CHAP MD5   A protocol for PPP encrypted authentication included with most PPP clients

CHAP MD80   A protocol for authentication for Windows NT RAS included with most PPP clients

child processes   Processes in Unix are controlled by the fork system call as initiated through the shell interface, which allows parent processes to spawn multiple sub-processes known as child processes

Chorus microkernel   Because microkernel-based operating systems can be built in a modular fashion, limited only by the requirement to interface to the microkernel through the minimal number of microkernel system calls, it is possible for different operating systems to be developed from the same microkernel. The Chorus microkernel developed by Chorus Systems (France) is one example of a microkernel which has been used as the nucleus for numerous operating systems

CICS   IBM's CICS (Customer Information Control System) was among the original mainframe-based transaction process monitoring systems.

CIF   A videoconferencing screen format .CIF (Common Intermediate Format) 288 lines × 352 pixels/line

ciphertext   Encryption involves the changing of data into an indecipherable form prior to transmission. In this way, even if the transmitted data is somehow intercepted, it cannot be interpreted. The changed, unmeaningful data is known as ciphertext

ciphertext   Encryption involves the changing of data into an unreadable or unmeaningful form, known as ciphertext prior to transmission

CIPX   A protocol for compression of IPX headers included with most PPP clients

circuit-switched cellular   Analog cellular service capable of supporting 14.4Kbps max

CISC   In the case of a CISC architecture, instructions are interpreted into executable code by microcode which is itself a small computer software program running on the CPU chip. In effect, CISC required one software program to translate another software program.

CISC-to-RISC decoder   In a process which Intel refers to as dynamic execution, the P6 breaks complex CISC instructions down into simpler RISC-like, but not true RISC, instructions known as micro-ops.

classical IP   See IP over ATM

Classical IP over ATM   IETF RFC (Request for Comment) 1577 is known as Classical IP over ATM. The goal of Classical IP over ATM is to allow IP networks, as well as all upper layer TCP/IP protocols, utilities, and APIs encapsulated by IP; to be delivered over an ATM network without requiring modification to the TCP/IP protocols

client   A client PC is a computer which a user logs into in order to access LAN-attached resources and services

client network operating systems   Client network operating systems integrate traditional operating system functionality with advanced network operating system features to enable communication with a variety of different types of network operating system servers

client software architecture   The overall organization of software categories within a typical client workstation would include presentation, application, data management, network operating system, and operating system categories.

client-agent-server   The overall objective of a Client-agent-server architecture, as opposed to the more common LAN-based client/server architecture, is to reduce the amount of mobile client to server network traffic by building as much intelligence as possible into the server-based agent so that it can act on behalf of the mobile client application

client/server e-mail systems   The server in a client/server e-mail messaging architecture executes back-end e-mail engine software which supports real-time communication links to e-mail clients and other post offices via remote procedure calls (RPC).

client/server information system   A client/server information system takes advantage of the processing power now available on desktop computers by splitting the job of delivering quality information to end-users among multiple computers

client/server network operating systems   Client/Server network operating systems offer the ability to support hundreds of users, and the ability to interact with other network operating systems via gateways. These client/server network operating systems are both considerably more expensive and considerably more complicated to install and administer than peer-to-peer network operating systems.

Client32 Requester   An upgrade to the NetWare DOS Requester known as the Client32 Requester is able to offer a wider variety of VLM-based services while using client memory resources more efficiently

clock multiplying   When clock speeds on a given CPU chip are doubled or tripled, the CPU chip works at the higher rate internally only as instructions are processed in the pipelines at the new, higher rate.

clock speed   Specialized clock circuitry within the CPU chip is used to keep precise timing of CPU operations. Clock speed is measured in Megahertz (MHz) which means millions of cycles per second

clock-divided frequency   The clock speed of a bus may be the full clock speed of the CPU, measured in MHz, or may be one-half, one-third, or one-fourth of the CPU clock speed which is known as clock-divided frequency.

cluster controller   A cluster controller is a device which allows connection of both 3270 terminals as well as

LANs with possible wide area links to packet switched networks (X.25) or high speed leased lines. A cluster controller concentrates the transmissions of its numerous input devices and directs this concentrated data stream to the FEP either locally or remotely

clustering   Clustering implies using the CPU power of multiple CPUs located in separate computing platforms to produce a single, more powerful, virtual computer. Clusters are also sometimes referred to as Virtual Parallel Machines (VPM)

co-processors   math co-processors are separate CPU chips which included floating-point logic and could be purchased separately at the discretion of the computer owner

CODEC   At the heart of the videoconferencing system is the video CODEC (COder-DECoder), which digitizes not only analog video signals but also analog voice signals.

collaborative worksessions   Collaborative or Interactive work sessions allow users connected via networks to participate in joint worksessions as if they were all in the same room working at the same whiteboard or conference table

collapsed backbone   Collapsed backbones, a more recent innovation, collapse the entire network backbone, which once spanned several floors of a building, into the backplane of a single internetworking device such as a router. The backplane of the router which is shared by numerous internetworking modules has enormous bandwidth capacity, usually in the gigabits per second range.

collapsed backbone network   A switched network architecture which employs backbone/data center switches to offer high capacity, fault tolerant, switching capacity with traffic management capabilities

color depth   The number of displayed colors, or color depth, is another performance criteria which differentiates monitors. Common color depths are: 16 colors, 256 colors, 65,000 colors, 16.7 million colors

Common Desktop Environment   See CDE

Common Gateway Interface   See CGI

Common Intermediate Format   See CIF

Common Object Request Broker Architecture   See CORBA

Common Transport Semantics   In the New SNA architecture, Common Transport Semantics layer offers independence between the applications and the transport protocols which deliver those applications across the internetwork

Communications Applications Specification   See CAS

communications server   Remote users could attach to a dedicated multi-user server, known as an access server or communications server through one or more modems. Depending on the software loaded on the communications server, it may deliver remote node functionality, remote control functionality, or both.

communications-based groupware   Communications-based Groupware deals with establishing, maintaining, and managing a variety of types of ad-hoc communications between networked group members

compatibility   Compatibility can be thought of as successfully bridging the gap or communicating between two or more technology components, whether hardware or software

Component Interface API   Part of DMI, The Component Interface API is designed to interface to the individual application programs or desktop components which are to be managed and monitored on the local client.

computer system   The following four sub-systems contribute to the overall performance characteristics of any computer system: Processor or CPU, Memory sub-system, Storage sub-system, Video or Input/Output sub-system.

computer telephony integration   See CTI

conditional branch routing   In workflow automation software, Conditional branch routing introduces multiple possible routes to a process dependent on results or outcomes at a particular step in the process. Exception handling and sophisticated rules-based or expert systems can all be supported or integrated into conditional branch routing workflow automation software.

configuration bridge protocol data unit   Spanning Tree Algorithm bridges accomplish path management by communicating with each other via configuration bridge protocol data units (Configuration BPDU)

Configuration Services   LES Configuration Services are responsible for keeping track of the types of virtual LANs which are being supported over the ATM switching fabric and which LECs belong to which type of LAN. MAC addresses and corresponding ATM addresses of attached workstations are stored by the configuration server

connection-oriented   implying that specific paths known as virtual circuits are explored and determined prior to the first packet being sent. Once the virtual circuit is established directly from the source host or node to destination node, then all packets bound for that address follow each other in sequence down the same physical path.

connection-oriented   The fact that TCP is considered connection-oriented implies that a point-to-point connection between source and destination computers must be established before transmission can begin and that the connection will be torn down after transmission has concluded

connectionless   implying individual, fully addressed IPX packets, or datagrams, are free to negotiate their way through the network in search of their final destination

connectionless   IP allows each packet to be processed individually within the network and does not provide any guarantees as to whether packets will arrive at their intended destination in sequence, if at all. As such, IP is described as a connectionless, unreliable protocol

ConnectView   An add-on product to NetWare Connect known as ConnectView is available which allows network managers to analyze usage trends to spot possible abuse or to prepare reports for cost analysis or chargeback purposes.

container objects   In NDS, organizational units such as companies, divisions, and departments are referred to as container objects. Container objects can be cascaded and can contain leaf objects. Leaf objects cannot be cascaded.

cooked interfaces   Both block-oriented and character-oriented I/O may use buffers and queues to organize the transfer of data from the operating system to the hardware device in question through their respective cooked interfaces

cooperative multitasking   Multitasking implies that an operating system can be running more than one program simultaneously. Cooperative multitasking implies that a given application has access to all required system resources until that program relinquishes that control.

Copper Distributed Data Interface   See CDDI

CORBA   CORBA (Common Object Request Broker Architecture) as proposed by the industry coalition known as the Object Management Group (OMG). A standard for object middleware. See OLE

CORBA 2.0   Interoperability between object request brokers from different vendors can be achieved by compliance with the CORBA 2.0 specification, otherwise known as UNO or Universal Networked Objects.

corporate downsizing   Corporate downsizing, not to be confused with information systems downsizing, has involved elimination of positions within a corporation through attrition, early retirement, closed operations, or forced lay-offs.

CPU   The processor chip or central processing unit (CPU) in which software instructions are actually executed

CRC A 32 bit cyclical redundancy check (CRC) is generated over the address, type, and data fields as a frame check sequence in Ethernet networks

CSMA/CA Part of the IEEE 802.11 standard, CSMA/CA (Carrier Sense Multiple Access with Collision Avoidance) is similar to CSMA/CD except that collisions cannot be detected in wireless environments as they can in wire-based environments. Before transmitting, workstations wait a pre-determined amount of time in order to avoid collisions, and set up a point-to-point wireless circuit to the destination workstation

CSMA/CD Carrier Sense Multiple Access with Collision Detection or CSMA/CD is the access methodology used by Ethernet media sharing LANs

CSS Card and Socket Services is the driver specification for PCMCIA devices that enables the following capabilities and is supposed to relatively self-configuring: hot swappable devices allowing PCMCIA cards to be removed and inserted while the notebook computer is powered up, automatic PCMCIA card configuration, multiple PCMCIA card management, standby mode, I/O conflict management

CTI CTI or Computer Telephony Integration seeks to integrate the two most common productivity devices, the computer and the telephone, to enable increased productivity not otherwise possible by using the two devices in a non-integrated fashion. CTI is not a single application, but an ever-widening array of possibilities spawned by the integration of telephony and computing

Customer Information Control System See CICS

cut-through routing Routing implemented on switches using protocols such as MPOA is sometimes referred to as cut-through routing and uses ATM LAN Emulation as its Layer 2 switching specification

cut-through switches Cut-Through Switches read only the address information in the MAC layer header before beginning processing. Cut-through switching is very fast. However, because the Frame Check Sequence on the forwarded frame was not checked, bad frames are forwarded

CVRAM Cached VRAM (Video RAM)

cybermalls A service offered by some Internet Presence Providers that enables the production of professional quality presentations which can then be incorporated into cybermalls with other professional quality Web pages adhering to the standards established by the cybermall management.

cyclical redundancy check See CRC

D channel In Isochronous Ethernet, 1 64Kbps ISDN D

channel is used for management tasks such as call control and signaling.

daemon The server piece of a TCP/IP utility is usually referred to as a daemon, and is named with a "d" suffix. For example, the client piece of the FTP utility is known as FTP while the server piece is known as ftpd.

DARPA TCP/IP was developed during the 1970's and widely deployed during the 1980's under the auspices of DARPA or Defense Advanced Research Projects Agency in order to meet the Department

DAS Dual Attachment Station devices attach to both of FDDI's rings

data bus The CPU's internal data bus is responsible for delivering data to/from the L1 cache and processing pipelines

data bus width How many bits of data the CPU can read from and write to the L2 cache for each tick of the memory bus clock is determined by the data bus width. This is most often 32 or 64 bits

data cache the results of the executed instruction are written out to a memory location or register usually in a special area called a data cache in the write-back stage

data display channel See DDC

data distribution In a distributed information system, data from the distributed computing environment is distributed and replicated as needed through the functionality delivered by the data distribution or data management sub-system.

data encryption standard See DES

Data Link Control See DLC

Data Link Switching See DLSw

data migration Data migration utilities manage the migration of data among different types of storage devices as part of a comprehensive hierarchical storage management (HSM) program

data migration Data migration features have been added to NetWare 4.1 which allow files to be automatically migrated and archived in a structured fashion to the archival storage media of choice such as optical drives. Which files get migrated and when is totally controlled by parameters set by the system manager.

data PBX Data PBXs allow flexible inter-connection of personal computers, Macs, printers, modems, fax machines, asynchronous terminals, minicomputers and mainframes. They provide port sharing ability and allow for the transfer of e-mail and files among connected devices provided that appropriate e-mail or file transfer software has been installed on the communicating Personal computers or computers

data switch   Data switches also offer greater overall capacity in terms of both expandability and total numbers of personal computers and printers which can be attached, as well as more advanced features such as serial/parallel conversion, file transfer, and e-mail

data transparency   In order to qualify as a true Distributed Database Management System, the product in question must offer data transparency to the end user without regard for: Front-end Tool or Distributed Application, Type of Server Computer (Intel-Based, Minicomputer, Mainframe, etc.), Physical Location of the Server, Physical details and protocols of the network path to the Server

data-link layer   The data-link layer (layer 2 of the OSI model) is responsible for providing protocols which deliver reliability to upper layers for the point-to-point connections established by the physical layer protocols. The data-link layer is of particular interest to the study of local area networks as this is the layer in which network architecture standards are defined

database connectivity software   Database connectivity software is concerned with connecting a variety of front-end tools with a variety of distributed DBMS engines

database distribution   Database distribution implies that while an enterprise's entire database is viewed as a single logical database which is centrally managed, it is in fact, physically distributed across multiple servers which may or may not be widely separated geographically

database MIB   The IETF has been working on a Database MIB specification which would allow any enterprise data management system to report performance statistics back to any SNMP-compliant enterprise network management system.

database middleware   Database Middleware offers transparent database interoperability between clients and database servers executing a variety of different database engines

database replication   Database replication implies that multiple copies of a database are stored on multiple servers. Database replication also assumes that sufficient data management routines are implemented in order to assure that these multiple copies of the same database are kept synchronized in order to assure data integrity and consistency

datagram sockets   Provides unreliable, connectionless, datagram interprocess communications through the use of UDP (User Datagram Protocol) as the transport layer protocol.

DCE   The Open Software Foundation (OSF) has devel-oped an entire architecture for the development of distributed applications known as the Distributed Computing Environment (DCE)

DCE   In order to bring some standardization to distributed information systems architectures in order to help assure enterprise-wide interoperability, the Open Software Foundation (OSF) has introduced the Distributed Computing Environment (DCE) model.

DCE-compatible   Although both Windows NT and Windows 95 support DCE-compatible RPC messaging services, the Microsoft client platforms do not include other DCE services for distributed computing and cannot therefore be considered DCE-compliant

DCE-compliant   DCE services are included or embedded within DCE-compliant client or server operating system or network operating system environments. As a result, end-user companies or organizations do not purchase or implement DCE code or services directly. Rather, end-users purchase DCE-compliant software technology from software developers who have purchased licenses to incorporate standardized DCE services within their products

DDC   PnP compliant monitors will be controlled and configured according to the PnP DDC or Data Display Channel standard.

de-encapsulation   In de-encapsulation, each successive layer of the OSI model removes headers and/or trailers and processes the data which was passed to it from the corresponding layer protocol on the source client.

decision support room   In electronic meeting support software, Meetings may be held in specially equipped decision support rooms in which all forum participants gather in what is known as a same-place, same-time meeting or may convene via a local or wide area network according to participants' availability in what is known as a different-place, different-time meeting

decode stage   The decode stage converts the fetched instruction into low-level code understood by the CPU.

dedicated backup server   A network backup architecture, dedicated server architectures allow multiple servers to be backed up across the network backbone onto a dedicated backup server linked to multiple backup devices

deferred printing   A feature of NetWare Mobile, Deferred printing allows requests for document printing to be queued within the laptop until such time as the laptop is linked back to the network with access to a printer.

definition variables   As part of the Application MIB, Definition variables would store background information concerning applications such as application name, manufacturer, version, release, installation date, license number, number of consecutive users, etc.

delta file synchronization Delta file synchronization is perhaps the most significant file synchronization option in terms of its potential impact on reducing required bandwidth and file transfer time to accomplish the synchronization. Rather than sending entire files across the dial-up or LAN link, delta file synchronization only transfers the changes to those files

delta file transfer Delta file transfer allows only changes to files to be transferred

demand paged virtual memory system See paging

demand paging In a process known as demand paging, the virtual memory manager moves program code and data between assigned physical RAM and the disk-based paging or swap file unbeknownst to the unsuspecting process

Demand Priority Access See DPP

Demand Priority Protocol See DPP

departmental image management See document management & imaging

DES DES (Data Encryption Standard) is an encryption standard which was originally approved by the National Institute of Standards and Technology (NIST) in 1977, allowing encryption devices manufactured by different manufacturers to interoperate successfully

DES A standard known as DES (Data Encryption Standard) originally approved by the National Institute of Standards and Technology (NIST) in 1977, is often used thereby allowing encryption devices manufactured by different manufacturers to interoperate successfully

desktop management interface See DMI

desktop management task force See DMTF

destination address Rather than merely transferring all data between LANs or LAN segments, a bridge reads the destination address (MAC layer address of destination NIC) of each data frame on a LAN, decides whether the destination is local or remote (on the other side of the bridge), and only allows those data frames with non-local destination addresses to cross the bridge to the remote LAN.

device driver Device drivers, otherwise known as hardware device drivers, are specifically written to support a particular hardware device such as a printer, keyboard, or mouse. Windows NT provides a standardized environment within the I/O manager in which these device drivers can execute

device drivers The operating system, or kernel, interfaces to the various hardware components and their controllers via small software programs known as device drivers which are specifically written to be compatible with a particular operating system and a particular type of hardware device.

DFS Distributed File Services (DFS) is a DCE service whose purpose is to offer a consistent interface and consistent services for allowing users to access files from any node on the DCE-based enterprise network. DFS acts as a sort of translator between the native file system of the DCE host node and the DCE requesting client

DHCP Dynamic Host Configuration Protocol allows NT servers using TCP/IP to dynamically assign TCP/IP addresses to NT workstations, Windows for Workgroups clients, Win '95 clients or DOS clients running the TCP/IP-32 protocol stack.

DHCP Dynamic Host Control dynamically assigns IP upon requests from clients. With DHCP, IP addresses are leased for a fixed length of time rather than being permanently assigned

dial-in server See LAN modem

dial-out modem applications This ability to redirect information for dial-out modem applications from LAN-attached PCs is a cooperative task accomplished by the software of the remote node server and its corresponding remote client software. Not all remote node servers support dial-out functionality.

dial-up router In those cases where the amount of inter-LAN traffic from a remote site does not justify the cost of a leased line, dial-up routers may be the appropriate choice of internetworking equipment

dial-up server See remote node server

different-place different-time meeting In electronic meeting support software, Meetings may be held in specially equipped decision support rooms in which all forum participants gather in what is known as a same-place, same-time meeting or may convene via a local or wide area network according to participants' availability in what is known as a different-place, different-time meeting

Digital Encryption Standard See DES

digital license certificates License servers issue access tokens, more formally known as digital license certificates to allow access to licensed applications.

digital signature Authentication uses digital signatures which are attached to transmitted documents in order to assure both the authenticity of the author and the document's message integrity which verifies that the document has not been tampered with.

Digital Signature Encryption With Digital Signature Encryption, a document digital signature is created by the sender using a private key and the encrypted document. To validate the authenticity of the received document, the recipient uses a public key associated with the apparent sender to regenerate a digital signature from the received encrypted document. The transmitted digital signature is then compared by the recipient to the regenerated digital signature produced by using the public key and the received document. If the two digital signatures match, the document is authentic and has not been tampered with.

digital signature encryption Digital Signature Encryption appends an encrypted digital signature to the encrypted document as an electronic means of guaranteeing authenticity of the sending party and assurance that encrypted documents have not been tampered with during transmission

DIMM DIMMs (Dual In-Line Memory Module) are memory modules in which the DRAMs are mounted on both sides of the small circuit board.

DIP Originally, individual DIP (Dual In-Line Pin) chips were attached to circuit boards as a means of packaging and selling RAM

direct enablers If compatible CSS drivers are not available for a particular PC Card/Controller combination, or if the amount of memory CSS drivers require is unacceptable, then lower-level drivers known as direct enablers must be configured and installed.

Direct Memory Access See DMA

direct sequence spread spectrum Direct sequence spread spectrum (DSSS) transmits at a particular frequency within the allowable range. In order to distinguish between transmissions from multiple wireless workstations, DSSS adds at least ten bits to the data message in order to uniquely identify a particular transmission. DSSS receivers must be able to differentiate between these bits, known as chips, in order to properly distinguish transmissions

directory schema X.500 does not define the types of information, or directory schema which should be stored in these directory databases. This allows flexibility of design for X.500 product vendors but leads to interoperability problems for the purchasers of those products.

Directory service Directory or Naming service is a DCE service whose purpose is to offer the consistent directory services required in order for all DCE compliant clients to quickly and easily access required services. Any service or device which can be accessed is referred to as an object, is described by a series of attributes, and is listed as an entry in a directory

directory services Network operating systems have always depended on some sort of directory or naming service in which to store information about users as well as systems resources such as disks, servers, and printers.

directory synchronization services Directory synchronization services protocols are particularly important in enterprise e-mail environments in which multiple different e-mail systems are supported with accompanying independent directories

directory synchronization software See file synchronization

discussion categories See sections

disk allocation blocks Disks in a NetWare environment are divided into disk allocation blocks which can range in size from 4KB to 64KB. In the past, when a file needed a portion of a disk allocation block in order to complete file storage, the remainder of the partially occupied disk allocation block could not be used by other files and was effectively wasted

disk block sub-allocation Disk Block Sub-Allocation is a process aimed at optimizing the use of disk space for file storage. By dividing all disk allocation blocks into 512 byte (.5KB) suballocation blocks, multiple files are allowed to occupy single disk allocation blocks and disk storage efficiency is maximized.

disk duplexing Disk duplexing seeks to overcome the single point of failure inherent in disk mirroring by linking a separate disk controller to each mirrored disk drive.

disk mirroring Disk mirroring involves two disks attached to the same controller acting as mirror images for one another. Everything written to one disk is identically written to the other. In the event that one disk fails, the other disk immediately takes over.

distance vendor RIP uses a distance vector algorithm which only measures the number of hops to a distant router, to a maximum of 16

distance vendor protocols Router to router protocols, such as RIP, which only consider the distance between networks in hops as a determination of the best internetwork path are known as distance vector protocols

distinct layer 2 switching & layer 3 routing An internetwork evolutionary design scenario in which separate Layer 2 switches and Layer 3 routers cooperatively contribute what each does best in order to deliver internetwork traffic as efficiently as possible.

distributed applications An application which has been divided to execute cooperatively across two or more computers.

distributed architecture Information systems constructed according to the distributed architecture paradigm are often referred to as client/server information systems because the overall information system's duties are shared between client and server computers

distributed backbone Distributed backbones were once the norm in which individual LAN segments are linked to a backbone LAN media via bridges and transceivers. These backbone networks often ran vertically between floors of a building while multiple, horizontal LAN segments were distributed throughout the building and attached to the backbone via bridges.

distributed computing Distributed computing, also known as distributed processing, is nothing more than dividing an application program into two or more pieces, and subsequently distributing and processing those distributed applications onto two or more computers, either clients or servers.

distributed computing In a distributed information system, the application layer functionality of the top down model is delivered by a distributed computing solution which is able to interact successfully with the numerous virtual workgroups

Distributed Computing Environment See DCE

distributed database management systems Distributed database management systems should allow a user to access data without regard for Front-end Tool or Distributed Application, Type of Server Computer (Intel-Based, Minicomputer, Mainframe, etc.), Physical Location of the Server, Physical details and protocols of the network path to the Server

Distributed File Services See DFS

distributed information systems The virtual corporation requires a distributed information system comprised of a number of major interacting components or sub-systems

distributed object technology Distributed object technology would enable distributed applications to be more easily developed thanks to the reusability and encapsulation quality of the objects themselves

distributed parallel processing See DPP

distributed routing An internetwork evolutionary design scenario in which layer 2 switching and layer 3 routing functionality are combined into a single device sometimes referred to as a multi-layer switch.

distributed routing An enterprise network physical topology using devices known alternatively as Layer 3 Switches or Multi-Layer switches, routing functionality between virtual LANs is performed without the need for conventional routers. Routing tables must be maintained in the multi-layer switches just as in conventional routers.

Distributed Time Service See DTS

distributed transaction processing See DTP

distributed transaction processing monitor See DTPM

DIY See Raw sockets

DLC DLC or Data Link Control is a Windows NT communication protocol that has been traditionally reserved for communication with IBM mainframe computers. Recently, this same communication protocol has been used to communicate between Windows NT servers and printers which are attached directly to the network by network interface cards such as the Hewlett-Packard LaserJet 4Si equipped with a JetDirect card

DLSw IBM's version of TCP/IP encapsulation is known as Data Link Switching or DLSw and has been proposed as a standard to the IETF (Internet Engineering Task Force) as FRC (Request for Comment) 1434. DLSw does not propose anything radically new but incorporates many vendor-specific TCP/IP encapsulation features into a single standard which will hopefully be widely supported

DLT Digital Linear Tape backup device with 10GB capacity & 90-150MB/min throughput

DLUR/S The specific APPN protocol which deals with SNA/LAN integration is known as DLUR/S (Dependent Logical Unit Requester/Server).

DMA Direct Memory Access or DMA is a data transfer that allows data to be transferred between the disk drive and system memory without intervention from the CPU. This allows for both faster data transfer and less CPU interruptions.

DMA Interoperability standards among document management packages are contained in a specification known as DMA, or Document Management Alliance

DMI See DMTF

DMI Desktop management systems will rely upon an architecture and associated protocols proposed the Desktop Management Task Force (DMTF), which is comprised of over 50 companies including Intel, Microsoft, IBM, Digital, Hewlett-Packard, Apple, Compaq, Dell, and Sun.

DMI services layer DMI Services Layer is the DMI application which resides on each desktop device to be managed. The DMI Services Layer does the actual processing of desktop management information on the client platform and serves as an interface to two APIs

DMTF The DMTF or Desktop Management Task Force, has developed a common management environment for the management of desktop devices known as the DMI (Desktop Management Interface). Specific aspects of the DMI are contained in MIF (Management Information File) definitions

DMTF   The overall desktop management architecture proposed by the DMTF is known as the DMI or Desktop Management Interface

DNS   The Internet uses a naming service known as DNS or Domain Name System to translate between host names and IP addresses

DNS   The Domain Name System or DNS has been created to provide the following key services: Uniquely identify all hosts connected to the Internet by name, Resolve, or translate, host names into IP addresses (and vice versa), Identify which services are offered by each host such as gateway or mail transfer, and to which networks these serves are offered

DNS server   DNS is physically implemented in a client/server architecture in which client-based DNS software known as the DNS or name resolver, sends requests for DNS name resolution to a DNS (or name) Server

document conferencing software   When electronic whiteboard software sessions involve collaborative development or review of documents by multiple users linked via LAN or WAN links, the software category is occasionally referred to as document conferencing software

document management & imaging   When workflow automation involves a great deal of handling, storage, indexing, and retrieval of documents, an ancillary document management & imaging software package may be required

Document Management Alliance   See DMA

document type definition   See DTD

document-based groupware   Document-based Groupware deals with the management, storage, retrieval, and transport of structured documents among participating networked co-workers.

domain directory services   Network operating systems have always depended on some sort of naming service or directory in which to store information about users as well as systems resources such as disks, servers, and printers. Windows NT uses a domain directory service.

Domain Name Service   See DNS

domain name system   See DNS

domain OS   In NetWare 4.1's ring memory protection scheme, the area reserved for the operating system is known as Ring 0, otherwise known as domain OS (operating system)

domain OSP   In NetWare 4.1's ring memory protection scheme, The area reserved for NLMs is known as Ring 3 or domain OSP (operating system protected).

domains   Domain directory services see the network as a series of linked sub-divisions known as domains.

domains   Windows NT networks are organized around the concept of domains. A domain is a collection of Windows NT servers which share a single security sub-system that controls access to all resources in that domain

DOS Partition   In order to install the NetWare server software in the first place, the native operating system of the server must be present in its own disk partition. This might be referred to as a DOS partition, but the native operating system could have just as easily been UNIX or Windows NT.

double speed   CD-ROM speed specifications yielding sustained avg. data throughput of 300KBps

downsizing   Downsizing implies that a mainframe-based application has been re-deployed to run a smaller computer platform. That smaller platform may or may not be a distributed client/server information system

DPA   See DPP

DPP   Future versions of NetWare will support clustering through a systems architecture which Novell refers to as distributed parallel processing (DPP).

DPP   Demand Priority Protocol (Demand Priority Access) is the access methodology of 100VG-AnyLAN. Ports can be designated as high priority, thereby giving priority delivery status to time-sensitive types of traffic such as video or voice which require guaranteed delivery times for smooth presentation. This makes 100VG-AnyLAN especially well suited for multimedia traffic.

DRAM   DRAM or Dynamic RAM is memory which requires refresh cycles every few milliseconds to preserve its data

DTD   SGML (Standard Generalized Markup Language allows higher-level programming than HTML and is able to define its own DTDs (Document Type Definitions).

DTP   With the advent of client/server information systems, multiple geographically dispersed computers are linked, allowing transactions to be posted across multiple, distributed computers. This process is known as Distributed Transaction Processing (DTP) and requires a distributed TP Monitor. DTP is sometimes also known as Enterprise Transaction Processing or ETP.

DTP API   The Distributed Transaction Processing Monitor is able to interface to the local Transaction Processing Monitor thanks to a Distributed Transaction Processing Application Program Interface (DTP API) protocol supported by both TP Monitors.

DTPM   Distributed Transaction Process Monitoring actually requires two levels of TP monitoring. First, the local TP Monitor must assure the integrity of local postings. However, these local postings are just part of a single distributed transaction posting which must be coordinated overall by the Distributed Transaction Processing Monitor (DTPM).

DTS Distributed Time Service (DTS) - DCE services such as DFS and security services depend on time and date stamps as part of their functionality. It is important given the distributed, multi-node nature of a DCE implementation, that there is a source for an "official" time by which all connected systems can be synchronized

Dual Attachment Station See DAS

dual homing In FDDI, a given server may be connected to more than one FDDI concentrator to provide redundant connections and increased fault tolerance. Dual connecting servers in this manner is known as dual homing.

dual ring of trees Multiple concentrators attaching multiple devices to the FDDI rings as illustrated in Figure 7-13 is known as a dual ring of trees.

dual-issue A CPU which has two pipelines can issue two instructions simultaneously and is often referred to as a dual-issue or two-way processor

dual-ported VRAM The primary modification made by VRAM is that a portion of memory is reserved for servicing the screen refresh function in order to optimize performance for high resolution graphics. RAM segmented in this manner is sometimes referred to as dual-ported VRAM

DX DX implies a built-in math co-processor (1989)

DX2 DX2 implies that the clock speed has been doubled above DX clock speeds (1992)

DX4 DX4 implies that the clock speed has been *tripled* above DX clock speeds (1994)

dynamic allocation A license optimization technique that gives out either single user or suite licenses based on the number of suite applications used.

dynamic execution In a process which Intel refers to as dynamic execution, the P6 breaks complex CISC instructions down into simpler RISC-like, but not true RISC, instructions known as micro-ops.

Dynamic Host Configuration Protocol See DHCP

dynamic link library A DLL or dynamic link library file is loaded into memory as needed at run time by Windows NT rather than having to be compiled into, and permanently added to the applications programs

Dynamic RAM See DRAM

dynamic reconfiguration PnP standards also include support for dynamic reconfiguration which will enable such things as: PCMCIA cards being inserted into and removed from computers without a need to reboot, Hot docking (powered up) of laptop computers into docking bays or stations. Dynamic reconfiguration-aware applications software which could automatically respond to changes in system configuration

DynaText On-line help The transparent integration of CD-ROMs into the NetWare 4.1 file system has enabled the use of the DynaText On-Line Help system as the means of accessing all of the NetWare 4.1 manuals

E-IDE Extended IDE disk drive standard to be known as ATA-2 once adopted by ANSI. Features: up to 8.4 GB capacity, 4 daisy chained devices, and 11.1MBps performance

e-mail Most surveys show e-mail (electronic mail) as the second most popular use of local area networks following printer and file services.

e-mail APIs E-Mail APIs are required to allow e-mail and other mail-enabled applications to access the messaging infrastructures established by enterprise e-mail systems

e-mail clients E-mail clients may be either LAN-attached or linked to post offices via remote access

e-mail gateways E-mail system-to-e-mail system translation is accomplished by specially written software known as e-mail gateways. E-mail systems vary in the number of e-mail gateways supported and whether or not the gateway software must be run on a dedicated server.

E-zines Global E-mail also affords access to specifically targeted electronic magazines (E-zines)

early token release mechanism 16Mbps Token Ring network architectures use a modified form of token passing access methodology known as early token release mechanism in which the token is set to free and released as soon as the transmission of the data frame is completed rather than waiting for the transmitted data frame to return to the source workstation.

ECC memory Error Checking & Correcting (ECC) memory, also known as error correction code memory, has the ability to detect and correct errors in data stored in and retrieved from RAM memory. It is more expensive than conventional RAM but is worth the added cost in the case of servers.

EDA/SQL A product known as EDA/SQL (Enterprise Data Access/SQL) from Information Builders Inc., calling itself a Universal Data Access System, acts as a database middleware layer trapping SQL requests from clients and reformatting them as necessary before transporting them to the appropriate server.

Edge devices   In an MPOA architecture, Edge Devices might be a kind of hybrid hub, switch, and router that would act as interfaces or gateways between LANs and the ATM network. Once the ATM address is known, edge devices would be capable of establishing new virtual circuits over the ATM network.

edge switches   Edge switches deployed within the LANs will be programmed with minimal routing information. Edge switches will consult distributed route servers for "directory assistance" when they encounter routing situations which they are not equipped to handle

edge switches   Since the edge switches primary task is packet forwarding, they are loaded with only a minimum of routing information which is most often kept in fast cache memory. Like multi-layer switches, edge switches make routing decisions based on the subnet IDs in the network layer destination addresses embedded within the data link layer frames. Edge switches query the route server when they encounter unknown addresses

EDORAM   Extended Data Out RAM. Extended Data Output (EDO) chips minimize or eliminate the time the CPU has to wait (zero-wait-state) for output from memory by reading the next stored data bit at the same time it's transferring the first requested bit to the CPU.

EDOSRAM   Extended Data Out SRAM

EDOVRAM   Extended Data Out VRAM

EDRAM   Enhanced DRAM

EIA/TIA 568   EIA/TIA 568 (Electronics Industry Association/Telecommunications Industry Association). In addition to specifying UTP specifications, EIA/TIA 568 also specifies: The topology, cable types, and connector types to be used in EIA/TIA 568 compliant wiring schemes, the minimum performance specifications for cabling, connectors and components such as wall plates, punch down blocks and patch panels to be used in an EIA/TIA 568 compliant installation.

EISA   Extended industry standard architecture bus specification features 32 bit bus width with 33MBps throughput

electronic conferencing & meeting support   Electronic conferencing & meeting support software offers opportunities for workers to interact electronically. Brainstorming or idea generation sessions are conducted via the network and managed by the workgroup conferencing software package

Electronic Software Distribution   A desktop mangagement application that is able to distribute, update, and install software in remote clients and servers via the network.

electronic switch   This device is especially important if a laser printer is among the printers to be shared.

The small voltage spike which can be generated during the physical switching of a manual switch can be potentially damaging to the circuit boards of the laser printer. Electronic switches are often manufactured with built in software which scans attached personal computers for waiting print jobs

electronic whiteboard software   Electronic White board software is a hybrid category of groupware software combining elements of electronic meeting support, document conferencing, and videoconferencing. As a result, many electronic whiteboard software packages are incorporated into a variety of different types of software packages

EMI   Electro Magnetic Interference

encapsulating bridges   The encapsulating bridge merely takes the entire Ethernet data link layer frame and stuffs it in an "envelope" (data frame) which conforms to the FDDI data link layer protocol.

encapsulation   a data message emerges from a client front end program and proceeds down the protocol stack of the network operating system installed in the client PC in a process known as encapsulation. Each successive layer of the OSI model adds a header according to the syntax of the protocol which occupies that layer

Encina   Tuxedo from Novell and Encina from Transarc are two of the more popular multi-platform OLTP monitors suitable for client/server applications

enclosures   In electronic meeting support software, User comments on topics are made up of a series of messages which may contain supporting material or documents known as enclosures

encryption   Encryption renders data indecipherable to any unauthorized users that might be able to examine packets of data traffic. Encryption is especially important when transmitting credit card numbers or other confidential information

encryption   Encryption is a security process which is complimentary rather than mutually exclusive to authentication and authorization. As one time token-generated passwords are traversing networks, encryption ensures that if these transmissions were intercepted, the contents of the transmissions would be meaningless.

End nodes   In APPN, end Nodes are end user processing nodes, either clients or servers without any information on the overall network, available internetwork links, or routing tables

end-to-end network links   The network layer protocols are responsible for the establishment, maintenance, and termination of end-to-end network links. Network layer protocols are required when computers which are not physically connected to the same LAN must communicate

engine The server portion of the program is often called the back-end or engine

enhanced paging A pager based wireless service capable of delivering one or two way messages of 100 characters or less

enterprise directory services A centralized source of information about all services and computing platforms attached to a given enterprise network. This central repository of information is referred to as enterprise directory services

enterprise e-mail Enterprise e-mail requires enterprise-wide distribution and support of enterprise directory services, should be scaleable, should integrate with mail-enabled applications, should support security procedures, and should support standard messaging architectures

enterprise hubs Enterprise hubs are modular by design, offering a chassis-based architecture to which a variety of different modules can be inserted. In some cases, these modules can be inserted and/or removed while the hub remains powered-up, a capability known as hot-swappable.

enterprise network The enterprise network is the transportation system of the client-server architecture. Together with middleware, it is responsible for the transparent cooperation of distributed processors and databases

enterprise network An enterprise network electronically enables a business phenomenon known as the virtual corporation that implies a business partnership among cooperating business entities. Without the enterprise network, the virtual corporation would not exist. All client to server and server to server messages are actually delivered via the enterprise network.

enterprise network management system Systems which are able to manage multi-vendor, multi-platform enterprise networks. Examples include HP Open View, IBM System View and Sun SunNet Manager

enterprise network management systems Enterprise network management systems such as HP Open-View, IBM NetView, Sun SunNet Manager, are able to manage a variety of multi-vendor network attached devices distributed throughout an enterprise network

enterprise network management systems Agents from the numerous individual networking devices forward network management information to Enterprise Network Management Systems which compile

and report network operation statistics to the end user, most often in some type of graphical format. Enterprise Network Management systems are really management application programs running on a management server

enterprise transaction processing See DTP

error-free cut-through switches Error-Free Cut-Through Switches read both the addresses and Frame Check Sequences for every frame. Frames are forwarded immediately to destinations nodes in an identical fashion to cut-through switch is able to reconfigure those individual ports producing the bad frames to use store-and-forward switching

ESCON A standard for high speed data channels between FEPs and IBM mainframes, ESCON II (Enterprise System CONnection) has a maximum transmission rate of 70Mbps, has been available since 1990, and is able to transmit up to 30 miles over fiber optic cable.

ESD See Electronic Software Distribution

ESMR Enhanced specialized mobile radio. Currently under development, this wireless WAN service offers one or two way voice, paging, or messaging at speeds up to 4.8Kbps over proprietary integrated voice/data devices.

Ethernet Although strictly speaking, Ethernet and IEEE 802.3 are conflicting standards, the term Ethernet is commonly used to refer to any IEEE 802.3 compliant network

Ethernet II The first Ethernet standard was developed by Digital, Intel and Xerox corporation in 1981 and was known as DIX 1.0, sometimes referred to as Ethernet I. This standard was superseded in 1982 by DIX 2.0, the current Ethernet standard, also known as Ethernet II.

ETP See DTP

exceptions Exceptions are error conditions or unexpected events which the operating system must be prepared to handle appropriately. These exceptions are generally related to the operating system's responsibility to effectively manage system resources

execute stage the instruction is executed in the execute stage

execution units pipeline execution stages can be especially written to be optimized for certain operations such as handling only: Floating point operations, Integer operations, Branch logic (If-then-else) operations. These operation-specific options are called execution units

expansion bus A computer's expansion bus is for the connection of add-in cards and peripheral devices such as modems, fax boards, sound cards, additional serial ports, and additional input devices

explorer packet   In an internetwork connected via source routing bridges, the PC sends out a special explorer packet which determines the best path to the intended destination of its data message. The explorer packets are continually propagated through all source routing bridges until the destination workstation is finally reached.

external bus   a bus located outside of a CPU chip is referred to as an external bus

External data representation   See XDR

FAQ groups   "frequently asked question" groups or FAQ groups are similar to ListServe groups that users can subscribe to via e-mail.

Fast & Wide SCSI-2   An expansion bus specification: 16 bit bus width, 10MHz clock speed, 20MBps throughput

fast packet forwarding   See packet overlapping

Fast SCSI-2   an expansion bus specification: 8 bit bus width, 10MHz clock speed, 10MBps throughput

FAT   FAT (File Allocation Table)—DOS operating system—only file system for diskettes

fat client   When the business logic is distributed on the client in a two-tiered architecture, that architecture is known as fat client

fat server   When the business logic is distributed on the server in a two-tiered architecture, that architecture is known as fat server

FAX APIs   Standards for FAX software APIs which define interfaces between FAX software and hardware components

fax servers   PCs equipped with fax boards or fax modems and specially written faxing software which are dedicated to network Faxing

fax-on-demand   By combining computer-based faxing with interactive voice response, users can dial in and request that specific information be faxed to their fax machine.

FaxBIOS   FaxBIOS is a FAX API developed and supported by the FaxBIOS Association which is comprised of FAX circuit board vendors.

FDDI   Fiber Distributed Data Interface (FDDI) is a 100Mbps network architecture which was first specified in 1984 by the ANSI (American National Standards Institute) subcommittee entitled X3T9.5.

FEP   A front end processor is a computer which offloads the communications processing from the mainframe, allowing the mainframe to be dedicated to processing activities. A high speed data channel connects the FEP to the mainframe locally although FEPs can be deployed remotely as well.

fetch stage   The fetch stage brings an instruction into the pipeline from a holding area in the CPU known as the instruction cache

Fiber Distributed Data Interface   See FDDI

file compression   File compression is incorporated into NetWare 4.1 and is controllable on a file-by-file basis. The file compression process is highly customizable with adjustable settings for how often compression takes place as well as minimum acceptable disk space gained by compression.

file synchronization software   File synchronization software is able to synchronize versions of files on laptops and desktop workstations and is now often included as a standard or optional feature in client network operating systems. Also known as version control software or directory synchronization software

file system drivers   In order for NT to communicate with multiple different file systems (NTFS, FAT, HPFS), an intermediate layer of software known as file system drivers which can interact with both NT and the particular file system must be written.

file transfer protocol   See FTP

file transfer software   A powerful and easy to use category of networking software known as File Transfer Software has developed to meet the need for occasional or temporary networking of personal computers.

filter   A filter is a program which examines the source address and destination address of every incoming packet to the firewall server. Network access devices known as routers are also capable of filtering data packets

filter tables   Filter tables are lists of addresses whose data packets and embedded messages are either allowed or prohibited from proceeding through the firewall server and into the corporate network. Filter tables can also limit the access of certain IP addresses to certain directories.

filtering   Filtering is when a bridge reads the destination address on an Ethernet frame or Token Ring packet and decides whether or not that packet should be allowed access to the internetwork through the bridge

filtering rate   Measured in Packets/sec or Frames/sec, a measure of the filtering performance of a given bridge

firewall   In order to prevent unauthorized access from the Internet into a company's confidential data, specialized software known as a firewall is often deployed. Firewall software usually runs on a dedicated server which is connected, but outside of the corporate network

Flash RAM Flash Memory or Flash RAM remembers its data contents until it is flashed by a larger voltage and is used widely as main memory for portable computers

flat gray modular flat gray modular wiring, also known as gray satin or silver satin contains either 4, 6 or 8 wires which get crimped into either RJ-11 (4 wire), RJ-12 (6 wire), or RJ-45 plugs (8 wire) using a specialized crimping rod

fork Processes in Unix are controlled by the fork system call as initiated through the shell interface, which allows parent processes to spawn multiple subprocesses known as child processes

format converter A special type of bridge which includes a format converter can bridge between Ethernet and Token Ring. These special bridges may also be called multiprotocol bridges or translating bridges.

forums In electronic meeting support software discussion groups are called forums

forward if not local Since only frames with destination addresses not found in the known local nodes table are forwarded across the bridge, bridges are sometimes known as a "Forward-if-not-local" devices.

forward if proven remote Once the router is satisfied with both the viability of the destination address as well as with the quality of the intended path, it will release the carefully packaged data packet via processing known as forward-if-proven-remote logic.

forwarding Forwarding is the bridge process necessary to load the packet onto the internetwork media whether local or remote.

forwarding rate Measured in Packets/sec or Frames/sec, a measure of the forwarding performance of a given bridge

FPM Fast Page Mode

FRAD The access device to the frame relay network, known as a frame relay access device or FRAD must be able to respond to requests from the frame relay network to "throttle back" or slow down the input to the network or risk losing transmitted packets due to network overload.

fragmentation As contiguous blocks of memory of varying sizes are continuously cut out of a finite amount of primary memory, that primary memory suffers from fragmentation where numerous, small leftover pieces of contiguous memory remain unused.

FRAM Ferroelectric RAM

frame check sequence The frame check sequence (FCS) is an error detection mechanism generated by the transmitting Ethernet network interface card

Frame Relay A WAN packet switched network service known as Frame Relay has become a popular alternative SNA/LAN integration WAN service. The key positive attribute of Frame Relay is that charges are based on actual amounts of traffic transmitted rather than fixed monthly rates

frame relay access device See FRAD

frame status flags In a token passing access methodology, Successful delivery of the data frame is confirmed by the destination workstation setting frame status flags to indicate successful receipt of the frame and continuing to forward the original frame around the ring to the sending PC

frames The data-link layer provides the required reliability to the physical layer transmission by organizing the bit stream into structured frames which add addressing and error checking information.

frequency hopping spread spectrum Frequency Hopping spread spectrum (FHSS) hops from one frequency to another throughout the allowable frequency range. The pattern of frequency hopping must be known by the wireless receiver so that the message can be reconstructed correctly

front end processor See FEP

front-end The client portion of the program is often called the front-end

front-end tools Front-End tools for database management systems fall into two major categories: Database Query and Reporting Tools, Multi-platform Client/Server Application Development Tools

FTP In order to download, or transfer, information back to their client PCs, users would access a TCP/IP protocol known as FTP (File transfer protocol).

FTP FTP or File transfer protocol provides a common mechanism for transferring files between a variety of different types of networked computers. Strictly speaking, FTP does not provide a user interface but rather an API for FTP services

FTP servers Servers which support FTP logon from client PCs are often called FTP servers or anonymous FTP servers

full-duplex Ethernet This switch dependent capability requires specialized full duplex Ethernet NICs and supports full-duplex communication between the two computers which serve as the endpoints of a switched dedicated connection thereby allowing them to both send and receive data simultaneously.

gateway A LAN server-based, shared protocol converted access to a mainframe is known as a gateway

gateway protocols Gateway protocols are specific to the e-mail systems that are being translated between by the gateway

gateways Gateways are sometimes included as part of the message transfer agent functionality. Gateways are designed to translate fully between two different e-mail systems

Generic Security Service API See GSS-API

global directory service NDS is a global directory service, organizing and managing all networked resources over an entire distributed enterprise

global directory services See NDS

global e-mail Millions of users are connected worldwide to the Internet via the global e-mail sub-system. From a business perspective, Internet e-mail offers one method of sending inter-company e-mail.

global license sharing

Gopher A menu-based client/server system which features search engines that comb through all of the information in all of these information servers is referred to as the Gopher system

Gopher server Gopher client software is most often installed on a client PC and interacts with software running on a particular Gopher server, which transparently searches multiple FTP sites for requested information and delivers that information to the Gopher client

grafted Entire branches of the tree, designated as partitions, and including all subordinate container objects and leaf objects, can be pruned (removed) from one point in the NDS structure and grafted to another branch. In fact two entire trees can be merged together into a single tree.

granularity How finely access can be controlled (by disk, directory, or file level) is sometimes referred to as the granularity of the access control scheme.

graphical user interfaces See GUI

graphics accelerator chip Key component of a graphics accelerator card commonly differentiated by data path width, either 32 or 64 bit

group scheduling software Group scheduling software or calendar packages can be a very efficient way to schedule electronic or face-to-face meetings or conferences and is often integrated with e-mail systems so that requests for meetings can be automatically sent and replied to via e-mail.

groupware Groupware is the name of a category of software which seeks to take advantage of the fact that workers are networked together electronically in order to increase communication and maximize worker productivity.

GSS-API An open API which would allow applications to communicate with a variety of security authorization programs is known as GSS-API (Generic Security Service-Applications Program Interface) and is documented in RFCs 1508 and 1509.

guest The terms remote and local are often replaced by guest (remote) and host (local), when referring to Remote Control Software.

GUI Client-based presentation is often handled through familiar graphical user interfaces (GUI) such as Windows, OS/2 Presentation Manager, X Windows-based systems such as Motif and OpenLook, or the Macintosh Desktop.

GUI Graphical User Interface. The monitor-based image with which the user interacts, as contrasted to a character-based interface or a social user interface

H.221 Framing and synchronization specification which standardizes the CODEC's handshaking and interface to WAN services such as ISDN used for videoconference transmission

H.230 Multiplexing specification which describes how audio and video information should be transmitted over the same digital WAN link.

H.231 Multipoint control unit (MCU) specification which defines standards for a device to bridge three or more H.320 compliant codecs together on a single multipoint videoconference

H.233 Specification for encryption of video and audio information transmitted through H.230 compliant codecs. Also known as H.KEY

H.242 Specification for call set-up and tear-down for videoconference calls

H.261 Also known as Px64, describes compression and decompression algorithms used for videoconferencing. Also defines two screen formats, CIF (Common Intermediate Format) 288 lines x 352 pixels/line and QCIF (Quarter Common Intermediate Format) 144 lines x 176 pixels/line.

H.320 The International Telecommunications Union (ITU) has overseen the development of a family of videoconferencing standards known collectively as H.320

HAL Windows NT is a microkernel based operating system with a minimum of hardware specific code confined to a portion of the microkernel known as HAL, or the hardware abstraction layer

HAL Most of the hardware specific portions of Windows NT are isolated in a subsection known as the hardware abstraction layer, or HAL. The hardware abstraction layer in Windows NT provides similar functionally to the BIOS in DOS. It is the hardware (CPU) specific HAL which affords Windows NT its portability

hardware abstraction layer See HAL

hardware cache A hardware cache is a disk cache made up of memory chips placed directly on the disk controller

hardware emulation In order to improve Windows application performance, Apple has introduced the DOS card for the PowerMacintosh. This add-on card contains a 486DX2 66MHz processor, and is an example of hardware emulation.

hardware independent operating systems Because all of the hardware specific code is restricted to the microkernel, modular operating systems can be ported to any processor which can communicate with the microkernel on which that modular operating system is based

hardware-based RAID Hardware-Based RAID is more expensive than software-based RAID, but is also more reliable and is able to support more operating systems

hardware/software solutions A network faxing architecture in which the user supplies the PC to which vendor-supplied FAX boards and bundled software are loaded.

header Additional information added to the front of data is called a header

hierarchical The NDS database is organized in a hierarchical fashion, which can be logically thought of as a tree. The hierarchical design of the NDS database can be roughly equivalent to the hierarchical and geographical organization of the corporation being modeled.

hierarchical networking An internetworking design strategy known as hierarchical networking isolates local LAN traffic on a local network architecture such as Ethernet or Token Ring while transmitting internetwork traffic over a higher speed network architecture such as FDDI or Fast Ethernet. Servers are often directly connected to the backbone network while individual workstations access the backbone network only as needed through routers.

hierarchical storage management See HSM

horizontal scalability Adding servers for additional processing power is more specifically known as horizontal scalability. Applications which support horizontal scalability must be able to support multi-server directory synchronization, naming services, and replication

horizontal software compatibility Horizontal software compatibility is concerned with transparency between *similar* software layers *between* different clients and servers

host The terms remote and local are often replaced by guest (remote) and host (local), when referring to Remote Control Software

host-controller RAID In the case of Host-Controller RAID, the controller board which contains the RAID intelligence is installed in an available expansion slot. This requires bus interface compatibility

hot swappable In some cases, enterprise hub modules can be inserted and/or removed while the hub remains powered-up, a capability known as hot-swappable.

HPFS HPFS (High Performance File System)—OS/2 operating system

HPR/AnyNET Recent enhancements to APPN known as HPR (High Performance Routing)/AnyNET now allow multiple transport protocols such as IP and IPX to travel over the APPN network simultaneously with SNA traffic. In such an implementation, APPN rather than TCP/IP serves as the single backbone protocol able to transport multiple LAN protocols as well as SNA traffic simultaneously.

HSM Hierarchical Storage Management (HSM) is a technology which seeks to make optimal, or most effective, use of available storage media while minimizing the need for human intervention

HTML Web pages are collections of text, graphics, sound and video elements and are programmed in the first place using Web publishing software which may run on either client or server platforms. The Web pages are programmed using text formatted with HTML (HyperText Markup Language). Since HTML is textbased, any text editor could be used to generate the HTML code which would then be interpreted by the HTTP server software

HTML conversion utilities HTML Conversion Utilities are add-on products which work with existing word processing packages such as Microsoft's Word. For example, the Internet Assistant for Word for Windows automatically creates HTML documents from Word documents without the need for users to learn the intricacies of HTML.

HTML Hyperlink Maintenance software As Web pages change and hyperlinks must be updated to reflect those changes, automated hyperlink maintenance software is able to assure that all hyperlinks for Web Pages contained in the hyperlink database are automatically updated. This prevents old hyperlinks remaining on Web Pages when the associated URLs are not longer valid

HTTP Web servers run specialized Web server software which supports HTTP (HyperText Transport Protocol) in order to handle the organization of servicing the multiple Web client requests for Web pages. These Web pages are collections of text, graphics, sound and video elements

hub The hub provides a connecting point through which all attached devices are able to converse with one another. Hubs must be compatible with both the attached media and the NCIs which are installed in client PCs

hubs Wiring centers for network architectures other than token ring are known as hubs

hypertext link URLs are also used within a given Web page to allow hypertext links to other related Web pages, documents, or services such as e-mail. The term hypertext merely refers to documents which have the ability to link to other documents

HyperText Markup Language See HTML

HyperText Transport Protocol See HTTP

I-P-O Model The I-P-O model provides a framework in which to focus on the difference between the data that came into a particular networked device (I) and the data that came out of that same device (O). By defining this difference, the processing (P) performed by the device is documented.

I/O manager The I/O Manager is in charge of managing all input and output for the Windows NT operating system and is particularly concerned with managing the communications between: Device drivers, Network drivers, Cache Manager, File Systems Drivers

I/O request packets The I/O manager oversees the interaction among the various categories of drivers in order to assure that applications programs are delivered requested services in a timely fashion. Communication among these various drivers is standardized by the I/O manager through the use of I/O request packets.

IAP Internet Access Providers (IAP) - (Also known as internet Connectivity Provider (ICP)) Are primarily concerned with getting a subscriber company physically hooked up to the Internet

IASG In a MPOA architecture, Routing tables within the route server are organized according to Layer 3 protocol specific subnets which are referred to as Internet Address Summarization Groups (IASG).

IBM3270 In micro-mainframe connectivity, the micro (Standalone or LAN-attached PC) pretends to be or "emulates" a mainframe terminal such as an IBM 3270 attached and logged into the mainframe

ICMP Although IP is by definition an unreliable transport mechanism, ICMP or Internet Control Message Protocol does deliver a variety of error status and control messages related to the ability of IP to deliver its encapsulated payloads

IDE IDE (Integrated Drive Electronics) Disk drives are distinguished from earlier offerings by the inclu-

sion of the drive controller with the disk drive in a single integrated unit and the use of a bus interface known as ATA (AT Attachment). The key limitation of IDE drives was their capacity limitation of 528MB and ATA's 2-3 MBps data transfer rate

IDEA In the Pretty Good Privacy encryption method, combined documents and digital signatures are then encrypted using IDEA (International Data Encryption Algorithm) which makes use of one-time 128-bit keys known as session keys.

idea generation The second of 3 major functional categories of workgroup conferencing software. The major purpose of an electronically supported meeting is to generate idea in a non-threatening, politically neutral environment

IEEE 802 Local area network architecture standards are defined, debated and established by the IEEE (Institute of Electrical and Electronic Engineers) 802 committee

IEEE 802.1 See Spanning Tree Algorithm

IEEE 802.10 One possibility for standardization of switch to switch communication in support of virtual LANs which span multiple switches is IEEE 802.10. The additional 32 bit header could hold virtual LAN identifiers.

IEEE 802.11 A lack of interoperability among the wireless LAN offerings of different vendors is a shortcoming being addressed by a proposal for a new wireless LAN standard known as IEEE 802.11

IEEE 802.12 Details of the 100VG-AnyLAN network architecture are contained in the proposed IEEE 802.12 standard

IEEE 802.2 The upper sub-layer of the data-link layer which interfaces to the network layer is known as the logical link control or LLC sub-layer and is represented by a single IEEE 802 protocol (IEEE 802.2)

IEEE 802.3 Although strictly speaking, Ethernet and IEEE 802.3 are conflicting standards, the term Ethernet is commonly used to refer to any IEEE 802.3 compliant network

IEEE 802.3u The details of the operation of 100BaseT are in the IEEE 802.3u proposed standard

IEEE 802.3x Full duplex Ethernet has gathered sufficient interest from the networking technology vendor and user communities as to warrant the formation of the IEEE 802.3x committee to propose standards for full duplex Ethernet.

IEEE 802.5 IBM has been the driving force behind the standardization and adoption of Token Ring with a prototype in IBM's lab in Zurich, Switzerland serving as a model for the eventual IEEE 802.5 standard.

IEEE 802.9a Details of the Iso-Ethernet network architecture are contained in the IEEE 802.9a standard which is officially known as Isochronous Ethernet Integrated Services

IETF   The IETF (Internet Engineering Task Force) is the group in charge of seeking approval for a printer management MIB (management information base) which would transport printer management information over TCP/IP networks in SNMP (Simple Network Management Protocol) format

IMAP   Mail server management protocols may be either POP (Post Office Protocol) or IMAP (Internet Mail Access Protocol). IMAP is a more recent standard and possesses features added in response to increased remote connectivity and mobile computing

In-Place Migration   In-Place Migration uses the INSTALL program included in NetWare 4.1. After building the NDS structure, NetWare 3.x bindery users, groups are moved to the NetWare 4.1 NDS database.

information consumers   Use of the Internet as a source of required information

information providers   Use of the Internet as a means of advertising or otherwise promoting one's company

information systems downsizing   Downsizing implies that a mainframe-based application has been redeployed to run on a smaller computer platform. That smaller platform may or may not be a distributed client/server information system

Infrared Data Association   In order to assure multi-vendor interoperability between laptops and mobile aware operating systems, the infra-red transmission should conform to the IrDA (Infrared Data Association) standards.

Infrared transmission   A wireless LAN transmission methodology limited by its line-of-sight requirement.

Institute of Electrical and Electronic Engineers 802 Committee   See IEEE 802

instruction cache   a holding area for instructions pending execution in the CPU

Int14   Int14, or Interrupt 14, is one of the supported dial-out software re-directors and is most often employed by Microsoft network operating systems. Int14 is actually an IBM BIOS serial port interrupt used for the purpose of redirecting output from the local serial port

integrated client/server management system   In addition to managing a multi-vendor enterprise network, an integrated client-server management systems must also be able to supply the following management capabilities: Enterprise Database Management, Enterprise Desktop Management, Enterprise Transaction Processing Management, Enterprise Distributed Processing Management

integrated messaging services   Application programs such as e-mail are also able to use the NDS databases for network resource information such as UserIDs, passwords, and security restrictions. These integrated messaging services offered by NDS allow network managers to maintain a single database of user information for both network services and e-mail services.

Integrated Services Digital Network   See ISDN

Integrated Services Terminal Equipment   See ISTE

integration   Integration refers to that transitionary period of time in the migration process when both network operating systems must be running simultaneously and interacting to some degree

integration/migration services   Integration refers to that transitionary period of time in the migration process when both network operating systems must be running simultaneously and interacting to some degree Migration features are aimed at easing the transition from NetWare 3.12 to either NetWare 4.1 or Windows NT.

intelligent agent   See agent event manager

intelligent software   Intelligent software, also known as smart software, utilizes agents which assist end-users in their quest for increased productivity

intelligent token authentication technology   The technology used to generate and authenticate single use passwords is known as intelligent token authentication technology and may be either hardware-based or software-based.

inter-realm   If a Kerberos client wishes to access a server in another realm, it requests an inter-realm ticket granting ticket from its local ticket granting server to authorize access to the remote ticket granting server which can authorize access to the remote applications server.

inter-ring gate calls   NLMs executing in Ring 3 access operating systems services in Ring 0 by issuing structured inter-ring gate calls, thereby protecting the operating system from mis-behaving NLMs overwriting its memory space.

interactive voice response   Interactive Voice Response systems differ from audiotex systems in that IVR systems support on-line transaction processing rather than just information hot-line applications. As an example, banks use IVR systems to allow users to transfer funds between accounts by using only a touch tone phone.

Interdomain Trust In the case of a domain directory service such as Windows NT 3.51, the remote or foreign server receives the user authentication from the user's primary domain controller (local server) in a process known as Interdomain Trust (IT).

interdomain trust accounts Interdomain trust accounts allow NT server domain controllers to perform passthrough authentication to other domains

interface The logical gap between hardware or software components is referred to as an interface.

interlacing See interleaving

interleaving Interleaving is a technique which allows the graphics accelerator controller chip to perform two different operations to adjacent rows of video memory with each tick of the clock

internal bus A bus which is located strictly within a CPU chip is referred to as an internal bus

international data encryption algorithm See IDEA

Internet The Internet is a wide area network linking over 4,000,000 host computers. Originally developed as a means for the research, education, and scientific communities to share information, the Internet has been opened up in recent years to more commercial uses as well as to access by individuals

Internet Access Providers See IAP

Internet Address Summarization Group See IASG

Internet control message protocol See ICMP

Internet E-Mail Gateway The Internet E-Mail Gateway acts a translator, speaking a LAN-specific e-mail software protocol on one side and speaking the Internet's SMTP (Simple MailTransport Protocol) on the other. Depending on the transport protocol used by the Local Area Network, the Internet E-Mail Gateway may also have to translate between transport protocols since the Internet uses strictly TCP/IP

Internet Engineering Task Force See IETF

Internet Gateway While Internet E-Mail Gateways offer translation strictly between different LAN-based E-mail packages, Internet Gateways offer a LAN-attached link for client PCs to access a multitude of Internet-attached resources including e-mail, FTP/Telnet, newsgroups, Gopher, and the WWW

Internet Mail Access Protocol See IMAP

Internet Packet Exchange See IPX

Internet Presence Providers See IPP

Internet Protocol See IP

Internet Server LAN-attached Client PCs accessing the Internet through the Internet gateway must seek the Internet services they desire from an Internet Server. An Internet server runs a server application and offers e-mail services, Gopher services, newsgroup services or World Wide Web services to all Internet-attached users.

Internet Suite of Protocols A suite or collection of protocols associated with TCP/IP that supports open systems internetworking

Internet Suite of Protocols TCP/IP (Transmission Control Protocol/Internet Protocol) generally refers to an entire suite of protocols used to provide communication on a variety of layers between widely distributed different types of computers. Strictly speaking, TCP and IP are just two of the protocols contained within the family of protocols more properly known as the Internet Suite of Protocols.

internetworking Linking multiple LANs together in such as way as to deliver information more efficiently from cost, business, and performance perspectives.

interprocess communication See IPC

interrupts An interrupt is when the CPU is interrupted to stop doing one thing to do something else. Key hardware components such as the system bus, the keyboard, the video controller, serial ports, etc. are all assigned interrupt numbers. Higher priority sub-systems such as the system bus, keyboard, and video receive lower interrupt numbers than serial port devices such as modems.

inverse multiplexing MLPPP compliant devices are able to deliver "bandwidth on demand" in a process referred to as inverse multiplexing

IP IP (Internet Protocol) is the network layer protocol of the TCP/IP suite of protocols. It is primarily responsible for providing the addressing functionality necessary to assure that all reachable network destinations can be uniquely and correctly identified

IP over ATM IP over ATM (Classical IP) adapts the TCP/IP protocol stack to employ ATM services as a native transport protocol directly. This is an IP specific proposal and is not an option for LANs using other protocol stacks such as NetWare's IPX/SPX.

IPC IPC (Interprocess Communication) is a mechanism which will allow the multiple pieces of the application to communicate with each other

IPng IPng (IP next generation), otherwise known as IPv6 (IP version 6), offers significant increases in functionality as well as increased address space in comparison to IPv4 (current version, IP version 4).

IPP Internet Presence Providers (IPP) - Are primarily concerned with designing, developing, implementing, managing, and maintaining a subscriber, and maintaining a subscriber company's presence on the Internet.

IPv4 IPv4 (current version, IP version 4).

IPv6 See IPng

IPX Internet Packet Exchange (IPX), like most OSI network layer protocols, serves as a basic delivery mechanism for upper layer protocols such as SPX, RIP, SAP, and NCP. It is connectionless and unreliable.

IrDA See Infrared Data Association

ISA Industry Standard Architecture bus specification with 16 bit bus width and 8MBps throughput

ISDN Integrated Services Digital Network is a circuit-switched digital WAN service which is the support network transport service for Isochronous Ethernet

Iso-Ethernet Isochronous Ethernet (Iso-Ethernet) offers a combination of services by dividing the overall 16.144 Mbps bandwidth delivered to each workstation into several service-specific channels.

isochronous The term isochronous refers to any signaling system in which all connections or circuits are synchronized using a single common clocking reference. This common docking mechanism allows such systems to offer guaranteed delivery times which are very important to streaming or time-sensitive traffic such as voice and video.

Isochronous Ethernet See Iso-Ethernet

ISTE A workstation with an Iso-Ethernet NIC installed is properly referred to as Integrated Services Terminal Equipment

IT See Interdomain Trust

Java Java is an object-oriented language which adds animation and real-time interaction through the use of independently executed mini-programs called applets. The object-oriented nature of the language allows the applets to be run in a variety of different orders depending on the interaction with the user.

Kerberos Authentication in DCE is based on Kerberos authentication system which provides multilevel authentication and encryption services dependent upon the level of security required

kernel The operating system is actually a computer program, at least part of which runs all of the time on any given computer. The operating system program itself is sometimes referred to as a kernel

kernel mode In order to access the I/O manager portion of the NT executive, applications must enter Ring 0, or kernel mode execution

known local nodes Data-Link protocols such as Ethernet contain source addresses as well as the destination addresses within the pre-defined Ethernet Frame

layout. A bridge checks the source address of each frame it receives and adds that source address to a table of known local nodes

L1 cache High-speed memory placed directly on the processor chip as a buffer between the slower system memory (RAM) and the fast pipelines is known as on-board cache. On-board cache is also known as on-chip, primary cache, or L1 (Level 1) cache

L2 cache a high speed memory cache not directly on, but closely connected to the CPU chip. This memory is known as off-chip, secondary cache or L2 (Level 2) cache. The L2 cache is connected to the CPU chip through a memory bus whose speed is also measured in MHz

LAN A Local Area Network (LAN) is a combination of hardware and software technology which allows computers to share a variety of resources such as: printers and other peripheral devices, data, application programs, storage devices

LAN caching See network caching

LAN emulation LAN Emulation provides a translation layer which allows ATM to emulate existing Ethernet and token ring LANs and allows all current upper-layer LAN protocols to be transported by the ATM services in an unmodified fashion

LAN emulation ATM's ability to switch LAN traffic without the need to make any hardware or software changes to LAN clients or servers, is known as LAN Emulation

LAN Emulation Client See LEC

LAN Emulation Server See LES

LAN Emulation Services LES LAN Emulation Services receive address resolution protocol (ARP) requests from LECs seeking the ATM addresses of destination LAN workstations for which the MAC address is known

LAN inventory management software Automatically figures out the characteristics of each workstation and reports gathered data in useful and flexible formats.

LAN modem LAN Modem, also known as a Dial-In Server, offers shared remote access to LAN resources. LAN modems come with all necessary software preinstalled and therefore, do not require additional remote control or remote node software. LAN Modems are often limited to a single network architecture such as Ethernet or Token Ring, and/or to a single network operating system protocol such as IP, IPX (NetWare), NetBIOS, NetBEUI, or Appletalk.

LAN productivity software Application software that contributes directly to the productivity of its users; in other words, this is the software that people use to not only get their work done, but more importantly, to get their work done more quickly, effectively, accurately, or at a lower cost than if they did not have the benefit of this software

LAN resource management software   LAN resource management software is concerned with providing access to shared network resources and services. Examples of such shared network-attached resources include printers, fax machines, CD-ROMs, modems and a variety of other devices and services.

LAN software architecture   In order to organize and illustrate the inter-relationships between the various categories of LAN software, a LAN Software Architecture can be constructed divided into two major categories: Network operating systems and applications software. Also included are security software and management software

LAN switch   See switching hub

Large Internet Packets   See LIP

Large Packet IPX   See LIP

latency   The time it takes for a firewall server to examine the address of each packet and compare those addresses to filter table entries is known as latency

Layer 2 switches plus independent routing   An enterprise network physical topology in which Layer 2 switches are employed to provide bandwidth and control broadcasts within virtual LANs while independent routers are employed for controlling traffic between virtual LANs and for connecting the switched virtual LANs to the enterprise backbone

Layer 2 Virtual LANs   Layer 2 Virtual LANs are built using LAN switches which act as microsegmenting bridges. A LAN switch which supports a layer 2 virtual LAN distinguishes only between the MAC addresses of connected workstations

Layer 3 switches   See distributed routing

Layer 3 Virtual LANs   Layer 3 Virtual LANs are built using LAN switches which are able to process layer 3 network addresses. Such devices may be called routing switches. Since these devices are able to perform filtering based on network layer protocols and addresses, they are able to support multiple virtual LANs using different network layer protocols

LCD   LCD (Liquid Crystal Display) technology employs a fluorescent backlight which shines through a "multi-layer sandwich" of polarizers, liquid crystals, color filters and an electrode grid to produce the image on the screen.

leaf objects   In NDS, network resources are considered leaf objects

lease duration   IP addresses issued by DHCP are leased, rather than being permanently assigned, and the length of time which IP addresses can be kept by DHCP clients is known as the lease duration.

least significant bit   Both Ethernet and token ring believe that bit 0 on byte 0, referred to as the least significant bit, should be transmitted first

LEC   LAN Emulation Client (LEC) software may physically reside within ATM-to-LAN conversion devices or may be included within a router that supports ATM interfaces. The job of the LEC is to appear to be an ATM end-station on behalf of the LAN clients it represents

legacy applications   See backward compatibility

LES   LAN Emulation Server (LES) software resides on a server or workstation which is directly attached to the ATM network and has a unique ATM address. LES software offers Configuration services, Broadcast & Unknown services, and LAN emulation services.

library services   Part of the DMA document management interoperability standards; will include interoperable version control and access control

license management software   See license metering software

license metering software   Monitors the number of executing copies of a particular software package vs. the number of licenses purchased for that package.

license optimization   Process by which license management software can dynamically allocate licenses to those users wishing to execute a particular software package.

license pooling   See load balancing

license server   LSAPI-compliant applications communicate with a specialized license server that issues digital license certificates based on the license information stored in the license server database.

licensing server API   Builds license metering capability into nework operating systems, eliminating the need for third-party license metering software.

limited size messaging   See LSM

line conditioner   a line conditioner protects computer equipment from "dirty" power conditions such as surges, brownouts, and static spikes.

line printer services   LPS or Line Printer Services are available in client (requests) and server (responses) versions. The client portion runs on the client PC requesting services and the server portion runs on the print server. LPS supplies the printer services typically supplied by network operating systems such as NetWare, Windows for Workgroups, or Windows NT

link state   OSPF protocol uses a more comprehensive link state algorithm which can decide between multiple paths to a given router based upon variables other than number of hops such as delay, and capacity, throughput, and reliability of the circuits connecting the routers

link state packets   See LSP

link state protocols   Routing protocols known as link state protocols take into account other factors regarding internetwork paths such as link capacity, delay, throughput, reliability, or cost

link support layer   A layer of the ODI Architecture. LSL.COM is the program which orchestrates the operation of ODI drivers

links   Links are a unique aspect of the Unix file system which allow a given file to be known by, and accessed by more than one name. A link is nothing more than an entry in a directory which points to a file stored in another directory, or another whole directory

LIP   LIP or Large Internet Packets only applies to NetWare 4.1 LANs which are linked to each other via a wide area network through routers. LIP, also known as Large Packet IPX, allows NetWare clients to negotiate with the routers as to the size of the IPX frame. From the NetWare client's perspective, the larger the IPX frame, the larger the IPX frame's data field, and the greater the amount of data that the client can cram into a single IPX frame.

LIS   IP subnets established over ATM networks using the Classical IP over ATM protocol are known as Logical IP Subnets or LIS.

LLC   In order for an IEEE 802.3 compliant network interface card to be able to determine the type of protocols embedded within the data field of an IEEE 802.3 frame, it refers to the header of the IEEE 802.2 Logical Link Control (LLC) data unit.

LLC sub-layer   The upper sub-layer of the data-link layer which interfaces to the network layer is known as the logical control or LLC sub-layer and is represented by a single IEEE 802 protocol (IEEE 802.2)

load balancing   When multiple CPU's are controlled by the SMP operating system and individual threads of application processes are assigned to particular CPUs on a first-available basis, all CPUs are kept equally busy in a process known as load balancing

load balancing   The effective use of a network's redundant paths allows routers to perform load balancing of total network traffic across two or more links between two given locations

local area network   See LAN

local bus   Strictly speaking, the term local bus refers to any bus which interfaces directly to the system bus

local hub management software   Local management software is usually supplied by the hub vendor and runs over either DOS or Windows. This software allows monitoring and management of the hub from a locally attached management console.

local procedure call facility   The internal communication within Windows NT between internal client requests and server responses is controlled by a message passing environment known as the Local Procedure Call Facility.

local security authority   In Windows NT, the platform-specific login process interacts with the local security authority which actually provides the user authentication services

local session number   A NetBIOS variable with typically limits NetBIOS and NetBEUI clients and servers to a 254 session limit.

locally-attached multiple tape drives   A network backup architecture in which locally-attached multiple tape drives are attached directly to each server. The multiple tape drives provide both faster backup performance and fault tolerance

location managers   A feature of NetWare Mobile, location managers are able to detect the closest network attached resources such as printers for nomadic computer users that may be unaware of local network resources.

log file service   File system activity is looked upon as a series of transactions which are documented by the log file service of NTFS

Logical IP subnets   See LIS

logical link control   See LLC

logical network design   The network performance criteria which could be referred to as *what* the implemented network must do in order to meet the business objectives outlined at the outset of the top-down analysis are also sometimes referred to as the logical network design.

Logical Ring Physical Star   IBM's Token Ring network architecture, adhering to the IEEE 802.5 standard, utilizes a star configuration, sequential message delivery, and a token passing access methodology scheme. Since the sequential logical topology is equivalent to passing messages from neighbor to neighbor around a ring, the token ring network architecture is sometimes referred to as: Logical Ring, Physical Star.

logical topology   The particular message passing methodology, or how a message will be passed from workstation to workstation until the message ultimately reaches its intended destination workstation, is more properly known as a network architecture's logical topology

logon process   The Logon process is responsible for the interaction with the user on whatever computer platform they may wish to log in on

lookahead cache   Lookahead buffer is the simplest or most generic buffer implying only that a sequence of data blocks beyond that requested by the CPU is stored in anticipation of the next data request.

loosely-coupled   Loosely-coupled systems architectures are characterized by each CPU interacting with its own pool of system memory and devices. Coordination among the loosely-coupled CPUs is achieved by some type of messaging mechanism such as interprocess communication between the separate CPUs and their individual copies of the operating system. Most AMP system architectures would be considered loosely-coupled.

LPS   See Line printer services

LSAPI   See licensing server API

LSL   See link support layer

LSM   By adding a protocol known as LSM (Limited Size Messaging), CDPD will be able to transport two-way messaging which will offer the following key services beyond simple paging: Guaranteed delivery to destination mobile users even if those devices are unreachable at the time the message was originally sent, Return receipt acknowledgments to the party which originated the message.

LSP   See LSP

MAC sub-layer   The media access control or MAC sub-layer is a sub-layer of the data-link layer that interfaces with the physical layer and is represented by protocols which define how the shared local area network media is to be accessed by the many connected computers

Mach microkernel   Because microkernel-based operating systems can be built in a modular fashion, limited only by the requirement to interface to the microkernel through the minimal number of microkernel system calls, it is possible for different operating systems to be developed from the same microkernel. The Mach microkernel developed at Carnegie-Mellon University is one example of a microkernel which has been used as the nucleus for numerous operating systems.

MacOS   The release of MacOS Version 8.0 achieves at least three important goals for Apple: Creates a powerful new microkernel-based operating system, Runs legacy applications well, Removes hard-coded hardware-to-operating system links to enable Mac Clone hardware vendors and third-party Mac software vendors to fully participate in the PowerMac market.

Magneto-Optical   Disk technology backup device with 13GB capacity and 48–96MB/min throughput

mailslot   Mailslot is an interprocess communication mechanism used by the OS/2 LAN Manager network operating system.

management information base   See MIB

management information file   See MIF

management information format   See MIF

Management Interface API   Part of DMI, The Management Interface API is designed to interface to the desktop system management program which will consolidate the information from this client with all other desktop information

manual switch   The simplest of printer sharing devices is a manual switch, sometimes also known as a mechanical switch or an A/B switch

marketectures   Single vendor migration paths through increasingly sophisticated and high performance enterprise network architectures are commonly referred to as marketectures

massively parallel processing   See MPP

master domain architecture   This is a hierarchical architecture in which a single master domain is established into which all users are defined. Multiple sub-domains all offer inter-domain trust accounts to the single master domain, but the master domain does not allow trusted access from the sub-domains

Master File Table   See MFT

matrix switch   A type of data switch known as a matrix switch allows all possible combinations of connections among attached input and output devices

MAU   Token Ring wiring centers are known as MAUs (Multistation Access Unit)

maximum video bandwidth   A performance criteria which is a direct result of desired resolution and refresh rate is maximum video bandwidth which can be computed with the following formula: Required Video Bandwith = resolution height x resolution with x refresh rate x 1.5

MCA   Microchannel Architecture bus specification featuring 32 bit bus width with 20MBps throughput

MD5   In Pretty Good Privacy encryption method, digital signature encryption is provided using a combination of RSA and MD5 (Message Direct Version 5) encryption techniques

media access control   See MAC

media sharing LANs   Local area networks which use access methodologies to control the access of multiple users to a shared media are known as media sharing LANs.

meeting creation   The first of 3 major functional categories for workgroup conferencing software. Meetings must first be created or established.

meeting results reporting   The third of 3 major functional categories of workgroup conferencing software. In order to benefit fully from the ideas generated at the meeting, results must be easily, accurately, and flexibly reported.

megahertz   millions of cycles per second

memory bus   The L2 cache is connected to the CPU chip through a memory bus whose speed is also measured in MHz

message   Transport layer protocols also provide mechanisms for sequentially organizing multiple network layer packets into a coherent message.

message gateway   One of three cooperating components of the agent portion of the client/agent/server architecture. The message gateway can execute on the local server or on a dedicated Unix or Windows workstation, and acts as an interface between the client's message manager and the intelligent agent on the local server. The gateway also acts as a holding station for messages to and from mobile clients which are temporarily unreachable

message integrity   Authentication uses digital signatures which are attached to transmitted documents in order to assure both the authenticity of the author and the document's message integrity which verifies that the document has not been tampered with.

message manager   One of three cooperating components of the agent portion of the client/agent/server architecture. The message manager executes on the mobile client and acts as an interface between client applications requesting services and the wireless link over which the requests must be forwarded

message passing   Message passing, also known as message delivery, message queuing, and distributed messaging, differs significantly from the previously mentioned middleware sub-categories in its ability to establish various types of inter-process communications modes other than the send-and-wait mode

message transfer agents   See MTA

message transfer agents   Message transfer agents are responsible for forwarding messages between post offices and to destination clients. Some e-mail systems require the message transfer agent software to execute on a separate physical server from the local post office software

message-oriented middleware   See MOM

messages   In electronic meeting support software, User comments on topics are made up of a series of messages which may contain supporting material or documents known as enclosures

messaging infrastructure   Enterprise e-mail has become an enabling technology for other applications providing standardized, real-time intelligent transport services

meta-directory   An overall directory service which could insulate client applications from these multiple enterprise directory services is known as a meta-directory.

MFT   Master File Table is an NTFS feature that attempts to accomplish two key objectives which are often contradictory: Fast performance and lookups, especially on small files and directories, Reliable performance thanks to numerous redundant features

MIB   The types of information to be gathered and stored for enterprise network management systems have been defined as MIBs or Management Information Bases

MIB   Performance statistics are often gathered and stored in databases known as MIBs (Management Information Base)

MIB   The decision as to which information should be requested, transported, and stored for a variety of different devices is defined by a protocol related to SNMP known as MIB or Management Information Base. These defined fields and quantities which are encapsulated by SNMP and delivered via UDP are known as MIB objects

MIB   The network management information gathered must be stored in some type of database with an index and standardized field definitions so that network management workstations can easily access this data. A MIB, or Management Information Base as these databases are known, can differ in the fields defined for different vendor's networking devices

micro-mainframe connectivity   In micro-mainframe connectivity, the micro (Standalone or LAN-attached PC) pretends to be or "emulates" a mainframe terminal such as an IBM 3270 attached and logged into the mainframe

micro-segmentation   When segmentation is taken to the extreme of limiting each LAN segment to only a single workstation, the internetworking design strategy is known as micro-segmentation. A micro-segmented internetwork requires a LAN switch which is compatible with the NICs installed in the attached workstations

microcell spread spectrum   Limited to those areas such as college and corporate campuses that are served by microcells, this wireless WAN service offers full-duplex transmission at rates up to 104.5Mbps via proprietary modems.

microkernel   A microkernel is a sub-set of the overall operating system. It contains a minimum of hardware-specific instructions written to interact with a particular CPU chip

Microsoft Directory Services Manager for NetWare   Microsoft offers the Microsoft Directory Services Manager for NetWare which uses NT to centrally manage NetWare 2.x or 3.x servers which would normally need to be individually managed.

middleware   Middleware resides in the middle of the distributed processing system, serving as a transparent insulator surrounding the enterprise network over which the client-server communication actually travels.

middleware   In a distributed information system, the client to server messaging from the distributed computing sub-system must be transparent to differences in computing platforms, operating systems, network operating systems, or data management systems. This messaging transparency is delivered by an important category of software known as middleware

middleware application development tools   Middleware application development tools provide the functionality to build separate client and server-based distributed applications with imbedded remote procedure calls

MIF   The DMTF or Desktop Management Task Force, has developed a common management environment for the management of desktop devices known as the DMI (Desktop Management Interface). Specific aspects of the DMI are contained in MIF (Management Information File) definitions

MIF   Since DMI-compliant desktop management systems store performance and configuration statistics in a MIF (Management Information Format), and enterprise management systems employ a MIB, a MIF-to-MIB Mapper is required in order to link desktop and enterprise management systems

migration   Migration features are aimed at easing the transition from NetWare 3.12 to either NetWare 4.1 or Windows NT.

MIME   A protocol known as MIME (Multipurpose Internet Mail Extension) allows documents to be attached to e-mail regardless of the source application program, operating system, or network operating system

MIME   MIME or Multipurpose Internet Mail Extension allows binary files to be attached to SMTP delivered e-mail messages.

MIME   MIME (Multipurpose Internet Mail Extension) is actually an extension of SMTP which provides each part of a multimedia e-mail message with its own header which defines not only the type of infor-

mation contained therein but also the method used to encode that information

MIP   Processing power is often measured in MIPs (Millions of Instruction/Second).

Mirrored Server Link   See MSL

MLID   Network interface card drivers are referred to as Multi-Link Interface Drivers or MLID in an ODI-compliant environment

MLPPP   Multilink Point-to-Point Protocol or MLPPP (RFC 1717) is able to support multiple simultaneous physical WAN links and is also able to combine multiple channels from a variety of WAN services into a single logical link.

mobile computing   Mobile computing, addresses the need for field representatives to be able to access corporate information resources in order to offer superior customer service while working on the road. These field reps may or may not have a corporate office PC into which to dial

Mobile IP   Mobile IP, under consideration by the IETF, may be the roaming standard which wireless LANs require. Mobile IP, limited to TCP/IP networks, employs two pieces of software in order to support roaming: A mobile IP client is installed on the roaming wireless client workstation, A mobile IP home agent is installed on a server or router on the roaming user's home network.

mobile IPX   Novell had combined the functionality of NetWare Connect with a new communications protocol known as mobile IPX into a new product known as NetWare Mobile in order to support remote access clients which must frequently change locations

mobile MIB   The Mobile Management Task Force (MMTF) has proposed a mobile MIB capable of feeding configuration and location information to enterprise network management systems via SNMP. A key to the design of the mobile MIB was to balance the amount of information required in order to effectively manage remote clients while taking into account the limited bandwidth and expense of the remote links over which the management data must be transmitted.

mobile middleware   The ultimate goal of mobile middleware is to offer mobile users transparent client/server access independent of the following variables: Client or server platform (operating system, network operating system), Applications (client/server or client/agent/server), Wireless transmission services

mobile-aware applications   The overall objective of mobile-aware applications is to reduce the amount of mobile client to server network traffic by building as much intelligence as possible into the server-based agent so that it can act on behalf of the mobile client application

mobile-aware operating systems Operating systems which are able to easily adapt to these different computing modes with a variety of included supporting accessory programs and utilities are sometimes referred to as mobile-aware operating systems

modular concentrators See enterprise hubs

modularity of design The NT architecture with structured communications between sub-systems affords NT an architectural characteristic known as modularity of design which allows entire sub-systems to be easily added or replaced. For example, the replacement of the current Windows NT security sub-system with the Kerberos authentication system would be a relatively straight forward modification.

MOM MOM or message-oriented middleware, also known as message delivery, message passing, message queuing, and distributed messaging, differs significantly from remote procedure call middleware in its ability to establish various types of inter-process communications modes other than RPC's send-and-wait or synchronous mode.

monolithic architecture A monolithic architecture exists if required operating system components such as the file management system or the input/output and disk storage sub-system were arranged in a layered architecture with each layer only communicating directly with the layers immediately above and below it.

monolithic drivers Network interface card drivers written for specific adapter card/network operating system combinations are known as monolithic drivers

Mosaic Internet information consumers wishing to access the World Wide Web will require a client PC configured with a front-end software tool or web browser such as Mosaic or NetScape

Motif Motif from the Open Software Foundation is X Window Manager that communicates with X server software and serves as a GUI for Unix environments.

MPC level 1 CD-ROM standard proposed by the Multimedia PC Marketing Council (MPC)—150KBps sustained transfer rate, 1 sec max. avg. seek time, & 40% max. CPU usage

MPC level 2 CD-ROM standard proposed by the Multimedia PC Marketing Council (MPC)—300KBps sustained transfer rate, 400 msec max. avg. seek time, & 60% max. CPU usage

MPOA The ATM Forum is currently working on MPOA (Multi Protocols Over ATM) which will not only support IP, IPX, Appletalk and other network

protocols over ATM, but will also be able to route data directly between virtual LANs, thereby precluding the need for additional external routers

MPP Massively parallel processing (MPP) systems architectures employ thousands of CPUs, each with their own system memory. These MPP system architectures may be installed in a single machine or may spin several machines

MPR Novell's software-only router

MPR Windows NT can also support simultaneous access to NetWare files stored on NetWare servers thanks to a layer of software which acts as a sort of redirector for file system requests known as the multiple provider router (MPR). The MPR is an open interface which accepts requests to any supported file system from application programs adhering to the Win32 API

MPS In order to allow greater freedom of choice in matching SMP server hardware with SMP server operating systems, a SMP specification for the hardware/software interface known as MultiProcessing Specification 1.1 (MPS) has been proposed by Intel and is widely supported by SMP hardware and software vendors

MPTN A layer of the New SNA architecture, the Multiprotocol Transport Networking Layer supports numerous transport protocols including SNA/APPN

MS-DOS MS-DOS, an acronym for Microsoft Disk Operating System was originally designed to work on standalone, single user PCs. DOS introduced multiuser networking capabilities such as record and file locking with the release of Version 3.1. Network operating systems are able to call these DOS commands transparently to the networking operating system users

MSL In NetWare 4.1 SFT III, the synchronization of the servers is accomplished through a dedicated link known as the Mirrored Server Link (MSL). The use of the dedicated MSL link and dedicated MSL adapters prevents the server duplexing from adversely effecting LAN traffic

MTA Mail messages are just files which are transferred to the proper destination post-office, or file server, by message transfer agent (MTA) software which is usually executed on a dedicated workstation.

multi-layer switch A single device in which layer 2 switching and layer 3 routing functionality are combined.

multi-layer switches See distributed routing.

multi-link interface drivers See MLID

multi-platform e-mail client software Multi-platform e-mail software varies by the number of different computing platforms for which client e-mail software is available

multi-processor server Although 2 or 4 supported processors is a common number for most multi-processor servers, some super-computer type multi-processor servers can employ 64 or more CPUs and cost well over $1,000,000. Although Intel's Pentium chip at various clock speeds is perhaps the most commonly used CPU chip in multiprocessor servers, several other chips are also employed

multi-protocol bridges See translating bridge

multilevel security services Part of the DMA document management interoperability standards, Multilevel security services provide a variety of security levels for individual documents regardless of which DMA compliant document management system they are stored in

Multilink Point-to-Point Protocol See MLPPP

multimode In a Multimode or Multimode Step Index fiber optic cable, the rays of light will bounce off of the cladding at different angles and continue down the core while others will be absorbed in the cladding. These multiple rays at varying angles cause distortion and limit the overall transmission capabilities of the fiber

multimode graded index By gradually decreasing a characteristic of the core known as the refractive index from the center to the outer edge, reflected rays are focused along the core more efficiently yielding higher bandwidth (3 GBps) over several kilometers in a type of fiber optic cable known as Multimode Graded Index Fiber.

multimode step index See multimode

multiple master domains architecture This two-tiered architecture supports multiple master domains, with up to 10,000 users each. All sub-domains offer inter-domain trust accounts to all master domains.

multiple non-trusting domains architecture If multiple divisions or departments within a given organization do not need access to each other's data or network resources, then multiple independently managed domains can be established without defining any trust relationships between the domains.

multiple personality op.sys. Multiple personality sub-systems are just further examples of the extendibility or customizability of a microkernel based operating system. As a specific example, Windows NT includes OS/2, 32-bit Windows, 16-bit Windows, and POSIX sub-systems which allow applications written for any of those environments to be run on a Windows NT Platform.

multiple provider router See MPR

multiple trust architecture In this idealistic, flat architecture, all domains offer inter-domain trust accounts to all other domains. The difficulty with this architecture is that all domains are independently administered and trust relationships must be established for every possible domain-domain combination

multiple workplace environments See multiple personality operating systems

multiprocessing An operating system which supports multiprocessing is able to split the processing demands of applications programs across more than one processor or CPU

multiprocessing specification 1.1 See MPS

Multiprotocol Encapsulation over ATM Adaptation Layer 5 The IETF is currently working on RFC 1483, Multiprotocol Encapsulation over ATM Adaptation Layer 5. One of the significant contributions of this proposal is that it defines two different ways in which multiple network protocols can be transmitted simultaneously over an ATM network.

multiprotocol network printing When shared printing services are required across multiple, different network operating systems, using multiple different types of printers, then specialized multiprotocol network printing hardware and software is required

Multiprotocol Over ATM See MPOA

Multiprotocol Router See MPR

multiprotocol routers Multiprotocol routers have the capability to interpret, process and forward data packets of multiple routable and non-routable protocols

multiprotocol routing Multiprotocol routing provides the functionality necessary to actually process and understand multiple network protocols as well as translate between them. Without multiprotocol routing software, clients speaking multiple different network protocols cannot be supported.

Multiprotocol Transport Networking Layer See MPTN

Multipurpose Internet Mail Extension See MIME

multistation access unit See MAU

multisync The term multisync refers to the monitor's ability to automatically adjust to the installed video card's specifications and display the desired resolution at the accompanying refresh rate

multithreaded a multithreaded operating system allows multiple threads per task to operate simultaneously. Each thread from a single task is free to communicate individually with other threads throughout the distributed environment

multiuser Multiuser operating systems allow more than one user to log in simultaneously. In addition, multiuser operating systems are able to run the multiple application programs of those multiple users simultaneously.

named pipes Named Pipes is included in NT as an interprocess communication mechanism used by the OS/2 operating system.

Naming service See directory service

NASI NASI , or NetWare Asynchronous Services Interface, is a software interrupt which links to the NetWare shell on NetWare clients. As with the Int14 implementation, a TSR intercepts all of the information passed to the NASI interrupt and forwards it across the network to the dial-out modem pool.

native messaging protocols Native messaging protocols are concerned with how the e-mail messages are addressed, encapsulated and delivered. Although proprietary messaging protocols are satisfactory in closed environments, in open enterprise-wide environments, a widely-supported messaging protocol is required.

NBF NetBEUI Frame (NBF) is the Windows NT version of the NetBEUI protocol stack included for backward compatibility purposes with such NetBEUI-based network operating systems as Microsoft LAN Manager and OS/2 LAN Server

NCB requests for network attached resources are formatted in an agreed upon NetBIOS API format or syntax known as NCB or Network Control Block

NCP NetWare Core Protocols (NCP) provide a standardized set of commands or messages which can be used to communicate requests and responses for services between clients and servers

NDIS NDIS (Network Driver Interface Specification) is a driver specification which offers standard commands for communications between NDIS-compliant network operating system protocol stacks (NDIS Protocol Driver) and NDIS-compliant network adapter card drivers (NDIS MAC Drivers). In addition NDIS specifies a binding operation which is managed by a separate program known as the Protocol Manager

NDS Network operating system has always depended on some sort of naming service or directory in which to store information about users as well as systems resources such as disks, servers, and printers. NetWare 4.1 employs a global directory service known as NDS or NetWare Directory Services.

NDS NDS is a single logical database containing information about all network-attached resources which replaces the independently maintained, server-specific bindery files. The term "single logical database" is used because portions of the NDS database may be physically distributed on different servers throughout the network.

NDS Agent for NT Novell has introduced the NDS Agent for NT which allows an NT server to act as a NDS client on either a NetWare NDS server or on UNIX servers such as HP or SCO running NetWare services over UNIX. This software allows NT's domain-based naming service and NetWare's NetWare Directory Services to exchange and synchronize directory information

near-end crosstalk see NExT

near-line In HSM Information which is less frequently accessed is stored on near-line or near-on-line devices such as optical jukeboxes

NEST NEST or Novell Embedded Systems Technology is Novell's common networking communications architecture that will allow non-computing devices to interact transparently with distributed information systems providing centralized monitoring and control capabilities

Net2000 Universal API An application development environment in which the difficulties of supporting multiple distributed applications standards and multiple operating systems are rendered transparent through the use of a single set of high-level, network-aware APIs. This single interface to all networking services has been named the Net2000 APIs

NetBEUI A Microsoft enhanced version of NetBIOS known as NetBIOS Extended User Interface

NetBEUI Frame See NBF

NetBIOS NetBIOS (Network Basic Input/Output System) is an API which has become the de facto standard of network APIs for PC based networks.

NetBIOS application program NETBIOS application programs, otherwise known as NETBIOS Protocols, which interface with the NETBIOS API have been developed to perform specialized tasks on client and server PCs in order to enable this client/server communication. Two of the most famous of these NETBIOS application programs or protocols are the NETBIOS Redirector, on the client, and the Server Message Block (SMB) Server, on the server

NetScape Internet information consumers wishing to access the World Wide Web will require a client PC configured with a front-end software tool or web browser such as Mosaic or NetScape

NetSync cluster By running NETSYNC NLMs on both the NetWare 4.1 and NetWare 3.12 servers, all administration of the NetWare 3.12 servers, or NetSync Cluster, is done through NDS on the NetWare 4.1 server with changes automatically replicated to the binderies on the NetWare 3.12 servers

NetWare 4.1 SFT III NetWare 4.1 SFT III offers a unique tolerant feature known as server duplexing. In such a case, not only are the contents of the disks synchronized, but the contents of the servers' memory and CPUs are also synchronized. In case of the failure of the primary server, the duplexed server takes over transparently

NetWare 4.1 SMP Since the original NetWare 4.1 did not have SMP capability, some way needed to be found to support SMP while still assuring backward compatibility with all existing NLMs. This was done by having NetWare 4.1 SMP load a second operating system kernel, known as the SMP kernel, which works cooperatively with the first or native operating system kernel.

NetWare Connect NetWare Connect is NetWare's software-only remote access server solution providing both dial-in and dial-out access capabilities for up to 128 simultaneous users

NetWare Core Protocol See NCP

NetWare Directory Services See NDS

NetWare DOS Requester The NetWare DOS Requester actually works through DOS by having a VLM management program known as VLM.EXE interrupt DOS as appropriate and request services.

NetWare I/O Subsystem See NIOS

NetWare Link Services Protocol see NLSP

NetWare Loadable Module See NLM

NetWare NFS NetWare NFS allows UNIX systems to access NetWare file servers as if they were native NFS servers. NetWare NFS is actually a group of NLMs which runs on a NetWare server.

NetWare NFS Gateway NetWare NFS Gateway allows NetWare users to access NFS file systems on UNIX servers as if they were NetWare file servers. The gateway software is available for DOS, OS/2 or Macintosh computers.

NetWare Partition The NetWare kernel resides in a section of the server's disk drive known as the NetWare partition. This is the only portion of the disk which the NetWare kernel is physically able to access

NetWare Shell Up through NetWare Version 3.11, the NetWare client software for DOS clients was usually referred to as the NetWare Shell, or as NETx, in reference to NETx.COM which was the primary file involved in creating the DOS client shell. The "x" refers to the version of DOS with which the NetWare client software is used.

NetWare/IP NetWare/IP Version 2.1 is currently included with NetWare 4.1, and layers NCP (NetWare Core Protocols) over TCP/IP

network access device Clients, servers, and local area networks are connected to the Internet via a network access device such as a modem, an ISDN network access device, or a router.

network byte order The IP header can be either 20 or 24 bytes long, with the bits actually being transmitted in network byte order or from left to right

network caching Network caching or LAN caching software is able to improve overall remote node performance up to five times by caching repetitive applications commands and system calls. These add-on packages are comprised of both client and server pieces which work cooperatively to cache application commands and reduce network traffic over relatively low-speed WAN links. Network caching software is network operating system and protocol dependent, requiring that compatibility be assured prior to purchase

Network Control Block See NCB

network device interface specification See NDIS

network driver Network drivers provide support for multi-layer communications over a network. Examples include: NetBIOS, Redirector, and the SMB server interface to applications and file systems. Communication protocols such as TCP/IP, NetBEUI, and IPX/SPX provide transport services, NDIS provides the ability for a network interface card to support multiple protocols as well as the ability for a network operating system to communicate with more than one NIC in a single computer.

Network File System See NFS

network interface card The network interface card (or adapter) provides a transparent interface between the shared media of the LAN and the computer into which it is physically installed. The NIC takes messages which the computer directs it to send to other LAN attached computers or devices and formats those messages in a manner appropriate for transport over the LAN

network interface card The data-link layer frames are built within the network interface card installed in a computer according to the pre-determined frame layout particular to the network architecture of the installed network interface card. Network interface cards are given a unique address in a format determined by their network architecture

network interface card drivers Network interface card drivers are small software programs responsible for delivering full interoperability and compatibility between the NIC and the network operating system installed in a given computer

network interface cards   See NICs

network layer   The network layer protocols are responsible for the establishment, maintenance, and termination of end-to-end network links. Network layer protocols are required when computers which are not physically connected to the same LAN must communicate

network level filter   A filtering program which only examines source and destination addresses and determines access based on the entries in a filter table is known as a port level filter or network level filter.

Network News Transfer Protocol   See NNTP

Network nodes   In APPN, Network Nodes are processing nodes with routing capabilities. They have the ability to locate network resources, maintain tables of information regarding internetwork links, and establish a session between the requesting end-node and the internetwork service requested.

network objects   In some cases, directory services may view all users and network resources as network objects with information concerning them stored in a single database, arranged by object type. Object attributes can be modified and new network objects can be defined

network operating system   The software which runs on personal computers and allows them to log into a LAN and converse with other LAN-attached devices. Examples of popular network operating systems are NetWare, Vines, and Windows NT (not to be confused with Windows)

network operating system   A layer of software installed on both clients and servers which is responsible for the successful transport of messages across the network. A NOS is responsible for network-based resource sharing.

network operating systems   network operating systems are concerned with providing an interface between LAN hardware, such as network interface cards, and the application software installed on a particular client or server. The network operating system's job is to provide transparent interoperability between client and server portions of a given application program.

network virtual terminal   See Telnet negotiation

network-network interface   See NNI

networked group presentations   Networked Group Presentations allow one individual to present a graphically oriented presentation to multiple network-attached group members as if all seminar participants were seated in a single room

New SNA   The New SNA architecture would allow customers to integrate multi-vendor, multi-platform, multi-protocol information systems without being locked into one vendor's proprietary network architecture.

NExT   Near-End Crosstalk (NExT) is signal interference caused by a strong signal on one-pair (transmitting) overpowering a weaker signal on an adjacent pair (receiving).

NFS   NFS or Network File System is the file system most often associated with UNIX

NFS   NFS or Network File System was originally developed by Sun Microsystems as part of their Open Network Computing (ONC) environment. NFS allows multiple, different computing platforms to share files

NIC   See Network Interface Card

NICs   Network Interface Cards (NIC) are installed either internally or externally to client and server computers in order to provide a connection to the local area network of choice.

NIOS   DOS, Windows, and Windows 95 versions of the NetWare client software are based on a new 32 bit architecture known as NetWare I/O Subsystem or NIOS.

NLMs   Additional functionality can be added to the basic NetWare kernel through the use of NetWare Loadable Modules or NLMs. NLMs are programs which are specially written to interact with and add functionality to the NetWare kernel

NLSP   NLSP or NetWare Link Services Protocol is introduced in NetWare 4.1 in an effort to overcome the inefficiencies introduced by RIP NLSP only broadcasts as changes occur, or every 2 hours at a minimum. Real world implementations of NLSP have reported 15 to 20 times (not %) reduction in WAN traffic with Novell claiming up to 40-fold decreases in router-to-router traffic as possible

NNI   NNI or Network-Network Interface defines interoperability standards between various vendors' ATM equipment and network services. These standards are not as well defined as UNI.

NNTP   UseNet servers transfer news items between each other using a specialized transfer protocol known as NNTP (Network News Transport Protocol) and are also known as NNTP servers. Users wishing to access NNTP servers and their newsgroups must have NNTP client software loaded on their client PCs

nomadic computing   Novell's description of the need to support remote access clients which must frequently change locations

non-routable   Protocols processed by some routers are actually data link layer protocols without network layer addressing schemes. These protocols are considered non-routable.

non-routable protocol   Non-routable protocols can be processed by routers by either having the routers act as bridges or by encapsulating the non-routable data link layer frame's upper layer protocols in a routable network layer protocol such as IP

NOS   See network operating system

Novell DOS   Originally known as DR (Digital Research)—DOS, Novell DOS Version 7 (ND7) is intended as an alternative to MS-DOS 6.22. ND7 is really three products in one: DOS, Universal NetWare Client, Personal NetWare

Novell Embedded Systems Technology   See NEST

NT Executive   Application programs and APIs are prohibited from interacting directly with hardware resources in Windows NT. Instead, applications and APIs must access hardware resources by requesting services through the collection of system services known as the NT Executive

NT Kernel   Communications between the various NT Executive sub-systems and the I/O manager are controlled by the NT Kernel, sometimes referred to as a microkernel.

NTFS   NTFS (NT File System)—Windows NT

NWLink   IPX/SPX is supported in the Windows NT environment through a protocol stack known as NWLink which allows IPX/SPX to serve as the native communications protocol for all communications between NT clients and NT servers

object   An object can be thought of as data and the logic and rules to process that data which is treated as a single, encapsulated entity which can subsequently interoperate with, or be included in (encapsulate) other objects

object   An object is a software entity which describes data in terms of its attributes as contained in fields, and its behavior as defined by the methods or procedures which can alter the object's attributes. Objects could be thought of as miniature, free-standing software components which interact with each other in a structured manner, in order to produce overall application software functionality.

Object Linking & Embedding   See OLE

object management layer   Objects and inter-object communication can be distributed transparently across an enterprise network without application development programmers being required to know the physical location of required objects. This Object Management Layer would reside between the Network Operating System layer and the distributed application layer in a Client/Server Technology Architecture

object manager   The object manager in Windows NT is responsible for overall management of all NT objects including enforcement of naming conventions and authorization for accessing and manipulating any object. In a very real sense, the object manager is responsible for object security.

object middleware   A category of middleware known as object middleware allows objects created in multiple vendors' environments to communicate and request services of each other via the mediation services of an object request broker (ORB)

object oriented user interfaces   Object Oriented User Interfaces present the user with a graphical desktop on which objects such as files, directories, folders, disk drives, programs, or devices can be arranged according to the user's whim

object request broker   See ORB

object-oriented user interface   With Object Oriented User Interfaces (OOUI) users will no longer work by executing a particular application program, but will choose to accomplish a particular task. The combination of application programs required to complete that task will execute without direct actions from the user.

objects   Objects can be thought of as the system resources which are to be controlled or managed. User groups, users, printers, print servers, print queues, and disk volumes can all be considered objects by bindery services.

objects   Files within the MIBs are known as objects.

ODI   Open DataLink Interface operates in a manner similar to the basic functionality of NDIS and is orchestrated by a program known as LSL.COM where LSL stands for Link Support Layer

ODSI   Open Directory Services Interface. Microsoft's API for directory services synchronization

ODSI   Microsoft has developed an enterprise directory API known as ODSI (Open Directory Services Interface) which interfaces between Windows clients and multiple different enterprise directory services supporting the ODSI API.

OLE   OLE (Object Linking & Embedding) developed by Microsoft. A standard for object middleware. See CORBA

OLE   OLE (Object Linking & Embedding) is a Microsoft protocol which allows documents, spreadsheets, graphical presentations, and other types of attachments to be linked with e-mail messages

OLTP   In order to keep information real-time, business transactions must be posted immediately, rather than in nightly batches, using systems known as On-Line Transaction Processing (OLTP) systems.

OLTP OLTP (On-Line Transaction Processing) monitors, were originally developed to monitor and control the posting of numerous simultaneous transactions across multiple computing platforms

on-board cache High-seed memory placed directly on the processor chip as a buffer between the slower system memory (RAM) and the fast pipelines is known as on-board cache. On-board cache is also known as on-chip cache, primary cache, or L1 (Level 1) cache

On-Line Transaction Processing See OLTP

OOUI See Object oriented user interface

open data-link interface See ODI

Open Directory Services Interface See ODSI

Open Look OpenLook from Sun Microsystems is a X Window Manager that communicates with X server software and serves as a GUI for Unix environments.

open shortest path first See OSPF

Open Software Foundation See OSF

OpenVMS Microsoft and DEC have reached an agreement which will enable DEC's operating system, known as OpenVMS to also support the Win32 API.

operands stage any additional data or numbers, the operands, which are required to complete the instruction are fetched in the operands stage

operating system architecture The manner in which the various components of an operating system interact is referred to as the operating system architecture. The two major categories of operating system architectures are monolithic architectures and microkernel architectures.

Oracle Mobile Agents Oracle Mobile Agents, formerly known as Oracle-in-Motion is perhaps the best example of the overall architecture and components required to produce mobile-aware applications. The Oracle Mobile Agents architecture adheres to an overall client-agent-server architecture, as opposed to the more common LAN-based client/server architecture

ORB See object middleware

OS/2 Warp Connect From an architectural standpoint, OS/2 Warp Connect is similar to Windows NT is that separate virtual machines are implemented for 16-bit and 32-bit applications. OS/2 Warp Connect can run 16-bit Windows and DOS applications as well as native OS/2 applications

OSF In order to bring some standardization to distributed information systems architectures in order to help assure enterprise-wide interoperability, the Open Software Foundation (OSF) has introduced the Distributed Computing Environment (DCE) model.

OSI Model A framework for organizing networking technology and protocol solutions has been developed by the International Standards Organization (ISO) and is known as the Open Systems Interconnection (OSI) model

OSI Model The OSI Model consists of a hierarchy of 7 layers which loosely group the functional requirements for communication between two computing devices. The power of the OSI Model lies in its openness and flexibility. It can be used to organize and define protocols involved in communicating between two computing devices in the same room as effectively as two devices across the world from each other.

OSPF OSPF or Open Shortest Path First (RFC 1247) is an example of a link state protocol which was developed to overcome some of RIP's shortcomings such as the 15 hop limit and full routing table broadcasts every thirty seconds. OSPF uses IP for connectionless transport

out-of-order execution Out-of-order execution allows other pipelines to continue processing if one stalls.

overdrive chips Overdrive chips are replacement CPU chips, manufactured by Intel, which offer clock multiplying capabilities

P channel In Isochronous Ethernet, A 10Mbps ISDN P channel is reserved for Ethernet traffic and is completely compatible with 10BaseT Ethernet

P-A-D Architecture The delivery of quality information to end-users depends on the interaction of three fundamental processes: Presentation (also known as User Interface), Application (also known as Application Logic or Processing), Data (also known as Data Management or Data Manipulation)

P6 The P6 or Pentium Pro CPU chip itself is just one of two chips mounted in separate cavities in a single die or chip container, sometimes referred to as a package. This second cavity is occupied by a 256KB SRAM L2, or secondary cache, linked directly to the neighboring Pentium Pro chip through a dedicated 64 bit bus known as the backside bus

P7 Next generation Intel chip featuring: 4 to 6 superscalar pipelined architecture, Larger primary caches, Integrated secondary caches, More execution units, larger buffers to support deeper paths of speculative execution, speculative execution down both branches of conditional branch statements, 20 million transistors?

packaged L2 cache   In a P6 CPU, the second cavity is occupied by a 256KB SRAM 12 L2, or secondary cache, linked directly to the neighboring Pentium Pro chip through a dedicated 64 bit bus known as the backside bus. This directly linked L2 cache is also known as packaged L2 cache

packet bursts   See Burst Mode IPX

packet overlapping   With packet overlapping technology, the next packet of information is immediately forwarded as soon as its start of frame is detected rather than waiting for the previous frame to be totally onto the network media before beginning transmission of the next packet.

packet signing   In NetWare 4.1, every packet transmitted from a particular client workstation can have a unique, encrypted digital signature attached to it which can be authenticated by the server in a process known as packet signing. However, a performance price of 5-7% is paid for the increased security as valuable CPU cycles are spent encrypting and decrypting digital signatures.

packets   Network layer protocols are responsible for providing network layer (end-to-end) addressing schemes and for enabling inter-network routing of network layer data packets. The term packets is usually associated with network layer protocols while the term frames is usually associated with data link layer protocols

pages   Fixed size portions of the process which are loaded into primary memory on demand are known as pages

paging   Paging seeks to eliminate, or at least minimize, fragmentation, by allowing processes to execute with only portions, rather than the entire process, physically present in primary memory

paradigm shift   The period of time when information systems professionals are madly scrambling to gain competitive advantage for their companies by implementing the "new" paradigm is known as a paradigm shift.

paradigms   Unique combinations of systems architectures and people architectures are often referred to as paradigms of the information age.

parallel networks model   A network design in which separate networks for SNA and LAN traffic had to be established between the same corporate locations.

parallel processing   Systems which support multiple CPUs are generally referred to as parallel processing systems because multiple program instructions can be executed in parallel simultaneously. The two primary alternative system architectures, or sub-categories of parallel processing are: symmetric multiprocessing, asymmetric multiprocessing

parallel routing   Parallel routing adds a layer of sophistication to workflow automation software by allowing sub-processes to be completed by multiple users simultaneously. Parallel routing may be combined with conditional branch routing.

parent processes   Processes in Unix are controlled by the fork system call as initiated through the shell interface, which allows parent processes to spawn multiple sub-processes known as child processes

partitions   Entire branches of the tree, designated as partitions, and including all subordinate container objects and leaf objects, can be pruned (removed) from one point in the NDS structure and grafted to another branch. In fact two entire trees can be merged together into a single tree.

passive matrix   Passive Matrix displays do not employ transistors and therefore do not have individual control over each point in the display grid. As a result, screens are painted and re-painted a line at a time in a serial fashion

passthrough authentication   Users allowed into domains based on the trust relationships established by domain controllers are considered to be authorized by passthrough authentication.

password authentication   A feature of NetWare Mobile, Password authentication is still enforced on laptop computers as if they were attached to the file server in order to prevent unauthorized access. Password encryption is supported with overall security still managed by NDS.

path names   Path names are used in Unix to identify the specific path through the hierarchical file structure to a particular destination file

PCI   The PCI (peripheral component interconnect) bus provides its own clocking signal at 33 MHz and has a bus-width of either 32 or 64 bits.

PCMCIA   PCMCIA (personal computer memory card international association) is actually a series of specifications which represent the physical and functional/electrical standards for technology adhering to these specs

PCS   Personal Communications Services will provide national full duplex digital voice and data at up to 25Mbps via 2-way pagers, PDAs, and PCS devices

PDA   Some scheduling packages can communicate directly with PDAs (Personal Digital Assistants) that combine scheduling and communication functionality

PDC   Domain directory services associate network users and resources with a primary server known as a PDC or Primary Domain Controller

peer-to-peer internetworking   With full peer to peer

internetworking, the PC can exchange data with any mainframe or any other PC on a host-to-host level rather than acting like a "dumb" terminal as in the case of micro-mainframe connectivity

peer-to-peer network operating systems Peer-to-peer network operating systems, also known as DOS-based LANs or Low-cost LANs offered easy to install and use file and print services for workgroup and departmental networking needs.

Pentium The Pentium chip includes a 64 bit on-chip data path which allows twice as much information to be fetched with each tick of the CPU clock as a 486 chip. The Pentium chip is superscalar, containing 2 processing pipelines with three execution units to choose from; two integer and one floating point. It contains the equivalent of 3.3 million transistors and implements branch prediction using a branch target buffer.

performance monitoring Performance monitoring software should offer the ability to set thresholds for multiple system performance parameters. If these thresholds are exceeded, alerts or alarms should notify network management personnel of the problem, and offer advice as to possible diagnoses or solutions. Event logging and audit trials are often included as part of the performance monitoring package.

periodic replication Periodic replication is done on a timed basis. All new transactions which have accumulated since the last replication update are stored and forwarded all at once to all replicated servers.

peripheral sharing device Refers to a large category of devices which allow multiple PCs to share one or more printers or other peripherals such as modems or mainframe ports without the need for LAN hardware & software

Perl language The Perl language (Practical Extraction & Reporting Language) adds the following functionality to that offered by the Korn and Bourne shells: list processing, associative arrays, modern subroutines & functions, more control statements, better I/O, full function library

personal digital assistant See PDA

pervasive computing Novell talks about a view of the future known as pervasive computing in which not just computers but household and industrial appliances are all part of the same communications network, NetWare-based of course

PGP An Internet E-Mail specific encryption standard which also uses digital signature encryption to guarantee the authenticity, security, and message integrity of received e-mail is known as PGP which stands for Pretty Good Privacy, PGP overcomes inherent secu-

rity loopholes with public/private key security schemes by implementing a Web of Trust in which e-mail users electronically sign each other's public keys to create an interconnected group of public key users.

PGP A public domain encryption system known as Pretty Good Privacy (PGP) combines digital signature encryption with public key encryption

photo CD Also known as Kodak Photo CD, this is a standard for displaying photographs proposed by Kodak.

physical layer The physical layer, also known as layer 1 of the OSI model, is responsible for the establishment, maintenance and termination of physical connections between communicating devices. These connections are sometimes referred to as point-to-point data links

physical network design The *technology* layer analysis will determine *how* various hardware and software components will be combined to build a functional network which will meet pre-determined business objectives. The delineation of required technology is often referred to as the physical network design.

physical topology Clients and servers must be physically connected to each other according to some configuration and be linked by the shared media of choice. The physical layout of this configuration can have a significant impact on LAN performance and reliability and is known as a network architecture's physical topology.

piggyback updates A dial-up router update mechanism in which updates are performed only when the dial-up link has already been established for the purposes of exchanging user data.

PIO See Programmed I/O

pipelines A pipeline is analogous to an assembly line in a manufacturing plant and typically divides the overall process of completing a computer instruction into the following five stages or sub-processes: Fetch, Decode, Operands, Execute, Write back

pipes In Unix, Pipes is an interprocess communication mechanism which allows the output of one process to be used as the input for another process. Pipes is limited to communication between two processes executing on the same local computer and is initiated by a pipes system call

pixels Resolution refers to the number of pixels (picture elements) contained in the viewable area of the monitor screen and is reported as resolution height x resolution width. In simple terms, a greater number of pixels on the screen will produce a sharper image

plotter emulation buffer Plotter Emulation Buffers allow personal computers running graphics software to download graphics output quickly, thereby freeing the PC for more productive uses.

Plug-n-play See PnP

PnP The goal of plug-n-play is to free users from having to understand and worry about such things as IRQs (Interrupt Requests), DMA (Direct Memory Access) channels, memory addresses, COM ports, and editing CONFIG.SYS whenever they want to add a device to their computer.

PnP BIOS A PnP BIOS (Basic Input Output System) is required to interface directly to both PnP and non-PnP compliant hardware.

point-to-point data links The physical layer, also known as layer 1 of the OSI model, is responsible for the establishment, maintenance and termination of physical connections between communicating devices. These connections are sometimes referred to as point-to-point data links

Point-to-Point Protocol See PPP

poll spoofing Poll Spoofing is the ability of an internetworking device, such as an SDLC converter or router, to respond directly to, or acknowledge, the FEP's constant polling messages to the remote cluster controller. By answering these status check messages locally, the inquiry and its answer never enter the wide area link portion of the internetwork

POP Mail server management protocols may be either POP (Post Office Protocol) or IMAP (Internet Mail Access Protocol).

port A port can be thought of as a queue, or communications pipe, through which computer resources can be assigned to a task.

port level filter A filtering program which only examines source and destination addresses and determines access based on the entries in a filter table is known as a port level filter or network level filter.

port mirroring Port mirroring copies information from a particular switch port to an attached LAN analyzer. The difficulty with this approach is that it only allows one port to be monitored at a time.

port sharing device Port sharing is a peripheral sharing feature which orchestrates the sharing of a limited number of mainframe or minicomputer ports among many PC users

portability Portability refers to the ability for client/server applications to be developed in one computing environment and deployed in others

portability Portability is evidenced by Windows NT's unique ability to execute over multiple different CPUs such as Intel x86, MIPs RISC, DEC Alpha, and PowerPC

ports TCP is able to offer reliable transport services to applications through the use of ports. Ports are specific 16 bit addresses which are uniquely related to particular applications

Post Office Protocol See POP

post offices Post offices are responsible for storage of received messages and initial hops for outbound messages. Post offices are server-based and may also be required to maintain and store user profiles, and routing information to other post offices

POTS Dial-up phone service is sometimes referred to as POTS (Plain Old Telephone Service)

PowerPC The PowerPC is a true RISC chip whose features include: 64 bit internal data paths, 64KB of on-chip L1 cache, Superscalar architecture with six execution units, Branch prediction, speculative execution, and out of order execution

PPP Point-to-Point protocol allows connection via a variety of WAN services between a client PC and a centrally located server running IP or other network protocols

PPP Point-to-Point protocol is a data-link layer WAN protocol which is supported by NetWare Connect

PPP PPP (Point-to-point protocol) is the wide area data-link layer protocol which encapsulates the upper layer protocols in Windows NT RAS

PPP PPP is a WAN data-link layer protocol which is able to support multiple network layer protocols simultaneously over a single WAN connection. In addition, PPP is able to establish connections over a variety of WAN services including: ISDN, Frame Relay, SONET, X.25, as well as synchronous and asynchronous serial links.

PPP clients Standardized remote clients with the ability to link to servers running a variety of different network operating systems are sometimes referred to as PPP clients. In general, they can link to network operating systems which support IP, IPX, NetBEUI, or XNS as transport protocols.

pre-emptive multitasking Pre-emptive multitasking operating systems prevent misbehaving applications from monopolizing system resources by allocating system resources to applications according to priority or timing

presentation layer The presentation layer protocols provide an interface between user applications and various presentation-related services required by those applications. For example, data encryption/decryption protocols are considered presentation layer protocols as are protocols which translate between encoding schemes such as ASCII to EBCDIC

Presentation-Application-Data See P-A-D architecture

Pretty Good Privacy See PGP

primary cache High-speed memory placed directly on the processor chip as a buffer between the slower system memory (RAM) and the fast pipelines is known as on-board cache. On-board cache is also known as on-chip cache, primary cache, or L1 (Level 1) cache

primary data cache Primary caches can be specialized for storing data in order to increase overall efficiency

primary domain controller See PDC

primary domain controller Information concerning the network resources in a domain and the users which are allowed access to those resources is housed in a Windows NT server designated as the primary domain controller

primary instruction cache Primary caches can be specialized for storing instructions in order to increase overall efficiency

Principle of Shifting Bottlenecks As one aspect of a system which had been identified as a bottleneck is optimized, the bottleneck shifts to some other interacting component of the system.

printer sharing device Refers to a large category of devices which allow multiple PCs to share one or more printers without the need for LAN hardware & software.

printer sharing system A printer sharing system includes buffered printer sharing device, spooling and queue management software, cables, and adapters to connect the cables to the personal computers and printers and is all put together and sold as one product

private key The encryption key customizes the commonly known algorithm to prevent anyone without this private key from possibly decrypting the document

Private key encryption In private key encryption, a private key must be known by the both the sending and receiving encryption devices and allows so many unique combinations (nearly 2 to the 64th power), that unauthorized decryption is nearly impossible. The safe and reliable distribution of these private keys among numerous encryption devices can be difficult

private packet radio Proprietary wireless WAN service offered by RAM and Ardis in most major US cities. Offers full duplex packet switched data at speeds of up to 4.8Kbps via proprietary modems.

privileged mode The microkernel runs in what is known as privileged mode which implies that it is never swapped out of memory and has highest priority for allocation of CPU cycles

privileged mode The NT kernel runs in privileged mode and is therefore never paged out of memory

process group In Unix, processes may be organized into a process group for the purpose of more easily or effectively accomplishing a common goal, and may communicate with each other via an interprocess communication mechanism known as pipes.

process manager The process manager is ultimately responsible for the creation, maintenance, and termination of processes within Windows NT and communicates with the object manager and virtual memory manager in order to provide required resources and protection for the process in question

Processor I/O Processor I/O (Input/Output)—Also known as Programmed I/O or PIO. This data transfer method relies on a shared memory location in system memory as a transfer point for data between the disk drive and the system or main memory. The CPU is involved with every data transfer between the disk drive and system memory

production workflow This category of workflow software automates complicated business processes which are performed on a regular basis, perhaps daily

productivity paradox In the past decade, over $1 trillion dollars has been invested by business in information technology. Despite this massive investment, carefully conducted research indicates that there has been little if any increase in productivity as a direct result of this investment. This dilemma is known as the productivity paradox

promiscuous listen Promiscuous listen means that transparent bridges receive all data packets transmitted on the LANs to which they are connected.

propagation Forwarding messages by bridges to all workstations on all intermittent LANs is known as propagation.

propagation delay propagation delay is the time it takes a signal from a source PC to reach a destination PC. Because of this propagation delay, it is possible for a workstation to sense that there is no signal on the shared media, when in fact another distant workstation has transmitted a signal which has not yet reached the carrier sensing PC.

properties Properties are associated with objects and those aspects of objects which can or must be controlled. Examples of properties include such things as login time restrictions, network address restrictions, e-mail address, print job configuration, file and directory access rights, or user group membership.

protected memory mode Client network operating systems may execute 32 bit applications in their own address space, otherwise known as protected memory mode

protocol A protocol is a set of rules which govern communication between hardware and/or software components.

protocol conversion Translation between protocols which may be necessary in order to get any two network nodes to communicate successfully

protocol conversion Protocol conversion must take place to allow the PC to appear to be a 3270 terminal in the eyes of the mainframe.

protocol discriminator In order to differentiate which particular non-compliant protocol is embedded, any packet with AA in the DSAP and SSAP fields also has a 5 octet SNAP header known as a protocol discriminator following the Control field

protocol manager The NDIS program which controls the binding operation that combines separate NDIS compliant software from NOS and NIC vendors into a single compatible driver.

protocol stack The sum of all of the protocols employed in a particular computer is sometimes referred to as that computer's protocol stack

protocols Protocols are nothing more than rules for how communicating hardware and software components bridge interfaces or talk to one another

proxy polling Proxy polling emulates the FEP's polling messages on the remote side of the network, thereby assuring the remote cluster controller that it is still in touch with an FEP.

proxy server Some Web server software supports Proxy servers which act as holding bins or repositories for previously requested Web pages from distant Internet servers.

pruned Entire branches of the tree, designated as partitions, and including all subordinate container objects and leaf objects, can be pruned (removed) from one point in the NDS structure and grafted to another branch. In fact two entire trees can be merged together into a single tree.

public key encryption Public Key Encryption, the sending encryption device encrypts a document using the intended recipient's public key. This public key is readily available in a public directory or is sent by the intended recipient to the message sender. However, in order to decrypt the document, the receiving encryption/decryption device must be programmed with the recipient's private key

public key encryption Public Key Encryption could perhaps more accurately be named Public/Private Encryption since it actually combines usage of both public and private keys

QCIF A videoconferencing screen format QCIF (Quarter Common Intermediate Format) 144 lines x 176 pixels/line.

QIC Quarter inch cartridge magnetic tape with 40MB-25GB capacity & 4-96MB/min throughput

quad speed CD-ROM speed specification yielding sustained avg. data throughput of 600KBps

quad-issue a CPU with four pipelines would be called a quad-issue or four-way processor.

Quarter Common Intermediate Format See QCIF

query services Part of the DMA document management interoperability standards,

queue management This software manages and monitors the distribution of print jobs to various printers. It also allows printers to be enabled or disabled, or assigned to different personal computers

quick synchronization A feature of NetWare Mobile which allows only the changed portions of files to be transmitted during file re-synchronization.

R commands R commands describes a group of application layer service commands which can be executed remotely. For example, rlogin allows a user to remotely login to another computer and rexec allows the same user to execute a program on that remote computer

RAID In an effort to provide large amounts of data storage combined with fault tolerance and redundancy, numerous small disk drives were joined together in arrays and controlled by software which could make these numerous disk appear as one gigantic disk to server operating systems according to a series of standards known as RAID. RAID originally stood for Redundant Array of Inexpensive Disks

RAID level 0 Disk Striping—stripes data across multiple disks without redundancy

RAID level 1 Disk mirroring—also known as shadowing

RAID level 2 Striped array plus hamming code—writes data across multiple disks, adding hamming code for error detection & correction

RAID level 3 Striped array plus parity disk—Stripes data a byte at a time. Parity is calculated on a byte by byte basis and stored on a dedicated parity drive

RAID level 4 Independent striped array plus parity drive—stripes data in sectors. Parity stored on parity drive. Disks can work independently.

RAID level 5 Independent striped array plus striped parity—stripes data in sectors. Parity is interleaved and striped across multiple disks

RAID level 6 Independent striped array plus striped double parity—striped data and parity with two parity drives

RARP RARP or Reverse Address Resolution Protocol is used if the datalink layer address of the workstation is known but the IP address of the same workstation is required

RAS Windows NT's remote access server software

RAS Windows NT offers a service known as RAS or Remote Access Service which consists of both client and server software

raw interfaces Both block-oriented and character-oriented I/O may also bypass all buffers and queues and interact directly with hardware devices through their respective raw interfaces

raw sockets Provides direct interprocess communication from sockets to other layer protocols such as IP on the network layer or Ethernet on the data-link layer. Raw sockets is sometimes referred to as the DIY (Do-it-Yourself) interface since the functionality supplied by higher (transport) layer protocols such as TCP or UDP must be supplied by the programmer.

RDRAM Rambus DRAM

read ahead cache buffering A NetWare 4.1 feature known as read ahead cache buffering improves performance by reading ahead in the sequentially accessed file and caching that information in anticipation of the next request for information from the user

read-through cache Read-through cache allows data stored in the cache to be forwarded directly to the CPU without performing a physical disk read.

real time e-mail Real-time e-mail systems depend on remote procedure call messaging

real-mode device drivers Programs or sub-routines which write directly to computer hardware are sometimes referred to as employing real-mode device drivers.

real-time systems Information systems which give up-to-the-minute information are sometimes known as real-time systems

realms Enterprise networks implementing Kerberos are divided into Kerberos realms, each served by its own Kerberos server.

recursion If the local DNS cannot resolve an address itself, it may contact the higher authority DNS server, thereby increasing its own knowledge while meeting the client request in a process known as recursion.

redirector For every request for services coming from a client application program, a software module known as the redirector determines whether those requested resources are locally attached or network-attached

redundant processor architecture A redundant processor architecture goes beyond traditional symmetrical multiprocessing design. In a redundant processor architecture, each primary CPU is shadowed by a secondary identical tandem processor which executes the exact same instructions

refresh rate refresh rate refers to the number of times per second a screen image is redrawn or refreshed. Refresh rate is measured in Hz with 72 Hz being the current recommended minimum refresh rate

relational networks An enterprise network physical topology, relational networks seeks to overcome the need for manual configuration and maintenance of virtual LAN configuration tables in multilayer switches and route servers through a process known as automatic configuration. This automatic configuration is only possible with the use of a hybrid hardware device known as a relational switch which combines the capabilities of multilayer switches and ATM switches

relational switch See relational networks

relationship variables As part of the Application MIB, Relationship variables would define all other network attached resources on which a given distributed application depends. This would include databases, associated client applications, or other network resources

relative path names In Unix, Absolute path names start at the root directory in the listing of the path to the destination directory while relative path names start at the current directory

reliable Reliable transmission for upper layer application programs or utilities is assured through the additional fields contained within the TCP header which offer the following functionality: flow control, acknowledgements of successful receipt of packets after error checking, retransmission of packets as required, proper sequencing of packets

remote access The term remote access is most often used to generally describe the process of linking remote PCs to local LANs without implying the particular functionality of that link (remote node vs. remote control). Unfortunately, the term remote access is also sometimes more specifically used as a synonym for remote node.

Remote Access Service See RAS

remote configuration Increased security in SNMP2 allows not just monitoring and management of remote network devices, but actual remote configuration of those devices as well

remote control In remote control mode, the remote PC is merely supplying input and output devices for the local client which interacts as normal with the local server and other locally attached LAN resources

remote control software Remote Control Software, especially designed to allow remote PC's to "take-over" control of local PCs, should not be confused with the Asynchronous Communications Software used for dial-up connections to asynchronous hosts via modems

remote e-mail client software Remote e-mail client software must strike a balance between the need to offer users the same services as locally connected users while delivering those services over the comparatively limited bandwidth offered by dial-up telecommunications services as compared to local area network bandwidth.

remote monitoring See RMON

remote node Remote node or remote client computing implies that, in theory, the remote client PC should be able to operate as if it were locally attached to network resources. In other words, the geographic separation between the remote client and the local LAN resources should be transparent

remote node client software Most of the remote node server software packages also include compatible remote node client software. A problem arises, however, when a single remote node client needs to login to a variety of different servers running a variety of different network operating systems or remote node server packages.

remote node server An alternative to server-based remote access software is a standalone device alternatively known as a dial-up server or remote node server. Such a self-contained unit includes modems, communications software, and NOS-specific remote access server software in a turnkey system.

remote node server software Traditionally remote node client and server software were supplied by the vendor of the network operating system on the server to be remotely accessed. Windows NT RAS (Remote Access Service) and NetWare Connect are two examples of such NOS-specific remote node server software

remote node servers Remote node servers are strictly concerned with controlling remote access to LAN attached resources and acting as a gateway to those resources. Applications services are supplied by the same LAN-attached applications servers that are accessed by locally attached clients

remote node software Remote node software requires both remote node server and compatible remote node client software in order to successfully initiate remote node sessions

remote procedure call See RPC

remote procedure call messaging Realtime e-mail systems depend on remote procedure call messaging

remote procedure calls See RPC

remote procedure calls Remote procedure call middleware works in a manner similar to a locally run application program which activates, or calls, as subroutine stored outside of the application program itself, but usually in a sub-routine library on the same computer. The major difference with the remote procedure call is that the call for the execution of a subroutine is made to a remote procedure located on a distributed processor via the enterprise network

Remote Procedure Calls Service See RPC

repeater A repeater's job is to: Repeat the digital signal by regenerating and retiming the incoming signal, Pass all signals between all attached segments, Do not read destination addresses of data packets, Allow for the connection of and translation between different types of media, Effectively extend overall LAN distance by repeating signals between

replicated One of the key characteristics of the NDS database is its ability to have partitions be replicated, or physically stored on multiple file servers. Replication implies that these multiple copies of the same NDS partition are kept synchronized

requester Unlike the DOS client software of previous NetWare versions known as the NETx shell which acted as a replacement redirector, the DOS client software NetWare 4.1 is referred to as the requester

resolution Resolution refers to the number of pixels (picture elements) contained in the viewable area of the monitor screen and is reported as resolution height x resolution width. In simple terms, a greater number of pixels on the screen will produce a sharper image

resolver DNS is physically implemented in a client/server architecture in which client-based DNS software known as the DNS or name resolver, sends requests for DNS name resolution to a DNS (or name) Server

reverse address resolution protocol See RARP

reverse poison See split horizon

Rexx The Rexx scripting language offers an easier to learn and use alternative to Perl which supports structured programming techniques such as modularity while still offering access to shell commands

RFI Radio Frequency Interference

RIF One very important limitation of source routing bridges as applied to large internetworks is known as the 7 Hop Limit. Because of the limited space in the RIF (Router Information Field) of the explorer packet, only 7 hop locations can be included in the path to any remote destination

rightsizing Rightsizing implies that applications are

designed for and deployed on the platform, or type and size of computer, which makes the most sense: the "right" size computer. The right computer or platform implies that the choice is based on maximizing the efficiency with which the application runs

Ring 0   In NetWare 4.1's ring memory protection scheme, the area reserved for the operating system is known as Ring 0, otherwise known as domain OS (operating system)

Ring 3   In NetWare 4.1's ring memory protection scheme, The area reserved for NLMs is known as Ring 3 or domain OSP (operating system protected). NLMs executing in Ring 3 access operating systems services in Ring 0 by issuing structured inter-ring gate calls, thereby protecting the operating system from mis-behaving NLMs overwriting its memory space.

ring logical topology   See sequential

ring memory protection   NetWare 4.1 introduces ring memory protection which seeks to isolate and protect the operating system from potentially dangerous NLMs which were able to crash the entire system in previous versions of NetWare

ring physical topology   In a ring physical topology, each PC is actually an active part of the ring, passing data packets in a sequential pattern around the ring. If one of the PCs dies, or a network adapter card malfunctions, the "sequence" is broken, the token is lost, and the network is down.

RIP   NetWare's RIP, or Routing Information Protocol, is a router-to-router protocol used to keep routers on a NetWare network synchronized and up-to-date. RIP information is delivered to routers via IPX packets.

RIP   RIP is a router-to-router protocol associated with TCP/IP. RIP uses UDP as a transport protocol and broadcasts its routing tables to all directly connected routers every thirty seconds

RISC   RISC architectures interpret instructions directly in the CPU chip itself without the added overhead of the executing microcode. As a result of this hardware based decoding, the speed of processing is increased.

RMON   The most commonly used MIB for network monitoring and management is known as the RMON (Remote Monitoring) MIB

RMON MIB   Remote Network Monitoring MIB

RMON probe   RMON2 compatible agent software which resides within internetworking devices and reports performance statistics to enterprise network management systems is referred to as an RMON probe.

RMON2   The original RMON MIB standard which was developed in 1991 has been updated as RMON2. While the original RMON MIB only required compatible technology to be able to collect and analyze statistics on the physical and data link layers, RMON2 requires collection and analysis of network layer protocols as well.

roaming   One important issue not included in the IEEE 802.11 standard is roaming capability which allows a user to transparently move between the transmission ranges of wireless LANs without interruption. Proprietary roaming capabilities are currently offered by many wireless LAN vendors

root object   In NDS, the tree hierarchy starts at the top with the root object. There is only one root object in an entire global NDS database. Branches off of the root object are represented by container objects

round robin polling scheme   In 100VG-AnyLAN, the Demand Priority Protocol access methodology uses a round robin polling scheme in which the hubs scan each port in sequence to see if the attached workstations have any traffic to transmit. The round robin polling scheme is distributed through a hierarchical arrangement of cascaded hubs.

Route server   In a MPOA architecture, a Route Server would supply edge devices with their routing information including ATM addresses and virtual circuit IDs. The route server may actually be located within one of the ATM switches in the ATM backbone

router servers   An internetwork evolutionary design scenario in which Route Servers will provide a centralized repository of routing information while edge switches deployed within the LANs will be programmed with minimal routing information.

Routing Information Field   See RIF

Routing Information Protocol   See RIP

routing switches   Layer 3 Virtual LANs are built using LAN switches which are able to process layer 3 network addresses. Such devices may be called routing switches. Since these devices are able to perform filtering based on network layer protocols and addresses, they are able to support multiple virtual LANs using different network layer protocols

routing tables   Routers consult routing tables in order to determine the best path on which to forward a particular data packet.

roving port mirroring   Roving port mirroring creates a roving RMON (Remote Monitoring) probe which gathers statistics at regular intervals on multiple switch ports. The shortcoming with this approach remains that at any single point in time, only one port is being monitored

RPC   Remote Procedure Call middleware works in a manner similar to a locally run application program which activates, or calls, a sub-routine stored outside of the application program itself, but usually in a sub-routine library on the same computer. The major difference with the Remote Procedure Call is that the call for the execution of a sub-routine is made to a remote procedure located on a remote distributed processor via the enterprise network

RPC   The interprocess communication service defined within DCE is known as RPC or Remote Procedure Call. Windows NT, along with many other operating systems, supports RPC. Remote Procedure Calls is more like a "super" interprocess communication mechanism in that it has the ability to use other interprocess mechanisms such as named pipes, NetBIOS, or Winsock, should that be what a particular application requires.

RPC   RPC (Remote Procedure Call) is a session layer protocol responsible for establishing, maintaining, and terminating communications sessions between distributed applications in an NFS environment

RPC   Remote Procedure Calls Service is the interprocess communications mechanism supplied with DCE. In order to assure consistency and interoperability, the RPC services in DCE are not alterable by users or licensees of DCE

rules-based message handling   Advanced e-mail client capabilities include rules-based message handling which allows the e-mail client to act as an agent on behalf of the user by automatically returning e-mail during vacation periods or by screening e-mail by source of priority

RYGB   The type of phone wire installed in most homes consists of a tan plastic jacket containing four untwisted wires: red, yellow, green, and black and is also known as 4 conductor station wire or RYGB

S-HTTP   Secure S-HTTP is a secure version of HTTP which requires both client and server S-HTTP versions to be installed for secure end-to-end encrypted transmission. S-HTTP uses Digital Signature Encryption to assure that the document possesses both authenticity and message integrity

Same Server Migration   Same Server Migration is used if the current 3.x server must be the 4.1 server but In-Place Migration is not an option. In this case, the DOS-based client becomes a temporary repository for 3.x system files while the 3.x server is reformatted and has 4.1 installed.

same-place same-time meeting   In electronic meeting support software, Meetings may be held in specially equipped decision support rooms in which all forum participants gather in what is known as a same-place, same-time meeting or may convene via a local or wide area network according to participants' availability in what is known as a different-place, different-time meeting

SAP   SAP, or Service Advertising Protocol, is used by all network servers to advertise the services they provide to all other reachable networked servers. SAP uses IPX packets as its means of delivering its service advertising requests or responses throughout the network.

SAP filtering   In order to eliminate the every 60 second broadcast of SAP packets, an associated feature of advanced IPX known as SAP filtering, assures that SAP broadcasts are synchronized to take place only with NLSP updates.

SAS   Single Attachment Stations attach to only one of FDDI's two rings

SBA   In FDDI, frames transmitted in a continuous stream are known as synchronous frames and are prioritized according to a methodology known as synchronous bandwidth allocation or SBA which assigns fixed amounts of bandwidth to given stations.

scalability   Scalability refers to the ability of distributed processing systems to add clients without degrading the overall performance of the system

scalability   Scalability is evidenced by the ability of Windows NT to support symmetrical multiprocessing.

scalability   Should a given distributed application require more processing power, additional servers can be added to the pool of processing power without any changes required to client portions of the distributed applications

scalar   A CPU chip with a single pipeline as described above is known as a scalar processor

SCAM   PnP compliant SCSI controllers will be configured according to a PnP standard known as SCAM or SCSI Configured Automatically.

scheduler   When multiple processes are all contending for the same limited amount of primary memory not occupied by the non-swappable Unix kernel, the scheduler process, also known as the swapper, decides which processes should be removed from primary memory to the swap partition and which should be moved from the swap partition into main memory

screen caching   Screen caching allows only changes to screens, rather than entire screens to be transmitted over the limited bandwidth WAN links. Screen caching will reduce the amount of actual traffic transmitted over the WAN link

screen scrapers   With the help of a category of software known as screen scrapers or screen emulation software, character-based screens which were formerly displayed on dumb terminals are re-formatted into GUI format.

SCSI   SCSI (Small Computer System Interface) is a specification for an expansion bus which is unique in its ability to daisy-chain up to seven SCSI devices together .8 bit bus width, 5MHz clock speed, 5MBps throughput

SCSI configured automatically   See SCAM

SCSI-2   An expansion bus specification: 8 bit bus width, 10MHz clock speed, 10MBps throughput

SCSI-to-SCSI RAID   SCSI-to-SCSI RAID keeps all the RAID intelligence in the disk array cabinet. The controller card is installed with the RAID sub-system cabinet and connects to the host server via a standard SCSI controller.

SDLC   IBM SNA's data link layer protocol. SDLC frames do not contain anything equivalent to the OSI network layer addressing information for use by routers which makes SDLC a non-routable protocol

SDLC conversion   SDLC frames are converted to Token Ring Frames by a specialized internetworking device known as a SDLC Converter.

SDLC converter   See SDLC conversion

SDRAM   Synchronous DRAM. Adding clock synchronization to RAM allows memory chips to work at the same clock speed as the CPU.

secondary cache   A high speed memory cache not directly on, but closely connected to the CPU chip. This memory is known as off-chip, secondary cache or L2 (Level 2) cache. The L2 cache is connected to the CPU chip through a memory bus whose speed is also measured in MHz

sections   In electronic meeting support software, each forum would probably contain multiple topics for discussion known alternatively as discussion categories or sections

sectors   Data is stored on disks which are broken up into concentric rings, known as tracks, and portions of those tracks, known as sectors

Secure Courier   Secure Courier is based on SSL and allows users to create a secure digital envelope for transmission of financial transactions over the Internet. Secure Courier also provides consumer authentication for the cyber-merchants inhabiting the commercial Internet.

Secure HyperText Transport Protocol   See S-HTTP

secure single login   This assurance that users are able to log into a network, rather than each individual server and application, and be only able to access resources for which they are properly authorized is known as secure single login

secure SNMP   SNMP2 or a variation of SNMP known as Secure SNMP, will allow users to access carriers' network management information and incorporate it into the wide area component of ban enterprise network management system

Secure Sockets Layer   See SSL

security access tokens   In Windows NT, the local security authority generates a security access token for authorized users which contains security Ids (SID) for this user and all of the user groups to which this user belongs.

security account manager   In Windows NT, all of the user and user group ID and permission level information is stored in and maintained by the security account manager which interacts with the local security authority to verify user Ids and permission levels

security IDs   See security access tokens

security reference monitor   The security reference monitor is primarily concerned with authorization or authentication for processes that wish to access objects and users that wish to access the system via the logon process. It is the only kernel mode portion of the NT security system.

Security services   Security Services for DCE are divided into two general categories. Authorization grants users access to objects based on the contents of ACLs (Access Control Lists) while authentication guarantees the identity or authenticity of a user or object. Authentication in DCE is based on Kerberos authentication system which provides multi-level authentication and encryption services dependent upon the level of security required

segmentation   Segmentation is usually the first internetworking approach employed to reduce shared media congestion. By having fewer workstations per segment, there is less contention for the shared bandwidth

segmented lookahead cache   Segmented Lookahead buffers create multiple smaller buffer in which the next sequential data blocks from several reads can be stored.

send window   With an adaptive sliding window protocol, the number of packets allowed to be sent before the receipt of an acknowledgment determines the size of the send window

send-and-wait   Whenever an application program branches to a subroutine, whether a local or a remote procedure, that application program waits for the local or remote procedure to complete execution and return either data or some type of status message before continuing with its own program execution. This style of interprocess communication could be categorized as send-and-wait, also known as synchronous communication

send-and-wait   See synchronous communication

Sequenced Packet Exchange   See SPX

sequential   In a sequential logical topology, also known as a ring logical topology, data is passed from one PC (or node) to another. Each node examines the destination address of the data packet to determine if this particular packet is meant for it. If the data was not meant to be delivered at this node, the data is passed along to the next node in the logical ring.

sequential routing   In workflow automation software, the simplest of the routing schemes in which business processes follow predictable paths with individual steps following each other in a linear fashion.

Serial Line Interface Protocol   See SLIP

Serial Line Internet Protocol   See SLIP

server duplexing   NetWare 4.1 SFT III offers a unique fault tolerant feature known as server duplexing. In such a case, not only are the contents of the disks synchronized, but the contents of the servers' memory and CPUs are also synchronized. In case of the failure of the primary server, the duplexed server takes over transparently.

server front-end LAN switch   A switched network architecture in which dedicated LAN switch ports are only necessary for servers, while client workstations share a switch port via a cascaded media-sharing hub.

server isolation   Instead of assigning all workstations to their own LAN segment as in microsegmentation, only selected high-performance devices such as servers can be assigned to their own segment in an internetworking design strategy known as server isolation. By isolating servers on their own segments, guaranteed access to network bandwidth is assured

Server Message Block Server   See SMB

server network operating systems   Server network operating systems are able to be chosen and installed based on their performance characteristics for a given required functionality. For example, NetWare servers are often employed as file and print servers whereas Windows NT, OS/2, or UNIX servers are more likely to be employed as application servers

server trust accounts   Server trust accounts allow NT servers to download copies of the master domain database from a domain controller. This trust relationship is what enables backup domain controllers.

servers   Servers such as application servers and print servers are usually dedicated computers accessed only through LAN connections. Whereas a client could be considered a service requester, servers are characterized as service providers

Service Advertising Protocol   See SAP

service-granting ticket   In Kerberos, if the ticket granting server determines that the request is valid, a ticket is issued which will allow the user to access the requested server. This ticket is known as a service-granting ticket

Services for Macintosh   See SFM

session keys   In the Pretty Good Privacy encryption method, combined documents and digital signatures are then encrypted using IDEA (International Data Encryption Algorithm) which makes use of one-time 128-bit keys known as session keys

session layer   The session layer protocols are responsible for establishing, maintaining, and terminating sessions between user application programs. Sessions are interactive dialogues between networked computers and are of particular importance to distributed computing applications in a client/server environment

session limits   The second major improvement of NBF over NetBEUI has to do with session limits. Since NetBEUI is NetBIOS-based, it was forced to support the 254 session limit of NetBIOS. With NBF, each client to server connection can support 254 sessions, rather than a grand total for all connections of 254 sessions

SFM   Services for Macintosh - These independently controlled services, which include File Server for Macintosh and Print Server for Macintosh, allow an NT server to act as an Appleshare server for Macintosh clients

SGML   HTML is actually a subset of SGML (Standard Generalized Markup Language). Whereas HTML supports a pre-defined set of core elements of a Web Page such as headlines, paragraphs, chapter headings, hyperlink anchors, and footnotes identified by tags, SGML allows higher-level programming which is able to define its own DTDs (Document Type Definitions).

shared file e-mail   Shared file e-mail systems depend on store-and-forward messaging

shared file e-mail systems   In a shared file e-mail system architecture, the e-mail software uses the native file system included with every different network operating system over which the e-mail software executes. This set-up allowed a single e-mail package to run over multiple different network operating systems

shared media LANs   The various connected computers and peripheral devices will all share some type of media to converse with each other. As a result, LANs are sometimes more specifically referred to as shared media LANs or media-sharing LANs.

Shared media network architecture   Shared media

network architectures employ media-sharing network wiring centers such as hubs which offer all attached workstations shared access to a single LAN segment

shell In Unix, the command interpreter which is the user's interface to the system is a specialized user process known as a shell.

shielding Shielding may be a metallic foil or copper braid. The function of the shield is rather simple. It "shields" the individual twisted pairs as well as the entire cable from either EMI (Electromagnetic Interference) or RFI (Radio Frequency Interference).

SIDF Storage Independent Data Format (SIDF) allows portability between tape media and SIDF-compliant backup devices

signals The exception and interrupt handling facility in Unix is known as signals

SIMM SIMM (Single In-Line Memory Module) has become the more common method of RAM packaging. SIMMs are small printed circuit boards with attached DRAMs and come in basically two varieties: 30 pin SIMMs comprised of 8-Bit DRAMs, 72 pin SIMMs comprised of 16-Bit or 32-Bit DRAMs

Simple Mail Transfer Protocol See SMTP

Simple Management Protocol See SNMP2

simple network management protocol See SNMP

simultaneous RMON view Simultaneous RMON View allows all network traffic to be monitored simultaneously. Such a monitoring scheme is only possible on those switches which incorporate a shared memory multi-gigabit bus as opposed to a switching matrix internal architecture. Furthermore, unless this monitoring software is executed on a separate CPU, then switch performance is likely to degrade.

Single Attachment Station See SAS

single domain architecture All users and network resources are organized into a single domain of up to 10,000 users. This is a flat architecture with no inter-domain trust relationships involved

single mode Fiber optic cable that is able to focus the rays of light so that only a single wavelength can pass through at a time is known as Single Mode. Without numerous reflections of rays at multiple angles, distortion is eliminated and bandwidth is maximized

single point of failure Any network attached device or piece of technology whose failure would cause the failure of the entire network

single solution gateway Single solution gateways can

actually offer improved performance due to optimally written code translating between a specific front-end tool and a specific distributed database management system or between two different database engines

single speed CD-ROM speed specification yielding sustained avg. data throughput of 150KBps

Single Unix Specification See Spec 1170 APIs

single-use passwords One way in which authentication technology and protocols improve upon the security offered by simple passwords is by implementing single-use passwords

site In a Chorus microkernel-based operating system, a given hardware platform or CPU is considered a site, with one nucleus executing at each site.

slices Each disk in Unix is divided into multiple slices each of which can be used to accommodate either a file system, a swap area, or a raw data area. A Unix slice is equivalent to a partition in DOS

SLIP Serial Line Internet Protocol allows dial-up connection to IP-based servers

SLIP Serial Line Internet Protocol is a data-link WAN protocol which is supported by NetWare Connect

SLIP Serial Line Interface Protocol is able to establish asynchronous serial links between two computers which support both SLIP and TCP/IP over any of the following connections: via modems and a dial-up line, via modems and a point-to-point private or leased line, via hard-wired or direct connections

slot time In Ethernet networks, The time required for a given workstation to detect a collision is known as slot time and is measured in bits.

slow convergence The delay which occurs while all of the routers are propagating their routing tables using RIP, known as slow convergence, could allow certain routers to think that failed links to certain networks are still viable

small business network operating systems Small business network operating systems have had to differentiate themselves from client network operating systems and peer-to-peer network operating systems by offering more advanced features such as: dedicated 32-bit server software, bundled workgroup software, and an easy migration path to server-based network operating systems

Small Office Home Office See SOHO

smart software See intelligent software

SmartCard Smart Cards or SmartIDs which are credit-card sized devices that generate a one-time non-reusable password

SmartDisks   SmartDisks incorporate SmartCard technology into a 3.5" diskette that can be read by standard disk drives.

SmartID   See SmartCard

smartsizing   Smartsizing implies another level of questioning or re-engineering beyond that of right-sizing. Rather than merely re-evaluating the application program, smartsizing goes a step further and re-evaluates and re-engineers the business process which motivated the application in the first place

SMB   NETBIOS application programs, otherwise known as NETBIOS Protocols, which interface with the NETBIOS API have been developed to perform specialized tasks on client and server PCs in order to enable this client/server communication. Two of the most famous of these NETBIOS application programs or protocols are the NetBIOS Redirector, on the client, and the Server Message Block (SMB) Server, on the server

SMP   Symmetric multiprocessing (SMP) is a system architecture in which multiple CPU's are controlled by the SMP operating system and individual threads of application processes are assigned to particular CPUs on a first-available basis

SMP   High powered application servers require network operating systems which can support multiple CPUs, otherwise known as symmetrical multiprocessing or SMP

SMP   See SNMP2

SMP kernel   Since the original NetWare 4.1 did not have SMP capability, some way needed to be found to support SMP while still assuring backward compatibility with all existing NLMs. This was done by having NetWare 4.1 SMP load a second operating system kernel, known as the SMP kernel, which works cooperatively with the first or native operating system kernel.

SMP scalability   SMP scalability refers to the percentage of increased performance achieved for each additional CPU

SMS   Storage Management System (SMS) defines an API for third-party backup software to interoperate transparently with NetWare servers.

SMTP   The Internet E-Mail Gateway acts as a translator, speaking a LAN-specific e-mail software protocol on one side and speaking the Internet's SMTP (Simple MailTransport Protocol) on the other. Depending on the transport protocol used by the Local Area Network, the Internet E-Mail Gateway may also have to translate between transport protocols since the Internet uses strictly TCP/IP.

SMTP   Simple Mail Transfer Protocol allows different computers which support the TCP/IP protocol stack to exchange e-mail messages. SMTP is able to establish connections, provide reliable transport of e-mail messages via TCP, notify users of newly received e-mail, and terminate connections.

SMTP   Simple Mail Transfer Protocol (SMTP) is defined in two RFCs; RFC 822 defines the structure of an SMTP message and RFC 821 defines how SMTP messages are delivered from source to destination workstations. Some enterprise e-mail systems use SMTP as their native messaging protocol while others use SMTP gateways to translate native messaging protocols into SMTP.

SNA   Systems Network Architecture, IBM's proprietary network architecture, was originally designed to link mainframes

SNAP   In order to ease the transition to IEEE 802 compliance, an alternative method of identifying the embedded upper layer protocols was developed, known as SNAP or Sub-Network Access Protocol. Any protocol can use SNAP with IEEE 802.2 and appear to be an IEEE 802 compliant protocol.

SNMP   Network management information is formatted according to the SNMP or Simple Network Management Protocol which is a member of the Internet Suite of Protocols (TCP/IP)

SNMP   Performance management information can be communicated to Enterprise Management Systems such as HP OpenView or IBM SystemView in the proper SNMP (Simple Network Management Protocol) format

SNMP   SNMP offers a standardized protocol for the transport of management information such as device status, device activity, an alarm conditions

SNMP   Partly due to the dominance of TCP/IP as the internetworking protocol of choice, SNMP (Simple Network Management Protocol) is the de facto standard for delivering enterprise management data.

SNMP2   The need to reduce network traffic caused by the SNMP protocol as well as to deal with other aforementioned SNMP shortcomings, led to a proposal for a new version of SNMP known as SNMP2, or SMP (Simple Management Protocol).

social interfaces   Social interfaces are the emerging paradigm of computer-to-user interfaces. The overall goal of social interfaces is to provide a computer-to-user interface which is more intuitive and easier to use than the current generation of graphical user interfaces

socket   The unique port address of an application combined with the unique 32 bit IP address of the computer on which the application is executing is known as a socket

socket services   The Socket services sub-layer of the

PCMCIA Card & Socket Services driver specification is written specifically for the type of PCMCIA controller included in a notebook computer

sockets In Unix, Sockets is a more powerful and flexible interprocess communications mechanism than Pipes and is able to provide interprocess communications across network interfaces to processes running on widely distributed computers

software cache A software cache is the use of system memory in the computer reserved for a disk cache

software emulation An additional layer of software which allowed both Macintosh and Windows programs to execute on PowerPC chips

software-based RAID Software-Based RAID uses the CPU of the server to execute the RAID software which controls the multiple disk drives contained in the redundant array of independent disks

software-only solutions A network faxing architecture in which the user supplies both the PC to execute the FAX software as well as compatible FAX boards or modems

SOHO See telecommuting

source address Data-Link protocols such as Ethernet contain source addresses as well as the destination addresses within the pre-defined Ethernet Frame layout. A bridge checks the source address of each frame it receives and adds that source address to a table of known local nodes

source routing bridge A source routing bridge is used to connect two source-routing enabled Token Ring LANs. Data messages arrive at a source routing bridge with a detailed map of how they plan to reach their destination

source routing transparent bridge Bridges which can support links between source routing Token Ring LANs or transparent LANs, are known as Source Routing Transparent (SRT) bridges

Spanning Tree Algorithm The Spanning Tree Algorithm (STA) has been standardized as IEEE 802.1 for the purposes of controlling redundant paths in bridged networks and thereby reducing the possibility of broadcast storms.

SPAP Shiva's proprietary authentication protocol which includes password encryption and callback capability.

Spec 1170 APIs In attempting to standardize the operating system elements of Unix, a consortium of vendors has been working on the single Unix specification, otherwise known as the Spec 1170 APIs. This is a collection of over 1,000 APIs which, hopefully, all versions of Unix will support.

speculative execution Speculative execution actually goes ahead and begins to execute and store results of predicted branches chosen by branch prediction algorithms

split horizon In order to reduce slow convergence in RIP based router networks, Split horizon and reverse poison prevent routers from wasting time broadcasting routing table changes back to the routers which just supplied them with the same changes in the first place.

spoofing Spoofing is a method of filtering chatty or unwanted protocols from the WAN link while assuring that remote programs which require on-going communication from these filtered protocols are still re-assured via emulation of these protocols by the local dial-up router.

spooler Standalone spoolers store copies of print jobs in their own buffer memory.

spooling Spooling software "spools" a copy of the print job either into the PC's RAM (Random Access Memory) or onto its hard drive. Spooling software also has the ability to send multiple copies of a given print job to multiple printers simultaneously

Spread spectrum transmission Spread spectrum transmission, as its name implies, spreads a data message across a wide range or spectrum of frequencies. This technique was originally employed as a security measure since a receiver would need to know exactly how the message was spread across the frequency spectrum in order to intercept the message in meaningful form

SPX SPX is NetWare's connection-oriented, reliable transport layer protocol

SQL SQL (Structured Query Language) is a standardized database command language

SQL SQL (Structured Query Language) is a standardized data manipulation and query language supported by most databases which is roughly equivalent to a database-specific remote procedure call.

SRAM SRAM or Static RAM does not require a refresh cycle between accesses and therefore can be accessed much faster than DRAM. SRAM is more expensive than DRAM

SRM See Security Reference Monitor

SSL SSL wraps an encrypted envelope around HTTP transmissions. Whereas S-HTTP can only be used to encrypt Web documents, SSL can be wrapped around other Internet service transmissions such as FTP and Gopher as well as HTTP

stackable hubs Stackable hubs add expandability and manageability to the basic capabilities of the stand-alone hub. Stackable hubs can be linked together, or cascaded, to form one larger virtual hub of a single type of network architecture and media

stand-alone hubs Stand-alone hubs are fully config-ured hubs offering a limited number (12 or fewer) ports of a particular type of network architecture (Ethernet, Token Ring) and media.

stand-alone LAN switches Stand-alone Workgroup/ Department LAN switches—offer dedicated connec-tions to all attached client and server computers via individual switch ports.

Standard Generalized Markup Language See SGML

star The star physical topology employs some type of central management device. Depending on the net-work architecture and sophistication of the device, it may be called a hub, a wiring center, a concentrator, a MAU (Multiple Access Unit), a repeater or a switch-ing hub

state variables As part of the application MIB, State variables would report on the current status of a given application. Three possible states are: up, down, or degraded.

Static RAM See SRAM

storage independent data format See SIDF

storage management system See SMS

store-and-forward messaging A store-and-for-ward messaging technology is one in which mes-sages are sent, received, replied to, and delivered in discrete steps performed in a disjointed fashion over a period of time. This series of events is sometimes also described as an asynchronous messaging system

store-and-forward messaging Shared file e-mail sys-tems depend on store and forward messaging

store-and-forward switches These switches read the entire frame into a shared memory area in the switch. The contents of the transmitted Frame Check Se-quence field are read and compared to the locally re-calculated Frame Check Sequence. Store-and-for-ward switching is slower than cut-through switching but does not forward bad frames.

stored procedures Rather than have the transaction posting application program trigger the integrity check, the database definition itself can be written in such a way that if any particular field in the distrib-uted database is updated, then the SQL database ini-tiates a Stored Procedure which would proceed to perform all necessary integrity checking on the dis-tributed databases involved

stream sockets Provides reliable, connection-oriented, two-way (full-duplex), sequenced packet inter-process communications through use of TCP (Trans-mission Control Protocol) as the transport layer pro-tocol.

Structured Query Language See SQL

stubs Client and server programs that wish to use the RPC service simply issue program calls for that ser-vice via specialized calls to the RPC mechanism known as stubs.

stubs Stubs are specially coded lines of the applica-tions program added by the middleware application development tool to allow the client and server por-tions of distributed application to interface to the en-terprise network which connect those clients and servers.

sub-network access protocol See SNAP

sub-systems In microkernel based operating systems, all additional functionality is written to operate ex-ternally to the microkernel in software modules known as servers. Groups of servers are known as sub-systems

suballocation blocks Disk Block Sub-Allocation is a process aimed at optimizing the use of disk space for file storage. By dividing all disk allocation blocks into 512 byte (.5KB) suballocation blocks, multiple files are allowed to occupy single disk allocation blocks and disk storage efficiency is maximized.

subnet mask By applying a 32 bit subnet mask to a Class B IP address, a portion of the bits which com-prise the host ID can be reserved for denoting sub-networks, with the remaining bits being reserved for host IDs per sub-network.

subnetworking Subnetworking allows organizations which were issued an IP address with a single net-work ID to use a portion of their host ID address field to provide multiple subnetwork IDs in order to implement internetworking.

superpipelines Some pipelines employ more than five stages to complete a given instruction and are called superpipelined architectures

superscalar CPU chips may employ more than one pipeline and are known as superscalar

SVRAM Synchronous VRAM. Adding clock synchro-nization to RAM allows memory chips to work at the same clock speed as the CPU.

swapper See Scheduler

swapping Swapping implies that entire processes are swapped in and out of physical memory and onto the swap space partition of one or more disk drives

switched LAN network architecture Switched LAN architecture depend on wiring centers called LAN switches or switching hubs which offer all attached workstations access to a switching matrix that pro-vides point-to-point, rather than shared, connections between any two ports.

switching hub The switching hub is actually able to create connections, or switch, between any two attached Ethernet devices on a packet by packet basis in as little as 40 milliseconds. The "one-at-time" broadcast limitation previously associated with shared media Ethernet is overcome with an Ethernet switch

SX   SX implies no built-in math co-processor

symmetric multi-processing   See SMP

symmetrical multiprocessing   See SMP

synchronous   See send-and-wait

synchronous bandwidth allocation   See SBA

synchronous communication   Send-and-wait messaging is also referred to as synchronous communication because the requesting program and responding program remain synchronized, executing simultaneously in real time. Send-and-wait messaging assumes total network and client/server platform reliability as the client program will wait indefinitely or terminate without a response from the requested server.

Synchronous Data Link Control   See SDLC

synchronous frames   In FDDI, frames transmitted in a continuous stream are known as synchronous frames and are prioritized according to a methodology known as synchronous bandwidth allocation or SBA which assigns fixed amounts of bandwidth to given stations.

synchronous I/O   Synchronous I/O or inter-process communication refers to the situation when a client application spawns a thread for information or processing and waits for the results of that thread before continuing with the execution of the client application. Synchronous I/O is sometimes also referred to as connection-oriented communication.

synchronous replication   Synchronous replication assumes 100% network reliability. Synchronous replication uses a process known as two-phase commit in order to assure that all replicated database servers are properly updated

system bus   The system bus should be considered the superhighway of the buses which leave the computer system's CPU as other buses such as the local, I/O and peripheral buses interface directly to the system bus.

system calls   Application programs request computer resources by interfacing to the operating system through mutually supported system calls.

Systems Network Architecture   See SNA

tags   HTML supports a pre-defined set of core elements of a Web Page such as headlines, paragraphs, chapter headings, hyperlink anchors, and footnotes identified by tags

tape changers   Tape changers are required in order to swap tapes into/out of backup devices for multi-Gigabyte backup sessions.

tape streaming   See interleaving

TAPI   TAPI or Telephony API is a computer telephony integration API that was jointly developed and sponsored by Intel and Microsoft.

task   A task is the basic addressable unit of program execution. It is sometimes referred to as an execution environment to which resources such as CPU cycles or virtual memory space can be assigned

TCP   TCP or Transmission Control Protocol is a transport layer protocol which provides connection-oriented, reliable transmission for upper layer application programs or utilities

TCP/IP   TCP/IP (Transmission Protocol/Internet Protocol) just two of many of the protocols included in the Internet Suite of Protocols. Also used as a name for the entire suite of associated protocols and utilities.

TCP/IP   TCP/IP (Transmission Control Protocol/Internet Protocol) is the term generally used to refer to an entire suite of protocols used to provide communications on a variety of layers between widely distributed different types of computers. Strictly speaking, TCP and IP are just two of the protocols contained within the family of protocols more properly known as the Internet Suite of Protocols.

TCP/IP encapsulation   Each non-routable SNA SDLC frame is "stuffed" into an IP "envelope" for transport across the network and processing by routers supporting TCP/IP internetworking protocol

TCP/IP Model   Although not identical to the OSI 7 layer model, the 4 layer TCP/IP Model is no less effective at organizing protocols required to establish and maintain communications between different computers.

TDP   An alternative two-way messaging architecture is proposed by the PCIA (Personal Communicator Industry Association). Rather than building on existing IP-based networks as the CDPD/LSM architecture did, the TDP (Telocator Data Protocol) architecture is actually a suite of protocols defining an end-to-end system for two-way messaging to and from paging devices

technical support   The third major usage of remote computing is for technical support organizations which must be able to dial-in to client systems with the ability to appear as a local workstation, or take control of those workstations, in order to diagnose and correct problems remotely

telecommuting   Telecommuting, or more simply, working from home with all the information resources of the office LAN at one's fingertips, is often referred to as SOHO, or Small Office Home Office.

telephony API   See TAPI

telephony services API   See TSAPI

Telnet   Text-based information stored in Internet-connected servers can be accessed by remote users logging into these servers via a TCP/IP protocol known as Telnet. Once they are successfully logged into an Internet-based information server using either previously assigned user accounts and passwords or general access "anonymous" user accounts, users are able to execute programs on the remote computer as they were locally attached.

Telnet   Telnet is a terminal access API which allows remote terminals to connect to hosts running Telnetd (the Telnet server program). If the remote terminal accessing the Telnet server is not truly a "dumb" terminal, then terminal emulation software must be executed in order to make it appear to be just a "dumb" terminal to the Telnet server host.

Telnet negotiation   Because Telnet must be able to operate with a variety of terminal types, it contains an adaptive negotiation mechanism known as Telnet negotiation which allows Telnet to establish sessions assuming very basic functionality known as the Network Virtual Terminal, and progressively negotiate those more advanced terminal features which must be supported for the particular terminal and application in question.

telocator data protocol   See TDP

TFTP   TFTP, or Trivial File Transfer Protocol, was designed to be a simpler and less memory intensive alternative to FTP. TFTP uses UDP rather than TCP as its transport layer protocol.

thread   A task can be accomplished or executed through the work accomplished by one or more threads. Threads are the basic unit of execution and are only assigned resources through a given task. Tasks spawn threads in order to accomplish their instructions

threads   In electronic meeting support software, Specific discussion topics on which participants are welcome to comment are generally referred to as threads

Threads service   Threads Services are provided to offer multi-threaded capabilities to those DCE nodes whose native operating systems are not multi-threaded. Threads services are stored as functions which can be called from within a threads library

three-tiered C/S architecture   Three-tiered client/server architectures deliver the presentation logic on the client, the business logic on a dedicated server of its own, and the database logic on a super-server or mainframe

ticket   In Kerberos, An encrypted ticket is issued for each server to client session and is valid only for a pre-set amount of time.

ticket-granting ticket   In Kerberos, Users are first authenticated by the Kerberos Authentication server which consults its database and grants a ticket for the valid user to communicate with the Ticket Granting Server (TGS). This ticket is known as a ticket-granting ticket.

tightly-coupled   Tightly-coupled systems architectures are characterized by CPUs which share a common pool of system memory as well as other devices and sub-systems. Coordination among the multiple CPUs is achieved by system calls to/from the controlling operating system. Most SMP system architectures would be considered tightly-coupled.

time synchronous   In a time synchronous authentication scheme, Due to time synchronization, the server authentication unit should have the same current random authentication number which is compared to the one transmitted from the remote client.

time synchronous authentication   With time synchronous authentication, due to the time synchronization, the server authentication unit should have the same current random authentication number which is compared to the one transmitted from the remote client.

timed updates   A dial-up router update mechanism in which updates are performed at regular predetermined intervals

timing limitation   The second SNA characteristic which can cause problems when run over a shared LAN backbone is that SNA has timing limitations for transmission duration between SNA hosts and end-user devices. Thus on wide area, internetworked LANs over shared network media, SNA sessions can "time-out," effectively terminating the session.

token   In a token passing access methodology, a specific packet (24 bits) of data is known as a token

token authentication   All token authentication systems include server components linked to the communications server, and client components which are used with the remote access clients. Physically, the token authentication device employed at the remote client location may be a hand-held device resembling a calculator, a floppy disk, or it may be an in-line device linked to either the remote client's serial or parallel port

token passing   Token Passing is an access methodology that assures that each PC User has 100% of the network channel available for their data requests and transfers by insisting that no PC accesses the network without first possessing a specific packet (24 bits) of data known as a token

token response   In a token response authentication scheme, a transmitted challenge response is received by the authentication server and compared to the expected challenge response number which was generated at the server. If they match, the user is authenticated and allowed access to network attached resources.

token response authentication   Token response authentication schemes begin when the transmitted challenge response is received by the authentication server and compared to the expected challenge response number which was generated at the server. If they match, the user is authenticated and allowed access to network attached resources.

top down model   The top down model is a graphical representation of the top down approach insisting that a top-down approach to network analysis and design is undertaken should assure that the network design implemented will meet the business needs and objectives which motivated the design in the first place.

TP monitors   Transaction processing requires careful monitoring in order to assure that all, and not just some, postings related to a particular business transaction are successfully completed. This monitoring of transaction posting is done by a specialized type of software known as TP (Transaction Posting) Monitors

TP-PMD   The official ANSI standard for CDDI is known as TP-PMD (Twisted Pair-Physical Media Department).

tracks   Data is stored on disks which are broken up into concentric rings, known as tracks, and portions of those tracks, known as sectors.

traffic duplication   Because switched LAN connections are established, used, and terminated in a matter of microseconds for most transmissions, it is difficult if not impossible to monitor these transmissions in real time by traditional means. One solution to this dilemma is known as traffic duplication in which traffic between two switch ports is duplicated onto a third port to which traditional LAN analyzers can be attached.

trailer   Information added to the back of data is called a trailer

transaction   A transaction is the sequence or series of pre-defined steps or actions, taken within an application program, in order to properly record that business transaction

transaction processing monitors   Transaction processing monitors, sometimes referred to as OLTP (On-Line Transaction Processing) monitors, were originally developed to monitor and control the posting of numerous simultaneous transactions across multiple computing platforms

transaction rollback   Should a network failure occur during the commit phase of a two-phase commit, most data management systems will perform a transaction rollback and will remove all previously made updates from this replication, thereby returning all replicated servers to their previous state.

transition costs   Costs associated with the transition from mainframe-based systems to client/server systems such as application re-development, management tool development, and expenses to run both systems simultaneously.

translating bridges   A special type of bridge which includes a format converter can bridge between Ethernet and Token Ring. These special bridges may also be called multi-protocol bridges or translating bridges.

Transmission Control Protocol   TCP or Transmission Control Protocol is a transport layer protocol which provides connection-oriented, reliable transmission for upper layer application programs or utilities. This reliability is assured through the additional fields contained within the TCP header

Transmission Control Protocol/Internet Protocol   See TCP/IP

transparency   Transparency refers to the ability of distributed processing systems to combine clients and servers of different operating systems, network operating systems, and protocols into a cohesive system processing distributed applications without regard to the aforementioned differences

transparency   The fact that any client portion of a distributed application can communicate with any server portion of the same distributed application regardless of computing platform is an important characteristic of distributed computing known as transparency

transparent   Bridges are passive or transparent devices, receiving every frame broadcast on a given LAN. Bridges are known as transparent due to their ability to only process data link layer addresses while transparently forwarding any variety of upper layer protocols safely embedded within the data field of the datalink layer frame

transparent bridge   Bridges the connect LANs of similar data link format are known as transparent bridges

transport driver interface   The transport driver interface is actually a protocol specification which provides a layer of transparency between session layer redirectors and transport layer protocols. This allows session layer redirector software to be written independently of the particular transport layer software with which the redirector software will need to communicate.

transport layer   The transport layer protocols are responsible for providing reliability for the end-to-end network layer connections. Transport layer protocols provide end-to-end error recovery and flow control and also provide mechanisms for sequentially organizing multiple network layer packets into a coherent message.

triggered replication   Triggered replication is done as necessary as determined by certain programmable events such as the number of queued database updates to be replicated

triggered updates   In order to reduce slow convergence in RIP based router networks, Triggered updates allows routers to immediately broadcast routing table updates regarding failed links rather than having to wait for the next 20 sec.periodic update

triggered updates   A dial-up router update mechanism in which updates are performed whenever a certain programmable event, such as a change in available services, occurs

triggers   The trigger would cause an "integrity-assurance subroutine" to run which would check all of the necessary distributed database fields involved and verify that their current contents are correct based on the latest transaction

triple speed   CD-ROM speed specification yielding sustained avg. data throughput of 450KBps

trivial file transfer protocol   See TFTP

trust   In order to accomplish access to network resources beyond local domains without the need to have all user account and security information for every domain on all domain controllers, domains interact in a relationship known as trust

trust relationship   As long as trust relationships have been established between the Windows NT primary domain controllers in a multi-domain environment, then authorized users within those domains can access the resources on the multiple domains without the need to have user accounts previously established on all domains.

trusted node   The authorization software can be workstation-based, also referred to as trusted node

TSAPI   TSAPI or Telephony Services API is a computer telephony integration API that was jointly developed and sponsored by Novell and AT&T.

TSR   Programs stored in this exhibited memory are often stored as TSRs, or terminate and stay resident, programs. Terminate and Stay Resident programs do not utilize any CPU processing time until they are reactivated.

TTY   The acronym TTY refers to terminals in general but actually stands for teletypewriter and is a holdover from the days before terminals had video monitors.

turnkey solutions   A network faxing architecture in which specially made LAN-attached devices which are pre-configured with both software and all necessary FAX hardware are employed.

Tuxedo   Tuxedo from Novell and Encina from Transarc are two of the more popular multi-platform OLTP monitors suitable for client/server applications

two-phase commit   When multiple distributed databases which are physical located on widely dispersed servers must all be updated as part of a transaction update, two-phase commit assures that either all required databases will be updated or none of the required databases will be updated.

two-phase commit   Synchronous replication uses a process known as two-phase commit in order to assure that all replicated database servers are properly updated

two-tiered C/S architecture   Two-tired client/server architectures deliver the presentation logic on the client and the database logic on the server

two-way messaging   Two-way messaging, sometimes referred to as enhanced paging, allows short text messages to be transmitted between relatively inexpensive transmission devices such as PDAs (Personal Digital Assistants) and alphanumeric pagers

UDP   UDP or User Datagram Protocol is used to provide unreliable, connectionless messaging services for applications

Ultra SCSI   An expansion bus specification: 32 bit bus width, 10MHz clock speed, 40MBps throughput

UNI   UNI or User-Network Interface defines standards for interoperability between end-user equipment and ATM equipment and networks. These standards are well defined and equipment is fairly widely available.

unicast   Unicast (point-to-point) transmission.

unified messaging   Perhaps the most interesting for the LAN-based user, unified messaging, also known as the Universal In-Box will allow voice mail, e-mail, faxes, and pager messages to all be displayed on a single graphical screen. Messages can then be forwarded, deleted, or replied to easily in point and click fashion. Waiting calls can also be displayed in the same Universal In-Box.

Uniform Resource Locator   See URL

uninterruptable power supply   See UPS

universal client   A client workstation's ability to interoperate transparently with a number of different network operating system servers without the need for additional products or configurations is described as a universal client capability.

universal data access system   A Universal Data Access System, such as EDA/SQL acts as a middleware layer, trapping SQL requests from clients and reformatting them as necessary before transporting them to the appropriate server.

Universal Networked Objects   See UNO

universal-in-box   See unified messaging

UNIX   UNIX as a client workstation operating system is limited primarily to implementations in high-powered scientific or engineering workstations. UNIX itself is actually not just a single operating system, but many, largely incompatible, variations of a single operating system.

Unix   Unix is, in fact, a large family of related operating systems which all descended from work initially done by Ken Thompson and Dennis Ritchie at Bell Laboratories in the late 1960's and early 1970's

Unix system kernel   The Unix system kernel fulfills requests for services from Unix systems programs by interacting with the hardware layer and returning requested functionality to the systems programs and utilities.

Unix systems programs   Unix systems programs and utilities deliver requested functionality to users by issuing system calls to the Unix system kernel

UnixWare   UNIXWare is a full implementation of NetWare which runs over UNIX. The advantage of such an implementation is that the inherent capabilities of UNIX such as symmetrical multiprocessing are immediately available

UNO   Interoperability between object request brokers from different vendors can be achieved by compliance with the CORBA 2.0 specification, otherwise known as UNO or Universal Networked Objects.

unreliable   Implying that IPX does not require error checking and acknowledgment of error-free receipt by the destination host.

unreliable   IP is described as a connectionless, unreliable protocol. Assurances as to reliable receipts of packets in the proper sequence must be offered by the use of upper layer protocols such as TCP.

unshielded twisted pair   See UTP

UPS   Uninterruptable power supplies (UPS) for server PCs serve two distinct purposes: They provide sufficient backup power in the event of a power failure to allow for a normal system shutdown, They function as a line conditioner during normal operation by protecting computer equipment from "dirty" power conditions such as surges, brownouts, and static spikes.

upsizing   Upsizing might be considered as a subset of rightsizing. When applications lack processing power on their existing computing platform, they may be re-designed and re-deployed on larger, more powerful platforms.

URL   Indexed Web pages which may be located throughout the Internet are accessible through LYCOS via hot-clickable links known as URLs or Uniform Resource Locators.

UseNet Servers   UseNet Servers or NewsGroup servers share text-based news items over the Internet. Over 10,000 Newsgroups covering selected topics are available

user accounts database   In Windows NT, the user accounts database is physically stored on the primary domain controller except in those cases when an individual workstation may have a need to verify specific User IDs for remote access to that workstation

User Datagram Protocol   See UDP

user mode   as opposed to privileged mode, user mode applications run in a non-privileged processor mode with a limited set of interfaces available and limited access to system data

user mode   Windows NT applications are normally executed in Ring 3, known as user mode, in which they are limited to their own protected memory area. This prevents applications from writing into each other's memory space and thereby causing general protection faults and system crashes

user-network interface   See UNI

UTP   Twisted pair wiring consists of one or more pairs of insulated copper wire which are twisted at varying lengths, from two to twelve twists per foot, to reduce interference both between pairs and from outside sources such as electric motors and fluorescent lights. No additional shielding is added before the pairs are wrapped in the plastic covering.

values   Values are associated with properties and, in turn, with objects. For example, a value of Monday through Friday, 8:00 a.m. to 5:00 p.m. would be a value associated with the login time restriction property associated with a particular user or user group object.

vector   Once a NDIS driver is bound and operating, packets of a particular protocol are forwarded from the adapter card to the proper protocol stack by a layer of software known as the vector

version control software   See file synchronization

vertical scalability   A server of lesser processing power can be replaced by a more powerful server if the distributed applications executing on that server support vertical scalability. Vertical scalability requires that a given application is able to operate over a variety of different computing platforms and operating systems

vertical software compatibility Vertical software compatibility is concerned with making sure that all necessary compatible protocols are in place in order for all of the software and hardware within a single client or server to operate harmoniously and transparently

video BIOS The Video BIOS (Basic Input Output System) is contained on a chip on the graphics accelerator card. Its main function is to identify itself and its operating specifications to the computer's operating system during system startup. The Video BIOS provides the interface between the graphics accelerator card (hardware) and the computer system's operating system (software).

video digitization Video Digitization is a process by which a sample of a video signal is digitized into an 8 bit binary code

video memory video memory is usually either VRAM or DRAM. VRAM is definitely more expensive than DRAM and is faster on high-end applications requiring high resolutions, high color depth, and high-refresh rates such as 3-D imaging. The amount of VRAM required on a graphics accelerator is dependent to some extent on the color depth desired

virtual corporation A network-enabled entity in which globally dispersed enterprises are able to function as if all network-attached users were physically located in the same building

virtual corporation A business phenomenon known as the virtual corporation implies a business partnership among cooperating business entities which is electronically enabled via an enterprise network. In most cases, the virtual corporation implies that these business entities are sufficiently distant from one another that constant travel between locations in order to accomplish business objectives would not be possible. In other words, without the enterprise network, the virtual corporation would not exist.

virtual device drivers See VxDs

virtual LANs Networks which can make geographically distributed users appear to be connected to the same local LAN are known as virtual LANs

virtual loadable modules See VLM

virtual machines Windows NT is able to run applications from other platforms such as OS/2 and 16-bit Windows through specially written multiple personality sub-systems. These sub-systems in which different types of applications are able to execute are sometimes referred to as virtual machines

virtual machines Some client network operating systems, such as Windows NT, have the ability to support multiple APIs and multiple different operating

system sub-systems, sometimes known as virtual machines

virtual memory manager In order to allow application programs easy access to large amounts of memory despite limited physically installed memory, Windows NT uses portions of the disk drive as a swap file in order to offer up to 4GB (gigabytes) of memory to every process. The fact that some of a process' allocated memory is physically located on a disk drive rather than in RAM is kept transparent to the process by the Virtual Memory Manager

virtual parallel machines See VPM

virtual reality markup language See VRML

virtual routing An enterprise network physical topology, a route server-based physical topology actually employs both a route server and a number of auxiliary devices known as edge switches. The route server-based physical topology is also sometimes referred to as virtual routing

virtual workgroups Virtual workgroups dynamically allocate people to projects based on expertise rather than location, thereby allowing the most qualified people to be more easily assigned to appropriate projects without concern for the expense and wasted productivity caused by extensive travel or frequent relocation.

VJ A protocol for compression of IP headers included with most PPP clients

VLMs Rather than remaining as a monolithic, stand-alone operating system, the requester has taken on a more flexible modular appearance. NetWare client functionality can be added or updated on an incremental basis thanks to the introduction of Virtual Loadable Modules or VLMs

VPM Clustering implies using the CPU power of multiple CPUs located in separate computing platforms to produce a single, more powerful, virtual computer. Clusters are also sometimes referred to as Virtual Parallel Machines (VPM)

VRML VRML (Virtual Reality Modeling Language) and VRML+ have the capability to produce graphical programs which portray three-dimensional images allowing the user to seem to move in three-dimensional space when programs are executed

VxDs More secure 32 bit operating systems control access to hardware and certain system services via virtual device drivers otherwise known as VxDs

WAIS WAIS indexers generate multiple indexes for all types of files which organizations or individuals wish to offer access to via the Internet.

WAIS servers WAIS Servers offer these multiple indexes to other Internet-attached WAIS servers. WAIS servers also serve as search engines which have the ability to search for particular words or text strings in the indexes located across multiple Inter-attached information servers of various types.

web browsers WWW servers are accessed via client-based front-end software tools commonly referred to as Web browsers

web server A Web server combines hardware and software components to offer primarily Web services, but increasingly Web servers are also offering links to Gopher, FTP, and News services making the terms Web server and Internet server more and more synonymous. Web servers may or may not also contain software to develop or program Web pages and Web applications

web site Companies wishing to use the World Wide Web as a marketing tool establish a web site on the Internet and publicize the address of that web site

Wide Area Information Services See WAIS

Wide SCSI-2 An expansion bus specification: 16 bit bus width, 5MHz clock speed, 20MBps throughput

Win32 API Win32 API—This is the full blown 32 bit API which was created for Windows NT

Win32c API Win32c API—The "c" stands for compatible. This is the API included with Windows 95 and it contains nearly all of the functionality offered by NT's Win32 API while still remaining backward compatible with 16-bit Windows 3.1 applications.

Win32s API Win 32s API—The "s" stands for subset. This API was created for applications which need the processing power of 32 bit applications but must still be able to execute under 16-bit Windows 3.1

Windows 95 Windows 95 could be considered an all-in-one client software product as it includes graphical user interface, network operating system, and operating system functionality all in a single package. Among the key operating system related features incorporated within Windows 95 are the following: New graphical user interface, 32-bit API (Applications Program Interface) in a pre-emptive multitasking environment, Plug-n-Play capability

Windows Internet Naming Service See WINS

Windows NT RAS Microsoft's remote node server software for Windows NT

Windows NT Workstation Windows NT is a top-to-bottom client software product. Windows NT is a true 32-bit, pre-emptive multitasking operating system. All 32-bit applications execute in protected memory space

windows sockets The Windows Sockets interprocess communications mechanism, more commonly known as WinSock is the most flexible of all of the interprocess mechanisms currently supported by Windows NT. It allows programs written to support this protocol to operate transparently over a variety of different vendors' TCP/IP protocol stacks

WINS Because users and their workstations are easier to remember and access by name rather than address, NT keeps track of user names and associated IP addresses with a service known as WINS (Windows Internet Name Service).

WinSock 2 WinSock2, due to be released in 1996, added to WinSock's TCP/IP functionality by allowing WinSock-compliant applications to operate transparently over IPX/SPX, Appletalk, DECnet, and OSI transport protocols as well

wireless bridge Wireless bridges use spread spectrum radio transmission between LAN sites (up to 3 miles) and are primarily limited to Ethernet networks at this time.

wireless WAN services A variety of wireless services are available for use across wider geographic spans. These wireless WAN services vary in many ways including availability, applications, transmission speed and cost

wizards Context-sensitive help programs or "walk-you-through-it" help characters are commonly referred to as wizards. In other operating environments wizards might be known as experts or agents.

wizards See advisory agents

workflow automation software Workflow automation software allow geographically dispersed co-workers to work together on project teams as documents and information are automatically routed according to pre-programmed rules or workflow directives

workgroup Windows NT computers, especially Windows NT Workstation clients, can alternatively belong to workgroups, rather than domains. The key difference between workgroups and domains is that in a workgroup, there is no domain controller, and therefore, each workgroup computer must maintain their own security sub-system. In a workgroup, users log into a particular computer, whereas in domains, users log into a domain.

workgroup conferencing software See electronic conferencing & meeting support

workstation trust accounts Workstation trust accounts allow the workstation to connect to a domain by providing passthrough authentication for a Windows NT server in the domain

World Wide Web See WWW

WRAM Windows RAM

write back cache   Cache which only services the Fetch stage is known as write through cache, while cache which also services the Write Back stage is logically known as write back cache. Write-back cache allows disk writes to be stored in the cache right away so that processing can continue rather than waiting for the disk to be idle before doing a physical write to the disk. The danger in using write-back caches is that if power is lost before physical writes are done to the disk, then that data is lost.

write through cache   Cache which only services the Fetch stage is known as write through cache, while cache which also services the Write Back stage is logically known as write back cache.

write-back stage   The results of the executed instruction are written out to a memory location or register usually in a special area called a data cache in the write-back stage

WWW   The World Wide Web (WWW) is a collection of servers accessed via the Internet which offer graphical or multimedia (audio, video, image) presentations about a company's products, personnel, or services. WWW servers are accessed via client-based front-end software tools commonly referred to as Web browsers

X Windows   X Windows itself is not a GUI and should not be confused with Microsoft Windows. X Windows is a standardized system which defines the underlying communication between X server and X client software modules which combine to present a multi-windowed graphical user interface on a specially designed X terminal or a client workstation running some type of X terminal emulation.

X.400   X.400 is an OSI e-mail messaging protocol which defines both addressing and message delivery standards. Like SMTP, some enterprise e-mail systems are able to use X.400 as the native messaging protocol while others are able to translate into X.400 through the use of gateways.

X.500   As enterprise networks become more heterogeneous comprised of network operating systems from a variety of different vendors, the need will arise for different network operating systems to share each other's directory services information. A directory services specification known as X.500 offers the potential for this directory services interoperability

X.500   X.500 is an open specification for enterprise directory services which can be deployed in a distributed, replicated, hierarchical manner. However, due to selective implementation of portions of the X.500 specification along with proprietary extensions to the standard, there is no guarantee that X.500 compliant directory services from different vendors will even interoperate

X/Open   Compliance with both the CDE and Spec 1170 API Specifications will be certified by X/Open which is an independent Unix standards organization located in Menlo Park, CA.

XA   Extended Architecture for CD-ROM is Microsoft's Level 2 CD-ROM specification which supports simultaneous playback of voice, video, image and text.

XDR   XDR (External Data Representation) is a presentation layer protocol responsible for formatting data in a consistent manner so that all NFS clients and servers can process it, regardless of the computing platform or operating system on which the NFS suite may be executing

zero slot LANs   The name "zero slot" refers to the fact that by using existing serial or parallel ports for network communications, zero expansion slots are occupied by network interface cards

zone   The scope of coverage, or collection of domains, for which a given DNS server can resolve names is known as a DNS zone.

Index